The SAGE Handbook of
Small Business and Entrepreneurship

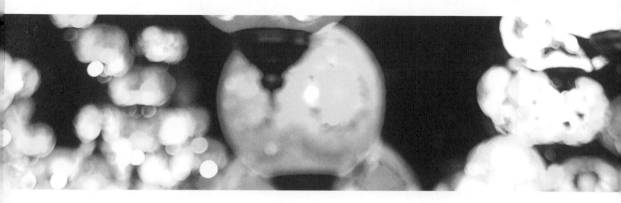

Sara Miller McCune founded SAGE Publishing in 1965 to support the dissemination of usable knowledge and educate a global community. SAGE publishes more than 1000 journals and over 800 new books each year, spanning a wide range of subject areas. Our growing selection of library products includes archives, data, case studies and video. SAGE remains majority owned by our founder and after her lifetime will become owned by a charitable trust that secures the company's continued independence.

Los Angeles | London | New Delhi | Singapore | Washington DC | Melbourne

The SAGE Handbook of
Small Business and Entrepreneurship

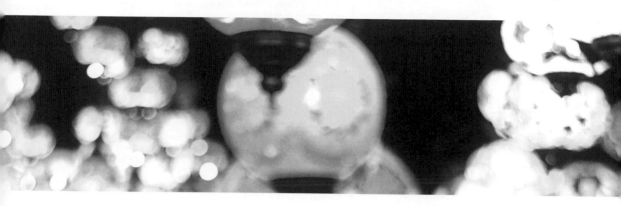

Edited by

Robert Blackburn,
Dirk De Clercq and
Jarna Heinonen

 reference

Los Angeles I London I New Delhi I Singapore I Washington DC I Melbourne

Los Angeles I London I New Delhi
Singapore I Washington DC I Melbourne

SAGE Publications Ltd
1 Oliver's Yard
55 City Road
London EC1Y 1SP

SAGE Publications Inc.
2455 Teller Road
Thousand Oaks, California 91320

SAGE Publications India Pvt Ltd
B 1/I 1 Mohan Cooperative Industrial Area
Mathura Road
New Delhi 110 044

SAGE Publications Asia-Pacific Pte Ltd
3 Church Street
#10-04 Samsung Hub
Singapore 049483

Editor: Delia Martinez-Alfonso
Editorial Assistant: Colette Wilson
Production Editor: Rudrani Mukherjee
Copyeditor: Sunrise Setting
Proofreader: Sunrise Setting
Indexer: Cathryn Pritchard
Marketing Manager: Alison Borg
Cover Design: Wendy Scott
Printed in the UK

Library of Congress Control Number: 2017938473

British Library Cataloguing in Publication data

A catalogue record for this book is available from the British Library

ISBN 978-1-4739-2523-6

At SAGE we take sustainability seriously. Most of our products are printed in the UK using FSC papers and boards. When we print overseas we ensure sustainable papers are used as measured by the PREPS grading system. We undertake an annual audit to monitor our sustainability.

Contents

List of Figures

List of Tables

Notes on the Editors and Contributors

THE EDITORS

Robert Blackburn is Associate Dean for Research, Kingston University Business School, Director of the Small Business Research Centre and Editor-in-Chief of the *International Small Business Journal*. He has undertaken research for private and public sector organizations worldwide on entrepreneurship and small business, including the OECD, the European Commission and Parliament, the UK's HM Treasury and HM Revenue and Customs, and banks and support agencies. Robert has held the Presidency of the European Council for Small Business and Entrepreneurship, is a Trustee and Treasurer of the Society for the Advancement of Management Studies, a member of the research committee of the Chartered Association of Business Schools, a Fellow of the Royal Society of Arts, a member of the Executive of the International Network of Business and Management Journals and is holder of the Queen's Award for Enterprise Promotion.

Dirk De Clercq is Professor of Management in the Goodman School of Business at Brock University, Canada. He is also Research Professor in the Small Business Research Centre at Kingston University, UK. His research interests are in the areas of entrepreneurship, innovation and organizational behaviour. He is Consulting Editor of *International Small Business Journal* and has published articles in *Entrepreneurship Theory and Practice*, *Journal of Business Venturing*, *Journal of International Business*, *Journal of Management Studies*, *Journal of Product Innovation Management* and *Strategic Entrepreneurship Journal*, among others.

Jarna Heinonen is Professor in Entrepreneurship and Director of the Entrepreneurship Unit within Turku School of Economics, University of Turku. In the field of entrepreneurship her research interests in particular include entrepreneurship education, corporate entrepreneurship and entrepreneurial behaviour, entrepreneurship policies and family business. She has conducted research for the European Commission, the OECD and various national ministries and other such bodies and is well connected to entrepreneurship stakeholders nationally and internationally. She is the book review editor at *International Small Business Journal* and has recently published in *Journal of Small Business Management*, *International Small Business Journal*, *European Educational Journal* and *Journal of Small Business and Enterprise Development*. She is also Visiting Professor at Kingston University in the UK and holds numerous positions of trust in the scientific community as well as in business and society.

THE CONTRIBUTORS

Samuel Adomako is Assistant Professor in Entrepreneurship and Innovation at the Entrepreneurship Institute, King Fahd University of Petroleum and Minerals, Saudi Arabia. Samuel has a multidisciplinary academic background and holds degrees in Sociology, Management and Entrepreneurship. His research examines the nexus of entrepreneurship, innovation and creativity within small and medium-sized enterprises (SMEs) and analyses the role of institutions in new venture creation or new business formation. Samuel received his PhD from University of Warwick.

Wafa N. Almobaireek, PhD in Business, Nottingham University, UK, is Associate Professor of Marketing and Entrepreneurship at King Saud University (KSU), the Dean of the Business School at Princess Nourah University (PNU) in Saudi Arabia, and a former Director of the Prince Salman Institute for Entrepreneurship (IPSE) at KSU. Research and teaching interests include marketing, small businesses and entrepreneurship. Dr Almobaireek is the author of a number of books in the area of small businesses and entrepreneurship. She is currently working on a number of projects in the same areas for several organizations in Saudi Arabia.

Ahmed Alshumaimeri, PhD in Marketing, Nottingham University, UK, is a practitioner and mentor for entrepreneurial innovation. He was one of the founders of Alsafat Capital, Almajd Satellite Channels and China Motors Company (CMC). Research and consulting interests include entrepreneurship, networking, business collaborations, business incubation and technology. Previously, Dr Alshumaimeri was the Assistant General-Director of the Saudi Credit Bank and served as the Dean of the Prince Salman Institute for Entrepreneurship and the Dean of Development at King Saud University. Dr Alshumaimeri is a bilingual author and has published eight books and numerous articles in academic and practitioner journals.

Bjørn Willy Åmo, PhD, is Associate Professor in Innovation at Nord University Business School. His research interests focus on corporate entrepreneurship, intrapreneurship, entrepreneurship education, social entrepreneurship and other aspects of entrepreneurship. He uses both qualitative and quantitative research methods. He teaches entrepreneurship courses and research methods at both bachelor and master levels. Dr Åmo is a member of the Norwegian Global Entrepreneurship Monitor team.

H. Shawna Chen, PhD, is Assistant Professor in the Goodman School of Business at Brock University. She teaches undergraduate and graduate entrepreneurship courses, such as business planning and creativity. Her research interests focus on entrepreneurial cognition and action. Before pursuing her PhD at Texas Tech University, Shawna was a serial entrepreneur involved in multiple Internet start-ups in the Washington DC area and a consultant in corporate finance and strategy.

Thomas M. Cooney is Professor in Entrepreneurship at the Dublin Institute of Technology, Academic Director of the DIT Institute for Minority Entrepreneurship and Adjunct Professor at the University of Turku (Finland). He is a former President of the International Council for Small Business (2012–13) and of the European Council for Small Business (2009–11) and was Chair of the ICSB 2014 World Entrepreneurship Conference. He was a Member of the Department of Enterprise, Jobs and Innovation 'Entrepreneurship Forum' (2013–14) and has been a policy advisor to the Irish government, the European Commission, OECD and other international organizations. He was a founding Director of Startup Ireland and works in various capacities with a range of businesses and not-for-profit organizations. He has researched and published widely on the topic of entrepreneurship and further details of his work can be found at www.thomascooney.com

Marc Cowling has a PhD in Business Economics from Warwick Business School and an MSc in Economics from London University. Before his appointment at Brighton (as Professor of

Entrepreneurship) he was Professor and Head of the Department of Management Studies at Exeter Business School. Prior to that, he held the posts of Chief Economist at the Institute for Employment Studies and The Work Foundation. He has also held positions at Warwick Business School, Birmingham Business School and London Business School. He is currently ranked in the top 11% of economists in the world by citations (H-index) according to Research Publications in Economics (REPEC, 6 November 2016) and in entrepreneurship he was ranked 23rd in the world during the period 1995–2006 according to 'Rankings of the Top Entrepreneurship Researchers and Affiliations'. Marc has spent the last 24 years researching in four core areas: The Dynamics of Early Stage Survival and Growth; The Financing of SMEs and Entrepreneurial Businesses; Labour Market Dynamics and Evaluating Public Policy.

Jonathan Deacon is Professor of Marketing at the South Wales Business School where he is Academic Director of the 'Exchange' at USW – an entrepreneurial Business Growth Hub and the Centre for Research in Entrepreneurship and Marketing (CREaM). Jonathan's career prior to academia was within business – especially high growth, new venture starts. Professor Deacon is an acknowledged 'thought leader' at the interface between Marketing, Entrepreneurship and Management. He is Global Vice Chair of the board of trustees and fellow of the Chartered Institute of Marketing, board member of the European Marketing Confederation and past editor of the international *Journal for Research in Marketing and Entrepreneurship* (JRME).

Cristina Díaz-García, PhD, is Associate Professor in the Department of Business Administration at the University of Castilla-La Mancha (Campus Albacete), Spain. She is author of the book Influencia del género en los recursos y resultados de las pequeñas empresas (Resources and performance of SMEs: The influence of gender), her dissertation was awarded a better dissertation prize in 2006 by the Economic and Social Council (consultative body of the Spanish Government). She is author and co-author of articles and book chapters on this topic. Her research focuses on gender, with a special interest on women's entrepreneurship and the effect of gender diversity in innovation, and ecoinnovation. She is co-editor of the 5th book of the Diana International Series by Edward Elgar titled 'Women's Entrepreneurship in Global and Local Contexts'. She is reviewer for many journals and part of the editorial review board of *International Journal of Entrepreneurial Behaviour and Research*.

Bob Doherty is Professor of Marketing at The York Management School, University of York and principal investigator on a four-year interdisciplinary research programme (£4.3m) on food resilience titled 'IKnowFood', funded by the Global Food Security Fund. In addition he holds a number of institutional-wide research positions including the research theme leader for sustainable food in the York Environmental Sustainability Research Institute (YESI). Bob specialises in research on hybrid organizations, namely the marketing and management aspects of fair trade organizations and social enterprises. Recently his research interests have developed to look at how hybrids can contribute to resilience in food systems. Bob has published in *Journal of Business Ethics, International Journal of Management Reviews, Business History* and *Journal of Social Policy*. For the past eight years he has been editor of the Emerald Group Publishing's *Social Enterprise Journal*.

Stephen Drinkwater is Professor of Economics at the Business School at the University of Roehampton, London. Stephen is also a research fellow at the IZA in Bonn, CoDE at the University of Manchester, CReAM at University College London and at the Wales Institute of Social and Economic Research, Data and Methods (WISERD). Stephen's main research interests lie in applied micro economics, particularly within the labour market. His research has primarily focused on self-employment, labour market discrimination, international and inter-regional migration. He has received research funding from several external organizations including the European Commission, the Joseph Rowntree Foundation, the OECD and the Economic and Social Research Council. He has published papers in a range of international peer-reviewed journals including *Economica, Economics Letters, International Small Business Journal, Journal of Population Economics, Journal of Regional Science, Labour Economics, Oxford Bulletin of Economics and Statistics, Regional Studies, Small Business Economics* and *Urban Studies.*

Fokko J. Eller is currently a PhD student and research assistant at the Institute of Management & Organization at the Leuphana University of Lüneburg, Germany. He received his Master of Arts in Management and Entrepreneurship from the Leuphana University of Lüneburg. Prior to his master programme he studied International Business at the University of Applied Sciences and Arts Dortmund, Germany and at the Guangdong University of Foreign Studies, China. His research focuses on sustainable entrepreneurship. He is particu-larly interested in how opportunities in sustainable entrepreneurship come to life and in the process of mission drift in hybrid organizations.

Mark Freel is the Royal Bank of Canada Professor for the commercialization of innovation at the Telfer School of Management and Professor of innovation and entrepreneurship at Lancaster University Management School.

Michael M. Gielnik is currently Professor for HR Development at the Leuphana University of Lüneburg, Germany. He studied psychology at the University of Giessen, Germany, and received his PhD from the Leuphana University of Lüneburg. He was a Visiting Senior Fellow at the National University of Singapore Business School. His research interest is entrepreneur-ship from a psychological perspective. Specifically, his research focuses on entrepreneurial learning and training, the entrepreneurial process and aging of entrepreneurs. He has taken a special interest in entrepreneurship in developing countries. He has conducted several research and practice projects on entrepreneurship in different countries in sub-Saharan Africa and Asia.

Alessandro Giudici is Lecturer in Strategy at Cass Business School (City, University of London, UK). His research focuses on organizations that support start-ups and SME growth, including venture associations, incubators, government agencies and the like, predominantly from a capability and business model perspective. His research has been published in *Business History, Long Range Planning* and *Strategic Organization* and is currently under review in a number of peer-reviewed journals. Before entering academia, Alessandro worked as a market-ing executive for a large multinational enterprise in the fast-moving consumer goods sector.

Paul Hannon is a graduate entrepreneur and has helped shape enterprise and entrepreneurship education, support and development in the UK and overseas during the past 35 years. He is a successful creator and innovator of local support initiatives for enterprise and entrepreneurship stimulation in the private and public sectors; he has won accolades for his innovative approaches to enterprise and entrepreneurship curricula design and delivery in higher educa-tion; and he is also an experienced entrepreneur with 10 years as the co-owner/director of a small growing firm in the food industry. In 2015 Paul was invited to be a member of Maserati 100, the top 100 individuals in the UK who actively support the next generation of future entrepreneurs. In 2016 he was appointed European Entrepreneurship Education Laureate by the Sten K. Johnson Centre for Entrepreneurship at Lund University, Sweden. At Swansea University in Wales Paul is Head of Section in Research, Engagement and Innovation Services. He is Director of the Institute for Entrepreneurial Leadership and is Director of Leading Business Growth, a body that supports leadership development and growth in hundreds of Welsh SMEs. The Institute for Entrepreneurial Leadership offers research, learning and development opportunities to stimulate cultures and practices of entrepreneurial leadership for individuals and organizations in highly uncertain, unpredictable and complex environments. Up to the end of March 2013 Paul was Chief Executive at the UK's National Centre for Entrepreneurship in Education (formerly NCGE) that supports long-term cultural change in UK universities and colleges.

Richard T. Harrison is Professor of Entrepreneurship and Innovation and Co-Director of the Centre for Strategic Leadership at the University of Edinburgh Business School. He was previously Dean of Queen's University Management School and Director of the Leadership Institute. He was Dixons Professor of Entrepreneurship and Innovation at the University of Edinburgh and has also held Chair-level appointments at the University of Aberdeen and University of Ulster. He has taught in China, Argentina, Australia, the US and Canada. His current research interests are linked by a unifying interest in the nature of the entrepreneurial process – in social and corporate as well as new venture contexts – as it is reflected in business development (particularly in the financing of innovation and growth) and in the implications of research and theorizing for practice and public policy. This includes the analysis of entrepreneurial finance, entrepreneurial learning and leadership processes, studies of the role of entrepreneurship and innovation in emerging economies (notably China, Malaysia) and examination of the nature of peace entrepreneurship in conflict societies (Northern Ireland, Rwanda, Kosova). In recognition of the importance of his research on entrepreneurial finance he was the 2015 recipient of the UK ESRC (Economic and Social Research Council) Award for Outstanding Research Impact on Business.

Helen Haugh is Senior Lecturer at Cambridge Judge Business School, Director of the Masters in Innovation, Strategy and Organizations, The Management of Technology and Innovation programme and Research Director for the Centre for Social Innovation. Helen's research interests focus on social and community entrepreneurship, family business and corporate responsibility. Her research in the social economy has examined community-led regeneration in rural communities, cross-sector collaboration and innovations in governance. Her work has been published in the *Academy of Management Education and Learning*, *Organization Studies*, *Entrepreneurship Theory and Practice*, *Journal of Business Ethics*, *Cambridge Journal of Economics* and *Entrepreneurship and Regional Development*.

Anders Hoffmann is now Deputy Permanent Secretary in the Ministry of Energy, Utilities and Climate in the government of Denmark. The work co-authored here is written in a personal capacity and relates to a previous role as Deputy Director General at the Danish Business Authority. There he was responsible for developing and implementing most of the business development policies in Denmark at the national, regional and local level. These policies covered entrepreneurship, EU structural funds, design, creative industry, second chance, clusters, market development, circular economy, sharing economy, social enterprises, CSR, offset, EU Leader approach and standardization. He was also responsible for the Authorities International division and the Danish approach to the reduction of economic burdens for firms. Dr Hoffmann holds a PhD in Economics and was a Senior Economist with the

OECD, supervising a team of economists and statisticians and coordinating activities related to micro-policy benchmarking. His academic output has been published in *Journal of International Economics* and *Economic Modelling*.

Louisa Huxtable-Thomas is the Research Lead for the Institute for Entrepreneurial Leadership at Swansea University, Wales. She has extensive experience in case study research and work-based learning, in facilitation of innovation and invention in supported companies, and in training and supervision of PhD students. In this role she undertakes research for a successful management and leadership programme aimed at improving leadership skills for owner-managers of small businesses. The role requires research into learning and teaching methods most suitable for this group of mature students, also into post-full-time education as well as analysis of the wider economic impacts that such learning has. In addition, Louisa has an academic role as advisor for two doctoral students and provides qualitative methodologies advice to a further five students at the recommendation of their Directors of Studies. As well as holding a doctorate in business and economics, Louisa holds a Postgraduate Certificate in Developing Higher Education and is a Fellow of the Higher Education Academy (FHEA). In previous roles she qualified as a Chartered Environmentalist (CEnv) and Member of the Institute of Ecology and Environmental Management (MIEEM) and Institute of Environmental Management and Assessment (AIEMA). Louisa has been considered a trusted advisor to the Welsh Assembly Government and local authorities in Wales.

Ulla Hytti is Research Director in the Entrepreneurship Unit at the University of Turku, Finland. She has taught entrepreneurship at undergraduate, graduate and post-graduate levels at the university, and has been conducting research into entrepreneurship education. Ulla was a founding member of the Finnish Scientific Association for Entrepreneurship Education and a President of the Association in 2014–15. She has organized and chaired several entrepreneurship and entrepreneurship education conferences nationally and internationally. Ulla is an Associate Editor at the *Journal of Small Business Management* and a Board Member in the European Council for Small Business (ECSB).

Bengt Johannisson is Professor Emeritus of Entrepreneurship at Linnaeus University. From 1998–2007, he was the Editor-in-Chief of Entrepreneurship & Regional Development and he himself has published widely on entrepreneurship, personal networking, family business as well as on local and regional development. His current research interests are process and practice theories and enactive methodology as applied to different arenas for entrepreneurship. In Sweden Bengt Johannisson has initiated several inter-university networks on research and post-graduate studies in entrepreneurship and for 15 years he was a co-director of the European Doctoral Programme in Entrepreneurship and Small Business Management. Bengt Johannisson is the first Scandinavian Winner of the Global Award for Entrepreneurship Research (2008) and in 2015 he received the European Entrepreneurship Education Award.

Rosalind Jones is Lecturer in Marketing and Program Director at Birmingham Business School, University of Birmingham. Her career until 2005 was in the public sector, prior to completion of a PhD in entrepreneurial marketing in small software technology firms at Bangor University, Wales. She is a Fellow of the Higher Education Academy and a 'Chartered Marketer' and Member of the Levitt Group of Senior Marketers for the Chartered Institute of Marketing. She is Co-Chair of the Academy of Marketing, Entrepreneurial & Small Business Marketing Special Interest Group and on the Steering Committee of the American Marketing Association (AMA) Special Interest Group in Research at the Marketing and Entrepreneurship Interface.

David J. Ketchen, PhD, The Pennsylvania State University, serves as Lowder Eminent Scholar and Professor of Management in the Harbert College of Business at Auburn University. His research interests include entrepreneurship and franchising, methodological issues in organizational research, strategic supply chain management, and the determinants of superior organizational performance. He has served as an Associate Editor for *Academy of Management Journal*, *Journal of Operations Management*, *Organizational Research Methods*, *Journal of Supply Chain Management*, *Journal of International Business Studies* and *Journal of Management*.

John Kitching is Professor in the Small Business Research Centre, Kingston University, UK. His research interests include the influence of regulation on small business activity and performance, and exploring the implications of critical realist philosophy of science for small business and entrepreneurship studies.

Lars Kolvereid, PhD, is Professor of Entrepreneurship. His research interests are entrepreneurship in general, especially new business creation processes and new business performance. Dr Kolvereid has published a large number of articles and books and has supervised more than 25 doctoral students and is the leader of the Norwegian Global Entrepreneurship Monitor team.

Sirpa Koskinen has a PhD in Education and works as a special education teacher. She has extensive experience from various forms of demanding special education. Currently she works in a hospital school in Hämeenlinna where her pupils are patients at a youth psychiatric ward. Previously Sirpa worked in a state reform school. She has also worked as a special education teacher in an upper secondary school with more than 500 pupils and in a Finnish school in Tallinn, Estonia.

Anne Kovalainen is Professor of Entrepreneurship at the School of Economics at the University of Turku, Finland. She has been visiting faculty fellow and visiting professor among others at Stanford University, London School of Economics, Technology University Sydney, and at Kingston University. Anne's intellectual background is in economic sociology, gender studies and business studies. Stemming from her disciplinary background, her publication track record is multidisciplinary. She established an international multidisciplinary conference on WORK in 2013, which runs biannually (latest on Work and Labour in the Digital Future WORK2017). She is editorial board member in International Small Business Journal (ECSB) and in Research in the Sociology of Work (ASA), among others. Her current research interests deal with science and technology studies, research methodology, transformation of economies, knowledge formation and changing relationships between entrepreneurship, work and gender. She leads a large research consortium on work and platform economy, currently analyzing the complexities of gig economy, sharing economy and platforms, including their transformational effects on work and entrepreneurship, academic work, self-employment and entrepreneurship (SWiPE). Professor Kovalainen holds several positions of trust and serves regularly national and international science institutions.

Christian Lechner is currently Full Professor of Strategy and Entrepreneurship at the Free University of Bolzano, Italy. He is the Director of the PhD programme in Economics and Management on Organizational and Institutional Outliers. He was former Professor in Entrepreneurship and Strategy for 12 years at Toulouse Business School where he was involved in entrepreneurship activities, the launch of an incubator and the coaching of small firms. He holds a PhD in business administration from the University of Regensburg, Germany, an MBA from the University of Georgia and degrees in business administration from the Ludwig-Maximilians-University in Munich and international business studies from the Università degli

Studi di Firenze, Florence, Italy. His research interests are inter-firm and inter-personal networks, habitual entrepreneurship, organizational configurations of new firms and growth, the resource-based view and entrepreneurial strategy.

Claire M. Leitch, DPhil, holds the Chair in Entrepreneurial Leadership at Lancaster University Management School, where she is also Head of Department, Leadership and Management. Her research interests concentrate on the development, enhancement and growth of individuals and organizations in an entrepreneurial context with a particular focus on leadership, leadership development and learning. She is an internationally recognized scholar whose work has shaped theoretical debate and had significant industrial and policy impact. She has published in *Journal of Small Business Management*, *Organization Research Methods*, *Academy of Management Learning and Education*, *British Journal of Management*, *Regional Studies* and *Entrepreneurship Theory and Practice*. Currently she is the Editor of *International Small Business Journal*.

Fergus Lyon is Professor of Enterprise and Organization and Director of the Centre for Enterprise and Economic Development Research at Middlesex University. His research focuses on social enterprise, hybrid organizations, enterprise support, innovation, trust and sustainability. He is Deputy Director of the ESRC Centre for the Understanding of Sustainable Prosperity (CUSP) and is leading a research theme on enterprise, the social economy and investment. He has a background in international development and enterprise support and is actively involved in conservation and farming enterprises in the UK. He has conducted research on enterprise issues in the UK, Ghana, Nigeria, Pakistan, India, Nepal and Bhutan. He has published on social enterprise and alternative organizational forms in a range of journals including *International Small Business Journal*, *International Journal of Management Reviews*, *Organization Studies*, *World Development* and *Entrepreneurship and Regional Development*. He published the Edward Elgar *Handbook of Research Methods on Trust*, now in its second edition.

Tatiana S. Manolova, DBA, Boston University, is Professor of Management at Bentley University, USA. Research interests include strategic management (competitive strategies of new and small companies), international entrepreneurship and management in emerging economies. She is affiliated with Diana International, an international research project exploring the growth strategies of women entrepreneurs worldwide. During 2010–11, she was a Visiting Professor at King Saud University, Riyadh, Saudi Arabia, and conducted research on entrepreneurship in Saudi Arabia in affiliation with the Prince Salman Institute for Entrepreneurship. Tatiana is the author of over 40 scholarly articles and book chapters. She serves on the editorial boards of *Entrepreneurship Theory and Practice*, *Journal of Business Venturing*, *International Small Business Journal* and the Babson College Entrepreneurship Research Conference Board of Reviewers (2015–17).

Colin Mason is Professor of Entrepreneurship in the Adam Smith Business School, University of Glasgow. He has held visiting positions at universities in Canada, Australia, New Zealand and Argentina. His research and teaching are in the areas of entrepreneurship and regional development. His specific research interests are in entrepreneurial finance and entrepreneurial ecosystems. He has written extensively on business angel investing and has been closely involved with government and private sector initiatives to promote business angel investment, both in the UK and elsewhere. He is the founder and co-editor of the journal *Venture Capital: An International Journal of Entrepreneurial Finance* (published by Taylor and Francis Ltd).

Catherine Matthews is currently Senior Lecturer in finance at the University of Brighton and has worked there since 1998 when she joined the staff as a graduate teaching assistant. She has since taught at post graduate and undergraduate levels across a number of subject areas, including economics, accounting and finance. Catherine has held external examiner and associate editor roles and enjoys being an active member of the research community at Brighton. Her research interests are in the area of small business finance and in particular trade credit management, which formed the focus of her doctoral research. Since being awarded her doctorate, Catherine has been working on publishing-related papers.

Maura McAdam is Professor in Management and Director of Entrepreneurship at Dublin City University, Dublin. She is a nationally and internationally recognized scholar within the area of entrepreneurship having particular expertise in gender, entrepreneurial leadership, technology entrepreneurship and family business. Accordingly, her research has been published in top rated North American and UK journals across a range of theoretical disciplines such as *Entrepreneurship Theory and Practice*, *Journal of Small Business Management*, *Regional Studies*, *Entrepreneurship and Regional Development* and *International Small Business Journal*. In addition, Maura has authored the book *Female Entrepreneurship* with Routledge publishing. Maura is an editorial board member of leading UK and US journals such as *International Small Business Journal* (ISBJ) and *Entrepreneurship, Theory and Practice* (ETP). In addition, Maura is an invited Fellow of the Royal Society of Arts (FRSA) and has held Visiting Scholar positions at Massey University and Babson College; she is currently a Visiting Scholar at the University of Nottingham and Princess Nourah Bint Abdulrahman University, Saudi Arabia.

Aaron F. McKenny, PhD, University of Oklahoma, is Assistant Professor of Management at the University of Central Florida. His research is primarily focused on the intersection of entrepreneurship and strategic management with an emphasis on the role of social and other non-economic phenomena in organizational settings. He is on the review boards for the *Journal of Management*, *Journal of Business Venturing* and *Family Business Review*. His research has been published in several journals, including *Journal of Management*, *Organizational Research Methods*, *Journal of Business Venturing*, *Strategic Entrepreneurship Journal*, *Entrepreneurship Theory and Practice*, *The Leadership Quarterly*, *Journal of the Academy of Marketing Science*, *Family Business Review*, *Business Communication Quarterly* and *Business Horizons*.

Morgan P. Miles is Professor at Charles Sturt University. Previously he had been Professor of Entrepreneurship and Innovation at the University of Canterbury, the Tom Hendrix Chair of Excellence at the University of Tennessee at Martin, Professor of Enterprise Development at the University of Tasmania and Professor of Marketing at Georgia Southern University. He has been a visiting scholar at Georgia Tech, Cambridge University, University of Stockholm, the University of Otago, University of Auckland and an Erskine Fellow at the University of Canterbury. He holds a DBA in Marketing from Mississippi State University. His research interests include entrepreneurial marketing and corporate social responsibility.

J. Robert Mitchell, PhD, is Associate Professor of Entrepreneurship and Strategy in the Department of Management at Colorado State University. He teaches undergraduate and graduate courses. Prior to joining Colorado State University, Rob was a Professor at the University of Oklahoma and at the Ivey School of Business, where he continues to hold an appointment as an adjunct research professor. He completed his doctoral studies in entrepreneurship and strategic management at the Kelley School of Business in Bloomington, Indiana. Before pursuing his PhD at Indiana University, Rob worked in a technology start-up in Salt Lake City, Utah and was involved in emerging enterprise consulting in Victoria, British Columbia. Rob was also the recipient of the NFIB Best Dissertation Award from the Entrepreneurship Division of the Academy of Management. Among other outlets, his research has been published in *Entrepreneurship Theory and Practice*, *Journal of Business Venturing*, *Strategic Entrepreneurship Journal* and *Strategic Management Journal*.

Ronald K. Mitchell is Professor of Entrepreneurship and JA Bagley Regents Chair in the Rawls College of Business at Texas Tech University, a Wheatley Institution Fellow and Distinguished Visiting Professor at the University of Victoria, in BC Canada. Previously, he was Winspear Chair in Public Policy and Business at the University of Victoria and Jointly-appointed Professor of Public Policy and Strategy at the Guanghua School of Management at Peking University. He is a CPA, former CEO, consultant and entrepreneur. He received his PhD from the University of Utah, winning the 1995 Heizer Dissertation Award. Ron publishes and serves in editorial review capacities in the top entrepreneurship and management journals, and was 2008–9 Chair of the Academy of Management Entrepreneurship Division. His academic mission focuses on problems and possibilities in opportunity emergence: understanding the core systems and institutions of society that enable greater human capacity. He researches, consults and lectures worldwide.

Kevin F. Mole is Associate Professor (Reader) in Entrepreneurship at Warwick Business School where he is associated with the Enterprise Research Centre (enterpriseresearch.ac.uk). His research interests include external support to small firms including policy choices in business support, the role of regulation and firm growth. He is published in journals such as the *Journal of International Business Studies*, *Journal of Business Venturing*, *International Small Business Journal*, *British Journal of Management* and *Environment and Planning*. He has worked for the Advanced Institute of Management and his client list includes OECD, Grant Thornton and the UK government department for business; past clients include the Small Business Service and Business Link University.

Michael H. Morris holds the James W. Walter Clinical Eminent Scholar Chair at the University of Florida. A pioneer in curricular innovation, he launched the first department and first school of entrepreneurship at major research universities. Dr Morris has published 11 books and over 200 articles, book chapters and other scholarly publications. His current research is focused on venture categories and their implications.

Sussie C. Morrish is Associate Professor of Marketing in the Department of Management, Marketing and Entrepreneurship at the University of Canterbury. Sussie teaches strategic marketing from basic to advanced levels. Sussie gained her PhD from the University of Canterbury while simultaneously teaching at the University of Auckland Business School. Her main research interests revolve around the marketing and entrepreneurship disciplines including various strategic approaches to portfolio entrepreneurship, airline alliances, internationalization, sustainability and country of origin effects. Her more recent research looks at the effects of the Canterbury Earthquakes on social enterprise, hospitality and related industries.

Xaver Neumeyer is currently Assistant Professor and Burwell Chair of Entrepreneurship at the School of Entrepreneurship, University of North Dakota, USA. His current research focuses on entrepreneurial ecosystems, specifically how these ecosystems are shaped by or shape entrepreneurs. He received his PhD in Mechanical Engineering from Northwestern University in 2014 and his MSc in Mechanical and Aerospace Engineering from the Illinois Institute of Technology in 2006. He also completed the Postdoctoral Bridge Program at the University of Florida in 2015, specializing in Entrepreneurship and International Business.

Mattias Nordqvist is Professor in Business Administration, the Hamrin International Professor of Family Business and Director of the Centre for Family Enterprise and Ownership (CeFEO) at Jönköping University. Mattias is also Visiting Professor at the Swedish University of Agricultural Sciences, Alnarp. Mattias is a former Co-Director of the Global STEP Project and Visiting Scholar at Babson College, USA, University of Alberta (Canada) and Bocconi University (Italy). He has served on the board of the International Family Enterprise Research Academy (IFERA) and is currently on the scientific committee of the Center for Young and Family Enterprise (Cyfe) at the University of Bergamo (Italy), on the scientific committee of the Family Business Centre at Lancaster University School of Management (UK) and on the scientific committee of the Dutch Centre of Expertise in Family Businesses at the Windesheim University of Applied Sciences (the Netherlands).

Niina Nummela is Professor of International Business at the Turku School of Economics, University of Turku, Finland, and Visiting Professor at the University of Tartu, Estonia. Her areas of expertise include international entrepreneurship, cross-border acquisitions and research methods. She has published widely in academic journals, has edited several academic books and serves on the editorial boards of *Journal of International Business Studies* and *International Small Business Journal*.

Kristina Nyström is Associate Professor in Economics with specialisation in entrepreneurship and industrial dynamics at the Division of Economics at the Department of Industrial Economics and Management at KTH, The Royal Institute of Technology and The Ratio Institute in Stockholm, Sweden. Kristina Nyström's research interests include firm dynamics in terms of entry, expansion, contraction of business and exit, industrial and regional dynamics, labour mobility associated with establishment and closure of businesses, regional resilience to displacements and institutional aspects of entrepreneurship and firm dynamics. Recent publications include articles in journals such as *Regional Studies*, *Small Business Economics* and *Labour*.

Abeer Pervaiz is a doctoral student in the PhD programme in management and economics on organizational and institutional outliers at the Free University of Bolzano-Bozen, Italy. Her educational background consists of an undergraduate degree in finance from the Lahore School of Economics (LSE), Pakistan and an MSc in Entrepreneurship and Innovation from the University of Amsterdam, the Netherlands on an Erasmus Scholarship. She has worked as a research assistant at the Lahore University of Management Sciences (LUMS), Pakistan. Her research interests include entrepreneurship, industry emergence, start-ups, strategy and social movements.

Luke Pittaway is the Copeland Professor of Entrepreneurship and Chair, Department of Management at Ohio University (Athens, OH) where he leads the academic programmes in the College of Business and the College's enhancements of university-wide programmes. He was formally the William A. Freeman Distinguished Chair in Free Enterprise and the Director of the Center for Entrepreneurial Learning and Leadership at Georgia Southern University where he managed programmes in entrepreneurship until May 2013. Dr Pittaway has previously worked at the University of Sheffield (UK), Lancaster University (UK) and the University of Surrey (UK). He has been a Research and Education Fellow with the National Council of Graduate Entrepreneurship and an Advanced Institute of Management Research Scholar. He is on a number of editorial boards including those for the *International Small Business Journal*, the *International Journal of Entrepreneurial Behaviour and Research* and the *Service Industries Journal*. Dr Pittaway's research focuses on entrepreneurship education and learning and he has a range of other interests, including entrepreneurial behaviour, networking, entrepreneurial failure, business growth and corporate venturing.

Seppo Poutanen is Senior Research Fellow and Docent of sociology at the Department of Management and Entrepreneurship, University of Turku, Finland. His areas of expertise include social epistemology, social theory, sociology of science, innovation studies, methodology of social sciences and economic sociology. Seppo Poutanen has acted as Visiting Professor and Visiting Fellow at several universities (e.g. Stanford University, LSE, University of Essex, Goldsmiths College, UTS Business School). One of his current research projects focuses on the rise of the entrepreneurial university. He has published his research in *Social Epistemology*, *Critical Public Health*, *Journal of Critical Realism*, *Sociological Research Online*, *International Journal of Gender and Entrepreneurship* and in several edited volumes. Seppo Poutanen's latest publication is a monograph with Anne Kovalainen: *Gender and Innovation in the New Economy – Women, Identity, and Creative Work*, New York: Palgrave Macmillan, 2017.

Christopher Pryor is Lecturer in Entrepreneurship at the University of Florida. He obtained his PhD from the School of Entrepreneurship at Oklahoma State University. His current research focuses on entrepreneurs' behaviours and the intersection of institutional contexts and entrepreneurship. His research has been published in *Strategic Entrepreneurship Journal*, among others.

Susana C. Santos is a Postdoctoral research fellow at the Center for Entrepreneurship & Innovation at Warrington College of Business at the University of Florida. She holds a PhD in Human Resources Management and Organizational Behaviour from Instituto Universitário de Lisboa (ISCTE-IUL), Portugal. Her main research interests are in the cognitive, affective and psychosocial processes of entrepreneurship, at individual and team levels.

Jeremy C. Short (PhD, Louisiana State University) is the Rath Chair in Strategic Management at the University of Oklahoma. His research focuses on multilevel determinants of firm performance, strategic decision processes, entrepreneurship, research methods, franchising and family business. He has served as Associate Editor for *Journal of Management* and *Family Business Review*. He currently serves on the review boards for *Journal of Management*, *Journal of Business Venturing*, *Strategic Entrepreneurship Journal*, *Organizational Research Methods* and *Family Business Review*. His research has appeared in a number of journals including the *Academy of Management Journal*, *Strategic Entrepreneurship Journal*, *Strategic Management Journal*, *Organization Science*, *Organizational Research Methods*, *Organizational Behavior and Human Decision Processes*, the *Journal of Management*, *Personnel Psychology*, *Entrepreneurship Theory & Practice*, *The Leadership Quarterly*, *Academy of Management Learning and Education*, the *Journal of Management Education*, the *Journal of Vocational*

Behavior, *Business Ethics Quarterly* and *Family Business Review*. He has published a strategic management textbook titled *Mastering Strategic Management*.

Danny Soetanto is Lecturer in Entrepreneurship and Innovation at Lancaster University Management School, the United Kingdom. His research interest covers the areas dealing with entrepreneurship, knowledge commercialization, incubator and incubation process and social networks. Danny has presented his works at national and international conferences and seminars and has published in several international journals. Danny is also a reviewer for several leading UK and US journals in the field of entrepreneurship and innovation.

Ben Spigel is Assistant Professor and Chancellor's Fellow at the University of Edinburgh Business School. He completed his PhD in the economic geography of entrepreneurship at the University of Toronto. He is interested in the relationships between regional cultural outlooks, institutional structures and high-growth, innovative entrepreneurship and how this contributes to the formation of resilient, sustainable economies.

Erik Stam is Full Professor at the Utrecht University School of Economics, where he holds the chair of Strategy, Organization and Entrepreneurship. Next to this he is co-founder and Academic Director of the Utrecht Centre for Entrepreneurship. He held positions at Erasmus University Rotterdam, the University of Cambridge, the Max Planck Institute of Economics (Jena, Germany), and the Netherlands Scientific Council for Government Policy (WRR). He is editor of *Small Business Economics*. He is interested in how socio-economic contexts (at the societal and organizational level) affect new value creation by individuals, and the consequences of this entrepreneurship for the performance of firms and society. He has co-authored more than a hundred books, book chapters and articles on these and related topics. In addition to his scientific work he is often consulted by governments, start-ups and corporates on innovation and entrepreneurship.

David J. Storey is Professor in the School of Business, Management and Economics at the University of Sussex, UK. His interest is in the factors influencing the performance of small, but especially new, firms. The theoretical underpinning for his work is a Gamblers Ruin model in which sales change is a random walk and survival depends upon both access to, and management of, financial resources. Empirical testing of these theories is undertaken using econometric analysis of large-scale panels of firms and individuals drawing upon data from the UK Census and from Barclays Bank. It confirms the very modest role in new firm performance played by factors such as traditional human capital, learning and strategy. Recently this work has appeared in *Journal of Business Venturing* (2014 with George Saridakis), *Small Business Economics* (2016 with Alex Coad and Julian Frankish), *Environment and Planning A* (2017 with Georgios Fotopulos) and *International Small Business Journal* (2016 with Alex Coad and Julian Frankish).

Hamid Vahidnia is a PhD candidate in the Rawls College of Business at Texas Tech University. He is interested in the dynamics of how and why actors – be they individuals, teams or organizations – take action to create (or even destroy) value for their various stakeholders. His research often deals with complexity, conflicting goals, multilevel factors and the simultaneous effects of the mind, body and social and situational factors on human action in entrepreneurial and business settings. Hamid's work has started to generate recognition, such as a 2015 Best Paper Award from the Emerald Publishing Group and the Critical Management Studies Division of the Academy of Management. His research is often influenced greatly by his multicultural experiences as well as his experiences as a new venture founder, industrial engineer and management consultant.

Judith van Helvert is a researcher at the Dutch Centre of Expertise in Family Businesses at the Windesheim University of Applied Sciences in the Netherlands and an external PhD student affiliated to the Centre for Family Enterprise and Ownership (CeFEO) at Jönköping University. Her dissertation focuses on advisory boards as a practice in strategising in family businesses.

Zhongming Wang is Professor of Industrial Psychology, Human Resource Management and Entrepreneurship at the School of Management, Zhejiang University, China. He received his MA degree in applied psychology from Gothenburg University and his PhD degree in industrial psychology at Hangzhou University. He is Director of the Global Entrepreneurship Research Centre and Centre for Human Resources and Strategic Development at Zhejiang University. His research interests are entrepreneurship competence, human resources, leadership, decision-making and organizational change. His publications include *Entrepreneurship Competence Development* (2015) and *Principles of Entrepreneurship and Research Methods in Psychology* (2017).

Miles A. Zachary, PhD, Texas Tech University, is Assistant Professor of Management at Auburn University. His research interests center on the sociocognitive elements of organizations that influence different organizational outcomes and stakeholder relationships over time, including organization identity/image, impression management and social evaluations. His research has been featured in professional journals including *Journal of Management, Strategic Entrepreneurship Journal, Family Business Review, Journal of the Academy of Marketing Science, Business Horizons, Journal of the Academy of Business and Economics* and the *Journal of International Business and Cultural Studies*.

Yanhai Zhao is Associate Professor of Management at the School of Management, Lanzhou University. He received his PhD in economics at the University of Paris III-Sorbonne nouvelle. His research interests are strategic management, business ethics, corporate social responsibility and entrepreneurship. He has conducted a number of important corporate consultation programmes in France and China (Chamber of Commerce Paris, Sinopec, National Grid, Gansu Bank, etc.).

Ivan Zupic is Lecturer in Entrepreneurship at Kingston Business School, London. He received his PhD degree in Management and Organization from the Faculty of Economics, University of Ljubljana, Slovenia. His research interests include high-growth firms, entrepreneurship policy, digital economy and research methods. His research has been published in peer-reviewed journals such as *Organizational Research Methods, Management Decision* and *European Management Journal*. Before entering academia he worked as a consultant in the IT industry and as a journalist/photographer in the media.

Acknowledgments

We would like to thank a number of individuals for their help in the production of this *Handbook*. First of all we would like to thank the team at SAGE Publishing, including Delia Martinez-Alfonso for her encouragement and advice, and Colette Wilson, Serena Ugolini and Rudrani Mukherjee for their excellent help in the editorial and production process. Second, we would like to thank Professor Zhongming Wang for his valuable time in giving us advice and input into the planning of the book. A big thank you goes to Valerie Thorne, who provided support throughout the process, particularly with the organization and editorial process of the chapters. Finally, a huge thank you goes to the authors of the main chapters without which this *Handbook* would not exist. These authors responded very positively to our critical reviews of their draft chapters and have produced excellent contributions to this exciting field of study.

Robert Blackburn
Small Business Research Centre, Kingston University, UK

Dirk De Clercq
Goodman School of Business, Brock University, Canada

Jarna Heinonen
University of Turku, School of Economics, Finland

Introduction

Robert Blackburn,
Dirk De Clercq and Jarna Heinonen

For some decades now, the field of entrepreneurship and small business studies has been one of the most vibrant and expansive in business and management, as well as the social sciences more broadly (see for example Carlsson, Braunerhjelm, McKelvey, Olofsson, Persson, & Ylinenpää, 2013; Fayolle, 2014; Landström, Parhankangas, Fayolle, & Riot, 2016; Shane & Venkataraman, 2000). Indeed, one estimate is that the number of Social Science Citation Index (SSCI) journals covering the field has expanded from four in 2003 to around 16 in 2016. Other estimates are much greater depending on the definitions used.[1] Entrepreneurship and small business special interest groups (SIGs) are now part and parcel of most mainstream business and management conferences, including the Academy of Management, and there has been a burgeoning of specialist entrepreneurship-related conferences and workshops, such as the Research in Entrepreneurship and Small Business (RENT) and a variety of doctoral and post-doctoral activities ensuring sustainability.[2]

Whether we know more about the phenomena under study than we did decades ago remains debatable but we believe this is the case. Certainly we have witnessed the increasing number of publications in the form of books series and specialist and mainstream international journals, as well as growing levels of engagement of academics with practitioners and policy makers at national and supra-national levels (Blackburn & Schaper, 2012; OECD/European Union, 2015; Storey, 2014). With this expansion and legitimization has come a growing fragmentation of the field, or specialization in sub-fields, in deepening our knowledge and levels of theorizing. Hence, the field spans topics ranging from entrepreneurial characteristics to the entrepreneurial process and behavioral issues, social entrepreneurship, family business, the management and organization of small businesses, the significance of context and many more (see: Fayolle, Landström, Gartner, & Berglund, 2016a; Ferreira, Reis, & Miranda, 2015; Hsu, Wiklund, Anderson, & Coffey, 2016; Meyer,

Libaers, Thijs, Grant, Glänzel, & Debackere, 2014; Volery & Mazzarol, 2015; Hsu, Wiklund, Anderson, & Coffey, 2016; Welter & Gartner, 2016). In some instances, particularly when studying a new area, researchers continue to borrow and develop concepts and approaches from other disciplines whilst, in others, specific theories have emerged (e.g. Aldrich, 2012). Davidsson, for example, in his analysis of the field, reports its 'considerable growth in volume, quality, and theory-drivenness' (Davidsson, 2016: p. 17). Certainly, the field cannot be accused of being narrow, insular or experiencing ossification! We thus concur with Landström and colleagues (2016) that the field is highly heterogeneous and multidisciplinary and addresses the phenomena at different levels.

The goal of this *Handbook* is to take stock of past research in the broad field of entrepreneurship and small business as well as push the agendas forward. This should be of particular interest to postgraduate students, researchers, and public and private analysts. The timing of a handbook such as this is relevant, as entrepreneurship programs have grown significantly in the past decades and virtually every higher education institution in the world has entrepreneurship within their curriculum, in some shape or form, irrespective of socio-political-economic context (see Davey, Hannon, & Penaluna, 2016; Valerio, Parton, & Robb, 2014),[3] as well as discussion over the complexities of 'entrepreneurship education', both conceptually and in practice (Fayolle, Verzat, & Wapshott, 2016b; Neck & Greene, 2011), or its impact on entrepreneurship levels (e.g. Walter & Block, 2016). Early career researchers are often required to publish numerous journal articles in order to develop, establish, and maintain their academic standing. Researchers of entrepreneurship also increasingly come from different disciplines – including psychology, finance, marketing, sociology, engineering, medicine, anthropology, and other fields – and hence there is need to be knowledgeable of the history of the field, as well as have insight into

fruitful areas for further research. Combining past and existing research with future orientation particularly helps younger scholars to identify researchers with similar interests and supports them to find new interesting questions to be asked in order to secure the future of entrepreneurship studies. Moreover, public policy-focused organizations and trade associations have for some time now drawn upon entrepreneurship and small business researchers to independently and critically assess the impact of policy interventions, such as growth policies and taxation incentives, as well as analyze entrepreneurial activity levels and a growing list of other topics (see for example Acs, Åstebro, Audretsch, & Robinson, 2016; Audretsch, Grilo, & Thurik, 2007; Bennett, 2014; Curran, 2000; Storey, 2014). Thus, a handbook such as this is also an essential tool to assist a varied set of stakeholders.

This brings us to the title of this *Handbook*. Of course, one of the earliest divisions in the field was the conceptual separation of 'entrepreneurs' from 'small business', essentially based on the observation of the different motivations of the people establishing an enterprise (Carland, Hoy, Boulton, & Carland, 1984). 'Small business owners' were classified as those that start the enterprise as an extension of the personality of the founder and the activities of the enterprise are inextricably bound with family needs. On the other hand, the 'entrepreneur' was regarded as one who starts an enterprise for the purpose of profit, or a risk taker, and the owners and managers utilize strategic management techniques. Such a separation is furthered by the argument that the domain should set out its boundaries in order to develop its own concepts as well as achieve external recognition. In examining the field as a whole, however, many empirical studies of 'entrepreneurship' involve analyses of human endeavor within new, small, or independent enterprises (e.g. Scase & Goffee, 1981). Furthermore, even when 'entrepreneurship' is in the foreground of articles and books, when the empirics of their studies are examined in detail, the arguments relating to 'risk-taking' often appear to disappear into thin air.[4] Indeed, this unraveling of entrepreneurs from the small business remains one of the Gordian knots of the field of study. Thus, although we recognize the significance of entrepreneurship as a focus of research, in the sense of new venture formation and risk-taking, we also recognize the importance of established and small firms, as well as the new areas of intellectual curiosity in the wider field.

In developing this *Handbook*, it has become even more obvious that the landscape of research has widened and deepened to include new and distinctive areas, such as entrepreneurial learning (e.g. Leitch & Vollery, 2017) and critical perspectives (e.g. Essers, Dey, Tedmanson, & Verduyn, 2017; Fletcher & Seldon, 2016), as well as to drill down into existing ones, such as family business (e.g. Hsu et al., 2017; López-Fernández, Serrano-Bedia, & Pérez-Pérez, 2016; Short, Sharma, Lumpkin, & Pearson, 2016), finance (e.g. Roberts, 2015; Short, Ketchen, McKenny, Allison, & Ireland, 2017), psychology (Brännback & Carsrud, 2017) and entrepreneurial 'exit' (e.g. DeTienne & Wennberg, 2016). The literature has also seen the production of more nuanced accounts and the utilization of a range of methodologies as sub-fields of study have emerged (see for example Shepherd & Patzelt, 2017), building upon earlier approaches to research (Curran & Blackburn, 2000; Davidsson, 2004). Furthermore, critical perspectives to entrepreneurship and small business research are becoming increasingly visible in conferences and publications, suggesting that 'mainstream' research (whatever is meant by that) has not been able to capture the phenomenon of entrepreneurship sufficiently.

Hence, we choose to use the title *Small Business and Entrepreneurship* to signal that this *Handbook* seeks to contribute to the field broadly defined. This provides the advantage of allowing new perspectives in the field whilst also facilitating further in-depth analyses of more mature sub-fields.

Set against this fertile research context, working with leading authors in their subject areas, we have aimed to produce a series of chapters that contribute empirically, conceptually, and methodologically to the discussion in the field. Of course, no publication can be exhaustive and cover all the challenges of this widening field. However, the book is truly multi-disciplinary, not restricted to one perspective or level, and approaches entrepreneurship and small business from various angles, using a variety of methodological stances, levels of analyses, and contexts. Classifying the field and its sub-fields is something of a challenge but we have sought to group the chapters into what we regard as having common areas of interest. Even so, we would not regard these sections as hermetically sealed from each other. Collectively, however, the chapters seek to provide a state-of-the-art on specific topics, established and new, and provide suggestions and platforms for future research.

CHAPTER OVERVIEWS

The book is divided into four parts.

Part I discusses issues related to *people and entrepreneurial processes*, focusing on how people, either as individuals or in groups, and their activities shape the nature of entrepreneurship activities in a variety of different ways.

Part II covers issues related to *entrepreneurship strategy, development, and organization,* providing contributions on the genesis of business development and the various ways in which small firms develop and the different ways in which entrepreneurship manifests itself in terms of organizational forms.

Part III focuses on the broader *entrepreneurial milieu* in which firms are embedded, entailing issues with respect to government, internationalization, and education.

Part IV focuses on issues related to *research methodologies* and trends in entrepreneurship research.

Part I: People and Entrepreneurial Processes

In Chapter 2, Leitch and Harrison provide a comprehensive review of research on entrepreneurial leadership. They identify five areas of concern, which in turn imply paths for further improvement: the incomplete ways in which entrepreneurial leadership has been informed by theories from either entrepreneurship or leadership; the lack of an overarching theory of the entrepreneurial leadership concept; the multitude of definitions; shortcomings in the measurement tools that have been used to assess the entrepreneurial leadership concept; and the limited understanding of how entrepreneurial leadership capability can be developed and enhanced. They suggest that entrepreneurship scholars with an interest in leadership could draw from recent developments in the field of leadership in order to generate expanded insights into the concept, for example by applying critical post-heroic perspectives and conceptualizing entrepreneurial leadership as a socially constructed and contested construct.

In Chapter 3, Vahidnia, Chen, Mitchell, and Mitchell focus on the potential dynamism of entrepreneurial action as far as it relates to and can be informed by insights offered by entrepreneurial cognition research. They argue that fixed conceptualizations hinder theory development and research on entrepreneurial action. They suggest how a socially situated cognition perspective can be used to help research on entrepreneurial action move beyond fixed conceptualizations-based explanations and better capture the dynamism associated with entrepreneurial action. They conclude with a discussion of methodological approaches that can be used in future research.

In Chapter 4, Nyström provides an extensive literature review on the pre- and post-entrepreneurship labor mobility of both entrepreneurs and employees in entrepreneurial firms. In terms of the labor mobility of entrepreneurs, she discusses research on individual characteristics and how these characteristics influence the performance of the entrepreneur and firm. She also highlights that relatively little is known about the post-entrepreneurship employment activity of entrepreneurs and how their previous experiences might have an impact on their future labor market careers. In terms of the labor mobility of employees in entrepreneurial firms, the author discusses recent literature on the individual characteristics of these employees, and points to the need for further examinations on how employment with an entrepreneurial firm is valued in the labor market, as well as what the future labor market performance might be of individuals who have been displaced from an entrepreneurial firm.

In Chapter 5, McAdam and Soetanto provide an in-depth discussion of the role of networks in the entrepreneurial process. They discuss the theoretical roots of the concept of entrepreneurial networks and the many benefits that accrue from network access, yet they also discuss the disadvantages or dark sides of networking. They offer several future research directions that challenge critical assumptions in extant network research. For example, they call for more research on the dynamic nature of networks, and the contextual influences on network development across different categories of entrepreneurs. They conclude with several case studies that illustrate how entrepreneurs can modify their network relationships during the entrepreneurial process.

In Chapter 6, Drinkwater examines the highly topical subject of the relationship between entrepreneurship and migration by first discussing the different ways in which these terms have typically been measured in the literature. He then provides evidence on the role of migration in entrepreneurship, using recent data for the UK, and provides a comprehensive discussion of how entrepreneurship in different groups of migrants might be affected by different factors. He concludes with various policy implications and recommendations for future research.

In Chapter 7, van Helvert and Nordqvist discuss entrepreneurship from a family business perspective and explain how the family business context impacts entrepreneurial activity. They discuss various relevant features of family business and how they connect to entrepreneurship. They provide particular attention to factors such as socio-emotional wealth, governance, values, organizational identity, trust, and conflict, which are each relevant to entrepreneurial activity in family businesses. They also distinguish the dynamics of family business from those of their non-family counterparts. They conclude the chapter by proposing various avenues of future inquiry on family business in relation to entrepreneurship.

In Chapter 8, Haugh, Lyon, and Doherty provide a discussion of the phenomenon of social entrepreneurship, with a particular focus on the relationship between social value creation and opportunity identification and exploitation. They seek to accomplish three objectives with their chapter. First, they review the rise to prominence of social entrepreneurship and the associated definitional and contextual debates. Second, they summarize the principal research findings with respect to social value creation and opportunity identification and exploitation. Third, they identify several critical topics that can advance knowledge and theory development in the area of social entrepreneurship.

Part II: Entrepreneurship and Small Business Management and Organization

In Chapter 9, Lechner and Pervaiz provide an in-depth discussion of the literature at the nexus between entrepreneurship and strategy. They draw from the notions of liability of newness and smallness to define entrepreneurial strategy and discuss the transferability of this concept to different contexts. They also discuss the relationship between entrepreneurial strategy and strategic entrepreneurship, and propose that cross-fertilization between the two concepts provides a fruitful avenue for future research. They further relate this discussion to concepts such as corporate entrepreneurship, corporate venturing, entrepreneurial orientation, and new venture strategy.

In Chapter 10, Eller and Gielnik provide an overview of different perspectives that have been used to explain new venture creation, namely, the psychological, team, resource, and institutional perspectives. They suggest that a more complete understanding of new venture creation requires an integrative model that combines these different perspectives into one single theoretical framework, and they underscore the central role of entrepreneurial action in this framework. They argue that the predictive value of empirical studies on new business creation can be significantly enhanced by combining theories that operate at different levels of analysis.

In Chapter 11, Zupic and Giudici provide a state-of-the-art literature review on new venture growth, and categorize this research into three topics: high-growth firms, antecedents of firm growth, and the growth process. They provide suggestions for how research on growth can move forward, including a reorientation from a focus on 'changes in amounts' to the processes underpinning firm growth, a combination of quantitative and qualitative studies, the leveraging of 'big data', and a clearer explanation of how various stakeholders can benefit from growth research.

In Chapter 12, Adomako and Mole provide complementary insights on the study of business growth. They discuss Penrose's view of firm growth, and highlight the different ways in which business growth has been measured, distinguishing between absolute and relative changes, and viewing growth as a process. They discuss different theories of business growth, including integrated models that explain the factors that drive business growth, as well as stage models that view business growth as a series of phases that a firm passes through during its life-cycle. They then elaborate on the different modes of business growth, as well as its drivers and constraints. They conclude by pointing out different areas of harmony and contention in the literature, from which they suggest several opportunities for future research.

In Chapter 13, Morris, Santos, Pryor, and Neumeyer review and critique the extant literature on entrepreneurial exit. They discuss the various definitions and conceptualizations of exit and associated constructs, and the major theories that are helpful in framing research on entrepreneurial exit. They identify key findings regarding the antecedents, processes, and outcomes surrounding an exit, and pinpoint several challenges in advancing our understanding of the exit phenomenon. The chapter concludes with a discussion of the priorities for ongoing research in the area of entrepreneurial exit.

In Chapter 14, Åmo and Kolvereid provide an extensive review of literature on corporate entrepreneurship, defined as entrepreneurship within established organizations. They develop a comprehensive model of corporate entrepreneurship, outlining different processes (strategic entrepreneurship, corporate entrepreneurship), antecedents (entrepreneurial orientation and entrepreneurial insight), context factors (managerial, organizational, and environmental) and outcomes (innovation, performance). They propose that future research in the realm of corporate entrepreneurship should be specific about the phenomena that are studied, provide precise definitions of core concepts, state its assumptions explicitly, and be clear about research context in order to compare research findings across studies.

In Chapter 15, Freel provides a critical review of literature on innovation in the context of SMEs. He argues that much of the research on the innovation in and by small firms has suffered from using a somewhat narrow perspective of innovation, by focusing on technology changes and applying rather static approaches. He argues, for example, that insufficient attention has been devoted to the importance of the individual entrepreneur and manager in the processes of small-firm innovation. He proposes that future research should acknowledge the ubiquity of innovation in small firms, put more emphasis on resource construction and deployment instead of resource stocks, and recognize the importance of organizational and social contexts in the process and outcomes of small-firm innovation.

In Chapter 16, Jones, Morrish, Deacon, and Miles provide a comprehensive overview of extant literature on the interface between marketing and entrepreneurship, with a focus on marketing in new or small firms. They discuss several relevant topics such as small firm marketing, entrepreneurial marketing orientation, entrepreneurial networks, and internationalization. They also highlight several areas of future research in the realm of entrepreneurial marketing: the role of entrepreneurial networks in internationalization, the application of entrepreneurial marketing concepts to emerging markets, and the relevance of entrepreneurial marketing for social entrepreneurship. They conclude by pinpointing different research opportunities with respect to entrepreneurial research methods and designs.

In Chapter 17, Mason uses the funding escalator as the binding framework to provide a comprehensive review of research on the financing of entrepreneurial ventures. He first discusses the main sources of finance used by entrepreneurial firms as they progress through different stages of development, and explains the role of government intervention in filling critical gaps in the funding escalator. He then elaborates on some of the fundamental changes in the practice of entrepreneurial finance that were caused by the dot.com crash and the 2008 global financial crisis. He argues that scholars must address current developments in the market for entrepreneurial finance, such as crowd-funding and business angel groups, in order to be relevant and impactful.

In Chapter 18, Cowling and Matthews provide an in-depth overview of research on the internal financing context for SMEs. They discuss how and why internal financial management is critical to the success and survival of smaller businesses, and emphasize the role and nature of SME financial management practice. They discuss why entrepreneurs often have a preference for internal over external funds. They point hereby to pecuniary factors such as lack of collateral and the relative price differential between internal and external funds, as well as to non-pecuniary factors such as the desire to maintain control and independence. They emphasize the need to investigate in more detail how and why smaller firms are capable, or incapable, of financing their daily operations, in order to fully understand their situation when they present themselves to external financiers.

Part III: Entrepreneurial Milieu

In Chapter 19, Hoffmann and Storey examine the key features of entrepreneurship policy and the specific role of business advice. They argue that the provision of publicly funded business advice to new and small firms is best theorized in a principal–agent framework in which the contract between the principal (central government) and the agent (the advice deliverer) is critical. The authors use the case of Denmark, and specifically Growth Houses, to illustrate this theoretical backdrop and to illustrate the important role played by an *evolving* policy context, whereby new information and changed circumstances lead to revisions of the principal–agent contract. They conclude with various implications for providers of other comparable policies.

In Chapter 20, Kitching discusses the effects of government regulation on entrepreneurship. He argues that government regulation should not merely be treated as a burden that imposes compliance cost or constraints on entrepreneurial action and performance. He demonstrates some of the conceptual and analytical limitations arising from using survey data to investigate *how* regulation impacts entrepreneurial action at the level of the firm. He discusses the usefulness of applying institutionalist approaches to the study of regulation, and presents an analytical framework on how regulation shapes, but does not determine, entrepreneurial action at the micro level. He provides various methodological considerations and concludes with different implications for researchers, theory development, and policy.

In Chapter 21, Stam and Spigel provide a critical review of the emerging literature on entrepreneurial ecosystems, conceptualized as a set of interdependent actors and factors that might be coordinated in such a way that they enable productive entrepreneurship within a particular territory. They discuss the relationships between ecosystems and relevant concepts such as industrial districts, clusters, and innovation systems. They present an integrative model that connects the functional attributes of entrepreneurial ecosystems with entrepreneurial outputs and welfare outcomes, and conclude by offering several implications for research and policy.

In Chapter 22, Wang and Zhao address the challenges of investigating corporate social responsibility, entrepreneurship, and small firms. They find that entrepreneurs' ethical behavior, social entrepreneurship practice, and sustainability face new challenges and as such require appropriate responses. They argue that new conceptual frameworks are needed if CSR is to be understood and developed in the field.

In Chapter 23, Nummela highlights the specific features of international entrepreneurship research. She identifies various areas that can serve as a bridge for scholars interested in advancing entrepreneurship, international business, and international entrepreneurship research. She emphasizes the need to account for the constant flux of temporal and spatial contexts when studying the phenomenon of international entrepreneurship, as well as the need to investigate the local roots and networks of entrepreneurs. She argues that the research fields of entrepreneurship and international business both offer opportunities for developing a deeper theoretical understanding of the mechanisms of how and why international ventures grow or fail, and she calls for an important role of international entrepreneurship scholars in this regard.

In Chapter 24, Almobaireek, Alshumaimeri, and Manolova explore the external and internal growth challenges of new and small ventures in the context of emerging economies. They provide a review of the literature on new and small business growth in emerging economies, and complement this review with illustrative evidence from field work and a large-scale nationally representative study on the state of small business in Saudi Arabia. The evidence of this study shows that the association between external challenges and growth in emerging economies is stronger in early stages of small firm development, while the association between internal challenges and growth is stronger in later stages. They conclude their chapter by offering various suggestions for future research and discussing implications for public policy and managerial practice in the emerging market context.

In Chapter 25, Pittaway, Huxtable-Thomas, and Hannon summarize recent studies on entrepreneurial learning in order to highlight their implications for the design of educational programs. They summarize key concepts and empirical contributions, with a particular focus on expanding the understanding of 'situated' social and contextual learning. They highlight critical concepts such as dynamic temporal phases, forms and characteristics of learning, and they lay out the underlying principles of each concept. They then present various conceptual and empirical contributions

to the topic of entrepreneurial learning. They conclude by highlighting the implications of current thinking on the design of development programs for entrepreneurs, and offer insights into future developments and lines of inquiry in entrepreneurial learning.

In Chapter 26, Cooney discusses the use of case studies in entrepreneurship education, and the benefits of writing and teaching case studies. He explains the background to the case study approach and highlights the benefits that such a teaching approach can offer to both students and educators. He also explores how case studies can be used most effectively in the classroom, and what the challenges are for instructors who design and write their own cases. He concludes by discussing the current and future position of the case study approach as a form of pedagogy.

In Chapter 27, Hytti and Koskinen discuss how enterprise education pedagogy can be implemented in compulsory education and how it can positively affect students' school motivation and learning. They expand the applicability of entrepreneurship education, by emphasizing entrepreneurship pedagogy as a way forward from viewing entrepreneurship education merely as content that is related to new venture creation. Based on an account of one reform school that followed the principles of enterprise education pedagogy, the authors provide concrete examples of how to implement such pedagogy in an extreme classroom context. They suggest that the development of self-regulation skills is an appropriate new metric (i.e. learning outcome) for enterprise education pedagogy and related assessments. They conclude by discussing the opportunities and challenges for teachers who experiment with entrepreneurial teaching methods.

Part IV: Researching Small Business and Entrepreneurship

In Chapter 28, McKenny, Zachary, Short, and Ketchen discuss the challenge of assessing causality in entrepreneurship research. They argue that this challenge is informed by the complexity of entrepreneurial phenomena, as well as by research design issues with respect to incomplete control over alternative explanations. They also posit that relatively little is known of how well entrepreneurship scholarship is performing in terms of methodological decisions that impact the ability to make causal claims. To illustrate their arguments, they focus on the causal relationship between corporate entrepreneurship and firm performance, and they discuss this relationship based on three criteria: the independent and dependent variables must co-vary, the independent variable must temporally precede the dependent variable, and alternative explanations must be eliminated. Based on their discussion of numerous articles on corporate entrepreneurship, they provide an interesting set of guidelines for how future entrepreneurship studies can make a stronger case for the presence of causality.

In Chapter 29 Kovalainen uses the term 'qualitative research strategy' as an umbrella concept that connects different qualitative methods. She discusses the different meanings given to qualitative research, the different methods used, and the overall content with a focus on entrepreneurship studies. She points out the strengths and pitfalls in using a qualitative research strategy, particularly in relation to issues in entrepreneurship. She concludes the chapter by providing various insights into future methods in entrepreneurship research, with a particular focus on the promise of qualitative research in entrepreneurship studies.

In Chapter 30, Díaz-García provides a critical examination of the main methodological approaches that have been used in studies of female entrepreneurship. She first discusses the dominant epistemological and ontological approaches that have been used in the study of gender in entrepreneurship. She then explains the benefits that can be derived from feminist and sociological approaches. Based on this analysis, she provides various suggestions for fruitful future research.

In Chapter 31, Johannisson discusses the possibility of a paradigm shift in entrepreneurship research. He identifies three critical issues that suggest the need for changing our understanding and modes of researching entrepreneurship: entrepreneuring is not about instigating change but temporarily arresting it; entrepreneuring is a processual phenomenon that crosses boundaries in time and space; and entrepreneuring is a multi-colored science. The author then reports a bibliometric analysis that maps how entrepreneurship research presents itself in relation to management studies, a field that is usually considered to embrace entrepreneurship. He considers entrepreneurship research as an entrepreneurial practice and argues that such enactive research is an appropriate methodology to capture the notion of entrepreneurship. He further argues that the entrepreneurship research community can strengthen its identity by promoting 'originality' as another dimension of quality in research, besides the established two dimensions of rigor and relevance.

In Chapter 32, Poutanen introduces certain critical perspectives in entrepreneurship research in relation to what is called 'mainstream' entrepreneurship research, while also acknowledging the blurring and constantly moving boundaries of 'mainstream' and 'non-mainstream' research. He discusses some methodological criticisms and flaws in entrepreneurship studies as well as the narrow ideology of entrepreneurialism. The author presents the 'avant-garde' of critical entrepreneurship research, which builds on complex ontological theories of processualist reality and unties 'entrepreneurship' from its narrow economy- and business-centered meanings. He also argues that the bold reconceptualization of 'entrepreneurship' in relation to 'creativity', for example, could offer opportunities for fruitful dialogue between the avant-gardists and more conventionally oriented researchers of entrepreneurship.

Notes

1 Estimates can vary. For example, Harzing has 13 journals listed with 'Entrepreneurship': http://www.harzing.com/download/jql_subject.pdf, whilst Google Scholar lists 20: https://scholar.google.co.uk/citations?view_op=top_venues&hl=en&vq=bus_entrepreneurshipinnovation, and in his analysis of core publications and related fields, Katz lists up to 129 journals: https://www.slu.edu/eweb/connect/for-faculty/infrastructure/core-publications-in-entrepreneurship-and-related-fields#RefereedScholarlyJournals.

2 Assessments of the quality of research in higher educational institutions, such as the UK HEFCE's Research Excellence Framework, also report on the growing quality and volume of work in the field (HEFCE, 2015).

3 Estimates of the number of entrepreneurship programs or courses in universities worldwide prove difficult to find because of the scale of the task this would involve and the spread of courses beyond business schools into other disciplines such as engineering and the arts (see for example Honig & Martin, 2014). However, based on our gleaning of many national higher education situations, we would stand by our contention that most universities have embraced some form of program.

4 One argument may be that 'entrepreneurship', because of its overtones of risk-taking and dynamism, may be a more attractive term to use than 'small business', with its potential image of 'mom and pop' or less dynamic economic entities.

REFERENCES

Acs, Z., Åstebro, T., Audretsch, D., and Robinson, D. T. (2016). Public policy to promote entrepreneurship: A call to arms. *Small Business Economics*, 47(1), 35–51.

Aldrich, H. E. (2012). The emergence of entrepreneurship as an academic field: A personal essay on institutional entrepreneurship. *Research Policy*, 41(7), 1240–1248.

Audretsch, D. B., Grilo, I., and Thurik, A. R. (Eds) (2007). *Handbook of research on entrepreneurship policy*. Edward Elgar, Cheltenham.

Bennett, R. J. (2014). *Entrepreneurship, small business and public policy*. Routledge, London and New York.

Blackburn, R. A., and Schaper, M. T. (Eds) (2012). *Government, SMEs and entrepreneurship development. Policy, practice and challenges*. Gower Publishing, Oxford.

Brännback, M., and Carsrud, A. L. (Eds) (2017). *Revisiting the entrepreneurial mind: Inside the black box: An expanded edition*. Springer, Cham, Switzerland.

Carland, J. W., Hoy, F., Boulton, W. R., and Carland, J. A. C. (1984). Differentiating entrepreneurs from small business owners: A conceptualization. *Academy of Management Review*, 9(2), 354–359.

Carlsson, B., Braunerhjelm, P., McKelvey, M., Olofsson, C., Persson, L., and Ylinenpää, H. (2013). The evolving domain of entrepreneurship research. *Small Business Economics*, 41(4), 913–930.

Curran, J. (2000). What is small business policy in the UK for? Evaluation and assessing small business policies. *International Small Business Journal*, 18(3), 36–50.

Curran, J., and Blackburn, R. (2000). *Researching the small enterprise*. Sage, London.

Davey, T., Hannon, P., and Penaluna, A. (2016). Entrepreneurship education and the role of universities in entrepreneurship: Introduction to the special issue. *Industry and Higher Education*, 30(3), 171–182.

Davidsson, P. (2004). *Researching entrepreneurship*. Springer, New York.

Davidsson, P. (2016). The field of entrepreneurship research: Some significant developments. In Bögenhold, D., Bonnet, J., Dejardin, M., and Garcia Perez de Lema, D. (Eds) *Contemporary entrepreneurship: Multidisciplinary perspectives on innovation and growth*. Springer, Cham, Switzerland, 17–28.

DeTienne, D., and Wennberg, K. (2016). Studying exit from entrepreneurship: New directions and insights. *International Small Business Journal*, 34(2), 151–156.

Essers, C., Dey, P., Tedmanson, D., and Verduyn, K. (Eds) (2017). *Critical perspectives on entrepreneurship: Challenging dominant discourses*. Routledge, London and New York.

Fayolle, A. (Ed.) (2014). *Handbook of research on small business and entrepreneurship*. Edward Elgar, Cheltenham.

Fayolle, A., Landström, H., Gartner, W. B., and Berglund, K. (2016a). The institutionalization of entrepreneurship: Questioning the status quo and re-gaining hope for entrepreneurship research. *Entrepreneurship & Regional Development*, 28(7–8), 477–486.

Fayolle, A., Verzat, C., and Wapshott, R. (2016b). In quest of legitimacy: The theoretical and methodological foundations of entrepreneurship education research. *International Small Business Journal*, 34(7), 895–904.

Ferreira, M. P., Reis, N. R., and Miranda, R. (2015). Thirty years of entrepreneurship research published in top journals: Analysis of citations, co-citations and themes. *Journal of Global Entrepreneurship Research*, 5(17), 1–22.

Fletcher, D., and Seldon, P. (2016). A critical review of critical perspectives in entrepreneurship research. In Landström, H., Parhankangas, A., Fayolle, A., and Riot, P. (Eds). *Challenging Entrepreneurship Research*. Routledge, London 131–154.

HEFCE (2015). Research Excellence Framework 2014: Overview Report by Main Panel C and Sub-panels 16 to 26, UOA 19, pp 53–69. http://www.ref.ac.uk/media/ref/content/expanel/member/Main%20Panel%20C%20overview%20report.pdf

Honig, B., and Martin, B. (2014). Entrepreneurship education. In Fayolle, A. (Ed.). *Handbook of research on small business and entrepreneurship*. Edward Elgar, Cheltenham, pp.127–146.

Hsu, D. K., Wiklund, J., Anderson, S. E., and Coffey, B. S. (2016). Entrepreneurial exit intentions and the business-family interface. *Journal of Business Venturing*, 31(6), 613–627.

Landström, H., Parhankangas, A., Fayolle, A., and Riot, P. (Eds) (2016). *Challenging entrepreneurship research*. Routledge, London and New York.

Leitch, C., and Vollery, T. (2017). Entrepreneurial leadership: Insights and directions. *International Small Business Journal*, 35(2), 147–156.

López-Fernández, M. C., Serrano-Bedia, A. M., and Pérez-Pérez, M. (2016). Entrepreneurship and family firm research: A bibliometric analysis of an emerging field. *Journal of Small Business Management*, 54(2), 622–639.

Meyer, M., Libaers, D., Thijs, B., Grant, K., Glänzel, W., and Debackere, K. (2014). Origin and emergence of entrepreneurship as a research field. *Scientometrics*, 98(1), 473–485.

Neck, H. M., and Greene, P. G. (2011). Entrepreneurship education: Known worlds and new frontiers. *Journal of Small Business Management*, 49(1), 55–70.

OECD/European Union (2015). *The Missing Entrepreneurs: Policies for self-employment and entrepreneurship*. Organisation for Economic Co-operation and Development Publishing, Paris.

Roberts, R. (2015). *Finance for small and entrepreneurial business*. Routledge, London and New York.

Scase, R., and Goffee, R. (1981). *The real world of the small business owner*. Croom Helm, London.

Shane, S., and Venkataraman, S. (2000). The promise of entrepreneurship as a field of research. *Academy of Management Review*, 25(1), 217–226.

Shepherd, D. A., and Patzelt, H. (2017). *Trailblazing in entrepreneurship*. Springer International Publishing, Cham, Switzerland.

Short, J. C., Ketchen, D. J., McKenny, A. F., Allison, T. H., and Ireland, R. D. (2017). Research on crowdfunding: Reviewing the (very recent) past and celebrating the present. *Entrepreneurship Theory and Practice*, 41(2), 149–160.

Short, J. C., Sharma, P., Lumpkin, G. T., and Pearson, A. W. (2016). 'Oh, the places we'll go!' Reviewing past, present, and future possibilities in family business research. *Family Business Review*, 29(1), 11–16.

Storey, D. J. (2014). Understanding the small business sector: Reflections and confessions. In Braunerhjelm, P. (Ed.) *20 years of entrepreneurship research – from small business dynamics to entrepreneurial growth and societal prosperity*. Swedish Entrepreneurship Forum, pp. 21–33.

Valerio, A., Parton, B., and Robb, A. (2014). *Entrepreneurship education and training programs around the world: Dimensions for success*. World Bank Publications, Washington DC.

Volery, T., and Mazzarol, T. (2015). The evolution of the small business and entrepreneurship field: A bibliometric investigation of articles published in the International Small Business Journal. *International Small Business Journal*, 33(4), 374–396.

Walter, S. G., and Block, J. H. (2016). Outcomes of entrepreneurship education: An institutional perspective. *Journal of Business Venturing*, 31(2), 216–233.

Welter, F., and Gartner, W. B. (Eds) (2016). *A research agenda for entrepreneurship and context*. Edward Elgar, Cheltenham, Northampton, MA.

PART I

People and Entrepreneurial Processes

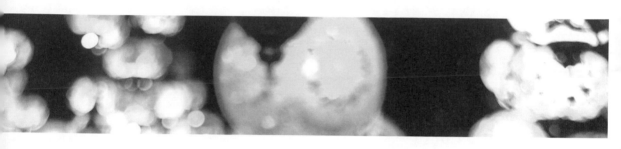

2

Entrepreneurial Leadership: A Critical Review and Research Agenda

Claire M. Leitch and Richard T. Harrison

INTRODUCTION

This chapter presents an overview of entrepreneurial leadership and suggests potential avenues for future research. While there may be no agreement as to what 'leadership' is, despite over fifty years of quantitative and qualitative research, there is a widespread consensus that it is important and that it is situational. Most leadership research has been conducted in corporate settings, and there has been much less attention given to issues of leadership and leadership development in the context of entrepreneurial and small and medium-sized enterprises (SMEs), high-tech settings or incubators. Accordingly, leadership in this context needs to be conceptualised differently from the corporate one, especially given the importance of entrepreneurship in economic development and restructuring.

We argue that it is important to understand more fully leadership in this setting for two interrelated reasons. First, the leadership capability of the founder/entrepreneur can have a significant impact on the success or failure of their firm (Jensen & Luthans, 2006; Leitch, McMullan & Harrison, 2013; Thorpe, Cope, Ram & Pedler, 2009). The pronounced imprinting effect of leaders of entrepreneurial ventures (Eisenhardt & Schoonhoven, 1990) has implications for our understanding of new venture viability and growth (Koryak, Mole, Lockett, Hayton, Ucbasaran & Hodgkinson, 2015). The higher likely impact of the entrepreneurial leader in their enactment of leadership is matched by the potentially greater challenges in developing appropriate and effective leadership capabilities and skills. For instance, the indistinct separation between leadership and managerial responsibilities and the tendency towards highly organic, non-formalised simple structures can result in less well-developed norms to guide appropriate behaviour (Ensley, Pearce & Hmieleski, 2006; Koryak et al., 2015). This can result in the potential dominance of an individual who themselves might be associated with a lack of flexibility, engagement, openness and responsiveness.

Second, small firms are not simply scaled-down versions of larger firms (Gibb, 2005). They are distinctive in terms of ambiguity, risk, uncertainty, innovation, organisational size and newness (Autio, 2013; Chen, 2007; Surie & Ashley, 2008) and are generally more sensitive than larger firms to external contexts, especially environmental dynamism and volatility. As such, the entrepreneurial setting places different demands on leaders. This is not a recent observation, as over twenty years ago Grant (1992) proposed what he called the 'entrepreneurial leadership' paradigm. Drawing on Burns's (1978) ideas of transformational leadership, he used the term 'entrepreneurial' to emphasise a particular approach to leadership in an entrepreneurial setting, thus introducing a new area of research.

The chapter is structured as follows: first, we provide an overview of current thinking on entrepreneurial leadership, identifying its limitations. Specifically, there are five areas of concern: first, the degree to which entrepreneurial leadership has been, or should be, shaped by theories and insights from either entrepreneurship or leadership; second, the absence of an overarching theory of the concept; third, the lack of definitional consensus; fourth, a deficiency in measurement tools to assess it; and fifth, little understanding of how entrepreneurial leadership capability might be developed and enhanced.

Second, drawing on the literature we present and discuss the key findings and lessons from four recent articles that have been chosen because they specifically address one or more of the key limitations highlighted above. With reference to the first article by Renko, El Tarabishy, Carsrud and Brännback (2015) we review the challenge of defining and measuring entrepreneurial leadership, distinguishing between approaches that are contextually oriented (focused on the characteristics of an entrepreneurial SME such as size, simplicity of organisational structures and environmental uncertainty) and content-oriented (focused on the nature and practice of leadership of entrepreneurial SMEs). We build on this, using Roomi and Harrison's (2011) paper, to explore the pedagogical challenge of developing and delivering effective entrepreneurial leadership education and development. In particular, we highlight the difference between leader development, which focuses on the de-contextualised development of the individual leader, and leadership development, which considers the situational development of the role. Drawing on an extended longitudinal study by Leitch et al. (2013) we illustrate the process of leadership development and emphasise the importance of human, social and institutional capital in developing entrepreneurial leadership among leaders of entrepreneurial small firms. Finally, we present Harrison, Leitch and McAdam's (2015) recent paper, which considered the role of gender in entrepreneurial leadership, to address concerns about the dominance of a male normative bias in both the entrepreneurship and leadership literatures.

In developing the argument of this chapter we take the view that in moving forward entrepreneurship scholars should take account of recent developments in the field of leadership, not least to avoid making the same assumptions and getting stuck in the same intellectual cul-de-sacs. In so doing, we argue that the concept of 'entrepreneurial leadership' exists at the interface of the two disciplines and that research into it can draw usefully on both. Thus, our aim in this chapter is to add to existing understandings by drawing on more recent developments in leadership including critical, post-heroic perspectives and emotional labour to develop the concept of entrepreneurial leadership more fully. Specifically our contribution is to reflect on the way forward for scholars interested in entrepreneurial leadership to present a research agenda which pays particular reference to its nature, role and development in a number of domains including family businesses and different cultural contexts.

OVERVIEW – CURRENT THINKING ON ENTREPRENEURIAL LEADERSHIP

In this section we present an overview of the concept of entrepreneurial leadership and critically reflect on three different perspectives evident in the literature. The differences between the first two perspectives are subtle but nevertheless important. Deriving mainly from the entrepreneurship literature, the first debate focuses on the entrepreneur as a leader and the second revolves around discussions about leaders having an entrepreneurial mindset. The third reflects the view that the concept sits at the intersection of both domains and draws on the similarities evident in debates and discussions about entrepreneurs and leaders.

The Rise of Entrepreneurial Leadership

Entrepreneurial leadership is ostensibly a 'new paradigm' (Fernald, Solomon & El Tarabisby, 2005; Lloyd, George & Ayman, 2005), emerging as an area of study to explore the common themes and linkages between entrepreneurship and leadership. The similarities between the two seem to be clear. In popular discourse, though perhaps less frequently in academia, both leaders in general and entrepreneurial leaders in particular tend to be presented in romantic terms as heroic, individual (generally white, male) change agents. Further, the processes of entrepreneurship and leadership are frequently heralded as major sources of competitive advantage and crucial for economic success, especially in VUCA (volatile, uncertain, complex, ambiguous) environments (Horney, Pasmore & O'Shea, 2010; Petrie, 2011). Parallels between the two domains include an early focus on traits and personality attributes to distinguish between who an entrepreneur or leader is and who is not and an interest in vision, influence, teams and strategy to achieve desired outcomes (Harrison & Leitch, 1994). Even though the

fields have followed similar evolutionary paths, debates in leadership, the more mature field, chronologically precede those in entrepreneurship (Perren & Burgoyne, 2003), prompting entrepreneurship scholars in particular to recognise the mutual benefits to be gained from amalgamating the two literatures: 'entrepreneurship could stand to gain from closer integration with leadership research' (Antonakis & Autio, 2007, p. 203). However, despite the apparent commonality and the potential benefits of a closer relationship the construct of 'entrepreneurial leader' remains contested.

The recent expansion of literature in this area is diffuse and has not been matched with the development of appropriate theoretical frameworks, conceptual analysis and theory building. Given the relative youth of the construct it is perhaps inevitable that conceptualisations of it are embryonic. Five main features characterise the literature. First, there is a lack of agreement on its boundaries: to what extent has the construct of entrepreneurial leadership drawn from either field or both? Second, it is atheoretical, and even though models and concepts from the entrepreneurship and leadership literatures have been drawn on they are not used to present a theory of entrepreneurial leadership (Leitch et al., 2013). Third, it lacks a formally agreed definition; the diversity of work has resulted in a plethora from which to choose (Harrison et al., 2015; Renko et al., 2015), as different researchers seek to establish the focus of their work. Fourth, few appropriate tools to assess its characteristics have been developed. Fifth, as a result of the diversity in understandings of entrepreneurial leadership there is a scarcity of knowledge about how it might be developed.

As Table 2.1 demonstrates the term tends to be employed by entrepreneurship scholars who have explored its application mainly in entrepreneurial and corporate settings. Less frequently the enactment of entrepreneurial leadership has been investigated in other contexts such as family businesses and

Table 2.1   Entrepreneurial leadership: focus of research

Focus of Research	Writers
The advocacy of an 'entrepreneurial' approach to leadership and appropriate in entrepreneurial or corporate organisations irrespective of size.	Renko et al., 2015; Greenberg et al., 2013; Ripoll et al., 2010; Surie and Ashley, 2008; Darling et al., 2007; Kuratko, 2007; Cohen, 2004; Gupta et al., 2004; Ireland et al., 2003; Nicholson, 1998; Swiercz and Lydon, 2002
Challenges and implications of entrepreneurial leadership in smaller, entrepreneurial companies.	Leitch et al., 2013; Wang et al., 2012; Kempster and Cope, 2010; Jones and Crompton, 2009; Chen, 2007; Jensen and Luthans, 2006; Ensley et al., 2006; Fernald Jr. et al., 2005; Koryak et al., 2015; Harrison et al., 2015
Identification of entrepreneurial leadership competencies and capabilities and the development of models and frameworks to cultivate and enhance these at undergraduate and postgraduate level.	Bagheri and Pihie, 2011, 2012; Roomi and Harrison, 2011; Buller and Finkle, 2013
The nature and process of entrepreneurial leadership in family firms to capitalise on entrepreneurial opportunities to grow family businesses.	Ng and Thorpe, 2010; Kansikas et al., 2012
The enactment of entrepreneurial leadership in the public sector as part of a modernising government agenda.	Currie et al., 2008; Young, 1991

political institutions. Most of the research can be divided into two main streams. In the first, the focus is on the leadership traits and styles of senior executives in entrepreneurial companies or on the advocacy of 'an entrepreneurial' approach to leadership more generally, and organisational scale is not specifically addressed. In the second, the challenges and implications of entrepreneurial leadership in the smaller entrepreneurial company are explicitly considered. A smaller body of work has sought to identify particular entrepreneurial leadership competencies and capabilities and propose models and frameworks to cultivate and enhance these amongst students and potential entrepreneurs.

The Relationship Between Entrepreneurship and Leadership

The relationship between entrepreneurship and leadership is concerned with establishing the parameters of the construct, resulting from the extent to which the terms 'entrepreneurship' or 'leadership' are privileged by the researcher and thus foregrounded. Three main questions can be asked (Table 2.2): first,

'is entrepreneurial leadership a particular style of leadership?'; second, 'does entrepreneurial leadership require specific entrepreneurial characteristics?'; and third, 'is entrepreneurial leadership an independent construct shaped by debates in both disciplines?'. The first two perspectives tend towards absolutism, while the third sits at the nexus of the fields of entrepreneurship and leadership. What is striking about the entrepreneurial leadership literature is that in practice the discussion is of the leader rather than of leadership. This raises two questions: first, are the terms 'entrepreneur' and 'leader' synonymous?; and second, is the study of leadership satisfactorily achieved through the study of leaders only? On the first of these the entrepreneurship literature still for the most part equates the two, and as such is behind the debate in leadership studies around alternative perspectives including distributed leadership (Thorpe, Gold & Lawler, 2011) and followership (Collinson, 2006; Crossman & Crossman, 2011). On the second the pre-eminent concern with the leader privileges the individual over context and reinforces, rather than challenges, heroic models of leadership (Collinson, 2011, 2014).

Table 2.2   Entrepreneurial leadership: establishing the boundaries

Perspective	As a type of leadership	As a mindset	At the interface
Key Features	Entrepreneurs are leaders by virtue of their position and the context in which they work With increasing formalisation and delegation of business functions and activities the entrepreneur's role evolves to become a leader	Entrepreneurial leaders who work in any organisation irrespective of size or sector and are not confined to the entrepreneurial context High-level corporate executives who promote entrepreneurial behaviours	Entrepreneurial leaders are distinctive Based on establishing commonalities in research conducted in entrepreneurship and leadership, such as traits, styles, behaviours and context
Disciplinary Origins	Entrepreneurship – the entrepreneurial domain is the context for the application of mainstream leadership theory	Strategic Management – resonances with intrapreneurship and intracorporate entrepreneurship	Grounded in both entrepreneurship and leadership but the two are not overlapping constructs
Writers	Covin and Slevin, 2002; Gupta et al., 2004; Ireland et al., 2003; McGrath and McMillan, 2000; Thornberry, 2006; Vecchio, 2003	Baum et al., 1998; Ensley et al., 2006; Gupta et al., 2004; Hmieleski and Ensley, 2007; Jensen and Luthans, 2006; Peterson et al., 2009; Soriano and Martínez, 2007; Swiercz and Lydon, 2002; Koryak et al., 2015	Baumol, 1968; Ensley et al., 2006; Coglister and Brigham, 2004

Source: Adapted from Renko et al., 2015; Leitch et al., 2013

Position 1: Entrepreneurial Leadership as a Style of Leadership

While entrepreneurship scholars have directly and indirectly examined the entrepreneur as a leader, discussions until recently have been episodic, lacking robust consideration. Recognition of the importance of the leader in the domain of entrepreneurship is not new and is often associated with the entrepreneur as being part of the formula for success (Koryak et al., 2015; Lloyd et al., 2005): 'at a common-sense level one can consider an entrepreneur offering leadership and a leader needing entrepreneurial flair' (Perren, 2002, p. 2). Indeed, a constant theme in Schumpeter's work is that the entrepreneur is a 'special case of the social phenomenon of leadership' (Prendergast, 2006; Schumpeter, 1928, p. 379). As an innovator and

a driver of change and creativity, Schumpeter (1949) considered the entrepreneur to be a natural-born leader also. For him, entrepreneurial innovation was a social function that permitted capitalist economies to develop. Individuals who possessed the leadership skills of appreciating possibilities, of doing things differently and bringing them to fruition were exceptional (Basilgan, 2011). In effect, entrepreneurs were regarded as the economic leaders of the market economy (Arena & Hagnauer, 2002; De Vecchi, 1995). Schumpeter did not regard such individuals as superior or 'great men' nor entrepreneurship a feat of intellect (Osterhammel, 1987). Instead, entrepreneurs were viewed as doers. Accordingly, the most important leadership characteristic of the Schumpeterian entrepreneur was the ability (through influence) to overcome psychological and social resistance (Sweezy, 1943, pp. 93–6).

In essence, such individuals were able to make the novel acceptable to the wider social grouping: 'leadership does not consist simply in finding or creating the new thing but in so impressing the social grouping with it as to draw it on in its wake' (Schumpeter, 1934, p. 88). Such leadership is not just dependent on intrinsic abilities but is also a function of its social context, suggesting that the entrepreneur performs different roles depending on the situation. For instance, of the twelve distinct entrepreneurial roles which Hébert and Link (1988) identified, that of the industrial leader is one.

For many writers, including Vecchio (2003), a number of the constructs used in entrepreneurship are also used in mainstream leadership theory. He is quite forthright in asserting that there is nothing distinctive about entrepreneurial leadership: 'it is more cogent and parsimonious to view entrepreneurship as simply a type of leadership that occurs in a specific context ... a type of leadership that is not beyond the reach or understanding of available theory in the areas of leadership and interpersonal influence' (Vecchio, 2003, p. 322). For him, entrepreneurs are leaders by virtue of their position, a view echoed by Cunningham and Lischeron (1991, p. 47), who believe that the central purpose of the entrepreneur is to lead and 'to adapt their style to the needs of the people'. In practice almost everything written on 'entrepreneurial leadership' comes from entrepreneurship: leadership scholars implicitly appear to accept Vecchio's argument and see the entrepreneurial domain as just another (not particularly interesting) context for the application of mainstream leadership theory.

The entrepreneurship position can be summarised as follows. Founders initially have to lead as there are no standard operating procedures and management practices and/or organisational structures are underdeveloped (Hmieleski & Ensley, 2007). As ventures grow and primary business functions are delegated the entrepreneur's role may more formally evolve to that of a leader (Jensen & Luthans, 2006) in keeping with the increasing formality of, and emphasis on, management and leadership practices associated with increasing organisational size (Perren & Grant, 2001). As such, entrepreneurship is regarded as simply a type of leadership that occurs in a specific setting, that is, the entrepreneurial or small business is the situation and available leadership theory can be applied to understanding it accordingly. Such a perspective implies a hierarchy of leadership orientations and the unidirectional transference of ideas from the leadership domain to entrepreneurship.

Position 2: Entrepreneurial Leadership as an Entrepreneurial Mindset

However, for others including Kuratko (2007) and Gupta, McMillan and Surie (2004) entrepreneurship is the essence of leadership and an entrepreneurial mindset and behaviours are essential for effective leadership. Thus, entrepreneurial leaders are neither entrepreneurs nor confined to entrepreneurial, small SMEs. Instead, such individuals possess an entrepreneurial leadership style and are able to work in any organisation, on any task and to lead teams and individuals entrepreneurially (Kansikas, Laakkonen, Sarpo & Kontinen, 2012; Young, 1991). For Gupta et al. (2004, p. 244) entrepreneurial orientation is a central element in their conception of entrepreneurial leadership, as firms adapt their resources or capabilities to meet emergent competition by translating 'emergent options into platforms for continuous value creation'. This approach builds on early work in strategic management (Smith & Peterson, 1988) where the potential for developing an entrepreneurial orientation within larger organisations through intracorporate entrepreneurship was recognised. The entrepreneurial leader as an employed leader has resonance with intrapreneurship and, indeed, the two concepts can overlap as intrapreneurs are frequently seen in leading positions in entrepreneurial projects and in new initiatives in companies (Kansikas et al., 2012).

Initial research in this stream explored the personality traits of leaders in senior positions in entrepreneurial companies, or advocated a more entrepreneurial approach to leadership including the development of creativity and innovation in business development (Chen, 2007). Such leadership was perceived to be distinctive and leaders were differentiated from managers: 'single-minded, thick-skinned dominating individuals … unlike managers' (Nicholson, 1998, pp. 529, 538). While this emphasises particular and innate traits and skills, others stress the importance of a set of behaviours such as the ability to influence and to achieve goals: entrepreneurial leadership is 'the ability to influence others to manage resources strategically in order to emphasise both opportunity-seeking and advantage-seeking behaviours' (Wang, Tee & Ahmed, 2012, p. 507). This distinguishes the entrepreneurial leader from the manager, where the capability to coordinate and plan is central (Michael, Storey & Thomas, 2002; Renko et al., 2015; Zaleznik, 1977). Going further, Darling, Gabrielsson & Seristo (2007, p. 5) propose a definition of 'entrepreneurial management leadership' that they view as a process of value creation that recognises and exploits opportunities. This increasing emphasis on opportunity is in keeping with the recent trends in entrepreneurship that have highlighted the importance of entrepreneurial orientation (Gupta et al., 2004; Surie & Ashley, 2008) and opportunity recognition (Chen, 2007; Renko et al., 2015; Wang et al., 2012). The focus on the latter is perhaps not surprising given that opportunity identification, development and exploitation has dominated entrepreneurship research for the past decade (Corbett, 2007; Dimov, 2011). There is a subtle distinction in this body of work from that which considers the entrepreneurial leader to be one of a number of leader styles in that it is not assumed to be superior or inferior to other styles, nor does it adopt the position that the constructs are essentially the same. Instead, entrepreneurship scholars have appropriated leadership models and concepts to advance thinking in their field.

Position 3: Entrepreneurial Leadership – at the Interface of Two Domains

While entrepreneurial leadership has been inspired by entrepreneurship, McKone-Sweet, Greenberg and Wilson (2011) stress that entrepreneurial leaders are different from entrepreneurs and highlight that researchers in both fields are adamant that the two constructs, while similar, are not the same. This view underpins the third body of work that sits at the interface/intersection of the two domains and is characterised by scholars identifying common themes. For example, Fernald et al. (2005) point to the importance of vision, problem-solving, decision-making, risk-taking and strategic initiatives in both domains while Coglister and Brigham (2004) highlight vision, influence, leading innovative/creative individuals and planning. While of value, work at the interface is limited in that it tends to be descriptive rather than providing analysis and explanatory insights, and has failed to provide guidance into how such commonalities might be built on. In particular, Coglister and Brigham are more concerned to warn entrepreneurship scholars of the pitfalls which leadership research has encountered instead of providing a definition of entrepreneurial leadership.

In a review of definitions generated by work at the interface Harrison et al. (2015) identified that the entrepreneurial leadership literature can be placed into four categories along two dimensions, orientation and disciplinary basis. From an orientation perspective there are internally driven studies that focus on traits, styles and behaviours of entrepreneurial leaders, while those with an external focus consider the role that context plays. From the disciplinary viewpoint studies can be grouped according to the degree to which they draw explicitly from one disciplinary tradition, leading to fragmentation, or those adopting a more integrated, multi-disciplinary position. As is clear from the discussion above, much work in this area comprises discipline-based studies that view entrepreneurship and leadership as separate domains. This is consistent with Becherer, Mendenhall and Eickhoff's belief (2008, p. 20) that entrepreneurship and leadership are not overlapping constructs, but are separate manifestations of a deeper phenomenon; entrepreneurial leadership, therefore, is the 'need to create', or 'the propensity to engage one's environment, to create something new, and to change craft within it'. This is reflected in a number of recent, more integrated studies characterised by holistic research that focuses on the internal, intrinsic elements of entrepreneurial leadership and the processes and circumstances by which it emerges.

In order to tease out more fully the issues underlying entrepreneurial leadership, in the following section we present and discuss four recently published papers. Reflecting the lack of agreement on a formal definition, all of the papers advance new definitions of 'entrepreneurial leadership'. Based on the categorisation employed by Harrison et al. (2015) all of the papers are externally focused, concentrating on the broader external domains in which entrepreneurial leadership is observed. Two (Roomi & Harrison, 2011 and Renko et al., 2015) are explicitly grounded in the disciplinary tradition of entrepreneurship while the other two (Leitch et al., 2013; Harrison et al., 2015) are located towards a more integrated perspective.

RECENT REFLECTIONS ON ENTREPRENEURIAL LEADERSHIP

We chose the papers discussed below (Table 2.3) (Renko et al., 2015; Roomi & Harrison, 2011; Leitch et al., 2013; Harrison et al., 2015) because they addressed one of the following limitations in the entrepreneurial leadership literature, namely its atheoretical nature, the lack of a formally agreed definition, an absence of measurement tools and insufficient knowledge about how to develop and/or enhance its capability.

How do we Measure Entrepreneurial Leadership?

Given the scarcity of protocols to measure the construct (exceptions include Gupta et al., 2004; Chen, 2007; Koryak et al., 2015), we have selected to review more thoroughly Renko et al.'s (2015) study that developed and subsequently tested the reliability and validity of the ENTRELEAD scale. In integrating elements from all three perspectives of entrepreneurial leadership (as a leadership style, an entrepreneurial mindset and as something distinctive) they conclude that entrepreneurial leadership is a unique style of leadership which can be found and developed in any organisation regardless of size, type or age. Further, they propose that it is a firm-wide phenomenon concerned with the development of entrepreneurial behaviours and attitudes of leaders at any level: the ability to influence and direct the performance of group members toward achieving those organisational goals incorporates the recognition and exploitation of entrepreneurial opportunities (Renko et al., 2015, p. 55). Specifically, they stress the importance of innovation and not just imitation in the recognition of opportunities involving both the perception of an opportunity as well as exploiting it. While they point to the importance of extending entrepreneurial behaviours and attitudes throughout an organisation, their focus, like much entrepreneurial leadership literature, remains on the individual. Their perspective of the construct is in response to demands for large organisations to act flexibly, responsively and entrepreneurially, i.e. to develop an entrepreneurial orientation. This is consistent with the view that entrepreneurial qualities of creativity, innovation, risk-taking and

Table 2.3   Featured studies: key characteristics

Papers\Features	Renko et al. (2015)	Roomi and Harrison (2011)	Leitch et al. (2013)	Harrison et al. (2015)
Limitation to be addressed	Absence of measurement tools	Insufficient knowledge about how to develop and/ or enhance entrepreneurial leadership capability	Atheoretical nature of entrepreneurial leadership	Atheoretical nature of entrepreneurial leadership
Key question	How do we measure entrepreneurial leadership?	How do we teach entrepreneurial leadership?	How do we move the thinking about entrepreneurial leadership forward?	How do we develop a gender-aware theory of entrepreneurial leadership?
Rationale for review	One of the few tools developed to assess and measure entrepreneurial leadership; integrates elements from all three perspectives of entrepreneurial leadership (as a style, a mindset and as something distinctive); introduces the role of followers	One of the first papers to highlight the lack of knowledge about how entrepreneurial leadership might be developed; discusses what capabilities need to be enhanced and how this might be achieved	One of the first attempts to introduce new theories from other disciplines to provide insights into the concept and to move away from a focus on transformational leadership; draws on institutional capital to augment ideas of human and social capital in entrepreneurial leadership development	Raises the importance of alternative perspectives; shifts focus from transformational leadership; aims to ensure that further development of entrepreneurial leadership takes cognisance of recent debates in leadership
Context	Entrepreneurial behaviour is appropriate in all organisations irrespective of size and sector	Behaviours to identify, develop and take advantage of entrepreneurial opportunities with a view to teaching and developing these in higher education	Leadership role performed in entrepreneurial (SME) ventures	The masculinisation on entrepreneurship and the role of gender in entrepreneurial leadership
Focus	Definition and metrics of the development of a research protocol to measure entrepreneurial characteristics and behaviours	Definition and pedagogy	Definition and conceptual development	Definition and conceptual development
Epistemology	Essentialist	Essentialist	Constructionist	Constructionist
Methods Employed	Two studies – in study one an instrument was developed, tested and revised and was subsequently cross-validated in study two	Survey of teaching practices at 51 higher education institutions in the UK	One-on-one interviews and focus groups with one cohort of eight participants on an entrepreneurial leadership development programme	N/A – conceptual paper

independent thinking are required for organisational success.

In explaining their definition and positioning of entrepreneurial leadership vis-à-vis other styles, Renko et al. draw on transformational leadership, creativity-enhancing leadership and the strategy literature and contrast it with management, which is concerned only with coordination and planning. Entrepreneurial leaders, on the other hand, act as role models who articulate a compelling vision for others in an organisation. Unusually, in the entrepreneurship field, specific reference is made to followers. However, they adopt a very traditional view of the relationship between followers and leaders that is unidirectional, privileging leaders and regarding followers for the most part as passive, unempowered and subordinate. This ignores much of the contemporary research in leadership studies, notably the long-established tradition of research on member–leader exchange (Harris, Li & Kirkman, 2014; Dienesch & Liden, 1986), and reinforces a heroic view of the individual as leader, which of course reflects their emphasis on vision and transformational leadership.

Notwithstanding the essentialist approach adopted in the paper, Renko et al. demonstrate that the success of entrepreneurial leadership depends on the interrelationships between leaders, followers and context, a fruitful area for further investigation. They also open the door to research consistent with the processual turn in entrepreneurship, as their study develops and validates an empirical tool for the measurement of entrepreneurial leadership that is focused on actions, processes and attributes.

How do we Teach Entrepreneurial Leadership?

The starting point for Roomi and Harrison's (2011) consideration of entrepreneurial leadership is that there has been little discussion in the literature of how to teach it. Accordingly,

their aim is to strengthen the connection between research and teaching and to provide suggestions for educators. Their fundamental question is to ask 'how leaders learn to be entrepreneurial and how entrepreneurs learn leadership?' (Roomi & Harrison, 2011, p. 1). Given the pedagogical focus of the paper, and its essentialist basis, the authors focus on integrating Kotter's (1990) definition of leadership and Stevenson and Gumpert's (1985, p. 2) definition of entrepreneurship to present entrepreneurial leadership as a fusion of the two: 'having and communicating the vision to engage teams to identify, develop and take advantage of opportunity in order to gain competitive advantage'. Their aim is to develop an approach to entrepreneurship education that provides students with a mindset to lead in an entrepreneurial way.

From their review of the entrepreneurial and leadership literatures, which in turn has been developed by Harrison et al. (2015), they identify a number of common features. These include: differences in leadership styles which are assumed be more effective in entrepreneurial settings; the role of context; and an emphasis on personality traits, environmental influences and/or learned behaviours. They argue that little attention has been paid to how entrepreneurial leadership behaviours can be learnt, if they can be taught and how this might be done. Specifically, they point to the paucity of literature on entrepreneurship education and the need to develop process models (Bagheri & Pihie, 2011, 2012), highlight the tendency of researchers to draw on the entrepreneurship education literature but not the leadership literature (Okudan & Rzasa, 2006) and propose a project-based, critically reflective approach which draws on Kempster and Cope's (2010) focus on experiential methods and call for 'entrepreneurial leadership learning'.

Their conclusion is that the role of leadership is under-emphasised in entrepreneurship education. Consequently, the educational challenge as they see it is of making leadership relevant to entrepreneurship and entrepreneurship relevant to leadership. If entrepreneurship is a way of contextualising leadership they suggest that pedagogy can draw on a variety of types of leadership theory including team-oriented leadership, value-based leadership and transformational and neo-charismatic leadership. While their aim to incorporate a wide-ranging number of ideas and theories into their model is commendable and their classification of existing literature is valuable they do not really address the challenges of operationalising entrepreneurial leadership. It is one thing to argue 'entrepreneurship education should teach students how to cultivate their entrepreneurial capability in leadership roles and their leadership capability in entrepreneurial contexts' (Roomi & Harrison, 2011, p. 29). It is quite another to specify how this might be done, and in this regard it would be valuable for entrepreneurship researchers to become more familiar with recent debates on the nature and process of leader and leadership development (Day, Fleenor, Atwater, Sturm & McKee, 2014).

How do we Move the Thinking about Entrepreneurial Leadership Forward?

In a recent paper, Leitch et al. (2013) draw on human and social perspectives in leadership development to inform the operationalisation of entrepreneurial leadership development and introduce the concept of institutional capital to provide the basis for future research in the area. They define entrepreneurial leadership as the leadership role performed in entrepreneurial ventures. In addressing concerns about the lack of emphasis of leadership in entrepreneurship education they develop the application of social capital theory within an entrepreneurial context. In particular, they note that the leadership and leadership development literatures, while following the same development paths, are separate and distinct in a way that is not evident in entrepreneurial leadership research.

Accordingly, they reflect on current perspectives in both domains. Specifically, they highlight the shift in attention from personal characteristics and an individualised and de-contextualised conceptualisation of a leader as a reified individual to one where leadership as a role is defined by the interaction of a leader with his/her social and organisational context. This attention to interaction increases the relevance of a process perspective as the emphasis moves from traits, behaviours and actions to leadership as a social process engaging everyone in the community. However, in the entrepreneurship leader development literature focus remains on leader development as the acquisition of skills and abilities, and not on leadership development as a socially situated practice. Following Iles and Preece (2006), Leitch et al. contend that entrepreneurial leaders need to focus on building company resources and capabilities (which depends on acquiring and developing knowledge and skills via human capital) and on stabilising relationships (which facilitate action and value creation through social capital). In bridging the gap between leader development and leadership development as a socially situated process Leitch et al. propose a social capital theory of entrepreneurial leader development. In so doing, they draw on debates of social capital theory in sociology and political science, where it is often viewed as a means of gaining access to resources through the interaction with others, and from political science and development economists where it is frequently used as a means of signalling group cohesion.

Leitch et al. explored the social capital theory of entrepreneurial leader development in their empirical study and discovered that the leadership development process requires the development of relationships, participation, engagement and trust to develop social cohesion and enhance social capital development. They found social capital is created at two levels – by peer-to-peer interaction within the programme and by peer-to-other via the programme facilitator to other networks. As such, it develops from mutual interactions and is mediated by the bridging role that the facilitator plays, which leads to the creation of a reservoir of social capital. The entrepreneurial leaders in the study were able to exploit this social capital, as during and after attendance on a leadership development programme they had formed into a tightly knit, cohesive group enabled by the establishment of a formally constituted community. The emergence of this social institution points to the potential importance of developing institutional capital in entrepreneurial leadership programmes. In this study the creation of an organisation and the rules by which it was governed encouraged sharing, collaboration and learning that enhanced human as well as social capital.

This research demonstrates that entrepreneurial leadership and leadership development is a social process. However, the dominant emphasis of research to date, including much of that referred to in this chapter, is on human capital. Future research could, therefore, usefully focus on exploring the concept of institutional capital more fully, and exploring its relationship to theories of human and social capital to understand capital as a collective property. In terms of the unit of analysis, social and institutional capital could be considered internally within organisations of different types and stages, on the basis that context matters (Welter, 2011; Zahra & Wright, 2011) to identify the facilitators and constraints on the dynamic relationships underlying entrepreneurial leadership development.

How do we Develop a Gender-Aware Theory of Entrepreneurial Leadership?

In their conceptual paper, Harrison et al. (2015) highlight the embedded masculinity of the entrepreneurial leadership domain, contending that it is gender blind, gender defensive and gender neutral (Patterson, Mavin & Turner, 2012). They argue that it is important to challenge prevailing gendered assumptions and conceptions, not least to avoid the danger that entrepreneurial leadership may be co-opted into the mainstream discourse without taking account of recent and relevant debates and discussions, particularly within leadership studies.

Neglecting the role of gender in entrepreneurial leadership is at odds with the considerable and growing attention to gender in leadership studies. There are two dimensions to this. First, the difficulty in separating the terms 'leadership' and 'men' (Eagly & Carli, 2007), as the languages of masculinity, leadership and entrepreneurship have effectively become synonymous (Schnurr, 2008). Second, this has been compounded by most research being conducted in Western industrialised cultures that expound these masculine ideals (Elliott & Stead, 2008). As a result, in entrepreneurial leadership the male/masculine is regarded as the universal, neutral subject against which the woman/female is judged (Ahl, 2006). In leadership research, however, two emerging literatures offer the possibility of a more nuanced treatment of gender. First, post-heroic models of leadership that emphasise leadership as a collaborative, relational process are often presented as gender neutral. Second, the notion of feminine leadership highlights apparently feminine attributes, attitudes and behaviours such as an interpersonal orientation, collaboration, empathy, kindness and more participatory and relational leadership styles (Due Billing & Alvesson, 2000). Even though masculine leadership has shown some signs of decline in recent years, aspiring leaders still appear to hold feminine leadership skills in low esteem (Holt & Marques, 2012).

Elaborating on Metcalfe and Woodham's (2012) recent review of new directions in gender, diversity and organisation theorising, Harrison et al. develop a research agenda for the gendered analysis of entrepreneurial leadership, which is undertaken at three levels.

At the micro level, they extend current gender research on social constructionism, critical management studies and intersectionality to contemporary entrepreneurial leadership research. Specifically, three themes are highlighted: the (in)visibility of women leaders negotiating their in/out-group status; the role of glass walls and ceilings in attenuating women's experience-building and career progression; and the role of gender fatigue in reinforcing masculinist conceptions of leadership. At the meso level, building on the critical social science literature on men's studies and race studies they highlight the importance of understanding intersectionality and the dangers of simply treating gender, ethnicity etc. as a variable to be analysed in an essentialist manner. At the macro level, they propose that post-colonial feminist studies, transnationalism and the geographies of place and space can provide a foundation for theoretically advancing the knowledge domain of a context-aware and situationally grounded entrepreneurial leadership research. This research agenda incorporating new frameworks and perspectives presents an opportunity for entrepreneurial leadership scholars to address wider issues concerning diversity, the generalisability of their findings and the inclusivity of the theories they develop.

Summary

The four papers discussed above have provided suggestions by which research into entrepreneurial leadership can be taken forward and have the potential to add fruitful insights to current knowledge. However, given that entrepreneurial leadership is complex, messy and unpredictable there remains scope for scholars to disclose or revitalise 'what is often buried beneath or contained within more taken-for-granted assumptions' (Verduijn, Dey, Tedmanson & Essers, 2014). To prevent perpetuating the mainstream and to ensure more holistic understanding we urge scholars studying entrepreneurial leadership to move away from drawing on more established theories and approaches in leadership such as transformational leadership and to embrace more recent developments. As research in entrepreneurial leadership is in its infancy scholars are well placed to ensure that its future theoretical development is informed by alternative and less orthodox perspectives.

NEW INFLUENCES ON ENTREPRENEURIAL LEADERSHIP RESEARCH

In calling for entrepreneurship scholars to explore the efficacy of other theories and concepts we urge a note of caution. Even though there is a tradition of importing theories from other disciplines into the field (Kenworthy & McMullan, 2012; Harrison & Leitch, 1996), the exogenous development of theory, in the sense of being derived from constructs and concepts developed elsewhere, rather than endogenously developed within the field, can pose a major challenge. Often, the interdisciplinary transfer of theories, concepts and constructs is incomplete in that their intellectual history, the current debates over their efficacy and developments in the evolution of thinking in the parent discipline are not taken fully into account. While valuable in enriching and providing a stimulus to the development of research, the de facto reliance on a snapshot of debates elsewhere rather than substantive engagement in the ongoing conversation about them may limit the benefits gained from this transfer (Pohl & Hadorn, 2008) and stymie understanding of, and knowledge about, entrepreneurial leadership.

The position we adopt in this chapter is that entrepreneurial leadership sits at the intersection of both leadership and entrepreneurship and emphasises the similarities evident between them. Thus, there is significant opportunity for theories and constructs in both to inform its development. To date transformational leadership has shaped most of the thinking in the area. However, most considerations of this theory in entrepreneurial leadership do not take into consideration critiques of it (see below for these) and with a few exceptions more recent developments in leadership theory are not reflected in current discussions. These more recent similarities in thinking between the two domains include an increasing awareness of the importance of context, and a move away from the 'great man', charismatic individualistic understanding of leader and entrepreneur as hero. This recognises the danger that an excessive focus on the individual has meant that there is less known about what makes leaders effective than about how they are perceived: in other words, in both domains there has, arguably, been too much focus on the individual and their qualities and less on how they change others and develop and revise processes in organisations to build leadership or entrepreneurial capability and capacity in an organisation. Fundamentally, contemporary research in both fields sees leadership and entrepreneurship as relational, based on the importance of interactions with others, benefiting from a critical approach (including acknowledgement of a social constructionist approach), in which separation of the individual (leader/entrepreneur) from the process (leadership/entrepreneurship) becomes an important issue in determining the appropriate object of study.

Despite these similarities, entrepreneurship scholarship focused on leadership still draws on outdated theory to try and build theory and provide conceptual underpinnings for the 'entrepreneurial leadership' construct; this restricts the extent to which the five limitations identified above can be addressed. Our approach here is to advocate that entrepreneurship scholarship should learn from and not perpetuate old theoretical debates in leadership, by carefully adopting new perspectives into entrepreneurial leadership and asking: what are the implications of building on these trends?

As an illustration of these issues, the case of transformational leadership is instructive. Derived from Burns's (1978) work which focused on examining the motivations and values underpinning how political leaders behave, transformational leadership, with its emphasis on charisma and affective elements, is one of the first systematic attempts in leadership to link leaders and followers (Bass, 1998; Bass & Avolio, 1994). While many would not necessarily disagree with the ultimate aim of transformational leadership there is a danger that the language employed in the theory tends towards the evangelical and idealistic in that transforming leaders are considered to provide a positive moral guide of working for the benefit of the team, organisation and/or community (Tourish, 2013).

Even though inspiring and influencing others is not inherently ethical or unethical (Howell & Avolio, 1992), relatively little attention has been paid in either the leadership or entrepreneurship literatures to the unethical facet of the theory, pseudo-transformational leadership. While authentic transformational leaders inspire and use their influence to empower others, pseudo-transformational leadership is characterised by self-serving, yet highly inspirational behaviour. By using their influence for self-gain, pseudo-transformational leaders abuse their positions of power by maximising self-interest, irrespective of followers' interest. Such leadership is antithetical to authentic transformational leadership (Christie, Barling & Turner, 2011). Further, recent critiques of transformational leadership have suggested that due to its multi-dimensionality it lacks a clear conceptual definition and a causal model to explain the relationship of influences on mediating processes and outcomes (van Knippenberg & Sitkin, 2013). While not explicitly stated, the theory is universalist in that its attributes are considered to be relevant in all situations: in essence, context is not considered. It also perpetuates a focus on personality traits and dispositions more in keeping with early approaches to understanding leadership.

Much of the research underpinning the theory is based on qualitative data gathered from male CEOs and MDs. Even though the role of followers is acknowledged the theory is leader-centric and based on highly gendered, heroic images of the great man. This is problematic for two reasons. First, few individuals are absolute leaders and many alternate between being a leader and a follower (Crossman & Crossman, 2011). Second, even though leaders would not exist without followers, leader and leadership dynamics are presented as asymmetrical.

While Renko et al. (2015) highlighted the role of followers in entrepreneurial leadership they did not develop it to specifically consider the role that they can play. This is perhaps not surprising in that in leadership studies more generally there has been little consideration of the role of the follower and how s/he might relate to or impact on a leader's attitudes or behaviours (Kelley, 1992, 2004; Uhl-Bien, Riggio, Lowe & Carsten, 2014). This has led recently to a growing acceptance of the idea of followership: indeed, the essence of leadership is followership (Bjerke, 1999). Part of the reason for this is increased awareness that leadership, like entrepreneurship, is a process and followers are crucial to it. Accordingly, to advance our understanding of leadership in any context we need to understand followership (Uhl-Bien et al., 2014). This emphasis on followership is highlighted in critical perspectives in which the relationship between leaders and followers is more explicitly acknowledged and there is an acceptance that the leadership role is fluid. Leadership is co-created in social and relational interactions between leaders and followers (Grint, 2000).

Critical leadership studies (CLS) are a relatively new approach to studying leadership. Similar to critical perspectives in entrepreneurship and management studies more generally, they question hegemonic approaches and beliefs in mainstream literature (Parker & Thomas, 2011). Specifically the focus is on critiquing rhetoric, tradition, authority and objectivity and on addressing what is neglected, absent or deficient in mainstream research (Collinson, 2011). Even though critical entrepreneurship research has challenged the hegemony of conventional approaches (including the ideological and practical privileging of maleness over femaleness, whiteness over colourness and Western over Africanness, Latinness) little research has engaged 'openly with the dark sides – the contradictions, paradoxes, ambiguities and tensions – at the heart of entrepreneurship' (Tedmanson, Verduijn, Essers & Gartner, 2012, p. 532). Indeed, entrepreneurship tends to be viewed as a desirable economic activity and an individualist phenomenon. In so doing, scholars are potentially in danger of ignoring its many different dimensions including those that are more negative (Verduijn et al., 2014). Implicit in much of the entrepreneurial discourse is the positive representation of the possibilities within entrepreneurial activity that is premised upon liberation of agentic potential open to all (McAdam, 2012). However, an emerging critique has challenged this stance (Ogbor, 2000; Armstrong, 2005).

Of particular relevance to entrepreneurial leadership is the focus in critical leadership studies on power (and the way it is reproduced in particular structures, relationships and practices) and identity constructions (through which leadership dynamics are reproduced, rationalised, sometimes resisted and occasionally transformed) (Collinson, 2005). Traditional approaches underestimate the complexity of leadership, specifically, the exercise and experience of power, which is central to all leadership dynamics. The orthodox view assumes a blunt and hierarchical, unidirectional relationship between leaders (who are portrayed as proactive agents) and their followers/employees (who passively respond to them) (Collinson, 2006). As such, leaders in their exercise of power and authority will reinforce and/or challenge dominant power relations. Arguably, this has been perpetuated by the dominance of transformational leadership, where the role of followers is viewed in relation to how susceptible they are to the leader and his/her style or behaviour. However, such an approach ignores that these relationships may not necessarily be unidirectional. Highlighting followers' agency is significant as it stresses that power relations are always two-way, contingent and interdependent, and that followers can influence the interaction, for instance, by resisting and dissenting.

To date, in entrepreneurial leadership research the role and impact of power and influence have largely been ignored. However, we argue the adoption of a critical perspective would bring a more nuanced understanding to leader/follower and other relationships. The critical turn recognises entrepreneurship as a socially constructed phenomenon that is given shape by its social, political and cultural context. This emphasis on the relationship between the entrepreneurial leader and the entrepreneurial system in which they and their business operate shapes and influences how they exercise power and authority. In particular, it throws light on the power relations between macro social relations and meso organisational practices and processes as well as the micro dynamics of entrepreneurial leaders and others. We suggest that there is opportunity to explore these issues in a variety of entrepreneurial settings, for instance, in new venture teams, in family businesses and in larger organisational settings in the context of intrapreneurship or corporate entrepreneurship. In the case of new venture teams scholars could investigate the entrepreneurial leadership dynamics involved in shared power and responsibility. Similarly, in the case of family businesses and family entrepreneurial teams, comprising related individuals (Discua Cruz, Howorth & Hamilton, 2013), exploring how authority and influence are exercised will extend knowledge about stewardship, trust and shared values. In larger organisational settings the likelihood that entrepreneurial leaders will emerge informally in more subordinated or dispersed relationships is greater than it would be in a smaller, entrepreneurial venture, thus providing researchers with the potential to draw on more relational and collective approaches to leadership such as shared leadership and distributed leadership.

Renko et al. (2015) argued that leadership is a firm-wide phenomenon which throws light on the importance of developing entrepreneurial leadership capability throughout an organisation instead of focusing on one or a handful of individuals in senior positions. Indeed, this is a challenge in the leadership development literature more generally where a distinction between 'leader' and 'leadership' has been made, which mirrors the move from individualistic to more relational understandings of leadership. In the case of leader development the emphasis is on developing an individual leader's human capital through the development and enhancement of individual-based knowledge, skills and abilities associated with formal leadership roles (Day, 2001; Day et al., 2014). Leadership development on the other hand is concerned with expanding an organisation's collective capacity so that all of its members are able to perform in formal and informal leadership roles effectively through engaging in leadership processes. In this perspective social capital and building networked relationships to enhance cooperation and resource exchange is highlighted and involves multiple individuals such as leaders and followers and peers in self-managed teams. In the context of entrepreneurial leadership development there is scope for a research agenda to be developed which includes multilevel and longitudinal studies, mapping reactions and patterns of exchange between groups, teams and organisation-wide initiatives.

This shift in focus from heroic and individualist perspectives to relational and collective ones, and the emergence of new theories of leadership including spiritual leadership (Fry, 2005), authentic leadership (Avolio & Gardner, 2005) and servant leadership (Spears & Lawrence, 2004) introduces an emotional dimension (Ashkanasy & Daus, 2002). In the leadership domain this has led to a stream of literature on leaders' emotional intelligence (Goleman, 1995) and the role of emotions on organisation performance (Fineman, 2000). In recent work Iszatt-White (2013) presents a detailed examination of the 'emotion work' performed by leaders in the accomplishment of their leadership activities. Much emotion work can be explored in the context of entrepreneurial leadership including the creation and elaboration of a vision, gaining buy-in to projects, building commitment and attempting to understand the ways in which it impacts on individual well-being, both of those in leadership positions and those who are not. Exploring the practice of emotion work and emotional labour experiences in entrepreneurial leaders will add insights into this emerging new agenda in leadership studies.

CONCLUSION

At the outset of this chapter we highlighted that most leadership research has been conducted in large organisational settings and relatively little attention has been paid to leadership and leadership development in the entrepreneurial and SMEs context. We argue that this is an oversight for two reasons. First, it has long been recognised that small firms are generally more sensitive than larger firms to external contexts, especially environmental dynamism and volatility, which places additional challenges on entrepreneurial leaders and their capabilities. Second, the imprinting effect of leaders of entrepreneurial ventures can have a significant impact, both positive and negative, on their businesses and it is thus important that we gain increased insights into how and in what ways these might impact on firm viability and growth.

We presented a critical analysis of the entrepreneurial leadership literature and identified three different perspectives: first, as a style of leadership; second, as a mindset; and third, as something distinctive. For us, entrepreneurial leadership sits at the interface of the disciplines of entrepreneurship and leadership and research into it can draw usefully from both. However, from the review above it is clear that the construct remains caught ambivalently at the interface (Harrison & Leitch, 1994). Thus, we caution scholars to be careful when borrowing or transferring constructs and theories from one discipline to the other. The circulation of knowledge among disciplines does not involve a simple, linear transfer of a concept, theory, or method from one disciplinary field to another and vice versa. What emerges from our review of both exemplar papers on entrepreneurial leadership and recent trends in leadership research itself is the very opposite, namely 'a complex, dynamic process of multidirectional exchanges, of knowledge production moving across and beyond disciplinary borders' (Darbellay, 2012, p. 16).

The entrepreneurial leadership literature is still heavily vested in the norms of mainstream leadership theory (whether trait, situational/contingency, path–goal theory, leader–member exchange, impression management, social identity theory or, as we have suggested above, transformational/transactional leadership theory). This tradition is leader/entrepreneur-centric, characterised by a focus on the individual and their qualities and on what makes an effective entrepreneurial leader, viewing the entrepreneurial leader as a proactive agent with largely passive followers and leadership itself as a top-down hierarchical influencing process. Accordingly, entrepreneurial leadership is a predictable practice and entrepreneurial leadership studies are a prescriptive endeavour.

In order to advance thinking in entrepreneurial leadership we suggest that scholars should draw on critical leadership studies that have emerged to challenge the hegemonic, orthodox perspective. From this viewpoint entrepreneurial leadership can be viewed as a socially constructed, contingent, integrative and contested construct, enacted as an emergent process through discourse and subject to the changing power dynamics between leaders and others. This recognises and responds to three weaknesses in the mainstream view: essentialism, romanticism and dualism (Collinson, 2011). First, in contrast to the psychological-based positivism and essentialism of traditional leadership research, a critical leadership studies perspective on entrepreneurial leadership emphasises that it is socially and discursively constituted through multiple discourses and meanings. Second, this perspective eschews the romanticism of the mainstream approach, archtypified in the notion of the heroic leader and the cult of individualism, and replaces this with an understanding of entrepreneurial leadership as social, relational and collective in nature. Third, in response to the dualistic nature of traditional approaches – leader/follower, transformational/transactional, individual/collective – a critical approach to entrepreneurial leadership emphasises its dialectical character embodied in the dynamic tension and interplay between categories.

The emerging research agenda we have signalled is to engage with contemporary leadership research that has evolved to post-heroic and critical leadership views, which see leadership as a collective plural activity based on the practices of many organisational members rather than a few leader-individuals. Beyond this, the detachment from individuals to plural forms, such as dyads, teams and collectives, offers additional opportunities for entrepreneurial leadership research to follow the emerging sociomaterial perspective in organisation and leadership studies (Hawkins, 2015; Pullen & Vachhani, 2013). In addition, it also permits a move beyond a human–human relations to a human–material relations perspective on entrepreneurial leadership to explore the connection between leadership and the materiality of artefacts, spaces, places and technology (Ropo, Salovaara, Sauer & de Paoli, 2015). In so doing, entrepreneurial leadership research has the potential to spearhead a new direction for entrepreneurship research more generally.

Embodied research on leadership and materiality is breaking new theoretical and empirical ground, questioning the taken-for-granted assumptions that underpin the relationships between materiality and leadership. Pullen and Vachhani (2013) have suggested three directions for research which might provide a stimulus to new entrepreneurial leadership research in this area: first, research that focuses on ways in which bodies and embodiment have, in part, been silenced but emerge in the performance, expression and enactment of leadership; second, research on materiality and the disruption, restriction and enabling of the taken-for-granted leadership function in organisations; and third, research that critically engages with these hitherto neglected dimensions of leadership (including cross-cultural differences and the problematic of materiality as it is expressed through language, bodies, discourses, technology, space and place). Research on entrepreneurial leadership is still in its infancy and, as our review has made clear, offers fertile ground for exploration and innovation and an opportunity to shape thinking in both its parent disciplines.

REFERENCES

Ahl, H. J. (2006) Why research on women entrepreneurs needs new directions, *Entrepreneurship Theory and Practice* 30 (5) pp. 595–621.

Antonakis, J. and Autio, E. (2007) Entrepreneurship and leadership, in J. R. Baum, M. Frese and R. Baron (eds) *The Psychology of Entrepreneurship*, London: Routledge, pp. 189–208.

Arena, R. and Hagnauer, D. (eds) (2002) *The Contribution of Joseph Schumpeter to Economics: Economic Development and Institutional Change*, London: Routledge.

Armstrong, P. (2005) *Critique of Entrepreneurship: People and Policy*, New York: Palgrave MacMillan.

Ashkanasy, N. M. and Daus, C. S. (2002) Emotion in the workplace: The new challenge for managers, *Academy of Management Executive* 16 (1) pp. 76–86.

Autio, E. (2013) Promoting Leadership Development in High-Growth New Ventures, Discussion Paper, Paris: OECD.

Avolio, B. J. and Gardner, W. L. (2005) Authentic leadership development: Getting to the root of positive forms of leadership, *The Leadership Quarterly* 16 (3) pp. 315–338.

Bagheri, A. and Pihie, Z. A. L. (2011) Entrepreneurial leadership: Towards a model for learning and development, *Human Resource Development International* 14 (4) pp. 447–463.

Bagheri, A. and Pihie, Z. A. L. (2012) Entrepreneurial leadership competencies development among Malaysian university students: The pervasive role of experience and social interaction, *Pertanika Journal of Social Science & Humanities* 20 (2) pp. 539–562.

Basilgan, M. (2011) The creative destruction of economic development: The Schumpeterian entrepreneur, *TOAiDe's Review of Public Administration* 5 (3) pp. 35–76.

Bass, B. M. (1998) *Transformational Leadership: Industrial, Military and Educational Impact*, Mahwah, NJ: Erlbaum.

Bass, B. M. and Avolio, B. J. (eds) (1994) *Improving Organizational Effectiveness through Transformational Leadership*, Thousand Oaks, CA: Sage.

Baum, J. R., Locke, E. A. and Kirkpatrick, S. A. (1998) A longitudinal study of the relation of vision and vision communication to venture growth in entrepreneurial firms, *Journal of Applied Psychology* 83 (1) pp. 43–54.

Baumol W. J. (1968) Entrepreneurship in Economic Theory, *The American Economic Review* 58 (2) pp 64–71.

Becherer, R. C., Mendenhall, M. E. and Eickhoff, K. F. (2008) Separated at birth: An inquiry on the conceptual independence of the entrepreneurship and the leadership constructs, *New England Journal of Entrepreneurship* 11 (2) pp. 13–27.

Bjerke, B. (1999) *Business leadership and culture: National management styles in the global economy*. Cheltenham: Edward Elgar.

Buller, P. F. and Finkle, T. A. (2013) The Hogan entrepreneurial leadership program: An innovation model of entrepreneurship education, *Journal of Entrepreneurship Education* 16 pp. 113–132.

Burns, J. M. (1978) *Leadership*, New York: Harper Row.

Chen, M-H. (2007) Entrepreneurial leadership and new ventures: Creativity in entrepreneurial teams, *Creativity and Innovation Management* 16 (3) pp. 239–249.

Christie, A., Barling, J. and Turner, N. (2011) Pseudo-transformational leadership: Model specification and outcomes, *Journal of Applied Social Psychology* 41 (1) pp. 2943–2984.

Coglister, C. C. and Brigham, K. H. (2004) The intersection of leadership and entrepreneurship: Mutual lessons to be learnt, *Leadership Quarterly* 15 (6) pp. 771–799.

Cohen, A. R. (2004) Building a company of leaders, *Leader to Leader* (34) pp. 16–20.

Collinson, D. L. (2005) Dialectics of leadership, *Human Relations* 58 (11) pp. 1419–1442.

Collinson, D. L. (2006) Rethinking followership: A post-structuralist analysis of follower identities, *The Leadership Quarterly* 17 (2), pp. 179–189.

Collinson, D. L. (2011) Critical leadership studies, in A. Bryman, D. L. Collinson, K. Grint, B. Jackson and M. Uhl-Bien (eds) *The Sage Handbook of Leadership*, London: Sage, pp. 179–192.

Collinson, D. L. (2014) Dichotomies, dialectics and dilemmas: New directions for critical leadership studies, *Leadership* 10 (1) pp. 36–55.

Corbett, A. C. (2007) Learning asymmetries and the discovery of entrepreneurial opportunities, *Journal of Business Venturing* 22 (1) pp. 97–118.

Covin, J. G. and Slevin, D. P. (2002) The entrepreneurial imperatives of strategic leadership, in M. A. Hitt, R. D. Ireland, S. M. Camp and D. L. Sexton (eds) *Strategic Entrepreneurship: Creating a New Mindset*, Oxford: Blackwell Publishers, pp. 309–327.

Crossman, B. and Crossman, J. (2011) Conceptualising followership: A review of literature, *Leadership* 7 (4) pp. 481–497.

Cunningham, J. B. and Lischeron, J. (1991) Defining entrepreneurship, *Journal of Small Business Management* 29 (1) pp. 45–61.

Currie, G., Humphreys, M., Ucbasaran, D. and McManus, S. (2008) Entrepreneurial leadership in the English public sector: Paradox or possibility, *Public Administration* 86 (4) pp. 987–1008.

Darbellay, F. (2012) The circulation of knowledge as an interdisciplinary process: Travelling concepts, analysis and metaphors, *Issues in Integrative Studies* 30, pp. 1–18.

Darling, J., Gabrielsson, M. and Seristo, H. (2007) Enhancing contemporary entrepreneurship: A focus on management leadership, *European Business Review* 19 (1) pp. 4–22.

Day, D. V. (2001) Leadership development: A review in context, *The Leadership Quarterly*, 11 (4) pp. 581–613.

Day, D. V., Fleenor, J. W., Atwater, L. E., Sturm, R. E. and McKee, R. A. (2014) Advances in leader and leadership development: A review of 25 years of research and theory, *The Leadership Quarterly* 25 (1) pp. 63–82.

De Vecchi, N. (1995) *Entrepreneurs, Institutions and Economic Change: The Economic Thought of J.A. Schumpeter (1905–1925)*. (A. J. Stone transl.), Cheltenham, UK and Northampton, MA: Edward Elgar Publishing.

Dienesch, R. M. and Liden, R. C. (1986) Leader-member exchange model of leadership: A critique and further development, *Academy of Management Review* 11 (3) pp. 618–634.

Dimov, D. (2011) Grappling with the unbearable elusiveness of entrepreneurial opportunities, *Entrepreneurship Theory and Practice* 35 (1) pp. 57–81.

Discua Cruz, A., Howorth, C. and Hamilton, E. (2013) Intrafamily entrepreneurship: The formation and membership of family entrepreneurial teams, *Entrepreneurship Theory and Practice* 37 (1) pp. 17–46.

Due Billing, Y. and Alvesson, M. (2000) Questioning the notion of feminine leadership: A critical perspective on the gender labelling of leadership, *Gender, Work and Organization* 7 (3) pp. 144–157.

Eagly, A. H. and Carli, L. L. (2007) *Through the Labyrinth: The Truth about how Women become Leaders*, Boston, MA: Harvard University Press.

Eisenhardt, K. M. and Schoonhoven, C. B. (1990) Organizational growth: Linking founding team, strategy, environment and growth among US semiconductor ventures, 1978–1988, *Administrative Science Quarterly* 35 (3) pp. 504–529.

Elliott, C. and Stead, V. (2008) Learning for leading women's experience: Towards a sociological understanding, *Leadership* 4 (2) pp. 159–180.

Ensley, M. D., Pearce, C. L. and Hmieleski, K. (2006) The moderating effect of environmental dynamism on the relationship between entrepreneur leadership behavior and new venture performance, *Journal of Business Venturing* 21 (2) pp. 243–263.

Fernald, L. W. Jr., Solomon, G. T. and El Tarabisby, A. (2005) A new paradigm: Entrepreneurial leadership, *Southern Business Review* 30 (2) pp. 1–10.

Fineman, S. (ed.) (2000) *Emotion in Organisations* (2nd ed), London: Sage.

Fry, L. W. (2005) Introduction to 'The Leadership Quarterly' special issue: Toward a paradigm of spiritual leadership, *The Leadership Quarterly* 16 (5) pp. 169–222.

Gibb, A. (2005) Meeting the development needs of owner managed small enterprise: a discussion of the centrality of action learning, *Action Learning: Research and Practice* 6 (3) pp 209–227.

Goleman, D. (1995) *Emotional Intelligence*, New York: Bantam Books.

Grant, A. (1992) The development of an entrepreneurial leadership paradigm for enhancing new venture success, paper presented at the 12th Annual Babson Entrepreneurial Research Conference, INSEAD, June.

Greenberg, D., McKone-Sweet, K. and Wilson, H. J. (2013) Entrepreneurial leaders: Creating opportunity in an unknowable world, *Leader to Leader* 2013(67) pp. 56–62.

Grint, K. (2000) *The Arts of Leadership*, Oxford: Oxford University Press

Gupta, V., McMillan, I. and Surie, G. (2004) Entrepreneurial leadership: Developing and measuring a cross-cultural construct, *Journal of Business Venturing* 19 (2) pp. 241–260.

Harris, T. B., Li, N. and Kirkman, B. L. (2014) Leader-member exchange (LMX) in context: How LMX differentiation and LMX relational separation attenuate LMX's influence on OCB and turnover intention, *The Leadership Quarterly* 25 (2) pp. 314–328.

Harrison, R. T. and Leitch, C. M. (1994) Entrepreneurship and leadership: The implications for education and development,

Entrepreneurship and Regional Development 6 (2) pp. 111–125.

Harrison, R. T. and Leitch, C. M. (1996) Discipline emergence in entrepreneurship: Accumulative fragmentalism or paradigmatic science?, *Entrepreneurship, Innovation and Change* 5 (2) pp. 65–83.

Harrison, R. T., Leitch, C. M. and McAdam, M. (2015) Breaking glass: Towards a gendered analysis of entrepreneurial leadership, *Journal of Small Business Management* (forthcoming)

Hawkins, B. (2015) Ship-shape: Materializing leadership in the British Royal Navy, *Human Relations* 68 (6) pp. 951–971.

Hébert, R. F. and Link, A. N. (1988) In search of the meaning of entrepreneurship, *Small Business Economics* 1 (1) pp. 39–49.

Hmieleski, K. M. and Ensley, M. D. (2007) A contextual examination of new venture performance: Entrepreneur leadership behaviour, top management team heterogeneity and environmental dynamism, *Journal of Organizational Behaviour* 28 (7) pp. 865–889.

Holt, S. and Marques, J. (2012) Empathy in leadership: Appropriate or misplaced? An empirical study on a topic that is asking for attention, *Journal of Business Ethics* 105 (1) pp. 95–105.

Horney, N., Pasmore, B. and O'Shea, T. (2010) Leadership agility: A business imperative for a VUCA world, *People & Strategy* 33 (4) pp. 34–41.

Howell, J. M. and Avolio, B. J. (1992) The ethics of charismatic leadership: Submission of liberation, *Academy of Management Executive* 6 (2) pp. 43–54.

Iles, P. and Preece, D. (2006) Developing leaders or developing leadership? The Academy of Chief Executives' programme in the north east of England, *Leadership* 2 (3) pp. 317–340.

Ireland, R. D., Hitt, M. A. and Sirmon, D. (2003) A model of strategic entrepreneurship: The construct and its dimensions, *Journal of Management* 19 (29), pp. 963–989.

Iszatt-White, M. (ed.) (2013) *Leadership as Emotional Labour* (Routledge Studies in Management, Organizations and Society), London: Routledge.

Jensen, S. M. and Luthans, F. (2006) Entrepreneurs as authentic leaders: Impact on employees' attitudes, *Leadership and Organisation Development Journal* 27 (8) pp. 646–666.

Jones, O. and Crompton, H. (2009) Enterprise logic and small firms: A model of authentic entrepreneurial leadership, *Journal of Strategy and Management* 2 (4) pp. 329–351.

Kansikas, J., Laakkonen, A., Sarpo, V. and Kontinen, T. (2012) Entrepreneurial leadership and familiness as resources for strategic entrepreneurship, *International Journal of Entrepreneurial Behaviour and Research* 18 (2) pp. 141–158.

Kelley, R. E. (2004) *Followership, Encyclopedia of Leadership*, Thousand Oaks, CA: Sage Publications.

Kelley, R. E. (1992) *The Power of Followership: How to Create Leaders People want to Follow and Followers who Lead Themselves*, New York: Double Day/Currency.

Kempster, S. and Cope, J. (2010) Learning to lead in the entrepreneurial context, *International Journal of Entrepreneurial Behaviour and Research* 16 (1) pp. 5–34.

Kenworthy, T. P. and McMullan, W. E. (2012) *Importing Theory*, paper presented to 2012 Babson College Entrepreneurship Research Conference, Texas, USA.

Koryak, O., Mole, K. F., Lockett, A., Hayton, J. C, Ucbasaran, D. and Hodgkinson, G. P. (2015) Entrepreneurial leadership, capabilities and growth, *International Small Business Journal* 33 (1) pp. 89–105.

Kotter, J. (1990) What leaders really do, *Harvard Business Review* 68 (3) pp. 103–112.

Kuratko, D. F. (2007) Entrepreneurial leadership in the 21st century, *Journal of Leadership and Organizational Studies* 13 (4) pp. 1–12.

Leitch, C. M., McMullan, C. and Harrison, R. T. (2013) The development of entrepreneurial leadership: The role of human, social and institutional capital, *British Journal of Management* 24 (3) pp. 347–366.

Lloyd, W. F. J., George, T. S. and Ayman, T. (2005) A new paradigm: Entrepreneurial leadership, *Southern Business Review* 30 (2) pp. 1–10.

McAdam, M. (2012) *Female Entrepreneurship*, London: Routledge.

McGrath, R. G. and MacMillan, I. C. (2000) *The Entrepreneurial Mindset*, Boston: Harvard Business School Publishing.

McKone-Sweet, K., Greenberg, D. and Wilson, H. J. (2011) Giving voice to a values approach to educating entrepreneurial leaders, *Journal of Business Ethics* 8 (1) pp. 337–342.

Metcalfe, B. D. and Woodham, C. (2012) Introduction: New directions in gender, diversity and organization theorizing – re-imagining feminist post-colonialism, transnationalism and geographies of power, *International Journal of Management Reviews* 14 (2) pp. 123–140.

Michael, S., Storey, D. and Thomas, H. (2002) Discovery and coordination in strategic management and entrepreneurship, in M. A. Hitt, R. D. Ireland, S. M. Camp and D. L. Sexton (eds) *Strategic Entrepreneurship: Creating a New Mindset*, Oxford: Blackwell Publishers, pp. 45–65.

Ng, W. and Thorpe, R. (2010) Not another study of great leaders: Entrepreneurial leadership in a mid-sized family firm for its further growth and development, *International Journal of Entrepreneurial Behaviour and Research* 16 (5) pp. 457–476.

Nicholson, N. (1998) Personality and entrepreneurial leadership: A study of the heads of the UK's most successful independent companies, *European Management Journal* 16 (5) pp. 529–539.

Ogbor, J. O. (2000) Mythicizing and reification in entrepreneurial discourse: Ideology-critique of entrepreneurial studies, *Journal of Management Studies* 37 (5) pp. 605–635.

Okudan, G. E. and Rzasa, S. E. (2006) A project-based approach to entrepreneurship, *Technovation* 26 (2) pp. 195–210.

Osterhammel, J. (1987) Varieties of social economics: Joseph A Schumpeter and Max Weber, in M. Wolfgang and J. Osterhammel (eds) *Max Weber and his Contemporaries*, London: Allen and Unwin, pp. 106–120.

Parker, M. and Thomas, R. (2011) What is a critical journal?, *Organization* 18 (4) pp. 419–427.

Patterson, N., Mavin, S. and Turner, J. (2012) Envisioning female entrepreneurs: Leaders from a gender perspective, *Gender in Management: An International Journal* 27 (6) pp. 395–416.

Perren, L. (2002) *Comparing Entrepreneurship and Leadership: A Textual Analysis*, Report from the SME Working Group, London: CEML.

Perren, L. and Burgoyne, J. (2003) *Management and Leadership Abilities: An Analysis of Texts, Testimony and Practice*, Report from the SME Working Group, London: CEML.

Perren, L. and Grant, P. (2001) Management and Leadership in UK SMEs, Council for Excellence in Management and Leadership.

Peterson, S. J., Walunbwa, F. O., Byron, K. and Myrowitz, J. (2009) CEO positive psychological traits, transformational leadership, and firm performance in high-technology start-up and established firms, *Journal of Management* 35 (2) pp. 348–368.

Petrie, N. (2011) *Future Trends in Leadership Development*, Greensboro, NC: Center for Creative Leadership.

Pohl, C. and Hadron, G. (2008) Methodological challenges of transdisciplinary research, *Natures Sciences Sociétés* 16 (2) pp. 111–121.

Prendergast, R. (2006) Schumpeter, Hegel and the vision of development, *Cambridge Journal of Economics* 30 (2) pp. 253–275.

Pullen, A. and Vachhani, S. (2013) The materiality of leadership, *Leadership* 9 (3) pp. 315–319.

Renko, M., El Tarabishy, A. Carsrud, A. L. and Brännback, M. (2015) Understanding and measuring entrepreneurial leadership, *Journal of Small Business Management* 53 (1) pp. 54–74.

Ripoll, M. M., Rodriguez, F. G., Barrasa, A. and Antino, M. (2010) Leadership in entrepreneurial organizations: Context and motives, *Psicothema* 22 (4) pp. 880–886.

Roomi, M. A. and Harrison, P. (2011) Entrepreneurial leadership: What is it and how should it be taught? *International Review of Entrepreneurship* 9 (3) pp. 1–43.

Ropo, A., Salovaara, P., Sauer, E. and de Paoli, D. (2015) *Leadership in Spaces and Places*, Cheltenham: Edward Elgar.

Schnurr, S. (2008) Surviving in a man's world with a sense of humour: An analysis of women leaders' use of humour at work, *Leadership* 4 (3) pp. 299–319.

Schumpeter, J. A. (1928) The instability of capitalism, *Economic Journal* 38 (151) pp. 361–386.

Schumpeter, J. A. (1934) *The Theory of Economic Development: An Inquiry into Profits, Capital, Credit, Interest and the Business Cycle* (transl. Redvers Opie), Cambridge, MA: Harvard University Press.

Schumpeter, J. A. (1949) Change and the entrepreneur, in R. V. Clemence (ed.) *Essays on Entrepreneurs, Innovations, Business Cycles, and the Evolution of Capitalism*, Cambridge, MA: Harvard University Press, pp. 63–84.

Smith, P. B. and Peterson, M. F. (1988) *Leadership, Organizations and Culture: An Event Management Model*, London: Sage.

Soriano, D. R. and Martinez, J. M. C. (2007) Transmitting the entrepreneurial spirit to the work team in SMEs: The importance of leadership, *Management Decision* 45 (7) pp. 1102–1122.

Spears, L. and Lawrence, M. (eds) (2004) *Practising Servant-Leadership: Succeeding through Trust, Bravery and Forgiveness*, San Francisco, CA: Jossey-Bass.

Stevenson, H. and Gumpert, D. (1985) The heart of entrepreneurship, *Harvard Business Review* 63 (2) pp. 85–94.

Surie, G. and Ashley, A. (2008) Integrating pragmatism and ethics in entrepreneurial leadership for sustainable value creation, *Journal of Business Ethics* 81 (1) pp. 235–246.

Sweezy, P. M. (1943) Professor Schumpeter's theory of innovation, *The Review of Economic Statistics* 25 (1) pp. 93–96.

Swiercz, P. M. and Lydon, S. R. (2002) Entrepreneurial leadership in high-tech firms: A field study, *Leadership and Organization Development Journal* 23 (7) pp. 380–389.

Tedmanson, D., Verduijn, K., Essers, C. and Gartner, W. B. (2012) Emancipation and/or oppression? Conceptualizing dimensions of criticality in entrepreneurship studies, *Organization* 19 (5) pp. 531–541.

Thornberry, N. (2006) *Lead like an Entrepreneur: Keeping the Entrepreneurial Spirit Alive within the Corporation*, Fairfield, PA: McGraw-Hill.

Thorpe, R., Cope, J., Ram, M. and Pedler, M. (2009) Editorial: Leadership development in small- and medium-sized enterprises: The case for action learning, *Action Learning Research and Practice* 6 (3) pp. 201–208.

Thorpe, R., Gold, J. and Lawler, J. (2011) Locating distributed leadership, *International Journal of Management Reviews* 13 (3) pp. 239–250.

Tourish, D. (2013) *The Dark Side of Transformational Leadership: A Critical Perspective*, London: Routledge.

Uhl-Bien, M., Riggio, R. E., Lowe, K. B. and Carsten, M. K. (2014) Followership theory: A review and research agenda, *The Leadership Quarterly* 25 (1) pp. 83–104.

van Knippenberg, D. and Sitkin, S. B. (2013) A critical assessment of charismatic-transformational leadership research: Back to the drawing board?, *The Academy of Management Annals* 7 (1) pp. 1–60.

Vecchio, R. P. (2003) Entrepreneurship and leadership: Common trends and common threads, *Human Resources Management Review* 13 (2) pp. 303–327.

Verduijn, K., Dey, P., Tedmanson, D. and Essers, C. (2014) Emancipation and/or oppression? Conceptualising dimensions of criticality in entrepreneurship studies, *International Journal of Entrepreneurial Behaviour and Research* 20 (2) pp. 98–107.

Wang, C. L., Tee, D. D. and Ahmed, P. K. (2012) Entrepreneurial leadership and context in Chinese firms: A tale of two Chinese private enterprises, *Asia Pacific Business Review* 18 (4) pp. 505–530.

Welter, F. (2011) Contexualizing entrepreneurship: Conceptual challenges and ways forward, *Entrepreneurship Theory and Practice* 35 (1) pp. 165–184.

Young, O. R. (1991) Political leadership and regime formation: On the development of institutions in international society, *International Organization* 45 pp. 281–308.

Zahra, S. A. and Wright, M. (2011) Entrepreneurship's next act, *Academy of Management Perspectives* 25 (4) pp. 67–83.

Zaleznik, A. (1977) Managers and leaders: Are they different?, *Harvard Business Review* 55 (3) pp. 67–78.

3

Entrepreneurial Action Research: Moving Beyond Fixed Conceptualizations

Hamid Vahidnia, H. Shawna Chen,
J. Robert Mitchell and Ronald K. Mitchell

INTRODUCTION

Apple, Inc. co-founder, Steve Wozniak, once suggested that: 'Entrepreneurs have to keep adjusting to [their situation] … everything's changing, everything's dynamic' (Livingston, 2007, p. 56). The idea here is that entrepreneurial action occurs in situations that are dynamic (e.g. Haynie & Shepherd, 2009; Mitchell, Randolph-Seng, & Mitchell, 2011). In this chapter, we focus on the potential dynamism of entrepreneurial action as far as it relates to and can be informed by insights offered by entrepreneurial cognition research (Mitchell, Busenitz, Lant, McDougall, Morse, & Smith, 2002, 2004; Mitchell, Busenitz, Bird, Marie Gaglio, McMullen, Morse, & Smith, 2007; Mitchell et al., 2011). We do so by taking into account this notion of 'adjusting' by understanding the adaptive action that is crucial in both explaining entrepreneurial action theoretically and in helping entrepreneurs to take more effective action

practically (e.g. Randolph-Seng, Mitchell, Vahidnia, Mitchell, Chen, & Statzer, 2015).

Ironically, entrepreneurial cognition research has not itself adjusted to this 'everything's changing, everything's dynamic' aspect of many entrepreneurial contexts. However, while this adjustment to cognitive dynamism has been gaining substantial momentum (e.g. Baker & Nelson, 2005; Baucus, Baucus, & Mitchell, 2014; Clarke & Cornelissen, 2014; Corbett, 2014; Drnovšek, Slavek, & Cardon, 2014; Forbes, 2014; Grégoire, 2014; Grégoire, Corbett, & McMullen, 2011; Cornelissen & Clarke, 2010; Haynie, Shepherd, Mosakowski, & Earley, 2010; McMullen, Wood, & Palich, 2014; Mitchell et al., 2011; Mitchell, Mitchell, Zachary, & Ryan, 2014; Randolph-Seng, Williams, & Hayek, 2014), much work prior to this acceleration has tended to treat the entrepreneurs, their actions, characteristics, tendencies, and other factors influencing their actions as being more monolithic, using fixed conceptualizations or 'boxologies'

(Mitchell et al., 2011; Smith & Semin, 2004). Additionally, fixed-conceptualization explanations often rely on some entity that relatively statically *influences* entrepreneurial action (e.g. Zahra & Wright, 2011) rather than using a conceptualization that captures entities dynamically *interacting* with entrepreneurs' cognitive resources and mental models to impact how entrepreneurs act when pursuing entrepreneurial opportunities. In this chapter we seek, therefore, to add to the developing dynamic-cognition-based explanations for entrepreneurial action.

To accomplish this task, the chapter is divided into two parts. In the first section, we look more closely at this general problem of fixed/stable conceptualizations, explaining how this 'fixed-ness' manifests itself in a variety of different forms, and thereby impedes the advancement of the management science of entrepreneurial action research. In the second section, using a socially situated cognition perspective (Mitchell et al., 2011, 2014; Smith & Semin, 2004, 2007), we suggest ways to apply this perspective to the further study of entrepreneurial action to enable researchers to incorporate dynamic cognition models in their analyses.

ENTREPRENEURIAL ACTION RESEARCH AND THE PROBLEM OF FIXED CONCEPTUALIZATIONS

Entrepreneurial action can be defined as any activities entrepreneurs undertake when pursuing entrepreneurial opportunities (Alvarez & Barney, 2007). Creating new opportunities, businesses, and/or entrepreneurial artifacts happens only over time and occurs as a result, not of a single activity, but of a course of action taken by entrepreneurs (Alvarez & Barney, 2007; McMullen & Dimov, 2013; Mitchell, Mitchell, & Smith, 2008; Venkataraman, Sarasvathy, Dew, & Forster, 2012). As individuals move from one action to the next, the context in which they operate

is likely to change (Welter, 2011). Studying entrepreneurial action is thus about understanding, in relation to this changing and dynamic context, what entrepreneurs do, how they do it, and why they perform certain activities but not others, in each situation. Thus, in this chapter, entrepreneurial action is conceptualized to be a process involving behavioral and cognitive activities taken within a changing situation in the pursuit of entrepreneurial opportunities (e.g. Chen, 2015).

While prior research has advanced understanding of entrepreneurial action, much of this research would seem to treat factors that influence entrepreneurial action in similar ways that, we believe, may yet hinder the development of more fine-grained understandings of entrepreneurial action. Specifically, much of the prior research provides explanations that primarily are based on what we term 'fixed conceptualizations' of entrepreneurs, their character, motivations, tendencies, and social contexts. In the existing research, these factors are seldom, if ever, assumed to change. This makes it difficult to explain the dynamic actions of entrepreneurs in response to their dynamic context, when constrained by these fixed conceptualizations. As we shall attempt to demonstrate, such fixed conceptualizations manifest themselves in specific ways. We suggest that identifying many of these fixed conceptualizations is an important part of understanding how entrepreneurs think and act. In doing so, we join other scholars who have criticized entrepreneurial action (and more generally entrepreneurship) research to stimulate more fruitful research in response to this criticism (e.g. Davidsson, 2003; Dimov, 2007; Gartner, Carter, & Hills, 2003; McMullen & Dimov, 2013; Zahra & Wright, 2011).

As a point of departure, we review the various forms that fixed conceptualizations have taken in the existing literature. In order to make our case, we only attempt to discuss higher-level assertions, treatments, and/or generalizations evident in these approaches.

In doing so, we acknowledge that not all the research we discuss and reference contains each and every type of fixed conceptualization issue; nor has this research necessarily made assertions that speak to these specific types of fixed conceptualization. Rather, in many cases, the research we discuss might only implicitly assume the fixed conceptualizations we assert to be problematic. We thus acknowledge that we have sacrificed some elements of precision, but we do so as a way of highlighting the broad nature of the challenges that fixed conceptualizations present, and demonstrate that they require attention and consideration in future research. We discuss, and in a descriptive way 'stylize', seven such 'fixed conceptualizations' in the following paragraphs.

Fixed Conceptualization #1: Entrepreneurs are Individuals with Fixed (and Heroic) Character/ Characteristics

In prior entrepreneurship research, entrepreneurs are treated as having stable, and often heroic characteristics. Traditionally, and following the lead of Knight (1921), the entrepreneur is conceptualized to be a risk-taker and 'bearer' of uncertainty. Earlier research on entrepreneurial traits attempted to describe the nature of such a hero (e.g. Hornaday & Bunker, 1970) or identify characteristics of this superman-entrepreneur (e.g. McClelland, 1965; Pickle, 1964), yet extensive subsequent research resulted in equivocal findings, not in a common and/or finite list of those traits (e.g. Brockhaus & Horwitz, 1986; Gartner, 1989).[1] More recent research goes beyond such heroic treatment (e.g. effectuation-focused research), but nonetheless often implicitly treats the entrepreneur as having heroic characteristics. For example, as Arend, Sarooghi, and Burkemper (2015) argue, the means by which effectuation entrepreneurs start ventures include relatively unalterable characteristics such as who the entrepreneur

is and what s/he wants. Additionally, in the effectuation approach, the entrepreneur may be seen to be a fully-in-charge heroic type who effectually creates the future, often from scratch (e.g. Sarasvathy, 2001). The entrepreneur is also portrayed to be so capable in dealing with others that in the majority of cases s/he 'cues in intelligent altruism in others' (Sarasvathy & Dew, 2008, p. 729; emphasis in original), thus at least partly eliminating the need for the entrepreneur to check constantly whether these other parties are trustworthy and can be relied upon as the situation changes.

Such heroic treatments, however, are reminiscent of institutional theorists' skepticism concerning the existence of 'hyper-muscular supermen' change agents (e.g. Suddaby, 2010, p. 15) and Rumelt's (1987, p. 136) tongue-in-cheek characterization of the entrepreneur: 'Where do new businesses come from? The textbooks say that the entrepreneur, like the stork, brings them.' This skeptical view is shared by scholars who increasingly have noted how others, such as founding teams (e.g. Ruef, Aldrich, & Carter, 2003), networks (e.g. Birley, 1986) and mentors (e.g. Ozgen & Baron, 2007), among other contributors, are also important to creating new businesses/opportunities and to high entrepreneurial performance. The danger of conceptualizing entrepreneurs as heroes is that it often leads to mystification of the way individuals think and act in the face of inevitable dynamism (e.g. Mitchell, 1996), thus hindering better identification and transmission of entrepreneurship-related skills, as well as empirical and theoretical work on entrepreneurial action.

While such a fixed conceptualization may be appealing *post hoc*, it is encumbered by survival/success bias (Davidsson, 2003; Dimov, 2007), is unrealistic (Shane, 2008), and misleading as to practical expectations (Arend et al., 2015). A more practical set of assumptions might conceptualize most entrepreneurial actors to have limited capacity and resources (e.g. limited capacity to process information) when facing the obstacles of opportunity pursuit (Arend et al., 2015; Busenitz & Barney, 1997) and to rely on other people's minds (such as mentors, potential customers, family and friends) and available tools (such as computer programs and information systems), among other resources, to deal with entrepreneurial challenges (e.g. Mitchell et al., 2011). Shane (2008, p. 160) agrees, stating: 'Our collective belief that the typical entrepreneur is a hero with special powers … is a myth'.

Fixed Conceptualization #2: Uncertainty Is Temporally and Contextually Fixed

Prior entrepreneurship research often implies that entrepreneurs deal with uncertainty all at once, as if the process of forming an opportunity or creating a new venture occurs in one action. The earlier work of Kirzner and the concept of entrepreneurial arbitrage is one such example (Kirzner, 1973, 2009). From this perspective, uncertainty generally is a constant variable (set at a high level), where this degree of uncertainty does not fluctuate often, and the effects of different types of uncertainty and fluctuations of uncertainty are not much included in explanations. Milliken (1987), however, has theorized that there exist three types of perceived uncertainty in the environment: state, effect, and response, and in a notable departure from the 'uncertainty as a fixed condition' conceptualization, McKelvie, Haynie, and Gustavsson (2011) have operationalized Milliken's (1987) notion of multidimensional uncertainty and have examined its implications for entrepreneurial action.

However, despite these improvements, scholars continue to treat uncertainty essentially as fixed, and its relationship with entrepreneurial action is therefore not entirely clear and/or explicit. Instead of dealing with fluctuating (and therefore conceptually messy) uncertainty, entrepreneurs are assumed to circumvent it. For example, by focusing on those aspects of the future that are under the control of the entrepreneur (e.g. in effectuation-based explanations) or by entering the field of entrepreneurship 'accidentally' (e.g. in user entrepreneurship), actors are conceptualized as able to experience some fixed level of uncertainty.

Yet, in the dynamic world, most entrepreneurs can neither be expected to accomplish all they must undertake in one event, nor can they be expected to remain undaunted by aspects of the world that are beyond their control (e.g. McGrath, 1999), in some cases preferring, for example, certain losses to uncertain gains (Kahneman & Tversky, 1979). Additionally, as entrepreneurs take action, new information inevitably becomes available about the supply and demand related to an opportunity (e.g. Mitchell et al., 2008), leading to variation in levels of uncertainty throughout the process. Similarly, when individuals invite others to join their venturing activities, the new team member may add much knowledge and information processing power to the team that may influence the level of uncertainty an individual or team perceives (Ruef et al., 2003). Therefore, we argue that accounting for variability in the level of perceived uncertainty in explanations is of theoretical and practical importance for studying entrepreneurial action.

Fixed Conceptualization #3: Entrepreneurs' Motivation Is Considered to Be Fixed

Much of our current understanding of entrepreneurial action comes from studying those who have succeeded (Davidsson, 2003). Yet, generalizing from this small portion of actors may or may not capture the real world as experienced by the majority of other actors. For example, in fixed-conceptualization approaches, most individuals generally are assumed not to enter into the realm of uncertainty represented by their taking entrepreneurial action (i.e. motivation = zero). But then something happens and an individual entrepreneur-actor decides now to 'bear' the uncertainties of taking entrepreneurial action; the motivation of that entrepreneur seems to have then been assumed to remain high and constant (i.e. motivation = fixed and high). For example, McMullen and Shepherd's (2006) account of entrepreneurial action, while providing an insightful synthesis of much previous work on entrepreneurial action, presupposes that, once having entered the realm of entrepreneurship, the entrepreneurs' motivation will remain (constant and) high. Shepherd, McMullen, and Jennings (2007) further imply that, once an individual overcomes ignorance and/or reduces doubt to believe that an opportunity is for him/her, entrepreneurial action 'ensues' thereafter.

Likewise, fixed conceptualizations of motivation can be seen in other work in the literature. For example, Shah and Tripsas (2007) and Baker, Miner, & Eesley (2003) generalize their models of user entrepreneurship and improvisation from data related to those who succeeded and thus focus on those entrepreneurs who have (by definition) high levels of motivation. While the primary focus of such work is to describe certain processes, when it comes to their generalizations, scholars often suggest (or assume) that entrepreneurs are sometimes so motivated that they frequently and readily act. In reality, however, we suggest that entrepreneurs' motivation may change frequently, e.g. depending even upon relatively minor sensory input (Baucus et al., 2014) or upon otherwise larger changes the entrepreneur may experience. We see inklings of this line of thinking in work that specifies several points in the entrepreneurial process where changes in mental processing may occur (Wood, Williams, & Grégoire, 2012).

Fixed Conceptualization #4: Actors Have Fixed (and Narrow) Criteria for Action

Past entrepreneurship research with strong roots in economics suggests that, when making choices or taking action in the pursuit of entrepreneurial opportunities, individuals mostly rely on certain fixed criteria, including, for example, seeking the objective of maximizing their expected return/utility (e.g. Casson, 1982) or judging if the 'risk/return dilemma' associated with an opportunity justifies pursuing it (McMullen & Shepherd, 2006, p. 141). Fixed-criteria (for action) research has been criticized on a number of grounds. First, reliance on fixed criteria such as maximizing expected return may not be feasible because, in many cases, one may not conceptually be able to calculate expected returns associated with entrepreneurial opportunities (e.g. see: Miller, 2007). Second, entrepreneurs can have multiple economic and non-economic criteria when acting, i.e. they are multi-objective when pursuing entrepreneurial opportunities (e.g. see: Baker & Pollock, 2007; Hamilton, 2000). For example, scholars have observed that entrepreneurs may pursue entrepreneurial opportunities because they have strong personal values for pursuing certain opportunities, seek independence, attempt to make a difference in the world, and/or want emancipation, among other things, while simultaneously trying to gain financial results (e.g. Rindova, Barry, & Ketchen, 2009). Some even argue that financial criteria themselves can be multi-faceted and changing as entrepreneurs' financial goals may change as they go through different stages of a business life cycle (e.g. Carter, 2011; Kammerlander, 2016). These arguments have led scholars to critique entrepreneurship research for becoming 'too narrowly focused' on maximizing financial returns/gains and/or on wealth maximization (e.g. see: Greenbank, 1999; Rindova et al., 2009, p. 478).

To address this narrow focus on some fixed criterion such as maximizing one's financial return, some research has offered alternative possibilities. For example, Sarasvathy (2001) proposes that, in contrast to causation-based entrepreneurial actions, which are based generally on maximizing expected returns, effectuation-based entrepreneurial actions are taken based on the criterion of affordable loss. In such cases the entrepreneur predetermines how much loss is affordable and focuses on what can be done by available means. Thus, effectuation theory replaces the fixed and unchanging criterion of maximizing one's return with the criterion of affordable loss, which itself appears to be of similar type in the sense that affordable loss is much like maximizing return in its tendency to restrict focus. To us, this substitution thus appears essentially to be substituting one type of static and fixed criterion in place of another. Thus, effectuation theory, in our view, does not easily accommodate the idea that entrepreneurs may have multiple and often changing criteria when making decisions and taking action (e.g. Carter, 2011; Hamilton, 2000; Rindova et al., 2009).

In sum, both theoretical and empirical research demonstrates that actors (such as entrepreneurs) utilize multiple criteria when acting (e.g. Gigerenzer, 1996; Hamilton, 2000; Rindova et al., 2009; Wood & Williams, 2014). Additionally, we take note also that the criteria that guide entrepreneurial action may change as the situation changes – e.g. in different stages of one's business (Carter, 2011; Gigerenzer & Goldstein, 1996; Miller, 2007). Wood and Williams (2014, p. 576), for example, found support for the notion that evaluation of opportunities 'takes the form of a multicriteria structured decision problem'. Thus, we argue that appreciating multiple and broader sets of criteria can help make entrepreneurial action research more productive and more connected to the real world of many entrepreneurs (e.g. Randolph-Seng et al., 2015; Shepherd, 2015). Accordingly, in future conceptualizations of the criteria that invoke entrepreneurial action, we suggest that actors be treated as agents that take into account multiple criteria when acting and that these criteria themselves also be conceptualized as changing.

Fixed Conceptualization #5: Social Situation/Context Is Fixed

In much of the literature, the context within which an entrepreneur is expected to work is generally assumed to be a market system, which itself provides an actor with little information (e.g. generally only price differences). In such a case, actors face Knightian uncertainty, where action is predicated upon various information-gaining strategies (Knight, 1921). But often it is not clear how these strategies relate to the specifics of the context in which they take place. Specifically, the market context generally is treated as being broad and homogeneous, detached from the actions of entrepreneurs (e.g. Zahra & Wright, 2011). Under such an assumption, it is mostly the differences between the cognitive resources residing inside the mind of the individual (Gaglio & Katz, 2001; Kirzner, 1973) that are suggested to impact entrepreneurial action.

In some research, the context is either: (1) included also in a very broad sense such as at the industry level not tightly connected to individual's actions (e.g. knowledge-intensive industries, as in Baker et al., 2003), or (2) essentially treated as irrelevant, as actors are expected to rely upon certain stable types of behavior no matter what the structure of the outer environment looks like (e.g. Sarasvathy, 2001). In either case, context is still fixed in our view. This assumption, while often convenient in specific research instances, is in sharp contrast to Simon's (1990) view that: '… human rational behavior … is shaped by a scissors whose two blades are the structure of task environments and the computational capabilities of the actor' (1990, p. 7).

Instead, then, for entrepreneurial action explanations to increase in their effectiveness, we suggest context be included as playing a major, dynamic, and changing role in entrepreneurial action. As the context of most entrepreneurs changes over time (e.g. Zahra & Wright, 2011; Welter, 2011) and as even slight changes in the environment can cause important changes in the behavior of the actors in that environment (e.g. Semin & Smith, 2013), more dynamic conceptualizations of the context and how its components influence entrepreneurial action are needed. Indeed, some scholars have even suggested ways of overcoming some of the methodological weaknesses of capturing the significance of changing context on action (Chalmers & Shaw, in press).

Fixed Conceptualization #6: Actors Have Fixed Tendencies toward Action

Synthesizing some of the work conducted earlier in entrepreneurship research (e.g. Casson, 1982; Knight, 1921, and others), McMullen and Shepherd (2006, p. 135) argue that, as these approaches suggest, individuals acting under uncertainty tend to be in a somewhat perpetual state of 'hesitancy, indecisiveness, and procrastination', leading these individuals to miss profit opportunities. We read this as a suggestion that there is a fixed tendency toward action that translates into no entrepreneurial action at all. Yet, once some individuals manage to escape this detrimental state (into entrepreneurial action at least), they are then expected to engage in entrepreneurial action and do so seemingly continuously thereafter, having assumedly adopted a fixed tendency toward entrepreneurial action.

Similarly, some research portrays entrepreneurs in ways that seem to have certain predispositions toward action. For example, Baker et al. (2003) suggest that some entrepreneurs are so ready to act that they readily improvise (or simultaneously plan and execute). Yet, no explanations as to *why* *some* entrepreneurs do improvise while others do not are offered, and – according to this account – we do not know what exactly was happening in either the internal (cognitive) world or in the external (outside) world that may have led to this type of behavior (e.g.

Zahra & Wright, 2011), leading to black-box-type explanations for entrepreneurial action (e.g. Mitchell et al., 2011).

It has long been suggested that many actors simply do not show a fixed tendency (coming solely from within their mind) when acting but, instead, that their behavior is more likely to also include a response component to the demands of their social situations (Gigerenzer & Goldstein, 1996; Granovetter, 1985; Simon, 1990). Not seriously accounting for the changes (or stability) in the context when theory building or theory testing can, we believe, undermine our ability to understand why such fixed tendencies are observed (e.g. Johns, 2006; Rousseau & Fried, 2001). We therefore argue that it is only when we fully appreciate the social situation of entrepreneurs (Liñán, Moriano, & Jaén, 2016; Mitchell et al., 2011; Mitchell et al., 2014; Randolph-Seng et al., 2015) that we may be able to move beyond these fixed conceptualizations of actors' tendencies toward action or inaction, to more fully explain *why* entrepreneurs take some actions and not others.

Fixed Conceptualization #7: Actors Have Fixed Foci of Attention

In both earlier and newer approaches to the study of entrepreneurial action, there seems to be portrayed an insensitivity of actors to the multi-faceted nature of entrepreneurial phenomena. At a conceptually higher level, Hayek (1937) points to the importance of foresight in action, suggesting that: 'before we can explain why people commit mistakes, we must first explain why they should ever be right' (1937, p. 34). He then argues that there are really two fundamentally different conditions of data (or knowledge available to the actor), which he argues are separate: (1) that individuals' subjective data are mutually compatible with each other; and (2) that this subjective, mutually compatible data possessed by involved individuals correspond to the objective, real world data (1937, pp. 39–40).

Traditional approaches generally focus on the objective side of the argument, that is, on market condition/imperfections, without sufficient discussion of how individuals act (e.g. Kirzner, 1973; for one exception, see Mises, 1949). Thus, actors are portrayed to have a limited focus: fixed at the system level, e.g. to identify profit opportunities. Some emergent approaches, however, typically portray actors that mostly or almost entirely focus on the subjective side of Hayek's argument. These actors are theorized to focus on what they think, with limited attention given to what the broader social system, such as a market, may value (see, most notably, Sarasvathy, 2001). Thus, the focus of the actor, generally, seems to be fixed on himself/herself. Accordingly, in our view, these potentially one-sided portrayals of actors that have fixed foci of attention do not fully take into account the effects of changes that occur as a result of the dynamics of the context on entrepreneurs' actions and the effects of those changes that occur as a result of the actions of entrepreneurs in the context (e.g. Johns, 2006; Welter, 2011). We therefore

suggest that in future work on entrepreneurial action, if we are to understand the mutual influence of entrepreneurs and their social situation on entrepreneurial action, actors be treated as agents who focus on both their subjective and objective worlds dynamically.

SUMMARY

In this section we have argued that approaches to entrepreneurial action often use fixed conceptualizations to characterize entrepreneurs and their attributes, tendencies, motivations, social contexts, etc. in explanations for entrepreneurial action. We have argued that this use of fixed conceptualizations leads to black-box-type explanations that cannot fully capture the dynamics and the changing nature of the thinking and doing of entrepreneurs in their social situations. Such fixed conceptualizations can take several forms, which we have discussed in the preceding paragraphs and summarize in the summary stylizations presented in Table 3.1.

Table 3.1   Examples of fixed conceptualizations in explaining entrepreneurs and their actions

Type of fixed conceptualization	Stylized understanding of earlier approaches	Stylized understanding of more recent approaches	Stylized understanding of issue(s)
1. Entrepreneurs are individuals with fixed (and heroic) character/ characteristics	The entrepreneur is the bearer of uncertainty (e.g. Knight, 1921) who shows 'boldness' (Kirzner, 1997, p. 72).	The entrepreneur is an 'effectuator' who creates the future, seemingly with little need to take its forces into account (e.g. Sarasvathy, 2001, p. 262).	Actors are not heroic, but do act in the face of limitations (e.g. Simon, 1990). Without an understanding of these nuances, the nature of entrepreneurial actions may remain mystical (e.g. Mitchell, 1996; Rumelt, 1987).
2. Uncertainty is temporally and contextually fixed	The entrepreneur apparently deals with high levels of uncertainty throughout the process (e.g. Knight, 1921).	The entrepreneur comes to the stage in an 'accidental' manner (Shah & Tripsas, 2007, p. 123), experiencing minimum uncertainty.	Process views (e.g. McMullen & Dimov, 2013) explain that time is important and that formation of an opportunity generally occurs in a sequence of actions, allowing the actors to deal, step by step, with varying levels of uncertainty (e.g. McGrath, 1999).

(Continued)

Table 3.1   (Continued)

3. Entrepreneurs' motivation is considered to be fixed	Having decided to bear uncertainty, the entrepreneur's motivation remains somewhat constant throughout the process (e.g. Kirzner, 1973).	The entrepreneur seems to have a rather fixed level of motivation while constantly improvising (e.g. Baker et al., 2003).	Actors' motivational levels change as they receive new information from the world. Survival bias (e.g. Davidsson, 2003) should not lead us to assume that all actors show high levels of motivation throughout the opportunity formation process.
4. Actors have fixed (and narrow) criteria for action	Criterion: How can the entrepreneur maximize his or her expected utility (e.g. see: Miller, 2007)?	Criterion: How much can the entrepreneur afford to lose (Sarasvathy, 2001)?	Ample empirics (e.g. on escalation of commitment; Staw, 1981) suggest that neither of the two criteria is entirely realistic. Human action cannot and should not be reduced to one single principle (Gigerenzer, 1996).
5. Social situation/ context is fixed	The context does not provide sufficient clue for the individual, leaving him or her in vacuum (e.g. Knight, 1921).	The context is discussed in broad and general terms, e.g. in terms such as 'new knowledge-based firms' (Baker et al., 2003, p. 256).	Lack of an understanding of the causal role of context results in an under-conceptualized understanding of '… human rational behavior [as]… scissors whose two blades are the structure of task environments and the computational capabilities of the actor' (Simon, 1990, p. 7).
6. Actors have fixed tendencies toward action	Actors almost always have doubt. This often undermines action (e.g. Knight, 1921).	Actors show a 'bias toward action' (Baker & Nelson, 2005, p. 334) or have certain principles to follow in almost all situations (Sarasvathy, 2001).	In reality, actors engage in different types of actions, not just one type, as the situation may demand (e.g. Gigerenzer, 1996).
7. Actors have fixed foci of attention	Actors mostly focus on understanding the objective reality (e.g. Kirzner, 1973).	Actors mostly focus on their own selves or worlds (e.g. Sarasvathy, 2001).	Entrepreneurial phenomena need to be viewed with a multi-faceted perspective (e.g. Hayek, 1937).

Overall, this review suggests that the study of entrepreneurial action can benefit by moving toward what we see to be more realistic conceptualizations. Such conceptualizations could provide accounts of action in which actors: (1) are viewed in more 'ordinary' ways as individuals with limited (cognitive and otherwise) resources; (2) experience varying levels of uncertainty, both temporally and contextually, as they proceed to create new value; (3) have motivations that vary at different points in the process; (4) have criteria for taking action or choosing among different courses of action that are variable or multi-faceted; (5) influence and are influenced by the nuances of their social situation and the other people/tools/objects with whom they interact; (6) have relatively complex sets of interests and changing tendencies that guide their actions; and (7) attend to both inner and outer demands of their environment, as these demands change.

In the second section of this chapter, we offer an approach that may assist in accomplishing a more robust conceptualization. We first introduce the socially situated cognition perspective as a broad approach to the task of offering more realistic explanations of entrepreneurial action. We then provide more specific 'future directions' in which this perspective can be used to assist researchers to develop more nuanced conceptualizations of the dynamics of entrepreneurial action, and we then conclude the chapter.

ENTREPRENEURIAL ACTION RESEARCH: TOWARD DYNAMIC CONCEPTUALIZATIONS

In the previous section we have argued for a more dynamic conceptualization of entrepreneurial action. The socially situated cognition perspective provides such a conceptualization, beginning with the notion that the most important function of cognition is to support action, where: 'thinking is for doing' (Fiske, 1992, p. 877). Socially situated cognition helpfully offers four themes or major assumptions for utilization by scholars when attempting to include this thinking-is-for-doing mechanism in better explanations: (1) cognition is action-oriented; (2) cognition is embodied; (3) cognition is situated; and (4) cognition is distributed (Smith & Semin, 2004).

That cognition is *action-oriented* means thinking does not merely occur for its own sake, but it has evolved to support and facilitate the capacity of individuals to take adaptive action within their environment, e.g. to achieve some goal or goals. That cognition is *embodied* suggests that thinking is heavily affected by the neurophysiology that produces a variety of different states of the body (e.g. Baucus et al., 2014, for a review of the neurophysiology of emotion and motivation). That cognition is *situated* suggests that the communicative (e.g. conversation with other individuals), relational, and group context in which an individual finds herself/himself influences the individual's thinking and doing. Thus, the content of thinking is thought to come not only from the individual's mind, but also from the environment in which one lives. That cognition is *distributed* means that not all thinking is done within the mind/brain of an isolated individual, but that, when acting, individuals also rely on other minds and tools that are disseminated across their social setting, including other actors and tools in the environment (Smith & Semin, 2004, 2007).[2]

In the remainder of this section, we focus on future directions: seven suggestions[3] for how a socially situated cognition perspective can assist in overcoming the potential problems of fixed conceptualizations of entrepreneurial action (as outlined in the first section) by enabling the development of more nuanced and fine-grained conceptualizations of entrepreneurial action. Specifically, we argue that a socially situated cognition perspective enables such fine-grained conceptualizations of human thought and behavior to be developed by taking into account critically important factors that go beyond the inner and mental resources of the individual actor and instead integrate explanations of the real world that most entrepreneurs experience (e.g. Randolph-Seng et al., 2015; Shepherd, 2015).

Future Direction #1: Examine Entrepreneurial Action from a Macroscopic View

The variety of forms that the problem of fixed conceptualization can take implies that research to date has focused tightly on certain attributes in isolation (e.g. personality, motivation, etc.) as part of deepening understanding of these factors and their role in entrepreneurial action. However, because of such a sharp focus on certain factors, we are somewhat disabled from more fully understanding the interaction among all of these factors. In other words, research has focused on a 'microscopic' view of social cognition, but also must attend to a 'macroscopic' view of social cognition. As Semin and Smith (2013) write:

> A microscopic perspective involves attending to traditional individual and representation-centered elements prevalent in mainstream psychology and social psychology, such as attention, motivation, representation, and categorization. In contrast, the phenomena to be explained and understood at a macroscopic level are social interaction in specific contexts and the processes driving it. This higher or macroscopic level organization has an entirely different quality than do the single units that compose and give rise to the phenomenon. (2013, p. 128)

For entrepreneurial action research, taking a macroscopic view can mean that, besides focusing on what entrepreneurs do (i.e. their 'observable' behaviors) or how they think (e.g. mental representations or cognitive resources they may have acquired through past experiences), we may need also to investigate a combination of factors that collectively and simultaneously, in the macro sense, influence entrepreneurial action (e.g. the combination of factors personal to the actor, such as their goals, together with the demands of the social and nonsocial situation, etc.). Under a macroscopic explanation, entrepreneurial action is likely to be taken in relation to the whole: the collective effects of such factors as opposed to their specific effects, e.g. being directed by some fixed and/or stable criteria such as maximizing utility or minimizing loss. As changes happen in any of these social and nonsocial factors (under the social situated view: where action, embodiment, situation, and distribution of cognitions merge macroscopically), the next actions might then, as a result, be expected to be influenced and thereby to be enacted differently. The 'whole', in this view, is conceptualized to be much more changeable and dynamic than previously conceptualized, as well as much broader (Semin & Smith,

2013). Thus, the macroscopic view, where entrepreneurial action is seen in its broader and changing social context, allows one to understand and explain how and why certain actions are taken, how and why the whole situation evolves as it does, and how behavioral responses to those situations, such as entrepreneurial action, are influenced accordingly.

Future Direction #2: Attend to the Specific Content of the Empirical World

Socially situated cognition suggests that, in many cases, human beings make decisions in real time, i.e. use mental representations that are constructed 'online' mentally, and they act based upon these representations as they interpret the environment, as opposed to acting based on 'offline' mental representations of the underlying structures (those not constructed in the moment) that are restored from cognitive resources such as long-term memory. For the most part, real-time use is the case because creating mental representations of the environment from mental storage at times can be costly (Semin & Smith, 2013). If, when pursuing entrepreneurial opportunities, entrepreneurs have to focus constantly on a variety of aspects of their environment that at times are highly novel (e.g. Teece, 2012), then it is problematic for these actors to rely constantly on previously stored cognitive resources, some of which may not apply to the current, immediate situation. Additionally, and at certain times, it may become too costly mentally or even impossible for entrepreneurs first to develop the cognitive resources applicable to the current situation and then, second, to use these resources to guide their actions, e.g. in cases where entrepreneurs have limited time and have to improvise. Theoretically, this future direction (of attending to the specific content of the empirical world) relies on the assumption that 'the world is its own best representation' (Agre, 1997, p. 63) and means that including in explanations attention to the specific content of the empirical world, as constructed 'online' in the mind of the entrepreneur, may improve the explanatory power of future research on entrepreneurial action.

Furthermore, it is likely that individuals will engage in different forms of action if 'online' mental representations are constructed differentially depending upon, for example, *both* environment and embodiment (due to the influence of group context, perception of the social environment, and/ or even slight differences in bodily states, etc.). Due to such path dependency in entrepreneurial action, among other factors, small initial differences can lead to considerable subsequent differences in results (Arthur, 1989; Baucus et al., 2014). Thus, a better understanding of how individuals create these mental 'online' representations based on their specific empirical world, and the effects of subtle differences in such 'online' constructions, are of theoretical and practical importance in future research on entrepreneurial action.

Future Direction #3: Work with Situated Concepts

A socially situated cognition perspective suggests that, in most cases, human beings create situated versions of concepts (Semin & Smith, 2013, pp. 131–2) – e.g. of success, cooperation, competition, morality, trust, etc. Thus, instead of working with fixed, universal, and objective concepts, such as acting, for example, based on having a fixed conceptualization of what success is, individuals are likely to construct situated versions of concepts they already know or learn as they interpret the context in the light of their entrepreneurial goals, such as in the case of an entrepreneurial opportunity that is being constantly developed and thus changed (e.g. Dimov, 2007). Further examination in future

studies, to detect the presence and influence of concepts that have been utilized in one way to guide the actions of entrepreneurs, but now are utilized in another way to guide, for example, follow-on entrepreneurial action, and furthermore to detect the way that meanings change as a result, is another theoretical direction for future research on entrepreneurial action. Where entrepreneurs are conceptualized to work with concepts that are malleable and thereby are changeable in their meanings, theorizing and empirical research might then also profit from the greater explanation of variance possible as these changes are captured in individuals, in their mind–body interaction, in the interface with other actors, and in the interaction with environments in the process of opportunity pursuit.

We suggest that one specific way to pursue this suggested line of research using situated concepts might be to examine how individuals interpret the world according to their current goals. Under the cognitive malleability assumptions of socially situated cognition, entrepreneurs' motivation would not be conceptualized as fixed throughout the entrepreneurial process. Nor should the criteria for entrepreneurs to take action be fixed or narrow. For example, unlike the motivation of many entrepreneurs to achieve monetary or other forms of success, at least early in the process, Spivack, McKelvie, and Haynie (2014) found that, later in the process of entrepreneurial action, some habitual entrepreneurs' behavioral and motivational factors showed similarities with those of 'addicted' individuals. Such changes, embodied in these entrepreneurs' brain and body, have been found to change the very content of their motivation and/or goals and were critical in those entrepreneurs' interpretation of the world, resulting even in negative influence of their behaviors on their family and friendships, among other factors. If, in researching entrepreneurial action, we conceptualize entrepreneurs as individuals who use situated concepts when acting, then we see as possible that these and other pluralistic views of factors motivating action can be captured effectively and the criteria for the invocation of action can thereby allow entrepreneurial action research to better explain differences in the actions of entrepreneurs.

Future Direction #4: Explore Entrepreneurial Action across Levels of Analysis

Although several scholars have stressed that it is the collective action, interaction, negotiation, and shared experience between entrepreneurs and their stakeholders that shape and reshape entrepreneurial opportunities (e.g. Alvarez & Barney, 2007; Mitchell, Mitchell, Mitchell, & Alvarez, 2012; Randolph-Seng et al., 2015; Venkataraman et al., 2012; Welter, 2011; Zahra, 2007; Zahra & Wright, 2011), research to date has failed sufficiently to explore entrepreneurial action across levels of analysis (Grégoire et al., 2011). As we explained in the first section of this chapter, this problem may have occurred at least in part because actors in entrepreneurial action research have been conceptualized to have fixed foci of attention. The socially situated cognition perspective suggests that cognition enables the adaptive regulation of self and others' behavior (Semin & Cacioppo, 2008; Smith & Semin, 2004), and that adaptive action requires examining cognitive and behavioral factors not only at the individual level but also at least at a social level of analysis (Semin, Garrido, & Palma, 2012; Semin & Smith, 2013). This cross-level examination in turn involves the examination of social interactions and functional purposes in a wider variety of social contexts.

We suggest that, from a socially situated cognition perspective, entrepreneurial action can be viewed across individual and social (e.g. team, community, and environment) levels of analysis (e.g. Autio, Dahlander, & Frederiksen, 2013; McGrath & MacMillan, 2000; Spedale & Watson, 2014; West, 2007). When viewed mostly at the individual level, cognition can involve static individual- and representation-centered elements, such as motivation and scripts that are activated in similar fashion across all situations (Smith & Semin, 2004, 2007). In contrast, when cognition is considered simultaneously at the individual and social levels, it involves social interactions and functional purposes in a variety of specifiable social contexts (Semin & Smith, 2013). Entrepreneurial action may thus be conceptualized to cross individual and social levels of analysis. For example, Autio et al. (2013) combined data collected from an online user community and found that both the interactions between entrepreneurs and the community and the interactions between the community and entrepreneurial opportunities (as forms of distributed cognition) regulate entrepreneurs' evaluation of entrepreneurial opportunities and their propensity to engage in entrepreneurial action (action at the level of the individual).

These cross-level engagements may occur in particular where entrepreneurs test potential opportunities through interacting with users in the Internet community; where feedback from the community motivates entrepreneurs to adapt or abandon potential opportunities; and where the adapted opportunities transform the community's validation and further encourage the entrepreneurs' engagement of entrepreneurial action (Autio et al., 2013). We suggest that, by using a socially situated cognition perspective and attending to real-world entrepreneurial action at multiple levels of analysis, and by parsing entrepreneurial action through an examination of social interactions at the levels of individuals, teams, communities, and institutions, we thereby may enable a better understanding of entrepreneurial action.

Future Direction #5:
Understand Action and Activities as the Whole and the Parts

As mentioned previously, future research opportunities exist where scholars examine entrepreneurial action from a macroscopic view. In this subsection we suggest an extension of this idea: research helping to explain and to understand the relationships between the 'whole' phenomenon and its 'parts'. This macroscopic view captures in entrepreneurial action the 'infinite diversity as the outcome of a recursively generated system … that [at] each level … displays a new emergent quality' (Semin et al., 2012, p. 140). Thus, when we conceptualize entrepreneurial action as syntheses of sets of discrete activities (Alvarez & Barney, 2007; Shepherd, 2015), we may then consider entrepreneurial action taken within a larger social process to represent the 'whole', and entrepreneurial activities to represent the constituent 'parts'. Entrepreneurial action may thus be conceptualized further to possess a substantively different quality than entrepreneurial activities, and vice versa. We argue that, where it is assumed that the parts cannot be comprehended without insights from explaining the whole, and that the whole cannot be analyzed without identifying and accessing the parts (Gazzaniga, 2010; Zacks & Tversky, 2001), then possibilities emerge for the explanation of additional variance in entrepreneurial action.

To date, scholars have mostly treated entrepreneurial action either as a single act (measured by attributes such as frequency, likelihood, and propensity) (e.g. McKelvie, Haynie, & Gustavsson, 2011; Mitchell & Shepherd, 2010) or as a series of activities (measured by magnitude, pace, and rhythm of event occurrence) (e.g. Autio et al., 2013; Delmar & Shane, 2004; Lichtenstein, Carter, Dooley, & Gartner, 2007). From a socially situated cognition perspective, we suggest that future research not only use entrepreneurial activity as 'the key unit of analysis' (Shepherd, 2015, p. 6) but also explore the relationships among activities as well as the relationships between constituent activities and entrepreneurial action (e.g. Spedale & Watson, 2014). As one example of such an approach, we note that Chen (2015) suggests that entrepreneurial activities can be organized under four ordinal degrees of abstractness and be considered together to better capture the dynamics of entrepreneurial action.

Future Direction #6:
Treat Entrepreneurial Action as a Process

Entrepreneurial cognition research has also fallen short in articulating entrepreneurial action as a process (Grégoire et al., 2011). In fact, one can argue that it is the lack of a process orientation in research on entrepreneurial cognition and action, such as, for example, lack of longitudinal studies, that contributes to the continued dependence in entrepreneurial action research on many of the fixed conceptualizations reported earlier in this chapter. Indeed, the socially situated cognition perspective is based on the assumption that the cognitive processes involve an inherently social process (Fiske, 1992; Robbins & Aydede, 2009) and are thus interactive (Semin et al., 2012).

For example, in studying the process whereby entrepreneurs move from one action to the next, we suggest that we may be able to use socially situated perspective or other dynamic cognition-based approaches to unbundle entrepreneurial action as an interactive, open-ended process, thereby to offer additional explanation and a better understanding, according to the following logic. Given that the socially situated cognition perspective emphasizes the significance of situational factors on cognition and action, and thus offers ways to unbundle the dynamic, interactive process among cognition, action, and the environment, we may argue that: (1) entrepreneurial action is interactive because action requires the social interactions between an entrepreneur's mind and other objects and persons in the social and physical environment; (2) entrepreneurial action is a process because social interactions between entrepreneurs and their stakeholders (e.g. family and friends, team members, customers, investors, suppliers, community, governments, and environment) take place over time; and (3) entrepreneurial action is open-ended because, as different factors may influence construction of 'online' mental representations, different entrepreneurial actions may be taken.

Theorized as an interactive open-ended process, entrepreneurial action should not therefore be treated as a fixed entity measured by attributes (e.g. more or less in frequency or propensity) but as a non-linear sequence of activities discerned by general patterns or mechanisms (Langley, 1999; McMullen & Dimov, 2013; Mohr, 1982; Van de Ven, 2007). Treating entrepreneurial action as a process thus opens another avenue for future research. For example, Lichtenstein et al. (2007) distinguish several patterns of entrepreneurial action that lead to better likelihood of venture creation and suggest that the sequence of entrepreneurial action is determined by the rate, dispersion, and concentration of entrepreneurial activities. Chen (2015) also found an underlying distance-abstractness mechanism that drives the entrepreneurial action process. As a result, she suggests that no particular sequence of entrepreneurial action should be deemed to be the best practice but instead that, within a changing situation, sequences simply unfold from the distance-abstractness mechanism over time.

Future Direction #7: Unbundle Entrepreneurial Action Using the Duality of Cognition

From the socially situated cognition perspective, cognition is described as being complex, dynamic, and changing (moment-to-moment),

especially as a result of factors at the social level (Heider, 1958; Lewin, 1951; Mitchell et al., 2014; Semin & Cacioppo, 2008; Simon, 1981). In the first section of this chapter, we argued that it is too costly cognitively for individuals to create mental representations of the world in many situations, and that, as such, the mind creates 'online' representations so as to respond and act based on the demands of the immediate situation. However, by 'online' representations we do not mean that cognition is an empty box that is refilled constantly by the content of the body, the environment, and/or other people with whom one's cognition interacts. Indeed, cognition and action should not be conceptualized to completely lack representativeness of situations, or as completely malleable (Semin et al., 2012). Thus, rather than conceptualizing cognition within a stability-change dichotomy, entrepreneurial action research might benefit from a conceptualization that views entrepreneurial cognition and its effects on entrepreneurial action as a 'duality' in which 'stability and change are fundamentally interdependent – contradictory but also mutually enabling' (Farjoun, 2010, p. 202).

For example, using an agent-based simulation, Mitchell, Mitchell, and Randolph-Seng (2014) suggested that the moment-to-moment interactions between a potentially more stable inner environment (internal cognition) and a potentially more dynamic outer environment (situations) drive the propensity and frequency of entrepreneurial action in the form of exchange creation. Shaver (2012) suggests that future studies can expand the stability-change and inner-outer dichotomies into a more refined two-by-two representation that more completely conceptualizes potential causes of entrepreneurial actions, where external task difficulty and internal dispositional ability are relatively stable (they can change over time but not from moment to moment), while external luck and internal effort can change rather quickly from moment to moment. In sum, the socially situated cognition perspective affords future research with additionally rich explanations of interdependency between stability and change in the inner and outer environment at individual and social levels.

CONCLUSION

In this chapter, we have focused on entrepreneurial action as it can be informed by a more complete awareness of the limitations of fixed conceptualizations, and by insights offered by entrepreneurial cognition research, especially the dynamic cognition approach offered by socially situated cognition theory. But how is this newly conceptualized research to be accomplished? As we conclude the chapter we briefly discuss some possible responses to this question. Looking forward, we see a few possible methodological approaches that can be adopted in future research to enable the application of a socially situated perspective to empirical work on entrepreneurial action, as we now discuss.

Because, as we have suggested, future research should treat entrepreneurs, their tendencies, motivations, contexts, etc. as dynamic and changing, researchers need to employ methods that are suitable for such a challenging task. For instance, quantitative longitudinal studies, measuring key variables and their variations, and the influence of variations (not just the absolute values) on key aspects of entrepreneurial action may provide additional explanations of entrepreneurial action. To further enrich such explanations, using qualitative longitudinal studies and either quantitatively coding theoretically important aspects of the context, or qualitatively identifying the how and why of the relationships identified can also be a promising research approach.

Future research can also use certain qualitative and quantitative methods that are capable of capturing the dynamics and the socially situated aspects of entrepreneurial action outlined above. For instance, visual mapping is a good strategy in tracing the overall temporal patterns and may be used to capture the *content* of a concept as well as the overall process of entrepreneurial action in limited space at a single glance. Visual maps may associate how an initial new idea that forms the basis of an entrepreneurial opportunity (Davidsson, 2015) evolves differently depending on who shapes the development of the opportunity, and in what ways (Dimov, 2007). Visual mapping thus can be used to explain the *situated* nature of entrepreneurial action. Conjoint analysis can be used by researchers who have the opportunity to collect a large number of attributes associated with the context, social actors, and other key aspects of entrepreneurial action. Conjoint analysis may show how and why even small changes in one or two of the factors tracked can influence or even transform the property of the whole process of entrepreneurial action. Thus, conjoint analysis offers a way to adapt empirically a *macroscopic* explanation of how and why entrepreneurs act the way they do.

In such ways, future research can capture empirically the cognitive aspects of entrepreneurial action, especially in terms of socially situated cognition theory. Our emphasis on this dynamism returns us to the quotation from Steve Wozniak with which we began this chapter: 'entrepreneurs have to keep adjusting to [their situation] … everything's changing, everything's dynamic' (Livingston, 2007, p. 56). As we have described above, this 'everything' can be understood in terms of the broader changing, social (macroscopic) context (future direction #1), especially as it relates to the 'online' interpretations that entrepreneurs develop in their interactions with the changing world (future direction #2) and the situation-specific nature of these understandings that are developed *within* and *across* each context (future direction #3).

We also note that this 'everything' needs to be understood more broadly, especially across levels of analysis, encompassing the decisions, individuals, teams, firms, communities, economies, and societies (future direction #4) and the specific actions that combine to affect each of these different levels (future direction #5). We therefore emphasize additionally the importance of Wozniak's suggestion that the 'everything' is also changing, and that this process of change is essential for understanding entrepreneurial action, but is also open-ended and uncertain (future direction #6). It is this duality of stability and change that represents a fundamental tension, but also opportunity in better understanding entrepreneurial action and cognition (future direction #7). In this way, through analyzing many of the key limitations in entrepreneurial action research imposed by fixed conceptualizations, and by speculating innovatively, we hope in this chapter to have articulated the implications of a socially situated cognition perspective for entrepreneurial action research.

Notes

1 But see also meta analyses by Collins, Hanges, and Locke (2004), Stewart and Roth (2001), and Zhao and Seibert (2006), which – through techniques of study aggregation – have been able to assert that traits or stable characteristics should not be so easily dismissed. Accordingly, it may be too early to draw a definitive conclusion on this line of inquiry. What can be offered, however, is that, even if certain entrepreneurial traits are found to be important in entrepreneurship, their influence on the new opportunity identification and exploitation may never be found to be so dominant to warrant entrepreneurs to be treated like heroes. This is the case because, in addition to traits, many other critical factors are also needed for entrepreneurs to identify and exploit opportunities successfully (e.g. learning capabilities, other people the entrepreneur interacts with, social setting and its constraints on entrepreneurs' actions, etc.).

2 For a more detailed review of the literature on human cognition and the key developments that led to work on a socially situated cognition perspective in entrepreneurial action research, see Randolph-Seng et al. (2015).

3 We note that these seven future directions do not necessarily directly correspond to the seven fixed conceptualizations we have outlined above. That is, they are not mutually exclusive in their applicability to resolving the problems associated with the fixed conceptualizations previously discussed.

REFERENCES

Agre, P. (1997). *Computation and human experience*. New York: Cambridge University Press.

Alvarez, S. A., & Barney, J. B. (2007). Discovery and creation: Alternative theories of entrepreneurial action. *Strategic Entrepreneurship Journal*, *1*(1–2), 11–26.

Arend, R. J., Sarooghi, H., & Burkemper, A. (2015). Effectuation as ineffectual? Applying the 3E theory-assessment framework to a proposed new theory of entrepreneurship. *Academy of Management Review*, *40*(4), 630–651.

Arthur, W. B. (1989). Competing technologies, increasing returns, and lock-in by historical events. *The Economic Journal*, *99*(394), 116–131.

Autio, E., Dahlander, L., & Frederiksen, L. (2013). Information exposure, opportunity evaluation, and entrepreneurial action: An investigation of an online user community. *Academy of Management Journal*, *56*(5), 1348–1371.

Baker, T., Miner, A. S., & Eesley, D. T. (2003). Improvising firms: Bricolage, account giving and improvisational competencies in the founding process. *Research Policy*, *32*(2), 255–276.

Baker, T., & Nelson, R. E. (2005). Creating something from nothing: Resource construction through entrepreneurial bricolage. *Administrative Science Quarterly*, *50*(3), 329–366.

Baker, T., & Pollock, T. G. (2007). Making the marriage work: The benefits of strategy's takeover of entrepreneurship for strategic organization. *Strategic Organization*, *5*(3), 297–312.

Baucus, D. A., Baucus, M. S., & Mitchell, R. K. (2014). Lessons from the neural foundation of entrepreneurial cognition: The case of emotion and motivation. In J. R. Mitchell, R. K. Mitchell, & B. Randolph-Seng (Eds)

Handbook of Entrepreneurial Cognition, 254–315, London: Edward Elgar.

Birley, S. (1986). The role of networks in the entrepreneurial process. *Journal of Business Venturing*, *1*(1), 107–117.

Brockhaus, R. H., & Horwitz, P. S. (1986). The psychology of the entrepreneur. In D. L. Sexton, & R. W. Smilor (Eds) *The Art and Science of Entrepreneurship*, 25–48, Cambridge, MA: Ballinger.

Busenitz, L. W., & Barney, J. B. (1997). Differences between entrepreneurs and managers in large organizations: Biases and heuristics in strategic decision-making. *Journal of Business Venturing*, *12*(1), 9–30.

Carter, S. (2011). The rewards of entrepreneurship: Exploring the incomes, wealth, and economic well-being of entrepreneurial households. *Entrepreneurship Theory and Practice*, *35*(1), 39–55.

Casson, M. (1982). *The entrepreneur: An economic theory*. Totowa, NJ: Barnes & Noble Books.

Chalmers, D. M., & Shaw, E. (in press). The endogenous construction of entrepreneurial contexts: A practice-based perspective. *International Small Business Journal*.

Chen, H. S. (2015). *Opportunity near or far: The theoretical structure and cognitive antecedents of entrepreneurial action* (Doctoral dissertation). Texas Tech University, Lubbock, TX.

Clarke, J. S., & Cornelissen, J. P. (2014). How language shapes thought: New vistas for entrepreneurship research. In J. R. Mitchell, R. K. Mitchell, & B. Randolph-Seng (Eds) *Handbook of Entrepreneurial Cognition*, 383–397, London: Edward Elgar.

Collins, C. J., Hanges, P. J., & Locke, E. A. (2004). The relationship of achievement motivation to entrepreneurial behavior: A meta-analysis. *Human Performance*, *17*(1), 95–117.

Corbett, A. (2014). Thinking big from the start: Entrepreneurial growth cognitions. In J. R. Mitchell, R. K. Mitchell, & B. Randolph-Seng, (Eds) *Handbook of Entrepreneurial Cognition*, 398–411, London: Edward Elgar.

Cornelissen, J. P., & Clarke, J. S. (2010). Imagining and rationalizing opportunities: Inductive reasoning and the creation and justification of new ventures. *Academy of Management Review*, *35*(4), 539–557.

Davidsson, P. (2003). The domain of entrepreneurship research: Some suggestions. *Advances in Entrepreneurship, Firm Emergence and Growth*, *6*(3), 315–372.

Davidsson, P. (2015). Entrepreneurial opportunities and the entrepreneurship nexus: A re-conceptualization. *Journal of Business Venturing*, *30*(5), 674–695.

Delmar, F., & Shane, S. (2004). Legitimating first: Organizing activities and the survival of new ventures. *Journal of Business Venturing*, *19*(3), 385–410.

Dimov, D. (2007). Beyond the single-person, single-insight attribution in understanding entrepreneurial opportunities. *Entrepreneurship Theory and Practice*, *31*(5), 713–731.

Drnovšek, M., Slavek, A., & Cardon, M. S. (2014). Cultural context, passion and self-efficacy: Do entrepreneurs operate on different 'planets'? In J. R. Mitchell, R. K. Mitchell, & B. Randolph-Seng (Eds) *Handbook of Entrepreneurial Cognition*, 227–253, London: Edward Elgar.

Farjoun, M. (2010). Beyond dualism: Stability and change as a duality. *Academy of Management Review*, *35*(2), 202–225.

Fiske, S. T. (1992). Thinking is for doing: Portraits of social cognition from daguerreotype to laser photo. *Journal of Personality and Social Psychology*, *63*(6), 877–889.

Forbes, D. P. (2014). The infrastructure of entrepreneurial learning. In J. R. Mitchell, R. K. Mitchell, & B. Randolph-Seng (Eds) *Handbook of Entrepreneurial Cognition*, 364–382, London: Edward Elgar.

Gaglio, C. M., & Katz, J. A. (2001). The psychological basis of opportunity identification: Entrepreneurial alertness. *Small Business Economics*, *16*(2), 95–111.

Gartner, W. B. (1989). Who is an entrepreneur? Is the wrong question. *Entrepreneurship Theory & Practice*, *13*(4), 47–68.

Gartner, W. B., Carter, N. M., & Hills, G. E. (2003). The language of opportunity. In C. Steyart, & D. Hjort (Eds) *New Movements in Entrepreneurship*, 103–124, Cheltenham, PA: Edward Elgar.

Gazzaniga, M. S. (2010). Neuroscience and the correct level of explanation for understanding mind. *Trends in Cognitive Sciences*, *14*(7), 291–292.

Gigerenzer, G. (1996). On narrow norms and vague heuristics: A reply to Kahneman and

Tversky. *Psychological Review*, *103*(3), 592–596.

Gigerenzer, G., & Goldstein, D. G. (1996). Reasoning the fast and frugal way: Models of bounded rationality. *Psychological Review*, *103*(4), 650–669.

Granovetter, M. (1985). Economic action and social structure: The problem of embeddedness. *American Journal of Sociology*, *91*(3), 481–510.

Greenbank, P. (1999). The pricing decision in the micro-business: A study of accountants, builders and printers. *International Small Business Journal*, *17*(3), 60–73.

Grégoire, D. (2014). Exploring the affective and cognitive dynamics of entrepreneurship across time and planes of influence. In J. R. Mitchell, R. K. Mitchell & B. Randolph-Seng (Eds) *Handbook of Entrepreneurial Cognition*, 182–225, Northampton, MA: Edward Elgar.

Grégoire, D. A., Corbett, A. C., & McMullen, J. S. (2011). The cognitive perspective in entrepreneurship: An agenda for future research. *Journal of Management Studies*, *48*(6), 1443–1477.

Hamilton, B. H. (2000). Does entrepreneurship pay? An empirical analysis of the returns to self-employment. *Journal of Political Economy*, *108*(3), 604–631.

Hayek, F. A. (1937). Economics and knowledge. *Economica*, *4*(13), 33–54.

Haynie, M., & Shepherd, D. A. (2009). A measure of adaptive cognition for entrepreneurship research. *Entrepreneurship Theory and Practice*, *33*(3), 695–714.

Haynie, J. M., Shepherd, D., Mosakowski, E., & Earley, P. C. (2010). A situated metacognitive model of the entrepreneurial mindset. *Journal of Business Venturing*, *25*(2), 217–229.

Heider, F. (1958). *The psychology of interpersonal relations*. New York: Wiley.

Hornaday, J. A., & Bunker, C. S. (1970). The nature of the entrepreneur. *Personnel Psychology*, *23*(1), 47–54.

Johns, G. (2006). The essential impact of context on organizational behavior. *Academy of Management Review*, *31*(2), 386–408.

Kahneman, D., & Tversky, A. (1979). Prospect theory: An analysis of decision under risk. *Econometrica: Journal of the Econometric Society*, *47*(2), 263–291.

Kammerlander, N. (2016). 'I want this firm to be in good hands': Emotional pricing of resigning entrepreneurs. *International Small Business Journal*, *34*(2), 189–214.

Kirzner, I. M. (1973). *Competition and entrepreneurship*. Chicago, IL: University of Chicago Press.

Kirzner, I. M. (1997). Entrepreneurial discovery and the competitive market process: An Austrian approach. *Journal of Economic Literature*, *35*(1), 60–85.

Kirzner, I. M. (2009). The alert and creative entrepreneur: A clarification. *Small Business Economics*, *32*(2), 145–152.

Knight, F. H. (1921). *Risk, uncertainty and profit*. New York: Hart, Schaffner and Marx.

Langley, A. (1999). Strategies for theorizing from process data. *Academy of Management Review*, *24*(4), 691–710.

Lewin, K. (1951). *Field theory in social science*. New York: Harper & Row.

Lichtenstein, B. B., Carter, N. M., Dooley, K. J., & Gartner, W. B. (2007). Complexity dynamics of nascent entrepreneurship. *Journal of Business Venturing*, *22*(2), 236–261.

Liñán, F., Moriano, J. A., & Jaén, I. (2016). Individualism and entrepreneurship: Does the pattern depend on the social context? *International Small Business Journal*, *34*(6), 760–776.

Livingston, J. (2007). *Founders at work: Stories of startups' early days*. New York: self-published.

McClelland, D. C. (1965). Need achievement and entrepreneurship: A longitudinal study. *Journal of Personality and Social Psychology*, *1*(4), 389–392.

McGrath, R. G. (1999). Falling forward: Real options reasoning and entrepreneurial failure. *Academy of Management Review*, *24*(1), 13–30.

McGrath, R. G., & MacMillan, I. C. (2000). *The entrepreneurial mindset: Strategies for continuously creating opportunity in an age of uncertainty*. Boston, MA: Harvard Business Press.

McKelvie, A., Haynie, J. M., & Gustavsson, V. (2011). Unpacking the uncertainty construct: Implications for entrepreneurial action. *Journal of Business Venturing*, *26*(3), 273–292.

McMullen, J. S., & Dimov, D. (2013). Time and the entrepreneurial journey: The problems and promise of studying entrepreneurship as a process. *Journal of Management Studies*, *50*(8), 1481–1512.

McMullen, J. S., & Shepherd, D. A. (2006). Entrepreneurial action and the role of uncertainty in the theory of the entrepreneur. *Academy of Management Review*, *31*(1), 132–152.

McMullen, J. S., Wood, M. S., & Palich, L. E. (2014). Entrepreneurial cognition and social cognitive neuroscience. In J. R. Mitchell, R. K. Mitchell, & B. Randolph-Seng (Eds) *Handbook of Entrepreneurial Cognition*, 316–363, London: Edward Elgar.

Miller, K. D. (2007). Risk and rationality in entrepreneurial processes. *Strategic Entrepreneurship Journal*, *1*(1–2), 57–74.

Milliken, F. J. (1987). Three types of perceived uncertainty about the environment: State, effect, and response uncertainty. *Academy of Management Review*, *12*(1), 133–143.

Mises, L. V. (1949). *Human action: A treatise on economics*. San Francisco, CA: Fox & Wilkes.

Mitchell, J. R., Mitchell, R. K., Mitchell, B. T., & Alvarez, S. (2012). Opportunity creation, underlying conditions and economic exchange. In A. C. Corbett, & J. A. Katz (Eds) *Entrepreneurial Action (Advances in Entrepreneurship, Firm Emergence and Growth, Volume 14)*, 89–123, London: Emerald Group Publishing Limited.

Mitchell, J. R., Mitchell, R. K., & Randolph-Seng, B. (Eds) (2014). *Handbook of entrepreneurial cognition*. London: Edward Elgar Publishing.

Mitchell, J. R., & Shepherd, D. A. (2010). To thine own self be true: Images of self, images of opportunity, and entrepreneurial action. *Journal of Business Venturing*, *25*(1), 138–154.

Mitchell, R. K. (1996). Oral history and expert scripts: Demystifying the entrepreneurial experience. *Journal of Management History*, *2*(3), 50–67.

Mitchell, R. K., Busenitz, L., Lant, T., McDougall, P. P., Morse, E. A., & Smith, J. B. (2002). Toward a theory of entrepreneurial cognition: Rethinking the people side of entrepreneurship research. *Entrepreneurship Theory and Practice*, *27*(2), 93–104.

Mitchell, R. K., Busenitz, L., Lant, T., McDougall, P. P., Morse, E. A., & Smith, J. B. (2004). The distinctive and inclusive domain of entrepreneurial cognition research. *Entrepreneurship Theory and Practice*, *28*(6), 505–518.

Mitchell, R. K., Busenitz, L. W., Bird, B., Marie Gaglio, C., McMullen, J. S., Morse, E. A., & Smith, J. B. (2007). The central question in entrepreneurial cognition research. *Entrepreneurship Theory and Practice*, *31*(1), 1–27.

Mitchell, R. K., Mitchell, J. R., & Smith, J. B. (2008). Inside opportunity formation: Enterprise failure, cognition, and the creation of opportunities. *Strategic Entrepreneurship Journal*, *2*(3), 225–242.

Mitchell, R. K., Mitchell, J. R., Zachary, M. A., & Ryan, M. R. (2014). Simulating socially-situated cognition in exchange creation. In J. R. Mitchell, R. K. Mitchell, & B. Randolph-Seng (Eds) *Handbook of Entrepreneurial Cognition*, 412–447, London: Edward Elgar.

Mitchell, R. K., Randolph-Seng, B., & Mitchell, J. R. (2011). Socially situated cognition: Imagining new opportunities for entrepreneurship research. *Academy of Management Review*, *36*(4), 774–776.

Mohr, L. B. (1982). *Explaining organizational behavior*. San Francisco, CA: Jossey-Bass.

Ozgen, E., & Baron, R. A. (2007). Social sources of information in opportunity recognition: Effects of mentors, industry networks, and professional forums. *Journal of Business Venturing*, *22*(2), 174–192.

Pickle, H. B. (1964). *Personality and success: An evaluation of personal characteristics of successful small business managers* (No. 4). Small Business Administration.

Randolph-Seng, B., Mitchell, R. K., Vahidnia, H., Mitchell, J. R., Chen, S., & Statzer, J. (2015). The microfoundations of entrepreneurial cognition research: Toward an integrative approach. *Foundations and Trends (R) in Entrepreneurship*, *11*(4), 207–335.

Randolph-Seng, B., Williams, W. A., Jr., & Hayek, M. (2014). Entrepreneurial self-regulation: Consciousness and cognition. In J. R. Mitchell, R. K. Mitchell, & B. Randolph-Seng (Eds) *Handbook of Entrepreneurial Cognition*, 132–153, London: Edward Elgar.

Rindova, V., Barry, D., & Ketchen, D. J. (2009). Entrepreneuring as emancipation. *Academy of Management Review*, *34*(3), 477–491.

Robbins, P. & Aydede, M. (2009). A short primer on situated cognition. In P. Robbins, & M. Aydede (Eds) *The Cambridge Handbook of Situated Cognition*, 3–10, Cambridge, UK: Cambridge University Press.

Rousseau, D. M., & Fried, Y. (2001). Location, location, location: Contextualizing organizational research. *Journal of Organizational Behavior*, *22*(1), 1–13.

Ruef, M., Aldrich, H. E., & Carter, N. M. (2003). The structure of founding teams: Homophily, strong ties, and isolation among US entrepreneurs. *American Sociological Review*, *68*(2), 195–222.

Rumelt, R. P. (1987). Theory, strategy, and entrepreneurship. In D. J. Teece (Ed.) *The Competitive Challenge*, 137–158, Cambridge, MA: Ballinger Publishing Company.

Sarasvathy, S. D. (2001). Causation and effectuation: Toward a theoretical shift from economic inevitability to entrepreneurial contingency. *Academy of Management Review*, *26*(2), 243–263.

Sarasvathy, S. D., & Dew, N. (2008). Effectuation and over-trust: Debating Goel and Karri. *Entrepreneurship Theory and Practice*, *32*(4), 727–737.

Semin, G. R., & Cacioppo, J. T. (2008). Grounding social cognition: Synchronization, entrainment, and coordination. In G. R. Semin, & E. R. Smith (Eds) *Embodied Grounding: Social, Cognitive, Affective, and Neuroscientific Approaches*, 119–147. Cambridge: Cambridge University Press.

Semin, G. R., Garrido, M. V., & Palma, T. A. (2012). Socially situated cognition: Recasting social cognition as an emergent phenomenon. In S. Fiske, & N. Macrea (Eds) *Sage Handbook of Social Cognition*, Seven Oaks, CA: Sage.

Semin, G. R., & Smith, E. R. (2013). Socially situated cognition in perspective. *Social Cognition*, *31*(2), 125–146.

Shah, S. K., & Tripsas, M. (2007). The accidental entrepreneur: The emergent and collective process of user entrepreneurship. *Strategic Entrepreneurship Journal*, *1*(1–2), 123–140.

Shane, S. A. (2008). *The illusions of entrepreneurship: The costly myths that entrepreneurs, investors, and policy makers live by*. New Haven, CT: Yale University Press.

Shaver, K. G. (2012). Entrepreneurial action: Conceptual foundations and research challenges. In A. C. Corbett, & J. A. Katz (Eds) *Entrepreneurial Action (Advances in Entrepreneurship, Firm Emergence and Growth,*

Volume 14), 281–306, London: Emerald Group Publishing Limited.

Shepherd, D. A. (2015). Party On! A call for entrepreneurship research that is more interactive, activity based, cognitively hot, compassionate, and prosocial. *Journal of Business Venturing*, *30*(4), 489–507.

Shepherd, D. A., McMullen, J. S., & Jennings, P. D. (2007). The formation of opportunity beliefs: Overcoming ignorance and reducing doubt. *Strategic Entrepreneurship Journal*, *1*(1–2), 75–95.

Simon, H. A. (1981). *The sciences of the artificial*. Cambridge, MA: The MIT Press.

Simon, H. A. (1990). Invariants of human behavior. *Annual Review of Psychology*, *41*, 1–19.

Smith, E. R., & Semin, G. R. (2004). Socially situated cognition: Cognition in its social context. *Advances In Experimental Social Psychology*, *36*, 57–121.

Smith, E. R., & Semin, G. R. (2007). Situated social cognition. *Current Directions in Psychological Science*, *16*(3), 132–135.

Spedale, S., & Watson, T. J. (2014). The emergence of entrepreneurial action: At the crossroads between institutional logics and individual life-orientation. *International Small Business Journal*, *32*(7), 759–776.

Spivack, A. J., McKelvie, A., & Haynie, J. M. (2014). Habitual entrepreneurs: Possible cases of entrepreneurship addiction? *Journal of Business Venturing*, *29*(5), 651–667.

Staw, B. M. (1981). The escalation of commitment to a course of action. *Academy of Management Review*, *6*(4), 577–587.

Stewart Jr, W. H., & Roth, P. L. (2001). Risk propensity differences between entrepreneurs and managers: A meta-analytic review. *Journal of Applied Psychology*, *86*(1), 145–153.

Suddaby, R. (2010). Challenges for institutional theory. *Journal of Management Inquiry*, *19*(1), 14–20.

Teece, D. J. (2012). Dynamic capabilities: Routines versus entrepreneurial action. *Journal of Management Studies*, *49*(8), 1395–1401.

Van de Ven, A. H. (2007). *Engaged scholarship: A guide for organizational and social research*. Oxford: Oxford University Press.

Venkataraman, S., Sarasvathy, S. D., Dew, N., & Forster, W. R. (2012). Reflections on the

2010 AMR decade award: Whither the promise? Moving forward with entrepreneurship as a science of the artificial. *Academy of Management Review*, *37*(1), 21–33.

Welter, F. (2011). Contextualizing entrepreneurship – conceptual challenges and ways forward. *Entrepreneurship Theory and Practice*, *35*(1), 165–184.

West, G. P., III. (2007). Collective cognition: When entrepreneurial teams, not individuals, make decisions. *Entrepreneurship Theory and Practice*, *31*(1), 77–102.

Wood, M. S., & Williams, D. W. (2014). Opportunity evaluation as rule-based decision making. *Journal of Management Studies*, *51*(4), 573–602.

Wood, M. S., Williams, D. W., & Grégoire, D. A. (2012). The road to riches? A model of the cognitive processes and inflection points underpinning entrepreneurial action. In A. Corbett & J. Katz (Eds) *Entrepreneurial action (Advances in Entrepreneurship, Firm Emergence and Growth, Volume 14)*, 207–252. London: Emerald Group Publishing Limited.

Zacks, J. M., & Tversky, B. (2001). Event structure in perception and conception. *Psychological Bulletin*, *127*(1), 3–21.

Zahra, S. A. (2007). Contextualizing theory building in entrepreneurship research. *Journal of Business Venturing*, *22*(3), 443–452.

Zahra, S. A., & Wright, M. (2011). Entrepreneurship's next act. *The Academy of Management Perspectives*, *25*(4), 67–83.

Zhao, H., & Seibert, S. E. (2006). The big five personality dimensions and entrepreneurial status: A meta-analytical review. *Journal of Applied Psychology*, *91*(2), 259–271.

4

Pre- and Post-entrepreneurship Labor Mobility of Entrepreneurs and Employees in Entrepreneurial Firms

Kristina Nyström

INTRODUCTION

In recent decades, the role of entrepreneurship for economic dynamics and economic growth has received a lot of attention from researchers and policymakers. Empirical studies show that, at least in the long run, there is a positive relationship between entrepreneurship, productivity, and economic growth (see e.g. reviews of the empirical literature by van Praag and Versloot (2007) and Nyström (2008a)). How does productivity increase and generate growth through the creation of entrepreneurial ventures? One reason is that many new ventures are innovation-based. Hence, entrepreneurship is claimed to be an important link to commercialization of innovations (Acs, Audretsch, Braunerhjelm, & Carlsson, 2009). Furthermore, entrepreneurship is an important part of the structural change process. Entrepreneurship induces reallocation of resources and hence improves the efficiency of the utilization of resources (Schumpeter, 1934, 1942). Finally, labor mobility induced

by the creation of new firms may create knowledge spillovers. According to endogenous growth theories, interactions between individuals result in knowledge spillovers. These knowledge spillovers are claimed to stimulate innovation and productivity growth and therefore be important for economic growth (Romer, 1986, 1990; Lucas, 1988). These knowledge spillovers are also expected to occur when individuals decide to start a new firm (see e.g. Fornahl, Zellner, & Audretsch, 2005).

Every year, there is a quite substantial turbulence of firms and labor mobility in an economy. International evidence shows that annual entry and exit rates usually are about 5 to 10 percent (see e.g. Baldwin, 1995; Geroski, 1991; Nyström 2006). However, international studies also identify substantial differences across industries and entry and exit rates are generally found to be higher in the service sectors compared with the manufacturing industry (see e.g. Dunne, Roberts, & Samuelson, 1988; Nyström, 2007).

In which labor mobility flows do entrepreneurial activities result? When a new firm is established, this induces labor mobility for the entrepreneur, who may leave employment to try out a new opportunity as an entrepreneur. Furthermore, if the entrepreneurial venture expands beyond the founder of the company, additional employees need to be recruited to the firm, which also induces labor mobility. These new employees need to be recruited from other firms or among individuals currently outside the labor market. They can be recruited from already existing firms, from firms closing down their business, or among individuals who are currently entrepreneurs. Recruitment among individuals currently not employed in the labor market may include recruitment of labor market entrants or individuals re-entering employment after a period of, for example, study or unemployment. Hence, the establishment of the entrepreneurial venture induces labor mobility of both entrepreneurs and employees in entrepreneurial firms. This chapter intends to provide a literature review of existing research related to the labor mobility of both entrepreneurs and employees in entrepreneurial ventures. Note that this literature review has no intention of being comprehensive, but rather aims at pointing to strands of literature covering the relevant aspects discussed. The chapter will also outline avenues for future research on this matter. I will focus on labor mobility related to both the period pre- and post-entrepreneurial activity as well as pre- and post-employment in an entrepreneurial firm. Hence, I will discuss a) pre-entrepreneurship labor mobility of entrepreneurs and b) post-entrepreneurship labor mobility of entrepreneurs, as well as c) pre-entrepreneurship labor mobility of employees in entrepreneurial firms and d) post-entrepreneurship labor mobility of employees in entrepreneurial firms. Furthermore, because the labor mobility of entrepreneurs and of employees in entrepreneurial firms is expected to be influenced by the institutional conditions in an economy, the role of institutions and, in particular, employment protection legislation (EPL) for labor mobility of entrepreneurs and employees in entrepreneurial firms will be discussed.

The chapter is structured as follows: The first part discusses labor mobility pre- and post-entrepreneurship. The second part discusses the recruitment process of employees in entrepreneurial firms and labor mobility pre- and post-employment in an entrepreneurial firm. The penultimate part discusses how EPL influences labor mobility of entrepreneurs and employees in entrepreneurial firms. Finally, in the last part conclusions and some final remarks are provided.

LABOR MOBILITY OF ENTREPRENEURS

Labor mobility patterns prior and post entrepreneurship may exist in several paths. Figure 4.1 illustrates the possible labor mobility transitions pre and post the entrepreneur starting his or her venture. The labor market transitions illustrated in this figure will act as a way of structuring the discussion on the current state of the literature and identification of research gaps.

If we start looking at the period prior to the creation of a new entrepreneurial venture at a certain point in time, illustrated by the left side of the figure, the entrepreneur could leave his/her existing employment to become an entrepreneur, exit an existing entrepreneurial venture or enter/re-enter the labor market by, for example, leaving educational activities or returning to the labor market for other reasons. Post-entrepreneurial labor mobility options, illustrated by the right side of the figure, include that the entrepreneur may start a new entrepreneurial venture (i.e. serial entrepreneurship), take a job in an incumbent firm (which may be a new venture or an incumbent firm) or leave the labor market (for studies, unemployment or other reasons).

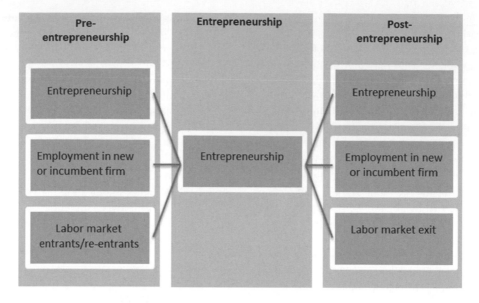

Figure 4.1   Labor mobility of entrepreneurs pre- and post-entrepreneurial activity

Pre-Entrepreneurship Labor Mobility

Starting with the literature on the period prior to the creation of a new entrepreneurial venture we can observe that, during recent decades, the literature on entrepreneurship has had a strong focus on individual characteristics, such as age, gender, education, and immigrant background, related to who becomes an entrepreneur. Furthermore, the literature has focused on how the individual characteristics of the entrepreneur influence the performance of the firm in terms of, for example, profitability, firm growth, and survival (see e.g. Parker, 2009 for a literature review).[1]

The literature on the determinants of entrepreneurship stresses the importance of human capital. One component of human capital is experience, which can be obtained through labor mobility prior to starting an entrepreneurial venture. Hence, we have knowledge about the pre-entrepreneurship employment activity of entrepreneurs with respect to how the entrepreneurs' prior experiences in the labor market may influence the propensity to become an entrepreneur and their subsequent performance as entrepreneurs. Human capital in terms of experience may, according to Shane (2003), include general business experience, functional experience, industry experience, start-up experience, and vicarious experience. Functional experience refers to, for instance, experience in marketing or management. Vicarious experience refers to, for example, having observed a relative's or a friend's entrepreneurial activities. With regard to general business experience, previous research shows that many entrepreneurs find their ideas at their previous employers (Bhide, 2000), and those entrepreneurs that identified their business ideas at a previous employer tend to have higher growth rates (Dunkelberg, Cooper, Woo, & Denis, 1987). Furthermore, diversity of experience is tested by the 'jack-of-all-trades' hypothesis, which implies, for example, that the number of different work roles and the number of different fields of experience are found to influence the probability of becoming an entrepreneur (Lazear, 2005; Wagner, 2003, 2006). Furthermore, varied job experience is associated with greater entrepreneurial aspirations (Hyytinen & Ilmakunnas, 2007a).

With regard to the performance indicator venture growth, having previous managerial experience seems more important than previous experience of entrepreneurship in the same sector (Storey, 1994). However, Hyytinen and Maliranta (2008) find that transition from employment to entrepreneurship is relatively rare. They also find that small firms spawn more new firms. However, we do not know the reason for this difference or the reason for the individuals' transition to entrepreneurship. We do not know if these transitions are necessity- or opportunity-based. Much of the literature on labor transitions between employment and self-employment has used individual-firm-level-based register data. The availability of this dataset gives us much detailed information about the individual and the firm. However, these datasets do not provide us with detailed information about whether the transition to entrepreneurship is necessity-based, for example, due to layoffs, or opportunity-based. Distinguishing between the different motives behind the transitions from employment to entrepreneurship would be interesting to explore further.

Regarding previous experience as entrepreneurs (serial entrepreneurship), previous empirical evidence suggests that individuals who have worked as entrepreneurs in the past and individuals with entrepreneurial aspirations are more likely to become entrepreneurs in the future (Hyytinen & Ilmakunnas, 2007b). On the performance of serial entrepreneurs, Parker (2013) finds that they obtain temporary benefits from entrepreneurship experience but that these benefits eventually disappear.

According to Figure 4.1 the third and last option of pre-entrepreneurial experience is entrepreneurs entering entrepreneurship as labor market entrants or re-entrants. There is quite extensive literature on the relationship between unemployment and entrepreneurship. Most of the evidence is on cross-section, time series or panel dimensions of this issue (see e.g. Parker (2009) for a literature review). However, we can also find some interesting studies regarding the transitions from unemployment to entrepreneurship. Regarding the frequency of transitions to self-employment, Cowling and Taylor (2001) find that most transition into paid employment or remain unemployed. However, the unemployed are more likely to transition into self-employment compared with the employed (Evans & Leighton, 1990). In addition, it is found that a history of job changes increases the willingness to become an entrepreneur (van Praag & van Ophem, 1995). What about the performance of ventures started by previously unemployed persons? Carrasco (1999) finds that, although unemployed people have a higher probability than employees of entering self-employment, their failure rate is higher. Andersson and Wadensjö (2007) find that previous employees who become entrepreneurs are more successful as entrepreneurs than unemployed people who become entrepreneurs. However, few studies on the transitions to entrepreneurship focus on entrepreneurship as a way to enter the labor market. As previously mentioned, there are numerous studies on the role of age and entrepreneurship, using age as a proxy for experience. However, few, if any, of these studies are able to explicitly study labor market entrants. This would be particularly interesting due to the focus on young entrepreneurs among many policymakers. Interesting research questions would, for instance, be to study whether entrepreneurship as a way to enter the labor market enhances or aggravates future career performance. How do employers perceive and value entrepreneurship as a way to enter the labor market?

To conclude this section we note that the prior experiences of entrepreneurs as employees and serial entrepreneurs are relatively well explored in the literature. We also have empirical knowledge about the transition from unemployment to entrepreneurship. Hence, the link between labor market entrants and re-entrants is identified as less explored and should be interesting for further empirical research.

Post-Entrepreneurship Labor Mobility

Looking at the labor mobility flows from entrepreneurship (the right part of Figure 4.1), transitions may include entrepreneurship (serial entrepreneurship), employment or exiting the labor market. As previously mentioned, we have knowledge about serial entrepreneurs continuing entrepreneurial activity. Comparably less is known about the post-entrepreneurial labor mobility to employment. Here, there are theoretical as well as empirical contributions to be made. Hence, knowledge about how the experience of entrepreneurship is valued in a future career as employee would be interesting to examine. It can be hypothesized that the role of entrepreneurship experience in future labor market careers may depend on the strength of the individual's current position in the labor market. For some entrepreneurs with a weaker position in the labor market (such as immigrants), experience of entrepreneurship may be a way to signal to the labor market that he or she possesses capabilities and competences that are attractive for employees. Hence, for immigrant entrepreneurs, entrepreneurship may act as an entry port to regular employment. Furthermore, the value of entrepreneurial experience in the 'regular' labor market would be interesting to study more extensively. Is experience of entrepreneurship a valuable resource in other positions in the labor market? Are persons with entrepreneurial experience perceived as more qualified to take on management positions? Do individuals with experience as entrepreneurs perform better or worse in terms of, for example, wage development or promotions compared with workers without entrepreneurial experience? There are a few studies on the effect of self-employment on wages. These studies generally find insignificant or negative effects of past self-employment on current wages. For instance, Brucea and Schuetze (2004) find that returning to wage employment after brief spells of self-employment does not increase earnings and probably rather decreases earnings. Kaiser and Malchow-Møller (2011) find that, on average, a spell of self-employment is associated with lower wages in dependent employment. However, interestingly enough they find that this negative effect disappears and is even positive for the self-employed, who switch to dependent employment in the same sector as their self-employment. The effect also disappears for the former self-employed earning a high income and for the former self-employed hiring more than one employee. These results indicate that opportunity- or necessity-based transitions from self-employment to dependent wage employment may be influential for these results.

Regarding exit from entrepreneurship, illustrated by the third option of post-entrepreneurial transition possibilities in Figure 4.1, we know that many exits are voluntary, i.e. they are not due to reasons related to the poor performance of the company. For instance, Cueto and Mato (2006) find that almost 50 percent of reported exits are due to bankruptcy, while the rest of the exits are voluntary, i.e. induced by, for example, the individual wanting to take on other opportunities, such as transitions into the labor market. However, in many of the statistical sources used for empirical analysis, voluntary and involuntary exits are not distinguishable. For the further research mentioned above, it is possible that the value of entrepreneurship experience is dependent on whether the exits were triggered by the high or low performance of the prior entrepreneurial activity.

Hence, to conclude the section on post-entrepreneurial labor transitions we identify the transition and valuation of entrepreneurial experience in the 'regular' labor market, as well as exit transitions, as links with great potential to explore further in empirical research.

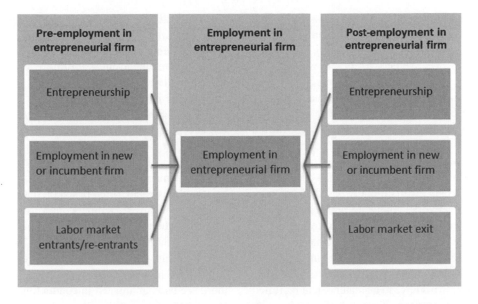

Figure 4.2   Labor mobility of employees pre- and post-employment in an entrepreneurial firm

LABOR MOBILITY OF EMPLOYEES IN ENTREPRENEURIAL FIRMS

In this section, I discuss labor mobility pre- and post-employment in an entrepreneurial firm. Figure 4.2 illustrates the possible labor mobility transitions pre- and post-employment in an entrepreneurial firm. Again, this figure will act as a starting point for the discussion on the current state of the literature and identification of research gaps. As illustrated by Figure 4.2 for employees who take a job in an entrepreneurial firm, labor mobility patterns prior to this employment may differ. The employee in the entrepreneurial firm may leave his/her existing employment for this employment, close his/her existing entrepreneurial venture to take employment with an entrepreneur or be a labor market entrant or re-entrant. Post-entrepreneurial labor mobility options include the entrepreneur starting a new entrepreneurial venture, taking a job in an incumbent firm (which may be a new venture or an incumbent firm) or leaving the labor market. However, before more explicitly discussing these different transition paths,

empirical evidence on the recruitment process in an entrepreneurial venture is discussed.

When an entrepreneurial venture needs to recruit employees, a matching process is needed, where both the entrepreneurial venture and the potential employee must find a satisfactory match. However, according to Behrends (2007) and Williamson, Cable, and Aldrich (2002), small and new firms have a competitive disadvantage in this recruitment process. Recruiting employees is difficult for entrepreneurial firms because they cannot rely on their reputation or market share to attract applicants (Aldrich, 1999). Firms with a good reputation may attract more applicants, which implies that they have a larger pool of applicants to select from, which probably increases the quality of the staff hired (Turban & Cable, 2003). Additional disadvantages of entrepreneurial ventures in the recruitment process are that the mortality rate of entrepreneurial firms is high and entrepreneurial firms often lack well-defined job descriptions, which may make them seem less legitimate and attractive to potential employees (Williamson, 2000).

Entrepreneurial firms may also be unable to provide supplementary benefits, such as social security benefits or training (Tumasjan, Strobel, & Welpe, 2011). These difficulties in the recruitment process imply that entrepreneurial ventures may have to rely more on social networks to obtain access to some resources required (see e.g. Aldrich & Zimmer, 1986; Greve & Salaff, 2003). However, during the transition from the start-up phase to the growth phase of a company, recruitment efforts initially based on personal social networks change to business networks in order to facilitate diversity in competencies among employees (Leung, Zhang, Wong, & Foo, 2006). Alternatively, in recruiting employees using social networks, entrepreneurial firms have to a greater extent recruited their employees among individuals with weaker positions in the labor market, such as labor market entrants. While the exploitation of social networks in the entrepreneurial process is relatively well explored in the literature, the latter perspective is, as I will discuss later on in this chapter, relatively unexplored.

Pre-Entrepreneurship Labor Mobility of Employees

Regarding the labor mobility of employees prior to employment in entrepreneurial firms, illustrated by the left part of Figure 4.2, there is an emerging stream of literature on the individual characteristics of employees (see e.g. Nyström, 2011; Dahl & Klepper, 2008; Ouimet & Zarutskie, 2014). For instance, Nyström (2011) finds that new firms hire a larger share of employees with immigrant backgrounds and that the share of employees with post-secondary education is lower among new firms compared with incumbent firms. Ouimet and Zarutskie (2014) find that young firms disproportionately hire young workers and in particular young firms with innovation potential. However, less is known about the employee's employment history prior to the employment in the new venture.

Nyström (2011) shows that employees of entrepreneurial ventures have a higher probability of being outsiders in the labor market. Hence, interesting avenues for future research would include studying to what extent employees in entrepreneurial firms come from firms closing down or whether employees accepting employment in a new venture have higher labor mobility compared with employees in incumbent firms. It should be noted that many of the studies that currently exist in this area are often based on data from countries such as Denmark and Sweden, countries where access to employer–employee matched data has enabled researchers to start investigating the employment history of employees in entrepreneurial firms. Hence there is clearly an interest in conducting similar studies for additional countries where access to these employer–employee datasets can be provided.

Another strand of literature explores the wage differential paid by new and incumbent firms. It is often argued that entrepreneurial firms pay lower wages and provide worse fringe benefits (see e.g. Shane, 2009). However, since, as previously mentioned, employees in new ventures tend to have a weaker position in the labor market, this wage differential can be partly explained by this selection mechanism (Nyström & Zhetibaeva Elvung, 2014). However, non–pecuniary factors influencing the decision to take an employment in an entrepreneurial firm may also be very important for the individual's decision to accept an employment. Empirical evidence shows that the non-pecuniary factors important for the decision to become an entrepreneur include, for instance, greater independence and job satisfaction (Hyytinen, Ilmakunnas, & Toivanen, 2013). However, the non-pecuniary factors associated with accepting an employment in an entrepreneurial firm remain relatively unexplored in the literature.

Other interesting avenues for future research to explore are the social network dimensions of hiring decisions in entrepreneurial firms. Quantitative studies based on large social network databases could provide further insights. In addition, further qualitative studies closely following recruitment processes in new ventures are of great interest. As previously mentioned, the recruitment processes of entrepreneurial firms are discussed in the literature. However, this strand of literature tends to focus on the entrepreneur's perspective. More research that remains to be done should study the motives and strategies of employees taking on employment in a new firm.

To conclude this section on pre-employment in entrepreneurial firms, all transition paths illustrated on the left side of Figure 4.2 (previous employment in new or incumbent firms, entrepreneurship, and coming from outside of the labor market) seem relatively unexplored, in particular using quantitative data such as employer–employee matched data. Another area worth stressing for future research is the importance of non-pecuniary factors for the decision to take an employment in an entrepreneurial firm.

Post-Entrepreneurship Labor Mobility of Employees

In this section, I discuss labor mobility transitions post-employment in an entrepreneurial firm. Klepper (2001) notes that studies on employee start-ups are rare. Since this article by Klepper was published, there have been some interesting studies on entrepreneurial spawning. However, regarding the transitions of previous employees to entrepreneurial firms, I think there is still a research gap to be filled. This literature tends to focus on the characteristics of the firms that generate start-ups and the performance of the spawned companies. In addition, these studies tend to be focused on the high-tech sector. Regarding the strand of literature on spin-offs, which focuses on the characteristics of the firms that generate spin-offs, the literature shows that successful parent firms, in terms of product leadership, are characterized by higher spin-off rates.

However, Andersson, Baltzopoulos, & Lööf (2012) find that firms with persistently high R&D activities tend to generate fewer spin-offs. This is explained by the observation that these employees may have a higher opportunity cost related to starting a firm on their own if the incumbent firm offers high wages and stable employment conditions. Furthermore, empirical evidence shows that spin-offs tend to outperform other start-ups with respect to survival rates, employment creation and growth performance (see e.g. Klepper, 2001; Klepper & Thompson, 2006).

What, then, drives individuals to leave their current company to create a spin-off? According to Klepper and Sleeper (2005) and Klepper and Thompson (2010), an important driver of spin-off activity is disagreement in the firm about the potential of opportunities or incongruity between the firm's current product or service offered or strategy and other opportunities that the employees have identified. Because disagreements on the future path of the company can become more pronounced in connection to a firm being involved in merger and acquisition activities (M&As), spin-off activities have shown to increase post M&A (Klepper, 2007). In the previous section, I discussed the distinction between involuntary and voluntary exits. A similar distinction would be interesting to make for entrepreneurial activities spurred by M&As and defined as spin-offs. A spin-off triggered by M&A activities can be induced by the fact that the new management of the company wants to outsource certain activities. Hence, the spin-off company may keep its primary customer base. Other entrepreneurial activities spawned from the company may be less voluntary and induced by the previously mentioned disagreement about future paths of the company or fear of being laid off in the aftermath of the M&A activity. Hence, these entrepreneurial activities may be more necessity-based, which probably has an effect on the expected performance of these spin-offs.

Given the previously mentioned literature on entrepreneurial spawning, I think there is a clear and interesting research gap to be filled. In most cases, the above-mentioned literature does not regard the extent to which the employees can be regarded as part of the entrepreneurial team, even though he/she is an employee. Hence, I think it would be interesting to place an increased focus on the individuals involved in the entrepreneurial spawning process and the experiences they have learned by specifically working in entrepreneurial firms. It can be argued that working for an entrepreneur provides a person with skills and experiences that can be used if one wants to try out entrepreneurial activities oneself. In addition, working for a successful entrepreneur may convince someone that, overall, entrepreneurship is a viable alternative to paid employment. (However, working for an unsuccessful entrepreneur may have the opposite effect). These arguments may be viable in both high-tech and low-tech industries.

A second option for the transition of employees of entrepreneurial firms is to take employment in another firm (the second option illustrated on the right part of Figure 4.2). This firm may again be an entrepreneurial firm or a firm with a more stable position in the market. Here, there is a clear research gap to be filled because the literature, to the best of my knowledge, does not explore the transition to paid employment after working in an entrepreneurial firm. Do individuals with experience working for an entrepreneurial firm perform better or worse in terms of, for example, wage development or promotion possibilities, compared with workers without experience working for an entrepreneurial firm?

Regarding the third option, the transition of employees that results in an exit from the labor market (illustrated by the last transition option on the right part of Figure 4.2), we have to consult the literature available on displacements if the individual faces a situation where the firm closes down. As noted by Nyström and Viklund Ros (2014), much of this literature is focused on the characteristics of the individuals who are affected by

displacements. According to this literature, older individuals, workers, women, less-educated workers, and employees with long tenures are found to suffer most from displacement (see, for instance, OECD, 2013). Less is known about the extent to which the characteristics of the closed firm influence transitions to new employment and the future labor market performance of displaced workers. Do displaced workers from an entrepreneurial firm find it more or less difficult to transition to a new job compared with employees from large incumbent firms? It is possible that larger and incumbent firms are able to provide better support for their employees in this transition process. In addition, it may be the case that the closures of large incumbent firms receive more attention from policymakers, which may induce additional policy measures aimed at reducing the problems associated with a large firm closure.

To conclude this section on post-employment in entrepreneurial firms, the transition to paid employment and valuation of this experience in the labor market is identified as an unexplored link. In addition, the labor market transition from employment in an entrepreneurial venture, in particular in the case of a firm closure, needs further attention from researchers.

INSTITUTIONS AND LABOR MOBILITY OF ENTREPRENEURS AND EMPLOYEES IN ENTREPRENEURIAL FIRMS

Institutions, defined as both the formal and informal rules of the game (North, 1991, 1994), are very important in shaping which entrepreneurial activities take place in a society (Baumol, 1990). Formal institutions include, for example, polity, judiciary, and bureaucracy. Informal institutions include, for example, norms and customs. The literature on the relationship between institutions and entrepreneurship is now rather extensive (see e.g. Boettke and Coyne (2009) for a literature review and Nyström (2008b), who shows a positive relationship between regulatory quality measured by the Economic Freedom of the World (EFW) index and self-employment). However, in this section, I will explicitly focus on the institutions that are particularly important for labor mobility and, in particular, employment protection legislation (EPL). From a theoretical perspective, one could expect strong EPL to discourage entrepreneurial activities. The arguments for such a relationship are, first, that small (and new) firms are disproportionately burdened by EPL. The argument here is that entrepreneurial firms have fewer possibilities to afford the costs of hiring and firing that EPL imposes. In addition, small and new firms are more vulnerable in cases of making less successful hiring decisions. Hence, it is argued that EPL both discourages entrepreneurship and lower survival rates (Parker, 2009). On the other hand, as argued by Acharya, Baghai, & Subramanian (2013), EPL provides employees with security in case of the short-term failure of their activities. This security may make employees more inclined to become involved in innovative activities that have the potential to create value for the firm in the long run. Hence, EPL may stimulate risky, but in the case of success, very profitable, activities, which may increase the chances of survival of the company.

For individuals employed in a firm, EPL may also influence their decisions to become an entrepreneur. EPL, which provides protection for employees with long tenure (such as those in Sweden), may make individuals less prone to trying out entrepreneurial activities. If they decide to leave a company to start a new firm, they will lose their tenure position in the firm, and if they return to positions as employees, they will be more exposed in the case of an economic downturn or in case the firm reduces its staff for other reasons. For policymakers, it is a difficult challenge to find the right balance between ensuring that sufficient labor mobility takes place at the same time as sufficient employment security for workers is provided.

Regarding the current empirical evidence on the relationship between entrepreneurship and EPL, the evidence is mixed. Among the studies that find a negative relationship between entrepreneurship and EPL, those by Kanniainen and Vesala (2005), Klapper, Laeven, and Rajan (2006) and van Stel, Storey, and Thurik (2007) can be mentioned. However, there are also a number of studies, such as Robson (2003) and Ciccone and Papaioannou (2007), finding insignificant statistical results for this relationship. Related to EPL and firm-level performance, Bassanini, Nunziata, and Venn (2009) find that dismissal regulations decrease total factor productivity (TFP). Conversely, Acharya et al. (2013) find that more stringent dismissal laws increase participation in innovative activities among employees, particularly those in innovation-intensive industries. Why do we have these ambiguous empirical results? As Parker (2009) notes, most of the previously mentioned evidence is based on cross-country data. In order to better understand the relationship with EPL, future studies should use disaggregate data. Furthermore, it would be interesting to more explicitly evaluate the consequences of changes in EPL schemes in individual countries and the effect on labor mobility and entrepreneurship; and the empirical evidence mentioned above is related to entrepreneurship in general and does not study the transitions to entrepreneurship and transitions to employment in entrepreneurial firms. An interesting research question to study would be whether entrepreneurs in countries with more or less relaxed EPL find that it is easier to recruit experienced workers compared with entrepreneurs in countries with stricter EPL.

CONCLUSION

This chapter has provided a literature review of existing research and identified research gaps related to the labor mobility of both entrepreneurs and employees in new firms before and after their activities as entrepreneurs or employees in entrepreneurial firms. Regarding the pre-entrepreneurship experience of entrepreneurs, the link between labor market entrants and re-entrants was identified as the least explored link. Regarding post-entrepreneurship transitions, exit transitions from the labor market as well as the transitions and valuation of entrepreneurial experience in the 'regular' labor market were identified as areas with research gaps interesting to explore further. In particular, it could be interesting to try to distinguish between voluntary and involuntary transitions. Regarding the valuation of entrepreneurial experience in the labor market, it should be possible using employer–employee matched data to study wage differentials between employees with and without entrepreneurial experience. Qualitative studies conducting interviews with persons responsible for recruitment of employees could also shed further light into how entrepreneurial experience is valued on the labor market.

Regarding pre-employment with an entrepreneurial firm, all transition paths (previous employment, entrepreneurship, and paths coming from outside of the labor market) seem relatively unexplored using quantitative data, even though there is currently an emerging quantitative literature stream exploring who new firms employ (e.g. Nyström, 2011; Dahl & Klepper, 2008). The empirical findings so far in this strand of literature indicate that entrepreneurial ventures seem important for labor market dynamics, in particular related to the employment of individuals with a weaker position in the labor market. Further empirical studies in this area would also include studies on the extent to which different types of entrepreneurial ventures are able to attract different types of employees and to what extent this influences firm performance. Such studies would, for instance, include distinguishing

between high-tech start-ups and low-tech start-ups, spin-offs versus non-spin-offs, academic spin-offs versus non-academic spin-offs, or large-firm spin-offs versus small-firm spin-offs. Finally, extending the literature on wage differentials between new and incumbent would include the study of the non-pecuniary benefits associated with employment in a new firm.

For post-employment in an entrepreneurial firm, the transition to entrepreneurial activity is relatively well explored in the entrepreneurial spawning and spin-off literature. However, the transition to paid employment was identified as an unexplored research area. Interesting research questions would, for example, be related to how employment with an entrepreneurial firm is valued in the labor market. Here, both quantitative and qualitative studies in a similar vein as mentioned above regarding the valuation of entrepreneurial experience should be of interest. In addition, given that employment in a new firm is very risky because mortality is high, it would be interesting to explore the future labor market performance of individuals displaced from an entrepreneurial firm.

Finally, in this chapter the role of EPL in the labor mobility of entrepreneurs and employees in entrepreneurial firms was discussed. Here, more empirical research based on micro-level data might be able to shed additional light on the currently relatively ambiguous empirical results on the relationship between EPL and entrepreneurship.

Note

1 In this chapter, I focus on the entrepreneur as having an economic function, i.e. the entrepreneur as a risk-taker, resource allocator or innovator (see e.g. Glancey and McQuaid, 2000). It should be noted that other strands of the entrepreneurship literature have focused on entrepreneurs as persons with a certain form of behavior (see e.g. Drucker, 1985) or persons with specific psychological traits (e.g. McClelland, 1961).

REFERENCES

Acharya, V. V., Baghai, R. P. and Subramanian, K. V. (2013), 'Labor laws and innovation', *Journal of Law and Economics,* Vol. 56, 4: 997–1037.

Acs, Z. J., Audretsch, D. B., Braunerhjelm, P. and Carlsson, B. (2009), 'The knowledge spillover theory of entrepreneurship', *Small Business Economics*, Vol. 32, 1: 15–30.

Aldrich, H. E. (1999), *Organizations Evolving*, Sage, London.

Aldrich, H. E. and Zimmer, C. (1986), 'Entrepreneurship through Social Networks', in Sexton, D. and Smiler, R. (eds), *The Art and Science of Entrepreneurship*, Ballinger, New York, pp. 3–23.

Andersson, M., Baltzopoulos, A. and Lööf, H. (2012), 'R&D strategies and entrepreneurial spawning', *Research Policy*, Vol. 41, 1: 54–68.

Andersson, P. and Wadensjö, E. (2007), 'Do the unemployed become successful entrepreneurs?' *International Journal of Manpower*, Vol. 28, 7: 604–626.

Baldwin, J. R. (1995), *The Dynamics of Industrial Competition: A North American Perspective*, Cambridge University Press, Cambridge.

Bassanini, A., Nunziata, L. and Venn, D. (2009), Job protection legislation and productivity growth in OECD countries, *Economic Policy*, Vol. 24, 58: 349–402.

Baumol, W. J. (1990), 'Entrepreneurship: Productive, unproductive and destructive', *Journal of Political Economy*, Vol. 98, 5: 893–921.

Behrends, T. (2007), 'Recruitment practices in small and medium size enterprises. An empirical study among knowledge-intensive professional service firms', *Management Revue*, Vol. 18, 1: 55–74.

Bhide, A. V. (2000), *The Origin and Evolution of New Businesses*, Oxford University Press, Oxford.

Boettke, P. and Coyne, C. (2009), 'Context matters: Institutions and entrepreneurship', *Foundations and Trends in Entrepreneurship*, Vol. 5, 3: 135–209.

Brucea, D. and Schuetze, H. J. (2004), 'The labor market consequences of experience in self-employment', *Labour Economics*, 11 (2004): 575–598.

Carrasco, R. (1999), 'Transitions to and from self-employment in Spain: An empirical analysis', *Oxford Bulletin of Economics and Statistics*, Vol. 61, 3: 315–41.

Ciccone, A. and Papaioannou, E. (2007), 'Red tape and delayed entry', *Journal of the European Economic Association*, Vol. 5, 2–3: 444–458.

Cowling, M. and Taylor, M. (2001), 'Entrepreneurial women and men: Two different species?' *Small Business Economics*, Vol. 16, 3: 167–175.

Cueto, B. and Mato, J. (2006), 'An analysis of self-employment subsidies with duration models', *Applied Economics*, Vol. 38, 1: 23–32.

Dahl, M. S. and Klepper, S. (2008), Whom Do New Firms Hire? (September 8, 2008). Available at SSRN: http://ssrn.com/abstract=2420122

Drucker, P. E (1985), *Entrepreneurship and Innovation*, Heinemann, London.

Dunkelberg, W., Cooper, A. C., Woo, C. and Denis, W. (1987), 'New firm growth and performance', in Churchill, N. et al. (eds), *Frontiers of Entrepreneurship Research*, Babson College, pp. 307–321.

Dunne, T. M., Roberts, J. and Samuelson, L. (1988), 'Patterns of firm entry and exit in US manufacturing industry', *Rand Journal of Economics*, Vol. 19, 4: 495–515.

Evans, D. S. and Leighton, L.-S. (1990), 'Small business formation by unemployed and employed workers', *Small Business Economics*, Vol. 2, 4: 319–330.

Fornahl, D., Zellner, C. and Audretsch, D. B. (2005), *The Role of Labour Mobility and Informal Networks for Knowledge Transfer*, Springer, Berlin.

Geroski, P. (1991), *Market Dynamics and Entry*, Blackwell, Oxford.

Glancey, K. S. and McQuaid, R. W. (2000), *Entrepreneurial Economics*, Palgrave, New York.

Greve, A. and Salaff, J. W. (2003), 'Social networks and entrepreneurship', *Entrepreneurship Theory and Practice*, Vol. 28, 1: 1–22.

Hyytinen, A. and Ilmakunnas, P. (2007a), 'Entrepreneurial aspirations: Another form of job search?' *Small Business Economics*, Vol. 29, 1: 63–80.

Hyytinen, A. and Ilmakunnas, P. (2007b), 'What distinguishes a serial entrepreneur?'

Industrial and Corporate Change, Vol. 16, 5: 793–821.

Hyytinen, A. and Maliranta, M. (2008), 'When do employees leave their job for entrepreneurship?' *Scandinavian Journal of Economics*, Vol. 110, 1: 1–21.

Hyytinen A., Ilmakunnas, P. and Toivanen, O. (2013), 'The return-to-entrepreneurship puzzle', *Labour Economics*, Vol. 20: 57–67.

Kaiser, K. and Malchow-Møller, N. (2011), 'Is self-employment really a bad experience? The effects of previous self-employment on subsequent wage-employment wages', *Journal of Business Venturing*, Vol. 26, 5: 572–588.

Kanniainen, V. and Vesala, T. (2005), 'Entrepreneurship and labour market institutions', *Economic Modelling*, 22: 828–847.

Klapper, L., Laeven, L. and Rajan, R. (2006), 'Entry regulation as a barrier to entrepreneurship', *Journal of Financial Economics*, Vol. 82, 3: 591–629.

Klepper, S. (2001), 'Employee startups in high-tech industries', *Industrial and Corporate Change*, Vol. 10, 3: 639–674.

Klepper, S. (2007), 'Disagreements, spin-offs and the evolution of Detroit as the capital of the U.S. automobile industry', *Management Science*, Vol. 53, 4: 616–631.

Klepper, S. and Sleeper, S. (2005), 'Entry by spinoffs', *Management Science*, Vol. 51, 8: 1291–1306.

Klepper, S. and Thompson, P. (2006), 'Spinoff entry in high-tech industries: motives and consequences', in Malerba, F. and Brussoni, S. (eds),*Economic Perspectives on Innovation*, Cambridge: Cambridge University Press, pp. 187–218.

Klepper, S. and Thompson, P. (2010), 'Disagreements and intra industry spin-offs', *International Journal of Industrial Organization*, Vol. 28, 5: 526–538.

Lazear, E. (2005), 'Entrepreneurship', *Journal of Labor Economics*, Vol. 23, 4: 649–680.

Leung, A., Zhang J., Wong P. K. and Foo, M. D. (2006), 'The use of networks in human resource acquisition for entrepreneurial firms: Multiple "fit" considerations', *Journal of Business Venturing*, Vol. 21, 5: 664–686.

Lucas, R. E. (1988), 'On the mechanisms of economic development', *Journal of Monetary Economics*, Vol. 22, 1: 3–42.

McClelland, D. C. (1961), *The Achieving Society*, Van Nostrand, Princeton, NJ.

North, D. (1991), 'Institutions', *Journal of Economic Perspectives*, Vol. 5, 1: 97–112.

North, D. (1994), 'Economic Performance through Time', *American Economic Review*, Vol. 84, 3: 359–68.

Nyström, K. (2006), Entry and Exit in Swedish Industrial Sectors, JIBS Dissertation series No 32, Jönköping International Business School, Jönköping, Sweden.

Nyström, K. (2007), 'Patterns and determinants of entry and exit in industrial sectors in Sweden', *Journal of International Entrepreneurship*, Vol. 5, 3–4: 85–110.

Nyström, K. (2008a), 'Is entrepreneurship the salvation for enhanced economic growth?', CESIS electronic working paper series no. 143, Royal Institute of Technology, Sweden.

Nyström, K. (2008b), 'The institutions of economic freedom and entrepreneurship: Evidence from panel data', *Public Choice*, Vol. 136, 3–4: 269–282.

Nyström, K. (2011), 'Labor mobility and entrepreneurship: Who do new firms employ?', *CESIS Electronic Working Paper Series*, Working Paper 250.

Nyström, K. and Viklund Ros, I. (2014), 'Exploring regional differences in the regional capacity to absorb displacements', Ratio Working Paper No. 235. Ratio, Stockholm.

Nyström, K. and Zhetibaeva Elvung, G. (2014), 'New firms and labor market entrants: Is there a wage penalty for employment in new firms?' *Small Business Economics*, Vol. 43, 2: 399–410.

OECD (2013), OECD Employment Outlook 2013, OECD, Paris. Retrieved from http://www.keepeek.com/ Digital-Asset-Management/ oecd/employment/oecd-employment-outlook-2013_ empl_outlook-2013-en#page214 (accessed May 02, 2015).

Ouimet, P. and Zarutskie, R. (2014) 'Who works for startups? The relation between firm age, employee age, and growth', *Journal of Financial Economics,* Vol. 112, 3: 386–407.

Parker, S. (2009), *The Economics of Entrepreneurship*, Cambridge University Press, Cambridge.

Parker, S. (2013), 'Do serial entrepreneurs run successively better-performing businesses?',

Journal of Business Venturing, 28, 5: 652–666.

Robson, M. T. (2003), 'Does stricter employment protection legislation promote self-employment?', *Small Business Economics*, Vol. 21, 3: 309–319.

Romer, P. M. (1986), 'Increasing returns and long-run growth', *Journal of Political Economy*, Vol. 94, 5: 1002–1037.

Romer, P. M. (1990), 'Endogenous technological change', *Journal of Political Economy*, Vol. 98, 5: 71–102.

Schumpeter, J. (1934), *The Theory of Economic Development*, Harvard University Press, Cambridge, MA.

Schumpeter, J. (1942), *Capitalism, Socialism and Democracy*, Harper and Row, New York.

Shane, S. (2003), *A General Theory of Entrepreneurship: The Individual-Opportunity Nexus*, Edward Elgar, Cheltenham.

Shane, S. (2009), 'Why encouraging more people to become entrepreneurs is bad public policy', *Small Business Economics*, 33, 2: 141–149.

Storey, D. J. (1994), *Understanding the Small Business Sector*, Routledge, London.

Tumasjan, A., Strobel, M. and Welpe, I. M. (2011), 'Employer brand building for start-ups: Which job attributes do employees value most?', *Zeitschrift für Betriebswirtschaft*, Vol. 81, 6: 111–136.

Turban, D. B. and Cable, D. M. (2003), 'Firm reputation and applicant pool characteristics', *Journal of Organizational Behavior*, Vol. 24, 6: 733–751.

van Praag, M. C. and van Ophem, H. (1995), 'Determinants of willingness and opportunity to start as an entrepreneur', *Kyklos*, Vol. 48, 4: 513–540.

van Praag, M. C. and Versloot, P. H. (2007), 'What is the value of entrepreneurship? A review of recent research', *Small Business Economics*, Vol. 29, 4: 351–382.

van Stel, A., Storey, D. J. and Thurik, A. R. (2007), 'The effect of business regulation on nascent and young business entrepreneurship, *Small Business Economics*, Vol. 24, 3: 311–321.

Wagner, J. (2003), 'Testing Lazear's Jack-of-all-trades view of entrepreneurship with German microdata', *Applied Economics Letters*, Vol. 10, 11: 687–689.

Wagner J. (2006), 'Are nascent entrepreneurs Jacks-of-all-trades? A test of Lazear's theory of entrepreneurship with German data', *Applied Economics*, Vol. 38, 20: 2415–2419.

Williamson, I. O. (2000), 'Employer legitimacy and recruitment success in small businesses', *Entrepreneurship Theory Practice*, Vol. 25, 1: 27–42.

Williamson, I. O., Cable, D. M., Aldrich, H. E. (2002), 'Smaller but not necessarily weaker: How small businesses can overcome barriers to recruitment', in Katz, J. and Lumpkin, T. (eds), *Managing People in Entrepreneurial Organizations*, Emerald Group Publishing Limited, London, pp. 83–106.

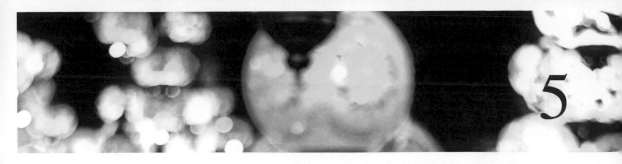

5

Networks and Entrepreneurship

Maura McAdam and Danny Soetanto

INTRODUCTION

In recent years, network theory and social relations research has emerged as a popular theme in explaining how entrepreneurs gain access to resources, obtain legitimacy and penetrate markets successfully (Hoang & Antoncic, 2003; Stuart & Sorenson, 2005; Sullivan & Ford, 2014). This line of enquiry rejects the traditional view of the entrepreneur as an isolated economic actor who is immersed in a lonely journey (Araujo & Easton, 1996; Farmer, Yao & Kung-McIntyre, 2011) and instead acknowledges the role of 'others' in supporting entrepreneurs during the entrepreneurial process (Dodd & Anderson, 2007; Slotte-Kock & Coviello, 2010; Batjargal, Hitt, Tsui, Arregle, Webb & Miller, 2013; Carnabuci & Diószegi, 2015). This emerging perspective argues that entrepreneurs are a product of their social context and their perception of opportunities is influenced by social relations (Greve & Salaff, 2003; Anderson, Park & Jack, 2007; Semrau & Werner, 2014). Accordingly, the entrepreneurial process should be understood as a complex social system where entrepreneurs actively engage in their social space to identify opportunities, gain legitimacy, access resources and overcome obstacles (Slotte-Kock and Coviello, 2010; Ozdemir, Moran, Zhong & Bliemel, 2014). Despite the increasing acknowledgement of the importance of networks within the entrepreneurial context (e.g. Parkhe, Wasserman & Ralston, 2006; Slotte-Kock & Coviello, 2010; Jack, 2010), there is a scarcity of research relating to the dynamic nature of networks. If networks are considered to be social arenas in which entrepreneurs manoeuvre and struggle in pursuit of scarce resources, we need to move beyond the current assumptions that networks are static. Instead, networks should be seen as dynamic and adaptive social systems which vigorously change according to contextual factors such as location and gender.

Within this chapter, we draw upon this notion that entrepreneurship is embedded in a social context, to explore the role of networks in the entrepreneurial process. In doing so, we first critically discuss the fundamental concept of entrepreneurial networks and its theoretical roots. Although acknowledging that networking is a particular entrepreneurial resource and the benefits that it can accrue therein, from a critical perspective, we also acknowledge the disadvantages or the dark side of networking. Building on this, we consider potential future research directions which challenge the assumptions in the current body of knowledge, in addition to the identification of innovative research methodologies. To augment this, we respond to calls for more work in relation to the dynamic nature of networks and the contextual dimensions and differences in the development of networks across different categories of entrepreneurs. Accordingly, we present four case studies to illustrate how entrepreneurs alter and modify their social relations during the entrepreneurial process.

NETWORKS AND ENTREPRENEURSHIP

Within the extant literature the role of networking in the entrepreneurial process is explored at length, focusing primarily upon the process of building and managing relationships in the business environment (Jack, 2005; Hoang & Antoncic, 2003). According to Aldrich, Rose & Woodward (1987) networks should be considered fundamental within the entrepreneurship context as a result of two principles. First, they act as a leveraging resource in enabling entrepreneurs to identify opportunities and gain access to scarce resources (Dubini & Aldrich, 1991; Ostgaard & Birley, 1996). Second, networks are a useful 'safety net' to test ideas, gain feedback and gather apposite information to exploit new opportunities (Johannisson, 1987; Hite, 2005). However, what is interesting about networks in the context of entrepreneurship is that, although

entrepreneurship is regarded as a single, independent and often solitary action, the process of entrepreneurship itself often emerges as a result of the intersection of several layers of networks, from social to professional networks (Araujo & Easton, 1996). So, while the common view might see entrepreneurship as being an individual act, it is in fact a social activity undertaken by individuals embedded in a social process (Steyaert & Katz, 2004; Downing, 2005).

In essence, the value of entrepreneurial networking lies in the supply of new ideas and information which supports the survival and growth of the venture (Hite & Hesterly, 2001; Witt, 2004). It is argued that these networks perform four important roles. First, they provide access to new ideas, information and other types of resources necessary during entrepreneurial activity. Second, they endorse the creation of legitimacy whereby entrepreneurs may gain credibility through the formation of alliances with established and reputable partners. Third, networks are utilised in order to exchange knowledge and so facilitate the generation of entrepreneurial learning. Finally, new networks help to strengthen existing relationships that, in turn, facilitate the achievement of entrepreneurial goals and enterprise growth (Shaw & Conway, 2000; Witt, 2004; Jack, 2005).

As mentioned previously, studies focusing on networks and entrepreneurship have increased exponentially in recent years (Hoang & Antoncic, 2003; Stuart & Sorenson, 2005; Parkhe et al., 2006). Table 5.1 illustrates some seminal network research in leading entrepreneurship journals. The articles were extracted from the Thomson Reuters' web of science where the top ten highest citations are presented. While they might not claim to use network theories, the table illustrates the important role of networks in the entrepreneurial context over a twenty-five-year period. Whilst some of the articles consider networks as a general phenomenon of relationships developed by individuals or firms, others have tried to contextualise networks

Table 5.1 Networking articles published since 1985 with highest citation metrics; articles selected were published between 1985 and 2010

Journal	Journal	Key findings
Davidsson and Honig (2003)	Journal of Business Venturing	Bridging and bonding, consisting of strong and weak ties, was a robust predictor for nascent entrepreneurs.
Hoang and Antoncic (2003)	Journal of Business Venturing	Review network studies according to the content of network relationship, governance and structure.
McDougall, Shane and Oviatt (1994)	Journal of Business Venturing	The role of networks in supporting the growth and market performance of international new ventures.
Ardichvili, Cardozo and Ray (2003)	Journal of Business Venturing	Social capital was identified as an antecedent of entrepreneurial alertness to business opportunities.
Oviatt and McDougall (2005)	Entrepreneurship Theory and Practice	Speed of entrepreneurial internationalisation is influenced by various forces including entrepreneurs' networks.
Dubini and Aldrich (1991)	Journal of Business Venturing	Describe the entrepreneur as embedded in a social context, channelled and constrained by their position in networks.
Westhead, Wright and Ucbasaran (2001)	Journal of Business Venturing	Networks as one of the driving factors for internationalising SMEs.
Greve and Salaff (2003)	Entrepreneurship Theory and Practice	Networks and networking in different contexts and stages of entrepreneurship.
Baron and Markman (2003)	Journal of Business Venturing	Entrepreneurs' social competence influences the outcomes of the entrepreneurial process.
Lechner and Dowling (2003)	Entrepreneurship and Regional Development	Strong and weak ties are important for the growth of the firm.

in more detail. However, the overall theme within these articles is the positive impact of network relationships on firm performance.

ENTREPRENEURIAL NETWORKING AND ITS THEORETICAL ROOTS

Network research in the entrepreneurship context has predominately relied upon social network theory as a framework for analysing the structure of whole social entities (Wasserman & Faust, 1994). Social network theory draws upon the constructs of social capital, network closures and structural holes, strong ties and weak ties (Hoang & Antoncic, 2003; Stuart & Sorenson, 2005; Parkhe et al., 2006). However, scholars have criticised network studies for failing to measure intervening mechanisms that link these constructs with entrepreneurial outcomes (Anderson et al., 2007; Gedajlovic, Honig, Moore, Payne & Wright, 2013). Indeed, both conceptual and empirical papers on networks to date have overlooked how these constructs are conceived and operationalised, which is deemed important given that each construct can have both a positive and negative effect on entrepreneurial outcomes (Gedajlovic et al., 2013). We will now describe the contribution of each construct.

The concept of social capital, which is grounded in sociology and anthropology studies, refers to the set of norms, networks and organisations through which people gain access to resources that are influential in empowering decision making and policy formulation (Nahapiet & Ghoshal, 1998; Kim & Aldrich, 2005; Hughes, Morgan, Ireland & Hughes, 2014; Sytch & Tatarynowicz, 2014). According to Coleman (1990, p. 302), social capital is defined as 'some aspects of social structure, facilitating certain actions in individuals who are within the structure'. There is a common consensus that social capital is a valuable asset whose value emerges from the access gained to resources through the social relationships of an actor (Lin, 2002; Liao & Welsch, 2003; Partanen, Chetty & Rajala, 2014; Semrau & Werner, 2014; Carnabuci & Diószegi, 2015). Social capital includes many aspects of the social context including social ties, trusting relationships and value systems which facilitate the actions of individuals located in a particular social context (Hoang & Antoncic, 2003; Nahapiet & Ghoshal, 1998). Hence, social capital is created within an embedding process whereby actors with more social capital are able to manage and access resources. In contrast, actors with less social capital are less able to engage in collaborative behaviour, which makes them more vulnerable to opportunistic behaviour (Lin, 2002).

At the level of the individual, the concept of social capital provides insights into how people enhance their career success (Adler & Kwon, 2002; Nahapiet and Ghoshal, 1998; Burt, 1997; 2004), and how entrepreneurship is facilitated (Anderson et al., 2007; Kim & Aldrich, 2005). At the firm level, the concept of social capital gives an additional explanation of the performance of firms and the emergence process of new firms (Shane, 2004; Steier & Greenwood, 2000; Kogut & Zander, 1992). In order to endow social capital, actors need to be embedded in social structures (Granovetter, 2005). However, taking a critical stance, Coleman (1988) argues

that network closures and their resultant social capital may give rise to environments whereby individual freedom of action is limited due to the rigid enforcement of norms. Regardless, social capital can be considered as a productive asset, resource or capability, without which certain ends would not be achievable (Coleman, 1990).

The next concept that has been used in explaining the advantage of networks in entrepreneurship is the structural dimension of networks (Tan, Zhang & Wang, 2015; Ozdemir et al., 2016; Nahapiet & Ghoshal, 1998). In relation to the structural dimension of networks, two main opposing views exist, namely network closure versus structural holes. The network closure argument (Ozdemir et al., 2014; Hoang & Antoncic, 2003; Coleman, 1990) proposes that close networks offer positive impacts as information in such networks is rapidly diffused to other people and interpreted in similar ways (Ozdemir et al., 2014; Hansen, 1999). Indeed, Granovetter (1983) argues that the positive effects of networks facilitate trust between people and reduce the risks of strategic behaviour as actors linked to such networks are more likely to conform to the norm of reciprocity (Simsek, Lubatkin & Floyd, 2003). Failure to reciprocate appropriately may result in strong sanctions and cause serious damage to reputation (Zaheer & McEvily, 1999; Gulati, 1995). However, close networks also have some disadvantages. In these networks, the autonomy of members is heavily restricted, since each decision taken by members is subject to the acceptance and influence of all interconnected contacts (Gargiulo & Benassi, 2000; Burt, 1997).

In contrast, the concept of structural holes refers to the hole or gap spanning between non-redundant contacts (Burt, 2004), with the number of non-redundant contacts important (Lechner & Leyronas, 2007). The structural holes argument claims that structural holes that are rich in non-redundant contacts provide access to more information about unique resources, opportunities and referrals to a wider scope of potential business partners (Zaheer & McEvily, 1999). The advantages of such networks can increase the range of networks in covering new information about opportunities, e.g. potential markets, investors and business ideas (Hite & Hesterly, 2001). Thus, structural holes offer greater payoffs through the exploitation of economic potentials (Hite & Hesterly, 2001; Zaheer & McEvily, 1999).

To date, the majority of studies investigating networks in the entrepreneurship domain have referred to the use and application of Granovetter's strong and weak ties hypothesis (Aldrich et al., 1987). Granovetter (1973) argued that an ideal network should consist of both strong and weak ties because the nature of these ties will impact on the operation of networks (Jack, 2005). Strong ties require frequent contacts that are usually long term, reciprocal and involve a strong degree of trust and emotional closeness (Patel & Terjesen, 2011). Furthermore, Hansen (1999) and Podolny (2001) argue that these types of relationships benefit from the transfer of complex information as individuals involved in close and emotional contact are generally more willing to expend time and effort in explaining and/or listening to complex ideas (Wuebker, Hampl & Wüstenhagen, 2015; Granovetter, 1985). Strong ties therefore shape the willingness of partners in the networks to provide resources as individuals are more likely to offer information, know-how or support to others who are close, than to those who are more distant (Nohria, 1992). Despite all these benefits, strong ties may constrain the search for new and novel information (Wuebker et al., 2015; Patel & Terjesen, 2011; Ruef, 2002).

Weak ties, on the other hand, represent heterogeneous ties and are perceived to be a critical element of the network structure, enabling information flow and dissemination (Hansen, 1999). A weak tie can be described both as temporary and as transient, and normally involves little emotional investment (Granovetter, 1973, 1983). Weak ties thus

provide information and resources beyond what is available in a close social circle (Granovetter, 1973, 1983) and can also be a source of unique opportunities and resources (Hansen, 1999).

From the above discussion, it is apparent that there is no consensus regarding which ties are more effective in influencing entrepreneurship. In fact, an emerging trend in the literature is the argument that both types of ties may provide benefits to individuals and firms (Gilsing & Duysters, 2008; Hite & Hesterly, 2001). It appears that both strong and weak ties provide the conduit, bridge and pathways to opportunities and resources; however, it is the characteristics of these ties that influence how they are identified, accessed, mobilised and exploited (Hite, 2005, 2008). In other words, the type of ties that constitute a network will have a significant impact on the type, nature and extent of resources (Jack, 2005).

A CRITICAL PERSPECTIVE

Undoubtedly, a substantial body of research has accumulated over the years devoted to enhancing our understanding of networks within the entrepreneurship context. However, network studies have been criticised for being too simplistic in explaining how entrepreneurs easily receive benefits from their networks. In fact, studies have tended to ignore the negative impact that may result from investing in particular network constructs and instead have portrayed networks in a purely positive manner. The current arguments tend to overlook networks as a process and a social context where entrepreneurs may suffer from barriers of homophily, social boundaries and bounded rationality. Therefore, there is arguably more research required on the negative or the dark side of networks within the entrepreneurship literature. For instance, a study by Maurer and Ebers (2006) found evidence that firms can realise performance benefits when their members repeatedly adapt the configuration of their social capital, while inertia turns a firm's social capital into a liability. Molina-Morales and Martínez-Fernández (2009) argue that social capital decreases beyond a certain point of development, with the effect of social interactions and trust on firm value creation being described as an inverted U-shaped curve. Putnam (2002) and Gottschalk (2009) also found that networks play an important role in illegal activities and crime.

Building on this critical perspective, it is important to recognise the risks associated with networking (Anderson & Jap, 2005). Whilst we assume that networks facilitate entrepreneurial actions by converting scarce resources into rich outcomes for entrepreneurs, this can involve both economic and social risks. Accordingly, trust is a key moderating factor in these exchanges (Bøllingtoft & Ulhøi, 2005). In fact, the literature states that trust in others and the process of building trust in relationships is deeply embedded in networks (Mønsted, 1995; Granovetter, 1983). According to Szarka (1990), trust is considered important in networked relationships as it facilitates cooperation. However, the issue of trust within networked relationships appears complex and somewhat difficult to assess. Furthermore, problems may arise in knowing who to trust and how much you can trust (Krishna, 2000), yet, once trust is developed, 'doing the party a favour is considered a privilege' (Johannisson, 1988). Overall the key theme emerging from the literature is that the successful development of relationships depends on mutual trust between the parties. Furthermore, pressure is placed on the receiving party to reciprocate by providing some benefit in return (Neergaard & Ulhøi, 2006). Trust allows each party to assume that each will take actions that are predictable and mutually acceptable (Uzzi, 1997).

Building on this theoretical grounding, in the next section we consider potential future research directions in order to move the current debate forward.

MOVING THE DEBATE FORWARD

Despite the growing body of evidence regarding the intersection between networks and entrepreneurship (Slotte-Kock & Coviello, 2010; Parkhe et al., 2006), there is scope for new and interesting research questions relating to the dynamic intersectional nature of networks. If networks are considered to be social arenas in which entrepreneurs manoeuvre and struggle in pursuit of desirable resources, we have to challenge current assumptions that networks and social relations are static (Jack, 2010; McAdam & McAdam, 2006). Instead, networks should be seen as an adaptive social system, which vigorously changes according to many factors such as context, learning, and obstacles experienced by the entrepreneurs. Networking is a process of identifying common interest, gaining knowledge and experience of other individuals while at the same time building trust (Jack, 2005). The actual process of networking should be seen as a continuous process which changes over time but also is determined by the social context in which it is embedded (Hite & Hesterly, 2001). For that reason, we aim to contribute to this endeavour through our identification of future research directions, namely: the dynamic nature of networks; the influence of gender upon networking; and networking in the context of business incubation.

Dynamic Nature of Entrepreneurial Networks

There is a growing body of evidence to support the relational and dynamic nature of networks whose content and structure can vary in response to entrepreneurial requirements at a specific point in time (Birley, 1987; Davidsson & Honig, 2003; Hite, 2008; Jack, 2005). This argument reconciles the current debate in network studies as to whether strong or weak ties, network closure or structural holes are more relevant for entrepreneurship.

Instead, as suggested by this dynamic perspective, each network characteristic may play a role depending on the context, stage of development and other external factors. Despite this, there is a scarcity of research which specifically deals with how networks change and evolve across different contexts and amongst different categories of entrepreneurs (Jack, 2010; Slotte-Kock & Coviello, 2010; Hoang & Antoncic, 2003). In addition to this, entrepreneurship studies have been criticised for producing contradictory and confusing evidence regarding how entrepreneurs should embed their networks and for overlooking the fact that networks develop over time (Slotte-Kock & Coviello, 2010).

In relation to the evolution of networks, Birley's (1985) seminal piece referred to the transition of informal to formal relationships and how these relationships changed when assembling key elements for the development of new firms. Ten years later Larson and Starr's (1993) conceptual work on the role of networks in the venture creation process provided a model illustrating three stages of activity used to secure critical economic and non-economic resources for entrepreneurship. These stages are 1) focus on essential dyadic ties, 2) convert dyadic ties to socioeconomic exchanges, and 3) layer the exchange with multiple exchange processes. In more recent work, Davidsson and Honig (2003) followed the development process of nascent entrepreneurs and found that interesting relationships exist among ties and the probability of market entry and success. In a similar vein, Hite (2008), Hite and Hesterly (2001), Jack (2005), Elfring and Hulsink (2003), Greve and Salaff (2003), and Jack (2010) all present accounts of network ties and how these can impact venture evolution, growth and development. In sum, these studies highlight the relational nature of networks and show that networks are not static but change and are dynamic as they evolve, and that the content and structure can vary in response to entrepreneurial requirements at a specific point in time (Burt, 1997; Johannisson, 1998; Hite, 2005).

Gender and Entrepreneurial Networks

Networking has the potential to provide significant advantages for female entrepreneurs, including access to advice, information, strategic alliances, membership of a professional community and the acquisition of credibility and legitimacy for their ventures (Carter & Shaw, 2006; Linehan & Scullion, 2008; Leitch, Harrison & Hill, 2014). However, to date, research on the discourse on gender and networking has been somewhat limited (Foss, 2010; Brush, De Bruin & Welter, 2009; Renzulli, Aldrich & Moody, 2000; Ibarra, 1993, 1997) and it is only recently that questions have been raised regarding the impact of gender on such activity (Foss, 2010; Díaz García & Carter, 2009; Neergaard, Shaw & Carter, 2005). Accordingly, some variations have been witnessed in the process of networking and what networks are used for between male and female entrepreneurs (Aldrich, Reese & Dubini, 1989; Carter, Brush, Greene, Gatewood & Hart, 2003). In fact, Starr and Yudkin (1996, p. 40) note that 'the few studies that compare the networking activities of women and men business owners show differences in the sex composition of the networks of women, but not in how men and women use their networks'. The composition of networks does vary by gender (Carter et al., 2003), with women tending to have networks composed entirely of other women, whom they use for emotional support. Consequently, attention has been drawn to the limited diversity of female entrepreneurs' networks (Renzulli et al., 2000; Minniti & Arenius, 2003; Foss, 2010) and often the term 'homophily' is used to describe such member selection, with homophily referring 'to the selection of other team members on the basis of similar ascriptive characteristics, such as gender, ethnicity, nationality, appearance and the like' (Ruef et al., 2003, p. 196).

However, three pertinent issues in the extant entrepreneurship literature currently restrict the discourse in this area

(Jennings & Brush, 2013). First, a normative masculine perspective currently dominates, which subsequently influences how research is conducted and findings presented. Second, there is a tendency to treat men and women as homogeneous groups that can be compared with each other. However, women business owners should not be treated as a homogeneous group, as there is more variation within than between the sexes when it comes to entrepreneurial networking (McGregor & Tweed, 2002; Foss, 2010; Harrison & Mason, 2007). For instance, recent research by Leitch et al. (2014) suggests that some women entrepreneurs use social networks strategically; some women, like some men, are effective networkers, while others may be less so; women do not necessarily favour the development of strong ties as opposed to weak ones; and only a small minority were concerned with developing relationships rather than business contacts. Third, to date, quantitative approaches have dominated the study of entrepreneurial networks (Schutjens & Stam, 2003; Greve & Salaff, 2003; Minguzzi & Passaro, 2001).

Business Incubator and Entrepreneurial Networks

Another future research direction is context, with one such context being the business incubator. For new and small firms, support mechanisms such as the business incubator may play a role in developing or creating entrepreneurial networks. In other words, the degree to which the networking opportunities provided by the business incubator support the small firm in its pursuit of sustainability and growth. Incubators provide an array of tailored support services such as accommodation, access to professional services, business advice and mentoring (Hackett & Dilts, 2004). As noted in recent studies (Ebbers, 2014; Grimaldi & Grandi, 2005), the focus of incubation provision has shifted from real estate to enterprise development with network access a main component of their

service. Whilst the literature has explored many of the tangible benefits of incubator placement in terms of credibility and support offered, there is little recognition that a context which ensures proximity between new firms is also a mechanism for embedding them within entrepreneurial networks whilst facilitating the development of new business and social networks. This is significant as the current literature would suggest that the development of such business and social networks is critical for firm survival and growth (Uzzi, 1997; Hisrich & Smilor, 1998). Applying social network theory to the business incubator context and the entrepreneurial process therefore would identify the business incubator's role in developing the entrepreneur's network in respect to gaining access to knowledge and resources in order to support entrepreneurial growth (Peters, Rice & Sundararajan, 2004). Furthermore, through this lens, a business incubator may be seen as a broker in terms of facilitating links between persons who are not directly connected, for example the establishment of links with consultants, other entrepreneurs or investors (Ebbers, 2014). Having identified the role of the university in facilitating such networks, future research needs to consider how proximity and tacit knowledge establishes the trust which underpins successful networking.

We now draw these future research directions through the presentation of case studies which illustrate how entrepreneurs alter and modify their networked relationships during the entrepreneurial process. The case studies presented here were collected through a network mapping approach where entrepreneurs were asked to visualise their networks in the form of drawing.

Innovative Data Collection Method for Network Study

There seems to be some debate in the literature about how networks should be studied. The dominant approach for understanding networks to date has been the use of quantitative approaches for data collection (Greve & Salaff, 2003). Yet calls for more qualitative work have been made (Hite, 2005; Hoang & Antoncic, 2003). The case for different research strategies that allow knowledge and understanding to be broadened and deepened and the use of tools and mechanisms that allow qualitative aspects to emerge has especially been made (Jack, 2010). Understanding the role of networks in entrepreneurial context is a challenge for researchers in terms of appropriately capturing the historical process of network development.

In this section, we respond to calls for alternative research strategies that allow knowledge and understanding of entrepreneurial networks to be broadened and deepened through the use of tools and mechanisms that allow qualitative aspects to emerge (Jack, 2010; Hite, 2005; Hoang & Antoncic, 2003). To meet this call, we now demonstrate an innovative research approach involving a network visualisation technique. This approach facilitates the capture of the complexities, intricacies, issues and changes that occur when developing networks. Irrespective of the focus of research, for clarity it is important that a study's unit of analysis is stated explicitly (Jack 2010; O'Donnell, Gilmore, Cummins & Carson, 2001), with our unit of analysis being the individual. So, our approach allowed our respondents to express their entrepreneurial journey and reflect on how their networks developed. To visualise the process of getting support and help from others, we asked the respondents to build a physical model in the form of network mapping. The participants were conditioned to imagine and later describe their networks by using drawing as a tool and guidance for the interview process. By constructing, such as building and drawing a network of personal contacts, the respondents produced a visual object that can be regarded as a reflection of their networks and networking activities. It was through the process of drawing that the respondents of our study experienced a growing understanding resulting from the feedback processes between the living mind and the encompassing world.

Using network mapping as a tool for data collection, a half-day interactive workshop was designed in which entrepreneurs were invited to visually present their networking strategy and demonstrate how their networks evolved in certain contexts or experiences. The respondents in this study were collected from a sample of small firms in the Northwest region of the United Kingdom (UK) that took part in a knowledge exchange workshop at Lancaster University. In total, there were 12 participants in the workshop. The participants were deliberately selected with a specific purpose in mind. Given our intention to explore their entrepreneurial networks, the nature of the study and the flexibility it offers, purposeful sampling was deemed an appropriate approach for identifying participants (Hoepfl, 1997). We are aware that one of the criticisms raised against this sampling method is that it can cause distortion through insufficient breadth (Patton, 1990). However, for this particular study it was deemed appropriate given that the participants on the workshop fitted our selection criteria. Accordingly, we were confident this sample would provide interesting insights into networking practices and the impact of their experiences on entrepreneurial activity.

Steps in the Workshop

In Step 1, participants were briefed about the objectives of the workshop. This was followed by an explanation about the role of networks in entrepreneurial activity.

In Step 2, participants were asked to generate names of their network contacts using the egocentric approach or name generator technique (Burt, 1997). However, the generation of names at this stage was not static as the participants could still add their contact names during the remaining activities. The workshop was meant to be interactive, so, rather than just generating names, participants were

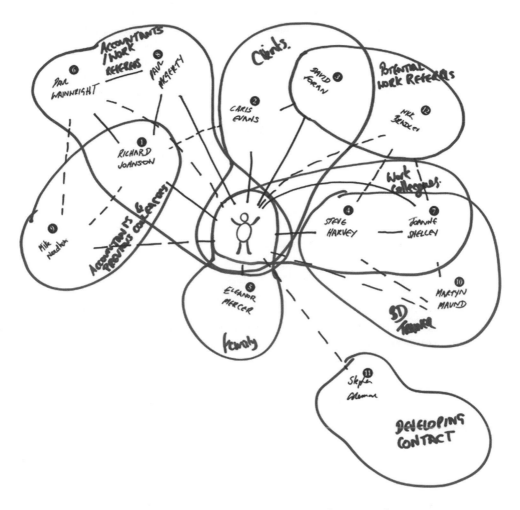

Figure 5.1 An example of network mapping produced by the respondents

encouraged to visualise their own network and at the same time reflect on the nature of their network through discussion and written notes. In this step, participants were also invited to note down some characteristics of their network contacts such as location and the way participants maintained their relationship with the contacts they identified.

In Step 3, we asked participants to reflect on what happened before they started their venture. Then participants were asked to draw a map of their initial network. There was no instruction on how to draw a network map. As a result, the network maps produced by each participant were individual to each participant. Figure 5.1 shows an example of a network map produced by the respondents. We guided the process by asking about the role of individual contacts and the context and situation of their business, as well as about the way the contacts were invited to the networks. We also investigated the contacts' backgrounds and how participants interacted with them. We then asked participants to reflect on a situation where they significantly changed their network (i.e. critical incidents). We continued this process for three or four cycles or until the participants told us that the network that they drew was the current or existing network.

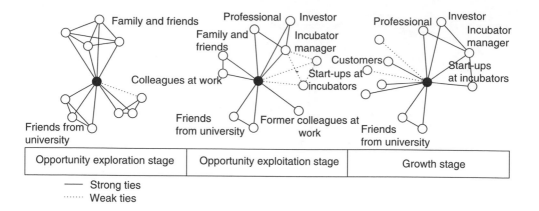

Figure 5.2   An illustration of Mark's networks

In Step 4, participants were asked to reflect on the role of the network in each development stage. This step also looked to increase the validity of this approach as the participants were encouraged to rethink the role of each network contact in several situations. During this process, some interviews were again carried out. The reason for the interviews was to deepen understanding about the networks and the role of contacts during the process of new product development.

Empirical Evidence

From the original sample of 12, we now present four case studies to illustrate patterns of change and characteristics of entrepreneurial networks.

Case 1: Mark

After graduating from university, Mark worked for a consultancy company. After two years, he decided to start his own business developing mobile apps for project management. The network mapping exercise revealed that Mark's early networks consisted of a small number of people who were separated into three clusters of networks, with those networks consisting of family, colleagues at work and small groups of friends from university. After receiving endorsement from

those close and strong networks, Mark then decided to leave his job and apply for an incubation programme. At the opportunity exploitation stage, Mark had built strong and large networks including contacts from diverse backgrounds, professionals and more significantly a new investor for his project. Mark praised the role of the incubator in helping him with this connection – 'The support from Tom (the manager of the incubator) was immense. The monthly networking event was so effective. I met a lot of interesting people. He has also introduced me to many of his contacts'. The network mapping (see Figure 5.2) demonstrates that Mark's networks were strongly connected, with most of his contacts familiar to each other. It was not until the growth stage that Mark developed a number of structural holes (Burt, 1997, 2004) that gave him advantages in building connections with potential clients. This case study clearly shows the advantages that Mark received as a result of different types of networks, strong and weak ties, and structural holes which allowed him not only to access much needed resources at the opportunity exploration stage but also supported the subsequent growth of his business.

Case 2: Kim

Kim had a background in computer science. She developed software for industrial

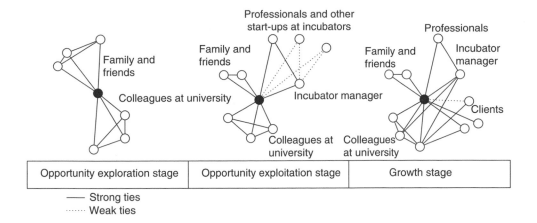

Strong ties
Weak ties

Figure 5.3   An illustration of Kim's networks

optimisation while working on her PhD project. At the opportunity exploration stage, Kim's network was quite limited, with her contacts being family and university colleagues. Kim started her business whilst locating at the incubator. Even at the opportunity exploitation stage, Kim's networks were still dominated by strong ties. The network mapping exercise shows that the development of her network was a relatively slow process. It appeared that Kim relied on the existing network with a few additional contacts as a result of the incubator's support. In evaluating her networking style, she expressed *'I had few supporters, but it was enough. I feel more comfortable talking about my business with someone that I know rather than a stranger.'* At the growth stage, her networks slightly expanded with the addition of new clients which she obtained as a result of her existing university contacts. Figure 5.3 illustrates the development of Kim's networks. It is evident that her networks were small and dominated by close contacts. Kim benefited from those contacts as they had offered emotional support, trust and some, albeit limited, new business opportunities. As a result of her tenancy in the incubator, her networks expanded; however, Kim's networks were still dominated by her strong ties, especially contacts from the university.

Case 3: John

John had worked as a laboratory assistant for more than 15 years at the university when he decided to start his own business. Having knowledge in designing and manufacturing bespoke laboratory tools, John saw an opportunity to offer his products to industry. As a result of the network mapping exercise, we found that John's networks were relatively large and consisted of a number of unconnected contacts. In articulating the nature of his networks, John remarked: *'I have accumulated a number of contacts. I worked for the university for a long time and had been involved in many projects. I know a lot of people from the university, even former PhD students who are now working in industry or other universities.'* At the opportunity exploration stage, John had managed to develop extensive networks as a result of previous involvement in projects with industrial partners and other European research institutes. Looking at the structure of John's networks, we found that they contained many structural holes. This type of network structure offers access to new information, knowledge and resources. In fact, John was able to attract investments from his contacts and secured several commission projects soon after leaving the university. Observing the dynamic nature of his network (Figure 5.4), we found that there were an increasing number of strong ties in the growth stage. In explaining these changes, John stated: '*I think I found what I called a core network ... of course, I keep other contacts ... but these people are really important for my business.*' John's position as a bridge of different clusters of networks had given him access to resources, information and opportunities.

Case 4: Toni

Toni was working in her family's business when she decided to start her own venture. Toni's business provides maintenance services for industrial and construction equipment. In developing her idea, Toni talked not only to family and friends but also to potential customers. She found these conversations were more organic in nature as opposed to planned or strategic, '*The new development or improvement of our product often occurred through discussions with our clients. Most of the time, I did not plan it. It just came out from the conversation when I met them. Their reactions were important for me to decide whether or not I would go for it. In general, I benefit a lot from having a lot of interactions.*' At the opportunity exploitation stage, Toni started to organise her internal and external resources by strengthening her networks. The importance of strong ties was encapsulated by the following comment: '*When I developed a new*

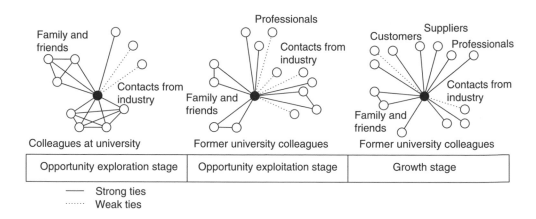

Figure 5.4   An illustration of John's networks

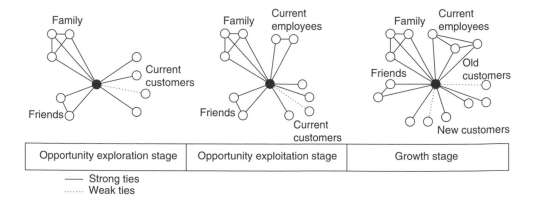

Figure 5.5   An illustration of Toni's networks

product, I usually got a lot of help from my close contacts. They were very helpful in solving my technical problems. I found them very important in this stage, especially in giving me feedback on how the market would react to my product.' At the growth stage, Toni's networks were again dominated by strong ties consisting of current employees, friends and family. Her ties with customers were getting more intense but some new and weak ties were also developed. From the network mapping (Figure 5.5), we found evidence that Toni benefited from networks consisting of both structural holes and strong ties. Toni's capability to maintain those networks helped her in realising the idea in a very short time period.

DISCUSSION

The presented case studies illustrate the role of networks in supporting entrepreneurial actions. They have also demonstrated that networks change as entrepreneurs adapt to the challenges associated with the development of a new venture. There was strong evidence that the entrepreneurs adapted their networks and activated strong and weak ties during their entrepreneurial journey. We also found a pattern whereby the entrepreneurs tended to develop networks with structural holes in the growth stage. While the findings confirmed that resources could be acquired through networks, we also found that networks have been used differently depending on the entrepreneur's socio-demographic context, such as gender and location. Comparing the approach adopted by the female and male entrepreneurs,

our study highlights that the female entrepreneurs developed their networks less aggressively compared with their male counterparts. Females are inherently good at networking, which means that they seek intrinsically to develop inclusive, reciprocal, collaborative, social relationships through their networking activities (Buttner, 1993; Martin, 2001). Accordingly, the female entrepreneurs had a high proportion of close networks and strong ties with family and friends whom they relied upon to provide much-needed moral support. For the male entrepreneurs, our study found that their networks were more dynamic with a high turnover of old and new contacts, indicating that they were more active and/or had different degrees of positionality when it came to accessing their networks compared with their female counterparts.

There are several reasons that may help explain the less dynamic nature of female entrepreneurs' networks. Our study found that the female entrepreneurs experienced higher barriers when developing their networks compared with their male counterparts, with such barriers influencing the characteristics of the subsequent networks formed. For example, Kim and Toni recognised that their family commitments had some negative impacts on the time available to dedicate to networking. Although the female entrepreneurs recognised that they had deliberately chosen to set up their own businesses, they were sometimes still overwhelmed with the challenge of balancing family and business demands. Another difficulty perceived by the female entrepreneurs was the penetration of male-dominated networks. Table 5.2 summarises the findings of the study.

Table 5.2 Female and male entrepreneurial networks

	Network closure and structural holes	Strong and weak ties	Network change
Female entrepreneur networks	Structural holes appear at later stage	Networks are dominated by strong ties	Less dynamic
Male entrepreneur networks	Structural holes emerge from the early stage	A mixture of strong and weak ties	More dynamic

Business Incubators and Entrepreneurial Networks

The network mapping also revealed that being located in a business incubator influenced the characteristics and dynamism of entrepreneurial networks. Scholars (Battisti & McAdam, 2012; McAdam & Marlow, 2008; McAdam & McAdam, 2008) suggest that the geographical proximity within a business incubator influences the frequency of contacts and endorses the development of networks. The physical and social proximity to other tenants plays a beneficial role as they can catalyse the entrepreneurial process while enhancing networking and collaboration amongst firms. An illustration of this can be seen visually from Mark's networks. He used a small number of close ties to discuss the feasibility of ideas in the opportunity exploration stage, which grew when he moved into the incubator. In the case of Kim's network, the role of the business incubator was significant for her venture's survival and growth. In addition to providing tenancy, the incubator helped Kim to develop relationships with business professionals. Overall, these two case studies revealed that the business incubators facilitated the development of networks with rich structural holes. In contrast, those entrepreneurs not located in the business incubator had to rely on their own networking capability in developing a network with structural holes. Table 5.3 summarises the findings of the study.

CONCLUSION

The aim of this chapter was to explore the changing role of network-based relationships in the entrepreneurial process. Accordingly, we drew upon the notion that entrepreneurship is embedded in a social context. This resulted in a critical discussion of the fundamental concept of entrepreneurial networks and its theoretical roots. Building on this, we then considered potential future research directions in order to move the current debate forward. To encapsulate the importance of entrepreneurship and how networks adapt and change to fulfil entrepreneurial needs, we presented case studies in the contrasting contexts of gender and location. In so doing, this chapter responded to calls for more qualitative enquiry into the study of entrepreneurial networks and accordingly adopted an innovative research approach involving a network visualisation technique. The case studies revealed that entrepreneurs not only have to build partnerships and network relations, but they must also ensure that the emerging social structure meets their resource needs. In particular, the findings revealed that networks are used differently depending on the entrepreneur's socio-demographic context, such as gender and location. This leads to a potential research avenue, namely the impact of those contexts on the outcomes of networks. Whilst we assume that networks facilitate entrepreneurial actions by converting limited resources into rich resources, for the entrepreneurs this requires undertaking strategic networking. Despite considerable empirical and theoretical

Table 5.3   Networks of entrepreneurs located at and outside incubators

	Network closure and structural holes	Strong and weak ties	The change in networks
Entrepreneurs located in the business incubator	Structural holes grow as a result of incubator support	A mixed network of strong and weak ties	Receive more opportunity to expand networks through incubator support
Entrepreneurs not located in the business incubator	Develop network of structural holes from the beginning	A mixed network of strong and weak ties	Rely on entrepreneurs' ability to change their network

development, greater understanding is still required of the impact of networking strategy on entrepreneurial actions, as we currently lack knowledge of the issues surrounding the entrepreneurs' decision to develop and maintain their networks.

REFERENCES

Adler, P. S., & Kwon, S. W. (2002). Social capital: Prospects for a new concept. *Academy of Management Review*, *27*(1), 17–40.

Aldrich, H., Reese, P. R., & Dubini, P. (1989). Women on the verge of a breakthrough: Networking among entrepreneurs in the United States and Italy. *Entrepreneurship & Regional Development*, *1*(4), 339–356.

Aldrich, H., Rosen, B., & Woodward, W. (1987). The impact of social networks on business founding and profit: A longitudinal study. *Frontiers of Entrepreneurship Research*, *7*(154), 68.

Anderson, A., Park, J., & Jack, S. (2007). Entrepreneurial social capital conceptualizing social capital in new high-tech firms. *International Small Business Journal*, *25*(3), 245–272.

Anderson, E., & Jap, S. D. (2005). The dark side of close relationships. *MIT Sloan Management Review*, *46*(3), 75–82.

Araujo, L., & Easton, G. (1996). Strategy: Where is the pattern? *Organization*, *3*(3), 361–383.

Ardichvili, A., Cardozo, R., & Ray, S. (2003). A theory of entrepreneurial opportunity identification and development. *Journal of Business venturing*, *18*(1), 105–123.

Baron, R. A., & Markman, G. D. (2003). Beyond social capital: The role of entrepreneurs' social competence in their financial success. *Journal of Business Venturing*, *18*(1), 41–60.

Batjargal, B., Hitt, M. A., Tsui, A. S., Arregle, J. L., Webb, J. W., & Miller, T. L. (2013). Institutional polycentrism, entrepreneurs' social networks, and new venture growth. *Academy of Management Journal*, *56*(4), 1024–1049.

Battisti, M., & McAdam, M. (2012). Challenges of social capital development in the university science incubator: The case of the graduate entrepreneur. *The International Journal of Entrepreneurship and Innovation*, *13*(4), 261–276.

Birley, S. (1985). The role of networks in the entrepreneurial process. *Journal of Business Venturing*, *1*(1), 107–117.

Birley, S. (1987). New ventures and employment growth. *Journal of Business Venturing*, *2*(2), 155–165.

Bøllingtoft, A., & Ulhøi, J. P. (2005). The networked business incubator – leveraging entrepreneurial agency? *Journal of Business Venturing*, *20*(2), 265–290.

Brush, C. G., De Bruin, A., & Welter, F. (2009). A gender-aware framework for women's entrepreneurship. *International Journal of Gender and Entrepreneurship*, *1*(1), 8–24.

Burt, R. S. (1997). The contingent value of social capital. *Administrative Science Quarterly*, *42*(2), 339–365.

Burt, R. S. (2004). Structural holes and good ideas. *American Journal of Sociology*, *110*(2), 349–399.

Buttner, E. H. (1993). Female entrepreneurs: How far have they come? *Business Horizons*, *36*(2), 59–65.

Carnabuci, G., & Diószegi, B. (2015). Social networks, cognitive style and innovative performance: A contingency perspective. *Academy of Management Journal*, *58*(3), 649–657.

Carter, N., Brush, C., Greene, P., Gatewood, E., & Hart, M. (2003). Women entrepreneurs who break through to equity financing: The influence of human, social and financial capital. *Venture Capital: An International Journal of Entrepreneurial Finance*, *5*(1), 1–28.

Carter, S., & Shaw, E. (2006). *Women's business ownership: Recent research and policy developments* (pp. 1–96). Report for BIS, Retrieved from https://strathprints.strath.ac.uk/8962/

Coleman, J. S. (1988). Social capital in the creation of human capital. *American Journal of Sociology*, S95–S120.

Coleman, J. S. (1990). *Foundations of social theory*. Cambridge, MA: Harvard University Press.

Davidsson, P., & Honig, B. (2003). The role of social and human capital among nascent entrepreneurs. *Journal of Business Venturing*, *18*(3), 301–331.

Díaz García, C., & Carter, S. (2009). Resource mobilization through business owners' networks: Is gender an issue? *International Journal of Gender and Entrepreneurship*, *1*(3), 226–252.

Dodd, S. D., & Anderson, A. R. (2007). Mumpsimus and the mything of the individualistic entrepreneur. *International Small Business Journal*, *25*(4), 341–360.

Downing, S. (2005). The social construction of entrepreneurship: Narrative and dramatic processes in the coproduction of organizations and identities. *Entrepreneurship Theory and Practice*, *29*(2), 185–204.

Dubini, P., & Aldrich, H. (1991). Personal and extended networks are central to the entrepreneurial process. *Journal of Business Venturing*, *6*(5), 305–313.

Ebbers, J. J. (2014). Networking behavior and contracting relationships among entrepreneurs in business incubators. *Entrepreneurship Theory and Practice*, *38*(5), 1159–1181.

Elfring, T., & Hulsink, W. (2003). Networks in entrepreneurship: The case of high-technology firms. *Small Business Economics*, *21*(4), 409–422.

Farmer, S. M., Yao, X., & Kung-Mcintyre, K. (2011). The behavioral impact of entrepreneur identity aspiration and prior entrepreneurial experience. *Entrepreneurship Theory and Practice*, *35*(2), 245–273. doi:10.1111/j.1540-6520.2009.00358.x

Foss, L. (2010). Research of entrepreneur networks: The case for a constructionist feminist theory perspective. *International Journal of Gender and Entrepreneurship*, *2*(1), 83–102.

Gargiulo, M., & Benassi, M. (2000). Trapped in your own net? Network cohesion, structural holes, and the adaptation of social capital. *Organization Science*, *11*(2), 183–196.

Gedajlovic, E., Honig, B., Moore, C. B., Payne, G. T., & Wright, M. (2013). Social capital and entrepreneurship: A schema and research agenda. *Entrepreneurship Theory and Practice*, *37*(3), 455–478.

Gilsing, V. A., & Duysters, G. M. (2008). Understanding novelty creation in exploration networks – structural and relational embeddedness jointly considered. *Technovation*, *28*(10), 693–708.

Gottschalk, P. (2009). *Entrepreneurship and organised crime: Entrepreneurs in illegal business*. Cheltenham, UK and Northampton, MA: Edward Elgar Publishing.

Granovetter, M. S. (1973). The strength of weak ties. *American Journal of Sociology*, *78*(6), 1360–1380.

Granovetter, M. (1983). The strength of weak ties: A network theory revisited. *Sociological Theory*, *1*(1), 201–233.

Granovetter, M. (1985). Economic action and social structure: The problem of embeddedness. *American Journal of Sociology*, *91*(3), 481–510.

Granovetter, M. (2005). The impact of social structure on economic outcomes. *The Journal of Economic Perspective*, *19*(1), 33–50.

Greve, A., & Salaff, J. W. (2003). Social networks and entrepreneurship. *Entrepreneurship Theory and Practice*, *28*(1), 1–22.

Grimaldi, R., & Grandi, A. (2005). Business incubators and new venture creation: An assessment of incubating models. *Technovation*, *25*(2), 111–121.

Gulati, R. (1995). Social structure and alliance formation patterns: A longitudinal analysis. *Administrative Science Quarterly*, *40*(4), 619–652.

Hackett, S. M., & Dilts, D. M. (2004). A systematic review of business incubation research. *The Journal of Technology Transfer*, *29*(1), 55–82.

Hansen, M. T. (1999). The search-transfer problem: The role of weak ties in sharing knowledge across organization subunits. *Administrative Science Quarterly*, *44*(1), 82–111.

Harrison, R. T., & Mason, C. M. (2007). Does gender matter? Women business angels and the supply of entrepreneurial finance. *Entrepreneurship Theory and Practice*, *31*(3), 445–472.

Hisrich, R. D., & Smilor, R. W. (1998). The university and business incubation: Technology transfer through entrepreneurial development. *Technology Transfer*, *13*(1), 14–19.

Hite, J. M. (2005). Evolutionary processes and paths of relationally embedded network ties in emerging entrepreneurial firms. *Entrepreneurship Theory and Practice*, *29*(1), 113–144.

Hite, J. M. (2008). The role of dyadic multidimensionality in the evolution of strategic network ties. *Advances in Strategic Management–Network Strategy*, *25*, 133–170.

Hite, J. M., & Hesterly, W. S. (2001). Research notes and commentaries. The evolution of firm networks: From emergence to early growth of the firm. *Strategic Management Journal*, *22*(3), 275–286.

Hoang, H., & Antoncic, B. (2003). Network-based research in entrepreneurship: A critical review. *Journal of Business Venturing*, *18*(2), 165–187.

Hoepfl, M. C. (1997). Choosing qualitative research: A primer for technology education researchers. *Journal of Technology Education*, *9*(1), 47–63.

Hughes, M., Morgan, R. E., Ireland, R. D., & Hughes, P. (2014). Social capital and learning advantages: A problem of absorptive capacity. *Strategic Entrepreneurship Journal*, *8*(3), 214–233.

Ibarra, H. (1993). Personal networks of women and minorities in management: A conceptual framework. *Academy of Management Review*, *18*(1), 56–87.

Ibarra, H. (1997). Paving an alternative route: Gender differences in managerial networks. *Social Psychology Quarterly*, *60*(1), 91–102.

Jack, S. L. (2005). The role, use and activation of strong and weak network ties: A qualitative analysis. *Journal of Management Studies*, *42*(6), 1233–1259.

Jack, S. L. (2010). Approaches to studying networks: Implications and outcomes. *Journal of Business Venturing*, *25*(1), 120–137.

Jennings, J. E., & Brush, C. G. (2013). Research on women entrepreneurs: Challenges to (and from) the broader entrepreneurship literature? *The Academy of Management Annals*, *7*(1), 663–715.

Johannisson, B. (1987). Anarchists and organizers: Entrepreneurs in a network perspective. *International Studies of Management & Organization*, *17*(1), 49–63.

Johannisson, B. (1988). Business formation – a network approach. *Scandinavian Journal of Management*, *4*(3), 83–99.

Kim, P., & Aldrich, H. (2005). *Social capital and entrepreneurship*. Foundations and Trends in Entrepreneurship, *1*(2), 55–104. doi: 10.1561/0300000002

Kogut, B., & Zander, U. (1992). Knowledge of the firm, combinative capabilities, and the replication of technology. *Organization Science*, *3*(3), 383–397.

Krishna, A. (2000). Creating and harnessing social capital. In P. Dasgupta & I. Serageldin, (Eds), *Social capital: A multifaceted perspective* (pp. 71–93). Washington, DC: The World Bank.

Larson, A., & Starr, J. A. (1993). A network model of organization formation. *Entrepreneurship Theory and Practice*, *17*(2), 5–15.

Lechner, C., & Dowling, M. (2003). Firm networks: External relationships as sources for the growth and competitiveness of entrepreneurial firms. *Entrepreneurship & Regional Development*, *15*(1), 1–26.

Lechner, C., & Leyronas, C. (2007). Network-centrality versus network-position in regional networks: What matters most? A study of a French high-tech cluster. *International Journal of Technoentrepreneurship*, *1*(1), 78–91.

Leitch, C., Harrison, R., & Hill, F. (2014). Women entrepreneurs' networking behaviours: Perspectives from entrepreneurs and network managers. In K. Lewis, C. Henry, E. Gatewood, & J. Watson (Eds), *Women's entrepreneurship in the 21st century: An international multi-level research analysis* (pp. 215–235). Cheltenham: Edward Elgar Publishing.

Liao, J., & Welsch, H. (2003). Social capital and entrepreneurial growth aspiration: A comparison of technology- and non-technology-based nascent entrepreneurs. *The Journal of High Technology Management Research*, *14*(1), 149–170.

Lin, N. (2002). *Social capital: A theory of social structure and action* (Vol. 19). Cambridge: Cambridge University Press.

Linehan, M., & Scullion, H. (2008). The development of female global managers: The role of mentoring and networking. *Journal of Business Ethics*, *83*(1), 29–40.

Martin, E. (2001). *The woman in the body: A cultural analysis of reproduction*. Boston, MA: Beacon Press.

Maurer, I., & Ebers, M. (2006). Dynamics of social capital and their performance implications: Lessons from biotechnology start-ups. *Administrative Science Quarterly*, *51*(2), 262–292.

McAdam, M., & McAdam, R. (2006). The networked incubator: The role and operation of entrepreneurial networking with the university science park incubator (USI). *The International Journal of Entrepreneurship and Innovation*, *7*(2), 87–97.

McAdam, M., & McAdam, R. (2008). High tech start-ups in University Science Park incubators: The relationship between the start-up's lifecycle progression and use of the incubator's resources. *Technovation*, *28*(5), 277–290.

McAdam, M., & Marlow, S. (2008). A preliminary investigation into networking activities within the university incubator. *International Journal of Entrepreneurial Behaviour and Research*, *14* (4), 219–241.

McDougall, P. P., Shane, S., & Oviatt, B. M. (1994). Explaining the formation of international new ventures: The limits of theories from international business research. *Journal of Business Venturing*, *9*(6), 469–487.

McGregor, J., & Tweed, D. (2002). Profiling a new generation of female small business owners in New Zealand: Networking, mentoring and growth. *Gender, Work & Organization*, *9*(4), 420–438.

Minguzzi, A., & Passaro, R. (2001). The network of relationships between the economic environment and the entrepreneurial culture in small firms. *Journal of Business Venturing*, *16*(2), 181–207.

Minniti, M., & Arenius, P. (2003). Women in entrepreneurship. Paper presented at The Entrepreneurial Advantage of Nations: First Annual Global Entrepreneurship Symposium, United Nations Headquarters, April 29, 2003.

Molina-Morales, F. X., & Martínez-Fernández, M. T. (2009). Too much love in the neighborhood can hurt: How an excess of intensity and trust in relationships may produce negative effects on firms. *Strategic Management Journal*, *30*(9), 1013–1023.

Mønsted, M. (1995). Processes and structures of networks: Reflections on methodology. *Entrepreneurship & Regional Development*, *7*(3), 193–214.

Nahapiet, J., & Ghoshal, S. (1998). Social capital, intellectual capital, and the organizational advantage. *Academy of Management Review*, *23*(2), 242–266.

Neergaard, H., & Ulhøi, J. P. (2006). Government agency and trust in the formation and transformation of interorganizational entrepreneurial networks. *Entrepreneurship Theory and Practice*, *30*(4), 519–539.

Neergaard, H., Shaw, E., & Carter, S. (2005). The impact of gender, social capital and networks on business ownership – a research agenda. *International Journal of Entrepreneurial Behaviour and Research*, *11*(5), 338–357.

Nohria, N. (1992). Introduction: Is a network perspective a useful way of studying organizations? In N. Nohria & R. G. Eccles (Eds), *Networks and organizations: Structure, form, and action* (pp. 1–22). Boston, MA: Harvard Business School Press.

O'Donnell, A., Gilmore, A., Cummins, D., & Carson, D. (2001). The network construct in entrepreneurship research: A review and critique. *Management Decision*, *39*(9), 749–760.

Ostgaard, T. A., & Birley, S. (1996). New venture growth and personal networks. *Journal of Business Research*, *36*(1), 37–50.

Oviatt, B. M., & McDougall, P. P. (2005). Defining international entrepreneurship and modeling the speed of internationalization. *Entrepreneurship Theory and Practice*, *29*(5), 537–554.

Ozdemir, S. Z., Moran, P., Zhong, X., & Bliemel, M. J. (2016). Reaching and acquiring valuable resources: The entrepreneur's use of brokerage, cohesion, and embeddedness. *Entrepreneurship Theory and Practice*, *40*(1), 49–79.

Parkhe, A., Wasserman, S., & Ralston, D. A. (2006). New frontiers in network theory development. *Academy of Management Review*, *31*(3), 560–568.

Partanen, J., Chetty, S. K., & Rajala, A. (2014). Innovation types and network relationships. *Entrepreneurship Theory and Practice*, *38*(5), 1027–1055.

Patel, P. C., & Terjesen, S. (2011). Complementary effects of network range and tie strength in enhancing transnational venture performance. *Strategic Entrepreneurship Journal*, *5*(1), 58–80.

Patton, M. Q. (1990). *Qualitative evaluation and research methods*. CA: Sage.

Peters, L., Rice, M., & Sundararajan, M. (2004). The role of incubators in the entrepreneurial process. *The Journal of Technology Transfer*, *29*(1), 83–91.

Podolny, J. M. (2001). Networks as the pipes and prisms of the market. *American Journal of Sociology*, *107*(1), 33–60.

Putnam, R. D. (2002). *Democracies in flux: The evolution of social capital in contemporary society*. Oxford: Oxford University Press.

Renzulli, L. A., Aldrich, H., & Moody, J. (2000). Family matters: Gender, networks, and entrepreneurial outcomes. *Social Forces*, *79*(2), 523–546.

Ruef, M. (2002). Strong ties, weak ties and islands: Structural and cultural predictors of organizational innovation. *Industrial and Corporate Change*, *11*(3), 427–449.

Ruef, M., Aldrich, H. E., & Carter, N. M. (2003). The structure of organizational founding teams: Homophily, strong ties, and isolation among U.S. entrepreneurs. *American Sociological Review*, *68*(2), pp. 195–222.

Schutjens, V., & Stam, E. (2003). The evolution and nature of young firm networks: A longitudinal perspective. *Small Business Economics, 21(2),* 115–134.

Semrau, T., & Werner, A. (2014). How exactly do network relationships pay off? The effects of network size and relationship quality on access to start-up resources. *Entrepreneurship Theory and Practice*, *38*(3), 501–525.

Shane, S. A. (2004). *Academic entrepreneurship: University spinoffs and wealth creation.* Cheltenham, UK and Northampton, MA: Edward Elgar Publishing.

Shaw, E., & Conway, S. (2000). Networking and the small firm. In S. Carter and D. Jones-Evans (Eds), *Enterprise and Small Business* (pp. 367–383). Harlow: Prentice Hall.

Simsek, Z., Lubatkin, M. H., & Floyd, S. W. (2003). Inter-firm networks and entrepreneurial behavior: A structural embeddedness perspective. *Journal of Management*, *29*(3), 427–442.

Slotte-Kock, S., & Coviello, N. (2010). Entrepreneurship research on network processes: A review and ways forward. *Entrepreneurship Theory and Practice*, *34*(1), 31–57.

Starr, J., & Yudkin, M. (1996). *Women entrepreneurs: A review of current research* (Vol. 15). Wellesley Centers for Women.

Steier, L., & Greenwood, R. (2000). Entrepreneurship and the evolution of angel financial networks. *Organization Studies*, *21*(1), 163–192.

Steyaert, C., & Katz, J. (2004). Reclaiming the space of entrepreneurship in society: Geographical, discursive and social dimensions. *Entrepreneurship and Regional Development*, *16* (3), 179–96.

Stuart, T. E., & Sorenson, O. (2005). Social networks and entrepreneurship. In S. A. Alvarez, R. Agarwal, & O. Sorenson (Eds), *Handbook of entrepreneurship research* (pp. 233–252). New York: Springer.

Sullivan, D. M., & Ford, C. M. (2014). How entrepreneurs use networks to address changing resource requirements during early venture development. *Entrepreneurship Theory and Practice*, *38*(3), 551–574.

Sytch, M., & Tatarynowicz, A. (2014). Exploring the locus of invention: The dynamics of network communities and firms' invention productivity. *Academy of Management Journal*, *57*(1), 249–279.

Szarka, J. (1990). Networking and small firms. *International Small Business Journal*, *8*(2), 10–22.

Tan, J., Zhang, H., & Wang, L. (2015). Network closure or structural hole? The conditioning effects of network-level social capital on innovation performance. *Entrepreneurship Theory and Practice*, *39*(5), 1189–1212.

Uzzi, B. (1997). Social structure and competition in interfirm networks: The paradox of embeddedness. *Administrative Science Quarterly*, *42*(1), 35–67.

Wasserman, S., & Faust, K. (1994). *Social network analysis: Methods and applications* (Vol. 8). Cambridge: Cambridge University Press.

Westhead, P., Wright, M., & Ucbasaran, D. (2001). The internationalization of new and small firms: A resource-based view. *Journal of Business Venturing*, *16*(4), 333–358.

Witt, P. (2004). Entrepreneurs' networks and the success of start-ups. *Entrepreneurship & Regional Development*, *16*(5), 391–412.

Wuebker, R., Hampl, N., & Wüstenhagen, R. (2015). The strength of strong ties in an emerging industry: Experimental evidence of the effects of status hierarchies and personal ties in venture capitalist decision making. *Strategic Entrepreneurship Journal*, *9*(2), 167–187.

Zaheer, A., & McEvily, B. (1999). Bridging ties: A source of firm heterogeneity in competitive capabilities. *Strategic Management Journal*, *20*(12), 1133–1156.

6

Migrant Entrepreneurship

Stephen Drinkwater

INTRODUCTION

Migration has become one of the most important contemporary public policy issues and topics for debate all over the world, as the movement of people across national boundaries has continued to increase. Evidence on the scale of global migration has recently been provided by the United Nations, who estimated that 244 million people lived outside the country of their birth in 2015, which represented a 41% increase in comparison to the estimate for 2000 (UN, 2015). Therefore, and perhaps not surprisingly, a large international literature has emerged over the last couple of decades on the relationship between entrepreneurship and migration. This literature initially started to emerge in sociology (Light, 1972; Bonacich, 1973), especially in relation to migrant enterprise in the United States (US), but has subsequently been augmented by studies from economics (Borjas, 1986; Yuengert, 1995) and then more recently from the expanding entrepreneurship literature

more generally (Levie, 2007; Kwong et al., 2009; Peroni, Riilo & Sarracino, 2016). However, it is not easy to summarise very succinctly the main findings from this literature because of the complexity of migration and therefore the range of possible ways in which it can impact on entrepreneurship – both positively and negatively. As a result, it is important to carefully consider how levels of entrepreneurship can vary for different groups of migrants and the factors that might account for such variations.

The growth in global migration that has been observed in recent decades is due to myriad factors (Castles, De Haas & Miller, 2013). However, of particular importance are those influences that underlie the continued process of globalisation. These include increased regional economic integration, which has enabled migrants from countries that are part of free-trade areas, such as the European Union (EU), to move to other member states often without restrictions. However, in some cases, migration policies that have been developed as a response to the increased migration due to the freedom of movement are likely to have influenced migrant entrepreneurship. For example, countries such as the United Kingdom (UK) have imposed certain restrictions on migration both before and after recent enlargements of the EU so that migrants from new member states could enter the labour market but only through certain routes, including by declaring themselves as self-employed (Clark, Drinkwater & Robinson, 2016). Governments have also actively encouraged immigration by particular groups, especially highly skilled workers and entrepreneurs more generally (Home Office, 2013). This is because of the desire of many modern governments to create a more dynamic and flexible economy, often driven by the continued objective of increasing economic growth rates. Given the view, dating back to Schumpeter (1942), that entrepreneurs can facilitate a more dynamic economy then migrant entrepreneurs are a group that countries have been particularly keen to attract. Different national governments have therefore introduced specific schemes aimed at enticing entrepreneurs to relocate in their countries (Desiderio, 2014).

This chapter examines the relationship between entrepreneurship and migration by firstly discussing the ways in which these terms have typically been measured in the literature. To illustrate some of the key features of this relationship, some initial evidence on entrepreneurship and migration is presented, using recent data for the UK. This is followed by a more detailed discussion of how entrepreneurship can be affected by a wide range of factors for different groups of migrants. Some of these factors may be general demographic influences, whereas others may be specific to particular migrant groups. The subsequent section then presents some up-to-date evidence on migrant entrepreneurship in the UK, focusing on some of the key drivers. The chapter culminates with a conclusion that briefly summarises the main findings from the review of the literature and empirical evidence, as well as providing some of the main policy implications and comments on future directions for research.

DEFINING AND MEASURING MIGRANT ENTREPRENEURSHIP

The section begins by considering different measures of entrepreneurship. The concept of entrepreneurship has been discussed and debated over several centuries and is thought to have originated in eighteenth-century France and to be derived from the term 'entreprendre' – meaning 'to do something' or 'to undertake' (Sobel, 2008). It has subsequently been refined, reshaped and adapted in several directions, including to encompass notions relating to the bearing of risk (Knight, 1921) and as a key source of innovation through a process of creative destruction (Schumpeter, 1942). However, for the purposes of this chapter, the definition of entrepreneurship emerges from a fairly pragmatic perspective and is to some extent determined by the available data. Such issues are particularly pertinent in relation to examining migrant entrepreneurship because migrant groups can be rather small with regards to the number of entrepreneurs that they contain, especially in relation to the majority population. Consequently, in order to undertake meaningful comparisons between groups, suitable data sources must be analysed.

Parker (2008) identifies two main broad approaches that have been used to measure entrepreneurship, especially with regards to making comparisons across countries. These are, firstly, estimates of entrepreneurship relating to self-employment, as obtained from large-scale population surveys such as the Labour Force Survey (LFS), and as reported in the Labour Force Statistics published by the Organisation for Economic Cooperation and Development (OECD), and secondly, more specific estimates of entrepreneurship as defined by the formation and operation of new firms from the Global Entrepreneurship Monitor (GEM). In particular, the GEM definition attempts to capture the total level of entrepreneurial activity. Parker (2008) notes that the two methods and approaches each have their advantages and disadvantages.

Estimates of self-employment from surveys are typically derived from a question that asks respondents about their main economic/labour market activity. The responses are then grossed up to provide estimates for the population as a whole by applying the appropriate weights. However, the types of jobs done by the self-employed vary widely in terms of status and earnings and they are likely to have become more irregular and precarious over time. This includes the increase in 'false' self-employment in Western European countries, which has been heavily influenced by migration from new member states following EU enlargement (Thornquist, 2015). Nevertheless, Faggio and Silva (2014) examine the relationship between self-employment and key features of entrepreneurship in the UK. Their measure of self-employment comes from the LFS, whilst entrepreneurship focuses on innovation and business creation. They find that the correlation between self-employment, innovation and business creation is strongly positive in urban areas but not in rural areas.

Moreover, there are several studies in which entrepreneurs have been directly identified with reference to whether a respondent participating in a social survey reports themselves as being self-employed. For example, in order to answer the question of 'What makes an entrepreneur?', Blanchflower and Oswald (1998) undertake a detailed analysis of survey data from the UK National Child Development Study to identify the sociodemographic characteristics of entrepreneurs and the factors that can facilitate entry, whilst, in attempting to establish whether individuals are 'born entrepreneurs', Viinikainen et al. (2016) examine whether an individual's personality in their childhood has an impact on whether they become self-employed in adulthood. This general approach, which utilises information on self-employment from large-scale surveys, is the one that will mainly be focused upon in the remainder of this chapter, particularly with regards to the empirical evidence that will be presented.

The concept of a 'migrant' can also be measured in a number of ways. The most common is using information on country of birth, with an individual defined as a migrant if they report that they were born outside the country in which they currently reside – regardless of when they moved to that country. Some studies have also considered second-generation migrants, in which the focus is on ethnic minorities more generally (Fairlie & Meyer, 1996; Clark & Drinkwater, 2000). Migrants can also be defined according to their nationality, which will include people who were born in the host country but consider themselves to have a different nationality but excludes those who assume the nationality of the host country having moved there from their country of origin. Differences between country of birth and nationality are small for some groups, such as migrants to the UK from other parts of the EU, but much larger for others, especially migrants to the UK from non-EU countries (ONS, 2015). For the purposes of this chapter, migration status will primarily be considered using the country of birth definition.

Regardless of how migrants and entrepreneurship are measured, entrepreneurship is found to vary considerably between migrants and the native-born across countries. For example, Levie (2007) and Peroni et al. (2016) report significant differences in entrepreneurial activity between migrants and the native-born using the GEM for the UK and Luxemburg respectively. Similarly, studies that have examined self-employment also identify large variations, including Borjas (1986) for the US, Clark and Drinkwater (2009) for the UK and Constant and Zimmermann (2006) for Germany. There is also some consistency across studies with regards to the diversity in the experience of different ethnic and migrant groups. This includes low levels of entrepreneurial activity among Black groups in both the UK and US, whereas far higher levels have typically been observed for many groups of Asian migrants (Fairlie & Meyer, 1996; Clark & Drinkwater, 2000).

Given the above discussion, as well as to motivate the analysis in the subsequent sections, there now follows an initial analysis of migrant entrepreneurship. This is measured by whether workers who were born outside the host country of birth identify themselves as primarily being self-employed, using recently collected data from the LFS for the UK.[1] The advantage of using such a data source is that it provides relatively large sample sizes, which is important since self-employment/entrepreneurship can be compared across a range of migrant groups. This is particularly relevant in countries such as the UK, which have experienced high levels of migration from an extremely diverse set of countries since the turn of the twenty-first century (Vertovec, 2007).

As in other countries, the composition of the migrant population in the UK has evolved over time following the arrival of distinct cohorts of migrants. For example, some of the main migrant groups originated from different parts of the British Commonwealth, after large-scale migration to the UK in the post-war period. In particular, there were relatively large population flows from the Indian sub-continent (especially from India, Pakistan and Bangladesh) to the UK in the 1960s and 1970s. Migration has continued from these countries in more recent times, although at a lower rate. Instead, migration to the UK over the last decade has been dominated by flows from other parts of Europe. This is particularly connected to the enlargements of the EU that took place in 2004 for A8 countries (the eight Central and Eastern European Countries that joined the EU in that year) and in 2007 from A2 countries (Bulgaria and Romania).[2] Furthermore, migration from other parts of the EU has also grown as a result of the relatively poor economic performance of several pre-2004 member states, such as Ireland, Italy, Greece, Portugal and Spain (Clark, Drinkwater and Robinson, 2016).

Background information on migration and entrepreneurship in the UK is provided in Table 6.1, which, in addition to summarising how overall self-employment rates (defined as the proportion of those in work whose main job is in self-employment) differ for the main migrant groups that are resident in the UK, also contains details on variations by (grouped) industrial sector and the percentage of self-employed who employ others. As previously indicated, Table 6.1 reveals that there continues to be considerable diversity in self-employment rates between migrant groups in the UK. In particular, whilst some groups have self-employment rates that are very similar to the UK-born, such as A8 migrants and those born in other EU countries and India, rates are more than twice as high for migrants from the A2 countries and Pakistan/Bangladesh.

These high rates of self-employment can partly be explained by the sectors that certain groups of migrants tend to work in, which are often low-skilled and do not require formal academic qualifications. In particular, almost a half of self-employed A2 migrants in the UK work in Construction, whilst over two-thirds of migrants from Pakistan/Bangladesh are employed in the Retail, Transport and Restaurants sectors. In contrast, the UK-born and other migrant groups display a more dispersed range of entrepreneurial activities. Table 6.1 does, however, reveal some further indications of an over-representation of the self-employed in certain sectors such as A8 migrants in Construction and Indian migrants in Retail, Transport and Restaurants. These findings may also be expected, to a certain degree, based on the sectoral concentrations observed for self-employed migrants from the A2 countries and Pakistan/Bangladesh. Sectoral variations in entrepreneurship will also impact on the percentage of self-employed employing others/working on their own. Migrants from A8 and A2 countries are most likely to work on their own, since 95% do not employ others, which is also related to the shorter amount of time that they have been resident in the UK. In contrast, migrants from India and other non-EU countries are least likely to work on their own, with over 20% of the self-employed from these groups employing others.

Table 6.1   Background statistics on self-employment in the UK by migrant group, 2014–15

	Self-Employment Rate	Percentage of Self-Employed Working in						Percentage with Other Employees	N (Self-Employed)
		Primary and Secondary Industries	Construction	Retail, Transport and Restaurants	Financial, Prof. & Support Services, ICT and Real Estate	Public Admin., Education and Health	Other Services		
UK-Born	13.8	10.2	20.9	16.0	27.7	13.2	12.1	17.3	12,259
Born in A8	13.4	5.5	35.4	14.3	22.7	7.7	14.5	4.8	381
Born in A2	32.8	1.8	46.8	15.8	21.6	4.1	9.9	5.9	171
Other EU-Born	13.8	6.3	12.5	9.8	35.7	23.4	12.3	16.4	367
Born in India	12.8	5.8	11.1	33.2	30.0	12.6	7.4	26.3	190
Born in Pakistan/ Bangladesh	28.9	1.6	7.2	66.6	12.8	8.8	3.1	14.0	322
Other Non-EU	15.8	4.3	10.5	29.8	30.1	14.9	10.5	21.3	1,093
All	14.1	9.2	20.2	18.2	27.5	13.2	11.8	17.2	14,783

Source: Labour Force Survey

Notes: A8 refers to the Czech Republic, Estonia, Hungary, Latvia, Lithuania, Poland, Slovakia and Slovenia; A2 countries are Bulgaria and Romania; Other EU-Born are migrants from the remaining 17 member states (these are mainly pre-2004 members but also include Malta, Cyprus and Croatia). Primary and Secondary Industries relates to Standard Industrial Classification (SIC) 2007 Sectors A–F; Retail, Transport and Restaurants relates to Sectors G–I; Financial, Professional & Support Services, ICT and Real Estate relates to Sectors J–N; Public Admin, Education and Health to Sectors O–Q; and Other Services relates to Sectors R–U.

EXPLAINING DIFFERENCES IN MIGRANT ENTREPRENEURSHIP

The background statistics that have been presented in the previous section provide a useful context for the subsequent discussion of key factors that are thought to explain the observed variations in entrepreneurship between immigrants and natives. Moreover, many of these influences are often able to account for the differences between groups of migrants. These include a range of general socio-demographic characteristics, which often have a similar effect on self-employment/ entrepreneurship for different migrant groups, although possibly to varying degrees (Le, 1999; Simoes, Crespo & Moreira, 2016). However, there are also a number of migration-specific influences on entrepreneurship, which can affect one or more groups of

migrants, again possibly to different degrees (Fairlie & Lofstrom, 2015).

In terms of general demographic influences, then, there are some characteristics that display a clear association with self-employment (Simoes et al., 2016). For example, rates of self-employment tend to be far lower for women. However, although self-employment is lower for women from virtually all migrant groups, there are large ethnic variations in the gender gap (Clark & Drinkwater, 2000). These differences may be partly explained by cultural and religious influences – since entrepreneurship may be viewed differently for women within certain migrant and religious groups. In terms of age, self-employment tends to be lowest amongst the youngest age groups and to peak amongst the middle aged (Simoes et al., 2016). This can be explained by younger age groups often lacking the necessary human capital, through more limited labour market experience, as well as financial capital to establish their own businesses. As a result, the age distribution of different migrant groups will impact on entrepreneurial activity, with there being a dampening effect for those groups that have a higher proportion of younger workers.

In addition to labour market experience, education plays a fundamental role in determining an individual's stock of human capital, which in turn can influence their entrepreneurial decisions. It can be argued that education can either have a positive or negative effect on self-employment (Simoes et al., 2016). For example, more highly educated individuals are typically presented with a larger range of opportunities in the paid labour market. In contrast, individuals with fewer formal educational qualifications may be able to achieve relatively higher returns by working for themselves. Lazear (2004) argues that entrepreneurs are 'jacks of all trades', in that they possess a more balanced set of skills rather than having a more specialised expertise. For migrants, proficiency in the host country's main language also makes an important contribution to human capital. Again, opposing arguments could be made with regards to the influence of poor language skills on entrepreneurship. These could result in a limited amount of opportunities in paid employment, thereby pushing individuals into self-employment (Clark & Drinkwater, 2000). On the other hand, it may be difficult for migrants with limited language skills to establish their own businesses, especially due to communication problems with potential customers and suppliers, as well as with regards to being sufficiently informed about the relevant regulations (Fairlie & Lofstrom, 2015). Recent empirical evidence is summarised by Fairlie and Lofstrom (2015), who report that Mexican migrants in the US who have poorer English language skills are more likely to be self-employed but this may not be the case for other groups of migrants.

Marital status and other family considerations, such as the presence of dependent children, can also impact on a person's decision of whether or not to enter, and then to remain in, self-employment. Simoes et al. (2016) review evidence on the relationship between entrepreneurship and family connections but report rather mixed results. This is because of possible offsetting influences of marriage as on the one hand it may encourage self-employment as spouses and children may be able to provide a cheap and reliable source of labour. On the other hand, self-employment may be seen as a less attractive option than a position in the paid labour market because it often provides a more variable and precarious source of income. Different effects may dominate for particular migrant groups, with cultural and religious factors again influencing the impact of family considerations and circumstances.

Geographical factors will also affect entrepreneurship amongst different migrant groups. Not only may some regions be more entrepreneurial than others (Cooke & Morgan, 1998) but entrepreneurship can also be affected by the geographical clustering of some migrant groups into ethnic enclaves. This is because these areas can provide members of migrant groups with a protected market, especially in the sale of ethnic-specific goods related to food and clothing (Aldrich et al., 1985), which is an idea that has received some empirical support (Lofstrom, 2002). However, this relationship may not hold in all settings and circumstances as ethnic enclaves can be relatively low income areas with high levels of deprivation as well as having the potential to produce high levels of competition (Clark & Drinkwater, 2010). Moreover, the changing nature of entrepreneurship – especially given the impact of technology – may further weaken the role of the protected market.

There are several other factors that may affect particular migrant groups. These include discrimination in the labour and credit markets (Clark & Drinkwater, 2000; Blanchflower, Levine & Zimmermann, 2003). In particular, employers, consumers and lenders may hold different levels of prejudice towards migrants from particular groups. Some individuals from those groups that are more discriminated against in the labour market may well have been pushed into self-employment, such as Pakistanis in the UK (Clark & Drinkwater, 2000). In contrast, discrimination in the credit market is likely to have restricted the realisation of business opportunities for more discriminated-against groups, as appears to be the case for Blacks in the US (Blanchflower et al., 2003). Moreover, access to the required financial capital is one of the most important factors in blocking potential entrepreneurs from establishing a business (Fairlie & Lofstrom, 2015). In particular, the low levels of personal wealth for some migrant groups can therefore impose a critical limit on obtaining a sufficient amount of financial capital. However, some migrant communities, such as Koreans and Chinese in the US, have a higher propensity to provide funds for business establishment (Bates, 1997).

Empirical studies from the US have also investigated the relationship between self-employment in the host and home countries. Evidence on this issue is mixed, with Yuengert (1995) indicating a positive and significant relationship, whereas no clear association is found by Fairlie and Meyer (1996), and Oyelere and Belton (2012) report that migrants from developing countries are less likely to be self-employed in the US than those from developed countries. Entrepreneurial aspirations may also be different for migrant groups, with education and family appearing to be important explanations for the observed diversity (Basu, 2004). In particular, Basu (2004) is able to distinguish between entrepreneurs whose aspirations are primarily driven by business, family, money and lifestyle considerations.

There are also interactions between demographic characteristics and some of the other influences that have been discussed. For example, higher levels of educational achievement have opened up new opportunities in paid employment for some of the groups that have tended to experience discrimination in

the labour market, such as Indians in the UK. This has had the effect of reducing levels of self-employment amongst these groups (Clark & Drinkwater, 2010). The amount of time that the migrant has been resident in the host country may also be important with regards to discrimination and credit constraints. This is because new arrivals may face greater levels of disadvantage in the labour market due to their initial disadvantages in terms of lacking country-specific skills (Chiswick, 1978), which may push them into self-employment. In contrast, those who have been in the host country for longer will have had more time to accumulate the capital that may be required to establish a business.

The above factors can also interact with one another to influence entrepreneurial outcomes for migrant and ethnic groups. In particular, Romero and Valdez (2016) use an intersectional approach to examine ethnic enterprise. They argue that no single experience can be used to explain ethnic entrepreneurship, even within a community that has the same migration and settlement patterns. Similarly, another approach that provides a broader perspective on migrant entrepreneurship is mixed embeddedness (Kloostermann, 2010), which incorporates market conditions and demand-side factors, especially those relating to the political, economic and legal environment. Kloostermann, Rusinovic and Yeboah (2016) use this approach to study Ghanaian entrepreneurs in the Netherlands. They find that, despite their relatively high levels of human capital and recent shifts in the urban economy, this group of migrant entrepreneurs are also concentrated towards the lower end of the labour market.

RECENT EVIDENCE ON MIGRANT ENTREPRENEURSHIP FROM THE UK

The empirical evidence that is provided below is intended to be illustrative of some of the key factors that determine migrant

Table 6.2 Self-employment rates for key demographic categories in the UK by migrant group, 2014–15

	Gender		Age			Education		
	Men	Women	16–29	30–44	45–64	Low	Medium	High
UK-Born	18.1	9.4	6.3	13.1	17.7	14.7	12.8	14.0
Born in A8	16.4	10.6	7.5	15.9	15.9	12.2	13.9	13.2
Born in A2	40.3	22.5	28.1	34.6	35.7	44.8	39.2	21.5
Other EU-Born	14.8	12.8	5.3	12.2	19.7	15.2	13.7	13.1
Born in India	16.1	8.2	5.6	11.5	17.8	14.3	16.8	11.1
Born in Pakistan/Bangladesh	33.8	12.2	10.1	29.4	35.1	32.7	29.5	26.4
Other Non-EU	19.6	11.9	8.8	14.8	19.1	17.2	16.2	15.4
All	18.4	9.7	6.6	13.8	18.0	15.0	13.6	14.3

Source: Labour Force Survey

Notes: Low Education relates to respondents who left full-time education before the age of 17, medium education for those who left full-time education between 17 and 20 and high education for those who left full-time education at the age of 21 or over. These definitions are consistent with those used by Dustmann, Frattini and Preston (2013), who discuss the reasons for classifying the education of migrants using the UK LFS in this way. Also see notes to Table 6.1 for details of the migrant groups.

entrepreneurship. Given the discussion of some of the main influences on migrant entrepreneurship that have been identified in the previous section, together with associated references from the literature, the evidence that is primarily provided in this section uses recently available information from the UK LFS for 2014–15 – as outlined in the discussion of Table 6.1. It is particularly important to provide recent statistics on migrant entrepreneurship because migration is a very dynamic process (Castles et al., 2013), especially in countries such as the UK (Vertovec, 2007). This implies that past empirical evidence can become out-dated, at least to a certain extent, including in relation to entrepreneurship. This is especially true in countries that have experienced high levels of diversity in recent inflows of migrants (Ram et al., 2013).[3]

Given the discussion from the previous section, the evidence that is presented in the following tables relates to differences in self-employment rates across the main migrant groups in the UK according to several influences. Firstly, Table 6.2 reports self-employment rates by gender, age and educational categories. The table reveals that the self-employment rate is higher for men than women for each of the migrant groups.

However, the gender gap does vary quite considerably between the groups. It is highest for people born in Pakistan and Bangladesh, at around 22 percentage points, and is lowest at just 2 percentage points for people born in Other EU countries (i.e. mainly pre-2004 member states). The gender gap is also relatively low for A8 migrants (6 percentage points) but considerably higher for A2 migrants (18 percentage points). These gaps reflect sectoral differences to some extent, given the concentration of men born in Romania/Bulgaria and Pakistan/Bangladesh in certain industries (Clark & Drinkwater, 2010).

Some similarities can also be observed with respect to variations by age across the migrant groups, with the self-employment rate increasing in the three age categories for each of the migrant groups.[4] The age differences are narrowest for A2 migrants, with less than an 8 point differential between the 16–29 and 45–64 age categories. For migrants born in Pakistan and Bangladesh, the self-employment rate strongly increases with age, reaching almost 30% for the 30–44 year olds compared with only 10% for the youngest age category. In addition to credit constraints, which tend to affect younger people to a greater extent, the age-related differences

Table 6.3   Self-employment rates by period of arrival in the UK by migrant group, 2014–15

	Before 2000	2000–3	2004–7	2008–11	2012–15
Born in A8	28.4	22.5	13.6	9.7	10.9
Born in A2	35.5	42.9	36.0	37.2	22.6
Other EU-Born	16.9	11.4	11.6	11.0	5.3
Born in India	19.1	11.6	10.5	7.3	4.0
Born in Pakistan/Bangladesh	31.8	27.3	32.6	15.7	18.2
Other Non-EU	18.2	14.4	13.9	12.7	9.1
All	19.6	16.1	14.9	12.9	10.2

Source: Labour Force Survey

Note: See notes to Table 6.1 for details of the migrant groups.

are also likely to be explained by higher levels of educational achievement amongst the younger members of most migrant groups.

There is a more mixed pattern with regards to the relationship between education and self-employment across the migrant groups, which is consistent with the different effects that human capital can have on self-employment, especially for migrants. For some groups, such as A2 migrants, self-employment decreases with educational attainment and is by far the lowest amongst the highly educated. This is again likely to reflect the activities that this group are mainly involved in in the UK, especially the construction industry. For A8 and Indian migrants, self-employment rates are highest in the medium education category, which is in contrast to the UK-born since rates are lowest in this category amongst natives.

In accordance with the discussion from the previous section, Table 6.3 indicates that self-employment rates tend to be higher for migrants who have been in the UK for longer periods of time. This pattern is fairly clear for migrants from other non-EU countries, with self-employment rates declining across each of the cohorts of arrival in the UK. The picture is more mixed for the other migrant groups. For example, self-employment rates are higher for migrants from A8 countries who arrived between 2012 and 2015 compared with those who arrived between 2008 and 2011, whilst, for A2 migrants, self-employment rates are far lower for those arriving after

2011. This is consistent with the migration policies that have affected this group because self-employment/entrepreneurship was the main route into the UK labour market during the transitional period that was in place between 2007 and 2013 (Clark et al., 2016). Self-employment rates are very low for recent migrants in other groups, especially those from other EU countries and India, as they are 5% or lower for migrant workers arriving between 2012 and 2015.

Table 6.4 summarises how self-employment rates vary across residents living in different parts of the UK. It shows that self-employment tends to be fairly well dispersed for some of the well-established migrant groups in the UK. Interestingly, the highest self-employment rates for people born in India, Pakistan and Bangladesh are observed in the Devolved Nations (Wales, Scotland and Northern Ireland). This is consistent with evidence and explanations provided by Clark and Drinkwater (2010) on the deprived and competitive nature of the areas where some groups of migrants tend to concentrate, especially in large cities. However, for other groups (especially A2 and A8 migrants), self-employment rates are by far the highest in London. In fact, around a half of A2 and almost a third of A8 migrant workers in London are self-employed. This is likely to be the result of strong demand conditions, especially in sectors such as construction that are associated with self-employment/entrepreneurship in particular parts of the UK.

Table 6.4   Self-employment rates by area of residence within the UK by migrant group, 2014–15

	North England	Midlands	South England	London	Devolved Nations
UK-Born	12.3	12.5	15.7	16.2	12.7
Born in A8	9.6	6.4	11.9	30.9	6.6
Born in A2	20.0	17.7	20.7	49.8	30.4
Other EU-Born	12.6	13.1	14.2	14.6	12.6
Born in India	12.3	12.1	14.0	12.0	14.9
Born in Pakistan/ Bangladesh	31.9	29.0	25.1	26.0	41.8
Other Non-EU	15.5	12.9	15.5	16.9	15.3
All	12.6	12.5	15.6	17.8	12.8

Source: Labour Force Survey

Notes: North England refers to the North West, North East and Yorkshire and the Humber regions. South England refers to the South East, South West and East of England regions. Devolved Nations refers to Northern Ireland, Scotland and Wales. See notes to Table 6.1 for details of the migrant groups.

CONCLUSION

This chapter has highlighted the diversity in the entrepreneurial experiences of migrants. Very high levels of entrepreneurship (in comparison with the native-born) are observed for some groups, whereas entrepreneurial activity is far lower for others. No single factor can account for these variations, partly due to the large differences that exist in the characteristics of migrants according to their countries of origin and their cohort of arrival in the destination country. These differences can relate to a wide range of factors including educational levels, cultural influences and location decisions within the host country, as well as interactions between these. In addition to the observed differences in rates of entrepreneurship, the types of activities that different groups tend to undertake also require careful consideration because of the influence of sectoral differences on entrepreneurial outcomes. Edwards et al. (2016) provide recent evidence for the UK on some of the new sectors in which migrant entrepreneurs are now observed and the emergence of entrepreneurs originating from different parts of the world. However, further analysis of these and related issues is required, especially for countries that have experienced high levels of migration flows.

Moreover, high rates of entrepreneurship should not necessarily be viewed positively if the entrepreneurship is concentrated within low-value activities, which require long hours of work for comparatively low rewards (Blanchflower, 2004). Rath and Swagerman (2016) undertake a detailed investigation of the policy measures and support schemes that have been introduced to encourage ethnic entrepreneurship in European cities. However, despite the range of measures identified, they argue that group-specific interventions are not that common. Moreover, given that migrant entrepreneurship has tended to have been viewed positively by policymakers in both host and sending countries, Naude, Siegel and Marchand (2015) review several relevant literatures on migrant entrepreneurship. They conclude that the evidence on issues such as the use of remittances to finance entrepreneurship and of entrepreneurial skills acquired overseas by return migrants, as well as immigrants being more entrepreneurial than natives, is rather mixed.

Therefore, government policy towards encouraging migrant entrepreneurship should pay close attention not just to the number of entrepreneurs but also to the sectors in which they operate. It follows that schemes could be introduced that aim to stimulate and incentivise entrepreneurship in particular sectors. These could encourage migrants away from the traditional sectors in which they have tended to concentrate, which are typically associated with low and volatile earnings. However, given that migration is a very dynamic process that will always continue to evolve, policy responses should not be too prescriptive with regards to migrant entrepreneurship. This is particularly because migration flows are influenced by a wide variety of factors – some of which are political and sometimes beyond the control of national governments such as in relation to intra-EU migration and movements for humanitarian reasons. Therefore, a key concern for government should relate to how they can better harness the entrepreneurial talent of migrants. Similarly, given the nature of migration flows, this also implies that it is difficult to predict the future direction of research on migrant entrepreneurship. Although lots of questions have been answered and explained, new issues will undoubtedly emerge as the prevalence for people to move to different countries continues to increase.

Notes

1 The particular sample of data used in this chapter is based on pooled quarters of unweighted LFS data from 2014 and 2015. For further information on the LFS, particularly in relation to how appropriate samples can be constructed to examine self-employment amongst migrant groups, see Clark and Drinkwater (2009) and Jones et al. (2015). Census data provide relatively similar definitions to surveys such as the LFS (Clark & Drinkwater, 2010).

2 Croatia also joined the EU in 2013. Transitional arrangements have also been imposed for migrants from Croatia – similar to those that existed for Bulgaria and Romania from January 2007 to December 2013. In contrast, there were essentially no restrictions on A8 migration to the UK from May 2004. Migrants from these countries could also enter the UK labour market through the self-employment route in the years leading up to the 2004 enlargement (Clark et al., 2016).

3 Fairlie and Lofstrom (2015) provide evidence on various aspects of immigrant entrepreneurship using US data.

4 Although the same self-employment rate is reported for A8 migrants in the 30–44 and 45–64 age categories, due to rounding.

ACKNOWLEDGEMENTS

Material from the Quarterly Labour Force Survey is Crown Copyright and has been made available by the Office for National Statistics (ONS) through the UK Data Service. I am grateful to Robert Blackburn for providing some helpful comments. The views expressed in this chapter and errors therein are those of the author.

REFERENCES

Aldrich, H., Cater, J., Jones, T., McEvoy, D. and Velleman, P. (1985), 'Ethnic residential concentration and the protected market hypothesis', *Social Forces,* 63(4), 996–1009.

Basu, A. (2004), 'Entrepreneurial aspirations among family business owners: An analysis of ethnic business owners in the UK', *International Journal of Entrepreneurial Behavior & Research,* 10(1/2), 12–33.

Bates, T. (1997), 'Financing small business creation: The case of Chinese and Korean immigrant entrepreneurs', *Journal of Business Venturing,* 12(2), 109–124.

Blanchflower, D. G. (2004), 'Self-employment: More may not be better', National Bureau of Economic Research Working Paper No. 10286.

Blanchflower, D. G. and Oswald, A. J. (1998), 'What makes an entrepreneur?', *Journal of Labor Economics,* 16(1), 26–60.

Blanchflower, D. G., Levine, P. and Zimmermann, D. (2003), 'Discrimination in the small-business credit market', *Review of Economics and Statistics,* 85(4), 930–943.

Bonacich, E. (1973), 'A theory of middleman minorities', *American Sociological Review,* 38(5), 583–594.

Borjas, G. J. (1986), 'The self-employment experience of immigrants', *Journal of Human Resources,* 21(4), 485–506.

Castles, S., De Haas, H. and Miller, M. J. (2013), *The Age of Migration: International Population Movements in the Modern World*, 5th Edition, Palgrave Macmillan, Basingstoke.

Chiswick, B. (1978), 'The effect of Americanization on the earnings of foreign-born men', *Journal of Political Economy*, 86(5), 897–921.

Clark, K. and Drinkwater, S. (2000), 'Pushed in or pulled out? Self-employment among ethnic minorities in England and Wales', *Labour Economics*, 7(5), 603–628.

Clark, K. and Drinkwater, S. (2009), 'Immigrant self-employment adjustment: Ethnic groups in the UK', *International Journal of Manpower*, 30(1), 163–175.

Clark, K. and Drinkwater, S. (2010), 'Patterns of ethnic self-employment in time and space: Evidence from British Census microdata', *Small Business Economics*, 34(3), 323–338.

Clark, K., Drinkwater, S. and Robinson, C. (2016), 'Labor mobility as an adjustment mechanism in the UK during the Great Recession', in M. Kahanec and K. F. Zimmermann (eds), *Labor Migration, EU Enlargement, and the Great Recession*, Springer, Berlin, 139–162.

Constant, A. and Zimmermann, K. F. (2006), 'The making of entrepreneurs in Germany: Are native men and immigrants alike?', *Small Business Economics*, 26(3), 279–300.

Cooke, P. and Morgan, K. (1998), *The Associational Economy: Firms, Regions, and Innovation*, Oxford University Press, Oxford.

Desiderio, M. V. (2014), *Policies to Support Immigrant Entrepreneurship*, Migration Policy Institute, Washington DC.

Dustmann, C., Frattini, T. and Preston, I. (2013), 'The effect of immigration along the distribution of wages', *Review of Economic Studies*, 80(1), 145–173.

Edwards, P., Ram, M., Jones, T. and Doldor, S. (2016), 'New migrant businesses and their workers: Developing, but not transforming, the ethnic economy', *Ethnic and Racial Studies*, 39(9), 1587–1617.

Faggio, G. and Silva, O. (2014), 'Self-employment and entrepreneurship in urban and rural labour markets', *Journal of Urban Economics*, 84, 67–85.

Fairlie, R. W. and Lofstrom, M. (2015), 'Immigrant entrepreneurship', in B. Chiswick and P. Miller (eds), *Handbook of the Economics of International Immigration*, Volume 1B, Elsevier, Amsterdam, 877–911.

Fairlie, R. W. and Meyer, B. D. (1996), 'Ethnic and racial self-employment differences and possible explanations', *Journal of Human Resources,* 31(4), 757–793.

Home Office (2013), 'New UK immigration rules aimed at attracting "best global talent"', Home Office, UK Government.

Jones, T., Ram, M., Li, Y., Edwards, P. and Villares, M. (2015), 'Super-diverse Britain and new migrant enterprises', IRiS Working Paper Series No. 8, University of Birmingham.

Kloosterman, R. C. (2010), 'Matching opportunities with resources: A framework for analysing (migrant) entrepreneurship from a mixed embeddedness perspective', *Entrepreneurship and Regional Development*, 22(1), 25–45.

Kloosterman, R. C., Rusinovic, K. and Yeboah, D. (2016), 'Super-diverse migrants – similar trajectories? Ghanaian entrepreneurship in the Netherlands seen from a mixed embeddedness perspective', *Journal of Ethnic and Migration Studies*, 42(6), 913–932.

Knight, F. H. (1921), *Risk, Uncertainty and Profit,* Houghton Mifflin, New York.

Kwong, C. C., Thompson, P., Jones-Evans, D. and Brooksbank, D. (2009), 'Nascent entrepreneurial activity within female ethnic minority groups', *International Journal of Entrepreneurial Behavior & Research*, 15(3), 262–281.

Lazear, E. P. (2004), 'Balanced skills and entrepreneurship', *American Economic Review, Papers & Proceedings,* 94(2), 208–211.

Le, A. T. (1999), 'Empirical studies of self-employment', *Journal of Economic Surveys*, 13(4), 382–416.

Levie, J. (2007), 'Immigration, in-migration, ethnicity and entrepreneurship in the United Kingdom', *Small Business Economics,* 28(2), 143–169.

Light, I. H. (1972), *Ethnic Enterprise in America: Business and Welfare Among Chinese, Japanese, and Blacks*, University of California Press, Berkeley, CA.

Lofstrom, M. (2002), 'Labor market assimilation and the self-employment decision of immigrant entrepreneurs', *Journal of Population Economics*, 15(1), 191–222.

Naude, W., Siegel, M. and Marchand, K. (2015), 'Migration, entrepreneurship and development: A critical review', IZA Discussion Paper No. 9284.

ONS (2015), *Population by Country of Birth and Nationality*, Office for National Statistics.

Oyelere, R. U. and Belton, W. (2012), 'Coming to America: Does having a developed home country matter for self-employment in the United States?', *American Economic Review, Papers & Proceedings*, 102(3), 538–542.

Parker, S. C. (2008), 'Statistical issues in applied entrepreneurship research: Data, methods and challenges', in E. Congregado (ed.), *Measuring Entrepreneurship: Building a Statistical System*, Springer, New York, 9–20.

Peroni, C., Riillo, C. A. and Sarracino, F. (2016), 'Entrepreneurship and immigration: Evidence from GEM Luxembourg', *Small Business Economics*, 46(4), 639–656.

Ram, M., Jones, T., Edwards, P., Kiselinchev, A., Muchenje, L. and Woldesenbet, K. (2013), 'Engaging with super-diversity: New migrant businesses and the research-policy nexus', *International Small Business Journal*, 31(4), 337–356.

Rath, J. and Swagerman, A. (2016), 'Promoting ethnic entrepreneurship in European cities: Sometimes ambitious, mostly absent, rarely addressing structural features', *International Migration*, 54(1), 152–166.

Romero, M. and Valdez, Z. (2016), 'Introduction to the special issue: Intersectionality and entrepreneurship', *Ethnic and Racial Studies*, 39(9), 1553–1565.

Schumpeter, J. (1942), *Capitalism, Socialism and Democracy*, Harper & Brothers, New York.

Simoes, N., Crespo, N. and Moreira, S. B. (2016), 'Individual determinants of self-employment entry: What do we really know?', *Journal of Economic Surveys*, 30(4), 783–806.

Sobel, R. S. (2008), 'Entrepreneurship', in D. R. Henderson (ed.), *The Concise Encyclopedia of Economics*, Liberty Fund, Indianapolis. www.econlib.org/Enc/Entrepreneurship.html

Thornquist, A. (2015), 'False self-employment and other precarious forms of employment in the "grey area" of the labour market', *The International Journal of Comparative Law and Industrial Relations*, 31(4), 411–430.

UN (2015), *International Migration Report 2015*, Department of Economic and Social Affairs, Population Division, United Nations, New York.

Vertovec, S. (2007), 'Super-diversity and its implications', *Ethnic and Racial Studies*, 30(6), 1024–1054.

Viinikainen, J., Heineck, G., Bockerman, P., Hintsanen, M., Raitakari, O. and Pehkonen, J. (2016), 'Born entrepreneur? Adolescents' personality characteristics and self-employment in adulthood', IZA Discussion Paper No. 9805.

Yuengert, A. M. (1995), 'Testing hypotheses of immigrant self-employment', *Journal of Human Resources*, 30(1), 194–204.

7

Entrepreneurship from a Family Business Perspective

Judith van Helvert and Mattias Nordqvist

INTRODUCTION

Over the last 30 years, research on family businesses has developed into a distinctive research field. The increased attention to and interest in family businesses is justified by the fact that 70 to 80 percent of European businesses are family businesses (Mandl, 2008). This implies that family businesses are important drivers of the economy (Martinez & Aldrich, 2014) in terms of both economic growth and employment. The academic community increasingly realizes that family businesses are systematically different from other businesses and organizations, paying attention to strategic themes such as top management teams (Minichilli, Corbetta, & Macmillan, 2010), finance and capital structure (Voordeckers, Le Breton-Miller, & Miller, 2014; Miller & Le Breton-Miller, 2005), resource management (Sirmon & Hitt, 2003), internationalization (Pukall & Calabrò, 2014), and relationships with stakeholders (Berrone, Cruz, & Gomez-Mejia,

2014). As argued by Fletcher (2014, p.137), 'the field has come a long way since rationalist and normative principles dominated the field and advocated the need to isolate family from business issues to ensure the effective working of the business'.

In this chapter, we discuss entrepreneurship from a family business perspective. In family businesses, family concerns and objectives are combined with entrepreneurial forces. The purpose of this chapter is to explain how the family business context impacts entrepreneurial activity. We start with a discussion of the unique features of family businesses. We proceed by explaining the link between entrepreneurship and family businesses. We continue by specifying the family influence that can be captured by numerous factors that are specifically relevant to entrepreneurial activity in family businesses and that distinguish them from their non-family counterparts. We conclude by proposing some future lines of research on family businesses in relation to entrepreneurship. Throughout the chapter,

---

Box 7.1

The H. Jansen Group, which is located in the eastern part of the Netherlands, is a prominent 4th-generation family business that celebrated its 100-year anniversary in 2013. The business offers services in three different sectors: insurance and risk management consultancy, automation solutions and cold stores. The company's cold store activities are performed in the Netherlands and in Germany. Additionally, the family has a separate business division in which the family capital is managed. The business has more than 175 employees and is financially sound. It has a down-to-earth culture in which the customer is put first.

The business is run by Vanessa Jansen, who has worked there since 2006. Formally, the directorship of the business's various divisions is shared by Vanessa and her father Hans. Previously, Hans took over his father's insurance activities and has grown the business through its automation and cold store divisions. The business is owned by Hans and his three daughters. Hans has slowly distanced himself from the divisions, passing the managing responsibilities on to Vanessa. Hans's youngest daughter also works in the business.

---

the various themes are illustrated by showing developments at H. Jansen Group, an entrepreneurial, fourth-generation family business from the Netherlands. An introduction to the case is given in Box 7.1.

UNIQUE FEATURES OF FAMILY BUSINESSES

Although some research activities were conducted in the 1950s and 1960s, research on family businesses began its rapid development in the 1980s, resulting in the launch of the Family Business Review in 1988 (Sharma, Melin, & Nordqvist, 2014). Early studies focused on defining a family business. Although various interesting views have been developed on what a family business is and how it is different from a non-family business, there is still no clear-cut definition. The difficulty of defining family businesses is primarily caused by the large variety within the population of family businesses (e.g. Melin & Nordqvist, 2007). For example, it is impossible to compare a local bakery man-

aged by a married couple with a fourth-generation international food producer such as Dr. Oetker. However, because empirical results are significantly affected by which definition of the family business is used, more attention should be paid to the consequences of various operationalizations and how empirical findings change according to the type and extent of family involvement in the business (Bettinelli, Fayolle, & Randerson, 2014; Sharma et al., 2014). Many studies, especially quantitative studies, draw on the *components* approach, defining family involvement in the business primarily in terms of ownership and management positions. The *essence* approach focuses on the family's influence over the business by looking at the psychological and behavioral aspects (e.g. transgenerational family control intention and commitment) of that influence. Chrisman, Chua, Pearson, and Barnett (2012) advocate a combination of both approaches to investigate and explain the behavior and performance of family businesses and how they are different from non-family businesses.

Research has identified the unique capabilities of family businesses such as the heightened effort of the family members working in the business, their long investment horizon, their superior reputation, and family-derived social capital. Other studies have focused on the specific challenges that confront family businesses. These challenges are attributable to negative efforts and abilities such as discouraged non-family managers and poor governance structures (Gedajlovic, Carney, Chrisman, & Kellermanns, 2012). These negative efforts and effects evolve from the tensions that arise from the overlap among the three interdependent subsystems of the family, the business, and ownership (Tagiuri & Davis, 1992). Each of these systems has its own interests and dynamics. The family system is internally oriented and consists of family members with deep, life-long emotional ties. Long-term loyalty, caring, and nurturing are highly valued. The focus of the business system is external and based on rationality. It values performance, skills, and productivity. The owners' primary interest is return on investment. When these interests align and things go well, additional challenges from family involvement do not arise. However, if there is a conflict of interest, the negative efforts and abilities to which Gedajlovic et al. (2012) refer may arise. An important challenge for the owner–manager is therefore to balance these interests and keep the actors in the different subsystems happy and involved.

The extent to which the various subsystems show overlap is different for every situation and is often related to the business's life-cycle phase. The business often develops from being managed by a controlling owner to a sibling partnership to a cousin consortium (Gersick, Lansberg, Desjardins, & Dunn, 1999). As family businesses enter second and later generations, family complexity increases because of the growing number of family members involved (children, grandchildren, and a host of cousins and in-laws) (Miller & Le Breton-Miller, 2006), often as owners (Lambrecht & Lievens, 2008). When the number of owners increases over the generations, shareholdings are progressively diluted (Gimeno Sandig, Labadie, Saris, & Mayordomo, 2006). Increased family complexity then has repercussions for the owners. However, it also has repercussions for the business and the family. For example, it potentially has a negative impact on family satisfaction when the nuclear family threshold is surpassed, resulting in less cohesiveness (more shareholders leads to a variety in personal goals, values, commitment to the business, and so forth) (Gimeno Sandig et al., 2006). This increase in family complexity and overlap of the systems can be addressed either by formalizing the governance structure (e.g. by creating either a family council or a board of directors that includes outsiders) or by pruning the family tree (Lambrecht & Lievens, 2008). By reducing the number of family shareholders, for example, to only the managing family members ('management-oriented' logic), the family brings simplicity back to the business's ownership structure (Lambrecht & Lievens, 2008). So, the family business is multifaceted, leading to diversity in governance structures and processes, depending on the age and size of the business, the family's involvement, the sector, and the legal context. Despite this heterogeneity among family businesses and consequently the diversity in structures and processes, it is only recently that research has begun to account for differences within the group of family businesses (Sharma et al., 2014).

Even if a family business is always started by an entrepreneur, the entrepreneurial spirit

---

Box 7.2

Although the H. Jansen Group is a 4th generation family business, it is still in the phase of a sibling partnership because ownership is shared by the three sisters. Over the past generation, ownership and management have passed to only one child of the next generation, thus minimizing the complexity of the overlap of the various subsystems.

is not guaranteed to survive in successive generations (Flören & Zwartendijk, 2008). The next section will elaborate on the link between family business and entrepreneurship and discuss the implications of family influence on entrepreneurial activity.

FAMILY ENTREPRENEURSHIP

For the most part, entrepreneurship and family business research have evolved in parallel as separate disciplines. Nevertheless, the two share an important interest, namely, how does the family influence entrepreneurial activity? The family business perspective focuses on the business's enhanced survivability and growth, whereas the entrepreneurship perspective focuses on venture creation (Rosa, Howorth, & Discua Cruz, 2014). In family businesses, entrepreneurship is often closely related to succession. In addition to entering a new market or industry by establishing a business, entrepreneurial entry can also involve taking over an established business by acquiring a business that someone else (often a family member) is exiting (Nordqvist, Wennberg, Bau, & Hellerstedt, 2013). Corporate entrepreneurship, which focuses on the processes by which established businesses create new organizations, initiate strategic renewal, and innovate within the organization, is another form of entrepreneurship relevant to family businesses because it is important to their sustained performance (McKelvie, McKenny, Lumpkin, & Short, 2014). Corporate entrepreneurship is believed to be different in family businesses because of their systems of governance and need for family harmony, the leverage of unique family business resources such as familiness ('the unique bundle of resources a particular business has because of the systems interaction between the family, its individual members and the business' (Habbershon & Williams, 1999, p. 11)), and specific agency problems (McKelvie et al., 2014).

It is interesting to note that family business scholars have paid relatively little attention to the understanding of families and their businesses as engines for new business activities, strategic renewal, and innovation (Nordqvist & Melin, 2010a). However, numerous studies have focused on this intersection in an attempt to generate a new research field in family entrepreneurship (Bettinelli et al., 2014). Family entrepreneurship is defined as 'the research field that studies entrepreneurial behaviors of families, family members, and family businesses' (Bettinelli et al., 2014, p. 164). An interesting perspective on the familial influence is provided by Heck, Danes, Fitzgerald, Haynes, Schrank, Stafford, & Winter (2006), who propose the family as the incubator for the generation of new business ideas, stressing home as the birthplace of entrepreneurial ventures.

The literature on the family's influence on opportunity recognition and entrepreneurial activity is diverse. It essentially provides two contradictory perspectives: one that presents the family business context as highly entrepreneurial (creative, dynamic, and oriented towards change) and one that presents the family business as an organization in which entrepreneurship is restricted by tradition and family-related power dynamics (conservative, risk averse, and inflexible) (Nordqvist & Melin, 2010a). Additionally, the family business has been positioned as a combination of three contrasting ideologies: paternalism, managerialism, and entrepreneurialism (Johannisson & Huse, 2000). These ideologies refer to a consistent and permanent cognition of the environment, which in combination with emotional commitment leads to a specific mode of behavior and economic activity. The paternalism ideology is the strongest in the family business because the family is recognized as an important universal institution in society. Paternalism is characterized by tradition maintenance and a focus on continuity by ensuring a safe future for subsequent generations. It involves acting in the best interests of others without their explicit consent

Table 7.1   A summary of ideological tensions (Koiranen, 2003)

	Paternalism	*Managerialism*	*Entrepreneurialism*
Rationalities	Caring	Being in charge	Venturing, creating
Characteristics	Protective, dominating, fatherly	Calculative, supervising, mechanistic	Initiative, innovating, organic
Parallel features	Emotionality, control	Intentionality, control	Intentionality, emotionality
Traps	Shared illusions	Inflexibility, shared rigidity	Foolhardiness, shared speculation
Justification of power	Seniority, superiority, being 'above'	Managerial competence, position	Ownership, risk-taking
Attitude toward keeping	Keeping traditions	Keeping business as controlled	Keeping business in change

(Flören & Zwartendijk, 2008). It can be considered an emotionally embedded clan structure in which the hierarchy is structured according to seniority and kinship ties. The ideology of managerialism relates to the structure and management of the business and its activities based on functional areas. It focuses on control through contractual agreements, institutional arrangements, and allocating resources in various stages of the process (Johannisson & Huse, 2000). The ideology of entrepreneurialism implies the organic organizing of resources combined with visionary abilities. It is characterized by trust relationships, willpower, intuition, and alertness (Flören & Zwartendijk, 2008). Whereas these ideologies have several features in common, they also have important differences, as identified by Koiranen (2003) (see Table 7.1).

According to Johannisson and Huse (2000), family businesses must accommodate all three ideologies to remain viable. Those authors argue that family businesses should attempt to capitalize both on the tensions that may arise among these three contrasting ideologies and on the energy that these tensions create. Although all three ideologies contain positive elements for the family business, it is important that they are present in their proper proportions. This ideological balance requires equilibrium between family and business interests.

Although the research field of family entrepreneurship is developing quickly, important

questions remain unanswered, including the following: Are family businesses more (or less) entrepreneurial than non-family businesses? How do family resources such as family social capital affect entrepreneurship over generations? Which family dynamics and considerations either enable or constrain entrepreneurial behavior? Does entrepreneurship in family businesses lead to value creation? Bettinelli et al. (2014) suggest exploring entrepreneurial behavior by studying the interplay between the individual, the family, and the family business as the three loci of entrepreneurial behavior in family businesses to disentangle the complex relationships that characterize the field. One example of such an interrelationship is the family's influence on individual family members. Through socialization, role modeling, and support for entrepreneurial activity, the family institution can, directly or indirectly, intentionally or unintentionally, influence its individual members, implying that, in family businesses, both individual and collective entrepreneurship are strongly rooted in the family context, whether positively or negatively (Bettinelli et al., 2014).

The importance of entrepreneurial practices for the continuity of family businesses is specifically acknowledged in the STEP research project. STEP refers to Successful Transgenerational Entrepreneurship Practices. This project is a collaborative effort of researchers from 44 universities all over the world and involves exploratory research (primarily case studies) on the nature of long-term

---

Box 7.3

The Jansen family thinks in generations in regard to the development and the continuity of the business. For that reason, the family needs to be entrepreneurial and develop new business activities. For example, when Vanessa's father entered the business, it was only involved in insurance activities. Hans then extended the business with the automation and cold store activities. Vanessa used her legal background to initiate the creation of a family office when she entered the company; the office is an organizational unit that performs centralized management and oversight of family investments, tax planning, estate planning, and philanthropic planning related to financial resources. Vanessa observed, '*My father and I have similar objectives and goals, it is the approach to reach those goals that differs. My father is a real entrepreneur, acting quickly without formalizing structures. I have a legal background, so I try to move things forward by integrating business units, making things more manageable, developing the conditions for corporate entrepreneurship.*'

---

entrepreneurial processes in larger family businesses. Transgenerational entrepreneurship refers to the practice of achieving continued growth and continuity by passing on the entrepreneurial mindsets and capabilities that enable the new generation to create new streams of wealth. The essence of transgenerational entrepreneurship practices relates to the entrepreneurial potential of the individual or the family, rather than the business (Rosa et al., 2014). In that sense, the project's emphasis switches from family businesses to business (or entrepreneurial) families. Entrepreneurial families often engage in habitual entrepreneurship, creating multiple businesses either serially (one at a time) or in a portfolio or group (Rosa et al., 2014; Nordqvist & Zellweger, 2010) in a manner similar to that of the H. Jansen Group (see Box 7.3).

Habitual entrepreneurship is heterogeneous and especially complex in a family context, including, for example, family members who pursue individual business activities that are not coordinated at the family level (Nordqvist & Melin, 2010b). However, our knowledge about what characterizes entrepreneurial families and what makes them successful in serial or portfolio ventures (compared with their mono-active counterparts) remains limited and invites future research (Rosa et al., 2014).

After this general discussion of the relationship between entrepreneurship and family businesses, we continue with a discussion of succession, which is a topic of crucial importance to family businesses and is closely related to entrepreneurship.

SUCCESSION FROM AN ENTREPRENEURIAL PROCESS PERSPECTIVE

Although management succession is an important event for every business, family businesses experience challenges that are unique to their organizational form (Long & Chrisman, 2014). Founders of family businesses often attempt to perpetuate their legacy and ensure continued family control via the exit of the current director(s) and the entry of the next generation. This act can therefore be considered to represent the family's continued commitment to entrepreneurship (Nordqvist et al., 2013). Numerous factors render management succession in family businesses problematic. For example, family business transitions must be accomplished within the confines of restricted candidate pools. Moreover, emotional and personal relationship ties among incumbents, successors, and the family itself represent a challenge to a successful succession (Miller, Steier, & Le Breton-Miller, 2006; Le Breton-Miller, Miller, & Steier, 2004). These additional challenges imply that succession must be planned well (Handler, 1994). Researchers agree that succession should be viewed as a multi-stage process over time, not an event. This process is often illustrated as a relay race in which the baton is passed to the next runner (Dyck, Mauws, Starke, & Mischke, 2002): order, timing, passing the baton, and communication are crucial elements that influence the success of a race. The principle of a relay race in which the next runner speeds up before the baton is passed is similar for management succession. When the incumbent takes the time to prepare the next generation to succeed, the likelihood of a successful succession increases. However, the incumbent must be ready to pass the management task to the next generation and should agree on how his or her successor will lead the business. Differences between the incumbent and successor in terms of experience, management style, etc. often make it difficult to agree on the successor's new role and the long-term vision of the business. Communication during the succession process is essential; if there is a lack of trust or joint vision, succession becomes problematic (Morris, Williams, Allen, & Avila, 1998). Communication is not only a matter of concern for the incumbent and the successor; employees and family members must be informed as much as possible. The successor needs the trust of these stakeholders to successfully complete his or her task.

Another challenge for the family business is that both management and ownership succession must be organized. This implies the possibility of a variety of combinations of ownership and management between family and professional managers for the business in transition (Handler, 1994). When the business is handed over to the next generation, the order of management and ownership succession must be decided; management can be transferred to the next generation first, ownership can be transferred first or both can transferred

at the same time. Next, it must be decided who is going to succeed in management and who is going to succeed in ownership. Of course, the manager(s) and owner(s) need not be the same persons. However, the manager is often also either the owner or one of the owners.

From an entrepreneurial process perspective, ownership succession can be defined as a 'process in which new owners, from within or outside the owner family, enter the business as owners and add new capital and resources that have consequences for business processes and outcomes such as innovation, entrepreneurial orientation and growth' (Nordqvist et al., 2013, p. 1090). The owners who leave the business while passing it on to the new owners have the ability to harvest the time, effort, and resources that they have put into the business. They might even be able to invest those resources in a new entrepreneurial venture (Nordqvist et al., 2013). Based on a literature review on succession in family businesses from an entrepreneurial process perspective, Nordqvist et al. (2013) illustrate the process as presented in Figure 7.1.

Nordqvist et al. (2013) categorize the current literature into four levels of analysis (environmental, organizational, interpersonal, and individual) and four main phases that characterize the succession process (start-up, owning and running the business, managing succession, and the post-succession phase). The different levels of analysis all involve factors and characteristics that might affect the entrepreneurial outcome in an ownership transition. For example, at the organizational level,

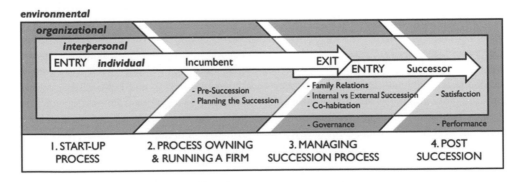

Figure 7.1 Succession from an entrepreneurial process perspective (Nordqvist et al., 2013)

specific governance modes have been found to emerge and change before, during, and after a succession (e.g. Barach & Ganitsky, 1995; Berenbeim, 1990; Chua, Chrisman, & Sharma, 2003; Poza, Hanlon, & Kishida, 2004). Moreover, Figure 7.1 shows that the business and the entrepreneur have their own lifecycles that can coincide but can also diverge. At the moment of exit, the entrepreneur or the family team can decide to sell, pass on or close the business. In the event of survival, the business will be run by another person or persons who enter the business. From an entrepreneurial perspective, the succession process then becomes a part of the entrepreneurial process (Nordqvist et al., 2013).

After having described the characteristics of family businesses, how the influence of the family impacts entrepreneurial activity, and how succession can be viewed from an entrepreneurial process perspective, we now proceed by narrowing down and specifying the family influence. The family influence can be captured by numerous factors that are specifically relevant to entrepreneurial activity in family businesses and that distinguish them from their non-family counterparts. The factors discussed have been studied by family business researchers from varied theoretical and methodological perspectives. For the purpose of this chapter, we will focus on the topics using an entrepreneurship lens.

SPECIFIC ISSUES IN FAMILY BUSINESSES IMPACTING ENTREPRENEURIAL ACTIVITY

Socio-Emotional Wealth

One of the reasons that the level of entrepreneurial activity might be negatively affected by the family influence involves socio-emotional wealth (Jaskiewicz, Combs, & Rau, 2015). The concept of socio-emotional wealth (SEW) refers to the utilities that family owners derive from the non-economic aspects of the business (Gomez-Mejia, Takacs-Haynes, Nunez-Nickel, Jacobsen, & Moyano-Fuentes, 2007). It is the sum of affective values that a family derives from controlling the business, including the preservation of dynastic family control, offering employment or resources for family members, building the family's reputation, and investing in environmental causes (Jaskiewicz et al., 2015). Family owners are unique in the sense that they are likely to see potential gains or losses in SEW as their primary frame of reference in the management of the business, efficiency or economic instrumentality considerations aside (Gomez-Mejia, Cruz, Berrone, & De Castro, 2011). This is not to say that this form of decision-making is irrational. Family businesses can be just as rational as non-family businesses when making managerial decisions; they simply have different criteria for judging whether these choices are good or bad. In essence, the SEW perspective explains both that family owners are motivated by non-financial aspects and that they are committed to preserving their SEW (Gomez-Mejia et al., 2011). This protection of SEW encourages risk-averse decisions (Jaskiewicz et al., 2015), thereby limiting the potential for entrepreneurial activity.

Governance

Research has shown that governance structure is an important contingency that affects entrepreneurial activity in family businesses (Le Breton-Miller, Miller, & Baresa, 2015). Governance and ownership are closely related and the research often treats them as synonymous. Being an owner provides special decision-making rights. It matters who owns what, when, how, and why. However, as argued by Gersick and Feliu (2014), to treat ownership as a synonym for governance is too limited for two reasons. First, governance is primarily an organizational issue, not a purely financial and legal one. Second, financial ownership is only one of the various forms of capital that must be governed. Governance in family businesses can be defined as 'the means of stewarding the multigenerational family organization. It establishes the processes whereby strategic goals are set, key relationships are maintained, the health of the family is safeguarded, accountability is maintained, and achievement and performance are recognized' (Goldbart & DiFuria, 2009, p. 7). These means mostly relate to various governance mechanisms: family councils, family assemblies, boards of directors, family offices, family foundations, shareholder agreements, and financial planning tools such as trusts and limited family partnerships (Gersick & Feliu, 2014). In essence, governance is about balancing the interests of the various stakeholders involved in the business (owners, family members, employees, customers, suppliers, the bank, etc.). For the owners, the governance system must protect both the security of the asset base and the return on those assets. These tasks are most often assigned to the board of directors (Gersick & Feliu, 2014), possibly extended to one or a few outsiders (Huse, 2007). For directors and employees, governance must support the business's management, including the articulation and evaluation of criteria, norms, and values for strategic decision-making, setting out the long- and short-term strategies, evaluating investments, etc. For the family members, the task of governance involves clarifying the demands and rewards of family membership with respect to the business, identifying opportunities for involvement in the business, facilitating information and communication flows, and enhancing the sense of belonging and commitment across generations and branches of the family (Gersick & Feliu, 2014). The management of these different interests via governance instruments influences the success or failure of entrepreneurial activities (Steier, Chrisman, & Chua, 2015).

Because there is great diversity within the family business population, those businesses' governance structures, along with the emotional and resource advantages and disadvantages associated with those structures, vary (Le Breton-Miller et al., 2015). Based on these differences, Le Breton-Miller et al. (2015) propose that governance structure influences a family business's entrepreneurial orientation (EO) in five ways. They focus on the characteristics of the board of directors, which is the governance mechanism that is most often discussed in the governance literature. First, they propose that the presence of family owners on the board of directors will be positively related to a business's EO because the owners intend to ensure that the business remains robust and profitable in the long run via renewal. Second, the presence of insiders on the board will be positively related to a business's EO because insiders have accurate knowledge of the business, its opportunities, and the competition presented by its rivals. Third, high levels of tenure among board members will be inversely related to a business's EO because those board members might lack both the incentive (tied to old traditions) and the knowledge (might have lost touch with current developments) to support entrepreneurship. Fourth, they propose that entrepreneurship in family businesses will vary inversely with the presence of later-generation CEOs and other executive positions. If recruitment is limited to the pool of family members, the chances of finding the best person decrease. Fifth, entrepreneurship in family businesses will be positively related to the presence of a founder and negatively related to the involvement of later-generation family members on the top management team and board of directors because later generations are likely to lack the founder's entrepreneurial talent. Box 7.4 illustrates the governance structure at the H. Jansen Group and the motivations why it is organized like this.

Values and Organizational Identity

Family values can significantly affect the values, behaviors, and attitudes of individual family members and therefore the social

Box 7.4

Governance is an important issue at the H. Jansen Group to safeguard the health of both the business and the family. Until recently, there was no specific agreement about the roles of various family members in the business. Vanessa wants to avoid conflict in case her father passes away; she and her sisters might have very different ideas about each other's roles in the business. Vanessa: '*I want to ensure the continuity of the family business. My sisters and I have to form a team, representing the fourth generation of the family. I want to keep my sisters involved and informed'*. For this reason she has asked a family business consultant to help develop a family constitution. A family constitution is a document in which the family's goals, norms and values in relation to the

business are written down. The document is intended to serve the fourth and later generations. Together with her father and the consultant, Vanessa has reviewed various topics that she specifically wants included in the constitution:

- governance (family council and advisory board, including the frequency and structure of meetings, topics to be discussed with the attendants);
- financial policies (dividend payments and fund management);
- the possibility for family members to work in the business;
- in-laws' involvement;
- the business's norms and values;
- external communication about the family business;
- management succession processes and the roles of the incumbent and successor;
- ownership succession;
- growth/performance principles;
- the duty to financially care for family members; and
- the possibility of modifying the constitution.

Vanessa explains the goal of the family constitution as follows: '*The family constitution forms the rules and regulations for the family business. It provides for good working relationships between the family members and the business by which the business can profit from the family overlap instead of it being a burden*'. Moreover, agreements about management succession processes will prevent situations in which a successor is selected solely because of family relationships. Instead, a competence test should support the notion that he or she is competent enough to take on the task.

In addition to the family constitution, Vanessa plans to have an advisory board to organize strategic decision-making support for herself in her role as the director of the family business. Although this board will not be empowered to make decisions, it can help to prepare and elaborate various scenarios and possibilities for managing strategic issues. Vanessa wants to ensure that she gets to choose the members of the advisory board herself. She does not want to involve persons from her father's network because she wants the board to support her path for the future. Also, Vanessa has decided that her father is not going to be one of the advisors on the advisory board, as he has already taken on that role in his relationship with Vanessa. Based on a job description in which she specifies the expertise that she is seeking, she attempts to attract three outsiders (preferably people currently unknown to her) who can therefore be truly independent in advising her.

Vanessa thinks that it is important to implement these organizational improvements as soon as possible: '*It is never too early to arrange a good governance structure, both for the family and the business. You need to make sure that good structures are in place to address potential conflict. If you are too late, relationships can be damaged, and a lot of money goes down the drain. You have to be prepared and be convinced of the urgency to arrange familial issues in time*'. Moreover, by clarifying the roles and responsibilities of the various family members and the firm's dividend policy, she provides more space and freedom to pursue new activities: '*One of the ways to guard the continuity of the family business is growth, autonomous growth, or taking over other businesses, or both. However, to do that, we need funds, so it is important for us to agree on the maximum amount of dividend to pay to the owners.*'

system of the family business (Bettinelli et al., 2014). Values are the implicit or explicit conception of what is desirable and therefore help participants of a social system agree on what is important (Koiranen, 2002). Explicit values are verbalized and implicit values are practised. These values, combined with common beliefs, meanings, norms, and symbols, comprise the culture of a family business. Values are proposed to be highly relevant in understanding the level of entrepreneurial activity in organizations (Davidsson & Wiklund, 1997; Fayolle, Liñán, & Moriano, 2014). Fayolle et al. (2014) suggest that values may help explain the formation of entrepreneurial intention antecedents such as attitude and moderate the effect of antecedents on the entrepreneurial intention. Moreover, values are proposed to play a role in the intention–action link by overcoming barriers and obstacles (Fayolle et al., 2014). Sorenson (2014), by building on social capital theory, explains that families establish common values and cultures through communication and information-sharing processes. However, the basic values of the family and the business can vary significantly. Whereas the family is an institution that fundamentally nurtures and sustains relationships, the business is an institution that fundamentally nurtures and sustains economies (Sorenson, 2014). Essentially, a family business is a combination of two social entities: it is a so-called hybrid-identity organization (Albert & Whetten, 1985). How do family values get integrated with business values or change into the business values?

The family business's identity is often considered an extension of the individual founder who creates the business (Dyer & Whetten, 2006). Sorenson (2014) argues that family values also become incorporated into the business by five other means: (1) multiple family members who own and work in the business use the family values to guide their business behavior; (2) family values are emphasized in succeeding generations; (3) family values become institutionalized over time in common symbols, rituals, stories, and heroes; (4) family values are written down in collaborative documents; and

(5) later-generation family owners stay actively involved in business governance. Essentially, these different means imply that the greater the interaction and communication between the family and the business (especially in later generations), the greater the likelihood that family values will become and remain an important part of the business and affect the business's level of entrepreneurial activity. Indeed, Craig, Dibrell, and Garrett (2014) find evidence that family influence positively influences family culture, family culture improves families' ability to be strategically flexible, and this flexibility positively impacts firm innovativeness. Discua Cruz, Howorth, and Hamilton (2013), studying entrepreneurial teams in family businesses, find that team membership is strongly influenced by the extent to which individuals share the same values, have shared understandings, have high levels of trust, and identify with each other. The importance of values is especially visible in social and sustainable entrepreneurship and philanthropy (Grenier, 2010). Research has shown that family businesses have always been at the forefront of such efforts and they represent an important percentage of the monetary contributions toward community well-being (Feliu & Botero, 2016). Important values at the H. Jansen Group are referred to in Box 7.5.

Trust and Conflict

Trust has been an important topic in entrepreneurship research because of its influence on reducing the transaction costs and risks involved

---

Box 7.5

Professionalism and expertise are important values at the H. Jansen Group and are strongly embedded into organizational activities. Vanessa Jansen notes, 'Whatever we do, we want to be good at it. We are constantly busy to educate and train our employees. Currently, we are working on professionalizing the HRM policies, structuring the meeting frequency of the management board and developing a management plan'.

with entrepreneurship (Welter, 2011). There are even important similarities between trust and entrepreneurship because, in both pursuing entrepreneurial activities and demonstrating trust, individuals address the unknown (Welter, 2012). Welter (2011) argues that trust is a conditional phenomenon that depends on contexts, situations, and cognitions. The context of the family business appears to be important. Trust is a feature central to family businesses because it represents a fundamental basis for stakeholder relationships (Sundarmurthy, 2008). Families can benefit from trust and transform it into a competitive advantage (Sundarmurthy, 2008), for example, through the availability of financial resources (Steier, 2003) that are required for entrepreneurial activity. However, trust also seems to be a feature that must be actively managed and sustained across generations because the trust inherent in the early stages of the business can be replaced by conflict and strife as businesses and their families evolve and grow (Steier & Muethel, 2014). Moreover, trust can potentially lead to opportunism, complacency, and blind faith (Eddleston & Morgan, 2014).

Trust, conflict, and emotions are highly interrelated concepts in family business research. Conflict has the potential to end the family business's existence. Because of the strong interrelationship between the family and the business, it is likely that conflict in the family domain also impacts the business domain and vice versa (Sharma, 2004). This potentially increases the intensity and frequency of conflicts compared with non-family businesses (McKee, Madden, Kellermanns, & Eddleston, 2014). Such conflict should be managed appropriately to limit the damage to both the family and the business. Various strategies can be used to manage conflict: ignore the conflict, force the implementation of an idea without concern for others, attempt to find a resolution that at least partially satisfies the parties involved, collaborate to come up with a mutually agreed-upon new solution, and third-party intervention. This final conflict-management strategy differs from the others

in the sense that new people (neutral outsiders) are introduced in an effort to mediate or resolve the conflict (McKee et al., 2014). It is interesting to note that some types and situations of conflict can enhance business performance. Cognitive conflict that results from disagreements about the pursuit of entrepreneurial action or process conflict resulting from the assignment of business tasks can improve decision-making and focus attention on alternatives related to what the business should do and how it should be done (McKee et al., 2014; Forbes & Milliken, 1999). Conflict situations can also lead to the creation of new businesses. A good example of this phenomenon is the story of the Dassler brothers, who ran a successful shoe factory located next to a river. However, a feud separated the brothers, dividing both their company and their family, leading to the creation of two rival, iconic businesses: Adidas and Puma.

The developments described in the Jansen case illustrate a number of the themes discussed above. Vanessa and her father are the directors of this fourth-generation family firm and must behave entrepreneurially to keep the business healthy and up to date. The case describes the succession process that Vanessa is experiencing. In this situation, succession has begun with the ownership transition to the next generation, which is represented by the three daughters. Management succession follows by transferring more responsibilities to Vanessa, step by step. This case shows that succession is not an event, but a process, and it takes years for formal changes to take place and for individuals to settle into their new roles. Vanessa struggles not only with her father's dominant role in the business but also with their private father–daughter relationship; she attempts to take charge by introducing changes to the governance structure and providing clarity in agreements between family members in relation to the business. This should also prevent conflict and keep family members who do not work in the business involved and informed. Vanessa is proud to be the fourth generation running the business. Professionalism and trustworthiness are considered key factors that have led to the firm's 100-year anniversary. Because the firm's name is similar to the family name, the reputation of individual family members is closely linked to firm activities, providing an additional reason to focus on quality.

THE FUTURE OF THE FIELD AND LINES OF INQUIRY

We now reflect on future research into entrepreneurial activity in family businesses. Whereas the link between entrepreneurship and family businesses has primarily been tackled through business-focused approaches, we would like to encourage a greater focus on the family. Because it is the family that distinguishes family businesses from non-family businesses, and because the family either is or provides the engine for new business activities, it is worthwhile to more closely examine questions raised earlier, including the following: How do family resources such as family social capital affect entrepreneurship over generations? Which family dynamics and considerations either enable or constrain entrepreneurial behavior? We have explained above that entrepreneurship is closely related to succession: therefore, a potential area for future inquiry would involve business families instead of family businesses. By focusing on the family and individual members, research attention shifts to activities that are unique to the family business situation. For example, scholars could consider the learning-in-practice that might take place either when business activities are discussed at the dinner table or when next-generation family members are involved in the business through summer jobs or other work activities. This learning can, in practice, eventually provide business innovation, change, and continuity (Hamilton, 2011). Another important line of research to pursue is the new generation's entrepreneurial orientation. Research among

students whose families own businesses (a project called the GUESSS survey) shows that today, the younger generations are both well-educated and increasingly likely to look elsewhere for employment. At the same time, this survey shows that these students are more entrepreneurial than other students, providing opportunities to develop new or related business activities (Sieger, Fueglistaller, & Zellweger, 2016).

Moreover, greater attention to the family's role in studying entrepreneurship can help address heterogeneity in the family business. For example, Chirico, Sirmon, Sciascia, and Mazzola (2011) have studied how performance in family businesses can be increased through entrepreneurship. They find that realizing the benefits of entrepreneurship in family businesses is a complicated matter affected by the synchronization of EO, generational involvement, and participative strategy. Although such studies are highly relevant to understanding the factors that impact entrepreneurial activity in family businesses in general, they cannot explain the specific influence of the family on entrepreneurship because the family business as such does not exist. Heterogeneity in today's family structures is significant and has changed significantly in recent decades (Sharma et al., 2014). For example, the notion of the nuclear family of the 1950s has been overshadowed by other forms of family, for example, individual family members who divorce, remarry, and give birth to children out of wedlock. These developments might have consequences for how entrepreneurial activities take place and how resources either are made available or are used in the business (Bettinelli et al., 2014). Accordingly, there is a need for a more nuanced understanding of family businesses and how they engage in entrepreneurial behavior. Instead of comparing family businesses with non-family businesses, more attention should be paid to differences among family businesses. For example, do family businesses with a longer history also adopt a longer-term perspective and, if so, what does that mean for their entrepreneurial behavior? Do family businesses become less risk averse because of a longer investment horizon or do they become more risk averse because they want to protect their legacy? Sharma et al. (2014) suggest that the concept of socio-emotional wealth can potentially help address the large variety of organizations within the group of family businesses. Other dimensions that can distinguish family businesses include, inter alia, the level of the family's involvement, the family's life stage (founder, siblings, or cousins), family values (including religion), and the family's overall level of unity. Additionally, as argued by Sharma et al. (2014), a clear definition of family is especially important for studies in which the family is the main unit of analysis, such as studies on habitual or portfolio entrepreneurship by enterprising families.

In addition to these suggestions for future studies in terms of content, we argue that it is important to collect data through direct interaction with key actors in the family and the business to obtain a better understanding of the family. For example, to enhance our understanding of the socialization of the family context and the entrepreneurial activities of family members, scholars should obtain access to process-oriented data and overcome empirical dogmatisms and narrow conceptualizations related to both the family and entrepreneurial behavior. By posing 'why' and 'how' questions, considering a diversity of methodological options (including combinations of methods and longitudinal studies) and choosing contextualized approaches, more insight can be gained into 'soft' issues (emotions, values, trust, etc.), which are difficult to grasp through the use of quantitative methods. An evidence-based entrepreneurship research approach, suggesting the combination of findings and contributions from the positive, narrative, and design research traditions, can potentially provide such an alternative research framework for better understanding of the role of the family in the business. This approach focuses on research

synthesis in terms of social mechanisms, contextual conditions, and outcome patterns (van Burg & Romme, 2014). Although this is a challenging task because the context and issues of each family are very different, we believe that more focus on the family variable could lead to a better understanding of entrepreneurial behavior in family businesses.

CONCLUSION

This chapter aimed to provide an overview of the various ways in which the context of the family business influences entrepreneurial activity. We have explained the challenges experienced by families that own a business caused by the overlap among the three systems (family, business, and ownership). This overlap results from individuals' involvement in playing different roles, for example, by being an owner and family member at the same time. Consequently, we discussed the link between entrepreneurship and family businesses, along with the different ideological tensions that are at play in family businesses. Moreover, we discussed the importance of transgenerational entrepreneurship, i.e. the challenge of passing on an entrepreneurial mindset to the next generation. We continued by elaborating on the family's influence on entrepreneurial activity by specifying the factors that distinguish family businesses from their non-family counterparts, including succession, socio-emotional wealth, governance, values, and trust. We ended the discussion by considering future developments and lines of inquiry for future research.

We hope that this chapter inspires not only family business researchers but also (and especially) entrepreneurship scholars to not only consider family businesses as a contextual factor in studying entrepreneurial activity but also to acknowledge the family business field's distinctive focus: the reciprocal influence of family and business.

REFERENCES

Albert, S.A. & Whetten, D.A. (1985). Organizational identity. In L.L. Cummings & B.M. Staw (Eds), *Research in Organizational Behavior* (pp. 263–295). Greenwich: CT JAI.

Barach, J. & Ganitsky, J. (1995). Successful succession in family business. *Family Business Review, 8*(2): 131.

Berenbeim, R. (1990). How business families manage the transition from owner to professional management. *Family Business Review, 3*(1): 69–110.

Berrone, P., Cruz, C. & Gomez-Mejia, L.R. (2014). Family-controlled firms and stakeholder management: A socio-emotional wealth preservation perspective. In L. Melin, M. Nordqvist & P. Sharma (Eds), *The Sage Handbook of Family Business* (pp. 179–195). London: Sage.

Bettinelli, C., Fayolle, A. & Randerson, K. (2014). Family entrepreneurship: A developing field. *Foundations and Trends in Entrepreneurship, 10*(3): 161–236.

Chirico, F., Sirmon, D.G., Sciascia, S. & Mazzola, P. (2011). Resource orchestration in family firms: Investigating how entrepreneurial orientation, generational involvement, and participative strategy affect performance. *Strategic Entrepreneurship Journal, 5*(4): 307–326.

Chrisman, J.J., Chua, J.H., Pearson, A.W. & Barnett, T. (2012). Family involvement, family influence, and family-centered non-economic goals in small firms. *Entrepreneurship Theory and Practice, 36*(2): 1–27.

Chua, J., Chrisman, J. & Sharma, P. (2003). Succession and nonsuccession concerns of family firms and agency relationship with nonfamily managers. *Family Business Review, 16*(2): 89–107.

Craig, J.B., Dibrell, C. & Garrett, R. (2014). Examining relationships among family influence, family culture, flexible planning systems, innovativeness and firm performance. *Journal of Family Business Strategy, 5*(3): 229–238.

Davidsson, P. & Wiklund, J. (1997). Values, beliefs and regional variations in new firm formation rates. *Journal of Economic Psychology, 18*(2): 179–199.

Discua Cruz, A., Howorth, C. & Hamilton, E. (2013). Intrafamily entrepreneurship: The formation and membership of family entrepreneurial teams. *Entrepreneurship: Theory and Practice, 37*(1): 17–46.

Dyck, B., Mauws, M., Starke, F.A. & Mischke, G.A. (2002). Passing the baton: The importance of sequence, timing, technique and communication in executive succession. *Journal of Business Venturing, 17*(2): 143–162.

Dyer, W.G. & Whetten, D.A. (2006). Family firms and social responsibility: Preliminary results from the S&P 500. *Entrepreneurship Theory & Practice, 30*(6): 785–802.

Eddleston, K.A. & Morgan, R.M. (2014). Trust, commitment and relationships in family business: Challenging conventional wisdom. *Journal of Family Business Strategy, 5*(3): 213–216.

Fayolle, A., Liñán, F. & Moriano, J.A. (2014). Beyond entrepreneurial intentions: Values and motivations in entrepreneurship. *International Entrepreneurship and Management Journal, 10*(4): 679–689.

Feliu, N. & Botero, I.C. (2016). Philanthropy in family enterprises: A review of literature. *Family Business Review, 29*(1): 121–141.

Fletcher, D. (2014). Family business inquiry as a critical social science. In L. Melin, M. Nordqvist & P. Sharma (Eds), *The Sage Handbook of Family Business* (pp. 137–154). London: Sage.

Flören, R. & Zwartendijk, G. (2008). Entrepreneurship and the family business. In W. Burggraaf, R. Flören & J. Kunst (Eds), *The Entrepreneur & the Entrepreneurship Cycle* (pp. 298–309). Assen: Koninklijke Van Gorcum BV.

Forbes, D.P. & Milliken, F.J. (1999). Cognition and corporate governance: Understanding boards of directors as strategic decision-making groups. *Academy of Management Review, 24*(3): 489–505.

Gedajlovic, E., Carney, M., Chrisman, J.J. & Kellermanns, F.W. (2012). The adolescence of family firm research: Taking stock and planning for the future. *Journal of Management, 38*(4): 1010–1037.

Gersick, K.E. & Feliu, N. (2014). Governing the family enterprise: Practices, performance and research. In L. Melin, M. Nordqvist & P. Sharma (Eds), *The Sage Handbook of Family Business* (pp. 196–225). London: Sage.

Gersick, K.E., Lansberg, I., Desjardins, M. & Dunn, B. (1999). Stages and transitions: Managing change in the family business. *Family Business Review*, *12*(4): 287–297.

Gimeno Sandig, A.G., Labadie, G.J., Saris, W. & Mayordomo, X.M. (2006). Internal factors of family business performance: An integrated theoretical model. In P.Z. Poutziouris, K.X. Smyrnios & S.B. Klein (Eds), *Handbook of Research on Family Business* (pp. 145–164). Cheltenham: Edward Elgar.

Goldbart, S. & DiFuria, J. (2009). Money and meaning: Implementation of effective family governance structures. *Journal of Practical Estate Planning*, *11*(6): 7–9.

Gomez-Mejia, L.R., Cruz, C., Berrone, P. & De Castro, J. (2011). The bind that ties: Socioemotional wealth preservation in family firms. *Academy of Management Annals*, *5*(1): 653–707.

Gomez-Mejia, L.R., Takacs-Haynes, K., Nunez-Nickel, M., Jacobson, K.J.L. & Moyano-Fuentes, J. (2007). Socioemotional wealth and business risks in family-controlled firms: Evidence from Spanish olive oil mills. *Administrative Science Quarterly*, *52*(1): 106–137.

Grenier, P. (2010). Vision and values: The relationship between the visions and actions of social entrepreneurs. In K. Hockerts, J. Mair & J.K. Robinson (Eds), *Values and Opportunities in Social Entrepreneurship* (pp. 52–70). Hampshire: Palgrave Macmillan.

Habbershon, T.G. & Williams, M.L. (1999). A resource-based framework for assessing the strategic advantages of family firms. *Family Business Review*, *12*(1): 1–25.

Hamilton, E. (2011). Entrepreneurial learning in family business: A situated learning perspective. *Journal of Small Business and Enterprise Development*, *18*(1): 8–26.

Handler, W. (1994). Succession in family business, a review of the research. *Family Business Review*, *7*(2): 133–157.

Heck, K.Z.R., Danes, M.S., Fitzgerald, A.M., Haynes, W.G., Schrank, L.H., Stafford, K. & Winter, M. (2006). The family's dynamic role within family business entrepreneurship. In P.Z. Poutziouris, K.X. Smyrnios & S.B Klein (Eds), *Handbook of Research on Family Business* (pp. 80–105). Cheltenham: Edward Elgar.

Huse, M. (2007). *Boards, Governance and Value Creation. The Human Side of Corporate Governance*. Cambridge: Cambridge University Press.

Jaskiewicz, P., Combs, J.G. & Rau, S.B. (2015). Entrepreneurial legacy: Toward a theory of how some family firms nurture transgenerational entrepreneurship. *Journal of Business Venturing*, *30*(1): 29–49.

Johannisson, B. & Huse, M. (2000). Recruiting outside board members in the small family business: An ideological challenge. *Entrepreneurship & Regional Development*, *12*(4): 353–378.

Koiranen, M. (2003). Understanding the contesting ideologies of family business: Challenge for leadership and professional services. *Family Business Review*, *16*(4): 241–250.

Koiranen, M. (2002). Over 100 years of age but still entrepreneurially active in the business: Exploring the values and family characteristics of old Finnish family firms. *Family Business Review*, *15*(3): 175–187.

Lambrecht, J. & Lievens, J. (2008). Pruning the family tree: An unexplored path to family business continuity and family harmony. *Family Business Review*, *21*(4): 295–313.

Le Breton-Miller, I., Miller, D. & Baresa, F. (2015). Governance and entrepreneurship in family firms: Agency, behavioral agency and resource-based comparisons. *Journal of Family Business Strategy*, *6*(1): 58–62.

Le Breton-Miller, I., Miller, D. & Steier, L.P. (2004). Toward an integrative model of effective FOB succession. *Entrepreneurship Theory and Practice*, *28*(4): 305–328.

Long, R.G. & Chrisman, J.J. (2014). Management succession in family business. In L. Melin, M. Nordqvist & P. Sharma (Eds), *The Sage Handbook of Family Business* (pp. 249–268). London: Sage.

Mandl, I. (2008). *Overview of family business relevant issues*. Contract No. 30-CE-0164021/00-51. Final Report. Vienna: KMU FORSCHUNG AUSTRIA, Austrian Institute for SME Research.

Martinez, M.A. & Aldrich, H. (2014). Sociological theories applied to family businesses. In L. Melin, M. Nordqvist & P. Sharma (Eds), *The Sage Handbook of Family Business* (pp. 83–99). London: Sage.

McKee, D.N., Madden, T.M., Kellermanns, F.W. & Eddleston, K.A. (2014). Conflict in family firms: The good and the bad. In L. Melin, M. Nordqvist & P. Sharma (Eds), *The Sage Handbook of Family Business* (pp. 514–528). London: Sage.

McKelvie, A., McKenny, A.F., Lumpkin, G.T. & Short, J.C. (2014). Corporate entrepreneurship in family businesses: Past contributions and future opportunities. In L. Melin, M. Nordqvist & P. Sharma (Eds), *The Sage Handbook of Family Business* (pp. 340–363). London: Sage.

Melin, L. & Nordqvist, M. (2007). The reflexive dynamics of institutionalization: The case of the family business. *Strategic Organization*, 5(3): 321–333.

Miller, D. & Le Breton-Miller, I. (2006). Family governance and firm performance: Agency, stewardship, and capabilities. *Family Business Review*, 19(1): 73–87.

Miller, D. & Le Breton-Miller, I. (2005). *Managing for The Long Run: Lessons in Competitive Advantage From Great Family Businesses*. Boston: Harvard Business School Press.

Miller, D., Steier, L.P. & Le Breton-Miller, I. (2006). Lost in time: Intergenerational succession, change and failure in family business. In P.Z. Poutziouris, K.X. Smyrnios & S.B Klein (Eds), *Handbook of Research on Family Business* (pp. 371–387). Cheltenham: Edward Elgar.

Minichilli, A., Corbetta, G. & Macmillan, I.C. (2010). Top management teams in family-controlled companies: 'Familiness', 'faultlines', and their impact on financial performance. *Journal of Management Studies*, 47(2): 205–222.

Morris, M.H., Williams, R.O., Allen, J.A. & Avila, R.A. (1998). Correlates of success in family business transitions. *Journal of Business Venturing*, 12(5): 385–401.

Nordqvist, M. & Melin, L. (2010a). Entrepreneurial families and family firms. *Entrepreneurship & Regional Development*, 22(3–4): 211–239.

Nordqvist, M. & Melin, L. (2010b). Entrepreneurial families and family firms. *Entrepreneurship & Regional Development*, 22(3–4): 211–239.

Nordqvist, M., Wennberg, K., Bau, M. & Hellerstedt, K. (2013). An entrepreneurial process perspective on succession in family firms. *Small Business Economics*, 40(4): 1087–1122.

Nordqvist, M. & Zellweger, T. (2010). *Transgenerational Entrepreneurship: Exploring Growth and Performance in Family Firms Across Generations*. Cheltenham: Edward Elgar.

Poza, E., Hanlon, S. & Kishida, R. (2004). Does the family business interaction factor represent a resource or a cost? *Family Business Review*, 17(2): 99–118.

Pukall, T.J. & Calabrò, A. (2014). The internationalization of family firms: A critical review and integrative model. *Family Business Review*, 27(2): 103–125.

Rosa, P., Howorth, C. & Discua Cruz, A. (2014). Habitual and portfolio entrepreneurship and the family in business. In L. Melin, M. Nordqvist & P. Sharma (Eds), *The Sage Handbook of Family Business* (pp. 364–382). London: Sage.

Sharma, P. (2004). An overview of the field of family business studies: Current status and directions for the future. *Family Business Review*, 17(1): 1–36.

Sharma, P., Melin, L. & Nordqvist, M. (2014). Introduction: Scope, evolution and future of family business studies. In L. Melin, M. Nordqvist & P. Sharma (Eds), *The Sage Handbook of Family Business* (pp. 1–22). London: Sage.

Sieger, P., Fueglistaller, U. & Zellweger, T. (2016). Student Entrepreneurship 2016: Insights From 50 Countries. St.Gallen/Bern: KMU-HSG/IMU.

Sirmon, D.G. & Hitt, M.A. (2003). Managing resources: Linking unique resources, management, and wealth creation in family firms. *Entrepreneurship Theory and Practice*, 27(4): 339–358.

Sorenson, R.L. (2014). Values in family business. In L. Melin, M. Nordqvist & P. Sharma (Eds), *The Sage Handbook of Family Business* (pp. 463–479). London: Sage.

Steier, L. (2003). Variants of agency contracts in family-financed ventures as a continuum of familial altruistic and market rationalities. *Journal of Business Venturing*, 18(5): 597–618.

Steier, L. & Muethel, M. (2014). Trust and family businesses. In L. Melin, M. Nordqvist & P. Sharma (Eds), *The Sage Handbook of Family Business* (pp. 498–513). London: Sage.

Steier, L.P., Chrisman, J.J. & Chua, J.H. (2015). Governance challenges in family businesses and business families. *Entrepreneurship Theory and Practice*, *39*(6): 1265–1280.

Sundarmurthy, C. (2008). Sustaining trust within family businesses. *Family Business Review*, *21*(1): 89–102.

Tagiuri, R. & Davis, J.A. (1992). On the goals of successful family companies. *Family Business Review*, *5*(1): 43–62.

Van Burg, J.C. & Romme, A.G.L. (2014). Creating the future together: Toward a framework for research synthesis in entrepreneurship. *Entrepreneurship Theory and Practice*, *38*(2): 369–397.

Voordeckers, W., Le Breton-Miller, I. & Miller, D. (2014). In search of the best of both worlds: Crafting a finance paper for the family business review. *Family Business Review*, *27*(4): 281–286.

Welter, F. (2012). All you need is trust? A critical review of the trust and entrepreneurship literature. *International Small Business Journal*, *30*(3): 193–212.

Welter, F. (2011). Trust and entrepreneurship. In L.P. Dana (Ed.), *World Encyclopedia of Entrepreneurship* (pp. 475–480). Cheltenham: Edward Elgar.

8

Social Entrepreneurship: Entrepreneurship and Social Value Creation

Helen Haugh, Fergus Lyon and Bob Doherty

INTRODUCTION

Scholar, policy and practitioner interest in social entrepreneurship has increased since the publication of influential books such as *The Rise of the Social Entrepreneur* (Leadbeater, 1998), *The Emergence of Social Enterprise* (Borzaga & Defourny, 2004) and *Managing and Measuring Social Enterprise* (Paton, 2003). During this period, articles in corporate publications (Boschee, 1995; Dees, 1998; Foster & Bradach, 2005) and academic books and journals helped the field to take shape (Austin, Stevenson & Wei-Skillern, 2006; Dart, 2004; Ridley-Duff & Bull, 2015; Seelos & Mair, 2005; Thompson, Alvy & Lees, 2000). At the same time policy developments were advanced in the United Kingdom (UK) (DTI, 2002; Sepulveda, 2015), European Union (EU) (Evers, 1995, 2005; Evers, Laville, Borzaga, Defourny, Lewis, Nyssens & Pestoff, 2004; Spear, 2008) and the United States (US) (Dees, 1998). More recent international comparisons further

indicate that social entrepreneurship is now an important entrepreneurial and development activity for economies around the world (Chandra & Wong, 2016; Jenner, 2016; Kerlin, 2006, 2010).

Recent reviews of the literature (Battilana & Lee, 2014; Doherty, Haugh & Lyon, 2014; Jones, Keogh & O'Leary, 2007; Peattie & Morley, 2008; Smith-Hunter, 2008) concur that social entrepreneurship describes the activities associated with the identification of opportunities to create social value and the creation of new ventures to pursue this goal in a financially sustainable way. Social entrepreneurship thus involves entrepreneurship – the establishment of sustainable organizations – and social purpose – processes and practices that create social value (Fowler, 2000; Mort, Weerawardena & Carnegie, 2003; Nicholls & Cho, 2006; Peredo & McLean, 2006).

Social enterprise organizations are faced with a choice of legal form but are distinguished from other organizational forms by the simultaneous presence of two characteristics: the generation of earned income from trading goods and services and the prominence of social mission in the goal structure of the enterprise (Peredo & McLean, 2006). Social enterprises thus comprise characteristics from at least two different categories of organizations. In common with organizations in the private sector they pursue commercial goals by the generation of a proportion of their income from trading in goods and services. With the public and nonprofit sectors they share in common the goal of creating social value. Social enterprises are thus private organizations committed to solving social problems (Mair & Martí, 2006; Weerawardena & Mort, 2006). Social enterprises are now widely accepted as playing an important role in addressing societal challenges of serving the disadvantaged and socially excluded (Blackburn & Ram, 2006; Defourny & Nyssens, 2006), unemployed (Pache & Santos, 2013), homeless (Teasdale, 2012) and the poor (Seelos & Mair, 2005), as well as tackling environmental issues such as climate change, biodiversity loss, pollution and recycling (Austin et al., 2006; Mair, Seelos & Borwankar, 2005). The impact of social entrepreneurship also extends beyond social value creation to stimulating more widespread societal change (Alvord, Brown & Letts, 2004; Lumpkin, Moss, Gras, Kato & Amezcua, 2013; Mair & Martí, 2006; Nicholls, 2006; Sen, 2007).

Three examples from practice illustrate how social enterprise business models combine commercial activity with the pursuit of social goals. Social firms employ the disabled and disadvantaged to make goods for and provide services to customers (DTI, 2002). The social firm business model involves employee training as well as individual support for personal recovery and development (Svandberg, Gumley & Wilson, 2010). Fair trade certified companies enable farmers and producers in developing countries to improve livelihoods by providing routes to markets and agricultural extension services (Davies, Doherty & Knox, 2010; Nicholls & Opal, 2005; Tiffen, 2002). In addition, the fair trade

premium paid to certified suppliers assists computer empowerment and development (Doherty, 2009). Finally, development trusts support community regeneration via asset-based development and a wide range of trading and service delivery activities (DTI, 2002; Westall, 2001). For social entrepreneurship, assets are broadly construed to include not just physical assets (Hart, 2001) but also knowledge, skills and emotions (Hopkins & Rippon, 2015).

The chapter is laid out as follows. We begin by summarizing the definitional debates and contextual influences on social entrepreneurship. This is followed by a review of the research on social entrepreneurship and opportunity identification. This section brings together opportunity recognition, construction and social innovation, and discusses processes of effectuation and bricolage in opportunity construction. We then appraise the research on opportunity exploitation by reviewing social enterprise business models, marketing, funding and human resource management. The final section advances ten suggestions for future research that will extend social enterprise theory and knowledge.

DEFINING SOCIAL ENTREPRENEURSHIP

Definitional debates feature prominently in the early social entrepreneurship literature and a standard definition has yet to be agreed upon (see for example Bacq & Janssen, 2011; Dacin, Dacin & Tracey, 2011). In the US the social entrepreneurship discourse is dominated by market-based approaches to income generation and social change (Alter, 2006; Austin et al., 2006; Dees, 1998). Although a spectrum of social purpose organizations from purely philanthropic to purely commercial has been advanced (Dees, 1998), social entrepreneurship is firmly anchored to social business models in which earned income is the principal source of organizational revenue. Dees, however, moderates the commercial focus by acknowledging that social enterprise business models should 'combine commercial and philanthropic elements in a productive balance' (Dees, 1998, p.60). The US perspective contrasts with the European social entrepreneurship discourse which is located in the cooperative tradition of collective social action (Borzaga & Defourny, 2004; Defourny & Nyssens, 2006; Evers et al., 2004). The UK borrows from both traditions and also stipulates that any surpluses from trading activity be principally reinvested in the business or disbursed for the benefit of the community (Amin, Cameron & Hudson, 2002; DTI, 2002).

The defining characteristic of earning income from trading differentiates social entrepreneurship from traditional nonprofit organizations and community and voluntary activities in which business models rely on funding from grants, donations and philanthropy (Alter, 2006; Dees, 1998). In philanthropy-dependent organizations the business model relies on income derived from donations and grants, the workforce includes volunteers and services to beneficiaries are provided free of charge. The pursuit of both commercial and social goals influences the types of social value-creating opportunities that can be exploited as well as the way that opportunities are employed to generate sustainable income. In practice, managing commercial and social goal achievement requires crafting a careful balance between resource utilization in order to build and maintain competitive advantage at the same time as serving beneficiaries and engaging with the key stakeholders (Moizer & Tracey, 2010).

CONTEXTUAL INFLUENCES ON SOCIAL ENTREPRENEURSHIP

Several political, economic and social trends in developed countries have encouraged policy and practitioner interest in social entrepreneurship. For example, the increasingly competitive international environment and rising domestic demand has increased pressure on government spending and pushed governments to find new ways of delivering health, social care and welfare services (Haugh & Kitson, 2007; Smith & Lipsky, 1993). This has led to policy-level promotion for suppliers to adopt entrepreneurial approaches to delivering health, social care and welfare services. At the same time, the decline in philanthropic giving, increased societal interest in social investing and the appeal of ethical capitalism has stimulated social entrepreneurship (Blackburn & Ram, 2006; Chell, 2007; Dacin et al., 2011; Defourny & Borzaga, 2001; Peattie & Morley, 2008; Shaw & Carter, 2007; Tickel & Peck, 2013).

In developing countries the trends to promote social entrepreneurship are anchored in intractable global problems of poverty and inequality, informal and corrupt political institutions and resource constraints (Lumpkin et al., 2013; Rivera-Santos, Holt, Littlewood & Kolk, 2015). The adverse environments found in sub-Saharan countries (Nega & Schneider, 2014; Thorgren & Omorede, 2015) have shifted the responsibility for economic and social development from the public to the private and nonprofit sectors (Thorgren & Omorede, 2015) and provided a fertile landscape for new social enterprise creation (Littlewood & Holt, 2015). Interest in social entrepreneurship has also increased in China as the economy has opened up to western influences (Chandra & Wong, 2016).

THEORIZING SOCIAL ENTREPRENEURSHIP

Although valuable contributions to a novel field of inquiry, many of the early contributions to social entrepreneurship were labelled as uncritical and lacking theoretical architecture (Haugh, 2005; Parkinson & Howorth, 2008; Sepulveda, Syrett & Calvo, 2013). The focus was to portray social entrepreneurship as an heroic activity in which the social entrepreneur was motivated by the desire to change the world (Alvord et al., 2004; Sen, 2007), implement solutions to global problems (Yunus, Moingeon & Lehmann-Ortega, 2010) and halt the hegemony of free market economics (Seelos & Mair, 2005).

More recent contributions have been anchored in a range of theoretical perspectives including institutional logics (Pache & Santos, 2013), institutional bridging (Tracey, Phillips & Jarvis, 2011), paradox and ambidexterity (Landsberg, 2004; Smith, Besharov, Wessels & Chertok, 2012; Smith, Gonin & Besharov, 2013), hybridity (Battilana & Dorado, 2010), and critiques of capitalism and free market economics (Amin, 2009; Laville & Nyssens, 2001; Ménard, 2004; Santos, 2012). Further, critical scholars have explored how the meaning of social entrepreneurship has been socially constructed from the dialectical discourse between politics and practice (Teasdale, 2012; Lyon & Sepulveda, 2009).

SOCIAL VALUE CREATION AND OPPORTUNITY IDENTIFICATION

The processes of social entrepreneurship are anchored in the practices of establishing a new venture to pursue commercial and social goals (Hockerts, 2006). Despite the centrality of opportunity identification to entrepreneurship (Vaghely & Julien, 2010) few studies have examined how opportunities to create social value are recognized (Corner & Ho, 2010; Hockerts, 2006) and discovered (Murphy & Coombes, 2008). Insights into how social value-creating opportunities are recognized or constructed (Luke & Chu, 2013) can be gleaned from the many case studies of social enterprise development; for example, opportunities might be evident in community economic and social deprivation (Haugh, 2007; Thompson et al., 2000), institutional voids (Mair & Martí, 2009), or discovered from the social entrepreneur's vision

and active searching for opportunities (Alvord et al., 2004; Thompson et al., 2000). In addition, entrepreneurial qualities of passion (Thorgren & Omorede, 2015), commitment (Sharir & Learner, 2006) and creativity (Sen, 2007) have been noted to drive social entrepreneurship opportunity identification.

The extent to which social entrepreneurs recognize or discover opportunities in different ways from commercial entrepreneurs is explored in a number of studies (Doherty, Foster, Mason, Meehan, Rotheroe & Royce, 2009; Mair & Martí, 2006; Corner & Ho, 2010; Nicholls, 2006). Doherty et al. (2009) found that the opportunity-seeking culture of fair trade certified organizations enabled them to identify opportunities that other third-sector organizations were unable to pursue. In particular, the culture of nonprofit organizations relies on philanthropic funds whereas social enterprise actively pursues income generation.

SOCIAL INNOVATION

Social innovation is the development and discovery of a novel solution to a social problem that is more effective, efficient, sustainable, or socially just than current solutions and in which the value created accrues primarily to society rather than to private individuals (Phills, Deiglmeir & Miller, 2008). The broad definition of social innovation embraces a range of novel services such as work integration (Pache & Santos, 2013), livelihood and income generation (Seelos & Mair, 2005; Yunus et al., 2010) and supporting the socially excluded (Blackburn & Ram, 2006; Svandberg et al., 2010); new organizational forms for social enterprise that blend knowledge, skills and resources from different economic sectors (Phills et al., 2008; Tracey et al., 2011); and new strategies for engaging and communicating with stakeholders (Chew & Lyon, 2012). However, social innovation is a social construct capable of multiple interpretations (Osborne, Chew & McLaughlin, 2008) and the innovativeness of social entrepreneurship is frequently asserted (Drayton, 2005) but rarely challenged.

The *Stanford Social Innovation Review* has been instrumental in raising the profile of social innovation by disseminating information about new developments in social enterprise business models (Phills et al., 2008). Grass roots social innovation capitalizes on traditional and community knowledge to develop innovations for communities (Gupta, Sinha, Koradia & Patel, 2003) and social alliances create opportunities for social innovation from pooling partners' knowledge and skills (Lyon, 2012). Public sector and philanthropic support for social innovation has been manifest in the flow of funds to assist the development of new products, services and delivery mechanisms for socially and environmentally beneficial goods and services (Osborne et al., 2008). An unintended consequence of the enhanced flow of funds to support social innovation has been to sacrifice tried and tested social, community and environmental products and services in favour of novel solutions (Amin, 2009).

PROCESSUAL APPROACHES TO OPPORTUNITY DISCOVERY

Three principal theories have been employed to advance social entrepreneurship opportunity research. First, effectuation theory describes a process in which opportunities emerge hand in hand with environmental and resource constraints (Sarasvathy, 2001). Corner and Ho (2010) show how social entrepreneurship opportunities develop in this way but also allude to linear opportunity development processes. Second, bricolage, in which the resources to hand are employed in novel ways to create goods and services, has proved insightful when analysing social entrepreneurship (Di Domenico, Haugh & Tracey,

2010; Fisher, 2012). Finally, structuration theory (Giddens, 1984) has shed light on how the interplay between context and social processes influences opportunities to create social value (Nicholls & Cho, 2006).

SOCIAL ENTREPRENEURSHIP AND OPPORTUNITY EXPLOITATION

Subsequent to opportunity identification, the next process in social entrepreneurship is to design the architecture for opportunity exploitation. Our review of social entrepreneurship research and opportunity exploitation is structured into four principal functions: social enterprise business models, marketing, finance and human resources management.

SOCIAL ENTERPRISE BUSINESS MODELS

An organization's business model comprises the structures and processes required to develop products and services as well as the mechanisms for generating income (Grassl, 2011; Yunus et al., 2010). The defining characteristic that social entrepreneurship involves both commercial and social value creation has challenged the design of business models incapable of managing the tensions between strategies that generate revenue and strategies that generate social value and societal change (Smith et al., 2013; Zahra, Gedajlovic, Neubaum & Shulman, 2009). Paton (2003) suggests that the pursuit of social goals can be in conflict with managerial rationality that prioritizes financial objectives. The search for multiple income streams and the imperative to be financially sustainable might lead the mission of the social enterprise to drift away from social value creation to focus on commercial revenue generation (Doherty et al., 2009).

Balancing Commercial and Social Goals

For social enterprises the strategic challenge is to balance the management of multiple sources of funds with the achievement of the social mission. The approach to resource mobilization is shaped by the organization's capabilities related to accessing income streams. To illustrate, the fair trade certified organizations Divine, Cafédirect and Liberation Nuts have been successful in developing commercial and own-label brands for their products. This contrasts with the experience of Oxfam when attempting to develop their own brand of fair trade-certified chocolate and coffee products. By restricting their own brand product distribution to Oxfam outlets, Oxfam failed to take advantage of the commercial distribution opportunities in mainstreet retail outlets. Despite investing in product development and market research, insufficient sales of the Oxfam branded products led to the products' withdrawal from the market (Doherty, 2009).

Stakeholder Engagement

Social and commercial business models differ in terms of the increased diversity of stakeholder groups that impact on, and are impacted by, the activities of the social enterprise (Di Domenico et al., 2010). Courtney (2002) suggests that social enterprise strategy development is more resource intensive due to the involvement of different stakeholder groups in consultation and decision-making processes. The collective approach to strategy formation raises new challenges of working with and governance of relationships with multiple stakeholders (Hudson, 2002).

Scaling Social Impact

The pursuit of commercial and social goals also impacts on the design of business models to achieve growth. Growth might be achieved by endogenous growth (Bloom & Smith, 2010) or diffusion of a successful business model through replication. In addition, growth might be achieved by either improving commercial performance or increasing social impact. Thus social enterprise growth necessitates a wider conceptualization of organizational performance when compared with commercial organizations (Lyon & Fernandez, 2012). The strategies of scaling and growth are further complicated by the difficulties in measuring commercial performance as well as social and environmental impact (Darby & Jenkins, 2006; Paton, 2003). To focus on profit as a single measure of success fails to capture the impact of social entrepreneurship on social value creation and broader societal change (Paton, 2003; Speckbacher, 2003).

Although scaling social impact through social franchising has been discussed (Bradach, 2003; Dees, Anderson & Wei-Skillern, 2004) the empirical data find that success of business model franchising in the private sector is difficult for social entrepreneurship to emulate. The challenges include identifying which components of the social business model to license (Dees et al., 2004), and recruiting franchisees willing to pay for the franchise, and who also have the motivation and capabilities to achieve both commercial and social goals (Tracey & Jarvis, 2007).

Social Alliances

An important strategy for social value creation is to work in partnership with other organizations from the same, or other, economic sectors (Austin et al., 2006; Di Domenico, Tracey & Haugh, 2009). Social alliances might be created horizontally to enhance capacity to bid for service delivery contracts, share social networks, resources and assets, and as a forerunner to mergers between social enterprises. Horizontal social alliances are built on relationships between more equal partners and are not hierarchical (Hardy, Phillips & Lawrence, 2003). Collaboration is one of the cooperative values set out by the cooperatives movement (ICA, 1994), although there has been limited research on how these forms of social enterprise implement this ideal in practice when operating in a more competitive environment.

Alternatively, vertical social alliances might be constructed to reap the benefits of closer supply chain integration or market creation. For example, a study of four locations in the UK found that collaborative relationships between social enterprise and commercial organizations were strongest and most effective where the local economies were stronger and was less effective in places where there were fewer economic opportunities and less economic growth (Amin et al., 2002).

In common with commercial entrepreneurship, access to resources is key to successful opportunity exploitation and competitive advantage (Barney, 1991). In the UK and US, an important income source for social entrepreneurship originates from the public sector either as grants and donations or contracts for the delivery of health, social care and welfare services. Thus building strong and productive relationships with decision makers with the power to award funds and contracts is strategically important. Relational contracting (Spear, 2008, p.44), in which the award of contracts is rooted in the strength and quality of social relationships between funders and recipients, has become an important social enterprise income generation strategy. Since the majority of social enterprises are small organizations (Lyon, Teasdale & Baldock, 2010) the relationships with stakeholders are based on trust and remain informal (Munoz & Tindsley, 2008, p.53). Social entrepreneurs reported they feared that efforts to formalize relationships would jeopardize future contracts. The unequal power relationship between contracting partners however undermines the capacity of social enterprises to negotiate beneficial contracts (Craig, Taylor, Wilkinson & Bloor, 2002). For example, Munoz and Tindsley (2008) also found that many social enterprises had trading relationships with partners without a formal contract between them, and that the agreement to trade

did not cover their full costs. The power differences between the two partners in the alliance meant that the social enterprise was powerless to resolve these issues.

SOCIAL ENTERPRISE MARKETING

Generating commercial income means that understanding how markets function is integral to social enterprise opportunity exploitation. Research has noted how social entrepreneurship has employed relationship and ethical differentiation strategies to appeal to customers and consumers (Doherty, 2009). In addition, social marketing has been instrumental in helping individuals to abandon antisocial habits and addictions such as smoking, and practise more healthy behaviour (Andreason, 2006).

Relationship Marketing

The important role that relationships play in building trust and cooperation to facilitate economic action is well established in the literature. When relationship marketing is anchored in ethical principles, markets reward organizational virtuousness and trustworthiness via customer and consumer loyalty (Murphy, Laczniak & Wood, 2007). Social enterprise values of equity, openness and mutuality embody the true spirit of relationship marketing (Murphy et al., 2007) and create an important marketing advantage when competing in the market place. In addition, relationship marketing extends the importance of building trusting relationships to all stakeholders, not just trading partners (Harker & Eagan, 2006).

Ethical Marketing

Insight into ethics, markets (Wagner-Tsukamoto, 2007) and marketing is gained from the increasing volume of research that has explored the principles, procedures and processes of fair trade certification (Davies et al., 2010). Fair trade scholarship highlighted how many early fair trade certified organizations were unsuccessful in achieving an effective balance between satisfying consumer expectations concerning product quality, availability and pricing at the same time as achieving the social mission to help farmers and producers in developing countries (Strong, 1997; Nicholls & Opal, 2005). Many of the first fair trade products to be certified did not succeed in the market place and were withdrawn. Subsequent to the product withdrawals, rigorous fair trade certification principles and procedures were introduced and professional product development processes designed. This was followed by the development of a range of fair trade-certified, good quality products with market appeal. Campaigns by activists to persuade major retailers to stock fair trade certified products leveraged new mainstream distribution outlets for fair trade products (Davies, 2009). For fair trade certified social enterprises, therefore, marketing involves balancing not just commercial and social goals but also crafting a balance between communicating ethical principles and achieving and maintaining consumer expectations concerning product quality (Golding, 2009; Golding & Peattie, 2005). In this way customers not only purchase the physical dimensions of products and services but also buy into the social mission of the seller or provider (Mann, 2008).

Social Marketing

Social marketing involves the application of 'marketing knowledge, concepts and techniques to enhance social as well as economic ends' (Andreason, 2006, p.9). Thus social marketing explicitly borrows commercial marketing practices and applies them to achieving social goals. Social marketing is, however, distinctive in that the sponsoring organization is not the beneficiary of the investment in marketing. Instead the audience

for marketing communications comprises the target market and broader society (Golding & Peattie, 2005). Take for example a social marketing campaign to reduce tobacco smoking by the UK charity Ash. The marketing campaign would be targeted at tobacco smokers and might be funded by philanthropic and public sector donations to an anti-smoking charity. In a second example, the UK social enterprise Little Angels invests in social marketing techniques to increase the prevalence of breastfeeding in mothers from disadvantaged backgrounds. The marketing campaign is complemented by workshops to provide advice and training to new mothers.

SOCIAL ENTERPRISE HUMAN RESOURCE MANAGEMENT

The social pursuit of social goals plays an important role in several aspects of social enterprise management of human resources. First, the commitment to creating social value and societal change are motivating factors for recruiting employees, volunteers and trustees (Borzaga & Solari, 2001; Royce, 2007). Ensuring that the balance between commercial and social goal achievement is maintained is thus important for ensuring that the supply of labour is sufficient to keep the social enterprise functioning. Second, the exploitation of opportunities to provide training services and employment skills to the long-term unemployed means that social enterprise human resource strategies comprise both skills-based and beneficiary recruitment. Social enterprises that adopt Intermediate Labour Market (ILM) and Worker Integration Social Enterprises (WISE) business models need therefore to respond to the needs of both categories of employee as well as, in some cases, the needs of volunteers (Smith et al., 2013). Finally, the cultural differences between commercial and nonprofit organizations impact on employee remuneration and compensation packages (Wilson & Post, 2013) which in turn shape the attractiveness of employment opportunities.

Employee and Volunteer Recruitment

The rapid growth in the population of social enterprises preceded the design and implementation of training and educational programmes for social enterprise leaders, volunteers and trustees. The inevitable employee skills gap (Salamon, Sokolowski & List, 2003) increased competition for the small pool of qualified and skilled staff. Volunteers comprise 43% of the global social economy workforce and are an important human resource for filling short-term and temporary skills gaps (Salamon et al., 2003).

For example, the social enterprise Liberation Nuts was originally established as a charity but the commercial exploitation of market opportunities to supply nuts and seeds to manufacturers and retailers meant that the charity's legal form was inappropriate (Mason & Doherty, 2016). During the period of initial growth Liberation Nuts struggled to achieve the balance between social and commercial skills. Despite much consumer demand for the organization's products, the management team's lack of marketing skills and failure to build commercial relationships with distributors impacted negatively on product availability. The sustainability of Liberation Nuts was later assured when the balance between commercial and social skills was achieved. In a second example, in a study of microfinance organizations in South America, the recruitment of employees and trustees with commercial and social skills was also instrumental to achieving sustainability (Battilana & Dorado, 2010).

Employee and Volunteer Motivation

Further, social enterprise leaders perform a critical role in motivating employees, volunteers and trustees (Young, 2006) to invest extra effort to help the organization achieve commercial and social success. The intrinsic rewards from working for a social enterprise are thus important for maintaining a committed and enthusiastic cohort of employees and unremunerated volunteers and trustees (Gennard & Judge, 2005). The recent trend for employees from the private sector to 'downshift' to more intrinsically rewarding work in the social economy has also increased the supply of skilled labour (Mason & Doherty, 2016). More cautiously, since volunteers are not contractually obliged to comply with organizational and managerial demands, they are at liberty to withdraw their labour, for example if they disapprove of the strategic direction pursued by the social enterprise (Royce, 2007).

Governance

Social enterprise dual mission means that board members are simultaneously exposed to institutional pressures to achieve financial sustainability, generate social value and build and maintain close relationships with a range of stakeholder groups (Mason & Doherty, 2016). Battilana and Lee (2014) propose that effective social enterprise governance plays a central role in ensuring accountability to all the organization's stakeholders and resisting pressures to drift towards either social or commercial objectives at the expense of the other. Drawing on paradox theory, Lüscher and Lewis (2008) proposed that social leaders and trustees who adopted paradoxical thinking at board level and faced up to the tensions were better able to adapt and integrate the competing social and commercial demands.

SOCIAL ENTERPRISE FINANCE

The sustainability of social enterprise business models is directly influenced by the establishment of a viable and effective financial architecture to maintain liquidity. Earned income strategies provide a flow of unrestricted funds which confers the maximum organizational autonomy over strategic and investment decisions. However, few social enterprises generate 100% of their income from trading and most rely on a mix of philanthropy, grants and income from trading. Social enterprise access to debt and loan finance has been noted to be restricted, and in response the institutionalization of the new field of social finance has recently begun to take root. For example, venture philanthropy (Scarlata & Alemany, 2010), social venture capital (Silby, 1997), community investment funds (Nicholls, 2010) and patient capital (Westall & Chalkley, 2007) are novel investment vehicles that provide funds for organizations to create social value and societal change. At the same time, new techniques to measure social performance have been developed to ensure that social enterprises are accountable to stakeholders (Emerson, 2003; Nicholls, 2010; Flockhart, 2005).

Social Investment

The social investment market comprises both the supply of and demand for funds. Social investors provide packages of finance, philanthropy and business support to organizations committed to social and environmental value creation (Doherty et al., 2014). The investment packages range from low-cost loans for social purpose organizations to innovative forms of philanthropic venture capital (Scarlata & Alemany, 2010). The diversity of packages reflects different investor expectations of financial, social and environmental returns on investment (Nicholls, 2010). In this new field of activity support programmes have been instituted to help prepare social enterprises build capacity in preparation for receiving social finance (Mason & Kwok, 2010) and measure social value creation (Flockhart, 2005; Nicholls, 2009). Social networks are also important for resource acquisition (Coleman, 1988) and social enterprise business models leverage strong social entrepreneur networks to access

funds to support social value creation. For example, relationships with philanthropists, social activists, campaigners, customers and volunteers can all be leveraged for commercial opportunities and access to low-cost capital (Peredo & Chrisman, 2006; Smith-Hunter, 2008; Mair & Martí, 2006).

Share Capital

The choice of legal structure impacts on permissible sources of funds. In the UK, for example, capital from the issuance of shares can be raised by three social enterprise organizational forms: community interest companies limited by share; industrial and provident societies trading as cooperatives; and benefit corporations (BCorps). In the US only the BCorp permits the issuance of share capital for social value creation. Registered charities, for example the low-profit limited liability company (L3C), are prohibited from issuing share capital; however, preferential tax and fiscal arrangements reduce the financial liabilities of this organizational form.

The new company and cooperative legal forms for social enterprise that have been established in the UK, US and Europe are indicative of policy recognition that social enterprises are a category of organizations that is distinguishable from commercial and nonprofits (Katz & Page, 2013). The new legal forms confer legitimacy on the simultaneous pursuit of commercial and social goals. However, despite the new legal forms for social entrepreneurship, opportunity exploitation continues to be challenging and fraught with tension (Battilana & Lee, 2014).

CONCLUSION

This chapter has reviewed the literature on social entrepreneurship opportunity identification and exploitation. It has drawn on a wide range of conceptual and empirical studies. Although a substantial body of work exists, there are many fruitful opportunities for further research to expand theory and knowledge of social entrepreneurship. In this final section of the chapter we outline ten research suggestions to keep social entrepreneurship research moving forward, making it theoretically interesting and of practical relevance.

1   Social entrepreneurship and opportunity identification: The few studies that have explored social entrepreneurship opportunity recognition and construction have opened up an important field for future social entrepreneurship research (Lehner & Kansikas, 2012; Short, Ketchen, Shook & Ireland, 2010; Short, Moss & Lumpkin, 2010). The current focus on defining and describing social opportunities can be complemented by analysis of how social entrepreneurs discover or create opportunities for social value creation. The role of social entrepreneur emotions (Goss, 2005) such as passion (Thorgren & Omorede, 2015) have begun to shed light on motivations for social entrepreneurship and further studies might examine other positive as well as negative emotions on the motivation for opportunity recognition and construction.

2   Social enterprise hybrids: Scholars have begun to investigate how tensions between commercial and social goal achievement are managed (Pache & Santos, 2013). Studies have found that successful strategies for managing conflicting demands include separation and integration (Alter, 2006) and selective coupling (Pache & Santos, 2013). However, our understanding of contextual influences on managing commercial and social goals is incomplete. Research that explored the mechanisms for achieving multiple goals when there is resource scarcity and competition would advance knowledge on the determinants and efficacy of strategies for goal alignment, and goal conflict resolution.

3   Social entrepreneurship identity and identification: Identity comprises the stable and enduring characteristics of an organization (Whetton, 2006). For social enterprise hybrids the pursuit of commercial and social goals means that crafting a stable identity comprises managing the tensions between two potentially conflicting goals and logics (Pache & Santos, 2013).

Research that analysed how identity differences can be employed to achieve competitive advantage would be valuable for the range of organizations that strive to reconcile competing goals, values and practices.

4   Social entrepreneurship and resource acquisition: Analysis of the resources for social entrepreneurship has been dominated by the challenges of acquiring and managing financial and human resources and few studies have considered how physical assets, such as business premises (Hart, 2001) and emotional assets (Hopkins & Rippon, 2015), are leveraged to generate revenue and create social value. Yet asset-based income generation has the potential to generate a reliable flow of income as well as security for debt and loan finance. Research that identified the determinants of successful asset-based social business models would have implications for both theory and practice.

5   Business models for social entrepreneurship: The intractability of global economic and social problems has led to policy and practitioner interest in supporting social enterprise growth and social business model replication (Bloom & Smith, 2010). The review by Battilana and Lee (2014) of social enterprise hybrids found that social enterprises in the US are less successful than commercial organizations when seeking to acquire start-up capital, register as a legal form and enter new markets. These constraints in turn hinder their prospects of long-term survival. Strategic management processes are noted to be underdeveloped in social enterprise (Paton, 2003), yet effective strategic management is fundamental to competitive advantage. Research to identify the determinants and components of successful social enterprise business models would advance both management theory and practice. Configurational analytical techniques such as Qualitative Comparative Analysis (QCA) (Ragin, 1987) would enable the effective combinations of practices to be identified and replicated by other organizations.

6   Social enterprise failure: As the volume of social entrepreneurship research accumulates, more attention to how social enterprises mature, decline and cease trading would assist both theory development and practice (Tracey et al., 2011). There is also potential to examine how social entrepreneurs learn from failure and draw

on past experience of both success and failure in future opportunity identification and exploitation. How the detritus from failed social enterprises is reused to either restart or found new social enterprises would advance theories of effectuation and bricolage.

7 Institutional influences on social entrepreneurship opportunity identification and exploitation: The opportunities for social value creation and the business models implemented by social enterprise managers will reflect changing consumer norms and attitudes. As culture shapes such preferences there is a need for international comparative research that explores national and international institutional influences on social entrepreneurship. Much research has focussed on health and employment sectors and there is a growing interest in environmental services and cultural industries. There is evidence that the role of the state in supporting social entrepreneurship may be decreasing in Europe and increasing in places such as East Asia (Defourny & Shin-Yang, 2011) and Africa (Thorgren & Omorede, 2015). Future research can also explore the changing nature of the role of the state and the evolution of social enterprise business models.

8 Social enterprise marketing: Social entrepreneurship marketing research has to date relied on theories developed from the study of commercial organizations (Doherty et al., 2009). The principles of relationship, ethical and social marketing appear to align with the defining characteristics of social entrepreneurship. However, the absence of the profit maximization motive and the centrality of stakeholder relationships have the potential to lead to new models of marketing which are oriented towards social and environmental value creation.

9 Information technology and social entrepreneurship: Advances in information technology and social media have been embraced by some, but not all, social enterprises. Community-based social enterprises have been successful in securing technological connectivity for rural communities, the disabled and the housebound. In addition, advances in technology have revolutionized health care, and payments systems in developing countries (van Rensburg, Veldsman & Jenkins, 2008). Further, innovations in social media have improved communications. How might information technology be employed to empower communities and release entrepre-

neurial potential to further economic and social development?

10 Social entrepreneurship and reinventing capitalism for the 21st century: Despite the benefits that capitalism has undoubtedly brought to people in many countries, the impacts of global economic crises, intractable social problems and climate change persist. Social entrepreneurship has been talked about as a mechanism for changing capitalism for the 21st century (Amin et al., 2002; Mort et al., 2003; Sen, 2007). What role might social entrepreneurship play in changing the central tenets of free market economics to reflect the needs of a world in which poverty, disease and environmental damage persist?

REFERENCES

Alter, K. (2006). *Social Enterprise Typology*. Virtue Ventures, Washington, DC.

Alvord, S.H., Brown, L.D., & Letts, C.W. (2004). Social entrepreneurship and societal transformation: An exploratory study. *The Journal of Applied Behavioural Science*, 40, 260–282.

Amin, A. (2009). Extraordinarily ordinary: Working in the social economy. *Social Enterprise Journal*, 5, 30–49.

Amin, A., Cameron, A., & Hudson, R. (2002). *Placing the Social Economy*. Routledge, London.

Andreason, R.A. (2006). *Social Marketing in the 21st Century*. Sage, London.

Austin, J.E., Stevenson, H., & Wei-Skillern, J. (2006). Social entrepreneurship and commercial entrepreneurship: Same, different, or both? *Entrepreneurship Theory and Practice*, 30, 1–22.

Bacq S., & Janssen, F. (2011). The multiple faces of social entrepreneurship: A review of definitional issues based on geographical and thematic criteria. *Entrepreneurship & Regional Development*, 5–6, 373–403.

Barney, J.B. (1991). Firm resources and sustained competitive advantage. *Journal of Management*, 17, 99–120.

Battilana, J., & Dorado, S. (2010). Building sustainable hybrid organizations: The case of commercial microfinance organizations. *Academy of Management Journal*, 53, 1419–1440.

Battilana, J., & Lee, M. (2014). Advancing research on hybrid organizing. Insights from the study of social enterprises. *The Academy of Management Annals,* 8, 397–441.

Blackburn, R., & Ram, M. (2006). Fix or fixation? The contribution and limitation of entrepreneurship and small firms to combating social exclusion. *Entrepreneurship and Regional Development,* 18, 73–89.

Bloom, P., & Smith, B. (2010). Identifying the drivers of social entrepreneurial impact: Theoretical development and an exploratory empirical test of SCALERS. *Journal of Social Entrepreneurship,* 1, 126–145.

Borzaga, C., & Defourny, J. (2004). *The Emergence of Social Enterprise.* Routledge, London.

Borzaga, C., & Solari, L. (2001). Management challenges for social enterprises. In C. Borzaga and J. Defourny (Eds), *The Emergence of Social Enterprise,* 333–349, Routledge, London.

Boschee, J. (1995). Social entrepreneurship. *Across the Board,* 32, 20–25.

Bradach, J. (2003). Going to scale: The challenge of replicating social programs. *Stanford Social Innovation Review,* 1, 19–25.

Chandra, Y., & Wong, L. (Eds) (2016). *Social Entrepreneurship in the Greater China Region: Policy and Cases.* Routledge, New York.

Chell, E. (2007). Social enterprise and entrepreneurship: Towards a convergent theory of the entrepreneurial process. *International Small Business Journal,* 25, 5–26.

Chew, C., & Lyon, F. (2012). Social enterprise and innovation in third sector organizations. In S. Osborne and L. Browne (Eds), *Handbook of Innovation and Change in Public Sector Services.* Routledge, London.

Coleman, J.S. (1988). Social capital in the creation of human capital. *American Journal of Sociology,* 94, 95–120.

Corner, P.D., & Ho, M. (2010). How opportunities develop in social entrepreneurship. *Entrepreneurship Theory and Practice,* 34, 635–659.

Courtney, R. (2002). *Strategic Management for Voluntary Nonprofit Organisations.* Routledge, New York.

Craig, G., Taylor, M., Wilkinson, M., & Bloor, K. (2002). *Contract or Trust: The Role of Compact in Local Governance.* The Policy Press, Bristol, UK.

Dacin, M.T., Dacin, P.A., & Tracey, P. (2011). Social entrepreneurship: Critique and future directions. *Organization Science,* 22, 1203–1213.

Darby, L., & Jenkins, H. (2006). Applying sustainability indicators to the social enterprise business model. *International Journal of Social Economics,* 33, 411–431.

Dart, R. (2004). The legitimacy of social enterprise. *Nonprofit Management and Leadership,* 14, 411–424.

Davies, I.A. (2009). Alliances and networks: Creating success in the UK fair trade market. *Journal of Business Ethics,* 86, 109–126.

Davies, I.A., Doherty, B., & Knox, S. (2010). The rise and fall of a fair trade pioneer. The story of Cafédirect. *Journal of Business Ethics,* 92, 127–147.

Dees, J.G. (1998). Enterprising nonprofits. *Harvard Business Review,* 76, 55–67.

Dees, J.G., Anderson, B.B., & Wei-Skillern, J. (2004). Pathways to social impact: Strategies for scaling out successful social innovations. *Stanford Social Innovation Review,* 2, 24–32.

Defourny, J., & Borzaga, C. (2001). *Social Enterprise and the Third Sector.* Routledge, London.

Defourny, J., & Nyssens, M. (2006). *Defining Social Enterprise: Social Enterprise at the Crossroads of Market, Public Policies and Civil Society.* Routledge, Taylor and Francis Group, London and New York.

Defourny, J., & Shin-Yang, K. (2011). Emerging models of social enterprise in eastern Asia: A cross country analysis. *Social Enterprise Journal,* 7, 86–111.

Di Domenico, M.L., Haugh, H., & Tracey, P. (2010). Social bricolage: Theorising social value creation in social enterprises. *Entrepreneurship Theory and Practice,* 43, 681–703.

Di Domenico, M.L., Tracey, P., & Haugh, H. (2009). The dialectic of social exchange: Theorizing corporate-social enterprise collaboration. *Organization Studies,* 30, 887–907.

Doherty, B. (2009). Resource advantage theory and fair trade social enterprises. *Journal of Strategic Marketing,* 19, 357–380.

Doherty, B., Foster, G., Mason, C., Meehan, J., Rotheroe, N., & Royce, M. (2009). *Management for Social Enterprise.* Sage, London.

Doherty, B., Haugh, H., & Lyon, F. (2014). Social enterprises as hybrid organizations. A review and research agenda. *International Journal of Management Reviews*, 16, 417–436.

Drayton, B. (2005). Where the real power lies. *Alliance*, 10, 29–30.

DTI (2002). *Social Enterprise: A Strategy for Success*. Department of Trade and Industry, London.

Emerson, J. (2003). The blended value proposition: Integrating social and financial returns. *California Management Review*, 45, 35–51.

Evers, A. (2005). Mixed welfare systems and hybrid organizations: Changes in the governance and provision of social services. *International Journal of Public Administration*, 28, 737–748.

Evers, A. (1995). Part of the welfare mix: The third sector as an intermediate area. *Voluntas*, 6, 159–182.

Evers, A., Laville, J.L., Borzaga, C., Defourny, J., Lewis, J., Nyssens, M., & Pestoff, V. (2004). Defining the third sector in Europe. In A. Evers and J.L. Laville (Eds), *The Third Sector in Europe*. Edward Elgar, London.

Fisher, G. (2012). Effectuation, causation, and bricolage: A behavioral comparison of emerging theories in entrepreneurship research. *Entrepreneurship Theory and Practice*, 36, 1019–1051.

Flockhart, A. (2005). The use of social return on investment (SROI) and investment ready tools (IRT) to bridge the financial credibility gap. *Social Enterprise Journal*, 1, 29–42.

Foster, W., & Bradach, J. (2005). Should non-profits seek profits? *Harvard Business Review*, 83, 92–100.

Fowler, A. (2000). NGDOs as a moment in history: Beyond aid to social entrepreneurship or civic innovation? *Third World Quarterly*, 21, 637–654.

Gennard, J., & Judge, G. (2005). *Employee Relations*. Chartered Institute of Personnel Development, London.

Giddens, A. (1984). *The Constitution of Society. Outline of a Theory of Structuration*. University of California Press, Berkeley, CA.

Golding, K. (2009). Fair trade's dual aspect: The communications challenge of fair trade marketing. *Journal of Macromarketing*, 29, 160–171.

Golding, K., & Peattie, K. (2005). In search of a Golden Blend: Perspectives on the marketing of fair trade coffee. *Sustainable Development*, 13, 154–165.

Goss, D. (2005). Entrepreneurship and 'the social': Towards a deference-emotion theory. *Human Relations*, 58, 617–636.

Grassl, W. (2011). Business models of social enterprise: A design approach to hybridity. *Journal of Entrepreneurship Perspectives*, 1, 37–60.

Gupta, A.K., Sinha, R., Koradia, D., & Patel, R. (2003). Mobilizing grassroots' technological innovations and traditional knowledge, values and institutions: Articulating social and ethical capital. *Futures*, 35, 975–987.

Hardy, C., Phillips, N., & Lawrence, T. (2003). Resources, knowledge and influence: The organisational effects of interorganisational collaboration. *Journal of Management Studies*, 40, 321–347.

Harker, M.J., & Eagan, J. (2006). The past, present and future of relationship marketing. *Journal of Marketing Management*, 22, 215–242.

Hart, L. (2001). *Developing an Asset Base*. Development Trusts Association, London.

Haugh, H. (2007). Community-led social venture creation. *Entrepreneurship Theory and Practice*, 31, 161–182.

Haugh, H. (2005). A research agenda for social entrepreneurship. *Social Enterprise Journal*, 1, 1–12.

Haugh, H., & Kitson, M. (2007). The third way and the third sector: New Labour's economic policy and the social economy. *Cambridge Journal of Economics*, 31, 973–994.

Hockerts, K. (2006). Entrepreneurial opportunity in social purpose ventures. In J. Mair, J. Robinson, & K. Hockerts (Eds), *Social Entrepreneurship*, Palgrave Macmillan, Basingstoke.

Hopkins, T., & Rippon, T. (2015). *Head, Hands and Heart: Asset Based Approaches to Healthcare*. The Health Foundation, London.

Hudson, M. (2002). *Managing Without Profit*. Second Edition. Penguin, London.

ICA (International Co-operative Alliance) (1994). Draft statement on cooperative identity. Geneva, ICA.

Jenner, P. (2016). Social enterprise sustainability revisited: An international comparison. *Social Enterprise Journal*, 12, 42–60.

Jones, D., Keogh, B., & O'Leary, H. (2007). *Developing the social economy: Critical review of the literature*. Social Enterprise Institute (SEI), Edinburgh.

Katz, R., & Page, A. (2013). Sustainable business. *Emory Law Journal*, 62, 851–884.

Kerlin, J. (2010). A comparative analysis of the global emergence of social enterprise. *Voluntas*, 21, 162–179.

Kerlin, J. (2006). Social enterprise in the United States and Europe: Understanding and learning from the differences. *Voluntas*, 17, 246–262.

Landsberg, B.E. (2004). The nonprofit paradox: For-profit business models in the third sector. *International Journal for Not-For-Profit Law*, 6, http://www.icnl.org/research/journal/vol6iss2/special_7.htm

Laville, J.L., & Nyssens, M. (2001). Then social enterprise: Towards a theoretical socio-economic approach. In C. Borzaga and J. Defourny (Eds), *The Emergence of Social Enterprise*, 312–332, Routledge, London.

Leadbeater, C. (1998). *The Rise of the Social Entrepreneur*. Demos, London.

Lehner, O., & Kansikas, J. (2012). Opportunity recognition in social entrepreneurship: A thematic analysis. *Journal of Entrepreneurship*, 21, 25–58.

Littlewood, D., & Holt, D. (2015). Social entrepreneurship in South Africa: Exploring the influence of environment. *Business & Society*. http://journals.sagepub.com/doi/pdf/10.1177/0007650315613293

Luke, B., & Chu, V. (2013). Social enterprise versus social entrepeneurship: An examination of the 'why' and 'how' of social change. *International Small Business Journal*, 31, 764–784.

Lumpkin, G.T., Moss, T.W., Gras, D.M., Kato, S., & Amezcua, A.S. (2013). Entrepreneurial processes in social contexts: How are they different, if at all? *Small Business Economics*, 40, 761–783.

Lüscher, L., & Lewis, M. (2008). Organizational change and managerial sensemaking: Working through paradox. *Academy of Management Journal*, 51, 221–240.

Lyon, F. (2012). Social innovation, co-operation and competition: Interorganizational relations for social enterprises in the delivery of public services. In A. Nicholls and A. Murdock (Eds), *Social Innovation*, Palgrave MacMillan, London.

Lyon, F., & Fernandez, H. (2012). Strategies for scaling up social enterprise: Lessons from early years providers. *Social Enterprise Journal*, 8, 63–77.

Lyon, F., & Sepulveda, L. (2009). Mapping social enterprises: Past approaches, challenges and future directions. *Social Enterprise Journal*, 5, 83–94.

Lyon, F., Teasdale, S., & Baldock, R. (2010). Approaches to measuring the scale of the social enterprise sector. Third Sector Research Centre, Working Briefing Paper 43, Birmingham.

Mair, J., & Martí, I. (2009). Entrepreneurship in and around institutional voids: A case study from Bangladesh. *Journal of Business Venturing*, 24, 419–435.

Mair, J., & Martí, I. (2006). Social entrepreneurship research: A source of explanation, prediction, and delight. *Journal of World Business*, 41, 36–44.

Mair, J., Seelos, C., & Borwankar, A. (2005). Social entrepreneurial initiatives within the sustainable development landscape. *International Journal of Entrepreneurship Education*, 2, 431–452.

Mann, S. (2008). Analysing fair trade in economic terms. *The Journal of Socio-Economics*, 37, 2034–2042.

Mason, C., & Doherty, B. (2016). A fair trade-off? Paradoxes in the governance of fair-trade social enterprise. *Journal of Business Ethics*, 3, 451–469.

Mason, C.M., & Kwok, J. (2010). Investment readiness programmes and access to finance: A critical review of design issues. *Local Economy*, 25, 269–292.

Ménard, C. (2004). The economics of hybrid organizations. *Journal of Institutional and Theoretical Economics*, 160, 345–376.

Moizer, J., & Tracey, P. (2010). Strategy making in social enterprise: The role of resource allocation and its effects on organisational sustainability. *Systems Research and Behavioural Science*, 27, 252–266.

Mort, G.S., Weerawardena, J., & Carnegie, K. (2003). Social entrepreneurship: Towards conceptualization. *International Journal of Nonprofit and Voluntary Sector Marketing*, 8, 76–89.

Munoz, S.A., & Tindsley, S. (2008). Selling to the public sector – prospects and problems for social enterprise in the UK. *The Journal of Corporate Citizenship*, 32, 43–62.

Murphy, E.P., Laczniak, R.G., & Wood, G. (2007). An ethical basis for relationship marketing: A virtue ethics perspective. *European Journal of Marketing*, 41, 37–57.

Murphy, P.J., & Coombes, S.M. (2008). A model of social entrepreneurial discovery. *Journal of Business Ethics*, 87, 325–336.

Nega, B., & Schneider, G. (2014). NGOs, the state and development in Africa. *Review of Social Economy*, 72, 485–503.

Nicholls, A. (2010). The institutionalization of social investment: The interplay of investment logics and investor rationalities. *Journal of Social Entrepreneurship*, 1, 70–100.

Nicholls, A. (2009). 'We do good things don't we?' Blended value accounting in social entrepreneurship. *Accounting, Organizations and Society*, 34, 755–769.

Nicholls, A. (2006). *Social Entrepreneurship: New Models of Sustainable Social Change*. Oxford University Press, Oxford.

Nicholls, A., & Cho, A.H. (2006). Social entrepreneurship: The structuration of a field. In A. Nicholls (Ed.), *Social Entrepreneurship: New Models of Sustainable Social Change*, 99–118, Oxford University Press, Oxford.

Nicholls, A., & Opal, C. (2005). *Fair Trade: Market-Driven Ethical Consumption*. Sage, London.

Osborne, S., Chew, C., & McLaughlin, K. (2008). The once and future pioneers? The innovative capacity of voluntary organisations and the provision of public services: A longitudinal approach. *Public Management Review*, 10, 51–70.

Pache, A.C., & Santos, F. (2013). Inside the hybrid organization: Selective coupling as a response to competing institutional logics. *Academy of Management Journal*, 56, 972–1001.

Parkinson, C., & Howorth, C. (2008). The language of social entrepreneurs. *Entrepreneurship & Regional Development*, 20, 285–309.

Paton, R. (2003). *Managing and Measuring Social Enterprise*. Sage, London.

Peattie, K., & Morley, A. (2008). Social enterprises: Diversity and dynamics, contexts and contributions. A research monograph. ESRC & BRASS Research Centre.

Peredo, A.M., & Chrisman, J.J. (2006). Towards a theory of community-based enterprise. *Academy of Management Review*, 31, 309–328.

Peredo, A.M., & McLean, M. (2006). Social entrepreneurship: A critical review of the concept. *Journal of World Business*, 41, 56–65.

Phills, J., Deiglmeir, K., & Miller, D. (2008). Rediscovering social innovation. *Stanford Social Innovation Review*, 6, 34–43.

Ragin, C.C. (1987). *The Comparative Method. Moving beyond Qualitative and Quantitative Strategies*. University of California Press, Berkeley, CA.

Ridley-Duff, R., & Bull, M. (2015). *Understanding Social Enterprise: Theory and Practice*. Sage, London.

Rivera-Santos, M., Holt, D., Littlewood, D., & Kolk, A. (2015). Social entrepreneurship in sub-Saharan Africa. *Academy of Management Perspectives*, 29, 72–91.

Royce, M. (2007). Using human resource management tools to support social enterprise: Emerging themes from the sector. *Social Enterprise Journal*, 3, 10–19.

Salamon, M.L., Sokolowski, W.S., & List, R. (2003). Global civil society: An overview. The John Hopkins Comparative Study for the Nonprofit sector project. Institute for Policy Studies, Centre for Civil Society, Baltimore, USA.

Santos, P. (2012). A positive theory of social entrepreneurship. *Journal of World Business*, 111, 335–351.

Sarasvathy, S.D. (2001). Causation and effectuation: Toward a theoretical shift from economic inevitability to entrepreneurial contingency. *Academy of Management Review*, 25, 243–263.

Scarlata, M., & Alemany, L. (2010). Deal structuring in philanthropic venture capital investments: Financing instruments, valuation and covenants. *Journal of Business Ethics*, 95, 121–145.

Seelos, C., & Mair, J. (2005). Social entrepreneurship: Creating new business models to serve the poor. *Business Horizons*, 48, 241–246.

Sen, P. (2007). Ashoka's big idea: Transforming the world through social entrepreneurship. *Futures*, 39, 534–553.

Sepulveda, L. (2015). Social Enterprise – A new phenomenon in the field of economic and social welfare? *Social Policy & Administration*, 49, 842–861.

Sepulveda, L., Syrett, S., & Calvo, S. (2013). Social enterprise and ethnic minorities: Exploring the consequences of the evolving British policy agenda. *Environment and Planning C (Government and Policy)*, 31, 633–648.

Sharir, M., & Learner, M. (2006). Gauging the success of social ventures initiated by individual social entrepreneurs. *Journal of World Business*, 41, 6–20.

Shaw, E., & Carter, S. (2007). Social entrepreneurship: Theoretical antecedents and empirical analysis of entrepreneurial processes and outcomes. *Journal of Small Business and Enterprise Development*, 14, 418–434.

Short, J., Ketchen, D., Shook, C., & Ireland, R. (2010). The concept of opportunity in entrepreneurship research: Past accomplishments and future challenges. *Journal of Management*, 36, 40–65.

Short, J., Moss, T., & Lumpkin, T. (2010). Research in social entrepreneurship: Past contributions and future opportunities. *Strategic Entrepreneurship Journal*, 3, 161–194.

Silby, D. (1997). Social venture capital: Sowing the seeds of a sustainable future. *Journal of Investing*, 6, 108–111.

Smith, S.R., & Lipsky, M. (1993). *Nonprofits for Hire: The Welfare State in the Age of Contracting*. Harvard University Press, Cambridge, MA.

Smith, W.K., Besharov, M.L., Wessels, A.K., & Chertok, M. (2012). A paradoxical leadership model for social entrepreneurs: Challenges, leadership skills and pedagogical tools for managing social and commercial demands. *Academy of Management Learning and Education*, 11, 463–478.

Smith, W.K, Gonin, M., & Besharov, M.L. (2013). Managing social-business tensions: A review and research agenda. *Business Ethics Quarterly*, 23, 407–442.

Smith-Hunter, A.E. (2008). Toward a multidimensional model of social entrepreneurship: Definitions, clarifications, and theoretical perspectives. *Journal of Business and Economics Research*, 6, 93–110.

Spear, R. (2008). European perspectives on social enterprise. In P. Hunter (Ed.), *Social Enterprise for Public Service: How does the Third Sector Deliver?* The Smith Institute, London.

Speckbacher, G. (2003). The economics of performance management in nonprofit organizations. *Nonprofit Management and Leadership*, 13, 267–281.

Strong, C. (1997). The problems of translating fair trade principles into consumer purchase behaviour. *Marketing Intelligence and Planning*, 15, 32–37.

Svandberg, J., Gumley, A., & Wilson, A. (2010). How do social firms contribute to recovery from mental illness? A qualitative study. *Clinical Psychology and Psychotherapy*, 17, 482–496.

Teasdale, S. (2012). What's in a name? Making sense of social enterprise discourses. *Public Policy and Administration*, 27, 99–119.

Thompson, J., Alvy, G., & Lees, A. (2000). Social entrepreneurship. A new look at people and potential. *Management Decision*, 38, 328–338.

Thorgren, S., & Omorede, A. (2015). Passionate leaders in social entrepreneurship: Exploring an African context. *Business & Society*. http://journals.sagepub.com/doi/pdf/10.1177/0007650315612070

Tickell, A., & Peck, J. (2013). Making global rules: Globalization or neoliberalization? In J. Peck and H. Yeung (Eds), *Remaking the Global Economy*, 163–181, Sage: London.

Tiffen, P. (2002). A chocolate-coated case for alternative international business models. *Development in Practice*, 12, 383–397.

Tracey, P., & Jarvis, O. (2007). Toward a theory of social venture franchising. *Entrepreneurship Theory & Practice*, 31, 667–685.

Tracey, P., Phillips, N., & Jarvis, O. (2011). Bridging institutional entrepreneurship and the creation of new organizational forms: A multilevel model. *Organization Science*, 22, 60–80.

Vaghely, I.P., & Julien, P.-A. (2010). Are opportunities recognized or constructed? An information perspective on entrepreneurial opportunity identification. *Journal of Business Venturing*, 25, 73–86.

van Rensburg, J., Veldsman, A., & Jenkins, M. (2008). From technologists to social enterprise developers: Our journey as 'ICT for development' practitioners in Southern

Africa. *Information Technology for Development*, 14, 76–89.

Wagner-Tsukamoto, S. (2007). Moral agency, profits and the firm: Economic revisions to the Friedman theorem. *Journal of Business Ethics*, 70, 209–220.

Weerawardena, J., & Mort, G.S. (2006). Investigating social entrepreneurship: A multidimensional model. *Journal of World Business*, 41, 21–35.

Westall, A. (2001). *Value-led, Market Driven*. Institute for Public Policy Research, London.

Westall, A., & Chalkley, D. (2007). *Social Enterprise Futures*. The Smith Institute, London.

Whetton, D.A. (2006). Albert and Whetten revisited: Strengthening the concept of organisational identity. *Journal of Management Inquiry*, 15, 216–234.

Wilson, F., & Post, J.E. (2013). Business models for people, planet (and profit): Exploring the phenomena of social business, a market-based approach to social value creation. *Small Business Economics*, 40, 715–737.

Young, D.R. (2006). Social enterprise in community and economic development in the USA: Theory, corporate form and purpose. *International Journal of Entrepreneurship and Innovation*, 6, 241–255.

Yunus, M., Moingeon, B., & Lehmann-Ortega, L. (2010). Building social business models: Lessons from the Grameen experience. *Long Range Planning*, 43, 308–325.

Zahra, S.A., Gedajlovic, E., Neubaum, D.O., & Shulman, J.M. (2009). A typology of social entrepreneurs: Motives, search processes and ethical challenges. *Journal of Business Venturing*, 24, 519–532.

PART II

Entrepreneurship and Small Business Management and Organization

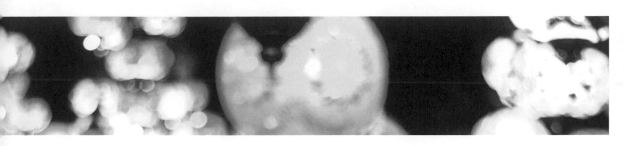

9

Entrepreneurial Strategy: A Contingency Review and Outlook for Future Research

Christian Lechner and Abeer Pervaiz

INTRODUCTION

Why do some firms survive and others not? Why do some firms develop faster than others? And why are some firms more profitable than others? These questions are at the heart of strategy and strategy research tries to understand the varying degree of competitiveness of firms. Generally, the outcome variable in strategy research, and thus also research on entrepreneurial strategy, is some form of organizational performance.

This chapter reviews selected literature on entrepreneurship and strategy. We outline what entrepreneurial strategy means, taking into consideration the concept of strategic entrepreneurship that began emerging around the year 2000, the ideas of corporate entrepreneurship developed in the 1990s, and the idea of an entrepreneurial orientation as a strategic process variable, which was initially proposed in the 1980s. While a firm's competitiveness is achieved through effectiveness, efficiency, and innovation, and requires

a relevant and not easily reversible commitment of people, energy, and resources, i.e. a strategy, it remains unclear why we need to study entrepreneurial strategy specifically. We elaborate why and how different understandings of entrepreneurial strategy are tied to different firm contexts and theoretical underpinnings, acknowledging thereby that an entrepreneurial firm is not a small big firm.

The field of strategic entrepreneurship tries to combine elements of opportunity seeking from the entrepreneurship side and elements of advantage seeking from the strategy side in order to better understand firm performance. We argue that the context and the starting situation of firms of different sizes and age differ widely and thus require different views of strategy making in organizations. Therefore, strategy in the entrepreneurial and SME context needs to be conceptualized differently from that in the corporate context. While the idea of strategic entrepreneurship is linked to ideas of an entrepreneurial mindset, or entrepreneurial behavior, and can be considered a part of corporate entrepreneurship, it is the context of entrepreneurial firms characterized by liability of newness and smallness that is the defining element of a strategy for entrepreneurial firms. We distinguish therefore between entrepreneurial strategy related to new venture performance and strategic entrepreneurship related to the performance of established firms.

Drawing on previous research, we discuss three key issues in this chapter. First, by focusing on the context of liability of newness and smallness (and thus resource scarcity), we define entrepreneurial strategy in a context-specific manner and discuss the transferability of this concept to different contexts. Second, we frame the literature on entrepreneurial behavior in strategy-making within the underlying theories, highlighting how the underlying theories might be contingent on organizational context. Third, based on the tensions and gaps in this research, we develop directions for future research.

BACKGROUND: ENTREPRENEURSHIP AND STRATEGIC MANAGEMENT

Shane and Venkataraman (2000, p. 218) defined the field of entrepreneurship as 'the scholarly examination of how, by whom, and with what effects opportunities to create future goods and services are discovered, evaluated, and exploited', including the study of 'the sources of opportunities; the processes of discovery, evaluation, and exploitation of opportunities; and the set of individuals who discover, evaluate, and exploit them'. Widely accepted, it basically extended (following animated discussions in the entrepreneurship community) the entrepreneurship concept to all forms of firms.

The intersection of entrepreneurship and management was introduced by Stevenson and Jarillo (1990) based on earlier work (Stevenson, 1983) that distinguished between entrepreneurial and administrative management style. Meyer, Neck, & Meeks (2002) conceive the interface of entrepreneurship and strategy management around four fields (see Table 9.1): entrepreneurship (creation side) and strategic management (performance side), and SMEs and large corporations. Generally, entrepreneurship is seen to be more about creation while strategic management places emphasis on having competitive advantage; entrepreneurship examines small businesses while strategic management is more concerned with large businesses (Meyer et al., 2002).

Before we discuss these intersections, we give an overview of the concepts of entrepreneurship and strategic management as they give rise to a variety of concepts that are somehow related, such as strategic entrepreneurship, corporate venturing, and entrepreneurial orientation. As a starting point, we will frame the concept of entrepreneurship and describe its distinctive characteristics.

Entrepreneurship from a Life Cycle Perspective of Firms

Overall, entrepreneurship can be divided into at least two essential stages using a life cycle

Table 9.1 Entrepreneurship and strategic management

	Entrepreneurship (Creation)	*Strategic Management (Performance)*
Large Corporation	F1: Corporate entrepreneurship, innovation in large firms, new product development in large firms	F2: The 'classical' field of strategic management
SMEs	F3: New venture creation, new product development in small firms, innovation in small firms, opportunity recognition	F4: New venture performance and strategy, small business performance and strategy, growth, small business strategic factors and resources

Source: Adapted from Meyer et al., 2002

perspective. The first stage is the entrepreneurial process that leads to the entrepreneurial event, that is, the creation of a new firm to capitalize on an opportunity (Gartner, 1989; Gartner, Bird, & Starr, 1992); it is the process of opportunity identification, recognition, the analysis of the opportunity, and the planning (that is manifested in the business plan) and setting up of the new firm (Kuratko & Hodgetts, 1998). It is about getting the product to the market and attaining the first customers, that is, placing the firm in a real-life context (see Table 9.1, quadrant F3). The main outcome variable of this first stage is the entrepreneurial event; issues of competitiveness are generally not yet addressed. Therefore, it is not the focus of this chapter. The second stage is about nourishing the growth of the entrepreneurial firm that is situated in the specific context of resource poverty, and deals with specific growth strategies and their implementation (see Table 9.1, F4). Compared with established firms, entrepreneurial firms face many challenges that have an impact on the probability of survival and growth. Entrepreneurial firms are characterized by liability of newness (Stinchcombe, 1965). New firms face two innovation problems: the firm itself is an innovation and the products or services it offers usually are too. The probability of failure increases further because of the lack of effective management practices and the lack of track records with outside buyers and suppliers (Stinchcombe, 1965). Liability of newness is a central hypothesis in entrepreneurship research and means that a new firm lacks legitimacy in the economic world, characterized, at best, by lack of trust and, at worst, by not being known at all.

Liability of smallness is the second defining characteristic (Baum, 1996). Entrepreneurial firms lack resources. Having only few resources, the company faces particular challenges to establish itself in the market place; lacking legitimacy, access to resources is not a trivial issue. Liability of smallness (Baum, 1996) and liability of

newness (Carroll, 1983; Freeman, Glenn, & Michael, 1983; Stinchcombe, 1965) are the context for the new venture; they determine the main strategic issues of the start-up. Research on entrepreneurial strategy needs to address these particular challenges. Before defining the concept of entrepreneurial strategy more precisely, it is essential to understand the concept of strategy in general. The next section explains strategy and strategic management in more detail.

Strategy and Strategic Management

'Strategy is about winning' (Grant, 1998, p. 3). For management, strategy is the art of gaining and sustaining a competitive advantage. If a firm has a competitive advantage, it receives above-average returns (Porter, 1980). Strategy is about a relevant commitment of resources and is not easily reversible (Grant, 1998). In business, strategy is about choices under uncertainty (Sutton, 1998): uncertainty about the future, the environment, and the competitive actions of other firms in order to improve the competitive position of the firm (Grant, 1998; Johnson & Scholes, 1997; Sutton, 1998).

The field of strategic management is clearly oriented towards the large integrated enterprise (Chandler, 1962, 1990; Penrose, 1959), and this type of firm is the norm in textbooks (Drucker, 1988). Chandler's strategy definition (Chandler, 1962) is an expression of this mindset: the firm is the locus for resource allocation and coordination assuming both the possession of the resources and the means to possess them. Other writings also confirm this view (Ansoff, 1979; Porter, 1987; Schendel & Hofer, 1979; Sutton 1998). Even Schumpeter's 'entrepreneur' (Schumpeter, 1980) was the innovative driver within the large firm (Burns, 1968). The business model of the large, often multinational integrated firm as an extreme pole of how to organize the business system (through vertical integration of the value chain) is the traditional model of economic theory (Chandler, 1962; Coase, 1937; Jarillo, 1993; Williamson, 1975; Witte, 1991). The development of this type of organization has been regarded as incremental, fueled by direct investment (Penrose, 1959), or mergers and acquisitions (Lorenzoni & Ornati, 1988).

Both entrepreneurship and strategy are concerned with the survival and development of firms requiring competitiveness. The next section therefore sheds some light on the competitiveness of firms as a common denominator for entrepreneurship and strategy.

The Competitiveness of Firms as a Common Theme in Entrepreneurship and Strategy

The notion of growth is central to entrepreneurship. To some extent, entrepreneurial strategy is the art of growing without resources (or with very little resources). Growth, however, is not possible without strategy. Thus, it appears that entrepreneurial firms need to assure firm survival (as a minimum goal) and then realize substantial growth. In any case, two questions emerge: Why do some firms survive while others don't? And why do some firms perform better than others?

A basic condition for a firm's performance is competitiveness. Competitiveness can be understood as the productivity with which human and other resources are used by a firm, region, or nation (Porter, 2005). Three components, as drivers of productivity, determine the competitiveness of a firm: effectiveness, efficiency, and innovativeness. Effectiveness means that a firm is able to deliver a desired output (Jarillo, 1993). Efficiency means that a company is able to perform the same activities better than its competitors (Porter, 1996). Innovation can drive both effectiveness and efficiency. To be competitive, a firm needs to achieve both effectiveness and efficiency, but effectiveness and efficiency are not sufficient to achieve a competitive advantage (Porter, 1996). A firm gains a competitive advantage by being unique in fulfilling the three determinants (effectiveness, efficiency, innovativeness) leading to differential firm performance. The competitiveness of a firm depends on the resource base of a firm (Amit & Schoemaker, 1993; Barney, 1991, 1996; Conner, 1991; Mahoney & Pandian, 1992; Penrose, 1959; Peteraf, 1993; Wernerfelt, 1984). It defines the performance potential on the business unit level in isolation of all other factors that might influence firm performance (Peteraf & Barney, 2003).

Firms are, however, not islands. They are embedded in larger socio-economic systems through relationships with other firms, through their location in a specific geographical area (Richardson, 1972), and through their 'membership' in industries (Porter, 1980; Rumelt, 1984). The competitiveness of firms cannot be fully understood if the firm's embeddedness in larger socio-economic systems is ignored (Lorenzoni, 1992). Apart from firm-level effects, a variety of factors exist that can drive firm-level performance (Meyer, 1991).

The question of 'Why do some firms perform better than others?' or 'Why do some firms survive while others don't?' is thus complex. For matters of simplicity, we can distinguish between three levels of effects on firm performance (see Lechner, 2000):

1 Firm-level effects
2 Firm-constellation effects
3 Regional- or national-level effects

Firm-level effects are industry effects, business strategy effects, and corporate effects (Bowman & Helfat, 2001; McGahan & Porter, 1997; Rumelt, 1984). Firm-constellation effects can be summarized under the relational view (Dyer & Singh, 1998), and they include positive effects that firms can achieve through relationships with other firms, for instance, through joint ventures, alliances, co-opetition, networks, etc. (Meyer, 1991). Finally, regional- or national-level effects are effects that stem from a firm's embeddedness in even larger socio-economic systems such as a firm's ecosystem, regions, or nations through, for example, beneficial national innovation systems (Dodgson, Gann, & Salter, 2005; Porter, 1990).

While competitiveness is a common denominator for strategy research for entrepreneurial and established firms, the distinctiveness of the two firm types leads to different forms of strategy. These differences are important as they suggest that the concepts might not be applied to a differing context. We can conclude that the entrepreneurial venture (and therefore its management) is a distinct form and is characterized by liability of newness, resource poverty, and liability of adolescence. The next section distinguishes between different variations of strategy and entrepreneurship in order to lay the ground for future research challenges.

VARIATIONS OF STRATEGY AND ENTREPRENEURSHIP: DEFINITIONS OF CONCEPTS

The different foci of strategic management and entrepreneurship and the distinct firm dimensions (large vs. small firms) lead to four main intersections (as shown in Table 9.1). From these intersections, we can define various concepts that have emerged in the field of entrepreneurship.

Corporate Entrepreneurship (F1)

The evolution of corporate entrepreneurship came into existence when managers and management scholars identified how the process of entrepreneurship might be introduced within an established organization (Corbett, Covin, O'Connor, & Tucci, 2013) with the objective of achieving sustainable competitive advantage, especially through continuous innovation (Covin & Slevin, 2002). The concept of corporate entrepreneurship has

always been rather ambiguous since most scholars use a variety of terms to define the entrepreneurial efforts (see Rensburg, 2013) of individuals working within an existing organization. Such terms include 'corporate entrepreneurship (Burgelman, 1983; Zahra, 1993), corporate venturing (Biggadike, 1979), intrepreneuring (Pinchot, 1985), internal corporate entrepreneurship (Jones & Butler, 1992), internal entrepreneurship (Schollhammer, 1982; Vesper, 1984), strategic renewal (Guth & Ginsberg, 1990) and venturing (Hornsby, Naffziger, Kuratko, & Montagno, 1993)' (Sharma & Chrisman, 1999, p. 13). Based on a review of the concept of corporate entrepreneurship from the 1980s till the mid 1990s (Burgelman, 1983; Chung & Gibbons, 1997; Covin & Slevin, 1991; Guth & Ginsberg, 1990; Schendel, 1990; Spann, Adams, & Wortman, 1988; Vesper, 1984; Zahra, 1993, 1995, 1996), Sharma and Chrisman (1999) defined corporate entrepreneurship as follows:

> *Corporate entrepreneurship* (F1) 'is the process whereby an individual or a group of individuals, in association with an existing organization, create a new organization or instigate renewal or innovation within that organization' (Sharma and Chrisman, 1999, p. 18).

In the corporate entrepreneurship domain, the distinction between corporate venturing and strategic renewal added more clarity (Corbett et al., 2013). They are two distinct phenomena: corporate venturing, which refers to 'the birth of new businesses within existing organizations' (Guth & Ginsberg, 1990, p. 5) and strategic renewal, which refers to 'the transformation of organizations through renewal of the key ideas on which they are built' (Guth and Ginsberg, 1990, p. 5).

Corporate Venturing (F1 and F2)

Corporate venturing is related to the idea that innovation changes a firm's product offerings and/or leads to entry into new markets.

Entry into a new market can be achieved by establishing a new organizational unit or within the existing structures of the firm. Considering that diversification is understood as offering new products to new markets (Ansoff, 1957), the concept of corporate venturing is closely related to the strategy of diversification.

> **Corporate venturing** *(F1 and F2) 'refers to corporate entrepreneurial efforts that lead to the creation of new business organizations within the corporate organization' (Sharma and Chrisman, 1999, p. 19).*

Strategic Entrepreneurship (F1)

Strategic entrepreneurship is an element of corporate entrepreneurship. Morris, Kuratko, and Covin (2011) and Phan, Wright, Ucbasaran and Tan (2009) proposed that corporate entrepreneurship is best understood by two factors: corporate venturing on the one side, and strategic entrepreneurship on the other. In essence, both corporate venturing and strategic entrepreneurship are supposed to inform corporate management of how to make organizations more entrepreneurial. Hitt, Ireland, Camp, and Sexton (2001, p. 2) propose that Strategic entrepreneurship is like strategic management with an opportunity focus (Hitt et al., 2001). Ireland, Hitt, Camp, and Sexton (2001) claim that, in order for firms to create maximum wealth, entrepreneurial and strategic actions need to be integrated.

> **Strategic entrepreneurship** *(F1) 'is the integration of entrepreneurial (i.e. opportunity-seeking actions) and strategic (i.e. advantage-seeking actions) perspectives to design and implement entrepreneurial strategies that create wealth' (Hitt et al., 2001, p. 481).*

According to the strategic entrepreneurship perspective, changes in the firm's environment create uncertainty, but also opportunities (Hitt et al., 2001). Strategic entrepreneurship embraces (see Companys & McMullen, 2007, p. 301) innovation as a driver of wealth creation (Kirzner, 1997;

Schumpeter, 1934) and competitive advantage (Ahuja & Katila, 2004), and combines it with the identification and exploitation of opportunities (Hitt et al., 2001). Entrepreneurship and strategic actions are perceived as being complementary to one another and, if combined, can create greatest wealth (Hitt et al., 2001). Firms need to find a balance between 'opportunity-seeking behaviors of "entrepreneurship" and the advantage-seeking behaviors associated with "strategic management"' (Hitt, Ireland, Sirmon, & Trahms, 2011). This combined perspective of entrepreneurship and strategic management expresses itself through an entrepreneurial mindset, entrepreneurial culture, and leadership, managing organizational resources in a strategic manner, applying creativity, and developing innovation (Ireland, Hitt, & Sirmon, 2003).

Strategic entrepreneurship has shifted entrepreneurship strategy strongly in the corporate domain (from F4 to F2). This has partially led to a conceptual confusion that might dissolve the distinctiveness of the two domains of strategy and entrepreneurship (Rensburg, 2013). While being criticized (Rensburg, 2013), for instance, for lacking robustness (Kyrgidou & Hughes, 2010), strategic entrepreneurship appears to have emerged as a growing topic of research (Klein, Barney, & Foss, 2012).

Entrepreneurial Orientation (F1)

Strategic entrepreneurship deals with the creation of competitive advantage through the identification of new opportunities (Ireland et al., 2003). Entrepreneurial orientation (EO) is understood as the strategy-making processes, structures, and behaviors of firms characterized by innovativeness, proactiveness, risk-taking, competitive aggressiveness, and autonomy, facilitating the pursuit of opportunities (Lumpkin, Cogliser, & Schneider, 2009; Lumpkin & Dess, 1996).

Entrepreneurial Orientation (F1) 'refers to the processes, practices, and decision-making activities that lead to new entry' as characterized by one or more of the following dimensions: 'a propensity to act autonomously, a willingness to innovate and take risks, and a tendency to be aggressive toward competitors and proactive relative to marketplace opportunities' (Lumpkin & Dess, 1996, pp. 136, 137).

In general, research indicates a positive impact of EO on firm performance, but associated analyses suggest that the EO–performance relationship is mediated or moderated by diverse variables (Messersmith & Wales, 2011; Rauch, Lumpkin, Wiklund, & Frese, 2009; Wales, Gupta, & Mousa, 2011). To some extent, the long-standing literature on EO captures the sort of entrepreneurial mindset claimed by strategic entrepreneurship (Hitt et al., 2001) and translated into firm behavior.

Entrepreneurial Strategy or New Venture Strategy (F4)

Entrepreneurial ventures are characterized by a series of liabilities (newness, resource poverty, adolescence) and occupy the initial phases of a firm's life cycle. The focus on new ventures and their subsequent development in a context of liabilities of newness and smallness remains a major line of entrepreneurship research (Shane & Venkataraman, 2000). Because of the specific characteristics of entrepreneurial firms, entrepreneurial strategies are distinct. Entrepreneurial strategies are thus a plan of action for young and small firms to enter markets and survive and grow (until the firms become established). Entrepreneurial strategy and new venture strategy can be treated as equals.

Entrepreneurial strategy or new venture strategy is a plan of action (emerging or developed) that comprises 'all the functions, activities, and actions associated with the perceiving of opportunities and the creation of organizations to pursue them' (Bygrave & Hofer, 1991, p. 14) in order to realize substantial growth despite the resources currently controlled.

The definitions and concepts have been described to create clarity and familiarity with the different concepts existing within the literature. The following section will discuss the relationship between entrepreneurial strategy and strategic entrepreneurship.

THE RELATIONSHIP BETWEEN ENTREPRENEURIAL STRATEGY AND STRATEGIC ENTREPRENEURSHIP: WHO INFORMS WHO?

We conceive entrepreneurial strategies as those series of strategic actions that allow firms characterized by liabilities of newness and smallness to enter markets and to survive and thrive. As the entrepreneurship concept has been extended to all forms of organizations and as different relationships have been established between entrepreneurship and strategy, the question arises of who informs who. The idea of cross-fertilization of the fields of strategy and entrepreneurship (Sandberg, 1992) is relevant for understanding the state of the art and future avenues of research. We could imagine a series of cross-influences and feedback loops that would benefit the two fields separately and fuel a potential shared field of strategy and entrepreneurship (see Table 9.1).

A first flow of influence could go from the (slightly more) established field of strategic management towards early entrepreneurship research (influence from F2 to F4). Indeed, pioneers in entrepreneurship (such as Day, 1992; Schendel & Hofer, 1979) initially related and borrowed concepts from the fellow young field of strategic management and adapted them for entrepreneurship research (such as Sandberg & Hofer, 1987). By applying strategic management thinking, it could be partially shown that the strategic fit of the opportunity and the company's resources and capabilities drives venture performance (Chandler & Hanks, 1994) and that the opportunity is largely dependent on market attractiveness (Chandler & Hanks, 1994; Sandberg & Hofer, 1987). Several studies in various industries confirmed the influence of industrial structure on the firm's growth and the choice of strategy (Chandler & Hanks, 1994; Covin, Prescott, & Slevin, 1990; McCann, 1991; Roure & Maidique, 1986; Siegel, Siegel, & Macmillan, 1993). Generally, the young field of entrepreneurship borrowed extensively from other disciplines (Plaschka & Welsch, 1990; Vesper, 1987) without developing its own conceptual framework (Shane & Venkataraman, 2000).

Subsequently, strategy scholars became more and more interested in the entrepreneurship phenomenon (such as Alvarez & Barney, 2004; Covin & Slevin, 1989; Hitt et al., 2001; Lumpkin & Dess, 1995). So did entrepreneurship research inform strategic management and thus strategic entrepreneurship (influence from F4 to F2)? Meyer et al. (2002) reviewed the literature from 1980 to 2000 and saw trends of strategic management research making inroads into entrepreneurship journals but not vice versa. The creation of the *Strategic Entrepreneurship Journal* in 2007 may be seen as an attempt to combine entrepreneurship and strategic management in a more balanced way. A review of articles since the inception of the journal (but also including articles from other journals in the time period) suggests, however, that the main topics of strategic entrepreneurship largely ignore SMEs. The main focus of the roughly 20 empirical articles are large corporations (such as Burgelman & Grove, 2007), public organizations (such as Luke & Verreynne, 2006), academic institutions (Patzelt & Shepherd, 2009), and corporate venture capital (Dew, Sarasathy, Read, & Wiltbank, 2009); others have leveraged classical theories and linked them to strategic entrepreneurship, such as agency theory (Audretsch, Lehamnn, & Plummer, 2009) or corporate governance (Phan et al., 2009). Research on family firms (see Lumpkin, Steier, & Wright, 2011) is mainly dedicated to well-established firms (with an average age of at least 30 years). While a focus on large firms is dominant (F4), research using the concept of strategic entrepreneurship with an SME perspective is rare (for example Shirokova, Vega, & Sokolova, 2013.

It appears that strategic entrepreneurship focused selectively on some characteristics of entrepreneurial firms, such as outcome variables of some form of organizational imprinting (innovation, flexibility, speed), behavioral or attitude outcomes (entrepreneurial mindset, EO), or context of opportunities (uncertainty), and tried to move some of these concepts from the individual level of the entrepreneur or, more precisely, from the entrepreneurial team level to the corporate level. This selective approach neglected, first, the specific situation of new ventures (the liabilities), as well as other important defining elements such as survival rates of start-ups, opportunity costs, and the essential link between entrepreneurial strategy and the financing of new ventures (Smith & Smith, 2000). The specific research in entrepreneurship on how established companies can become, for instance, more flexible, act faster, be more alert to opportunities, organize opportunity exploitation in the face of uncertainty etc has basically not informed strategic entrepreneurship. On the other hand, there is 'by definition' a certain tendency to transfer findings from strategic entrepreneurship to all types of firms, including new venturing, neglecting the specific characteristics of those firms. In the following comparative analysis of interrelated concepts, we will see how some of these incompatibilities create tensions but also opportunities for future research.

Entrepreneurial Strategy vs. Strategic Entrepreneurship: The Question of Context

The link between entrepreneurship and strategic management seems to be relatively logical as both commonly investigate firm performance as an outcome variable (see Meyer et al., 2002;

Summer, Bettis, Duhaime, Grant, Hambrick, Snow, & Zeithaml, 1990). As Venkatraman and Ramanujam state: 'For the strategy researcher, the option to move away from defining (and measuring) performance of effectiveness is not a viable one. This is because performance improvement is at the heart of strategic management' (1986, p. 801). Even if opinions have been raised that a single-minded focus on firm performance in entrepreneurship might be too narrow and should be broadened to wealth generation in general (Hitt et al., 2001; Venkataraman, 1997), the performance, and particularly the exceptional performance of new firms (for example in terms of growth), is an essential topic in entrepreneurship research (Meyer et al., 2002) since it will eventually have an impact on the wealth of societies (Baumol, 1996; Birch, 1987; Sen, 1999).

Claims about changing economic conditions have led to the general call for all firms to become more entrepreneurial and for strategic entrepreneurship (Hitt et al., 2001). It is evident that there is an interaction between entrepreneurial strategy and strategic entrepreneurship. Basic strategy tools might be adapted to serve as tools for entrepreneurial strategy (from F2 to F4), even if some do not address the primary preoccupations of entrepreneurial firms: how to gain legitimacy, how to enter new markets, how to initially position products or services in order to gain first customers, how to accelerate break-even or assure additional financing until the break-even, etc.

More interesting is how elements of entrepreneurial strategy can be transferred to established corporations (from F4 to F1). If corporate management can learn something from entrepreneurial firms, then the context of liabilities of newness and smallness has two important implications for strategic management. First, established firms would be able to enter emerging markets more efficiently if new activities were set up with reduced resources. However, to what extent do size differences matter? Research on disruptive technologies appears to suggest that the performance criteria make it difficult for large firms to enter

emerging markets the way entrepreneurial firms do (Christensen, 1997). Second, the way entrepreneurial firms overcome liability of newness might inform corporate management on how to develop strategies of unrelated diversification more efficiently and effectively. Indeed, unrelated diversification means that firms enter new markets where existing firm resources (including reputation) are of little use. It appears, however, that these two topics have not made inroads into strategic management research. There appear to be limits to generalization. On one hand, new entry is for start-ups the reason of existence and strategic actions will determine the survival of the firm; it involves high levels of risk-taking. On the other hand, diversification in itself can be seen as a risk diversification strategy, questioning thus the notion of entrepreneurial risk-taking in corporate venturing (Smith & Smith, 2000).

Strategic Entrepreneurship vs. Entrepreneurial Strategy: The Question of Process

Strategic entrepreneurship is supposed to combine the advantage-seeking orientation of strategic management and the opportunity-seeking orientation of entrepreneurship (Hitt & Ireland, 2002). In this sense, the processes of new entry strategy and competitive strategy are unified in one set of strategies but to what extent can strategic entrepreneurship be applied to new ventures? The resource-based view claims that a competitive advantage is based on differentials in resources that a firm possesses. It is about firm-specific resources that lead to firm-specific competitive advantage. Penrose (1959) formulated that the growth of firms depends on the resource base of the firm and the efficient and effective management of these resources by able managers. If we accept, however, the view that new ventures are characterized by liability of newness and smallness, then we arrive at a growth paradox: if we put resource-poor new ventures and relatively inefficient start-up management into Penrose's growth formula, then there would be no fast-growing entrepreneurial firms. It is this growth paradox that can drive efforts in research: how do entrepreneurial strategies (that differ from resource-based advantage-seeking behavior) enable firms to enter into new markets? And, how do growth processes of entrepreneurial firms unfold over time?

From a process perspective, we can develop new insights. If we accept the fundamental starting conditions of new ventures, then strategic entrepreneurship would be a sequential, not concurrent concept for entrepreneurial strategy. New ventures do not have the resource base necessary to find and exploit an opportunity through new market entry and at the same time to seek to establish a competitive advantage. New ventures will first need to develop a series of actions for entering into a new market given its liabilities. Only after the implementation of an effective entry strategy can firms seek to establish a competitive advantage. We can thus think of an entrepreneurial strategy process as having three phases: 1) the entry strategy (F4); 2) a transitional phase between entry strategy and competitive strategy; and 3) the competitive strategy of the firm (F1 & F2). In all three areas vast research opportunities still exist.

Competitive Strategy vs. Entrepreneurial Orientation: The Question of Content and Process

Entrepreneurial orientation (EO) is understood as the strategy-making processes, structures, and behaviors of firms characterized by innovativeness, proactiveness, risk-taking, competitive aggressiveness, and autonomy, facilitating the pursuit of opportunities (Lumpkin & Dess, 1996; Lumpkin et al., 2009). Competitive strategy explores how a firm operates (Schendel & Hofer, 1979) in order to increase firm performance (Porter, 1980). Both EO and competitive strategy are strategic business unit-level concepts (Covin & Lumpkin, 2011), the former being the strategy-making process and the latter describing the content. In this sense, competitive strategy adds content to EO and channels it. In other words, EO would not be sufficient for firm performance without a competitive strategy (Ireland et al., 2003).

Both EO and competitive strategies have their own inner logic; they are distinct theoretical constructs (Lumpkin & Dess, 1996) and their conceptual separation should help to advance the understanding of the transformation of EO into firm performance (Wales et al., 2011). Lechner and Gudmundsson (2014) investigated the relationship between EO and competitive strategy and came to the conclusion that, while both types of competitive strategies (differentiation and cost leadership) had a positive impact on firm strategy, the different dimensions of EO had opposite influences on firm strategy, that is, EO as a unilateral concept did not have unambiguous performance effects if channeled through strategy.

Macro-Level vs. Micro-Level: The Question of Level of Analysis

Most strategy concepts in entrepreneurship, be it corporate entrepreneurship, strategic entrepreneurship, or entrepreneurial orientation, have a macro-perspective: they consider the general entrepreneurial behavior of firms but do not reach down to the action level (Shepherd, 2015). Lumpkin and Dess (1996, p. 136) noted that the 'essential act of entrepreneurship is new entry. New entry can be accomplished by entering new or established markets with new or existing goods or services. New entry is the act of launching a new venture, either by a start-up firm, through an existing firm, or via internal corporate venturing'. They go on to say that EO is a behavior that favors new entry. However, research on the actions through which new ventures (in particular) enter into markets is thin. Literature from a micro-perspective on effective actions can be traced back to the beginning of the entrepreneurship field. Drucker (1985) names a few entrepreneurial strategies that entrepreneurial firms can partially apply. The most comprehensive work on entrepreneurial action is most likely Karl Vesper's book on new venture strategies (1980, and the revised version in 1990); this book contains anecdotal evidence and develops a theory, i.e. it could be qualified as a series of hypotheses that would all need to be tested. Bhide (2000) addresses a few questions on how resource-deprived entrepreneurial firms enter into the market but the evidence is rather descriptive. In the end, we know very little about the actions or series of actions entrepreneurial firms take to establish a position in the market in order to survive and grow.

Entrepreneurial Strategy as Research on Outliers: The Question of Methodology

Entrepreneurial strategies deal with firms that have at least some growth potential. Fast-growing firms are only a fraction of all firms and, of these, only a small fraction are financed by venture capital firms (Lechner, 2000). The subject of entrepreneurship, i.e. entrepreneurial firms are exceptions to the rule: they are outliers. One long-held and seldom questioned assumption in (strategic) management research is that normal (i.e. Gaussian) distributions characterize variables of interest for both theory and practice (Meyer, Gaba, & Colwell, 2005). In this respect, scores on variables such as firm resources (e.g. intellectual capital, or superior processes) and firm performance and outcomes (e.g. competitive advantage, or growth) are assumed to aggregate around the mean, which is stable and meaningful, suggesting that observations can be accurately characterized by some combination of the mean and standard deviation (Crawford, Aguinis, Lichtenstein, Davidsson, & McKelvey, 2015). Today, however, there is various evidence that

data follow a Power Law Distribution (PLD) (Boisot & McKelvey, 2010). PLDs are highly skewed, with 'long tails' that identify extreme events, i.e. data that are outside the range of the normal curve (Crawford, McKelvey, & Lichtenstein, 2014). In this respect, Andriani and McKelvey (2009) list 101 examples of power law phenomena in management, providing evidence that data are mostly not distributed normally. Crawford et al. (2015) showed that 48 out of 49 variables playing a central role in resource-, cognition-, action-, and environment-based entrepreneurship theories exhibit highly skewed distributions.

Against this background, it is astounding that researchers today still treat the Gaussian curve as a given fact for social data distribution. The assumption of Gaussian normality leads to serious issues for theory development if empirical data follow a PLD (Delbridge & Fiss, 2013).

FUTURE RESEARCH

Entrepreneurial Strategy: Back to the Future

The field of entrepreneurship has made important progress in understanding why individuals create firms or not (the question of nascent entrepreneurship), and how the behavior of entrepreneurs shapes the emerging organization. As firm competitiveness is influenced by firm-level effects, firm-constellation effects, and regional- or national-level effects, we can also conclude that research has made important advances in understanding firm-constellation effects. While entrepreneurship scholars had initially studied firm-level effects, most progress has been made concerning firm-constellation and regional-level effects with an accumulated body of research that stresses different streams and approaches. For instance, the strategic use of external resources through inter-firm networks in many different industries

(Jarillo, 1989; Lorenzoni & Ornati, 1988; Powell, 1987) that are often embedded in regional clusters (Lechner & Dowling, 2000) has been shown to be an effective means for overcoming these liabilities. In this context, inter-firm networks are considered an important model of organization development (Powell, 1987, 1990; Richardson, 1972) to enable an entrepreneurial firm to grow and survive (Freel, 2000; Jarillo, 1988; Johannisson, 1998; Lorenzoni & Ornati, 1988; Nohria, 1992; Venkataraman & Van de Ven, 1998). The accumulated research body has advanced our knowledge on how entrepreneurial firms can effectively use inter-firm networks to overcome liabilities and to enable growth.

Finally, the impact of entrepreneurship on the economy has been demonstrated and increased the interest of policymakers but also of corporate management in the phenomenon of entrepreneurship: the policymaker asks how entrepreneurship can be increased while corporate management ponders what could be learned from entrepreneurship or how more entrepreneurship could be installed in all forms of firms. More and more research efforts in a widened field of entrepreneurship have become inclusive for all forms of organizations; however, while interesting as a development of a new paradigm, we need to ask ourselves if we already know enough about entrepreneurial strategy understood as the sequence of actions (constituting thus a developed or emerging plan of actions), i.e. a strategy on how to enter markets and to survive and grow given the context of entrepreneurial firms? Our critical assessment suggests that relevant strategic questions of entrepreneurship have not been explored sufficiently beyond the early work of the pioneers in the field. It appears that our understanding of new venture entry strategies and new venture competitive strategies, especially on the micro-level, is not exhaustive.

From the relation between entrepreneurial strategies and strategic entrepreneurship, new streams for future research are emerging. First, a stream dedicated to entrepreneurial strategies, which we could consider a return to the origins of entrepreneurship research; second, a stream investigating the transfer from entrepreneurial strategies to strategic entrepreneurship; it would lead to entrepreneurship research that informs corporate management; third, research taking into account the quest for exceptional outcomes as the result of entrepreneurship (radical innovation, exponential growth, etc.); it would require alternative methodological approaches. In the following, we will highlight future research opportunities in these areas.

Future Research Dedicated to Entrepreneurial Strategies (F4)

Opportunities for future research on entrepreneurial strategy lie in adopting a micro-perspective, i.e. research that reaches down to the action level and analyzes how new ventures enter markets or create new markets despite liabilities of smallness and newness under uncertainty. First, strategic entrepreneurship states that uncertainty is an advantage of entrepreneurial firms. We argue that uncertainty is a problem for all forms of organizations but we do not know enough about what entrepreneurial firms are doing to deal with this problem. More in-depth and longitudinal case studies might help to uncover other mechanisms of how entrepreneurial firms deal with uncertainty and act upon opportunities. While lean start-up techniques appear to be a means for dealing with the problem of uncertainty, there is little research that has shown the effects of these behaviors. Other emerging practitioner concepts (minimum viable product, rapid customer validation techniques, etc.) are still largely ignored in research. This might be because they are theoretically fuzzy or less elegant and thus riskier to study. For instance, we could not find yet a single study that investigated whether early prototyping or the use of minimum viable products have positive impacts on firm development.

Second, market entry is a core issue in entrepreneurship. Given the lack of resources (liability of smallness) necessary to develop a (resource-based) competitive advantage, future research can explore how entrepreneurial firms enter new markets and survive before they thrive. A relatively forgotten strategy concept in this regard is that of strategic groups (Hunt, 1972) and its application to new ventures. Understood 'as a group of firms within the same industry making similar decisions in key areas' (Porter, 1980, p. 129), they appear – despite unresolved conceptual framing issues (Leask & Parker, 2006) – an interesting rediscovery for entrepreneurial entry strategies. Research could address the question of how the creation of a new strategic group by a firm entering a new market influences its survival probability and growth potential. Given resource constraints, resource attraction remains a major topic in entrepreneurship research: this partially covers questions of entrepreneurial financing, but also resource access strategies through inter-firm networking, or the recombination of available factors in order to go on within constraints, as in the case of bricolage (Baker & Nelson, 2005) but also bootstrapping (Brush, 2008). Bricolage and bootstrapping are still underdeveloped areas in entrepreneurship research.

Third, liability of newness poses additional challenges for market entry. Research on signaling effects (Stuart, Hoang, & Hybels, 1999) and inter-firm networks (Lechner & Dowling, 2003) could identify some factors that enable firms to gain legitimacy with customers and investors. However, research on market entry could further explore how firms gain legitimacy with other stakeholders and through other legitimacy strategies.

Fourth, related research questions concern the firm development from disadvantaged positions: if entrepreneurial firms enter new markets by offering special conditions to customers or by occupying niches considered unattractive by other firms (Bhide, 2000), then how can firms move out of these unfavorable positions? In this sense, the back-transfer of the concept of strategic entrepreneurship towards entrepreneurial strategies opens new avenues for future research. If opportunity seeking and advantage seeking do not occur at the same time for entrepreneurial ventures, then a new field of studies investigating the transition phase from entry strategies to competitive strategy emerges. If firms enter markets in particular conditions, then the final competitive position of the firm will be different from its initial positioning. Research questions thus include the process of resource development while venturing (given the resource poverty of entrepreneurial firms) as a premise for later development of competitive advantage. This view can also enrich the existing body of research on learning by entrepreneurial teams. Since entrepreneurs often act in markets that are not well developed, the question of market creation arises under the severe constraints of entrepreneurial firms. Given that opportunities to enter are not always the most attractive ones, the move to more attractive opportunities would lead to a series of short-term strategic moves. This suggests that strategy making in entrepreneurial firms is about sequences of relatively short-term strategic actions rather than about long-term strategies. More investigation is needed into the patterns of strategy making and the sequences of differing strategies in the development of entrepreneurial firms that extend classical life cycle models (for example Greiner, 1972).

Fifth, entrepreneurial firms not only enter into existing markets but can also participate in the creation of new markets. Concerning market creation, a shift away from the single entrepreneur to a community of like-minded entrepreneurs might be also a promising road of inquiry. If industry emergence is community driven, then the question arises of how some entrepreneurial firms stand out in the crowd. A rediscovery of population ecology (Aldrich & Fiol, 1994; Hannan & Freeman, 1977) could be a promising road.

Future Research Dedicated to Strategic Entrepreneurship (F1 and F2)

We have highlighted how cross-fertilization between entrepreneurial strategy and strategic entrepreneurship can lead to future research; taking stock of the dedicated research on new ventures and the possible transfer of strategies (understood as a series of actions) in order to thrive in the difficult start-up context appears a promising direction. For instance, the idea of staged investments and option thinking can be intensified in research on corporate venturing. Generally, the field of strategic entrepreneurship could benefit from the integration of concepts from entrepreneurial finance, a sub-discipline that has made substantial progress in taking into account the specificities of new venture management. They include the insep-arability of investment decisions from the financing package decisions, the limited role of diversification for wealth creation, the importance of real options reasoning, exit strategies as a factor of new venture valuation, and the substantial role of information prob-lems (Smith & Smith, 2000). These substan-tial issues alone would create a series of inconsistencies with the idea of strategic entrepreneurship, one being, for example, the management of diversification from a strate-gic entrepreneurship perspective.

Strategic entrepreneurship embraces inno-vation as a core topic. Radical innovation and the development of new product categories can lead to the creation of new industries. New industry emergence surpasses, however, the boundaries of the individual firm. Similar to a community of entrepreneurs, the focus shifts from the individual firm to an enabling eco-system (Mason & Brown, 2013). In strat-egy, the focus in research mainly investigated the patterns of collaboration and competition in high-tech industries (Adner & Kapoor, 2010; Iansiti & Levien, 2004). Therefore, future research could relate strategic eco-systems to entrepreneurship and industry emergence.

Strategic entrepreneurship tries to combine opportunity- and advantage-seeking behav-ior; does this imply that the two behaviors need to be accomplished by the same actor? The long history of Google, Microsoft, and others in acquiring young firms might actu-ally suggest that it could be more attractive for large firms to leave entrepreneurship to the entrepreneurial firms and to pick up the winners later on instead of trying to play the entrepreneurship game. Similar arguments could be made for corporate venture capital. Future research could investigate if and how a separation of actors for the different behav-iors creates value.

In addition, opportunity orientation requires an entrepreneurial mindset and influences thus strategic posture and strategy processes. Research that combines strategy process with strategy content is still rare. In particular, concepts such as EO or, in a more restricted fashion, an entrepreneurial mindset appear to be incomplete, calling for more research on complementors (whether moderators or mediators). Future research could investigate, for instance, the different configurations of EO and their relationship to strategy and firm performance. While EO research has made substantial progress in analyzing the environ-mental factors that explain EO, more research is needed to investigate what constructs medi-ate EO (Wales et al., 2011).

Future Research Dedicated to Outliers

Research (Crawford et al., 2015) could show that means-based approaches in research may not only exclude the interesting phe-nomena but may also be questionable from a methodological point of view. In 'traditional' statistics, extreme events, which are outside the range of the normal curve, are 'mistakes' or outliers that need to be removed from the data sample. But, for strategy, these outliers are the interesting subjects since they find new solutions outside the norm, have high creativity, go new ways, or develop an idiosyncratic approach to a common problem (Andriani & McKelvey, 2009). To put it differently: if strategy is about understanding why some firms outperform others, then strategy research should dedicate more attention to studying outliers than variances close to the mean. For research on entrepreneurial strategy, this means that researchers need to reflect on different quantitative methods in order to study outliers. An alternative could be more and more rigorous, longitudinal qualitative research in entrepreneurship (Suddaby, Bruton, & Si, 2015) for studying outliers in entrepreneurship while at the same time avoiding survival bias, which frequently affects entrepreneurship research (Lechner & Gudmundsson, 2014).

Entrepreneurship deals a lot with those entrepreneurs 'who made it' and thus with the outliers of the general population of entrepreneurs. The study of outliers in entrepreneurship could draw from existing theory of star power effects in labor economics (Menger, 1999). From a strategy perspective, the research question is how minimal differences in initial endowments can lead to the nonproportional growth differences of entrepreneurial firms. Future research could, for instance, explore the strategic commonalities of the so-called unicorns (start-ups with a market valuation of more than 1 billion US dollars).

CONCLUSION

Entrepreneurship and strategic management research share a common denominator: the competitiveness of firms. While strategic management is dedicated to large firms, entrepreneurship is dedicated to new ventures (and thus temporary small firms). Therefore, it appears reasonable to distinguish between entrepreneurial strategies (focus on entrepreneurial firms characterized by liability of newness and smallness) and strategic entrepreneurship (focus on large

firms). In this chapter, we framed the concepts of strategic management and entrepreneurship and defined related concepts such as corporate entrepreneurship, corporate venturing, strategic entrepreneurship, entrepreneurial orientation, and entrepreneurial or new venture strategy.

When discussing the relationship between entrepreneurial strategy and strategic entrepreneurship, we proposed that cross-fertilization between the two concepts would be a fruitful road of inquiry since the distinction between entrepreneurial strategy and strategic entrepreneurship creates theoretical inconsistencies that can inform future research endeavors. One important topic is, for instance, the transition of small firms from entry to competitive strategy. Moreover, the phenomenon of outliers raised questions about research methodologies but also creates opportunities for future scientific inquiry. In conclusion, research on entrepreneurial strategies would benefit from going back to the basics (including studying the pioneers of the entrepreneurial strategies) while strategic entrepreneurship could benefit from integrating more the findings of entrepreneurial strategies for developing its own agenda.

REFERENCES

Adner, R. and Kapoor, R. (2010) 'Value creation in innovation ecosystems: How the structure of technological interdependence affects firm performance in new technology generations', *Strategic Management Journal*, 31(3): 306–333.

Ahuja, G. and Katila, R. (2004) 'Where do resources come from? The role of idiosyncratic situations', *Strategic Management Journal*, 25(8–9): 887–907.

Aldrich, H. and Fiol, M. (1994) 'Fools rush in? The institutional context of industry creation', *The Academy of Management Review*, 19(4): 645–670.

Alvarez, S. and Barney, J. (2004) 'Organizing rent generation and appropriation: Toward theory of the entrepreneurial firm', *Journal of Business Venturing*, 19(5): 621–635.

Amit, R. and Schoemaker, P. J. (1993) 'Strategic assets and organizational rent', *Strategic Management Journal*, 14(1): 33–46.

Andriani, P. and McKelvey, B. (2009) 'Perspective – From Gaussian to Paretian thinking: Causes and implications of power laws in organizations', *Organization Science*, 20(6): 1053–1071.

Ansoff, I. (1957) 'Strategies for diversification', *Harvard Business Review*, 35(5): 113–124.

Ansoff, I. (1979) 'The changing shape of the strategic problem', in D. Schendel and C. Hofer (eds), *Strategic Management: A New View of Business Policy and Planning*. Boston, MA: Little Brown and Co. pp. 37–44.

Audretsch, D. B., Lehmann, E. E. and Plummer, L. A. (2009) 'Agency and governance in strategic entrepreneurship', *Entrepreneurship Theory and Practice*, 33(1): 149–166.

Baker, T. and Nelson, R. E. (2005) 'Creating something from nothing: Resource construction through entrepreneurial bricolage', *Administrative Science Quarterly*, 50(3): 329–366.

Barney, J. (1991) 'Firm resources and sustained competitive advantage', *Journal of Management*, 17(1): 99–120.

Barney, J. (1996) 'The resource-based theory of the firm', *Organizational Science*, 7(5): 3–22.

Baum, J. A. C. (1996) 'Organizational ecology', in S. Clegg, C. Hardy and W. Nord (eds), *Handbook of Organization Studies*. London: Sage. pp. 77–114.

Baumol, W. (1996) 'Entrepreneurship: Productive, unproductive, and destructive', *Journal of Business Venturing*, 11(1): 3–22.

Biggadike, R. (1979) 'The risky business of diversification', *Harvard Business Review*, 57(3): 103–111.

Birch, D. (1987) *Job creation in America: How our smallest companies put the most people to work*. New York: Free Press.

Boisot, M. and McKelvey, B. (2010) 'Integrating modernist and postmodernist perspectives on organizations: A complexity science bridge', *Academy of Management Review*, 35(3): 415–433.

Bowman, H. E. and Helfat, E. C. (2001) 'Does corporate strategy matter?', *Strategic Management Journal*, 22(1): 1–23.

Brush, G. C. (2008) 'Pioneering strategies for entrepreneurial success', *Business Horizons*, 51(1): 21–27.

Burgelman, A. R. (1983) 'A process model of internal corporate venturing in the diversified major firm', *Administrative Science Quarterly*, 28(2): 223–244.

Burgelman, A. R. and Grove, A. S. (2007) 'Let chaos reign, then rein in chaos-repeatedly: Managing strategic dynamics for corporate longevity', *Strategic Management Journal*, 28(10): 965–979.

Burns, A. (1968) 'The nature and causes of business cycles', *International Encyclopedia of the Social Sciences*, 2: 226–245.

Bygrave, W. and Hofer, C. (1991) 'Theorizing about entrepreneurship', *Entrepreneurship Theory and Practice*, 16(2): 13–22.

Carroll, A. B. (1983) 'Corporate social responsibility: Will industry respond to cut-backs in social program funding?', *Vital Speeches of the Day*, 49(19): 604–608.

Chandler, A. D. (1962) *Strategy and structure: Chapters in the history of American industrial enterprise*. Cambridge, MA: MIT Press.

Chandler, A. D. (1990) *Strategy and structure: Chapters in the history of the industrial enterprise*. Cambridge, MA: MIT Press.

Chandler, G. N. and Hanks, S. H. (1994) 'Founder competence, the environment, and venture performance', *Entrepreneurship, Theory and Practice*, 18(3): 77–89.

Christensen, C. M. (1997) *The innovator's dilemma*. Boston, MA: Harvard Business School Press.

Chung, L. H. and Gibbons, P. T. (1997) 'Corporate entrepreneurship: The roles of ideology and social capital', *Group and Organization Management*, 22(1): 10–30.

Coase, R. (1937) 'The nature of the firm', *Economica*, 4(16): 386–405.

Companys, Y. E. and McMullen, J. S. (2007) 'Strategic entrepreneurs at work: The nature, discovery, and exploitation of entrepreneurial opportunities', *Small Business Economics*, 28(4): 301–322.

Conner, K. R. (1991) 'A historical comparison of resource-based theory and five schools of thought within industrial organization economics: Do we have a new theory of the firm?', *Journal of Management*, 17(1): 121–154.

Corbett, A., Covin, G. J., O'Connor, C. G. and Tucci, L. C. (2013) 'Corporate entrepreneurship: State-of-the-art research and a future research agenda', *Journal of Product Innovation Management*, 30(5): 812–820.

Covin, J. G. and Lumpkin, G. T. (2011) 'Entrepreneurial orientation theory and research: Reflections on a needed construct', *Entrepreneurship Theory and Practice*, 35(5): 855–872.

Covin, J. G. and Slevin, D. P. (1989) 'Strategic management of small firms in hostile and benign environments', *Strategic Management Journal*, 10(1): 75–87.

Covin, J. G. and Slevin, D. P. (1991) 'A conceptual model of entrepreneurship as firm behavior', *Entrepreneurship Theory and Practice*, 16(1): 7–25.

Covin, J. G. and Slevin, D. P. (2002) 'The entrepreneurial imperatives of strategic leadership', in M. A. Hitt, R. D. Ireland, S. M. Camp and D. L. Sexton (eds), *Strategic Entrepreneurship: Creating a New Mindset*. Oxford: Blackwell Publishers. pp. 309–327.

Covin, J. G., Prescott, J. E. and Slevin, D. P. (1990) 'The effects of technological sophistication on the strategic profiles, structure, and performance of firms', *Journal of Management Studies*, 27(5): 485–510.

Crawford, G. C., Aguinis, H., Lichtenstein, B., Davidsson, P. and McKelvey, B. (2015) 'Power law distributions in entrepreneurship: Implications for theory and research', *Journal of Business Venturing*, 30(5): 696–713.

Crawford, G. C., McKelvey, B. and Lichtenstein, B. (2014) 'The empirical reality of entrepreneurship: How power law distributed outcomes call for new theory and method', *Journal of Business Venturing Insights*, 1: 3–7.

Day, D. L. (1992) 'Research linkages between entrepreneurship and strategic management', in D. L. Sexton and J. D. Kasarda (eds), *The State of the Art of Entrepreneurship*. Boston: PWS-Kent.

Delbridge, R. and Fiss, P. C. (2013) 'Editors' comments: Styles of theorizing and the social organization of knowledge', *Academy of Management Review*, 38(3): 325–331.

Dew, N., Sarasathy, S., Read, S. and Wiltbank, R. (2009) 'Affordable loss: Behavioral economic aspects of the plunge decision', *Strategic Entrepreneurship Journal*, 3(2): 105–126.

Dodgson, M. J., Gann, D. and Salter, A. (2005) *Think, play, do: Innovation, technology, and organization*. Oxford: Oxford University Press.

Drucker, F. P. (1985) 'Entrepreneurial strategies', *California Management Review*, 27(2): 9–25.

Drucker, F. P. (1988) The coming of the new organization, *Harvard Business Review*, 66: 45–53.

Dyer, J. H. and Singh, H. (1998) 'The relational view: Cooperative strategy and sources of inter-organizational competitive advantage', *The Academy of Management Review*, 23(4): 660–679.

Freel, M. S. (2000) 'Do small innovating firms outperform non-innovators?', *Small Business Economics,* 14(3): 195–210.

Freeman, J., Glenn, R. C. and Michael, T. H. (1983) 'The liability of newness: Age dependence in organizational death rates', *American Sociological Review,* 48(5): 692–710.

Gartner, W. B. (1989) 'Who is an entrepreneur? Is the wrong question', *Entrepreneurship Theory and Practice,* 13(4): 47–68.

Gartner, W. B., Bird, B. J. and Starr, J. A. (1992) 'Acting as if: Differentiating entrepreneurial from organizational behavior', *Entrepreneurship Theory and Practice*, 16(3): 13–32.

Grant, R. M. (1998) Contemporary strategy analysis. Malden, MA: Blackwell Publishers Ltd.

Greiner, L. (1972) *'Evolution and revolution as organizations grow'*, *Harvard Business Review*, 50(4): 37–46.

Guth, W. D. and Ginsberg, A. (1990) 'Guest editors' introduction: Corporate entrepreneurship', *Strategic Management Journal*, 11: 5–15.

Hannan, M. and Freeman, J. (1977) 'The population ecology of organizations', *American Journal of Sociology*, 82(5): 929–964.

Hitt, M. A., Ireland, R. D., Camp, M. and Sexton, D. L. (2001) 'Guest editor's introduction to the special issue strategic entrepreneurship: Entrepreneurial strategies for wealth creation', *Strategic Management Journal*, 22(6–7): 479–491.

Hitt, M. A., Ireland, R. D., Sirmon, D. G. and Trahms, C. A. (2011) 'Strategic entrepreneurship: Creating value for individuals, organizations, and society', *Academy of Management Perspectives*, 25(2): 57–75.

Hornsby, J. S., Naffziger, D. W., Kuratko, D. F. and Montagno, R. V. (1993) 'An integrative model of the corporate entrepreneurship process', *Entrepreneurship Theory and Practice*, 17(2): 29–37.

Hunt, M. S. (1972) Competition in the major home appliance industry 1960–1970. Unpublished PhD dissertation, Harvard University.

Iansiti, M. and Levien, R. (2004) 'Strategy as ecology', *Harvard Business Review*, 82(3): 68–79.

Ireland, R. D., Hitt, M. A., Camp, S. M. and Sexton, D. L. (2001) Integrating entrepreneurship and strategic management action to create firm wealth, *Academy of Management Executive*, 15(1): 49–63.

Ireland, R. D., Hitt, M. A. and Sirmon, D. G. (2003) 'A model of strategic entrepreneurship: The construct and its dimensions', *Journal of Management*, 29(6): 963–989.

Jarillo, J. C. (1988) 'On strategic networks', *Strategic Management Journal*, 9(1): 31–41.

Jarillo, J. C. (1989) 'Entrepreneurship and growth: The strategic use of external resources', *Journal of Business Venturing*, 4(2): 133–147.

Jarillo, J. C. (1993) *Strategic networks: Creating the borderless organization*. Bodmin, Cornwall: MPG Books Ltd.

Johannisson, B. (1998) *Entrepreneurship as a collective phenomenon*. Lyon, France: RENT XII.

Johnson, G. and Scholes, K. (1997) *Exploring corporate strategy*. Pennsylvania, PA: Prentice Hall.

Jones, G. R. and Butler, J. E. (1992) 'Managing internal corporate entrepreneurship: An agency theory', *Journal of Management*, 18(4): 733–749.

Kirzner, I. (1997) 'Entrepreneurial discovery and the competitive market process: An Austrian approach', *Journal of Economic Literature*, 35(1): 60–85.

Klein, P. G., Barney, J. B. and Foss, N. J. (2012) Strategic entrepreneurship, papers SSRN. Available at SSRN: https://ssrn.com/abstract= 2137050

Kuratko, D. F. and Hodgetts, M. R. (1998) *Effective small business management*. Fort Worth, TX: Dryden Press.

Kyrgidou, L. P. and Hughes, M. (2010) 'Strategic entrepreneurship: Origins, core elements and research directions', *European Business Review*, 22(1): 43–63.

Leask, G. and Parker, D. (2006) 'Strategic group theory: Review, examination and application

in the UK pharmaceutical industry', *Journal of Management Development*, 25(4): 386–408.

Lechner, C. (2000) *The competitiveness of firm networks*. New York: Gabler.

Lechner, C. and Dowling, M. (2000) 'The evolution of industrial districts and regional networks: The case of the biotechnology region Munich/Martinsried', *Journal of Management and Governance*, Special Issue, 3(99): 309–338.

Lechner, C. and Dowling, M. (2003) 'Firm networks: External relationships as sources for the growth and competitiveness of entrepreneurial firms', *Entrepreneurship and Regional Development*, 15(1): 1–26.

Lechner, C. and Gudmundsson, S. (2014) 'Entrepreneurial orientation, firm strategy and small firm performance', *International Small Business Journal*, 32(1): 36–60.

Lorenzoni, G. (1992) *Accordi, reti e vantaggio competitivo*. Milan, Italy: Etas Libri.

Lorenzoni, G. and Ornati, A. O. (1988) 'Constellation of firms and new ventures', *Journal of Business Venturing*, 3(1): 41–57.

Luke, B. and Verreynne, M. L. (2006) 'Exploring strategic entrepreneurship in the public sector', *Qualitative Research in Accounting & Management*, 3(1): 4–26.

Lumpkin, G. T. and Dess, G. G. (1995) 'Simplicity as a strategy-making process: The effects of stage of organizational development and environment on performance', *Academy of Management Journal,* 38(5): 1386–1407.

Lumpkin, G. T. and Dess, G. G. (1996) 'Clarifying the entrepreneurial orientation construct and linking it to performance', *The Academy of Management Review*, 21(1): 135–172.

Lumpkin, G. T. Cogliser, C. and Schneider, D. (2009) 'Understanding and measuring autonomy: An entrepreneurial orientation perspective', *Entrepreneurship Theory and Practice*, 33(1): 47–69.

Lumpkin, G. T., Steier, L. and Wright, M. (2011) 'Strategic entrepreneurship in family firms', *Strategic Entrepreneurship Journal*, 5(4): 285–306.

Mahoney, J. T. and Pandian, J. R. (1992) 'The resource-based view within the conversation of strategic management', *Strategic Management Journal*, 13(5): 363–380.

Mason, C. and Brown, R. (2013) 'Creating good public policy to support high growth firms', *Small Business Economics*, 40(2): 211–225.

McCann, J. E. (1991) 'Patterns of growth, competitive technology, and financial strategies in young ventures', *Journal of Business Ventures*, 6(3): 189–203.

McGahan, M. A. and Porter, E. M. (1997) 'How much does industry matter really?', *Strategic Management Journal*, 18 (Summer Special Issue): 15–30.

Menger, P. M. (1999) 'Artistic labor markets and careers', *Annual Review of Sociology*, 24 (1): 541–571.

Messersmith, G. J. and Wales, J. W. (2011) 'Entrepreneurial orientation and performance in young firms: The role of human resource management', *International Small Business Journal,* 31(2): 115–136.

Meyer, A. D. (1991) 'What is strategy's distinctive competence?', *Journal of Management*, 17(4): 821–833.

Meyer, A. D., Gaba, V. and Colwell, K. A. (2005) 'Organizing far from equilibrium: Nonlinear change in organizational fields', *Organization Science*, 16(5): 456–473.

Meyer, G. D., Neck, H. M. and Meeks, M. D. (2002) 'The entrepreneurship–strategic management interface', in M. A. Hitt, R. D. Ireland, S. M. Camp and D. L. Sexton (eds), *Strategic Entrepreneurship: Creating a New Mindset*. Oxford: Blackwell Publishing. pp. 19–44.

Morris, M. H., Kuratko, D. F. and Covin, J. G. (2011) *Corporate entrepreneurship and innovation*. Mason, OH: South-Western, Cengage Learning.

Nohria, N. (1992) 'Is a network perspective a useful way of studying organizations?', in N. Nohria and R. G. Eccles (eds), *Networks and Organizations: Structure, Form, and Action*. Boston, MA: Harvard Business School Press. pp. 1–22.

Patzelt, H. and Shepherd, D. A. (2009) 'Strategic entrepreneurship at universities: Academic entrepreneurs' assessment of policy programs', *Entrepreneurship Theory and Practice*, 33(1): 319–340.

Penrose, E. (1959) *The theory of the growth of the firm*. Oxford: Oxford University Press.

Peteraf, M. (1993) 'The cornerstones of competitive advantage: A resource-based view', *Strategic Management Journal*, 14(3): 79–92.

Peteraf, M. and Barney, J. (2003) 'Unraveling the resource-based tangle', *Managerial and Decision Economics*, 24(4): 309–323.

Phan, P. H., Wright, M., Ucbasaran, D. and Tan, W. L. (2009) 'Corporate entrepreneurship: Current research and future directions', *Journal of Business Venturing*, 24(3): 197–205.

Pinchot, G. III. (1985) *Intrapreneuring*. New York: Harper & Row.

Plaschka, G. and Welsch, H. (1990) 'Emerging structures in entrepreneurship education: Curricular designs and strategies', *Entrepreneurship Theory and Practice,* 14(3): 55–71.

Porter, M. E. (1980) *Competitive strategy*. New York: Free Press.

Porter, M. E. (1987) From competitive advantage to corporate strategy, *Harvard Business Review*, May (online edition).

Porter, M. E. (1990) The competitive advantage of nations. *Harvard Business Review, March–April (online edition)*.

Porter, M. E. (1996) What is strategy? *Harvard Business Review, November–December: 61–80*.

Porter, M. E. (2005) 'What is competitiveness? Notes on globalization and strategy', 1(1): 2–3.

Powell, W. W. (1987) 'Hybrid organizational arrangements: New form or transitional development?', *California Management Review*, 30(1): 67–87.

Powell, W. W. (1990) 'Neither market nor hierarchy: Network forms of organization', *Research in Organization Behavior*, 12: 295–336.

Rauch, A., Lumpkin, G. T., Wiklund, J. and Frese, M. (2009) 'Entrepreneurial orientation and business performance: An assessment of past research and suggestions for the future', *Entrepreneurship Theory and Practice*, 33(3): 761–787.

Rensburg, D. J. (2013) 'Is strategic entrepreneurship a pleonasm?', *Journal of Management and Strategy*, 4(1): 15–21.

Richardson, G. B. (1972) 'The organization of industry', *The Economic Journal*, 82(327): 883–896.

Roure, J. B. and Maidique, M. A. (1986) 'Linking prefunding factors and high-technology venture success: An exploratory study', *Journal of Business Venturing*, 1(3): 295–306.

Rumelt, R. (1984) 'Towards a strategic theory of the firm', in R. Lamb (ed.), *Competitive Strategic Management*. Englewood Cliffs, NJ: Prentice-Hall: 556–570.

Sandberg, W. (1992) 'Strategic management's potential contributions to a theory of entrepreneurship', *Entrepreneurship Theory and Practice*, 16(3): 73–90.

Sandberg, W. and Hofer, C. (1987) 'Improving new venture performance: The role of strategy, industry, structure and the entrepreneur', *Journal of Business Venturing*, 2(1): 5–28.

Schendel, D. (1990) 'Introduction to the special issue on corporate entrepreneurship', *Strategic Management Journal*, 11: 1–3.

Schendel, D. and Hofer, C. (1979) *Strategic management: A new view of business policy and planning*. Boston, MA: Little Brown and Co.

Schollhammer, H. (1982) 'Internal corporate entrepreneurship', in C. A. Kent, D. L. Sexton and K. H. Vesper (eds), *Encyclopedia of Entrepreneurship*. Englewood Cliffs, NJ: Prentice Hall. pp. 209–229.

Schumpeter, J. A. (1934). *The theory of economic development: An inquiry into profits, capital, credit, interest and the business cycle, translated from the German by Redvers Opie*. New Brunswick, NJ and London: Transaction Publishers.

Schumpeter, J. A. (1980) Methodological Individualism Brussels: Institutum Europæum. English translation by Michiel van Notten of the corresponding chapter of Joseph Schumpeter (1908) Das Wesen und der Hauptinhalt der theoretischen Nationalökonomie, with a preface by F. A. Hayek and a summary by Frank van Dun.

Sen, A. (1999) *Development as freedom*. Oxford: Oxford University Press.

Shane, S. and Venkataraman, S. (2000) 'The promise of entrepreneurship as a field of research', *Academy of Management Journal*, 25(1): 217–226.

Sharma, P. and Chrisman, J. J. (1999) 'Toward a reconciliation of the definitional issues in the field of corporate entrepreneurship', *Entrepreneurship Theory and Practice*, 23(3): 11–27.

Shepherd, D. A. (2015) 'Party On! A call for entrepreneurship research that is more interactive, activity based, cognitively hot, compassionate, and prosocial', *Journal of Business Venturing*, 30(4): 489–507.

Shirokova, G., Vega, G. and Sokolova, L. (2013) 'Performance of Russian SMEs: Exploration, exploitation and strategic entrepreneurship', *Critical Perspectives on International Business*, 9(1–2): 173–203.

Siegel, R., Siegel, E. and Macmillan, I. (1993) 'Characteristics distinguishing high-growth ventures', *Journal of Business Venturing*, 8(2): 169–180.

Smith, R. L. and Smith, J. K. (2000) *Entrepreneurial finance*. New York: John Wiley.

Spann, M. S., Adams, M. and Wortman, M. S. (1988) 'Entrepreneurship: Definitions, dimensions, and dilemmas', *Proceedings of the US Association for Small Business and Entrepreneurship*, 147–153.

Stevenson, H. H. (1983), *A perspective on entrepreneurship*, Harvard, MA: Harvard Business School Press.

Stevenson, H. H. and Jarillo, J. C. (1990) 'A paradigm of entrepreneurship: Entrepreneurial management', *Strategic Management Journal*, 11: 17–27.

Stinchcombe, A. L. (1965) 'Social structure and organizations', in J. G. March (ed.), *Handbook of Organizations*. Chicago, IL: Rand McNally. pp 142–193.

Stuart, T. E., Hoang, H. and Hybels, R. C. (1999) 'Inter organizational endorsements and the performance of entrepreneurial ventures', *Administrative Science Quarterly*, 44(2): 315–349.

Suddaby, R., Bruton, G. D. and Si, S. X. (2015) 'Entrepreneurship through a qualitative lens: Insights on the construction and/or discovery of entrepreneurial opportunity', *Journal of Business Venturing*, 30(1): 1–10.

Summer, C. E., Bettis, R. A., Duhaime, I. H., Grant, J. H., Hambrick, D. C., Snow, C. C. and Zeithaml, C. P. (1990) 'Doctoral education in business policy and strategy', *Journal of Management*, 16(2): 361–398.

Sutton, J. (1998) *Technology and market structure: Theory and history*. Cambridge, MA: MIT Press.

Venkataraman, S. (1997) 'The distinctive domain of entrepreneurship research: An editor's perspective', in J. Katz and R. Brockhaus (eds), *Advances in Entrepreneurship, Firm Emergence and Growth*. Greenwich, CT: JAI Press, 3(1): 119–138.

Venkataraman, S. and Van de Ven, A. H. (1998) 'A hostile environmental jolts, transaction set, and new business', *Journal of Business Venturing*, 13(3): 231–255.

Venkatraman, N. and Ramanujam, V. (1986) 'Measurement of business performance in strategy research: A comparison of approaches', *Academy of Management Review*, 11(4): 801–814.

Vesper, K. H. (1984) 'Three faces of corporate entrepreneurship', in J. A. Hornaday et al. (eds), *Frontiers of 'Entrepreneurship Research*. Wellesley, MA: Babson College. pp. 294–320.

Vesper, K. H. (1987) 'Entrepreneurship academics: How can we tell when the field is getting somewhere?' *Journal of Business Venturing*, 3(1): 1–10.

Wales, W., Gupta, V. and Mousa, F. T. (2011) 'Empirical research on entrepreneurial orientation: An assessment and suggestions for future research', *International Small Business Journal*, 31(4): 357–383.

Wernerfelt, B. (1984) 'A resource-based view of the firm', *Strategic Management Journal*, 5(2): 171–180.

Williamson, O. (1975) *Markets and hierarchies: Analysis and antitrust implications*. New York: Free Press.

Witte, E. (1991) 'Betriebswirtschaftliche Forschung – wohin?, Konsequenzen aus der Institutionenökonomik', in D. Ordelheide, B. Rudolph, E. Büsselmann, *Betriebswirtschaftslehre und ökonomische Theorie*. Stuttgart: Poeschl. pp. 445–469.

Zahra, S. A. (1993) 'A conceptual model of entrepreneurship as firm behavior: A critique and extension', *Entrepreneurship Theory and Practice*, 17(4): 5–21.

Zahra, S. A. (1995) 'Corporate entrepreneurship and financial performance: The case of management leveraged buyouts', *Journal of Business Venturing*, 10(3): 225–247.

Zahra. S. A. (1996) 'Governance, ownership, and corporate entrepreneurship: The moderating impact of industry technological opportunities', *Academy of Management Journal*, 39(6): 1713–1735.

10

Perspectives on
New Venture Creation

Fokko J. Eller and Michael M. Gielnik

INTRODUCTION

In this chapter, we provide an overview of theories useful to understand new venture creation. In particular, we focus on theories from four broader perspectives: the psychological, team, resource, and institutional perspective. This allows us to consider individual-level factors as well as interpersonal factors and societal-level factors. The four perspectives we discuss in this chapter cover the main theoretical approaches scholars have adopted to explain new venture creation. Against this background, we will first outline and explain the different theoretical frameworks. Second, we will clarify what the main research questions for each perspective are, and how previous research has sought to address these questions. In the third part, we will highlight specific gaps in the literature and how future research could address these gaps. We propose a theoretical model that combines the different perspectives in an integrative model (see Figure 10.1). At the center of this integrative model we place the entrepreneur, whose actions are fundamental to the creation of new ventures (Baron, 2007a; Frese, 2009). We thus understand new venture creation as a process in which entrepreneurial action is the only factor directly influencing new venture creation. The other factors either indirectly influence new venture creation through the entrepreneurs' actions or interact with the entrepreneurs' actions on new venture creation (Frese & Gielnik, 2014). The last part of this chapter will provide a specific approach that future researchers can use to study new venture creation.

NEW VENTURE CREATION AS AN OUTCOME OF THE ENTREPRENEURIAL PROCESS

We understand new venture creation as an outcome of the entrepreneurial process. According to Gartner (1988), new venture

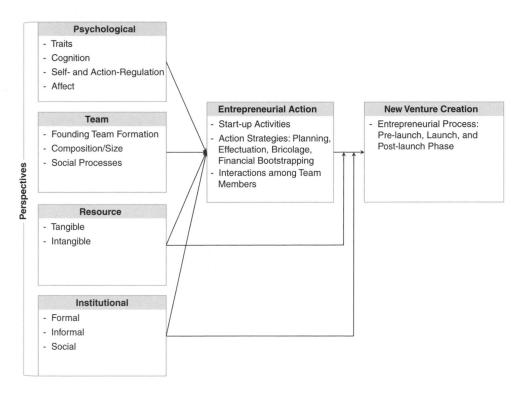

Figure 10.1   The integrative model of new venture creation

creation or the process by which new ventures and organizations come into existence is the 'primary phenomenon of entrepreneurship' (p. 57). The entrepreneurial process comprises the discovery, evaluation, and exploitation of a business opportunity (Baron, 2007b; Shane & Venkataraman, 2000). Baron (2007b) defines three major phases in the entrepreneurial process, distinguishing between the pre-launch, launch, and post-launch phase. In the pre-launch phase entrepreneurs identify opportunities, and develop these into a viable and feasible product or service. In the launch phase, they create an overall strategy to advance the business idea and start with the acquisition of resources necessary for starting the venture. Finally, the post-launch phase refers to managing the new venture.

The central research questions to understand the entrepreneurial process can be summarized as follows: (1) What are the specific tasks and steps in the entrepreneurial process

(Baron, 2007b; Carter, Gartner, & Reynolds, 1996; Gartner, 1988; Hisrich, Langan-Fox, & Grant, 2007; Shane, 2003)? (2) What are the main factors driving success in the entrepreneurial process (Baron, 2007b)? Scholars have approached these two questions from different perspectives. Scholars adopting a psychological perspective have examined micro-level factors, such as entrepreneurs' competencies (including knowledge, skills, cognitions, motivations, and personal characteristics) that are required in the different phases of the entrepreneurial process (psychological perspective) (Baron, 2007b; Hisrich et al., 2007; Jack & Anderson, 2002; Zhou, 2008). On a macro level, scholars have examined the role institutional and resource factors play in the entrepreneurial process (institutional and resource perspective) (Aldrich & Zimmer, 1986; Alvarez & Busenitz, 2001; Jack & Anderson, 2002; Meek, Pacheco, & York, 2010; Welter, 2011).

Finally, on a meso level, scholars have adopted a team perspective examining team processes that influence the entrepreneurial process (team perspective) (Cooney, 2005; Cooper, Woo, & Dunkelberg, 1989; Kamm, Shuman, Seeger, & Nurick, 1990).

In the next sections, we describe in more detail the different perspectives that explain new venture creation and the entrepreneurial process.

NEW VENTURE CREATION FROM A PSYCHOLOGICAL PERSPECTIVE

Brandstätter (2011) stated that the psychological perspective on entrepreneurship substantially contributed to the understanding of how entrepreneurs think, what they aim for, what they do, and what they actually achieve. Central to the psychological perspective of new venture creation is (a) the trait approach, (b) the cognitive approach, (c) the self- and action-regulation approach, and (d) the affect approach. Essentially, the psychological perspective emphasizes the importance of psychological mechanisms underlying and leading to entrepreneurial action (see Figure 10.1).

The Trait Approach

The trait approach can be described as the search for characteristics and traits of the entrepreneur (Gartner, 1988). 'In this approach the entrepreneur is the basic unit of analysis and the entrepreneur's traits and characteristics are the key to explaining entrepreneurship as a phenomenon […]' (Gartner, 1988, p. 48). The general assumption of the trait approach is that traits and individual characteristics have an effect on entrepreneurs' actions through motivation and decision making (cf. Judge & Ilies, 2002). The trait approach combines a number of different theories, for example, the big five personality traits concept, which describes the following

five personality dimensions: openness, conscientiousness, extraversion, agreeableness, and neuroticism (Norman, 1963). Zhao and Seibert (2006) show in their meta-analytical study that entrepreneurs differ substantially from managers with regard to conscientiousness, openness to experience, neuroticism, and agreeableness. The results suggest that entrepreneurs are more conscientious and open to new experiences as well as less neurotic and less agreeable. However, scholars agree that the five factor model is too distal to explain entrepreneurship (Baum & Frese, 2007). Consequently, the trait approach has developed more specific constructs that go beyond the big five and are more proximal to entrepreneurship (Baum & Frese, 2007; Frese & Gielnik, 2014; Rauch & Frese, 2007). An example is McClelland's (1965) need theory. McClelland's theory is based on three basic needs: need for achievement, need for power, and need for affiliation, which affect peoples' actions. McClelland (1965) has argued that entrepreneurs are especially high in need for achievement because they strive for situations in which they can excel. In fact, meta-analytic research has supported this theory, showing that need for achievement is related to entrepreneurship (Collins, Hanges, & Locke, 2004; Rauch & Frese, 2007). An interesting finding from the trait approach is that risk propensity, a trait commonly associated with entrepreneurship in the popular media, is only weakly related to entrepreneurship (Rauch & Frese, 2007; Stewart & Roth, 2004). This finding indicates that the role of risk propensity is either overrated or the relationship between risk propensity and entrepreneurship is more complex than a purely linear relationship. In recent years, the trait approach has lost some of its appeal to explain entrepreneurship. In fact, Gartner (1988) has noted that asking 'Who is an entrepreneur?' is the wrong question and does not help much to understand successful entrepreneurship and venture creation. Although traits are related to entrepreneurship, traits do not elucidate the underlying processes and mechanisms that lead to new venture creation. Consequently, traits do not help to develop leverage points to promote entrepreneurship. To gain deeper insights into the processes and mechanisms involved in entrepreneurship, scholars have turned to a cognitive and self-/action-regulatory perspective on entrepreneurship.

The Cognitive Approach

The cognitive approach has focused on entrepreneurial cognition (Baron, 2004). Entrepreneurial cognition is defined as the knowledge structures that entrepreneurs use to think, reason, and behave in order to evaluate opportunities, create new ventures, and grow their ventures (Mitchell, Busenitz, Lant, McDougall, Morse, & Smith, 2002; Mitchell, Busenitz, Bird, Gaglio, McMullen, Morse, & Smith, 2007). The cognitive approach assumes that entrepreneurs' actions and decisions are heavily influenced by cognitive factors and mechanisms (Baron & Ward, 2004). For example, opportunity identification and exploitation depend on people's capacities to acquire and process relevant information (Shane & Venkataraman, 2000). Scholars have therefore suggested that a cognitive approach is particularly helpful to understand why some people are more successful in the entrepreneurial process than others (Mitchell et al., 2002, 2007). Central cognitive factors are knowledge (including experience and expertise) (Keh, Foo, & Lim, 2002; Shane, 2000; Simon, Houghton, & Aquino, 2000; Zhou, 2008), cognitive capabilities (e.g. general mental ability and creativity), and decision-making biases or heuristics (e.g. overconfidence or illusion of control). Knowledge is central to the entrepreneurial process as it helps entrepreneurs to identify new business opportunities, proceed more efficiently through the launch phase, and develop better strategies to grow their ventures. Meta-analytic evidence has provided extensive support for the important role of knowledge in the entrepreneurial process (Crook, Todd, Combs, Woehr, & Ketchen, 2011; Martin, McNally, & Kay, 2013; Unger, Rauch, Frese, & Rosenbusch, 2011). Similarly, cognitive capabilities, such as creativity, help entrepreneurs to process and combine new information with positive effects on generating business ideas and problem solutions (Gielnik, Frese, Graf, & Kampschulte, 2012; Gielnik, Krämer, Kappel, & Frese, 2014a). Finally, scholars have linked decision-making biases and heuristics, such as overconfidence and illusion of control (the overestimation of one's skills to control the outcome of a certain situation (Keh et al., 2002; Simon et al., 2000)) to entrepreneurship. Overconfidence is a cognitive bias and as such leads to flawed decisions. Research has shown that overconfidence has a positive effect on starting a business but a negative effect on survival (Dawson & Henley, 2012). On the one hand, overconfidence helps to overcome the initial uncertainty inherent in new venture creation, because people are overly confident that their venture will be successful. On the other hand, overconfidence has a negative effect on venture performance and survival because overconfidence leads to flawed decisions, biased forecasts, and escalation of commitment (Frese & Gielnik, 2014). In general, the cognitive approach has great potential in explaining new venture creation by providing insights into the decision-making processes of entrepreneurs and how they identify and exploit opportunities.

The Self- or Action-Regulation Approach

The self- or action-regulation approach focuses on regulatory and motivational aspects influencing entrepreneurs' actions (Frese, 2007; McMullen & Shepherd, 2006). A central assumption in literature is that any form of entrepreneurship requires action (Frese, 2007; McMullen & Shepherd, 2006).

Entrepreneurs have to identify and develop business opportunities, they have to acquire the necessary resources and equipment to build viable business structures, and they have to manage the business to ensure growth and survival of the new venture. Several theories in entrepreneurship consider action to be the key success factor (Baron, 2007a; Frese, 2009; McMullen & Shepherd, 2006). Action is goal-oriented behavior (Frese, 2009). Given the importance of action, scholars have suggested that self- and action-regulatory factors are central to understanding entrepreneurship. Self-regulation is defined as an internal or transactional process that enables a person to guide his or her goal-directed activities over time and across changing circumstances (Karoly, 1993). Similarly, action-regulation refers to how individuals regulate their actions to achieve goals actively (Frese, 2007). Important theories in this domain are control theories (Carver & Scheier, 1982), social cognitive theory (Bandura, 1991), and action-regulation theory (Frese & Zapf, 1994). These theories seek to explain how people initiate and maintain action. Building on these theoretical frameworks, entrepreneurship scholars have particularly focused on constructs such as goal-setting, goal intentions, action planning, and entrepreneurial self-efficacy (Brinckmann, Grichnik, & Kapsa, 2010; Castrogiovanni, 1996; Delmar & Shane, 2003; Gielnik, Frese, Kahara-Kawuki, Wasswa Katono, Kyejjusa, Ngoma et al., 2015; Gielnik et al., 2014a; Gruber, 2007; Honig & Samuelsson, 2012). Goal intentions reflect what entrepreneurs want to achieve. The strength of entrepreneurs' goal intentions is an indicator of the effort they are willing to invest (Bird, 1988). Action plans are mental simulations of actions outlining how to achieve a goal (Frese, 2009). Entrepreneurial self-efficacy is rooted in social cognitive theory (Bandura, 1991) and reflects entrepreneurs' confidence in their skills to successfully complete entrepreneurial tasks (Chen, Greene, & Crick, 1998).

Goal-setting and action planning helps to initiate and maintain entrepreneurial action; accordingly, goal-setting and action planning have been consistently linked to entrepreneurial success across all phases of the entrepreneurial process (Baron, 2007b; Baum, Locke, & Kirkpatrick, 1998; Brinckmann et al., 2010; Frese & Zapf, 1994; Frese, 2007; Frese, Krauss, Keith, Escher, Grabarkiewicz, Luneng, & Friedrich, 2007; Gielnik, Barabas, Frese, Namatovu-Dawa, Scholz, Metzger, & Walter, 2013). Similarly, entrepreneurial self-efficacy has a motivational function with positive effects in all phases of the entrepreneurial process (Rauch & Frese, 2007). The self-/action-regulatory approach is particularly useful to understand new venture creation insofar as it specifically looks at the processes underlying entrepreneurs' actions to create a new venture.

The Affect Approach

Finally, the affect approach examines how feelings or emotions influence entrepreneurs' actions and thus new venture creation (Foo, Uy, & Baron, 2009). Emotion is conceptualized as a construct with two dimensions: activation and valence (Russell, 1980). Activation describes the state of wakefulness or attention and is usually indicated as high or low; valence describes whether an emotion is pleasant or unpleasant (Baron, Hmieleski, & Henry, 2012). We can thus distinguish between positive and negative affect, and high and low activation. In entrepreneurship, scholars have mainly focused on the motivating function of positive affect with high activation. An example of a positive and activating affect is entrepreneurial passion. Entrepreneurial passion describes strong and positive feelings that entrepreneurs experience when they are engaged in key activities that are important to the self-identity of the entrepreneur (Cardon, Sudek, & Mitteness, 2009). In regard to new venture creation, scholars have proposed that entrepreneurial passion can promote creativity, the discovery and exploitation of opportunities, the acquisition of resources, and other activities important for launching a new venture (Cardon, Grégoire, Stevens, & Patel, 2013). However, further research has shown that not only positive affect but also negative affect increases entrepreneurs' efforts to create a new venture. Whereas positive affect is positively related to effort in tasks that go beyond immediately required tasks, negative affect is positively related to effort in tasks that are immediately required (Foo et al., 2009). The beneficial function of negative affect has also been demonstrated by Bledow, Schmitt, Frese, and Kühnel (2011) and Bledow, Rosing, and Frese (2013), who have shown that a shift from negative to positive affect increases people's creativity. In conclusion, both positive and negative affect play an important role in influencing several mechanisms important for entrepreneurship, such as opportunity identification, effort, and creativity (Baron, 2008).

After focusing on the individual-level we will now turn to the team level and its role in the entrepreneurial process.

NEW VENTURE CREATION FROM A TEAM PERSPECTIVE

Prior research concentrated mostly on the single entrepreneur as the driving force behind new venture creation (Baron, 2007a). However, a large percentage of new ventures are created and led by teams (Cooper et al., 1989; Kamm et al., 1990). These are usually described as founding teams. Founding teams are two or more persons, who have a common interest in actively establishing a new venture, leading the venture, and having the final decision-making authority regarding the venture (Brinckmann & Hoegl, 2011; Cooney, 2005; Kamm et al., 1990).

The team perspective focuses on four general research questions. First, how do founding teams form or what are the factors that influence the formation of teams (Bird, 1989; Forbes, Borchert, Zellmer-Bruhn, & Sapienza, 2006; Kamm et al., 1990)? Second, how does the composition of the team affect new venture creation? More precisely, how does team diversity in terms of background (gender, age, race) and functional (experience, education) variables influence new venture creation (Ensley & Hmieleski, 2005; Hoogendoorn, Oosterbeek, & van Praag, 2013; Kamm et al., 1990; Klotz, Hmieleski, Bradley, & Busenitz, 2013)? Third, how does team size affect new venture creation (Brinckmann & Hoegl, 2011; Brinckmann, Salomo, & Gemuenden, 2011; Cooper et al., 1989; Kamm et al., 1990; West, 2007)? Fourth, what are the social processes in founding teams and how do they affect performance (Brinckmann & Hoegl, 2011; Brinckmann et al., 2011; Ensley & Hmieleski, 2005; Lechler, 2001)? The fourth question is particularly important as it looks at the underlying mechanisms and processes relevant for new venture creation. We suggest that team members' interactions and the entrepreneurial actions by the teams are mediating mechanisms in the relationship to new venture creation (see Figure 10.1). In the following, we describe this perspective in more detail.

The Formation of Founding Teams

The first research question deals with the formation of teams. Although there is no recipe on how to create the perfect new venture team, scholars have identified some standard influences on how teams come together. For example, Kamm et al. (1990) adopted social network theory and argued that team members are not selected based on the complementarity of each individual's skills and knowledge, but that new venture teams typically develop out of existing relationships. The interpersonal attraction theory has a similar approach and posits that the inherent human desire for interpersonal attraction and social connection is the main driver influencing team formation (Forbes et al., 2006). Likeability, proximity, enjoyment of each other's company, alikeness, and complementarity of characteristics are central factors to this theory and influence whether people are attracted to each other or not (Kamm et al., 1990). However, Bird (1989) showed that economic rationalism can also be a factor in team formation. In this context, factors such as willingness to invest money, or know-how in new venture creation, are the main drivers of the formation process (Bird, 1989). In conclusion, interpersonal attraction, economic rationalism, and further factors like social networks or shared backgrounds are factors explaining formation of founding teams.

Founding Team Diversity

The second research question deals with team diversity, which describes the degree to which team members differ, with regard to factors such as gender, age, or nationality. The relationship between team diversity and performance is however inconsistent: there are positive as well as negative effects of team diversity (van Knippenberg, De Dreu, & Homan, 2004). The apparent advantage of diversified teams is that they have access to more information and expertise. One reason why diversity results in negative effects is intergroup bias, referring to the categorization of team members into similar in-group members or dissimilar out-group members (van Knippenberg et al., 2004; van Knippenberg & Schippers, 2007). This categorization is usually accompanied by less positive reactions to members with an out-group status, which can result in relational conflicts, low identification with and commitment to the group, low satisfaction, and high turnover (van Knippenberg et al., 2004). Ensley and Hmieleski (2005) analyzed the difference between new venture teams with a shared background and independent new venture teams, finding positive relationships between diversity and performance. In

particular they found that independent (diverse) teams showed advanced group dynamics and performed better in terms of revenue growths and cash flow. These independent teams were more heterogeneous in terms of education, experience, expertise, and skills compared with teams with a shared background. This helped them in the process of new venture creation by being more efficient in planning and problem-solving, as well as reacting faster and being more flexible. Similarly, Hoogendoorn et al. (2013) analyzed the composition of founding teams with regard to the gender distribution. Their findings suggest that an equal gender distribution results in better performance in terms of sales and profits compared with male-dominated teams. In conclusion, research findings suggest that independent and diverse founding teams have an advantage over homogeneous founding teams with a shared background.

The Initial Team Size

The third question deals with the initial team size. Several studies have focused on the initial team size as a predictor of new venture performance (Cooper et al., 1989; Feeser & Willard, 1990; Klotz et al., 2013; Lechler, 2001). The theoretical consideration is that larger teams have a greater pool of resources. In fact, research shows that a founding team with more members has access to a wider range of resources, including the initial capital and the available networks, as well as individual experience and expertise (Cooper et al., 1989; Eisenhardt & Schoonhoven, 1990; Sine, Mitsuhashi, & Kirsch, 2006; Teach, Tarplay, & Schwartz, 1986). The consistent result of these studies is that the size of the founding team is related to the venture's success in terms of opportunity recognition and exploitation, survival, and performance. However, larger teams may be more susceptible to process loss. Process loss is the team's inability to realize their full potential (Kerr & Tindale, 2004). One reason for process loss is that the team fails to identify members' competencies and thus fails to utilize their resources (Kerr & Tindale, 2004). Especially in larger teams process loss is usually due to redundant communication and conflict, resulting in reduced productivity (Haleblian & Finkelstein, 1993).

Social Processes within Founding Teams

The fourth question deals with social processes and the actions and interactions taking place in teams. Recently, research shifted its focus from team composition factors to the social processes and interactions within teams in order to explain new venture performance (Baron & Tang, 2008; Brinckmann & Hoegl, 2011; Ensley & Hmieleski, 2005; Ensley, Pearson, & Amason, 2002; Hoegl & Gemuenden, 2001). This shift is based on the consideration that team composition represents an easy to observe factor, which, however, is too distal from the processes and actions influencing new venture performance. Team composition constitutes the input, which is less proximal to the outcome (new venture performance) than the social processes. Thus, in order to understand how new venture performance is achieved, it is necessary to analyze how and which social processes occur in teams (van Knippenberg & Schippers, 2007).

Important social processes that occur among the team members are, for example, team cohesion, shared strategic cognition, team potency, and conflicts (Ensley & Hmieleski, 2005). Team cohesion describes the internal solidarity and affects the team's performance by influencing the members' motivation and commitment (Ensley & Hmieleski, 2005). Shared strategic cognition refers to the degree of agreement on the venture's future development. A high level of agreement entails a high level of commitment with positive effects on new venture creation

(Ensley & Hmieleski, 2005). Team potency is similar to self-efficacy, as both describe the degree to which the team or self is convinced to successfully realize their plans. A founding team with high team potency thus strongly believes that they can start and manage a new venture (Pearce, Gallagher, & Ensley, 2002). Conflicts within teams received much attention. Ensley and Pearce (2001) divided conflicts into two categories: a) cognitive conflicts and b) affective conflicts. Cognitive conflicts refer to the members' disagreement about the activities, strategies, and goals necessary to implement the new venture and as such can contribute to a positive exchange of ideas (Pearce et al., 2002). Affective conflicts have personal differences as the subject of discussion and as such are more likely to lead to discord (Ensley and Hmieleski, 2005; van Knippenberg et al., 2004).

In summary, the team perspective is able to explain phenomena in new venture creation that have not been addressed by the psychological perspective, which has mainly focused on the individual entrepreneur. However, it is important to note that team formation, composition, and size are only distal factors. In the same way as individual characteristics (see psychological perspective), team characteristics have an indirect effect on new venture creation through actions and interactions of the team members (see Figure 10.1).

NEW VENTURE CREATION FROM A RESOURCE PERSPECTIVE

Scholars agree that the availability of resources is a central factor for the creation of new ventures (Alvarez & Busenitz, 2001; De Mel, McKenzie, & Woodruff, 2008; Evans & Leighton, 1989; Ho & Wong, 2007). Resources are necessary to establish business structures in order to be able to pursue and exploit business opportunities, and they substantially contribute to the venture's success and survival (Chrisman, Bauerschmitt, &

Hofer, 1998). Scholars have even suggested that combining resources in novel ways to deliver superior value is the very essence of entrepreneurship (Ardichvili, Cardozo, & Ray, 2003). Resources play two roles (see Figure 10.1): on the one hand, the availability of resources influences entrepreneurs' actions and new venture creation (main effect of resources). On the other hand, the absence of resources makes it less likely that entrepreneurs' actions lead to new venture creation. In the following, we will explain to what extent tangible and intangible resources promote entrepreneurial action to create new ventures (main effect). Moreover, we will focus on new venture creation under resource constraints and how concepts like financial bootstrapping, bricolage, and effectuation might help to overcome a lack of resources (integrative effect).

The resource-based view explains and analyzes the sources of competitive advantages for existing enterprises (Barney, 1991). It introduces two assumptions, which are that: a) resources among the different firms of an industry are heterogeneously distributed, and b) these strategic resources are to a certain degree immobile, which guarantees that competitive advantages can be maintained over time (Barney, 1991). Alvarez and Busenitz (2001) identify the concept of resource heterogeneity as the connecting link between entrepreneurship and resource-based theory. The term resource encompasses a multitude of factors that are usually classified as tangible or intangible assets or physical, human, and organizational capital (Barney, 1991; Chrisman et al., 1998; Katz & Gartner, 1988).

General research questions from the resource perspective are: First, what role do tangible and intangible resources play for new venture creation and performance (Barney, 1991; Chrisman et al., 1998; Ho & Wong, 2007; Katz & Gartner, 1988; Kwon & Adler, 2002)? Second, how do resources come into existence and how do entrepreneurs utilize them to exploit business opportunities (Alvarez & Busenitz, 2001)? Third, how do resource constraints affect new venture creation (Castrogiovanni, 1991; Ho & Wong, 2007)? Fourth, what are the specific mechanisms with which entrepreneurs overcome resource constraints (Shane & Venkataraman, 2000; Venkataraman, Sarasvathy, Dew, & Forster, 2012)?

The Role of Tangible and Intangible Resources in New Venture Creation

Tangible resources are primarily a venture's material assets; a common example is the company's financial capital. Intangible resources refer to the immaterial assets such as social capital. Chrisman et al. (1998) argue that, in order to sustain or to create a competitive advantage, the venture depends particularly on its intangible resources. This follows from the fact that tangible resources are simple to understand and easy to acquire or imitate (Barney, 1991). Intangible resources on the other hand are path-dependent, socially complex and firm-specific (Alvarez & Busenitz, 2001; Barney, 1991; Peteraf, 1993). As such they are more likely to fulfill Barney's (1991) conditions of being valuable, rare, imperfectly imitable, and non-substitutable for generating a sustained competitive advantage. The most important intangible resource is the venture's unique competence, the one thing the company does best and that distinguishes it from every other company (Alvarez & Busenitz, 2001).

In this chapter we focus on financial capital and social capital as the main representatives of tangible and intangible resources. Financial capital refers to the availability of money. Different sources of financial capital are traditional debt financing, venture capital financing, and informal investments (Ho & Wong, 2007). However, during the entrepreneurial process entrepreneurs usually have to rely on alternative financing methods, such as informal investors like family and friends (Ho & Wong, 2007). Social capital represents a social resource and refers to the goodwill that arises through social relations and can be used to facilitate action (Kwon & Adler, 2002). Meta-analytic research has provided evidence for the importance of social capital in entrepreneurship (Stam, Arzlanian, & Elfring, 2014).

Tangible and intangible resources play an important role across all three phases of the entrepreneurial process (Alvarez & Busenitz, 2001; Baron, 2007a; Chrisman et al., 1998; Gartner, 1985; Shane, 2000). The pre-launch phase requires activities like raising financial capital to develop a business idea into a viable and feasible business opportunity, and to overcome entry barriers like economies of scale or product differentiation (Baron, 2007b; Ho & Wong, 2007). Social capital helps to raise financial capital, because it offers access to the support and assistance of people (Kwon & Adler, 2002). During the launch phase there is a need for tangible and intangible resources to implement the idea and to set up the new venture by establishing viable business structures and acquiring the necessary equipment (Ho & Wong, 2007). A surplus of financial capital thereby serves as a buffer against initial mistakes (Chrisman et al., 1998). At the same time social capital facilitates the access to distribution and supply channels, as well as to the labor market (Adler & Kwon, 2002). Finally, during the post-launch phase entrepreneurs need resources to grow their ventures. Entrepreneurs gain access to traditional financing sources by building up tangible assets and credibility that can be pledged as collateral (Ho & Wong, 2007). Intangible resources remain relevant, since they continue to fulfill the conditions of being valuable, rare, imperfectly imitable, and non-substitutable.

The Effects of Resource Constraints on New Venture Creation

Resource constraints affect new venture creation in several ways. Firstly, resource constraints act as an entry barrier. As such they prevent new venture creation because the capital requirements exceed the entrepreneur's financial capabilities to initiate and maintain start-up activities (Ho & Wong, 2007). One explanation is that the industry's prevailing economies of scale impede the entrepreneur from reaching an efficient production level (Ho & Wong, 2007; Wright, 1987). Second, resource constraints affect launch and post-launch performance. This is, for example, due to a lack of financial capital, which hinders the acquisition of necessary assets to build viable organizational structures and production processes (Gartner, 1985). Furthermore, initial mistakes cannot be compensated for and wrong choices cannot be reversed when insufficient resources are available (Chrisman et al., 1998). Furthermore, it restricts the choice of strategies that entrepreneurs can choose from (Chrisman et al., 1998; Wright, 1987). A strategy of cost leadership or differentiation is not feasible for new ventures, when cost advantages or high initial investments cannot be realized (Wright, 1987). Resources and resource constraints thus have a direct effect on the actions entrepreneurs can take and thus affect new venture creation (see Figure 10.1).

Overcoming Resource Constraints

Although resource constraints complicate new venture creation they do not prevent it. This may be a) due to an environment or industry in which economies of scale, and other cost advantages, do not protect already existing companies (Shane & Venkataraman, 2000); b) due to the fact that some entrepreneurs are able to secure the necessary financial resources through traditional sources of capital (Holtz-Eakin, Joulfaian, & Rosen, 1994); or c) due to specific action strategies like effectuation, bricolage, and financial bootstrapping, which help entrepreneurs to attenuate or overcome the negative effect of resource constraints (Baker & Nelson, 2005; Sarasvathy, 2001; Winborg & Landström, 2001). These concepts are briefly described as examples of how previous research has sought to address the problem of resource constraints in new venture creation. These concepts also illustrate how resources and entrepreneurs' actions interact in the new venture creation process (see Figure 10.1).

Effectuation is a concept based on four core principles and an underlying logic developed by Sarasvathy (2001). The four principles state that entrepreneurs who apply effectuation start with the means at hand, shift their focus from possible profit to affordable loss, form strategic alliances to cooperate with third parties, and exploit contingencies whenever they arise as possible opportunities to enter new markets and industries. The underlying logic of effectuation says that the future cannot be predicted and therefore the entrepreneur should concentrate on those parts that can be controlled (Read, Song, & Smit, 2009; Sarasvathy, 2001). In the context of resource constraints, effectuation offers an approach that facilitates taking action and the creation of a new venture. For example, the vast acquisition of capital or the need for a large employee base is bypassed by concentrating on the means at hand (Sarasvathy, 2001). The entrepreneur thus might forgo the optimal set-up of the company and assemble only the minimum set of resources. Eventually, however, a new business is launched even under resource constraints.

Bricolage is another concept that supports new venture creation under resource constraints (Baker & Nelson, 2005). It is built on similar principles to effectuation, insofar as it strives to always make do with whatever is at hand by recombining it in new ways (Baker & Nelson, 2005). Bricoleurs thus rely on their skill set, knowledge, and any kind of tangible resource in their possession (Baker & Nelson, 2005). Recombining resources in new ways means that bricoleurs find new and originally unintended purposes for existing resources (Baker & Nelson, 2005). Accordingly, ventures experiment with material inputs and try out new solutions (Baker & Nelson, 2005). Bricolage is often associated with penurious environments (Baker & Nelson, 2005; Fisher, 2012). Making do by creatively recombining the resources at hand constitutes an approach

for new venture creation that assumes an extreme form of resource constraint.

Financial bootstrapping describes the different methods used by entrepreneurs in order to secure financial resources whilst avoiding traditional sources of capital (Freear & Wetzel, 1990; Van Auken & Neeley, 1996; Winborg & Landström, 2001). Winborg and Landström (2001) conducted an empirical study in Sweden and identified six different groups of bootstrapping methods. They labeled the different groups as follows: 1) owner financing methods (an exemplary method is withholding the manager's salary); 2) minimization of accounts receivable (using interest on overdue payment); 3) joint utilization (sharing and borrowing resources from other businesses); 4) delaying payments (delaying payments to suppliers); 5) minimization of capital invested in stock (seeking the best conditions possible with the supplier); 6) subsidy finance (applying for funding) (Winborg & Landström, 2001). Financial bootstrapping helps to overcome resource constraints insofar as entrepreneurs can get access to alternative sources of funding and thus engage in start-up activities although they lack traditional sources of funding.

In summary, tangible and intangible resources constitute important enabling or hindering factors in the new venture creation process by affecting the actions entrepreneurs can take (direct effect). However, entrepreneurs can attenuate the hindering effect by using adequate action strategies, such as effectuation, bricolage, or financial bootstrapping. We therefore assume an interaction between resources and entrepreneurs' actions (see Figure 10.1).

NEW VENTURE CREATION FROM AN INSTITUTIONAL PERSPECTIVE

The institutional perspective plays an important role insofar as institutions provide the context in which entrepreneurship happens. Scott (1987) and Welter (2011) established a threefold division of formal (laws, regulations), informal (culture and norms of society and the market) and social (networks and family) institutions. These institutions set the framework in which the entrepreneur operates, and therefore have to be considered as important factors influencing entrepreneurial action and new venture creation (Gartner, 1995; North, 1990; Shane, 2003; Welter, 2011).

The most recurring research question from the institutional perspective is: How do the different institutional contexts enable as well as constrain the new venture creation process (Gartner, 1995; Manolova, Eunni, & Gyoshev, 2008; North, 1990; Welter & Smallbone, 2011; Welter, 2011)? Second and third interesting questions are: How does institutional change affect new venture creation (Manolova et al., 2008; Meek et al., 2010; Smallbone & Welter, 2010; Welter & Smallbone, 2011; Welter, 2011)? And how does entrepreneurship affect institutional change (Johnstone & Lionais, 2004; Pacheco, Dean, & Payne, 2010; Spence, Gherib, & Biwolé, 2011; Welter & Smallbone, 2011)? The following sections will provide answers to these questions.

The Role of Formal, Informal and Social Institutions in New Venture Creation

The first question asks how formal, informal, and social institutions enable and constrain new venture creation. Formal or regulatory institutions represent the officially codified, enacted, and enforced structure of laws in a community, society, or nation (Manolova et al., 2008). Formal institutions determine the ease of starting a business and set the legal framework the business is operating in (North, 1990). They account for a majority of opportunity creations and restrictions (Welter, 2011), for example by providing a legal infrastructure that reduces the transaction costs (Welter & Smallbone, 2011). Research has shown that the introduction of property rights promotes new venture creation since it decreases the risk

of property loss (Baughn & Neupert, 2003; Luthans, Stajkovic, & Ibrayeva, 2000). Additionally, entrepreneurs can exploit opportunities that emerge from new regulations and rules (Welter, 2011). Yang (2004) describes how entrepreneurs became successful by exploiting poorly defined and enforced rules, allowing them to take advantage of tax deductions. Yet formal institutions can also constrain entrepreneurship by erecting entry barriers through laws and regulations, as well as regulating market exits, and limiting strategic choices by enacting laws that regulate the economic, constitutional, and legal framework (Manolova et al., 2008; North, 1990; Welter & Smallbone, 2011).

Informal institutions like social norms and cultural values compel the entrepreneur to behave in certain ways and influence the decision about whether or not someone engages in an entrepreneurial activity and what type of business is initiated (Meek et al., 2010; Scott, 1987; Welter, 2011). For example, Meek et al. (2010) have shown that social norms in terms of sustainability influence the rate of ecologically sustainable businesses created in a specific region. Furthermore, society's norms and values determine whether a new venture is tolerated and whether the entrepreneur can acquire legitimacy (Zimmerman & Zeitz, 2002).

Social institutions refer to the entrepreneur's networks, such as family and friends (Welter, 2011). They enable entrepreneurial action by providing additional resources, ranging from financial capital, information, potential employees, clients, and business partners, to emotional understanding and support (Welter & Smallbone, 2011; Welter, 2011). Social institutions can also constrain entrepreneurial action by perpetuating prevailing gender roles or stereotypes that prevent individuals from starting their own venture (e.g. age discrimination) (Funken & Gielnik, 2015; Welter, 2011). Social discrimination, for example, can complicate the formation of strategic alliances with third parties as well as entering new markets.

The Effects of Institutional Change on New Venture Creation

The second question pertains to institutional change and how it affects entrepreneurs' actions and new venture creation. Social, societal, and geographical contexts can change over time. In general, entrepreneurship scholars have noted that changing conditions, such as advancements in technology, or economic, political, social, and demographic change, are the source of new opportunities and thus facilitate opportunity identification (Baron, 2006). Opportunity identification and new venture creation can thus be regarded as a consequence of a juxtaposition of new situations or conditions (Baron, 2006). Furthermore, changing contexts have additional effects on new venture creation. First, formal institutional change means changes in laws or regulations (North, 1990; Welter, 2011). As mentioned above, these changes constitute a main source and repression of entrepreneurial opportunities, since they may remove, erect, lower or raise market entry and exit barriers overnight (Smallbone & Welter, 2010). The World Bank's (2010) report on the ease of doing business highlights how such changes affect new venture creations. For example, countries that reduce the necessary time to register a business increase the rate of new venture creations. Further findings show that heavy-handed regulation increases start-up costs. This results in lower profit margins, which discourage entrepreneurs to take action, thus decreasing the rate of new venture creation.

Changes in informal institutions are less frequent and rapid. Whereas political or judicial decisions may become valid instantaneously and thus change the formal institutional context abruptly, informal institutions are more constant (North, 1990). One of the main reasons for this is that informal institutions are based on social norms, which are deeply embedded in society (Manolova et al., 2008; Meek et al., 2010; North, 1990). A change in social institutions, for example a change in local traditions, can promote entrepreneurship by providing more autonomy and freedom to take entrepreneurial action (Welter, 2011). One example is the efforts by the Indian government to reduce the negative effects of the caste system on class mobility in order to increase entrepreneurship (Dana, 2000). Similarly, changes in norms towards environmental or sustainable behavior have resulted in a trend of pro-environmental and social entrepreneurship (Shepherd and Patzelt, 2011).

New Venture Creation as a Driver of Institutional Change

Just as institutional change can drive entrepreneurial action and new venture creation, entrepreneurial action and new venture creation can drive institutional change. This is because institutions and entrepreneurship are mutually dependent (Johnstone & Lionais, 2004). Institutions can, for example, be changed by the process of path-dependent institutional evolution. This process states that informal institutions are either being changed gradually by adding new procedures or structures, or through the reorientation or recombination toward new purposes (Welter & Smallbone, 2011). Boas (2007) describes this as the layering process, in which an institution is changed incrementally by adding further rules to the pre-existing ones. He argues that this process can result in an eventual change of the institution's fundamental nature (Boas, 2007). The process of reorientation or recombination may be particularly applicable for sustainable entrepreneurs. Sustainable entrepreneurs focus on the preservation of nature, life support, and community, while pursuing business opportunities in order to develop future products and services (Shepherd & Patzelt, 2011). Sustainable entrepreneurs are further being described as the engine of sustainable development which will cause the next industrial revolution and a more sustainable future (Pacheco et al., 2010). Entrepreneurs may change institutions through acting as role models for others to adopt and implement social or environmental practices (Spence et al., 2011). Furthermore, entrepreneurs change institutions by altering and creating norms, government legislation, and property rights (Pacheco et al., 2010). One way of doing this is the use of collective action (Pacheco et al., 2010). These examples emphasize that entrepreneurs can act as change agents who interact with and change their institutional environment (Welter & Smallbone, 2011).

In short, institutions can constitute drivers as well as obstacles of new venture creation. However, this does not represent a single-sided dependency, since entrepreneurs and the process of creating new ventures can change the institutional context.

FUTURE RESEARCH

Based on the previous sections we will now explain the specific gaps that emerged for each perspective and offer suggestions on how future research can address these gaps. We use our overview of the theoretical perspectives and the phases of the entrepreneurial process to develop an outline of future research questions. In total, we suggest that there are five broad areas for future research. This includes questions with regard to 1) the psychological and team perspective, 2) the resource perspective, 3) the institutional perspective, 4) the process perspective (questions about how certain effects change along the entrepreneurial process), and 5) the integrative perspective (combining perspectives within each phase of the entrepreneurial process).

Future Research Directions for Different Perspectives

First, although the trait approach has received less consideration in recent years, scholars argue that the psychology of entrepreneurs requires further attention (Baron, 2007a; Baum & Frese, 2007; Rauch & Frese, 2007). Future research should therefore refocus on the effects of traits and investigate the mediating mechanisms underlying the relationship between traits and new venture creation (Baum & Frese, 2007; Hisrich et al., 2007; Rauch & Frese, 2007). Rauch and Frese (2007) thereby emphasized the need to a) study specific traits such as achievement motive, and b) match the traits to specific tasks. For example, Baum and Locke (2004) examined how entrepreneurial traits, such as tenacity, affected new venture growth through the motivational constructs of goal-setting and self-efficacy. An additional avenue for future research is considering personality not only as a predictor but also as an outcome of entrepreneurship. For example, Gielnik, Spitzmuller, Schmitt, Klemann, and Frese (2014b) found that changes in passion are an outcome of entrepreneurial effort. Moreover, personality may change as a consequence of certain events. For example, Judge, Simon, Hurst, and Kelley (2014) provide evidence that work experiences shape personality traits. Consequently, future research should ask the following two questions: To what extent does entrepreneurship positively or negatively affect personality? And to what extent are individual characteristics an outcome of the entrepreneurial process? Future research adopting the trait approach should thus consider Bandura's (1978) concept of reciprocal determinism when analyzing new venture creation.

Furthermore, the field of entrepreneurial cognition offers a multitude of directions for future research. The main question is: What are important cognitive factors in new venture creation and how do they influence the success in the various phases of the entrepreneurial process? For example, Haynie, Shepherd, and Patzelt (2012) analyzed how differences in individuals' metacognitive ability, the ability to reduce the negative consequence of a knowledge deficit, and feedback type affect cognitive adaptability.

They found that individuals who scored high on metacognitive ability were more effective in adapting their decisions when new information became available. This suggests that individuals inexperienced in the entrepreneurial process can substitute this knowledge deficit to a certain degree. Grégoire, Corbett, and McMullen (2011) proposed an agenda for future research in the cognitive perspective. They emphasize the need to further analyze the relationship between mind, environment, and entrepreneurial action and to study the role and interactions of different cognitive variables at the same time on different levels of analysis.

With regard to the self-regulatory approach, scholars should research within-person changes of self-regulation and motivation. Lord, Diefendorff, Schmidt, and Hall (2010) point out several promising research opportunities including the analysis of the simultaneous pursuit of multiple goals and the levels of self-regulation involved. Furthermore, important motivational constructs, such as entrepreneurial passion, are not stable but change over time (Gielnik et al., 2014b). Lord et al. (2010) found that 50 percent of the variance in motivation and self-regulation is within-person variability. Thus, a dynamic approach as a direction for future research seems promising. Future research on fluctuations of constructs like entrepreneurial passion would contribute to our understanding of the temporal dynamics inherent in motivational factors.

Regarding entrepreneurial teams, empirical research provides evidence that founding teams are responsible for the majority of new venture creations and are generally more successful than single entrepreneurs (Cooper et al., 1989; Kamm et al., 1990; Lechler, 2001). Hence, it would be of great interest to gain a deeper understanding of the relational and cognitive dynamics and social processes in founding teams. We propose to analyze social processes and how they change along the different entrepreneurial phases and over time. This would allow for a better understanding of how social processes affect new venture creation.

Resources and their effects on new venture creation have been thoroughly studied. However, there is still potential for future research by focusing on how entrepreneurs overcome resource constraints. In this regard future research could analyze the relationship between bricolage, effectuation, and financial bootstrapping as well as which method to apply under what circumstances. Furthermore, cognitive factors might similarly attenuate the negative effect of capital constraints on new venture creation. For example, Bischoff, Gielnik, Frese, and Dlugosch (2013) provide evidence that entrepreneurs can overcome financial constraints through training that promotes financial mental models. Thus, analyzing moderating effects on the relationship between financial constraints and new venture creation offers a promising direction for future research.

Considering the institutional perspective, Welter (2011) calls for a stronger contextualization of entrepreneurship research in general and stresses that new venture creation not only takes place within a precise context but also carries its own context to the research project. Hence, interesting questions for future research from the institutional perspective are: How do the different institutional contexts enable as well as constrain the venture creation process? How does institutional change affect new venture creation? And how does entrepreneurship affect institutional change (Meek et al., 2010; Welter & Smallbone, 2011)? Since institutions not only constitute market entry barriers but also affect the growth and development of new ventures, we propose it would be interesting to conduct future research that incorporates all phases of the entrepreneurial process. In this context, future research could use longitudinal studies to gain a more nuanced understanding of new venture creation from an institutional perspective, and how the different institutions influence new venture performance across the phases of the entrepreneurial process.

Future Research: Combining the Different Perspectives and Taking an Integrative Approach

We propose that future research should consider a) the combined roles, and possible integrative effects, of the four categories and b) the intermediate role of entrepreneurial action in this process. Combining the different perspectives into an integrative perspective is the most promising avenue for future research. In this integrative perspective on new venture creation, the actions by the entrepreneur/the entrepreneurial team are at the center of factors predicting new venture creation (see Figure 10.1). We suggest placing entrepreneurs and their actions center stage because entrepreneurs are the ones who discover, evaluate, and exploit opportunities for new venture creation (Shane & Venkataraman, 2000; Shane, 2000). Entrepreneurs engage in start-up activities (developing business strategies, acquiring equipment, hiring employees, etc.) to establish viable business structures and operational procedures (Gartner, 1985). New venture creation is thus the outcome of the actions and decisions taken by entrepreneurs to exploit opportunities (Baron, 2007b; Lichtenstein, Carter, Dooley, & Gartner, 2007; McMullen & Shepherd, 2006).

The psychological perspective provides antecedents for entrepreneurial action (see Figure 10.1). For example, the personality trait creativity is related to entrepreneurial action and the resource perspective. This is because creativity will help entrepreneurs to process and combine new information, which has a positive effect on the generation of creative solutions to overcome resource constraints (Zhao & Seibert, 2006; Gielnik et al., 2012, 2014a). In a similar way, factors from the cognitive, self-regulation and affect approach act as antecedents for entrepreneurial action. Illusion of control, as an example of the cognitive approach, is a bias that indicates how likely it is that an individual overstates his or her ability to control a situation

that is mostly determined by chance (Keh et al., 2002). Hence, illusion of control lowers the perceived level of risk when entrepreneurs take action, resulting in more favorable opportunity evaluations (Keh et al., 2002). Illusion of control can therefore lead to a positive orientation resulting in greater effort (McKenna, 1993). In regard to formal institutions an entrepreneur might thus show more persistence to work his way around unfavorable regulations. Entrepreneurial passion, as an example of the affect approach, offers a further explanation of how entrepreneurs overcome uncertainties or unfavorable conditions. Entrepreneurial passion becomes particularly important when entrepreneurs are confronted with resource constraints, since passion leads to a higher degree of energy and effort (Baum & Locke, 2004). A specific example is the entrepreneur's passion for developing his venture. Passion for development is characterized by activities such as acquiring new customers, entering new markets, and adapting and improving organizational processes (Breugst, Domurath, Patzelt, & Klaukien, 2012). These activities affect the venture's employees and increase their motivation and commitment, which is imperative when faced with a lack of financial resources and the inability to pay competitive salaries (Breugst et al., 2012).

The team perspective provides further antecedents for entrepreneurial action, visualized in Figure 10.1 as the line connecting the team perspective with entrepreneurial action. For example, the initial team size affects the pool of available resources that the team can use to start its business. Hence, a smaller team with a smaller pool of resources may have to invest more effort into overcoming resource constraints. Correspondingly, a homogeneous team, with similar skills and a similar knowledge background, may have to invest more time into searching for information and developing business strategies. Additionally, relational capabilities such as the team's social competence decide how successfully the team is connected to third parties (Baron & Markman, 2003). This can affect the team's capability to exploit opportunities that emerge from new regulations, laws, or strategic alliances, for instance, gaining access to new distribution channels or securing the support and services of different stakeholders.

The resource perspective and especially the existence of resource constraints is a common approach to explain new venture creation or why it may be limited (Chrisman et al., 1998). However, we argue that financial resources are important but constraints can be overcome through entrepreneurial actions and action strategies. For example, the lack of financial capital can be overcome by engaging in financial bootstrapping (Winborg & Landström, 2001). In other words, the lack of financial capital induces the entrepreneur to engage in alternative actions such as borrowing resources from other businesses. The above mentioned concepts of bricolage and effectuation offer two further pathways to create a new venture under financial resource constraints. Effectuation suggests that entrepreneurs achieve their aims by concentrating on their given means (Sarasvathy, 2001). In this context, entrepreneurs may utilize their networks and form alliances or partnerships in order to acquire the necessary financial capital (Sarasvathy, 2001). Bricolage suggest that entrepreneurs improvise and continuously adapt in order to achieve their aims (Garud & Karnøe, 2003). This is done by using existing resources and applying them in creative and useful ways (Gundry, Kickul, Griffiths, & Bacq, 2011). For instance, in their comparative study Garud and Karnøe (2003) follow a Danish producer of wind turbines, who successfully applies a bricolage approach by using modest resources and local knowledge, in order to progressively build up a viable product. Thus, resource constraints may not hinder new venture creation but lead to the application of new or different action strategies.

Institutions play a significant role in new venture creation. Manolova et al. (2008),

Meek et al. (2010) and Welter (2011) show that formal, as well as informal, and social institutions can promote the creation of new ventures. Meek et al.'s (2010) findings further suggest that institutions affect the type of new venture that is created. This is in line with Welter's (2011) notions that local traditions define gender roles, which in turn affect the nature and extent of female entrepreneurship. However, we argue that entrepreneurs are not merely influenced by institutions, but act as change agents who create and alter existing institutions. This becomes especially apparent when looking at social or ecological venture creations, where entrepreneurs are more prone to question the existing paradigms, attempt to do more with less, and focus on long-term sustainability rather than short-term gain (Spence et al., 2011). Pacheco et al. (2010) identified three ways in which entrepreneurial action can change existing institutions. First, by changing industry norms; Pacheco et al. (2010) provide examples from the coffee, tourism, and nanotechnology industry, in which social norms were changed by entrepreneurs through the introduction of formal and informal codes of conduct. Second, entrepreneurs can establish self-enforced property rights (Pacheco et al., 2010). In their study Pacheco et al. (2010) offer an example of how local fishermen established property rights in order to maintain the lobster population and thus create an environment for sustained venture survival. Third, entrepreneurs can act as change agents by obtaining support from governmental legislation in order to implement cooperative behavior. In this case, Pacheco et al. (2010) refer to the solar energy industry, which achieves the intervention of the government through the Solar Energy Industries Association. This association acts as a voice for the solar energy industry, lobbying its interests. In all three cases, entrepreneurs' actions change institutions. Figure 10.1 depicts this interplay as the intersection between institutions, entrepreneurial actions, and new venture creation.

Hence, the integrative perspective suggests that the psychological, team, institutional, and resource perspective alone do not sufficiently explain new venture creation. Instead it is the combination of these perspectives and the entrepreneur's actions that provide a comprehensive idea of the interplay between the different factors.

CONCLUSION

In this chapter, we sought to demonstrate that there have been different perspectives which scholars have used to explain new venture creation. These perspectives are the psychological, team, resource, and institutional perspectives. The psychological perspective deals with how entrepreneurs think, how they regulate and take control of their actions to achieve their goals, and how emotions affect their actions. The team perspective replaces the concept of the single entrepreneur with the founding team and its members; the team perspective thus moves research to an interpersonal level, looking at how the team's size and composition as well as the social processes affect the team's action. The resource perspective looks at the role of tangible and intangible resources and their effects on new venture creation. Finally, the institutional perspective deals with new venture creation from a macro-perspective, distinguishing between formal (e.g. laws and regulations), informal (e.g. culture and norms), and social institutions (e.g. networks). Although these different perspectives make their unique contributions, we suggest that a thorough understanding of new venture creation requires an integrative model combining the different perspectives into a single theoretical framework. Only an integrated theoretical model gives due consideration to the complexities entrepreneurs deal with when engaging in new venture creation. This model is depicted in Figure 10.1, with entrepreneurial action at the center. The other factors either indirectly influence new venture

creation through the entrepreneurs' actions or interact with the entrepreneurs' actions on new venture creation.

The review of the literature presented in this chapter has several theoretical implications. We can infer that factors on the individual, team, and societal level influence new venture creation. Scholars can use a theoretical framework from each level to examine and explain new venture creation. However, a more promising approach resulting in theoretical models with higher predictive value is to combine and integrate theories from different levels. For example, Hmieleski and Baron (2009) have used social cognitive theory (Bandura, 1989) to explain growth of new ventures. Social cognitive theory proposes that there is a reciprocal determinism between factors on the individual level (e.g. personality), individuals' actions, and the environment (e.g. resources and institutions). Hmieleski and Baron (2009) showed that entrepreneurs' optimism (a construct rooted in the psychological perspective) interacts with environmental dynamism (an environmental construct) in predicting new venture growth. This study demonstrates the value of taking an integrative perspective. Besides social cognitive theory (Bandura, 1989), the action-characteristic model of entrepreneurship (Frese & Gielnik, 2014) explicitly considers factors on different levels to explain new venture creation. We hope that future research builds on these theories and develops new theoretical frameworks, integrating the different perspectives into a comprehensive model of new venture creation.

The chapter also has several practical implications. While each theoretical perspective (psychological, team, resource, and institutional) provides its own recommendations to promote new venture creation, there are two approaches, which follow from the theoretical model presented in Figure 10.1. First, the model puts action center stage. This means that interventions focusing on facilitating action should be particularly effective. Recently, scholars have presented training interventions to enhance personal initiative and entrepreneurial action with beneficial effects on new venture performance and new venture creation (Gielnik et al., 2015; Glaub, Frese, Fischer, & Hoppe, 2014). Second, these training interventions should complement interventions which have been implemented on macro levels. For example, reports by the World Bank (2010) on the ease of doing business show that governments are constantly changing the regulatory requirements to facilitate entrepreneurship. Similarly, several measures have been taken to provide entrepreneurs with easy access to capital (De Mel et al., 2008). An integrative perspective combining the individual/team perspective with the resource and institutional perspective should provide better results in promoting new venture creation. In fact, the study by De Mel et al. (2008) provides evidence that providing financial resources works best when entrepreneurs have acquired the necessary abilities to effectively use the financial capital. Similarly, changing regulatory frameworks so that they become more conducive to entrepreneurship only translates into successful entrepreneurship when people take the necessary actions to benefit from the new laws and regulations.

Although an integrative perspective may complicate things in research on new venture creation because it assumes that no single theoretical perspective is sufficient, we think that adopting such a perspective is most promising in advancing our understanding of new venture creation.

REFERENCES

Adler, P. S., and Kwon, S. (2002). Social capital: Prospects for a new concept. *Academy of Management*, 27(1), 17–40.

Aldrich, H., and Zimmer, C. (1986). Entrepreneurship through social networks. In D. Sexton & R. Smilor (Eds), *The Art and Science of Entrepreneurship* (pp. 3–23). Cambridge: Ballinger.

Alvarez, S. A., and Busenitz, L. W. (2001). The entrepreneurship of resource-based theory. *Journal of Management*, 27(6), 755–775.

Ardichvili, A., Cardozo, R., and Ray, S. (2003). A theory of entrepreneurial opportunity identification and development. *Journal of Business Venturing*, 18(1), 105–123.

Baker, T., and Nelson, R. E. (2005). Creating something from nothing: Resource construction through entrepreneurial bricolage. *Administrative Science Quarterly*, 50(3), 329–366.

Bandura, A. (1978). The self system in reciprocal determinism. *American Psychologist*, 33(4), 344–358.

Bandura, A. (1989). Human agency in social cognitive theory. *American Psychology Association*, 44(9), 1175–1184.

Bandura, A. (1991). Social cognitive theory of self-regulation. *Organizational Behavior and Human Decision Processes*, 50(2), 248–287.

Barney, J. (1991). Firm resources and sustained competitive advantage. *Journal of Management*, 17(1), 99–120.

Baron, R. A. (2004). The cognitive perspective: A valuable tool for answering entrepreneurship's basic 'why' questions. *Journal of Business Venturing*, 19(2), 221–239.

Baron, R. A. (2006). Opportunity recognition as pattern recognition: How entrepreneurs 'connect the dots' to identify new business opportunities. *The Academy of Management Perspectives*, 20(1), 104–120.

Baron, R. A. (2007a). Behavioral and cognitive factors in entrepreneurship: Entrepreneurs as the active element in new venture creation. *Strategic Entrepreneurship Journal*, 1(1–2), 167–182.

Baron, R. A. (2007b). Entrepreneurship: A process perspective. In J. R. Baum, M. Frese, & R. A. Baron (Eds), *The Psychology of Entrepreneurship* (pp. 19–40). Mahwah, NJ: Lawrence Erlbaum.

Baron, R. A. (2008). The role of affect in the entrepreneurial process. *Academy of Management Journal*, 33(2), 328–340.

Baron, R. A., Hmieleski, K. M., and Henry, R. A. (2012). Entrepreneurs' dispositional positive affect: The potential benefits – and potential costs – of being 'up'. *Journal of Business Venturing*, 27(3), 310–324.

Baron, R. A., and Markman, G. D. (2003). Beyond social capital: The role of entrepreneurs' social competence in their financial success. *Journal of Business Venturing, 18*(1), 41–60.

Baron, R. A., and Tang, J. (2008). Entrepreneurs' social skills and new venture performance: Mediating mechanisms and cultural generality. *Journal of Management, 35*(2), 282–306.

Baron, R. A., and Ward, T. B. (2004). Expanding entrepreneurial cognition's toolbox: Potential contributions from the field of cognitive science. *Entrepreneurship: Theory and Practice, 28*(6), 553–573.

Baughn, C., and Neupert, K. (2003). Culture and national conditions facilitating entrepreneurial start-ups. *Journal of International Entrepreneurship, 1*(3), 313–330.

Baum, J. R., and Frese, M. (2007). Entrepreneurship as an area of psychology study: An introduction. In J. R. Baum, M. Frese, & R. A. Baron (Eds), *The Psychology of Entrepreneurship* (pp. 1–18). Mahwah, NJ: Lawrence Erlbaum.

Baum, J. R., and Locke, E. A. (2004). The relationship of entrepreneurial traits, skill, and motivation to subsequent venture growth. *The Journal of Applied Psychology, 89*(4), 587–598.

Baum, J. R., Locke, E. A., and Kirkpatrick, S. A. (1998). A longitudinal study of the relation of vision and vision communication to venture growth in entrepreneurial firms. *Journal of Applied Psychology, 83*(1), 43–54.

Bird, B. J. (1988). Implementing entrepreneurial ideas: The case for intention. *Academy of Management Review, 13*(3), 442–453.

Bird, B. J. (1989). *Entrepreneurial Behavior* (Volume 8). Glenview, IL: Scott Foresman & Company.

Bischoff, K. M., Gielnik, M. M., Frese, M., and Dlugosch, T. J. (2013). Limited access to capital, start-ups, and the moderating effect of an entrepreneurship training: Integrating economic and psychological theories in the context of new venture creation. *Presented at Babson College Entrepreneurship Research Conference, June 5–8, Lyon, France.*

Bledow, R., Rosing, K., and Frese, M. (2013). A dynamic perspective on affect and creativity. *Academy of Management Journal, 56*(2), 432–450.

Bledow, R., Schmitt, A., Frese, M., and Kühnel, J. (2011). The affective shift model of work engagement. *Journal of Applied Psychology, 96*(6), 1246–1257.

Boas, T. C. (2007). Conceptualizing continuity and change: The composite-standard model of path dependence. *Journal of Theoretical Politics, 19*(1), 33–54.

Brandstätter, H. (2011). Personality aspects of entrepreneurship: A look at five meta-analyses. *Personality and Individual Differences, 51*(3), 222–230.

Breugst, N., Domurath, A., Patzelt, H., and Klaukien, A. (2012). Perceptions of entrepreneurial passion and employees' commitment to entrepreneurial ventures. *Entrepreneurship Theory and Practice, 36*(1), 171–192.

Brinckmann, J., Grichnik, D., and Kapsa, D. (2010). Should entrepreneurs plan or just storm the castle? A meta-analysis on contextual factors impacting the business planning-performance relationship in small firms. *Journal of Business Venturing, 25*(1), 24–40.

Brinckmann, J., and Hoegl, M. (2011). Effects of initial teamwork capability and initial relational capability on the development of new technology-based firms. *Strategic Entrepreneurship Journal, 5*(1), 37–57.

Brinckmann, J., Salomo, S., and Gemuenden, H. G. (2011). Financial management competence of founding teams and growth of new technology-based firms. *Entrepreneurship: Theory and Practice, 35*(2), 217–243.

Cardon, M. S., Grégoire, D. A., Stevens, C. E., and Patel, P. C. (2013). Measuring entrepreneurial passion: Conceptual foundations and scale validation. *Journal of Business Venturing, 28*(3), 373–396.

Cardon, M. S., Sudek, R., and Mitteness, C. (2009). The impact of perceived entrepreneurial passion on angel investing. *Frontiers of Entrepreneurship Research, 29*(2), 1–15.

Carter, N. M., Gartner, W. B., and Reynolds, P. D. (1996). Exploring start up event sequences. *Journal of Business Venturing, 11*(3), 151–166.

Carver, C. S., and Scheier, M. F. (1982). Control theory: A useful conceptual framework for personality-social, clinical, and health psychology. *Psychological Bulletin, 92*(1), 111–135.

Castrogiovanni, G. J. (1991). Environmental munificence: A theoretical assessment. *The Academy of Management Review, 16*(3), 542–565.

Castrogiovanni, G. J. (1996). Pre-startup planning and the survival of new small businesses: Theoretical linkages. *Journal of Management, 22*(6), 801–822.

Chen, C. C., Greene, P. G., and Crick, A. (1998). Does entrepreneurial self-efficacy distinguish entrepreneurs from managers? *Journal of Business Venturing, 13*(4), 295–316.

Chrisman, J. J., Bauerschmidt, A., and Hofer, C. W. (1998). The determinants of new venture performance: An extended model. *Entrepreneurship: Theory & Practice, 23*(1), 5–29.

Collins, C. J., Hanges, P. J., and Locke, E. A. (2004). The relationship of achievement motivation to entrepreneurial behavior: A meta-analysis. *Human Performance, 17*(1), 95–117.

Cooney, T. M. (2005). Editorial: What is an entrepreneurial team? *International Small Business Journal, 23*(3), 226–235.

Cooper, A. C., Woo, C. Y., and Dunkelberg, W. C. (1989). Entrepreneurship and the initial size of firms. *Journal of Business Venturing, 4*(5), 317–332.

Crook, T. R., Todd, S. Y., Combs, J. G., Woehr, D. J., and Ketchen, D. J. (2011). Does human capital matter? A meta-analysis of the relationship between human capital and firm performance. *The Journal of Applied Psychology, 96*(3), 443–456.

Dana, L. P. (2000). Creating entrepreneurs in India. *Journal of Small Business Management, 38*(1), 86–92.

Dawson, C., and Henley, A. (2012). Over-optimism and entry and exit from self-employment. *International Small Business Journal, 31*(8), 938–954.

Delmar, F., and Shane, S. A. (2003). Does business planning facilitate the development of new ventures? *Strategic Management Journal, 24*(12), 1165–1185.

De Mel, S., McKenzie, D., and Woodruff, C. M. (2008). Returns to capital in microenterprises: Evidence from a field experiment. *The Quarterly Journal of Economics, 123*(4), 1329–1372.

Eisenhardt, K. M., and Schoonhoven, C. B. (1990). Organizational growth: Linking founding team, strategy, environment, and growth among U.S. semiconductor ventures, 1978–1988. *Administrative Science Quarterly, 35*(3), 504–529.

Ensley, M. D., and Hmieleski, K. M. (2005). A comparative study of new venture top management team composition, dynamics and performance between university-based and independent start-ups. *Research Policy, 34*(7), 1091–1105.

Ensley, M. D., and Pearce, C. L. (2001). Shared cognition in top management teams: Implications for new venture performance. *Journal of Organizational Behavior, 22*(2), 145–160.

Ensley, M. D., Pearson, A., and Amason, A. (2002). Understanding the dynamics of new venture top management teams: Cohesion, conflict, and new venture performance. *Journal of Business Venturing, 17*(4), 365–386.

Evans, D. S., and Leighton, L. S. (1989). Some empirical aspects of entrepreneurship. *American Economic Review, 79*(3), 519–535.

Feeser, H. R., and Willard, G. E. (1990). Founding strategy and performance: A comparison of high and low growth high tech firms. *Strategic Management Journal, 11*(2), 87–98.

Fisher, G. (2012). Effectuation, causation, and bricolage: A behavioral comparison of emerging theories in entrepreneurship research. *Entrepreneurship: Theory and Practice, 36*(5), 1019–1051.

Foo, M. D., Uy, M. A., and Baron, R. A. (2009). How do feelings influence effort? An empirical study of entrepreneurs' affect and venture effort. *The Journal of Applied Psychology, 94*(4), 1086–1094.

Forbes, D. P., Borchert, P. S., Zellmer-Bruhn, M. E., and Sapienza, H. J. (2006). Entrepreneurial team formation: An exploration of new member addition. *Entrepreneurship: Theory and Practice, 30*(2), 225–248.

Freear, J., and Wetzel, W. E. (1990). Who bankrolls high-tech entrepreneurs? *Journal of Business Venturing, 5*(2), 77–89.

Frese, M. (2007). The psychological actions and entrepreneurial success: An action theory approach. In J. R. Baum, M. Frese, & R. A. Baron (Eds), *The Psychology of Entrepreneurship* (pp. 151–189). Mahwah, NJ: Lawrence Erlbaum.

Frese, M. (2009). Toward a psychology of entrepreneurship: An action theory perspective. *Foundations and Trends® in Entrepreneurship, 5*(6), 437–496.

Frese, M., and Gielnik, M. M. (2014). The psychology of entrepreneurship. *Annual Review of Organizational Psychology and Organizational Behavior*, *1*(1), 413–438.

Frese, M., Krauss, S. I., Keith, N., Escher, S., Grabarkiewicz, R., Luneng, S. T., and Friedrich, C. (2007). Business owners' action planning and its relationship to business success in three African countries. *The Journal of Applied Psychology*, *92*(6), 1481–1498.

Frese, M., and Zapf, D. (1994). Action as the core of work psychology: A German approach. In H. C. Triandis, M. D. Dunnette, & L. M. Hough (Eds), *Handbook of Industrial and Organizational Psychology, Vol. 4 (2nd ed.)* (pp. 271–340). Palo Alto, CA: Consulting Psychologists Press.

Funken, R., and Gielnik, M. M. (2015). Entrepreneurship and aging. In N. A. Pachana (Ed.), *Encyclopedia of Geropsychology* (pp. 1–7). Singapore: Springer.

Gartner, W. B. (1985). A conceptual framework for describing the phenomenon of new venture creation. *Academy of Management Review*, *10*(4), 696–706.

Gartner, W. B. (1988). Who is an entrepreneur? Is the wrong question. *American Journal of Small Business*, *12*(4), 11–32.

Gartner, W. B. (1995). Aspects of organizational emergence. In I. Bull, H. Thomas, & G. Willard (Eds.), *Entrepreneurship: Perspectives on Theory Building* (pp. 67–86). Oxford: Pergamon.

Garud, R., and Karnøe, P. (2003). Bricolage versus breakthrough: Distributed and embedded agency in technology entrepreneurship. *Research Policy*, *32*(2), 277–300.

Gielnik, M. M., Barabas, S., Frese, M., Namatovu-Dawa, R., Scholz, F. A., Metzger, J. R., and Walter, T. (2013). A temporal analysis of how entrepreneurial goal intentions, positive fantasies, and action planning affect starting a new venture and when the effects wear off. *Journal of Business Venturing*, *29*(6), 755–772.

Gielnik, M. M., Frese, M., Graf, J. M., and Kampschulte, A. (2012). Creativity in the opportunity identification process and the moderating effect of diversity of information. *Journal of Business Venturing*, *27*(5), 559–576.

Gielnik, M. M., Frese, M., Kahara-Kawuki, A., Wasswa Katono, I., Kyejjusa, S., Ngoma, M.,

… Dlugosch, T. J. (2015). Action and action-regulation in entrepreneurship: Evaluating a student training for promoting entrepreneurship. *Academy of Management Learning & Education*, *14*(1), 69–94.

Gielnik, M. M., Krämer, A. C., Kappel, B., and Frese, M. (2014a). Antecedents of business opportunity identification and innovation: Investigating the interplay of information processing and information acquisition. *Applied Psychology*, *63*(2), 344–381.

Gielnik, M. M., Spitzmuller, M., Schmitt, A., Klemann, D. K., and Frese, M. (2014b). I put in effort, therefore I am passionate: Investigating the path from effort to passion in entrepreneurship. *Academy of Management Journal*, *58*(4), 1012–1031.

Glaub, M. E., Frese, M., Fischer, S., and Hoppe, M. (2014). Increasing personal initiative in small business managers or owners leads to entrepreneurial success: A theory-based controlled randomized field intervention for evidence-based management. *Academy of Management Learning & Education*, *13*(3), 354–379.

Grégoire, D., Corbett, A., and McMullen, J. S. (2011). The cognitive perspective in entrepreneurship: An agenda for future research. *Journal of Management Studies*, *48*(6), 1443–1477.

Gruber, M. (2007). Uncovering the value of planning in new venture creation: A process and contingency perspective. *Journal of Business Venturing*, *22*(6), 782–807.

Gundry, L. K., Kickul, J. R., Griffiths, M. D., and Bacq, S. C. (2011). Entrepreneurial bricolage and innovation ecology: Precursors to social innovation? *Frontiers of Entrepreneurship Research*, *31*(19), 659–673.

Haleblian, J., and Finkelstein, S. (1993). Top management team size, CEO dominance, and firm performance: The moderating roles of environmental turbulence and discretion. *Academy of Management Journal*, *36*(4), 844–863.

Haynie, J. M., Shepherd, D. A., and Patzelt, H. (2012). Cognitive adaptability and an entrepreneurial task: The role of metacognitive ability and feedback. *Entrepreneurship: Theory and Practice*, *36*(2), 237–265.

Hisrich, R., Langan-Fox, J., and Grant, S. (2007). Entrepreneurship research and practice:

A call to action for psychology. *The American Psychologist*, *62*(6), 575–589.

Hmieleski, K. M., and Baron, R. A. (2009). Entrepreneurs' optimism and new venture performance: A social cognitive perspective. *Academy of Management Journal*, *52*(3), 473–488.

Ho, Y. P., and Wong, P. K. (2007). Financing, regulatory costs and entrepreneurial propensity. *Small Business Economics*, *28*(2–3), 187–204.

Hoegl, M., and Gemuenden, H. G. (2001). Teamwork quality and the success of innovative projects. *Organization Science*, *12*(4), 435–449.

Holtz-Eakin, D., Joulfaian, D., and Rosen, H. S. (1994). Sticking it out: Entrepreneurial survival and liquidity constraints. *Journal of Political Economy*, *102*(1), 53–75.

Honig, B., and Samuelsson, M. (2012). Planning and the entrepreneur: A longitudinal examination of nascent entrepreneurs in Sweden. *Journal of Small Business Management*, *50*(3), 365–388.

Hoogendoorn, S., Oosterbeek, H., and van Praag, M. (2013). The impact of gender diversity on the performance of business teams: Evidence from a field experiment. *Management Science*, *59*(7), 1514–1528.

Jack, S. L., and Anderson, A. R. (2002). The effects of embeddedness on the entrepreneurial process. *Journal of Business Venturing*, *17*(5), 467–487.

Johnstone, H., and Lionais, D. (2004). Depleted communities and community business entrepreneurship: Revaluing space through place. *Entrepreneurship & Regional Development*, *16*(3), 217–233.

Judge, T. A., and Ilies, R. (2002). Relationship of personality to performance motivation: A meta-analytic review. *The Journal of Applied Psychology*, *87*(4), 797–807.

Judge, T. A., Simon, L. S., Hurst, C., and Kelley, K. (2014). What I experienced yesterday is who I am today: Relationship of work motivations and behaviors to within-individual variation in the five-factor model of personality. *The Journal of Applied Psychology*, *99*(2), 199–221.

Kamm, J. B., Shuman, J. C., Seeger, J. A., and Nurick, A. J. (1990). Entrepreneurial teams in new venture creation: A research agenda. *Entrepreneurship: Theory and Practice*, *14*(4), 7–17.

Karoly, P. (1993). Mechanisms of self-regulation: A systems view. *Annual Review of Psychology*, *44*(1), 23–52.

Katz, J., and Gartner, W. B. (1988). Properties of emerging organizations. *Academy of Management Review*, *13*(3), 429–441.

Keh, H., Foo, M. D., and Lim, B. (2002). Opportunity evaluation under risky conditions: The cognitive processes of entrepreneurs. *Entrepreneurship Theory and Practice*, *27*(2), 125–148.

Kerr, N. L., and Tindale, R. S. (2004). Group performance and decision making. *Annual Review of Psychology*, *55*(1), 623–655.

Klotz, A. C., Hmieleski, K. M., Bradley, B. H., and Busenitz, L. W. (2013). New venture teams: A review of the literature and roadmap for future research. *Journal of Management*, *40*(1), 226–255.

Lechler, T. (2001). Social interaction: A determinant of entrepreneurial team venture success. *Small Business Economics*, *16*(4), 263–278.

Lichtenstein, B. B., Carter, N. M., Dooley, K. J., and Gartner, W. B. (2007). Complexity dynamics of nascent entrepreneurship. *Journal of Business Venturing*, *22*(2), 236–261.

Lord, R. G., Diefendorff, J. M., Schmidt, A. M., and Hall, R. J. (2010). Self-regulation at work. *Annual Review of Psychology*, *61*(1), 543–568.

Luthans, F., Stajkovic, A. D., and Ibrayeva, E. (2000). Environmental and psychological challenges facing entrepreneurial development in transitional economies. *Journal of World Business*, *35*(1), 95–110.

Manolova, T. S., Eunni, R. V., and Gyoshev, B. S. (2008). Institutional environments for entrepreneurship: Evidence from emerging economies in Eastern Europe. *Entrepreneurship: Theory and Practice*, *32*(1), 203–218.

Martin, B. C., McNally, J. J., and Kay, M. J. (2013). Examining the formation of human capital in entrepreneurship: A meta-analysis of entrepreneurship education outcomes. *Journal of Business Venturing*, *28*(2), 211–224.

McClelland, D. C. (1965). N achievement and entrepreneurship: A longitudinal study. *Journal of Personality and Social Psychology*, *1*(4), 389–392.

McKenna, F. P. (1993). It won't happen to me: Unrealistic optimism or illusion of control? *British Journal of Psychology*, *84*(1), 39–50.

McMullen, J. S., and Shepherd, D. A. (2006). Entrepreneurial action and the role of uncertainty in the theory of the entrepreneur. *Academy of Management Review*, *31*(1), 132–152.

Meek, W. R., Pacheco, D. F., and York, J. G. (2010). The impact of social norms on entrepreneurial action: Evidence from the environmental entrepreneurship context. *Journal of Business Venturing*, *25*(5), 493–509.

Mitchell, R. K., Busenitz, L. W., Bird, B. J., Gaglio, M. G., McMullen, J. S., Morse, E. A., and Smith, J. B. (2007). The central question in entrepreneurial cognition research. *Entrepreneurship Theory and Practice*, *31*(1), 1–27.

Mitchell, R. K., Busenitz, L. W., Lant, T., McDougall, P. P., Morse, E. A., and Smith, J. B. (2002). Toward a theory of entrepreneurial cognition: Rethinking the people side of entrepreneurship research. *Entrepreneurship Theory and Practice*, *27*(2), 93–104.

Norman, W. T. (1963). Toward an adequate taxonomy of personality attributes: Replicated factors structure in peer nomination personality ratings. *Journal of Abnormal and Social Psychology*, *66*(6), 574–583.

North, D. C. (1990). *Institutions, Institutional Change and Economic Performance*. Cambridge: Cambridge University Press.

Pacheco, D. F., Dean, T. J., and Payne, D. S. (2010). Escaping the green prison: Entrepreneurship and the creation of opportunities for sustainable development. *Journal of Business Venturing*, *25*(5), 464–480.

Pearce, C. L., Gallagher, C. A., and Ensley, M. D. (2002). Confidence at the group level of analysis: A longitudinal investigation of the relationship between potency and team effectiveness. *Journal of Occupational & Organizational Psychology*, *75*(1), 115–119.

Peteraf, M. A. (1993). The cornerstones of competitive advantage: A resource-based view. *Strategic Management Journal*, *14*(3), 179–191.

Rauch, A., and Frese, M. (2007). Let's put the person back into entrepreneurship research: A meta-analysis on the relationship between business owners' personality traits, business creation, and success. *European Journal of Work and Organizational Psychology*, *16*(4), 353–385.

Read, S., Song, M., and Smit, W. (2009). A meta-analytic review of effectuation and venture performance. *Journal of Business Venturing*, *24*(6), 573–587.

Russell, J. A. (1980). A circumplex model of affect. *Journal of Personality and Social Psychology*, *39*(6), 1161–1178.

Sarasvathy, S. D. (2001). Toward causation and effectuation: A theoretical shift from inevitability to economic entrepreneurial contingency. *The Academy of Management Review*, *26*(2), 243–263.

Scott, W. R. (1987). The adolescence of institutional theory. *Administrative Science Quarterly*, *32*(4), 493–511.

Shane, S. A. (2000). Prior knowledge and the discovery of entrepreneurial opportunities. *Organization Science*, *11*(4), 448–469.

Shane, S. A. (2003). *A General Theory of Entrepreneurship: The Individual-Opportunity Nexus*. Cheltenham: Edward Elgar Publishing.

Shane, S. A., and Venkataraman, S. (2000). The promise of entrepreneurship as a field of research. *The Academy of Management Review*, *25*(1), 217–226.

Shepherd, D. A., and Patzelt, H. (2011). The new field of sustainable entrepreneurship: Studying entrepreneurial action linking 'what is to be sustained' with 'what is to be developed'. *Entrepreneurship: Theory and Practice*, *35*(1), 137–163.

Simon, M., Houghton, S. M., and Aquino, K. (2000). Cognitive biases, risk perception, and venture formation. *Journal of Business Venturing*, *15*(2), 113–134.

Sine, W. D., Mitsuhashi, H., and Kirsch, D. A. (2006). Revisiting Burns and Stalker: Formal structure and new venture performance in emerging economic sectors. *Academy of Management Journal*, *49*(1), 121–132.

Smallbone, D., and Welter, F. (2010). *Entrepreneurship and Small Business Development in Post-Socialist Economies*. London: Routledge.

Spence, M., Gherib, J. B. B., and Biwolé, V. O. (2011). Sustainable entrepreneurship: Is entrepreneurial will enough? A north-south comparison. *Journal of Business Ethics*, *99*(3), 335–367.

Stam, W., Arzlanian, S., and Elfring, T. (2014). Social capital of entrepreneurs and small firm performance: A meta-analysis of contextual and methodological moderators. *Journal of Business Venturing*, *29*(1), 152–173.

Stewart, W. H., and Roth, P. L. (2004). Data quality affects meta-analytic conclusions: A response to Miner and Raju (2004) concerning entrepreneurial risk propensity. *The Journal of Applied Psychology*, *89*(1), 14–21.

Teach, R. D., Tarplay, F. A., and Schwartz, R. G. (1986). Software venture teams. In R. Ronstadt, J. A. Hornaday, R. Peterson, & K. Vesper (Eds), *Frontiers of Entrepreneurship Research* (pp. 546–562). Wellesley: Babson College.

Unger, J., Rauch, A., Frese, M., and Rosenbusch, N. (2011). Human capital and entrepreneurial success: A meta-analytic review. *Journal of Business Venturing*, *26*(3), 341–358.

Van Auken, H. E., and Neeley, L. (1996). Evidence of bootstrap financing among small start-up firms. *The Journal of Entrepreneurial and Small Business Finance*, *5*(3), 235–249.

Van Knippenberg, D., De Dreu, C. K. W., and Homan, A. C. (2004). Work group diversity and group performance: An integrative model and research agenda. *Journal of Applied Psychology*, *89*(6), 1008–1022.

Van Knippenberg, D., and Schippers, M. C. (2007). Work group diversity. *Annual Review of Psychology*, *58*(1), 515–541.

Venkataraman, S., Sarasvathy, S. D., Dew, N., and Forster, W. R. (2012). Whither the promise? Moving forward with entrepreneurship as a science of the artificial. *Academy of Management Review*, *37*(1), 1–34.

Welter, F. (2011). Contextualizing entrepreneurship-conceptual challenges and ways forward. *Entrepreneurship: Theory and Practice*, *35*(1), 165–184.

Welter, F., and Smallbone, D. (2011). Institutional perspectives on entrepreneurial behavior in challenging environments. *Journal of Small Business Management*, *49*(1), 107–125.

West, G. P. (2007). Collective cognition: When entrepreneurial teams, not individuals, make decisions. *Entrepreneurship: Theory and Practice*, *31*(1), 77–102.

Winborg, J., and Landström, H. (2001). Financial bootstrapping in small businesses. *Journal of Business Venturing*, *16*(3), 235–254.

World Bank. (2010). *Doing Business 2011: Making a difference for entrepreneurs*. Washington DC: World Bank.

Wright, P. (1987). Research notes and communications: A refinement of Porter's strategies. *Strategic Management Journal*, *8*(1), 93–101.

Yang, K. (2004). Institutional holes and entrepreneurship in China. *The Sociological Review*, *52*(3), 371–389.

Zhao, H., and Seibert, S. E. (2006). The big five personality dimensions and entrepreneurial status: A meta-analytical review. *The Journal of Applied Psychology*, *91*(2), 259–271.

Zhou, J. (2008). New look at creativity in the entrepreneurial process. *Strategic Entrepreneurship Journal*, *2*(1), 1–5.

Zimmerman, M. A., and Zeitz, G. J. (2002). Beyond survival: Achieving new venture growth by building legitimacy. *Academy of Management Review*, *27*(3), 414–431.

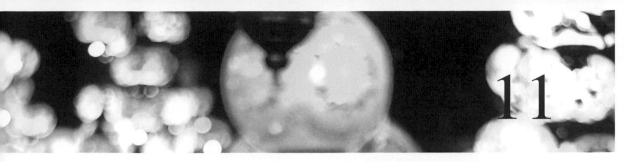

11

New Venture Growth: Current Findings and Future Challenges

Ivan Zupic and Alessandro Giudici

INTRODUCTION

Everybody seems to be interested in growth. Politicians and policymakers love growth because it brings new jobs and helps economic development. Startup founders want advice on growing their ventures into multibillion dollar companies. Academics want to understand growth in order to help entrepreneurs and politicians achieve it. From a practice point of view, the recently established Future 50 program backed by the UK government to accelerate the growth of a selected group of high-growth digital startups represents a case in point. A thorough understanding of new venture growth is therefore critical when establishing these kinds of programs.

New venture growth is one of the founding topics of entrepreneurship research. Growth is a multidimensional and complex phenomenon (Davidsson, Achtenhagen, & Naldi, 2010; Delmar, Davidsson, & Gartner, 2003). It can be viewed as the development of the firm or simply as quantitative change in the size of the

firm (Penrose, 1959). Growth is also one of the most frequently used measures of firm performance. A number of studies, whose explicit aim was not to study firm growth, have used growth as a measure of firm performance. This chapter focuses on new venture growth and is organized in two sections.

First, we review the state-of-the-art of the literature on new venture growth and classify this into three perspectives: the research on high-growth firms, which comes mainly from an economic perspective; the research on factors driving firm growth (i.e. antecedents of growth), which represents the entrepreneurial perspective; and research on the growth process. Research on high-growth firms primarily utilizes large-scale secondary databases to research stylized facts about populations of high-growth new ventures and their effect on the wider economy, mainly in relation to GDP growth and the employment rate. The second perspective uses quantitative and qualitative methods to investigate questions relating to how different factors (e.g. human capital, social capital, finance, and strategy) influence new venture growth levels. Finally, the third perspective investigates the process of new venture growth. Process research comes primarily in the form of stages-of-growth models (e.g. Churchill & Lewis, 1983; Hanks, Watson, Jansen, & Chandler, 1993; Kazanjian, 1988). These models have, however, been heavily criticized as overly deterministic (Levie & Lichtenstein, 2010) and are thus less diffused in contemporary research. Arguably, new research approaches are needed to reinvigorate this latter stream, which is also likely to be most useful to entrepreneurs in practice.

Finally, we outline our suggestions for moving the research agenda forward. We summarize the suggestions of previous major reviews and discuss methodological and measurement challenges in designing growth studies. Further, we argue that the extant research is not sufficiently useful to policy-makers and entrepreneurs and thus pay specific attention to proposing future research directions that might address this gap.

New venture growth research is a vast and fragmented landscape that is impossible to cover in-depth in one chapter. We focused on summarizing the core contributions, but space constraints have meant the exclusion of some nuanced discussions. We will therefore occasionally point the reader to more extensive discussions of specific subject matter.

NEW VENTURE GROWTH: CURRENT FINDINGS

This section summarizes current findings in firm growth research. We divide the literature into three sections: (1) research on high-growth firms; (2) antecedents of growth (the most thoroughly researched area with the largest number of studies); and (3) growth process. We conclude by examining how growth is measured. Our visualization of the landscape of new venture growth research is presented in Figure 11.1.

(WHAT WE KNOW ABOUT) HIGH-GROWTH FIRMS

Interest in high-growth firms (HGFs) is driven by the recognition that the bulk of job creation is the consequence of the fast growth of a small number of firms while the average firm's contribution is negligible (Coad, Daunfeldt, Hölzl, Johansson, & Nightingale, 2014). The HGF literature is largely empirical, and emerged as a large distinct research stream only weakly connected to other literature on firm growth (Zupic & Drnovsek, 2014). Research on HGFs usually comes from an economic perspective, is mostly conducted on large-scale secondary databases, and tends to be published in journals like *Small Business Economics* and *Industrial and Corporate Change*.

High-growth firms are most often defined in one of the following two ways: (1) as a percentage of firms recording the highest growth (e.g. the top 5% of the fastest growing firms) or (2) as all firms surpassing an annual predetermined level (e.g. all firms growing at least 20% annually in a three-year period) (Coad et al., 2014). The OECD and Eurostat's recommended definition of HGFs is that annual growth (measured in sales or number of employees) should exceed 20% for a period of three years and that the firm should have at least ten employees in the starting year (Eurostat-OECD, 2007). There are significant differences in how firms grow, and different growth measures are weakly correlated. This suggests that firms are often considered high growth only according to one measurement criterion. The consequence of the choice of growth measure is that different firms will be classified as high growth.

The literature on HGFs has mostly been guided by these firms' supposed *outsized contribution to job creation*. As most small firms do not have the capability or even motivation to grow, there is a small minority of firms that create most new jobs, which seems to be confirmed by the literature. Henrekson and Johansson (2010) performed an analysis of recent studies and found that

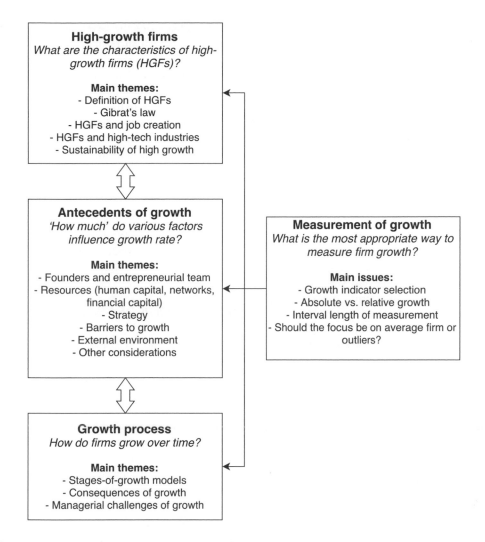

Figure 11.1   Map of the new venture growth literature

gazelles are indeed outstanding job creators. The term 'gazelles' should be used only for young high-growth firms, specifically those that are less than five years old. Since Birch (1979), small firms have been identified as creating the majority of new jobs. Recent studies, however, seem to imply that the relationship between the age of the firm and growth is more important than the relationship between size and growth (Haltiwanger, Jarmin, & Miranda, 2013). Therefore, young firms, not small ones, create the majority of jobs (Lawless, 2014).

Gibrat's law (Gibrat, 1931; Sutton, 1997) – the law of proportionate effect – states that firm size and growth rate are independent and that growth has no correlation through time. This represents the most researched issue in the HGF literature. HGFs tend to be smaller in size, which runs contrary to Gibrat's law (Moreno & Casillas, 2007). Most empirical studies now tend to reject Gibrat's law for smaller firms. However, the law appears to hold for larger firms. The law is a good first approximation of growth rate distribution, indicating that growth in HGFs has a large random component (Coad et al., 2014). Firms' growth rate distributions tend to be tent-shaped, meaning that the majority of firms do not grow at all while a small number of firms experience high-growth episodes.

It seems to be that high-growth firms are *one-hit wonders* (Daunfeldt & Halvarsson, 2015) as most are unable to sustain high growth beyond a brief period. Coad and Hölzl (2009) found a negative autocorrelation of annual growth in small growing firms, which means that sustained fast growth is a very rare occurrence. Furthermore, the R^2 values of studies that aim to explain high growth are very low; the explained variation by these models is usually below 10% (Coad et al., 2014).

HGFs are not necessarily high-tech. The often assumed association between high-growth firms and high-tech industries is not empirically supported. HGFs come from all sectors (Henrekson & Johansson, 2010). Technology-based firms are represented roughly equally in high-growth as in all firms. However, service sectors seem to have a slightly larger proportion of HGFs. High-growth SMEs in countries closer to the technological frontier have a higher R&D intensity than others while, in other countries, there is no difference in R&D intensity between high-growth SMEs and others (Hölzl, 2009). Hölzl investigated the connection between investment and R&D on European-wide data from a CIS survey and concluded that R&D seems to be important only for high-growth SMEs in countries close to the technological frontier.

It is difficult to conclude from the HGF literature what policymakers should do to spur economic growth and increase employment. As noted earlier, HGFs cannot be reliably predicted; high growth is not usually a persistent phenomenon; and there is a significant random component in growth rates. The explanatory power of models is low. Young small firms do create the majority of jobs but also have the highest rates of churn (Anyadike-Danes, Hart, & Du, 2015). Furthermore, Nightingale and Coad (2014) listed several methodological and political biases in the research on entrepreneurial firms, which resulted in positive bias in assessments of the impact of startups on the economy. This leads us to the conclusion that, although research on HGFs has produced several important stylized facts, its lessons for policy are mostly in relation to 'what not to do' and that 'it's complicated' as opposed to concrete advice on specific policies that work.

This section briefly summarized the research on HGFs (for an in-depth treatment of the HGF literature, see Coad, 2009; for other recent reviews and summaries, see Coad et al., 2014; Henrekson & Johansson, 2010; Moreno & Coad, 2015).

ANTECEDENTS OF GROWTH

This section reviews research into various factors that drive firm growth: founders and the entrepreneurial team, resources, strategy, the external environment, barriers to growth, and other considerations. Most of the studies in this section examine the effects of antecedents on growth rates and are sometimes labeled as the 'change of amount' research stream. Growth is viewed here as the dependent variable. This research tends to be published in general management or specialty entrepreneurship and strategy journals.

FOUNDER AND ENTREPRENEURIAL TEAM FACTORS

Motivation and ambition are important drivers of firm growth (Baum, Locke, & Smith, 2001). Entrepreneurs with higher growth ambitions are more likely to create a high-growth venture. However, it is inaccurate to assume that most entrepreneurs have high-growth ambitions. On the contrary, the majority of small business founders have limited intentions to grow their ventures and are motivated by other goals (e.g. to provide for family or to enable certain lifestyles). Starting a new venture with the motivation of financial success is significantly connected with future growth (Cassar, 2007). However, growth motivation can be both a growth predictor and an acquired taste as the managers of firms that have experienced past episodes of high growth are more likely to be motivated by future high growth (Delmar & Wiklund, 2008).

A number of studies have examined the connection between entrepreneurial teams and growth. One issue in this regard is the association between leadership behavior and growth. Ensley, Hmieleski, and Pearce (2006) found that shared leadership (stemming from within a team by emergent formal and informal leaders) is more strongly associated with growth than vertical leadership (from an appointed formal leader as commander). Transformational and empowering dimensions of vertical leadership are even negatively associated with growth.

Founding top-management team (TMT) characteristics have important consequences for a venture's subsequent growth. Previous experience in the same industry seems to be strongly associated with growth (Colombo & Grilli, 2005; Cooper, Gimeno-Gascon, & Woo, 1994). For instance, a content analysis of company narratives found that 76% of high-growth companies had founders with previous industry experience compared with just 24% of slow-growth firms (Barringer, Jones, & Neubaum, 2005). Specific competences and technical skills are linked to growth while general competences (e.g. organizing and managerial skills) appear not to be (Baum et al., 2001).

Colombo and Grilli (2005) found that founders with previous management experience gained easier access to private equity investment but that having that experience, on average, did not positively affect growth. However, obtaining private equity itself has a positive effect on future growth. Does this mean that venture capitalists are misguided by betting on ex-managers? Founders'

education in economics or business fields positively affects growth. Their past joint work experience and heterogeneity in industry experience (founders with experience from both within and outside the new venture industry) have been linked to higher growth (Eisenhardt & Schoonhoven, 1990; Vissa & Chacar, 2009). University-based high-tech startups have been found to be slower growing than their independent counterparts (Ensley & Hmieleski, 2005).

Company founders can have common prior company affiliation (e.g. an entrepreneurial team working together before founding the firm) or diverse prior company affiliation (founders worked for different companies). Companies whose founding team has both common and diverse company affiliation are more likely to grow (Beckman, 2006). This finding suggests that shared understanding following common history encourages exploitation strategies (efficiency and speed of implementation) while creativity associated with diverse prior company affiliations encourages exploration behavior (innovation and change). Both of these contribute toward making firms more ambidextrous (i.e. able to handle both exploration and exploitation simultaneously) (Raisch & Birkinshaw, 2008). Similarly, Beckman, Burton, and O'Reilly (2007) found that diverse prior company affiliation and diverse functional experiences lead to a higher probability of venture capital investment, which is one of the predictors of growth. Adding experienced top-management team members when developing a venture is also associated with higher growth.

High growth in itself can lead to top-management team change because different managerial capabilities are needed to handle the increased complexity of managing the venture (Boeker & Wiltbank, 2005). This need can be counterbalanced by TMT functional diversity to ensure that the capabilities needed for growth are already present in the team. However, low growth can also lead to management team change as it is often perceived as a failure on the part of management.

RESOURCES

The founding work of resource-based explanations of firm growth is *The Theory of the Growth of the Firm* (Penrose, 1959). Penrose suggested that there are managerial limits to firm growth. Experienced managers need to train new managers, thus diverting time and attention away from their work, suggesting that there are adjustment costs to growth. The availability of experienced managers puts an upper limit on the rate a firm is able to grow, the so-called 'Penrose effect'. The second central tenet of Penrose's theory is the productive opportunity set (POS) facing the firm. The identification and exploitation of growth opportunities is dependent on managers' subjective evaluation of POS. The POS is influenced by a firm's current resources and knowledge and the ways in which managers can recombine them to develop new products and services. The legacy of Penrose's work was later further developed within the resource-based view (RBV) (Barney, 1991; Wernerfelt, 1984). Resources that are valuable, rare, inimitable, and non-substitutable (VRIN) are considered to be sources of competitive advantage. Acquiring and orchestrating the right resources is thus crucial for firm success.

Capabilities are firm-level constructs that reflect a firm's ability to use its resources. Growth-related capabilities can be divided into substantive growth capabilities (those that enable the firm to compete and grow, e.g. new product development) and dynamic capabilities (those that extend, change, or create new substantive capabilities) (Koryak, Mole, Lockett, Hayton, Ucbasaran, & Hodgkinson, 2015). For instance, one study found that marketing and financial capabilities can be associated with market expansion and innovation as two ways of achieving high growth (Barbero, Casillas, & Feldman, 2011). Another study based on 212 young technology firms established that technology and marketing management competences are linked to higher development speed (Salomo, Brinckmann, & Talke, 2008). Developed

capabilities are a key growth enabler as high levels of resources cannot compensate for weak capabilities (O'Cass & Sok, 2014).

The most researched resources in the growth literature are human, financial, and social capital (i.e. networks). The performance of new ventures is often dependent on the initial human and financial resource base at startup (Cooper et al., 1994). *Human capital* includes both the human capital of the founders (covered in the previous section) and employee capabilities that help founders achieve their goals. A meta-analysis of human capital studies showed that the outcomes of human capital (e.g. knowledge, skills) are more strongly connected to entrepreneurial success than human capital investments (e.g. education, experience) (Unger, Rauch, Frese, & Rosenbusch, 2011). The connection between human capital and success is also stronger for young businesses but not for high-tech firms. Human capital thus seems to be important for both technology and non-technology new ventures.

Another highly researched topic is the importance of *networks* in firm growth. Two different kinds of networks are examined: entrepreneurs' personal networks and firm networks. Personal networks refer to the social capital of the entrepreneurial team while firm networks are strategic alliances that small firms have with other firms. Social capital can also be a way for entrepreneurs to compensate for the lack of other forms of resources (e.g. human, financial), and social networks can also be a source of advice and emotional support. Networks allow entrepreneurs to access resources and capabilities they do not possess. Moreover, they can enhance the effectiveness of existing financial and human resources (Florin, Lubatkin, & Schulze, 2003). A variety of weak ties that bridge otherwise disconnected groups (Burt, 1992; Granovetter, 1973) make it more likely for entrepreneurs to acquire new information and knowledge.

It is mostly acknowledged that the *social capital of entrepreneurs* has a positive effect on growth. In their longitudinal study, Davidsson and Honig (2003) found that bridging and bonding social capital consisting of both strong and weak ties plays an important role in new venture development. Lechner and Dowling (2003) also found that both strong and weak ties are positively associated with firm growth. Indeed, as Pirolo and Presutti (2010) suggested, finding the optimal configuration of strong and weak ties is one of the major challenges for startups. Structural holes in entrepreneurial teams' external networks are positively correlated with new venture performance (Vissa & Chacar, 2009). Additionally, specific human capital in the form of domain knowledge seems to enable entrepreneurs to leverage bridging ties (i.e. connecting otherwise separate networks) for growth (Scholten, Omta, Kemp, & Elfring, 2015). The combination of network centrality and extra-industry bridging ties in entrepreneurial teams with high entrepreneurial orientation has also been found to enhance new venture performance (Stam & Elfring, 2008).

Khaire (2010) showed that new ventures can overcome lack of legitimacy and status by mimicking the structures and ceremonial activities of established players and becoming affiliated with them. In this way, new ventures can grow and overcome their lack of resources. Notwithstanding, some studies have found that social networks at founding seem to have a negative effect on sales in subsequent years (Lechner, Dowling, & Welpe, 2006).

While the majority of network studies are based on data from developed economies, several have explored *networks and institutions in emerging economies*. Batjargal's (2010) survey of software entrepreneurs in China and Russia discovered a negative effect of structural holes on the profit growth of new ventures. Somewhat conflictingly, a study of 637 entrepreneurs in four developed and emerging economies linked structural holes with revenue growth (Batjargal, Hitt, Tsui, Arregle, Webb, & Miller, 2013). This link was stronger in the presence of weak and inefficient institutions. Another study (based on the same data collection) investigated how the proportion of family ties in different types of networks

(business advice, emotional support, or business resources) helps or undermines firm growth (Arregle, Batjargal, Hitt, Webb, Miller, & Tsui, 2015). Network capabilities can also strengthen the relationship between entrepreneurial orientation and growth performance (Walter, Auer, & Ritter, 2006). Finally, strategic alliances are another form of network (this is discussed in the strategy section).

Another extensively researched predictor of growth is finance. Fast growth usually requires increasing amounts of capital that can be sourced from venture capitalists, banks, or customers. Finance studies on growth have examined how startups use various types of financing (Cassar, 2004), credit constraints faced by new technology-based firms (Colombo & Grilli, 2006), growth-cycle theory of small business financing (Gregory, Rutherford, Oswald, & Gardiner, 2005), and how bootstrapping new ventures affects their growth (Vanacker, Manigart, Meuleman, & Sels, 2011). The role of venture capitalists has been thoroughly examined, and several studies have found that firms supported by venture capital investment experience higher growth (Inderst & Mueller, 2009). However, a recent meta-analysis challenged this view (Rosenbusch, Brinckmann, & Müller, 2013) and, after controlling for industry selection, found that the venture capital effect on growth is small. Nevertheless, the working venture capital industry is considered to be one of the cornerstones of the successful technology entrepreneurial ecosystem (Grilli, 2014).

Nason and Wiklund (2015), in their meta-analysis of growth studies, made the distinction between VRIN resources characteristic of RBV (Barney, 1991) and Penrosean versatile resources. VRIN resources enable firms to distinguish themselves from competitors that do not possess such resources as a way of facilitating sustained growth. Conversely, resource versatility allows managers to use them in a variety of ways to develop a broad range of new products and services, thus increasing a firm's productive opportunity set and enabling its managers to take broader strategic actions. A meta-analysis of 113 studies showed that VRIN resources have no effect on growth while more versatile resources can be linked to higher growth (Nason & Wiklund, 2015). This spells bad news for RBV-based growth explanations. The authors thus recommend that future studies build on Penrose's theory instead.

STRATEGY

A sub-stream of the growth literature examines the connection between firm strategy and growth. Studies on the effects of competitive strategies on growth have produced conflicting findings. Some studies have shown that higher levels of competitive strategy (focus, low-cost, or differentiation) are positively associated with higher growth (Lechner & Gudmundsson, 2014). Others have found that the differentiation strategy has a positive effect on growth while focus or low-cost strategies have no effect on growth (Baum et al., 2001), that no single generic competitive strategy can be linked to higher growth (Leitner & Güldenberg, 2009), and that combined strategies perform better.

Strategic decision speed has been connected with higher growth, an effect that has been especially pronounced in dynamic environments (Baum & Wally, 2003). This finding might encourage managers to follow the strategy of simple rules (Sull & Eisenhardt, 2012) but, in dynamic industries, higher growth is also associated with higher strategic variety (Larrañeta, Zahra, & Galán González, 2014).

Entrepreneurship orientation (EO) (Miller, 1983) has also been shown to be one of the most robust predictors of growth (Wiklund, Patzelt, & Shepherd, 2009). EO captures the entrepreneurial aspects of firms' operations (Lumpkin & Dess, 1996) and is usually defined as a multidimensional construct that includes risk-taking, proactiveness, and innovativeness. Managers of firms with high EO tend to more frequently engage in entrepreneurially uncertain activities (Wales, 2016). Nonetheless, EO cannot be expected to be universally beneficial as its effects might be contextually dependent, and different dimensions of EO might generate different effects on firm performance. In particular, innovativeness has been independently examined as a possible factor influencing growth.

Business models have emerged as an important new perspective in strategy (Aversa, Haefliger, Rossi, & Baden-Fuller, 2015; Baden-Fuller & Haefliger, 2013; Teece, 2010). However, the role of business models in new venture growth remains largely uncharted territory, with the exception of one study. High-growth firms in declining industries have been shown to have different value propositions (a central component of a business model) than incumbent firms (Chandler, Broberg, & Allison, 2014). High-growth firms are able to grow in spite of adverse conditions by creating one of the three unique value propositions: meeting the needs of an underserved market segment, identifying a new market segment by focusing on product/service characteristics that appeal to that segment, or providing a total customer solution.

Alliances are one way in which new ventures can access strategic resources (Gulati, 1998). They are specifically attractive to entrepreneurs who do not want to cede control over their ventures. Complementary resources from partners can compensate for the lack of internal resources and enable market access, and endorsements from well-known established firms can signal quality and help overcome legitimacy barriers faced by new ventures. Alliances can predict growth and seem to be the vehicle through which venture capital investment can promote growth (Mohr, Garnsey, & Theyel, 2013). They can mitigate the negative effects of bootstrapping on new venture growth as bootstrapping has been found to have an inverted-U relationship with new venture performance (Patel, Fiet, & Sohl, 2011). Collaborating with big firms might also impact new ventures negatively as external partnerships can influence the link between internal capabilities and growth. Having too many partnerships can limit growth as partners' resources, rather than complement, can act as substitutes for internal resources and capabilities (Vandaie & Zaheer, 2014). Power relations between partners can also be asymmetric. New ventures thus need to be selective and cautious when entering strategic alliances.

The question of mode of growth – whether it is internal (i.e. organic) or external (i.e. acquisitive) – is a strategic issue (McKelvie & Wiklund, 2010). Acquisitive growth enables firms to grow more quickly and can – under certain conditions – even spur subsequent organic growth (Lockett & Wild, 2013). Acquisitive growth can also enable firms to embark on new development paths that might not be available organically from these firms' current resource base and POS. This is a consequence of path dependency as a firm's future market opportunities depend on current opportunities, and acquisitions might be a way of breaking that limit to growth. This proposition seemed to be confirmed by a study on a 10-year panel of Swedish firms, which found that previous organic growth acts as a limit on current growth (Lockett, Wiklund, Davidsson, & Girma, 2011). Previous acquisitive growth, however, has a positive influence on current organic growth.

Moreover, exportation and internationalization are another frequently used mode of growth. This topic is generally well covered within the international business literature and does not merit further discussion here (for a recent review of the internationalization process literature, see Welch & Paavilainen-Mäntymäki, 2014).

EXTERNAL FACTORS

The characteristics of the organizational environment substantially influence the amount and modes of firm growth. Dess and Beard (1984) proposed three dimensions of the organizational environment: munificence, complexity, and dynamism. The munificence concept states that organizations seek environments that enable them to grow and generate slack resources that allow them to survive periods of scarcity (Cyert & March, 1963). Dynamism represents both environmental turbulence and the stability–instability axis. Highly dynamic environments are characterized by unpredictable change and heightened uncertainty. Environmental complexity refers to the heterogeneity and range of activities that organizations need to perform (Child, 1972).

Some studies have conducted thorough investigations of strategic decision speed and firm performance under different combinations of organizational and environmental characteristics (Baum & Wally, 2003). They examined entrepreneurs' growth intentions as they change through time under different competitive conditions (Dutta & Thornhill, 2008). Other studies have also scrutinized the moderating influence of environmental dynamism on the relationship between leadership behavior and venture performance (Ensley, Pearce, & Hmieleski, 2006), entry modes when internationalizing (Rasheed, 2005), and opportunity exploitation under conditions of risk and uncertainty (Hmieleski & Baron, 2008). Clarysse, Bruneel, and Wright (2011) examined how firms develop and structure their portfolios of resources in different kinds of environments.

BARRIERS TO GROWTH

Barriers to growth are factors that constrain growth in new ventures. Although barriers can be viewed as mirror images of drivers of growth, some factors are more frequently discussed as constraints and limiters of growth (Davidsson et al., 2010). Several studies found that financial constraints (e.g. lack of access to credit) are the most common impediments to growth (Pissarides, 1999). Institutional barriers like taxation and regulation are also often considered as important impediments. Andersson (2003) found that rules and taxation make it difficult to attract foreign talent to Sweden. Budak and Rajh (2014) examined how the business sector is dealing with corruption in seven Western Balkans countries. They found that some entrepreneurs understand corruption as 'greasing the wheels' and that a key component in fighting corruption was to raise anti-corruption awareness. Interestingly, some studies (Xheneti & Bartlett, 2012) reported that firms with a greater awareness of corruption grew faster. Aidis (2005) implemented a study on 332 Lithuanian SMEs and found interrelations between formal and informal barriers.

A considerable amount of barriers-to-growth research is geographically focused on Eastern European transitional countries. Barriers to growth have been researched in the context of Lithuania (Aidis, 2005), Albania (Hashi, 2001; Xheneti & Bartlett, 2012), Kosovo (Hoxha & Capelleras, 2010), Slovenia (Bartlett & Bukvič, 2001), Russia (Doern, 2009), Bulgaria (Pissarides, Singer, & Svejnar, 2003), developing countries (Coad & Tamvada, 2012; Das & Das, 2014; Robson & Obeng, 2008), as well as specific contexts in developed countries (e.g. Lee & Cowling, 2013). However, the barriers-to-growth literature is fragmented and theoretically underdeveloped (Doern, 2009). Extant studies are based on quantitative surveys with theoretically weakly founded questionnaires. A shift from prediction towards understanding is thus needed to advance knowledge on barriers to growth.

OTHER CONSIDERATIONS

Some growth-related studies cannot be easily classified into the abovementioned categories. This section briefly reviews these studies. Formal human resource management practices have been linked to higher performance in SMEs (Sheehan, 2014). High-performance work systems (HPWS) are usually referred to as a set of practices designed to improve employees' skills and effort. These practices include recruitment and selection, monetary performance incentives, performance appraisal processes, and employee training processes. HPWS have been found to improve growth prospects in young firms that also exhibit high entrepreneurial orientation (EO) (Messersmith & Wales, 2013). Opportunity spin-offs (initiated by the former employees of incumbents to exploit an opportunity) have been found to grow faster than incumbent-backed and necessity spin-offs (Bruneel, Van de Velde, & Clarysse, 2013). In a comparative case study, Hansen and Hamilton (2011) isolated factors that distinguish growing from non-growing firms.

Some studies suggest that there is a significant random component to the growth process. The proposition that firm growth is best approximated by a random walk and that its survival depends on the stock of resources at startup or that accumulated thereafter is part of Gambler's ruin theory (Coad, Frankish, Roberts, & Storey, 2013). Firms are here compared to gamblers whose wins are based on chance, but they must stop playing when they run out of money. Coad and colleagues tested this theory on a sample of 6,247 new ventures and found its explanations superior to resource-based predictions. They also found that each growth path in the observed four-year period occurs with roughly equal probability and that growth has a positive effect on subsequent survival. Growth rates are nearly random, but survival is not. Therefore, according to this study, even though firm growth is not a pure random walk, chance is the most dominant component.

This account was disputed by Derbyshire and Garnsey (2014) who wrote that Coad and colleagues' result was an artefact of measurement and that comparing entrepreneurship to indeterminate processes such as gambling was incorrect and counterproductive. The concept of deterministic chaos in complexity science provides an explanation for the failure to identify factors that are closely linked to firm performance. Therefore, while it might seem like the growth process is largely indeterministic (i.e. it has no cause and is random), there is an underlying process that involves iterative matching of a firm's resources to external opportunities. Firm growth is thus not a random process, but entrepreneurial skill and a firm's resources affect its growth. Viewing firms as complex adaptive systems would explain the failure of decades of entrepreneurship research on firm growth and would offer a new lens for further research (Derbyshire & Garnsey, 2015).

GROWTH PROCESS

While the previous research streams reviewed in this chapter are primarily concerned with the 'amount' of growth, studies in this section adopt a processual view of growth. The main focus of this literature is on how firms grow, the problems caused by growth, and how to solve them.

New venture growth process research is dominated by *stage models of growth* that first appeared in the early 1970s and dominated the growth discussion throughout the 1980s and early 1990s (e.g. Churchill & Lewis, 1983; Greiner, 1972; Hanks et al., 1993; Kazanjian, 1988). The stages-of-growth models assume that there are a certain number of stages in the development of a company and that all firms move through these stages. The development of a biological organism is used as a metaphor for growing organizations, so these models are sometimes also called organizational life-cycle models.

For example, in Greiner's model (1972), the organization develops in a successive series of interchanging evolutions (periods of steady growth and stability) and revolutions (periods of substantial organizational turmoil and change). Revolutionary periods are characterized by crises and practices that no longer work for a larger organization. Management

thus needs to establish a new set of management practices and organizational structures that will become the basis for the next period of evolutionary growth. Greiner's model features five stages of evolutionary growth (creativity, direction, delegation, coordination, and collaboration) punctuated by revolutionary leadership crises, autonomy, control, and red tape. If organizations wish to move to the next stage, they need to undergo some kind of revolutionary transformation and solve the crisis at hand.

One reason for the popularity of stage models among practitioners is their high face validity. The majority of entrepreneurs can identify the stage their company is in at a certain point in time (Eggers, Leahy, & Churchill, 1994). The problems discussed in the stages literature are real-world organizational challenges that are relevant to founders and managers of growing firms.

Few contemporary studies still utilize the stages-of-growth paradigm. It has been criticized as overly deterministic (Phelps, Adams, & Bessant, 2007). New ventures are supposed to linearly advance through different stages, and there is supposed to be an optimal configuration for each stage, which is an obviously unrealistic assumption considering the significant differences between individual firms. Levie and Lichtenstein (2010) assessed 104 stages-of-growth models published between 1962 and 2006 and reached worrying conclusions. There is no agreement in the literature of what exactly is a stage, and every definition was used only by a handful of authors without wide-reaching consensus. The number of stages in these models varies a great deal, and three to six stages are usually proposed. There is no consensus on the number of stages and the relationships between stages. The theoretical foundations and conceptual origins of the models are weak. Furthermore, all stage models assumed that organizations have a growth imperative, which is contrary to empirical findings that many organizations have no desire or capabilities to grow. The proliferation of models continued even though half of them were presented as 'universal', supposedly covering all kinds of firms. The assessment concluded that stage models do not accurately represent the growth and development of new ventures and should 'no longer be used by scholars of entrepreneurship, for they act as a barrier to advancement of research on the growth of entrepreneurial organizations' (Levie & Lichtenstein, 2010, p. 336).

This judgement is pretty harsh; how therefore do we get out of this conundrum? Levie and Lichtenstein (2010) proposed a *dynamic states model* that builds on stage models but modifies two unrealistic assumptions: that businesses develop like organisms through a specific number of stages and that these stages represent a fixed program of development. The authors define a dynamic state as 'a network of beliefs, relationships, systems, and structures that convert opportunity tension into tangible value for an organization's customers/clients'. Opportunity tension, in this context, means the tension between the perceived untapped market potential and the commitment to act on that potential. Dynamic states thus represent the best perceived match between a firm's business model and the market potential. In an organization's existence, there can be any number of dynamic states in any sequence. Levie and Lichtenstein (2010) laid the foundations for the dynamic states approach in a very abstract and general way. Further work should thus focus on elaborating on these and specifying the details in particular contexts.

Phelps, Adams, and Bessant (2007) proposed an alternative model by discarding stages and introducing six tipping points that characterize qualitative changes in developing organizations: (1) people management (developing the skills to encourage delegation, communication, and teamwork); (2) strategic orientation (moving away from an opportunistic to a more deliberate strategy); (3) formalized systems (when existing informal systems fail to adequately cope with changed environmental conditions); (4) new market entry (replicating existing business models in new markets or developing new products

for existing customers requires stronger customer awareness and is constrained by the lack of marketing and sales skills); (5) obtaining finance (growing firms need to move to external capital providers); and (6) operational improvement (moving towards a better understanding of process capabilities and the implementation of best practices for efficiency gains). These tipping points are the consequence of growth and need to be overcome by developing and applying new knowledge to resolve the challenges posed. Absorptive capacity (Cohen & Levinthal, 1990) is a critical capability in this regard.

Studies examining the growth process outside of the stage models paradigm are few and far between. Prashantham and Dhanaraj (2010) used a process lens within the grounded theory approach to study a three-year evolution of social capital in four internationalizing Indian software firms. They found that initial social capital rapidly diminishes and that, when that happens, a broad variety of searches for new network relationships becomes necessary for growth. Raisch (2008) examined the organizational design challenges of growing firms and inductively developed a process model of balanced structural designs that enable firms to pursue profitable growth while simultaneously balancing exploration and exploitation activities in different situations. Rindova, Yeow, Martins, and Faraj (2012) examined how Google and Yahoo utilized their partnering portfolios in their distinct approaches to growth. Clarysse et al. (2011) analyzed the growth paths of young technology firms and showed that different growth paths result from firms' attempts to structure resource portfolios in accordance with environmental demands.

MEASUREMENT OF GROWTH

Different indicators can be used to measure growth: sales growth, employment growth, asset growth, or profit growth, among others.

The two most utilized indicators in the extant research are sales (or turnover) growth and growth in the number of employees. Low concurrent validity has been found among different growth indicators (Shepherd & Wiklund, 2009; Weinzimmer, Nystrom, & Freeman, 1998). For instance, sales and employment growth are only modestly correlated. It is thus questionable whether the universal theory of growth can be achieved. It would need to explain several measures of growth that are not necessarily correlated (Shepherd & Wiklund, 2009).

Most studies do not explain why a particular indicator was used. Indicator choice needs to be substantiated by the theoretical focus of the investigation. Greater attention to the context specificity of both measures and theories is warranted. Entrepreneurs, for example, are interested in developing their business, not necessarily employing more people, so measures of most use to them would be sales or profit growth. An additional measure of interest specifically in high-tech startups would be the value of the firm (Achtenhagen, Naldi, & Melin, 2010). However, generating higher employment is one of the major objectives of policymakers; therefore, research that aims to inform policy would tend to use employment growth measures.

A multiple-year time window is usually used for measuring growth. This reduces the amount of noise and one-off growth events. Another dilemma is to choose between absolute and relative growth indicators. Relative growth is most frequently measured as a percentage or log change. Absolute growth is a raw number change of selected indicators in the measured time period. Relative measures tend to be biased towards smaller firms (i.e. small firms seem to grow faster when relative measures are used) while absolute measures favor larger firms. This dilemma has led to the construction of compound indexes, such as the Birch Index, that include both relative and absolute measures of growth. These indicators have, however, been criticized as conceptually empty (Davidsson, Delmar, & Wiklund, 2006) since it is difficult to determine exactly what they measure. Furthermore, the Birch Index is driven by absolute growth in large firms, so it cannot resolve the issue of absolute or relative measure selection (Coad et al., 2014). Developing absolute growth hypotheses based on the findings of studies using relative growth (and vice versa) is thus not recommended (Shepherd & Wiklund, 2009).

A further complication is that most measures of growth (and entrepreneurship in general) are not normally distributed but exhibit highly skewed power law distributions (Crawford, Aguinis, Lichtenstein, Davidsson, & McKelvey, 2015). For instance, most of the central constructs in resource-based explanations of performance – human, social, and financial capital – are found to be power law distributed. As a consequence, the workhorses of Gaussian statistics – means and standard deviations – are relatively meaningless in many cases and do not provide apt descriptions of the variables. Thus, the results of studies relying on unjustified normality assumptions often have little relevance for policymakers and practitioners. A greater focus should be on the outliers (e.g. fast-growing firms), which are usually thought of as exceptions to be squeezed by transformations into normal distributions in the traditional approach.

The measurement of organizational growth is a significant topic in itself, and space considerations do not allow us to do justice to it (readers may wish to consult several excellent reviews of growth measurement (cf. Delmar, 2006; Shepherd & Wiklund, 2009; Weinzimmer et al., 1998) as well as extensive treatments of measurement issues in Davidsson et al., 2010; Coad et al., 2014).

SUMMARY OF CURRENT FINDINGS

We have divided the new venture growth literature into three sections: research on high-growth firms (HGFs), antecedents of growth, and growth process.

The research on HGFs is guided by their important contribution to job creation. It examines the characteristics of fast-growing firms and has so far established the following stylized facts: (1) young firms, not small ones, create the majority of jobs; (2) Gibrat's law (growth rate is independent of size) holds for large firms but not for small ones; (3) the majority of firms do not grow at all; (4) HGFs are often one-hit wonders as high growth is extremely difficult to sustain; (5) HGFs are often young but not necessarily small; (6) HGFs are not necessarily high-tech; (7) concrete policy advice remains thin.

Antecedents of growth represents the largest research stream among the three examined. It investigates the effects that various factors have on the rate of growth. This literature is dominated by resource-based explanations of growth that were first established by Penrose (1959) and thereafter elaborated within the RBV. The most researched factors are the founding team characteristics; human, social, and financial resources; strategy; and the external environment. A recent meta-analysis found that Penrosean versatile resources are more useful for growth than the RBV's VRIN resources (Nason & Wiklund, 2015). The outsized attention on the amount of growth suggests that other aspects of growth remain neglected (Davidsson et al., 2010).

The growth process research has been dominated by the stages-of-growth models. These models assume that firms move linearly through a specific number of stages that are punctuated by crises. Firms need to overcome crises at certain stages of development if they want to continue on the growth path. These models have high face validity among entrepreneurs but have received only scant empirical support. A recent review (Levie & Lichtenstein, 2010) concluded that these models are not appropriate for further research. However, lessons from the stages literature can be used in the dynamic states approach, which discards the unsupported

assumptions of the stages literature. Studies that examine the growth process outside of the stages paradigm are very rare.

There are two major deficiencies of the extant literature. First, there is not enough accumulation of knowledge, which is partly a consequence of an insufficient number of replications being conducted (Shepherd & Wiklund, 2009). The exception is research on HGFs, where issues are typically examined across multiple datasets in different studies. Although some direct effects of major factors on growth are well researched, more nuanced findings are typically one-off. This is not characteristic only of the growth field; it is a problem that plagues much of management research. The academic incentives and publication preferences of the top outlets are structured so that they seek novel findings and theoretical contributions. Replication and confirmations of past findings are thus being neglected. However, a single study, regardless of how well executed, cannot provide final and conclusive resolutions to any issue (Davidsson, 2015).

Second, the explained variance of growth studies is typically low. Firm growth is a complex phenomenon, and it is perhaps a bit naïve to expect that a small number of factors at founding or later stages can significantly impact growth paths. Although firm growth is not a completely random process, it has a significant stochastic component.

The following section outlines a future research program aimed at alleviating these shortcomings.

NEW VENTURE GROWTH: FUTURE CHALLENGES

At the start of the discussion on future research relating to firm growth, we examined the research suggestions of previous major reviews in the firm growth literature. The findings of this meta-review of reviews published between 2006 and 2015 are summarized in Table 11.1.

Table 11.1 Findings and suggestions for further research from previous reviews

Review	Focus	Selected main findings	Suggestions for further research
Gilbert et al., 2006	New venture growth	The two resources most often found connected with new venture growth are human capital and financial capital.	Examine the impact of specific forms of entrepreneur competences on growth. Conduct more in-depth explorations of the role of teams and leadership. There are several opportunities to research the relationship between resources and different types of growth (internal, external). Explore how financial capital enables or constrains decision-making, which in turn influences growth.
Macpherson & Holt, 2007	Knowledge and learning in small-firm growth	Most studies favor high-tech and manufacturing industries. A significant subsection of research examines new ventures rather than old firms. The growth process is significantly more complex than the stage models portray.	Use of epistemological approaches that are sensitive to relational qualities; for instance, activity theory or practice theory might provide useful frameworks for research. Researchers should use methodologies that are able to get close to practice (e.g. ethnography, processual research). More sophisticated heuristics targeting policy initiatives are needed. These should address the idiosyncratic and contextual nature of growth as opposed to blanket and best-practice approaches.
Dobbs & Hamilton, 2007	Small business growth	The growth literature uses a wide range of measures and models, i.e. knowledge development is fragmented rather than cumulative. New theoretical perspectives are needed to understand the growth process.	Focus on growth as a process and incorporate more longitudinal theories and research designs. Use the learning perspective to study growth paths and tipping points in the growth of small businesses in the same industry and region.
Coad, 2009	High-growth firms	Gibrat's law is a useful model of firm growth even though it is not perfectly accurate in all contexts and for all firms. The nature of growth is remarkably random. Financial performance and productivity are poor predictors of growth. No single theoretical perspective can explain firm growth. The standard regression approach, which focuses on 'the average effect for the average firm', is not an appropriate method for analyzing the growth phenomenon because few firms grow rapidly and the 'average firm' will barely grow at all.	Use cohort studies to explore the relationship between financial performance and growth, which feature the significant gap between theoretical predictions and empirical results. Use techniques that go beyond 'average firm' characteristics (e.g. quantile regression). More research is needed on the relationship between innovation and growth. Empirical work should first provide 'stylized facts', which should then be explained using theory.

(Continued)

Table 11.1 (Continued)

Davidsson et al., 2010	Small business growth	Small-firm growth is a complex phenomenon that addresses both the 'change in amount' of growth and the growth process. The literature is fragmented and develops along separate lines of inquiry. There is lack of integration of existing findings into a comprehensive theory of growth. The knowledge on growth modes and growth processes is underdeveloped. There is a dearth of high quality in-depth studies. There is little need for new studies seeking to identify antecedents of growth.	Conduct theory-driven studies within more homogeneous samples of firms. Rigorous, theoretically sampled case-based growth process studies are needed. More effort should be put into researching the management challenges of growth.
McKelvie & Wiklund, 2010	Growth mode	Researchers prematurely began addressing 'how much' questions before adequately answering 'how' questions.	The research focus should be changed to growth modes (organic, acquisition, or hybrid). Researchers should strive to explain which growth modes firms choose and why. The relationships among different growth modes should be examined. Penrose's theory should be extended to include hybrid modes of growth. Real-time longitudinal case studies could be used to focus on how growing firms utilize and combine different growth mechanisms.
Levie & Lichtenstein, 2010	Stage models of growth	Stage models are overly deterministic. There is no agreement on what stages are and how they are related. The biological metaphor of the firm as a developing organism is inappropriate. Stage models are not appropriate for explaining business growth.	Stage models should no longer be used for further research. They should be replaced with dynamic states models, which have their foundations in complexity theory. These models offer theoretical support for research on business sustainability.
Wright & Stigliani, 2013	Entrepreneurial growth	The growth literature is overly focused on 'how much' studies and neglects 'how' and 'why' questions.	More research is needed into how entrepreneurs' cognitive processes influence growth, how entrepreneurs obtain and configure resources needed for growth, how important are contextual factors for these questions, and whether they influence types and patterns of growth.

Table 11.1 (Continued)

Moreno & Coad, 2015	High-growth firms	High-growth episodes in firms are rare and most often not repeated. High-growth firms generate most of the new jobs in developed economies; they tend to be young and present in all industries.	Explore the differences among regions and countries – how contextual factors influence the prevalence of HGFs. Look into the different firm strategies and growth. Explore the internal characteristics of high-growth firms. Investigate the role of different strategies in high growth.
Wright, Roper, Hart, & Carter, 2015	The *IJSB* special issue containing evidence-based reviews of growth policy focused on five areas: job creation, innovation and exporting, ethnic and gender diversity, finance, and management and leadership	The majority of jobs in the UK are created by small firms. Internal enablers (skills, research and development (R&D), capital investment, and liquidity) have a major influence in shaping SME innovation and exports. Targeted supply-side and demand-side policies are effective in promoting SME innovation and export. SME growth depends on substantive growth capabilities, which are shaped by leadership and capability development issues.	More research is needed on the processes that drive job creation in different types of firms in order to develop appropriate policy interventions. How do entrepreneur objectives (growth/lifestyle) and the importance of retaining control affect venture capital or equity funding decisions? There is a need to better understand how psychological factors influence the selection and implementation of growth goals. Little is known about how dynamic capabilities evolve in emerging ventures and how entrepreneurial cognition and growth intentions shape the development of dynamic capabilities in supporting sustained growth.

Several previous reviews found that the research on growth is fragmented and that findings are often conflicting. Our effort largely confirms that this is still the case. A comprehensive universal theory of growth might not be possible, or at least we are very far from it. Our better bet would be to produce a variety of context-dependent mid-range theories that work for certain types of firms.

Here, we outline a strategy for the further development of new venture growth research. We suggest three strategies to improve the field: (1) reorient the focus of research from 'change in amount' to the process of firm growth; (2) use fewer questionnaire-based quantitative studies and more qualitative, in-depth studies as well as studies that leverage big data; and (3) pay more attention to the usefulness of growth research for other stakeholders: entrepreneurs and policymakers.

Several authors suggested that the mode of growth should be the focus of future studies (e.g. McKelvie & Wiklund, 2010). They argued that growth research has focused predominantly on 'how much' questions while neglecting 'how' questions. Future focus should thus be on examining how firms grow – whether organically or by acquisition. However, with the exception of a few examples (Clarysse et al., 2011; Lockett et al., 2011; Naldi & Davidsson, 2014), these studies are yet to materialize. The reason might be the scarcity of secondary data, including modes of growth, and the difficulty of gathering new data on this topic. Of necessity therefore are longitudinal research designs that require significant time and resource investments. It is easy to observe the dearth of longitudinal designs in the literature review; however, it is considerably more difficult, time-consuming, and expensive to rigorously implement them in real-world research.

A major part of firm growth research is dominated by the RBV perspective. We suggest that future firm growth researchers should aim to bring more diversity in their research questions so that the foundations of

other theoretical perspectives, such as behavioral theory (Cyert & March, 1963), that have proven their utility in prior management research can be utilized. An important aspect of behavioral theory underscores an orientation toward processes rather than outcomes of organizational growth. Cyert and March (1963), in their initial contribution, emphasized the actual process of making business decisions so that imperfectly rationalized organizational goals, which can be seen as consequences of different coalitions within firms, can be attained.

Human resource management (HRM) is another topic that has so far been neglected within the firm growth literature and should be given greater credence in the future. Most of the existing studies on the role of people in firm growth focus on the role of human capital (of the individual/entrepreneur) and the impact that this personal capability has on firm growth. While managing and motivating employees, finding new talent, and recruiting the right people are widely discussed themes among practitioners, entrepreneurs, and investors of high-potential firms, there is a lack of scholarly discourse on these questions in the particular context of high-growth firms. Some of these questions consider how HRM practices and different HR systems (e.g. high-performance work systems) at the firm level change during the process of growth. Further research is needed to investigate the specifics of these issues. When focusing on the outcomes of different modes of growth (McKelvie & Wiklund, 2010), researchers could explore how and why the productivity of human research practices differ across organic, acquisition, and hybrid modes of growth.

Finally, by 'over-focusing' on RBV arguments, the existing research on firm growth has neglected the role of customers as sources of growth (Zander & Zander, 2005). The role of customers was already noted in Penrose's (1959) concept of 'inside track', which allows firms to sense and capture value from existing customers. The underestimation of demand-side arguments is visible not only in the context of firm growth research but also in the broader management literature (Priem, Li, & Carr, 2012). There are future research opportunities associated with using demand-side theoretical foundations and exploring firm growth from the business model viewpoint. Indeed, the concept of business model (Baden-Fuller & Morgan, 2010) is an integrative perspective that combines both supply- and demand-side arguments. Firm growth research from the business model perspective (Baden-Fuller & Mangematin, 2013) could explore the role of the institutional environment and opportunity co-creation (George & Bock, 2011) in the context of firm growth. By using institutional theory in entrepreneurship and sense-making (Daft & Weick, 1984), institutional pressures on the business models that shape firm growth could be analyzed. Business models may be an important component in the co-evolution of stories that determine legitimacy as a necessary component of firm survival (George & Bock, 2011; Lounsbury & Glynn, 2001).

MEASUREMENT AND METHODS

Cross-sectional studies of the influence of various factors on firm growth explain only a limited amount of the variance in growth rates. These factors are assumed to be stable and context-free. It is questionable whether a comprehensive model of firm growth based on these factors can be developed (Dobbs & Hamilton, 2007). Factors that vary over time would have a better chance of explaining differences in growth rates. Moreover, cross-sectional studies are only able to identify the factors that accompany growth spurts, which are not necessarily those generating the growth.

As the saying goes, 'not everything that counts can be counted'. We are not the first to suggest that the field needs more case studies (cf. Davidsson et al., 2010; Leitch, Hill, &

Neergaard, 2010; Wright & Stigliani, 2013) that delve deeper into growth phenomena than our limited capability – which measures what goes on inside firms – is able to explain.

Qualitative methods are relatively little used in contemporary growth research. Arguably, this deficiency has two explanations: (1) a fair number of researchers believe that qualitative studies are difficult to publish; and (2) rigorous qualitative studies are difficult and time-consuming to conduct, especially in an environment in which most academics are under increasing pressure to publish quickly and extensively. This does not mean that there are no robust qualitative studies. Some recent excellent examples include Bamiatzi and Kirchmaier (2014), Hansen and Hamilton (2011), and Rindova et al. (2012). Lockett and Wild (2014) also noted that, while Penrose (1959) used historical case studies for the development of *The Theory of the Growth of The Firm*, this method has been neglected in contemporary studies on RBV and firm growth. Penrose used a hybrid approach, including both inductive and deductive logic, a research process in which history played a major role.

As Wright and Stigliani (2013) argued, the field needs to embrace more innovative research methodologies. This could be implemented on either side of the qualitative–quantitative continuum. Ethnographic, narrative, and case study approaches have so far been neglected in growth research. Notwithstanding, one such opportunity is the availability of (big) data from the internet, which calls for the use of alternative methods of data collection such as web scraping. Recent advancements in computerized text analysis (e.g. Blei, 2012) that can be used to content-analyze large amounts of text documents make this a potentially fruitful avenue for further research that is currently completely untapped.

If the critique of Crawford and colleagues (2015) concerning power law distribution effects is accurate, it would imply that a large part of existing research, which is based on average effects for average firms – to put it politely – is not very useful. There is a need for additional research into how power law distributions shape results in growth studies and what methods would be more appropriate for studying new venture growth. Some authors suggest that techniques like quantile regression might be more appropriate (Coad, 2009).

FUTURE CHALLENGES – HIGH-GROWTH FIRMS

Research on high-growth firms represents a dynamic and vibrant field that has produced a number of stylized facts about HGFs. There is a considerable push among policymakers to concentrate support for HGFs in the hope of increasing employment. More research is thus needed on the evaluation of policy approaches for supporting HGFs. What policy measures increase the frequency of HGFs? Are these effective at boosting employment? Having more HGFs also implies a higher number of declining and failing firms, with its attendant negative effects. Are these offset by the good effects? The danger is that by supporting HGFs, as defined on the basis of employee growth, policymakers will encourage labor-intensive enterprises that weaken economic productivity. One new phenomenon that warrants further investigation is the appearance of venture accelerators (Cohen, 2013). Do these really accelerate growth?

A fruitful avenue is further exploitation of matched employer–employee databases that can now be constructed for a number of advanced economies. Some advanced innovative approaches warrant attention. For instance, labor flow networks – networks where nodes represent firms and connections represent labor flows among firms (Guerrero & Axtell, 2013) – could be constructed for whole economies and utilized to examine the role of HGFs in employment.

FUTURE CHALLENGES – ANTECEDENTS OF GROWTH

The research on 'growth amount' almost completely dominates the entrepreneurial perspective of firm growth studies. Extant research has placed too much emphasis on the question of 'how much' companies grow while neglecting questions on 'how' they grow (Davidsson et al., 2010; Leitch et al., 2010; McKelvie & Wiklund, 2010). We believe the research on antecedents of growth has hit a wall similar to that of the stages-of-growth literature. As Davidsson et al. (2010) noted, there is little chance that additional factors that explain growth beyond what we now know will be found. Growth rates have been shown to be nearly random (Coad et al., 2014), so it is perhaps futile to try to improve explained variance (McKelvie & Wiklund, 2010). Therefore, the first issue would be for researchers to reorient their perspective to other more fruitful avenues like growth process.

For researchers who would like to continue their work within this orientation, rigorous longitudinal studies in specific industries might be of value. Large-scale context-specific and theoretically driven studies that would follow a cohort of firms in their growth and repeatedly gather data from this cohort would further contribute to knowledge on antecedents of growth. The effort, scale, and time required for such a project are probably beyond the realm of most entrepreneurship researchers.

FUTURE CHALLENGES – GROWTH PROCESS

Stages-of-growth models do not currently constitute a very active stream of research and have been heavily criticized (Levie & Lichtenstein, 2010). We think, however, that it would be unwise to dismiss the stage models literature too soon. The criticism might have a point that organizational development is never linear through a fixed number of stages. Firms are too different in character and development path to be described by a single universal stage model. The problems addressed in this literature are nevertheless real and important. The decline in process studies is also unfortunate for entrepreneurs and managers as this research has a greater potential to inform practice than merely studying 'the amount of growth' in relation to various antecedents that are not under the influence of the entrepreneur. Stage models are a metaphor that functions for a subset of firms. By transforming them along the lines of Levie and Lichtenstein's dynamic states model, it generalizes them onto a larger population of firms. Further theoretical work is needed to elaborate this perspective.

McKelvie and Wiklund (2010) suggested that future researchers examining the growth process by focusing on different modes of growth can build on the theoretical foundations of behavioral theory. This would allow researchers to explore how firms achieve growth-related goals through organic, acquisition, and hybrid modes of growth. A selected mode of growth defines the variety of coalitions that are present in the firm, which in turn influence routines and processes in the firm (Argote & Greve, 2007), such as decision-making processes. Decision-making processes in the context of firm growth can be analyzed on several levels. On the individual level of analysis, the cognitive biases and heuristics (Busenitz & Barney, 1997) of entrepreneurs/managers in the context of firm growth can be analyzed. The mezzo level of inquiry could explore the functionality of decision-making processes within top management teams (Amason, 1996) while, at the firm level of analysis, researchers could analyze how a firm's slack resources associated with growth goals facilitate a search for new ends and means through innovation (Geiger & Cashen, 2002).

Contemporary digital enterprises (e.g. Google, Twitter, WhatsApp) are able to scale much faster than the previous generation of companies. Does this mean that the 'Penrose effects' do not hold for such firms? These companies go through periods of hypergrowth; it would therefore be interesting to investigate the consequences of such growth and how such incredibly high growth rates are sustained. This line of inquiry (studying the management challenges and effects of growth) would be fruitful not just for digital but for all kinds of new ventures.

CONCLUSION

This chapter presented a summary of the contemporary growth literature and its most influential foundations and theoretical perspectives. It also outlined several opportunities for future research. The new venture growth landscape is fragmented but extremely important for scholars, entrepreneurs, and policymakers. This chapter is our small contribution to moving the field forward.

REFERENCES

Achtenhagen, L., Naldi, L., & Melin, L. (2010). 'Business growth' – do practitioners and scholars really talk about the same thing? *Entrepreneurship Theory and Practice, 34*(2), 289–316. doi:10.1111/j.1540-6520.2010.00376.x

Aidis, R. (2005). Institutional barriers to small- and medium-sized enterprise operations in transition countries. *Small Business Economics, 25*(4), 305–317. doi:10.1007/s11187-003-6463-7

Amason, A. C. (1996). Distinguishing the effects of functional and dysfunctional conflict on strategic decision making: resolving a paradox for top management teams. *Academy of Management Journal, 39*(1), 123–148. doi:10.2307/256633

Andersson, S. (2003). High-growth firms in the Swedish ERP industry. *Journal of Small Business and Enterprise Development, 10*(2), 180–193. doi:10.1108/14626000310473201

Anyadike-Danes, M., Hart, M., & Du, J. (2015). Firm dynamics and job creation in the United Kingdom: 1998–2013. *International Small Business Journal*, *33*(1), 12–27. doi:10.1177/0266242614552334

Argote, L., & Greve, H. R. (2007). A behavioral theory of the firm – 40 years and counting: introduction and impact. *Organization Science*, *18*(3), 337–349. doi:10.1287/orsc.1070.0280

Arregle, J.-L., Batjargal, B., Hitt, M. A., Webb, J. W., Miller, T., & Tsui, A. S. (2015). Family ties in entrepreneurs' social networks and new venture growth. *Entrepreneurship Theory and Practice*, *39*(2), 313–344. doi:10.1111/etap.12044

Aversa, P., Haefliger, S., Rossi, A., & Baden-Fuller, C. (2015). From business model to business modelling: modularity and manipulation. In C. Baden-Fuller & V. Mangematin (Eds), *Business Models and Modelling* (Vol. 33, pp. 151–185). UK: Emerald Group Publishing Limited. doi:10.1108/S0742-332220150000033022

Baden-Fuller, C., & Haefliger, S. (2013). Business models and technological innovation. *Long Range Planning*, *46*(6), 419–426. doi:10.1016/j.lrp.2013.08.023

Baden-Fuller, C., & Mangematin, V. (2013). Business models: a challenging agenda. *Strategic Organization*, *11*(4), 418–427. doi:10.1177/1476127013510112

Baden-Fuller, C., & Morgan, M. S. (2010). Business models as models. *Long Range Planning*, *43*(2–3), 156–171. doi:10.1016/j.lrp.2010.02.005

Bamiatzi, V. C., & Kirchmaier, T. (2014). Strategies for superior performance under adverse conditions: a focus on small and medium-sized high-growth firms. *International Small Business Journal*, *32*(3), 259–284. doi:10.1177/0266242612459534

Barbero, J. L., Casillas, J. C., & Feldman, H. D. (2011). Managerial capabilities and paths to growth as determinants of high-growth small and medium-sized enterprises. *International Small Business Journal*, *29*(6), 671–694. doi:10.1177/0266242610378287

Barney, J. (1991). Firm resources and sustained competitive advantage. *Journal of Management*, *17*(1), 99–120.

Barringer, B. R., Jones, F. F., & Neubaum, D. O. (2005). A quantitative content analysis of the characteristics of rapid-growth firms and their founders. *Journal of Business Venturing*, *20*(5), 663–687. doi: http://dx.doi.org/10.1016/j.jbusvent.2004.03.004

Bartlett, W., & Bukvič, V. (2001). Barriers to SME growth in Slovenia. *MOST: Economic Policy in Transitional Economies*, *11*(2), 177–195. doi:10.1023/A:1012206414785

Batjargal, B. (2010). The effects of network's structural holes: polycentric institutions, product portfolio, and new venture growth in China and Russia. *Strategic Entrepreneurship Journal*, *4*(2), 146–163. doi:10.1002/sej.88

Batjargal, B., Hitt, M. A., Tsui, A. S., Arregle, J.-L., Webb, J. W., & Miller, T. L. (2013). Institutional polycentrism, entrepreneurs' social networks, and new venture growth. *Academy of Management Journal*, *56*(4), 1024–1049. doi:10.5465/amj.2010.0095

Baum, J. R., Locke, E. A., & Smith, K. G. (2001). A multidimensional model of venture growth. *Academy of Management Journal*, *44*(2), 292–303. doi:10.2307/3069456

Baum, R. J., & Wally, S. (2003). Strategic decision speed and firm performance. *Strategic Management Journal*, *24*(11), 1107–1129. doi:10.1002/smj.343

Beckman, C. M. (2006). The influence of founding team company affiliations on firm behavior. *Academy of Management Journal*, *49*(4), 741–758. doi:10.5465/AMJ.2006.22083030

Beckman, C. M., Burton, M. D., & O'Reilly, C. (2007). Early teams: the impact of team demography on VC financing and going public. *Journal of Business Venturing*, *22*(2), 147–173. doi:http://dx.doi.org/10.1016/j.jbusvent.2006.02.001

Birch, D. L. (1979). *The job generation process*. Cambridge, MA: M.I.T. Program on Neighborhood and Regional Change. Retrieved from http://books.google.si/books?id=fsQTAQAAMAAJ

Blei, D. M. (2012). Probabilistic topic models. *Communications of the ACM*, *55*(4), 77–84.

Boeker, W., & Wiltbank, R. (2005). New venture evolution and managerial capabilities. *Organization Science*, *16*(2), 123–133. doi:10.1287/orsc.1050.0115

Bruneel, J., Van de Velde, E., & Clarysse, B. (2013). Impact of the type of corporate spin-off on growth. *Entrepreneurship Theory and Practice*, *37*(4), 943–959. doi:10.1111/j.1540-6520.2012.00517.x

Budak, J., & Rajh, E. (2014). Corruption as an obstacle for doing business in the Western Balkans: a business sector perspective. *International Small Business Journal*, *32*(2), 140–157. doi:10.1177/0266242613498882

Burt, R. S. (1992). *Structural holes: the social structure of competition*. Cambridge, MA: Harvard University Press. Retrieved from https://books.google.si/books?id=_gjtAAAAMAAJ

Busenitz, L. W., & Barney, J. B. (1997). Differences between entrepreneurs and managers in large organizations: biases and heuristics in strategic decision-making. *Journal of Business Venturing*, *12*(1), 9–30. Retrieved from http://www.sciencedirect.com/science/article/pii/S0883902696000031

Cassar, G. (2004). The financing of business start-ups. *Journal of Business Venturing*, *19*(2), 261–283. Retrieved from http://www.sciencedirect.com/science/article/pii/S0883902603000296

Cassar, G. (2007). Money, money, money? A longitudinal investigation of entrepreneur career reasons, growth preferences and achieved growth. *Entrepreneurship & Regional Development*, *19*(1), 89–107. doi:10.1080/08985620601002246

Chandler, G. N., Broberg, J. C., & Allison, T. H. (2014). Customer value propositions in declining industries: differences between industry representative and high-growth firms. *Strategic Entrepreneurship Journal*, *8*(3), 234–253. doi:10.1002/sej.1181

Child, J. (1972). Organizational structure, environment and performance: the role of strategic choice. *Sociology*, *6*(1), 1–22. doi:10.1177/003803857200600101

Churchill, N. C., & Lewis, V. (1983). The five stages of small business growth. *Harvard Business Review*, *61*(3), 30–50.

Clarysse, B., Bruneel, J., & Wright, M. (2011). Explaining growth paths of young technology-based firms: structuring resource portfolios in different competitive environments. *Strategic Entrepreneurship Journal*, *5*(2), 137–157. doi:10.1002/sej.111

Coad, A. (2009). *The growth of firms: a survey of theories and empirical evidence*. Cheltenham: Edward Elgar Publishing.

Coad, A., Daunfeldt, S.-O., Hölzl, W., Johansson, D., & Nightingale, P. (2014). High-growth firms: introduction to the special section. *Industrial and Corporate Change*, *23*(1), 91–112. doi:10.1093/icc/dtt052

Coad, A., Frankish, J., Roberts, R. G., & Storey, D. J. (2013). Growth paths and survival chances: an application of Gambler's Ruin theory. *Journal of Business Venturing*, *28*(5), 615–632. doi:http://dx.doi.org/10.1016/j.jbusvent.2012.06.002

Coad, A., & Hölzl, W. (2009). On the autocorrelation of growth rates. *Journal of Industry, Competition and Trade*, *9*(2), 139–166. doi:10.1007/s10842-009-0048-3

Coad, A., & Tamvada, J. P. (2012). Firm growth and barriers to growth among small firms in India. *Small Business Economics*, *39*(2), 383–400. doi:10.1007/s11187-011-9318-7

Cohen, S. (2013). What do accelerators do? Insights from incubators and angels. *Innovations*, *8*(3–4), 19–25.

Cohen, W. M., & Levinthal, D. A. (1990). Absorptive capacity: a new perspective on learning and innovation. *Administrative Science Quarterly*, *35*(1), 128–152.

Colombo, M. G., & Grilli, L. (2005). Founders' human capital and the growth of new technology-based firms: a competence-based view. *Research Policy*, *34*(6), 795–816. doi:http://dx.doi.org/10.1016/j.respol.2005.03.010

Colombo, M. G., & Grilli, L. (2006). Funding gaps? Access to bank loans by high-tech start-ups. *Small Business Economics*, *29*(1–2), 25–46. doi:10.1007/s11187-005-4067-0

Cooper, A. C., Gimeno-Gascon, F. J., & Woo, C. Y. (1994). Initial human and financial capital as predictors of new venture performance. *Journal of Business Venturing*, *9*(5), 371–395. doi:http://dx.doi.org/10.1016/0883-9026(94)90013-2

Crawford, G. C., Aguinis, H., Lichtenstein, B., Davidsson, P., & McKelvey, B. (2015). Power law distributions in entrepreneurship: implications for theory and research. *Journal of Business Venturing*, *30*(5), 696–713. doi:http://dx.doi.org/10.1016/j.jbusvent.2015.01.001

Cyert, R. M., & March, J. G. (1963). *A behavioral theory of the firm*. Englewood Cliffs, NJ: Prentice-Hall.

Daft, R. L., & Weick, K. E. (1984). Toward a model of organizations as interpretation systems. *Academy of Management Review*, *9*(2), 284–295. doi:10.5465/AMR.1984.4277657

Das, S. S., & Das, A. (2014). India shining? A two-wave study of business constraints upon micro and small manufacturing firms in India. *International Small Business Journal, 32*(2), 180–203. doi:10.1177/0266242613488790

Daunfeldt, S.-O., & Halvarsson, D. (2015). Are high-growth firms one-hit wonders? Evidence from Sweden. *Small Business Economics, 44*(2), 361–383. doi:10.1007/s11187-014-9599-8

Davidsson, P. (2015). Data replication and extension: a commentary. *Journal of Business Venturing Insights, 3*, 12–15. doi:http://dx.doi.org/10.1016/j.jbvi.2015.02.001

Davidsson, P., Achtenhagen, L., & Naldi, L. (2010). Small firm growth. *Foundations and Trends in Entrepreneurship, 6*(2), 98–166. doi:10.1561/0300000029

Davidsson, P., Delmar, F., & Wiklund, J. (2006). Conceptual and empirical challenges in the study of firm growth. In P. Davidsson, F. Delmar, & J. Wiklund (Eds), *Entrepreneurship and the Growth of Firms* (p. 240). Cheltenham: Edward Elgar Publishing. doi:10.4337/9781781009949.00010

Davidsson, P., & Honig, B. (2003). The role of social and human capital among nascent entrepreneurs. *Journal of Business Venturing, 18*(3), 301–331. doi:http://dx.doi.org/10.1016/S0883-9026(02)00097-6

Delmar, F. (2006). Measuring growth: methodological considerations and empirical results. In P. Davidsson, F. Delmar, & J. Wiklund (Eds), *Entrepreneurship and the Growth of Firms* (Vol. 1, pp. 62–84). Cheltenham: Edward Elgar.

Delmar, F., Davidsson, P., & Gartner, W. B. (2003). Arriving at the high-growth firm. *Journal of Business Venturing, 18*(2), 189–216. doi:http://dx.doi.org/10.1016/S0883-9026(02)00080-0

Delmar, F., & Wiklund, J. (2008). The effect of small business managers' growth motivation on firm growth: a longitudinal study. *Entrepreneurship Theory and Practice, 32*(3), 437–457. doi:10.1111/j.1540-6520.2008.00235.x

Derbyshire, J., & Garnsey, E. (2014). Firm growth and the illusion of randomness. *Journal of Business Venturing Insights, 1–2*, 8–11. doi:http://dx.doi.org/10.1016/j.jbvi.2014.09.003

Derbyshire, J., & Garnsey, E. (2015). Are firm growth paths random? A further response regarding Gambler's Ruin theory. *Journal of Business Venturing Insights, 3*, 9–11.

doi:http://dx.doi.org/10.1016/j.jbvi.2014.12.001

Dess, G. G., & Beard, D. W. (1984). Dimensions of organizational task environments. *Administrative Science Quarterly, 29*(1), 52–73.

Dobbs, M., & Hamilton, R. T. (2007). Small business growth: recent evidence and new directions. *International Journal of Entrepreneurial Behavior & Research, 13*(5), 296–322. doi:10.1108/13552550710780885

Doern, R. (2009). Investigating barriers to SME growth and development in transition environments: a critique and suggestions for developing the methodology. *International Small Business Journal, 27*(3), 275–305. doi:10.1177/0266242609102275

Dutta, D. K., & Thornhill, S. (2008). The evolution of growth intentions: toward a cognition-based model. *Journal of Business Venturing, 23*(3), 307–332. Retrieved from http://www.sciencedirect.com/science/article/pii/S0883902607000250

Eggers, J. H., Leahy, K. T., & Churchill, N. C. (1994). *Stages of small business growth revisited: insights into growth path and leadership/management skills in low- and high-growth companies.* Fontainebleau: INSEAD.

Eisenhardt, K. M., & Schoonhoven, C. B. (1990). Organizational growth: linking founding team, strategy, environment, and growth among US semiconductor ventures, 1978–1988. *Administrative Science Quarterly, 35*(3), 504–529.

Ensley, M. D., & Hmieleski, K. M. (2005). A comparative study of new venture top management team composition, dynamics and performance between university-based and independent start-ups. *Research Policy, 34*(7), 1091–1105. doi:http://dx.doi.org/10.1016/j.respol.2005.05.008

Ensley, M. D., Hmieleski, K. M., & Pearce, C. L. (2006). The importance of vertical and shared leadership within new venture top management teams: implications for the performance of startups. *The Leadership Quarterly, 17*(3), 217–231.

Ensley, M. D., Pearce, C. L., & Hmieleski, K. M. (2006). The moderating effect of environmental dynamism on the relationship between entrepreneur leadership behavior and new venture performance. *Journal of Business Venturing, 21*(2), 243–263.

Retrieved from http://www.sciencedirect. com/science/article/pii/S0883902605000418

Eurostat-OECD. (2007). *Eurostat – OECD Manual on Business Demography Statistics.* Luxembourg. Retrieved from http://www. oecd.org/std/business-stats/eurostat-oecdmanualonbusinessdemographystatistics.htm

Florin, J., Lubatkin, M., & Schulze, W. (2003). A social capital model of high-growth ventures. *Academy of Management Journal, 46*(3), 374–384. doi:10.2307/30040630

Geiger, S. W., & Cashen, L. H. (2002). A multidimensional examination of slack and its impact on innovation. *Journal of Managerial Issues, 14*(1), 68–84.

George, G., & Bock, A. J. (2011). The business model in practice and its implications for entrepreneurship research. *Entrepreneurship Theory and Practice, 35*(1), 83–111. doi:10.1111/j.1540-6520.2010.00424.x

Gibrat. (1931). *Les inégalités économiques. applications: aux inégalités des richesses, a la concentration des entreprises, aux populations des villes, aux statistiques des familles, etc., d'une loi nouvelle: la loi de l'effet proportionnel.* Paris: Sirey.

Gilbert, B. A., McDougall, P. P., & Audretsch, D. B. (2006). New venture growth: a review and extension. *Journal of Management, 32*(6), 926–950. doi:10.1177/0149206306293860

Granovetter, M. S. (1973). The strength of weak ties. *American Journal of Sociology, 78*(6), 1360–1380. Retrieved from http://www.jstor.org/stable/2776392

Gregory, B. T., Rutherford, M. W., Oswald, S., & Gardiner, L. (2005). An empirical investigation of the growth cycle theory of small firm financing. *Journal of Small Business Management, 43*(4), 382–392. doi:10.1111/j.1540-627X.2005.00143.x

Greiner, L. E. (1972). Evolution and revolution as organizations grow. *Harvard Business Review, 50*(4), 37–46.

Grilli, L. (2014). High-tech entrepreneurship in Europe: a heuristic firm growth model and three '(un-)easy' pieces for policy-making. *Industry and Innovation, 21*(4), 267–284. doi:10.1080/13662716.2014.939850

Guerrero, O. A., & Axtell, R. L. (2013). Employment growth through labor flow networks. *PLoS ONE, 8*(5), e60808. Retrieved from http://dx.doi.org/10.1371%2Fjournal.pone.0060808

Gulati, R. (1998). Alliances and networks. *Strategic Management Journal, 19*(4), 293–317. doi:10.1002/(SICI)1097-0266(199804) 19:4<293::AID-SMJ982>3.0.CO;2-M

Haltiwanger, J., Jarmin, R. S., & Miranda, J. (2013). Who creates jobs? small versus large versus young. *Review of Economics and Statistics, 95*(2), 347–361. doi:10.1162/REST_a_00288

Hanks, S. H., Watson, C. J., Jansen, E., & Chandler, G. N. (1993). Tightening the life-cycle construct: a taxonomic study of growth stage configurations in high-technology organizations. *Entrepreneurship: Theory and Practice, 18*(2), 5–29.

Hansen, B., & Hamilton, R. T. (2011). Factors distinguishing small firm growers and non-growers. *International Small Business Journal, 29*(3), 278–294. doi:10.1177/0266242610381846

Hashi, I. (2001). Financial and institutional barriers to SME growth in Albania: results of an enterprise survey. *MOST: Economic Policy in Transitional Economies, 11*(3), 221–238. doi:10.1023/A:1013157127524

Henrekson, M., & Johansson, D. (2010). Gazelles as job creators: a survey and interpretation of the evidence. *Small Business Economics, 35*(2), 227–244. doi:10.1007/s11187-009-9172-z

Hmieleski, K. M., & Baron, R. A. (2008). Regulatory focus and new venture performance: a study of entrepreneurial opportunity exploitation under conditions of risk versus uncertainty. *Strategic Entrepreneurship Journal, 2*(4), 285–299. doi:10.1002/sej.56

Hölzl, W. (2009). Is the R&D behaviour of fast-growing SMEs different? Evidence from CIS III data for 16 countries. *Small Business Economics, 33*(1), 59–75. doi:10.1007/s11187-009-9182-x

Hoxha, D., & Capelleras, J. L. (2010). Fast growing firms in a transitional and extreme environment: are they different? *Journal of Small Business and Enterprise Development, 17*(3), 350–370. doi:10.1108/14626001011068671

Inderst, R., & Mueller, H. M. (2009). Early-stage financing and firm growth in new industries. *Journal of Financial Economics, 93*(2), 276–291.

Kazanjian, R. K. (1988). Relation of dominant problems to stages of growth in technology-based new ventures. *Academy of Management Journal*, *31*(2), 257–279. doi:10.2307/256548

Khaire, M. (2010). Young and no money? Never mind: the material impact of social resources on new venture growth. *Organization Science*, *21*(1), 168–185. doi:10.1287/orsc.1090.0438

Koryak, O., Mole, K. F., Lockett, A., Hayton, J. C., Ucbasaran, D., & Hodgkinson, G. P. (2015). Entrepreneurial leadership, capabilities and firm growth. *International Small Business Journal*, *33*(1), 89–105. doi:10.1177/0266242614558315

Larrañeta, B., Zahra, S. A., & Galán González, J. L. (2014). Strategic repertoire variety and new venture growth: the moderating effects of origin and industry dynamism. *Strategic Management Journal*, *35*(5), 761–772. doi:10.1002/smj.2103

Lawless, M. (2014). Age or size? Contributions to job creation. *Small Business Economics*, *42*(4), 815–830. doi:10.1007/s11187-013-9513-9

Lechner, C., & Dowling, M. (2003). Firm networks: external relationships as sources for the growth and competitiveness of entrepreneurial firms. *Entrepreneurship & Regional Development*, *15*(1), 1–26. doi:10.1080/08985620210159220

Lechner, C., Dowling, M., & Welpe, I. (2006). Firm networks and firm development: the role of the relational mix. *Journal of Business Venturing*, *21*(4), 514–540. Retrieved from http://www.sciencedirect.com/science/article/pii/S088390260500025X

Lechner, C., & Gudmundsson, S. V. (2014). Entrepreneurial orientation, firm strategy and small firm performance. *International Small Business Journal*, *32*(1), 36–60. doi:10.1177/0266242612455034

Lee, N., & Cowling, M. (2013). Place, sorting effects and barriers to enterprise in deprived areas: different problems or different firms? *International Small Business Journal*, *31*(8), 914–937. doi:10.1177/0266242612445402

Leitch, C., Hill, F., & Neergaard, H. (2010). Entrepreneurial and business growth and the quest for a 'comprehensive theory': tilting at windmills? *Entrepreneurship Theory and Practice*, *34*(2), 249–260. doi:10.1111/j.1540-6520.2010.00374.x

Leitner, K.-H., & Güldenberg, S. (2009). Generic strategies and firm performance in SMEs: a longitudinal study of Austrian SMEs. *Small Business Economics*, *35*(2), 169–189. doi:10.1007/s11187-009-9239-x

Levie, J., & Lichtenstein, B. B. (2010). A terminal assessment of stages theory: introducing a dynamic states approach to entrepreneurship. *Entrepreneurship Theory and Practice*, *34*(2), 317–350. doi:10.1111/j.1540-6520.2010.00377.x

Lockett, A., Wiklund, J., Davidsson, P., & Girma, S. (2011). Organic and acquisitive growth: re-examining, testing and extending Penrose's growth theory. *Journal of Management Studies*, *48*(1), 48–74. doi:10.1111/j.1467-6486.2009.00879.x

Lockett, A., & Wild, A. (2013). A Penrosean theory of acquisitive growth. *Business History*, *55*(5), 790–817. doi:10.1080/00076791.2013.790370

Lockett, A., & Wild, A. (2014). Bringing history (back) into the resource-based view. *Business History*, *56*(3), 372–390. doi:10.1080/00076791.2013.790371

Lounsbury, M., & Glynn, M. A. (2001). Cultural entrepreneurship: stories, legitimacy, and the acquisition of resources. *Strategic Management Journal*, *22*(6–7), 545–564. doi:10.1002/smj.188

Lumpkin, G., & Dess, G. (1996). Clarifying the entrepreneurial orientation construct and linking it to performance. *Academy of Management Review*, *21*(1), 135–172.

Macpherson, A., & Holt, R. (2007). Knowledge, learning and small firm growth: a systematic review of the evidence. *Research Policy*, *36*(2), 172–192. doi:http://dx.doi.org/10.1016/j.respol.2006.10.001

McKelvie, A., & Wiklund, J. (2010). Advancing firm growth research: a focus on growth mode instead of growth rate. *Entrepreneurship Theory and Practice*, *34*(2), 261–288. doi:10.1111/j.1540-6520.2010.00375.x

Messersmith, J. G., & Wales, W. J. (2013). Entrepreneurial orientation and performance in young firms: the role of human resource management. *International Small Business Journal*, *31*(2), 115–136. doi:10.1177/0266242611416141

Miller, D. (1983). The correlates of entrepreneurship in three types of firms. *Management Science*, *29*(7), 770–791.

Mohr, V., Garnsey, E., & Theyel, G. (2013). The role of alliances in the early development of high-growth firms. *Industrial and Corporate Change*, 23(2), 233–259.

Moreno, A. M., & Casillas, J. C. (2007). High-growth SMEs versus non-high-growth SMEs: a discriminant analysis. *Entrepreneurship & Regional Development*, 19(1), 69–88. doi:10.1080/08985620601002162

Moreno, F., & Coad, A. (2015). High-growth firms: stylized facts and conflicting results. In A. C. Corbett, J. Katz, & A. McKelvie (Eds), *Advances in Entrepreneurship, Firm Emergence and Growth* (Volume 17, pp. 187–230). Bingley: Emerald Group Publishing Limited.

Naldi, L., & Davidsson, P. (2014). Entrepreneurial growth: the role of international knowledge acquisition as moderated by firm age. *Journal of Business Venturing*, 29(5), 687–703. doi:http://dx.doi.org/10.1016/j.jbusvent.2013.08.003

Nason, R. S., & Wiklund, J. (2015). An assessment of resource-based theorizing on firm growth and suggestions for the future. *Journal of Management*. doi:10.1177/0149206315610635

Nightingale, P., & Coad, A. (2014). Muppets and gazelles: political and methodological biases in entrepreneurship research. *Industrial and Corporate Change*, 23(1), 113–143. doi:10.1093/icc/dtt057

O'Cass, A., & Sok, P. (2014). The role of intellectual resources, product innovation capability, reputational resources and marketing capability combinations in firm growth. *International Small Business Journal*, 32(8), 996–1018. doi:10.1177/0266242613480225

Patel, P. C., Fiet, J. O., & Sohl, J. E. (2011). Mitigating the limited scalability of bootstrapping through strategic alliances to enhance new venture growth. *International Small Business Journal*, 29(5), 421–447. doi:10.1177/0266242610396622

Penrose, E. (1959). *The theory of the growth of the firm*. Oxford: Oxford University Press.

Phelps, R., Adams, R., & Bessant, J. (2007). Life cycles of growing organizations: a review with implications for knowledge and learning. *International Journal of Management Reviews*, 9(1), 1–30. doi:10.1111/j.1468-2370.2007.00200.x

Pirolo, L., & Presutti, M. (2010). The impact of social capital on the start-ups' performance growth. *Journal of Small Business Management*, 48(2), 197–227. doi:10.1111/j.1540-627X.2010.00292.x

Pissarides, F. (1999). Is lack of funds the main obstacle to growth? EBRD's experience with small- and medium-sized businesses in Central and Eastern Europe. *Journal of Business Venturing*, 14(5–6), 519–539. doi:10.1016/S0883-9026(98)00027-5

Pissarides, F., Singer, M., & Svejnar, J. (2003). Objectives and constraints of entrepreneurs: evidence from small and medium size enterprises in Russia and Bulgaria. *Journal of Comparative Economics*, 31(3), 503–531. doi:http://dx.doi.org/10.1016/S0147-5967(03)00054-4

Prashantham, S., & Dhanaraj, C. (2010). The dynamic influence of social capital on the international growth of new ventures. *Journal of Management Studies*, 47(6), 967–994. doi:10.1111/j.1467-6486.2009.00904.x

Priem, R. L., Li, S., & Carr, J. C. (2012). Insights and new directions from demand-side approaches to technology innovation, entrepreneurship, and strategic management research. *Journal of Management*, 38(1), 346–374. doi:10.1177/0149206311429614

Raisch, S. (2008). Balanced structures: designing organizations for profitable growth. *Long Range Planning*, 41(5), 483–508. doi:http://dx.doi.org/10.1016/j.lrp.2008.06.004

Raisch, S., & Birkinshaw, J. (2008). Organizational ambidexterity: antecedents, outcomes, and moderators. *Journal of Management*, 34(3), 375–409. doi:10.1177/0149206308316058

Rasheed, H. S. (2005). Foreign entry mode and performance: the moderating effects of environment. *Journal of Small Business Management*, 43(1), 41–54. doi:10.1111/j.1540-627X.2004.00124.x

Rindova, V. P., Yeow, A., Martins, L. L., & Faraj, S. (2012). Partnering portfolios, value-creation logics, and growth trajectories: a comparison of Yahoo and Google (1995 to 2007). *Strategic Entrepreneurship Journal*, 6(2), 133–151. doi:10.1002/sej.1131

Robson, P. J. A., & Obeng, B. A. (2008). The barriers to growth in Ghana. *Small Business Economics*, 30(4), 385–403. doi:10.1007/s11187-007-9046-1

Rosenbusch, N., Brinckmann, J., & Müller, V. (2013). Does acquiring venture capital pay off for the funded firms? A meta-analysis on the relationship between venture capital investment and funded firm financial performance. *Journal of Business Venturing, 28*(3), 335–353. doi:http://dx.doi.org/10.1016/j.jbusvent.2012.04.002

Salomo, S., Brinckmann, J., & Talke, K. (2008). Functional management competence and growth of young technology-based firms. *Creativity and Innovation Management, 17*(3), 186–203. doi:10.1111/j.1467-8691.2008.00485.x

Scholten, V., Omta, O., Kemp, R., & Elfring, T. (2015). Bridging ties and the role of research and start-up experience on the early growth of Dutch academic spin-offs. *Technovation, 45–46,* 40–51. doi:http://dx.doi.org/10.1016/j.technovation.2015.05.001

Sheehan, M. (2014). Human resource management and performance: evidence from small and medium-sized firms. *International Small Business Journal, 32*(5), 545–570. doi:10.1177/0266242612465454

Shepherd, D., & Wiklund, J. (2009). Are we comparing apples with apples or apples with oranges? Appropriateness of knowledge accumulation across growth studies. *Entrepreneurship Theory and Practice, 33*(1), 105–123. doi:10.1111/j.1540-6520.2008.00282.x

Stam, W., & Elfring, T. (2008). Entrepreneurial orientation and new venture performance: the moderating role of intra- and extraindustry social capital. *Academy of Management Journal, 51*(1), 97–111. doi:10.5465/AMJ.2008.30744031

Sull, D., & Eisenhardt, K. M. (2012). Simple rules for a complex world. *Harvard Business Review, 90*(9), 68–74.

Sutton, J. (1997). Gibrat's legacy. *Journal of Economic Literature, 35*(1), 40–59. doi:10.2307/2729692

Teece, D. J. (2010). Business models, business strategy and innovation. *Long Range Planning, 43*(2–3), 172–194.

Unger, J. M., Rauch, A., Frese, M., & Rosenbusch, N. (2011). Human capital and entrepreneurial success: a meta-analytical review. *Journal of Business Venturing, 26*(3), 341–358. doi:http://dx.doi.org/10.1016/j.jbusvent.2009.09.004

Vanacker, T., Manigart, S., Meuleman, M., & Sels, L. (2011). A longitudinal study on the relationship between financial bootstrapping and new venture growth. *Entrepreneurship &*

Regional Development, 23(9–10), 681–705. doi:10.1080/08985626.2010.502250

Vandaie, R., & Zaheer, A. (2014). Surviving bear hugs: firm capability, large partner alliances, and growth. *Strategic Management Journal, 35*(4), 566–577. doi:10.1002/smj.2115

Vissa, B., & Chacar, A. S. (2009). Leveraging ties: the contingent value of entrepreneurial teams' external advice networks on Indian software venture performance. *Strategic Management Journal, 30*(11), 1179–1191. doi:10.1002/smj.785

Wales, W. J. (2016). Entrepreneurial orientation: a review and synthesis of promising research directions. *International Small Business Journal, 34*(1), 3–15. doi:10.1177/0266242615613840

Walter, A., Auer, M., & Ritter, T. (2006). The impact of network capabilities and entrepreneurial orientation on university spin-off performance. *Journal of Business Venturing, 21*(4), 541–567. doi:http://dx.doi.org/10.1016/j.jbusvent.2005.02.005

Weinzimmer, L. G., Nystrom, P. C., & Freeman, S. J. (1998). Measuring organizational growth: issues, consequences and guidelines. *Journal of Management, 24*(2), 235–262. doi:10.1177/014920639802400205

Welch, C., & Paavilainen-Mäntymäki, E. (2014). Putting process (back) in: research on the internationalization process of the firm. *International Journal of Management Reviews, 16*(1), 2–23. doi:10.1111/ijmr.12006

Wernerfelt., B (1984). A resource-based view of the firm. *Strategic Management Journal, 5*(2), 171–180.

Wiklund, J., Patzelt, H., & Shepherd, D. (2009). Building an integrative model of small business growth. *Small Business Economics, 32*(4), 351–374. doi:10.1007/s11187-007-9084-8

Wright, M., Roper, S., Hart, M., & Carter, S. (2015). Joining the dots: building the evidence base for SME growth policy. *International Small Business Journal, 33*(1), 3–11. doi:10.1177/0266242614558316

Wright, M., & Stigliani, I. (2013). Entrepreneurship and growth. *International Small Business Journal, 31*(1), 3–22. doi:10.1177/0266242612467359

Xheneti, M., & Bartlett, W. (2012). Institutional constraints and SME growth in postcommunist Albania. *Journal of Small Business* and *Enterprise Development*, *19*(4), 607–626. doi:10.1108/14626001211277424

Zander, I., & Zander, U. (2005). The Inside track: on the important (but neglected) role of customers in the resource-based view of strategy and firm growth. *Journal of Management Studies*, *42*(8), 1519–1548. doi:10.1111/j.1467-6486.2005.00555.x

Zupic, I., & Drnovsek, M. (2014). Firm growth: research front and intellectual structure. *Academy of Management Proceedings*, *2014*(1), 12367.

12

Small Business Growth and Performance

Samuel Adomako and Kevin F. Mole

INTRODUCTION

Entrepreneurship, economics and strategy scholars have studied business growth for a number of years (e.g. Coad, Segarra & Teruel, 2016; Davidsson & Wiklund, 2000; Delmar, 1997; Delmar & Wiklund, 2008; McKelvie & Wiklund, 2010). Despite these substantial scholarly efforts in business growth, theoretical developments have been notably slow (Davidsson & Wiklund, 2000; Delmar, 1997; McKelvie & Wiklund, 2010), making it difficult to distil a clearer picture of the small business growth phenomenon (Ardichvili, Cardozo, Harmon & Vadakath, 1998; Storey, 1994; Wiklund, 1998). Extant reviews have accounted for this negative status quo in business growth research, suggesting that, despite many scholarly studies on business growth, our knowledge on the phenomenon is still limited (e.g. Coad, 2007; Davidsson & Wiklund, 2000; Macpherson & Holt, 2007; McKelvie & Wiklund, 2010; Shepherd & Wiklund, 2009; Weinzimmer,

Nystrom & Freeman, 1998). The difficulty in distilling a clearer picture of the business growth phenomenon has been attributed to how scholars approach the theoretical and epistemological issues and interpretations; operationalisation; empirical contexts; modelling; and analysis of the small business growth literature (Davidsson, Achtenhagen & Naldi, 2010).

The focus of this chapter is, therefore, to contribute to further understanding of business growth by reviewing extant literature. To achieve this objective, this review is organised as follows: first, we highlight the Penrose theory of firm growth. Second, we examine the evidence of how business growth is measured. Third, we review evidence relating to theories of business growth: (1) integrated models and (2) stage models. Fourth, we review what is known about modes of business growth. Fifth, we examine drivers of, and constraints to, business growth. In the final section, we highlight areas of consensus and contention.

PENROSEAN VIEW OF FIRM GROWTH

Penrose's (1959/1995) theory of the growth of the firm has received overwhelming scholarly support (e.g. Garnsey, 1998; Lockett, Wiklund, Davidsson & Girma, 2011; Mahoney & Michael, 2005; Naldi & Davidsson, 2014; Obeng, Robson & Haugh, 2014; Pitelis, 2007). These are all substantial and critical empirical works which have attempted to use Penrose's theory of growth as a theoretical lens to explain small business growth. According to Penrose's (1959, p. 217) theory, the process of firm growth is influenced by the extent of the firm's resources, that the 'amount of resources administered by a firm has in itself a significant influence on the opportunities for expansion open to the firm'. This suggests that larger firms or firms with access to more resources tend to grow more rapidly than smaller firms.

The entrepreneurship and small business literature recognises resources as physical, financial and human capital resources (Obeng et al., 2014). The contribution of Penrose's resource-based theory in explaining small business growth can be attributed to the importance the theory places in distinguishing between the internal resources of businesses and their capacity to achieve high growth (Davidsson & Wiklund, 1999). That is, the resource-based view (RBV) of the firm is based on the assumption that the internal resources of the business can affect its capacity to achieve higher growth (Davidsson & Wiklund, 1999).

Wider scholarly enquiry on RBV (e.g. Barney, 1986, 1991; Wernerfelt, 1984) emanated from Penrose's (1959) seminal work, which has contributed immensely to the strategic management literature. The RBV views organisations as bundles of resources. For example, assets, capabilities, organisational resources, information and knowledge can be classified as resources within an organisation.

Several empirical studies have highlighted the importance of the internal resources of the firm to the achievement of competitive advantage over its rivals (e.g. Barney, 1991; Wernerfelt, 1984). These resources are important for generating competitive advantage (Barney, 1991; Penrose, 1959). Accordingly, Barney (1991, p. 102) stressed that, to achieve a competitive advantage, a firm should 'implement value creating strategy not simultaneously being implemented by any current or potential competitors'.

However, some scholars suggest that, while resources are important to achieving competitive advantage, firms do not have to own these resources themselves (Dhanaraj & Beamish, 2003). Instead, firms can form alliances with other organisations by establishing trade relationships and inter-firm alliances (Hessels & Parker, 2013). Thus, the RBV provides a useful theoretical lens for explaining how small businesses can gain competitive advantage and enhance firm performance through leveraging external networks (Street & Cameron, 2007).

It is arguable that Penrose's contribution fails to fully address the issue of knowledge-related intra-firm advantages. Penrose took for granted that knowledge-related intra-firm advantages predict firm growth. Yet, this is not clear in her theory. A contentious issue is to pose a question as to why firms do not sell their (intangible) assets in the open market (Pitelis, 2009). Clearly, it can be argued that there are differential capabilities, i.e. firms are better in making use of their own assets than other firms (i.e. the market). Yet Penrose did not discuss this issue in the theory of the growth of the firm.

MEASURING BUSINESS GROWTH

Measuring business growth has generated diverse views (e.g. Achtenhagen, Naldi & Melin, 2010; Birley & Westhead, 1990; Delmar, 2000; Shepherd & Wiklund, 2009; Weinzimmer et al., 1998). Scholars have measured business growth from two main perspectives: change in amount and growth as a process (Davidsson et al., 2010; Penrose, 1959). In her seminal work, Penrose (1959,

p. 1) positioned the phenomenon of growth as follows:

> The term 'growth' is used in ordinary discourse with two different connotations. It sometimes denotes merely increase in amount; e.g., when one speaks of 'growth' in output, export, sales. At other times, however, it is used in its primary meaning implying an increase in size or improvement in quality as a result of a *process* of development … in which an interacting series of internal changes leads to increase in size accompanied by changes in the characteristics of the growing object.

This suggests that growth can be defined as an increase in amount or as an internal process development.

From the change-in-amount perspective, different measures of growth such as sales, employment, assets, physical output, market share and profits have been employed in the literature (e.g. Ardichvili et al., 1998; Barringer, Jones & Neubaum, 2005; Davidsson & Wiklund, 2000; Delmar, 1997; Delmar, Davidsson & Gartner, 2003; Delmar & Wiklund, 2008; Wiklund, 1998). These measures offer particular advantages and disadvantages in distilling the picture of the phenomenon of growth (Delmar, 1997). Yet there seems to be a controversy in the literature as to which indicator is appropriate in measuring business growth (McKelvie & Wiklund, 2010; Weinzimmer et al., 1998). Indeed, the notion of growth as 'increase in amount' dominates empirical studies that measure business growth in the entrepreneurship field (Achtenhagen et al., 2010). Thus, previous empirical development tends to place much emphasis on outcome-based predictors which denote an increase in size or amount.

There is a growing consensus on the use of sales as a measure of growth over a time period of 5 years in the literature (e.g. Ardichvili et al., 1998; Barkham, Gudgin, Hart & Hanvey, 1996; Barringer et al., 2005; Dunne & Hughes, 1994; Miller, 1987; Weinzimmer et al., 1998). A major conclusion is that sales often precede other indicators (e.g. Davidsson et al., 2010; Flamholtz, 1986). For example, it is the increase in sales that calls for increase in assets and employees, which leads to higher

profits or market share (Flamholtz, 1986). Other researchers contend that sales can be measured with ease across various countries and industry and are also the preferred measure for business owners (e.g. Hoy, McDougall & Dsouza, 1992). Owner–managers use sales figures most and sales figures are preferred by entrepreneurs (Barkham et al., 1996).

Another indicator that has received much attention in measuring growth is employment (Delmar, 1997). Scholarly studies mostly use relative employment growth over a three-year period (Peters & Brush, 1996; Vaessen & Keeble, 1995; Zahra, 1993). However, according to Davidsson and Wiklund (2000), employment as an indicator of growth is highly relevant to policymakers because they tend to focus on employment rather than sales growth of businesses within an economy. Yet, because some businesses employ an outsourcing strategy, employment growth is not always highly related to sales growth (e.g. Chandler, McKelvie & Davidsson, 2009; Delmar et al., 2003; Shepherd & Wiklund, 2009).

Indeed, the use of one indicator as a measure of growth may or may not actually reflect growth when using another indicator as a measure (Delmar et al., 2003). Therefore, some scholars have advocated the use of multiple measures to account for variations in model testing and theory development (Weinzimmer et al., 1998). There appears to be no consensus or universally accepted measure of business growth and employing multiple measures is likely to provide a complete picture of business growth and a way to test the robustness of any theoretical model (Delmar et al., 2003). A major shortcoming of the use of multiple indicators is that the assumption of common cause may be incorrect (Delmar et al., 2003). Further, some scholars are of the view that different growth measures and calculations of business growth influence model-building and theory development differently and advocate for the use of a single measure of business growth (Chandler & Hanks, 1993; Delmar, 1997; Weinzimmer et al., 1998). Table 12.1

Table 12.1 Summary of studies measuring business growth

Author(s)	How growth is measured	Time frame of the study (in years)	Sample size
Coad et al. (2016)	Sales growth, employment growth and productivity growth	8	26,660
Beck et al. (2015)	Sales	1	344
Capasso et al. (2015)	Employment	4	13,236
García-Posada and Mora-Sanguinetti (2014)	Sales and employment	8	2,861,174
Arregle et al. (2015)	Sales	2	515
Federico and Capelleras (2015)	Sales	14	926
Fafchamps et al. (2014)	Profits	4	781
O'Cass and Sok (2014)	Sales, profit, customer satisfaction and financial growth	1	171
Obeng et al. (2014)	Employment	0.6	441
Mai and Zheng (2013)	Market share	2	905
Schoonjans et al. (2013)	Employment, net assets and added value growth	5	108,241
Didier and Schmukler (2013)	Total assets, sales and employment	20	214,271
Hamelin (2013)	Sales	6	22,237
Anderson and Eshima (2013)	Sales, employment and market share	1	207
Rahaman (2011)	Sales and employment	10	52,140
Barringer et al. (2005)	Sales and employment	3	100
Chandler and Baueus (1996)	Sales	1	66
Becchetti and Trovato (2002)	Financial growth	8	4,000
Carpenter and Petersen (2002)	Total assets	3	372
Davidsson and Delmar (1997)	Employment	1	11,748
Delmar et al. (2003)	Sales and employment	1	11,748
Freel and Robson (2004)	Employment	3	1,347
Glancey (1998)	Employment	1	38
Davidsson and Henrekson (2002)	Employment	1	8,173
Kelley and Nakosteen (2005)	Sales revenue	11	67
Kangasharju (2000)	Employment	7	26,057
Johnson et al. (1999)	Employment	2	75
Littunen and Tohmo (2003)	Sales growth	7	200
Locke (2004)	Employment	1	170
North and Smallbone (2000)	Sales and employment	5	1,050
O'Gorman (2001)	Sales turnover and employment	20	2 (Longitudinal study)
Yasuda (2005)	Employment	6	14,000
Wiklund and Shepherd (2003)	Employment and sales	3	326
Pena (2002)	Employment, sales and profit	1	119
Reichstein and Dahl (2004)	Sales turnover and employment	1	9,000
Donaldson (1987)	Sales	3	48
Chrisman and Leslie (1989)	Sales	1	86
Kazanjian (1988)	Sales	1.5	71
Davidsson (1991)	Sales and employment	3	322
Miller and Friesen (1983)	Sales and profit	5	86

(Continued)

Table 12.1   (Continued)

Miller and Toulouse (1986)	Sales	5	97
Orser et al. (2000)	Sales	2	1,004
Olson and Bokor (1995)	Sales	5	91
LeBrasseur et al. (2003)	Sales	2	145
Dess and Davis (1984)	Sales	1	22
Hamilton and Shergill (1992)	Sales, earnings per share (EPS), dividends and assets	11	67
Nkomo (1987)	Sales	5	264
Morrison and Roth (1992)	Sales	3	306
Weinzimmer et al. (1998)	Sales and employment	5	193

summarises empirical studies and the ways growth is conceptualised. As can be seen from Table 12.1, sales and employment have been used extensively in measuring business growth in the literature.

THEORIES OF BUSINESS GROWTH

Business growth has much attention from scholars in the business literature (e.g. Smallbone & Wyer, 2000; Storey, 1994; Yasuda, 2005), with several studies attempting to explain the dynamics of business growth (e.g. Hanks & Chandler, 1992; Hanks, Watson, Jansen & Chandler, 1993) and associating many factors with business growth (e.g. Obeng et al., 2014; Orser, Hogarth-Scott & Riding, 2000; Sleuwaegen & Goedhuys, 2002). However, evidence from the literature indicates that various theories that predict business growth have been sparse and scattered (Garnsey, 1998). For example, Davidsson et al. (2002, p. 1) described economic theories that predict business growth as 'crude and contradictory'. The reason may be that the literature is broad in scope (McMahon, 1998) and not confined to a single discipline.

Similarly, Penrose (1959, 1995) indicated that many factors influence the growth of businesses and as such it is difficult to explain small business growth with a single one-fits-all model. Theories of business growth can be broadly divided into: (1) integrated model theories, which explain the factors that drive business growth; and (2) stage models, which view firm growth as a series of phases or stages of development through which a firm must pass in its life-cycle.

INTEGRATED MODELS OF BUSINESS GROWTH

A growing list of internal and external factors that could affect business growth creates a challenge for studies that attempt to explain business growth. Several theories have been proposed to examine business growth and these include Gibrat's (1931) law of proportionate effect, Penrose's (1959) theory of firm growth, Jovanovic's (1982) learning theory, Storey's (1994) growth determinants model, Davidsson's (1991) growth determinants model and Wiklund's (1998) growth model. These theories have received reasonable validity assessment in both advanced economies (e.g. Orser et al., 2000; Stam, 2010; Weinzimmer et al., 1998; Wiklund, Patzelt & Shepherd, 2009) and less developed market economies (e.g. Masakure, Hensen & Cranfield, 2009; Obeng et al., 2014). A point of convergence of most of these theories is that they suggest internal and external factors that could affect business growth. Notwithstanding the fact that a large body of research on business growth theories has been conducted, there seems to be a controversy as to which theory is appropriate in predicting business growth (e.g. Barringer et al., 2005; Delmar & Wiklund, 2008; Delmar et al., 2003; McKelvie & Wiklund, 2010; Weinzimmer et al., 1998). While individual studies cover an array of factors on different levels (e.g. Eisenhardt & Schoonhoven, 1990; Sandberg & Hofer, 1987), other scholars (e.g. Davidsson, 1991; Wiklund, 1998) attempt to formally integrate a broad range of growth drivers in a causal model. Thus, Davidsson's and Wiklund's models capture many factors with mediated relationships, which represents an important area of examination in management research.

LIFE-CYCLE AND STAGE MODELS

Apart from scholarly attempts to examine the factors that influence business growth, there is a large body of literature that is concerned with growth processes. These models are often presented in the form of life-cycle or stage models that encompass the entire lifespan of a business (e.g. Barringer et al., 2005; Dodge & Robbins, 1992; Gibb & Davies, 1990; Gill, 1985; Greiner, 1972; Hanks, 1990a, 1990b; Hanks & Chandler, 1994; Hanks, Watson & Jansen, 1991; Hanks et al., 1993; Kazanjian, 1988; Kazanjian & Drazin, 1989, 1990; O'Farrell & Hitchens, 1988; Scott & Bruce,1987; Steinmetz, 1969). These models attempt to explain the dynamic nature of growth of small businesses.

The main difference between life-cycle models and stage models is that, whilst life-cycle models represent a cycle of emergence, growth, maturity and decline (e.g. Adizes, 1989; Whetten, 1987), stage models focus on the problems encountered by small businesses (e.g. Kazanjian, 1988; Moy & Luk, 2003; Walsh, 1988). According to Kimberly and Miles (1980) organisations are born, grow and decline. These have been referred to as life-cycle models. This raises contentious issues in economics, business and sociology (Kimberly & Miles, 1980; McMahon, 1998; Penrose, 1952).

Stage or developmental models, on the other hand, consider mainly the firm's development process (emergence, growth, maturity and decline) and the generic problems firms go through during growth. Indeed, stage models show that there are certain problems associated with each stage of business growth and these problems are unique at each stage of firm development (Kazanjian, 1988; Moy & Luk, 2003; Olson, 1987; Walsh, 1988). Accordingly, O'Gorman (2001) indicated that it is important to overcome obstacles at each stage so that small businesses can move through different stages in order to achieve growth. However, recent empirical work (Delmar et al., 2003) suggests that research must focus on the heterogeneous patterns of growth outcomes. In this case, the primary motives of the entrepreneurs tend to be mediated by different factors, leading to numerous growth paths.

Of the models discussed so far, the work of Hanks et al. (1993) appears to be most suitable for explaining business growth. This is because the model provides evidence to suggest that, with reference to increasing age and size, there is a sequential progression of organisations through the stages in the evolvement and development of enterprises. A similar assumption has been raised by Kazanjian and Drazin (1989), suggesting that there is a sequential progression of enterprises through stages as they evolve. Although Hanks et al. (1993) suggested some limitations of their study, such as it being based on one particular industry and geographic setting, it represents one of the most significant attempts to elucidate research-based stage models.

MODES OF BUSINESS GROWTH

Small businesses grow in a number of ways including internal organic growth (e.g. organic and acquisitions) and external growth (e.g.

internationalisation or multiple locations). Entrepreneurs are likely to embark on different forms of growth based on their wider motivations (Delmar et al., 2003). For example, entrepreneurs of acquired businesses are more likely to embark on high growth than owners of independent businesses. In the sections that follow next, modes of growth of small business are discussed.

ORGANIC GROWTH VS ACQUISITIONS

Growth through acquisitions depicts a strategy in which a firm buys another firm or business (Park & Jang, 2010). In her seminal work, Penrose (1959) stressed the existence of different routes to growth, notably organic growth versus growth by acquisitions. She highlighted that organic growth can be limited by three factors: internal factors (e.g. managerial ability), external factors (e.g. product or factor markets) and a combination of internal and external factors (e.g. risk or uncertainty).

Indeed, regarding individual and strategy-related factors, organic growth does not take place automatically, but depends on growth opportunities in the market and specialised resources and managerial abilities in order to plan and allocate the resources efficiently (Penrose, 1959). For example, businesses that want to grow organically may embark on specialised technological training that can enhance the day-to-day operational strength of the companies. The new skills acquired by the employees can provide additional value to the existing operational capacity of the business, which in turn allows the business to grow its market. It has been argued by a number of scholars (e.g. Davidsson et al., 2010) that this experience and knowledge will remain unused if the business fails to grow further.

Indeed, Penrose (1959) espoused several arguments for explaining why firms might decide to acquire existing firms for growth. When entering new markets, the costs as well as managerial and technical difficulties could

be reduced by acquiring another firm. Thus, using acquisition strategy small businesses are likely to overcome market deficiencies and achieve faster growth. Accordingly, Penrose (1959, p. 129) highlighted, 'thus the existing resources of a firm will not limit the extent to which successful expansion can be effected through acquisition, but will also influence the direction of external expansion'.

Research evidence suggests that motives behind acquisitions include market access; expansion; diversification; sustainable competitive advantage; response to revolutionary change in the industry; and/or acquisition of knowledge of other businesses, firms and industries (Deiser, 1994; Kruger & Muller-Stewens, 1994; Lockett et al., 2011; UNCTAD, 2000; von Krogh, Sinatra & Singh, 1994). Acquisitions can be defensive strategy aimed at protecting market share in a declining or consolidating industry. The rationale behind acquiring another business may be to help the acquirer attain its strategic goals more quickly and inexpensively than if the company acted on its own. Such moves may help the small business to overcome barriers associated with competition and market deficiencies.

Research on the effects of acquisitions on business growth has produced mixed results. While several scholars have reported a negative relationship between acquisitions and business growth (e.g. Cosh, Hughes & Lee, 1989; Mueller, 1985; Odagiri & Hase, 1989), other scholars have reported a strong positive relationship between the two concepts (Taketoshi, 1984). However, acquisitions are advantageous because their results are likely to be seen more quickly than internal growth (Park & Jang, 2010).

According to Penrose (1959), growth through acquisitions enables the business to acquire tangible and intangible assets. This may help alleviate managerial constraints, leading to the growth of the business. Further, Marks and Mirvis (2001) argued that the outcomes of acquisitions allow businesses to gain flexibility, leverage competencies, share resources, and create opportunities that otherwise would be impossible.

GROWTH THROUGH NETWORKS AND ALLIANCES

Research on networks has a long-standing history in the management and organisational theory literature (Lechner, Dowling & Welpe, 2006), as well as discussion of entrepreneurs' personal networks (e.g. Birley, 1985) and firm networks (e.g. Butler & Hansen, 1991). Network theory offers important understanding into how businesses relate to each other and grow. Indeed, several researchers have developed typologies of networks (e.g. Aldrich & Zimmer, 1986; Johannisson, 1987; Knoke & Kuklinski, 1983; Lechner et al., 2006; Melin, 1987; Uzzi, 1997). Further, a number of empirical studies have indicated that networks lead to business growth (Donckels & Lambrecht, 1995; Hansen, 1995), for example, research in the field of economic sociology (Grabher & Stark, 1997).

According to Yli-Renko, Autio and Sapienza (2001), through external linkages entrepreneurs acquire knowledge, especially in the knowledge-intensive industries. It has also been argued that alliances provide the platform for a collective learning process in which ideas related to business development are exchanged and further developed as well as given the opportunity for knowledge-sharing among individual businesses (Hardy, Philips & Lawrence, 2003; Kale, Singh & Perlmutter, 2000).

Moreover, research evidence indicates that small business managers continuously learn from other small business counterparts instead of the formal classroom learning process (Kitching, 2008). Indeed, a number of scholars have explicitly converged on the above notion, suggesting that licensing, alliances and joint ventures are important for high-growth firms (e.g. Blundel, 2002; Killing, 1978; Roberts & Berry, 1985; Street & Cameron, 2007; Watson, 2007). Thus, the evidence points to the role of networks and alliances in enhancing business growth.

GROWTH THROUGH INTERNATIONALISATION

Growth through internationalisation is perhaps the most complex strategy that any business can opt for in the quest to grow. However, internationalisation strategy may be adopted by entrepreneurs to counter the local market inefficiencies and barriers in the local business environment. The expansion of small businesses is viewed as an entrepreneurial act because it involves the setting-up of product markets (Ibeh, 2003; Thorelli, 1987). A large body of literature exists on the internationalisation process of small businesses (Andersen, 1993; Leonidou & Katsikeas, 1996). According to Westhead, Wright and Ucbasaran (2001), the way to understand internationalisation was as a consequence of the resources that the firm held.

Much of the early empirical evidence on internationalisation behaviours has concluded that the route to internationalisation involves a series of incremental 'stages' with exporting as an initial route to internationalisation. In this regard, internationalisation can be seen as a part of a firm's growth and development strategy as it is involved in cross-border and market-related activities (Jones, 1999). This resonates with Penrose's (1959, p. 1) fundamental meaning of growth as: 'an increase in size or an improvement in quality as a result of a process'.

Indeed, growth through internationalisation which centres on exporting, foreign direct investment (FDI) and alliances has been recognised as a strategy for enhancing performance of high-growth firms (Lu & Beamish, 2001). Small businesses that enter new geographical markets may have the opportunity to expand their customer base. Further, internationalisation may lead to increase in revenue that can provide the possibility of an increased production volume and increased production capabilities of the firm to fulfil the demands of its customers (Lu & Beamish, 2001). Engaging in exporting allows businesses to commit greater resources to foreign markets and focus on countries that are 'physically' distant (Bell, Crick & Young, 2004).

In his seminal work, Ansoff (1965) developed a product–market matrix that identifies new market development, and also referred to as internationalisation as a forward-looking strategy for fast small business growth. Accordingly, small business may regard the international market as secondary to the domestic market activities. Thus, domestic markets and international markets are often viewed as divergent strategic options rather than complementary strategies for growth (Bell et al., 2004). Resource constraints may also stop small firms from entering the international market (Carson, Cromie, McGowan & Hill, 1995).

Though internationalisation may be the riskiest business growth strategy, entrepreneurs may use it as a reaction to market constraints in the domestic market. Small businesses may adopt internationalisation as a strategy to minimise risk in the business environment. Thus, for small businesses to minimise variations in sales and profits, firms enter international markets to take advantage of business cycle differences among countries. Some scholars have argued that small firms export because they have a unique product and a technological edge over competitors (e.g. Pope, 2002). Small businesses might also use the internationalisation strategy as a defensive strategy to fight rivals in the international market rather than in the home market.

Interestingly, research on internationalisation as a route to growth acknowledges that the process of growth is not always unidirectional (Davidsson et al., 2010). Rather, scholarly studies direct our attention to how businesses reduce their international activities or withdraw from international operations (Benito & Welch, 1997). Indeed, research on international growth of new and small businesses has so far not yielded many strong generalisations (Davidsson, Achtenhagen & Naldi, 2005). Thus, internationalisation as a route to growth provides a fresh area for future scholarly work.

DETERMINANTS OF BUSINESS GROWTH

The issue of whether business growth is determined internally, externally or both remains to a large extent an unanswered question in the literature. The extant literature that classifies external and internal factors that influence small business growth has categorised them in different ways. For example, some previous studies have differentiated between the individual and environmental variables that influence small business growth (Bygrave, 1994; Ronstadt, 1984). Storey (1994) categorised variables that affect small business growth under three broad headings, namely: the entrepreneur, the characteristics of the firm and the strategy of the firm. Storey (1994) indicated that these categorisations are based on starting resources of the entrepreneur, characteristics of the business and the strategy developed by the business. Table 12.2 below depicts Storey's (1994) classification of factors that affect business growth.

Storey (1994) identified key variables to each component and advanced the importance of combining all the components appropriately for rapid growth to take place. Each component provides a unique offering; the entrepreneur can be recognised prior to start-up, the business manifests decisions made at start-up, while strategy reflects its growth rate. However, exact prediction is more important to the entrepreneur than historical accounts. Storey's (1994) mechanistic approach contributes little to providing the chemistry that puts together these perspectives for growth to occur. The issue here is to determine whether internal influences such as owner–managers' growth aspirations matter or whether external variables matter in determining small business growth. Moreover, Storey's (1994) variables are all individually and empirically derived variables that have consistent impact on growth but there is no suggestion of which combination of factors is important.

Table 12.2   Storey's (1994) variables influencing small business growth

Entrepreneur	Firm	Strategy
Motivation	Age	Workforce training
Unemployment	Sector	Management training
Education	Legal form	External training
Management experience	Location	External equity
Number of founders	Size	Technology
Prior self-employment	Ownership	Market positioning
Family history		Market adjustments
Social marginality		Planning
Functional skills		State support
Training		New products
Age		Management recruitment
Prior business failure		Customer concentration
Prior sector experience		Competition
Prior firm size experience		Information and advice
Gender		Exporting

Source: Storey (1994)

Similarly, several studies have reported high growth in businesses with a variety of size and age characteristics (Rutherford, McMullen & Oswald, 2001; Smallbone & North, 1995). Thus, the evidence provides solid grounds to argue that younger businesses are not likely to grow more than older businesses. For this reason, older businesses' potential to grow should not be ignored.

Indeed, a complex array of external variables that influence small business growth as suggested by the population ecology perspective (Hannan & Freeman, 1977) could be located around the structure of industries and markets. Previous research indicates that there is a rapid growth of businesses in dynamic industries and regions (Carroll & Hannan, 2000; Davidsson & Delmer, 1997). Thus, there is convincing evidence to suggest that business growth is externally determined to some extent. Conversely, there is compelling evidence to argue that owner–managers' growth aspirations or willingness to grow, their growth motivation and communicated vision influence business growth (Baum, Locke & Smith, 2001; Kolvereid & Bullvåg, 1996).

A review of the literature suggests that growth is to some extent an issue of willingness and skill, but basic enablers and constraints in the environment cannot be ignored. Thus, prevailing scholarly studies have concluded that business growth is influenced by many factors including the management strategies, characteristics of the entrepreneur, environment-/industry-specific factors and characteristics of the business (Dobbs & Hamilton, 2007). However, this classification is not new as many of the elements in the classification have been professed in previous studies (Barkham et al., 1996; Baum et al., 2001; Delmar et al., 2003; Edelman, Brush & Manolova, 2005; Smallbone & North, 1995; Smallbone & Wyer, 2006; Storey, 1994; Street & Cameron, 2007; Wiklund & Shepherd, 2003). However, a major conclusion that can be derived from prevailing scholarly reviews is that business growth is influenced by a mirage of internal and external factors.

A wide array of internal factors that affect business growth has been cited in the entrepreneurship literature. For example, internal factors include factors related to firm strategy (Bamford, Dean & McDougall, 1997; Freel & Robson, 2004; McMahon, 1998; Olson &

Bokor, 1995; Wiklund & Shepherd, 2005), factors related to the characteristics of the entrepreneur (e.g. Barringer & Jones, 2004; Davidsson, 1989a; Smallbone & Wyer, 2000; Storey, 1994) and characteristics of the business. The characteristics of the business relate to key decisions made on starting the business which are deemed to impact on the growth of the business. Extant literature shows that firm age and size, legal status, sector affiliation and firm location all relate to growth (Storey, 1994). Significantly, the discussion of age and size as drivers of business growth has long been examined in the literature following the formulation of 'Gibrat's Law' (Gibrat, 1931). According to Gibrat's law, the rate of growth of a firm is independent of its size at the beginning of the period and the probability of a given growth rate during a specific time interval is the same for any business within the same industry. However, the influences of age on business growth are mixed (Davidsson, et al., 2010).

With regards to external factors that drive business growth, the population ecology perspective (Hannan & Freeman, 1977) suggests that external environmental forces affect a firm's growth. Indeed, several other studies indicate that the external business environment influences the success of businesses (Dess & Beard, 1984; Hawawini, Subramanian & Verdin, 2003; Kangasharju, 2000).

CONSTRAINTS TO GROWTH

In the small business literature, constraints are frequently part of studies on characteristics of business growth. Additionally, constraints have been used to distinguish between firms which are likely to grow or not (Aidis, 2005; Robson & Obeng, 2008). The concept of barriers tends to be a growth deterrent (Davidsson 2004). Accordingly, research has documented the existence of such constraints in the entrepreneurship and small business literature where scholars have differentiated between

'internal' (e.g. lack of managerial/technical know-how, vision, capacity, finance) and 'external' constraints (e.g. adverse market conditions, economic/institutional arrangements) (Allinson, Braidford, Houston & Stone, 2013; Robson & Obeng 2008). However, the idea of 'internal' constraints seems to concern the knowledge and ability of the small business managers, which seems closer to concepts of the knowledgeable agent (Giddens, 1984), whereas external constraints go beyond individuals (Mole & Mole, 2010).

FINANCE BARRIERS

Finance barriers constitute one of the main barriers that hinder business growth. The entrepreneurship literature suggests that there is a general consensus that access to finance is a major problem for entrepreneurship (Keyser, de Kruif & Frese, 2000; Moy & Luk, 2003; Robson & Obeng, 2008; Schiffer & Weder, 2001; Tagoe, Nyarko & Anuwa-Amarh, 2005). The main issue for most entrepreneurs is whether to go for equity financing and dilute ownership or rely on debt financing or internal financing. This has spurred two streams of research on financial barriers. These are (i) external barriers, which are mostly related to the supply of finance and (ii) internal barriers, which are related to demand for finance. The barriers connected to the supply of finance include difficulty in accessing capital and high cost of capital. The difficulty in accessing capital has been attributed to factors such as attitudes of lenders or to the information gap between suppliers of money and small business owners (Binks & Ennew, 1996). On the demand side of the argument, most entrepreneurs believe that accessing finance from an external source dilutes ownership. The unwillingness of owner–managers of small businesses to relinquish power to external parties serves as a constraint to small business growth (Storey, 1994; Burns, 2001).

MANAGERIAL AND TECHNICAL KNOW-HOW

Managerial and technical know-how are considered valuable assets to small businesses because it is not possible to take away knowledge from individuals as tangible and financial assets can be taken (Barney, 1991; Becker, 1975; Chandler and Jansen, 1992; Cooper, Gimeno-Gascon and Woo, 1994). Lack of skilled managers and absence of business skills in marketing and business development contribute to the problems of small business growth (Bartlett & Bukvič, 2001; Robson & Obeng, 2008). Small businesses may find it difficult to attract skilled employees, train and retain them. Because small businesses are unable to attract skilled labour due to high wages and other factors, the focus on training becomes relevant in small businesses. The evidence on the relationship between training and performance is conflicting. While some studies have failed to make a link between training and improved performance (Storey & Westhead, 1997), other studies (Cosh et al., 1989; Mano, Iddrisu, Yoshino & Sonobe, 2012) support the view that training could lead to improved performance. Yet small businesses' investment in training has not been encouraging. The reason may be that entrepreneurs fear losing trained employees to larger organisations that offer high remuneration and better conditions of service. It can also be attributed to the fact that smaller businesses do not have strong financial muscle to invest in training (Carter & Jones-Evans, 2006). This suggests that financial backing in the form of funding is needed in small businesses to allow them to undertake training for their staff.

REGULATORY AND ECONOMIC CONSTRAINTS

Previous empirical studies on institutions and regulatory barriers tend to examine the kinds of institutions that hamper business growth (Bartlett & Bukvič, 2001; Baumol, 1990; Krasniqi, 2007; Roxas, Lindsay, Ashill & Victorio, 2007). Some governments' institutions and regulatory policies have equally been identified as a source of constraint to small business growth. Certain institutions pose a burden on small business and may discourage entrepreneurial activities (Carter & Jones-Evans, 2006; Davidsson & Henderson, 2002; Smallbone & Welter, 2001). Legislation which demands the preparation and delivery of documents where expert assistance will be needed creates compliance costs which will probably pose a greater burden for SMEs, since they do not usually have such resources on their payroll (Smallbone & Welter, 2001b).

The focus on regulatory and institutional barriers has been that they influence decisions and actions of businesses (Aldrich & Fiol, 1994). However, the literature is silent on how regulations and institutions affect small business decisions and actions (Peng & Heath, 1996). While there appears to be an agreement on what constitutes a negative environment, little is known about what constitutes a positive environment.

MARKET CONSTRAINTS

The market environment in which the business operates is associated with certain barriers that hamper its growth. These constraints include those that reflect the market structures and competitors' behaviour (ACOST, 1990) and other factors such as cost of advertising and market research obstacles (Robson & Obeng, 2008). Factors such as low demand for products/services, exporting difficulties and a highly competitive environment can hinder the growth of small businesses. Market constraints can be approached in two ways: external barriers and internal barriers. External barriers vary depending upon the extent of market competition and the sector in which the business operates (Bartlett &

Bukvič, 2001). Several studies have revealed that competition or market challenges adversely affect small business growth (e.g. Gill & Biger, 2012; Hay & Kamshad, 1994; Kazanjian, 1988; Moy & Luk, 2003).

Internal market barriers, on the other hand, involve identification of market opportunities (Davidsson, 2004), choosing a market segment (McGee, 1989) and the business's weakness in extending resources and opportunities to the market segment (ACOST, 1990). Business opportunity is created when the firm's market, services and product are expanded. In a recent study, Robson and Obeng (2008) reported that smaller businesses are likely to encounter less demand than larger businesses.

CONCLUSION

This review has examined the phenomenon of business growth, including a definition of small business growth, ways of measuring growth, theories of business growth, and drivers of and constraints to growth. The review suggests that models of business growth have been portrayed in a fragmented and inconsistent manner (Weinzimmer et al., 1998) and that growth is now regarded as an episode rather than a classification of a firm. We note that there is lack of consensus regarding which model is appropriate in addressing business growth. Furthermore, existing studies have explicitly failed to define growth models and no effort has been made to distinguish between life-cycle, growth stages or development stages (Hanks et al., 1993). Moreover, our review suggests that stage models of growth only depict symptoms of growth and do not reflect the underlying causes of growth.

We note that business growth measurement has been mixed and inconsistent. However, the two most common ways of measuring business growth are sales and employment. It is important to acknowledge that, notwithstanding this notion of growth conceptualisation, other scholars equate growth with 'mere' increase in volume (e.g. Barringer et al., 2005; Delmar & Wiklund, 2008; Delmar et al., 2003; Shepherd & Wiklund, 2009). We note that several studies use multiple measures to examine business growth. The evidence suggests that, notwithstanding the several advantages associated with the use of multiple indicators, such as sales and employment, a major shortcoming of the use of multiple indicators is that the assumption of common cause may be incorrect (Delmar et al., 2003). Further, some scholars are of the view that different growth measures and calculations of business growth influence model-building and theory development differently and advocate for the use of a single measure of business growth (Chandler & Hanks, 1993; Delmar, 1997; Weinzimmer et al., 1998).

Regarding modes of growth, robust evidence suggests organic versus. acquisition growth, growth through networks and alliances, and growth through internationalisation. The literature suggests that business owners embark on different forms of growth based on their wider motivations (Delmar et al., 2003). We know little about which mode of growth is much more efficacious in driving business growth. To date, studies have generally ignored the mode of growth which best spurs business growth. As a result, our understanding regarding which mode achieves business growth best is constrained and possibly takes an overly simplistic view of this phenomenon.

With specific regards to factors that drive business growth, the extant literature has classified external and internal factors. Yet the issue of whether business growth is determined internally, externally or both remains to a large extent an unanswered question in the literature. Therefore, future studies may examine the extent to which business growth is determined internally, externally or both. It should, however, be acknowledged that it is sometimes difficult to determine what factors are truly 'external' and 'internal' (e.g. Davidsson, 1989a, 1991).

Lastly, the literature suggests that some factors influence business as growth deterrents (Davidsson, 1989b), which have a negative influence on business growth (Barber, Metcalfe & Porteous, 1989). Accordingly, constraints have been used to distinguish between firms which are likely to grow or not (Aidis, 2005, Robson & Obeng, 2008). However, research on constraints to business growth limits our understanding on how entrepreneurs deal with or react to constraints to growth by 'writing individuals out of the story' (Jennings, Perren & Carter, 2005, p. 147). Such treatment of constraints gives an incomplete picture of the role of entrepreneurs in dealing with constraints. We suggest that there exists a significant opportunity for understanding how entrepreneurs react to business constraints. Such an understanding holds potential for policy and practical interventions to mitigate constraints in the business growth process. Therefore, future research should focus on how entrepreneurs react to constraints to growth.

REFERENCES

Achtenhagen, L., Naldi, L. & Melin, L. (2010). 'Business growth' – do practitioners and scholars really talk about the same thing? *Entrepreneurship Theory and Practice*, 34(2): 289–316.

ACOST. (1990). The enterprise challenge: Overcoming barriers to growth in small firms. *The Advisory Council on Science and Technology, UK*. London: HMSO.

Adizes, I. (1989). *Corporate Lifecycles: How and Why Corporations Grow and Die and What To Do About It*. Englewood Cliffs, NJ: Prentice-Hall.

Aidis, R. (2005). Institutional barriers to small- and medium-sized enterprise operations in transition countries. *Small Business Economics*, 25(4): 305–317.

Aldrich, H. E. & Fiol, M. C. (1994). Fools rush in? The institutional context of industry creation. *Academy of Management Review*, 19(4): 645–670.

Aldrich, H. W. & Zimmer, C. (1986). Entrepreneurship through social networks. In D. Sexton & R. Smilor (Eds), *The Art and Science of Entrepreneurship*. Cambridge, MA: Ballinger, 3–23.

Allinson, G., Braidford, P., Houston, M. & Stone, I. (2013). Understanding growth in microbusinesses. London: BIS Research paper Number 114.

Andersen, O. (1993). On the internationalization process of firms: a critical analysis. *Journal of International Business Studies*, 24(2): 209–231.

Anderson, B. S. & Eshima, Y. (2013). The influence of firm age and intangible resources on the relationship between entrepreneurial orientation and firm growth among Japanese SMEs. *Journal of Business Venturing*, 28(3): 413–429.

Ansoff, H. I. (1965). *Corporate Strategy*. New York: McGraw-Hill.

Ardichvili, A., Cardozo, S., Harmon, S. & Vadakath, S. (1998). *Towards a theory of new venture growth*. Paper presented at the 1998 Babson Entrepreneurship Research Conference, Ghent, Belgium.

Arregle, J. L., Batjargal, B., Hitt, M. A., Webb, J. W., Miller, T. & Tsui, A. S. (2013). Family ties in entrepreneurs' social networks and new venture growth. *Entrepreneurship Theory and Practice*, 39(2): 313–344. doi: 10.1111/etap.12044

Arregle, J. L., Batjargal, B., Hitt, M. A., Webb, J. W., Miller, T. & Tsui, A. S. (2015). Family ties in entrepreneurs' social networks and new venture growth. *Entrepreneurship Theory and Practice*, 39(2), 313–344.

Bamford, C. E., Dean, T. J. & McDougall, P. P. (1997). Initial strategies and new venture growth: an examination of the effectiveness of broad vs. narrow breadth strategies. In P. D. Reynolds, W. D. Bygrave, N. M. Carter, P. Davidsson, W. B. Gartner, C. M. Mason & P. P. McDougall (Eds), *Frontiers of Entrepreneurship Research*. Wellesley, MA: Babson College, 375–389.

Barber, J., Metcalfe, J. S. & Porteous, M. (1989). *Barriers to Growth in Small Firms*. London: Routledge.

Barkham, R., Gudgin, G., Hart, M. & Hanvey, E. (1996). *The determinants of small firm growth: an inter-regional study in the United Kingdom* 1986–1990. London: Jessica Kingsley Publishers.

Barney, J. (1991). Firm resources and sustained competitive advantage. *Journal of Management*, 17(1): 99–120.

Barney, J. (1986). Strategic factor markets: expectations, luck, and business strategy. *Management Science*, 32(10): 1231–1241.

Barney, J.B. (1986). Strategic factor markets: expectations, luck, and business strategy. *Management Science*, 32(10): 1231–1241.

Barringer, B. R. & Jones, F. F. (2004). Achieving rapid growth – revisiting the managerial capacity problem. *Journal of Developmental Entrepreneurship*, 9(1): 73–87.

Barringer, B. R., Jones, F. F. & Neubaum, D. O. (2005). A quantitative content analysis of the characteristics of rapid growth firms and their founders. *Journal of Business Venturing*, 20(5): 663–687.

Bartlett, W. & Bukvić, B. (2001). Barriers to SME growth in Slovenia. *Economic Policy in Transition Economies*, 11(2): 177–195.

Baum, J. R., Locke, E. A. & Smith, K. G. (2001). A multidimensional model of venture growth. *Academy of Management Journal*, 44(2): 292–303.

Baumol, W. (1990). Entrepreneurship: productive, unproductive and destructive. *Journal of Political Economy*, 98(5): 893–921.

Becchetti, L. & Trovato, G. (2002). The determinants of growth for small and medium sized firms. The role of the availability of external finance. *Small Business Economics*, 19(4): 292–306.

Beck, T., Lu., L. & Yang, R. (2015). Finance and growth for microenterprises: evidence from rural China. *World Development*, 67: 38–56.

Becker, G., (1975). *Human Capital*. Chicago, IL: Chicago University Press.

Bell, J., Crick, D. & Young, S. (2004). Small firm internationalisation and business strategy: an exploratory study of 'knowledge-intensive' and 'traditional' manufacturing firms in the UK. *International Small Business Journal*, 22(1): 23–56.

Benito, G. R. G. & Welch, L. S. (1997). De-internationalisation. *Management International Review*, 37(2): 7–25.

Binks, M. R. & Ennew, C. T. (1996). Growing firms and the credit constraint. *Small Business Economics*, 8(1): 17–25.

Birley, S. (1985). The role of networks in the entrepreneurial process. *Journal of Business Venturing*, 3(1): 107–117.

Birley, S. & Westhead, P. (1990). Growth and performance contrasts between 'types' of small business. *Strategic Management Journal*, 11(7): 535–557.

Blundel, R. (2002). Network evolution and the growth of artisanal firms: a tale of two regional cheese makers. *Entrepreneurship & Regional Development*, 14(10): 1–30.

Burns, P. (2001). *Entrepreneurship and Small Business*. Basingstoke: Palgrave.

Butler, J. E. & Hansen, G. S. (1991). Network evolution, entrepreneurial success, and regional development. *Entrepreneurship and Regional Development*, 3(1): 1–16.

Bygrave, W. D. (1994). *The Portable MBA in Entrepreneurship*. Chichester: John Wiley.

Capasso, M., Treibich, T. & Verspagen, B. (2015). The medium-term effect of R&D on firm growth. *Small Business Economics*, 45(1): 39–62.

Carpenter, R. E. & Petersen, B. C. (2002). Capital market imperfections, high-tech investment, and new equity financing. *The Economic Journal*, 112(477): F54–F72.

Carroll, G. R. & Hannan, M. T. (2000). *The Demography of Corporations and Industries*. Princeton, NJ: Princeton University Press.

Carson, D., Cromie, S., McGowan, P. & Hill, J. (1995). *Marketing and Entrepreneurship in SMEs: An Innovative Approach*. London: Prentice Hall.

Carter, S. & Jones-Evans, D. (2006). *Enterprise and Small Business*. Harlow: FT Prentice-Hall.

Chandler, G. N. & Baueus, D. A. (1996). Gauging performance in emerging businesses: longitudinal evidence and growth patterns analysis. In P. D. Reynolds et al. (Eds), *Frontiers of Entrepreneurship Research* (pp. 491–504). Center for Entrepreneurial Studies, Babson College, Babson Park, MA.

Chandler, G. N. & Hanks, S. H. (1993). Measuring the performance of emerging businesses: a validation study. *Journal of Business Venturing*, 8(5): 391–408.

Chandler, G. N. & Jansen, E. (1992). The founder's self-assessed competence and venture performance. *Journal of Business Venturing*, 7(3): 223–236.

Chandler, G. N., McKelvie, A. & Davidsson, P. (2009). Asset specificity and behavioural uncertainty as moderators of the sales growth-employment relationship in emerging ventures. *Journal of Business Venturing*, 24(4): 373–387.

Chrisman, J. J. & Leslie, J. (1989). Strategic, administrative, and operating problems: the impact of outsiders on small firm performance. *Entrepreneurship Theory & Practice*, 13(3): 37–51.

Coad, A. (2007). *Firm growth: A survey*. CES Working Papers 2007.24, University Sorbonne, Paris.

Coad, A., Segarra, A. & Teruel, M. (2016). Innovation and firm growth: does firm age play a role? *Research Policy*, 45(2): 387–400.

Cooper, A. C., Gimeno-Gascon, F. J. & Woo, C. Y. (1994). Initial human and financial capital as predictors of new venture performance. *Journal of Business Venturing*, 9(5): 371–395.

Cosh, A. D., Hughes, A. & Lee, K. (1989). Institutional investment, mergers and the market for corporate control. *International Journal of Industrial Organisation*, 7(1): 73–100.

Davidsson, P. (2004). *Researching Entrepreneurship*. New York: Springer.

Davidsson, P. (1991). Continued entrepreneurship: ability, need, and opportunity as determinants of small firm growth. *Journal of Business Venturing*, 6(6): 405–429.

Davidsson, P. (1989a). *Continued Entrepreneurship and Small Firm Growth*. Stockholm: Stockholm School of Economics.

Davidsson, P. (1989b). Entrepreneurship – and after? A study of growth willingness in small firms. *Journal of Business Venturing*, 4(3): 211–226.

Davidsson, P., Achtenhagen, L. & Naldi, L. (2010). Small firm growth. *Foundations and Trends in Entrepreneurship*, 6(2): 69–166.

Davidsson, P., Achtenhagen, L. & Naldi, L. (2005). *Research on Small Firms: A Review*. Proceedings of the European Institute of Small Growth Business. Available at: http://eprints.qut.edu.au/archive/00002072/0 1/EISB_version_Research_on_small_firm_growth.pdf. Accessed 23/07/2013.

Davidsson, P. & Delmar, F. (1997). High-growth firms and their contribution to employment: the case of Sweden 1987–96. Paris: OECD Working Party on SMEs.

Davidsson, P. & Henrekson, M. (2002). Determinants of the prevalence of start-ups and high-growth firms. *Small Business Economics*, 19(2): 81–100.

Davidsson, P. & Wiklund, J. (2000). Conceptual and empirical challenges in the study of firm growth. In D. Sexton & H. Landström (Eds), *Handbook of Entrepreneurship* (pp. 39–61). Oxford: Blackwell Publishers.

Davidsson, P. & Wiklund, J. (1999). Theoretical and methodological issues in the study of firm growth. Jönköping International Business School, Working Paper Series: 99–6.

Deiser, R. (1994). Post-acquisition management: a process of strategic and organizational learning. In G. von Krogh, A. Sinatra & H. Singh (Eds), *The Management of Corporate Acquisitions: International Perspectives* (pp. 359–390). UK: Palgrave Macmillan.

Delmar, F. (2000). *Measuring Growth: Methodological Considerations and Empirical Results*. Stockholm: Entrepreneurship and Small Business Research Institute (ESBRI).

Delmar, F. (1997). Measuring growth: methodological considerations and empirical results. In R. Donckels & A. Miettinen (Eds), *Entrepreneurship and SME Research: On its Way to the Next Millennium* (pp. 199–216). Aldershot and Brookfield, VA: Ashgate.

Delmar, F. & Wiklund, J. (2008). The effect of small business managers' growth motivation on firm growth: a longitudinal study. *Entrepreneurship Theory and Practice*, 32(3): 437–453.

Delmar, F., Davidsson, P. & Gartner, W. (2003). Arriving at the high-growth Firm. *Journal of Business Venturing*, 18(2): 189–216.

Dess, G. G. & Beard, D. W. (1984). Dimensions of organisational task environment. *Administrative Science Quarterly*, 29(1): 52–73.

Dess, G. G. & Davis, P. S. (1984). Porter's (1980) generic strategies as determinants of strategic group membership and organizational performance. *Academy of Management Journal*, 27(3): 467–488.

Dhanaraj, C. & Beamish, P. W. (2003). A resource-based approach to the study of export performance. *Journal of Small Business Management*, 41(3): 242–261.

Didier, T. & Schmukler, S. L. (2013). The financing and growth of firms in China and India: evidence from capital markets. *Journal of International Money and Finance*, 39: 111–137.

Dobbs, M. & Hamilton, R. T. (2007). Small business growth: recent evidence and new directions. *International Journal of Entrepreneurial Behaviour and Research*, 13(5): 296–322.

Dodge, H. R. & Robbins, J. E. (1992). An empirical investigation of the organisational life-cycle model for small business development and survival. *Journal of Small Business Management*, 30(1): 27–34.

Donaldson, L. (1987). Strategy and structural adjustment to regain fit and performance: in defence of contingency theory. *Journal of Management Studies*, 24(1): 1–24.

Donckels, R. & Lambrecht, J. (1995). Networks and small business growth: an explanatory model. *Small Business Economics*, 7(4): 273–289.

Dunne, P. & Hughes, A. (1994). Age, size, growth and survival: UK companies in the 1980s. *The Journal of Industrial Economics*, 42(2), 115–140.

Dunne, P. & Hughes, A. (1986). Age, size, growth and survival revisited. Working Paper No. 23. University of Cambridge: Small Business Research Centre.

Edelman, L. F., Brush, C. G. & Manolova, T. (2005). Co-alignment in the resource-performance relationship: strategy as mediator. *Journal of Business Venturing*, 20(3): 359–383.

Eisenhardt, K. M. & Schoonhoven, C. B. (1990). Organizational growth: linking founding team, strategy, environment, and growth among US semiconductor ventures, 1978–1988. *Administrative Science Quarterly*, 35(3): 504–529.

Fafchamps, M., McKenzie, D., Quinn, S. & Woodruff, C. (2014). Microenterprise growth and the flypaper effect: evidence from a randomized experiment in Ghana. *Journal of Development Economics*, 106: 211–226.

Federico, J. S. & Capelleras, J. L. (2015). The heterogeneous dynamics between growth and profits: the case of young firms. *Small Business Economics*, 44(2): 231–253.

Flamholtz, E. G. (1986). *Managing the Transition from an Entrepreneurship to a Professionally Managed Firm*. San Francisco, CA: Jossey-Bass.

Freel, M. S. & Robson, P. J. A. (2004). Small firm innovation, growth and performance. *International Small Business Journal*, 22(6): 561–575.

García-Posada, M. & Mora-Sanguinetti, J. S. (2014). Does (average) size matter? Court enforcement, business demography and firm growth. *Small Business Economics*, 44(3): 639–669.

Garnsey, E. (1998). A theory of the early growth of the firm. *Industrial and Corporate Change*, 7(3): 523–556.

Gibb, A. A. & Davis, L. (1990). In pursuit of the frameworks of growth models of the small business. *International Small Business Journal*, 9(1): 15–31.

Gibrat, R. (1931). *Les Inegalites Economiques*. Paris: Librairie du Recueil Sirey.

Giddens, A. (1984). *The Constitution of Society. Outline of the Theory of Structuration*. Cambridge: Polity.

Gill, A. & Biger, N. (2012). Barriers to small business growth in Canada. *Journal of Small Business and Enterprise Development,* 19(4): 656–668.

Gill, J. (1985). *Factors Affecting the Survival and Growth of the Smaller Company*. Aldershot: Gower.

Glancey, K. (1998). Determinants of growth and profitability in small entrepreneurial firms. *International Journal of Entrepreneurial Behaviour and Research*, 4(1): 18–25.

Grabher, G. & Stark, D. (1997). Organizing diversity: evolutionary theory, network analysis, and postsocialist transformations. In G. Grabher & D. Stark (Eds), *Restructuring Networks: Legacies, Linkages, and Localities in Postsocialism* (pp. 23–39). Oxford: Oxford University Press.

Greiner, L. E. (1972). Evolution and revolution as organisations grow. *Harvard Business Review*, 50(4): 37–46.

Hamelin, A. (2013). Influence of family ownership on small business growth. Evidence from French SMEs. *Small Business Economics*, 41(3): 563–579. doi: 10.1007/s11187-012 9452-x

Hamilton, R. T. & Shergill, G. S. (1992). The relationship between strategy-structure fit and financial performance in New Zealand: evidence of generality and validity with enhanced controls. *Journal of Management Studies*, 29(1): 95–113.

Hanks, S. H. (1990a). *An Empirical Examination of the Organization Life Cycle in High Technology Organizations*, Doctor of Philosophy Dissertation, University of Utah, Salt Lake City, Utah.

Hanks, S. H. (1990b). The organization life cycle: integrating content and process. *Journal of Small Business Strategy*, 1(1): 1–13.

Hanks, S. H. & Chandler, G. (1994). Patterns of functional specialization in emerging high tech firms. *Journal of Small Business Management*, 32(2): 23–36.

Hanks, S. H. & Chandler, G. N. (1992). The growth of emerging firms: a theoretical framework and research agenda. Paper to the 7th Annual National Conference of the United States Association for Small Business and Entrepreneurship, Chicago, IL.

Hanks, S. H., Watson, C. J. & Jansen, E. (1991). Toward a configurational taxonomy of the organization life cycle. In G. E. Hills & R. W. LaForge (Eds), *Research at the Marketing/Entrepreneurship Interface* (pp. 24–39). Chicago, IL: University of Illinois Press.

Hanks, S. H., Watson, C. J., Jansen, E. & Chandler, G. N. (1993). Tightening the life-cycle construct: a taxonomic study of growth stage configurations in high-technology organizations. *Entrepreneurship Theory and Practice*, 18(2): 5–29.

Hannan, M. T. & Freeman, J. H. (1977). The population ecology of organizations. *American Journal of Sociology,* 82(5): 929–964.

Hansen, E. L. (1995). Entrepreneurial network and new organization growth. *Entrepreneurship Theory & Practice*, 19(4): 7–19.

Hardy, C., Philips, N. & Lawrence, T. B. (2003). Resources, knowledge and influence: the organizational effects of interorganisational collaboration. *Journal of Management Studies*, 40(2): 321–347.

Hawawini, G., Subramanian, V. & Verdin, P. (2003). Is performance driven by industry- or firm-specific factors? a new look at the evidence. *Strategic Management Journal,* 24(1): 1–16.

Hay, M. & Kamshad, K. (1994). Small firm growth: intentions, implementation and barriers. *Business Strategy Review*, 5(3): 49–68.

Hessels, J. & Parker, S. C. (2013). Constraints, internationalization and growth: a cross-country analysis of European SMEs. *Journal of World Business,* 48(1): 137–148.

Hoy, F., McDougall, P. P. & Dsouza, D. E. (1992). Strategies and environments of high growth firms. In D. L. Sexton & J. D. Kasarda (Eds), *The State of the Art of Entrepreneurship.* Boston: PWS-Kent Publishing.

Ibeh, N. (2003). Toward a contingency framework of export entrepreneurship: conceptualisations and empirical evidence. *Small Business Economics*, 20(1): 49–68.

Jennings, P. L., Perren, L. & Carter, S. (2005). Guest editors' introduction: alternative perspectives on entrepreneurship research. *Entrepreneurship Theory and Practice*, 29(2): 145–152.

Johannisson, B. (1987). Anarchists and organizers: entrepreneurs in a network perspective. *International Studies of Management and Organization*, 17(1): 49–63.

Johnson, P., Conway, C. & Kattuman, P. (1999). Small business growth in the short run. *Small Business Economics*, 12(2): 103–112.

Jones, M. V. (1999). The internalisation of small high-technology firms. *Journal of International Marketing*, 7(4): 15–41.

Jovanovic, B. (1982). Selection and the evolution of industry. *Econometrica*, 50(3): 649–670.

Kale, P., Singh, H. & Perlmutter, H. (2000). Learning and protection of proprietary assets in strategic alliances: building relational capital. *Strategic Management Journal*, 21(3): 217–237.

Kangasharju, A. (2000). Growth of the smallest: determinants of small firm growth during strong economic fluctuations. *International Small Business Journal*, 19(1): 28–43.

Kazanjian, R. K. (1988). Relation of dominant problems to stages of growth in technology-based new ventures. *Academy of Management Journal*, 31(2): 257–279.

Kazanjian, R. K. & Drazin, R. (1990). A stage-contingent model of design and growth for technology based ventures. *Journal of Business Venturing*, 5(3): 137–150.

Kazanjian, R. K. & Drazin, R. (1989). An empirical test of stage of growth progression model. *Management Science*, 35(12): 1489–1503.

Kelley, D. J. & Nakosteen, R. A. (2005). Technology resources, alliances, and sustained growth in new, technology-based firms. *IEEE Transactions on Engineering Management*, 52(3): 292–300.

Keyser, M., de Kruif, M. & Frese, M. (2000). The psychological strategy process and socio-demographic variables as predictors of success for micro- and small-scale business owners in Zambia. In M. Frese (Ed.), *Success and Failure of Micro Business Owners in Africa: A Psychological Approach* (pp. 31–54). Westport, CT: Quorum Books.

Killing, J. P. (1978). Diversification through licensing. *R&D Management*, 8(3): 159–163.

Kimberly, J. R. & Miles, R. H. (1980). Preface. In J. R. Kimberly, R. H. Miles et al. (Eds), *The Organizational Life Cycle: Issues in the Creation, Transformation, and Decline of Organizations* (pp. ix–xiii). San Francisco, CA: Jossey-Bass.

Kitching, J. (2008). Rethinking UK small employers' skills policies and the role of workplace learning. *International Journal of Training and Development*, 12(2): 100–120.

Knoke, D. & Kuklinski, J. H. (1983). *Network Analysis*. Beverly Hills: Sage.

Kolvereid, L. & Bullvåg, E. (1996). Growth intentions and actual growth: the impact of entrepreneurial choice. *Journal of Enterprising Culture*, 4(1): 1–17.

Krasniqi, B. (2007). Barriers to entrepreneurship and SME growth in transition: evidence from Kosova. *Journal of Developmental Entrepreneurship*, 12(1): 71–94.

Kruger, W. & Muller-Stewens, G. (1994). Matching acquisition policy and integration style. In G. von Krogh, A. Sinatra & H. Singh (Eds), *The Management of Corporate Acquisitions: International Perspectives* (pp. 50–87). UK: Palgrave Macmillan UK.

LeBrasseur, R., Zanibbi, L. & Zinger, T. J. (2003). Growth momentum in early stages of small business start-ups. *International Small Business Journal*, 21(3): 315–330.

Lechner, C., Dowling, M. & Welpe, I. (2006). Firm networks and firm development: the role of the relational mix. *Journal of Business Venturing*, 21(4): 514–540.

Leonidou, L. C. & Katsikeas, C. S. (1996). The export development process: an integrative review of empirical models. *Journal of International Business Studies*, 27(3): 517–551.

Littunen, H. & Tohmo, T. (2003). The high growth firm in new metal-based manufacturing and business services in Finland. *Small Business Economics*, 21(2): 187–200.

Locke, S. (2004). ICT adoption and SME growth in New Zealand. *Journal of American Academy of Business,* 4(1/2): 93–102.

Lockett, A., Wiklund, J., Davidsson, P. & Girma, S. (2011). Organic and acquisitive growth: re-examining and extending Penrose's Growth Theory. *Journal of Management Studies*, 48(1): 48–74.

Lu, J. W. & Beamish, P. W. (2001). The internationalization and performance of SMEs. *Strategic Management Journal*, 22(6/7): 565–586.

Macpherson, A. & Holt, R. (2007). Knowledge, learning and SME growth: a systematic review of the evidence. *Research Policy*, 36(2): 172–192.

Mahoney, J. T. & Michael, S. C. (2005). A subjectivist theory of entrepreneurship. In Alvarez, S. A., Agarwal, R. and Sorenson, O. (Eds), *Handbook of Entrepreneurship* (pp. 33–53). Boston, MA: Springer.

Mano, Y., Iddrisu, A., Yoshino, Y. & Sonobe, T. (2012). How can micro and small enterprises in sub-saharan Africa become more productive? The impacts of experimental basic managerial training. *World Development*, 40(3), 458–468.

Marks, M. L. & Mirvis, P. H. (2001). Making mergers and acquisitions work: Strategic and psychological preparation. *The Academy of Management Executive*, 15(2), 80–92.

Marks, M. L. & Mirvis, P. H. (2010). *Joining Forces: Making One Plus One Equal Three in Mergers, Acquisitions, and Alliances* (pp. 34–43). San Francisco, CA: Jossey-Bass Publishers.

Masakure, O., Henson, S. & Cranfield, J. (2009). Performance of micro-enterprises in Ghana: a resource-based view. *Journal of Small Business and Enterprise Development*, 16(3): 466–484.

McGee, J. (1989). Barriers to growth: the effects of market structure. In J. Barber, J. S. Metcalfe & M. Porteous (Eds), *Barriers to Small Business Growth* (pp. 173–195). London: Routledge.

McKelvie, M. & Wiklund, J. (2010). Advancing firm growth research: a focus on growth mode instead of growth rate. *Entrepreneurship Theory and Practice*, 34(2): 261–288.

McMahon, R. G. P. (1998). Stage models of SME growth reconsidered: small enterprise research. *The Journal of SEAANZ*, 6(2): 20–35.

Melin, L. (1987). The field-of-force metaphor: a study in industrial change. *International Studies of Management and Organization*, 17(1): 24–33.

Miller, D. (1987). Strategy making and structure: analysis and implications for performance. *Academy of Management Journal*, 30(1): 7–32.

Miller, D. & Friesen, P. (1983). Strategy-making and environment: the third link. *Strategic Management Journal*, 4(3): 221–235.

Miller, D. & Toulouse, J. M. (1986). Chief executive personality and corporate strategy and structure in small firms. *Management Science*, 32(11): 1398–1409.

Mole, K. F. & Mole, M. (2010). Entrepreneurship as the structuration of individual and opportunity: a response using a critical realist perspective. Comment on Sarason, Dean and Dillard. *Journal of Business Venturing*, 25(2): 230–237.

Morrison, A. J. & Roth, K. (1992). A taxonomy of business-level strategies in global industries. *Strategic Management Journal*, 13(6): 399–418.

Moy, J. W. & Luk, V. W. M. (2003). The life-cycle model as a framework for understanding barriers to SME growth in Hong Kong. *Asia Pacific Business Review,* 10(2): 199–220.

Mueller, D. C. (1985). Mergers and market share. *The Review of Economics and Statistics*, 67(2): 259–267.

Naldi, L. & Davidsson, P. (2014). Entrepreneurial growth: the role of international knowledge acquisition as moderated by firm age. *Journal of Business Venturing*, 29(5): 687–703.

Nkomo, S. M. (1987). Human resource planning and organizational performance: an exploratory analysis. *Strategic Management Journal*, 8(4): 387–392.

North, D. & Smallbone, D. (2000). The innovativeness and growth of rural SMEs during the 1990s. *Regional Studies*, 34(2): 145–157.

Obeng, B. A., Robson, P. & Haugh, H. (2014). Strategic entrepreneurship and small firm growth in Ghana. *International Small Business Journal*, 32(5): 501–524.

O'Cass, A. & Sok, P. (2014). The role of intellectual resources, product innovation capability, reputational resources and marketing capability combinations in firm growth. *International Small Business Journal*, 32(8): 996–1018. doi: 10.1177/0266242613480225

Odagiri, H. & Hase, T. (1989). Are mergers and acquisitions going to be popular in Japan too? An empirical study. *International Journal of Industrial Organisation*, 7(1): 49–72.

O'Farrell, P. & Hitchens, D. (1988). Alternative theories of small firm growth: a critical review. *Environmental Planning*, 20(10): 1365–1383.

O'Gorman, C. (2001). The sustainability of growth in small and medium sized enterprises. *International Journal of Entrepreneurship Behaviour & Research*, 7(2): 60–71.

Olson, P. D. (1987). Entrepreneurship and management. *Journal of Small Business Management*, 25(3): 7–13.

Olson, P. D. & Bokor, D. W. (1995). Strategy process-content interaction: effects on growth performance in small start-up firms. *Journal of Small Business Management*, 33(1): 34–44.

Orser, B. J., Hogarth-Scott, S. & Riding, A. L. (2000). Performance, firm size, and management problem solving. *Journal of Small Business Management*, 38(4): 42–58.

Park, K. & Jang, S. (2010). Mergers and acquisitions and firm growth: investigating restaurant firms. *Journal of Hospitality Management*, 23(7): 141–149.

Pena, I. (2002). Intellectual capital and business start-up success. *Journal of Intellectual Capital*, 3(2): 180–198.

Peng, M. W. & Heath, P. (1996). The growth of the firm in planned economies in transition: institutions, organizations, and strategic choice. *Academy of Management Review*, 21(2): 492–528.

Penrose, E. T. (1995). *The Theory of the Growth of the Firm*, 3rd ed. Oxford: Oxford University Press.

Penrose, E. T. (1959). *The Theory of the Growth of the Firm*. Oxford: Oxford University Press.

Penrose, E. T. (1952). Biological analogies in the theory of the firm. *American Economic Review*, 42(5): 804–819.

Peters, M. P. & Brush, C. G. (1996). Market information scanning activities and growth in new ventures: a comparison of service and manufacturing businesses. *Journal of Business Research*, 36(1): 81–89.

Pitelis, C. (2009). Edith Penrose's 'The theory of the growth of the firm' fifty years later. MPRA Paper No. 23180. Available at: http://mpra.ub.unimuenchen.de/23180/. Accessed 20/06/2015.

Pitelis, C. (2007). Edith Penrose and a learning-based perspective on the MNE and OLI1. *Management International Review*, 47(2): 207–235.

Pope, R. A. (2002). Why small firms export: another look. *Journal of Small Business Management*, 40(1): 17–26.

Rahaman, M. M. (2011). Access to financing and firm growth. *Journal of Banking and Finance*, 35(3): 709–723.

Reichstein, T. & Dahl, M. S. (2004). Are firm growth rates random? Patterns and dependencies. *International Review of Applied Economics*, 18(2): 225–246.

Roberts, E. B. & Berry, C. A. (1985). Entering new businesses: selecting strategies for success. *Sloan Management Review*, 26(Spring), 3–17.

Robson, P. J. A. & Obeng, B. A. (2008). The barriers to growth in Ghana. *Small Business Economics*, 30(4): 385–403.

Ronstadt, R. (1984). *Entrepreneurship*. Dover, Lord Publishing.

Roxas, H., Lindsay, V., Ashill, N. & Victorio, A. (2007). An institutional view of local entrepreneurial climate. *Journal of Asia Entrepreneurship and Sustainability*, 3(1): 1–28.

Rutherford, M. W., McMullen, P. & Oswald, S. (2001). Examining the issue of size and the small business: a self-organising map approach. *The Journal of Business and Economic Studies*, 7(2): 64–81.

Sandberg, W. R. & Hofer, C. W. (1987). Improving new venture performance: the role of strategy, industry structure, and the entrepreneur. *Journal of Business Venturing*, 2(1): 5–28.

Schiffer, M. & Weder, B. (2001). Firm size and the business environment: worldwide survey results. IFC discussion paper number 43.

Schoonjans, B., Cauwenberge, P. V. & Bauwhede, H. V. (2013). Formal business networking and SME growth. *Small Business Economics*, 41(1): 169–181. doi: 10.1007/s11187-011-9408-6

Scott, M. & Bruce, R. (1987). Five stages of growth in small business. *Long Range Planning*, 20(3): 45–52.

Shepherd, D. & Wiklund, J. (2009). Are we comparing apples with apples or apples with oranges? Appropriateness of knowledge accumulation across growth studies. *Entrepreneurial Theory and Practice*, 33(1): 105–123.

Sleuwaegen, L. & Goedhuys, M. (2002). Growth of firms in developing countries, evidence from Cote d'Ivoire. *Journal of Development Economics*, 68(1): 117–135.

Smallbone, D. & North, D. (1995). Targeting established SMEs: does their age matter? *International Small Business Journal*, 13(3): 4–22.

Smallbone, D. & Welter, F. (2001). The role of government in SME development in transition countries. *International Small Business Journal*, 19(4): 63–77.

Smallbone, D. & Wyer, P. (2000). Growth and development in the small firm. In S. Carter & D. James-Evans (Eds), *Enterprise and Small Business* (pp. 100–126). Harlow: Prentice Hall.

Stam, E. (2010). Growth beyond Gibrat: firm growth processes and strategies. *Small Business Economics*, 35(2): 129–135.

Steinmetz, L. L. (1969). Critical stages of small business growth: when they occur and how to survive them. *Business Horizons*, 12(10): 29–36.

Storey, D. & Westhead, P. (1997). Management training in small firms – a case of market failure? *Human Resource Management Journal*, 7(2): 61–71.

Storey, D. J. (1994). *Understanding the Small Business Sector*. London: Routledge.

Street, C. T & Cameron, A. F. (2007). External relationships and the small business: a review of small business alliance and network research. *Journal of Small Business Management*, 45(2): 239–266.

Tagoe, N., Nyarko, E. & Anuwa-Amarh, E. (2005). Financial challenges facing urban SMEs under financial sector liberalization in Ghana. *Journal of Small Business Management*, 43(3): 331–343.

Taketoshi, R. (1984). *A Study on the Mergers in Japanese Manufacturing Industry*. University of Tsukuba, Japan.

Thorelli, H. B. (1987). Entrepreneurship in international marketing: some research opportunities. In G. E. Hills (Ed.), *Research at the Marketing/Entrepreneurship Interface*. Marrietta, GA: USASBE.

UNCTAD, World Investment Report. (2000). *United Nations Conference on Trade and Development,* United Nations, New York.

Uzzi, B. (1997). Social structure and competition in interfirm networks: the paradox of embeddedness. *Administrative Science Quarterly*, 42(1): 35–67.

Vaessen, P. & Keeble, D. (1995). Growth-oriented SMEs in unfavourable regional environments. *Regional Studies*, 29(6): 489–505.

von Krogh, G., Sinatra, A. & Singh, H. (Eds). (1994). *The Management of Corporate Acquisitions: International Perspectives.* London: The Macmillan Press.

Walsh, J. P. (1988). Selectivity and selective perception: an investigation of managers' belief structures and information processing. *Academy of Management Journal*, 31(4): 873–896.

Watson, J. (2007). Modelling the relationship between networking and firm performance. *Journal of Business Venturing*, 22(6): 852–874.

Weinzimmer, L. G., Nystrom, P. C. & Freeman, S. J. (1998). Measuring organizational growth: issues, consequences and guidelines. *Journal of Management*, 24(2): 235–262.

Wernerfelt, B. (1984). A resource-based view of the firm. *Strategic Management Journal*, 5(2): 171–180.

Westhead, P., Cowling, M. & Howorth, C. (2001). The development of family companies: management and ownership issues. *Family Business Review*, 14(4): 369–385.

Westhead, P., Wright, M. & Ucbasaran, D. (2001). The internationalization of new and small firms: A resource-based view. *Journal of Business Venturing*, 16(4): 333–358.

Whetten, D. A. (1987). Organisational growth and decline processes. *Annual Review of Sociology*, 13(1): 335–358.

Wiklund, J. (1998). Small firm growth and performance. Entrepreneurship and beyond. Dissertation, Jonkoping International Business School, Jonkoping, Sweden.

Wiklund, J. & Shepherd, D. (2005). Entrepreneurial orientation and small business performance: a configurational approach. *Journal of Business Venturing*, 20(1): 71–91.

Wiklund, J. & Shepherd, D. (2003). Aspiring for and achieving growth: the moderating role of resources and opportunities. *Journal of Management Studies*, 40(8): 1919–1941.

Wiklund, J., Patzelt, H. & Shepherd, D. A. (2009). Building an integrative model of small business growth. *Small Business Economics*, 32(4): 351–374.

Yasuda, T. (2005). Firm growth, size, age and behaviour in Japanese manufacturing. *Small Business Economics*, 24(1): 1–15.

Yli-Renko, H., Autio, E. & Sapienza, H. J. (2001). Social capital, knowledge acquisition, and knowledge exploitation in young technology-based firms. *Strategic Management Journal*, 22(6–7): 587–613.

Zahra, S. A. (1993). Environment, corporate entrepreneurship, and financial performance: a taxonomic approach. *Journal of Business Venturing*, 8(4): 319–340.

13

The Nature of Entrepreneurial Exit

Michael H. Morris, Susana C. Santos,
Christopher Pryor and Xaver Neumeyer

INTRODUCTION

All entrepreneurs eventually exit their ventures. Exit refers to the process by which founders of privately held firms depart the organization they created (Wennberg & DeTienne, 2014). Regardless of the form it takes, or the extent to which it is planned, exit has long been viewed as a relevant stage in the entrepreneurial process (DeTienne, McKelvie, & Chandler, 2015; Stevenson, Roberts, & Grousbeck, 1989).

Exit research has tended to focus on types, predictors, and consequences of exit (e.g. Gimeno, Folta, Cooper, & Woo, 1997; Ucbasaran, Wright, & Westhead, 2003). An array of personal and organizational factors influence when and how the entrepreneur exits (Delmar, Hellerstedt, & Wennberg, 2006; Taylor, 1999). It can occur at all stages of a venture's life, though probabilities of exit vary across stages. Further, the implications of a given exit strategy vary depending on timing and circumstances inside

and outside the venture (DeTienne, 2010). Moreover, exit produces a wide range of psychological, emotional, operational, and financial outcomes at individual, organizational, and societal levels (Wennberg, Wiklund, DeTienne, & Cardon, 2010).

In this chapter, we review the extant work on entrepreneurial exit. The definition and conceptualization of exit and associated constructs are examined. Major theories helpful in framing research on entrepreneurial exit are investigated. Key findings regarding antecedents, processes, and outcomes surrounding an exit are explored. Significant challenges in advancing our understanding of exit are identified, and priorities are established in terms of ongoing research.

CONCEPTUALIZING EXIT STRATEGY

Entrepreneurial exit is the process by which the founders of privately held firms leave the firm they helped to create, thereby removing them-selves, in varying degrees, from the ownership and decision-making structure (DeTienne, 2010). Yet some confusion exists, as three types of exit are possible: the exit of the entre-preneur from the venture, the exit (and payoff) of investors from the firm, and the exit of the venture from the marketplace. In this chapter, we focus on the entrepreneur's exit from the venture.

Exit strategy refers to a particular mode of exit from the firm. Several modes are empha-sized in the extant literature, including sale to a third party or another business, merger, man-agement or employee buy-out, family (or third party) succession, initial public offering, liq-uidation, and discontinuance (DeTienne et al., 2015; Hsu et al., 2016; Wennberg & DeTienne, 2014). Some also distinguish a distress sale and distress liquidation (Amaral, Baptista, &

Lima, 2007). Box 13.1 below provides a sum-mary of these various exit modes.

Attempts at classification suggest these strategies fall into three categories (DeTienne & Chirico, 2013; Ryan & Power, 2012): financial-based exit strategies such as IPO or trade sale, which represent the highest potential financial return to an entrepreneur; stewardship-based strategies, such as family or employee succession, which are pro-social and pro-organizational approaches allow-ing founders to influence the firm's longer-term viability (DeTienne et al., 2015); and cessation-based strategies such as closing or liquidation. In general, founders of growth-oriented firms are more inclined toward financial-based strategies, whereas lifestyle small business owners more often choose stewardship and cessation-based strategies (Ryan & Power, 2012). Financial-based

---

Box 13.1: Summary of key exit strategies

Sale to a third party: In a *harvest sale*, the venture continues doing business while the entrepreneur exits. Usually, the business is performing well and the entrepreneur is able to extract some or all of the firm's economic value by selling his/her equity stake to private buyer(s). A *distress sale* finds the entrepreneur selling his/her equity but only able to extract a small amount of value generated. The business may be losing money and the entrepreneur is unable to stop the losses, or has significant debt he/she is unable to repay.

Merger or acquisition: A variation on a sale to a third party where the buyer is another company.

Management or Employee Buy-out: A variation on a sale to a third party where the buyer is either one or more managers within the venture, or the employees of the venture.

Initial Public Offering: A variation on a sale to a third party where the venture, or a significant portion of the equity in the venture, is sold over a public stock exchange such as the NASDAQ or the New York Stock Exchange.

Family (or Third Party) Succession: Family succession is when the entrepreneur gives his or her equity stake to family members who continue the business, while the entrepreneur completely or partially exits. Succession can also involve turning the business over to a non-family member, such as a trusted colleague.

Liquidation: *Harvest liquidation* refers to the termination of a profitable firm and distribution of the value of its assets to the entrepreneur and/or any creditors. Personal reasons (e.g. divorce, career change, and health issues), or business reasons (e.g. obsolete technology, capital-intensive assets with the value of the firm locked into the assets, and a lack of available buyers) are drivers of this exit strategy. *Distress liquidation* refers to the termination of an unprofitable firm, often one with significant liabilities, where the distribution of any asset value is made to the firm's creditors (and the entrepreneur). This can involve bankruptcy.

Discontinuance: Closing of the firm involves a decision to shut down and lose any value in the business.

strategies require the most advance planning, while cessation-based strategies require the least (DeTienne et al., 2015). Stewardship-based strategies likely fall in the middle.

Entrepreneurial exit is a path-dependent process (Taylor, 1999). Thus, elements involved in launching and growing a venture (e.g. motives, resources, strategies) have an impact on how and when the entrepreneur exits. Further, exit strategies developed early in the life of a venture can influence subsequent decisions and behaviors (DeTienne et al., 2015). The optimal strategy depends on the unique situation of the entrepreneur and their context (DeTienne, 2010). In purely economic terms, one might expect the entrepreneur to prefer a sale over liquidation and liquidation over closing the firm or bankruptcy. In practice, a complex mix of motives affects approaches to exit. As a case in point, Mitchell (1994) found the attachment entrepreneurs have to their ventures transcended the economic value that might derive from a sale or liquidation.

THEORETICAL PERSPECTIVES USED TO EXAMINE EXIT STRATEGY

The most prevalent theoretical lenses used in research on entrepreneurial exit have been concerned with the formation of behavioral intentions to pursue an exit and with how individuals perceive the value of their ventures. Context may also drive the theoretical framework scholars choose to use. In the following discussion, we describe some of the prominent approaches.

Intentions and Value

An individual's intentions to engage in a particular behavior are a dependable predictor of that behavior (Ajzen & Fishbein, 1980). According to the theory of planned behavior, intentions are driven by attitudes, social norms, and the individual's perceived control

over the focal behavior. All three affect the choice of exit strategy (Soleimanof, Morris & Syed, 2014). For instance, while entrepreneurs may prefer to exit via IPO or acquisition, they do not have exclusive control over their ability to do so, which could reduce their intentions toward potentially lucrative exit paths.

The value entrepreneurs place on their ventures and on their continued venture involvement can influence exit strategy. Prospect theory (Kahneman & Tversky, 1979) explains how individuals assess value by relying on reference points. What one entrepreneur perceives as high performance and another perceives as low performance depends on a reference point, or threshold, set by the entrepreneurs (Gimeno et al., 1997). Prospect theory suggests that those business owners whose ventures are high-performing relative to a reference point will accelerate their exit, and those with underperforming firms will delay exit. The latter tends to exacerbate the likelihood of negative possibilities (e.g. distress liquidation), since these entrepreneurs hang on longer, hoping performance will eventually improve (Wennberg et al., 2010). Expected utility theory suggests entrepreneurs are driven to maximize their returns. So long as their venture provides better personal returns than alternative activities, they will persist in their venture.

When Context Matters

Scholars have employed different theoretical perspectives to examine influences on exit decisions and outcomes in particular contexts. DeTienne and Chirico (2013) employ a socioemotional wealth perspective and threshold theory to explain how exit strategies vary in family firms. The greater the benefit the family derives from ownership, the lower their threshold level of performance for the venture and the more likely they are to seek an exit that would ensure family control after transfer (Hsu, Wiklund, Anderson, & Coffey, 2016; Sharma, Chrisman, & Chua, 2003). Elsewhere, Justo, DeTienne, and Sieger

(2015) draw on social feminist theory to challenge the notion that females are exiting at higher rates than males due to underperformance, noting that, instead, they are more often exiting voluntarily and/or in pursuit of lucrative opportunities outside the venture.

A Theory of Entrepreneurial Exit

Some exit studies have implicitly or explicitly eschewed the adoption of a particular theoretical lens, while attempting to develop new theory. For instance, DeTienne and her colleagues (2015) draw on existing literature to develop a typology in which entrepreneurs exit via lucrative financial remuneration (i.e. harvest strategy), by successfully transitioning the firm to new ownership while maintaining a degree of influence (i.e. stewardship strategy),

---

Box 13.2: Antecedents of exit strategy

Individual Level Characteristics

- Industry experience
- Gender
- Age
- Education
- Outside employment
- Intentions to exit
- Satisfaction with venture
- Thinking style (analytic vs. intuitive)
- Motivation (intrinsic vs. extrinsic)
- Entrepreneurship 'style' (effectual vs. causal)

Venture Level Characteristics

- Age
- Additional equity investment
- Lifecycle stage
- Size of founding team
- Innovativeness
- Number of employees
- Performance (financial/non-financial)
- Resource portfolio breadth and depth

Environmental Characteristics

- Barriers to exit
- Relationships among market/industry players
- Innovativeness of competitive environment

---

or by terminating the venture's activities (i.e. voluntary cessation strategy). Their typology was a continuation of DeTienne's (2010) earlier work, which also implicitly avoided existing theoretical frameworks to set the boundary conditions of exit phenomena.

RESEARCH INSIGHTS: ANTECEDENTS AND DETERMINANTS OF EXIT

Exit strategy choices are influenced by a number of factors, which can be grouped into characteristics of the entrepreneur, the venture, and the external environment (see Box 13.2 below). These factors are further elaborated upon below.

Entrepreneur Characteristics

Among the demographic variables examined in exit research are age, education, and gender, as well as prior experience and whether the entrepreneur has supplemental employment outside the venture. As an entrepreneur's age and timeframe related to expected returns shorten, they may become more sensitive to short-term variations in venture value, which will increase the likelihood they exit rather than expose themselves to unnecessary risks. Education would help them acquire higher-paying jobs compared to less-educated entrepreneurs, which means they expect greater returns from their ventures and would exit faster than others when expectations are not met (Wennberg et al., 2010). Gender also has an effect, with women tending to place lower value on monetary outcomes and deriving fewer psycho-emotional benefits from the venture, such as identity and psychological ownership. It is argued that women place greater value on personal relationships outside work and are less risk tolerant than men. Therefore, they are more likely to exit the venture voluntarily, due to personal reasons, or to pursue other opportunities, than due to venture failure (Justo et al., 2015).

Prior entrepreneurial experience can influence exit strategy in at least two ways. Experienced entrepreneurs tend to start with fewer resource constraints, have greater access to financing, and are better able to identify lucrative opportunities when compared with novice entrepreneurs (Hayward, Forster, Sarasvathy, & Fredrickson, 2010; Ucbasaran, Westhead, & Wright, 2009). Additionally, experienced entrepreneurs have better employment alternatives outside the venture, increasing their opportunity costs. Both dynamics lead experienced entrepreneurs to place higher performance thresholds on their ventures, which means they are more willing to exit when the venture fails to meet performance standards (DeTienne & Cardon, 2012). Experienced entrepreneurs are also likely to pursue more lucrative exit strategies than others due to the venture's higher growth potential and institutional investors' preference for experienced founders (Wennberg et al., 2010). Finally, entrepreneurs who have been involved with prior acquisitions are able to put this experience to use and obtain more favorable exit outcomes than those lacking such experience (van Teeffelen & Uhlaner, 2013). Research suggests that many entrepreneurs hold an outside job while starting their ventures. Wennberg and colleagues (2010) found that entrepreneurs who had an outside job were less likely to exit their ventures in financially stressful situations (e.g. distress liquidation, fire sales) but that taking an outside job did not influence the likelihood they would follow more lucrative exit strategies.

Effort has been devoted to understanding the influence of internal, personal characteristics on exit. DeTienne and colleagues (2015) explore how extrinsic or autonomy-seeking motivation influences exit strategy. Entrepreneurs who were motivated by the potential for financial gain were more likely to seek an exit strategy that maximized their returns, while entrepreneurs driven to seek autonomy were more likely to pursue strategies that allowed them continued involvement with the firm as they are loathe to hand their ventures to successors who would use them to pursue short-term gains.

DeTienne et al. (2015) suggest that entrepreneurs who exhibit a causal cognitive style pursue exit strategies differently from those relying on an effectual cognitive style. The authors demonstrate that entrepreneurs who use causal decision making are more likely to see exit as a culmination of planning and effort. Therefore, for the causal entrepreneur, exit strategies more often feature a harvest (e.g. IPO, acquisition), and are less likely to involve a cessation-based exit.

Brigham, De Castro, and Shepherd (2007) draw on person-organizational fit research to argue that entrepreneurs whose cognitive style, personal motivations, goals, and values become misaligned with their venture will become dissatisfied and seek to exit. Misalignment can occur when entrepreneurs, who may rely initially on an intuitive cognitive style, find themselves constrained by a venture that is developing more organizational structure and routines. These entrepreneurs may be less suited for later stages of the venture lifecycle, with their fit declining over time. One implication is that entrepreneurs' thresholds for their businesses may decline with time, making them more likely to adopt less lucrative exit strategies.

Venture Characteristics

DeTienne (2010) links the formation of exit strategies to the life cycle stage of the venture. She posits that entrepreneurs who are driven by extrinsic motivation will develop an exit strategy at the earliest stages of the venture. In the gestation phase, should the entrepreneur determine the venture will not meet growth expectations, they will abandon the idea. During infancy, exit strategy can come to have pervasive effects within the venture, as the expected means of exit affects decisions related to financing, growth, and strategy. For instance, the entrepreneur seeking a lucrative financial exit strategy will tend to push harder to identify and capture new opportunities, while the one seeking a stewardship-type strategy may pursue managed growth and a less aggressive stance toward markets and competitors. At later stages, two factors influence formation of exit strategy. First, for ventures that encounter growth and attract investors, entrepreneurs' chances of realizing a significant financial return, such as IPO or acquisition, become greater (DeTienne, 2010). Second, entrepreneurs may come to personally identify with their venture and develop relationships with key stakeholders (e.g. Cardon, Zietsma, Saparito, Matherne, & Davis, 2005). As a consequence, these entrepreneurs may develop a sense of responsibility for their venture that drives them to pursue a strategy that affords them some control after exit. Finally, DeTienne (2010) posits that, in maturity, few entrepreneurs who desired a financially lucrative exit strategy are still managing their ventures; instead, those still managing tend to be entrepreneurs who either identify strongly with their venture or are managing it as a lifestyle business. At this point, exit strategies are often aimed at transitioning the business to an employee, manager, or buyer upon the founder's retirement.

The attachment that forms between entrepreneurs and aging ventures is emphasized by Dehlen, Zellweger, Kamerlander, and Halter (2014) who find that firm age influences efforts to pursue a successor-type strategy. Their emotional attachment to the venture can lead entrepreneurs to develop a status quo bias, blinding them to cues that potential external succession candidates are available. Even if the entrepreneur perceives the existence of an able external candidate, a preference for the status quo compels a downplaying of such information in favor of internal candidates. Other research suggests that older ventures with proven business models and stable returns are more likely to be sold than liquidated (Amaral et al., 2007); however, the idiosyncratic resources acquired by older firms may make finding a suitable buyer more challenging.

The number of employees in a venture has been positively associated with preference for a stewardship strategy (DeTienne et al., 2015). Entrepreneurs with many employees can develop strong concern for their welfare, especially where employees comprised the team that helped launch the venture. Their exit strategies are influenced by a desire to address employee needs and what is best for the organization, rather than for the entrepreneur or investors (DeTienne et al., 2015). Similarly, smaller ventures are more likely than larger ventures to close outright, given the smaller number of stakeholders to be considered (Battisti & Okamuro, 2010). Aside from employees, Collewaert (2012) considered the effect that angel investors have on exit. She found that, when entrepreneurs and angel investors had conflicting goals related to the venture, both were more likely to exit. This suggests greater complexity in setting an exit strategy, at least after a venture has acquired significant investment. With venture capitalist involvement, there is evidence to indicate an 'exit-centric' approach to investment decisions (Mason & Botelho, 2016).

Finally, DeTienne and Cardon (2008) argue that the breadth and depth of a venture's initial resource position can influence exit strategy. Ventures that offered more innovative products or that had higher initial investments were more likely to choose an exit strategy that resulted in an IPO or a sale.

Environmental Characteristics

Another set of antecedents concern the external environment, including barriers to exit, competitive rivalry, and innovation pressures. Barriers to exit are factors that deter entrepreneurs from removing resource commitments from their ventures and the markets within which they operate. Examples include undervaluation of resource portfolios, lack of a resale market for such resources, hesitation to terminate promising venture activities (e.g. product development), and future expectations about market developments (Harrigan, 1981). By delaying timely exit, barriers can result in selection of substandard exit strategies. Thus, external conditions can encourage entrepreneurs to persist with venture activities beyond an economically optimal point, resulting in unfavorable liquidation or outright termination of ventures. Competition can also play a role. High levels of competition can mask the cooperation (or relationships) that exist among competitors in a market (Boeker, Goodstein, Stephan, & Murmann, 1997). A venture may maintain points of contact with competitors out of strategic concerns, such as maintaining a presence in competitors' markets (Gimeno, 1994). Contacts with larger competitors or other industry players may also help entrepreneurs overcome resource constraints (e.g. Howorth & Moro, 2006). Entrepreneurs with more contacts may tend to delay exiting longer than entrepreneurs without such contacts. Although delay may be associated with less optimal exit strategies, contacts may also help identify potential buyers when one does exit.

The level of innovativeness in one's competitive environment has been shown to influence exit strategy. Sarkar, Echambadi, Agarwal, and Sen (2006) approach environmental innovativeness along two dimensions: technological regime and intensity. The technological regime is the extent to which technical knowledge is shared among key industry players: the less the sharing, the more 'entrepreneurial' the regime and the greater advantage for industry newcomers. Technological intensity refers to the centrality of technology in an industry and the number of investments firms make to pursue technological solutions. These two dimensions can align in a way that affects exit of newer ventures (Sarkar et al., 2006). Industries that have 'entrepreneurial' technical regimes while also being technologically intense are least likely to see new venture entrants that exit quickly; conversely, industries with 'routinized' technical

regimes (i.e. where incumbents benefit from accumulated scientific knowledge and other non-transferable resources) and that have low technological intensity also have fewer opportunities for new entrants, accelerating exit.

RESEARCH INSIGHTS: THE EXIT PROCESS

The actual anatomy of an exit has not received much scholarly attention, with the exception of family business succession. Hence, the process of exiting is not well understood. On one level, it involves a set of steps that differ based on the type of exit strategy. Here, particular activities involved when, say, selling a business or pursuing an IPO have been specified (e.g. Draho, 2004). Yet, on another level, exit processes can be messy, disjointed, ambiguous, uncertain, and extend over indeterminate amounts of time. As such, it would seem that the exit process involves personal dynamics, cognitive and emotional processing, learning, conflict, unexpected developments, and obstacles to be overcome.

In a succession context, Dehlen et al. (2014) describe how an entrepreneur's exit decision is hampered by information asymmetry between the incumbent and successor candidate. Because neither party is fully aware of the other's competencies and post-succession intentions, and because the successor candidate is unable to completely ascertain the quality of the venture, both parties can assume worst-possible outcomes, which threatens the venture's transition. To overcome these challenges, Dehlen and colleagues (2014) argue the incumbent entrepreneur relies on signals (e.g. the successor candidate's education, work experience) to evaluate the successor's suitability. Additionally, the effort an incumbent dedicates to screening can enhance or mitigate the effectiveness of the candidate's signals. As the incumbent's screening efforts increase, the potential successor's signals are more effective. However, prolonged screening may discourage the successor candidate, who may withdraw altogether. These effects are particularly relevant to exit strategies in family firms: the information asymmetries between an incumbent entrepreneur and family members would be lower than they would be between the incumbent and outside candidates. Therefore, incumbents may be more likely to pursue a stewardship-type exit strategy and select a family member as successor as an efficacious solution to information asymmetries.

A key variable in the exit process is exit planning and preparation. This is another area that has received limited focus from researchers (with the exception of family business succession planning). The entrepreneur engages in some level of 'exit effort', or devotion of time, effort, and money to various activities that can facilitate a successful exit. These activities include researching, learning, reflecting, planning, and strategizing efforts. Exit is not something the single-venture entrepreneur has ever done before, or a type of activity where they are highly knowledgeable. It is a novel experience. As such, the effort required to accomplish a successful exit can be considerable. The range of activities that constitute exit effort is extensive, some of which command significant resource commitments (see Box 13.3 below).

Exit effort enables the identification of exit routes, associated risks and outcomes, ways to enhance venture value prior to exit, and formulation of plans for wealth transfer, business succession, business sustainability, and the entrepreneur's post-exit life. Involvement in exit preparation activities is a critical factor in navigating what can be a complex and unpredictable process. Such activities likely receive serious attention once the entrepreneur has formulated an exit strategy, and the amount of effort devoted will be associated with the type of strategy. Closing or liquidating a business may require relatively less preparation, while transferring a business may be more time-consuming and costly, and selling a business or going public place even greater demands on the entrepreneur (Leroy,

---

Box 13.3: Activities that comprise exit effort

- Attend seminars on exit
- Consult with exit specialists
- Meet with business broker
- Consult with banker
- Construct a succession plan
- Engage in wealth transfer planning
- Work with attorney on legal aspects of exit
- Manage expectations of key internal and external stakeholders
- Conduct financial audit of company
- Have valuations of business performed
- Ensure equipment and facilities are well-maintained
- Establish well-documented operations and systems
- Examine and enhance transferability of clients, internal systems, contracts, leases
- Address pending or potential litigation surrounding the business
- Establish clear ownership of assets
- Ensure ongoing copyright, trademark and patent protection of intellectual property
- Create balanced portfolio of products and services
- Assess business model viability for coming decade
- Work to protect brand image
- Establish active advisory board
- Ensure tax payments are up to date
- Work to mitigate risks, such as from over-dependence on certain suppliers or customers

Manigart, & Collewaert, 2015). Further, there is evidence to suggest lack of exit effort results in inefficient exit, often at significant cost not only to those involved with the venture, but to society at large (European Commission, 2013).

As entrepreneurs differ in their outlooks, experiences, and capabilities, we can expect them to differ in the effort they apply towards completion of an exit. Consider the notion of the entrepreneur's work-role. Work-role comprises job involvement, company identification, and professional attachment (Feldman, 1994). Entrepreneurs high on these dimensions may have less incentive to dedicate extensive effort toward actions that lead them to lose a valued set of role activities and a source of self-identity (Feldman, 1994). In a similar vein, psychological ownership (Pierce, Kostova, & Dirks, 2001), where individuals feel that the venture is theirs, is a force countering the motivation to engage in exit effort.

RESEARCH INSIGHTS: OUTCOMES OF EXIT STRATEGY

What happens after the exit strategy is executed? It would appear there are effects at multiple levels: the individual, firm, industry, and larger economy (community, regional, and national levels). At the individual level, outcomes are strongly influenced by the perception and experience of either a successful or unsuccessful exit. For example, Bates (2005) demonstrated that both successful and unsuccessful closures can be differentiated based on owner and firm traits. Owners of high opportunity cost businesses were found to be more likely to perceive and experience successful closures.

Some exits result in the launch of a new venture, or 'serial entrepreneurship' (Westhead, Ucbasaran, Wright, & Binks, 2005). Stokes and Blackburn (2002) found this to be commonplace, with 60% of exit entrepreneurs starting a new business. In many instances, then, it is a voluntary exit driven by the recognition of a new opportunity (Westhead et al., 2005). Hessels, Grilo, Thurik, and van der Zwan (2011) provide evidence that a recent exit increases the probability of involvement in new and different entrepreneurial activities, which can produce several levels of entrepreneurial engagement. Using Global Entrepreneurship Monitor data, they show that the probability of entrepreneurial engagement after exit is higher for males, who demonstrate lower fear of failure, and for those who have other entrepreneurs as role models. Exited entrepreneurs may also be more capable of detecting and realizing new opportunities (Hessels et al., 2011). Previous venture experience can make serial entrepreneurs more skillful and socially connected, enhancing their abilities to attract investment funding and create better-performing businesses (Hsu, 2007). Moreover, with exits due to failure, serial entrepreneurs use the failure experience to make sense of the process and facilitate learning (Baumard & Starbuck, 2005). Learning from successful and unsuccessful exits is one of the most significant outcomes for the entrepreneur and, if it survives, the firm (Burgelman, 1994). Other individual outcomes include the emotional and psychological reactions to exit. Exit can mean loss of an entity to which the individual was intrinsically attached (Cardon et al., 2005). The individual can experience loss of identity, and struggle with how to define their legacy. Grief has been studied as a reaction to exit. Shepherd (2003) demonstrated the moderating role of grief on the relation between feedback information and self-employment knowledge, suggesting grief can diminish the ability to learn from the events of loss. In his multilevel, meso-level theory of grief recovery, Shepherd (2009) suggests individuals with higher emotional intelligence are better able to use grief to process information about exit or loss, and are more likely to help and coach others on a similar process. Jenkins, Wiklund, and Brundin (2014) found that grief feelings vary among entrepreneurs after firm failure, and the effect is moderated by loss of self-esteem. These results highlight the role of psychological and human capital as an outcome of exit (e.g. Leroy et al., 2015).

Additional social-psychological factors, such as anxiety, equity, mood, evaluation of self and partner, and level of agreement, are also outcomes of exit (Kushnir, 1984). There are potential social costs, as the exit can impact the nature and extent of the entrepreneur's personal and professional relationships. Evidence exists of a negative impact on marriages and close relationships of an unsatisfactory exit (Singh, Corner, & Pavlovich, 2007). Further, exit can involve subsequent financial cost to the entrepreneur, as it can represent a loss or decrease in personal income.

Let us turn to firm-level outcomes. Statistics on the types of exits that are executed produce an unclear picture. Ronstadt (1986) concluded the largest percentage of exits involved selling out (46%), followed by liquidation (43%), bankruptcy (5%), and undetermined/unclear (5%). Balcaen, Manigart, Buyze, and Ooghe (2012) examined distress-related exits in Belgium, revealing that 44% were voluntary liquidations, 41% were court-driven, mainly due to bankruptcy, and 14% were mergers and acquisitions. There is also lack of clarity when it comes to a) how many firms can be considered successful at the time of exit, and b) how successful those exits can be considered. Hence, a matrix might be considered, with one axis devoted to successful and unsuccessful ventures, and the other to successful and unsuccessful exits. In this context, Ucbasaran, Westhead, and Wright (2006) found that about 30% of entrepreneurs considered their venture successful at the time of exit (see also Headd, 2003). Alternatively, Coad (2013) concludes that most business exits are not successful.

Limited research has been conducted on firm-level outcomes for ventures that are not liquidated. Consider venture acquisition, where there are implications for both the acquired and acquiring firm. The acquired venture will experience changes in operating procedures, strategic priorities, and workplace culture. Studies suggest that employees in entrepreneurial firms engage in more informal employer–employee relationships than those in larger, established firms (Jack, Hyman, & Osborne, 2006). Exits can also cause uncertainty and fear among employees. As a result, employees of the acquired venture may tend to leave. Similarly, some sales require the founder of the acquired firm to remain for a period of time following acquisition. These entrepreneurs are frequently unhappy with their new role and the changes being implemented in their former company.

Entrepreneurial firms absorbed by established companies face three possible outcomes. First, the parent company keeps organizational structures and hierarchy intact, preserving the newly acquired firm's entrepreneurial orientation and organizational identity. Second, the parent company fully integrates the new acquisition into its corporate structure. The success rate of such an integration will depend on a range of factors, such as the level of corporate entrepreneurship (Thomson & McNamara, 2001), speed of integration (Homburg & Bucerius, 2006), and organizational culture (Schraeder & Self, 2003). A study of 253 horizontal mergers and acquisitions in European and US manufacturing industries showed that asset divestiture and resource redeployment contributed to the acquisition's performance (Capron, 1999). Third, the acquiring firm might only be interested in certain assets such as patents, inventory, or real estate, thereby dissolving the firm upon purchase and forcing employees of the acquired firm to look for new employment opportunities.

The dyadic relationship between a new owner and the acquired firm can also have varying effects on firm strategy, growth, and innovation capability. For instance, exit can prompt modifications in the distribution of resources and changes in how production systems are organized (Robins, 1993). Acquisitions can also help large and established firms counter the familiarity, maturity, and propinquity (i.e. kinship) traps, and develop unique capabilities that give them a sustainable competitive advantage (Ahuja & Lampert, 2001). Overall, the long-term effects of acquisitions on entrepreneurial firms remain largely unknown. Impacts on such variables as organizational identity, strategic orientation, or innovation performance require more attention.

Succession within family businesses is an exit possibility that has generated considerable attention. While the need for well-formulated succession and wealth transfer plans has received the greatest emphasis from researchers (Notwani, Levenburg, & Schwarz, 2006), Morris, Williams, Allen, and Avila (1997) provide evidence that post-succession performance is also affected by the preparation level of heirs and internal family relationships, with the latter explaining the largest proportion of the variance in performance. When there is a lack of suitable family successors, a possible outcome is management buyout. An empirical study with 104 former private European family firms showed that there were higher efficiency advantages for succession in businesses with no pre-buyout equity holding by non-family managers (Scholes, Wright, Westhead, & Bruining, 2010).

With IPOs, a stronger body of evidence has been produced regarding firm performance and, specifically, the tendency for firms to underperform in the years following an IPO. For example, Ahmad-Zaluki (2008) reported clear evidence of declining performance in the IPO year and up to three years following the IPO relative to the pre-IPO period. Others suggest this relationship is affected by equity retention by the founding entrepreneurs (Jain & Kini, 1994), the relative performance of the firm prior to the IPO (Peristiani & Hong, 2004), and the age of the firm at the time of the IPO (Clark, 2002).

Exit also poses outcomes at the industry level and within the aggregate economy. Research has proposed that a constant flux of births and deaths of entrepreneurial firms can act as a 'seedbed' for more innovative industries. In the context of new industry formation, (voluntary and involuntary) business exits provide critical resources and learning at lower costs, fueling industry growth (Beesley & Hamilton, 1984). In fact, intra-industry firm movements or turbulence are better measures of an industry's dynamic behavior than market concentration (Grossack, 1965).

At the level of the economy, the net effect of different types of exit strategies is unclear. Shutting down or liquidating firms can mean less productive resources are transferred to more productive ones, but can also result in loss of jobs and economic value (Knott & Posen, 2005). Business sales to other parties and IPOs can find companies revitalized, resulting in sustained growth. The magnitude of exit effects will also depend on the level of analysis. Local economies will be more affected by voluntary or involuntary exits than the national economy. For example, the decline of the car industry in Detroit led to the involuntary exits of specialized industry suppliers as well as a range of lifestyle businesses such as restaurants, grocery stores, or medical offices, triggering a cascade of economic and population decline.

The economy benefits when entrepreneurs pursue new ventures following an exit. A case study of Scottish technology-based firms found this sort of serial entrepreneurship has a positive impact on regional economic development (Mason & Harrison, 2006). Separately, Pe'er and Vertinsky (2008) verified that the exit of firms stimulates the entry of new, more productive enterprises in the same location. The entry of new firms generates the possible release of new resources, such as knowledge, allowing existing firms to increase productivity (Burke & van Stel, 2014).

Another largely unexplored aspect of entrepreneurial exits is how entrepreneurs subsequently connect with their environments as investors, advisors, mentors, or community organizers. This process, called entrepreneurial recycling, will increase in magnitude as the growing proportion of aging entrepreneurs feel the need to pass on their operational responsibilities to other parties. Consequently, we will see an increased influx of 'retirement' capital that will create new impulses for the overall economy (DeTienne & Cardon, 2012). Exiting entrepreneurs also produce unseen economic benefits to local entrepreneurial ecosystems by providing social capital to novice entrepreneurs critical for their development (Mason & Harrison, 2006).

FUTURE RESEARCH CHALLENGES AND PRIORITIES

Exit strategy research is slowly gaining traction within the broader entrepreneurship literature (e.g. Wennberg & DeTienne, 2014; DeTienne, McKelvie, & Chandler, 2015). With increased attention come a number of challenges, including conceptual, theoretical, and methodological concerns. Scholars still lack conceptual agreement with regard to fundamental concepts as well as the tools to measure them. For instance, the conceptualization of a 'successful outcome' from an exit likely has a number of dimensions depending on the type of exit strategy. Once specified, these dimensions require valid and reliable measures. The same can be said about the notion of 'voluntariness'. Exit strategies vary in the degree to which they are completely voluntary or effectively imposed on the entrepreneur. Another underdeveloped construct is 'exit planning' or preparation. Planning activities take numerous and varied forms and are pursued in differing degrees over time. We have little insight into what constitutes a well or poorly planned exit. A fourth example might be termed 'execution quality', or the degree to which a given exit strategy is well-executed. It may be that there are instances where the type of strategy matters less than how well it is pursued. Again, both conceptual and measurement problems require attention. Until scholars develop exit-specific concepts and associated measures,

they will be compelled to rely on less accurate measures as proxies.

At the broader theoretical level, a process-based perspective on exit remains elusive, which hampers efforts to more fully understand how entrepreneurs move from the initial start-up act, or from the point when they begin to consider an exit, to the moment they relinquish control and depart the venture. It may be important to integrate exit literature with a process-based, opportunity-centric understanding of entrepreneurship. For instance, what are the relationships between an entrepreneurs' recognition, evaluation, and exploitation of opportunities and exit strategy? Is exit strategy an important antecedent to the entrepreneurship process, might exit strategy follow as an outcome of entrepreneurs' exploitation efforts, or do opportunities and exit strategies emerge together? In short, what is 'entrepreneurial' about exit? Although exit is an important part of the entrepreneurship process, theorists have yet to explicate the importance of the entrepreneurship process for exit strategy.

Another challenge in terms of theory development lies with boundary setting. The definition of exit offered by DeTienne (2010, p. 204) suggests that entrepreneurial exit can only exist when the founders of privately held firms leave the firm they helped to create. Does this include all types of entrepreneurial ventures (e.g. survival, lifestyle and growth-oriented firms, franchises) and ventures at any stage of development beyond founding? If so, do we need different theories to reflect each of these contexts? Further, the definition suggests we must exclude from consideration social or non-profit ventures or corporate ventures, areas receiving considerable attention in contemporary entrepreneurship research. Similarly, from a boundary perspective, when does the exit process begin and end? Can it commence as early as the launch of a venture, and does it endure well after the actual exit takes place?

Studying entrepreneurial exit also presents a variety of methodological challenges, especially given that, in many cases, the venture of interest no longer exists and the founding entrepreneur is no longer involved and may be difficult to locate. This is more than a sampling issue. It can be reflected in the choice of dependent variables (i.e. exit intentions rather than actual exit), and in the use of archival data (Wennberg et al., 2010) and other secondary data, such as the Global Entrepreneurship Monitor (e.g. Justo et al., 2015). The nature of exit also presents difficulties in using qualitative methodologies. These methodologies, such as case studies, are especially important when the objective is to develop a rich understanding of the complexities, interactions, and relationships at play in a phenomenon (Eisenhardt & Graebner, 2007). Although exit research would benefit from the use of such methodologies, the challenge is to find firms in the midst of an exit (which itself can be delineated in various ways).

Yet another methodological challenge lies with research designs. Most exit research has been conducted using cross-sectional and panel designs. Nevertheless, longitudinal and experimental designs are relevant approaches that can contribute to our understanding of exit. For example, the question 'how does exit strategy emerge or change over time?' requires a longitudinal design that tracks founders' paths and measures variables over time in order to depict process evolution. Longitudinal studies can be demanding and resource consuming, but are especially useful in providing insights into 'why' and 'how' questions for an activity that occurs over time. However, executing longitudinal designs is constrained by the inability to predict in advance which entrepreneurs will exit, when, and how. Additionally, answering why and how questions necessitates the use of different sources of data. It is critical to access perceptions of various actors involved in exit, including founders, employees, family members, customers, and suppliers, among others.

With such research challenges in mind, what are the priorities for ongoing work in the exit area? Clearly, many fundamental questions remain unaddressed. Consider just a few of these questions:

- Which demographic and background variables best explain exit preferences, actual exit routes, and subsequent outcomes, and why?
- How, why, and under which conditions do founding strategies determine exit options and outcomes?
- If we consider the anatomy of a particular exit, can patterns in activities and behaviors be identified based on type of exit strategy? Which of these are common across exit strategies?
- What are the determinants of successful exit, and how do these determinants vary based on type of exit strategy?
- How do exit strategies and subsequent outcomes vary across survival, lifestyle, managed-growth, and aggressive-growth ventures?
- Which characteristics of exit planning have the greatest impact on exit outcomes and in what ways?
- How do suboptimal exit outcomes impact subsequent behaviors of the stakeholders in a venture?
- What are the societal costs in terms of lost value from unplanned or suboptimal exits?
- What are the implications, at a societal level, of changes in exit rates and the proportion of different types of exits over time? Are there environmental factors (e.g. the business cycle, the nature of entrepreneurial ecosystems) that impact these rates and proportions?
- Can public policy be designed in ways to enhance societal welfare by influencing exit decisions of entrepreneurs?

These and other questions make clear that exit is a fertile scholarly arena with rich opportunities for varied streams of research. Yet the volume of research remains limited. This may be due to the large number of other pressing scholarly issues affecting earlier stages in the entrepreneurial process. Or, perhaps the questions surrounding creating and growing a venture are simply viewed as more central to entrepreneurial behavior than are issues surrounding how one exits that venture. It is critical that exit receives more priority, as it represents the culmination of the entrepreneurial journey. Moreover, exit can have implications at the individual, organizational, and societal levels that are every bit as significant as the implications of entry.

CONCLUSION

Exit research is a young, relevant, and promising research domain within entrepreneurship. It is an emerging field that has to date attracted a small group of scholars who have produced most of the published work. While some governments track aggregate exit activity, it is a phenomenon for which there is little in the way of statistical databases that capture types or causes of exit at the industry, regional, or national levels. In spite of this, pioneering scholars have established a solid foundation upon which researchers can build.

To date, the evidence suggests exit approaches and related issues are not topics entrepreneurs typically take into account when deciding to launch a venture, although the conventional argument is that they should do so. Exit is often a topic of focus only when circumstances surrounding the entrepreneur, venture, or external environment dictate that it receive consideration. For various reasons, many entrepreneurs resist the need to formulate an exit strategy or engage in exit planning and preparation. This tendency can result in exits having suboptimal or less than desirable outcomes for the individual, the venture, and society. Advances have been made in delineating and categorizing exit strategies, and in identifying elements that go into properly executing types of strategies. Further, key factors influencing the choice of a given exit approach have been specified, and types of positive and negative exit outcomes have been clarified.

At the same time, many key constructs surrounding exit have not been well-conceptualized and/or valid measures of these constructs have not been fully developed and operationalized. The dynamics within the exit process are not well understood, while capturing the actual outcomes and corresponding implications of various exit behaviors remains a struggle. Progress has been limited by conceptual and methodological challenges and, while some of these are particularly vexing, they would appear surmountable. The greater need is for more scholars to become involved with the conduct of exit research. In the final analysis, the exit arena contains a rich array of intriguing research questions having significant implications for different levels of analysis and policy interventions.

REFERENCES

Ahmad-Zaluki, N. A. (2008). Post-IPO operating performance and earnings management. *International Business Research*, *1*(2), 39–48.

Ahuja, G., & Lampert, M. C. (2001). Entrepreneurship in the large corporation: A longitudinal study of how established firms create breakthrough inventions. *Strategic Management Journal*, *22*(6–7), 521–543.

Ajzen, I., & Fishbein, M. (1980). *Understanding attitudes and predicting social behavior.* Englewood Cliffs, NJ: Prentice Hall.

Amaral, A. M., Baptista, R., & Lima, F. (2007). Entrepreneurial exit and firm performance. *Frontiers of Entrepreneurship Research*, *27*(5). Available at: http://digitalknowledge. babson.edu/fer/vol27/iss5/1

Balcaen, S., Manigart, S., Buyze, J., & Ooghe, H. (2012). Firm exit after distress: Differentiating between bankruptcy, voluntary liquidation and M&A. *Small Business Economics*, *39*(4), 949–975.

Bates, T. (2005). Analysis of young, small firms that have closed: Delineating successful from unsuccessful closures. *Journal of Business Venturing*, *20*(3), 343–358.

Battisti, M., & Okamuro, H. (2010). Selling, passing on or closing? Determinants of entrepreneurial intentions on exit modes (November 18, 2010). Massey U. College of Business Research Paper Paper No. 27. Available at SSRN: https://ssrn.com/abstract=1711336 or http://dx.doi.org/10.2139/ssrn.1711336

Baumard, P., & Starbuck, W. H. (2005). Learning from failures: Why it may not happen. *Long Range Planning, 38*(3), 281–298.

Beesley, M. E., & Hamilton, R. T. (1984). Small firms' seedbed role and the concept of turbulence. *Journal of Industrial Economics, 33*(2), 217–232.

Boeker, W., Goodstein, J., Stephan, J., & Murmann, J. P. (1997). Competition in a multimarket environment: The case of market exit. *Organization Science, 8*(2), 126–142.

Brigham, K. H., De Castro, J. O., & Shepherd, D. A. (2007). A person–organization fit model of owner-managers' cognitive style and organizational demands. *Entrepreneurship Theory and Practice, 31*(1), 29–51.

Burgelman, R. A. (1994). A process theory of strategic business exit in dynamic environments. *Administrative Science Quarterly, 39*(1), 24–56.

Burke, A., & van Stel, A. (2014). Entry and exit in disequilibrium. *Journal of Business Venturing, 29*(1), 174–192.

Capron, L. (1999). The long-term performance of horizontal acquisitions. *Strategic Management Journal, 20*(11), 987–1018.

Cardon, M. S., Zietsma, C., Saparito, P., Matherne, B. P., & Davis, C. (2005). A tale of passion: New insights into entrepreneurship from a parenthood metaphor. *Journal of Business Venturing, 20*(1), 23–45.

Clark, D. (2002). A study of the relationship between firm age at IPO and aftermarket stock performance. *Financial Markets, Institutions, & Instruments, 11*(4), 385–400.

Coad, A. (2013). Death is not success: Reflections on business exit. *International Small Business Journal, 22*(4), 331–348. doi:10.1177/0266242612475104

Collewaert, V. (2012). Angel investors' and entrepreneurs' intentions to exit ventures: A conflict perspective. *Entrepreneurship Theory and Practice, 36*(4), 753–779.

Dehlen, T., Zellweger, T., Kamerlander, N., & Halter, F. (2014). The role of information asymmetry in the choice of entrepreneurial exit routes. *Journal of Business Venturing, 29*(2), 193–209.

Delmar, F., Hellerstedt, K., & Wennberg, K. (2006). The evolution of firms created by the science and technology labor force in Sweden 1990–2000. In J. Ulhoi, & P. Christensen (Eds),

Managing Complexity and Change in SMEs (pp. 69–102). Cheltenham, UK and Northampton, MA: Edward Elgar Publishing.

DeTienne, D. R. (2010). Entrepreneurial exit as a critical component of the entrepreneurial process: Theoretical development. *Journal of Business Venturing, 25*(2), 203–215.

DeTienne, D. R., & Cardon, M. S. (2008). Entrepreneurial exit strategies: The impact of human capital. Babson College Entrepreneurship Research Conference *Frontiers of Entrepreneurship Research.* Available at SSRN: http://ssrn.com/abstract=1310922 or http://dx.doi.org/10.2139/ssrn.1310922

DeTienne, D. R., & Cardon, M. S. (2012). Impact of founder experience on exit intentions. *Small Business Economics, 38*(4), 351–374.

DeTienne, D. R., & Chirico, F. (2013). Exit strategies in family firms: How socioemotional wealth drives the threshold of performance. *Entrepreneurship Theory and Practice, 37*(6), 1297–1318.

DeTienne, D. R., McKelvie, A., & Chandler, G. N. (2015). Making sense of entrepreneurial exit strategies: A typology and test. *Journal of Business Venturing, 30*(2), 255–272.

Draho, J. (2004). *The IPO decision: Why and how companies go public.* Cheltenham: Edward Elgar.

Eisenhardt, K. M., & Graebner, M. E. (2007). Theory building from cases: Opportunities and challenges. *Academy of Management Journal, 50*(1), 25–32.

European Commission (2013). *Dynamics of the business population – Business Demography,* https://ec.europa.eu/eurostat/cros/content/dynamics-business-population-business-demography-pdf-file_en

Feldman, D. C. (1994). The decision to retire early: A review and conceptualization. *Academy of Management Review, 19*(2), 285–311.

Gimeno, J. (1994). Multipoint competition, market rivalry and firm performance: A test of the mutual forbearance hypothesis in the airline industry, 1984–1988. Unpublished doctoral dissertation, Purdue University, West Lafayette, IN.

Gimeno, J., Folta, T. B., Cooper, A. C., & Woo, C. Y. (1997). Survival of the fittest? Entrepreneurial human capital and the persistence of underperforming firms. *Administrative Science Quarterly, 42*(4), 750–783.

Grossack, I. M. (1965). Towards an integration of static and dynamic measures of industry concentration. *The Review of Economics and Statistics*, *47*(3), 301–308.

Harrigan, K. R. (1981). Barriers to entry and competitive strategies. *Strategic Management Journal*, *2*(4), 395–412.

Hayward, M. L., Forster, W. R., Sarasvathy, S. D., & Fredrickson, B. L. (2010). Beyond hubris: How highly confident entrepreneurs rebound to venture again. *Journal of Business Venturing*, *25*(6), 569–578.

Headd, B. (2003). Redefining business success: Distinguishing between closure and failure. *Small Business Economics*, *21*(1), 51–61.

Hessels, J., Grilo, I. Thurik, A. R., & van der Zwan, P. (2011). Entrepreneurial exit and entrepreneurial engagement. *Journal of Evolutionary Economics*, *21*(3), 447–470.

Homburg, C., & Bucerius, M. (2006). Is speed of integration really a success factor of mergers and acquisitions? An analysis of the role of internal and external relatedness. *Strategic Management Journal*, *27*(4), 347–367.

Howorth, C. A., & Moro, A. (2006). Trust within entrepreneur bank relationships: Insights from Italy. *Entrepreneurship Theory and Practice*, *30*(4), 495–517.

Hsu, D. K. (2007). Experienced entrepreneurial founders, organizational capital, and venture capital funding. *Research Policy*, *36*(5), 722–741.

Hsu, D. K., Wiklund, J., Anderson, S. E., & Coffey, B. S. (2016). Entrepreneurial exit intentions and the business–family interface. *Journal of Business Venturing*, *31*(6), 613–627.

Jack, S. L., Hyman, J., & Osborne, F. (2006). Small entrepreneurial ventures culture, change and the impact on HRM: A critical review. *Human Resource Management Review*, *16*(4), 456–466.

Jain, B., & Kini, O. (1994). The post-issue operating performance of IPO firms. *Journal of Finance*, *49*(5), 1699–1726.

Jenkins, A. S., Wiklund, J., & Brundin, E. (2014). Individual responses to firm failure: Appraisals, grief, and the influence of prior failure experience. *Journal of Business Venturing*, *29*(1), 17–33.

Justo, R., DeTienne, D. R., & Sieger, P. (2015). Failure or voluntary exit? Reassessing the female underperformance hypothesis. *Journal of Business Venturing*, *30*(6), 775–792.

Kahneman, D., & Tversky, A. (1979). Prospect theory: An analysis on decision under risk. *Econometrica*, *47*(2), 263–292.

Knott, A. M., & Posen, H. E. (2005). Is failure good? *Strategic Management Journal*, *26*(7), 617–641.

Kushnir, T. (1984). Social-psychological factors associated with the dissolution of dyadic business partnerships. *The Journal of Social Psychology*, *122*(2), 181–188.

Leroy, H., Manigart, S., Meuleman, M., & Collewaert, V. (2015). Understanding the continuation of firm activities when entrepreneurs exit their firms. *Journal of Small Business Management*, *53*(2), 400–415.

Mason, C., & Botelho, T. (2016). The role of the exit in the initial screening of investment opportunities: The case of business angel syndicate gatekeepers. *International Small Business Journal*, *34*(2), 157–175.

Mason, C. M., & Harrison, R. T. (2006). After the exit: Acquisitions, entrepreneurial recycling and regional economic development. *Regional Studies*, *40*(1), 55–73.

Mitchell, W. (1994). The dynamics of evolving markets: Effects of business sales and age on dissolutions and divestitures. *Administrative Science Quarterly*, *39*(4), 575–602.

Morris, M. H., Williams, R., Allen, J., & Avila, A. (1997). Correlates of success in family business transitions. *Journal of Business Venturing*, *12*(5), 385–401.

Notwani, J., Levenburg, N. M., & Schwarz, R. V. (2006). Succession planning in SMEs. *International Small Business Journal*, *24*(5), 471–495.

Pe'er, A., & Vertinsky, I. (2008). Firm failures as a determinant of new entry: Is there evidence of local creative destruction? *Journal of Business Venturing*, *23*(3), 280–306.

Peristiani, S., & Hong, G. (2004). Pre-IPO financial performance and aftermarket survival. *Current Issues in Economics and Finance*, *10*(2), 1–7.

Pierce, J. L., Kostova, T., & Dirks, K. T. (2001). Toward a theory of psychological ownership in organizations. *Academy of Management Review*, *26*(2), 298–310.

Robins, J. A. (1993). Organization as strategy: Restructuring production in the film industry.

Strategic Management Journal, 1(Summer Special Issue), 103–118.

Ronstadt, R. (1986). Exit, stage left: Why entrepreneurs end their entrepreneurial careers before retirement. *Journal of Business Venturing*, *1*(3), 323–338.

Ryan, G., & Power, B. (2012). Small business transfer decisions: What really matters? Evidence from Ireland and Scotland. *Irish Journal of Management*, *31*(2), 99–125.

Sarkar, M. B., Echambadi, R. A. J., Agarwal, R., & Sen, B. (2006). The effect of the innovative environment on exit of entrepreneurial firms. *Strategic Management Journal*, *27*(6), 519–539.

Scholes, L., Wright, M., Westhead, P., & Bruining, H. (2010). Strategic changes in family firms post management buyout: Ownership and governance issues. *International Small Business Journal*, *28*(5), 505–521.

Schraeder, M., & Self, D. R. (2003). Enhancing the success of mergers and acquisitions: An organizational culture perspective. *Management Decision*, *41*(5), 511–522.

Sharma, P., Chrisman, J. J., & Chua, J. H. (2003). Predictors of satisfaction with the succession process in family firms. *Journal of Business Venturing*, *18*(5), 667–687.

Shepherd, D. A. (2003). Learning from business failure: Propositions about the grief recovery process for the self-employed. *Academy of Management Review*, *28*(2), 318–329.

Shepherd, D. A. (2009). Grief recovery from the loss of a family business: A multi- and meso-level theory. *Journal of Business Venturing*, *24*(1), 81–97.

Singh, S., Corner, P., & Pavlovich, K. (2007). Coping with entrepreneurial failure. *Journal of Management & Organization*, *13*(4), 331–344.

Soleimanof, S., Morris, M. & Syed, I. (2014). The role of retirement intention in entrepreneurial exit. In D. DeTienne & K. Wennberg, (Eds), *Handbook on Enrepreneurial Exit* (pp. 157–183). Cheltenham, UK: Edward Elgar.

Stevenson, H. H., Roberts, M. J., & Grousbeck, H. I. (1989). *New business ventures and the entrepreneur*. Homewood, IL: R. D. Irwin.

Stokes, D., & Blackburn, R. (2002). Learning the hard way: The lessons of owner-managers who have closed their businesses. *Journal of Small Business and Enterprise Development*, *9*(1), 17–27.

Taylor, M. P. (1999). Survival of the fittest? An analysis of self-employment durations in Britain. *Economic Journal*, *109*(454), C140–C155.

Thomson, N., & McNamara, P. (2001). Achieving post-acquisition success: The role of corporate entrepreneurship. *Long Range Planning*, *34*(6), 669–697.

Ucbasaran, D., Westhead, P., & Wright, M. (2006). Habitual entrepreneurs. In A. Basu, M. Casson, N. Wadeson, & B. Yeung (Eds), *The Oxford Handbook of Entrepreneurship* (pp. 461–483). Aldershot: Edward Elgar.

Ucbasaran, D., Westhead, P., & Wright, M. (2009). The extent and nature of opportunity identification by experienced entrepreneurs. *Journal of Business Venturing*, *24*(2), 99–115.

Ucbasaran, D., Wright, M., & Westhead, P. (2003). A longitudinal study of habitual entrepreneurs: Starters and acquirers. *Entrepreneurship and Regional Development*, *15*(3), 207–228.

van Teeffelen, L., & Uhlaner, L. (2013). Firm resource characteristics and human capital as predictors of exit choice: An exploratory study of SMEs. *Entrepreneurship Research Journal*, *3*(1), 84–108.

Wennberg, K., & DeTienne, D. R. (2014). What do we really mean when we talk about 'exit'? A critical review of research on entrepreneurial exit. *International Small Business Journal*, *32*(1), 4–16.

Wennberg, K., Wiklund, J., DeTienne, D. R., & Cardon, M. S. (2010). Reconceptualizing entrepreneurial exit: Divergent exit routes and their drivers. *Journal of Business Venturing*, *25*(4), 361–375.

Westhead, P., Ucbasaran, D., Wright, M., & Binks, M. (2005). Novice, serial, and portfolio entrepreneur behaviour and contributions. *Small Business Economics*, *25*(2), 109–132.

14

Corporate Entrepreneurship

Bjørn Willy Åmo and Lars Kolvereid

INTRODUCTION

Entrepreneurship can be defined as the pursuit of opportunities by individuals or groups of individuals in order to create wealth (Ireland, Hitt, & Sirmon, 2003). Corporate Entrepreneurship (CE) is entrepreneurship within established organizations. In order to meet the need for renewal, managers and scholars have recognized that, by enacting entrepreneurial processes within the organization, established corporations can achieve competitive advantages (Covin & Slevin, 2002). CE can be viewed as a way of taking advantage of the creativity of managers and employees in order to innovate and to achieve organizational renewal, increased competitiveness, and increased performance.

Sharma and Chrisman (1999, p. 18) defined CE as 'the process whereby an individual or a group of individuals, in association with an existing organization, create an organization or instigate renewal or innovation within that organization'. This definition suggests that the CE concept consists of two related but distinguishable phenomena: (1) corporate venturing, which concerns the development of new businesses in association with the organization, and (2) strategic entrepreneurship, which concerns the innovation and renewal of the organization in other entrepreneurial ways.

Corporate venturing can be further divided into internal and external corporate venturing (Kuratko, Hornsby, & Hayton, 2015a). Internal corporate venturing concerns the creation of new businesses within the corporation. Such new businesses are typically owned by the corporation, and can be spun-off as separate entities, such as corporate or university spin-offs, but often reside within the structure of the corporation. In external corporate venturing new businesses are created outside the organization and subsequently invested in or bought by the corporation. These businesses are usually very young firms or firms with a large growth potential. External corporate venturing also includes activities such as corporate venture capital investments, licensing, acquisitions, start-ups by former employees, and joint ventures (Phan, Wright, Ucbasaran, & Tan, 2009).

While corporate venturing concerns new business or business units connected to the corporation, strategic entrepreneurship usually involves the entire organization or at least a significant part of it. Strategic entrepreneurship encompasses a broad array of entrepreneurial activities that are adopted by an organization in order to innovate and pursue competitive advantage (Kurato et al., 2015a). These activities can lead to significant changes in the way the organization is structured and does business, or can result in efforts leading to innovations that exploit new markets or new product offerings (Sharma & Chrisman, 1999).

The desired outcomes of CE can be renewal or innovativeness (Baden-Fuller, 1995; Guth & Ginsberg, 1990), internationalization (Birkinshaw, 1997), improved profitability (Vozikis, Bruton, Prasad, & Merikas, 1999), and increased competitiveness (Borch, Huse, & Senneseth, 1999; Covin & Miles, 1999). Miles and Covin (2002) divided the primary purposes of engaging in CE into three: (1) to build innovative capacity, (2) to gain greater value from current organizational

competencies or to expand the scope of the organization to new areas of strategic importance, and (3) to generate increased financial returns.

Entrepreneurial orientation (EO) has been described as the engine that drives CE (Morris, Webb, & Franklin, 2011). However, the organization's ability to discover or create opportunities is not explicitly included in the EO concept. The EO concept misses the necessary link to entrepreneurial learning in order to fully capture the dynamic of the CE process. Bloodgood, Hornsby, Burkemper, and Saroogh (2015) argue that entrepreneurial insight, which concerns the adaption of ideas into innovative practices, is the starting point of CE processes.

Several contextual factors in the organization's external environment can influence the relationship between process inputs and outputs from the CE process (Kurato et al., 2015a). Environments can vary with regard to dimensions such as dynamism, complexity, and hostility. This concerns the industry the firm is operating in, as well as the spatial location of the firm.

Based on the discussion above, we arrive at a model of CE shown in Figure 14.1. We will use this model to structure the review of the literature in the section that follows.

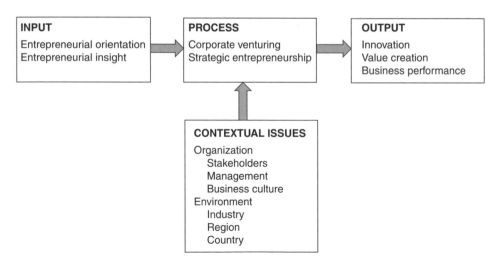

Figure 14.1   An input, process, context and output model of corporate entrepreneurship

Entrepreneurial orientation, entrepreneurial insight, or opportunities which are discovered or created are the primary input factors to the CE process. This process can involve internal or external corporate venturing or any form of strategic entrepreneurship. The outcomes of the process are innovation and organizational performance. Various factors in the organization and the management of the corporate venturing process as well as the environment surrounding the organization can all have an impact on the process, and influence the extent to which the desired outcomes are met.

STATE OF THE ART REVIEW

In this section we will describe and discuss the different elements in our model. We start with entrepreneurial orientation and entrepreneurial insight, followed by a discussion of the different types of organizational entrepreneurship: strategic entrepreneurship and corporate venturing. We then introduce the various characteristics of the organization and the organizational environment that can influence the CE process. Finally, we discuss the various outcomes of the process, in particular, innovation and organizational performance.

Process Inputs

Entrepreneurial orientation refers to the strategy-making processes and styles of firms that engage in entrepreneurial activities (Lumpkin & Dess, 1996). EO is therefore a characteristic of the firm and includes the following five dimensions: risk-taking, innovativeness, proactiveness, autonomy, and competitive aggressiveness (Covin & Lumpkin, 2011).

Risk-taking is associated with the firm's willingness to make large resource allocations involving unknown outcomes. A firm's innovativeness is characterized by its tendency to engage in and support new ideas, originality, opportunity testing, and creative processes that may lead to new routines, new products or services or new market developments. Proactiveness refers to the organizational processes aimed at predicting the future, enabling the organization to position itself for fulfilling future needs. Therefore, proactiveness also concerns opportunistic behavior where firms actively create and shape market opportunities. Autonomy refers to the independent action of an individual or a team in the pursuit to gather support for a business idea. Competitive aggressiveness refers to how a firm relates to its competitors and fights for its place in established markets.

The feedback loop of building new behavioral patterns based upon previous experience where novel business ideas emerge is not strongly prominent in the EO concept (Wang, 2008). A response to this weakness is the system dynamics model of CE developed by Bloodgood et al. (2015). In this model the starting point is entrepreneurial insight, a concept which is similar to entrepreneurial orientation, but where the emphasis is on the organization's ability to discover or create opportunities. Entrepreneurial insight is embedded in the organization and influences the adaption of ideas into innovation practices (Lanza & Passarelli, 2014). The entrepreneurial insight of an organization is continuously updated by feedback from prior exposure to opportunities, including earlier experience from opportunity recognition, assessment, legitimation, and implementation. In the Bloodgood et al. (2015) model this insight triggers the recognition of new opportunities. Opportunity recognition is the starting point of CE, since CE concerns the 'discovery and pursuit of new opportunities through innovation, new business creation or the introduction of new business models' (Hayton & Kelly, 2006, p. 407). Short, Ketchen, Combs, and Ireland (2010) defined an opportunity in the context of CE as a potentially lucrative idea which is discovered or created by an organization.

CE: Strategic Entrepreneurship

Covin and Miles (1999) distinguish between four archetypical forms of strategic entrepreneurship: domain redefinition, strategic renewal, sustained regeneration, and organizational rejuvenation.

Domain redefinition

Domain redefinition is based upon disruptive innovations in order to achieve competitive advantages. Domain redefinition usually combines new products or services produced through new routines and where the organization controls and tunes unique resources in a complex way. Disruptive innovations go beyond radical innovations by transforming business practice and rewriting rules for an industry (Kuratko et al., 2015a). Domain redefinition is often based upon technical superiority in combination with other unique knowledge-based resources. A quick response often provides first mover advantages for the producer.

A disruptive innovation often requires a substantial change in the organization. The organization needs to change the business model, the resource base, and the production procedures in order to succeed (Cucculelli & Bettinelli, 2015). In domain redefinition both the organization and its customers change their production/consumption patterns substantially. The innovation creates more value for the customer than previous means in order to satisfy customer needs. The increased customer value is greater than the cost of purchasing, using, and adjusting to the new product. This exploitation of disruptive innovations results in a redefinition of the value creation system, and a new industry then emerges.

Domain redefinition is a rare event, but some world-leading organizations manage to carry out such change processes more than once (Finkle, 2012). These world leaders proactively invent new industries or 'blue oceans' (Kim & Maubourgne, 2005) through a process of creative destruction. To pursue

domain redefinition means putting in a 'big bet' and involves high risks for the organization. Cucculelli and Bettinelli (2015) compared Italian firms that have changed their business models with firms where no such change had occurred. Their results indicated that business model reconfiguration had a positive effect on the ability of the firm to perform well.

Strategic renewal

Strategic renewal has an internal focus on the organization itself. Strategic renewal relates to the activities an organization undertakes to alter its path dependency in order to achieve a better fit between the organization and its environment (Kwee, Van Den Bosch, & Volberda, 2011). The change that follows from a strategic renewal affects the whole organization, including the borders of the organization, the products, and the production procedures. The strategic renewal often includes internal change via reorganization, resulting in renewed offerings. The core of strategic renewal is changing the organizational identity and cognition to fit with a new context (Macpherson & Jones, 2008; Tripsas, 2009). It is usually a reactive response to deteriorating market shares, intended to lead to new and improved ways of gaining terrain in an old industry (Agarwal & Helfat, 2009).

Strategic renewal occurs more frequently and is less risky than domain regeneration (Covin & Miles, 1999). The potential gain is correspondingly lower. There is a risk that the change effort will conflict with established routines that enable the organization to perform its current tasks well (Nelson & Winter, 1982). The findings reported by Glaser, Fourné, and Elfring et al. (2015) suggest that a top-down approach to strategic renewal is most effective.

Sustained regeneration

An even less risky and more common approach is that of sustained regeneration (Kuratko & Audretsch, 2009). Sustained regeneration seeks to exploit a differentiation strategy (Porter, 1985) in order to gain competitive advantages. An organization or department pursuing sustained regeneration improves offerings and seeks to create or control market niches (Morris, Kuratko, & Covin, 2008). Large organizations are often more able than smaller firms to refine or improve their offerings. Big organizations produce more, they interact more often with customers and suppliers, learn more about their possibilities and opportunities, are more resourceful, and can more often reap benefits from economies of scale.

It is possible for some parts of an organization to pursue sustained regeneration through differentiation by offering new products and services or approaching new markets while other parts of the same organization do not. These new offerings can stem from a bottom-up initiative, but should align with the overall product portfolio and the policy of the organization in order to be accepted and incorporated in the production lines of the corporation. The more internal stakeholders that need to be involved, the more convincing the innovation champions need to be for the initiative to be successful. Sometimes the new product offerings are implemented in existing organizational structures and sometimes new organizational structures are created to support the new initiative.

Organizational rejuvenation

Organizational rejuvenation is based on cost leadership (Porter, 1985) as a competitive advantage. Organizational rejuvenation often entails changes to value chain activities (Dess, Ireland, Zahra, Floyd, Janney, & Lane, 2003). These initiatives can have a profound immediate impact on the organization. However, they may also include smaller routine improvements and enhanced efficiency schemas through micro changes (Höglund, 2011), since 'even small scale innovations initiated by individuals – "micro changes" – can eventually add up to "macro-changes"' (Kanter, 1984, p. 18). Such efforts are relatively common as the realm of the individual

employees' empowerment largely decides which initiatives the employee can implement without asking for resources or disturbing their co-workers.

The inclusion of minor individual 'intrapreneurial' initiatives does not exclude major routine improvements initiated and controlled from the top. The hierarchical level and, inherently, the work domain of the manager or worker decide which improvement cues the person perceives and feels responsible to act on. In the case where the innovation cue needs support from other organizational stakeholders it will turn into a political process about how the innovation cue is interpreted and acted on.

CE: Corporate Venturing

There are several ways in which new corporate venturing initiatives can be linked to the mother organization. A corporate venturing initiative can be organized as a new business entity, as a new project, or materialized as an entrepreneurial philosophy influencing parts of or the total organization. Johnson (2012) argues that the new venture's assignment has to be distinct from the mother company's existing business in order to be considered as corporate venturing. Internal corporate venturing is a process where new businesses are created by 'intrapreneurs' in the organization and subsequently owned by the organization (Kuratko, Covin, & Hornsby, 2014).

External corporate venturing refers to new businesses created outside organizations' borders and eventually incorporated into the organization in one way or another. In external corporate venturing the individuals in charge of the process are sometimes referred to as 'expreneurs' (Chang, 1998; Christensen, 2004). Cooperative or joint venturing occurs when two or more parent organizations combine their resources and create a new business (Kuratko et al., 2014). The literature on mergers and acquisitions discusses why and how firms obtain new technology through merging with or acquiring a company that already possesses the technology or entering into some sort of alliance (Lambe & Spekman, 1997).

Westhead, Wright, and McElwee (2011) include corporate venture capital initiatives under the corporate venturing umbrella. Lin and Lee (2011) show that firms that manage to increase their corporate venturing investments' diversity while maintaining strategic linkages add value to the investing firm's future growth. Corporate venture capital investments are direct minority equity investments made by established companies in privately held ventures (Basu, Phelps, & Kotha, 2011). The primary goal for corporate investors is usually strategic rather than merely financial returns (Allen & Hevert, 2007). Investments in emerging firms which possess high-growth potential innovations allow corporate investors to probe into new technologies (Maula, Keil, & Zahra, 2013). The choice of corporate venture capital investment modus depends on risk perceptions and learning aims. Separating the new venture from the corporate agenda fosters explorative learning, whereas tight integration may induce exploitative learning (Schildt, Maula, & Keil, 2005).

Larger organizations can mimic the advantages of smaller firms by dedicating separate organizational units to entrepreneurship through internal corporate venturing (Kollmann & Stöckmann, 2008). For the manager in charge of organizing such a business opportunity one major issue is the degree of structural autonomy suitable for the new venture (Garrett & Covin, 2013). This concerns the amount and type of managerial attention given to the new initiative and the allocation of resources. Other relevant issues are how to protect the new initiative from envy and the red tape of the mother organization, how information and knowledge should flow between the new venture and its mother organization, and how goals and achievements are determined and evaluated. The degree of structural autonomy has implications for how costs and revenues can be accounted for and measured. A higher degree of structural autonomy allows other incentive systems than in the mother organization.

From the employees' perspective, taking part in entrepreneurial ventures often entails higher job risk, pay risk, and demands more effort. It is usually more time-consuming than doing ordinary paid work. Incentive contracts may then induce a higher level of effort and risk-taking behavior in the corporate venturing team (Douglas & Shepherd, 2000). Monsen, Patzelt, and Saxton (2010) find that profit-sharing appears to be a good instrument to motivate employee participation in entrepreneurial venturing and they advise: 'As attracting employees to participate in corporate venturing is essential in dynamic environments, firms must recognize the complexity of the decision that employees face to volunteer for such posts, and must design not just pay but other job factors accordingly' (Monsen et al., 2010, pp. 120–1). Profit-sharing schemes do not just affect performance in the new venture. Biniari (2012) shows how affective reactions such as envy and lack of cooperation from significant employees in the mother organization influence the success of a new venture under different structural autonomy configurations.

Process Outcomes

The ultimate goal of engaging in a CE process is organizational survival and increased performance. As with regular entrepreneurship a central objective of CE is to create value. A central assumption is that increased performance is achieved by gaining competitive advantages through increasing organizations' innovative capacity and by exploiting innovations.

Rogers (1995, p. 11) defines an innovation as 'an idea, practice, or object that is perceived as new by an individual or other unit of adoption'. When an organization engages in CE, a desired output from the process is some kind of innovation. There are many different kinds of innovations. The type of innovation has implications for the way resources should be organized around the innovation in order to be exploited. Different types of innovations need different types of resources to be organized and structured in different ways. There is a high degree of overlap between research on innovation management and CE. Phan et al. (2009) argued for a clearer distinction between the two, emphasizing that CE processes are driven by market opportunities rather than new technologies.

Sometimes the innovation is groundbreaking, but most often it is only a modest improvement of what already has proven to work. We find innovations all along this continuum. Dewar and Dutton (1986) classify innovations as radical or incremental. This distinction is important since it determines the amount of resources needed to implement the innovation and the magnitude of change needed in the organization. The more radical the innovation, the more change takes place and the more resources are needed.

Daft and Becker (1978) distinguish between administrative and technical innovations. Many firms organize themselves in line and staff departments where line produces the goods sold and staff assist through back office support. Van De Veen, Polley, Garud, and Venkataraman (2008) point out that most innovations include both a technical and an administrative element. When an organization or an organizational unit of adoption adopts a technical innovation, the new technology often requires some routine changes in order to adjust to the new way of operation.

It is also possible to distinguish between externally oriented innovations, in the form of new products and markets to expand the business territory, and internally oriented innovations, such as new routines and procedures in order to reduce costs or enhance effectiveness. The innovation concept encompasses externally oriented innovations towards markets as well as internal improvements of routines. Porter (1985) suggests that firms can improve their competitive power

by diversifying away from their competitors by offering new products to new markets, or by achieving cost leadership through routine improvement.

Managerial and Organizational Issues

Many factors inside the organization can have an impact on CE processes. Below we focus on some of the most important factors and discuss the influence of stakeholders and the role of management, organizational culture, and resources.

Stakeholders

Many players are often involved in the CE process. Those who regularly interact with an organization and who depend on the output of the endeavor are called stakeholders. Stakeholders provide resources to an organized effort and they will then expect some rewards in return for this effort (Freeman, 1984). The main actors in the CE process, i.e. stakeholders, are owners, top managers, middle managers, workforce managers, and workers (Atkinson, Waterhouse, & Wells, 1997). A common overall goal shared by all these stakeholders is the survival of the organization. The different stakeholders have other goals in addition to this for their engagement (Coff, 1999). The owners would like to see that the firm produces shareholder profit, and the workforce would like to receive salaries and other benefits.

An organization or a project can only exist as long as this exchange of effort and benefit is balanced (Näsi, 1994). In addition, stakeholders need to have a common aim for the endeavor in order to persist with the said endeavor in the long run. Organizations, as well as the people who work there, have several, often inconsistent, goals. Sometimes an innovation can hamper or affect how these goals are achieved, leaving the implantation of an innovation to an uncertain organizational internal political process. Even if different stakeholders to some extent do have coherent overall goals, they do not always agree on all goals or the means to reach these goals. This can lead to a conflict amongst stakeholders as to the actions that are appropriate to reach the goal (Mitroff, 1983). As a result, stakeholders may well inherently pursue somewhat different types of objectives or expectations (Vaara, 1994).

Management

CE can be a strategic approach initiated and controlled by the top management team. Upper echelon literature has pointed to the role of top managers in strategy formation and the resulting organizational effects (Hambrick, 2007). A top-down perspective takes the corporate strategy put in place by top management as a point of departure. However, CE can also be a bottom-up approach. Domain redefinition and strategic renewal are most often top-down processes, while organizational rejuvenation, sustained regeneration, and intrapreneurship can be bottom-up processes. As domain redefinition and strategic renewal are strategic decisions concerning the total organization, they are usually top-down processes where top management provides directions to which other organizational members try to adjust and contribute. Key mechanisms in these processes are control and leadership.

The argument for investigating CE from a top-down perspective is that such initiatives have to be supported from top management in order to become a reality (Nielsen, Klyver, Rostgaard, & Bager, 2012). Using a top-down perspective, CE becomes a strategy where the top management team taps creativity from human resources in the organization. It is then the responsibility of the top management team to formulate and implement a strategy aimed at achieving the goals of the organization, as well as to evaluate the progress towards the strategic objectives (Kuratko, Hornsby, & Goldsby, 2004).

Dess et al. (2003) describe this process as creating consensus on the dominant logic: an agreement that change is needed and about the type of change needed. The top management team gives the initiative name and content. The management team assigns members, responsibilities, and resources to a CE group in charge of defining the problem. In turn, the venture team group suggests an innovation that solves the problem and implements the change. The role of top management is directing the innovation process and sponsoring the appropriate solution. This requires articulating a vision, gaining acceptance of this vision within the organization, and gaining congruence between the vision and the followers' self-interest. Top management bears a particular responsibility for creating an organizing architecture that facilitates the CE process.

The role of middle management is to implement, facilitate, and synthesize the process of innovation in the organization (Dess et al., 2003). Middle managers become the main contributors to CE (Kuratko, Ireland, & Hornsby, 2001). Middle managers can act as innovation champions, expressing enthusiasm and stamina and getting the right people involved (Howell, Shea, & Higgins, 2005). Employees should provide managers with innovation ideas for evaluation. New business ideas should be delegated to a person or a group of persons with the right set of skills and qualities in order to succeed with the task on behalf of the organization. Innovation champions can promote entrepreneurial initiatives by shielding the intrapreneurs from organizational norms and by acquisition of resources (Kanter, 1984).

Employees at the operational level are claimed to be the motor of autonomous strategic CE initiatives (Burgelman, 1983, p. 241). The bottom-up perspective takes the view that successful CE is created by organizational members with the enthusiasm and self-confidence that pulls the initiative through (Nielsen et al., 2012). These people are often referred to as 'intrapreneurs' (Pinchot & Pellman, 1999).

Combining a top-down and bottom-up approach has some advantages. Managers can provide employees with cues regarding the desirability of entrepreneurial initiatives, even if such initiatives are not actively requested by management. When employees offer suggestions or engage in a discussion about how to improve certain aspects of the business process of the firm, they learn more about the desired development path for the firm. This process is a dialogue rather than detached independent projects run by employees or a process totally controlled and planned by the top management team. The CE process thus becomes a form of interplay between the corporate strategy and employees' willingness to contribute. There is some empirical support for the claim that a combination of approaches can be useful. Åmo and Kolvereid (2005) investigated the effect of intrapreneurial personality and the presence of a strategic orientation towards CE formulated by top management on employee innovation behavior. Both intrapreneurial personality and CE strategy contributed to the explanation of innovative behavior, but a combination of these had a stronger effect than each factor alone.

Culture

A culture stimulates or blocks certain kinds of behavior, but it does not amount to behavior in itself. Culture, according to Schein (2010, p. 18), is a pattern of shared basic assumptions learned by a group as it solves its problems and corrects the group's way to perceive, think, and feel in relation to these problems. Business culture can be developed and nurtured by management in order to promote CE amongst its employees. In order for a firm to engage in CE managers should create a corporate culture or pro-entrepreneurship architecture where employees are encouraged to contribute with innovation (Crawford & Kreiser, 2015). Jones-Evans (2000) argues that managers cannot command entrepreneurial initiatives from their subordinates; people self-select and will only develop their ideas if proper organizational arrangements are offered.

Kuratko et al. (2014) identify five dimensions that are conducive to entrepreneurial behavior among employees: top management support, work autonomy, rewards, slack resources, and internal and external organizational boundaries that allow sharing of information. There need to be slack resources in order to allowing experimenting and the testing of ideas in a learning environment rich in information. Proactive employees risk facing organizational resistance from co-workers and managers who may feel their position threatened (Zahra, 2015). Therefore, employees committing effort to an innovation idea take personal risks. Managers wanting CE efforts from their employees should then actively ask for such initiatives, and ensure empowerment together with incentives to step forward.

Resources

The resources an organization controls are of central importance to the CE process. Entrepreneurship entails a process of creating value by combining resources in order to exploit an opportunity (Stevenson, Roberts, & Grousbeck, 1992). Barney (1991) defines resources as those assets, capabilities, processes, attributes, information, and knowledge controlled by an entity, thus enabling it to conceive and implement strategies that allow it to improve its competitive power. Resources can be grouped into human resources, financial resources, and operating resources. The resource base of the organization consists of the intellectual, operating, and financial capital that the organization controls, plus the sum of the human and social capital of its employees, together with the organizational architecture and business culture that allow it to exploit this sum of capital. Large organizations control more resources than small ones. Therefore, large organizations are more often capable of pulling off more radical innovations. However, large organizations often suffer from structural inertia, and are often more rigid and less dynamic. Larger organizations may have more stakeholders than smaller organizations that need to be involved in releasing and coordinating resources in order to build the necessary support system around an innovation.

Power and control over resources are important when engaging in intrapreneurship. Human capital as education, training, and business experience is a resource commonly linked to CE. The employees' human and social capital blended with the individuals' creativity, proactivity, and capability will tempt the organization to ask for entrepreneurial initiatives. Similarly, it is the vast array of resources controlled by the organization and available for the intrapreneurial employee that tempts the employee to pursue an innovation idea inside the organization instead of pursuing the business idea by starting an independent business outside the organization. The higher ranked the managers or workers are in the organization, the more resources they control. The more resourceful, the more capable they usually are in engaging in CE. This suggests that higher ranked employees more often engage in CE. Research also indicates that empowering work units working in complex and dynamic environments can enhance individuals' performance (D'Innocenzo, Luciano, Mathieu, Maynard, & Chen, 2016). The top management team can decide which level of empowerment different positions in the organizations have, allowing employees at different levels to contribute to the process.

CE depends on people. The actions of these people are influenced by many factors at different levels. At the individual level, people are different in skills, personality, motivation, background, and education. If we study CE from an organizational perspective, we see that people have different positions in the organization, where they have different responsibilities and powers and experience different expectations from their colleagues and managers regarding how they should respond to a given challenge. This explains then to a large extent their entrepreneurial behavior.

Issues in the Organizational Environment

Contingency theory suggests that there needs to be a fit between environment, organizational structure, and business strategy in order to obtain optimal performance (Miller, 1988). Some industries offer more challenges than other industries and some industrial sectors are richer with regard to opportunity cues than others. In a spatial perspective, national legislations and cultures also affect corporate entrepreneurial activity.

Industry

Scant research exists with regard to comparing and explaining differences in CE across different industries. Even so, some research does indicate that the industry the firm operates in also influences CE. For example, Davidsson, Kirchhoff, Hatemi, and Gustavsson (2002) link industry to differences in growth rates. Other scholars, for example Zahra (1996, 2012) and Sciascia, D'Oria, Bruni, and Larrañeta (2014) use industry as a control variable or concentrate their research on a single industry (Ahuja & Lampert, 2001; Phillips & Messersmith, 2013). The use of industry as a control variable suggests that industry itself may influence the choice of level and type of CE, and the outcomes associated with this choice. Some industries are more knowledge intensive with more empowered employees than other industries. Moreover, industries differ regarding competitive intensity, fragmentation, and technological turnover (Ireland, Covin, & Kuratko, 2009). Some industries are therefore more innovative than others (von Hippel, 1988).

Region

There are institutional environments (Scott, 1995) constituted in regional and national conditions as well that also influence the manifestations of CE. Gómez-Haro, Aragón-Correa, and Cordón-Pozo (2011) find regional differences within the country of

Spain regarding entrepreneurship in established firms. They put these differences down to the regulatory, cognitive, and normative institutional frameworks (Scott, 1995) in which these firms operate and argue that the normative and the cognitive dimensions both influence entrepreneurial orientation while the regulatory dimension influences the type of entrepreneurial activity the organization involves itself in.

Country

Others have investigated how national culture and institutional frameworks influence aspects of CE. Turró, Urbano, and Peris-Ortiz (2014) found that living in an entrepreneurial culture where the media exposes entrepreneurship positively contributes to CE. They also found that institutional factors such as bureaucracy and access to finance influence CE. Morris, Davis, and Allen (1994) found that Hofstede's (1980) individualism–collectivism contributed to explaining CE in their study of how CE differs between Portugal, the USA, and South Africa. Further, Bosma, Stam, and Wennekers (2011) found a negative correlation between intrapreneurship and early-stage independent entrepreneurial activity at the macro level. They also revealed that the prevalence of intrapreneurship is about twice as high in high-income countries than in low-income countries.

FUTURE RESEARCH

We structure our suggestions for future research on CE according to our conceptual model in Figure 14.1, and start with suggestions for research on CE inputs, followed by CE processes, outcomes, and contextual issues.

Research on CE Inputs

Baron (2006) asks for studies that investigate why some people, but not others, identify specific opportunities and how to train people to be better in recognizing opportunities. Related to this, there is a call for studying CE from a learning organization perspective (Zahra, 2015). Recognizing that CE is a knowledge and conversation process, research on CE can also gain from investigating the transformative process from knowledge into business activity. If we knew more about what taking part in CE processes does to the knowledge base of the employee, we might learn more about how such processes can be managed and stimulated. We need to know more about how it builds experiences, skills, and entrepreneurial confidence in employees individually and as a group.

We have previously argued that the current EO framework does not link strongly to entrepreneurial learning (Wang, 2008). Entrepreneurial learning is a central element in opportunity creation (Nielsen et al., 2012). Therefore, more scholarly work on extending the EO construct is needed in order to increase its usefulness in studies of CE. The Bloodgood et al. (2015) study with their entrepreneurial insight construct could inspire such theoretical developments.

Another theoretical issue associated with entrepreneurial learning relates to whether the individual or the organization is the proper level of analysis. Wang (2008) advises researchers who investigate learning in micro and small firms to build theory that takes account of individual entrepreneurs' learning when studying organizational learning, as the individual and the firm are often very much the same thing – for small firms.

In their review of 109 studies on human capital and entrepreneurship, Marvel, Davis, and Sproul (2016) also raise the issue of analysis level. They notice that firm-level human capital has usually been treated as an extension of individual-level human capital, missing the importance of managed inter-individual interaction present in transforming human capital into knowledge and abilities relative to organizational competencies. They further argue that an increased understanding of such processes is needed within the CE research field. This implies a need for revisiting the human capital construct and building understandings on how firm-level human capital constructs a link to elements of CE. The Marvel et al. (2016) review also raises methodological issues as they find that general measures of investments in human capital are commonly employed in CE research. They recommend future research to focus on the usefulness of human capital and not its mere presence. They believe that authors often oversimplify human capital and mask its influence on entrepreneurial performance.

Research on CE Processes

Heinonen and Toivonen (2008) claim that balancing top-down management and bottom-up initiatives through control and autonomy is a major challenge for managers. Current research provides little advice about how this balance should be handled in order to reap the full benefit of employee innovation initiatives. Research in intrapreneurship should help us to understand more about how opportunities are identified, how employees search for solutions to the opportunities, how they gather resources in order to test out their visionary solutions, and how they build alliances and seek protection from the bureaucracy of the firm (Nielsen et al., 2012).

Zahra, Filatotchev, and Wright (2009) ask how CE evolves over time within an organization. We do not know much about what firms do to implement their decision to adopt a CE strategy. We still do not know what kind of firms adopt CE and how they make this decision. As an organization evolves over time, its perception of risks and how it handles risks changes. Organizational informality evolves into more formal approaches to tasks and relationships and delegation becomes more prominent. This has consequences for how the organization relates to entrepreneurship over time (Kuratko, Morris, & Schindehutte, 2015b). Similarly, there is

a call for research on how and why corporate venture unit activity and roles evolve over time (Hill & Birkinshaw, 2008). There could be hidden development paths that, once unveiled, could be leapfrogged, allowing firms to reach higher levels of competitive advantages faster.

Business model innovation studies are limited to the context of large, leading firms, leaving such studies in small and medium enterprises largely unexplored despite their contribution to the economy (Cucculelli & Bettinelli, 2015). Kuratko et al. (2015a) also call for scholarly work contributing to an improved understanding of the SME sector and their involvement in CE. The corporate entrepreneurial process is likely to differ between small and micro firms and larger firms due to their differing managerial challenges (Greiner, 1972), and how they organize for control and governance.

We need to learn how family firms differ from other firms with regard to CE. Specifics of a family culture (Burns, 2011) might influence the processes leading to CE as well as its manifestations and the desired outcomes. Recent research argues that family firm and CE literature would gain from informing one another (McKelvie, McKenney, Lumpkin, & Short, 2014). Strategic management in family businesses might differ from non-family businesses based upon their system of governance and the influence of family culture, their unique stock of resources, and their distinct agency issues.

Research on mergers and acquisitions focuses on strategic fit, organizational fit, and how and why such processes fail or succeed (Cartwright & Schoenberg, 2006). Research on corporate venturing could be fertilized by this rich literature about mergers and acquisitions as corporate venturing investigates how an established business organizes and links a new business initiative to its existing operations. Firms conduct external corporate venturing as mergers and acquisitions to enable exploitation of new business opportunities (Ireland & Webb, 2007). This is the case even as acquisitions very often fail to achieve the desired results for the acquiring firm (Koryak, Mole, Lockett, Hayton, Ucbasaran, & Hodgkinson, 2015). Small firms may benefit from the existence of private information in the valuation of companies (Lockett, Wiklund, Davidsson, & Girma, 2011), while larger firms are more resourceful and more able to bridge sense-making from one acquisition process to the next (Brueller, Carmeli, & Drori, 2014).

Much research on CE equals the opinion of the CEO on the homogeneously experienced overall corporate culture. This does not take account of important diverging sub-cultures and personal experiences among the middle managers and workers who usually translate the corporate strategy into action. Similarly, asking the employees, co-workers or managers also introduces measurement issues. As managers and colleagues do not necessarily know or appreciate the entrepreneurial effort of a co-worker (Dess & Lumpkin, 2005), it is challenging to measure this by asking managers and colleagues (Zahra, 2015). Rodell and Lynch (2016) report that colleagues gave credit to employees volunteering when they attributed this to intrinsic reasons and stigmatized employees when they believed the initiative was to impress management. Using the employee as the respondent of course adds social desirability, at least, to the equation. Heinonen and Toivonen (2008) further argue that the interpretation and understanding of the experienced CE phenomenon depend on whether the management or the individual perspective is taken as the starting point in the analysis.

Crawford and Kreiser (2015) argue that CE processes are highly skewed to the right, i.e. a small proportion of the population possesses the ability to act truly entrepreneurially. This implies that outliers become the most important and useful cases for researchers to study as these individuals or firms will wield a disproportionate influence on the outcome. This insight will influence how measurements should be constructed as well

as how we define our population of objects to study. Another methodological issue raised by Ireland et al. (2009) is that CE strategies may not be stable and are thus difficult to capture empirically.

Research on CE Outputs

There are also some troublesome conceptual issues related to the definition of innovation. We do not call it an innovation unless it is already a success (Van de Veen et al., 2008). Innovation is something that *has* succeeded; failed attempts are nameless. Hence, we have no system for studying failures, indicating that it is difficult to study how innovation relates to success. There is a need to develop intellectual tools that allow us to see the dark side of the moon, i.e. innovation efforts that have failed (Bloodgood et al., 2015). Kim and Pennings (2009) demonstrate in their study of strategic renewal in the tennis racket industry that only a small proportion of introduced innovative products become an immediate success. They find failed innovations that evoked new mental dispositions and behavioral practices that later on gave cues to industry revolutions benefiting the firm that introduced the failed innovation. This issue relates to how long we should wait before we measure the accumulated costs and benefits. If we measure this too soon, we may miss many of the benefits. If we wait too long, the results become uninteresting – as there is nothing to learn from them. The context has changed and the world has moved on. Similarly, not all results are easily and accurately accounted for. Some failures result in organizational learning that is utilized in later successes. Measuring success introduces measurement problems, as it is difficult to separate all the costs and revenues related to an innovation initiative from the mother organization.

The discussion about goals for engaging in CE mainly focuses on reaching financial goals. However, corporate actors pursue other goals in addition to financial goals. There are also issues related to stakeholders' goals regarding CE that have methodological implications. The multitude of stakeholders and the organizational political bargaining inherent in and affecting the CE process raise issues about who to ask when claiming success.

Research on CE Contexts

Kollman and Stöckmann (2008) ask which environmental and organizational conditions call organizations to engage in CE. They claim that, even if we know a great deal about how organizations arrange themselves in order to be able to conduct different CE activities, we do not know much about how firms develop a desire to engage in CE in the first place. We do not fully know what causes firms to move beyond the 'brink' and start seeing CE as the answer to their perceived problem.

There is considerable empirical evidence for a positive relationship between CE and organizational performance. Bierwerth, Schwens, Isidor, and Kabst (2015) synthesized the findings from 43 different samples. Their results revealed that strategic renewal, innovation, and corporate venturing positively influence subjective as well as objective organizational performance. The effect of innovation on performance was particularly strong in high-tech industries, suggesting that industry plays an important role in the expected outcomes of engaging in CE. Even so, there are still research possibilities in relation to how industry influences conditions for CE. Industries differ as to how knowledge intensive they are, some industries depend more on knowledgeable and empowered employees than other industries, and industries differ regarding competitive intensity, fragmentation, and technological turnover, implying different conditions for CE.

Recent research asks if there are cultural differences shaping how opportunities are perceived and acted upon (Short et al., 2010). Amongst those addressing this issue are Bosma, Wennekers, Guerrero, Amorós,

Martiarena, and Singer (2013). They show substantial national differences regarding continued entrepreneurship, indicating that there are research opportunities in the field to explain how different national cultures and legal structures can affect these differences, reaching beyond our current understanding.

Despite the increasing academic interest in international entrepreneurship there are underexplored issues linked to CE and internationalization. In an increasingly globalized world, there is an issue related to CE that has received less attention than deserved. There is a lack of research as to how international organizations utilize different institutional or national frameworks in order to increase their stock of innovation initiatives, and how they seek to cross-fertilize between their international subdivisions.

There are calls for studies of CE that have methodological implications. Westhead et al. (2011) ask for more large-sample studies in order to tease out the interplay between environment, diverse types of CE, and financial performance. The wide variety of manifestations of corporate entrepreneurial activity, as well as the many influences on such behavior, call for considerations on sample selection as well as on sample size. Another methodological issue is raised by Zahra (1991) when he asks for studies taking account of the lag effect that might exist between antecedent variables and entrepreneurship. This has implications for how we measure cause and effect, and implies a call for more longitudinal studies. Hence, Kwee et al. (2011) ask for longitudinal studies of strategic renewal in order to capture the contribution from the organizational antecedents.

The current framework of CE is developed for private organizations. This leads Kuratko et al. (2015a) to ask for research on CE to be extended into the public and non-profit sector. The public and non-profit sector is large in many countries and makes substantial contributions to the well-being of the population. The entrepreneurship processes within these types of organizations are not completely understood yet. We might expect these processes to differ from CE processes in the private sector as the goals of the organization and its stakeholders differ from those in the private sector.

CONCLUSION

In this chapter we have referred to CE as entrepreneurship within established organizations. A central element of the CE process is that members of the organization structure resources in order to exploit opportunities to achieve organizational renewal and competitive advantages through innovation. The process is triggered by entrepreneurial insight and the organization's ability to discover or create opportunities. CE initiatives include various forms of strategic entrepreneurship and corporate venturing. The key outputs from the process are innovations and subsequently organizational renewal, believed to increase competitiveness and organizational performance. The CE process is influenced by a number of contextual factors, both internal and external to the organization.

Our general, quite abstract, model of CE, is of course a simplification of reality. Organizations are faced with many different opportunities, and it is a challenging task to determine which opportunities to pursue. The choice between different types of strategies of entrepreneurship and corporate venturing is also complicated. The fact that there are many different types of innovations, organizations, resources, and contexts also complicates matters. We have chosen to focus on a few aspects of the CE process that we believe are important.

It hampers research that the CE phenomenon is so complex and contains so many subcategories. The distinction between the subcategories is fuzzy and there are challenging measurement issues. In their review of current CE studies, Nason, McKelvie, and Lumpkin (2015) argue that most researchers investigate CE under a uniform umbrella without focusing on a specific phenomenon. Ireland et al. (2009) stress the lack of research on different manifestations of CE outcomes.

Not all research studies state their presumptions and explicitly detail their contexts. This makes it difficult to compare research findings and subtract the overlying learning. We need more precise definitions to limit the type of activity we study so that we know what we see. We also need more knowledge about CE issues in order to better prepare students to become 'intrapreneurs' or champions of CE processes and innovations in organizations.

REFERENCES

Agarwal, R. and Helfat, C.E. (2009) 'Strategic renewal of organizations', *Organization Science*, 20(2): 281–293.

Ahuja, G. and Lampert, M.C. (2001) 'Entrepreneurship in the large corporation: Longitudinal study of how established firms create breakthrough inventions', *Strategic Management Journal*, 22(6–7): 521–543.

Allen, S.A. and Hevert, K.T. (2007) 'Venture capital investing by information technology companies: Did it pay?', *Journal of Business Venturing*, 22(2): 262–282.

Åmo, B.W. and Kolvereid, L. (2005) 'Organizational strategy, individual personality and innovation behavior', *Journal of Enterprising Culture*, 13(1): 7–19.

Atkinson, A.A., Waterhouse, J.J., and Wells, R.B. (1997) 'A stakeholder approach to strategic performance measurements', *Sloan Management Review*, 38(3): 25–37.

Baden-Fuller, C. (1995) 'Strategic innovation, corporate entrepreneurship and matching outside-in to inside-out approaches to strategy research', *British Journal of Management*, 6(1): 3–16.

Barney, J. (1991) 'Firm resources and sustained competitive advantage', *Journal of Management*, 17(1): 99–120.

Baron, R.A. (2006) 'Opportunity recognition as pattern recognition: How entrepreneurs "Connect the dots" to identify new business opportunities', *Academy of Management Perspectives,* 20(1): 104–119.

Basu, S., Phelps, C., and Kotha, S. (2011) 'Towards understanding who makes corporate venture capital investments and why', *Journal of Business Venturing*, 26(2): 153–171.

Bierwerth, M., Schwens, C., Isidor, R., and Kabst, R. (2015) 'Corporate entrepreneurship and performance: A meta-analysis', *Small Business Economics*, 45(2): 255–278.

Biniari, M.G. (2012) 'The emotional embeddedness of corporate entrepreneurship: The case of envy', *Entrepreneurship Theory and Practice*, 36(1): 141–170.

Birkinshaw, J. (1997) 'Entrepreneurship in multinational corporations: The characteristics of subsidiary initiatives', *Strategic Management Journal*, 18(3): 207–229.

Bloodgood, J.M., Hornsby, J.S., Burkemper, A.C., and Saroogh, H. (2015) 'A system dynamic perspective of organizational entrepreneurship', *Small Business Economics*, 45(2): 393–402.

Borch, O.J., Huse, M., and Senneseth, K. (1999) 'Resource configuration, competitive strategies, and corporate entrepreneurship: An empirical examination of small firms', *Entrepreneurship Theory and Practice*, 24(1): 49–70.

Bosma, N.S., Stam, E., and Wennekers, S. (2011) 'Intrapreneurship versus independent entrepreneurship: A cross-national analysis of individual entrepreneurial behavior', *Tjalling C. Koopmans Institute Discussion Paper Series*, 11(4): 1–32.

Bosma, N.S., Wennekers, S., Guerrero, M., Amorós, J.E., Martiarena, A., and Singer, S. (2013) Global Entrepreneurship Monitor: Special report on entrepreneurial employee activity. GERA: London.

Brueller, N.N., Carmeli, A., and Drori, I. (2014) 'How do different types of mergers and acquisitions facilitate strategic agility?' *California Management Review*, 56(3): 39–57.

Burgelman, R.A. (1983) 'A process model of internal corporate venturing in the diversified major firm', *Administrative Science Quarterly*, 28(2): 223–244.

Burns, P. (2011) *Entrepreneurship and small business: Start-up, growth & maturity*, 3rd ed. New York: Palgrave Macmillan.

Cartwright, S. and Schoenberg, R. (2006) 'Thirty years of mergers and acquisitions research: Recent advances and future opportunities', *British Journal of Management*, 17(1): 1–5.

Chang, J. (1998) 'Model of corporate entrepreneurship: Intrapreneurship and exopreneurship', *Borneo Review*, (9)2: 187–213.

Christensen, K.S. (2004) 'A classification of the corporate entrepreneurship umbrella: Labels and perspectives', *International Journal of Management and Enterprise Development*, 1(4): 301–315.

Coff, R.W. (1999) 'When competitive advantage doesn't lead to performance: The resource-based view and stakeholder bargaining power', *Organization Science*, 10(2): 119–133.

Covin, J.G. and Lumpkin, G.T. (2011) 'Entrepreneurial orientation theory and research: Reflections on a needed construct', *Entrepreneurship Theory and Practice*, 35(5): 855–872.

Covin, J. and Miles, M. (1999) 'Corporate entrepreneurship and the pursuit of competitive advantages', *Entrepreneurship Theory and Practice*, 23(3): 47–63.

Covin, J.G. and Slevin, D.P. (2002) 'The entrepreneurial imperatives of strategic leadership'. In M.A. Hitt, R.D. Ireland, S.M. Camp and D.L. Sexton (Eds), *Strategic entrepreneurship: Creating a new mindset*. Oxford: Blackwell Publishers, 309–327.

Crawford, G.C. and Kreiser, P.M. (2015) 'Corporate entrepreneurship strategy: Extending the integrative framework through the lens of complexity science', *Small Business Economics*, 45(3): 403–423.

Cucculelli, M. and Bettinelli, C. (2015) 'Business models, intangibles and firm performance: Evidence on corporate entrepreneurship from Italian manufacturing SMEs', *Small Business Economics*, 45(2): 329–350.

D'Innocenzo, L., Luciano, M.M., Mathieu, J.E., Maynard, M.T., and Chen, G. (2016) 'Empowered to perform: A multilevel investigation of the influence of empowerment on performance in hospital units', *Academy of Management Journal*, 59(4), 1290–1307.

Daft, R.L. and Becker, S. (1978) *Innovations in organizations*. New York: Elsevier.

Davidsson, P., Kirchhoff, B., Hatemi, J.A., and Gustavsson, H. (2002) 'Empirical analysis of business growth factors using Swedish data', *Journal of Small Business Management*, 40(4): 332–349.

Dess, G.G. and Lumpkin, G.T. (2005) 'The role of entrepreneurial orientation in stimulating effective corporate entrepreneurship', *The Academy of Management Executive*, 19(1): 147–156.

Dess, G.G., Ireland, R.D., Zahra, S.A., Floyd, S.W., Janney, J.J., and Lane, P.J. (2003) 'Emerging issues in corporate entrepreneurship', *Journal of Management*, 29(3): 351–378.

Dewar, R.D. and Dutton, J.E. (1986) 'The adoption of radical and incremental innovations: An empirical analysis', *Management Science*, 31(11): 1422–1433.

Douglas, E.J. and Shepherd, D.A. (2000) 'Entrepreneurship as a utility maximizing response', *Journal of Business Venturing*, 15(3): 231–251.

Finkle, T.A. (2012) 'Corporate entrepreneurship and innovation in Silicon Valley: The case of Google, Inc.', *Entrepreneurship Theory and Practice*, 36(4): 863–884.

Freeman, R.E. (1984) *Strategic management: A stakeholder approach*. Marchfield, MA: Pitman Publishing.

Garrett, R.P. and Covin, J.G. (2013) 'Internal corporate venture operations independence and performance: A knowledge-based perspective', *Entrepreneurship Theory and Practice*, 39(4): 763–790.

Glaser, L., Fourné, S.P., and Elfring, T. (2015) 'Achieving strategic renewal: The multi-level influences of top and middle managers' boundary-spanning', *Small Business Economics*, 45(2): 305–327.

Gómez-Haro, S., Aragón-Correa, J.A., and Cordón-Pozo, E. (2011) 'Differentiating the effects of the institutional environment on corporate entrepreneurship', *Management Decision*, 49(10): 1677–1693.

Greiner, L. (1972) 'Evolution and revolution as organizations grow', *Harvard Business Review*, 50(4): 37–46.

Guth, W.D. and Ginsberg, A. (1990) 'Guest editors' introduction: Corporate entrepreneurship', *Strategic Management Journal*, 11(4): 5–15.

Hambrick, D.C. (2007) 'Upper echelons theory: An update', *Academy of Management Review,* 32(4): 334–343.

Hayton, J.C. and Kelley, D.J. (2006) 'A competency-based framework for promoting corporate entrepreneurship', *Human Resource Management*, 45(3): 407–428.

Heinonen, J. and Toivonen, J. (2008) 'Corporate entrepreneurs or silent followers?', *Leadership & Organization Development Journal*, 29(7): 583–599.

Hill, S.A. and Birkinshaw, J. (2008) 'Strategy–organization configurations in corporate venture units: Impact on performance and survival', *Journal of Business Venturing*, 23(4): 423–444.

Hofstede, G. (1980) *Culture's consequences: International differences in work-related values*. London: Sage.

Höglund, L. (2011) 'Entrepreneurship in established firms from a strategic entrepreneurship perspective'. In E. Segelod, K. Berglund, E. Bjurström, E. Dahlquist, L. Hallèn and U. Johanson (Eds), *Studies in industrial renewal*. Sweden: Mälardalen University Press, 317–327.

Howell, J.M., Shea, C.M., and Higgins, C.A. (2005) 'Champions of product innovations: Defining, developing, and validating a measure of champion behavior', *Journal of Business Venturing*, 20(5): 641–661.

Ireland, R.D. and Webb, J.W. (2007) 'Strategic entrepreneurship: Creating competitive advantage through streams of innovation', *Business Horizons*, 50(1): 49–59.

Ireland, R.D., Covin, J.G., and Kuratko, D.F. (2009) 'Conceptualizing corporate entrepreneurship strategy', *Entrepreneurship Theory and Practice*, 33(1): 19–46.

Ireland, R.D., Hitt, M.A., and Sirmon, D.G. (2003) 'A model of strategic entrepreneurship: The construct and its dimensions', *Journal of Management*, 29(6): 963–989.

Johnson, K.L. (2012) 'The role of structural and planning autonomy in the performance of internal corporate ventures', *Journal of Small Business Management*, 50(3): 469–497.

Jones-Evans, D. (2000) 'Intrapreneurship'. In S. Carter and D. Jones-Evans (Eds), *Enterprise and small business*. New York: Prentice Hall, 242–258.

Kanter, R.M. (1984) *The change master.* New York: Simon & Schuster.

Kim, H.E. and Pennings, J.M. (2009) 'Innovation and strategic renewal in mature markets: A study of the tennis racket industry', *Organization Science*, 20(2): 368–383.

Kim, W.C. and Mauborgne, R. (2005) *Blue ocean strategy*. MA: Harvard Business Review Press.

Kollmann, T. and Stöckmann, C. (2008) 'Corporate entrepreneurship'. In C. Wankel (Ed.), *21st century management: A reference handbook*. Thousand Oaks, CA: Sage Publications, Inc, 11–21.

Koryak, O., Mole, K.F., Lockett, A., Hayton, J.C., Ucbasaran, D., and Hodgkinson, G.P. (2015) 'Entrepreneurial leadership, capabilities and firm growth', *International Small Business Journal*, 33(1): 89–105.

Kuratko, D.F. and Audretsch, D.B. (2009) 'Strategic entrepreneurship: Exploring different perspectives of an emerging concept', *Entrepreneurship Theory and Practice*, 33(1): 1–17.

Kuratko, D.F., Covin, J.G., and Hornsby, J.S. (2014) 'Why implementing corporate innovation is so difficult', *Business Horizons*, 57(5): 647–655.

Kuratko, D.F., Hornsby, J.S., and Goldsby, M.G. (2004) 'Sustaining corporate entrepreneurship: Modelling perceived implementation and outcome at organizational and individual level', *Entrepreneurship and Innovation*, 5(2): 77–89.

Kuratko, D.F., Hornsby, J.S., and Hayton, J. (2015a) 'Corporate entrepreneurship: The innovative challenge for a new global economic reality', *Small Business Economics*, 45(2): 245–253.

Kuratko, D.F., Ireland, R.D., and Hornsby, J.S. (2001) 'Improving firm performance through entrepreneurial actions: Acordia's corporate entrepreneurship strategy', *The Academy of Management Executive*, 15(4): 60–71.

Kuratko, D.F., Morris, M.H., and Schindehutte, M. (2015b) 'Understanding the dynamics of entrepreneurship through framework approaches', *Small Business Economics*, 45(1): 1–13.

Kwee, Z., Van Den Bosch, F.A.J., and Volberda, H.W. (2011) 'The influence of top management teams on corporate governance orientation on strategic renewal trajectories: A longitudinal analysis of Royal Dutch Shell plc, 1907–2004', *Journal of Management Studies*, 48(5): 984–1014.

Lambe, C.J. and Spekman, R.E. (1997) 'Alliances, external technology acquisition, and discontinuous technological change', *Journal of Product Innovation Management*, 14(2): 102–116.

Lanza, A. and Passarelli, M. (2014) 'Technology change and dynamic entrepreneurial capabilities', *Journal of Small Business Management*, 52(3): 427–450.

Lin, S.J. and Lee, J.R. (2011) 'Configuring a corporate venturing portfolio to create growth value: Within-portfolio diversity and strategic linkage', *Journal of Business Venturing*, 26(4): 489–503.

Lockett, A., Wiklund, J., Davidsson, P., and Girma, S. (2011) 'Organic and acquisitive growth: Re-examining, testing and extending Penrose's growth theory', *Journal of Management Studies*, 48(1): 48–74.

Lumpkin, G.T. and Dess, G.G. (1996) 'Clarifying the entrepreneurial orientation construct and linking it to performance', *Academy of Management Review*, 21(1): 135–172.

Macpherson, A. and Jones, O. (2008) 'Object mediated learning and strategic renewal in a mature organization', *Management Learning*, 39(2): 177–201.

Marvel, M.R., Davis, J.L., and Sproul, C.R. (2016). 'Human capital and entrepreneurship research: A critical review and future directions', *Entrepreneurship Theory and Practice*, 40(3): 599–626.

Maula, M.V., Keil, T., and Zahra, S.A. (2013) 'Top management's attention to discontinuous technological change: Corporate venture capital as an alert mechanism', *Organization Science*, 24(3): 926–947.

McKelvie, A., McKenney, A.F., Lumpkin, G.T., and Short, J.C. (2014) 'Corporate entrepreneurship in family businesses: Past contributions and future opportunities'. In L. Melin, M. Nordqvist and P. Sharma (Eds), *SAGE Handbook of family business*. London: Sage, 340–363.

Miles, M.P. and Covin, J.G. (2002) 'Exploring the practice of corporate venturing: Some common forms and their organizational implications', *Entrepreneurship Theory and Practice*, 26(3): 21–40.

Miller, D. (1988) 'Relating Porter's business strategies to environment and structure: Analysis and performance implications',

Academy of Management Journal, 31(2): 280–308.

Mitroff, I.I. (1983) *Stakeholders of the organizational mind*. San Francisco, CA: Jossey-Bass Publishers.

Monsen, E., Patzelt, H., and Saxton, T. (2010) 'Beyond simple utility: Incentive design and trade-offs for corporate employee-entrepreneurs', *Entrepreneurship Theory and Practice*, 34(1): 105–130.

Morris, M.H., Davis, D.L., and Allen, J.W. (1994) 'Fostering corporate entrepreneurship: Cross-cultural comparisons of the importance of individualism versus collectivism', *Journal of International Business Studies*, 25(1): 65–89.

Morris, M.H., Kuratko, D.F., and Covin, J.G. (2008) *Corporate entrepreneurship and innovation*. South Western: Thomson Higher Education.

Morris, M.H., Webb, J.W., and Franklin, R.J. (2011) 'Understanding the manifestation of entrepreneurial orientation in the nonprofit context', *Entrepreneurship Theory and Practice*, 35(5): 947–971.

Näsi, J. (1994) 'What is stakeholder thinking? A snapshot of a social theory of the firm'. In J. Näsi (Ed.), *Understanding stakeholder thinking*. Helsinki: LSR-Publications, 19–31.

Nason, R.S., McKelvie, A., and Lumpkin, G.T. (2015) 'The role of organizational size in the heterogeneous nature of corporate entrepreneurship', *Small Business Economics*, 45(2): 279–304.

Nelson, R.R. and Winter, S.G. (1982) *An evolutionary theory of economic change*. Cambridge, MA: Belknap Press of Harvard University Press.

Nielsen, S.L., Klyver, K., Rostgaard, M., and Bager, T. (2012) *Entrepreneurship in theory and practice: Paradoxes in play*. Cheltenham: Edward Elgar.

Phan, P., Wright, M., Ucbasaran, D., and Tan, W. (2009) 'Corporate entrepreneurship: current research and future directions', *Journal of Business Venturing*, 24(3): 197–205.

Phillips, J.M. and Messersmith, J.G. (2013) 'Are professional service firms uniquely suited for corporate entrepreneurship? A theoretical model connecting professional service intensity and corporate entrepreneurship', *Journal of Business and Entrepreneurship*, 24(2): 79–96.

Pinchot, G. and Pellman, R. (1999) *Intrapreneuring in action: A handbook for business innovation*. San Francisco, CA: Berrett-Koehler Publishers.

Porter, M.E. (1985) *Competitive advantage*. New York: The Free Press.

Rodell, J.B. and Lynch, J.W. (2016) 'Perceptions of employee volunteering: Is it "credited" or "stigmatized" by colleagues?', *Academy of Management Journal*, 59(2), 611–635.

Rogers, E.M. (1995) *Diffusion of innovations*. 4th ed., New York: The Free Press.

Schein, E.H. (2010) *Organizational culture and leadership* (Vol. 2). New York: John Wiley & Sons.

Schildt, H.A., Maula, M.V., and Keil, T. (2005) 'Explorative and exploitative learning from external corporate ventures', *Entrepreneurship Theory and Practice*, 29(4): 493–515.

Sciascia, S., D'Oria, L., Bruni, M., and Larrañeta, B. (2014) 'Entrepreneurial orientation in low-and medium-tech industries: The need for absorptive capacity to increase performance', *European Management Journal*, 32(5): 761–769.

Scott, W.R. (1995) *Institutions and organizations*. Thousand Oaks, CA: Sage.

Sharma, P. and Chrisman, J.J. (1999) 'Toward a reconciliation of the definitional issues in the field of corporate entrepreneurship', *Entrepreneurship Theory and Practice*, 23(3): 11–17.

Short, J.C., Ketchen, D.J., Combs, J.G., and Ireland, R.D. (2010) 'Research methods in entrepreneurship opportunities and challenges', *Organizational Research Methods*, 13(1): 6–15.

Stevenson, H., Roberts, M., and Grousbeck, H.I. (1992) *New business ventures and the entrepreneur*. Chicago, IL: Irwin Publishing.

Tripsas, M. (2009) 'Technology, identity, and inertia: Through the lens of "The Digital Photography Company"', *Organizational Science*, 20(2), 441–460.

Turró, A., Urbano, D., and Peris-Ortiz, M. (2014) 'Culture and innovation: The moderating effect of cultural values on corporate entrepreneurship', *Technological Forecasting and Social Change*, 88(1): 360–369.

Vaara, E. (1994) 'Linking social construction of success and stakeholder thinking: An analysis of a merger case'. In J. Näsi (Ed.),

Understanding stakeholder thinking. Helsinki: LSR-Publications, 215–235.

Van de Veen, A.H., Polley, D.E., Garud, R., and Venkataraman, S. (2008) *The innovation journey*. New York: Oxford University Press Inc.

Von Hippel, E. (1988) *The sources of innovation*. New York: Oxford University Press.

Vozikis, G.S., Bruton, G.D., Prasad, D., and Merikas, A.A. (1999) 'Linking corporate entrepreneurship to financial theory through additional value creation', *Entrepreneurship Theory and Practice*, 24(2): 33–44.

Wang, C.L. (2008) 'Entrepreneurial orientation, learning orientation, and firm performance', *Entrepreneurship Theory and Practice*, 32(4): 635–656.

Westhead, P., Wright, M., and McElwee, G. (2011) *Entrepreneurship: Perspectives and cases*. New York: Prentice Hall.

Zahra, S.A. (1991) 'Predictors and outcomes of corporate entrepreneurship: An exploratory study', *Journal of Business Venturing*, 6(4): 259–285.

Zahra, S.A. (1996) 'Governance, ownership, and corporate entrepreneurship: The moderating impact of industry technological opportunities', *Academy of Management Journal*, 39(6): 1713–1735.

Zahra, S.A. (2012) 'Organizational learning and entrepreneurship in family firms: Exploring the moderating effect of ownership and cohesion', *Small Business Economics*, 38(1): 51–65.

Zahra, S.A. (2015) 'Corporate entrepreneurship as knowledge creation and conversation: The role of entrepreneurial hubs', *Small Business Economics*, 44(4): 727–735.

Zahra, S.A., Filatotchev, I., and Wright, M. (2009) 'How do threshold firms sustain corporate entrepreneurship? The role of boards and absorptive capacity', *Journal of Business Venturing*, 24(3): 248–260.

15

Entrepreneurship, Innovation and Small Business

Mark Freel

INTRODUCTION

The prevailing idea that entrepreneurship and innovation are strongly associated with new and small firms owes much to Schumpeter's (1934) early identification of new firms as the primary sources of new combinations in competitive capitalism. This is often termed 'Schumpeter Mark I' (e.g. Malerba & Orsenigo, 1995; Nelson & Winter, 1982) and represents a 'widening' pattern of innovation (Breschi, Malerba & Orsenigo, 2000). Here, innovation activities are diffused; the source of innovation frequently changes; the prospects of innovators fluctuate; innovative entry is commonplace; and, crucially, innovators are typically of small economic size.

This is the Schumpeter who takes pride of place in our undergraduate entrepreneurship classes and in our textbooks. Leveraging new ideas, new products or new processes, entrepreneurs enter an industry, launch new enterprises and challenge incumbent firms. This process undermines existing ways of producing, organising and distributing and competes away profits associated with previous innovations. It is the process of 'creative destruction' that situates the entrepreneur as 'the pivot on which everything turns' (Schumpeter, 1954, p. 555). It is concerned with substantial changes and not with incremental innovation (Hagedoorn, 1996) and it figures large when we talk about entrepreneurship (Gartner, 1990).

Yet, as it appears in the entrepreneurship literature, it is generally ahistorical. It elides Schumpeter's (1942) later change of emphasis. If our 'early' Schumpeter was influenced by nineteenth-century business cycles and European industrial structure, this 'later' Schumpeter – Schumpeter Mark II – was inspired by characteristics of American industry in the first half of the twentieth century. The pattern of innovation proposed in *Capitalism, Socialism and Democracy* is associated with 'deepening' (Malerba & Orsenigo, 1996). Innovation activities are concentrated; the same firms are frequently the main sources of innovation; barriers to innovative entry are high; and innovators are frequently characterised by large economic size. Schumpeter (1942) emphasised the relevance of the industrial R&D laboratory and the importance of large firms for technological innovation.

This emphasis prevailed over the following decades. It is captured in J.K. Galbraith's (Galbraith, 1956) reflection on a small firm innovation advantage as a 'pleasant fiction.'[1] And it presaged the general neglect of the innovative potential of small firms throughout the middle part of the twentieth century. This was the view that 'big is best'. That the costliness (and riskiness) of technology development was such that it could only be carried out by firms (or public organisations) that had the resources associated with considerable size.

However, paralleling the new interest in small firms as sources of job creation (Birch, 1979), the final quarter of the last century also saw new research on the relative role of small and large firms in innovation and on the distinctive patterns of innovation identified by Schumpeter. Some of it was concerned with testing the market structure implications of Schumpeter's work (see Kamien & Schwartz, 1975; Soete, 1979). However, an important stream of research emerged which helped reconcile the patterns. Richly drawn industry case studies considerably nuanced the often sterile large firm *versus* the small debate. This work revealed a 'dynamic complementarity' (Nooteboom, 1994; Rothwell, 1983;) between large and small firms in the innovation process (see also Abernathy & Utterback, 1978; Utterback & Abernathy, 1975), affording both firm classes central roles at different stages of the industry lifecycle. In contrast to the body of work which sought to test 'later' Schumpeter's market power hypothesis, this work was clear that comparative advantage in innovation was 'unequivocally associated with neither large nor small scale' (Rothwell, 1984, p. 19).

It has been observed that the question of how firm size relates to innovation has motivated the second largest body of empirical

work in the field of industrial organisation (Cohen, 2010). Its inspiration lies, in large part, with Schumpeter's (1934, 1942) contrasting hypotheses. Reconciling 'early' Schumpeter and 'older' Schumpeter (Hagedoorn, 1996) has involved understanding the dynamic context to many innovations, on the one hand, and the coexistence of modes of innovation, on the other. This chapter will take the work on dynamic complementarities as both its point of departure and the basis of its research agenda. The chapter will begin with a reflection upon the early work, identifying dynamic complementarities and the key implications that flow from it. This is followed by a broad (not deep) review of the empirical literature on innovation in, and by, small firms. My contention is that much of the empirical work on small firm innovation has only taken 'static' inspiration from earlier 'dynamic' work – constrained, in large part, by prevailing research designs. Moreover, it has focused on a narrow perspective of innovation – one bound up in significant changes in technologies. The limitations of this approach will inform a research agenda which seeks to place resource deployment and management at the heart of a discussion that recognises the dynamism of resources and constraints in innovative firms and in innovative environments. And, importantly, recognises the ubiquity of innovation in small firms.

DYNAMIC COMPLEMENTARITY

In an influential paper, Rothwell (1983) suggested that the relative importance of firms of different sizes to innovation in a particular industry was likely to depend upon the *age* of that industry. Drawing on rich case studies of the evolution of the CAD industry (Kaplinsky, 1983) and the US semiconductor industry (Rothwell, 1984), Rothwell sketched some general patterns.

In the first instance he noted that, in the evolution of both of these industries, established large firms or large public institutions played a crucial role in early invention and innovation. Large size appeared to 'matter' for the highly speculative work involved. Importantly, however, initial development activity was geared towards 'own use'. In the development of CAD, for instance, the early running was made by large, technologically advanced, mechanical engineering firms in the defence, aerospace and automotive industries (involving collaborations with mainframe computer manufacturers such as IBM). This was process innovation, with little or no market for CAD beyond the firms themselves.

However, as the technology diffused a second stage began. This second stage was characterised by the entry of new, small, specialised firms. Many of these were spun off from the large firms or public laboratories that pioneered the early technology development, as engineers and scientists recognised the broader application of the technologies. Others involved wholly new entrants from related fields, attracted by the prospects of profit. Importantly, these new firms were typically small and their offerings varied considerably.

In both instances, large firms and venture capital played a significant role in funding the start-up and growth of these new technology-based firms (NTBFs).

Finally, as both industries matured, product offerings became more standardised and scale economies became increasingly important. Some of the smaller firms grew, others were acquired and many others exited. Stable oligopolies were formed, with a relatively few large firms dominating the industries. Innovation activity was limited and directed at small changes to meet specific customer demands or at minor process improvements. Only specialist market niches were left for new and small firms.

In the broad picture, innovative advantage appeared to shift from large, to small and back to large firms – although the nature and rate of innovation changed and fell through the industry evolution. Figure 15.1, adapted from Kaplinsky (1983), illustrates the development for the CAD industry.

This pattern also underpins the 'lifecycle' thesis developed across multiple industry

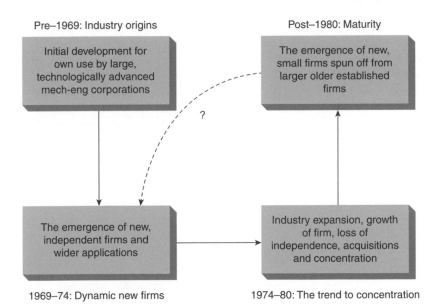

Figure 15.1   The evolution of the CAD industry

Source: Adapted from Kaplinsky (1983)

case studies by Abernathy and Utterback (Abernathy & Utterback, 1978; Utterback & Abernathy, 1975) and elaborated in Utterback's seminal text (Utterback, 1996). In this view, the early stages of the industry are characterised by considerable radical product innovation. Firms are said by Utterback (1996) to be 'unencumbered by universal technical standards or by uniform product expectations in the marketplace [and] experiment freely with new forms and materials' (p. 81). In other words, firms are not sure what is technically possible and customers are unable to clearly articulate their wants. Markets are small, but growing, and competition is often against consumer scepticism, rather than against competitors' offerings. Development work is skill-intensive, relying upon the ingenuity of the entrepreneurs and key employees and employing general purpose equipment and machinery. This provides the basis for the flexibility required by frequent product changes, with each new offering acting as a market experiment, and rapid customer feedback driving further innovation.

This is the era of small firm innovation. The industry quickly blossoms from one, or a few, initial entrants, through an explosion of competition, to a vibrant competitive landscape marked by considerable product variety. In the US automobile industry, for instance, the number of producers rose from four in 1895 to a peak of 274 in 1909 (Simon, 1995). These firms offered open- and closed-body automobiles; steered with wheels and levers; and powered by steam, electricity and internal combustion. The firms were largely craft producers, employing skilled workforces to hand-craft vehicles for the few wealthy customers who could afford them (Holweg, 2008). Successful innovation was skill-intensive and required rapid internal and external communication process and considerable process flexibility.

However, as in Rothwell's model, the period of small firm advantage is transitory. Customer expectations coalesce and technical advances become more difficult and more costly to discover. Firms' priorities shift towards reducing costs and increasing sales. The emphasis shifts from product innovation to process innovation. As scale economies become more important, competitive advantage shifts to those firms adept at scaling up production and at marketing and customer relations. The explosion of competition quickly becomes an implosion as the industry moves towards a stable oligopoly, with a handful of large producers dominating mainstream markets. A few specialised niches may remain, typified by unusually high or low performance and inhabited by smaller firms with limited growth prospects. The apogee of 274 automotive firms in 1909 had quickly become 30 by 1929 and had fallen to a low of seven by 1960 (Simon, 1995).

The research underpinning these 'dynamic' models is extensive and the findings are compelling. The simple conclusion one might draw is that entrepreneurial small firms appear to have a comparative advantage in the earlier stages of commercialisation and market making, whereas large firms have an advantage in the later stages and in the improvement and scaling up of early breakthroughs (Freeman & Soete, 1997). This is the essence of Rothwell's (1983) 'dynamic complementarity'.

Of course, it is not always easy to identify the stage of an industry or, indeed, its likelihood of transitioning from one stage to another. In which case, it may make more sense to simply observe that small firms make a greater contribution in fields characterised by radical, but relatively inexpensive, innovation and where both development costs and entry barriers are low and in industries where the total rate of innovation is high, R&D intensity is low, and there is a large component of skilled labour. In contrast, large firms appear to enjoy relative innovation advantages in industries that are concentrated, capital and advertising intensive, and where development costs are high (Acs & Audretsch 1990, 1988, 1987).

Identifying *when* and *where* small firms may enjoy a comparative advantage is clearly important.[2] However, more important still is identifying *why* that advantage may exist. As Autio and colleagues observe (Autio, Kenney, Mustar, Siegel & Wright, 2014), '… not all entrepreneurs innovate'. These authors call attention to the '… regulating effects of context on innovation activities' and the important contingencies these impose. In this vein, one wonders what it is about the firms themselves or about the environments they occupy that permits or compels them to innovate, or discourages or retards innovation. Improving our understanding of these is likely to be the basis of replicability and of extending the lessons of dynamic models to the population of small firms more generally.

RESOURCES AND BEHAVIOURS

Despite the promise of dynamic models, much of the subsequent empirical literature has been characterised by a more 'static' approach. The observation that both large and small firms may be innovative at different stages of the lifecycle and to different ends indicates the existence of broadly differing capabilities for innovation. It is the bases of these differing capabilities that have occupied much of the subsequent academic literature. In large part, research has taken its lead, often explicitly, from Rothwell's (e.g. Rothwell, 1983, 1989) early listing of the advantages and disadvantages of large and small firms for innovation.

Small firms, Rothwell suggested, had advantages in marketing, management and internal communications. These advantages were bound up in their nearness to customers, their lack of bureaucracy and their flexibility. On the other hand, small firms faced a number of challenges associated with attracting finance, recruiting specialist labour, managing growth and dealing with regulation. From these, one could infer that small firms were behaviourally advantaged, but resource-constrained in their contribution to innovation

(Nooteboom, 1994). And, as large-scale survey data became more widely available, it is a broad focus on resource constraints and, albeit to a lesser extent, behavioural advantages that has dominated the literature. The literature on small firm innovation is replete with, *inter alia*, studies of access to finance (e.g. Chemmanur & Fulghieri, 2014; Revest & Sapio, 2012); access to human capital (McGuirk, Lenihan & Hart 2015); employment of distinctive appropriation strategies (Leiponen & Byma, 2009); market orientation (Keskin, 2006; Verhees & Meulenberg, 2004); environmental influences (Freel, 2005b; Katila & Shane, 2005); and engagement in networks (Gronum, Verreynne & Kastelle, 2012) or, more recently, adoption of open innovation techniques (Vahter, Love & Roper, 2014).

Effectively reviewing this larger body of work is clearly beyond a short chapter such as this. However, there is some merit in reflecting upon two of the more prominent themes – to the extent that they typify much of the work on resources and behaviours. To this end, the next two sections briefly consider the general tenor of research on the financing of small firm innovation (as the most commonly identified resource constraint) and on the use of networks (as a frequently encouraged behaviour). My contention is that these two topics are central to understanding the advantages and disadvantages that small firms face in trying to innovate. However, the existing literature has, in large part, approached them in such a way as to exclude the majority of small firms and the dynamic perspective that provided much of the rich insight in earlier studies has largely receded.

Financing Innovation in Small Firms

Access to finance is amongst the most commonly cited and enthusiastically debated 'barriers' to innovation in the small firms literature (e.g. Mina, Lahr & Hughes, 2013;

Revest & Sapio, 2012) and the focus of much policy rhetoric (see Colombo, Cumming & Vismara, 2014). Invariably, academics and policymakers alight on improving the supply of or, more recently, the demand for venture capital (in both its formal and informal guises) as a means to ameliorating this deficiency. To this end, the standard argument runs something like the following:

Innovation is essentially a speculative process. In the main, resources must be committed prior to receipt of revenues from the sale of products or services which these resources generate (Brophy & Shulman, 1993). Yet costs and revenues are inevitably difficult to anticipate with any precision (Moore & Garnsey, 1993). As Arrow (1971) noted, a rational organisation's likelihood of investing in high-risk projects will invariably be a function of their ability to transfer or spread risk. Firms commonly transfer risk through insurance. Unfortunately, in the classic Knightian sense (Knight, 1921), the success or failure of an innovative venture cannot be assigned some probability value and cannot be insured against. Yet, for the large firm, risk may be effectively spread through a portfolio of investments. That is, '… large firms may diversify their innovative projects and obtain more stable cashflows' (Giudici & Paleari, 2000, p. 40). By contrast, small firms more often develop single research projects that require considerable funding, relative to turnover base. Moreover, if finance is required (i.e. factor inputs must be paid for) in advance of receipt of revenues from the sale of project outcomes, '… then the growth of the project will always require funding from outside the project' (Brophy & Shulman, 1993, p. 65). In the latter case, this may include investment of retained profits from other income streams. However, on the simplest level, firm size is likely to mean, of itself, that internally generated funds, for the financing of an innovation project of a given size, will be less available in smaller firms than larger firms (Canepa & Stoneman, 2007).

Accordingly, in the face of such internal cash constraints, firms must either abandon or reject the innovation project, or seek access to external finance. Since debt finance cannot be classified as 'genuine' risk capital – requiring periodic payment of interest and ultimate repayment of the principal – the most common means by which risk is spread is through the sale of equity claims in the given project. Moreover, relative tolerance of failure and for experimentation is a key feature of external finance, allowing it to promote or stifle innovation (Chemmanur & Fulghieri, 2014). This, again, speaks to the pertinence of equity versus debt. Inevitably, the need for firms to have better access to equity funding for innovation has invariably been among the central conclusions of policy studies (Murray, 2007).

This focus on venture capital (in its various forms) to fund innovation is problematic for a couple of reasons. In the first instance, very few firms get venture capital funding. Only a tiny percentage of US start-ups raise funds from venture capitalists (Mulcahy, 2013), and the numbers are likely to be smaller elsewhere. Beyond that, VC investment typically does not fund the sorts of innovation that commentators have in mind. Historically, less than half of one per cent of venture capital investments fund early-stage technology development. As the venture capitalist Bob Zider noted, venture capitalists 'avoid early-stages, when the technologies are uncertain, and market needs are unknown' (Zider, 1998). If our concern is with funding small firm innovation, we have alighted on a topic that is of limited relevance to the sector as a whole. Even for technology-based firms, venture capital plays a limited role (Revest & Sapio, 2012).

What is clear is that a pecking order prevails in the financing of innovation in small firms. Internal funding is the preferred method and, where external finance is required, debt forms the major source. Indeed, debt may be, at least from the perspective of the best small firms, the most suitable source of external funding for innovation. For instance, it is suggested that, in addition to allowing individual entrepreneurs to maintain control, the acceptance of debt may act as a positive market signal (Giudici & Paleari, 2000; Goodacre & Tonks, 1995; Myers & Majluf, 1984; Ross, 1977). That is, '… high-quality managers [of high-quality projects] will signal their quality by choosing a capital structure involving a large percentage of debt, that will not be copied by the low-quality manager' (Goodacre & Tonks, 1995, p. 321). This debt cannot be assumed without a high degree of confidence in the profitability of the project and the ability of the firm to make periodic repayments. Moreover, acceptance of debt may also signal the entrepreneur's unwillingness to share in the expected gains from any investment.

The effect of this 'signalling' is similar to that of the 'pecking-order' hypothesis (Myers, 1984). That is, firms are likely to opt for self-financing, where possible (since this sends the most positive signal to the market), and thereafter debt financing. Again, equity is likely to be issued rarely. However, since the scope for signalling only exists in the presence of information asymmetries, it is likely that over time, as reputation is built and asymmetries diminish, firms will switch from debt to equity. Thus, firms with little or no track record, for successful innovation, are more likely to employ debt than firms with an established track record. Again, this is likely to hold for many small innovators.

Finally, where interest payments are tax deductible, debt is likely to be a less costly means of financing innovation. That is, '[s]ince equity holders bear risk which debt holders do not, the expected returns on holding equity will be higher than the returns (which are the interest payment) on debt' (Goodacre & Tonks, 1995, pp. 318–19). It is important to note, however, that a highly geared (or leveraged) firm presents a greater risk to both equity holders and creditors, due to the greater probability of bankruptcy (see classically Modigliani & Miller, 1958). Accordingly, to compensate for the high probability of failure, debt providers are likely to require higher returns on debt (i.e.

higher rates of interest), to such an extent that debt and equity become equally costly.

Regardless of the nuances of these issues, recent work has begun to better reflect the importance of banks as funders of innovation in the small firm sector. The small firms' literature has seen a number of contributions aimed at better understanding the role bank funding may play in stimulating innovation. However, most of these have followed a fairly standard format: employing cross-sectional survey data to estimate the likelihood of loan turndowns (Lee, Sameen & Cowling, 2015); loan scaling (Freel, 2007); and loan rates (Nitani & Riding, 2013). Typically these studies indicate a tougher financial environment for innovative small firms. The studies are important, but one wonders at the extent to which they have advanced earlier studies (Giudici & Paleari, 2000; Westhead & Storey, 1997) in highlighting financial constraints that are particularly acute for innovative small firms.

Certainly, calls for greater diversity in banking services (Lee, Sameen & Cowling, 2015) or for schemes that improve the 'debt readiness' of small firms (Freel, 2007) make sense. There is undoubtedly scope for reducing information asymmetries and the associated transaction costs – perhaps facilitated by the gradual move towards a more relational rather than transactional banking service. In this, there may also be a role for government as an information, or goodwill, broker. There may also be a role for government in mitigating the risk profile of innovative ventures from the perspective of the lender – a role that the Small Firms Loan Guarantee Scheme (SFLGS) seems well-suited for. However, the SFLGSs are often viewed as 'funding of last resort' and suffer from poor visibility, lack targeting and impose an interest rate premium upon firms – which may in fact be associated with an increased failure/default rate as the more marginal projects are pushed to the scheme (Cowling & Mitchell, 2003). Regardless, most policy interventions are on the supply side or are indirect. For instance, in the latter case, developed economies invariably vest the larger part of their innovation budgets in R&D tax credit schemes. Such policies disproportionately reward large firms engaged in systematic R&D (Czarnitzki, Hanel & Rosa, 2011). The effect of shifting policy resources towards grant and advice schemes is a question worth exploring further (see, for example Audretsch, 2003 and Qian and Haynes, 2014 on the US SBIR programme).

However, the real limitation in the extant literature is not in what has been done, but in what is not being done. The resource constraint in small firms is not simply one of resource stocks, but of the deployment of the stocks. Whilst studies of debt finance for innovation speak to issues of relevance to a greater set of small firms, they also elide key issues. For instance, whilst credit scoring techniques have reduced the role of negotiation in debt contracting (Berger & Frame, 2007), price and non-price terms still vary (Rostamkalaei & Freel, 2016) and entrepreneurs have scope to influence these in a variety of ways (e.g. information management, shopping around, advice-seeking and so on). Our understanding of lending and borrowing *processes* is poorly served by current work. In addition, our understanding of banking relationships over time is limited. How do reputation and track record influence borrowing decisions and outcomes? Likewise, our understanding of the different loan instruments and how they are used to stimulate innovation is limited. Overdrafts and credit cards differ from term loans and mortgages, and my intuition is that all of these are used to fund innovation. However, the scope and scale of innovation may vary. Crucially, all of these imply the exercise of management. Successful innovation requires capable management. In this case it entails, at a minimum, the management of banking relationships, the management of information and the management of funds. In examining financial constraints to innovation, the role of the manager and management is virtually absent from the existing literature.

Networking, Collaboration and Learning

Turning to the issue of behavioural advantages: this section takes the fashion for studies of cooperative or networked innovation as emblematic of a behaviour to be encouraged in small innovative firms. It is certainly the case that industrial innovation is increasingly viewed as a distributed activity, with few firms able to innovate in isolation. Tether argues that, in consequence, 'the old debates about firm-size, market structure and innovation are becoming outmoded, as the boundaries of the firm are becoming increasingly "fuzzy"' (Tether, 2002, p. 947). However, perhaps a more elemental consideration is the view that successful innovation relies upon accessing external knowledge, rather than information (Rothwell, 1991). The emphasis on knowledge rather than information, in which arm's-length contacts are insufficient, underpins the conception of innovation as an iterative, cumulative and cooperative phenomenon, in which '… interactive learning and collective entrepreneurship are fundamental' (Lundvall, 1992, p. 9). Since 'the technological and market knowledge which underpins innovation is often tacit and idiosyncratic … [it is] … therefore often learned by doing, using and *interacting* with customers, suppliers and related industries' (Utterback & Afuah, 2000, p. 170, emphasis added). Indeed, many commentators now hold that innovation is no longer the province of individual firms, but is a matter of collective action. In other words, innovation may, more appropriately, be considered the product of networks of related actors. The issue, then, is how firms and organisations of various sizes work together to innovate.

This view is compelling. Contemporary products and services are typically parts of larger systems of use. And, as products and services are systemic, so are likely developments in products and services. Moreover, for resource-constrained small firms, networks and collaboration may offer vital access to resources that would be otherwise unobtainable (Pittaway, Robertson, Munir, Denyer & Neely, 2004). However, whilst the conceptual literature talks in process terms about *learning* or *interacting*, the empirical literature has been much less ambitious. Earlier work was dominated by production function approaches (explicitly or otherwise) that viewed innovations as outputs driven by stocks of inputs, amongst which networks and cooperation were one category (e.g. Bougrain & Haudeville, 2002; Freel, 2003; Rogers, 2004; Romijn & Albu, 2002). More recent work has followed a similar format, albeit with the better work employing panel data (e.g. Gronum et al., 2012; Vahter et al., 2014). The general conclusion, with a few caveats, is that networking and cooperation are beneficial for innovation.

In many respects, inter-firm networks, most especially in the context of innovation and innovation-related activities, have been presented as a 'blueprint' for economic success for small firms. The evidence that successful innovators were more likely to have been engaged in cooperative ventures, or to be widely networked, is pervasive. However, this observation is more appropriately couched in conditional terms: cooperation in *certain types* of innovation activities, with *particular organisations* appears to be associated with higher levels of innovation in *some small firms* – conversely, many sources of innovation-related collaboration do not correlate with higher levels of firm-level innovativeness. This, again, talks to the importance of contingencies. And, as I note at the end of the chapter, these contingencies are as likely to relate to management attitudes and actions as to the external environment. For instance, Baker, Grinstein and Harmancioglu (2015) recently observed that the marginal value of external networking increases as entrepreneurial orientation weakens, and that the relationship is particularly acute in small firms. As these authors conclude, '… the ability to utilize market knowledge, ideas, and interpretations from external networks provides

a means for firms that cannot or will not develop a strong entrepreneurial culture to more successfully innovate' (p. 13).

Clearly, blanket collaboration imperatives overstate the case and misunderstand the various dynamics at work. Cooperation for innovation carries higher risk (Lhuillery & Pfister, 2009), with some firms succeeding and others failing. Moreover, there is some evidence of eventually diminishing returns to networking (Laursen & Salter, 2006), which are often rationalised in terms of an increasing information and managerial burden. The complex relationship between networking and innovation in small firms is further indicated by the generally low levels of interaction one observes (survey-based studies suggest cooperation for innovation is a minority activity amongst small firms). And by the noted primacy of 'trust' as the foundation of successful cooperation (Nooteboom, 1999), which suggests, in turn, an essentially interpersonal dimension to innovation-related cooperation.

Obviously, there is a limit to what may be learned about innovation in small firms by simply counting network partners and placing them on the right-hand side of a regression equation. Simply put, there is a great discrepancy between a general agreement that innovation should be understood as an interactive learning process (that may permit resource and risk-sharing), on the one hand, and very limited knowledge about the nature of interactions (how relationships emerge and evolve; how they are managed; what underpins success and failure, and so on) and why they matter so much, on the other.

There is also a tendency in the empirical literature (and the accompanying policy work) to overemphasise inter-organisational activities and to neglect the important intra-organisational interactions and capabilities. In contrast, it seems clear that innovation, even in smaller firms, is primarily a process built on internal capabilities (Dosi, 1988). That is, in most industries the bulk of innovation effort is undertaken by firms themselves and occurs within firms themselves. Indeed, even in circumstances where the requirement for collaborative effort is identified, it is thought to be essential that firms have developed internal competencies that facilitate the effective recognition, appraisal, negotiation and assimilation of external expertise (Tether, 2002). Only rarely will firms be mere passive receptors of exogenous technology (broadly defined). In other words, the interactivity of the innovation process may also refer to collaborations and iterations involving departments and individuals within the firm as well as, perhaps less frequently, external cooperation and networking – though the issue is by no means clear-cut.

What does seem clear, however, from the large number of innovators consistently recording no cooperative linkages for innovation, is that external collaboration is unquestionably neither a necessary nor a sufficient condition for innovation. Where 'connectivity' is evident it takes a much 'softer' form. To this end, there is a parallel literature that holds that successful knowledge transfer through networks requires particular social skills (Macpherson & Holt, 2007; Yli-Renko, Autio & Sapienza, 2001). This literature points to the importance of relational skills (Perren, 2002) and attitudinal skills (Tjosvold & Weicker, 1993) underpinning successful networking. On the whole, however, it is much less prominent and addresses innovation more obliquely. Disappointingly, the same charges may be laid at the limited literature on knowledge management (e.g. Alegre, Sengupta & Lapiedra, 2013; Desouza & Awazu, 2006; Gray, 2006). Although I believe the latter offers considerable prospect for improving our understanding of innovation in small firms.

To the extent that innovation involves the creation and use of new knowledge (or new use of existing knowledge), it is fundamentally about learning. Learning involves the creation of both tacit and codified knowledge concerned with the technical characteristics of processes and products, but also with knowledge of how and why to search

in particular ways, and where to find key (problem-solving) people within relevant networks (Lundvall & Johnson, 1994). An important corollary of this observation is that any firm-level strategy for innovation must be, at its heart, a human resources strategy (Smith, 2000) – a strategy for the recruitment, retention and development of the firm's human resources. There is plenty of empirical support for this, with recent work on 'innovative human capital' in small firms (McGuirk et al., 2015) providing evidence of the particular importance of training to both product and process innovation. This is not a particularly new observation, and echoes earlier work that observed a significant effect of training on the introduction of 'new to the market' products (Freel, 2005a). It is also consistent with Thornhill's (2006) observations on the coincidental effect of training and innovation on small firm performance in low-technology sectors. However, Thornhill offers further nuance: in high-technology sectors it is the combination of highly skilled employees and innovation which drive growth. It also appears that the types of skills and the manner of skills acquisition is contingent. The incremental and cumulative nature of learning and innovation for most firms is likely to require literate and numerate employees, particularly in technical and marketing areas, and not necessarily the university-trained people upon which strength in 'high-tech' depends. Though there is some evidence of a greater high-skilled employment in innovative small firms in more dynamic sectors, perhaps allowing these firms to achieve process improvements and keep pace with advancing technology – '… to progress from what we may term a "know how" culture to a "know why" culture' (Scott, Jones, Bramley & Bolton, 1996, p. 86).

Of course, other studies find no effect of training on innovation in small firms and point instead to the importance of entrepreneurial motivation and management (e.g. Romero & Martínez-Román, 2012). And this inconsistency should give us pause. It is not the mere presence of 'innovative human capital', highly-skilled employees, or the activity of training that 'matters'. Rather, it is the processes involved in the acquisition of human capital, in the deployment of highly skilled employees and in the design and delivery of training. It is about 'how' and not simply about 'what' and 'how many'. This speaks to the importance of 'institutional logics' in the deployment of resources (Pahnke, Katila & Eisenhardt, 2015).

Ultimately, however – as with the financing of small firm innovation, or innovation networking – the gaps in our know-how appear to involve a better understanding of the dynamics of the firm generally, and of management specifically. If certain behaviours are more or less likely to encourage innovation in small firms, one wonders how easily observed they are in the cross-section.

BETTER 'DYNAMICS', BROADER PERSPECTIVES AND THE MANAGEMENT OF INNOVATION

Whilst studies of financial constraints and of innovation networking and learning speak, in a general sense, to resources and behaviours, most studies continue to rely upon limited case studies or larger cross-sections. The dynamic perspective that provided much of the rich insight in earlier studies has largely receded. Moreover, the conception of innovation that is adopted is typically narrow – bound up in products and processes and requiring some larger degree of 'novelty'. 'Softer' forms of innovation, in business models or in the organisation of work, have received much less focus (Autio et al., 2014). Both of these observations suggest scope for research and researchers.

In the latter case, part of the challenge concerns the performance effects of innovation. Modelling performance is fraught. However, most studies of the impact of innovation on small firm performance suggest that, on average, innovators outperform non-innovators

(Audretsch, Coad & Segarra, 2014). Yet there is an important limitation to much of the extant work. These studies usually compare successful innovators (i.e. those who have managed to get a new product to the market) with a mixed bundle of unsuccessful innovators and genuine non-innovators. Innovation is a risky strategy and, to the extent that we would expect unsuccessful innovators to perform more poorly than non-innovators, this empirical work is likely to overstate the performance benefits of innovation on average. Moreover, we know that, even amongst successful innovators, performance premiums are highly skewed and evidence suggests that an aggressive innovation strategy only really benefits a handful of 'superstar firms' (Coad & Rao, 2008). That some firms benefit more than others from innovation once more suggests the existence of important contingencies (Autio et al. (2014) call them 'contexts'). Identifying these and understanding their influence is an important avenue for future research. Recent examples in this vein include work on the effects of learning and unlearning, through innovation, on firm performance (Leal-Rodríguez, Eldridge, Roldán, Leal-Millán & Ortega-Gutiérrez, 2015).

However, focusing on higher risk, higher reward innovation also runs the risk of ignoring the wider innovation potential of small firms. The generation of variety may be the single most important role that small firms play in economies. And, at the level of the firm, the creation of value is central to competitiveness. Variety and value creation will more often entail innovations that are poorly captured in standard questions about new product or process introductions or R&D expenditures. Rather, it is likely to be better represented by recent work on business model innovation (George & Bock, 2011; Trimi & Berbegal-Mirabent, 2012), organisational innovation (Gallego, Rubalcaba & Hipp, 2013; Laforet, 2011) and service innovation (Salunke, Weerawardena & McColl-Kennedy, 2013). Fully understanding small firms' contribution to innovation requires this broader perspective.

Nonetheless, a greater part of the recent work on small firm innovation is familiar. The sophistication of the econometrics has improved, as has the quality of data – at least in the better work. However, much of the research still has a flavour of a 'characteristics of …' approach. This is the approach that has dominated our studies of important output phenomena, such as growth, internationalisation and, of course, innovation. Progress has been made with the use of panel data (e.g. Audretsch, Segarra & Teruel, 2014; Vahter et al., 2014) and the increasing concern for contingencies (e.g. Baker et al., 2015; Berchicci, de Jong & Freel, 2015; Yang, Zheng & Zhao, 2014). However, managers and management continue to go largely unobserved. For instance, in their excellent introduction to a special issue on 'Entrepreneurial Innovation', Autio et al. (2014) use the word 'management' only once (in a passing reference to management buyouts). This is despite identifying 'organizational context' as one of six contextual influences on innovation.[3]

Yet, in an intriguing contribution to the innovation debate, Volberda and van den Bosch (2005) argued that '… Management Matters Most'. Much of our concern in understanding innovation has been with measuring the availability of macro- or micro-technological variables (e.g. R&D expenditures, graduate employment, patents) and promoting or studying particular technology sectors. Disappointingly, this is true in the small firms' literature as well, where it makes even less sense. This bias towards technological innovation has seen administrative innovation (i.e. improvements in management ideas and management practices) neglected. Yet it is likely that management (the effective acquisition and deployment of resources) matters at least as much as technological factors and perhaps more. Improving our understanding of small firm innovation – of how resource constraints are overcome and behavioural advantages are exploited – is likely to require a return to rich case studies and an employment of mixed methods.

There are a few examples of this kind of work (Berends, Jelinek, Reymen & Stultiëns, 2014), but they are notable for their rarity. A return to dynamism and the beginning of a broader perspective on small firm innovation requires more of an effort to get inside the 'black box' (Rosenberg, 1982) of innovation processes in small firms. It is likely to be a story of management and managers.

CONCLUSION

The theme of this chapter has been the tendency to neglect important contingencies in small firm innovation processes. In a similar vein, Autio et al. (2014) lament the tendency of the entrepreneurship literature to focus on the individual or the firm and to neglect structure and institutions. This speaks to the contingency of context. And, to the extent that the firm is often treated as a black box, where resources go in and innovations come out, it is easy to sympathise with the former view and celebrate the latter. However, it is not immediately clear that industry and technology contexts, institutional and policy contexts, or spatial contexts have been especially neglected. One need only think of the array of industry-specific studies, or the vast body of work inspired by the related systems or innovation literatures (Howells, 1999; Lundvall, 1992; Malerba, 2004) to recognise both the contributions and limitations in these areas. Indeed, although appropriately situating our research in its temporal context has become rarer, the early work discussed at the beginning of this chapter provides us with solid foundations to explore temporal contingencies.

Rather, I believe that it is the 'organisational' and 'social' contexts that have been most overlooked. The importance of the individual entrepreneur and manager, and of management practice, to small firm innovation processes ought not to be understated. Past research has suggested that, in the overwhelming majority of small firms, the owner–manager was central to the initiation and development of innovations (North & Smallbone, 2000). Moreover, there is ample evidence that the patterns of innovation – in rates, sources and directions of innovation – strongly associate with differences in strategies and business practices in small firms (De Jong & Marsili, 2006).

Recent work has begun to illustrate the importance of organisational and social contexts (i.e. of managers and management) to small firm innovation. Nelson (2014), for instance, observed the attempted commercialisation of an innovation initially within a university context and subsequently in a start-up setting. He reported that the same individuals exhibited different behaviours in the different organisational contexts, marked by different rewards structures and incentive systems. In a related contribution, Pahnke et al. (2015) demonstrate that partners' institutional logic influences the success of innovative projects in young firms, observing that venture capital partners are more likely to strengthen innovation in focal firms than either Corporate Venture Capitalists or government agencies. These authors attribute this to the differing partners' institutional logics, which enable different resource deployment strategies. These are illuminating studies, but they are relatively rare.

Rather, much of the empirical work on small firm innovation has been concerned with essentially static consideration of small firms' behavioural advantages and resource constraints. This is despite a promising early literature that recognised the dynamic contributions of small and large firms to innovation and recognised the changing nature of management and organisation. This, of course, is not to suggest that behaviours and resources are not at the heart of understanding small firm innovation. Rather, given the inconsistency of behaviours, our concern ought to be with how certain behaviours are encouraged and constrained and not on simply recording behaviours and associating them with

outcomes. And, in light of the socially constructed nature of resource environments (Baker & Nelson, 2005), our focus might more fruitfully be on resource construction and deployment, than on resource stocks. Although these approaches suggest multiple contingencies, I believe that management and organisation will feature prominently.

Notes

1 The full quote is: 'There is no more pleasant fiction than that technical change is the product of the matchless ingenuity of the small man forced by competition to employ his wits to better his neighbor' (p. 86).
2 Indeed, these are exactly the questions that Autio et al. (2014) consider to be the 'real' questions.
3 The others are 'industry and technological', 'institutional and policy', 'social', 'temporal' and 'spatial' contexts.

REFERENCES

Abernathy, William J., and James M. Utterback. 1978. 'Patterns of Industrial Innovation'. *Technology Review* 80 (7): 40–47.

Acs, Zoltan J., and David B. Audretsch. 1987. 'Innovation, Market Structure, and Firm Size'. *The Review of Economics and Statistics* 69 (4): 567–74.

Acs, Zoltan J., and David B. Audretsch. 1988. 'Innovation in Large and Small Firms: An Empirical Analysis'. *The American Economic Review* 78 (4): 678–90.

Acs, Zoltan J., and David B. Audretsch. 1990. *Innovation and Small Firms*. MIT Press. https://books.google.ca/books?hl=en&lr= &id=yqpr53a0R74C&oi=fnd&pg=PR7&dq=a udretsch+and+acs&ots=gPKL0YG5K_&sig= mUO9MPUBqljuoCdFcPiloxSAd_g.

Alegre, Joaquín, Kishore Sengupta, and Rafael Lapiedra. 2013. 'Knowledge Management and Innovation Performance in a High-Tech SMEs Industry'. *International Small Business Journal* 31 (4): 454–70.

Arrow, Kenneth. 1971. 'Economic Welfare and the Allocation of Resources for Invention'. Republished in: Rosenberg, N. (ed.) The

Economics of Technological Change. Harmondsworth: Penguin Books Ltd.

Audretsch, David B. 2003. 'Standing on the Shoulders of Midgets: The US Small Business Innovation Research Program (SBIR)'. *Small Business Economics* 20 (2): 129–35.

Audretsch, David B., Alex Coad, and Agustí Segarra. 2014. 'Firm Growth and Innovation'. *Small Business Economics* 47 (1): 1–7.

Audretsch, David B., Agustí Segarra, and Mercedes Teruel. 2014. 'Why Don't All Young Firms Invest in R&D?' *Small Business Economics* 43 (4): 751–66.

Autio, Erkko, Martin Kenney, Philippe Mustar, Don Siegel, and Mike Wright. 2014. 'Entrepreneurial Innovation: The Importance of Context'. *Research Policy* 43 (7): 1097–108.

Baker, Ted, and Reed E. Nelson. 2005. 'Creating Something from Nothing: Resource Construction through Entrepreneurial Bricolage'. *Administrative Science Quarterly* 50 (3): 329–66.

Baker, William E., Amir Grinstein, and Nukhet Harmancioglu. 2015. 'Whose Innovation Performance Benefits More from External Networks: Entrepreneurial or Conservative Firms?' *Journal of Product Innovation Management*. http://onlinelibrary.wiley.com/doi/10.1111/jpim.12263/full.

Berchicci, Luca, Jeroen PJ de Jong, and Mark Freel. 2016. 'Remote Collaboration and Innovative Performance: The Moderating Role of R&D Intensity'. *Industrial and Corporate Change* 25 (3): 429–46.

Berends, Hans, Mariann Jelinek, Isabelle Reymen, and Rutger Stultiëns. 2014. 'Product Innovation Processes in Small Firms: Combining Entrepreneurial Effectuation and Managerial Causation'. *Journal of Product Innovation Management* 31 (3): 616–35.

Berger, Allen N., and W. Scott Frame. 2007. 'Small Business Credit Scoring and Credit Availability'. *Journal of Small Business Management* 45 (1): 5–22.

Birch, David GW. 1979. 'The Job Generation Process'. http://papers.ssrn.com/sol3/papers.cfm?abstract_id=1510007.

Bougrain, Frédéric, and Bernard Haudeville. 2002. 'Innovation, Collaboration and SMEs Internal Research Capacities'. *Research Policy* 31 (5): 735–47.

Breschi, Stefano, Franco Malerba, and Luigi Orsenigo. 2000. 'Technological Regimes and Schumpeterian Patterns of Innovation'. *Economic Journal* 110 (463): 388–410.

Brophy, D., and J. Shulman. 1993. 'Financial Factors Which Stimulate Innovation'. *Entrepreneurship Theory and Practice* 17 (2): 61–73.

Canepa, Alessandra, and Paul Stoneman. 2007. 'Financial Constraints to Innovation in the UK: Evidence from CIS2 and CIS3'. *Oxford Economic Papers*, 60 (4): 711–30.

Chemmanur, Thomas J., and Paolo Fulghieri. 2014. 'Entrepreneurial Finance and Innovation: An Introduction and Agenda for Future Research'. *Review of Financial Studies* 27 (1): 1–19.

Coad, Alex, and Rekha Rao. 2008. 'Innovation and Firm Growth in High-Tech Sectors: A Quantile Regression Approach'. *Research Policy* 37 (4): 633–48.

Cohen, Wesley M. 2010. 'Fifty Years of Empirical Studies of Innovative Activity and Performance'. *Handbook of the Economics of Innovation* 1: 129–213.

Colombo, Massimo G., Douglas J. Cumming, and Silvio Vismara. 2014. 'Governmental Venture Capital for Innovative Young Firms'. *The Journal of Technology Transfer*, 41, 10–24.

Cowling, Marc, and Peter Mitchell. 2003. 'Is the Small Firms Loan Guarantee Scheme Hazardous for Banks or Helpful to Small Business?' *Small Business Economics* 21 (1): 63–71.

Czarnitzki, Dirk, Petr Hanel, and Julio Miguel Rosa. 2011. 'Evaluating the Impact of R&D Tax Credits on Innovation: A Microeconometric Study on Canadian Firms'. *Research Policy* 40 (2): 217–29.

De Jong, Jeroen PJ, and Orietta Marsili. 2006. 'The Fruit Flies of Innovations: A Taxonomy of Innovative Small Firms'. *Research Policy* 35 (2): 213–29.

Desouza, Kevin C., and Yukika Awazu. 2006. 'Knowledge Management at SMEs: Five Peculiarities'. *Journal of Knowledge Management* 10 (1): 32–43.

Dosi, Giovanni. 1988. 'Sources, Procedures, and Microeconomic Effects of Innovation'. *Journal of Economic Literature* 26 (3): 1120–71.

Freel, Mark S. 2003. 'Sectoral Patterns of Small Firm Innovation, Networking and Proximity'. *Research Policy* 32 (5): 751–70.

Freel, Mark S. 2005a. 'Patterns of Innovation and Skills in Small Firms'. *Technovation* 25 (2): 123–34.

Freel, Mark S. 2005b. 'Perceived Environmental Uncertainty and Innovation in Small Firms'. *Small Business Economics* 25 (1): 49–64.

Freel, Mark S. 2007. 'Are Small Innovators Credit Rationed?' *Small Business Economics* 28 (1): 23–35.

Freeman, Christopher, and Luc Soete. 1997. *The Economics of Industrial Innovation*. Psychology Press. https://books.google.ca/books?hl=en&lr=&id=5AJ7IIHCJNAC&oi=fnd&pg=PP2&dq=freeman+and+soete&ots=_k7SRGyhQE&sig=V1BfvWp9Lx4Ei1OJ6CVOo9YhSvU

Galbraith, John Kenneth. 1956. *American Capitalism: The Theory of Countervailing Power*. Boston, MA: Houghton Mifflin.

Gallego, Jorge, Luis Rubalcaba, and Christiane Hipp. 2013. 'Organizational Innovation in Small European Firms: A Multidimensional Approach'. *International Small Business Journal* 31 (5): 563–79.

Gartner, William B. 1990. 'What Are We Talking About When We Talk About Entrepreneurship?' *Journal of Business Venturing* 5 (1): 15–28.

George, Gerard, and Adam J. Bock. 2011. 'The Business Model in Practice and Its Implications for Entrepreneurship Research'. *Entrepreneurship Theory and Practice* 35 (1): 83–111.

Giudici, Giancarlo, and Stefano Paleari. 2000. 'The Provision of Finance to Innovation: A Survey Conducted among Italian Technology-Based Small Firms'. *Small Business Economics* 14 (1): 37–53.

Goodacre, Alan, and Ian Tonks. 1995. 'Finance and Technological Change'. *Handbook of the Economics of Technological Change*. Oxford: Basil Blackwell, 298–341.

Gray, Colin. 2006. 'Absorptive Capacity, Knowledge Management and Innovation in Entrepreneurial Small Firms'. *International Journal of Entrepreneurial Behavior & Research* 12 (6): 345–60.

Gronum, Sarel, Martie-Louise Verreynne, and Tim Kastelle. 2012. 'The Role of Networks in Small and Medium-Sized Enterprise Innovation and Firm Performance'. *Journal of Small Business Management* 50 (2): 257–82.

Hagedoorn, John. 1996. 'Innovation and Entrepreneurship: Schumpeter Revisited'. *Industrial and Corporate Change* 5 (3): 883–96.

Holweg, Matthias. 2008. 'The Evolution of Competition in the Automotive Industry'. In *Build To Order*, 13–34. Springer. http://link.springer.com/chapter/10.1007/978-1-84800-225-8_2.

Howells, Jeremy. 1999. 'Regional Systems of Innovation?' in: Jeremy Howells and Jonathan Michie (eds) *Innovation Policy in a Global Economy*, Cambridge: Cambridge University Press, Cambridge, 67–93.

Kamien, Morton I., and Nancy L. Schwartz. 1975. 'Market Structure and Innovation: A Survey'. *Journal of Economic Literature* 13 (1): 1–37.

Kaplinsky, Raphael. 1983. 'Firm Size and Technical Change in a Dynamic Context'. *The Journal of Industrial Economics* 32 (1): 39–59.

Katila, Riitta, and Scott Shane. 2005. 'When Does Lack of Resources Make New Firms Innovative?' *Academy of Management Journal* 48 (5): 814–29.

Keskin, Halit. 2006. 'Market Orientation, Learning Orientation, and Innovation Capabilities in SMEs: An Extended Model'. *European Journal of Innovation Management* 9 (4): 396–417.

Knight, Frank H. 1921. *Risk, Uncertainty and Profit*. New York: Hart, Schaffner and Marx.

Laforet, Sylvie. 2011. 'A Framework of Organisational Innovation and Outcomes in SMEs'. *International Journal of Entrepreneurial Behavior & Research* 17 (4): 380–408.

Laursen, Kjeld, and Amon. Salter. 2006. 'Open for Innovation: The Role of Openness in Explaining Innovation Performance among UK Manufacturing Firms'. *Strategic Management Journal* 27 (2): 131–50.

Leal-Rodríguez, Antonio Luis, Stephen Eldridge, José Luis Roldán, Antonio Genaro Leal-Millán, and Jaime Ortega-Gutiérrez. 2015. 'Organizational Unlearning, Innovation Outcomes, and Performance: The Moderating Effect of Firm Size'. *Journal of Business Research* 68 (4): 803–9.

Lee, Neil, Hiba Sameen, and Marc Cowling. 2015. 'Access to Finance for Innovative SMEs since the Financial Crisis'. *Research Policy* 44 (2): 370–80.

Leiponen, Aija, and Justin Byma. 2009. 'If You Cannot Block, You Better Run: Small Firms, Cooperative Innovation, and Appropriation Strategies'. *Research Policy* 38 (9): 1478–88.

Lhuillery, Stephane, and Etienne Pfister. 2009. 'R&D Cooperation and Failures in Innovation Projects: Empirical Evidence from French CIS Data'. *Research Policy* 38 (1): 45–57.

Lundvall, Bengt-äke. 1992. National Systems of Innovation: Toward a Theory of Innovation and Interactive Learning. London and New York: Pinter.

Lundvall, Bengt-äke, and Björn Johnson. 1994. 'The Learning Economy'. *Journal of Industry Studies* 1 (2): 23–42.

Macpherson, Allan, and Robin Holt. 2007. 'Knowledge, Learning and Small Firm Growth: A Systematic Review of the Evidence'. *Research Policy* 36 (2): 172–92.

Malerba, Franco. 2004. Sectoral Systems of Innovation: Concepts, Issues and Analyses of Six Major Sectors in Europe. Cambridge: Cambridge University Press.

Malerba, Franco, and Luigi Orsenigo. 1995. 'Schumpeterian Patterns of Innovation'. *Cambridge Journal of Economics* 19 (1): 47–65.

Malerba, Franco, and Luigi Orsenigo. 1996. 'Schumpeterian Patterns of Innovation Are Technology-Specific'. *Research Policy* 25 (3): 451–78.

McGuirk, Helen, Helena Lenihan, and Mark Hart. 2015. 'Measuring the Impact of Innovative Human Capital on Small Firms' Propensity to Innovate'. *Research Policy* 44 (4): 965–76.

Mina, Andrea, Henry Lahr, and Alan Hughes. 2013. 'The Demand and Supply of External Finance for Innovative Firms'. *Industrial and Corporate Change* 22 (4): 869–901.

Modigliani, Franco, and Merton H. Miller. 1958. 'The Cost of Capital, Corporation Finance and the Theory of Investment'. *The American Economic Review* 48 (3): 261–97.

Moore, Ian, and Elizabeth Garnsey. 1993. 'Funding for Innovation in Small Firms: The Role of Government'. *Research Policy* 22 (5): 507–19.

Mulcahy, Diane. 2013. 'Six Myths about Venture Capitalists'. *Harvard Business Review*. http://hbr.org/2013/05/six-myths-about-venture-capitalists/ar/1

Murray, Gordon C. 2007. 'Venture Capital and Government Policy'. In Landström H. (ed.) *Handbook of Research on Venture Capital,* Cheltenham: Edward Elgar, 113–51.

Myers, Stewart C. 1984. 'The Capital Structure Puzzle'. *The Journal of Finance* 39 (3): 574–92. doi:10.1111/j.1540-6261.1984.tb03646.x.

Myers, Stewart C., and Nicholas S. Majluf. 1984. 'Corporate Financing and Investment Decisions When Firms Have Information That Investors Do Not Have'. *Journal of Financial Economics* 13 (2): 187–221.

Nelson, Andrew J. 2014. 'From the Ivory Tower to the Startup Garage: Organizational Context and Commercialization Processes'. *Research Policy* 43 (7): 1144–56.

Nelson, Richard R., and Sidney G. Winter. 1982. *An Evolutionary Theory of Economic Change*. Harvard University Press. https://books.google.ca/books?hl=en&lr=&id=6Kx7s_HXxrkC&oi=fnd&pg=PA1&dq=nelson+and+winter&ots=7v0ULEC2EF&sig=RyRmcrkEgHDO5O5agXD4HfOL0TE.

Nitani, Miwako, and Allan Riding. 2013. 'Growth, R&D Intensity and Commercial Lender Relationships'. *Journal of Small Business & Entrepreneurship* 26 (2): 109–24.

Nooteboom, Bart. 1999. 'Innovation and Inter-Firm Linkages: New Implications for Policy'. *Research Policy* 28 (8): 793–805.

Nooteboom, Bart. 1994. 'Innovation and Diffusion in Small Firms: Theory and Evidence'. *Small Business Economics* 6 (5): 327–47.

North, David, and David Smallbone. 2000. 'Innovative Activity in SMEs and Rural Economic Development: Some Evidence from England'. *European Planning Studies* 8 (1): 87–106.

Pahnke, Emily Cox, Riitta Katila, and Kathleen M. Eisenhardt. 2015. 'Who Takes You to the Dance? How Partners' Institutional Logics Influence Innovation in Young Firms'. *Administrative Science Quarterly* 60 (4): 596–633.

Perren, Lew. 2002. 'The Entrepreneurial Process of Network Development in Small Biotechnology Firms: The Case of "Destiny Pharma Ltd"'. *International Journal of Entrepreneurship and Innovation Management* 2 (4–5): 390–405.

Pittaway, L., M. Robertson, K. Munir, D. Denyer, and A. Neely. 2004. 'Networking and Innovation: A Systematic Review of the Evidence'.

International Journal of Management Reviews 5 (3–4): 137–68.

Qian, Haifeng, and Kingsley E. Haynes. 2014. 'Beyond Innovation: The Small Business Innovation Research Program as Entrepreneurship Policy'. *The Journal of Technology Transfer* 39 (4): 524–43.

Revest, Valerie, and Alessandro Sapio. 2012. 'Financing Technology-Based Small Firms in Europe: What Do We Know?' *Small Business Economics* 39 (1): 179–205.

Rogers, Mark. 2004. 'Networks, Firm Size and Innovation'. *Small Business Economics* 22 (2): 141–53.

Romero, Isidoro, and Juan A. Martínez-Román. 2012. 'Self-Employment and Innovation. Exploring the Determinants of Innovative Behavior in Small Businesses'. *Research Policy* 41 (1): 178–89.

Romijn, Henny, and Mike Albu. 2002. 'Innovation, Networking and Proximity: Lessons from Small High Technology Firms in the UK'. *Regional Studies* 36 (1): 81–86.

Rosenberg, Nathan. 1982. *Inside the Black Box: Technology and Economics*. Cambridge University Press. https://books.google.ca/books?hl=en&lr=&id=GSyGBicq1NIC&oi=fnd&pg=PR7&dq=inside+the+black+box+innovation&ots=Vnbb4UTj_Y&sig=8aZQuwCfktQywvuBxrm48u3HPO4.

Ross, Stephen A. 1977. 'The Determination of Financial Structure: The Incentive-Signalling Approach'. *The Bell Journal of Economics* 8 (1): 23–40.

Rostamkalaei, Anoosheh, and Mark Freel. 2016. 'The Cost of Growth: Small Firms and the Pricing of Bank Loans'. *Small Business Economics* 46 (2): 255–72.

Rothwell, Roy. 1983. 'Innovation and Firm Size – a Case for Dynamic Complementarity – Or, Is Small Really So Beautiful?' *Journal of General Management* 8 (3): 5–25.

Rothwell, Roy. 1984. 'The Role of Small Firms in the Emergence of New Technologies'. *Omega* 12 (1): 19–29.

Rothwell, Roy. 1989. 'Small Firms, Innovation and Industrial Change'. *Small Business Economics* 1 (1): 51–64.

Rothwell, Roy. 1991. 'External Networking and Innovation in Small and Medium-Sized Manufacturing Firms in Europe'. *Technovation* 11 (2): 93–112.

Salunke, Sandeep, Jay Weerawardena, and Janet R. McColl-Kennedy. 2013. 'Competing through Service Innovation: The Role of Bricolage and Entrepreneurship in Project-Oriented Firms'. *Journal of Business Research* 66 (8): 1085–97.

Schumpeter, Joseph A. 1934. *The Theory of Economic Development: An Inquiry into Profits, Capital, Credit, Interest, and the Business Cycle*. Vol. 55. Transaction Publishers, New Brunswick, NJ and London. http://books.google.ca/books?hl=en&lr=&id=-OZwWcOGeOwC&oi=fnd&pg=PR6&dq=schumpeter+1934&ots=iM5WtXujFa&sig=t6K1CSKJQdDt1jqXwwUGqyinMI4.

Schumpeter, Joseph A. 1942. Socialism, Capitalism and Democracy. New York: Harper and Brothers.

Schumpeter, Joseph A. 1954. *History of Economic Analysis*. London: Routledge. https://books.google.ca/books?hl=en&lr=&id=HZ1WpT5cbgcC&oi=fnd&pg=PR3&dq=History+of+Economic+Analysis+schumpeter&ots=GVsq7dzrt8&sig=UCwONP1Elr6Kexu5PlVVdpJf9Sk.

Scott, Peter, Bryn Jones, Alan Bramley, and Brian Bolton. 1996. 'Enhancing Technology and Skills in Small- and Medium-Sized Manufacturing Firms: Problems and Prospects'. *International Small Business Journal* 14 (3): 85–99.

Simon, Kenneth L. 1995. `Shakeouts: firm survival and technological change in new manufacturing industries', unpublished dissertation, Carnegie Mellon University. www.rpi.edu/~simonk/pdf/ksimonsphd.pdf

Smith, Keith. 2000. 'Innovation as a Systemic Phenomenon: Rethinking the Role of Policy'. *Enterprise and Innovation Management Studies* 1 (1): 73–102.

Soete, Luc LG. 1979. 'Firm Size and Inventive Activity: The Evidence Reconsidered'. *European Economic Review* 12 (4): 319–40.

Tether, Bruce S. 2002. 'Who Co-Operates for Innovation, and Why: An Empirical Analysis'. *Research Policy* 31 (6): 947–67.

Thornhill, Stewart. 2006. 'Knowledge, Innovation and Firm Performance in High- and Low-Technology Regimes'. *Journal of Business Venturing* 21 (5): 687–703.

Tjosvold, Dean, and David Weicker. 1993. 'Cooperative and Competitive Networking by Entrepreneurs: A Critical Incident Study'.

Journal of Small Business Management 31 (1): 11–21.

Trimi, Silvana, and Jasmina Berbegal-Mirabent. 2012. 'Business Model Innovation in Entrepreneurship'. *International Entrepreneurship and Management Journal* 8 (4): 449–65.

Utterback, James M. 1996. *Mastering the Dynamics of Innovation*. Harvard Business Press.

Utterback, James M., and William J. Abernathy. 1975. 'A Dynamic Model of Process and Product Innovation'. *Omega* 3 (6): 639–56.

Utterback, James M., and A. Afuah. 2000. 'Sources of Innovative Environments: A Technological Evolution Perspective'. In: Acs Z. (ed.) *Regional Innovation, Knowledge and Global Change*, London: Pinter, 169–85.

Vahter, Priit, James H. Love, and Stephen Roper. 2014. 'Openness and Innovation Performance: Are Small Firms Different?' *Industry and Innovation* 21 (7–8): 1–21.

Verhees, Frans J.H.M, and Matthew T.G. Meulenberg. 2004. 'Market Orientation, Innovativeness, Product Innovation, and Performance in Small Firms'. *Journal of Small Business Management* 42 (2): 134–54.

Volberda, Henk, and Frans van den Bosch. 2005. 'Why Management Matters Most'. In *European Business Forum* 22: 36–40. http://repub.eur.nl/pub/10939/.

Westhead, Paul, and David J. Storey. 1997. 'Financial Constraints on the Growth of High Technology Small Firms in the United Kingdom'. *Applied Financial Economics* 7 (2): 197–201. doi:10.1080/096031097333763.

Yang, Haibin, Yanfeng Zheng, and Xia Zhao. 2014. 'Exploration or Exploitation? Small Firms' Alliance Strategies with Large Firms'. *Strategic Management Journal* 35 (1): 146–57.

Yli-Renko, Helena, Erkko Autio, and Harry J. Sapienza. 2001. 'Social Capital, Knowledge Acquisition, and Knowledge Exploitation in Young Technology-Based Firms'. *Strategic Management Journal* 22 (6–7): 587–613.

Zider, Bob. 1998. 'How Venture Capital Works'. *Harvard Business Review* 76 (6): 131–39.

16

Entrepreneurial Marketing in Small Enterprises

Rosalind Jones, Sussie C. Morrish,
Jonathan Deacon and Morgan P. Miles

INTRODUCTION

This chapter introduces state-of-the-art viewpoints from established researchers in the study of entrepreneurship and marketing in small and growing enterprises. Researchers in small business emphasize the significance of marketing along with management and money for effective entrepreneurial growth strategies (for example, Brush, Ceru, & Blackburn, 2009), while marketing researchers acknowledge the importance of entrepreneurship, which leads to innovation in the firm's market orientation (Webb, Ireland, Hitt, & Tihanyi, 2011). Marketing and entrepreneurship are acknowledged as two distinct disciplines. The entrepreneurial marketing (EM) concept has created cross-disciplinary fertilization of ideas, yet is firmly grounded in the study of marketing within small firms. EM is an approach to marketing that seeks to create or discover new market opportunities and then successfully exploit these opportunities by leveraging innovation, risk management, and first-mover advantage to create a superior market position. While mainstream marketing over the last century has tended to focus on large organizations selling products and services to static markets with defined segments, entrepreneurial marketing seeks to create new markets or serve existing markets with innovative and often disruptive offerings (Morrish, Miles, & Deacon, 2010). This chapter discusses pioneering work on entrepreneurial marketing by authors such as Carson (1990), Hills (1995), and Morris, Schindehutte, and LaForge (2002), along with contemporary research in the field.

The chapter begins by introducing existing ideas, opinions, and empirically based evidence from global research on the phenomenon of entrepreneurial marketing, which commenced in 1982 with invited researchers led by Professor Gerry Hills in the United States, with the first research milestone being a marketing and entrepreneurship interface (MEI) meeting taking place at Babson College's Frontiers of Entrepreneurship Research in 1984.

It then introduces and explains contemporary themes emanating from the study of entrepreneurial marketing in new ventures and small- to medium-sized enterprises (SMEs), which often operate in challenging marketplaces. Clarification of key differences and overlaps in the study of marketing in small enterprises are presented and discussed. Themes presented in the first part include differences between marketing in new ventures and SMEs (as opposed to the study of marketing in larger organizations meeting the needs of mass-consumer or business-2-business markets). Common substantive topics emerge from this body of research, these being: marketing and business challenges and limitations for SMEs, growth strategies for SMEs, and entrepreneurial marketing orientation (EMO). Entrepreneurial networks are also a pivotal theme of EM, with a considerable body of network literature emanating from the SME marketing field, including research of entrepreneurs and their personal contact networks (PCNs) or *entrepreneurial networks.* The study of marketing and growth strategies in new ventures and small high-growth firms has also spawned significant networking research within the internationalization literature.

On this basis, the final section of the chapter suggests future research opportunities in the EM field in the small-firm context. These include the further study of SMEs and entrepreneurial networks, EM in emerging markets, social entrepreneurship, and entrepreneurial methods of research which take into account the firm as a social construct. The chapter provides several figures and tables to support knowledge in this area and proposes research avenues and questions for the future.

CURRENT THINKING ON ENTREPRENEURIAL MARKETING RESEARCH

EM is now considered an established research domain. In 2006 Hills and Hultman described EM as an umbrella strategy which acknowledges three broad areas of research: marketing that takes place in new ventures or SMEs, entrepreneurial marketing activity that takes place in large organizations, and innovative and cost-effective marketing strategies that provoke market change (Hills & Hultman, 2006). EM research is derived from two key research arenas: entrepreneurship and marketing. The area of study that is of interest to EM research is found at the interface (overlap) of marketing and entrepreneurship. The role of innovation is a central theme of this *marketing/entrepreneurship interface* as it plays a significant role in creating or stimulating 'disruptive' markets. Hills and Hultman (2006) illustrate its significance by providing a Venn diagram which includes entrepreneurship, marketing, and innovation (and their overlaps as the *interface* of research). Innovation in relation to EM provides new opportunity creation that is driven by entrepreneurial action and Schumpeterian behavior.

A substantial body of EM research focuses on marketing which takes place in new and small firms. More recently, with the development of e-commerce, the role of e-marketing and digital marketing together with social media has become of increased interest (Alford & Page, 2015; Harrigan, 2013; Harrigan, Ramsey, & Ibbotson, 2009). EM researchers have studied aspects in larger organizations such as the role of entrepreneurial teams in firm marketing capability and relationships between entrepreneurial orientation and market orientation and their outputs.

There is much debate about whether EM research should be via a 'lens' and, if so, from which domain or emphasis: that of 'marketing' or that of 'entrepreneurship'? Or, should it be viewed differently as a combination of activities where entrepreneurship and marketing overlap? For further knowledge, researchers new to this area are advised to read the report on the Charleston Summit paper (Hansen & Eggers, 2010). The paper summarizes past and future research at the marketing/entrepreneurship interface, providing an abundant source of ideas for future research and a helpful platform on which to base the focus of new studies. These four perspectives of the marketing/entrepreneurship interface identified at the Summit are outlined below.

(a) Marketing and entrepreneurship: Commonalities between both disciplines.
(b) Entrepreneurship in marketing: Entrepreneurship issues framed in the field of marketing or viewed through a marketing theoretical lens.
(c) Marketing in entrepreneurship: Marketing issues framed in the field of entrepreneurship or viewed through an entrepreneurship theoretical lens.
(d) Unique interface concepts: Concepts that are distinct to the interface and evolve out of the combination of entrepreneurship and marketing (Hansen & Eggers, 2010).

The Charleston Summit highlighted small business marketing to be at the foundation of the marketing/entrepreneurship interface, with Carson referring to Gardner's model (1994) and depicting a Venn diagram with circles representing marketing, entrepreneurship, and small business characteristics. 'This suggests that future researchers that want to work in the second perspective, entrepreneurship within marketing, should consider small business or SME issues within the research framework or context of marketing' (Hansen & Eggers, 2010, p. 46).

Researchers may also like to note the summit group's observation of the dominance of literature from the third perspective (marketing in entrepreneurship) in top management and entrepreneurship journals. As every small business employs marketing and selling of products and services in the firm, entrepreneurship and small business researchers may find it extremely beneficial to consider research which focuses on this area, for it has resonance in all areas of entrepreneurship and enterprise research, and it has much to offer in areas such as the study of female and ethnic entrepreneurs as well as the study of finance in start-up firms. Conversely, EM researchers who have a general background in either marketing or entrepreneurship have produced research which naturally takes into account existing research on entrepreneurs and enterprise

research, given that marketing in SMEs is acknowledged as being an implicit activity driven by the personality of the entrepreneur and highly influenced by their vision for the firm's future (Carson, Cromie, McGowan, & Hill, 1995; Jones & Rowley, 2011).

THE RESEARCH CONTEXT OF MARKETING

Over the last three decades, the study of mainstream marketing (and aspects which we see as having critical relevance to the study of EM and marketing in SMEs) has focussed on administrative marketing, market orientation, and strategic marketing. The majority of this research has emanated from studies of large organizations selling products and/or services in mass markets. There is of course a myriad of other specific areas of research contained within the marketing discipline, such as consumer behavior, branding etc. However, in this chapter, we will be identifying and discussing relevant mainstream marketing theory and EM. Most importantly, we will focus on how and why small firms' marketing practices differ and also the importance of deploying appropriate research methodologies in the entrepreneurial small-firm context.

Traditionally, marketers are educated or trained to adopt a strategic perspective. They are expected to evaluate and plan long-term marketing strategies to meet the predicted norms of the prevailing marketplace and to identify large similar groups of customers who are likely to respond to similar stimuli through production, promotion, advertising, and sales methods (see Morrish, 2011). Indeed, marketing strategy models still in use are very similar, overlapping with well-known business strategy models such as those by Ansoff and Porter. Such marketing and business models still in use in management education are largely inappropriate for the small, growing firm (Jones & Edwards, 2013). Marketing in such a way requires a significant marketing budget, an assumed market share, and a fairly static marketplace involving fewer market opportunities with a few large players. Without more flexible entrepreneurial marketing approaches to markets, large firms are ceasing to keep ahead of the marketplace and failing to innovate, as the demise of the traditional music store and bookstore demonstrates.

More recently, larger firms have been influenced by successful entrepreneurs and entrepreneurial marketers who are able to (a) create new markets rapidly where there is little or no competition through new product or service innovations, (b) identify new market opportunities in existing markets by offering new ways of doing things (either by new ways of marketing or by promotional activities), (c) having a unique company ethos that customers can relate to or other novel means of attracting new custom, or (d) create and seize new opportunities from serendipitous encounters. The rise of e-commerce and e-marketing has created new industries and markets for technology-competent entrepreneurs; the smaller firm is able to take advantage of digital marketing, social media, and cost-effective approaches to reaching and communicating with larger, more geographically distant customers. (For a detailed list and discussion on entrepreneurial marketing approaches to different types of innovative marketing techniques on a limited budget, such as guerrilla marketing, see Schindehutte, Morris, and Pitt, 2009). Despite the obvious benefit of marketing using websites and the internet, entrepreneurs are still faced with a myriad of issues and challenges which make marketing in the new start-up business venture and the smaller firm very distinct from marketing for established large organizations.

RESEARCH CHALLENGES: THE SME MARKETING CONTEXT

Many commentators have attempted to define marketing within the dynamic, entrepreneurial small-firm context only to fall foul of the inadequacies of lexicography and conceptualization. As Hills (1995) argues, 'just as a child is not a small adult, a small firm is not a small Fortune 500 company'. Debate within academic symposia as to the nature of marketing within the small firm and marketing's relationship with entrepreneurship appears to be increasing (Whalen et al., 2016). Areas of debate concern issues relating to the entrepreneurial adaptation of administrative marketing approaches (formal marketing methods deployed by larger organizations) or the complete abandonment of such frameworks in favor of a more adaptive, fluid, and socially constructed (situation-specific and culturally sensitive) entrepreneurial marketing approach (see for example the outcome of the Charleston Summit in Hansen and Eggers, 2010). The central feature of a situation-specific approach and application of marketing is that it is contextualized to the individual focal firm, and therefore has both a uniqueness and inherent complexity (Deacon & Harris, 2011). Carson and Gilmore (2000) identify three inherent dimensions of SME marketing which are implicitly carried out in the firm: networking, competencies, and innovation. They also identify a fourth dimension of adapting marketing tools and techniques to suit the characteristics of the SME. While this activity is complex, Carson and Gilmore (2000) contend that there are 'essential key factors' that can be identified that allow an insight into how marketing is performed within each context. These factors are interdependent, interrelated, and synergistically influential in that for successful interface to take place between the firm and the market, firms 'simply have to perform' (Carson & Gilmore, 2000, p. 5) as such activities form the contextual entrepreneurial ecosystem of the SME situation-specific network.

SME MARKETING

As we have intimated earlier, researchers have discovered over the last three decades that marketing activities are very different in the new and small firm (Carson, 1990; Carson & Gilmore, 2000). Early SME marketing research offered very few insights as it had been previously assumed that textbook marketing (administrative marketing) was applicable to the small-firm context. In reality, only very basic marketing activity can be used by an inexperienced entrepreneur and so the small firm focuses on basic survival needs before there is hope of implementing any growth strategies (Jones & Parry, 2011). The entrepreneur or owner–manager (for there is debate as to whether all small business owners are entrepreneurial in nature) all too often has little knowledge or understanding of marketing and little business expertise (Carson et al., 1995). The firm's focus is often on financial aspects at start-up and using boot-strapping methods, while technology entrepreneurs who are 'experts' in their own field often disregard marketing, market/consumer awareness, and market readiness; this is often a reason for market and firm failure at the start (Jones & Parry, 2011). However, over time successful entrepreneurs become naturally adept at developing close relationships with their customers (Carson et al., 1995; Stokes, 2000) and develop highly effective local markets through becoming embedded in the local market and industry (Carson et al., 1995).

Surprisingly, there is very limited research on the differences between small- and large-firm marketing, with the exceptions of Hill (2001) and Jones and Rowley (2009b). Differences emanating from Jones and Rowley's educational software sector study include attitudinal and behavioral differences associated with company size and professional business and market expertise. Smaller firms lack awareness of market competition; however, entrepreneurs are adept at establishing close relationships with customers and swift to react to customer demands, which leads to smaller firms being customer-oriented but less market-oriented. In an effort to develop deeper knowledge and understanding

of small-firm growth in relation to entrepreneurship and marketing activity, recently there have been moves towards SME orientation research. Although there are established studies on entrepreneurial orientation and market orientation, these have largely been carried out in larger organizations, and, as our earlier discussions suggest, marketing is very different in the small firm.

ENTREPRENEURIAL MARKETING ORIENTATION IN SMEs

In an effort to understand the contribution and constituents of effective marketing over the last three decades, mainstream marketing researchers have developed market (or marketing) orientation (MO) measures and scales. Popular scales include those developed by Narver and Slater (1990) and Kohli, Jaworski, and Kumar (1993). A significant number of entrepreneurship researchers have studied entrepreneurial orientation (EO) in firms. An interesting example of this can be found with Morris and Paul (1987), who measured the roles of both EO and MO in small firms with at least 100 employees. They found that those firms which scored higher in terms of EO were also more market-oriented, having a formal marketing department and marketing personnel in senior executive positions. These marketing departments tend to be a key source of strategic direction in terms of innovation, and they tend to significantly act on the strategic direction of the firm. Morris and Paul note that the skills of those in marketing need to reflect the entrepreneurial dimensions of innovation, risk-taking, and proactiveness, with marketers not only being able to understand customers, but being able to inform development of innovative products and services, research and development (R&D), etc.

Perhaps surprisingly, very few researchers have created or adapted MO scales or measures for the study of small firms. Notable exceptions include Pelham (2000) and Pelham and Wilson's (1995) scales, both of which produced statistically valid measures. Despite this gap in research, the significance of EM and marketing activity and its impact on firm growth is well documented in the SME marketing literature (Carson, 1990; Carson et al., 1995; Stokes, 2000). More recently, mainstream MO researchers have recognized that firms which adopt other strategic orientations combined with MO are likely to perform better than firms adopting only a market orientation (Grinstein, 2008). Notably, the absence of MO and other skills and competencies in SMEs often leads to lower performance levels and higher risks of business failure (Jones, Suoranta, & Rowley, 2013b).

EM is defined as the proactive identification and exploitation of opportunities for 'acquiring and retaining profitable customers through innovative approaches to risk management, resource leveraging and value creation' (Morris et al., 2002, p. 5). EM tends to be responsive and reactive to competition and opportunistic in nature (Carson et al., 1995). It is also highly dependent on networking (Carson et al., 1995; Miller, Besser, & Malshe, 2007) and the opportunities it provides for the generation of social capital (Bowey & Easton, 2007; Cope, Jack, & Rose, 2007; Miller et al., 2007; Shaw, 2006). Networks facilitate the formation and generation of customer contacts where word-of-mouth recommendation is facilitated through use of interorganizational network relationships and personal contact networks (Gilmore, Carson, & Grant, 2001; Hill & Wright, 2001).

Hills and Hultman (2006, p. 222) identified EM behavioral characteristics which included 'marketing tactics often two-way with customers' and 'marketing decisions based on daily contacts and networks'. Empirical evidence suggests that there exists a significant correlation between an enterprise's marketing and entrepreneurial orientations, both of which are widely responsible for corporate success (Miles & Arnold, 1991), and the relatively recent development of EM theory has generated a substantial body of literature surrounding the interface between marketing and entrepreneurship (Kraus, Filser, Eggers, Hills, & Hultman, 2012).

Jones and Rowley (2011) propose an EM paradigm should be advanced to include an approach to marketing that is grounded in the knowledge bases of not only marketing, but also of innovation, entrepreneurship, and customer engagement and relationships. This philosophical standpoint is operationalized through a focus on *orientations*. Thus, the conceptual model (Jones & Rowley, 2011) seeks to integrate key facets of the MO scales with facets from customer orientation (CO), entrepreneurial orientation (EO), and innovation orientation (IO). In particular, the case is argued for the inclusion of the notion of customer orientation as a distinct component of EM, rather than being subsumed under MO. Also, while prior studies on MO use the firm's interdepartmental communications in their measures (for example Kohli et al., 1993), Jones and Rowley (2011) propose that small firms do not have departments and use internal (within the firm) networks to communicate. Innovation orientation is in its early stage of development but is an acknowledged aspect of EM, and is hence included within the conceptual model. For further details of how the conceptual model (see Figure 16.1) is constructed please refer to Jones and Rowley (2011).

The entrepreneurial marketing conceptual model (Jones & Rowley, 2011), although published later, was subsequently used to inform development of an empirically based model and qualitative research framework known as the 'EMICO' framework (Jones & Rowley, 2009a). 'EMICO' is an acronym of the orientations identified in the earlier conceptual model, which allowed for investigation of activities, attitudes, and behaviors in SMEs; in this case, in a sample of small technology firms in Wales, UK

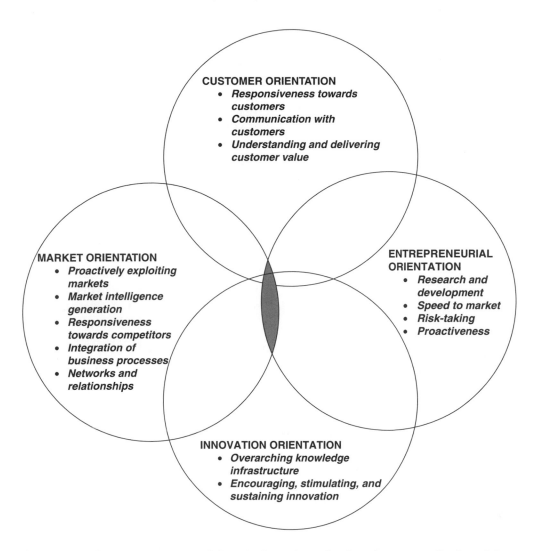

Figure 16.1   The SME entrepreneurial marketing orientation (EMO) conceptualized model (Jones & Rowley, 2011)

(Jones & Rowley, 2009a), and it was later used in a comparative study in Silicon Valley, US (Jones et al., 2013a).

The 'EMICO' framework was informed using existing EO, MO, CO, and IO literature together with empirically based evidence from a sample of UK software technology firms, and by finally comparing research findings with EM concepts: the seven EM dimensions outlined by Morris et al. (2002) and the 23 EM characteristics identified by Hills and Hultman (2005, cited

in Hills & Hultman, 2006, p. 222). As part of the iterative process for the 'EMICO' framework's development, relevant aspects from these authors were incorporated into the final framework.

The seven EM dimensions outlined by Morris et al. (2002, p. 10) are listed below.

- Opportunity-driven.
- Proactiveness.
- Innovation-focused.
- Customer intensity.

- Risk management.
- Resource leveraging.
- Value creation.

The 23 EM characteristics identified by Hills and Hultman (2005, cited in Hills & Hultman, 2006, p. 222) are as follows:

1 Marketing permeates all levels and functional areas of the firm.
2 Marketing decisions are linked to personal goals and long-term performance.
3 There is a flexible, customization approach to market.
4 There is speedy reaction to shifts in customer preference.
5 The firm exploits smaller market niches.
6 There is customer knowledge based on market immersion/interaction.
7 Marketing tactics are often two-way with customers.
8 Planning, or lack of, occurs in short incremental steps.
9 Vision and strategy are driven by tactical successes.
10 Founders and other personalities are central to marketing.
11 Marketing decisions are made based on daily contacts and networks.
12 Formal market research is rare.
13 The firm is focused on proactively creating and exploiting markets.
14 There is an inherent focus on recognition of opportunities.
15 There is calculated risk-taking in new ventures.
16 There is reliance on intuition and experience.
17 Product/venture creation is interactive, incremental, informal, and with little research analysis.
18 There is a role for passion, zeal, and commitment.
19 The firm strives to lead customers.
20 There is value creation through relationships and alliances.
21 Marketing is based on personal reputation, trust, and credibility.
22 There is innovation in products/services and strategies.
23 There is a heavy focus on selling and promotion.

The final 'EMICO' framework model (Jones & Rowley, 2009a) contains 15 dimensions in total related to EMO together with descriptors for each dimension based on qualitative interview statements of research participants in the sample of firms (both employees and entrepreneurs). The model therefore reflects participants' activities and behaviors in the firms in relation to EM in their own words. Both the EMO conceptual model and the 'EMICO' framework provide implications for future researchers which are discussed later in the chapter.

ENTREPRENEURIAL NETWORKS

Entrepreneurial network research has developed as a central theme in the SME marketing field from the observations of researchers such as Carson (1990), Carson et al. (1995), and Shaw (2006). Network research from the economics and management literature, such as that by Granovetter (1985), has informed network studies from a social network perspective. An interesting development in the research of internationalization of SMEs is the common and substantive theme of marketing using networks and network capabilities, a particular interest to researchers studying the swift growth and expansion of new ventures and *born globals*. So networks are a central theme not only in the SME marketing literature, but also in the EM literature (Collinson & Shaw, 2001). Networks, and the ability to leverage them to create new partnerships, have been identified to be a foundation for successful entrepreneurs (Sarasvathy, 2001) as well as a foundation of entrepreneurial marketing, while Gilmore and Carson define social networks as 'a collection of individuals who may or may not be known to each other and who in some way contribute something to the entrepreneur, either passively, reactively or proactively whether specifically elicited or not' (Gilmore & Carson, 1999, p. 31). Networks have a central actor which may be an individual or an organization. In entrepreneurial firms, this is usually driven by the founder; thus, the firm's network configuration is really a reflection of the founder's relationships. Many small high-technology firms often fall into this category (Knight & Cavusgil, 2004; Oviatt & McDougall, 1994). If we accept that the entrepreneurial or small-firm orientation is linked inevitably to the orientation of the entrepreneurial individual, forming the focal point of the firm as suggested by Carson et al. (1995), then we should also accept that the network of social connections that make up the perceived 'market' are likely to be social contacts of the individual and that any interactions between these are thus socially constructed and personal in nature (Starr & MacMillan, 1990). Furthermore, it has been observed that such network activities are natural, as part of an interactive society, and have the possibility of being enhanced in a specific way – that is, for marketing purposes.

As networking has an intuitive sociological basis, it is therefore possible to suggest that the entrepreneur may not be fully aware of the extent and value of the network that has been built up within the context of the individual firm within a specific commercial sector; indeed, the network is likely to have been developed over time and with differing motivations, and yet not in any formal or demonstrable way (Deacon, 2008). Some have likened the development of a network to that of a cloud – when observed it can be seen, but it is difficult to make tangible contact with all its dimensions. It will appear to be in constant flux, but at the same time it is always recognizable (Gilmore & Carson, 1999). Complexity theorists hold a similar view in that they suggest that a social network is critical to being able to navigate a course through the turbulence that sits in the space between chaos and order (Lewin, 1993).

Networking, then, is seen to fit with the entrepreneurial ethos of the small firm in that, to maintain a viable position in an ever-changing environment, the firm will seek to match internal resource strengths with external entrepreneurial opportunities (McGowan & Rocks, 1995; Timmons, 1994).

As marketing activities within the small firm differ from 'conventional' approaches in that the entrepreneur will be constantly making decisions 'at the edge' (Hill & McGowan, 1996), and that such decisions are characterized by their non-linear, time-compressed, and intuitive nature (Hill, McGowan, & Drummond, 1999), then the entrepreneurial response to this is for the entrepreneur to use network contacts in order to obtain the necessary 'fit' between the firm and the market (Dubini & Aldrich, 1991; Johanson & Vahlne, 2003; Keene, 2000). The characteristics of the SME's approach to networking are somewhat similar to that of an SME's marketing characteristics, with both displaying informality, reaction, spontaneity, and some conformity to industry norms (Gilmore et al., 2001). In a similar vein, Jones et al. (2013b) developed the Strategic Network Marketing Model from a qualitative study of small UK and US software technology firms. The ecosystem in Silicon Valley, US provided a more extensive ecosystem leading to much more network capability in Silicon Valley firms.

The Strategic Network Marketing Model demonstrates that entrepreneurs develop strategic clusters of networks, namely, social networks, business networks, sales and marketing networks, innovation networks, customer networks, and a central intra-firm network, from which information flows inwardly and outwardly (as opposed to operating within departments as with large firms). A personalized network will be trusted by the entrepreneur and will act as the 'dependable guide for understanding the turbulent and dynamic environment' (Carson et al., 1995, p. 201). Networking represents a great advantage for the entrepreneur; it represents a way of marketing that is inseparable from 'doing business' and is compatible with the resources available. However, competencies in relationship-building, maintenance, and interpersonal communication are central to the success of this type of marketing activity (Bjerke & Hultman, 2002). It is the linguistic *touch points* at the marketing/networking interface and communication competencies, the personal interaction and making of 'marketing meaning', that bonds them together and allows for 'progress and growth' (Hill et al., 1999, p. 72) through market development. The SME internationalization literature also contains considerable network research, as networks are a highly effective method of moving into cross-boundary or overseas markets. The role of networks, appropriate research methods, and implications for future research will be discussed later in the chapter.

ENTREPRENEURIAL NETWORKS AND INTERNATIONALIZATION

Vasilchenko and Morrish (2011) classify an entrepreneur's networks into social networks or business networks, both consisting of a set of actors linked by relationships (Hoang & Antoncic, 2003). Networks and relationships are essential to the EM concept, whereby they are utilized for leveraging resources, and value is created through the relationships and alliances that entrepreneurs create (Jones & Rowley, 2011, 2009a). Networks work well to complement the founder's experience (Cooper, 1981) where internationalization is concerned as they provide linkages that the founder may not necessarily directly have access to and they avoid the liability of sameness (Starr & Bygrave, 1991), especially when starting new ventures.

Internationalization poses many challenges and the barriers to this process can be daunting to small start-up firms, given that they are characteristically scant in resources and may be a considerable distance from the markets they wish to enter. Vesper (1980) proposes that start-up experience can enable network-building and may act as proxy for skills and competencies not readily available to the firm. Speed to market is especially important for high-technology firms given the nature of their products (Bell, McNaughton, & Young, 2001; Litvak, 1990; Smallbone & North,

1995), making networks an appropriate vehicle toward internationalization (Elfring & Hulsink, 2003), and suggesting that networks are widely recognized as an important aspect of internationalization success.

An important strategic decision in internationalization is market selection and entry, and this is where networks play a significant role (Coviello & Munro, 1995). This is manifested in the founder's choice of countries whereby the presence of networks appears to influence the decision even more than the perceived distance from their home country. Thus it makes sense to suggest that networks support international aspirations. In internationalization, an entrepreneur's networks are useful in finding information about opportunities or potential international business partners (Johanson & Vahlne, 2003) and in relation to location (Coviello & Munro, 1997). The uncertainties associated with entering a new market could be reduced if the entrepreneur can access local market information from personal or business contacts (Vasilchenko & Morrish, 2011), thus they are instrumental in a firm's development of international business activities. As firms expand into foreign markets, business networks can facilitate the acquisition of experiential knowledge about international markets; therefore, business networks can be strongly relied upon, especially during the international opportunity exploitation stage (Eriksson & Johanson, 1997). Business networks can provide synergistic relationships with other firms that complement their resources at various stages in the value chain (Jones, 1999; Nummela, 2002) and can speed up the internationalization process.

Vasilchenko and Morrish (2011) have developed an internationalization model (see Figure 16.2) that captures how social and business networks impact on an internationalizing firm's opportunity for exploration and exploitation, to better understand the network mechanisms underlying internationalization. In their New Zealand research, Vasilchenko and Morrish (2011) used in-depth case studies of four firms (no older than six years) who were

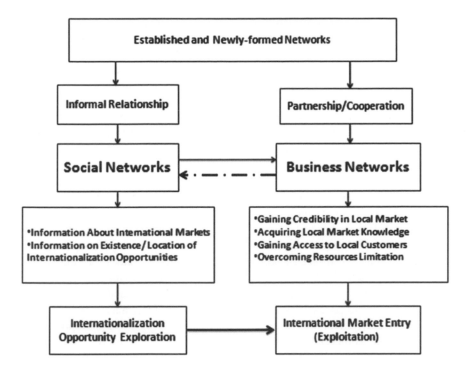

Figure 16.2   Network-based internationalization model (Vasilchenko & Morrish, 2011)

all born global and initiated their international activities within the first year of inception. All case study firms were in the high-technology sector with core activities in online accounting software, Wi-Fi hotspot software, phone backup software, and artificial intelligence software. Three of the companies were privately held and one was a public company. In all cases, the founding entrepreneurs were interviewed as they were the individuals best able to articulate their company's internationalization strategies. The companies were fast-growth firms and had presence in the UK, Australia, Fiji, India, and Canada. Through these case studies, the researchers investigated the role of entrepreneurial networks in the exploration and exploitation of internationalization opportunities in information and communication technology (ICT) firms.

This research culminated in the development of the Network-based Internationalization Model, which proposes that social networks, as well as business networks, can be a source of actual international opportunity (Vasilchenko & Morrish, 2011). The Network-based Internationalization Model shown in Figure 16.2 emphasizes the significance of both social and business networks in newly formed and also established networks of the internationalizing small entrepreneurial firm. It also demonstrates the relationships and touch points between both types of network relationships.

Networks consisting of a multitude of people and organizations to create innovation and commercialize products to international markets (Coviello & Munro, 1995, 1997; Elfring & Hulsink, 2003; Kelly, 2000) are fast becoming a necessity for firms to effectively execute strategies, most notably those that involve internationalization. For smaller businesses that are often significantly resource-constrained, networking could substantially improve their ability to take advantage of new opportunities in the marketplace and quickly exploit these fully, therefore improving their competitiveness and, consequently, their like-lihood of survival. The New Zealand study highlighted EM characteristics which are particularly visible in small internationalizing firms. The respondent owner–managers of small software technology firms were adept at entrepreneurially leveraging resources for their firms, a facet of EM particularly identi-fied by Morris et al. (2002). Networks, part-nerships, and alliances were prevalent in this sector, and resources for business, innova-tion, and marketing were obtained by implic-itly using network and relationship-building approaches (Hills & Hultman, 2006).

How the entrepreneur instigates his or her networks can be explained in part by recent *effectual reasoning* research. For example, Galkina and Chetty (2015) explored the inter-nationalization process by integrating effec-tual theory (Sarasvathy, 2001) with a revisit to the Uppsala internationalization process model to help understand the implicit aspects of networking by internationalizing SMEs. The findings confirmed Vasilchenko and Morrish's (2011) study in that entrepreneurs were found to network with interested part-ners rather than by predefined network goals, while entrepreneurs who were effective at networking entered a market when the oppor-tunity emerged and committed to network relations that increased their means. The fol-lowing section of the chapter suggests fruitful future research avenues for research based on the material discussed above and based on the surfacing of key areas of current research and highlighted omissions in the current literature.

FUTURE RESEARCH OPPORTUNITIES FOR SME MARKETING RESEARCH

The first part of this chapter introduced an overview of research in the domain of entre-preneurial marketing (EM), and the overlaps between concepts and any differences were extrapolated and explained. While the area is too broad to cover every detail of the topic,

we have sought to provide new inspiration for the study of EM and some interesting avenues of research for the future based on calls in the developing literature by eminent researchers in the field. Core concepts of EM include the entrepreneur's implicit use of networks to carry out marketing activity and to create or identify new market opportuni-ties. EM is specifically linked to opportunity recognition, assessment, and exploitation and is based on a combination of studies (Miles & Darroch, 2006; Miles, Verreynne, Luke, Eversole, & Barraket, 2013; Morrish et al., 2010; Shane & Venkataraman, 2000). Looking forward, and in addition to current research, four avenues for future research are offered in this chapter: (1) entrepreneurial networks and internationalization, (2) appli-cation of EM to emerging markets, (3) appli-cation of EM in social entrepreneurship, and (4) research opportunity which has a focus on entrepreneurial methods.

ENTREPRENEURIAL NETWORKS AND INTERNATIONALIZATION

We included the role of EMO, networks, and internationalization as having a bearing on the way new ventures grow and establish them-selves in domestic and overseas/cross-boundary markets. As networking has an intui-tive basis, it can be suggested that the entrepre-neur may not be fully aware of the extent and value of the network that has been built up within the context of the individual firm and within a specific commercial sector; the net-work is likely to have been developed over time, with differing motivations, and yet not in any formal or demonstrable way (Deacon, 2008). As mentioned earlier in this chapter, networks are core to EM as successful entre-preneurs leverage additional firm resources and create value (Jones & Rowley, 2011, 2009a). Over time the entrepreneur develops marketing experience and network competencies. These networks provide important linkages for the

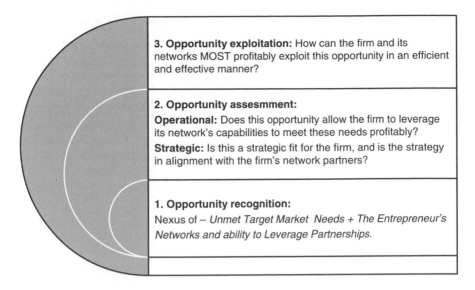

3. Opportunity exploitation: How can the firm and its networks MOST profitably exploit this opportunity in an efficient and effective manner?

2. Opportunity assesmment:
Operational: Does this opportunity allow the firm to leverage its network's capabilities to meet these needs profitably?
Strategic: Is this a strategic fit for the firm, and is the strategy in alignment with the firm's network partners?

1. Opportunity recognition:
Nexus of – *Unmet Target Market Needs + The Entrepreneur's Networks and ability to Leverage Partnerships.*

Figure 16.3   Entrepreneurial marketing[1] from a networking perspective[2]

[1] Shane & Venkataraman (2000) and Miles & Darroch (2006)

[2] Model adapted from Miles et al. (2013)

firm in the industry in which they are embedded. SMEs carry out marketing activities using networks (such as customer networks, university networks, business networks, and web-based networks) for implicitly gathering market research data from personal contacts working in other technology firms. For example, Jones et al. (2013b) found that, in micro firms, the entrepreneur is often the firm's salesperson who performs multiple other tasks, complemented by a significant amount of networking.

The example of research in New Zealand technology markets provides an opportunity to explore how born global firms market in high-speed, challenging, global marketplaces. Vasilchenko and Morrish (2011) offer an internationalization opportunity exploration–exploitation model that emanates from the entrepreneur's network configuration and that provides insight into the logic behind the non-sequential and non-linear patterns of network-driven internationalization. Further research needs to carried out in this area as to how entrepreneurs who focus on internationalization (either at or before firm inception, or as part of a progressive entry into new markets) activate and facilitate these networks, whether it be from effectual reasoning or perhaps driven by their strategic orientation (EMO). Furthermore, it is necessary to understand which activities and behaviors create the environment whereby internationalization can take place, for example, when two firms internationalize, but only one has high growth.

Figure 16.3 articulates how networks impact the recognition, assessment, and exploitation of opportunities. The work of Shane and Venkataraman (2000) was chosen to form part of the basis of the model shown in Figure 16.3 as their research is the primary source of the opportunity recognition (discovery/creation), opportunity assessment, and opportunity exploitation process. It was also informed by Miles and Darroch (2006).

Table 16.1 illustrates the potential research topics and linkages between networks and entrepreneurial marketing and is also informed by the work of Shane and Venkataraman (2000) and Miles and Darroch (2006).

Table 16.1   Research questions pertaining to networks in entrepreneurial marketing[3]

Elements of entrepreneurial marketing[1]	Entrepreneurial marketing as opportunity creation and discovery[2]	Entrepreneurial marketing as opportunity assessment[2]	Entrepreneurial marketing as opportunity exploitation[2]
Customer focus and intensity	How can the entrepreneur leverage networks to create new customers and meet new customer needs?	How do networks impact the assessment of markets and firms' capacity to exploit them?	How do firms leverage other network partners in the pursuit of creating competitive advantage?
Value creation	Can an entrepreneur's networks alter the value position?	Can the proposed value proposition be delivered profitably – leveraging the network partners to manage downside risk?	What type of business model will allow the firm to most effectively leverage its network to create advantage?
Resource leveraging	How can a firm maximize the use of other people's money using its networks?	Would a firm change its assessment of an opportunity based on knowledge of its network partners?	Do networks allow resource leveraging?
Risk management	How can networks be exploited to manage risk?	How do networks reduce risks?	How can networks be best structured to manage downside risk?
Innovation	Can the ability to innovate be enhanced with partners?	Are networks sources of advantage in innovation?	Can networks be used to more effectively exploit the opportunity through co-branding or joint marketing?
Opportunity-driven	How can firms use contacts of their networks as economic opportunities?	How do networked firms select the opportunities that they will pursue?	What are the network-based solutions to exploiting the opportunities available?

1 Morris, Schindehutte, & LaForge (2002)

2 Shane & Venkataraman (2000)

3 Table adapted from Miles & Darroch (2006)

ENTREPRENEURIAL MARKETING IN EMERGING MARKETS

Entrepreneurial marketing has been recently applied in the context of emerging markets such as India (Ahmadi & O'Cass, 2015) and Papua New Guinea (Bonney, Collins, Verreynne, & Miles, 2013). EM in an emerging market context is often a much more useful paradigm than traditional administrative marketing due to: (1) its grounding in effectual logic with a focus on entrepreneurs and their means, networks, and ability to leverage partnerships, contingencies, and manage downside risks (Morrish, 2009); (2)

its foundation being based on resource constraints; and (3) its application of the dimensions of value creation and innovation (Morris et al., 2002). However, EM in an emerging market context must be adapted to reflect the realities of the local environment. For example, in an ongoing study of EM applied to agricultural value chains in Vietnam, what is considered an innovative practice for subsistence cattle farmers (a formal system of value chain coordination) would not be classified as a process innovation in more sophisticated beef-producing nations, such as Australia. Figure 16.4 illustrates EM processes in an emerging

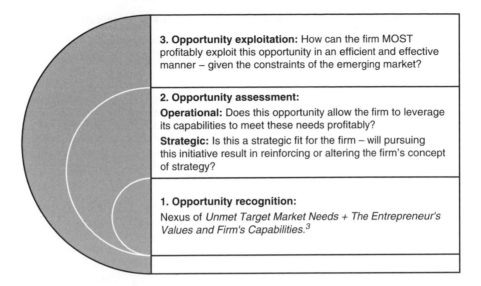

Figure 16.4   Entrepreneurial marketing[1] from an emerging market perspective[2]

[1] Shane & Venkataraman (2000) and Miles & Darroch (2006)

[2] Model adapted from Miles et al. (2013)

[3] Morrish, Miles & Deacon et al. (2010)

market context and articulates how recognition, assessment, and exploitation of opportunities are shaped by the emerging market context. EM in emerging markets offers a more efficient and effective set of processes to pursue competitive advantage in resource- and market-constrained environments. Emerging market firms could leverage EM by adapting Shane and Venkataraman's (2000) model of opportunity creation (discovery) and opportunity/organization fit assessment, and profitably exploiting the opportunity (Shane & Venkataraman, 2000) combined with the seven EM dimensions proposed by Morris et al. (2002) and outlined earlier in the first part of this chapter. Table 16.2 illustrates how EM can be used by entrepreneurs in an emerging market context to build and renew competitive advantage. Potential research questions are offered in each cell to stimulate additional work in the area of entrepreneurial marketing in emerging markets.

ENTREPRENEURIAL MARKETING AND SOCIAL ENTREPRENEURSHIP

Social entrepreneurial marketing (SEM) is the application of entrepreneurial marketing to enhance the effectiveness and efficiency of social enterprises. Social entrepreneurial marketing has become a critical social enterprise competency as globally governments have abdicated their responsibilities in society's most vulnerable communities to non-governmental organizations and social enterprises, such as churches and charities. Bennett (2008) found that social enterprises have emerged to provide social welfare services as state-provided services in the UK diminished. These social enterprises are non-profit organizations established to fulfill a social mission that is supported by commerce.

EM offers more efficient and effective marketing processes for social enterprises seeking to create *contributive advantage*, or the ability of the social enterprise (SE) to

Table 16.2   Research questions pertaining to the adoption of entrepreneurial marketing in an emerging market context[3]

Elements of entrepreneurial marketing[1]	Entrepreneurial marketing as opportunity creation and discovery[2]	Entrepreneurial marketing as opportunity assessment[2]	Entrepreneurial marketing as opportunity exploitation[2]
Customer focus and intensity	How can customer focus and deep understanding of customer needs result in the discovery of additional economic opportunities?	How do firms in emerging markets evaluate their ability to address these opportunities with their own organizational values, mission, strategy, and capacity?	How do firms in emerging markets identify and work with other organizational partners in the pursuit of creating competitive advantage?
Value creation	What are the current value offerings that address the expressed need and how can they be improved or disrupted?	Can the proposed value proposition be delivered profitably – leveraging partners and contingencies to manage downside risk?	What type of business model will allow the firm to create a superior marketing position and gain advantage?
Resource leveraging	How can firms in emerging markets use new technologies such as social media and IT to leverage their scarce resources?	How do firms in emerging markets use effectual logic?	Does resource leveraging result in new business models in emerging markets?
Risk management	How can downside risks be best managed in emerging markets with often high levels of corruption, crime, and poverty?	Are pre-commitments viable risk management strategies when there are less than adequate legal and regulatory institutions?	How can a business model be structured to manage downside risk while still allowing profitable upside opportunities to be exploited?
Innovation	How does the typology of innovation change in an emerging market context?	What are the risks of performance failure, liability, and negative unintended consequences that a for-profit firm might be exposed to in exploiting opportunities?	How can emerging market firms use innovations that are context relevant during the exploitation phase?
Opportunity driven	How can for-profits use the tremendous social and economic needs of emerging marketing as economic opportunities?	How do firms select the opportunities that they will pursue?	What are various alternatives to exploiting the opportunities available?

1 Morris, Schindehutte & LaForge (2002)

2 Shane & Venkataraman (2000)

3 Table adapted from Miles & Darroch (2006)

satisfy the beneficiary's needs in an effective and efficient manner (see Robb-Post, Stamp, Brannback, Carsrud, & Hacker, 2010). While entrepreneurial marketing has been introduced in a social enterprise context (see Miles, Verreynne, & Luke, 2014), it has also been recently applied in a variety of unique contexts, such as community disaster recovery and renewal (Miles, Lewis, Hall-Phillips, Morrish, Gilmore, & Kasouf, 2015), museum marketing (Lehman, Fillis, & Miles, 2014), and agricultural value chains analysis (Lewis, Miles, Crispin, Bonney, Woods, Fei, & Ayala, 2014). All these studies have applied an entrepreneurial marketing framework in each context.

Social enterprises in this new era of reduced government support can, and should, leverage entrepreneurial marketing for contributive advantage, such that social enterprises adopting social entrepreneurial marketing will engage in marketing processes that are based on opportunity creation and/or discovery, evaluation, and exploitation (Shane & Venkataraman, 2000) to meet their beneficiaries' expressed and latent needs.

Miles et al. (2013) proposed a process model of social entrepreneurship that offers insight into some of the issues and challenges of social enterprises being more entrepreneurial. Figure 16.5 illustrates this process model and articulates how opportunity recognition, assessment, and exploitation are shaped by the values and mission of a social enterprise.

Miles and Darroch (2006) offer a framework for large for-profits that might be adapted to guide social enterprises in their adoption of entrepreneurial marketing processes. Table 16.3 illustrates how entrepreneurial marketing processes can be used by social

enterprises to build and renew contributive advantage as well as the potential topics and linkages between social enterprise and entrepreneurial marketing. The interaction between the process model of entrepreneurship proposed by Shane and Venkataraman (2000) and the seven dimensions of entrepreneurial marketing proposed by Morris et al. (2002), as articulated by Miles and Darroch (2006), for large for-profit firms are adapted for the context of social enterprises. Potential research questions are offered in each cell to stimulate additional work in the area of social entrepreneurial marketing.

ENTREPRENEURIAL METHODS

Finally, we offer a research opportunity which has a focus on entrepreneurial methods. Within the emerging field of EM, there should be encouragement and support for researchers themselves to adopt entrepreneurial research designs in order to uncover insight that more normative quantitative methodologies

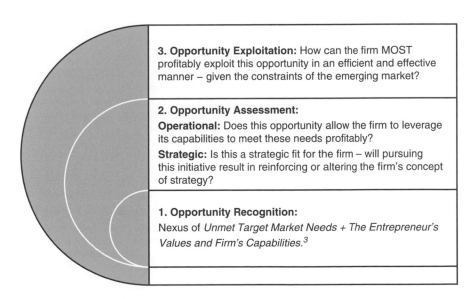

Figure 16.5   Entrepreneurial marketing[1] from an SEM perspective[2]

[1] Morris, Schindehutte, & LaForge (2002)

[2] Shane & Venkataraman (2000)

Table 16.3 Research questions pertaining to social entrepreneurial marketing (SEM) and the process of entrepreneurship[3]

Elements of SEM[1]	SEM as opportunity creation and discovery[2]	SEM as opportunity assessment[2]	SEM as opportunity exploitation[2]
Beneficiary focus and intensity	How can a focus on the explicit and latent needs of a social enterprise's beneficiaries result in the discovery of additional opportunities to serve?	How do social enterprises evaluate their ability to meet beneficiary needs that fit with their own organizational values, mission, and capacity?	How can social enterprises leverage other organizations in the pursuit of creating contributive advantage?
Value creation	Should social enterprise create value propositions that will allow the maximum number of beneficiaries to take advantage of the offering or that best meet a smaller number of beneficiaries' needs?	Can the proposed value proposition be delivered in an economically and socially sustainable manner?	What type of social enterprise business models allows the maximum number of beneficiaries to take advantage of the offering?
Resource leveraging	How can social enterprise accomplish what both Stevenson and Gumpert (1985) and Sarasvathy (2001) propose – to leverage their scarce resources by maximizing the use of external resources?	How are social enterprises using effectual logic in opportunity assessment?	How does resource leveraging result in partnerships that: (1) minimize the direct risk to the social enterprise, while (2) enhancing the set of available resources that will result in (3) new unpredictable opportunities to serve?
Risk management	How can risk management be accomplished while the social enterprise focuses on serving their beneficiaries?	Do social enterprises use pre-commitments to manage risk?	How much risk should a social enterprise be willing to accept?
Innovation	How do social enterprises perceive innovation and its capability to build the number and range of problems that can be addressed?	What are the risks of performance failure, liability, and negative unintended consequences that a social enterprise might be exposed to?	How can social enterprise use innovations and technologies that are context relevant during the exploitation phase?
Opportunity-driven	How can social enterprise better see needs as opportunities to serve in crises, problems, and community challenges?	No one social enterprise can meet all a beneficiary community's needs – how do they pick the needs to address?	What opportunities should be exploited?
Proactive	How do emerging issues and challenges that impact a social enterprise's beneficiaries often stimulate opportunity creation or discovery?	How do social enterprises match their capabilities to adapt to the changing needs of their beneficiaries?	Should social enterprises exploit profitable marketable opportunities to generate resources to better serve their beneficiaries?

1 Morris, Schindehutte, & LaForge (2002)

2 Shane & Venkataraman (2000)

3 Table adapted from Miles & Darroch (2006)

overlook; in western culture the prevailing causal, neoclassical microeconomic research approaches will tell us some things about phenomena under investigation, but will they enable a depth of insight and a true understanding?

Researching a complex entrepreneurial ecosystem clearly cannot be undertaken without an acceptance that the EM function within the focal firm is first and foremost a social construct. Such research will deal with the everyday life experience of the business owner–manager or entrepreneur; these everyday experiences only exist as a relational artifact at a point of contact with others within the social system of the focal firm and are of course central to the development of a network, be it local or international. For meaning to be developed we cannot reduce the study to just an individual, but will need to consider the contacts, connections, group attachments, and social meetings that relate one person to another, as well as practice-based research (Gross, Carson, & Jones, 2014; Saunders, 2005). As a consequence, the key factors in a situation-specific study of the meaning and operation of EM are, and will be, socially constructed, and it is impossible to treat business owners as separate from their social contexts and environments (Gilmore, Carson, & O'Donnell, 2004). The linguistic nature of such contexts will be desirous to understand if we are to cartographically make socially constructed connections to aid theoretical development, and, ontologically, a greater emphasis should therefore be placed upon the capture, interpretation, and understanding of narrative in context. Thus, we encourage researchers to seek insight and gain understanding of the psychological and sociological context of EM through ethnographic interpretation.

CONCLUSION

This chapter explored the existing and emerging topics of SME marketing that are encapsulated within the research domain of entrepreneurial marketing: that is, research at the marketing/entrepreneurship interface. We have introduced and discussed different and important viewpoints emerging from the SME marketing literature and highlighted the overlaps in research themes and their differences. These differences particularly lie in the way marketing activity is carried out in larger firms versus smaller firms or new ventures. New and small firms are often limited by business, financial, and employee resources (as also noted in SME management literature); thus, innovative approaches to marketing which are implicitly carried out in the firm and are often closely intertwined with other firm activities, being influenced by the personality of the entrepreneur, dominate the way the firm markets itself. Noting these differences is important as the use of inappropriate research methods, or the application of inappropriate mainstream models, may render the research of the SME invalid or, at least, lacking in essential detail relevant to the entrepreneur, the small firm, and the industry context. There is also the danger of the entrepreneur attempting to apply marketing tools and models made for the large firm and finding them inappropriate and expensive to apply in the small-firm context. The upside for larger entrepreneurial firms in relation to the study of SME marketing and entrepreneurial marketing activity in the small firm is that such identified *adaptive capabilities* of successful entrepreneurial firms, who often operate in very challenging, dynamic marketplaces (such as technology sectors), are seemingly being adopted in larger firms in order for them to survive and grow.

The chapter highlighted the significance of firm orientation research in the field, as firms who adopt both an entrepreneurial orientation and marketing orientation often have more significant growth, and hence the study of entrepreneurial marketing orientation as a distinct topic of current research. Networks and networking are also pivotal themes within entrepreneurial marketing and SME internationalization literature, essential for the entrepreneur who seeks new opportunities and for value creation activities.

The chapter has also described the relationships and linkages between entrepreneurial marketing and networking, emerging markets, and social enterprise, respectively. Tables 16.1, 16.2, and 16.3 offer scholars a series of potential research questions that should be addressed to more fully articulate the effectiveness and efficiency of entrepreneurial marketing. In these tables, entrepreneurial marketing is matched to potential areas of research that specifically address EM as opportunity creation and discovery, EM as opportunity assessment, and EM as opportunity exploitation. While there are other contexts in which entrepreneurial marketing can be applied, these areas of research mentioned above highlight areas that are of interest to both entrepreneurial marketing and entrepreneurship researchers, and areas where answers to these questions can contribute to theory, practice, and policy. Entrepreneurial marketing is a powerful notion in that marketing does not have to be the same in all businesses, or in any one business, as the context and situation changes. Entrepreneurial marketing embodies the spirit of entrepreneurship with its pragmatic approach: that is, marketing by employing innovation as a lever on marketing practices. We hope that this overview and introduction to these topics of interest in entrepreneurial marketing will stimulate additional research and a more programmatic approach to scholarship in the subject.

REFERENCES

Ahmadi, H. and O'Cass, A. (2016) 'The role of entrepreneurial marketing in new technology ventures first product commercialisation', *Journal of Strategic Marketing*, 24(1): 47–60.

Alford, P. and Page, S.J. (2015) 'Marketing technology for adoption by small business', *The Service Industries Journal*, 35(11–12): 655–69.

Bell, J., McNaughton, R. and Young, S. (2001) 'Born-again global firms: An extension to the born global phenomenon', *Journal of International Management*, 7(3): 173–89.

Bennett, R. (2008) 'Marketing of voluntary organizations as contract providers of national and local government welfare services in the UK', *Voluntas*, 19(3): 268–95.

Bjerke, B. and Hultman, C. (2002) *Entrepreneurial Marketing: The Growth of Small Firms in the New Economic Era*. Cheltenham: Edward Elgar.

Bonney, L., Collins, R., Verreynne, M.-L. and Miles, M.P. (2013) 'A short note on entrepreneurship as an alternative logic to address food security in the developing world', *Journal of Developmental Entrepreneurship*, 18(3): 1350016–25.

Bowey, J.L. and Easton, G. (2007) 'Entrepreneurial social capital unplugged: An activity-based analysis', *International Small Business Journal*, 25(3): 273–306.

Brush, C.G., Ceru, D.J. and Blackburn, R. (2009) 'Pathways to entrepreneurial growth: The influence of management, marketing, and money', *Business Horizons*, 52(5): 481–91.

Carson, D. (1990) 'Some exploratory models for assessing small firms' marketing performance: A qualitative approach', *European Journal of Marketing*, 24(11): 8–51.

Carson, D. and Gilmore, A. (2000) 'Marketing at the interface: Not "what" but "how"', *Journal of Marketing Theory and Practice*, 8(2): 1–7.

Carson, D., Cromie, S., McGowan, P. and Hill, J. (1995) *Marketing and Entrepreneurship in SMEs: An Innovative Approach*. Essex: Prentice Hall.

Collinson, E. and Shaw, E. (2001) 'Entrepreneurial marketing: A historical perspective on development and practice,' *Management Decision*, 39(9): 761–66.

Cooper, A. (1981) 'Strategic management: New ventures and small business', *Long Range Planning*, 14(5): 39–45.

Cope, J., Jack, S. and Rose, M.B. (2007) 'Social capital and entrepreneurship: An introduction', *International Small Business Journal*, 25(3): 213–19.

Coviello, N. and Munro, H. (1997) 'Network relationships and the internationalisation process of small software firms', *International Business Review*, 6(4): 361–86.

Coviello, N. and Munro, H. (1995) 'Growing the entrepreneurial firm: Networking for internal market development', *European Journal of Marketing*, *29*(7): 49–61.

Deacon, J.H. (2008) 'A study of the meaning and operation of the language for marketing in context'. *PhD thesis*, University of Ulster, Northern Ireland.

Deacon, J.H. and Harris, J.A. (2011) 'A conceptualisation of the meaning and operation of a language for marketing in context', *Journal of Research in Marketing and Entrepreneurship*, *13*(2): 146–60.

Dubini, P. and Aldrich, H. (1991) 'Personal and extended networks are central to the entrepreneurial process', *Journal of Business Venturing*, *6*(5): 305–13.

Elfring, T. and Hulsink, W. (2003) 'Networks in entrepreneurship: The case of high-technology firms', *Small Business Economics*, *21*(4): 409–22.

Eriksson, K. and Johanson, J. (1997) 'Experiential knowledge and cost in the internationalisation process', *Journal of International Business Studies*, *28*(2): 337–60.

Galkina, T. and Chetty, S. (2015) 'Effectuation and networking of internationalizing SMEs', *Management International Review*, *55*(5): 647–76.

Gardner, D. (1994) 'Marketing/entrepreneurship interface: A conceptualization', in G.E. Hills (ed.), *Marketing and Entrepreneurship: Research Ideas and Opportunities*. Westport, CT: Quorum Books. pp. 35–54.

Gilmore, A. and Carson, D. (1999) 'Entrepreneurial marketing by networking', *New England Journal of Entrepreneurship*, *2*(2): 31–38.

Gilmore, A., Carson, D. and Grant, K. (2001) 'SME marketing in practice', *Marketing Intelligence & Planning*, *19*(1): 6–11.

Gilmore, A., Carson, D. and O'Donnell, A. (2004) 'Small business owner–managers and their attitude to risk', *Marketing Intelligence and Planning*, *22*(3): 349–60.

Granovetter, M. (1985) 'Economic action and social structure: The problem of embeddedness', *American Journal of Sociology*, *91*(3): 481–510.

Grinstein, A. (2008) 'The relationships between market orientation and alternative strategic orientations: A meta-analysis', *European Journal of Marketing*, *42*(1/2): 115–34.

Gross, N., Carson, D. and Jones, R. (2014) 'Beyond rhetoric: Re-thinking entrepreneurial marketing from a practice perspective', *Journal of Research in Marketing and Entrepreneurship*, *16*(2): 105–27.

Hansen, D. and Eggers, F. (2010) 'The marketing/entrepreneurship interface: A report on the Charleston Summit', *Journal of Research in Marketing and Entrepreneurship*, *12*(1): 42–53.

Harrigan, P. (2013) 'Social media, customer relationship management, and SMEs', in Z. Sethna, R. Jones and P. Harrigan (eds), *Entrepreneurial Marketing: Global Perspectives*. Bingley: Emerald Group Publishing. pp. 221–41.

Harrigan, P., Ramsey, E. and Ibbotson, P. (2009) 'Investigating the e–CRM activities of Irish SMEs', *Journal of Small Business and Enterprise Development*, *16*(3): 443–65.

Hill, J. (2001) 'A multidimensional study of the key determinants of effective SME marketing activity: Part 1', *International Journal of Entrepreneurial Behavior & Research*, *7*(5): 171–204.

Hill, J. and McGowan, P. (1996) 'Marketing development through networking: A competency based approach for small firm entrepreneurs', *Journal of Small Business and Enterprise Development*, *3*(3): 148–56.

Hill, J., McGowan, P. and Drummond, P. (1999) 'The development and application of a qualitative approach to researching the marketing networks of small firm entrepreneurs', *Qualitative Market Research: An International Journal*, *2*(2): 71–81.

Hill, J. and Wright, L.T. (2001) 'A qualitative research agenda for small to medium-sized enterprises', *Marketing Intelligence & Planning*, *19*(6): 432–43.

Hills, G.E. (1995) 'Foreword', in D. Carson, S. Cromie, P. McGowan and J. Hill (eds), *Marketing and Entrepreneurship in SMEs: An Innovative Approach*. London: Prentice Hall. pp. xiii–xiv.

Hills, G.E. and Hultman, C.M. (2006) 'Entrepreneurial marketing', in S. Lagrosen and G. Svensson (eds), *Marketing: Broadening the Horizons*. Denmark: Studentlitteratur. pp. 219–34.

Hills, G.E. and Hultman, C.M. (2005) 'Marketing, Entrepreneurship and SMEs: Knowledge and Education Revisited', paper presented at

The Academy of Marketing SIG on Entrepreneurship and SME Marketing, Southampton, UK.

Hoang, H. and Antoncic, B. (2003) 'Network-based research in entrepreneurship: A critical review', *Journal of Business Venturing*, *18*(2): 165–87.

Johanson, J. and Vahlne, J.E. (2003) 'Business relationship, learning and commitment in the internationalisation process', *Journal of International Entrepreneurship*, *1*(1): 83–101.

Jones, M.V. (1999) 'The internationalisation of small high-technology firms', *Journal of International Marketing*, *7*(4): 15–41.

Jones, R. and Edwards, R. (2013) 'Developing successful international management education programs: Meeting the requirements of entrepreneurial ventures and their business environments', in D. Tsang, H.H. Kazeroony, and G. Ellis (eds), *The Routledge Companion to International Management Education*. Oxon, New York: Routledge. pp. 374–88.

Jones, R. and Parry, S. (2011) 'Business support for new technology-based firms: A study of entrepreneurs in North Wales', *International Journal of Entrepreneurial Behavior & Research*, *17*(6): 645–62.

Jones, R. and Rowley, J. (2011) 'Entrepreneurial marketing in small businesses: A conceptual exploration', *International Small Business Journal*, *29*(1): 25–36.

Jones, R. and Rowley, J. (2009a) 'Presentation of a generic "EMICO" framework for research exploration of entrepreneurial marketing in SMEs', *Journal of Research in Marketing and Entrepreneurship*, *11*(1): 5–21.

Jones, R. and Rowley, J. (2009b) 'Marketing activities of companies in the educational software sector', *Qualitative Market Research: An International Journal*, *12*(3): 337–54.

Jones, R., Suoranta, M. and Rowley, J. (2013a) 'Entrepreneurial marketing: A comparative study', *The Service Industries Journal*, *33*(7–8): 705–19.

Jones, R., Suoranta, M. and Rowley, J. (2013b) 'Strategic network marketing in technology SMEs', *Journal of Marketing Management*, *29*(5–6): 671–97.

Keene, A. (2000) 'Complexity theory: The challenging role of leadership', *Industrial and Commercial Training*, *32*(1): 15–18.

Kelly, S.J. (2000) 'The role of relationship marketing and networking in foreign market entry and sustained competitiveness by Australian SMEs', in G. Ogunmokun and R. Gabbay (eds), *Advances in International Marketing and Global Strategy*. Perth, WA: Academic Press International. pp. 24–36.

Knight, G.A. and Cavusgil, S.T. (2004) 'Innovation, organizational capabilities, and the born-global firm', *Journal of International Business Studies*, *35*(2): 124–141.

Kohli, A.K., Jaworski, B.J. and Kumar, A. (1993) 'MARKOR: A measure of market orientation', *Journal of Marketing Research*, *30*(4): 467–77.

Kraus, S., Filser, M., Eggers, F., Hills, G.E. and Hultman, C.M. (2012) 'The entrepreneurial marketing domain: A citation and co-citation analysis', *Journal of Research in Marketing and Entrepreneurship*, *14*(1): 6–26.

Lehman, K., Fillis, I. and Miles, M.P. (2014) 'The art of entrepreneurial market creation', *Journal of Research in Marketing and Entrepreneurship*, *16*(2): 163–82.

Lewin, R. (1993) *Complexity: Life on the Edge of Chaos*. London: Phoenix.

Lewis, G., Miles, M.P., Crispin, S., Bonney, L., Woods, M., Fei, J. and Ayala, S. (2014) 'Branding as innovation within agribusiness value chains', *Journal of Research in Marketing and Entrepreneurship*, *16*(2): 146–62.

Litvak, I.A. (1990) 'Instant international: Strategic reality for small high-technology firms in Canada', *Multinational Business*, *2*(2): 1–12.

McGowan, P. and Rocks, S. (1995) Entrepreneurial marketing networking and small firm innovation. *Proceedings of Research at the Marketing/Entrepreneurship Interface*, University of Illinois, Chicago, pp. 43–54.

Miles, M.P. and Arnold, D.R. (1991) 'The relationship between marketing orientation and entrepreneurial orientation', *Entrepreneurship Theory and Practice*, *15*(4): 49–65.

Miles, M.P. and Darroch, J. (2006) 'Large firms, entrepreneurial marketing and the cycle of competitive advantage', *European Journal of Marketing*, *40*(5/6): 485–501.

Miles, M.P., Lewis, G.K., Hall-Phillips, A., Morrish, S.C., Gilmore, A. and Kasouf, C. (2016) 'The influence of entrepreneurial marketing processes and entrepreneurial self-efficacy on community vulnerability, risk and resilience', *Journal of Strategic Marketing*, *24*(1): 1–13.

Miles, M.P., Verreynne, M-L., and Luke, B. (2014) 'The development of a social value marketing orientation scale', *Journal of Business Ethics*, *123*(4): 549–56.

Miles, M.P., Verreynne, M-L., Luke, B., Eversole, R. and Barraket, J. (2013) 'The development of a social value orientation scale: The nexus of Vincentian social values and entrepreneurship in social enterprises', *Review of Business*, *33*(2): 91–102.

Miller, N.J., Besser, T. and Malshe, A. (2007) 'Strategic networking among small businesses in small US communities', *International Small Business Journal*, *25*(6): 631–65.

Morris, M., Schindehutte, M. and LaForge, R.W. (2002) 'Entrepreneurial marketing: A construct for integrating emerging entrepreneurship and marketing perspectives', *Journal of Marketing Theory and Practice*, *10*(4): 1–18.

Morris, M.H. and Paul, G.W. (1987) 'The relationship between entrepreneurship and marketing in established firms', *Journal of Business Venturing*, *2*(3): 247–59.

Morrish, S.C. (2011) 'Entrepreneurial marketing: A strategy for the twenty–first century?', *Journal of Research in Marketing and Entrepreneurship*, *13*(2): 110–19.

Morrish, S.C. (2009) 'Portfolio entrepreneurs: An effectuation approach to multiple venture development', *Journal of Research in Marketing and Entrepreneurship*, *11*(1): 32–48.

Morrish, S.C., Miles, M.P. and Deacon, J.H. (2010) 'Entrepreneurial marketing: Acknowledging the entrepreneur and customer-centric interrelationship', *Journal of Strategic Marketing*, *18*(4): 303–16.

Narver, J.C. and Slater, S.F. (1990) 'The effect of a marketing orientation on business profitability', *Journal of Marketing*, *54*(4): 20–35.

Nummela, N. (2002) Change in SME internationalisation: A network perspective. *Proceedings of the 28th EIBA Conference*, Athens (December 8–10).

Oviatt, B.M. and McDougall, P.P. (1994) 'Toward a theory of international new ventures', *Journal of International Business Studies*, *25*(1): 45–64.

Pelham, A.M. (2000) 'Market orientation and other potential influences on performance in small and medium-sized manufacturing firms', *Journal of Small Business Management*, *38*(1): 48–67.

Pelham, A.M. and Wilson, D.T. (1995) 'A longitudinal study of the impact of market structure, firm structure, strategy, and market orientation culture on dimensions of small-firm performance', *Journal of the Academy of Marketing Science*, *24*(1): 27–43.

Robb-Post, C., Stamp, J., Brannback, M., Carsrud, A. and Hacker, R. (2010) 'Social rent generation in social entrepreneurship: How competitive advantage becomes contributive advantage'. *Proceedings of the ICSB World Conference*, Cincinnati, Ohio.

Sarasvathy, S. (2001) 'Causation and effectuation: Toward a theoretical shift from economic inevitability to entrepreneurial contingency', *Academy of Management Review*, *26*(2): 243–63.

Saunders, V. (2005) 'The meaning of marketing in Welsh SMEs', *PhD dissertation,* University of Wales, Newport, UK.

Schindehutte, M., Morris, M.H. and Pitt, L.F. (2009) *Rethinking Marketing: The Entrepreneurial Imperative*. New Jersey: Pearson Prentice Hall.

Shane, S. and Venkataraman, S. (2000) 'The promise of entrepreneurship as a field of research', *Academy of Management Review*, *25*(1): 217–26.

Shaw, E. (2006) 'Small firm networking: An insight into contents and motivating factors', *International Small Business Journal*, *24*(1): 5–29.

Smallbone, D. and North, D. (1995) 'Targeting established SMEs: Does their age matter?', *International Small Business Journal*, *13*(3): 47–64.

Starr, J.A. and Bygrave, W.D (1991) 'The assets and liabilities of prior start–up experience: An exploratory study of multiple venture entrepreneurs', in N.C. Churchill, W.D. Bygrave, J.G. Covin, D.L. Sexton, D.P. Slevin, and W.E. Wetzel (eds), *Frontiers of Entrepreneurial Research*. Wellesley, MA: Babson College. pp. 213–27.

Starr, J. and Macmillan, I. (1990) 'Resource co-optation via social contracting: Resource acquisition strategies for new ventures', *Strategic Management Journal*, *11*(Summer): 79–92.

Stevenson, H. and Gumpert, D. (1985) 'The heart of entrepreneurship', *Harvard Business Review*, *63*(2): 85–94.

Stokes, D. (2000) 'Putting entrepreneurship into marketing: The process of entrepreneurial marketing', *Journal of Research in Marketing and Entrepreneurship*, *2*(1): 1–6.

Timmons, G. (1994) *New Venture Creation*. 4th edn. Burr Ridge: Irwin.

Vasilchenko, E. and Morrish, S. (2011) 'The role of entrepreneurial networks in the exploration and exploitation of internationalisation opportunities by information and communication technology firms', *Journal of International Marketing*, *19*(4): 88–105.

Vesper, K. (1980) *New Venture Strategies*. Englewood Cliffs: Prentice-Hall.

Webb, J.W., Ireland, R.D., Hitt, G.M. and Tihanyi, L. (2011) 'Where is the opportunity without the customer? An integration of marketing activities, the entrepreneurship process, and institutional theory', *Journal of the Academy of Marketing Science*, *39*(4): 537–54.

Whalen, P., Uslay, C., Pascal, V.J., Omura, G., McAuley, A., Kasouf, C.J., Jones, R., Hultman, C.M., Hills, G.E., Hansen, D.J. and Gilmore, A. (2016) 'Anatomy of competitive advantage: Towards a contingency theory of entrepreneurial marketing', *Journal of Strategic Marketing*, *24*(1): 5–19.

17

Financing Entrepreneurial Ventures

Colin Mason

INTRODUCTION

The pecking order theory is a long-standing feature in the entrepreneurial finance literature (Myers, 1984). It suggests that firms adopt a ranking of sources of finance. For cost and control reasons firms will prefer internal finance (personal funds, retained profits) over external finance. When external finance is required then debt will be preferred over equity, which requires the sale of shares in the business and hence dilutes control by bringing external investors into its ownership. But in reality new businesses with growth ambitions – which we will term *entrepreneurial businesses* – are likely to encounter the 'valley of death' (Figure 17.1), which describes the situation in which they encounter a period of negative cash flow resulting from heavy expenditure on research and development, product development and scaling up before their product or service brings in sufficient revenue from customers to generate profits. Banks seek to lend to established businesses

that are profitable, have collateral as security for the loan and strong cash flow to repay the loan. Businesses in the 'valley of death' do not meet any of these criteria. This means that entrepreneurial businesses – and new technology-based firms in particular – will turn to equity finance at a much earlier stage in their development than predicted by the pecking order hypothesis (Riding, Orser & Chamberlin, 2012; Sjögren & Zackrisson, 2005). However, even providers of equity finance – primarily business angels and venture capital funds – are unlikely to invest in firms at the start-up stage because they are too 'informationally opaque' (Berger & Udell, 1988). Collecting the necessary information is too expensive, difficult to interpret, or simply not available, all of which increases the risks of adverse selection and moral hazard. Investors want to see a proven business model and evidence of market traction before they will consider investing.

The funding escalator model illustrates the funding context encountered by entrepreneurial businesses (Figure 17.2). It shows the

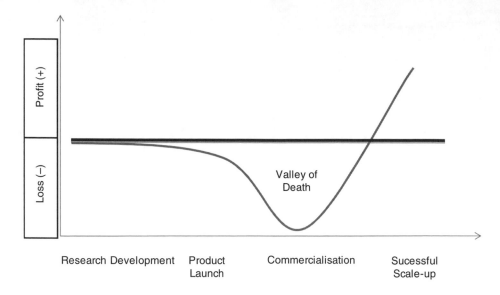

Figure 17.1   The valley of death

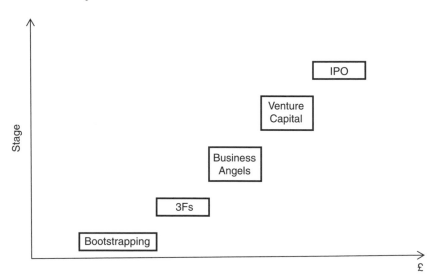

Figure 17.2   Traditional funding escalator

different sources of finance available to such companies as they progress from the start-up phase, through the infant stage and on the route to becoming established. These are complementary rather than competing and, although having distinct positions in the life cycle of the firm, can be stretched between different phases of a firm's development, and hence overlap (Klonowski, 2015).

At the seed stage firms will be reliant on the '3Fs' – the founder's own financial resources (including credit cards) and investment from family and friends. Typically these sources, along with bootstrapping, finance the seed and start-up phases. Grants might also be used. Without a trading record bank debt is inaccessible, other than in the form of an overdraft. As the business starts to gain market traction, indicating proof-of-concept, it requires finance for market development. The lack of a sufficiently long trading record means that bank funding continues to be unavailable. Here the main source is business angels – high net worth individuals who are investing their own money. The emergence of equity crowdfunding platforms now offers a further source of finance. Businesses that are scaling up their activities will seek venture capital – professional managers who raise finance from third parties (pension funds, banks, family trusts, etc.) to invest in businesses with high growth potential. Fast-growing businesses may raise several rounds of venture capital, with later rounds syndicated between several funds. The final stage in the funding escalator – which few firms reach – is the Initial Public Offering (IPO), in which the firm's shares are traded on a stock market. This is an opportunity to raise even larger amounts of finance but also provides a liquidity opportunity for existing shareholders (founders, management teams, key employees and investors), enabling them, over a period of time, to sell some or all of their shares. This puts cash into the hands of both business angels and the investors in venture capital funds, enabling them to reinvest in other early-stage businesses. However, it is much more common for angel and venture capital investors to seek a 'harvest event' at an earlier stage in the development of their investee businesses by means of a sale to a larger, often international, company, in what is termed a trade sale. Strategic sales have the added benefit of providing the business with access to a range of non-financial resources, notably distribution channels and professional management.

This chapter uses the funding escalator as its framework. The structure is as follows. The next section discusses the main sources of finance used by entrepreneurial firms as they progress from the start-up stage – bootstrapping, business angels, venture capital and public markets (crowdfunding is discussed later). In reality this is not a smooth progression. There are gaps in the supply of finance – which are typically attributed to market failures arising from transaction costs.

Because of the importance that governments attribute to entrepreneurial businesses, notably in terms of their job creation (Anyadike-Danes et al., 2009; Henrekson & Johansson, 2010; Mason & Brown, 2013), they have been active in seeking to close such gaps with a variety of interventions. These will be examined later in the chapter. The supply of entrepreneurial finance is influenced by macroeconomic conditions and is therefore subject to change over time. Specifically it has been suggested that the funding escalator has changed fundamentally as a result of the impact of the dotcom crash and the post-2008 global financial crisis on investors, and this evidence will be reviewed. In the final section the preceding material is synthesised in order to offer an agenda for future research.

SOURCES OF ENTREPRENEURIAL FINANCE

Bootstrapping

Despite the emphasis on raising finance from business angels and venture capital firms the reality is that most entrepreneurs self-finance the pre-start-up, start-up and early growth phases of their businesses. This reflects the enormous information asymmetries that any potential investor will encounter in attempting to evaluate the merits of a start-up venture. However, Bhide (1992) argues that the funding gap is more to do with the asymmetry of *expectations* between the prospective investor and the entrepreneur. As he observes, 'most start-ups don't have the assets that an objective investor would consider valuable'. This is because 'in many start-ups the founders … have little to offer investors besides their hopes and dreams … The entrepreneurs believe that they can somehow make a profit, but the investors do not' (Bhide, 1992, p. 110) As a consequence, most entrepreneurial businesses must bootstrap in order to start and grow their business. Indeed, Bhide (1992, p. 110) suggests that the biggest challenge for

Table 17.1   Types of bootstrapping techniques

Finance	Operations and production	Human resources	Research and development
Retain current job	Start business from home	Hire young and inexperienced employees	Develop products and services at the weekends and evenings
Offer related services to help pay for product development	Barter to acquire services and products	Under-staff operations	
Purchase used equipment	Ship products early (without perfecting them) – engage with early customers to identify problems	Pay employees with stock or stock options	Rely on external research and development
Stretch suppliers and offer discounts for early payment to clients		Hire relatives and friends at below-market rates	Focus on commercialising university-based research
Lease instead of buy	Purchase used equipment	Rent managers and employees for a short term	Use clients to pay development costs
Rely on peer-to-peer and social lending	Use resources jointly (e.g. production facilities, employees)		
Take inventory on consignment	Co-ordinate purchases with other firms		
Use personal savings			
Entrepreneur does not take salary	Focus on quick-to-break-even products		
Use government salary and grants	Avoid investing in real estate		

Source: Amended from Klonowski (2015) table 6.1

entrepreneurs is not raising money, but 'having the wits and hustle to do without it'.

There are two approaches to bootstrapping. One is creative ways of acquiring the use of resources at either little or no cost. The other is ways of organising the business to minimise or avoid the need for such resources (Freear, Sohl & Wetzel, 1995). Table 17.1 provides examples of bootstrapping techniques. However, there is considerable diversity in how firms use bootstrapping. Winborg and Landström (2001) identified six clusters of bootstrapping firms based on the bootstrapping methods used and the characteristics of the business: (1) delaying bootstrappers; (2) relationship-oriented bootstrappers; (3) subsidy-oriented bootstrappers; (4) minimising bootstrappers; (5) non-bootstrappers; and (6) private owner-financed bootstrappers. Malmström's (2014) taxonomy identified three types of bootstrapping strategies: 'quick-fix bootstrappers', which emphasise temporary access to resources and prefer internally oriented activities for such purposes; 'proactive bootstrappers', which focus on operational resource issues; and 'efficient bootstrappers', which prefer activities that are externally and vertically oriented, up or down in the value creation chain. Winborg (2009) suggests that there are three reasons why firms bootstrap: to reduce costs; because of capital constraints; and to reduce risks. There are geographical variations in the types of bootstrapping used (Harrison, Mason & Girling, 2004). Jones and Jayawarna (2005) emphasise that social networks play a key role in accessing resources though networking.

Nearly all entrepreneurial businesses use bootstrapping in their early stages. Indeed, Timmons (1999, p. 37) describes bootstrapping as 'a way of life in entrepreneurial companies'. Hofman (1997, p. 54) adds that even 'great companies … get started this way'. However, whereas many firms will use bootstrapping as a means of getting to a positive cash flow and then seek to raise external finance, some will continue to use bootstrapping out of choice as a philosophy of operating a business in a frugal manner to minimise cash burn. Indeed, studies confirm that, although bootstrapping is especially important for start-ups (Brush, Carter, Gatewood, Greene & Hart, 2006; Jones & Jayawarna, 2005), it is used by firms of all ages (Ebben & Johnson, 2006).

Bootstrapping has various advantages. It is the most inexpensive and flexible means of generating capital. No financial obligations are involved. It minimises the founder's 'walk away costs' should the business fail. It creates a culture of financial discipline, efficiency and flexibility. It does not involve relinquishing ownership. And it enables value to be created so that its shares will be worth more if it raises equity finance at some point in the future. However, bootstrapping limits resource inputs, which may constrain the ability to pursue growth opportunities (Mac an Bhaird & Lynn, 2015). But Vanacker, Manigart and Meuleman (2011) find that the association between bootstrapping and venture growth is either non-existent or positive.

Business Angels

Businesses that go on to seek equity finance are likely to turn in the first instance to business angels – high net worth individuals who invest their own finance in businesses in which they may play a hands-on role and in the hope of financial gain. The typical business angel is male, in their 50s or 60s and has an entrepreneurial background (many are serial entrepreneurs) who will invest anywhere from £10,000 to £250,000 and over in a single investment. Their investments represent just a small proportion of their overall wealth (typically 5% to 15%). Most business angels make just a handful of investments (fewer than five) but there is a small proportion of much more active angels. Various studies have developed typologies of angels (e.g. Lahti, 2011; Sørheim & Landström, 2001). Angels are increasingly organising themselves into managed or self-managed angel groups both to make bigger and follow-on investment and to pool the expertise of individual angels in sourcing deal flow, deal evaluation and post-investment support. It also enables individual angels to achieve greater diversification (Carpentier & Suret, 2015a; Croce, Tenca & Ughetto, 2016;

Mason, Botelho & Harrison, 2016). Most angels play hands-on roles, contributing their skills, knowledge and networks to the support of their investee businesses (Politis, 2008). Returns are skewed. The high failure rate is high (over 40%) but 20–30% of investments generate high returns (Mason & Harrison, 2002a; Wiltbank, 2009; Wiltbank & Boeker, 2007). Most exits are achieved through a trade sale – the acquisition of the investee business by another company. Stock market flotations of angel-backed companies are rare (Carpentier & Suret, 2015b; Johnson & Sohl, 2012). Angels also have a high proportion of 'living dead' investments in their portfolios. These are companies that generate sufficient profits to survive but are unlikely to be acquisition targets. In these cases the only exit is likely to be a sale of the shares back to the management at a nominal price.

Angel investing is a private activity (there are no directories of angel investing) and their investments are below the radar so tracking their investment activity through official sources is challenging (Mason & Harrison, 2008); hence, as Wetzel (1981), the pioneer of business angel research, noted, the size of the angel population and its investment activity are unknown and unknowable. However, it is clear that, after family sources, angels are the largest source of start-up and early-stage risk capital, making substantially more investments than venture capital companies (perhaps 20–40 times) and the aggregate amount that they invest is also substantially greater (Gaston, 1989a; Mason & Harrison, 2000; Sohl, 2012). EBAN (2014) estimates that in Europe business angels invest €3 for every €1 invested by venture capital funds in the early-stage investment market. Moreover, angel investing has been quite resilient during and after the global financial crisis (GFC) in comparison with bank lending to SMEs and venture capital (Mason & Harrison, 2015) and is ahead of pre-GFC levels (EBAN, 2014). Angel investing is now found throughout the world (May & Liu, 2016; Landström & Mason, 2016).

Despite this, angel investing has attracted substantially less research attention compared with the much smaller – in terms of investments – venture capital industry. Early research focused on the characteristics of angels and their investment decision-making (e.g. Brettel, 2003; Freear et al., 1994, 1995; Gaston, 1989b; Haar, Starr & MacMillan, 1988; Landström, 1993; Lumme, Mason & Suomi, 1998; Mason & Harrison, 1994; Paul, Whittam & Johnston, 2003; Wetzel, 1981, 1983). The business angel's investment decision-making comprises various stages: deal sourcing, initial screen, due diligence, negotiation and contracting, post-investment support and the exit. It has been suggested that the source of the investment opportunity has a significant initial influence on the angel's decision whether to consider the opportunity further (Mason & Rogers, 1997; Riding, Duxbury & Haines, 1995), with referrals from close associates having lower rejection rates than those that come from sources that are not known to the angel. Angels will then consider how well the proposal 'fits' their knowledge domain and personal investment criteria (Mason & Rogers, 1997; Mitteness, Baucus & Sudek, 2012). It is only from this point that the attributes of the opportunity are considered.

The entrepreneur/management team is the most important consideration, with the growth potential of the market and product/service attributes ranked second and third, but of considerably less importance (e.g. Brettel, 2003; Hindle & Wenban, 1999; Mason & Harrison, 1994; Mason & Rogers, 1997; Maxwell, Jeffrey & Lévesque, 2011; Stedler & Peters, 2003; Sudek, 2006). The competence, motivation and integrity of the entrepreneur (Lumme et al., 1998) and their trustworthiness (Harrison, Dibben & Mason, 1997; Maxwell, Jeffrey & Lévesque, 2014) are all particularly significant. Angels use a non-compensatory approach to deal with evaluation (Jeffrey, Lévesque & Maxwell, 2016). In other words, they do not allow weaknesses in some aspects of the business to be offset by strengths elsewhere. Reasons why angels reject investment

opportunities are overwhelmingly associated with perceived weaknesses in the entrepreneur and management team (e.g. Haar et al., 1988; Lumme et al., 1998; Mason, Botelho & Zygmunt, 2017; Mason & Harrison, 1994; Riding et al., 1995).

However, the significance of specific investment criteria changes as the opportunity passes from the initial screening stage to detailed evaluation (Croce et al., 2016; Feeney, Haines & Riding, 1999; Mitteness et al., 2012; Riding et al., 1995). For example, it has also been noted that, whereas the initial screening is based on quantifiable criteria, in the later stages when angels increase their scrutiny they focus on less quantifiable intangibles, such as the trustworthiness of the entrepreneur, their commitment and passion (Brush, Edelman & Manolova, 2012). A further observation is that opportunities that fail to get past the initial screening stage tend to be rejected because of an accumulation of deficiencies, what Mason and Rogers (1997) term a 'three strikes and you're out' approach, whereas rejections later in the process tend to be associated with a single deal killer (Mason & Harrison, 1996). Nevertheless, the reality is that most angels do only limited research and due diligence before investing and spend relatively little time on deliberation and negotiation (Mason & Harrison, 1996), making their decisions more on 'feelings than analysis' (Shane, 2009). Indeed, the quality of the 'pitch' has a major influence on how angels respond to investment proposals (Clark, 2008; Mason & Harrison, 2003; Parhankangas & Ehrlich, 2014).

Less is known about the other stages in the investment process. Kelly and Hay (2003) remains the only study of the contract and the structure of the investment. There are few studies of the post-investment relationship of angels and entrepreneurs or of the nature and effectiveness of the value-added contribution that angels make (for a review see Politis, 2008). Finally, the exit process has largely been ignored. Mason and Botelho (2016) highlight the lack of 'exit-centricness' amongst angel

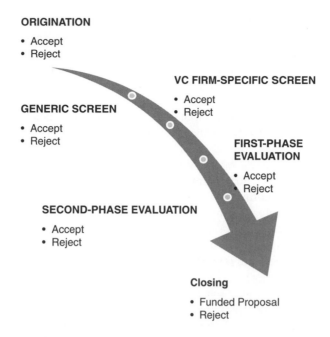

ORIGINATION
- Accept
- Reject

GENERIC SCREEN
- Accept
- Reject

VC FIRM-SPECIFIC SCREEN
- Accept
- Reject

FIRST-PHASE EVALUATION
- Accept
- Reject

SECOND-PHASE EVALUATION
- Accept
- Reject

Closing
- Funded Proposal
- Reject

Figure 17.3   The venture capital investment process (based on Fried & Hisrich, 1994)

group managers. There are just a handful of studies of investment returns (Capizzi, 2015; Mason & Harrison, 2002a; Wiltbank, 2009; Wiltbank & Boeker, 2007). The subsequent fortunes of the business after the exit have not attracted any attention from researchers.

Venture Capital

Venture capital firms are financial intermediaries which attract finance from various investors – termed limited partners – such as financial institutions (banks, pension funds, insurance companies), large companies, wealthy families and endowments – into fixed life investment vehicles ('funds') with a specific investment focus (location, technology, stage of business development). These investors are passive. The venture capital firm – the general partner – is responsible for the identification of promising investment opportunities which offer the prospects of high reward, supporting them through the provision of advice, information

and networking and ultimately managing an exit from the investment. The proceeds from the fund are returned to the limited partners. The venture capital firm is compensated by a management fee (typically 2% of the value of the fund) and carried interest (a system of reward based on the performance of the fund upon its realisation). Fried and Hisrich (1994) identify the various stages of the investment process (Figure 17.3). This is similar to the investment process of business angels.

Venture capital firms invest at all stages of a firm's development including seed and start-up stages, first stage (or series A), second stage (series B) and mezzanine (a combination of debt and equity for expansion). The traditional role of venture capital is to provide two types of funding: finance to enable a firm that has demonstrated market traction to scale up to full production (series A), and expansion finance for firms that are already up and running (series B). In fact, venture capital investors typically make several rounds of investment in their investee businesses and so will be investing across several stages in their development. Their follow-on investments are likely to be syndicated with other investors that the original investor brings in, especially in later rounds of investment when the amounts are larger (DeClercq & Dimov, 2004; Lerner, 1994; Lockett & Wright, 1999). This is both to spread their financial risk and access the specific resources of these other investors. Most venture capital firms are independent organisations. Some are subsidiaries of financial institutions (termed 'captives'). A few large non-financial companies, particularly technology companies, have their own venture capital subsidiaries which invest for strategic reasons to complement their own internal R&D activities (corporate venture capital).

Venture capital funds are highly selective as to the businesses in which they invest. The need to generate a large return on their investment in a five- to seven-year time frame through an IPO or acquisition means that only certain types of businesses are candidates for this type of funding. Management needs to be capable of rapidly building an enterprise. The numerous studies of the venture capitalists' investment criteria have established that they 'bet' on the jockey (entrepreneur) rather than the horse (business) (Hisrich & Jankowicz, 1990; MacMillan, Kulow & Khoylian, 1988; MacMillan, Siegal and Subba Narasimba 1985; Smart, 1999; Zacharakis & Meyer, 1998). However, because angels and venture capitalists differ in their ability to manage agency costs they attach different levels of importance to the entrepreneur and emphasise different attributes of the entrepreneur (Fiet, 1995; Hsu, Haynie, Simmons & McKelvie, 2014; Van Osnabrugge, 2000).

Venture capitalists (VCs) avoid companies that are developing ground-level technologies and businesses that are trying to create a market (Bhide, 2008). Rather, they seek to build on the high-level knowledge that the business has already secured. Typically this means a business that has technological foundations in the form of their own or someone else's patents (usually obtained

prior to raising venture capital) and an incipient technological advantage. Finally, venture capitalists look to invest in businesses where rapid expansion has significant payoffs. Their 'sweet spot' is businesses that have sizeable sales but can also show evidence of a large number of potential users who have not yet become customers (Bhide, 2008). They generally avoid investing in mature markets. A handful of studies have examined how entrepreneurs choose venture capitalists (Falik, Lahti & Keinonen, 2016; Valliere & Peterson, 2007). A significant omission is the lack of studies of institutional investors in venture capital (Barnes & Menzies, 2005).

The importance of venture capitalists is not just the money that they provide but their hands-on involvement in their investee businesses. Various studies have examined the venture capital–entrepreneur relationship (Busenitz, Fiet & Moesel, 2004; De Clercq & Sapienza, 2001; Shepherd & Zacharakis, 2001; St-Pierre, Nomo & Pilaeva, 2011; Yitshaki. 2012). Several studies have examined the nature of the hands-on contribution of venture capitalists, whether this involvement adds value and how they specifically add value. A review of these studies concludes that there is little consensus in the definition and management of value-added inputs and outcomes and little consensus on which inputs are most important (Large & Muegge, 2008). Of course, one of the challenges is the attribution of the superior performance of VC-backed firms if such an effect can be identified. Does it reflect the ability of VCs to select and invest in firms with above average levels of innovation or their ability to enhance the performance of their investee businesses? Peneder (2010) argues that there is a selection effect, which can be interpreted as indicating that VCs are allocating finance to innovative firms, but there is also a distinct value-added effect. Other studies have explored whether the effectiveness of the value-added contributions is influenced – for better or worse – by the quality of the relationship, looking specifically at the effects of disappointed expectations (Parhankangas & Landström, 2004) and VC–entrepreneur conflict (Brettel, Mauer & Appelhoff, 2013; Higashide & Birley, 2002; Sapienza, 1992).

One of the specific value-added contributions of venture capital is to take their investee companies to a stock market flotation (an IPO). A major theme in the finance literature is on the pricing of IPO – the difference between the offer or opening price and the subsequent price after short-term (e.g. one day) and longer-term (e.g. one month) trading. There is a weight of academic evidence that the short-term performance of IPOs is positive, relative to the market as a whole, meaning that they are underpriced and so 'leave money on the table', while their longer-term performance is worse than the market as a whole. The amount of underpricing is related to the extent of information asymmetry. However, venture capital-backed IPOs are less likely to suffer either problem. The companies they bring to market may be of better quality because of their skills in selecting companies to invest in and the value-added that they contribute. It may also reflect a certification effect. Venture capital firms repeatedly bring companies to the market so have reputational capital to protect. They also have strong relationships with underwriters to sell the shares. All of this reduces information asymmetry (Bessler & Seim, 2012; Dolvin, 2005; Dolvin & Pyles, 2006; Pennacchio, 2014).

The importance of venture capital lies in its 'powerful influence on innovation' (Lerner & Watson, 2008, p. 7) in its investee companies which, in turn, is a driver for economic growth (Hellmann & Puri, 2000; Kortum & Lerner, 2000). Venture capital funds focus their investments on companies with innovation ability – and hence with powerful potential for patenting – and are able to support these firms to innovate both financially and through their support and guidance, for example, by spotting potential for further applications. Venture capital backing is associated with a significant reduction in time to market. However, the uneven geography of venture capital investing both globally and within countries (Mason, 2007) means that these benefits are geographically restricted. That said, there has been a spatial diffusion of venture capital beyond its US and NW Europe origins, notably to Israel (Avnimelech & Harel, 2012), central and eastern Europe (Bliss, 1999; Klonowski, 2011) and China (Lu & Tan, 2012). Venture capital is also emerging in developing countries (Lingelbach, 2012; Landström & Mason, 2016). Cross-border investing has been an important driver of this internationalisation process, with local investors partnering with US VC firms to help their expansion into the USA (Nitani & Riding, 2013) and international investors seeking out local partners to overcome the 'liability of foreignness' (Huang, Martin Kenne & Patton, 2015; Mäkelä & Maula, 2005).

Initial Public Offering

Acquiring a listing on a public stock market – often termed an IPO – may be the logical final step for a fast-growing company which can offer a good track record of profitability and prospects of significant further growth. An IPO is primarily an opportunity for a business to raise significant amounts of additional finance from the general public and financial institutions at the IPO and subsequently through secondary issues (Baldock, 2015). Raising debt finance also becomes easier with a public listing. Public companies can also use their shares to make acquisitions. A stock market listing also enables existing shareholders – notably the founders and their families, business angels and venture capital funds – to sell their shares to realise their capital gains. However, shareholders who are insiders in the business (entrepreneurs and investors) are often subject to a 'lock-in' period both before and after the IPO before they are allowed to sell their shares because of the price-sensitive information that they possess.

Companies have to be a significant size to achieve and maintain a flotation and seek to raise significant amounts of additional finance on account of the high costs involved (lawyer, accountant and broker fees and commissions, joining fees and an annual charge, and ongoing compliance regulations, disclosure requirements and shareholder communications). There is also a need for increased corporate governance and reporting to instill shareholder confidence in the company (Baldock, Supri, North, Macauley & Rushton, 2013). They also need to offer the prospect of strong future growth prospects (Baldock, 2015). Hence, the number of companies achieving IPOs is small. However, these companies are of disproportionate economic significance on account of their size (turnover, employment) (Kenney, Patton & Ritter, 2012).

A high proportion of IPOs have been venture capital-backed. In Johnson and Sohl's (2012) study of US IPOs between 2001 and 2007, 56% had previously raised finance from venture capital funds or, less frequently, just from business angels. This underlines the strong interdependence between venture capital and the stock market. Indeed, there is considerable academic evidence that active stock markets significantly stimulate venture capital activity because they enable venture capital firms to exit faster and more profitably. We also noted in the previous section that VCs play a certification role which reduces the degree of underpricing in the companies they bring to market compared with other IPOs.

Summary

In well-developed entrepreneurial economies, various sources of equity finance will be present. The concept of the funding escalator suggests that entrepreneurial businesses will use these different sources of finance at different stages in their development. However, the discussion of the funding escalator is incomplete without the inclusion of government, which has intervened at a macro scale

to create the appropriate framework conditions to stimulate the venture capital industry and subsequently at the micro scale with direct interventions to 'fix' gaps in the availability finance that emerge periodically in response to economic crises. Discussion of the funding escalator is therefore incomplete without the inclusion of government interventions. This is the focus of the next section.

GOVERNMENT INTERVENTION IN THE SUPPLY OF ENTREPRENEURIAL FINANCE

Government intervention has been at two levels. First, governments have played a significant role in pump-priming the inception of venture capital in several countries, notably the US and Israel (see Lerner, 2009, chapter for other examples). A venture capital industry requires a supportive legal and tax system. A well-developed set of legal rules and effective court enforcement are essential to enable entrepreneurs and investors to enter into complex contracts. Complex securities (notably preferred stock), stock options, capital gains tax, partnership laws (which allow tax follow-through), an active IPO market and rules on the ownership of university research (to facilitate commercialisation) are also critical to the emergence of a venture capital industry (Lerner, 2009; Lingelbach, 2015). In recent years, governments have also sought to promote business angel activity. Key interventions have been, first, to define 'accredited' investors who are not constrained by rules on the promotion of investments; second, tax incentives to change the risk–reward balance; and, third, to subsidise angel networks to provide a forum to enable investors and entrepreneurs to more easily find one another (Mason, 2009a; Collewaert, Manigart & Aernoudt, 2010; OECD, 2011).

Governments have also intervened directly in response to the identification of gaps in the supply of risk capital with mechanisms to increase its supply. These gaps are both structural (size-related) and geographical, arising from the concentration of venture capital in 'core' regions (Avdeitchikova, 2012; Mason, 2007; Mason & Pierakkis, 2013). Direct interventions have mainly focused on creating government-sponsored venture capital funds (GSVCFs). The form of intervention has evolved over time with governments becoming less directly involved and instead favouring hybrid schemes which use government funding to leverage private sector funding into a fund comprising both public and private money and managed by private sector managers (Murray, 2007). This hybrid fund concept has been extended with the creation of business angel co-investment funds which invest alongside business angel groups on a £1 for £1 basis, usually on a passive basis, relying on the business angel group to find the investment opportunities and negotiate the investment which they bring to the co-fund. The co-fund arrangement therefore enables angels either to participate in larger investments in specific businesses or to spread their investments over a larger number of businesses (Owen & Mason, 2016).

However, there is growing evidence that, regardless of the approach, GSVCFs have been ineffective in stimulating entrepreneurship-led economic development (Alperovych, Hübner & Lobet, 2015; Bertoni & Tykvová, 2015; Brander & Hellman, 2014; Cumming & MacIntosh, 2006; Cumming, Grilli & Murtinu, 2014; Grilli & Murtinu, 2014; Munari & Toshi, 2015; Nightingale, Murray, Cowling, Baden-Fuller, Mason, Siepel, Hopkins & Dannreuther, 2009). This is attributable to several factors (Mason, 2016): (i) their design – notably size, sector and geographical limits on their investment focus; (ii) their ineffectiveness in adding value to their investments (Schäfer & Shilder, 2009; Luukkonen, Deschryvere & Bertoni, 2013); and (iii) the lack of high-quality demand for equity finance, especially in peripheral regions where many such schemes are focused. Because of the weak entrepreneurial ecosystem of such regions there is not necessarily a large number of businesses that either want or need to access venture capital or that can offer the type of returns that venture capital funds seek.

RECENT DEVELOPMENTS IN ENTREPRENEURIAL FINANCE: IMPLICATIONS FOR THE FUNDING ESCALATOR

The basic funding escalator model is no longer an accurate portrayal of the supply of finance (Baldock & Mason, 2015; Gill, 2015; Harrison, 2013; North, Baldock & Ullah, 2013). Two particular discontinuities are now apparent. The first is the breakdown in the complementary relationship between business angels and venture capital funds whereby businesses would raise their first round of finance from business angels and raise subsequent rounds of funding from venture capital funds. Benjamin and Margulis (2000, p. 76) describe this relationship as follows: 'It boils down to this. Angel investment runs the critical first leg of the relay race, passing the baton to venture capital only after a company has begun to fund its stride. Venture capitalists focus … on expansion and later stages of development, when their contribution is most effective'. Several studies provide empirical confirmation of this relationship, notably Freear and Wetzel (1989; 1990), Harrison and Mason (2000), and Madill, Haines and Rising (2005). The second discontinuity is the declining number of entrepreneurial companies that have chosen to go down the IPO route. In addition, several new sources of finance have emerged, of which crowdfunding is by far the most important.

The Impact of the Post-2000 Technology Crash

The origins of these changes go back to the dotcom frenzy of the late 1990s – the period in which the World Wide Web emerged (Valliere & Peterson, 2004). Successful investments in early internet-related businesses as a result of high IPO valuations and buoyant M&A markets raised the returns of venture capital funds during the second half of the 1990s. This, in turn, increased the attractiveness of venture capital as an asset class, drawing more and more money into the industry, and enabled both existing and new fund managers to launch bigger and bigger funds. Meanwhile these early successes created hype around specific sectors ('you don't want to be missing out on something hot') which encouraged further investment activity, further driving up valuations which investors rationalised on the basis that 'the rules of the investment game had changed'. Moreover, when failures emerged these were attributed to poor selection rather than the sector and to poor execution rather than deals that should never have been funded. These attitudes acted 'to suppress normal risk assessment controls that might otherwise have slowly deflated the bubble' (Valliere & Peterson, 2004, p. 19). The bubble was only sustainable as long as share prices on public markets were also rising. Once the NASDAQ market began to fall, prompted by the realisation that the valuations were not justified, this had knock-on effects all the way down the 'food chain' with significant implications for both business angels and venture capital firms and for the funding escalator.

The huge fall in public markets meant that venture capital funds had no option but to write down the value of the investments that they retained in their portfolios, often to zero. Those companies that did raise further funding were refinanced at much lower prices ('down rounds'). This affected all of the investors in the business. However, as the first external investors in a business the angels were the biggest casualties. At best their investments were massively diluted, but if they were unwilling or unable to provide new cash in the next funding round they faced 'cram down', in which case their investment was likely to be wiped out. The consequence was that the angel community collectively 'lost trust' in VCs (GP Capital, 2004). Angels saw VCs 'as guys who would cram them down' and so were no longer willing to invest in deals that would require more than one round of funding from a venture capital firm. Evidence from angels in an early review of the UK's Angel Co-Investment Scheme suggests that this antipathy between angels and venture capital funds persists to the present day (Owen & Mason, 2016). This undermined the complementary relationship that business angels and venture capitalists have traditionally held in funding entrepreneurial businesses.

Impact on the Venture Capital Industry

VCs suffered a massive loss in the value of their portfolios as a result of a combination of the failure of many of their investee businesses and the need to revalue their remaining portfolio companies which the decline in the NASDAQ had revealed to be overvalued. Nevertheless, most VCs were sitting on large amounts of finance when the crash occurred, having taken advantage of the large returns that they were making in the run-up to the crash to raise large amounts of new money (1998/99 were peak years for fundraising by the venture capital industry). However, the money that was invested prior to the tech crash was lost when the tech economy collapsed. VCs with funds to invest in the immediate aftermath of the crash found few investment opportunities. The overall effect of this oversupply of capital and declining demand was to lower the average returns of funds. Indeed, for over a decade most venture capital funds have returned less cash to their investors than they had raised (after fees were paid) and failed to outperform the stock market (Mulcahy, Weeks & Bradley, 2012). This has had a long-term detrimental effect on the ability of VCs to raise new funds and make new investments (Mason, 2009b).[1] Google's IPO in 2004 prompted a revival in the US VC sector. Limited Partners (LPs) started returning to the VC sector from 2005 but this recovery was cut short by the financial crisis in 2008 (Block & Sander, 2009; Clark, 2014).

The current nature of venture capital is now very different. First, it is much smaller. Venture capital fundraising remains nowhere near the amounts raised at the peak of the dotcom boom. Second, there is a clear trend to bigger venture capital funds, in excess of $1bn. In the USA the key driver for this is the trend for companies going public later. It has been estimated that compared with the dotcom era firms are waiting twice as long before they go to an IPO and have triple the revenue when they do achieve an IPO (Clark, 2014). However, they still need finance to continue growing, so VCFs need to be able to continue to invest until the IPO to avoid dilution, hence the need for bigger funds. Just 10 funds in the US accounted for 48% of all funds raised in 2012 (Clark, 2014). In Europe the trend has been driven by the switch to private equity investment, investing in large established companies to facilitate corporate restructuring (e.g. management buyouts) (Wright, Hoskisson & Busenitz, 2001; Wright, Gillingham & Amess, 2009). The overall effect has been to reduce the number of venture capital funds and the amount of conventional VC available to emerging entrepreneurial companies.

Impact on Business Angels

Those angels who remained in the market learnt from their experiences and changed their practices in two critical respects. First, they no longer consider businesses that need several millions of dollars of investment that will require several follow-on rounds of investment from venture capital firms to get to an exit. Instead they now look to invest in companies that can become cash positive without the need for several rounds of follow-on venture capital and can achieve an exit via trade sale in around three years (Peters, 2009). This approach has been aided by

reductions in the costs of starting a technology business. Second, they recognised the advantages of working together; hence individual angels have increasingly joined with one another to invest via managed angel groups. This enables them to aggregate their investment capacity to make bigger investments and follow-on investments, and potentially take businesses to an exit without the need for follow-on funding from venture capital funds, and hence fill at least part of the gap created by the shrinkage of the venture capital industry. Some of the larger and longer-established US groups have gone on to establish sidecar funds – that is, committed sources of capital that invest alongside the angel group. Other benefits that individual angels derive from investing as part of a group include the opportunity to build a more diversified investment portfolio, and the pooling of individual networks, skills and knowledge to generate better deal flow, undertake superior evaluation and due diligence of investment opportunities and enhance their post-investment support of investee companies. (For examples, see Gregson, Mann & Harrison, 2013; May & Simmons, 2001.) It is important to emphasise that these angel groups are not collective investment vehicles. Individual angels continue to make their own investment decisions, although the opportunities they see are likely to have been pre-screened by the group manager, and they will invest alongside other group members in specific businesses. However, they will only play a hands-on role in a small number of investee businesses, on behalf of the group, where there is a good fit between their expertise and the nature of the business (Carpentier & Suret, 2015a; Croce et al., 2016; Mason, Botelho & Harrison, 2016).

Implications for the Funding Escalator

These developments have significantly changed both angel investing and the angel–VC relationship and hence the funding escalator from what it was prior to the technology bubble. There has been a bifurcation of the market. Angel groups are now increasingly the only source of funding for new and emerging businesses seeking investments in the range £250,000 to £1 million (under $1m in the USA: Sohl, 2012). Moreover, as a consequence of their greater financial resources angel groups have the ability to provide follow-on funding. Indeed, 60–80% of the investments made by Scottish angel groups have been follow-on investments (Mason, Botelho & Harrison, 2016). Meanwhile a smaller number of companies seeking larger amounts of funding go straight to venture capital firms.

Government Co-Investment Funds

As noted earlier, governments have been active players in the provision of seed, start-up and early growth finance for some time. However, several studies have questioned the effectiveness of these funds. Accepting this criticism, but at the same time recognising the widening gap between the size of the typical angel investment and the increase in the minimum investment by venture capital funds, governments have developed a new funding model – the co-investment fund – with the intention of raising the funding capacity of angel groups. In the Scottish Co-investment Fund (SCF) model – the first scheme of its type – accredited co-investment partners (angel groups and smaller venture capital funds) can raise matched investment on a deal-by-deal basis up to a maximum of 50% of the total funding package on a commercial basis and ranging from £10,000 up to £1.5 million, as part of a total deal size ranging from £20,000 up to £10 million. The SCF, which is part of the Scottish Investment Bank, invests on equal terms with the investment partner ('pari passu'). The majority of investments by angel groups (85%) in Scotland are made in conjunction with the co-investments fund. However, there are a variety of other models.

The UK's Angel Co-Investment Fund (ACF), launched in November 2011 (and initially restricted to England), makes investments of between £100,000 and £1 million alongside syndicates of business angels in order to support high-potential businesses and give them the capital they need to develop and propel growth. In this model a business angel syndicate that has agreed to invest in a business brings the proposal to the co-investment fund. The investment decision of the ACF is critically based on its judgement of the capability of the angel group that is promoting the investment. Early evaluation of the ACF indicated that it is meeting its aim of addressing the funding gap for early-stage potential high-growth businesses, particularly in generating step-change stretch funding of £500,000 to £2 million, an amount that is beyond the normal range of angel syndicates. The scheme exhibits high levels of additionality and attribution, very low levels of potential crowding out and supported the preference of entrepreneurs for 'smart angel money' over 'controlling VCs' (Owen & Mason, 2016). However, there was no evidence that the ACF's other objectives – to spread good investment practice, and encourage more formal angel group activity – were being achieved. The European Investment Bank also has a co-investment fund that operates on the Scottish model in pre-approving investment partners but, unlike the other schemes, co-invests alongside individual angels (who have the capacity to invest a minimum of €250,000). Launched in 2012, the scheme currently operates in Germany, Austria and Spain but is to be rolled out across the EU.

Equity Crowdfunding

Crowdfunding has emerged within the past decade as a new and rapidly growing source of finance. It is typically used by firms at the seed and early stages but can be used at later stages (Tomczak & Brem, 2013). It is an

Table 17.2 Types of crowdfunding

Donations model	The donations model is typically used by social, environmental and charitable ventures which seek purely philanthropic donations from individuals who identify with the cause and believe that it is a worthy undertaking. Individual contributions are generally very small (around $25). Investors do not expect a financial return. Instead they derive an intrinsic return from identification with, and participation in, a worthy project.
Rewards model	The rewards model is most commonly used by artistic, theatrical, film and music ventures. Investors derive a 'token' return (e.g. T-shirt, signed CD) or special privilege (e.g. tickets to a new show or concert; backstage access).
Pre-purchase model	The pre-purchase model is, in effect, a form of bootstrapping strategy in which customers provide the financing that is necessary for the business to produce its first generation of products.
Lending model	The lending model (or peer-to-peer lending) involves the investors in providing finance in the form of loans which they expect to be repaid along with a specified rate of interest over a specified period of time. The platform will organise a standardised loan agreement and reporting procedures.
Equity model	The equity model enables businesses to raise finance from investors who will receive an ownership stake in the business. In theory, this model allows anyone to become a business angel – although in practice in many countries investors have to be accredited. Each investor may have full shareholder powers (e.g. to vote, exercise rights, appoint management, decide upon distribution of profits, etc.). However, the need to engage with multiple shareholders on an ongoing basis can create a major administrative burden for the business; hence some platforms will take on these roles as a nominee shareholder. In other cases these shareholders may have a separate category of shares with fewer rights.

aggregation model that raises small amounts of money from numerous members of the general public, normally via a web-based intermediary platform. These crowdfunding platforms represent a new and increasingly influential institution in the entrepreneurial finance market. Some companies have undertaken their own direct crowdfunding campaigns which have either targeted the general public or their own 'supporters' (e.g. bands pitching to their fans; companies pitching to their customers). These individual crowdfunding campaigns can be structured more flexibly, for example regarding investor compensation and involvement (Belleflamme, Lambert & Schwienbacher, 2013). Crowdfunding is not confined to business but is also used by not-for-profit organisations (e.g. social enterprises, charities) and communities to bring various assets into community ownership (e.g. football clubs).

There are five distinct forms of crowdfunding – donation, reward, pre-purchase, lending and equity (Table 17.2). Globally, crowdfunding in all of its forms has overtaken the venture capital industry in terms of funding

for smaller companies (*Financial Times*, 2016). Equity crowdfunding – or crowdinvesting – remains the smallest category, dwarfed by peer-to-peer lending (Collins & Pierrakis, 2012). It has attracted people with relatively small amounts to invest (£20 is a common minimum stake). Some 62% of investors interviewed by Collins and Pierrakis said they had no previous experience of investing. Each investor may have full shareholder powers (e.g. to vote, exercise rights, appoint management, decide upon distribution of profits, etc.). However, the need to engage with multiple shareholders on an ongoing basis can create a major administrative burden for the business; hence some platforms will take on these roles as a nominee shareholder. In other cases these shareholders may have a separate category of shares with fewer rights. Most companies have raised relatively small amounts but the occasional £1 million plus investment has occurred (*Financial Times*, 2015).

The crowdfunding process begins when the entrepreneur registers his or her proposal on the online platform with a call for finance and provides information about the business and the purpose of the fundraising (e.g. business plan, financial projections, legal documents, video, etc.). Investors have little opportunity to do their own due diligence and must rely on this information to make their investment decision. Platforms typically require firms to set a target for the amount of finance that they seek to raise. This target amount of finance has to be reached or exceeded for the money to be released. If not, it is returned to the investors. The majority of companies are unsuccessful in reaching their target figure – 60% in the case of Crowdcube (*Financial Times*, 2015). Other platforms pass on the money regardless of whether the target is reached. The platforms will take a commission (typically 7%) of the funds raised by the entrepreneur (Klonowski, 2015).

Firms may derive non-financial benefits from raising finance through equity crowdfunding. First, crowdfunding platforms can become alternative distribution channels. Second, it provides an excellent pre-market test of the legitimacy and acceptance of the product. Third, it has the potential for powerful word-of-mouth marketing. Fourth, it provides a quicker time to market because of the immediate global access provided by the platform. Fifth, the crowd may be able to solve problems that the firm subsequently encounters. However, there are also negatives. In particular, if the crowdfunding campaign is successful then there is immediate pressure on the firm to scale up. But too rapid an expansion strategy may result in business failure. In addition, firms may not be able to handle the corporate governance implications of dealing with a large group of investors. There is also a reputational risk for the business if it is not able to achieve its target funding threshold.

The Decline in the IPO Market

There has been a significant decline in IPOs in both the USA and Europe since the dotcom crash. In the USA the average number of IPOs per annum has declined from over 500 in the 1990s to just 126 between 2001 and 2009 (Weild & Kim, 2010) and has remained low since then. This has been attributed to the introduction of an array of regulatory changes designed to advance low-cost trading which has had the unintended consequence of removing the value components that are required to support the market, and smaller caps in particular, such as quality sell-side research, capital commitment and sale. In other words, higher transaction costs actually subsidised services that supported investors (Weild & Kim, 2010).

An alternative explanation for the decline in IPOs is structural. The VC investment model was designed to invest in capital-intensive manufacturing sectors (e.g. semiconductors) which would then be taken onto the stock market to continue their growth. However, over the past two decades the majority of technology start-ups have been software-based as the digital revolution has taken hold. Their costs of doing business have fallen dramatically as a result of several developments: reductions in the cost of hardware; the availability of open source software with no licence fees or maintenance costs; access to the global labour markets; search engine marketing to enable small markets to be reached and served affordably; and the lower costs of advertising and distribution costs on the Internet. As a result, these companies need to raise a smaller amount of money than was the norm for high-growth businesses in the past.

A further explanation for the decline in IPOs is the behaviour of venture capital funds which now routinely expect to sell out to existing firms rather than take their companies public (Merrill, 2009). IPOs have fallen from 40% to 20% as a proportion of VC exits between the 1990s and the 2000s (Bessler & Seim, 2012). To put this another way, VC-backed IPOs have accounted for less than one-third of IPOs in recent years compared with over half in 1999. This is linked to the emergence of alternative buyers of their investee companies, specifically large cash-rich companies which have increasingly been following a 'buy-to-build' strategy rather than relying on internal R&D for new products to remain competitive. Examples include Microsoft, IBM, Cisco and Google, which have each been involved in acquiring substantial numbers of technology companies around the world, many of which were VC-backed. Most of their acquisitions are under $30 million and only a few years from start-up (Peters, 2009). This is reflected in the steady rise in the acquisition rate since 2001.

Many commentators have expressed disquiet about the decline in the number of IPOs over the past two decades. First, they are a major source of jobs. Kenney et al. (2012) note that entrepreneurial growth companies that went public between 2001 and 2012 increased their aggregate employment by 156% compared with their pre-IPO level. Second, the preference of VCs to exit through a trade sale – which Weild and Kim (2010, p. 7) describe as 'big companies … eating our young' – raises the concern that established large firms may retard innovation in their acquired businesses or direct it to incremental products, services and products. Third, the drop in the proportion of IPOs is claimed to reduce the chances of technological breakthroughs and hence less chance of a Google, Microsoft, Yahoo!, Genentech, Oracle or Cisco emerging. Fourth, acquisitions generate lower returns for venture capitalists compared with IPOs, which limits their ability to raise new funds and, in turn, reduces the amount of venture capital available in the future. Fifth, by limiting their investment options it also hurts the pension funds which are the main investors in venture capital funds. The *Financial Times* columnist Luke Johnson (2010) therefore stresses that 'a vigorous pipeline of IPOs is a sure sign of a healthy and expanding economy, and successful flotations create a positive feedback loop that stimulates entrepreneurship, jobs and invention'.

Summary

These developments are changing the way in which entrepreneurial companies are being financed (Figure 17.4). First, there is emerging evidence (Mason & Harrison, 2015; Owen & Mason, 2016) that entrepreneurial companies will use bootstrapping and a seed capital round to get off the ground and establish proof-of-concept, and then raise second-round funding in the £0.5 to £2 million range as a 'bundle' of finance from angel groups, along with one or more co-investors (e.g. a co-fund, side car fund, other angel groups, specialist venture capital fund) which, perhaps, with follow-on funding from these investors, will provide a sufficient runway for the business to become profitable and achieve an 'early exit' (Peters, 2009).

Second, instead of growing by means of several further rounds of venture capital on their way to an IPO, companies will increasingly be sold through a trade sale often whilst still quite small. There are several reasons for this. First, there is a buyer's market as global technology companies have increasingly been seeking to grow through acquisition of young innovative businesses. Second, it may reflect the adoption by angel groups of the 'early exit' strategy advocated by Basil Peters (2009) in which he advocates that angels invest in businesses that can achieve an exit within a few years rather than the riskier approach of attracting follow-on investment from venture capital funds who will seek a 'home run'. Third, in some cases it will reflect a lack of alternative options for companies that are unable to raise follow-on funding. Finally, it reflects the reduced costs of growing a technology company as noted above, although with the caveat that labour costs are spiralling upwards. Whatever the reason, the consequence is that fewer companies go to an IPO.

Finally, the big unknown is the future role of crowdinvesting. It is still too new for sufficient performance measures to emerge. Some commentators expect that it will be

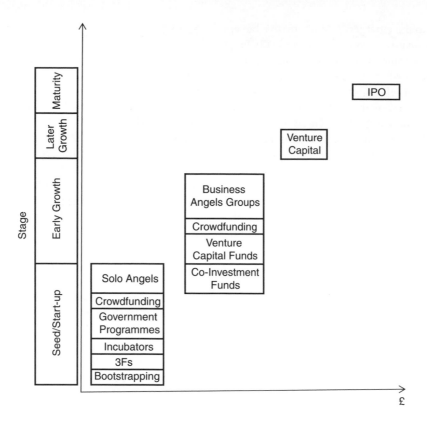

Figure 17.4   The new funding escalator – the 'bundling' approach

a 'flash in the pan' once the expected large number of failures emerge. Others see it as ultimately being usurped by institutions as a new investment channel. Another perspective sees venture capital firms (and business angel groups) developing complementary relationships with platforms which, on the one hand, overcomes the outdated VC model which has been shown to be ineffective in raising new funds and in making successful investments in tech start-ups, and on the other hand can build on the 'social proof' indicators that platforms generate (Salomon, 2016). Fred Wilson, a prominent US VC, has suggested that VCs need to build businesses on top of crowdinvesting platforms, so that where they spot an interesting deal on such a platform they can offer to sponsor it with an investment, potentially making it easier for the business to raise the remaining finance

to meet its target. The VC could also join the board (quoted in Salomon, 2016). More straightforwardly, VCs and BAs could co-invest with the crowd, providing their management skills and investment experience. Indeed, predictions of growing collaboration and even mergers between VCs and crowdfunding platforms are increasing (*Financial Times*, 2016).

ENTREPRENEURIAL FINANCE: A RESEARCH AGENDA

An underlying theme of this chapter has been that of change. The real world is not static. However, this is a challenge for scholars. The research sources that we use – datasets, interviews, surveys, documents – are inevitably historic to a greater or lesser extent. So we need to be aware of what is changing in the world of entrepreneurial finance as we are writing about it – both to contextualise our research appropriately and to ensure the relevance of our research questions for policy and practice. Entrepreneurship scholars do not want to be writing business history by accident! To give just one example, scholars have been slow to observe and examine the changing nature of business angel investing. Mason, Botelho and Zygmunt (2017) have suggested that the emergence of angel groups might have resulted in the creation of 'communities of practice' who share common approaches to investing. This suggests that groups of angels and solo angels are becoming increasingly different in the ways in which they invest. Meanwhile Sohl (2007, 2012) has questioned whether these groups are evolving into venture capital funds, resulting in the demise of angel-style investing.

Another broad theme is to understand the geographies of entrepreneurial finance. The demand for entrepreneurial finance and its supply are not the same in all locations. The geographical concentration of both venture capital investments (Florida & Kenney, 1988; Martin, 1992; Mason & Harrison, 2002b; Mason & Pierrakis, 2013) and IPO firms (e.g. Amini, Keasey & Hudson, 2012; Kenney et al., 2012) have been documented. Can venture capital-deficient regions 'import' venture capital from other regions and countries? Angel investing also exhibits geographical variations reflecting both the underlying geographical distribution of angel investors (which is linked to geographies of entrepreneurial activities) and also investment flows which favour large urban areas in core regions (Avdeitchikova, 2009). And we noted earlier that there are geographical variations in bootstrapping strategies (Winborg & Landström, 2001; Harrison et al., 2004). All of this suggests that the funding escalator takes different forms in different places – and has more gaps – in some places than in others.

Turning to specific research themes, several can be identified that should comprise part of an entrepreneurial finance research agenda. The first is the ongoing evolution of the angel market. Specifically there is a need for further research on the operation and evolution of angel groups and the role that the individual members of the groups now play in the investment and post-investment processes. More than half of all investments by business angel groups are now follow-on investments; this occurs in a very different context to that of the original investment decision (e.g. information availability, personal relationships). Some studies have examined these decisions in a venture capital context using escalation of commitment as a framework (e.g. Birmingham, Busenitz & Arthurs, 2003; Devigne, Manigart & Wright, 2016) but have not been the subject of study in the business angel context.

A second theme is equity crowdinvesting. We need to know more about the investors – what are their characteristics, what motivates them, how do they make their investment decisions, what returns do they achieve? Similarly, we need to understand why businesses go down the crowdfunding route for funding. Would such businesses have been potential candidates for angel or venture capital funding, or are they distinctive and, if so, in what ways? Where does equity crowdfunding fit into the funding escalator? Would business angels or venture capital funds be willing to make follow-on investments in businesses that had raised equity via crowdfunding? The operations of the crowdfunding platforms also require greater scrutiny. And returns data need to be monitored as they start to emerge. Crowdcube had its first exit in July 2015.

The exit process is another topic that has attracted less attention than its importance warrants. There have been few studies of investment returns especially for business angel investments. Moreover, the reliability of those studies that have been based on self-report data by angels has been questioned on the grounds that angels bias their responses to their successful investments – although there is no evidence that this occurs. In recent years exits have assumed prominence in the general entrepreneurship literature (Wennberg, Wiklund, DeTienne & Cardon, 2010; Wennberg & DeTienne, 2014; DeTienne & Wennberg, 2016). However, this research agenda has had an entrepreneur-centric view of the exit and ignored contexts where external investors are involved. Venture capital investors are thought to play an active role in the exit process. The equivalent role of business angels is much less clear. The practitioner literature advocates that angel investors need to take an exit-centric perspective from the very start of the investment process, with opportunities for exit being part of the investment decision-making process and then influencing ongoing strategic decisions (Mason, Harrison & Botelho, 2015). However, the limited evidence suggests that business angel group managers are not particularly exit-centric (Mason & Botelho, 2016).

The declining trend in IPOs, and the wider economic consequences, is another topic requiring further research. The reasons why companies are shunning IPOs need to be explained. Does it reflect the negative views of entrepreneurs on being a public company (e.g. costs, short-termism of the investment community)? Is it because investors are less interested in smaller stocks? Does it reflect the smaller number of companies that scale up? If so, this begs the question why? Is it because more entrepreneurs are motivated by a build-to-sell approach? Have economic and technical changes – such as the declining significance of economies of scale, and the shift from physical to digital products and services – reduced the need to grow to the size at which an IPO becomes an option? The wider implications of fewer public companies on economic development and the investment community (e.g. venture capital firms, pension funds) also need to be examined. And as the converse of fewer IPOs is more trade sales then what are the consequences for the entrepreneurial businesses

that are absorbed into larger companies in terms of their job creation, innovation and physical identity? This is a particularly important issue for peripheral regions which already have a deficiency of stock market listed companies. What happens to the entrepreneurs? How extensive is 'entrepreneurial recycling' (Mason & Harrison, 2006)?

Finally, in view of the prominence of government in the supply of entrepreneurial finance, there is a need for better evaluations. Of course, the time that it takes to exit from an investment (and bearing in mind that 'lemons ripen before plums') means that the question of the effectiveness of such schemes can only be addressed after several years, by which time they have often been discontinued by a new government. However, issues such as additionality and displacement can be examined from an early stage in the operation of such schemes. It would be useful to understand what influences and shapes government intervention in the first place, looking in particular at the process from 'idea' to 'policy' and on to 'implementation' (cf. Arshed, Carter & Mason, 2014; Arshed, Mason & Carter, 2016).

CONCLUSION

This chapter has examined the financing of entrepreneurial ventures from a funding escalator perspective. It discussed the basic model, highlighting the progression of a fast-growing start-up from bootstrapping, to angel funding, one or more rounds of venture capital and ultimately to an IPO. The nature of each of these sources of finance was reviewed. The discussion then moved on to the role of government intervention, both at the macro scale to create the appropriate 'framework conditions' for venture capital and at the micro scale with interventions designed to fill gaps in the funding escalator. The second half of the chapter highlighted changes in the supply of entrepreneurial finance that can be traced back to the fall-out from the dotcom boom and crash at the turn of the century. The repercussions of this crisis undermined the critical complementarities between business angels and venture capital funds as venture capital firms largely abandoned early-stage investing. There has also been a decline in the number of IPOs. This is at least partially linked to the preference of venture capitalists to exit through a trade sale (preferably to a Fortune 500 tech company) rather than an IPO. Meanwhile, new sources of seed finance have emerged, notably crowdfunding. Angels have organised themselves into managed groups to make larger investments, including follow-on investments, to fill the gap created by the contraction of early stage venture capital and to avoid being diluted. The creation of Government Co-Investment Funds appears to be a positive contribution. Thus, the funding escalator has been transformed to a 'bundling' model in which companies that have proved proof-of-concept will put together a funding package from several sources, typically with a business angel group at the core and also comprising funding from a co-investment fund, crowdfunding platform, or corporate venture capital to create a sufficiently large investment and a financial runway to get them to an exit. The final section highlighted the range of research questions that have arisen as a result of these developments. The critical point is that if scholars are to produce research that is relevant and influential they must be aware of current developments in the market for entrepreneurial finance. This can only occur through engagement with the actors in the market.

Note

1 In the USA VCs raised over $100 billion in 2000 but only 10% of this total in 2003. UK VCs, which had joined the dotcom investment frenzy later than their US counterparts, continued to fundraise in 2001, raising over $4.2 billion and hence investing this money in less propitious economic conditions. However, this dropped to $400 million by 2004 (Clark, 2014).

REFERENCES

Alperovych, Y, Hübner, G and Lobet, F (2015), How does governmental versus private venture capital backing affect a firm's efficiency? Evidence from Belgium, *Journal of Business Venturing*, 30 (4), 508–535.

Amini, S, Keasey, K and Hudson, R (2012), The equity funding of smaller growing companies and regional stock exchanges, *International Small Business Journal*, 30 (8), 832–849.

Anyadike-Danes, M, Bonner, K, Hart, M and Mason, C (2009), *Measuring Business Growth: High Growth Firms and Their Contribution to Employment in the UK*, NESTA: London. https://www.nesta.org.uk/sites/default/files/vital-six-per-cent.pdf

Arshed, N, Carter, S and Mason, C (2014), The ineffectiveness of entrepreneurship policy in the UK: is policy formulation to blame? *Small Business Economics*, 43 (3), 639–659.

Arshed, N, Mason, C and Carter, S (2016), Exploring the disconnect in policy implementation: a case of enterprise policy in England, *Environment and Planning C: Government and Policy*, 34 (8), 1582–1611.

Avdeitchikova, S (2009), False expectations: reconsidering the role of informal venture capital in closing the regional equity gap, *Entrepreneurship and Regional Development*, 21 (2), 99–130.

Avdeitchikova, S (2012), The geographic organization of 'venture capital' and 'business angels', in H Landström and C Mason (eds) *Handbook of Research on Venture Capital: Volume 2, A Globalizing Industry*. Cheltenham: Edward Elgar, pp. 175–208

Avnimelech, G and Harel, S (2012), Global venture capital 'hotspots': Israel, in H Landström and C Mason (eds) *Handbook of Research on Venture Capital: Volume 2, A Globalizing Industry*. Cheltenham: Edward Elgar, pp. 209–226.

Baldock, R (2015), What is the role of public feeder markets in developing technology-based small firms? An exploration of the motivations for listing on AIM since the GFC, *Venture Capital: An International Journal of Entrepreneurial Finance*, 17 (1–2), 87–112.

Baldock, R and Mason, C (2015), Establishing a new UK finance escalator for innovative SMEs: the roles of the Enterprise Capital

Funds and Angel Co-Investment Fund, *Venture Capital: An International Journal of Entrepreneurial Finance*, 17 (1–2), 59–86.

Baldock, R, Supri, S, North, D, Macauley, P and Rushton, S (2013), Investigation into the Motivations Behind the Listing Decisions of UK Companies, BIS Research Paper Number 126.

Barnes, S and Menzies, V (2005), Investment into venture capital funds in Europe: an exploratory study, *Venture Capital: An International Journal of Entrepreneurial Finance*, 7 (3), 209–226.

Belleflamme, P, Lambert, T and Schwienbacher, A (2013), Individual crowdfunding practices, *Venture Capital: An International Journal of Entrepreneurial Finance*, 15 (4), 313–333.

Benjamin, G A and Margulis, J B (2000), *Angel Financing: How to Find and Invest in Private Equity*. New York: Wiley.

Berger, A N and Udell, G F (1988), The economics of small business finance: the roles of private equity and debt markets in the financial growth cycle, *Journal of Banking and Finance*, 22 (6–8), 613–673.

Bertoni F and Tykvová, T (2015), Does governmental venture capital spur invention and innovation? Evidence from young European biotech companies, *Research Policy*, 44 (4), 925–935.

Bessler, W and Seim, M (2012), The performance of venture capital backed IPOs, *Venture Capital: An International Journal of Entrepreneurial Finance*, 14 (4), 215–239.

Bhide, A (2008), *The Venturesome Economy*. Princeton, NJ: Princeton University Press.

Bhide, A V (1992), Bootstrap finance: the art of start-ups, *Harvard Business Review*, 70 (6), 109–117.

Birmingham, C, Busenitz, L and Arthurs, J. (2003), The escalation of commitment by venture capitalists in reinvestment decisions, *Venture Capital: An International Jou rnal of Entrepreneurial Finance*, 5 (3), 217–230.

Bliss, R T (1999), A venture capital model for transitioning economies: the case of Poland, *Venture Capital: An International Journal of Entrepreneurial Finance*, 1 (3), 241–257.

Block, J and Sandner, P (2009), What is the effect of the financial crisis on venture capital financing? Empirical evidence from US Internet start-ups, *Venture Capital: An International Journal of Entrepreneurial Finance*, 11 (4), 295–309.

Brander, J, Du, Q and Hellman, T (2014), The effects of government sponsored venture capital: international evidence, *Journal of Finance*, doi: 10.1093/rof/rfu009

Brettel, M (2003), Business angels in Germany: a research note, *Venture Capital: An International Journal of Entrepreneurial Finance*, 5 (3), 251–268.

Brettel, M, Mauer, R and Appelhoff, D (2013), The entrepreneur's perception in the entrepreneur–VCF relationship: the impact of conflict types on investor value, *Venture Capital: An International Journal of Entrepreneurial Finance*, 15 (3), 173–197.

Brush, C G, Carter, N M, Gatewood, E J, Greene, P G and Hart, M M (2006), The use of bootstrapping by women entrepreneurs in positioning for growth, *Venture Capital: An International Journal of Entrepreneurial Finance*, 8 (1), 15–31.

Brush, C, Edelman, L F and Manolova, T S (2012), Ready for funding? Entrepreneurial ventures and the pursuit of angel financing, *Venture Capital: An International Journal of Entrepreneurial Finance*, 14 (2–3), 111–129.

Busenitz, L W, Fiet, J J and Moesel, D D (2004), Reconsidering the venture capitalists' 'value added' proposition: An interorganizational learning perspective, *Journal of Business Venturing*, 19 (6), 787–807.

Capizzi, V (2015), The returns of business angel investments and their major determinants, *Venture Capital: An International Journal of Entrepreneurial Finance*, 17 (4), 271–298.

Carpentier, C and Suret, J-M (2015a), Angel group members' decision process and rejection criteria: a longitudinal analysis, *Journal of Business Venturing*, 30 (6), 808–821.

Carpentier, C and Suret, J-M (2015b), Canadian business angel perspectives on exit: a research note, *International Small Business Journal*, 33 (5), 582–593.

Clark, C (2008), The impact of entrepreneurs' oral 'pitch' presentation skills on business angels' initial screening investment decisions, *Venture Capital: An International Journal of Entrepreneurial Finance*, 10 (4), 257–279.

Clark, J (2014), VC evolved: How VC has adapted in the 15 tumultuous years since the dotcom boom, London: BVCA. http://www.bvca.co.uk/Portals/0/library/documents/

VC%20Evolved/VC%20Evolved.pdfhttp://
www.bvca.co.uk/Portals/0/library/docu-
ments/VC%20Evolved/VC%20Evolved.pdf

Collewaert, V, Manigart, S and Aernoudt, R
(2010), An assessment of government funding of business angel networks in Flanders,
Regional Studies, 44 (1), 119–130.

Collins, L and Pierrakis, Y (2012), *The Venture
Crowd: Crowdfunding Equity Investments
into Business*. London: NESTA. 3.

Croce, A, Tenca, F and Ughetto, E (2016), How
business angel groups work: rejection criteria
in investment evaluation, *International Small
Business Journal*, 35 (4), 405–426.

Cumming, D J and MacIntosh, J G (2006),
Crowding out private equity: Canadian evidence, *Journal of Business Venturing*, 21 (5),
569–609.

Cumming, D J, Grilli, L and Murtinu, S (2014),
Governmental and independent venture capital investments in Europe: a firm-level performance analysis, *Journal of Corporate Finance*,
/dx.doi.org/10.1016/j.jcorpfin.2014.10.016

De Clercq, D and Dimov, D (2004), Explaining
venture capital firms' syndication behaviour:
a longitudinal study, *Venture Capital: An
International Journal of Entrepreneurial
Finance*, 6 (4), 243–225.

De Clercq, D and Sapienza, H J (2001), The
creation of relational rents in venture capitalist-
entrepreneur dyads, *Venture Capital: An
International Journal of Entrepreneurial
Finance*, 3 (2), 107–127.

DeTienne, D and Wennberg, K (2016), Studying exit from entrepreneurship: new directions and insights, *International Small
Business Journal*, 34 (2), 151–156.

Devigne, D, Manigart, S and Wright, M (2016),
Escalation of commitment in venture capital
decision making: differentiating between
domestic and international investors, *Journal
of Business Venturing*, 31 (3), 253–271.

Dolvin, S (2005), Venture capitalist certification
of IPOs, *Venture Capital: An International
Journal of Entrepreneurial Finance*, 7 (2),
131–148.

Dolvin, S and Pyles, M (2006), Venture capitalist quality and IPO certification, *Venture
Capital: An International Journal of Entrepreneurial Finance*, 8 (4), 353–371.

Ebben, J and Johnson, A (2006), Bootstrapping
in small firms: an empirical analysis of change

over time, *Journal of Business Venturing*, 21
(6), 851–865.

European Business Angel Network (EBAN) (2014),
Statistic Compendium 5.5b, Brussels: European
Business Angels Network http://www.eban.org/
wp-content/uploads/2014/09/13.-Statistics-
Compendium-2014.pdf

Falik, Y, Lahti, T and Keinonen, H (2016), Does
startup experience matter? Venture capital
selection criteria among Israeli entrepreneurs,
*Venture Capital: An International Journal of
Entrepreneurial Finance*, 18 (2), 149–174.

Feeney, L, Haines, G H and Riding, A L (1999),
Private investors' investment criteria: insights
from qualitative data, *Venture Capital: An
International Journal of Entrepreneurial
Finance*, 1 (2), 121–145.

Fiet, J O (1995), Risk avoidance strategies in
venture capital markets, *Journal of Management Studies*, 32 (4), 551–574.

Financial Times. (2015), AngelList equity crowdfunding platform to launch in UK, 13, February.

Financial Times. (2016), Crowdfunding sites to
do battle with VC firms, 14 June.

Florida, R and Kenney, M (1988), Venture capital, high technology and regional development, *Regional Studies*, 22 (1), 33–48.

Freear, J and Wetzel, W E (1989), Equity capital
for entrepreneurs, in R H Brockhaism Sr, N C
Churchill, J A Katz, B A Kirchhoff, K H Vesper
and W E Wetzel, Jr (eds) *Frontiers of Entrepreneurship Research 1989*. Wellesley, MA:
Babson College.

Freear, J and Wetzel, W E (1990), Who bankrolls high-tech entrepreneurs? *Journal of
Business Venturing*, 5 (2), 77–89.

Freear, J, Sohl, J E and Wetzel, W E Jr (1994),
Angels and non-angels: are there differences?
Journal of Business Venturing, 9 (2), 109–123.

Freear, J, Sohl, J E and Wetzel, W E Jr (1995),
Angels: personal investors in the venture
capital market, *Entrepreneurship and
Regional Development*, 7, 85–94.

Fried, V H and Hisrich, R D (1994), Toward a model
of venture capital investment decision making,
Financial Management, 23 (3), 28–37.

Gaston, R J (1989a), The scale of informal capital markets, *Small Business Economics*, 1,
223–230.

Gaston, R J (1989b), *Finding Private Venture
Capital for Your Firm: A Complete Guide*.
New York: Wiley.

Gill, D (2015), Consolidating the gains, *Venture Capital: An International Journal of Entrepreneurial Finance*, 17 (1–2), 43–58.

GP Capital (2004), *The Disconnect: What Can be Done to Improve the Working Relationship Between UK Business Angels and Venture Capitalists?* London: GP Capital in association with London Business Angels.

Gregson, G, Mann, S and Harrison, R (2013), Business angel syndication and the evolution of risk capital in a small market economy: evidence from Scotland, *Management and Decision Economics*, 34 (2), 95–107.

Grilli, L and Murtinu, S (2014), Government, venture capital and the growth of European high-tech entrepreneurial firms, *Research Policy*, 43 (9), 1523–1543.

Haar, N E, Starr, J and MacMillan, I C (1988), Informal risk capital investors: investment patterns on the east coast of the USA, *Journal of Business Venturing*, 3 (1), 11–29.

Harrison, R T (2013), Crowdfunding and the revitalisation of the early stage risk capital market: catalyst or chimera? *Venture Capital: An International Journal of Entrepreneurial Finance*, 15 (4), 283–287.

Harrison, R T and Mason, C M (2000), Venture capital market complementarities: the links between business angels and venture capital funds in the UK, *Venture Capital: An International Journal of Entrepreneurial Finance*, 2, 223–242.

Harrison, R T, Dibben, M R and Mason, C M (1997), The role of trust in the informal investor's investment decision: an exploratory analysis, *Entrepreneurship Theory and Practice*, 21 (4), 63–82.

Harrison, R T, Mason, C M and Girling, P (2004), Financial bootstrapping and venture development in the software industry, *Entrepreneurship and Regional Development*, 16 (4), 307–333.

Hellmann, T and Puri, M (2000), The interaction between product market and financing strategy: the role of venture capital, *Review of Financial Studies*, 13 (4), 959–984.

Henrekson, M and Johansson, D (2010), Gazelles as job creators: a survey and interpretation of the evidence, *Small Business Economics*, 35 (2), 227–244.

Higashide, H and Birley, S (2002), The consequences of conflict between the venture capitalist and the entrepreneurial team in the United Kingdom from the perspective of the venture capitalist, *Journal of Business Venturing*, 17 (1), 59–81.

Hindle, K and Wenban, R (1999), Australia's informal venture capitalists: an exploratory profile, *Venture Capital: An International Journal of Entrepreneurial Finance*, 1 (2), 169–186.

Hisrich, R D and Jankowicz, A D (1990), Intuition in venture capital decisions: an exploratory study using a new technique, *Journal of Business Venturing*, 5 (1), 49–62.

Hofman, M (1997), Desperation capitalism: a bootstrapper's hall of fame, *Inc.* August, pp. 54–58.

Hsu, D K, Haynie, M, Simmons, S and McKelvie, A (2014), What matters, matters differently: a conjoint analysis of the decision policies of angel and venture capitalists, *Venture Capital: An International Journal of Entrepreneurial Finance*, 16 (1), 1–25.

Huang, X, Martin Kenne, M and Patton, D (2015), Responding to uncertainty: syndication partner choice by foreign venture capital firms in China, *Venture Capital: An International Journal of Entrepreneurial Finance*, 17 (3), 215–235.

Jeffrey, S, Lévesque, M and Maxwell, A L (2016), The non-compensatory relationship between risk and return in business angel investment decision making, *Venture Capital: An International Journal of Entrepreneurial Finance*, 18 (3), 189–209.

Johnson, L (2010), Tragic tale of the vanishing IPO market, *Financial Times*, 30 November.

Johnson, W C and Sohl, J E (2012), Angels and venture capitalists in the initial public offering market, *Venture Capital: An International Journal of Entrepreneurial Finance*, 14 (1), 27–42.

Jones, O and Jayawarna, D (2005), Resourcing new businesses: social networks, bootstrapping and firm performance, *Venture Capital: An International Journal of Entrepreneurial Finance*, 12 (2), 127–152.

Kelly, P and Hay, M (2003), Business angel contracts: the influence of context, *Venture Capital: An International Journal of Entrepreneurial Finance*, 5 (4), 287–312.

Kenney, M, Patton, D and Ritter, J R (2012), *Post IPO Employment and Revenue Growth for US IPOs: June 1996–2010*. Kansas City: Kauffman Foundation.

Klonowski, D (2011), Private equity in Poland after two decades of development: evolution, industry drivers, and returns, *Venture Capital: An International Journal of Entrepreneurial Finance*, 13 (4), 295–311.

Klonowski, D (2015), *Strategic Entrepreneurial Finance*. London: Routledge.

Kortum, S and Lerner, J (2000), Assessing the contribution of venture capital to innovation, *Rand Journal of Economics*, 31 (4), 674–692.

Lahti, T (2011), Categorization of angel investments: an explorative analysis of risk reduction strategies in Finland, *Venture Capital: An International Journal of Entrepreneurial Finance*, 13 (1), 49–74.

Landström, H (1993), Informal risk capital in Sweden and some international comparisons, *Journal of Business Venturing*, 8 (6), 525–540.

Landström, H and Mason, C (eds) (2016), *Handbook of Research on Business Angels*. Cheltenham: Edward Elgar.

Large, D and Muegge, S (2008), Venture capitalists' non-financial value-added: an evaluation of the evidence and implications for research, *Venture Capital: An International Journal of Entrepreneurial Finance*, 10 (1), 21–53.

Lerner, J (1994), The syndication of venture capital investments, *Financial Management*, 23 (3), 16–27.

Lerner, J (2009), *Boulevard of Broken Dreams*. Princeton, NJ: Princeton University Press.

Lerner, J and Watson, B (2008), The public venture capital challenge: the Australian case, *Venture Capital: An International Journal of Entrepreneurial Finance*, 10 (1), 1–20.

Lingelbach, D (2012), Global venture capital 'hotspots': developing countries, in H Landström and C Mason (eds) *Handbook of Research on Venture Capital: Volume 2, A Globalizing Industry*. Cheltenham: Edward Elgar, pp. 251–279.

Lingelbach, D (2015), Developing venture capital when institutions change, *Venture Capital: An International Journal of Entrepreneurial Finance*, 17 (4), 327–363.

Lockett, A and Wright, M (1999), The syndication of private equity: evidence from the UK, *Venture Capital: An International Journal of Entrepreneurial Finance*, 1 (4), 303–324.

Lu, H and Tan, Y (2012), Global venture capital 'hotspots': China, in H Landström and C Mason (eds) *Handbook of Research on Venture Capital: Volume 2, A Globalizing Industry*. Cheltenham: Edward Elgar, pp. 227–250.

Lumme, A, Mason, C and Suomi, M (1998), *Informal Venture Capital: Investors, Investments and Policy Issues in Finland*. Kluwer.

Luukkonen, T, Deschryvere, M and Bertoni, F (2013), The value added by government venture capital funds compared with independent venture capital funds, *Technovation*, http://dx.doi.org/10.1016/j.dechnovation.2012.11.007

Mac an Bhaird, C and Lynn, T (2015), Seeding the cloud: financial bootstrapping in the computer software sector, *Venture Capital: An International Journal of Entrepreneurial Finance*, 17 (1–2), 151–170.

MacMillan, I C, Kulow, D M and Khoylian, R (1988), Venture capitalists' involvement in their investments: extent and performance, *Journal of Business Venturing*, 4, 27–47.

MacMillan, I C, Siegal, R and Subba Narasimba, P N (1995), Criteria used by venture capitalists to evaluate new venture proposals, in J A Hornaday, E B Shils, J A Timmons and K H Vesper (eds) *Frontiers of Entrepreneurship Research 1985*. Wellesley MA: Babson College, pp. 126–141.

Madill, J J, Haines, G H Jr and Rising, A L (2005), The role of angels in technology SMEs: a link to venture capital, *Venture Capital: An International Journal of Entrepreneurial Finance*, 7 (2), 107–129.

Mäkelä, M M and Maula, M V J (2005), Cross-border venture capital and new venture internationalization: an isomorphism perspective, *Venture Capital: An International Journal of Entrepreneurial Finance*, 7 (3), 227–257.

Malmström, M (2014), Typologies of bootstrap financing behavior in small ventures, *Venture Capital: An International Journal of Entrepreneurial Finance*, 16 (1), 27–50.

Martin, R L (1992), Financing regional enterprise: the role of the venture capital market, in R Townroe and R L Martin (eds) *Regional Development in the 1990s: The British Isles in Transition*. London: Jessica Kingsley, pp. 161–171.

Mason, C M (2007), Venture capital: a geographical perspective, in H Landström (ed.) *Handbook of Research on Venture Capital*. Cheltenham: Edward Elgar, pp. 86–112.

Mason, C M (2009a), Public policy support for the informal venture capital market in Europe: a critical review, *International Small Business Journal*, 27 (5), 536–556.

Mason, C (2009b), Venture capital in crisis? *Venture Capital: An International Journal of Entrepreneurial Finance,* 11 (4), 279–285.

Mason, C (2016), Promoting high growth entrepreneurship in peripheral regions: a critique of government sponsored venture capital funds, *Welsh Economic Review*, 24 (Spring), 36–41.

Mason, C and Botelho, T (2016), The role of the exit in the initial screening of investment opportunities: the case of business angel syndicate gatekeepers, *International Small Business Journal*, 34 (2), 157–175.

Mason, C and Brown, R (2013), Creating good public policy to support high growth firms, *Small Business Economics*, 40 (2), 211–225.

Mason, C M and Harrison, R T (1994), The informal venture capital market in the UK, in A Hughes and D J Storey (eds) *Financing Small Firms*. London: Routledge, pp. 64–111.

Mason, C M and Harrison, R T (1996), Informal venture capital: a study of the investment process and post-investment experience, *Entrepreneurship and Regional Development*, 8 (2), 105–126.

Mason, C M and Harrison, R T (2000), The size of the informal venture capital market in the United Kingdom, *Small Business Economics,* 15 (2), 137–148.

Mason, C M and Harrison, R T (2002a), Is it worth it? The rates of return from informal venture capital investments, *Journal of Business Venturing*, 17 (3), 211–236.

Mason C M and Harrison, R T (2002b), The geography of venture capital investments in the UK, *Transactions, Institute of British Geographers*, 27 (4), 427–451.

Mason, C M and Harrison, R T (2003), 'Auditioning for money': what do technology investors look for at the initial screening stage? *Journal of Private Equity*, 6 (2), 29–42.

Mason, C M and Harrison, R T (2006), After the exit: acquisitions, entrepreneurial recycling and regional economic development, *Regional Studies*, 40 (1), 55–73.

Mason, C M and Harrison, R T. (2008), Measuring business angel investment activity in the United Kingdom: a review of potential data sources, *Venture Capital: An International Journal of Entrepreneurial Finance*, 10 (4), 309–330.

Mason, C M and Harrison, R T (2015), Business angel investment activity in the financial crisis: UK evidence and policy implications, *Environment and Planning C: Government and Policy,* 33 (1), 43–60

Mason, C and Pierrakis, Y (2013), Venture capital, the regions and public policy: the United Kingdom since the post-2000 technology crash, *Regional Studies*, 47 (5), 1156–1171.

Mason, C and Rogers, A (1997), The business angel's investment decision: an exploratory analysis, in D Deakins, P Jennings and C Mason (eds) *Entrepreneurship in the 1990s*. London: Paul Chapman Publishing, pp. 29–46.

Mason, C, Botelho, T and Harrison, R (2016), 'The transformation of the business angel market: evidence and research implications', *Venture Capital: An International Journal of Entrepreneurial Finance*, 18 (4), 321–344.

Mason, C, Botelho, T and Zygmunt, J (2017), 'Why business angels reject investment opportunities: Is it personal? *International Small Business Journal,* 35(5), 519–534.

Mason, C, Harrison R and Botelho, T (2015), Business angel exits: strategies and processes, in J G Hussain, J G and J M Scott (eds) *Research Handbook on Entrepreneurial Finance*. Cheltenham: Edward Elgar, pp. 102–124.

Maxwell, A, Jeffrey, S A and Lévesque, M (2011), Business angel early stage decision making, *Journal of Business Venturing*, 26 (2), 212–225.

Maxwell, A, Jeffrey, S A and Lévesque, M. (2014), Trustworthiness: a critical ingredient for entrepreneurs seeking investors, *Entrepreneurship Theory and Practice,* 38 (5), 1057–1080.

May, J and Liu, M M (2016), *Angels Without Borders: Trends and Policies Shaping Angel Investment Worldwide*. Singapore: World Scientific.

May, J and Simmons, C (2001), *Every Business Needs An Angel: Getting the Money you Need to Make your Business Grow*. New York: Crown Business.

Merrill, S A (2009), Investor Exits, Innovation, and Entrepreneurial Firm Growth: Questions for Research. Kauffman Foundation Large Research Projects Research. Available at SSRN: https://ssrn.com/abstract=1581483

Mitteness, C R, Baucus, M S and Sudek, R (2012), Horse vs. jockey? How stage of funding process and industry experience affect the evaluations of angel investors, *Venture Capital: An International Journal of Entrepreneurial Finance*, 14 (4), 241–267.

Mulchay, D, Weeks, B and Bradley, H S (2012), *'We Have Met The Enemy … And He Is One Of Us.' Lessons from Twenty Years of the Kauffman Foundation's Investment in Venture Capital Funds and the Triumph of Hope over Experience*. Kansas City: Kauffman Foundation.

Munari, F and Toshi, L (2015), Assessing the impact of public venture capital programmes in the United Kingdom: do regional characteristics matter? *Journal of Business Venturing*, 30 (2), 205–226.

Murray, G C (2007), Venture capital and government policy, in H Landström (ed.) *Handbook of Research on Venture Capital*. Cheltenham: Edward Elgar, pp. 113–151.

Myers, S C (1984), The capital structure puzzle, *Journal of Finance*, 39 (3), 574–592.

Nightingale, P, Murray, G, Cowling, M, Baden-Fuller, C, Mason, C, Siepel, J, Hopkins, M and Dannreuther C (2009), *From Funding Gaps to Thin Markets: UK Government Approaches for Early Stage Venture Capital*. London: NESTA.

Nitani, M and Riding, A (2013), Fund size and the syndication of venture capital investments, *Venture Capital: An International Journal of Entrepreneurial Finance*, 15 (1), 53–75.

North, D, Baldock, R and Ullah, F (2013), Funding the growth of UK technology-based small firms since the financial crash: are there breakages in the finance escalator? *Venture Capital: An International Journal of Entrepreneurial Finance*, 15 (3), 237–260.

OECD (2011), *Financing High Growth Firms: The Role of Angel Investors*. Paris: OECD Publishing. http://dx.doi.org/10.1787/9789264118782-en

Owen (Baldock), R and Mason, C (2016), The Role of Government Co-investment Funds in the Entrepreneurial Finance Market: An early assessment of the UK Angel Co-investment Fund, Working Paper: CEEDR, University of Middlesex and Adam Smith Business School, University of Glasgow.

Parhankangas, A and Ehrlich, M (2014), How entrepreneurs seduce business angels: an impression management approach, *Journal of Business Venturing*, 29 (4), 543–564.

Parhankangas, A and Landström, H (2004), Responses to psychological contract violations in the venture capitalist-entrepreneur relationship: an exploratory study, *Venture Capital: An International Journal of Entrepreneurial Finance*, 6 (4), 217–242. doi:10.1080/1369106042000258526

Paul, S, Whittam, G and Johnston, J (2003), The operation of the informal venture capital market in Scotland, *Venture Capital: An International Journal of Entrepreneurial Finance*, 5 (4), 313–335.

Peneder, M (2010), The impact of venture capital on innovation behaviour and firm growth, *Venture Capital: An International Journal of Entrepreneurial Finance*, 12 (2), 83–107.

Pennacchio, L (2014), The causal effect of venture capital backing on the underpricing of Italian initial public offerings, *Venture Capital: An International Journal of Entrepreneurial Finance*, 16 (2), 131–155.

Peters, B (2009), *Early Exits: Exit strategies for Entrepreneurs and Angel Investors (but maybe not Venture Capitalists)*. Vancouver: Meteor Bytes.

Politis, D (2008), Business angels and value added: what do we know and where do we go? *Venture Capital: An International Journal of Entrepreneurial Finance*, 10 (2), 127–147.

Riding, A L, Duxbury, L and Haines, G, Jr (1995), *Financing Enterprise Development: Decision-making by Canadian Angels*. School of Business, Carleton University, Ottawa.

Riding, A, Orser, B and Chamberlin, T (2012), Investing in R&D: small- and medium-sized enterprise financing preferences, *Venture Capital: An International Journal of Entrepreneurial Finance*, 14 (2–3), 199–214.

Salomon, V (2016), Emergent models of financial intermediation for innovative companies:

from venture capital to crowdinvesting platforms in Switzerland, *Venture Capital: An International Journal of Entrepreneurial Finance*, 18 (1), 21–41.

Sapienza, H J (1992), When do venture capitalists add value? *Journal of Business Venturing*, 7 (1), 9–27.

Schäfer, D and Schilder, D (2009), Smart capital in German start-ups: an empirical analysis, *Venture Capital: An International Journal of Entrepreneurial Finance*, 11 (2), 163–183.

Shane, S (2009), *Fool's Gold: The Truth Behind Angel Investing in America*. New York: Oxford University Press.

Shepherd, D A and Zacharakis, A (2001), The venture capitalist-entrepreneur relationship: control, trust and confidence in co-operative behaviour, *Venture Capital: An International Journal of Entrepreneurial Finance*, 3 (2), 129–141.

Sjögren, H and Zackrisson, M (2005), The search for competent capital: financing of high technology small firms in Sweden and USA, *Venture Capital: An International Journal of Entrepreneurial Finance*, 7 (1), 75–97.

Smart, G H (1999), Management assessment methods in venture capital: an empirical analysis of human capital valuation, *Venture Capital: An International Journal of Entrepreneurial Finance*, 1 (1), 59–82.

Sohl, J (2007), The organization of the informal venture capital market, in H Landström (ed.) *Handbook of Research on Venture Capital*. Cheltenham: Edward Elgar, pp. 347–368.

Sohl, J (2012), The changing nature of the angel market, in H Landström and C Mason (eds) *The Handbook of Research on Venture Capital: Volume II*. Cheltenham: Edward Elgar, pp. 17–41.

Sørheim, R and Landström, H (2001), Informal investors: a categorization with policy implications, *Entrepreneurship and Regional Development*, 13 (4), 351–370.

Stedler, H R and Peters, H H (2003), Business angels in Germany: an empirical study. *Venture Capital: An International Journal of Entrepreneurial Finance*, 5 (3), 269–276.

St-Pierre, J, Nomo, T S and Pilaeva, K (2011), The non-financial contribution of venture capitalists to VC-backed SMEs: the case of traditional sectors, *Venture Capital: An*

International Journal of Entrepreneurial Finance, 13 (2), 103–118.

Sudek, R (2006), Angel investment criteria, *Journal of Small Business Strategy*, 17 (2–3), 89–103.

Timmons, J A (1999), *New Venture Creation: Entrepreneurship For the 21st Century*. Boston, MA: Irwin-McGraw Hill, 5th edition.

Tomczak, A and Brem, A (2013), A conceptualized investment model of crowdfunding, *Venture Capital: An International Journal of Entrepreneurial Finance*, 15 (4), 335–359.

Valliere, D and Peterson, R (2004), Inflating the bubble: examining dot-com investor behaviour, *Venture Capital: An International Journal of Entrepreneurial Finance*, 6 (1), 1–22.

Valliere, D and Peterson, R (2007), When entrepreneurs choose VCs: experience, choice criteria and introspection accuracy, *Venture Capital: An International Journal of Entrepreneurial Finance*, 9 (4), 285–309.

Vanacker, T, Manigart, S and Meuleman, M (2011), A longitudinal study on the relationship between financial bootstrapping and new venture growth, *Entrepreneurship and Regional Development*, 23 (9–10), 681–705.

Van Osnabrugge, M (2000), A comparison of business angel and venture capitalist investment procedures: an agency theory-based analysis, *Venture Capital: An International Journal of Entrepreneurial Finance*, 2 (2), 91–109.

Weild, D and Kim, E (2010), *Market Structure is Causing the IPO Crisis and More*, Grant Thornton Capital Market Series.

Wennberg, K and DeTienne, D R (2014), What do we really mean when we talk about 'exit'? A critical review of research on entrepreneurial exit, *International Small Business Journal*, 32 (1), 4–16.

Wennberg, K, Wiklund, J, DeTienne, D R and Cardon, M S (2010), Reconceptualising entrepreneurial exit: divergent exit routes and their drivers, *Journal of Business Venturing*, 25 (4), 361–375.

Wetzel, W E (1981), Informal Risk Capital In New England, in K H Vesper (ed.) *Frontiers of Entrepreneurship Research 1981*. Wellesley, MA: Babson College, pp. 217–245.

Wetzel Jr, W E (1983), Angels and informal venture capital, *Sloan Management Review*, 24 (4), 23–34.

Wiltbank, R E (2009), *Siding With the Angels. Business Angel Investing – Promising Outcomes and Effective Strategies*. London: NESTA.

Wiltbank, R E and Boeker, W (2007), *Returns To Angel Investors in Groups*. Kansas City: Kauffman Foundation.

Winborg, J (2009), Use of financial bootstrapping in new businesses: a question of last resort? *Venture Capital: An International Journal of Entrepreneurial Finance*, 11 (1), 71–83.

Winborg, J and Landström, H (2001), Financial bootstrapping in small businesses: examining small business managers' resource acquisition behaviors, *Journal of Business Venturing*, 16 (3), 235–254.

Wright, M, Gillingham, J and Amess, K (2009), The economic impact of private equity: what

we know and what we would like to know, *Venture Capital: An International Journal of Entrepreneurial Finance*, 11 (1), 1–21.

Wright, M, Hoskisson, R E and Busenitz, L W (2001), Firm rebirth: buyouts as facilitators of strategic growth and entrepreneurship, *The Academy of Management Perspectives*, 15 (1), 111–121.

Yitshaki, R (2012), Relational norms and entrepreneurs' confidence in venture capitalists' cooperation: the mediating role of venture capitalists' strategic and managerial involvement, *Venture Capital: An International Journal of Entrepreneurial Finance*, 14 (1), 43–59.

Zacharakis, A L and Meyer, G D (1998), A lack of insight: do venture capitalists really understand their own decision process? *Journal of Business Venturing*, 13 (1), 57–75.

18

Internal Financial Management in Smaller, Entrepreneurial Businesses

Marc Cowling and Catherine Matthews[1]

INTRODUCTION

Smaller businesses face unique problems when seeking to access financial capital from external markets due to their informational opacity (Stiglitz & Weiss, 1981), closely held ownership structures (Cressy & Olofsson, 1997) and lack of physical assets to place as security against loans (Cowling, 2010). This presents a particular problem if combined with a relative lack of financial sophistication, informal accounting methods, poor internal cash-flow management and a reluctance to take specialist professional advice. A key outcome of these internal competency constraints, and their potential to cause external finance barriers, is that smaller businesses exhibit a preference for, and an over-reliance upon, internally generated funds to capitalise their operations. For these reasons, internal financial management is critical to the success and survival of smaller businesses. Within this chapter these issues are explored and discussed in the first part with a review of the extant literature concerning the internal financing context for SMEs (Small- and Medium-Sized Enterprises) and the role and nature of SME financial management practice. The second part of the chapter is concerned with drawing out the implications of the evidence reviewed for small businesses and identifying a research agenda for the future that fills existing gaps in our knowledge and understanding of internal financial management practices within SMEs. The chapter closes with a brief conclusion.

CONTEXT

The external financing and internal financial management of small- and medium-sized firms has been an issue of concern for both policymakers and researchers for a considerable time. In the UK, the government has been interested in financial issues relevant to SMEs for 80 years since the Macmillan Committee

(1931) identified the existence of a financing gap for small firms, whilst further evidence of gaps in finance emerged from subsequent government-commissioned reports, for example the Bolton Committee (1971) and the Wilson Committee (1979). As the economic importance of SMEs also became more fully recognised (for example, Bolton (1971) and Wilson (1979)), the availability of finance for the inception and growth of small firms received increased attention. In Canada and the US, policy action in the small firm finance arena began as early as the 1950s and 1960s when each country set up its core loan guarantee programmes, both of which remain in existence today. Central to much of the research concerning finance and small firms has therefore been the investigation of the nature and extent of the 'finance gap' for both equity and debt (for example, Berger & Udell, 1998; Berry, Grant & Jarvis, 2003; Binks & Ennew, 1996; Binks, Ennew & Reed, 1992; Cosh & Hughes, 1994; Hamilton & Fox, 1998; Hancock & Wilcox, 1998; Keasey & Watson, 1994). This review initially explores demand- and supply-side issues associated with the provision of finance to SMEs, establishing a backdrop to the subsequent discussion of the financial characteristics of SMEs as manifested within their capital structures. These distinct, emergent financial characteristics imply the importance of internal financial management within SMEs for their continued survival and development.

THE PROVISION OF FINANCE AND SMES: DEMAND- AND SUPPLY-SIDE ISSUES

Debt Finance: Supply-Side Issues

The existence of a finance gap has been evaluated with reference to both supply- and demand-side factors. On the supply side, it has been argued that some small firms with sound investment propositions may be unable to raise finance as a result of information asymmetry between the providers of finance and the small firm (Binks et al., 1992). As Fraser (2004, p. 27) identifies, 'fundamentally the problem arises because lenders are imperfectly informed about the characteristics of potential borrowers'. For the providers of debt finance to small, private firms, problems of information asymmetry are particularly pronounced due to the costs and difficulties associated with the selection, appraising and monitoring of 'appropriate' borrowers; lenders to small firms are exposed to both adverse selection and moral hazard. Adverse selection occurs as a result of lenders' inability to rely upon the price mechanism used to identify viable projects; increasing the interest rate simply results in low-risk borrowers, with viable projects, leaving the market, with only high-risk borrowers remaining (Binks et al., 1992; Fraser, 2004). This situation is further compounded by the moral hazard problem, which results from difficulties in monitoring borrowers, with lenders unable to ensure that small firms will behave in a manner consistent with the contract.

Information asymmetries therefore imply that lenders to small firms are exposed to high risk and will incur disproportionate monitoring costs, independent of the size of the loan. In order to mitigate conditions of information asymmetry lenders may adapt their terms for smaller firms by requiring higher levels of collateral, and charging higher interest rates. Banks may attempt to 'bond' borrowers by requiring high levels of collateral to secure lending against, which can be onerous, particularly if personal collateral is used where business collateral may not be sufficient (Binks & Ennew, 1996). Assuming access to collateral, it has also been argued that borrowers themselves can signal the strength and viability of a project by selecting a secured loan from a 'menu' of terms (Bester, 1985). Borrowers with riskier projects would be more inclined to select higher interest payments on an unsecured loan, through fear of losing their collateral (Bester, 1985). Evidence of the role of collateral in signalling information to the lender is provided by Berry, Faulkner, Hughes and Jarvis (1993), who found that bankers considered the provision of personal collateral by small firm owners signalled their strength of commitment. Information asymmetry for lenders will also be lower where a track record can be observed by the lender (Paul, Whittam & Wyper, 2007).

The implications for small firm financing are that banks may rely heavily upon the provision of collateral, and charge high interest rate premiums. As monitoring costs are unrelated to the size of the loan, agency costs will be at their highest for smaller loans to new ventures (Hamilton & Fox, 1998). Finance gaps for unsecured debt could therefore potentially occur where there is a viable project, but a lack of collateral (Binks et al., 1992), or where the business venture is new and lacks a trading history (Fraser, 2004). For growing firms the provision of collateral can also be problematic where security is already committed to existing borrowing, with none available against which to raise additional finance (Berry et al., 1993; Binks et al., 1992).

In the years prior to the recent global financial crisis of 2007/2008, there was evidence of improvements in the relationships between banks and small firms (see for example, Berry, 2006; Berry et al., 1993; Fraser, 2004; Wilson, 2004), and subsequent changes in the financing of SMEs, with small firms appearing to reduce their short-term exposure and utilise a wider range of sources of finance (Bank of England, 2004; Fraser, 2004). Despite a reduction in small firm reliance upon the overdraft (see Bank of England, 2004), overdrafts and credit cards remained, however, the most popular form of finance for small firms (Fraser, 2004), whilst some aspects of the provision of debt finance to SMEs remained problematic. Information asymmetries determined that for start-up firms, described as 'informationally opaque' by Paul et al. (2007, p. 10), and for firms with a high proportion of intangible assets, finance gaps persisted (Berry, 2006; Graham, 2004a;

Graham, 2004b). In addition, the wider use of sources of finance was associated with the size of the small firm (Bank of England, 2004; Cosh & Hughes, 2003; Fraser, 2004). A change in the financing of small firms, as observed by Graham (2004a, p. 20), was the growth in the use of personal sources of finance, such as credit cards and consumer loans, which were driven by the previously buoyant macro-economy and provided 'quicker and more straightforward financing options than other bank finance'. An ACCA policy briefing paper published in 2006 also identified access to finance issues for the following: women setting up new businesses; ethnic minority businesses; entrepreneurs from deprived backgrounds; and high technology businesses (ACCA, 2006). Even in times of relative macroeconomic prosperity, supply-side issues remained.

In 2007/2008, the world experienced a financial crisis of unprecedented scale, leading to a massive constriction in the availability of credit and bank lending (Buckley, 2011). The impact of this financial turbulence exacerbated supply-side issues regarding the provision of debt finance to SMEs. Fraser (2009) identified increased rejection rates for overdrafts and term loans, higher loan margins and a decline particularly in the supply of credit for higher-risk firms without collateral. Further evidence highlights increased rejection rates of a range of forms of credit (Cowling & Liu, 2011; Fraser, 2009; FSB, 2012b).

The number of credit-rationed firms during a three-month period in 2009 was estimated by Cowling and Liu (2011) as being 119,000, with the main reason cited for attempting to access finance reported as working capital/cash-flow requirements. The FSB's 2011 members' survey (published in 2012) similarly reports that the use of external sources of finance had fallen 19% from 2009, and that ensuring cash flow was the main reason for attempting to secure financial help (FSB, 2012a). A further FSB report concerning small firms and access to finance highlighted a fall in successful loan applications in the UK during 2007 to 2010 of 24%, compared with a corresponding 9% fall observed in Germany (FSB, 2012b).

The role of information asymmetries was aggravated by the financial crisis; collateral requirements and the intangible nature of knowledge-based assets important to innovative firms created particular problems for SMEs in accessing finance (Lee, Sameen & Martin, 2013). Funding that was provided appeared to be targeted at larger SMEs more likely to be able to provide security (Cowling, Liu & Ledger, 2012; Fraser, 2009). The constriction of credit within the banking system thus instigated several coalition government responses to facilitating access to finance for small firms including project Merlin, the launch of the Enterprise Finance Guarantee Scheme, and the Business Bank, whose main purpose was intended to facilitate lending to viable businesses otherwise unable to secure finance as the result of a lack of collateral or the inability to provide a track record. It is evident that supply-side issues associated with the provision of external debt finance moved up the agenda of SME problems.

External Equity Finance: Supply-Side Issues

External equity finance could potentially provide an appropriate source of risk capital for some SMEs, whereby the provider of funds participates in capital appreciation, growth and a share of the profits, in recognition of their exposure to higher risk. However, evidence of external, private equity investment in the financing of start-ups and early-stage investments has clearly demonstrated limited involvement; only 3% of total private equity was invested at start-up stage and only 5% in early stage development (HM Treasury and Small Business Service, 2003).

A number of supply-side issues explain the lack of provision of equity finance to SMEs. The provision of small amounts of equity (below £1 million) is seen as unprofitable; there are high costs regarding arrangement,

monitoring and ongoing management that are fixed regardless of the size of investment (Harris, 1995; HM Treasury and Small Business Service, 2003) and accentuated by the existence of information asymmetries. Risk for the equity provider is high, and rewards are generally related to the size of the investment. Lack of an exit route implies the equity investor can be tied to an illiquid investment. As a result the UK government introduced schemes over the years to encourage and support the provision of small amounts of equity; these included the Enterprise Investment Scheme, Venture Capital Trusts and the Regional Venture Capital Funds. However, survey evidence from Fraser (2004) indicates that private equity continues to play only a minor role in the financing of small firms, with only 3% of small firms using equity finance from any source in the past three years, and 25% of this being provided by directors.

Debt and External Equity Finance: Demand-Side Issues

The capital structures of small firms cannot be explained solely with reference to supply-side issues of access and provision. The most prominent demand-side factor appears to be the desire of owner–managers to maintain, and avoid dilution of, control of their business (Cosh & Hughes, 2003; Robson Rhodes, 1984). This implies a preference of owner–managers for internal funds, sources of finance that offer a minimum level of intrusion to the business, and an aversion to external equity (for example, Hamilton & Fox, 1998; Michaelas, Chittenden & Poutziouris, 1998; Wilson, 2004). Indeed, the desire to maintain control has been identified within the research as a key factor in establishing a 'pecking order' (Myers, 1984) of sources of finance for SMEs (Hamilton & Fox, 1998; Michaelas et al., 1998). Small firms first use internally generated funds, next they will turn to debt finance, and only as a last resort will they choose equity. This helps to explain the dominance of internal funds as a source of finance,

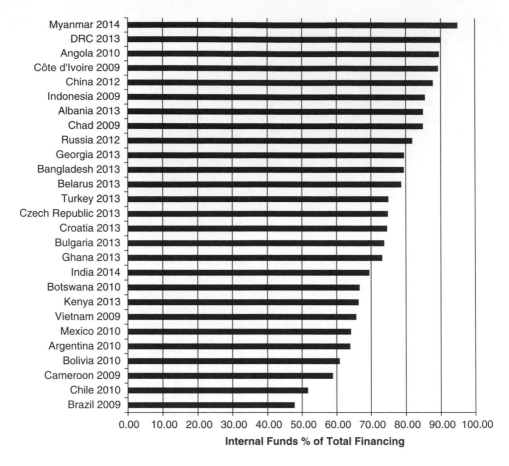

Figure 18.1   The importance of internal funds in developing country SMEs' financing

Source: World Bank, BEEPS Survey, 2014

the popularity of debt for small firms when compared with equity (Bank of England, 2004; Fraser, 2004), and their reliance upon short-term sources, such as overdrafts and credit cards, rather than secured debt (Fraser, 2004). Figure 18.1 above illustrates the significance of internal funds in the financing of SMEs in developing countries, whilst Figure 18.2 illustrates the use of internal funds in financing European SMEs. For the vast majority of both developing and developed countries, internal funds represent over 50% of the total financing of SMEs.

Attitudes to risk and personal goals and beliefs have also been identified as characteristics of owner–managers that may influence their demand for debt finance (Cosh & Hughes,

2003; Kotey, 1999; Michaelas et al., 1998). These research findings suggest that the entrepreneurial values of owner–managers, their personal goals and their attitudes to risk may all impact upon demand for debt financing.

What has been characterised as a 'knowledge gap' (Hutchinson, 1999) has also been identified as a possible demand-side factor affecting small firms' access to both debt and external equity. Fraser (2004) identifies that SMEs may suffer from skills shortages that could impact upon the quality of their business plans, and inhibit their access to finance, finding that, of business loan applications that were rejected, 15% resulted from inadequate business plans. Similarly, the 'poor quality and presentation of business plans'

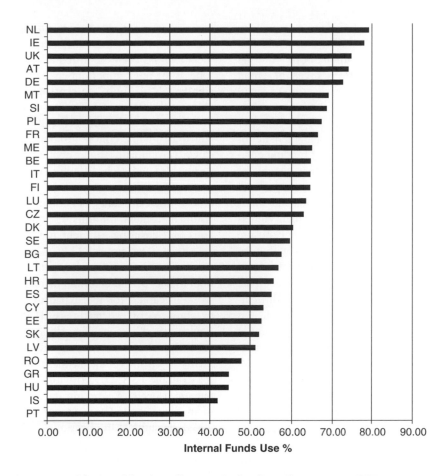

Figure 18.2   Use of internal funds to finance the business in European SMEs

Source: World Bank, BEEPS Survey, 2014

(HM Treasury and Small Business Service, 2003, p. 12) has been attributed to reducing the access of potentially high-growth SMEs to equity finance. The Bank of England (2004, p. 24) discusses a 'lack of investment readiness', referring to the findings of the Global Entrepreneurship Monitor (Harding, 2003, p. 43) that found equity investors complained that 'there is not a supply of equity problem as such, but there is a problem in the supply of decent investor-ready propositions', when questioned regarding the lack of investment in the lower end of the market. Equity investors 'cited the inadequacy of investment propositions … as the predominant reason' why they chose not to invest in SMEs (Bank of England, 2004, p. 25).

THE CAPITAL STRUCTURES OF SMEs AND IMPLICATIONS FOR INTERNAL FINANCIAL MANAGEMENT

The demand- and supply-side factors discussed above interact to determine the capital structures of SMEs with important implications for small firms' management of financial resources. Internal resources emerge as the most significant form of finance, with debt the dominant source of external finance, when external finance is sought (Chittenden, Hall & Hutchinson, 1996; Michaelas et al., 1998). Evidence from Fraser (2009) identifies overdrafts and credit cards as remaining the most popular form of external finance available to small firms, and highlights that the use of asset-based finance fell back to just 2.2% of small firms between 2005 and 2008. This reliance upon both internal resources and short-term sources of credit can result in the undercapitalisation of small firms (Michaelas et al., 1998) and cause financial problems (Kotey, 1999).

As a result of the financial characteristics of small firms and the challenging funding environment, effective financial management of internal resources is of vital importance. Small firms' reliance upon internal funds and short-term sources of finance increases their vulnerability to liquidity problems and their exposure to external factors, such as changes within the macroeconomy (Kotey, 1999; Michaelas et al., 1998). Undercapitalisation will exacerbate these problems and present particular difficulties for businesses wishing to grow (Michaelas et al., 1998). Efficient internal management of financial resources eases reliance upon short-term sources of finance, and aids those small firms who find it difficult to access funds. When considering the motivations of small businesses in using external finance, 50% of businesses reported using overdrafts to fund working capital (Fraser, 2004), whilst 16% of small businesses raised their largest term loan to finance working capital (Fraser, 2004). The FSB survey 2011 reported that the second greatest barrier to success for members was cash flow, with 43% of respondents reporting that their reason for attempting to secure financial help was to ensure cash flow (FSB, 2012a). The effective internal management of financial resources within SMEs is therefore a particularly significant aspect of firm practice.

INTERNAL FINANCIAL MANAGEMENT PRACTICE WITHIN SMEs: ISSUES AND EVIDENCE

Working capital management, which refers to the management of current assets and current liabilities and is primarily concerned with the short-term financial position of a business (Arnold, 2013), constitutes the key focus for a firm's internal financial management and has been identified as representing 'one of the most important challenges facing small to medium enterprises (SMEs)' (Mazzarol, 2014, p. 2). The key components of working capital are generally acknowledged as: trade creditors (amounts payable), stock (inventory), trade debtors (amounts receivable) and cash. Effective management of these short-term assets and liabilities is crucial to ensure that cash continues to flow within a business, minimising liquidity problems and ensuring efficient use of internal resources. The financial characteristics of small firms have been shown to imply the importance of the internal management of working capital for the expansion, success, or failure of a business (Chittenden, Poutziouris & Michaelas, 1998). However, cash flow has been consistently cited by SMEs as an important business barrier (see for example FSB, 2012a) whilst other problematic aspects of working capital management, for example late payment (see Wilson, 2008), have direct implications for liquidity.

It is not surprising therefore that the effective financial management of small firms has been the focus of a number of studies, which have largely concluded that various aspects of financial management are poor, or requiring improvement (see: Bolton, 1971; Jindrichovska, 2013; Mungal & Garbharran, 2014; Nayak & Greenfield, 1994; Storey, Keasey, Watson & Wynarczyk, 1987). However, methodological issues are apparent that have important implications for the evaluation of existing research (see Deakins, Morrison & Galloway, 2002; Jarvis, Kitching, Curran & Lightfoot, 1996; Perren & Grant, 2000) concerning internal financial management within SMEs, and that resonate with wider paradigmatic issues within SME research (see Blackburn & Kovalainen, 2009; Grant & Perren, 2002). Prior to reviewing research concerned particularly with working capital management within SMEs, the following section will discuss these key methodological issues within the context of the broader SME financial management literature and outline findings from research that has adopted an alternative methodological perspective to the dominant paradigm.

FINANCIAL MANAGEMENT WITHIN SMEs AND METHODOLOGICAL ISSUES

This section of the chapter seeks to establish a discussion of the broad methodological issues related to research concerned with financial management within SMEs. Discussion of these issues, and of the apparent contradictions within the literature that emerge, is a useful backdrop to the subsequent review of research focused upon working capital management as it enables the findings of the research to be evaluated in light of these concerns. The discussion below reviews critiques of the dominant paradigmatic positioning of SME financial management research, and discusses evidence from qualitative research studies that illuminate overlooked dimensions of firm practice and provide evidence contrary to the view that financial management practice within SMEs is often poor.

Research concerning the internal financial management practices of SMEs has been observed as dominated by hypothetical deductive methodological approaches, underpinned with a positivist ontology and largely concerned with the uptake of normative practice (Jarvis et al., 1996). Yet the uniqueness of SMEs and the characteristics that distinguish them from their larger counterparts have been identified as generating different types of financial problems (Abdulsaleh & Worthington, 2013; Ang, 1991). In addition, the assumption that small firms should be assessed against normative, large-firm practice underpins much of the survey-based research, for which it has been criticised. Jarvis et al. (1996) identify three arguments as to why this assumption is inappropriate for small firms. First, it is identified that what

is currently accepted as 'best practice' is in itself a fluid concept, with consensus shifting with favoured practices. Second, it is argued that many larger enterprises do not adhere strictly to the techniques and methods identified as 'best practice', and that several well-publicised failings in financial management have occurred within expertly staffed treasury departments. Finally, the environmental conditions that small firms operate under are recognised to be substantially different from those of larger enterprises (Curran, 1990; Rainnie, 1989; Shutt & Whittington, 1987). The widely disparate operating conditions of small firms will have implications for the type of financial management that is appropriate.

Qualitative research studies have reported contrasting findings with regards to financial management and decision-making within small firms. Curran, Jarvis, Kitching & Lightfoot (1997) used a qualitative, grounded theory approach to consider the factors taken into account by small firms when setting prices, finding evidence that SME practice incorporated different forms of rationality, and demonstrated sophisticated understanding of markets. Similarly, Jarvis et al. (1996) adopted a qualitative, grounded approach to the investigation of financial management practices within small firms. They found that small business owners are motivated by a range of factors and pursue a variety of objectives in the financial management of their business, concluding that the research offered a contrasting view to the widely held perspective that small business owner–managers lacked sophistication and skills with regards to financial management when compared with normative, formal notions of large firm 'best practice'.

Using a comparative case study methodology, Perren, Berry and Partridge (1998) found that, in the early history of a business, owner–managers used informal mechanisms of information and control, appropriate and effective for the scale of the business. As growth occurred, formal systems evolved, dependent upon the 'dynamic interplay of factors' (Perren et al., 1998, p. 359). Deakins et al. (2002, p. 7) also used a case study approach to investigating financial management with their research findings supporting Jarvis et al. (1996) regarding small firm owner/manager's rationality, and Perren et al. (1998) regarding the evolutionary development of formal systems in small firm development. Ekanem (2005, p. 315) investigated investment appraisal within small firms using a qualitative research methodology to collect 'insider accounts', concluding that 'none of the case study firms employed any conventional methods in their investment decision-making process' but that they did demonstrate 'systematic and logical thought' that resulted in benchmarking. The research identifies the use of informal routines that provided 'satisficing solutions' and were conceptualised as 'bootstrapping'.

The choice of methodological paradigm implies differences in research findings with regards to the financial management practices of small firms (Perren et al., 1998). Perren and Grant (2000) distinguish between research that adopts a subjectivist perspective, focusing upon the micro world of the owner–manager, and research focused upon macro-level, objectified management accounting procedures, arguing that differences in perspective account for differences in findings. The focus for researchers at a macro-level is upon the adoption of formalised management accounting practices, with little consideration of informal practice, whilst subjectivist approaches reveal informal aspects of practice, but may not recognise the influence of formalised knowledge (Perren & Grant, 2000). Objectivist perspectives have tended to identify poor financial management practices and control within SMEs, but have been criticised for assuming that small firms should necessarily adopt normative practices, and for failing to recognise the diverse objectives of small firm owner–managers (Jarvis et al. 1996; Jarvis et al., 2000; Curran et al., 1997). As outlined above, inductive, qualitative research has however provided evidence to suggest informal aspects of practice are particularly relevant to owner–managers in

small firms and can support sophisticated decision-making. Research regarding financial management within SMEs has tended to focus upon formalised financial management practices, arguably resulting in a constrained and one-dimensional understanding. With these methodological issues in mind, the discussion now focuses specifically upon working capital management within SMEs.

WORKING CAPITAL MANAGEMENT IN SMEs

The following discussion reviews research that has investigated aspects of working capital management practice within SMEs. Empirical research concerned with working capital management is reviewed initially and can be seen to be mainly concerned with the role of formal practice. Other research has been primarily concerned with the deductive testing of theoretical explanations for SME working capital management practices, and a discussion of the approach and findings of such studies is also included within this section. Research that considers the working capital management practices of SMEs within developing countries is also discussed, as firms within these countries can face distinct environmental circumstances. This section closes by drawing together the emergent issues for future research.

Descriptive empirical research concerning working capital management in SMEs has tended to emphasise the characteristics of small firms and the adoption of working capital management practices, as identified from normative practice. Peel and Wilson (1996) conducted a postal survey concerning the capital budgeting and working capital management practices of small firms, which included asking respondents to indicate on a scale of 1–5 the frequency with which they reviewed formal aspects of working capital management. Peel and Wilson (1996) conclude that to some extent capital budgeting techniques were associated with firm size, but that this was not the case for working capital practices. Their findings implied that a high proportion of the SMEs surveyed reported using formal capital budgeting techniques, and that those firms were also more active in their working capital management. This type of research strategy is primarily concerned with normative, formal practice, and results could be affected by the respondent's perception that they *should* be reviewing these aspects of practice frequently. The potential problems with such a research approach are recognised by the authors, who suggest the use of in-depth case studies for the future investigation of financial management within SMEs.

Peel, Wilson and Howorth (2000) undertook further survey-based research that considered the credit management practices of small UK manufacturing firms, and factors perceived to be impediments to improving business performance. Creditor and debtor characteristics of small firms were identified, with micro firms appearing to be suffering less from problems of late payment, in comparison with the 'larger' small firms. Wilson and Summers (2002) also support these findings, identifying that small firms experiencing growth use the extension of trade credit to signal financial strength. With regards to credit management, owner–managers were surveyed as to which credit management procedures were used, whilst working capital management is again assessed according to the frequency of review of particular components. Findings identify that smaller firms review working capital less frequently. Peel et al. (2000) therefore provided further empirical evidence of credit management within small firms, in terms of normative practices.

Howorth and Wilson (1999) extended previously collected survey data using both quantitative and qualitative data to consider late payment and the small firm. This aspect of working capital management has been the particular subject of research in the UK due to recognition of the problem caused to small firms by late payment, and the subsequent

ineffectual legislation (Wilson, 2008). Howorth and Wilson (1999) identify that surveys have documented the extent of the late payment problem, but there has been little research considering the payment behaviours of small firms. Survey data established the extent of the late payment problem for small firms, from both the demand and supply side. Multivariate techniques identified factors that were 'shown to impact on firms' perceptions of the late payment problem' (Howorth & Wilson, 1999, p. 310). The case studies were used to explore whether late payment arises from dominant suppliers, poor financial management, or the firm's financing strategy. Dominance of customers did not appear to be a major problem, whilst the small firms that suffered most from late payment were characterised by undercapitalisation and poor credit management. Assessment of working capital management practices is again undertaken against a backdrop of normative practice. The case studies identify interesting aspects, yet the focus remains upon formalised manifestations of firm practice.

Also using a combination of case studies and a large postal survey Chittenden et al. (1998) undertook a detailed review of the financial management practices of SMEs that included consideration of particular aspects of working capital management. This research recognised that motivational drivers of practice for owner–managers are often ignored, and that 'best practice' might not be appropriate, concluding that proactive credit management and systematic benchmarking should be encouraged by business support agencies.

Howorth and Reber (2003) utilised survey data alongside qualitative case studies, to explore the habitual late payment of trade credit by small firms, taking a demand-side position. The case studies were used to 'investigate unexpected results' (Howorth & Reber, 2003, p. 480) from a multivariate analysis that considered the hypothetical positive relationship between small firm late payment and bank financing, relationships with suppliers, firm size and growth, with a negative association expected between 'habitual late paying firms and use of long term sources of finance, customers paying on time and take up of early payment discounts' (Howorth & Reber, 2003, p. 474), concluding that there is 'strong evidence of a financing demand for late payment'(p. 480). The findings are generated from hypothesised explanations of late payment, whereby unexpected results are investigated further with the use of case studies. Howorth and Reber (2003, p. 480) recognise the potential limitations of a research strategy that is reliant upon proxy variables to operationalise hypothesised explanations, stating that the 'number of customers/suppliers is a poor proxy for the quality or closeness of the relationship between suppliers and customers'. It could also be argued that asking owner–managers how often they review working capital management practices is a poor proxy for identifying 'active' working capital management in small firms.

Late payment and small firms was also the subject of Chittenden and Bragg's (1997) research that considered the impact from a macroeconomic perspective. In particular, the research considers the reasons for granting credit; the importance of payment practices; and the impact that late payment has upon SMEs and the economy. Analysis of 500 company accounts was conducted to determine the impact on working capital. The reasons for granting trade credit are explored from a top-down position whereby the extension of trade credit is considered with reference to theoretical, conceptual explanations. Chittenden and Bragg (1997) find from their discussion of the impact of economic motivations, administrative reasons, and the influence of dominant customers that economically beneficial motivations for extending trade credit have declined, concluding that dominant customers are imposing payment terms. The focus of Chittenden and Bragg's (1997, p. 33) research was to consider the potential economic impact of the late payment problem; they found that a late

payment multiplier effect existed and that 'well drafted legislation' for a statutory right to interest would be effective.

Much of the research undertaken into working capital management within small firms has been concerned with a deductive research strategy and testing theory. Petersen and Rajan (1997, p. 689) used a national database of small business finance to test finance advantage theories, price discrimination theories and transaction cost theories, finding evidence of an information advantage to the supplier of trade credit over financial institutions in the form of built-in 'trip wires' that provided early signals regarding the financial distress of a customer. In addition, the opportunity for price discrimination was identified as a further incentive.

Theories of trade credit extension were also tested by Wilson and Summers (2002), but with firms of a smaller size than Petersen and Rajan (1997). Wilson and Summers (2002) consider the different influences upon credit granting for firms with an average of 10 employees. Survey data from a postal questionnaire were used to model small firms' choices of credit terms and credit period as a function of transaction costs, economies of scale, marketing objectives and the use of trade credit to provide finance. Findings suggested that firm size affected credit policy, both directly and indirectly, as did industry norms, lack of access to finance and the nature of the relationship with the client. Wilson and Summers (2002) identify that industry norms influence the credit period, but that this is limited by access to resources and finance. Additionally, relationships with clients can reduce problems with monitoring, leading to longer credit periods for repeat customers.

Summers and Wilson (2003) extend their investigation of explanatory theories for trade credit, considering the role of trade credit as a strategic tool in supporting corporate objectives. The theories of trade credit extension and credit terms offered that are tested include: marketing motivations; financial motivations;

transaction costs; contract compliance; and the impact of specific investments. The credit granting decision was tested using multivariate models. Summers and Wilson (2003) find that trade credit management is an important means of developing relationships with clients and encouraging repeat business, in spite of the influence of industry norms. Firms were found to vary their terms primarily for marketing-related rationales that enabled them to secure business.

Howorth and Westhead (2003) also adopted a multivariate approach, developing testable hypotheses from a resource-based view of the firm, agency theory and transaction cost theory, in order to address whether there are different 'types' of small firms with regards to the take-up of working capital management routines. Howorth and Westhead (2003, p. 107) identify four different 'types' of firms from a cluster analysis, concluding that 'small firms are not a homogenous group with regard to the take up of working capital management routines', and that due to time constraints working capital management practice may well reflect assessment of marginal returns; owner–managers undertake to proactively manage working capital only when it is considered worthwhile. The focus of this research however remains upon the take up of working capital management routines representative of normative practice; again this is determined by the frequency of review of different aspects of working capital. These routines are then modelled against independent firm variables, which consist of some dummy variables.

Given the limited resources available to SMEs, research undertaken by Tauringana and Afrifa (2013), which considered SMEs listed upon AIM (Alternative Investment Market), focused upon the relative importance of working capital management for firm profitability. The research utilised panel data analysis of financial data for 133 firms, and a questionnaire survey with 19 respondents which was used to establish the relative importance of working capital and its constituent elements. Tauringana and Afrifa (2013) found that, of the component elements of working capital (identified as inventory, accounts receivable and accounts payable), accounts payable and accounts receivable were relatively more important for firm profitability. As a result, Tauringana and Afrifa (2013) argued firms with restricted resources should direct their efforts towards these aspects of working capital.

The determinants of trade credit were analysed across seven European countries by Garcia-Teruel and Martinez-Solano (2010). This study looked to examine both the role of trade credit in European SMEs and the factors that determined levels of trade credit across European countries, identifying any differences. The paper identifies three broad theoretical explanations for the extension of trade credit: financial motives, operational motives and commercial motives. Their findings show that, despite differences between the countries in terms of levels of trade credit, the determinants of trade credit were generally consistent across the countries. The extension of trade credit is explained with reference to availability and cost of funds, and the size of the firm. Evidence also suggested that trade credit was used as a marketing tool, supporting the notion of price discrimination. In terms of SME use of trade credit, the larger SMEs, and those with growth opportunities, received more trade credit. However, where SMEs had access to external financing, trade credit was used to a lesser extent.

The contribution of SMEs to the economies of developing countries in Africa has prompted several studies that examine financial management, particularly as the high failure rate of SMEs in these regions (see for example, Tushabomwe-Kazooba, 2006) has been in part attributed to failings in financial management and associated aspects of firm practice. Research, with a notable exception, is again largely characterised by the use of structured questionnaires to collect data and an emphasis upon formalised practice. Uwonda, Okello and Okello (2013) argue that the 50% failure rate amongst newly established Ugandan SMEs is in part attributable to issues associated with poor cash flow management, despite Uganda ranking highly in terms of entrepreneurial characteristics. Cash flow management therefore forms the focus of their research, which uses a structured questionnaire to investigate cash flow planning, monitoring and control within 120 service sector SMEs. Overall, this research identified poor cash flow management. Tax planning, working capital management and the determination and interpretation of financial statements were identified as significant obstacles to cash flow planning, whilst the monitoring of cash flows and lack of budgetary and cash flow control were identified as key issues for Ugandan SMEs. The authors point to a need for the involvement of suitably qualified personnel, and to the responsibilities of government in creating and nurturing an appropriate environment within which SMEs receive the support required to improve their financial management.

Similarly Abanis (2013) investigated the financial management practices of SMEs in Uganda, prompted by their high failure rate. Questionnaires were used to establish the extent of financial management within Ugandan SMEs, assessing financial management across working capital management, investment decisions, financing, accounting information systems and financial reporting and analysis. As with Uwonda et al. (2013), consideration was given to formalised aspects of financial management practice and findings identified reliance upon internal funds consistent with pecking order theory (Myers, 1984) and evidence of poor financial management practice, with the extent of financial management described as low. A research study undertaken in Ghana by Amoako (2013) utilised a structured questionnaire to consider the role of accounting practices and record keeping, identifying the significance of this information in terms of accessing finance and managing an SME successfully. Amoako (2013) found that the respondent SMEs failed to keep formal accounting records, citing key reasons as being a lack of understanding of the need for them, deficiencies in accounting knowledge and the perceived cost of engaging an accountant. Understandably, Amoako (2013) argues that the financial performance of Ghanaian SMEs is severely impeded by the quality and availability of accounting information and calls for government involvement in creating guidelines for SMEs and in making the preparation of accounts mandatory. Figure 18.3 below identifies the proportion of SMEs with audited financial statements in developing countries, and provides further evidence to support the issues raised by Amoako (2013) above.

Research conducted in Uganda by Orobia, Byabashaija, Munene, Sejjaaka and Musinguzi (2013) provides qualitative evidence regarding working capital management, in contrast to the evidence reviewed above, taking a process perspective informed by action theory. Semi-structured interviews were conducted and interview data coded deductively, utilising prior research. The research concludes that a key difference between small and large firms is in the processes involved in working capital management, whereby for the owner–managers of SMEs it is informal practices that dominate, with intuitive planning and control evident. Orobia et al. (2013) therefore argue that owner–managers are better supported with tailor-made advice and an increased awareness of working capital processes, rather than generic advice focused upon the introduction of conventional practices.

The above review of working capital management research within SMEs highlights the same emphasis upon formalised, normative practice as identified in the broader literature concerning SME financial management, with explanations of SME working capital management behaviour largely derived deductively from theory testing. As discussed earlier, these approaches have been questioned in terms of their appropriateness; small firms are different from each other, and their larger counterparts, with varying

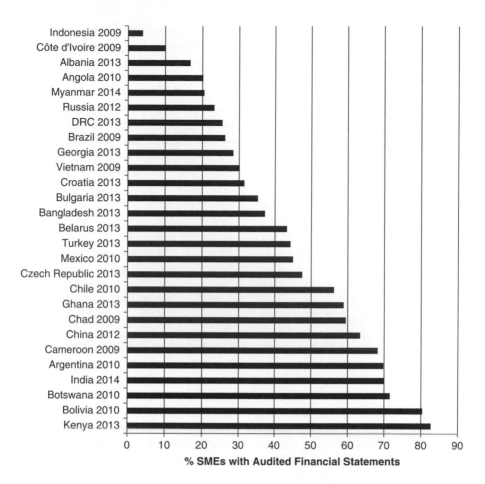

Figure 18.3   SMEs with audited financial statements in developing countries

Source: World Bank, BEEPS Survey, 2014

aspects of environmental exposure and distinct financial structures, whilst small firm owner–managers have been shown to have complex motivations and rationalities that extend beyond profit maximisation (Curran et al., 1997; Jarvis et al., 1996; Jarvis et al., 2000). Subsequently, the internal financial management practices of SMEs are understood largely in terms of formal, normative practice, from an objectivist position that has particular associated limitations. The second part of this chapter follows with discussion of an agenda for future research and will begin by exploring the implications of the issues outlined here.

CONCLUSION

Paradigmatic Debates and Methodological Approaches: Formal and Informal Dimensions of Financial Management Practice

The review of the internal financial management practices of SMEs has highlighted how differences within research findings have been attributed to differences in methodological approach and ontological positioning. However, the vast majority of the existing research assesses SME financial management against normative practice using deductive, quantitative approaches. Normative financial management practices are derived from neo-classical economic theory that assumes profit maximisation is the objective of the firm, and that an actor's behaviour is determined by instrumental rationality. Given that SMEs are widely acknowledged to exhibit distinct financial characteristics (Abdulsaleh & Worthington, 2013) and have a wide and complex range of rationality directing their decision-making (Curran et al., 1997; Jarvis et al., 1996), these assumptions have, however, been criticised. Whilst potentially representing 'best practice' for large companies, there are a number of characteristics of small firms that imply normative practices may not be effective or appropriate for SMEs, and that actual practice might be better understood from an alternative perspective (Jarvis et al., 1996).

The dominance of quantitative, positivist research has in part been explained within discussion of the broader methodological issues associated with SME research. Curran and Blackburn (2001, p. 124) discuss qualitative and quantitative research paradigms, identifying the dominance of quantitative, positivist SME research and 'a need to engage more positively with the epistemological principles underlying qualitative research'. Issues of paradigmatic constriction were also identified by Grant and Perren (2002, p. 185), who used 'Burrell and Morgan's (1979) paradigmatic taxonomy to conduct a systematic meta-theoretical analysis of articles published in 2000', within selected SME journals. Their findings highlighted the dominance of research with a functionalist ontology and called for a wider range of paradigmatic perspectives within SME research.

Blackburn and Kovalainen (2009, p. 133) similarly argue that, as the result of attempts to 'satisfy practical audiences', ontological and epistemological issues are often ignored, and that SME research suffers from a limited range of paradigmatic perspectives. This is partly explained by Blackburn and Kovalainen (2009, p. 139) as being driven by government policymakers' preferences, and resulting in research with an emphasis

upon 'reporting rather than analysing, and describing rather than explaining'. As well as identifying a need to broaden methodological perspectives, Blackburn and Kovalainen (2009, p. 136) identify the increased significance of this where particular aspects of SME research might be considered as 'mined out'; where this is the case researchers are encouraged to, amongst other things, consider in-depth 'existing methodological approaches'.

There are therefore methodological issues within research concerning the internal financial management of SMEs which reflect wider concerns within the SME research arena. Research concerned with financial management has tended to assess small firms against 'best practice', and provide explanations of behaviour based upon the testing of hypotheses derived from neoclassical economic theory. Such research has tended to identify a lack of financial management skill within small firms. In contrast, the few research studies underpinned with a qualitative research methodology that have been undertaken have discovered evidence of sophisticated and effective informal decision-making and practice. Very little research however has been undertaken that explores both informal and formal financial management practices within SMEs using inductive, qualitative methods. As SMEs are acknowledged to 'differ significantly from large firms in terms of their financial decisions and behaviour' (Abdulsaleh & Worthington, 2013, p. 36), future research could address the lack of emphasis upon informal dimensions of internal financial management practice and avoid imposing normative assumptions of 'best practice' by carefully considering the paradigmatic position adopted and the methodological approaches used. A broadening of methodological approach should result in a richer and deeper understanding of the internal financial management practices of SMEs, allowing for recognition of both informal and formal dimensions of practice and of the complex, contextual conditions within which internal financial management practice occurs.

Gaps in Existing Knowledge

A future research agenda

Whilst the association between internal financial management in SMEs, the demand for external capital and the willingness of external financiers to meet these demands cannot be ignored, the evidence is fairly clear in two aspects. First, entrepreneurs have a preference for internal funds over all external sources of financial capital and this is related to pecuniary factors such as lack of collateral and the relative price differential between internal and external funds, but also non-pecuniary factors such as the desire to maintain control and independence. These two stylised facts mean that how entrepreneurs manage their internal finances is paramount.

Yet it is clear that the vast majority of theoretical and empirical research to date has focused on interactions with external capital markets and simply assumed that, due to their information opacity and wider issues around informational asymmetries and the relative quality of information that is presented to external financiers which favours the private information available to the entrepreneur, finance constraints are likely to be present in SME finance markets.

The literature relating to internal financial management and the lack of financial acumen amongst many entrepreneurs is relatively sparse by comparison. This leaves many important research questions unanswered and requires a significant body of new research to rectify this imbalance between research on smaller firms' engagement with external capital markets and the process by which cash is generated and managed within the business and by whom. In one sense, research has focused too far down the path on smaller firms fulfilling their financing needs. As we have highlighted, not only do the majority of smaller firms have a clear preference for internally generated funds, but their contribution to total financing is large. It is only when the firms' financing needs cannot be met from internal sources that they seek recourse to

the external market. In this respect, we need to know more about how and why smaller businesses are capable (or incapable) of financing their day-to-day operations and investments to fully understand what happens when they present themselves to external financiers. With this in mind we offer a menu of questions which future research might address from both a theoretical and empirical perspective. These are:

Human capital

- What level of financial skills and competencies do smaller firms possess internally and to what extent do they engage with external financial professionals?
- How does internal learning occur in the context of financial competencies? And as firms evolve (grow bigger and get older) do they hire in more capability?

The centrality of the entrepreneur or entrepreneurial team to decision-making in SMEs means that their human capital, both formal (education), informal (experiential learning), particularly in respect of financial matters, plays an important role in how their firms manage their cash flows and the way that their businesses structure their capital. Further, they also have a direct effect on their ability to access capital from external financiers. Where the entrepreneurial team is deficient in financial skills and expertise, there is a requirement for building relationships with external finance professionals, including accountants, auditors and suppliers of finance. This proposed human capital strand of new research would capture elements of internal and external financial management skills and add more insight into the relationships between the two.

Internal finance

- What is the decision-making process by which the entrepreneur chooses to take cash out of their firm or leave it in the firm to finance future operations? The unique context of the family business may be a particularly interesting area to research and compare.
- How does the relative cash position of the firm change as it evolves over time (gets bigger and

older)? Is it the absolute cash position or the variability in cash flows that is most important?
- Does the preference for internal finance over external finance change as firms evolve (get bigger and older)?
- How important are directors' loans and equity as an additional source of internal financing?

There are many life-cycle theories which outline how firms capitalise their businesses and how they progressively use more sophisticated sources of finance as they become older and more stable. But the empirical evidence shows very clearly that only a tiny minority of SMEs actually use, or even consider, many of the more sophisticated and higher-order financial instruments. Even venture capital, despite its disproportionate attention in the literature, is largely an irrelevance to 99% of SMEs. We propose that more research attention is devoted to how entrepreneurs make their decisions about whether or not to build up cash reserves within their businesses, thus removing the need for external finance, or withdraw free cash from the business to realise the cash returns to their entrepreneurial efforts. We also suggest that the unique closely held ownership structure of SMEs, and particularly where a single extended family retains a majority stake, allows new work to be conducted at the interface of the entrepreneur as an owner of a firm and as an individual, or a member of a family group. Here the entrepreneur, or family, faces a different set of choices in relation to profit reinvestment or disbursement than is the case for firms owned by external shareholders.

Technology and innovation

- To what extent have smaller businesses engaged with new technologies to support their internal financial management (e.g online tax payments, accounting software, invoicing, internet banking etc.) and the preparation of external finance applications?
- Have crowdfunding and P2P lending platforms changed the relative preferences of entre-

preneurs in terms of internal versus external financing?

The technology revolution in the banking sector began in the mid to late 1990s and has continued apace. This has changed the way core financial services are provided and delivered to SMEs. In particular, the increasingly widespread use of internet banking applications has enabled entrepreneurs to conduct many basic financial transactions on their mobile phones or portable computers. But this technology shift has also meant that entrepreneurs can also access other financial services using a variety of IT applications, such as accounting software, online submission tax returns, automated invoicing software linked to internal work management systems etc. In this sense entrepreneurs have a much greater level of knowledge and control over their internal finances than was the case a generation ago. Further, there are also more obvious time savings. It is clear that there are many gaps in our basic knowledge about the uptake and use of these new technologies and new ways of accessing and engaging with financial services as research data and evidence have struggled to keep pace with the rapid changes in IT in financial services. And this has also been apparent in terms of alternative sources and providers of capital with the huge growth in P2P lending and crowdfunding platforms. More research is needed to (a) establish how prevalent these new technologies are in the SME sector, and (b) what they mean for SMEs and the way we think about the financial life-cycle of the firm.

Note

1 Discussion within this chapter draws upon material within the PhD thesis by Catherine Matthews entitled 'Trade credit management within small professional firms: practice, agency and structure' (2013). The author of this chapter wishes to acknowledge this and thank her supervisors, Professor Aidan Berry and Professor Lew Perren, for their invaluable input to the development of the arguments.

REFERENCES

Abanis, T. (2013). Financial management practices in small and medium sized enterprises in selected districts in western Uganda. *Research Journal of Finance and Accounting*. Vol. 4, No. 2, pp. 29–43.

Abdulsaleh, A. M. and Worthington, A. C. (2013). Small and medium-sized enterprises financing: a review of the literature. *International Journal of Business and Management*. Vol. 13, No. 14, p. 36.

ACCA. 2006. Improving access to finance for small firms. Policy Briefing Paper. London: ACCA.

Amoako, G. K. (2013). Accounting practices of SMEs: a case study of Kumasi Metropolis in Ghana. *International Journal of Business and Management*. Vol. 8, No. 24, pp. 73–83.

Ang, J. (1991). Small business uniqueness and the theory of financial management. *The Journal of Small Business Finance*. Vol. 1, No. 1, pp. 1–13.

Arnold, G. (2013). *Corporate financial management*. (5th ed). Harlow: Pearson.

Bank of England. (2004). *Finance for small firms – an eleventh report*. London: Bank of England.

Berger, A. and Udell, G. (1998). The economics of small business finance: the roles of private equity and debt markets in the financial growth cycle. *Journal of Banking and Finance*. Vol. 22, No. 6–8, pp. 613–673.

Berry, A. (2006). Banks, SMEs and accountants: an international study of SMEs' banking relationships. London: The Association of Chartered Certified Accountants.

Berry, A., Faulkner, S., Hughes, M. and Jarvis, R. (1993). Financial information, the banker and small business. *British Accounting Review*. Vol. 25, No. 2, pp. 131–150.

Berry, A., Grant, P. and Jarvis, R. (2003). *Can European banks plug the finance gap for UK SMEs?* ACCA Research Report No. 81. London: Association of Chartered Certified Accountants.

Bester, H. (1985). Screening vs. rationing in credit markets with imperfect information. *The American Economic Review*. Vol. 75, No. 4, pp. 850–855.

Binks, M. and Ennew, C. (1996). Growing firms and the credit constraint. *Small Business Economics*. Vol. 8, No. 1, pp. 17–25.

Binks, M., Ennew, C. and Reed, G. (1992). Information asymmetries and the provision of finance to small firms. *International Small Business Journal*. Vol. 11, No. 1, pp. 35–46.

Blackburn, R. and Kovalainen, A. (2009). Researching small firms and entrepreneurship: past, present and future. *International Journal of Management Reviews*. Vol. 11, No. 2, pp. 127–148.

Buckley, A. (2011). *Financial crisis: causes, context and consequences*. Harlow: Financial Times Prentice Hall.

Burrell, G. and Morgan, G. (1979). *Sociological paradigms and organisational analysis*. Aldershot: Ashgate Publishing Ltd.

Chittenden, F. and Bragg, R. (1997). Trade credit cash-flow and SMEs in the UK, Germany and France. *International Small Business Journal*. Vol. 16, No. 1, pp. 22–35.

Chittenden, F., Hall, G. and Hutchinson, P. (1996). Small firm growth, access to capital markets and financial structure: review of issues and an empirical investigation. *Small Business Economics*. Vol. 8, No. 1, pp. 59–61.

Chittenden, F., Poutziouris, P. and Michaelas, N. (1998). *Financial management and working capital practices in UK SMEs*. Manchester: Manchester Business School.

Cosh, A. and Hughes, A. (1994). Size, financial structure and profitability: UK companies in the 1980s. In: A. Hughes & D. Storey (eds) *Finance and the small firm*, pp. 18–63. London: Routledge.

Cosh, A. and Hughes, A. (2003). The British SME sector 1991–2002. In: A. Cosh and A. Hughes (eds) *Enterprise challenged: Policy and performance in the British SME sector 1999–2002*. pp. 103–113. Cambridge: ESRC. Centre for Business Research. University of Cambridge.

Cowling, M. (2010). The role of loan guarantee schemes in alleviating credit rationing in the UK. *Journal of Financial Stability*. Vol. 6, No. 1, pp. 36–44.

Cowling, M. and Liu, W. (2011). *Business growth, access to finance, and performance outcomes in the recession*. Sheffield: Department for Business Innovation & Skills.

Cowling, M., Liu, W. and Ledger, A. (2012). Small business financing in the UK before and during the current financial crisis.

International Small Business Journal. Vol. 30, No. 7, pp. 778–800.

Cressy, R. and Olofsson, C. (1997). European SME financing: an overview. *Small Business Economics*. Vol. 9, No. 2, pp. 87–96.

Curran, J. (1990). Rethinking economic structure: exploring the role of the small firm and self employment in the British economy. *Work, Employment and Society*. Special Issue, Vol. 4, pp. 125–146.

Curran, J. and Blackburn, R. (2001). *Researching the small enterprise*. London: Sage.

Curran, J., Jarvis, R., Kitching, J. and Lightfoot, G. (1997). The pricing decision in small firms: complexities and the deprioritising of economic determinants. *International Small Business Journal*. Vol. 15, No. 2, pp. 17–37.

Deakins, D., Morrison, A. and Galloway, L. (2002). Evolution, financial management and learning in the small firm. *Journal of Small Business and Enterprise Development*. Vol. 9, No. 1, pp. 7–16.

Ekanem, I. (2005). 'Bootstrapping': The investment decision-making process in small firms. *The British Accounting Review*. Vol. 37, No. 3, pp. 299–318.

Federation of Small Businesses (2012a). *The FSB 'voice of small business' membership survey*. London: FSB.

Federation of Small Businesses (2012b). *ALT+ finance: small firms and access to finance*. London: FSB.

Fraser, S. (2004). Finance for small and medium-sized enterprises: a report on the 2004 UK survey of SME finances. Warwick: Warwick Business School.

Fraser, S. (2009). Small firms in the credit crisis: evidence from the UK survey of SME finances. Warwick: Warwick Business School.

Garcia-Teruel, P. J. and Martinez-Solano, P. (2010). Determinants of trade credit: a comparative study of European SMEs. *International Small Business Journal*. Vol. 28, No. 3, pp. 215–233.

Grant, P. and Perren, L. (2002). Small business and entrepreneurial research: meta-theories, paradigms and prejudices. *International Small Business Journal*. Vol. 20, No. 2, pp. 185–211.

Hamilton, R. and Fox, M. A. (1998). The financing preferences of small firm owners. *International Journal of Entrepreneurial Behaviour & Research*. Vol. 4, No. 3, pp. 239–248.

Hancock, D. and Wilcox, J. A. (1998). The 'credit crunch' and the availability of credit to small business. *Journal of Banking and Finance*. Vol. 22, No. 6–8, pp. 983–1014.

Harding, R. (2003). Global Entrepreneurship Monitor United Kingdom. 2002. London Business School.

Harris, S. (1995). Managing organizations to address the finance gap: a study of organizations that are doing so. *International Journal of Entrepreneurial Behaviour & Research*. Vol. 1, No. 1, pp. 63–82.

HM Government. (1931). *Report of the committee on finance and industry*. Macmillan Report cmnd 3897. London: HMSO.

HM Government. (1971). *Report of the committee of inquiry on small firms*. Bolton Report cmnd 4811. London: HMSO.

HM Government. (1979). *Interim report on the financing of small firms*. Wilson Report cmnd 7503. London: HMSO.

HM Government. (2004a). Graham review of the small firms loan guarantee scheme. Interim report. London: HMSO.

HM Government. (2004b). Graham review of the small firms loan guarantee scheme. Recommendations. London: HMSO.

HM Treasury and Small Business Service (SBS). (2003). Bridging the finance gap: a consultation on improving access to growth capital for small businesses. London: HMSO.

Howorth, C. and Reber, B. (2003). Habitual late payment of trade credit: an empirical examination of UK small firms. *Managerial and Decision Economics*. Vol. 24, No. 6–7, pp. 471–482.

Howorth, C. and Westhead, P. (2003). The focus of working capital management in UK small firms. *Management Accounting Research*. Vol. 14, No. 2, pp. 94–111.

Howorth, C. and Wilson, N. (1999). Late payment and the small firm: an examination of case studies. *Journal of Small Business and Enterprise Development*. Vol. 5, No. 4, pp. 307–315.

Hutchinson, P. (1999). Small enterprise: finance, ownership and control. *International Journal of Management Reviews*. Vol. 1, No. 3, pp. 343–365.

Jarvis, R., Curran, J., Kitching, J. and Lightfoot, G. (2000). The use of quantitative and qualitative criteria in the measurement of performance in small firms. *Journal of Small Business and Enterprise Development*. Vol. 7, No. 2, pp. 123–134.

Jarvis, R., Kitching, J., Curran, J. and Lightfoot, G. (1996). *The financial management of small firms: an alternative perspective.* (Research Report 49). London: Certified Accountants Educational Trust.

Jindrichovska, I. (2013). Financial management in SMEs. *European Research Studies*. Volume XV1, Special Issue on SMEs, pp. 79–96.

Keasey, K. and Watson, R. (1994). The bank financing of small firms in UK: issues and evidence. *Small Business Economics*. Vol. 6, No. 5, pp. 349–362.

Kotey, B. (1999). Debt financing and factors internal to the business. *International Small Business Journal*. Vol. 17, No. 3, pp. 11–29.

Lee, N., Sameen, H. and Martin, L. (2013). Credit and the crisis: access to finance for innovative small firms since the recession. Lancaster: The Big Innovation Centre.

Mazzarol, T. (2014). Research review: a review of the latest research in the field of small business and entrepreneurship. *Small Enterprise Research*. Vol. 21, No. 1, pp. 2–13.

Michaelas, N., Chittenden, F. and Poutziouris, P. (1998). A model of capital structure decision making in small firms. *Journal of Small Business and Enterprise Development*. Vol. 5, No. 3, pp. 246–260.

Mungal, A. and Garbharran, H. L. (2014). The perceptions of small businesses in the implementation of cash management techniques. *Journal of Economics and Behavioural Studies*. Vol. 6, No. 1, pp. 75–83.

Myers, S. C. (1984). The capital structure puzzle. *Journal of Finance*. Vol. 39, No. 3, pp. 574–592.

Nayak, A. and Greenfield, S. (1994). The use of management accounting information for managing micro businesses. In: A. Hughes & D. Storey (eds) *Finance and the small firm*, pp. 182–231. London: Routledge.

Orobia, L. A., Byabashaija, W., Munene, J. C., Sejjaaka, S. K. and Musinguzi, D. (2013). How do small business owners manage working capital in an emerging economy? A qualitative enquiry. *Qualitative Research in Accounting and Management*. Vol. 10, No. 2, pp. 127–143.

Paul, S., Whittam, G. and Wyper, J. (2007). The pecking order hypothesis: does it apply to start up firms? *Journal of Small Business and Enterprise Development*. Vol. 14, No. 1, pp. 8–21.

Peel, M. and Wilson, N. (1996). Working capital and financial management practices in the small firm sector. *International Small Business Journal*. Vol. 14, No. 2, pp. 52–68.

Peel, M., Wilson, N. and Howorth, C. (2000). Late payment and credit management in the small firm sector: some empirical evidence. *International Small Business Journal*. Vol. 18, No. 2, pp. 17–37.

Perren, L., Berry, A. and Partridge, M. (1998). The evolution of management information, control and decision-making processes in small growth-orientated service sector businesses: exploratory lessons from four cases of success. *Journal of Small Business and Enterprise Development*. Vol. 4, No. 4, pp. 351–361.

Perren, L. and Grant, P. (2000). The evolution of management accounting routines in small businesses: a social construction perspective. *Management Accounting Research*. Vol. 11, No. 4, pp. 391–411.

Petersen, M. and Rajan, R. (1997). Trade credit: theories and evidence. *The Review of Financial Studies*. Vol. 10, No. 3, pp. 661–691.

Rainnie, A. (1989). Industrial relations in small firms: small isn't beautiful. London: Routledge.

Robson Rhodes. (1984). A study of businesses financed under the small firms loan guarantee scheme. Department of Trade and Industry. London: HMSO.

Shutt, J. and Whittington, R. (1987). Fragmentation strategies and the rise of small units. *Regional Studies*. Vol. 21, No. 1, pp. 13–23.

Stiglitz, J. and Weiss, A. (1981). Credit rationing in markets with imperfect information. *The American Economic Review*. Vol. 71, No. 3, pp. 393–410.

Storey, D., Keasey, K., Watson, R. and Wynarczyk, P. (1987). *The performance of small firms*. London: Croom Helm.

Summers, B. and Wilson, N. (2003). Trade credit and customer relationships. *Managerial and Decision Economics*. Vol. 24, Nos. 6 & 7, pp. 439–455.

Tauringana, V. and Afrifa, G. A. (2013). The relative importance of working capital management and its components to SME's profitability. *Journal of Small Business and Enterprise Development*. Vol. 20, No. 3, pp. 453–469.

Tushabomwe-Kazooba, C. (2006). Cases of small business failure in Uganda: a case study from Bushenyi and Mbarara Towns. *African Studies Quarterly*. Vol. 8, No. 4, pp. 27–35.

Uwonda, G., Okello, N. and Okello, N. G. (2013). Cash flow management utilization by small medium sized enterprises (SMEs) in northern Uganda. *Merit Research Journal of Accounting, Auditing, Economics and Finance*. Vol. 1, No. 5, pp. 67–80.

Wilson, N. (2008). *An investigation into payment trends and behaviour in the UK: 1997–2007*. Leeds: Credit Management Research Centre.

Wilson, N. and Summers, B. (2002). Trade credit terms offered by small firms: survey evidence and empirical analysis. *Journal of Business Finance & Accounting*. Vol. 29, Nos. 3 & 4, pp. 317–351.

Wilson, R. (2004). *Business finance 2004*. London: Institute of Directors.

World Bank. (2014). World Bank Business Environment and Enterprise Performance Survey (BEEPS).

PART III

Entrepreneurial Milieu

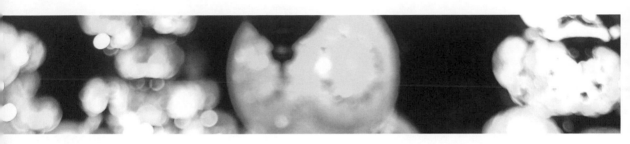

19

Can Governments Promote Gazelles? Evidence from Denmark

Anders Hoffmann and David J. Storey

INTRODUCTION

Governments in virtually all developed economies appear to believe that entrepreneurship – or elements of entrepreneurship – is socially sub-optimal in their country. As a consequence, entrepreneurship policy – defined as the efforts of government to raise the creation rate and performance of new and small businesses[1] – has expanded in scale and scope in the last two decades (Bennett, 2015).

This policy shift has been paralleled by an increase in scholarly interest in the subject. For example, Robson, Wijbenga and Parker (2009) and Bridge (2010) all provide helpful reviews, noting the shift in focus away from mere policy description to something closer to careful justification and appraisal. The justifications for policy interventions are now more carefully scrutinised by scholars (Lundström & Stevenson, 2005; Acs, Astebro, Audretsch & Robinson, 2016). Perhaps as a consequence, policy interventions have become more clearly articulated

by some governments in their own policy documents (DECA, 2009).

In this chapter we refer to these as 'front-end' policy issues, since they comprise the strategic decisions on whether to intervene and the form of that intervention. In contrast, at the other end of the policy spectrum – the 'back end' – there has also been a huge expansion in the number of studies evaluating the effectiveness of policy interventions. These studies now cover most continents (see Chrisman & McMullan, 2004; Chrisman, McMullan & Hall, 2005 for the US; Pons Rotger, Gortz & Storey, 2012 for Denmark; Cumming & Fischer, 2015 for Canada; Wren & Storey, 2002 for the UK; Morris & Stevens, 2010 for New Zealand; Kosters & Obschonka, 2010 for Germany; Lambrecht & Pirnay, 2005 for Belgium; Eurofound, 2016 for the EU; Acevedo & Tan, 2010 for Latin America and the Caribbean; OECD, 2007 for high-income countries). We refer to these as 'back-end' policy issues, since these evaluations can only take place once the policy has been in operation for some period of time.

If the 'front' and 'back' issues are well covered in scholarly literature, what appears to be almost uncharted territory[2] are the 'middle' issues of policy implementation, and how and why this evolves over time. This omission is unfortunate for three reasons. First, even when a decision has been made by governments to 'intervene', the policymaker faces a wide range of choices in deciding upon both the objectives of policy and how these objectives are to be achieved. The large diversity of policies (OECD, 2007), their often only short-lived existence (Greene, Mole & Storey, 2008) and their frequent recycling between countries[3] and even in the same country some years later,[4] imply that poorly framed policies, despite possibly having noble objectives, risk being ineffective. A theoretical framework and an evidence base for highlighting and guiding such policy choices have to be established. Second, even when objectives are agreed and formally stated, numerous more operational decisions have to be made, all of which can influence the overall effectiveness of the policy. The absence of theory, combined with a very limited evidence base, means the policymaker receives little help in making these decisions. Third, policymakers in countries newly embarking on such policies, or developing new policy areas, may fail to realise the wide spectrum of choices that are open to them about both the objectives and the delivery of policy.

This chapter explicitly addresses these 'middle' issues, although for it to be persuasive it also has to reliably document outcomes. Its starting point is the decision by the Danish government to shift entrepreneurship policy away from a focus on new firms and towards seeking to increase the number of 'gazelles' – fast-growing new and small firms (Nielsen, 2016), This policy was to be implemented through the establishment of 'Growth Houses', which provided free counselling for entrepreneurs and small firms with growth ambitions.

How that policy on 'Growth Houses' evolved is the case at the heart of this chapter. What it does not address is arriving at the decision to intervene – a front-end issue covered by Nielsen (2016). It also only provides a partial evaluation of the programme, although one which is considerably more sophisticated than the norm.[5]

Instead, given its focus on the middle policy issue, it has two audiences. The first is scholars of entrepreneurship policy – concerned with how governments may influence, positively or negatively, the quality and/or quantity of entrepreneurship in an economy. Developing the early ideas of Mole (2002a), the theoretical framework is a Principal–Agent Model. This framework is appropriate since the central government (Principal) does not deliver the policy itself but has to rely on Agents – in this case hybrid, public–private, organisations – to deliver the counselling to the potential gazelles. The generalisability of the framework is that national governments almost always devolve the delivery of any form of entrepreneurship policy to local agents (OECD, 1998). The Principal–Agent framework therefore has wide applicability.

Our second audience is policymakers in the field of entrepreneurship – ranging from those in countries seeking to develop entrepreneurship policy instruments for the first time to those with established policies, but which are continually seeking refinement. It emphasises that, even after the key political 'front-end' decisions have been made, the implementation of the policy provides continual challenges reflecting a combination of changed circumstances and learning on the part of both Principal and Agent. This interaction is captured through observing changes in the regulatory contract.

The Danish gazelles case is relevant to both audiences. The policy on developing gazelles clearly emerges from a long-established research result – that a small proportion of new firms contribute disproportionately to job creation (Birch, 1987; Storey, 1985, 1994). The case therefore describes taking a 'clear-cut result' and developing a policy from it. The novelty of the chapter is to provide both a theoretical context, and a description linked to that theory showing how and why this 'clear-cut result' evolved into operational policy – but only after a considerable number of iterations.

The chapter begins by articulating, in the second section, the key features of entrepreneurship policy and the specific role of business advice. It then argues that the provision of publicly-funded business advice to new and small firms is best theorised in a Principal–Agent framework in which the contract between the Principal (central government) and the Agent (the advice deliverer) is critical. The following section provides a brief description of regional government and its changes in Denmark, since we make the case that entrepreneurship and business advice are strongly intertwined and influenced by the regional and national context. Next is the section describing the operations and governance of Growth Houses, linking them closely with the theoretical issues of the second section. The fifth section describes how the policy context evolves and then shows how new information and changed circumstances lead to revisions of the contract. The sixth section presents the collected data and the following section links the performance of Growth House clients with the evolution of the contract over time. The main arguments and the implications for other providers of comparable policies are presented in the Conclusion.

ENTREPRENEURSHIP POLICY AND THE DELIVERY OF BUSINESS ADVICE

There appear to be five common features that characterise entrepreneurship policy.

The first is the decision to spend taxpayer funds. This is justified on the grounds that such expenditure has economic benefits, such as enhancing competitiveness or job creation (CEC, 2003). In other cases the benefits are stated to be primarily social – such as providing opportunities for disadvantaged groups such as the unskilled, the unemployed, in-migrants or those living in areas of deprivation.

A second key feature is the scale of this expenditure. Although it is extremely difficult to obtain comprehensive data on this matter, where such data are available the sums are considerable. For example in the US, the Small Business Innovation Research (SBIR) Program alone had an annual outlay in 2004 of in excess of 2 billion USD. In the UK estimates of small business 'support' have ranged up to 10 billion GBP annually. This means public expenditure is either slightly more than, or broadly similar to, that on the police service and exceeds that on universities (Storey & Greene, 2010). The most recent estimates are provided by Lundström, Vikström, Fink, Meuleman, Głodek, Storey and Kroksgård (2014). These cover Sweden in detail, but also provide coverage of other countries and regions. They conclude that, on a per capita basis, Sweden expenditure is broadly similar to that of the UK. The scale of this expenditure emphasises the importance of ensuring it generates value for money.

The third key feature of entrepreneurship policy is that funding is spent in very different ways in developed countries. The OECD (2007) distinguishes between six key spending areas: regulatory framework; R&D and technology; entrepreneurial capabilities; culture; access to finance; and market conditions. It is clear that the focus of expenditure is very different amongst developed countries, but why these priorities differ is rarely articulated.

The fourth feature is that, in some countries, policy changes often quite radically over time (Greene et al., 2008). Such changes may reflect changed political priorities, but they may also result from learning about how to deliver policies more effectively. This learning can be derived from experience, policy evaluations or from policy instruments that appear successful elsewhere. Despite these frequent organisational changes there also remain instances of how little the basic modus operandi of those delivering the policy changes over time with the same individuals remaining in post in newly-named organisations.

The final, and most relevant feature for this chapter is that in virtually all developed economies a key element of entrepreneurship policy is the provision of advice to nascent, new and small businesses. Pons Rotger et al. (2012) argue that using public funds to provide subsidised advice and guidance to individuals who are in the process of creating a new venture – guided preparation – is justified from two theoretical perspectives. The first is the dynamic capability perspective (Chrisman et al., 2005; Cumming & Fischer, 2015) which links knowledge with competitive advantage. According to Chrisman and McMullan (2004), once the need for new knowledge is recognised by the venture founder, the value of outside assistance comes primarily from the opportunity for enhancing knowledge generation. The experienced outsider directs and facilitates a contextual learning process that leads to the creation of a combination of tacit knowledge (which is primarily experience-based) and explicit knowledge (based on facts and theories).

The second perspective views publicly funded external advice primarily as a 'badge' (Bell, Taylor & Thorpe, 2002). It argues that, because new ventures have very uncertain outcomes, the founder has to send signals to resource providers such as banks, suppliers or even employees to emphasise their qualities. It is this 'badge' or certification – meaning it can be shown to others – which is its key value. 'Badging' is therefore analytically separate from knowledge: a venture founder, for example, may gain no additional knowledge by being required to develop a business plan from a public advice provider – yet without that badge provided by the plan commercial funding is less likely to be provided (Burke, Fraser & Greene, 2010). This

difficulty of separating the effect of badging, funding and knowledge on the performance of new and small firms recurs frequently in 'back-end' assessments of entrepreneurship policy measures.

Nevertheless the overriding theoretical perspective is the economic concept of market failure. Public funding is normally justified on grounds of information imperfections and positive externalities (Storey & Greene, 2010). Information imperfections reflect the limited knowledge that founders of new ventures have of their own skills prior to start-up. It also reflects the inability of resource suppliers to accurately judge those abilities. It is argued that public funding of these activities is justified because knowledge-benefits accrue not only to venture founders and resource suppliers but also to those external to the transaction who benefit from additional wealth creation. The reservations of the economist are whether, without the subsidy, information provision is socially sub-optimal (Parker, 2007) and whether guided preparation actually enhances the performance of new ventures.

Given this context, our case is that policy impact is also likely to be strongly influenced by how that intervention takes place. To address the 'how to' question it is crucial to recognise that policy delivery is normally not under the direct control of the government department responsible for the funding. So, although central government funds the provision of the advice, its employees do not normally directly provide the advice. This is for two reasons. The first is that business circumstances can differ markedly from one locality to another and so the advice provided has to be tailored to the local circumstances about which local or regional organisations are likely to be better informed. The second reason is that it is assumed that public servants are less likely to be credible suppliers of advice than individuals either with prior experience of, or currently working in, small private sector enterprises.

For both these reasons advice is frequently directly provided by private sector

Table 19.1   Principal Agent: the delivery of business advice

Central Government [Principal] wants:	Growth Houses [Agent] want:
1. To show funding is distributed in line with stated public policies. 2. To show expenditure was in line with the policy areas specified by the legislators. 3. To show policies contributed to achieving the overall government objective of enhancing enterprise. 4. To ensure the public provision of advice did not lead to private sector consultants being 'crowded out'. 5. To show the taxpayer got 'value for money' from the expenditure. This means it has to be related to firm performance. 6. To ensure an appropriate distribution of funding amongst the regions. 7. To have a funding distribution system that is flexible when circumstances change and which rewards good performance from Agents.	1. The opportunity to exercise discretion on how money is to be spent because of variations in local circumstances which are imperfectly understood by the Principal. 2. To have discretion over the selection of their client group of firms. 3. To demonstrate the impact of working with a small group of firms with growth potential. 4. To have the opportunity to enhance the performance of their clients, without having to 'hand them over' to private sector consultants prematurely. 5. To have a reward system that is based upon factors under their control – such as number of hours of support. 6. To avoid having an uncertain reward system which is heavily dependent on firm performance – over which they have less control.

consultants under contract from a quasi-public organisation, but ultimately funded by government. The task of government, acting on behalf of the taxpayer, is to ensure the advice is provided in a cost-effective manner. It is therefore a classic Principal–Agent relationship (Miller, 2008) in which the interest of the two parties may not be identical and, in many respects, may differ markedly.

The problem faced by the central government (Principal) is to ensure regional organisations delivering business support (Agent) do so in the way required by the Principal, given that the latter can only monitor the Agent to a limited degree. According to Principal–Agent theory, the Principal seeks to ensure the interests of the two are as closely aligned as possible, most notably in a contract that links the performance of the Agent, and hence payment, to objectives specified by the Principal. The terms and enforceability of the contract lie at the heart of Principal–Agent Theory.

Table 19.1 sets out the differing objectives of the Principal and the Agent, assuming that both parties are committed to delivering the best possible service for the taxpayer (Principal) and for the business client (Agent).

It assumes the Principal has to demonstrate the funding was spent in accordance with the intentions of the national legislators.

The Principal also wishes to demonstrate the taxpayer obtained value for such funding – presumably in the form of additional employment or wealth creation and wishes to ensure the Agent is incentivised to deliver this support in a cost-effective manner. Finally, the Principal is concerned to ensure that the provision of publicly-funded business advice does not lead to private-sector advice being 'crowded out'.

To demonstrate this has been achieved the Principal seeks to impose, in return for the funding, a contract that specifies performance measure(s) capable of being transparently monitored. However, from the Agent's perspective, such a contract can be onerous or even misguided. It can be onerous in the sense that to demonstrate compliance requires the collection of information and data on clients, with three potentially negative consequences. The first is that some clients may view the information on sales, profitability or even employment as private, and so be unwilling to divulge them to an outsider. The second is that it takes time to collect such information. This risks the Agent getting a reputation amongst its clients for being 'bureaucratic' and so alienating both them and other potential clients. Third, the collection and processing of information is costly and, where budgets are fixed, so removes funding from the direct provision of client services.

Table 19.2   Timetable of key events leading to the creation of Growth Houses

February 2005: A Liberal-Conservative government is re-elected in Denmark

March 2005: Denmark in the Global Economy report published

April 2005: The Globalisation Council is created, with the Prime Minister as Chair

Autumn 2005: The concept of Growth Houses as a mechanism for promoting Entrepreneurship is developed

April 2006: Danish Globalisation Strategy launched

June 2006: Official launch of five Growth Houses: one per region

January 2007: Growth Houses formally open their doors

January 2011: Responsibility for the Growth Houses is transferred from Central government to the municipalities

However the contract may be viewed as misguided by the Agent for reasons set out on the left-hand side of Table 19.1. The first is that a contract specifying detailed performance metrics for the Agent conflicts with viewing the latter as being in the best position to deliver local services in an appropriate manner. In short, local discretion is removed. The second is that, although the Principal sees enhancing client performance as the key performance measure, the Agent may not wish to be judged by a metric over which it has only a partial influence. Specifically, the Agent may provide its services effectively but the client performance may be weak for a variety of reasons outside the control of the Agent – most notably, as we shall see later, the state of the macro-economy. Third, the subjective view of Agents is that they can most easily demonstrate impact by working intensively over an extended period of time with a small group of clients. Unfortunately, it is then these successful clients that are passed on to the private sector clients – risking the contribution of the Agent being underestimated by the Principal

The public funding of business support delivered by regional agencies can therefore be seen within a Principal–Agent theoretical context. We now turn to the specific case of promoting gazelles in Denmark through publicly-sponsored Growth Houses. Danish Growth Houses are of wide interest for two main reasons. First, the Growth Houses are governed by yearly contracts, which changed over time reflecting the Principal–Agent problems discussed above. Second, data on both Growth House users and non-users is available in Denmark, so it is possible to gain powerful insights into both the management and the effectiveness of the programme.

DEVELOPING THE GROWTH HOUSES POLICY IN DENMARK

This section provides an historic timeline of how the Danish Growth Houses policy evolved as crucial background for interpreting the case. It provides only a brief description of how the political decision was made, because the core of this chapter focuses on the implementation, rather than the taking of, the policy decision.

The time-line of the decision-making is set out in Table 19.2. It shows the Danish focus on entrepreneurship policy effectively began in February 2005 when a Liberal-conservative government was re-elected to power and, two months later, it launched its policy statement: *New Goals – Denmark in the Global Economy*. It stated: 'We must prepare the Danish society, the individual Dane and the individual enterprise to become better at responding to the challenges posed by an increasingly open international economy.'

The strategy set four goals – one of which was: 'Denmark as a leading entrepreneurial society: Our goal is for Denmark, by 2015, to be one of the societies in the world where most growth enterprises are launched.'

In April 2005, the government appointed a Globalisation Council to implement the policy statement. Amongst the aims of the Council, one was to make Denmark 'a leading entrepreneurial society'. The evidence available at the time reported: 'The Danish start-up rate was 10% which is on a level with the United States and is among the best in Europe' (Danish Entrepreneurship Index, 2004).

Crucially however, when a measure of new firm growth was used, the results were less impressive. Only 3.3% of new firms in Denmark in 2000–2002 had a growth rate of 60% or more. This was not only well below that for Korea or the US, but it was also less than half that of EU countries such as the UK, Spain and Holland.

The Globalisation Council discussions therefore focused on how to increase the number of new high-growth entrepreneurs/ firms, rather than more firms in total. This marked a sharp change of policy focus.

Prior to the implementation of a Growth Policy, all 13 Danish regions (*Amter*) had an *Erhvervsservicecenter* (ESC) offering up to four hours of free advice to entrepreneurs and SMEs, but this system did not have growth as a key success parameter. Two thirds of funding came from regional, and the remainder from central, government. The sense was that its effectiveness probably varied across Danish regions, but no data on the survival or growth of ESC clients was available to adequately document this subjective view.

The new policy emphasis on gazelles was taking place at the same time as a re-organisation of regional government. The number of regions was reduced from 13 to five. It was also decided that responsibility for business development would move from the regions to the municipalities. All ESC centres were therefore closed, but the budget for the business support system was not immediately transferred to the municipalities. This enhanced the bargaining position of central government and enabled more 'radical' organisational forms to be explored.

By early 2006, it had become clear that there was political support for having a Growth House in each of the five new regions. The proposal for the creation of Growth Houses, together with many other new initiatives, was presented in the Globalisation Strategy in April 2006. This proposal was then converted into an official agreement between the government and the municipalities that set out the main principles (June 2006). The budget for the Growth Houses was to be managed by the central government until the end of 2010 and was to be identical to that spent on the old system.

The official agreement did not specify how the Growth Houses would be financed after 2011, but there seems to have been an understanding that the annual budget of 90 million DKK would be transferred to the municipalities. The Globalisation Strategy also allocated an additional 162 million DKK for the period 2007–2009 for developing supporting initiatives in the Growth Houses.

The Growth Houses were finally established in 2007 – with there being at least one set of premises in each of the five regions. However, what made Growth Houses internationally distinctive was their governance structure, linked closely to Principal–Agent theory discussed in the second section above. It is to this that we now turn.

THE OPERATIONS AND GOVERNANCE OF GROWTH HOUSES

Several factors influenced the discussions between the Danish Enterprise and Construction Authority (DECA) and the municipalities about the governance of Growth Houses. The first was a desire to ensure that the focus of Growth Houses was on new and small firms with growth potential, as opposed to providing advice to all new/small firms. The second was a recognition that local circumstances varied and so it was helpful for there to be some involvement of municipalities in choosing how to implement the initiative. Furthermore, municipalities were responsible for providing the basic advice to all new enterprises. The third was a sense of unease that this form of specialised business advice was best provided by public agencies. The fourth was a concern by the central government to ensure demonstrable value for money in terms of clear enhancement of job creation amongst the clients of Growth Houses.

To obtain operational guidance the Danish government looked closely at the English Business Links which had encountered many of the same issues (Mole, 2002a, 2002b). These were 'one stop shop' organisations supplying advice to new and small enterprises. Each was operated by independent private or quasi-private businesses based on long-term contracts where funding for business advice provision came from central government.[6] This made it similar to the proposed Danish system, giving the government the key advantage that the contract could be terminated if the provider did not meet given standards.

Despite its overall attractions, there were two aspects of the Business Link system which the Danish government wished to avoid. The first was changing providers, because this was felt to exclude long-term learning and so was only to be used as a last resort. Second, Business Links were competitive, rather than collaborative organisations, which again the Danish government thought was undesirable.

Growth Houses, therefore, tried to combine the desirable elements of Business Links – their independence and their ability to deliver advice in a cost-effective manner – whilst avoiding the less desirable elements – most notably their lack of contact with the municipalities and their competitive structures. These principles were embodied in the contract between DECA and the Growth Houses. The latter began life on 1 January 2007 as five independent private foundations of the state, in cooperation with their relevant municipality. They were fully financed by the government and their board comprised politicians from the municipalities, representatives from local businesses and an employee from DECA.

THE EVOLVING CONTRACT WITH THE GROWTH HOUSES

This section sets out the key elements of the contract between the Principal (DECA) and the Agent (the Growth Houses) and how, in line with the expectations of a Principal–Agent Model, these evolved over time. The contract specified clear performance goals. Table 19.3 shows these goals for 2007 but also, most importantly for this chapter, how they evolved over the period until 2010 based upon experience.

After 2010 only two significant changes were made – the user satisfaction was changed so it was based on a net-promoter score[7] and the total number of users was changed in 2013. This followed an internal evaluation showing that the Growth Houses could increase their impact by devoting more time to each firm. DECA accepted this by reducing the total number of clients from 2,500 to 2,000 but then introduced a new activity, in which the Growth Houses were expected to engage with 2,000 additional firms through events and other short-term activities. However, because these engagements were short-term, it meant the Growth Houses had more time for their prime clients.

Core to the early contract was a bonus linked to performance, constituting up to 10% of total funding. The contract specified, for each performance goal, both the measure of success and a weighting for the goal, with the aggregate weights summing to unity. At the end of each year, payments to the Growth House were based on an aggregate score comprising the weighted performance goals in the contract, with the bonus paid depending on this score.

From 2008 onwards, a key Growth House performance metric was the performance of its clients, compared with that of otherwise similar firms that had not received business advice. These firms were referred to as the 'control group' firms.

Finally, in line with Principal–Agent Theory, the contract was changed annually as the Principal assessed impact and tried

Table 19.3 Goals for the regional Growth Houses, 2007–10

	2007	2008	2009	2010
Recruiting Director	1 April	—	—	—
Cooperation agreements with local business units	Min. 90%	—	—	—
Cooperation agreements with other public actors	Minimum 15 agreements	—	—	—
Conclusion of cooperation agreements with private operators	Minimum 10 agreements	—	—	—
Deadline for development of the website	1 December	—	—	—
Mentor networks	The goal is to establish mentor networks with more than 50 associated mentors.	—	—	—
Competence development for advisors	Completed first stage of competence development programme	There are, across the Growth Houses, established specialised networks in at least four areas of focus. These networks shall have completed competency development over two days.	—	—
Number of users of the Growth Houses	5,075	2,500	2,000	2,500
Share referred to private consultants, public operators etc.	Min. 75%	Min. 75%	Min. 75%	Min. 75%
Share referred to private consultants	—	—	—	70%
Users satisfaction with the Growth Houses (satisfied or very satisfied with the services)	Min. 80%	Min. 80%	Min. 80%	Min. 80%

(Continued)

Table 19.3 (Continued)

User satisfaction with the counsellors (satisfied or very satisfied)	—	—	Min. 70%	Min. 80%
Cooperative partner satisfaction with the Growth Houses (satisfied or very satisfied)	—	Min. 80%	Min. 80%	Min. 80%
Cooperation with private consultants	—	The Growth Houses shall create competency profiles on at least 50 private consultants, who are highly qualified and have specialised skills to consult new and small growth enterprises in the region.	—	—
Employment growth in the counselled enterprises	—	Min. +10 percentage points (compared to non-counselled enterprises)	Same growth rate as in the year of counselling	Min. +10 percentage points (compared to the year of counselling)
Turnover growth in the counselled enterprises	—	Min. +20 percentage points (compared to non-counselled enterprises)	Min. +20 percentage points (compared to non-counselled enterprises)	Min. +15 percentage points (compared to the year of counselling)
Export growth in the counselled enterprises	—	Min. +20 percentage points (compared to non-counselled enterprises)	Min. +20 percentage points (compared to the year of counselling)	Min. +10 percentage points (compared to the year of counselling)
Share of high-growth enterprises in the region	—	Min. +2 percentage points (compared to last year)	Min. +1 percentage points (compared to last year)	Min. +2 percentage points (compared to last year)
Development of new activities/services	Arrange or co-arrange minimum 40 activities	—	The Growth Houses jointly develop and implement at least 3 new programmes/initiatives for entrepreneurs and businesses with growth ambitions.	The Growth Houses must jointly conduct 5 new projects to develop the quality of their services
Events etc.	—	The Growth Houses fulfils its role as regional coordinator of a nationwide growth campaign from 17 to 23 November 2008.	The Growth Houses have at least the equivalent of 20% of their clients participating in regional events.	—
Press coverage and the knowledge rate to the regional Growth Houses	—	—	—	+ 10%

new approaches to influence the performance of the Agent. This learning is reflected in changes in the terms of the contract.

In 2007 the key task was to get the Growth Houses up and running – so the emphasis in the contract was on establishing the agreements and networks necessary for delivering the services. These are often referred to as Input-Based targets such as the hours of counselling provided. However, by 2008, Table 19.3 shows there was a much greater emphasis on performance – or Output-Based – targets such as growth in employment, turnover and exports amongst the Growth Houses' clients. These targets were heavily weighted by the Principal, constituting 30% of the aggregate score.[8]

In order to demonstrate impact, Table 19.3 shows the contract specified that Growth House clients were expected to grow 10% faster in terms of employment and 20% faster in terms of sales and exports than firms that had not received assistance – the control group firms.

These contractual changes were met with considerable concern by the Agents – the municipalities and the Growth Houses. As emphasised in the theories in the section headed 'Entrepreneurship Policy' above, there were strong reservations expressed about their funding being based on the performance of clients over which they had only a partial influence, particularly because 10% of their income depended on this performance indicator.

By the end of 2008, two further problems emerged in assessing whether the contract goals had been met. First, the contract specified the customers' performance was to be evaluated in the same year as they received the advice. This meant there might have been insufficient time for the impact of the advice to be reflected in additional sales or employment. Second, the control group initially comprised only those firms with positive growth in either metric, and within this group there were often a small number which had experienced hyper-growth. This raised the

arithmetic mean for the control group well above the median.

Table 19.3 shows how these issues were addressed in the 2009 contract. The control group was expanded to include all firms (including those with negative growth) and the targets were related to growth in the calendar year 2009 of clients receiving advice in 2008. In addition, the employment goal was 'simplified' to exclude any comparison with a control group, so Growth House clients only had to generate the same number of jobs as in the previous year.

Unfortunately, this 'simplification' had the opposite of its intended effect because measuring performance in 2009 was based on the 2008 contracts being signed prior to the onset of the severe global financial crisis of that year. It meant Growth House clients were, in fact, net job-shedders.

To address this, Table 19.3 shows the 2010 contract then reintroduced the concept of the control groups but in a different way. The performance of Growth Houses in 2010 was evaluated based on the performance in 2009 of their clients. The control group were firms that did not differ from the Growth House clients in terms of region, sector and size.

Finally, Table 19.3 shows that, reflecting their diverse objectives, there are areas of performance, other than those of their clients, on which Growth Houses are judged. Some have changed over time as reflected in their inclusion in, or removal from, the contract, whereas others are present throughout the period – such as the share of customers referred to private consultants, public operators, etc.

The final contract performance measure is client satisfaction. As with almost all programmes of business advice throughout the developed world, reported satisfaction is rarely less than 75% (OECD, 2007).[9] However, although it is strongly favoured by the suppliers of advice as an appropriate performance metric, it fails to capture whether the advice influences client performance and for that reason is not given a high weighting in this contract.

DATA SOURCES

We now describe the data used by DECA to assess the extent to which Growth Houses met the conditions of their contracts.

First, DECA developed a customer relations management system (CRM) that enabled the clients of the Growth Houses to be tracked. The CRM served the dual purpose of enabling the Growth Houses to manage their customers and business partners and for DECA to access data for the contract monitoring and impact assessment. The CRM system is based on the Danish CVR number, which is a unique identification number for Danish firms used for a wide variety of transactions with the public sector and with financial institutions. The legitimacy of the enterprise can be assessed via a mathematical algorithm of the CVR number. The CRM also has a direct link to a private business databank, so the address, the sector and other basic data on the enterprise do not have to be collected by the Growth Houses.

The CVR number of the client is sent, quarterly, to Statistics Denmark to update information on age, legal status, activity and size. It is also used for the annual calculation of the contract conditions. Until the end of 2009 all Danish firms with employees were required to pay into a pension scheme and this data was used to check employment data, but this is no longer in place. Sales and export data are derived from the Value Added Tax (VAT) system. Both sets of data are normally released 60 days after the quarter to which they referred.

Both registers are highly reliable because they include all firms having either turnover or employees or both and any errors negatively impact either the employees' pension or the VAT revenue for the state. Export data is also derived from the VAT sources – although of course not all firms have export sales. All these sources are then linked to the CVR number of the Growth House clients each quarter.

We noted in the previous section that three contract performance goals were formulated for comparison with a control group. For example, Table 19.3 shows that one goal in 2010 was 'Growth in employment in firms that were Growth House clients in 2009, is at least 10 percentage points higher than in other firms in the region'.

The control group (other firms) is drawn so as to control for region, size and industry. It includes all 'active' firms with less than 250 employees and sales below a threshold which varies by sector. Data on client satisfaction was collected differently. Here the client mail address was sent automatically to an independent private firm commissioned to seek client views on the Growth Houses and on any private consultants to which they were referred.

GROWTH HOUSE CLIENT PERFORMANCE

This section shows how the data sources described in the previous section were used by the Principal to assess the performance of the Agent as specified in the 'Evolving Contract' section. The evolution reflects changes in both macro-economic circumstances and the experience of the two parties.

Table 19.4 shows the results of the initial approach to estimating impact, showing employment change amongst Growth House clients 2008–2009. The shaded boxes in the table shows the number of employees in Growth House clients at the time they receive their advice. So, in Quarters 1–2 2008, aggregate employment in Growth House clients was 4,240 employees. However, when employment in that cohort of firms is tracked over time, it falls in each subsequent period, ending with 3,533 by the third quarter of 2009.

The shaded box in the row for Q3–Q4 2008 shows employment in enterprises that become clients in Q3–Q4 2008. Employment rises from 15,047 in the previous quarter to 15,140 when they become clients – which might be interpreted as evidence of the Growth Houses selecting the appropriate clients. However, in

Table 19.4   Number of employees in firms using the Growth Houses

		Observation period			
		Q1–Q2 2008	Q3–Q4 2008	Q1–Q2 2009	Q3–Q4 2009
Counselling period	Q1–Q2 2008	4,240	4,261	3,744	3,533
	Q3–Q4 2008	15,047	15,140	13,419	12,521
	Q1–Q2 2009	9,408	9,778	8,960	8,443
	Q3–Q4 2009	8,164	8,498	8,056	7,978

Source: Statistics Denmark

Table 19.5   Sales change for Growth House clients and control group firms

	Change 2008		Change 2009	
	Clients	Control group	Clients	Control group
Clients in 2008	9.1	7.1	−12.8	−15.2
Clients in 2009	9.2	8.9	−8.6	−14.5

Note: The control group reflects location, sector and size of clients in Q3 in the year. The control period is therefore constant going from left to right in the table. The growth rate for 2008 is calculated as sales in 2008 divided by sales in 2007.

both the later time periods after receiving the advice, their employment falls.

Similar findings emerge from the third and fourth rows, with employment rising between Q1–2 and Q3–4 2008 but then declining in both later time periods – with this pattern characterising firms both when they become Growth House clients and prior to becoming clients. It is, therefore, difficult from this basic data to directly identify a Growth House employment effect. In fact the most obvious interpretation is that becoming a Growth House client is associated with employment reductions – making it an area of real concern for the Principal.

As a result of discussions between the Principal and the Agents it was agreed that the former should commission further statistical analysis. As noted in the 'Evolving Contract' section, the novelty was the introduction of 'control groups' of firms that were observably comparable to Growth House clients but which were not clients.[10] Unfortunately, the employment data series on which Table 19.4 is based was discontinued in Q3 2009 so the analysis for this period which uses control groups is limited to sales data.

Table 19.5 provides a comparison of sales change for Growth House clients and control group firms in both 2008 and 2009. In 2008 Growth House clients sales rose by an average of 9.1%, compared with those of the control group that rose by 7.1%. Reflecting the macroeconomic situation, and paralleling the results in Table 19.4, in 2009 both groups experience falling sales, but the drop is greater (14.5%) for the control group than for the clients (8.6%). In this sense Growth House clients out-perform the controls in the year in which they receive the advice.

Table 19.5 also shows that the Growth House clients receiving their advice in 2008 experienced smaller sales falls in 2009 (12.8%) than the control firms (15.2%) – perhaps indicating that the advice had a lasting impact. Some of this better performance, of course, could reflect selection, with Growth Houses attracting and selecting firms likely to perform well, and there is some evidence of this in the table. It shows that, in the year before they became clients, those receiving advice in 2009 had sales rises of 9.1% – higher than the controls which had a rise of only 7.1%. This implies that, at least for the year for which data are available, the Growth Houses were attracting and selecting better-performing firms. So, whilst it was reassuring that the Agents were selecting 'better' firms, the better performance

Table 19.6   Comparing Growth House clients and control group firms, 2008–9 to 2013–14

Performance year	Metric	Annual % change in employment in Growth House clients	Annual % change in employment in control group	Difference	No. of Growth House clients	No. in control group
2008–9	Sales and employment					
2010–11	Employment	+4.5	+1.2	+3.3	1,341	103,077
2011–12	Employment	+ 6.3	+1.9	+4.4	1,611	152,269
2012–13	Employment	+4.7	0.1	+4.8	1,767	168,540
2012–14	Employment	+10.3	+2.6	+7.7	1,628	151,981
2013–14	Employment	+6.8	+2.1	+4.7	1,405	166,785

of Growth House clients does not necessarily reflect the impact of the assistance received. The challenge to the Principal was then to enhance the quality of the statistical work to obtain reassurance that the Agents were genuinely 'adding value' to their clients.

The other elements of the contract were much less problematic. Reported client satisfaction rates rose over time from about 77% in 2007 to close to 90% in 2011. There was also very little variation in these rates between the five Growth Houses. This meant that these input-based elements of the contract raised the proportion of total bonus paid to close to 70% – whereas this would have been up to 10% lower if based exclusively on output-based metrics. So, whatever reservations there may have been over the validity of the statistical tests, the Agents could justifiably claim their bonus which was duly paid in February 2011.

We now turn to the period from 2010 onwards. During this time Statistics Denmark has been able to provide employment data for both Growth House clients and for a control group of firms matched by region, sector, size (in terms of full-time employees), age and prior growth.

Table 19.6 shows that, in all five years in which the analysis has been undertaken, the Growth House firms have grown faster in terms of employment than the control sample. In most years this difference in growth rate exceeds 4% and suggests that the service provided by the Growth House

has been performance-enhancing. It suggests that, although the implementation of the programme was time-consuming and at times even adversarial, its long-run impact was positive. However, these differences in employment growth rates were less than half of the 10% specified in the 2010 contract.

An evaluation of the Growth Houses in 2013 (only available in Danish[11]) tried to control for selection bias by introducing questions to the clients on their perceived impact of their use of Growth House services. It aggregated the total amount of employment generated and then removed that in those firms who said the Growth House had no impact on its performance. It found this excluded 50% of the growth – implying that some part of the remaining 50% could be attributable to the Growth House.

CONCLUSION

The introduction to this chapter made the case that scholars of entrepreneurship and SME policy have had three main foci – policy description, examining the case for intervention and impact assessment. It was argued that less attention has been devoted to 'middle' issues such as how public policies are implemented, how they evolve over time and their long-run impact. We also made the case that those developing public policy would benefit from seeing how policy evolves over time in an exemplar advanced economy. The interests of both scholars and policymakers are addressed in this case of the Danish 'Growth Houses'.

The chapter documents the iterations in the evolution of the 'Growth Houses' policy between 2007 and 2010 and then traces impact up until 2014. The key theoretical novelty of the chapter is modelling policy implementation using a Principal–Agent framework. Specifically, we highlight the role of an evolving contract between the central government (Principal) providing the funding and the Growth Houses (Agent) providing advice to their clients. The Principal sees the contract as incentivising the Agent to provide advice that 'makes a difference' to the target group of firms – gazelles or firms capable of becoming gazelles. The case illustrates that the evolution of the policy was lengthy but that, almost a decade after it was first mooted, there is evidence that Growth House clients benefit from the advice and assistance they receive.

Ideally, we would like to place the Growth House findings alongside those of other entrepreneurship support policies and compare their effectiveness, but this is not possible. This is because of the varying level of sophistication employed in these evaluations, so making comparisons invalid (OECD, 2007). So, acknowledging these problems, we now conclude by highlighting issues where the lessons are fairly clear but then turn to those requiring further work.

The first clear lesson from this case is confirmation that entrepreneurship policy provision is a classic local and regional issue. The vast bulk of new enterprises are started by individuals in their own locality – because they were born there, worked there, or currently live there. Policy is therefore a local political issue with the expectation that advisory and other support services are delivered by locally or regionally accountable organisations. Since entrepreneurship is heavily embedded in, and reflective of, local conditions it is appropriate for local and regional organisations to be at the heart of shaping the

entrepreneurial environment. So, if this environment was to change, as the central government in Denmark decided in 2005 that it must, then this also required a change at the regional and local level.

A second important lesson is that, when formulating policy, Denmark drew heavily upon those countries with a long experience of providing business advice. It made the decision that it did not wish these services to be provided by a publicly-owned organisation and then carefully examined the case of Business Link. The model it chose was similar to, but with a larger municipal governance role than its English comparator.

A third lesson is that policy evolution is strongly linked to the availability of reliable data on the economic performance of the customers of the Growth Houses. Denmark, together with other Nordic countries, has reliable and current data on key firm metrics, such as sales and employment. It has also invested heavily in ensuring the presence of a single serial number that ensures the linkage of records. This investment means that Danish policymakers can monitor the impact of policy changes quickly. This has clearly enabled Denmark to modify policy in the light of changed events.

Although there are clear lessons, there are also key challenges that remain. The Denmark case shows that although business advice is delivered regionally, and with regional accountability, the bulk of the funding is provided centrally, making it a classic Principal–Agent issue. The Principal seeks to ensure, although the services provided by the Agent are regionally 'customised', that they also satisfy a high minimum standard and have impact – defined as improving the performance of the clients of the Agent. To ensure this takes place a contract has to be brokered between the Principal and the Agent and has to evolve to take account of both changed external circumstances and learning on the part of both parties.

On the central question of whether the evolving contract has incentivised the Agents to focus their advice on firms with growth potential, and whether the performance of their clients was enhanced as a result, the results are broadly positive. Recalling that Growth Houses were a new initiative and one being developed during a global recession, it is unsurprising that, until 2010–11 it was difficult to identify an employment impact of the policy. However, since that time the employment growth rate of Growth House firms has exceeded that of the control group over each of four years – although by considerably less than the 10% initially specified in the 2010 contract.

Our conclusion is that the formulation of incentives to business advice providers in the form of a performance-related contract appears to be a promising approach but perhaps the central lesson for both scholars and policymakers is the scale, duration and nature of the iterations needed for successful policy implementation. In this case, moving from developing the concept in 2005 to assessment in 2011 has had to overcome problems of scepticism, world recession, discontinuance of data-sets and ultimately recognition of the importance of undertaking advanced statistical work.

Even so, formulating a contract that provides appropriate incentives for publicly-funded advice providers to enhance client performance is a valued prize, but one requiring continuous review. The challenge for scholars is to provide more such reviews of SME and entrepreneurship policy implementation. The case made here is that the Principal–Agent framework is applicable to SME and entrepreneurship policies beyond the provision of business advice. The obvious examples are the provision of access to finance in the form of loan guarantees or equity programmes where the Agent is normally a formal financial institution but the Principal is perhaps the Department of Finance in the government. A second example might be policies to provide employee training in new and small firms – where the Agent providing the training is a private

supplier. A third example of an Agent might be charities that are funded to encourage the disadvantaged to begin their own enterprises. A fourth example is SME innovation policies where science parks or research institutes act as Agents to government. In all these cases, charting how this Principal–Agent relationship has evolved in delivering policy would considerably enhance the richness of our understanding of SME and entrepreneurship policy impact.

Notes

1   Lundström and Stevenson (2005) distinguish between entrepreneurship and SME policy. The former they restrict to policies that influence the creation process, whereas the latter policies seek to enhance the performance of existing or established firms. This distinction can be helpful but in this chapter we will assume that entrepreneurship policy also includes SME policy.

2   Important exceptions are political scientists such as Dannreuther (2007) or McHugh and May (2002) and, more recently, Arshad et al. (2014).

3   For example, policies to provide financial incentives to the unemployed to start a business began in the UK in 1981 with the Enterprise Allowance Scheme (Storey, 1994). This was followed by Germany in the later 1980s with the *Überbrückungsgeld* [Bridging Allowance] and then by the Start-Up Subsidy in 2003 (Baumgartner & Caliendo, 2008). This was also used in Denmark between 1987 and 1997. Here, unemployed individuals who started their own business could get up to half of their unemployment benefits for 3½ years.

4   The clearest example is the UK Business Expansion Scheme (BES) which enabled (wealthy) individuals to obtain tax relief upon investments in new businesses. BES was closed in 1993 because it had become a vehicle for flagrant tax avoidance and yet was effectively reinstated as the Enterprise Investment Scheme within eighteen months (Storey, 1994). A later review of EIS by Cowling, Bates, Jagger and Murray (2008) concluded that its 'effects remain very small at present'. A second UK example is the Enterprise Allowance which, despite being abolished in 1993, was resurrected in 2011.

5   Despite not being the most sophisticated it is considerably more extensive than that available for many enterprise programmes in many countries. The GAO in the US and the NAO in the UK are scathing about the reluctance to evaluate enterprise programmes and, even when they are

evaluated, the reluctance to use the appropriate techniques leading to a strong likelihood that impact is over-estimated (GAO, 2012; NAO, 2013).

6   In practice the income to Business Links (BLs) came not only from central government for the provision of business advice, but also from other public and private sources such as the delivery of EU programmes. The dependency of the BLs on central government funding for provision of business advice therefore varied markedly from one BL to another and this meant that often very different 'types' of BL existed (Mole et al., 2011). This also applies to the Growth Houses, with two of them being very good at accessing EU programmes.

7   The net-promoter score is based on the following question: 'How likely is it that you would recommend the Growth House to a friend or colleague?' The scoring is based on a 0 to 10 scale – 9 or 10 are Promoters, 0 to 6 are Detractors, 7 and 8 are Passives, The net-promoter score is calculated by subtracting the percentage of customers who are Detractors from the percentage of customers who are Promoters.

8   On top of these three goals there is a fourth one (weighted 10) that is related to the share of gazelles in the region. The motive for this is that the Growth Houses should contribute to the government's goals.

9   The average for the Growth Houses is even higher – 86%.

10 This is classified as a Step V procedure by Storey (1999). It is not the most advanced of statistical approaches – Step VI – since it fails to control for 'unobservables'. Pons Rotger et al. (2011) in their analysis of North Jutland, however, do use Step VI.

11 https://erhvervsstyrelsen.dk/sites/default/files/media/evalueringafvaeksthusene2013.pdf

REFERENCES

Acevedo, G.L. and Tan, H. (2010), *Evaluation of SME Programs in Latin America and the Caribbean*, International Bank for Reconstruction and Development, The World Bank, Washington, DC.

Acs, Z.J., Astebro, T., Audretsch, D.B. and Robinson, D.T. (2016), Public policy to promote entrepreneurship: a call to arms, *Small Business Economics*, 47(1), 35–51.

Arshad, N., Carter, S. and Mason, C. (2014), The ineffectiveness of entrepreneurship policy: is policy formulation to blame? *Small Business Economics*, 43(3), 639–659.

Baumgartner, H.J. and Caliendo, M. (2008), Turning unemployment into self-employment: effectiveness of two start-up programmes, *Oxford Bulletin of Economics and Statistics*, 70(3), 347–373.

Bell, E., Taylor, S. and Thorpe, R. (2002), Organizational differentiation through badging: investors in people and the value of the sign, *Journal of Management Studies*, 39(8), 1071–1085.

Bennett, R.J. (2015), *Entrepreneurship, Small Business and Policy: Evolution and Revolution*, Routledge, London.

Birch, D.L. (1987), *Job Creation in America*, Free Press, New York.

Bridge, S. (2010), *Re-Thinking Enterprise Policy*, Palgrave, Basingstoke.

Burke, A., Fraser, S. and Greene, F.J. (2010), Multiple effects of business plans on new ventures, *Journal of Management Studies*, 47(3), 391–415.

CEC (Commission of the European Communities) (2003), Green Paper: Entrepreneurship in Europe, CEC, Brussels.

Chrisman, J.J. and McMullan, W.E. (2004), Outsider assistance as a knowledge resource for new venture survival, *Journal of Small Business Management*, 42, 229–244.

Chrisman, J.J., McMullan, E. and Hall, J. (2005), The influence of guided preparation on the long-term performance of new ventures, *Journal of Business Venturing*, 20, 769–791.

Cowling, M., Bates, P., Jagger, N. and Murray, G. (2008), *Study of the Impact of Enterprise Investment Scheme (EIS) and Venture Capital Trusts (VCTs) on Company Performance*, HM Revenue and Customs, Research Report 44, London.

Cumming, D. and Fischer, E. (2015), Assessing the impact of publicly funded business advisory services on entrepreneurial internationalization, *International Small Business Journal*, 33(8), 824–839.

Danish Entrepreneurship Index (2004), DECA, Copenhagen.

Dannreuther, C. (2007), EU SME policy: on the edge of governance, *CESifo Forum*, 8(2), 7–13.

DECA (Danish Enterprise and Construction Authority) (2009), *Entrepreneurship Conditions in Denmark*, DECA, Copenhagen.

Eurofound (European Foundation for the Improvement of Living and Working Conditions)

(2016), *Start-Up Support for Young People in the EU: From Implementation to Evaluation*, Eurofound, Dublin.

GAO (Government Accountability Office) (2012), *Opportunities to Reduce Duplication, Overlap and Fragmentation, Achieve Savings, and Enhance Revenue*, GAO, Washington, DC.

Greene, F.J., Mole, K.F. and Storey, D.J. (2008), *Three Decades of Enterprise Culture: Entrepreneurship, Economic Regeneration and Public Policy*, Palgrave, Basingstoke.

Kosters, S. and Obschonka, M. (2010), *Building Winners? An Empirical Evaluation of Public Business Assistance in the Founding Process*, Jena Economic Research Papers, No. 5.

Lambrecht, J. and Pirnay, F. (2005), An evaluation of public support measures for private external consultancies to SMEs in the Walloon region of Belgium, *Entrepreneurship and Regional Development*, 17(2), 89–108.

Lundström, A. and Stevenson, L. (2005), *Entrepreneurship Policy: Theory and Practice*, Springer, Dordrecht.

Lundström, A., Vikström, P., Fink, M., Meuleman, M., Głodek, P., Storey, D.J. and Kroksgård, A. (2014), Measuring the costs and coverage of SME and entrepreneurship policy: a pioneering study, *Entrepreneurship Theory and Practice*, 38(4), 941–957.

McHugh, J. and May, T. (2002), Small business policy: a political consensus? *The Political Quarterly*, 73(1), 76–85.

Miller, G.J. (2008), Solutions to Principal–Agent Problems in Firms, in C. Menard and M.M. Shirley (eds), *Handbook of New Institutional Economics*, Springer, Dordrecht, pp. 349–370.

Mole, K.F. (2002a), Business advisors impact on SMEs, *International Small Business Journal*, 20(2), 139–162.

Mole, K.F. (2002b), Street-level technocracy in UK small business support: business links, personal business advisors and the small business service, *Environment and Planning C*, 20(2), 179–194.

Mole, K.F., Hart, M., Roper, S. and Saal, D. (2011), Broader or deeper? Exploring the most effective intervention profile for public business support, *Environment and Planning A*, 43(1), 87–106.

Morris, M. and Stevens, P. (2010), Evaluation of a New Zealand business support programme using firm performance micro-data, *Small Enterprise Research*,17(1), 30–42.

NAO (National Audit Office) (2013), *Evaluation in Government*, National Audit Office, London.

Nielsen, P-S. (2016), An organizational taxonomy of entrepreneurship policy delivery structures, *Journal of Small Business and Enterprise Development*, 23(2), 514–527.

OECD (Organization for Economic Cooperation and Development) (1998), *Fostering Entrepreneurship*, OECD, Paris.

OECD (Organization for Economic Cooperation and Development) (2007), *OECD Framework for the Evaluation of SME and Entrepreneurship Policies and Programmes*, OECD, Paris.

Parker, S.C. (2007), Policymakers Beware!, in D.B. Audretsch, I. Grillo and R. Thurik (eds), *Handbook of Research on Entrepreneurship Policy*, Edward Elgar, Cheltenham, pp. 54–63.

Pons Rotger, G., Gortz, M. and Storey, D.J. (2012), Assessing the effectiveness of guided preparation for new venture creation: theory and practice, *Journal of Business Venturing*, 27(4), 506–521.

Robson, P.J.A., Wijbenga, F. and Parker, S.C. (2009), Introduction to Special Issue: Entrepreneurship and policy: challenges and directions for future research, *International Small Business Journal*, 27(5), October, 531–535.

Storey, D.J. (1985), Manufacturing Employment Change in Northern England, 1965–78: The Role of Small Business, in D.J. Storey (ed.), *Small Firms in Regional Economic Development: Britain, Ireland and the United States*, Cambridge University Press, Cambridge.

Storey, D.J. (1994), *Understanding the Small Business Sector*, Routledge, London.

Storey, D.J. (1999), Six Steps to Heaven: Evaluating the Impact of Public Policies to Support Small Businesses in Developed Economies, in D. Sexton and H. Landström (eds), *Handbook of Entrepreneurship*, Blackwell, Oxford, pp. 176–194.

Storey, D.J. and Greene, F.J. (2010), *Small Business and Entrepreneurship*, Pearson, London.

Wren, C. and Storey, D.J. (2002), Evaluating the effect of soft business support upon small firm performance, *Oxford Economic Papers*, 54(2), 334–365.

20

Exploring Firm-Level Effects of Regulation: Going Beyond Survey Approaches

John Kitching

INTRODUCTION

The law is widely regarded as one of the important institutional forces impacting entrepreneurship (Boettke & Coyne, 2009; Smallbone & Welter, 2009; Campbell, 2012), often conceptualised as one component in entrepreneurial ecosystems (Spigel, 2015; Stam, 2015) or entrepreneurial regimes (Dilli & Elert, 2016). Legislation is widely regarded as a means of tackling market failure (e.g. Minniti, 2008), an attempt to remove or mitigate the negative externalities generated by the activities of market agents that are not reflected in the price of goods. Market failure arguments underpin regulatory reform initiatives in developed and developing economies (OECD, 2015; World Bank, 2016). Yet such a view implicitly treats market and state as independent and opposed forces rather than as necessarily intertwined and mutually supportive (Polanyi, 1957; Hutton & Schneider, 2008; Mazzucato, 2013). Governments regulate for many reasons: to facilitate market

exchange; to provide, or enable the provision of, public goods; to pursue distributive goals; and to constrain market irrationality, all of which impact market functioning (Stiglitz, 2009; Feintuck, 2010). Beyond economic objectives, governments also regulate to manage socio-cultural *perceptions* of risk, as distinct from dealing with the risks themselves, and to enhance government legitimacy and power (Habermas, 1976; Haines, 2011). There is no guarantee, of course, that regulators will succeed in their endeavours. Intervention outcomes are necessarily contingent upon how regulated entities and their stakeholders respond.

Public choice and public interest theories of regulation might be distinguished (Shleifer, 2005) and related to entrepreneurial action. Public choice theories emphasise the socially suboptimal character of regulation and the potential for 'capture' by powerful interest groups: laws restricting market entry and competition favour incumbent firms (Stigler, 1971), while also fostering corruption of public officials in their roles as legislator, inspector and enforcer (Djankov, La Porta, Lopez-de-Silanes & Shleifer, 2002). Public interest theories, in contrast, argue for the social benefits of regulation, in terms of enabling the provision of public goods that enhance market functioning but which markets themselves cannot supply, or supply in sufficient quantity. Stricter entry regulation, for instance, might prevent 'excess entry' of 'inefficient' or 'lower quality' firms that might lead to a loss of welfare in the wider economy (Ghosh & Saha, 2007; Carpentier & Suret, 2012) and/or enhance consumer and market confidence (Carpenter, 2009). Both theories, however, focus on the *macro*-level outcomes of regulation rather than on the mechanisms shaping entrepreneurs' micro-level adaptations to the legal landscape.

Legal relations are partly constitutive of the social world. Regulation does not simply distort pre-existing market signals but, rather, plays a crucial *constitutive* role in shaping what markets are (Hodgson, 2003; Hodgson, 2015). Property rights permit entrepreneurs to acquire finance (Johnson, McMillan & Woodruff, 2002; Djankov, McLiesh & Shleifer, 2007) and to mobilise resources in pursuit of profit, while the institutions of contract and money enable entrepreneurs to trade and to secure the proceeds from trading. Competition and antitrust laws prohibit price-fixing, cartels, bid-rigging and other forms of market collusion that disadvantage consumers. Consumer rights to receive goods that are fit for purpose protect buyers from misleading sales practices and thereby support consumption. Mandatory credit reporting systems improve financial intermediation and access. Codified legal systems are necessary preconditions for the complex global markets of today (Stiglitz, 2009). This broader lens on the entrepreneurship/regulation link encompasses the enabling and motivational influences of regulation on action that can contribute to higher levels of entrepreneurial performance *as well as* legal constraints on activities. Because businesses are immersed in a sea of law (Edelman & Suchman, 1997), the influence of regulation is substantial, pervasive and enduring. Regulatory regimes constitute a condition of all forms of entrepreneurial action and the outcomes that ensue.

In this chapter, a wider panorama on the links between state regulation and entrepreneurial action and performance is presented, one that extends beyond treating regulation simply as a burden, compliance cost or constraint on action. If regulation was only a constraint, one wonders how business ventures might exist at all. The chapter is organised as follows. First, the key concepts of entrepreneurship and regulation are defined. Second, institutionalist approaches to studying the influence of regulation on entrepreneurial action, commonly used by entrepreneurship researchers, are briefly discussed. Third, an analytical framework is presented setting out how regulation shapes, but does not determine, entrepreneurial action at the micro-level. Subsequent sections discuss survey approaches to exploring the connection between entrepreneurship and regulation, and qualitative studies. A primary aim of the chapter is to demonstrate some of the conceptual and analytical limitations arising from using survey data to investigate *how* regulation impacts entrepreneurial action at the level of the firm. To conclude, the key arguments are summarised and implications for theory and for policy discussed.

KEY CONCEPTS

To begin, the key concepts entrepreneurship and regulation, whose relationship is the subject of the chapter, are defined. There is a large literature on the meaning of the term 'entrepreneurship' (Schumpeter, 1934; Kirzner, 1973; Shane & Venkataraman, 2000; Hebert & Link, 2006; Alvarez & Barney, 2007; Sarasvathy, 2008). Broadly speaking, scholars separate on whether entrepreneurship refers to particular types of activity or to particular types of actor. Different definitions of entrepreneurship lead to divergent research findings; some of these are discussed later. For the purposes of the chapter, entrepreneurship refers to the panoply of activities surrounding the creation of new goods and services (Venkataraman, 1997),[1] although the scope is further narrowed to the context of small, for-profit organisations. The term 'new' connotes no profound novelty and includes products imitating those already in existence supplied by others. The term 'entrepreneurial activities' encompasses resource acquisition and mobilisation practices, and forming and developing relationships with important stakeholders such as investors, suppliers and customers that enable such resourcing practices.

To be clear, the term 'regulation' refers to a binding set of legal rules; it does not include all forms of government action designed to influence behaviour or to wider state and non-state attempts to exert social control or influence (Baldwin & Cave, 1999). This definition excludes fiscal, monetary and other policies that incorporate no regulatory element as defined here, although in practice such measures are often integrated. Regulation might be defined as:

> the legal and administrative rules created, applied and enforced by state and state-supported organisations – at local, national and supra-national level – that both mandate and prohibit actions by individuals and organisations, with infringements subject to criminal, civil and administrative penalties.

Regulation refers to state-authorised and -enforced rules, existing as texts in statutes or other legal and administrative instruments, mandating or prohibiting particular activities by individuals and organisations (Kitching, Hart & Wilson, 2015a). Sources of regulation might be national, supranational or subnational in origin. Responsibility for designing legal rules, information gathering and enforcement may be delegated to independent or private sector agencies but the state underwrites such powers. Regulation, as

conceptualised here, is synonymous with the entirety of the legal framework, incorporating the criminal and civil law codes that protect the person, private property and contract, and their enforcement. Regulation is, therefore, ubiquitous; there are no regulation-free spaces where entrepreneurs or stakeholders stand outside the law.

INSTITUTIONALIST APPROACHES TO STUDYING THE IMPACT OF REGULATION ON ENTREPRENEURIAL ACTION

The law is a dynamic institutional force possessing the power to influence the activities of entrepreneurs and the various stakeholders with whom they interact (including investors, suppliers, customers, competitors, infrastructure providers and regulatory authorities) (Hodgson, 2015; Kitching et al., 2015a). Several studies specify institutions, including state regulation, as drivers of, or constraints on, entrepreneurial action (Tolbert, David & Sine, 2011). Regulation is one of the institutional 'rules of the game', influencing the distribution of entrepreneurial effort between productive, unproductive and destructive forms of activity (Baumol, 1990; Sobel, 2008). Legal rules may divert activity from productive into unproductive and destructive practices such as rent-seeking or organised crime with limited or no benefits for the wider society. Too much regulation might inhibit some entrepreneurs from entering the formal economy at all (Williams & Martinez, 2014).

Drawing on the new institutional economics approach of North (1990) or the more sociological approach of Scott (2014), many researchers apply institutional theories to various aspects of entrepreneurial behaviour. North defines institutions as the human-devised constraints that shape human interaction, to create order and reduce uncertainty, and which provide the incentive structure of an economy. North (1991) distinguishes formal rules, including state regulation, constitutions and property rights, from informal constraints (sanctions, taboos, customs, traditions and codes of conduct). Laws are purposely created rules whereas social customs arise largely as the unintended by-product of social interaction. One problem with the North conception is that he assumes a rational wealth-maximising market agent consciously adapting behaviour to the institutional framework. Yet, arguably, market agents act, and choose to comply (or not) with the law, for normative and moral motives as well for 'economic' reasons (Hodgson, 2013).

Scott (2014) proposes a wider set of institutional 'pillars' that encompass, but also extend beyond, the legal framework: regulative; normative; and cultural-cognitive. Scott conceives of institutions as multifaceted, durable social structures made up of symbolic elements, social activities and material resources. The regulatory pillar, incorporating rule-setting, monitoring and sanctioning activities, is the one most relevant to state regulation as defined here but Scott's definition seems to incorporate non-state as well as state organisations. Sanctioning, for instance, is argued to operate through informal mechanisms such as shaming as well as state-authorised mechanisms such as courts. Informal mechanisms are important but incorporating them takes us beyond a strict concern with how the law moulds entrepreneurial action. Moreover, Scott's (2014: 56) definition of institutions as rules *and* activities *and* resources conflates quite distinct entities. If the law as a set of rules is conflated with the practices the rules ostensibly govern, then it becomes impossible to separate the law from what entrepreneurs actually do. Laws and entrepreneurial activities must be kept separate in analysis.

Entrepreneurship researchers have drawn on institutionalist ideas to develop arguments linking macro-level indices of regulatory quality to measures of entrepreneurship but say little about the specific mechanisms through which regulation influences entrepreneurial action at the micro-level. Studies often do not specify precisely *how* the law affects what entrepreneurs do. Focusing on the processes through which regulation generates effects is important because without a theory specifying the mechanisms, it is not possible to explain the connections between regulation, entrepreneurial action and venture performance. Macro-level arguments regarding the properties of the wider institutional context do not suffice to demonstrate how individual entrepreneurs, or their firms, adapt to the regulatory regime. Analyses must also pay attention to the part played by agents' subjective beliefs, motivations and choices in such adaptive processes. The following section elaborates a framework to explain such processes.

THEORISING THE INFLUENCE OF REGULATION ON ENTREPRENEURIAL ACTION

The conception of regulation and its effects on entrepreneurial action presented here possesses a number of features other studies neglect or do not fully appreciate (Kitching et al., 2015a). First, regulation distributes possibilities for action, and exposure to harm, between entrepreneurs and their stakeholders by endowing the parties with particular powers (legal rights) and liabilities (legal obligations). By creating expectations of market agents' behaviour, the law can stabilise market conditions, facilitating investment, innovation and trade. By transforming rights and obligations, regulatory reform shifts the balance of power between entrepreneurs and stakeholders – who may include competitor entrepreneurs – creating possibilities for action (Shane, 2003). Prohibiting anti-competitive practices, for instance, enables new entrants to compete better with incumbent firms, while increased consumer rights shift power towards buyers in relation to producers/suppliers.

Second, the law only makes certain actions *possible*; regulation only produces effects through the exercise of human agency. There is no fixed connection between the existence of a regulation and what market agents do; there is always some scope for choice. If entrepreneurs, or their stakeholders, do not act differently as a consequence of regulation, its effect is zero. The regulatory framework constitutes part of the broader context of entrepreneurial action which shapes, but does not determine, what entrepreneurs do, or the consequences that flow from their activities. But because regulation distributes capacities for action variably between entrepreneurs and stakeholders, some might be better placed to pursue profitable projects than others. Favourable conditions, however, never suffice to ensure an event occurs, given agents' powers to choose to act otherwise (Ramoglou, 2013). Entrepreneurs, like other agents, must choose how to deploy their finite resources; they cannot pursue all possible projects they believe are open to them simultaneously.

Third, by mandating and prohibiting actions on the part of those regulated, the law, simultaneously, enables and motivates *as well as* constrains entrepreneurs' activities (Mayer-Schönberger, 2010; Kitching et al., 2013; Kitching, Kašperová & Collis, 2015b). Property rights, for example, enable entrepreneurs to mobilise assets in pursuit of profit, but also constrain them by prohibiting unauthorised use of *others'* resources. Contracts enable resource owners to trade with others but also bind them legally to the deals they make. Moreover, by restricting certain courses of action or imposing certain costs, regulation can motivate entrepreneurs to implement product and process innovations in order to cut costs and/or increase revenue. Consequently, regulatory regimes produce variable firm-level performance effects because entrepreneurs and stakeholders adapt to the law in different ways (e.g. Edwards, Ram & Black, 2004; Henrekson, 2007), not simply by complying with regulation or not, but also by acting to further their aims within limits permitted by law.

Fourth, from the standpoint of an individual entrepreneur, regulation produces effects directly and indirectly (Kitching, 2007; Kitching, 2016a). These two types of effect are only distinguishable analytically; in practice, they intertwine. Regulation impacts entrepreneurs directly by placing obligations on them with which they must comply or suffer legal sanctions. Indirect effects arise from entrepreneurs' interactions with stakeholders who adapt *their* behaviour as a consequence of the law. Where entrepreneurs adjust their own activities as a response to stakeholder adaptations to the law, then regulation generates indirect effects on that entrepreneur's activities and performance. Indirect regulatory influences might be complex, and difficult to detect. Studies focusing solely on direct effects, such as those concentrating on compliance costs (e.g. Chittenden, Kauser & Poutziouris, 2002), miss the indirect influences arising from stakeholder action. Relationships with stakeholders mediate the effects of regulation on entrepreneurs in at least three ways (Kitching, 2016b): first, by shaping the processes through which entrepreneurs discover, interpret and adapt to their legal obligations; second, by influencing stakeholder adaptations to entrepreneurs' responses to legal obligations in their role as suppliers, customers and competitors, for instance; and, third, because stakeholders are regulated entities too, they face pressures to comply with their own legal mandates and prohibitions or risk sanctions for non-compliance. Indirect impacts are often overlooked by researchers yet they are just as much a consequence of regulation as are direct influences.

Fifth, the influence of regulation on entrepreneurial action does *not* depend upon agents' full awareness of their own legal rights and obligations or those of stakeholders (Kitching et al., 2015a). Regulatory regimes constitute conditions of action, in part unacknowledged, generating real effects on behaviour without explicitly entering agents' reasoning or motivations. Property and contract rights enabling entrepreneurs to acquire and deploy resources are essential for trade, irrespective of whether these rights are recognised and reported as causally significant. Stakeholder actions (and inactions) moulded by *their* regulatory obligations might influence the entrepreneurs with whom they interact, whether or not those entrepreneurs are aware of them. Changes in competitor, supplier and customer activity arising from regulatory reform may stimulate entrepreneurs to adapt behaviour but may not be attributed by those entrepreneurs to the law. Entrepreneurs may have no idea how stakeholder decisions affect them or even who these stakeholders are. The effects of regulation may, therefore, only be *partly* visible to entrepreneurs. Neither entrepreneurs nor stakeholders possess perfect information concerning regulatory processes and outcomes; entrepreneurs' perceptions of regulatory effects are fallible and corrigible. In research surveys and interviews, therefore, entrepreneurs may *mis*perceive and *mis*report the impact of regulation. Explanation of regulatory impacts must allow for respondents' partial awareness.

Through its influence on entrepreneurs' micro-level adaptations, regulation contributes to macro-level effects. Regulation shapes the kinds of relations entrepreneurs form and transform, and the governance mechanisms that regulate these relations. Because entrepreneurs and stakeholders have some degree of discretion over whether, and how, to adapt their behaviour as a consequence of regulation, its effects both at the micro-level of the individual venture and at the macro-level of the market, industry or nation are difficult to predict. A favourable business environment cannot be assumed to serve all entrepreneurs equally well; some will create successful ventures, while others will fail.

SURVEY APPROACHES

Quantitative studies investigating the entrepreneurship/regulation connection are of several types (Kitching, 2006). Some focus on the micro-level, investigating entrepreneurs' perceptions of regulatory burdens (Carter, Mason & Tagg, 2009) and to what extent they constitute an obstacle to business success in comparison with other potential barriers such as market competition or lack of access to finance (Department for Business, Energy & Industrial Strategy, 2016). Such perception studies offer partial insights into regulatory processes and outcomes because they tell us what entrepreneurs *think* about regulation but not necessarily what they *do* about it. Finding entrepreneurs perceive regulation as burdensome tells us nothing about whether and how they discover, interpret or act upon it. Perceiving regulation to be burdensome might motivate entrepreneurs to abandon their ventures or, alternatively, may spur them to act in ways that overcome the costs and constraints imposed, for instance, by seeking more efficient processes or by developing new products.

More sophisticated survey approaches seek to quantify the costs of compliance with regulation (Chittenden et al., 2002; Crain & Crain, 2010, 2014; Schoonjans, Van Cauwenberge, Reekmans & Simoens, 2011). Regulation is argued to impose compliance costs, diverting entrepreneurial effort and resources away from productive, profit-generating uses towards 'unproductive' compliance. Studies usually involve estimating the money and time resources consumed in complying with a particular regulation. Such estimates are treated as the opportunity costs of regulation: as the resources entrepreneurs would have had available to devote to their productive, profit-generating activities. Compliance costs are usually found to be regressive, with small firms suffering disproportionately. The assumption underpinning compliance cost studies is that regulation necessarily impedes, rather than facilitates, economic activity.

Cross-national comparative surveys typically focus on the macro-level, seeking to identify relationships between the regulatory and institutional environment and some measure of entrepreneurship. Several find a strong link between property rights protection and level of entrepreneurship (e.g. Estrin, Korostoleva & Mickiewicz, 2013). Some find a positive association between lighter levels of entry regulation (in the form of the number of registration or administrative procedures, the time and money costs of registration, or skill/educational standards) and entrepreneurship, defined in various ways (Djankov et al., 2002; Klapper, Laeven & Rajan, 2006; Prantl & Spitz-Oener, 2009; Troilo, 2011; Ciriaci, 2014; Urbano & Alvarez, 2014; Bailey & Thomas, 2015; Aparicio, Urbano & Audretsch, 2016), while others do not (van Stel, Storey & Thurik, 2007; Bowen & de Clercq, 2008; Autio, 2011; Valdez & Richardson, 2013). Spencer and Gómez (2004) demonstrate mixed findings depending on the definition of entrepreneurship adopted. Without a precise conception of what entrepreneurship is, specifying clear connections between entry regulation and entrepreneurship is likely to prove extremely challenging.

Evidence on the relationship between entry regulation and the *quality* of business start-ups suggests a complex link. Consistent with Baumol's (1990) argument, some suggest that more stringent regulation increases informal entrepreneurial activity (Djankov et al., 2002; Capelleras, Mole, Greene & Storey, 2008), while others claim that it reduces opportunity (Ho & Wong, 2007), high-growth aspiration (Troilo, 2011) and strategic entrepreneurship (Levie & Autio, 2011). Others, conversely, find that tougher entry requirements restrict entry to better-performing businesses. Branstetter, Lima, Taylor and Venâncio (2014) found the expected association between regulatory reforms reducing the cost of market entry and increases in new firm formation, but they also discovered that the increase was confined largely to 'marginal firms' that were typically very small, owned by poorly educated entrepreneurs, operating in low-technology sectors and less likely than other firms to survive the first two years. Simplistic assertions that

lighter entry regulation *necessarily* increases entrepreneurship, or that this translates into improved public welfare, ought therefore to be avoided. The impact of regulation might depend on the interaction between the law and many other non-legal factors (Eberhart, Eesley, Cheng & Skousen, 2015).

Size-contingent regulations may impact upon business growth by encouraging or discouraging expansion beyond some size threshold. Garicano, Lelarge and Van Reenen (2016) note how larger (with 50 or more employees) employers' legal obligations, including those of creating a works council, establishing a health and safety committee and appointing a union representative, are associated with a 'bulge' in the business size distribution just below the threshold at 50. This is argued to entail a misallocation of resources to smaller firms, with implications for productivity. Such 'distortions' are treated as the welfare cost of the legislation. In the US, small firms are obliged to offer state small-group health insurance (varying by state from 25 to 100 employees); larger employers are not affected by this regulation (Kapur, Karaca-Mandic, Gates & Fulton, 2012). The authors suggest that the reform led firms to expand employment in order to avoid the greater regulation of smaller employers.

Regulation influencing the activities of stakeholders with whom entrepreneurs interact necessarily impacts entrepreneurs' activity and performance indirectly. Legislation relaxing controls on US banks' ability to set up, or acquire, new branches outside their home state, for instance, has been found to increase the supply of cheap credit to small firms (Rice & Strahan, 2010). On the other hand, strict capital market entry requirements limiting stock exchange listing have been argued to enhance investor confidence and returns (Black, 2001; La Porta, Lopez-de-Silanes & Shleifer, 2006; Carpentier & Suret, 2012; Cumming & Knill, 2012) and to prevent the emergence of a 'lemon market' (Akerlof, 1970). Regulation clearly exerts diverse effects.

Bankruptcy laws impact entrepreneurs directly and indirectly. They influence entrepreneurs and their creditors directly by specifying how the remaining assets of a distressed venture are to be distributed between entrepreneurs and suppliers, financiers and the tax authorities. Laws differ between countries, specifically in terms of the money and time costs of following bankruptcy procedures, the availability of a reorganisation option or a 'fresh start' with debts discharged, whether they grant an automatic stay of assets or whether incumbent managers are allowed to continue in post (Peng, Yamakawa & Lee, 2010). Debtor-friendly bankruptcy legislation is associated with higher levels of self-employment (Armour & Cumming, 2008), controlling for other legal, economic and social factors, although this link is claimed to be mediated by level of wealth (Fossen, 2014). But bankruptcy rules can also influence how financiers adapt their behaviour in order to allow for difficulties recovering money from borrowers in default; these activities impact entrepreneurs indirectly. Variations in bankruptcy codes influence bank lending practices, with French banks more likely to ask for higher levels of collateral than their UK and German counterparts because of greater difficulties in recovering assets from defaulting businesses (Davydenko & Franks, 2008) or by charging higher interest rates (Armour & Cumming, 2008).

PROBLEMS WITH SURVEY APPROACHES

Developing a coherent explanation linking macro-level properties of the institutional context, including the legal framework, to entrepreneurial action at the micro-level using survey data is difficult for various reasons. First, researchers conceptualise and operationalise entrepreneurship in diverse ways; for example, as self-employment, as new firm start-up registration, as

nascent/early stage start-up activity, as listed (or newly-listed) companies on a stock exchange, as opportunity- or necessity-motivated venture creation, as strategic-entry entrepreneurship and as high-aspiration businesses. Unsurprisingly, perhaps, these related but distinct definitions of entrepreneurship give rise to contradictory research findings (Spencer & Gómez, 2004; Chowdhury, Terjesen & Audretsch, 2015), making generalisation difficult.

Second, survey studies often rely on quite crude indices of 'regulatory quality'. Several studies examining the links between regulation and entrepreneurship have constructed indices using data drawn from the Index of Economic Freedom published by the *Wall Street Journal* and the Heritage Foundation (e.g. McMullen, Bagby & Palich, 2008; Troilo, 2011; Estrin et al., 2013; Stenholm, Acs & Wuebker, 2013; Valdez & Richardson, 2013; Chowdhury et al., 2015), the Fraser Institute's Economic Freedom of the World Index (e.g. Bjørnskov & Foss, 2013; Sambharya & Musteen, 2014; Dilli & Elert, 2016) or the World Bank 'Doing Business' indicators (e.g. Ho & Wong, 2007; van Stel et al., 2007; Autio, 2011; Levie & Autio, 2011; Troilo, 2011; Stenholm et al., 2013; Aparicio et al., 2016). Studies based on these indices inevitably share in their weaknesses to some extent.

The purpose of these indices is to reduce a complex variety of regulatory and other institutional and behavioural factors to a number in order to be able to compare and rank individual countries in terms of economic freedom or the ease of doing business. Each index uses a combination of data sources, including statistics provided by international organisations, business surveys and expert opinion, as well as the provider's own interpretation of the data used. The Heritage Foundation's Index of Economic Freedom 2016 ranks 186 countries on the basis of 10 equally weighted components, related to four broad pillars (rule of law, limited government, regulatory efficiency, open markets).[2] The Fraser

Institute's Economic Freedom of the World Index provides 42 data points across five broad areas (size of government; legal structure and security of property rights; access to sound money; freedom to trade internationally; and regulation of credit, labour, and business) to rank 159 countries and territories (Gwartney, Lawson & Hall with others, 2016). The World Bank (2016) benchmarks 190 economies against best practice for 10 dimensions (starting a business, dealing with construction permits, getting electricity, registering property, getting credit, protecting minority investors, paying taxes, trading across borders, enforcing contracts, and resolving insolvency) in order to calculate a distance-to-frontier measure for each country; this measure provides the basis for the country rankings. Each of these three indices inevitably incorporates assumptions regarding what constitutes a high or low score on each dimension of interest.

Such indices, arguably, provide limited insight into how regulation shapes entrepreneurial action at the micro-level. By defining the national-level properties of the institutional framework for each country, surveys thereby implicitly conceive of the regulatory regime in each country in an undifferentiated way, as if it exerts identical influences on all entrepreneurs within territorial borders. Moreover, many studies combine regulation, as defined here, with broader aspects of state intervention, for example, the size of government expenditure (e.g. Estrin et al., 2013; Valdez & Richardson, 2013) or some other feature of the business environment such as access to finance (e.g. Urbano & Alvarez, 2014; Chowdhury et al., 2015). These studies thereby conflate regulatory influences with other institutional and behavioural factors.

Beyond macro-level characterisations of legal frameworks, cross-national surveys rarely specify the precise mechanisms through which regulation moulds entrepreneurial action (contrast Frontier Economics, 2012, for an attempt to do this with regard to UK product and labour market regulation).

Macro-level indices are unable to explain whether, and how, particular entrepreneurs discover, interpret and adapt to particular laws. Surveys seek to identify the aggregate effects of compliance/adaptation, implicitly assuming entrepreneurs to be fully aware of their regulatory obligations, that they interpret them similarly and also adapt to them in identical ways. Yet regulations exert multiple, often contradictory, influences on individual entrepreneurs. There is no single regulatory effect on entrepreneurs (Kitching, 2006). Regulation is likely to impact entrepreneurs quite differently contingent upon not only their particular exposure to specific laws but also in relation to their capacity to discover, comply with and adapt to them. Such impacts are profoundly contingent on time, space and the entrepreneur's social-structural positioning. Entrepreneurs' awareness and understanding of particular regulations, and their capacity and willingness to adapt to them are highly variable. Reducing the regulatory regime to a single number does scant justice to the diverse influences regulation exerts on particular entrepreneurs in specific industrial, market and regional contexts. Indeed, surveys of business owners find massive variation in the amount of time reported to comply with the same regulation, and that official indicators can seriously overstate the experience of dealing with regulation for many (Hallward-Driemeier & Pritchett, 2011).

QUALITATIVE STUDIES OF REGULATORY PROCESSES

Qualitative studies are better placed to explore the forces that shape entrepreneurial action at the micro-level, including explaining how individual entrepreneurs discover, interpret and adapt to the regulatory obligations placed upon them; and to demonstrate how regulation shapes relationships with stakeholders, enabling and motivating access to resources such as finance, labour and information and to facilitating market exchange. Property and contract rights are essential preconditions for market exchange, although where these are deeply-institutionalised, entrepreneurs might not report them as drivers, or enablers, of their activity. Similar arguments might be made with regard to other long-established legal obligations that have come to constitute a taken for granted part of doing business.

Entry regulations permit entrepreneurs to create new goods and services by licensing them to undertake particular activities. Business registration and minimum capital requirements are common examples (van Stel et al., 2007) but, in addition to this, entry to certain professions and occupations is also licensed (Koumenta et al., 2014). From the standpoint of an individual entrepreneur, entry regulations and licensing practices influence them directly by authorising them to operate, and indirectly by permitting or prohibiting others to do the same. Whatever levels of performance entrepreneurs achieve subsequently is facilitated by these fundamental regulatory enablements – and by the regulatory constraints prohibiting entry by prospective competitors.

Beyond these basic enablements, regulation creates possibilities for entrepreneurs to act where stakeholders are mandated or motivated to act in particular ways: where consumers are mandated or motivated to purchase goods and services, or where competitors are motivated to exit (Kitching et al., 2015a). This emphasises the importance of *indirect* regulatory influences on entrepreneurial action and demonstrates how regulatory reform *redistributes* capacities for action and exposure to particular market risks. For instance, regulation requiring those participating in sailing activities to wear safety clothing, for instance, stimulates consumer demand, creating a market for safety clothing manufacturers and suppliers.

Regulation also stimulates entrepreneurial action where it encourages but does not compel clients to purchase. The US Sarbanes-Oxley Act, 2002 sought to restore investor confidence following the collapse of Enron by imposing harsh penalties on corporations for failure to present truthful accounts. A UK recruitment agency owner reported that the Act had encouraged US companies based in the UK to hire agency staff in order to ensure compliance and thereby boosted his agency's sales (Kitching et al., 2015a). Recent UK legislation increasing new obligations on retail travel insurance providers encouraged many smaller providers to exit the market, arguably improving the prospects of the remaining incumbents. It should be emphasised that regulation only makes action *possible*; it cannot guarantee successful outcomes because stakeholders acting in pursuit of their own goals may frustrate the entrepreneur's aims. Competitors, for instance, may adapt more effectively to the changing legal landscape, and entrepreneurs may be unable to exploit the possibilities regulation affords.

Kitching et al. (2013, 2015b) investigated the impacts of legislation permitting small companies to file abbreviated accounts at Companies House, the UK public register; these require limited balance sheet information and no profit and loss account. Ostensibly intended to enhance company performance by reducing the administrative burden of preparing and filing accounts, the legislation was found to generate a wide variety of adverse effects arising from the lack of readily accessible public information as well as benefits arising from confidentiality. Adverse effects include discouraging suppliers and customers from trading with small companies, poorer credit ratings/scores awarded by credit reference agencies, reduced access to trade credit, and poorer credit insurance cover for those looking to trade with small companies. These undesirable consequences may occur without the awareness of the small company directors choosing to file abbreviated accounts, even where they report benefits. Tabone and Baldacchino (2003) note how the requirement for a statutory audit might generate benefits by imposing financial discipline upon business owners as well as protecting society from business malpractice.

In summary, qualitative studies of regulatory processes, though limited in number, support the argument that regulation is a dynamic force shaping entrepreneurial action and performance in diverse ways. Regulation enables and motivates entrepreneurs – and their stakeholders – to act in particular ways as well as constraining their activities. These diverse influences generate a range of effects at the level of the firm with regard to resource acquisition and mobilisation which, in turn, contribute to variable levels of venture performance. Research should reflect these conflicting regulatory tendencies.

CONCLUSIONS AND IMPLICATIONS

This chapter has sought to demonstrate the diverse influences of regulation on entrepreneurial action and performance in a small firm setting. Regulation impacts entrepreneurs directly, by mandating and prohibiting action on their part, and indirectly, by shaping the behaviour of the various stakeholders (including investors, suppliers, customers, competitors, infrastructure providers and regulatory authorities) with whom entrepreneurs interact. As stakeholders are regulated entities too, regulation permeates all entrepreneurs' market and non-market relationships. Direct and indirect regulatory influences interact to enable, motivate and constrain entrepreneurial action.

This argument suggests two important implications, one for theory and research, and one for public policy. First, researchers should adopt a more open-ended approach to investigating the impact of the law on entrepreneurial processes and outcomes; researchers should not restrict themselves solely to identifying those legal obligations, or associated activities, that entrepreneurs perceive to be a burden. Regulation generates diverse effects on entrepreneurs, largely through the

medium of their relationships with a wide range of close and distant stakeholders, whether or not entrepreneurs perceive such influences. Entrepreneurs' experiences of dealing with the legal mandates and prohibitions placed directly upon them are important but are just the tip of the iceberg for explaining how regulation impacts their activities and performance. The effects of regulation are irreducible to entrepreneurs' fallible experiences of them.

Conceptualised this way, the effects of regulation on entrepreneurial action are ubiquitous. Regulatory regimes constitute a condition of all forms of entrepreneurial action – resource acquisition and mobilisation – and the ensuing business performance outcomes. Legal frameworks enable entrepreneurs to trade, distributing capacities to act between entrepreneurs and their stakeholders (including other entrepreneurs acting as suppliers, customers and competitors) to access resources and to generate sales. Legal relations are partly constitutive of market relations between entrepreneurs and stakeholders but do not determine how entrepreneurs – or their stakeholders – exercise their agency. Researchers must also investigate the material and symbolic resources available to entrepreneurs, and how these are drawn upon in interaction with stakeholders, to generate specific economic outcomes.

A second implication is that unless policymakers recognise the full range of regulatory influences on entrepreneurs, and the wider social conditions that promote or retard them, reform policies intended to boost entrepreneurship are likely to produce unintended and/or unwanted consequences. Initiatives presupposing the law to be solely a burden, cost or constraint on action not only overlook its variable impacts on individual entrepreneurs, they also ignore entrepreneurs' adaptive capabilities. Deregulation policies might also be much less important than other levers policymakers might use to support entrepreneurial action. Policies to develop entrepreneurs' capabilities to access and use valuable resources (finance, skilled labour, information) or broader fiscal and monetary programmes to support investment and consumption might be preferable. Reducing regulatory requirements may do little to enable or motivate investment, innovation and trade if they encourage entrepreneurs to adopt business models centring on cost-cutting rather than on product innovation to enhance competitiveness. Regulatory reform might not generate the desired public policy ends if, by facilitating extensive cost-cutting, it undermines market confidence and the capacity of entrepreneurs to produce goods consumers want to buy.

Notes

1 Entrepreneurial activities so defined may occur in new ventures or in established enterprises.
2 http://www.heritage.org/index/about

REFERENCES

Akerlof, G. (1970), 'The market for "lemons": quality uncertainty and the market mechanism', *Quarterly Journal of Economics*, 84(3): 488–500.

Alvarez, S. and Barney, J. (2007), 'Discovery and creation: alternative theories of entrepreneurial action', *Organizações em Contexto*, 3(6): 123–152.

Aparicio, S., Urbano, D. and Audretsch, D. (2016), 'Institutional factors, opportunity entrepreneurship and economic growth: panel data evidence', *Technological Forecasting & Social Change*, 102, January, 45–61.

Armour, J. and Cumming, D. (2008), 'Bankruptcy law and entrepreneurship', *American Law and Economics Review*, 10(2): 303–350.

Autio, E. (2011), 'High-aspiration entrepreneurship', in M. Minniti (ed.), *The Dynamics of Entrepreneurship: Evidence from the Global Entrepreneurship Monitor Data*, Oxford, Oxford University Press, pp. 259–275.

Bailey, J. and Thomas, D. (2015), *Regulating Away Competition: The Effect of Regulation on Entrepreneurship and Employment*, Mercatus Working Paper, online at: https://www.mercatus.org/system/files/Bailey-Regulation-Entrepreneurship.pdf

Baldwin, R. and Cave, M. (1999), *Understanding Regulation*, Oxford, Oxford University Press.

Baumol, W. (1990), 'Entrepreneurship: productive, unproductive, and destructive', *Journal of Political Economy*, 98(5): 893–921.

Bjørnskov, C. and Foss, N. (2013), 'How strategic entrepreneurship and the institutional context drive economic growth', *Strategic Entrepreneurship Journal*, 79(1): 50–69.

Black, B. (2001), 'The legal and institutional preconditions for strong securities markets', *UCLA Law Review*, 48(4): 881–855.

Boettke, P. and Coyne, C. (2009), 'Context matters: institutions and entrepreneurship', *Foundations and Trends® in Entrepreneurship*, 5(3): 135–209.

Bowen, H. and de Clercq, D. (2008), 'Institutional context and the allocation of entrepreneurial effort', *Journal of International Business Studies*, 39(4): 747–767.

Branstetter, L., Lima, F., Taylor, L. and Venâncio, A. (2014), 'Do entry regulations deter entrepreneurship and job creation? Evidence from recent reforms in Portugal', *Economic Journal*, 124(577): 805–832.

Campbell, N. (2012), 'Entrepreneurial action and the rules of the game: an editorial to introduce the Journal of Entrepreneurship and Public Policy', *Journal of Entrepreneurship and Public Policy*, 1(1): 4–11.

Capelleras, J-L., Mole, K., Greene, F. and Storey, D. (2008), 'Do more heavily regulated economies have poorer performing new ventures? Evidence from Britain and Spain', *Journal of International Business Studies*, 39(4): 688–704.

Carpenter, D. (2009), 'Confidence games: how does regulation constitute markets?', in E. Balleisen and D. Moss (eds), *Government and Markets: Toward a New Theory of Regulation*, Cambridge, Cambridge University Press, pp. 164–190.

Carpentier, C. and Suret, J-M. (2012), 'Entrepreneurial equity financing and securities regulation: an empirical analysis', *International Small Business Journal*, 30(1): 41–64.

Carter, S., Mason, C. and Tagg, S. (2009), 'Perceptions and experience of employment regulation in UK small firms', *Environment and Planning C: Government and Policy*, 27(2): 263–278.

Chittenden, F., Kauser, S. and Poutziouris, P. (2002), *Regulatory Burdens of Small Business: A Literature Review*, Small Business Service, online at: http://webarchive.nationalarchives.gov.uk/+/http://www.berr.gov.uk/files/file38324.pdf

Chowdhury, F., Terjesen, S. and Audretsch, D. (2015), 'Varieties of entrepreneurship: institutional drivers across entrepreneurial activity and country', *European Journal of Law and Economics*, 40(1): 121–148.

Ciriaci, D. (2014), *Business Dynamics and Red Tape Barriers*, European Commission, Economic Papers 532, online at: http://ec.europa.eu/economy_finance/publications/economic_paper/2014/pdf/ecp532_en.pdf

Crain, N. and Crain, W.M. (2010), *The Impact of Regulatory Costs on Small Firms*, Small Business Administration Office of Advocacy, online at: https://www.sba.gov/sites/default/files/The%20Impact%20of%20Regulatory%20Costs%20on%20Small%20Firms%20%28Full%29_0.pdf

Crain, W.M. and Crain, N. (2014), *The Cost of Federal Regulation to the US Economy, Manufacturing and Small Business*, report for the National Association of Manufacturers, online at: http://www.nam.org/Data-and-Reports/Cost-of-Federal-Regulations/Federal-Regulation-Full-Study.pdf

Cumming, D. and Knill, A. (2012), 'Disclosure, venture capital and entrepreneurial spawning', *Journal of International Business Studies*, 43(6): 563–590.

Davydenko, S. and Franks, J. (2008), 'Do bankruptcy codes matter? A study of defaults in France, Germany, and the UK', *Journal of Finance*, 63(2): 565–608.

Department for Business, Energy and Industrial Strategy (2016), *Business Perceptions Survey 2016 Report*, BEIS Research Paper No. 293, online at: https://www.gov.uk/government/publications/business-regulation-perception-survey-2016

Dilli, S. and Elert, N. (2016), *The Diversity of Entrepreneurial Regimes in Europe*, IFN Working Paper No. 1118, online at: http://www.ifn.se/wfiles/wp/wp1118.pdf

Djankov, S., La Porta, R., Lopez-de-Silanes, F. and Shleifer, A. (2002), 'The regulation of entry', *Quarterly Journal of Economics*, 117(2): 1–37.

Djankov, S., McLiesh, C. and Shleifer, A. (2007), 'Private credit in 129 countries', *Journal of Financial Economics*, 84(2): 299–329.

Eberhart, R., Eesley, C., Cheng, J. and Skousen, B. (2015), *Institutions and Types of Entrepreneurship: Interactive Influence of Regulatory and Non-Regulatory Institutions*, online at: https://papers.ssrn.com/sol3/papers.cfm?abstract_id=2608793

Edelman, L. and Suchman, M. (1997), 'The legal environments of organizations', *Annual Review of Sociology*, 23(1): 479–515.

Edwards, P., Ram, M. and Black, J. (2004), 'Why does employment legislation not damage small firms?', *Journal of Law and Society*, 31(2): 245–265.

Estrin, S., Korostoleva, J. and Mickiewicz, T. (2013), 'Which institutions encourage entrepreneurial growth aspirations?', *Journal of Business Venturing*, 28(4): 564–580.

Feintuck, M. (2010), 'Regulatory rationales beyond the economic: in search of the public interest', in R. Baldwin, M. Cave and M. Lodge (eds), *The Oxford Handbook of Regulation*, Oxford, Oxford University Press, pp. 39–63.

Fossen, F. (2014), 'Personal bankruptcy law, wealth, and entrepreneurship – evidence from the introduction of a "fresh start" policy', *American Law and Economics Review*, 16(1): 269–312.

Frontier Economics (2012), *The Impact of Regulation on Growth*, report prepared for the Department of Business Innovation and Skills, online at: https://www.gov.uk/government/publications/the-impact-of-regulation-on-economic-growth

Garicano, L., Lelarge, C. and Van Reenen, J. (2013), 'Firm size distortions and the productivity distribution: evidence from France', *American Economic Review*, 106(11): 3439–3479.

Ghosh, A. and Saha, S. (2007), 'Excess entry in the absence of scale economies', *Economic Theory*, 30(3): 575–586.

Gwartney, J., Lawson, R. and Hall, J. with Murphy, R., Butler, R., Considine, J., Faria, H.,

Fike, R., McMahon, F., Montesunas-Yufa, H., Stansel, D. and Tuszynski, M. (2016), *Economic Freedom of the World 2016 Annual Report*, Fraser Institute, online at: https://www.fraserinstitute.org/studieseconomic-freedom-of-the-world-2016-annual-report

Habermas, J. (1976), *Legitimation Crisis* (trans. T. McCarthy), London, Heinemann.

Haines, F. (2011), *The Paradox of Regulation*, Cheltenham, Edward Elgar.

Hallward-Driemeier, M. and Pritchett, L. (2011), *How Doing Business is Done and the 'Doing Business' Indicators: The Investment Climate When Firms Have Climate Control*, Policy Research Working Paper 5563, online at: https://openknowledge.worldbank.org/bitstream/handle/10986/3330/WPS5563.pdf?sequence=1&isAllowed=y

Hebert, R. and Link, A. (2006), 'Historical perspectives on the entrepreneur', *Foundations and Trends® in Entrepreneurship*, 2(4): 261–408.

Henrekson, M. (2007), 'Entrepreneurship and institutions', *Comparative Labor Law & Policy Journal*, 28(4): 717–742.

Ho, Y-P. and Wong, P-K. (2007), 'Financing, regulatory costs and entrepreneurial propensity', *Small Business Economics*, 28(2–3): 187–204.

Hodgson, G. (2003), 'The enforcement of contracts and property rights: constitutive versus epiphenomenal conceptions of law', *International Review of Sociology*, 13(2): 375–391.

Hodgson, G. (2013), *From Pleasure Machines to Moral Communities: An Evolutionary Economics without Homo Economicus*, London, University of Chicago Press.

Hodgson, G. (2015), *Conceptualizing Capitalism: Institutions, Evolution, Future*, London, University of Chicago Press.

Hutton, W. and Schneider, P. (2008), *The Failure of Market Failure: Towards a 21st Century Keynesianism*, NESTA Provocation No. 8, online at: http://www.nesta.org.uk/sites/default/files/the_failure_of_market_failure.pdf

Johnson, S., McMillan, J. and Woodruff, C. (2002), 'Property rights and finance', *American Economic Review*, 92(5): 1335–1356.

Kapur, K., Karaca-Mandic, P., Gates, S. and Fulton, B. (2012), 'Do small-group health insurance regulations influence small business size?', *Journal of Risk and Insurance*, 79(1): 231–259.

Kirzner, I. (1973), *Competition and Entrepreneurship*, Chicago, IL, University of Chicago Press.

Kitching, J. (2006), 'A burden on business? Reviewing the evidence base on regulation and small business performance', *Environment and Planning C: Government and Policy*, 24(6): 799–814.

Kitching, J. (2007), 'Is less more? Better regulation and the small enterprise', in S. Weatherill (ed.), *Better Regulation*, Oxford, Hart, pp. 155–173.

Kitching, J. (2016a), 'Between vulnerable compliance and confident ignorance: small employers, regulatory discovery practices and external support networks', *International Small Business Journal*, 34(5): 601–617.

Kitching, J. (2016b), 'The ubiquitous influence of regulation on entrepreneurial action: how relations with accountants mediate small company adaptation to financial reporting legislation', *International Journal of Entrepreneurial Behaviour and Research*, 22(2): 215–233.

Kitching, J., Kašperová, E. and Collis, J. (2013), 'The bearable lightness of the administrative burden – UK financial reporting regulation and small company performance', in F. Welter, R. Blackburn, E. Ljunggren and B. Åmo (eds), *Entrepreneurial Business and Society*, Cheltenham, Edward Elgar, pp. 58–78.

Kitching, J., Hart, M. and Wilson, N. (2015a), 'Burden or benefit? Regulation as a dynamic influence on small business performance', *International Small Business Journal*, 33(2): 130–147.

Kitching, J., Kašperová, E. and Collis, J. (2015b), 'The contradictory consequences of regulation: the influence of filing abbreviated accounts on UK small company performance', *International Small Business Journal*, 33(7): 671–688.

Klapper, L., Laeven, L. and Rajan, R. (2006), 'Entry regulation as a barrier to entrepreneurship', *Journal of Financial Economics*, 82(3): 591–629.

Koumenta, M., Humphris, A., Keliener, M. and Pagliero, M. (2014), *Occupational Regulation in the EU and UK: Prevalence and Labour Market Impacts*, online at: https://www.gov.uk/government/uploads/system/uploads/attachment_data/file/343554/bis-14-999-occupational-regulation-in-the-EU-and-UK.pdf

La Porta, R., Lopez-de-Silanes, F. and Shleifer, A. (2006), 'What works in securities laws?', *Journal of Finance*, 61(1): 1–32.

Levie, J. and Autio, E. (2011), 'Regulatory burden, rule of law and entry of strategic entrepreneurs: an international panel study', *Journal of Management Studies*, 48(6): 1392–1419.

Mayer-Schönberger, V. (2010), 'The law as stimulus: the role of law in fostering innovative entrepreneurship', *I/S: A Journal of Law and Policy for the Information Society*, 6(2): 153–188.

Mazzucato, M. (2013), *The Entrepreneurial State: Debunking Public vs. Private Sector Myths*, London, Anthem Press.

McMullen, J., Bagby, R. and Palich, L. (2008), 'Economic freedom and the motivation to engage in entrepreneurial action', *Entrepreneurship Theory and Practice*, 32(5): 875–895.

Minniti, M. (2008), 'The role of government policy on entrepreneurial activity: productive, unproductive, or destructive?', *Entrepreneurship Theory and Practice*, 32(5): 779–790.

North, D. (1990), *Institutions, Institutional Change and Economic Performance*, Cambridge, Cambridge University Press.

North, D. (1991), 'Institutions', *Journal of Economic Perspectives*, 5(1): 97–112.

OECD (Organization for Economic Cooperation and Development) (2015), *Regulatory Policy Outlook 2015*, online at: http://www.oecd.org/gov/oecd-regulatory-policy-outlook-2015-9789264238770-en.htm

Peng, M., Yamakawa, Y. and Lee, S-H. (2010), 'Bankruptcy laws and entrepreneur friendliness', *Entrepreneurship Theory and Practice*, 34(3): 517–530.

Polanyi, K. (1957), *The Great Transformation*. Boston, MA, Beacon Press.

Prantl, S. and Spitz-Oener, A. (2009), 'How does entry regulation influence entry into self-employment and occupational mobility?', *Economics of Transition*, 17(4): 769–802.

Ramoglou, S. (2013), 'Who is a "non-entrepreneur"? Taking the "others" of entrepreneurship seriously', *International Small Business Journal*, 31(4): 432–453.

Rice, T. and Strahan, R. (2010), 'Does credit competition affect small-firm finance?', *Journal of Finance*, 65(3): 861–889.

Sambharya, R. and Musteen, M. (2014), 'Institutional environment and entrepreneurship: an empirical study across countries', *Journal of International Entrepreneurship*, 12(4): 314–330.

Sarasvathy, S. (2008), *Effectuation: Elements of Entrepreneurial Expertise*, Cheltenham, Edward Elgar.

Schoonjans, B., Van Cauwenberge, P., Reekmans, C. and Simoens, G. (2011), 'A survey of tax compliance costs of Flemish SMEs: magnitude and determinants', *Environment and Planning C: Government and Policy*, 29(4): 605–621.

Schumpeter, J. (1934), *The Theory of Economic Development*, New Brunswick, NJ, Transaction Books.

Scott, W. (2014), *Institutions and Organizations: Ideas, Interests and Identities* (4th edn), Sage, London.

Shane, S. (2003), *A General Theory of Entrepreneurship: The Individual-Opportunity Nexus*, Cheltenham, Edward Elgar.

Shane, S. and Venkataraman, S. (2000), 'The promise of entrepreneurship as a field of research', *Academy of Management Review*, 25(1): 217–226.

Shleifer, A. (2005), 'Understanding regulation', *European Financial Management*, 11(4): 439–451.

Smallbone, D. and Welter, F. (2009), *Entrepreneurship and Small Business Development in Post-Socialist Economies*, Abingdon, Routledge.

Sobel, R. (2008), 'Testing Baumol: institutional quality and the productivity of entrepreneurship', *Journal of Business Venturing*, 23(6): 641–655.

Spencer, J. and Gómez, C. (2004), 'The relationship among national institutional structures, economic factors, and domestic entrepreneurial activity: a multicountry study', *Journal of Business Research*, 57(10): 1098–1107.

Spigel, B. (2015), 'The relational organization of entrepreneurial ecosystems', *Entrepreneurship Theory and Practice*, 41(1): 49–72.

Stam, E. (2015), 'Entrepreneurial ecosystems and regional policy: a sympathetic critique', *European Planning Studies*, 23(9): 1759–1769.

Stenholm, P., Acs, Z.J. and Wuebker, R. (2013), 'Exploring country-level institutional arrangements on the rate and type of entrepreneurial activity', *Journal of Business Venturing*, 28(1): 176–193.

Stigler, G. (1971), 'The theory of economic regulation', *Bell Journal of Economics and Management*, 2(1): 3–21.

Stiglitz, J. (2009), 'Government failure vs. market failure: principles of regulation', in E. Balleisen and D. Moss (eds), *Government and Markets: Toward a New Theory of Regulation*, Cambridge, Cambridge University Press, pp. 13–51.

Tabone, N. and Baldacchino, P. (2003), 'The statutory audit of owner-managed companies in Malta', *Managerial Auditing Journal*, 18(5): 387–398.

Tolbert, P., David, R. and Sine, W. (2011), 'Studying choice and change: the intersection of institutional theory and entrepreneurship research', *Organization Science*, 22(5): 1332–1344.

Troilo, M. (2011), 'Legal institutions and high-growth aspiration entrepreneurship', *Economic Systems*, 35(2): 158–175.

Urbano, D. and Alvarez, C. (2014), 'Institutional dimensions and entrepreneurial activity: an international study', *Small Business Economics*, 42(4): 703–716.

Valdez, M. and Richardson, J. (2013), 'Institutional determinants of macro-level entrepreneurship', *Entrepreneurship Theory and Practice*, 37(5): 1149–1175.

van Stel, A., Storey, D. and Thurik, A.R. (2007), 'The effect of business regulations on nascent and young business entrepreneurship', *Small Business Economics*, 28(2–3): 171–186.

Venkataraman, S. (1997), 'The distinctive domain of entrepreneurship research', in J. Katz and R. Brockhaus (eds), *Advances in Entrepreneurship, Firm Emergence and Growth: Volume 3*, Greenwich, CT, JAI Press, pp. 119–138.

Williams, C. and Martinez, A. (2014), 'Entrepreneurship in the informal economy: a product of too much or too little state intervention?', *International Journal of Entrepreneurship and Innovation*, 15(4): 227–237.

World Bank, The (2016), *Doing Business 2017: Equal Opportunity for All*, online at: http://www.doingbusiness.org/reports/global-reports/doing-business-2017

21

Entrepreneurial Ecosystems[1]

Erik Stam and Ben Spigel

INTRODUCTION

In recent years the fields of entrepreneurship studies, economic geography, urban economics, and the economics of entrepreneurship have moved closer to each other through research on the context of entrepreneurship (Ucbasaran, Westhead & Wright, 2001; Welter, 2011; Zahra, Wright & Abdelgawad, 2014; Autio, Kenney, Mustar, Siegel & Wright, 2014), the growing recognition that not all types of entrepreneurship are equally important for economic growth (Henrekson & Sanandaji, 2014; Stam, Suddle, Hessels & Van Stel, 2009; Stam, Hartog, Van Stel & Thurik, 2011; Wong, Ho & Autio, 2005), and the increasing interest in the entrepreneurial actor within urban and regional economics (Acs & Armington, 2004; Feldman, 2001; Glaeser, Rosenthal & Strange, 2010). These developments have culminated in an emerging entrepreneurial ecosystem approach that explicitly focuses on how urban and regional contexts affect ambitious entrepreneurship. In

this chapter we will review and discuss this emergent entrepreneurial ecosystem approach. We define entrepreneurial ecosystems as *a set of interdependent actors and factors coordinated in such a way that they enable productive entrepreneurship within a particular territory*. We see productive entrepreneurship (Baumol, 1990) as an outcome of successful ambitious entrepreneurship. Ambitious entrepreneurs are individuals exploring opportunities to discover and evaluate new goods and services and exploit them in order to add as much value as possible (Stam, Bosma, Van Witteloostuijn, de Jong, Bogaert, Edwards & Jaspers, 2012). That means more than just 'being your own boss' or 'pursuing self-fulfilment' through business ownership; ambitious entrepreneurs attach importance to the performance and success of their ventures and seek to quickly scale up (Stam et al., 2012). In practice, ambitious entrepreneurs are more likely to achieve substantial firm growth, innovation or internationalization than the 'average' entrepreneur.

Though recent interest in entrepreneurial ecosystems amongst academic researchers is driven by its popularity with policymakers and entrepreneurs, it is part of a larger trend in entrepreneurship studies. The fundamental ideas behind entrepreneurial ecosystems were first developed in the 1980s and 1990s as part of a shift in entrepreneurship studies away from individualistic, personality-based research towards a broader perspective that incorporated the role of social, cultural, and economic forces in the entrepreneurship process (Dodd & Anderson, 2007). This was part of a wider movement away from conceptions of the entrepreneur as a solitary Schumpeterian 'economic superman' and towards a more nuanced view of entrepreneurship as a social process embedded in broader contexts (Nijkamp, 2003; Steyaert & Katz, 2004). In particular, the place that entrepreneurship takes within is seen as having a crucial impact over the entire entrepreneurship process, from the ability and willingness of nascent entrepreneurs to start a firm to their ability to find venture capital and eventually structure an exit from the firm. Works by Pennings (1982), Dubini (1989), Van de Ven (1993) and Bahrami and Evans (1995) developed the concept of an 'entrepreneurial environment' or ecosystem in order to explain the influence regional economic and social factors have over the entrepreneurship process. Building on previous movements that decentred the individual entrepreneur as the sole locus of value creation, the new contextual turn emphasizes the importance of situating the entrepreneurial phenomenon in a broader field that incorporates temporal, spatial, social, organizational and market dimensions of context (Zahra, 2007; Zahra et al., 2014). While the past decade has seen entrepreneurship researchers become more sensitive to some contexts such as location, too often context is 'taken for granted, its influence underappreciated or … controlled away' (Welter, 2011, pp. 173–174). That is, previous work in entrepreneurship has tended to attempt to eliminate the role of context in order to produce generalizable models of entrepreneurial activity when instead context should be the specific focus of investigation. A context such as location should not be treated as a simple control variable or proxy; a deeper examination is required of how the cultural, social, political and economic structures and processes associated with a place influence all aspects of the entrepreneurial journey. A context like location is not a *cause* of particular entrepreneurial practices but rather reflects a much more complex influence on entrepreneurship (Johannisson, 2011).

The purpose of this chapter is to critically investigate the emerging literature on entrepreneurial ecosystems. Current work on ecosystems is underdeveloped, focusing more on superficial generalizations based on successful case studies such as Silicon Valley or Boulder, Colorado rather than on rigorous social science research. The next section provides a review of the multiple definitions of ecosystems found within the literature. Next, we discuss the relationships between ecosystems and allied concepts such as industrial districts, clusters and innovation systems. The chapter concludes by discussing an integrative model that connects the functional attributes of entrepreneurial ecosystems with entrepreneurial outputs and welfare outcomes.

THE ENTREPRENEURIAL ECOSYSTEM DEFINED

The concept of entrepreneurial ecosystems has gained popularity in recent years due to mainstream business books such as Feld's (2012) *Startup Communities* and work by Isenberg (2010) in the *Harvard Business Review*. These works have popularized the idea amongst entrepreneurial leaders and policymakers that a place's community and culture can have a significant impact on the entrepreneurship process. But despite its popularity, there is not yet a widely shared definition of entrepreneurial ecosystems amongst researchers or practitioners. The first component of the term is *entrepreneurial*: a process in which opportunities for creating new goods and services are explored, evaluated and exploited (Schumpeter, 1934; Shane & Venkataraman, 2000). The entrepreneurial ecosystem approach often narrows this entrepreneurship down to 'high-growth start-ups' or 'scale-ups', claiming that this type of entrepreneurship is an important source of innovation, productivity growth and employment (World Economic Forum, 2013; Mason & Brown, 2014). Empirically, this claim seems too exclusive: networks of innovative start-ups or entrepreneurial employees can also be forms of productive entrepreneurship (Baumol, 1990) and in that way the source of earlier mentioned welfare outcomes. But it is clear that the entrepreneurial ecosystem approach does not by definition include the traditional statistical indicators of entrepreneurship, such as 'self-employment' or 'small businesses'. This distinction between the traditional measures of entrepreneurship and the conceptually more adequate measures of entrepreneurship such as innovative and growth-oriented entrepreneurship, is increasingly emphasized in the entrepreneurship literature (Shane, 2009; Stam et al., 2012; Mason & Brown, 2013; Henrekson & Sanandaji, 2014).

The second component of the term is *ecosystem*. The biological interpretation of this concept in which the interaction of living organisms with their physical environment is at the centre is obviously not to be taken too literally. Rather, the entrepreneurial ecosystem approach emphasizes that entrepreneurship takes place in a community of interdependent actors (cf. Freeman & Audia, 2006). In particular the literature on entrepreneurial ecosystems focuses on the role of the (social) context in allowing or restricting entrepreneurship and in that sense is closely connected to other recent 'systems of entrepreneurship' or systemic entrepreneurship research approaches (Neck, Meyer, Cohen & Corbett, 2004; Sternberg, 2007; Ylinenpää, 2009; Acs, Autio & Szerb, 2014), which often aim to bridge the innovation system approach

and entrepreneurship studies. Unlike previous uses of the term 'ecosystem' in the management literature such as by Moore (1993) and Iansiti and Levien (2004) that focus on the organization of a single industry or value chain, entrepreneurial ecosystems are an inherently geographic perspective. That is to say, entrepreneurial ecosystems focus on the cultures, institutions and networks that build up within a region over time rather than the emergence of order within global markets.

Entrepreneurial activity, as an *output* of the entrepreneurial ecosystem, is considered the process by which individuals create opportunities for innovation. This innovation will eventually lead to new value in society and this is therefore the ultimate *outcome* of an entrepreneurial ecosystem while entrepreneurial activity is a more intermediary *output* of the system. This entrepreneurial activity has many manifestations, such as innovative start-ups, high-growth start-ups and entrepreneurial employees (Stam, 2014). Especially entrepreneurial employees seem to be of great importance for new value creation in developed economies like Europe (Bosma, Wennekers & Amorós, 2012; Stam, 2013; Bosma, Stam & Wennekers, 2014). The term 'productive entrepreneurship' refers to 'any entrepreneurial activity that contributes directly or indirectly to net output of the economy or to the capacity to produce additional output' (Baumol, 1993, p. 30); this we interpret as entrepreneurial activity that creates aggregate welfare increases. Productive entrepreneurship might also include failed enterprises that have provided a fertile breeding ground for subsequent ventures or inspired them, creating net social value ('catalyst ventures': Davidsson, 2005). Technically speaking this means that the total (social) value created by entrepreneurial activity should be more than the sum of the (private) value created for the individual entrepreneurs (leaving distributional issues aside).

While work on entrepreneurial ecosystems is still in its infancy there are already several empirical studies showing how a rich entrepreneurial ecosystem enables entrepreneurship and subsequent value creation at the regional level (Fritsch, 2013; Tsvetkova, 2015). For example, Mack and Mayer (2016) explore how early entrepreneurial successes in Phoenix, Arizona have contributed to a persistently strong entrepreneurial ecosystem based on visible success stories, a strong entrepreneurial culture and supportive public policies. Similarly, Spigel's (2017) study of entrepreneurial ecosystems in Waterloo and Calgary, Canada suggests that while ecosystems can have different structures and origins, their success lies in their ability to create a cohesive social and economic system that supports the creation and growth of new ventures. Other work on regions such as Silicon Valley (Saxenian, 1994; Patton & Kenney, 2005), Washington DC (Feldman, 2001) and Kyoto (Aoyama, 2009) – even if not using the precise term 'entrepreneurial ecosystem' – described how interlocking historically produced, place-based elements created the conditions for long-term entrepreneurial success. Works such as Acs et al. (2014) have employed large-scale quantitative methods, rather than qualitative case studies, to identify strong entrepreneurial ecosystems.

PREDECESSORS TO THE ENTREPRENEURIAL ECOSYSTEM APPROACH

What the entrepreneurial ecosystem approach has in common with other established concepts – such as industrial districts, clusters, and innovation systems – is the focus on the external business environment: that there are forces beyond the boundaries of an organization but within those of a region that can contribute to a firm's overall competitiveness (see Table 21.1). The industrial district approach emphasizes the local division of labour of an industry (Marshall, 1920 [1890]) and the interaction between the community of people and a population of firms within a socio-territorial entity (Becattini, 1990) in order to

be successful on international markets. The cluster approach focuses on 'geographic concentrations of interconnected companies, specialised suppliers, service providers, firms in related industries, and associated institutions … in particular fields that compete but also co-operate' (Porter, 1998, p. 197). Regional innovation systems (RIS) refer to the networks and institutions linking knowledge-producing hubs such as universities and public research labs within a region and innovative firms. These linkages allow knowledge to spill over between different organizations, increasing a region's overall innovativeness (Cooke, Gomez Uranga & Etxebarria, 1997).

The entrepreneurial ecosystem approach differs from industrial district, cluster and innovation system approaches by the fact that the entrepreneur, rather than the firm, is the focal point of analysis (Spigel & Harrison, forthcoming). The entrepreneurial ecosystem approach thus begins with the entrepreneurial individual instead of the company but also emphasizes the role of the social and economic context surrounding the entrepreneurial process. Most cluster studies focus on firms and industries, including their dynamics (Frenken, Cefis & Stam, 2015). As opposed to the clusters, district and innovation systems literature, the focus of ecosystems research is placed firmly on the entrepreneur and the start-up rather than larger, more established firms or slower-growing SMEs. The high-growth start-ups that make up the basis of entrepreneurial ecosystems are not necessarily included in all cluster and industrial district models (Markusen, 1996). While frameworks of industrial districts, clusters and innovation systems do include a role for entrepreneurs (e.g. Henry & Pinch, 2000; Cooke, 2001; Ylinenpää, 2009), the focus is not specifically on them but rather on the role of entrepreneurs and start-ups within larger systems of value creation and innovation. As a result, these existing approaches often see start-ups as smaller versions of larger, international firms rather than as unique organizational entities with different (and often more constrained) capabilities and resources.

Table 21.1 Comparison of industrial district, cluster and innovation system literature

	Key actors	Key concepts	Input into entrepreneurial ecosystem approach	Key outcome	Key references	Key references entrepreneurship
Marshallian industrial district	SMEs	Labour market pooling; specialized goods and services; knowledge spillovers; market competition	Talent (labour market pooling), intermediate services (specialized goods and services), knowledge (spillovers)	Regional economic growth (productivity)	Marshall, 1920 [1890]; Krugman, 1991; Markusen, 1996	—
Italianate industrial district	SMEs; local government	Flexible specialization, interfirm cooperation, trust (social embeddedness)	Networks between entrepreneurs and enterprises	Regional economic growth (employment)	Piore & Sabel, 1984; Becattini, 1990; Harrison, 1992	Johannisson et al., 1994; Malecki, 1997; Lazerson & Lorenzoni, 1999
Cluster	Innovative firms	Factor conditions; demand conditions; related and supporting industries; firm structure, strategy and rivalry	Talent, finance, knowledge, physical infrastructure (factor conditions); demand (demand); support services/ intermediaries (related and supporting industries); etc.	National/regional competitiveness (productivity of particular industries)	Porter, 1990; Porter, 1998	Rocha, 2004; Rocha & Sternberg, 2005; Delgado et al., 2010
Innovation system	Innovative firms; national government	Networks, inter-organizational learning system	Knowledge, finance, formal institutions, demand	Innovation	Freeman, 1987; Lundvall, 1992; Braczyk et al., 1998	Sternberg, 2007; Ylinenpää, 2009

Beyond this, the role of knowledge differs between ecosystems and allied concepts like clusters and innovation systems. Within traditional models knowledge refers to the technical know-how necessary to develop new products and technologies and the market knowledge necessary to know which new products will succeed in the marketplace (see Cooke, 2001). This knowledge is key in ecosystems, but ecosystems approaches also highlight a new type of knowledge: knowledge about the entrepreneurship process itself. This includes knowledge about the challenges facing entrepreneurs as they scale, how to design business plans and pitch ideas to angel investors and venture capitalists, and how to overcome the liability of newness when working with potential clients and suppliers. Thus, the mentoring and networking between entrepreneurs are critical to sharing entrepreneurial knowledge within an ecosystem (Lafuente, Yancy & Rialp, 2007).

Table 21.2   Differences and similarities between entrepreneurial ecosystems and related concepts

Approach	Industrial district, cluster, innovation systems	Entrepreneurial ecosystem
Main focus	Main focus is on economic and social structures of a place that influence overall innovation and firm competitiveness. In many cases, little distinction made between (fast-growing) start-ups and other types of organizations.	Start-ups explicitly at centre of ecosystem. Seen as distinct from established large firms and (lower-growth) SMEs in terms of conceptual development and policy formation.
Role of knowledge	Focus on knowledge as source of new technological and market insights. Knowledge from multiple sources is recombined to increase firm competitiveness. Knowledge spillovers from universities and other large research intensive organizations are crucial.	In addition to market and technical knowledge, entrepreneurial knowledge is crucial. Knowledge about the entrepreneurship process is shared between entrepreneurs and mentors through informal social networks, entrepreneurship organizations and training courses offered.
Locus of action	Private firms and state form primary locus of action in building and maintaining industrial district/cluster/innovation system. Little room for individual agency in their creation.	Entrepreneur is the core actor in building and sustaining the ecosystem. While state and other sources might support ecosystem through public investment, entrepreneurs retain agency to develop and lead the ecosystem.

Another significant contrast with other concepts is that the entrepreneurial ecosystem approach not only sees entrepreneurship as a result of the system, but also sees the importance of entrepreneurs as central players (leaders) in the creation of the system and in keeping the system healthy (Feldman, 2014). This 'privatization' of entrepreneurship policy diminishes the role of the state compared with previous policy approaches. However, this does not remove its role but rather shifts it to that of a 'feeder' of the ecosystem than as a 'leader' (Feld, 2012). Entrepreneurs with a long-term commitment to the ecosystem are often best positioned to recognize the opportunities and restrictions of the ecosystem and to deal with them together with other 'feeders' of the ecosystem (such as professional service providers and the financial infrastructure). These successful businesspeople and philanthropists can act as 'dealmakers', using their own social networks and capital to improve the entrepreneurial environment of their home region (Feldman & Zoller, 2012). However, the government retains an important role as a

'feeder' who acts to create a conducive economic and social environment for entrepreneurship, for example in adjusting laws and regulations or providing training and educational opportunities. Market failures and system failures are not necessarily rationales for government intervention: even here, entrepreneurs can find opportunities, for example by reducing information asymmetry and organizing collective action to create public goods.

As illustrated in Table 21.2, there are significant differences between entrepreneurial ecosystems and allied concepts such as industrial districts, clusters and innovation systems. See Acs, Stam, Audretsch & O'Connor (2017) for a similar comparison, also including the strategy literature on innovation and business ecosystems. This does not mean that work on ecosystems cannot draw on the decades of research underlying these concepts, but that the findings from this work must be reinterpreted through the agent-centred approach that is at the heart of the entrepreneurial ecosystem approach.

ATTRIBUTES OF SUCCESSFUL ENTREPRENEURIAL ECOSYSTEMS

The recent popular literature on entrepreneurial ecosystems is directly aimed at the key stakeholders of the ecosystem, mainly entrepreneurial leaders and policymakers rather than an academic audience. The recent entrepreneurial ecosystem literature provides several lists of factors which are deemed to be important for the success of an entrepreneurial ecosystem. Naturally, entrepreneurs (being visible and connected) are considered to be the heart of a successful ecosystem, but successful entrepreneurial ecosystems have multiple attributes (Feld, 2012, pp. 186–7). Next to the key role of entrepreneurs themselves (in leading the development of the ecosystem and as mentors or advisors), the nine attributes by Feld (2012) emphasize the interaction between the players in the ecosystem (with high network density, many connecting events, and large companies collaborating with local start-ups) and access to all kinds of relevant resources (talent, services, capital), with an enabling role of government in the background.

An important input is a broad, deep talent pool of employees in all sectors and areas of expertise. This includes both technical workers as well as more business-oriented workers such as salespeople, marketers and business development professionals. Universities are an excellent resource for start-up talent and should be well connected to the community. Next to human capital, financial capital is key: a strong, dense and supportive community of Venture Capitalists, business angels, seed investors and other forms of financing should be available, visible, and accessible across sectors, demographics and geography. A successful ecosystem necessitates leadership, consisting of a strong group of entrepreneurs who are visible, accessible and committed to the region being a great place to start and grow a company. It also requires many well-respected mentors and advisors giving back across all stages, sectors, demographics and

geographies as well as a solid presence of effective and well-integrated accelerators and incubators (i.e. intermediaries). In addition, it requires professional services (legal, accounting, real estate, insurance, consulting) that specialize in the unique needs of start-ups and scale-ups and are appropriately priced (such as offering equity-for-service arrangements). For an ecosystem to be successful, large established organizations should also be supportive. This includes large anchor firms, which should create specific departments and programmes to encourage cooperation with high-growth start-ups, and it also includes strong government support for and understanding of start-ups to economic growth. Additionally, supportive policies should be in place covering economic development, tax and investment vehicles. Another prerequisite is a large number of events for entrepreneurs and community to connect and engage, with highly visible and authentic participants (e.g. meet-ups, pitch days, start-up weekends, boot camps, hackatons and competitions). Finally, a thriving ecosystem is said to depend on a deep, well-connected community of start-ups and entrepreneurs along with engaged and visible investors, advisors, mentors and supporters (indicated by high network density). Optimally, these people and organizations cut across sectors and demographics. Everyone must be willing to give back to their community.

Isenberg (2010) also discusses the concept of the entrepreneurial ecosystem. He notes that there is no exact formula for the creation of such an ecosystem but that (public) leaders should follow nine principles when building an entrepreneurial ecosystem. These principles first emphasize the role of local conditions and bottom-up processes: (1) stop emulating Silicon Valley; (2) shape the ecosystem around local conditions; (3) engage the private sector from the start; (4) stress the roots of new ventures; (5) don't over-engineer clusters; help them grow organically. Second, they emphasize ambitious entrepreneurship: (6) favour the high potentials; (7) get a big win on the board. And third, they should focus on institutions: (8) tackle cultural change head-on; (9) reform legal, bureaucratic and regulatory frameworks). These principles are claimed to lead to 'venture creation', the 'creation of an ecosystem' and a 'vibrant business sector' (Isenberg, 2010). It is unclear how the causal mechanisms work to realize these different results. Even though this might be a practitioner's point of view, the emphasis on the role of local conditions and bottom-up processes is largely in line with recent academic work on regional innovation and growth (cf. Boschma & Martin, 2010; Cooke, Asheim, Boschma, Martin, Schwartz & Tödtling, 2011), while the focus on ambitious entrepreneurship and institutions is also a key feature of recent entrepreneurship research (Henrekson & Johansson, 2009; Stam et al., 2012; Acs et al., 2014).

Based on this, Isenberg (2011) formulates six distinct domains of the ecosystem: policy, finance, culture, support, human capital and markets. This largely overlaps with the previously mentioned nine attributes and the eight pillars distinguished by the World Economic Forum (2013, pp. 6–7) for a successful ecosystem, each with a number of components. These pillars also focus on the presence of key factors (resources) like human capital, finance and services; the actors involved in this (talent, investors, mentors/advisors, entrepreneurial peers); the formal ('government and regulatory framework') and informal institutions ('cultural support') enabling entrepreneurship; and finally, access to customers in domestic and foreign markets.

The listed attributes, principles and pillars show that the entrepreneurial ecosystem approach contains a shift of traditional economic thinking about businesses, and especially on markets and market failure, to a new economic view on people, networks and institutions. The common denominator appears to be the fact that entrepreneurs create new value, organized by a wide variety of governance modes, enabled and confined within a specific institutional context. This does not mean that companies and markets (and market failure) are irrelevant. But markets and companies are governance modes which, like all other forms of governance, will always be imperfect. Moreover, entrepreneurship is often about companies and markets 'in the making', and not about situations that come close to a 'fully efficient market equilibrium', as in the ideal of the market failure approach.

Drawing on these studies, Spigel (2017, p. 50) defines entrepreneurial ecosystems as 'combinations of social, political, economic, and cultural elements within a region that support the development and growth of innovative startups and encourage nascent entrepreneurs and other actors to take the risks of starting, funding, and otherwise assisting high-risk ventures'. He groups these attributes into three categories – cultural, social, and material – that explain the level of entrepreneurial activity as the output of entrepreneurial ecosystems: cultural attributes (supportive culture and histories of entrepreneurship), social attributes (worker talent, investment capital, networks, mentors and role models), and material attributes (policy and governance, universities, support services, physical infrastructure, open markets). Importantly, these categories of attributes are not isolated from one another but are created and reproduced through their interrelationships. For example, networking programmes sponsored by a regional government (a material attribute) depends on the pre-existence of existing knowledge-sharing networks within the region to build on (a social attribute), which in turn requires the effort of business networking and knowledge sharing to be legitimized within the local culture (a cultural attribute). But while the operation of the programme depends on these social and cultural attributes, it also strengthens and reproduces them by helping to create successful new ventures who see networking with other entrepreneurs as a normal business activity. This relationship is illustrated in Figure 21.1.

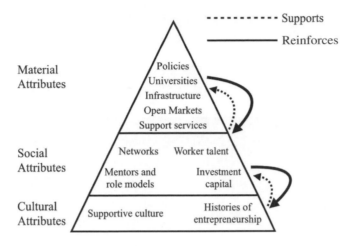

Figure 21.1   Relationships between attributes within entrepreneurial ecosystems (Spigel, 2017)

SHORTCOMINGS OF THE ENTREPRENEURIAL ECOSYSTEM APPROACH

The mere popularity of the entrepreneurial ecosystem approach is no guarantee of its profundity. Seductive though the entrepreneurial ecosystem concept is, there is much about it that is problematic and the rush to employ the entrepreneurial ecosystem approach has run ahead of answering many fundamental conceptual, theoretical and empirical questions. The phenomenon at first appears rather tautological: entrepreneurial ecosystems are systems that produce successful entrepreneurship, and where there is a lot of successful entrepreneurship there is apparently a good entrepreneurial ecosystem. Such tautological reasoning ultimately offers little insight for research or public policy. Second, the approach as yet provides only long laundry lists of relevant factors without a clear reasoning of cause and effect nor how they are tied to specific place-based histories. These factors do provide some focus but they offer no consistent explanation of their coherence or their interdependent effects on entrepreneurship – and, ultimately, on aggregate welfare. And third, it is not clear which level of analysis this approach is targeting.

Geographically, it could be a city, a region or a country. It can also be other systems less strictly defined in space, such as sectors or corporations, which create opportunities for firm creation and growth.

Such approaches do not offer sufficient explanations for economic outcomes and have not been clearly demarcated. Nor do they provide useful insights into the fundamental causes of the entrepreneurial ecosystems. The World Economic Forum (2013) study, for example, concludes that access to markets, human capital and finance are most important for the growth of entrepreneurial companies. But these can best be seen as superficial perquisites, not as the fundamental causes for the success of ecosystems – for human resources and finance are, after all, largely dependent on the underlying institutions regarding education and financial markets (Acemoglu, Johnson & Robinson, 2005). For an adequate explanation we must distinguish between the necessary and contingent conditions of an ecosystem and clearly define the role of the government and other public organizations. This has not yet been accomplished. The question remains: how do entrepreneurial ecosystems perform with the different forms of entrepreneurship (as output) and in terms

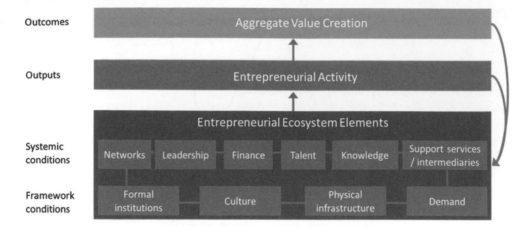

Figure 21.2   Key elements, outputs and outcomes of the entrepreneurial ecosystem (based on Stam, 2015)

of aggregate welfare effects (as final outcome)? After more elaboration, the tautology will probably disappear. Constructive synthesis of, on the one hand, the previously mentioned elements of the entrepreneurial ecosystem approach and, on the other hand, the insights from the existing empirical studies on entrepreneurship and (regional) economic development (Stam & Bosma, 2015a; Fritsch, 2013) could provide a better framework for policy.

The question of the level at which entrepreneurial ecosystems operate has not been answered yet. This would depend on the spatial scale on which the elements are achieved, on the one hand, and how they are limited, on the other hand. For most system elements it seems possible to demarcate them at a regional (sub-national) level (e.g. regional labour markets), while the conditions can be designed on both regional and national level (e.g. national laws and regulations) (cf. Stam & Bosma, 2015b). In addition, entrepreneurs of high-growth firms and especially entrepreneurial employees in large established firms could act as ecosystem connectors on a global scale, connecting distinct regional entrepreneurial ecosystems in their role as knowledge integrators (Sternberg, 2007; Malecki, 2011).

AN ENTREPRENEURIAL ECOSYSTEM MODEL

In response to these critiques we have developed a new entrepreneurial ecosystem model, as shown in Figure 21.2. The new model includes insights from the previous literature (i.e. the aspects that have been deemed important elements of entrepreneurial ecosystems), but most importantly it provides more causal depth with four ontological layers (framework conditions, systemic conditions, outputs and outcomes), including the upward and downward causation, and intra-layer causal relations. Upward causation reveals how the fundamental causes of new value creation are mediated by intermediate causes, while downward causation shows how outcomes and outputs of the system over time also feed back into the system conditions. Intra-layer causal relations refer to the interaction of the different elements within the ecosystem, and how the different outputs and outcomes of the ecosystem might interact.

The elements of the entrepreneurial ecosystem that can be distinguished are framework conditions and systemic conditions. Both are summarized in Figure 21.2. The framework conditions include the social (informal and formal institutions) and physical conditions enabling or constraining human interaction. In addition, access to a more or less exogenous demand for new goods and services is also of great importance. This access to buyers of goods and services, however, is likely to be more related to the relative position of the ecosystem than its internal conditions (in contrast to, for example, the important role of 'home demand' in Porter's (1990) cluster approach). These conditions might be regarded as the fundamental causes of value creation in the entrepreneurial ecosystem. However, in order to fully understand how these fundamental causes lead to this outcome, we first need to gain insight into how systemic conditions lead to entrepreneurial activity.

Systemic conditions are the heart of the ecosystem: networks of entrepreneurs, leadership, finance, talent, knowledge and support services. The presence of these elements and the interaction between them are crucial for the success of the ecosystem. Networks of entrepreneurs provide an information flow, enabling an effective distribution of knowledge, labour and capital. Leadership provides direction and role models for the entrepreneurial ecosystem. This leadership is critical in building and maintaining a healthy ecosystem. This involves a set of 'visible' entrepreneurial leaders who are committed to the region. Access to financing – preferably provided by investors with entrepreneurial knowledge – is crucial for investments in uncertain entrepreneurial projects with a long-term horizon (see e.g. Kerr & Nanda, 2009). But perhaps the most important element of an effective entrepreneurial ecosystem is the presence of a diverse and skilled group of workers ('talent': see e.g. Acs & Armington, 2004; Lee, Florida & Acs, 2004; Qian, Acs & Stough, 2013). An important source of opportunities for entrepreneurship can be found in knowledge, from both public and private organizations (see e.g. Audretsch & Lehmann, 2005). Finally, the supply of support services by a variety of intermediaries can substantially lower entry barriers for new entrepreneurial projects, and reduce the time to market of innovations (see e.g. Zhang & Li, 2010).

CONCLUSIONS AND POLICY IMPLICATIONS

The concept of entrepreneurial ecosystems is very attracting to regional policymakers and leaders. The idea that a certain mixture of public policy options, social attitudes and financing can catalyse long-lasting entrepreneurial and innovation activity is a seductive promise to leaders looking to create a foundation for more sustainable growth. Authors like Feld (2012) are quick to point out that examples like Silicon Valley are not replicable. The growth of places like Silicon Valley is tied directly into particular events (e.g. the founding of Stanford University with an explicitly industrial orientation), historical trends (the US government shifting defence research away from the east coast in the 1930s and 1940s, the emergence of the venture capital industry in the 1950s and 1960s), and the existence of a long-lasting culture that encourages risk-taking, rebellion and innovation throughout the place (Saxenian, 1994; Lécuyer, 2006; Kenney, 2011). Taking one aspect of this complex ecosystem, such as an effective university technology transfer office, will not replicate the other factors, actors and institutions that make it up.

However, other cases of successful ecosystems offer more reasonable approaches for policymakers. Spigel's (2017) discussion of Waterloo, Ontario is an instructive example of how a mid-sized city can develop a strong and supportive entrepreneurial ecosystem. The city was historically an industrial economy, but the establishment of the University of Waterloo in the 1950s helped move the region towards a more advanced, knowledge-based economy. Crucially, the university has had an applied, industry-focused research orientation from its founding. As the university emerged as a world leading centre for computer science and electrical engineering research, entrepreneurial faculty and students were attracted to the university and the region. This pool of highly skilled workers was instrumental to the creation and growth of Research in Motion, maker of the Blackberry smartphone, as well as numerous other smaller high-tech start-ups. While the region has a highly effective entrepreneurship support organization, its role is secondary to the strong networks of entrepreneurs, mentors and financers. These networks help new entrepreneurs learn the formal and informal skills associated with being a high-tech entrepreneur and help knowledge about new markets, technologies and opportunities to flow through the region. This helps to reproduce and strengthen the region's overall cultural orientation towards entrepreneurship, ensuring that it survives the recent decline of local anchor firms like Research in Motion. This effective ecosystem was not created overnight nor through a purposeful effort by the state or an individual. Rather, numerous actors and factors have contributed to creating an ecosystem that supports innovative, high-growth entrepreneurship which in turn has helped the region avoid the decline and population loss that commonly afflicts old industrial regions in the new knowledge-based economy.

The entrepreneurial ecosystem approach intuitively evokes recognition and acknowledgement among public and private stakeholders of regional economies. A critical review reveals that many insights of decades of research into entrepreneurship and regional development in the past can be used as input to the new approach. It might even be said that the entrepreneurial ecosystem approach contains no new separate insights. However, the entrepreneurial ecosystem approach provides a framework for integration of insights from the academic literature on regional entrepreneurship and the approach includes several valuable novel contributions to our understanding of the entrepreneurship process and its impact on regional economic development. First, the system approach builds up from the level of the entrepreneur in order to better understand the context of the entrepreneurship. Such a system approach also centres on the weakest link that mostly limits the performance of the entrepreneurial ecosystem (Acs et al., 2014). A second novel contribution is the prominent place given to the entrepreneurs themselves to build the entrepreneurial ecosystem and keep it

healthy, fed by the other stakeholders relevant to the ecosystem. Although causal relations within the system and the effects on entrepreneurship and value creation have not yet been studied sufficiently, the entrepreneurial ecosystem approach offers valuable elements for an improved understanding of the performance of regional economies. The approach emphasizes interdependencies within the entrepreneurship context, and it provides a bottom-up analysis of the performance of regional economies, without fixating on individual entrepreneurs.

The approach also feeds the shift in entrepreneurship policy from a focus on the quantity to a focus on the quality of entrepreneurship. In line with Thurik, Stam and Audretsch (2013), the next shift would be from 'entrepreneurship policy' to policy for an 'entrepreneurial economy', i.e. an entrepreneurial ecosystem. So policy will not be about maximizing a certain indicator of entrepreneurship, but about creating a context, a system, in which productive entrepreneurship can flourish. This shift also necessitates a shift in thinking about the rationales for policy. The economic policy perspective has been reduced to examining the extent to which markets function optimally, in order to reach the maximum (allocative) efficiency. Or, in policy language, is this a case of market failure? The textbook rationales for government intervention are externalities, abuse of market power, public goods and asymmetric information. Markets are an important mode of governance in economic systems. In the context of innovation and entrepreneurship, the failure of that mode of governance may also be a reason for government intervention (see e.g. Jacobs & Theeuwes, 2005). Public policy based on insights of the industrial district and cluster approaches also uses the market failure rationale for public policy interventions, such as externalities arising from knowledge spillovers or coordination failures due to information asymmetries. This mode of governance, however, also has substantial constraints for innovation and entrepreneurship policies (Nooteboom & Stam, 2008). Market failure plays a role, but not everything in the innovation system can be reduced to market contexts:

the non-market interaction is seen not only as market failure, but often as a necessity for the realization of innovations (Teece, 1992). For innovation and knowledge sharing in general, especially non-codified knowledge, informal interaction is of great importance. Cooperation makes it possible to exchange much more knowledge than can be specified contractually. This was the reason to create a wider framework for this type of policy: the innovation system approach. The focus of this approach is the so-called system failure: the lack of sufficient elements in the innovation system (e.g. certain types of financing or knowledge) or a non-optimal interaction between these elements (e.g. between companies and knowledge institutes). An innovation system works well if there is a sufficient variety of organizations that fulfil the required functions in such an innovation system, and as a result create an optimal interaction between these elements (Nooteboom & Stam, 2008). The innovation system approach not only examines at markets, but also, and especially, organizations and their interaction, and not only through market transactions, but also otherwise. However, in the innovation system approach, the role of entrepreneurs remains a black box, as does the market failure approach, for that matter. This makes the entrepreneurial ecosystem approach more desirable, as it appears to be able to solve the shortcomings of the market failure approach and the system failure approach, and seems better applicable to policies for an entrepreneurial economy.

Note

1   This chapter is partly based on Stam (2015).

REFERENCES

Acemoglu, D., Johnson, S. & Robinson, J.A. (2005), Institutions as a Fundamental Cause of Long-Run Growth. In Aghion, P. & Durlauf, S. (eds), *Handbook of Economic Growth*. Amsterdam: Elsevier.

Acs, Z.J. & Armington, C. (2004), The impact of geographic differences in human capital on service firm formation rates. *Journal of Urban Economics* 56(2): 244–278.

Acs, Z.J., Autio, E. & Szerb, L. (2014), National systems of entrepreneurship: measurement issues and policy implications. *Research Policy* 43(3): 476–449.

Acs, Z.J., Stam, E., Audretsch, D.B. & O'Connor, A. (2017), The lineages of the entrepreneurial ecosystem approach. *Small Business Economics* 49(1): 1–10.

Aoyama, Y. (2009), Entrepreneurship and regional culture: the case of Hamamtsu and Kyoto, Japan. *Regional Studies* 43(3): 495–512.

Audretsch, D.B. & Lehmann, E.E. (2005), Does the knowledge spillover theory of entrepreneurship hold for regions? *Research Policy* 34(8): 1191–1202.

Autio, E., Kenney, M., Mustar, P., Siegel, D. & Wright, M. (2014), Entrepreneurial innovation: the importance of context. *Research Policy* 43(7): 1097–1108.

Bahrami, H. & Evans, S. (1995), Flexible re-cycling and high-technology entrepreneurship. *California Management Review* 37: 62–89.

Baumol, W.J. (1990), Entrepreneurship: productive, unproductive, and destructive. *Journal of Political Economy* 98(5): 893–921.

Baumol, W.J. (1993), *Entrepreneurship, Management and the Structure of Payoffs*. MIT Press: London.

Becattini, G. (1990), The Marshallian Industrial District as a Socio-Economic Notion. In Pyke, F., Becattini, G. & Sengenberger, W. (eds), *Industrial Districts and Inter-Firm Co-Operation in Italy*. International Institute for Labour Studies: Geneva.

Boschma, R. & Martin, R. (2010), *The Handbook of Evolutionary Economic Geography*. Cheltenham: Edward Elgar.

Bosma, N., Stam, E. & Wennekers, S. (2014), Intrapreneurship Versus Entrepreneurship in High and Low Income Countries. In Blackburn, R., Delmar, F., Fayolle, A. & Welter, F. (eds), *Entrepreneurship, People and Organisations. Frontiers in European Entrepreneurship Research*. Cheltenham: Edward Elgar. pp. 94–115.

Bosma, N., Wennekers, S. & Amorós, J.E. (2012), *Global Entrepreneurship Monitor 2011 Extended Report: Entrepreneurs and Entrepreneurial Employees Across the Globe*. Babson College, Babson Park, MA, United States: Global Entrepreneurship Research Association.

Braczyk, H.J., Cooke, P.N. & Heidenreich, M. (1998), *Regional Innovation Systems: The Role of Governances in a Globalized World*. London: Routledge.

Cooke, P. (2001), Regional innovation systems, clusters, and the knowledge economy. *Industrial and Corporate Change* 10: 945–974.

Cooke, P., Asheim, B., Boschma, R., Martin, R., Schwartz, D. & Tödtling, F. (2011), *Handbook of Regional Innovation and Growth*. Cheltenham: Edward Elgar.

Cooke, P., Gomez Uranga, M. & Etxebarria, G. (1997), Regional innovation systems: institutional and organizational dimensions. *Research Policy* 26: 475–491.

Davidsson, P. (2005), *Researching Entrepreneurship*. New York: Springer-Verlag.

Delgado, M., Porter, M.E. & Stern, S. (2010), Clusters and entrepreneurship. *Journal of Economic Geography* 10(4): 495–518.

Dodd, S.D. & Anderson, A.R. (2007), Mumpsimus and the mything of the individualistic entrepreneur. *International Small Business Journal* 25: 341–360.

Dubini, P. (1989), The influence of motivations and environment on business start-ups: some hints for public policies. *Journal of Business Venturing* 4(1): 11–26.

Feld, B. (2012), *Startup Communities: Building an Entrepreneurial Ecosystem in Your City*. New York: Wiley.

Feldman, M.P. (2001), The entrepreneurial event revisited: firm formation in a regional context. *Industrial and Corporate Change* 10(4): 861–891.

Feldman, M.P. (2014), The character of innovative places: entrepreneurial strategy, economic development, and prosperity. *Small Business Economics* 43: 9–20.

Feldman, M. & Zoller, T.D. (2012), Dealmakers in place: social capital connections in regional entrepreneurial economies. *Regional Studies* 46(1): 23–37.

Freeman, C. (1987), *Technology and Economic Performance: Lessons from Japan*. London: Pinter.

Freeman, J.H. & Audia, P.G. (2006), Community ecology and the sociology of organizations. *Annual Review of Sociology* 32: 145–169.

Frenken, K., Cefis, E. & Stam, E. (2015), Industrial dynamics and clusters: a survey. *Regional Studies* 49(1): 10–27.

Fritsch, M. (2013), New business formation and regional development – a survey and assessment of the evidence. *Foundations and Trends in Entrepreneurship* 9: 249–364.

Glaeser, E.L., Rosenthal, S.S. & Strange, W.C. (2010), Urban economics and entrepreneurship. *Journal of Urban Economics* 67(1): 1–14.

Harrison, B. (1992), Industrial districts: old wine in new bottles? *Regional Studies* 26(5): 469–483.

Henrekson, M. & Johansson, D. (2009), Competencies and institutions fostering high-growth firms. *Foundations and Trends in Entrepreneurship* 5(1): 1–80.

Henrekson, M. & Sanandaji, T. (2014), Small business activity does not measure entrepreneurship. *Proceedings of the National Academy of Sciences* 111(5): 1760–1765.

Henry, N. & Pinch, S. (2000), Spatialising knowledge: placing the knowledge community of Motor Sport Valley. *Geoforum* 31(2): 191–208.

Iansiti, M. & Levien, R. (2004), *The Keystone Advantage: What the New Dynamics of Business Ecosystems Mean for Strategy, Innovation, and Sustainability*. Boston, MA: Harvard Business School Press.

Isenberg, D.J. (2010), How to start an entrepreneurial revolution. *Harvard Business Review* 88(6): 41–50.

Isenberg, D.J. (2011), Introducing the Entrepreneurship Ecosystem: Four Defining Characteristics. http://www.forbes.com/sites/danisenberg/2011/05/25/introducing-the-entrepreneurship-ecosystem-four-defining-characteristics/

Jacobs, B. & Theeuwes, J. (2005), Innovation in the Netherlands: the market falters and the government fails. *De Economist* 153(1): 107–124.

Johannisson, B. (2011) Towards a practice theory of entrepreneuring. *Small Business Economics* 36: 135–150.

Johannisson, B., Alexanderson, O., Nowicki, K. & Senneseth, K. (1994), Beyond anarchy and organization: entrepreneurs in contextual networks. *Entrepreneurship & Regional Development* 6(4): 329–356.

Kenney, M. (2011), How venture capital became a component of the US national system of innovation. *Industrial and Corporate Change* 20(6): 1677–1723.

Kerr, W.R. & Nanda, R. (2009), Democratizing entry: banking deregulations, financing constraints, and entrepreneurship. *Journal of Financial Economics* 94(1): 124–149.

Krugman, P. (1991), *Geography and Trade*. Cambridge, MA: MIT Press.

Lafuente, E., Yancy, V. & Rialp, J. (2007), Regional differences in the influence of role models: comparing the entrepreneurial process of rural Catalonia. *Regional Studies*, 41(6): 779–795.

Lazerson, M.H. & Lorenzoni, G. (1999), The firms that feed industrial districts: a return to the Italian source. *Industrial and Corporate Change* 8(2): 235–266.

Lécuyer, C. (2006), *Making Silicon Valley: Innovation and the Growth of High Tech, 1930–1970*. Cambridge, MA: MIT Press.

Lee, S.Y., Florida, R. & Acs Z.J. (2004), Creativity and entrepreneurship: a regional analysis of new firm formation. *Regional Studies* 38(8): 879–891.

Lundvall, B. (1992), *National Systems of Innovation. Towards a Theory of Innovation and Interactive Learning*. London: Anthem Press.

Mack, E. & Mayer, H. (2016), The evolutionary dynamics of entrepreneurial ecosystems. *Urban Studies* 53(10): 2118–2133.

Malecki, E.J. (1997), Entrepreneurs, Networks, and Economic Development: a Review of Recent Research. In Katz, J.A. (ed.), *Advances in Entrepreneurship, Firm Emergence, and Growth*, Vol. 3, pp. 57–118. Greenwich, CT: JAI Press.

Malecki, E.J. (2011), Connecting local entrepreneurial ecosystems to global innovation networks: open innovation, double networks and knowledge integration. *International Journal of Entrepreneurship and Innovation Management* 14(1): 36–59.

Markusen, A. (1996), Sticky places in slippery space: typology of industrial districts. *Economic Geography* 72(3): 293–313.

Marshall, A. (1920 [1890]), *Principles of Economics*. London: Macmillan.

Mason, C. & Brown, R. (2013), Creating good public policy to support high-growth firms. *Small Business Economics* 40(2): 211–225.

Mason, C. & Brown, R. (2014), Entrepreneurial ecosystems and growth oriented entrepreneurship. Background paper prepared for the workshop organised by the OECD LEED Programme and the Dutch Ministry of Economic Affairs on Entrepreneurial Ecosystems and Growth Oriented Entrepreneurship, The Hague, Netherlands.

Moore, J.F. (1993), Predators and prey: a new ecology of competition. *Harvard Business Review*, May–June: 75–86.

Neck, H.M., Meyer, G.D., Cohen, B. & Corbett, A.C. (2004), An entrepreneurial system view of new venture creation. *Journal of Small Business Management* 42(2): 190–208.

Nijkamp, P. (2003), Entrepreneurship in a modern network economy. *Regional Studies* 37(4): 395–405.

Nooteboom, B. & Stam, E. (2008), *Micro-Foundations for Innovation Policy*. Amsterdam: Amsterdam University Press.

Patton, D. & Kenney, M. (2005), The spatial configuration of the entrepreneurial support network for the semiconductor industry. *R&D Management* 35(1): 1–17.

Pennings, J.M. (1982), The urban quality of life and entrepreneurship. *Academy of Management Journal* 25(1): 63–79.

Piore, M.J. & Sabel, C.F. (1984), *The Second Industrial Divide: Possibilities for Prosperity*. New York: Basic Books.

Porter, M.E. (1990), *The Competitive Advantage of Nations*. London: Macmillan.

Porter, M.E. (1998), *On Competition*. Boston, MA: Harvard Business School Press.

Qian, H., Acs, Z.J. and Stough, R.R. (2013), Regional systems of entrepreneurship: the nexus of human capital, knowledge and new firm formation. *Journal of Economic Geography* 13(4): 559–587.

Rocha, H.O. (2004), Entrepreneurship and development: the role of clusters. *Small Business Economics* 23(5): 363–400.

Rocha, H.O. & Sternberg, R. (2005), Entrepreneurship: the role of clusters theoretical perspectives and empirical evidence from Germany. *Small Business Economics* 24(3): 267–292.

Saxenian, A. (1994), *Regional Advantage: Culture and Competition in Silicon Valley and Route 128*. Cambridge, MA: Harvard University Press.

Schumpeter, J.A. (1934), *The Theory of Economic Development*. Cambridge, MA: Harvard University Press.

Shane, S. (2009), Why encouraging more people to become entrepreneurs is bad public policy. *Small Business Economics* 33(2): 141–149.

Shane, S. & Venkataraman, S. (2000), The promise of entrepreneurship as a field of research. *Academy of Management Review* 25(1): 217–226.

Spigel, B. (2017), The Relational Organization of Entrepreneurial Ecosystems. *Entrepreneurship Theory and Practice* 41: 49–72.

Spigel, B. & Harrison, R. (Forthcoming), Towards a Process Theory of Entrepreneurial Ecosystems. *Strategic Entrepreneurship Journal.*

Stam, E. (2013), Knowledge and entrepreneurial employees: a country level analysis. *Small Business Economics* 41(4): 887–898.

Stam, E. (2014), The Dutch Entrepreneurial Ecosystem. Available at SSRN: http://dx.doi.org/10.2139/ssrn.2473475

Stam, E. (2015), Entrepreneurial ecosystems and regional policy: a sympathetic critique. *European Planning Studies* 23(9): 1759–1769.

Stam, E. & Bosma, N. (2015a), Growing Entrepreneurial Economies: Entrepreneurship and Regional Development. In Baker, T. and Welter, F. (eds), *The Routledge Companion to Entrepreneurship*. London: Routledge. pp. 325–340.

Stam, E. & Bosma, N. (2015b), Local Policies for High-Growth Firms. In Audretsch, D., Link, A. & Walshok, M. (eds), *Oxford Handbook of Local Competitiveness*. Oxford: Oxford University Press. Chapter 14.

Stam, E., Bosma, N., Van Witteloostuijn, A., de Jong, J., Bogaert, S., Edwards, N. & Jaspers, F. (2012), *Ambitious Entrepreneurship. A Review of the Academic Literature and New Directions for Public Policy*. The Hague: Adviesraad voor Wetenschap en Technologie-beleid (AWT).

Stam, E., Hartog, C., Van Stel, A. & Thurik, R. (2011), Ambitious Entrepreneurship and Macro-Economic Growth. In Minniti, M. (ed.), *The Dynamics of Entrepreneurship. Evidence from the Global Entrepreneurship Monitor Data*. Oxford: Oxford University Press.

Stam, E., Suddle, K., Hessels, J. & Van Stel, A. (2009), High-Growth Entrepreneurs, Public Policies and Economic Growth. In Leitao, J. & Baptista, R. (eds), *Public Policies for Fostering Entrepreneurship: A European Perspective*. New York: Springer. pp. 91–110.

Sternberg, R. (2007), Entrepreneurship, proximity and regional innovation systems. *Tijdschrift voor Economische en Sociale Geografie* 98(5): 652–666.

Steyaert, C. & Katz, J. (2004), Reclaiming the space of entrepreneurship in society: geographical, discursive and social dimensions. *Entrepreneurship and Regional Development*, 16(3): 179–196.

Teece, D. (1992), Competition, cooperation, and innovation: organizational arrangements for regimes of rapid technological progress. *Journal of Economic Behavior and Organization* 18(1): 1–25.

Thurik, R., Stam, E. & Audretsch, D. (2013), The rise of the entrepreneurial economy and the future of dynamic capitalism. *Technovation* 33(8–9): 302–310.

Tsvetkova, A. (2015), Innovation, entrepreneurship, and metropolitan economic performance: empirical test of recent theoretical propositions. *Economic Development Quarterly* 29(4): 299–316.

Ucbasaran, D., Westhead, P. & Wright, M. (2001), The focus of entrepreneurial research: contextual and process issues. *Entrepreneurship Theory and Practice* 25(4): 57–80.

Van de Ven, A. (1993), The development of an infrastructure for entrepreneurship. *Journal of Business Venturing* 8(3): 211–230.

Welter, F. (2011), Contextualizing entrepreneurship – conceptual challenges and ways forward. *Entrepreneurship Theory and Practice* 35: 165–184.

Wong, P., Ho, Y. & Autio, E. (2005), Entrepreneurship, innovation and economic growth: evidence from GEM data. *Small Business Economics* 24(3): 335–350.

World Economic Forum (2013), *Entrepreneurial Ecosystems Around the Globe and Company Growth Dynamics*. Davos: World Economic Forum.

Ylinenpää, H. (2009), Entrepreneurship and innovation systems: towards a development of the ERIS/IRIS concept. *European Planning Studies* 17(8): 1153–1170.

Zahra, S.A. (2007), Contextualizing theory building in entrepreneurship research. *Journal of Business Venturing* 22(3): 443–452.

Zahra, S.A., Wright, M. & Abdelgawad, S.G. (2014), Contextualization and the advancement of entrepreneurship research. *International Small Business Journal* 32(5): 479–500.

Zhang, Y. & Li, H. (2010), Innovation search of new ventures in a technology cluster: the role of ties with service intermediaries. *Strategic Management Journal* 31(1): 88–109.

22

Entrepreneurial Social Responsibility

Zhongming Wang and Yanhai Zhao

INTRODUCTION

In the twenty-first century, businesses have become more entrepreneurial, connected, global and innovative. However, the rapid development of small business and various kinds of entrepreneurship calls for more responsible organizations, in the form of corporate social responsibility (CSR). Hence a focus on CSR and small firms is both highly pertinent and timely: CSR is increasingly recognized as a key to competitive advantage and small business and entrepreneurship are identified as the engines of sustainable growth and social change (e.g. Porter & Kramer, 2006; Carroll & Shabana, 2010; Casson & Pavelin, 2016; Panwar et al., 2016; Soto-Acosta et al., 2016; Stoian & Gilman, 2017).

However, the current models of 'business + CSR' do not adequately allow for the dynamics of social responsibility practices in entrepreneurial or small firms. In order to effectively produce creative solutions and sustainable development, a 'business × CSR' approach, or an entrepreneurial social responsibility approach, may need to be developed to produce a better understanding and solutions. A growing body of research shows that entrepreneurs' ethical behaviour, social entrepreneurship practice and sustainable entrepreneurship are presenting key challenges in developing effective CSR strategies.

As a result, new conceptual frameworks are needed to further investigate CSR in entrepreneurship and small businesses because of their unique competitive challenges and institutional constraints (e.g. Vazquez-Carrasco & Lopez-Perez, 2013; Stoian & Gilman, 2017). An integrated conceptualization of *entrepreneurial social responsibility* (ESR) is needed in order to incorporate CSR into small business and entrepreneurship. In this chapter, we will address the conceptual evolution of entrepreneurship in relation to the social responsibility dimension of entrepreneurship and small business, and present new directions in developing ESR strategies.

CONCEPTUAL DEVELOPMENT: LOCAL AND GLOBAL

Although the concept of CSR has emerged in modern times, social responsibility thinking and its conceptualization has had a long history. The underpinning thinking of responsibility and social responsibility, it can be argued, is largely rooted in ancient Chinese business thinking and practice, as well as early Western management development. Philosophies such as Confucianism, Buddhism and Taoism emphasized that benevolence, philanthropy, humaneness and social norms were social expectations for legitimate behaviour (Gao, 2009). Confucian businessmen, for instance, sought to integrate *li* (profits) with *yi* (righteousness), and concepts such as fairness, honesty, integrity and trust are considered as essential to reputation and business success (Hao, 2004). Businesses in Anhui and Shanxi provinces were thus known for their professionalism, diligence, modesty and generosity (Yu & Xiao, 2012). In the 1930s and 1940s, group responsibility was a key element of workgroups under Chinese plant management. In the 1960s, group social responsibility was built into work competition activities. Since the opening up and reform in China in 1978, the development of contracted responsibility systems emphasized a set of comprehensive responsibilities, including people responsibility, production responsibility and leadership responsibility. Organizational and social responsibility were written into business contracts.

In its early stages, CSR was mostly seen as a personal effort (Bowen, 1953), a construct originated from managerial discretion (Ackermann & Bauer, 1976). The concept was then further integrated through the notions of organizational legitimacy and the iron law of responsibility (Davis & Blomstrom, 1975). CSR is now regarded as a much more dynamic, multi-level and multi-dimensional concept, involving corporate social performance, stakeholder approaches, and aiming to throw light on societal expectations of corporations (Carroll, 1979; Carroll, 1991; Freeman, 1984; Wood, 1991; Aguilera et al., 2007).

More recently, the Company Law of the People's Republic of China of 2005 outlined the needs for Chinese firms in regard to their social responsibilities. State-owned enterprises (SOEs), in particular, have taken the lead in CSR practices (Yin & Zhang, 2012). Meanwhile, the Chinese business environment has involved frequent ethically questionable decisions (Lu, 2009) such as *guanxi*, relationship-building based on mutual personal favours and connections, which need addressing (Chen & Chen, 2004). Thus, it is recommended that government, industrial organizations, business networks and media, as well as consumer groups, should work together to promote Chinese firms to engage in CSR (Campbell, 2007).

Entrepreneurship is seen as a special means of promoting economic, technical and social advancements, creating important economic and social value (Sarasvathy et al., 2014). Entrepreneurs are creating new products and new services and generating new jobs that are essential to economic growth and social advancement. Yet the ethical and social implications of entrepreneurship have only recently been recognized as significantly important to entrepreneurial success (Harris, Sapienza & Bowie, 2009).

At present, policymakers, corporate practitioners and academic researchers are emphasizing the importance of entrepreneurship, not only as a contributor to economic advancement but also as a driving force of social change (Spence, 2016). Consequently, new concepts and forms of entrepreneurship, such as social entrepreneurship, environmental and sustainable entrepreneurship, sustainable corporate entrepreneurship and international entrepreneurship, are gaining attention in the literature.

Social Entrepreneurship and Responsibility

Social entrepreneurship is gaining acceptance in theory and practice as a means of helping to address market and government failures as well as promote social development (Choi, 2009). However, various terms and concepts exist, including social entrepreneurship, social entrepreneur and social enterprise/venture (Bacq & Janssen, 2011; Mort, Weerawardena & Carnegie, 2013). The phenomenon is multifaceted (Bacq & Janssen, 2011) and highly contextualized (Dacin, Dacin & Matear, 2010). Mair, Marti and Ventresca (2012) suggest that a better understanding of social entrepreneurship involves looking at it from a broader angle. In general, studies of social entrepreneurship consider three areas:

1 The definition;
2 The key components; and
3 The innovativeness or ultimate goal of social entrepreneurship.

Social entrepreneurship involves solving social problems and satisfying social needs, rather than profit maximization (Zahra et al., 2009). Hence, having a social mission and social value creation are widely accepted as the essential dimensions of social entrepreneurship (Peredo & Mclean, 2006; Mair & Mati, 2006). Problems claimed to be addressed by social entrepreneurship include health care, education, disaster relief, social justice and reform, poverty, environment protection and employment (Choi, 2009).

Sustainable Entrepreneurship and Responsibility

By applying the 'triple bottom line', business sustainability has become integral to corporate strategy and is regarded as a symbol of good corporate citizenship (Elkington, 1998; Hoivik & Mele, 2009; Spence, 2016). Yet the majority of the sustainability literature has focused on established and larger organizations although more recently research has begun to identify entrepreneurship as a means of addressing market failures under sustainability

pressures (Hall, Daneke & Lenox, 2010; Hockerts & Wüstenhagen, 2010; York & Venkataraman, 2010).

Sustainable entrepreneurship tends to cover a wide range of activities including community sustainability and the development of enterprises for non-economic gains (Shepherd & Patzelt, 2011). Parrish (2010) differentiated the primary profit-motivation of opportunity-driven entrepreneurs from the primary social motivation of sustainability-driven entrepreneurs. In fact, entrepreneurs who have high entrepreneurial responsibilities should have higher 'entrepreneurial alertness', not only to overcome imperfections within their own business, but also to develop a more balanced allocation of sustainable resources and business practices. Indeed, a framework of sustainable corporate entrepreneurship (SCE) has been developed to reflect balancing the efforts for sustainability, corporate entrepreneurship and financial performance (Miles, Munilla & Darroch, 2009; Hall et al., 2010).

A key issue in the literature is whether firms with different levels of commitment to sustainability may produce higher firm-level environmental and economic performance (Miles & Covin, 2000; Waddock, 2000). To be effective at firm level, sustainability is recommended to be explicitly integrated into a firm's strategy (Menon, 1997) in order to gain long-term competitive advantage. Miles et al. (2009) defined entrepreneurial initiatives directed at solving sustainability issues as 'sustainable corporate entrepreneurship (SCE)'. SCE has three components: responsible environmental management, social accountability and long-term economic performance. SCE was further defined as a corporate entrepreneurial process to identify, evaluate and make use of business possibilities related to social and environmental issues. As such, SCE can be categorized into sustainable product development, manufacturing process reengineering, strategy renewal, domain redefinition and business model rejuvenation.

International Entrepreneurship and Responsibility

A further dimension to entrepreneurial social responsibility is its links with the growing international dimension of entrepreneurship and small business. The development of new international ventures has four essential factors: the formation of the organization by way of the internationalization of transactions, a flexible governance structure for resource management, a geographic advantage at the international level, and a sustainable competitive advantage due to the control of unique resources. Two important aspects of this research field in relation to social responsibility are international entrepreneurs and international opportunity (Ahmad, Amran & Halim, 2011; Shepherd & Patzelt, 2011; Shane & Nicolaou, 2013; Zahra, Wright & Abdelgawad, 2014; Nordman & Tolstoy, 2016).

The study of international entrepreneurs includes their psychological traits, such as international orientation, opportunity identification and risk-taking (Noor & Kuivalainen, 2015), and social demographic traits, such as linguistic ability, technical experiences and entrepreneurial experiences (McGaughey, 2007; Kropp, Lindsay & Shoham, 2008). Entrepreneurial opportunity is also one of the major themes of entrepreneurship research, and international entrepreneurship, in turn, is driven by cross-border opportunities (Mainela, Puhakka & Servais, 2013). However, these opportunities are not necessarily driven by the pursuit of profits or economical interests. A few studies have explored the non-economic opportunities. For example, Zahra and colleagues (2008; 2014) found that some social opportunities are by nature international. For instance, to bridge the poverty gap across countries or to cope with the challenges of climate change, there is the need for joint efforts worldwide. The associated environmental sustainable opportunities are often international (Shepherd & Patzelt, 2011). Meanwhile, other opportunities, such as community environment protection or water pollution may be more of a regional concern. Even in this case, these opportunities may still have an international dimension, because the creation of new products, services, materials or organizational approaches may need skills, techniques or solutions at an international level (Shane, 2012).

It may be argued that for the pursuit of social entrepreneurial opportunities, the institutional context plays a more important role than that in the case of conventional international business opportunities. Zahra and colleagues (2008) noticed that institutional failure was quite common across countries, especially when entrepreneurial social responsibility is weak, because entrepreneurs tend to overlook multicultural contextual opportunities. Fernhaber, Mcdougall-Covin and Shepherd (2009) also showed that with rich international experience and knowledge, it is easier for new ventures to find more international opportunities, because they have access to relevant information, ideas, technology and institutional networks.

We summarize the key characteristics of these entrepreneurship forms in Table 22.1, adapted from Schaltegger and Wagner (2011).

RESEARCH PROGRESS: CSR, ETHICS AND ENTREPRENEURSHIP

While entrepreneurial studies focused on sustainability have made remarkable progress, attention to social responsibility issues are less developed (Lepoutre & Heene, 2006; Perrini, Pogutz & Tencati, 2007). Recent studies have sought to explore the specific ethical issues that entrepreneurs face and to demonstrate the reasons for the differences in entrepreneurial firms' actions in regard to CSR and business ethics (Fassin, 2008; Fassin, Van Rossem & Buelens, 2011; Baumann-Pauly et al., 2013).

Table 22.1   Comparison of entrepreneurship responsibility characteristics

	Environmental Entrepreneurship	Social Entrepreneurship	Sustainable Entrepreneurship	International Entrepreneurship
Main objectives	Tackling environmental problems and creating market value	Dealing with societal issues and creating value for society	Solving societal/ environmental problems while achieving business success	Promoting global business and creating cross-border social value
Social responsibility	Integrating social, environmental and economic responsibilities	Enhancing societal and non-profit goals of responsibility	Embedding corporate value/ responsibilities into sustainability	Developing cross-border responsibilities for customers/business development
Challenge and key issues	How to link short-term and long-term responsibilities	How to balance social and economic values	How to integrate multiple resources to achieve sustainability	How to overcome cross-cultural and regional barriers for entrepreneurship

CSR in Small Business

Although SMEs account for the majority of business worldwide, they have tended to be less involved in CSR and attract less attention compared with large organizations (Baden, Harwood & Woodward, 2011; Fassin et al., 2011). This has been attributed to their size, resource poverty and/or simplicity of strategies (Fitzgerald et al., 2010). However, SMEs' participation in CSR has been shown to vary with culture, corporate environment, financial conditions, business size and stakeholder interests (Laudal, 2011; Lepoutre & Heene, 2006; Pirsch, Gupta & Grau, 2007). Some authors have highlighted the importance of legislation to promote compliance and stakeholder pressure from customers, local communities, environmental interest groups and others as key drivers of CSR, and have also explored the economic opportunities arising from pro-environmental behaviour (Gonzalez-Benito & Gonzalez-Benito, 2006; Lepoutre & Heene, 2006; Kehbila, Ertel & Brent, 2009).

In contrast to large corporations, CSR development and implementation in small business is both enabled and constrained. On one hand, because small businesses tend to be managed by their owners, where ownership and control lies with the same person, these owner-managers may have greater freedom for decision-making than managers in a large firm (Hamann, Habisch & Pechlaner, 2009). Small business owners will, therefore, have a strong influence on shaping the goals of the enterprise and these may include values other than profit and dividends for shareholders (Nicholson, 2008). Engagement in CSR tends to be more personalized, reflecting owner-managers' personal ethics and values as well as the needs of the surrounding community (Jamali, Zanhour & Keshishian, 2009; Looser & Wehrmeyer, 2016; Stoian & Gilman, 2017). On the other hand, because of their high dependence on a small number of customers and greater embeddedness in the local community, small businesses are often found to have limited ability and willingness to engage in CSR or related social or environmental issues (Hamann et al., 2009; Spence, 2016). Their involvement in CSR, therefore, has been found to focus more on internal dimensions, prioritizing issues that are closer to themselves and their primary stakeholders, and to be more personal and informal in nature (Spence & Rutherfoord, 2003; Jenkins, 2006; Perrini, 2006; Russo & Tencati, 2009; Santos, 2011; Baumann-Pauly et al., 2013).

Overall, CSR practices are less systematic, formalized and structured than in large organizations (Matten & Moon, 2008; Looser & Wehrmeyer, 2016). However, the literature tends to suggest that CSR in small firms takes place for different reasons than in larger organizations and there is no simple size-effect (Baumann-Pauly et al., 2013). Other factors, including the context of the enterprise, such as regulation density of the sector and ownership characteristics are important (Wickert, Scherer & Spence, 2016).

CSR in New Ventures

One interesting aspect of CSR and entrepreneurship is its relationship with the age of the enterprise. Focusing on entrepreneurs' personal value approach, Longenecker and colleagues (2006) found that entrepreneurs' personal values are essential in forming their new ventures' ethical climate. Although new ventures are regarded as drivers of growth by creating new jobs and fostering innovations, they may also have more harmful effects on the environment or operate in illegal ways, compared with already established corporations (Worthington & Patton, 2005; Webb, et al., 2009). The cause of this phenomenon lies in the liability of newness of new ventures (Wang & Bansal, 2012), which may have a negative impact on the development of their CSR. New ventures may lack the sophisticated operating processes and routines, systems and structures necessary for them to realize the economic returns from CSR investments (Wang & Bansal, 2012). Indeed, in order to build stakeholder relationships and a positive image from CSR, significant time is often required (Fombrun, Gardberg & Barnett, 2000; Barnett, 2007). The capital costs associated with CSR activities are often high (Brammer & Millington, 2008), and engagement with CSR may distract entrepreneurs' efforts from their primary new business activities and ambition (Wang & Bansal, 2012).

Nonetheless, some studies show that new ventures can benefit from CSR activities. Crick and Spence (2005) underline the fact that new ventures have goals that are often different from those of established, large corporations and that new ventures are often more dependent on their local community for resources, and thus their CSR efforts may help them in their resource endowment. Zahra et al. (2008) combined the notions of sympathy, institutional theory and harmony and found that entrepreneurs often have the motivation to start companies with a social purpose. Surie and Ashley (2008) integrated the notion of pragmatism into the study of entrepreneurial leadership, showing that entrepreneurship and ethics are not necessarily incompatible, and that entrepreneurial leadership needs to involve ethical actions to build legitimacy. Moreover, the impact of perceived unethical behaviour by entrepreneurs, angel investors and venture capitalists on their conflict process was significant. Unethical behaviour was shown to trigger not only conflict between venture partners, but may also affect their choice of conflict management strategy and increase the likelihood of conflict escalation (Collewaert & Fassin, 2013).

Entrepreneurs' Ethical Preference

The literature on entrepreneurs' ethical responsibility considerations initially asked the question whether entrepreneurs differed from other individuals. Chau and Siu (2000), for instance, examined ethical decision-making behaviour in corporate entrepreneurial organizations and showed that work, organization and individual characteristics were conducive to entrepreneurial ethical decisions. According to Solymossy and Masters (2002), the difference between entrepreneurs and others may lie in their moral judgement and behaviour, and even in their level of cognitive moral development. Carr (2003) argued that how entrepreneurs understood their business and ethical behaviour is a reflection of the way in which they lead their individual lives. Hannafey (2003) found that entrepreneurs faced 'uniquely complex moral problems' in regard to their understanding of basic fairness, personnel and customer relationships and distribution dilemmas.

A second major question that arises in understanding ethical preference is *how* is an entrepreneur different from 'ordinary' people in terms of their understanding of individual responsibility and effort? Recent studies demonstrate that entrepreneurs are more individually oriented and as such show a heterogeneity in their ethical values, as well as in their cognitive styles toward moral issues (Beugelsdijk & Noorderhaven, 2005; Trevino, Weaver & Reynolds, 2006; Bryant, 2009). Payne and Joyner (2006) found that while making decisions, entrepreneurs faced ethical dilemmas in balancing their own values against organizational factors such as profit division, organizational culture, employee well-being, customer satisfaction and external accountability. Focusing on the cognition of small-business owner-managers, Fassin et al. (2011) found that they differentiated among the various concepts related to CSR and business ethics. Ginghina (2012) pointed out that the main qualities characterizing successful entrepreneurship (initiative, perseverance, imagination, creativity, passion, courage, justice) were crucial to their ethical decision-making.

A further strand of the literature has examined the differences between small business owners and those in other work settings. Longenecker and others (2006) found that entrepreneurs offered differentiated ethical responses to managers in large organizations. Burton and Goldsby (2009) showed that small business owners were more likely to translate their attitudes into behaviour than those in larger organizations. Hence, those that had a higher CSR orientation would be more CSR-orientated in their enterprise; whereas those who placed an emphasis on economic aspects would be more economically orientated. The results also showed that small business owners tended to possess higher levels of economic and social responsibility than larger organizations operating in a more profit-orientated

domain. These results were, however, subject to a number of caveats and as such, research on the ethical performance of small business owners remains under development. As a result, when the entrepreneurs are engaged in the 'destructive innovation' process or an 'ethically pioneering' situation, they have to reflect on and even review their ethical standards (Harting, Harmeling & Venkataraman, 2006; McVea, 2009). This is supported by Baumann-Pauly et al. (2013) who propose that small firms have organizational characteristics that are favourable for '… promoting internal *implementation* of CSR-related practices in core business functions' (p. 693). On the other hand, large organizations were found to be better positioned to communicate externally their CSR practices.

Contextual Studies

An increasing emphasis is being placed on contextualized studies in entrepreneurship and small business with regard to corporate social responsibility. Welter (2011) defined a context as the summary of subjective environment and existence conditions and then proposed four contextual conditions of entrepreneurship studies: business, social, spatial and institutional. Zahra et al. (2014) included four interconnecting contextual elements into entrepreneurship (spatial, temporal, social and institutional). Oliver and Paul-Shaheen (1997) found that the resource advantages were often formed in a particular institutional context and the choice and use of resources is based on certain internal and external institutional factors. Anokhin and Schulze (2009), through an analysis of longitudinal data among 64 nations, showed that better control of corruption would be associated with rising levels of innovation and entrepreneurship, although the relationship was complex. Maurer, Bansal & Crossan, (2011) point out that a company's institutional environment can create or destroy the economic value. Keig, Brouthers & Marshall

(2015) showed that ignoring resource allocation responsibility, or the responsible usage of resources, in a country's institutional environment would lead to poor results. Wickert et al. (2016) emphasize the context of the enterprise rather than pure size-effects, although they argue that large organizations have cost advantages in terms of CSR 'talk, whilst small firms have cost advantages in terms of "walking the talk"'.

Contextual studies are often focused on less developed or emerging countries, while others try to place the interplay of entrepreneurship and business ethics in distinctive cultures. Ahmad et al. (2011), for example, proposed a model connecting entrepreneurs' personal values, perceived role of ethics and social responsibility, as well as ethical and socially responsible practices, to SME performance. Based on the Confucian concept of *ren* (love and compassion) and *yi* (righteousness or rightness), Zhu (2015) studied the practical manifestation in *qing* (positive emotions) and *li* (rationality) for decision-making. To reach a balanced outcome in their everyday business practices, Chinese entrepreneurs had to deal with the dilemma relating to *qing* and *li* holistically.

A FRAMEWORK OF ENTREPRENEURIAL SOCIAL RESPONSIBILITY

It is now widely recognized that research on CSR has tended to ignore the difference between managers and entrepreneurs, and between large corporations and small business. This gap leads to the need for new conceptual developments to address social responsibility issues in entrepreneurship and small business (Lepoutre & Heene, 2006; Perrini et al., 2007; Wickert et al., 2016).

Entrepreneurs face unique moral issues and behave differently concerning social responsibility (Solymossy & Masters, 2002).

This uniqueness necessitates a distinctive approach that is different from the dominant conceptual frameworks of corporate social responsibility. Such a framework should allow a better understanding of the dynamic nature and connections of an entrepreneur, entrepreneurship and social responsibility as well as sustainability. In this section, the core issues and challenges will be discussed and help underpin the development of an integrated framework of *entrepreneurial social responsibility* (ESR).

Essence of ESR

As discussed earlier, studies of CSR have mainly focused upon large companies or corporate organizations. However, small firms and new ventures are not just 'little big firms' (Tilley, 2000): they fundamentally differ in a number of ways from large firms but they also differ from each other. Within the small business population there is also substantial heterogeneity: across regions, sectors, culture, owner ambition and capabilities and ownership structure (Jenkins, 2006). Perrini (2006) suggested that the theoretical models developed for large firms such as the stakeholder theory (Freeman, 1984) may not be generalized to the SME's context (Spence & Rutherfoord, 2003). Indeed, what evidence we have suggests that the practice of CSR and business ethics in small firms is different from that of large and established firms. There appear to be four different features, which we will now examine.

First, small businesses and their owner-managers are not only smaller in size or in formation, but also appear to be characteristically different in their commitment and approaches to CSR and sustainability (Lepoutre & Heene, 2006; Wickert et al., 2016). In addition, there are organizational and industrial differences: industry sector, legal forms, historical background, business context and institutional structure, as well as cultural differences, resources, capabilities, owner-manager characteristics and strategic directions (see, for example, Murillo & Lozano, 2006; Perrini, 2006).

Second, entrepreneurs appear to play a more significant role in a firm's development trajectory, including its sustainability efforts. They face constant pressure from market competition (Robinson et al., 2007) but have relatively limited financial resources (De Clercq & Dakhli, 2009). As entrepreneurs create and build their firms in alignment with their personal aspirations and philosophies (Werner, 2008; Hamann et al., 2009), they may encounter ambiguity in their decision-making, which will affect their ethical standards and behaviour (Fassin et al., 2011).

Third, CSR and business ethics may well have greater impact on entrepreneurial firms than on other firms. Sarbutts (2003) noted that the alignment may position SMEs in a better place to adopt socially responsible practices than larger organizations as well as enhancing their reputation. While large organizations tend to have clear strategies, the implementation of CSR in small firms is largely dependent on the basic motivations of owners and managers. Enjoying relatively greater autonomy and flexibility, entrepreneurial firms that do engage in CSR will do so with a greater level of honesty and integrity (Jenkins, 2006; Baden et al., 2011; Russo & Tencati, 2009). This can also help them not only to create market opportunities, reduce costs and increase efficiency (Jenkins, 2006; Hamman et al., 2009), but also to foster innovation and attract and retain qualified employees (Perrini, 2006; Russo & Perrini, 2010).

Fourth, entrepreneurial firms engage in CSR and business ethics differently. Their success is dependent on their close community connections as well as reputation in local communities (Waddock, 2000). They can be more responsive to the demands of companies in their supply chain or financial institutions (e.g. Fassin, 2008; Russo & Tencati, 2009). Although often conducted in a more personalized and informal manner, entrepreneurial firms have been shown to take sustainability seriously, and thus their contributions are of more value for the local community (Spence & Rutherfoord, 2003; McCaffrey & Kurland, 2015).

Core Elements of ESR

A large number of entrepreneurship and small business studies have focused on 'entrepreneurial opportunities' (see, for example, Léger-Jarniou & Tegtmeier, 2017). From this perspective, entrepreneurship is understood to be inherently engaged in solving problems of risk, innovation and action, ultimately involving resource allocation. As entrepreneurs conduct their business within different contexts and environments, they may think differently from managers (Baron, 2007). The above three elements are the key areas where entrepreneurs will contribute to sustainability in a unique manner and therefore, it is argued, provide the core components of ESR.

Risk

Risk is recognized both as an attribute differentiating entrepreneurs from other managers and as an essential component of entrepreneurship. Shapero (1984) argued that entrepreneurs need to share the risk of success or failure and manage the organizations with a certain degree of autonomy. By examining how entrepreneurs experience and deal with ethical dilemmas, Robinson et al. (2007) suggested that, with limited financial resources and high levels of competition, entrepreneurs had to live with the 'ever-present threat of business failure' and, in these conditions, face dilemmas on deciding what is the right choice.. According to York and Venkataraman (2010), the exploration of entrepreneurial opportunities is, by definition, under circumstances of uncertainty and by taking action in the face of uncertainty, entrepreneurial action transforms uncertainty into opportunity. Fassin and others (2011) also confirm that the bearing of risk is an essential distinguishing factor between entrepreneurs and managers.

Innovation

Innovation in a responsible and sustainable manner is a further essential aspect of ESR (Brenkert, 2009). Harting et al. (2006) affirmed that there was a dynamic interplay between stakeholder relationships, innovation and competitive advantage. Hall and Rosson (2006) investigated examples of Internet innovation, including spam (destructive), music file sharing (unproductive) and Internet pharmacies (potentially productive) and the ethical dilemmas that technological turbulence and innovation presented. While discussing social innovation, Nicholls and Cho (2008) considered that innovation orientation was the feature that distinguishes social entrepreneurship from conventional social service programmes. Hochgerner (2011) found that innovation was not limited to technological innovation and increases in productivity, but was found also in the new combinations of social practices, organizational forms and nodes of behaviour. Cajaiba-Santana (2014) further found that to promote social change, innovation should be realized through the reconfiguration of how social goals are accomplished.

Action

Firms can engage in CSR through a number of internal and external actions, such as business philanthropy and community investment, environmental management and corporate governance (Blowfield & Murray, 2008). Although CSR is often depicted as informal and fragmented in entrepreneurial firms (Fassin, 2008), their social responsibility practice can be realized at both strategic and operational levels. Social responsibility was identified and confirmed as a useful tool in the strategic management literature (Santos, 2011; Porter & Kramer, 2006) and can help improve an entrepreneurial firm's 'bottom-line' (Coppa & Sriramesh, 2013; Stoian & Gilman, 2017) as well as its leadership (Quinn & Dalton, 2009). On the other hand, an entrepreneurial firm's engagement in CSR action is often personalized (Jamali

et al., 2009), and their social responsibility is found to be more orientated on the internal dimension (Santos, 2011; Baumann-Pauly et al., 2013). Evidence from Italy found CSR practices to be relational and informal rather than strategic and formal, prioritizing issues closer to owner-managers and their primary stakeholders (Perrini, 2006; Perrini et al., 2007), including addressing employee recruitment and retention.

Embeddedness

It is now recognized that innovation is not limited to technological advancements, as it can also be realized through the formation of new markets, the distribution of information to consumers and new methods of organizing (Dean & McMullen, 2007; Lisetchi & Brancu, 2014). In this regard, the embeddedness of CSR, both internally and externally, is a fundamental component of ESR in SMEs. Granovetter (1985) affirmed that entrepreneurs' activities are embedded into, and strongly influenced by, social relationships, and the various networks can set behavioural norms for firms (Granovetter, 2005). Zahra (2005) showed that the society and the market in which firms operate were two important sources of technology learning for new ventures. Spence, Gherib and Biwole (2011) considered that networks provided a source of unique competencies for entrepreneurial firms, especially SMEs, where they can benefit from the experience of others. This embeddedness also helps shape the CSR behaviour of small firms, through their industry norms and stakeholder networks (Spence & Rutherfoord, 2003).

ESR Frameworks

The review of the literature in this chapter has shown a range of CSR behaviours amongst SMEs and their underpinning rationales. Spence and Rutherfoord (2001) argue that entrepreneurial firms and SMEs can have four types of motivation frames in CSR: profit

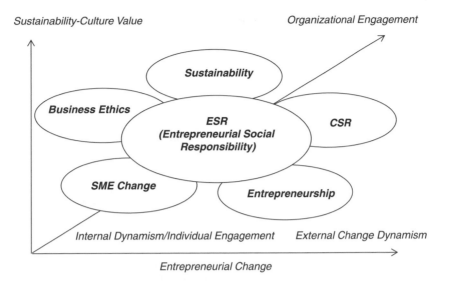

Figure 22.1   Dimensions of ESR

maximization, subsistence (long-term survival), enlightened self-interest (being active
in social issues) and social priority (work as a
long-term choice of lifestyle). These different
possibilities are put into a 2 × 2 matrix along
the two dimensions of profit (maximization or
satisficing) and social practice (active or inac-
tive). Austin, Stevenson and Wei-Skillern
(2006) found that social value creation could
occur along a continuum of commercial to
social entrepreneurship. They show the similarities and differences of commercial and
social entrepreneurship and the relative difficulties that social entrepreneurs have in terms
of resource mobilization. Bierly, Kolodinsky
and Charette (2009) investigated the relationship between creativity and ethical ideologies
and found that highly creative people were
'situationists', i.e. they had both an ethic of
caring and a pragmatic, moral decision-
making style.

Recent studies have shown that the ethics-
focused dynamic capabilities are positively
related to SMEs' ethical performance, and
that the performance effects were contingent
on SMEs' entrepreneurial orientation and
sensitivity to changes in the business context
(Arend, 2013).

Based on this literature, we propose a
multi-dimensional construct: ESR (Figure
22.1). The ESR framework is designed to
integrate multiple levels of analysis (individual and organizational, internal and external)
and organizational contexts (new ventures,
SMEs, larger organizations). This framework is helpful in depicting the dynamic
and essentially creative process of ESR,
involving the discovery and exploitation of
value-creating opportunities (social and commercial). In addition, the ESR framework
can help to extend entrepreneurship beyond
purely financial returns to a broader sustainable contribution, while integrating notions
of sustainability, CSR, business ethics, entrepreneurship and small business.

Based on the literature and the practice of
CSR and entrepreneurship, we conceive of
ESR as a construct with three core dimensions (innovation, risk and action) and three
peripheral embedded elements that are
subject to change and cultural integration
(Figure 22.2). The three elements range
from internal–external dynamism, individual–organizational engagement; and entrepreneurial change value and sustainability
culture value. These are embedded in the

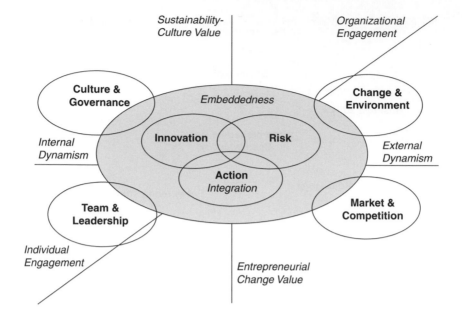

Figure 22.2   Key components of ESR under change and cultural integration

firms' internal (governance and team-building) and external environment (market and ecological and social environment).

The three core components of risk, innovation and action function within this broader framework. *Risk* involves a strong risk-taking and proactive tendency during the entrepreneurial process. To realize collective and personal value, entrepreneurs should be enterprising whilst being conscious of risks, paying attention to various social risks, assuming responsibilities and adapting to a changing environment.

Innovation comprises novel measures and approaches and the changing of the status quo. This dimension is not limited to simple innovations in products or processes, but the value-creating approach to realize unique productive factor combinations. Entrepreneurs innovatively promote social changes, highlighting the social value creation and establishing social value examples.

Action includes results-oriented pursuits and is regarded as a differentiating factor in social entrepreneurial success. It becomes

concrete through an inclusive culture construction, active stakeholder communication and interaction, and stakeholder community involvement.

Moreover, entrepreneurs have a need to embed themselves internally by building constructive teams and efficient governance structures, and externally by creating a favourable entrepreneurial environment through offering products, services and solutions that carry both social and commercial value in the competitive market, and by being actively engaged in environment protection efforts.

The above dimensions and components are inevitably interdependent. Ethical decision-making and social considerations can have significant impacts on entrepreneurial opportunity discovery, identification and exploitation processes. These processes, in turn, are embedded in the internal, external and institutional environments which may hinder or encourage efficient governance, team-building, market development and integration of sustainability-culture value as well as entrepreneurial change value.

CONCLUSION: NEW DIRECTIONS

With the emergence of interest and increased legitimization of sustainable development within business and policy circles (Cajaiba-Santana, 2014; Nybakk & Panwar, 2015), this chapter has demonstrated the inherent connections between business ethics/CSR, entrepreneurship and sustainability. In doing so, it has provided an overview of the literature on CSR in relation to entrepreneurship and small businesses. Although it is not possible to do justice to the vast literature in the field, the review provides a basis for suggestions and new directions in the field of study. The proposed ESR framework strives to cope with a number of academic and practical challenges which has implications for new research directions. This framework can help draw academic, professional and public attention to new areas of research and practice, in terms of ethical and social dimensions and process of entrepreneurial social responsibility, as well as relatively unexplored developing economies. In addition to the resource-based view (Maurer et al., 2011), institutional theory (Tracey, Phillips & Jarvis, 2011), social network theory (Granovetter, 2005; Siltaoja & Lahdesmaki, 2015), knowledge and learning theory (Arend, 2013) and stakeholder theory (Dew & Sarasvathy, 2007), it is worth emphasizing that the ESR research framework helps to provide a more comprehensive understanding of the complex interaction between entrepreneurship, small business and its dynamic, societal context. With this framework, the following directions can be investigated to further our understanding of CSR in relation to entrepreneurship and small business.

First, contributions can be developed from the internal context of entrepreneurial organizations, around the impact of ethical and social norms, rules and values on entrepreneurial 'opportunity' discovery, evaluation and exploitation. Special concern may be paid to questions such as: What are the influences of existing ethical rules on technical innovation? How will new ventures deal with CSR dilemmas whilst being engaged in 'destructive innovation'? How will entrepreneurs identify and distinguish appropriate value creation from business opportunities? Addressing these concerns will also help entrepreneurs to better understand the ethical and social norms, values and systems in which they operate and thus help shape their activities toward developing entrepreneurial opportunities for sustainable development.

Second, research may be conducted to understand the interaction of the internal and external environment, and the contextual dynamism that boosts and hinders entrepreneurs from pursuing sustainable ventures. This may address questions such as: Under what conditions will entrepreneurs pursue sustainability objectives? What are the structural barriers or incentives to adopting such entrepreneurial practices?

Third, the proposed ESR framework may also provide insights for large organizations to influence how they can innovate their current practices and shape how the industry in which they are situated will evolve. If large organizations follow the lead and logic of CSR-driven entrepreneurial enterprises, they will be able to improve their own ethical orientation, team cohesion and governance efficiency so as to construct competitive advantage from diversified innovative activities. This enhanced CSR awareness and practice amongst large organizations has the potential to then exert influence on smaller enterprises, through their product and service developments, supply networks and the setting of industry norms.

Fourth, the ESR framework shows the embeddedness and integration of sustainability-culture value and entrepreneurial change value, as an engine for business growth and social advancement. Questions can be asked such as: What kind of embeddedness model and integration strategy can support and enhance ESR? What kind of measurement of ESR effectiveness can be used to incentivize entrepreneurship for sustainable development? How can we develop an ESR approach to fully accommodate both internal–external dynamism and individual–organizational engagements for transformational and sustainable growth among small business and entrepreneurial firms? The answers to these questions will, in part, be conditional on what drives entrepreneurs to adopt a sustainable orientation and innovative strategies.

ACKNOWLEDGEMENT

This chapter is based upon studies supported by the grant from NSF China (No. 71232012) on organizational change and cultural integration among entrepreneurial firms and small business. We would like to thank the two reviewers for helping us to develop this chapter.

REFERENCES

Ackermann, R. and Bauer, R. (1976). *Corporate Social Performance: The Modern Dilemma*. Reston: Reston Publishing.

Aguilera, R.V., Rupp, D.E., Williams, C.A. and Ganapathi, J. (2007). Putting the s back in corporate social responsibility: A multilevel theory of social change in organizations. *Academy of Management Review*, 32, 836–863.

Ahmad, N.H., Amran, A. and Halim, H.A. (2011). Intercultural variations in ethical and socially responsible practices among SME owner-managers: A proposed model. In Soliman, K.S., *Creating Global Competitive Economies: A 360-Degree Approach*, Vols 1–4. Milan: IBIMA.

Anokhin, S. and Schulze, W.S. (2009). Entrepreneurship, innovation, and corruption. *Journal of Business Venturing*, 24, 465–476.

Arend, R.J. (2013). Ethics-focused dynamic capabilities: A small business perspective. *Small Business Economics*, 41, 1–24.

Austin, J., Stevenson, H. and Wei-Skillern, J. (2006). Social and commercial entrepreneurship: Same, different, or both? *Entrepreneurship Theory and Practice*, 30, 1–22.

Bacq, S. and Janssen, F. (2011). The multiple faces of social entrepreneurship: A review of definitional issues based on geographical and thematic criteria. *Entrepreneurship and Regional Development*, 23, 373–403.

Baden, D., Harwood, I.A. and Woodward, D.G. (2011). The effects of procurement policies on 'downstream' corporate social responsibility activity: Content-analytic insights into the views and actions of SME owner-managers. *International Small Business Journal*, 29, 259–277.

Barnett, M.L. (2007). Stakeholder influence capacity and the variability of financial returns to corporate social responsibility. *Academy of Management Review*, 32, 794–816.

Baron, D.P. (2007). Corporate social responsibility and social entrepreneurship. *Journal of Economics and Management Strategy*, 16, 683–717.

Baumann-Pauly, D., Wickert, C., Spence, L.J. and Scherer, A.G. (2013). Organizing corporate social responsibility in small and large firms: Size matters. *Journal of Business Ethics*, 115(4), 693–705.

Beugelsdijk, S. and Noorderhaven, N. (2005). Personality characteristics of self-employed: An empirical study. *Small Business Economics*, 24, 159–167.

Bierly, P.E., Kolodinsky, III, R.W. and Charette, B.J. (2009). Understanding the complex relationship between creativity and ethical ideologies. *Journal of Business Ethics*, 86, 101–112.

Blowfield, M. and Murray, A. (2008). *Corporate Responsibility – A Critical Introduction*. Oxford: Oxford University Press.

Bowen, H.R. (1953). *Social Responsibility of the Businessman*. New York: Harper & Row.

Brammer, S. and Millington, A. (2008). Does it pay to be different? An analysis of the relationship between corporate social and financial performance. *Strategic Management Journal*, 29, 1325–1343.

Brenkert, G.G. (2009). Innovation, rule breaking and the ethics of entrepreneurship. *Journal of Business Venturing*, 24, 448–464.

Bryant, P. (2009). Self-regulation and moral awareness among entrepreneurs. *Journal of Business Venturing*, 24, 505–518.

Burton, B.K. and Goldsby, M. (2009). Corporate social responsibility orientation, goals, and behavior: A study of small business owners. *Business and Society*, 48, 88–104.

Cajaiba-Santana, G. (2014). Social innovation: Moving the field forward: A conceptual framework. *Technological Forecast and Social Change*, 82, 42–51.

Campbell, J.L. (2007). Why would corporations behave in socially responsible ways? An institutional theory of corporate social responsibility. *Academy of Management Review*, 32, 946–967.

Carr, P. (2003). Revisiting the protestant ethic and the spirit of capitalism: Understanding the relationship between ethics and enterprise. *Journal of Business Ethics*, 47, 7–16.

Carroll, A.B. (1979). A three dimensional conceptual model of corporate social performance. *Academy of Management Review*, 4, 497–505.

Carroll, A.B. (1991). The pyramid of corporate social responsibility: Toward the moral management of organizational stakeholders. *Business Horizons*, 34, 39–48.

Carroll, A.B. and Shabana, K.M. (2010). The business case for corporate social responsibility: A review of concepts, research and practice. *International Journal of Management Reviews*, 12, 85–105.

Casson, M.C. and Pavelin, S. (2016). The social performance and responsibilities of entrepreneurship. *Business and Society*, 55, 11–13.

Chau, L.L.F. and Siu, W.S. (2000). Ethical decision-making in corporate entrepreneurial organizations. *Journal of Business Ethics*, 23, 365–375.

Chen, X.P. and Chen, C.C. (2004). On the intricacies of the Chinese guanxi: A process model of guanxi development. *Asia Pacific Journal of Management*, 21, 305–324.

Choi, H. (2009). The relation between corporate governance and corporate social responsibility. *Management and Information Systems Review*, 28, 45–66.

Collewaert, V. and Fassin, Y. (2013). Conflicts between entrepreneurs and investors: The impact of perceived unethical behavior. *Small Business Economics*, 40, 635–649.

Coppa, M. and Sriramesh, K. (2013). Corporate social responsibility among SMEs in Italy. *Public Relations Review*, 39, 30–39.

Crick, D. and Spence, M. (2005). The internationalisation of 'high performing' UK high-tech SMEs: A study of planned and unplanned strategies. *International Business Review*, 14, 167–185.

Dacin, P.A., Dacin, M.T. and Matear, M. (2010). Social entrepreneurship: Why we don't need a new theory and how we move forward from here. *Academy of Management Perspectives*, 24, 37–57.

Davis, P.K. and Blomstrom, L.R. (1975). *Business and Society: Environment and Responsibility* (3rd edn). New York: McGraw-Hill.

Dean, T.J. and McMullen, J.S. (2007). Toward a theory of sustainable entrepreneurship: Reducing environmental degradation through entrepreneurial action. *Journal of Business Venturing*, 22, 50–76.

De Clercq, D. and Dakhli, M. (2009). Personal strain and ethical standards of the self-employed. *Journal of Business Venturing*, 24, 477–490.

Dew, N. and Sarasvathy, S.D. (2007). Innovations, stakeholders and entrepreneurship. *Journal of Business Ethics*, 74, 267–283.

Elkington, J. (1998). *Cannibals with Forks – The Triple Bottom Line of the Twenty-First Century Business*. Oxford: Capstone.

Fassin, Y. (2008). SMEs and the fallacy of formalising CSR. *Business Ethics – a European Review*, 17, 364–378.

Fassin, Y., Van Rossem, A. and Buelens, M. (2011). Small-business owner-managers' perceptions of business ethics and CSR-related concepts. *Journal of Business Ethics*, 98, 425–453.

Fernhaber, S.A., Mcdougall-Covin, P.P. and Shepherd, D.A. (2009). International entrepreneurship: Leveraging internal and external knowledge sources. *Strategic Entrepreneurship Journal*, 3, 297–320.

Fitzgerald, M.A., Haynes, G.W., Schrank, H.L. and Danes, S.M. (2010). Socially responsible processes of small family business owners: Exploratory evidence from the national family business survey. *Journal of Small Business Management*, 48, 524–551.

Fombrun, C.J., Gardberg, N.A. and Barnett, M.L. (2000). Opportunity platforms and safety nets: Corporate citizenship and reputational risk. *Business and Society Review*, 105, 85–106.

Freeman, R.E. (1984). *Strategic Management: A Stakeholder Approach*. Boston, MA: Pittman.

Gao, Y. (2009). Corporate social performance in China: Evidence from large companies. *Journal of Business Ethics*, 89, 23–35.

Ginghina, A. (2012). Entrepreneurship and ethics: A closer look over the entrepreneur's behavior. *Entrepreneurship Education – a Priority for the Higher Education Institutions*, 95–98, proceedings of the International Conference Entrepreneurship Education, Edited by Catalin Martin and Elena Druica, University of Bucharest, Romania, 8–9 October. Bologna: Medimond.

González-Benito, J. and González-Benito,Ó. (2006). A review of determinant factors of environmental proactivity. *Business Strategy and the Environment*, 15, 87–102.

Granovetter, M. (1985). Economic action and social structure: The problem of embeddedness. *American Journal of Sociology*, 91, 481–510.

Granovetter, M. (2005). The impact of social structure on economic outcomes. *Journal of Economic Perspectives*, 19, 33–50.

Hall, J. and Rosson, P. (2006). The impact of technological turbulence on entrepreneurial behavior, social norms and ethics: Three Internet-based cases. *Journal of Business Ethics*, 64, 231–248.

Hall, J.K., Daneke, G.A. and Lenox, M.J. (2010). Sustainable development and entrepreneurship: Past contributions and future directions. *Journal of Business Venturing*, 25, 439–448.

Hamann, E.M., Habisch, A. and Pechlaner, H. (2009). Values that create value: Socially responsible business practices in SMEs – empirical evidence from German companies. *Business Ethics – a European Review*, 18, 37–51.

Hannafey, F.T. (2003). Entrepreneurship and ethics: A literature review. *Journal of Business Ethics*, 46, 99–110.

Hao, H.T. (2004). Business ethics system in the period of Ming and Qing dynasties. *Journal of ShanXi Finance and Economics University*, 26, 17–21.

Harris, J.D., Sapienza, H.J. and Bowie, N.E. (2009). Ethics and entrepreneurship. *Journal of Business Venturing*, 24, 407–418.

Harting, T.R., Harmeling, S.S. and Venkataraman, S. (2006). Innovative stakeholder relations: When 'ethics pays' (and when it doesn't). *Business Ethics Quarterly*, 16, 43–68.

Hochgerner, J. (2011). The analysis of social innovations as social practice. Bridges, 30. http://www. socialinnovation2011. eu/wp-conten1/uploads/2011/04.The-Analysis-of-Social-Innovations-as-Social-Practice. pdf [doste̞ p 20.05. 2013]

Hockerts, K. and Wüestenhagen, R. (2010). Greening goliaths versus emerging davids – theorizing about the role of incumbents and new entrants in sustainable entrepreneurship. *Journal of Business Venturing*, 25, 481–492.

Hoivik, H.V. and Mele, D. (2009). Can an SME become a global corporate citizen? Evidence from a case study. *Journal of Business Ethics*, 88, 551–563.

Jamali, D., Zanhour, M. and Keshishian, T. (2009). Peculiar strengths and relational attributes of SMEs in the context of CSR. *Journal of Business Ethics*, 87, 355–377.

Jenkins, H. (2006). Small business champions for corporate social responsibility. *Journal of Business Ethics*, 67, 241–256.

Kehbila, A.G., Ertel, J. and Brent, A.C. (2009). Strategic corporate environmental management within the South African automotive industry: Motivations, benefits, hurdles. *Corporate Social Responsibility and Environmental Management*, 16, 310–323.

Keig, D.L., Brouthers, L.E. and Marshall, V.B. (2015). Formal and informal corruption environments and multinational enterprise social irresponsibility. *Journal of Management Studies*, 52, 89–116.

Kropp, F., Lindsay, N.J. and Shoham, A. (2008). Entrepreneurial orientation and international entrepreneurial business venture startup. *International Journal of Entrepreneurial Behavior and Research*, 14(2), 102–117.

Laudal, T. (2011). Drivers and barriers of CSR and the size and internationalization of firms. *Social Responsibility Journal*, 7, 234–256.

Léger-Jarniou, C. and Tegtmeier, S. (eds) (2017). *Research Handbook on Entrepreneurial Opportunities: Reopening the Debate*. Cheltenham: Edward Elgar.

Lepoutre, J. and Heene, A. (2006). Investigating the impact of firm size on small business social responsibility: A critical review. *Journal of Business Ethics*, 67, 257–273.

Lisetchi, M. and Brancu, L. (2014). The entrepreneurship concept as a subject of social innovation. *Procedia – Social and Behavioral Sciences*, 124, 87–92.

Longenecker, J.G., Moore, C.W., Petty, J.W., Palich, L.E. and Mckinney, J.A. (2006). Ethical attitudes in small businesses and large corporations: Theory and empirical findings from a tracking study spanning three decades. *Journal of Small Business Management*, 44, 167–183.

Looser, S. and Wehrmeyer, W. (2016). Ethics of the firm, for the firm or in the firm? Purpose of extrinsic and intrinsic CSR in Switzerland. *Social Responsibility Journal*, 12, 545–570.

Lu, X. (2009). A Chinese perspective: Business ethics in China now and in the future. *Journal of Business Ethics*, 86, 451–461.

Mainela, T., Puhakka, V. and Servais, P.P. (2013). The concept of international opportunity in international entrepreneurship: A review and a research agenda. *International Journal of Management Reviews*, 16, 105–129.

Mair, J. and Marti, I. (2006). Social entrepreneurship research: A source of explanation, prediction, and delight. *Journal of World Business*, 41, 36–44.

Mair, J., Marti, I. and Ventresca, M.J. (2012). Building inclusive markets in rural Bangladesh: How intermediaries work institutional voids. *Academy of Management Journal*, 55, 819–850.

Matten, D. and Moon, J. (2008). 'Implicit' and 'explicit' CSR: A conceptual framework for a comparative understanding of corporate social responsibility. *Academy of Management Review*, 33, 404–424.

Maurer, C.C., Bansal, P. and Crossan, M.M. (2011). Creating economic value through social values: Introducing a culturally informed resource-based view. *Organization Science*, 22, 432–448.

McCaffrey, S.J. and Kurland, N.B. (2015). Does 'local' mean ethical? The US 'buy local' movement and CSR in SMEs. *Organization and Environment*, 28, 286–306.

McGaughey, S.L. (2007). Hidden ties in international new venturing: The case of portfolio entrepreneurship. *Journal of World Business*, 42, 307–321.

McVea, J.F. (2009). A field study of entrepreneurial decision-making and moral imagination. *Journal of Business Venturing*, 24, 491–504.

Menon, A. (1997). Enviropreneurial marketing strategy: The emergence of corporate environmentalism as market strategy. *Journal of Marketing*, 61, 51–67.

Miles, M.P. and Covin, J.G. (2000). Environmental marketing: A source of reputational, competitive, and financial advantage. *Journal of Business Ethics*, 23, 299–311.

Miles, M.P., Munilla, L.S. and Darroch, J. (2009). Sustainable corporate entrepreneurship. *International Entrepreneurship Management*, 5, 65–76.

Mort, G.S., Weerawardena, J. and Carnegie, K. (2003). Social entrepreneurship: Towards conceptualization. *International Journal of Nonprofit and Voluntary Sector Marketing*, 8, 76–88.

Murillo, D. and Lozano, J.M. (2006). SMEs and CSR: An approach to CSR in their own words. *Journal of Business Ethics*, 67, 227–240.

Nicholls, A. and Cho, A.H. (2008). Social entrepreneurship: The structuration of a field. In Nicholls, A. (ed.), *Social Entrepreneurship: New Models of Sustainable Social Change*. Oxford: Oxford University Press, pp. 99–118.

Nicholson, N. (2008). Evolutionary psychology and family business: A new synthesis for theory, research, and practice. *Family Business Review*, 21, 103–118.

Noor, I. and Kuivalainen, O. (2015). The effect of internal capabilities and external environment on small- and medium-sized enterprises' international performance and the role of the foreign market scope: The case of the Malaysian halal food industry. *Journal of International Entrepreneurship*, 13, 418–451.

Nordman, E.R. and Tolstoy, D. (2016). The impact of opportunity connectedness on innovation in SMEs' foreign-market relationships. *Technovation*, 47–57.

Nybakk, E. and Panwar, R. (2015). Understanding instrumental motivations for social responsibility engagement in a micro-firm context. *Business Ethics – a European Review*, 24, 18–33.

Oliver, T.R. and Paul-Shaheen, P. (1997). Translating ideas into actions: Entrepreneurial leadership in state health care reforms. *Journal of Health Politics, Policy and Law*, 22, 721–788.

Panwar, R., Nybakk, E., Hansen, E. and Pinkse, J. (2016). The effect of small firms' competitive strategies on their community and environmental engagement. *Journal of Cleaner Production*, 129, 578–585.

Parrish, B.D. (2010). Sustainability-driven entrepreneurship: Principles of organization design. *Journal of Business Venturing*, 25, 510–523.

Payne, D., and Joyner, B. E. (2006). Successful US entrepreneurs: Identifying ethical decision-making and social responsibility behaviors. *Journal of Business Ethics*, 65(3), 203–217.

Peredo, A.M. and Mclean, M. (2006). Social entrepreneurship: A critical review of the concept. *Journal of World Business*, 41, 56–65.

Perrini, F. (2006). SMEs and CSR theory: Evidence and implications from an Italian perspective. *Journal of Business Ethics*, 67, 305–316.

Perrini, F., Pogutz, S. and Tencati, A. (2007). Corporate social responsibility in Italy: State of the art. *Journal of Business Strategies*, 23, 65–91.

Pirsch, J., Gupta, S. and Grau, S.L. (2007). A framework for understanding corporate social responsibility programs as a continuum: An exploratory study. *Journal of Business Ethics*, 70, 125–140.

Porter, M.E. and Kramer, M.R. (2006). Strategy and society. *Harvard Business Review*, 84, (12), 78–92.

Quinn, L. and Dalton, M. (2009). Leading for sustainability: Implementing the tasks of leadership. *Corporate Governance*, 9, 21–38.

Robinson, D.A., Davidsson, P., Van Der Mescht, H. and Court, P. (2007). How entrepreneurs deal with ethical challenges – an application of the business ethics synergy star technique. *Journal of Business Ethics*, 71, 411–423.

Russo, A. and Perrini, F. (2010). Investigating stakeholder theory and social capital: CSR in large firms and SMEs. *Journal of Business Ethics*, 91, 207–221.

Russo, A. and Tencati, A. (2009). Formal vs. informal CSR strategies: Evidence from Italian micro, small, medium-sized, and large firms. *Journal of Business Ethics*, 85, 39–53.

Santos, F.M. (2011). CSR in SMEs: Strategies, practices, motivations and obstacles. *Social Responsibility Journal*, 7, 490–508.

Sarasvathy, S., Kumar, K., York, J.G. and Bhagavatula, S. (2014). An effectual approach to international entrepreneurship: Overlaps, challenges, and provocative possibilities. *Entrepreneurship Theory and Practice*, 38, 71–93.

Sarbutts, N. (2003). Can SMEs 'do' CSR? A practitioner's view of the ways small and medium-sized enterprises are able to manage reputation through corporate social responsibility. *Journal of Communication Management*, 7, 340–347.

Schaltegger, S. and Wagner, M. (2011). Sustainable entrepreneurship and sustainability innovation: Categories and interactions. *Business Strategy and the Environment*, 20, 224.

Shane, S. (2012). Reflections on the 2010 AMR Decade Award: Delivering on the promise of entrepreneurship as a field of research. *Academy of Management Review*, 37, 10–20.

Shane, S. and Nicolaou, N. (2013). The genetics of entrepreneurial performance. *International Small Business Journal*, 31, 473–495.

Shapero, A. (1984). The entrepreneurial event. In C. Kent (ed.), *The Environment for Entrepreneurship*. Toronto: Lexington Books, pp. 21–39.

Shepherd, D.A. and Patzelt, H. (2011). The new field of sustainable entrepreneurship: Studying entrepreneurial action linking 'what is to be sustained' with 'what is to be developed'. *Entrepreneurship Theory and Practice*, 35, 137–163.

Siltaoja, M. and Lahdesmaki, M. (2015). From rationality to emotionally embedded relations: Envy as a signal of power in stakeholder relations. *Journal of Business Ethics*, 128, 837–850.

Solymossy, E. and Masters, J.K. (2002). Ethics through an entrepreneurial lens: Theory and observation. *Journal of Business Ethics*, 38, 227–241.

Soto-Acosta, P., Cismaru, D.M., Vatamanescu, E.M. and Ciochina, R.S. (2016). Sustainable entrepreneurship in SMEs: A business performance perspective. *Sustainability*, 8(4), 342.

Spence, L.J. (2016). Small business social responsibility: Expanding core CSR theory. *Business and Society*, 55, 23–55.

Spence, L.J. and Rutherfoord, R. (2001). Social responsibility, profit maximisation and the small firm owner-manager. *Journal of Small Business and Enterprise Development*, 8(2), 126–139.

Spence, L.J. and Rutherfoord, R. (2003). Small business and empirical perspectives in business ethics: Editorial. *Journal of Business Ethics*, 47, 1–5.

Spence, M., Gherib, J.B.B. and Biwole, V.O. (2011). Sustainable entrepreneurship: Is entrepreneurial will enough? A north–south comparison. *Journal of Business Ethics*, 99, 335–367.

Stoian, C. and Gilman, M. (2017). Corporate social responsibility that 'pays': A strategic approach to CSR for SMEs. *Journal of Small Business Management*, 55(1), 5–31.

Surie, G. and Ashley, A. (2008). Integrating pragmatism and ethics in entrepreneurial leadership for sustainable value creation. *Journal of Business Ethics*, 81, 235–246.

Tilley, F. (2000). Small firm environmental ethics: How deep do they go? *Business Ethics – a European Review*, 9, 31–41.

Tracey, P., Phillips, N. and Jarvis, O. (2011). Bridging institutional entrepreneurship and the creation of new organizational forms: A multilevel model. *Organization Science*, 22, 60–80.

Trevino, L.K., Weaver, G.R. and Reynolds, S.J. (2006). Behavioral ethics in organizations: A review. *Journal of Management*, 32, 951–990.

Vazquez-Carrasco, R. and Lopez-Perez, M.E. (2013). Small and medium-sized enterprises and corporate social responsibility: A systematic review of the literature. *Quality and Quantity*, 47, 3205–3218.

Waddock, S. (2000). The multiple bottom lines of corporate citizenship: Social investing, reputation, and responsibility audits. *Business and Society Review*, 105, 323–345.

Wang, T. and Bansal, P. (2012). Social responsibility in new ventures: Profiting from a long-term orientation. *Strategic Management Journal*, 33(10), 1135–1153.

Webb, J.W., Tihanyi, L., Ireland, R.D. and Sirmon, D.G. (2009). You say illegal, I say legitimate: Entrepreneurship in the informal economy. *Academy of Management Review*, 34, 492–510.

Welter, F. (2011). Contextualizing entrepreneurship-conceptual challenges and ways forward. *Entrepreneurship Theory and Practice*, 35, 165–184.

Werner, A. (2008). The influence of Christian identity on SME owner-managers' conceptualisations of business practice. *Journal of Business Ethics*, 82, 449–462.

Wickert, C., Scherer, A.G. and Spence, L.J. (2016). Walking and talking corporate social responsibility: Implications of firm size and organizational cost. *Journal of Management Studies*, 53(7), 1169–1196.

Wood, D.J. (1991). Corporate social performance revisited. *Academy of Management Review*, 16, 691–718.

Worthington, I. and Patton, D. (2005). Strategic intent in the management of the green environment within SMEs: An analysis of the UK screen-printing sector. *Long Range Planning*, 38, 197–212.

Yin, J. and Zhang, Y. (2012). Institutional dynamics and corporate social responsibility (CSR) in an emerging country context: Evidence from China. *Journal of Business Ethics*, 111, 301–316.

York, J.G. and Venkataraman, S. (2010). The entrepreneur–environment nexus: Uncertainty, innovation, and allocation. *Journal of Business Venturing*, 25, 449–463.

Yu, J.T. and Xiao, G.R. (2012). *Business Ethics. Theories and Cases*. Beijing: Tsinghua University Press, pp. 37–40.

Zahra, S.A. (2005). A theory of international new ventures: A decade of research. *Journal* of *International Business Studies*, 36, 20–28.

Zahra, S.A., Gedajlovic, E., Neubaum, D.O. and Schulman, J. (2009). A typology of social entrepreneurs: Motives, search processes and ethical challenges. *Journal of Business Venturing*, 24, 519–532.

Zahra, S.A., Rawhouser, H.N., Bhawe, N., Neubaum, D.O. and Hayton, J.C. (2008). Globalization of social entrepreneurship opportunities. *Strategic Entrepreneurship Journal*, 2, 117–131.

Zahra, S.A., Wright, M. and Abdelgawad, S.G. (2014). Contextualization and the advancement of entrepreneurship research. *International Small Business Journal*, 32, 479–500.

Zhu, Y. (2015). The role of qing (positive emotions) and li (rationality) in Chinese entrepreneurial decision making: A Confucian *Ren-Yi* wisdom perspective. *Journal of Business Ethics*, 126, 613–630.

23

Bringing 'I' into 'E' – What Could It Mean? Reflections on the Past, Present and Future of International Entrepreneurship Research

Niina Nummela

INTRODUCTION

The emergence of international entrepreneurship (IE) as a research topic was recognised in the early 1990s (Wright & Ricks, 1994) and later specified as a field which lies at the intersection of two existing streams of research: entrepreneurship and international business (McDougall & Oviatt, 2000). The focus of the field has been elusive, but according to the most established definition, international entrepreneurship refers to 'the discovery, enactment, evaluation, and exploitation of opportunities – across national borders – to create future goods and services' (Oviatt & McDougall, 2005, p. 540). This implies that acting entrepreneurially and becoming international are two tightly intertwined but overlapping processes (Fletcher, 2004).

International entrepreneurship research deviates from its parent disciplines in its emphasis on *time*. Although the definition of IE does not explicitly refer to it, the temporal dimension has always been inherent in it.

While time in internationalisation is a very complex issue (Hurmerinta-Peltomäki, 2003), in international entrepreneurship research it typically refers to either the early start of international activities or the speed or pace of international growth (Zucchella, Palamara & Denicolai, 2007). Interest in the *early* internationalisation of the firm emerged in the late 1980s when researchers interested in SME internationalisation began to notice this phenomenon emerging from large data sets (Christensen, 1991; Hurmerinta-Peltomäki, 2004). However, international entrepreneurship scholars have been particularly interested in firms that are 'born' with the intent to serve markets quickly and less in accidental internationalisers (Coviello, 2015). These early internationalising firms may be labelled international new ventures (INVs), born globals, global start-ups or something else, depending on the definition used (Madsen, 2013).[1]

Another temporal dimension that has aroused particular interest among IE scholars is the *pace* of internationalisation. One of the key early arguments of IE researchers was that international new ventures deviate from other new ventures because of their fast foreign expansion, and speed has often been used as a proxy for international entrepreneurial behaviour (Acedo & Jones, 2007). However, IE researchers have typically taken a limited view of speed, as it is usually conceptualised and measured as the time between the inception of the firm and the start of internationalisation (Chetty, Johanson & Martin, 2014; Casillas & Acedo, 2013). It is only recently that scholars have paid attention to the complexity of speed and how it changes during internationalisation (see, e.g. Johanson & Kalinic, 2016).

Adding a temporal perspective is not a sufficient basis to claim that there is a need for a new approach or field. In the past, both international business and entrepreneurship have struggled to obtain legitimacy as a relevant and rigorous research field. Therefore, it is not surprising that IE has also experienced similar debates (Jones, Coviello & Tang, 2011; Keupp & Gassmann, 2009; Wright, Westhead & Ucbasaran, 2007). This is a natural phase in the development of a field, and it seems that during the last 25-plus years, IE has managed to differentiate itself and gain some legitimacy (Coviello, Jones & McDougall-Covin, 2016; Servantie, Cabrol, Guieu & Boissin, 2016). However, building a research field on two disciplines is not easy, as it requires considerable effort in combining different epistemological and ontological backgrounds. Unfortunately, there are cases where researchers have taken shortcuts in the process, e.g. by using measures from entrepreneurship and just adapting them slightly by adding the word 'international'. This has resulted in a number of measurement challenges (e.g. on challenges in measuring international entrepreneurial orientation, see Covin & Miller, 2014) and a failure to capture the true nature of the phenomenon.

In the future, the progress of IE as a research field depends on two key issues: (1) IE scholars' ability to continuously improve the rigour of research, and (2) their competence in

combining the best elements of both parent disciplines to create *something new*. In order to be sustainable, the field needs to provide value added to both academic and practitioner audiences – preferably through multitheoretic and multimethodological research designs (cf. Ireland & Webb, 2007). Consequently, the aim of this chapter is to highlight the specific features of international entrepreneurship research and identify areas of common interest which could serve as a bridge for scholars interested in advancing entrepreneurship, international business or international entrepreneurship research.

In addition to highlighting the complementarities, this chapter underlines the potential which the combination of international business and entrepreneurship holds in terms of contextualisation – something which has been called for in both fields (Michailova, 2011; Welter, 2011). International entrepreneurship as a phenomenon is deeply embedded in multiple contexts, which are the building blocks of a rigorous theory (Zahra, Wright & Abdelgawad, 2014). Researchers need to contextualise – i.e. to link empirical observations with relevant facts, events or points of view (Rousseau & Fried, 2001) – in order to obtain deeper understanding of the phenomenon. This chapter suggests how merging knowledge from international business and entrepreneurship fields would facilitate answering context-related questions, such as who, where, when and why (cf. Johns, 2006).

The chapter starts by introducing international business (IB) and IE research from the viewpoint of time and process, suggesting that this understanding could be built in when describing the temporal context of IE phenomena. Next, discourse on location and cross-border behaviour is presented to highlight the link between IE and the spatial context. The discussion is then brought to the level of the individual, i.e. the entrepreneur, to address cross-level contextualisation. The chapter concludes by synthesising the many faces of context from the viewpoint of future research.

CAPTURING THE DYNAMICS: A PROCESS VIEW ON ENTREPRENEURIAL INTERNATIONALISATION

A review of the IE research verifies that scholars in the field have focused on new ventures and their international growth process. The early works in the field in the late 1980s and the 1990s studied the characteristics of international new ventures and compared them with other types of organisations (Jones et al., 2011). The conclusion was that a number of factors related to the founder(s), the organisation and the business environment were identified as drivers of early internationalisation (Madsen & Servais, 1997). Another theme which has continued to be of interest is the internationalisation patterns of these firms (Jones et al., 2011). Typically, the focus has been on the description, comparison and explanation of start-up patterns and early internationalisation (see, e.g. Kuivalainen, Saarenketo & Puumalainen, 2012). However, in recent years, researchers' interest has increasingly turned from early internationalisation to survival and subsequent international growth (Mudambi & Zahra, 2007; Prashantham & Young, 2011). Independent of the focus, a critical reader may conclude that within the IE field the discussion on the behavioural process underlying internationalisation has remained rather descriptive. A more constructive, analytical debate regarding the mechanisms underlying international growth has been limited. The following question thus remains: What is entrepreneurial internationalisation? Answering this question requires a closer look at international business literature.

When discussing the internationalisation process, a common starting point is a reference to the work of scholars at Uppsala University in the 1970s. The well-known Uppsala model of the internationalisation process (Johanson & Vahlne, 1977) is a theory-based conceptual model arguing that internationalisation of a firm is characterised by risk management, experiential learning and a combination of resources and knowledge. It is expected to be applicable across companies of different sizes. The model resonates well with the growth of international new ventures, provided it is accepted that (a) internationalisation is a cyclical, time-based behaviour (Jones & Coviello, 2005) and that (b) experiential learning may occur already before the inception of the venture (Kontinen, 2014; Hewerdine & Welch, 2008). Thus, although the 'traditional' approach to internationalisation and IE are often contrasted, they can also be seen as complementary to each other.

Another common juxtaposition is related to entrepreneurial internationalisation as entrepreneurial behaviour, which is considered to be proactive and risk-taking (Covin & Slevin, 1991). Again, at first glance, this seems contradictory to internationalisation process research, which often assumes that the firm strives to keep risks related to internationalisation at a low level. However, a closer look at Johanson and Vahlne's (1977) seminal work reveals that instead of a low level of risk, they focus on tolerable risk, a concept which is very similar to the concept of affordable loss in entrepreneurship (Dew, Sarasvathy, Read & Wiltbank, 2009). Thus, entrepreneurial internationalisation involves risk-taking, albeit on the level that the decision maker is able to handle. IE research indicates that risk-taking and the pace of internationalisation are interrelated: firms with decision makers who have lower levels of risk perception are more likely to internationalise quickly (Acedo & Jones, 2007). Entrepreneurial internationalisation is a constant balancing act of risk and uncertainty: the perceived risk may increase due to growing resource commitment to international markets, but experienced uncertainty may decrease due to experiential learning (Liesch, Welch & Buckley, 2011).

Recently, entrepreneurial internationalisation has also been described as a process of international opportunity recognition and exploitation. When entering international markets for the first time, firms undergo a process of opportunity recognition (Hurmerinta,

Nummela & Paavilainen-Mäntymäki, 2015; Chandra, Styles & Wilkinson, 2009), and this process is repeated each time the firm enters a new market. Over time, internationalisation becomes a process of opportunity, portfolio processing and management (Chandra, Styles & Wilkinson, 2015).

From a theoretical point of view, internationalisation is about knowledge development and commitment to an opportunity (Johanson & Vahlne, 2009). Commitment to an opportunity occurs through a learning process, which may sometimes be quite rapid. Accelerated learning is possible due to three main reasons. First, it may be that international new ventures (INVs) benefit from the learning advantage of newness, i.e. they are faster to adapt and compete in new, dynamic environments because they are not burdened by old organisational routines and structures (Autio, Sapienza & Almeida, 2000). Second, INVs seem to be able to increase their absorptive capacity by improving knowledge acquisition, assimilation and transformation processes in order to exploit the knowledge more efficiently to facilitate rapid learning (Zahra & George, 2002). Third, INVs' ability to combine and benefit from different types of learning may compensate for their lack of experiential learning (Hewerdine & Welch, 2013; Bruneel, Yli-Renko & Clarysse, 2010). Usually, the congenital (i.e. pre-start-up) learning is highlighted, but interorganisational learning is also important (Fletcher & Harris, 2012). After the initial access to international markets, the ability to build weak ties, extend networks and obtain social capital is considered important for sustaining the speed of internationalisation (Prashantham & Young, 2011). Thus, while firms continue to learn from their partners, the impact of this interorganisational learning diminishes as the level of experiential learning increases (Bruneel et al., 2010). It is noteworthy that all three drivers of accelerated learning are related to organisational capabilities.

For quite some time, IE scholars have agreed that internationalisation may be considered an entrepreneurial process (Schweizer, Vahlne & Johanson, 2010; Jones & Coviello, 2005). The discussion above also shows that international business and entrepreneurship research complement each other when trying to understand entrepreneurial internationalisation. Introducing the insights from international business theories might facilitate our understanding of why entrepreneurial internationalisation may sometimes be accelerated. It also provides at least partial understanding of how the process takes place. Thus, the combination of the two research fields allows us to provide a richer picture of the temporal context in which international growth takes place.

Entrepreneurial internationalisation also seems to be a learning process which aims to identify and develop opportunities *across borders*. Consequently, in addition to the temporal context, the spatial context of the process also needs to be highlighted.

HITTING THE SCENE: ENTREPRENEURSHIP CROSSING BORDERS

Entrepreneurial internationalisation is embedded in a dynamic and constantly evolving spatial context. It has multiple layers, including the broader, *location-based context* and the more focused layer of the *firm-level interaction context*, both of which have gone through a notable change during the last decade.

The discussion on location has taken two opposite directions: on the one hand, focusing on the borderless world and pointing out that the role of location is diminishing, and on the other hand, highlighting the counterforces that lead to geographic clustering and the increasing importance of location. The first stream hit full speed after Thomas Friedman published *The World is Flat* in 2005, in which he argues that, due to globalisation and technological advancement, the geographic location of a firm has lost its relevance. This conclusion was quickly challenged by other scholars, who argued that innovations and industries tend to cluster (Florida, 2005; Florida, Gulden & Mellander, 2008), that globalisation touches only a fraction of the world's population (Ghemawat, 2007) and that MNC headquarters and subsidiaries are concentrated in a few cities in the world (Alcacer, Cantwell & Piscitello, 2016). The issue is much more complex, and thus in a way, both parties are right, but their argumentation covers only half of the truth.

Friedman's arguments have received support, particularly from the advocates of the information and communication technology (ICT) revolution and digitalisation. It is clear that these advancements will revolutionise the business models in some traditional industries and create completely new types of business, in which the business environment is more or less virtual. We have already witnessed the emergence of international business opportunities which are no longer location-based (see, e.g. Brouthers, Geisser & Rothlauf, 2016; Reuber & Fischer, 2011), and this is bound to have profound impacts on how business is conducted in the future.

Nevertheless, although very few areas of business remain completely intact, the degree of digitalisation's impact varies considerably. Today and in the future, we will still have international business operations which are strongly characterised by physical space. Thus, boundaries still do exist and location does matter in some cases. However, recent studies indicate that perhaps we should transfer our locus of interest from the nation state as a spatial context to the regions in which entrepreneurial, internationally growing companies are embedded (e.g. Sasaki & Yoshikawa, 2014; Zahra et al., 2014). This is particularly relevant for IE scholars since clusters and regions support accelerated entrepreneurial internationalisation, as co-location provides improved access to the resources needed (Zander, McDougall-Covin & Rose, 2015).

In the turbulent business environment, location has also become less unidimensional:

it can often be quite challenging to define the location or geographic space in which a company operates. Instead of a single entity, both small and large companies operate as globally dispersed value networks which jointly generate activities as 'global factories' (Eriksson, Nummela & Saarenketo, 2014; Buckley & Ghauri, 2004). The value chain of a company is globally dispersed: the upstream and downstream activities with the most value-adding elements are located in advanced economies, which are close to customers and advanced technology, while the least value-adding activities are located in the emerging markets to ensure cost efficiency (Mudambi, 2008). In this respect, the role and importance of location has increased in international business. Unfortunately, researchers quite often ignore the existence of multiple layers of spatial context and do not adapt their theoretical frameworks accordingly.

Then again, digitalisation does challenge existing concepts and theories related to international business. For example, many of these concepts and theories are based on the idea that successful internationalisation requires firms to overcome their liability of foreignness (LOF) related to the new markets. In the borderless world and in virtual markets, the LOF concept becomes obsolete, and thus alternative concepts and theories need to be introduced in order to understand how international 'location-free' opportunities are captured. Brouthers et al. (2016) suggest that the liability of outsidership could explain the variation in the internationalisation of Internet-based firms. Successful internationalisation would require membership in relevant networks, and the process of internationalisation depends on whether the company is able to become an insider (Johanson & Vahlne, 2009).

It is essential to understand that the liability of outsidership as a concept does not have a link to physical location or national boundaries (Johanson & Vahlne, 2009); on the contrary, it is linked more to the *firm-level context for firm-level interaction*. Although national or regional borders may appear as significant discontinuities in space (Beugelsdijk & Mudambi, 2013), from the viewpoint of interaction, other boundaries are of greater importance. In particular, sociocultural norms and perceptions may create frontiers which are difficult to overcome, and what makes them particularly challenging is that they are constantly changing (Ojala, 2015). Sociocultural norms exist in virtual environments as well, as interaction takes place between individuals. Their cultural backgrounds and cognitive schemas play a crucial role in how the interaction unfolds (Obadia, 2013; Elo, Benjowsky & Nummela, 2015). Again, international business theories offer tools explaining how to better understand the firm-level interaction crossing sociocultural boundaries.

Nevertheless, all this makes the contextualisation in IE research increasingly challenging. The 'entrepreneurial space' in which entrepreneurial firms operate is becoming more inclusive and interdependent. International entrepreneurial behaviour is embedded in a context which is characterised by the strong interdependence of actors. The markets develop towards multicultural marketplaces, i.e. spatial units – either physical or virtual – in which consumers, marketers, brands and ideas from multiple cultures interact continuously (Demangeot, Broderick & Craig, 2015). Thus, the multiple layers of contexts become increasingly intertwined. At the same time, contextualised theorising requires that we are also able to read across different levels of contexts. This means that besides understanding the organisation context, we also need to link our findings with the key actors, i.e. the individuals who are the focus of our interest.

BRINGING IT TO THE GRASS-ROOTS LEVEL

In addition to the constant flux of spatial and temporal contexts, we can also assume that the actors, i.e. the entrepreneurs, adapt themselves to fit the environment. Thus, contextualisation

requires that we take into account who is being studied (Johns, 2006). The majority of IE studies take a rather traditional view on the actor in entrepreneurial internationalisation, assuming that s/he starts business operations in her/his country of origin and faces the challenges which a new international environment poses there. If the liabilities of foreignness and/or outsidership are overcome, the route to international markets is clear.

Yet we know that the entrepreneurs of today are not a homogeneous group, including actors beyond just the profit-seeking entrepreneurs with strong roots in their home market. They include, for example, ethnic entrepreneurs who operate in their new home country, transnational entrepreneurs or diasporans who migrate from one country to another and maintain business relationships between the two countries (Riddle, Hrivnak & Nielsen, 2010; Drori, Honig & Wright, 2009). Variance in entrepreneurs' motivation, identity and cultural background leads to variance in internationalisation patterns – something we already see in practice. Therefore, we cannot automatically assume that the same theoretical frameworks would accurately capture all this variation.

Furthermore, it has also become increasingly challenging to define who actually is an entrepreneur. For example, the multicultural marketplaces also bring together consumers who act as international entrepreneurs (Chandra & Coviello, 2010). This leads to a revolutionary change in our understanding of how (international) opportunities emerge: they may also be created in the mutual relationship between the individual and the community in which s/he is a part (Shepherd, 2015). Thus, an entrepreneurial ecosystem and its members are no longer only the support structure which facilitates growth the of new ventures (cf. Spigel, 2015), but also active participants of the opportunity recognition and capture. In the future, it may be necessary to extend our view from the firm as the unit of analysis to the entrepreneurial ecosystem and study its relationship with (international) entrepreneurial behaviour (cf. Wright & Stigliani, 2013).

From the viewpoint of international entrepreneurship, the theoretical lenses which we apply to understand the key actors, i.e. the entrepreneurs, are limited. The classic entrepreneurship and international business theories were developed in Western economies, and although recent studies have shed more light on entrepreneurial behaviour in emerging and developing economies, it is fair to say that our understanding is very much Western-based. Additionally, we tend to consider entrepreneurs as individuals with strong local roots and networks, which they draw upon to build their operations. However, international entrepreneurship research in particular has shown that a growing number of entrepreneurs start their businesses not only with a global mindset, but are also supported by considerable international experience and exposure through studying, living and working abroad. Therefore, it is about time to bring in the contextualisation to the level of individual.

CONCLUSION

International entrepreneurship is a very phenomenon-driven research field and thus follows the tradition of its parent disciplines. While this chapter has demonstrated that international entrepreneurship has its own particular features, it also highlights multiple areas of research where entrepreneurship and international business scholars would have common interests. Additionally, there are areas in which one of the disciplines is more advanced than the other, and building on this knowledge would facilitate the other field's ability to take a leap forward. An example of such beneficial bridge-building could be the cognitive drivers of entrepreneurial behaviour, as conceptual discussions of such drivers have been more advanced in entrepreneurship research than in internationalisation literature (Acedo & Jones, 2007).

On the other hand, neither entrepreneurship nor international business as a field has been very successful in developing theoretical understanding of *how* firms grow. In both fields, scholars have concentrated on developing diverse frameworks and identifying patterns. For example, Delmar, Davidsson and Gartner (2003) found seven different growth patterns and Kuivalainen et al. (2012) found ten alternative internationalisation patterns among knowledge-intensive SMEs. In other words, scholars have been searching for answers for the same questions, but without much success. At this point one can ask the following question: Why not join forces and try to explain how growth differs according to different entrepreneurial contexts (cf. Wright & Stigliani, 2013)?

Another example of a phenomenon of mutual interest is failure. Although it has been discussed in entrepreneurship, international business and international entrepreneurship literature, an implicit assumption of continuous growth dominates. Failures are typically treated as separate events or periods during the company's life cycle, again stressing the descriptive, pattern-searching approach. At the same time, our understanding of the underlying mechanisms remains superficial and limited.

Besides the potential for collaboration, the prospects for contextualisation through combining insights from entrepreneurship and international business are also noteworthy. The world is more complex than ever and the phenomena of interest are spread over space, time and all possible boundaries. Wicked problems are here to stay, and they need to be tackled – also by international entrepreneurship scholars.

Note

1 It should be stressed that the terms 'international new venture' and 'born global' are not to be used interchangeably, as the definitions of the concepts differ significantly. The IE field generally suffers from conceptual confusion and therefore it is essential to define the key concepts explicitly.

ACKNOWLEDGEMENTS

This work was supported by the Estonian Research Council's grant PUT 1003.

REFERENCES

Acedo, F.J. & Jones, M.V. (2007), Speed of internationalization and entrepreneurial cognition: Insights and a comparison between international new ventures, exporters and domestic firms. *Journal of World Business*, 42 (3), 236–252.

Alcacer, J., Cantwell, J. & Piscitello, L. (2016), Internationalization in the information age: A new era for places, firms, and international business networks? *Journal of International Business Studies*, 47 (5), 499–512.

Autio, E., Sapienza, H.J. & Almeida, J.G. (2000), Effects of age at entry, knowledge intensity, and imitability on international growth. *Academy of Management Journal*, 43 (5), 909–924.

Beugelsdijk, S. & Mudambi, R. (2013), MNEs as border-crossing multi-location enterprises: The role of discontinuities in geographic space. *Journal of International Business Studies*, 44 (5), 413–426.

Brouthers, K.D., Geisser, K.D. & Rothlauf, F. (2016), Explaining the internationalization of ibusiness firms. *Journal of International Business Studies*, 47 (5), 513–534.

Bruneel, J., Yli-Renko, H. & Clarysse, B. (2010), Learning from experience and learning from others: How congenital and interorganizational learning substitute for experiential learning in young firm internationalization. *Strategic Entrepreneurship Journal*, 4 (2), 164–182.

Buckley, P.J. & Ghauri, P.N. (2004), Globalisation, economic geography and the strategy of multinational enterprises. *Journal of International Business Studies*, 35 (2), 81–98.

Casillas, J.C. & Acedo, F.J. (2013), Speed in the internationalization process of the firm. *International Journal of Management Reviews*, 15 (1), 15–29.

Chandra, Y. & Coviello, N. (2010), Broadening the concept of international entrepreneurship: Consumers as international entrepreneurs. *Journal of World Business*, 45 (3), 228–236.

Chandra, Y., Styles, C. & Wilkinson, I. (2009), The recognition of first time international entrepreneurial opportunities. Evidence from firms in knowledge-based industries. *International Marketing Review*, 26 (1), 30–61.

Chandra, Y., Styles, C. & Wilkinson, I.F. (2015), Opportunity portfolio: Moving beyond single opportunity explanations in international entrepreneurship research. *Asia Pacific Journal of Management*, 32 (1), 199–228.

Chetty, S., Johanson, M. & Martin, O.M. (2014), Speed of internationalization: Conceptualization, measurement and validation. *Journal of World Business*, 49 (4), 633–650.

Christensen, P.R. (1991), The small and medium sized exporters squeeze: Empirical evidence and model reflections. *Entrepreneurship and Regional Development*, 3 (1), 49–65.

Coviello, N. (2015), Re-thinking research on born globals. *Journal of International Business Studies*, 46 (1), 17–26.

Coviello, N.E., Jones, M.V. & McDougall-Covin, P.P. (2016), Is international entrepreneurship research a viable spin-off from its parent disciplines? In A. Fayolle & P. Riot (eds), *Rethinking Entrepreneurship: Debating Research Orientations*, pp. 78–99. Oxford and New York: Routledge.

Covin, J.G. & Miller, D. (2014), International entrepreneurial orientation: Conceptual considerations, research themes, measurement issues, and future research directions. *Entrepreneurship Theory and Practice*, 38 (1), 11–44.

Covin, J.G. & Slevin, D.P. (1991), A conceptual model of entrepreneurship as firm behavior. *Entrepreneurship Theory and Practice*, 16 (1), 7–25.

Delmar, F., Davidsson, P. & Gartner, W.B. (2003), Arriving at the high-growth firm. *Journal of Business Venturing*, 18 (2), 189–216.

Demangeot, C., Broderick, A.J. & Craig, C.S. (2015), Multicultural marketplaces. *International Marketing Review*, 32 (2), 118–140.

Dew, N., Sarasvathy, S.D., Read, S. & Wiltbank, R. (2009), Affordable loss: Behavioral economic aspects of plunge decision. *Strategic Entrepreneurship Journal*, 3 (2), 105–126.

Drori, I., Honig, B. & Wright, M. (2009), Transnational entrepreneurship: An emergent field of study. *Entrepreneurship Theory and Practice*, 33 (5), 1001–1022.

Elo, M., Benjowsky, C. & Nummela, N. (2015), Intercultural competences and interaction schemes – four forces regulating dyadic encounters in international business. *Industrial Marketing Management*, 48 (5), 38–49.

Eriksson, T., Nummela, N. & Saarenketo, S. (2014), Dynamic capability in a small global factory. *International Business Review*, 23 (1), 169–180.

Fletcher, D. (2004), International entrepreneurship and the small business. *Entrepreneurship and Regional Development*, 16 (4), 289–305.

Fletcher, M. & Harris, S. (2012), Knowledge acquisition for the internationalization of the smaller firm: Content and sources. *International Business Review*, 21 (4), 631–647.

Florida, R. (2005), The world is spiky. *The Atlantic Monthly*, 296 (3), 48–51.

Florida, R., Gulden, T. & Mellander, C. (2008), The rise of the mega-region. *Cambridge Journal of Regions, Economy and Society*, 1 (3), 459–476.

Friedman, T. (2005), *The World is Flat: A Brief History of the Globalized World in the Twenty-First Century*. London: Allen Lane.

Ghemawat, P. (2007), Why the world isn't flat. *Foreign Policy*, 159 (March/April), 54–60.

Hewerdine, L. & Welch, C. (2008), Reinterpreting a 'prime example' of a born global: Cochlear's international launch. In M.P. Feldman & G. Santangelo (eds), *New Perspectives in International Business Research. Progress in International Business Research*, Vol. 3, pp. 189–206. Bingley: Emerald Group.

Hewerdine, L. & Welch, C. (2013), Are international new ventures really new? A process study of organizational emergence and internationalization. *Journal of World Business*, 48 (4), 466–477.

Hurmerinta, L., Nummela, N. & Paavilainen-Mäntymäki, E. (2015), Opening and closing doors: The role of language in international opportunity recognition and exploitation, *International Business Review*, 25 (6), 1082–1094.

Hurmerinta-Peltomäki, L. (2003), Time and internationalisation. Theoretical challenges set by rapid internationalisation. *Journal of International Entrepreneurship*, 1 (2), 217–236.

Hurmerinta-Peltomäki, L. (2004), Conceptual and methodological underpinnings in the study of rapid internationalisers. In M.V. Jones & P. Dimitratos (eds), *Emerging Paradigms in International Entrepreneurship*, pp. 64–88. Cheltenham: Edward Elgar.

Ireland, R.D. & Webb, J.W. (2007), A cross-disciplinary exploration of entrepreneurship research. *Journal of Management*, 33 (6), 891–927.

Johanson, J. & Vahlne, J.E. (1977), The internationalization process of the firm: A model of knowledge development and increasing foreign market commitment, *Journal of International Business Studies*, 8 (1), 23–32.

Johanson, J. & Vahlne, J.E. (2009), The Uppsala internationalization process model revisited: From liability of foreignness to liability of outsidership. *Journal of International Business Studies*, 40 (9), 1411–1431.

Johanson, M. & Kalinic, I. (2016), Acceleration and deceleration in the internationalization process of the firm. *Management International Review*, 56 (6), forthcoming.

Johns, G. (2006), The essential impact of context on organizational behavior. *Academy of Management Review*, 31 (2), 386–408.

Jones, M.V. & Coviello, N.E. (2005), Internationalization: Conceptualizing an entrepreneurial process of behaviour in time. *Journal of International Business Studies*, 36 (3), 284–303.

Jones, M.V., Coviello, N. & Tang, Y.K. (2011), International entrepreneurship research (1989–2009): A domain ontology and thematic analysis. *Journal of Business Venturing*, 26 (6), 632–659.

Keupp, M.M. & Gassmann, O. (2009), The past and the future of international entrepreneurship: A review and suggestions for developing the field. *Journal of Management*, 35 (3), 600–633.

Kontinen, T. (2014), Biohit: A global, family-owned company embarking on a new phase. *Entrepreneurship Theory and Practice*, 38 (1), 185–203.

Kuivalainen, O., Saarenketo, S. & Puumalainen, K. (2012), Start-up patterns of internationalization: A framework and its application in the context of knowledge-intensive SMEs. *European Management Journal*, 30 (4), 372–385.

Liesch, P.W., Welch, L.S. & Buckley, P.J. (2011), Risk and uncertainty in internationalisation and international entrepreneurship studies. Review and conceptual development. *Management International Review*, 51 (6), 851–873.

Madsen, T.K. (2013), Early and rapidly internationalizing ventures: Similarities and differences between classifications based on the original international new venture and born global literatures. *Journal of International Entrepreneurship*, 11 (1), 65–79.

Madsen, T.K. & Servais, P. (1997), The internationalization of born globals: An evolutionary process? *International Business Review*, 6 (6), 561–583.

McDougall, P.P. & Oviatt, B.M. (2000), International entrepreneurship: The intersection of two research paths. *Academy of Management Journal*, 43 (5), 902–906.

Michailova, S. (2011), Contextualizing in international business research: Why do we need more of it and how can we be better at it? *Scandinavian Journal of Management*, 27 (1), 129–139.

Mudambi, R. (2008), Location, control and innovation in knowledge-intensive industries, *Journal of Economic Geography*, 8 (5), 699–725.

Mudambi, R. & Zahra, S.A. (2007), The survival of international new ventures. *Journal of International Business Studies*, 38 (2), 333–352.

Obadia, C. (2013), Foreigness-induced cognitive disorientation. *Management International Review*, 53 (3), 325–360.

Ojala, A. (2015), Geographic, cultural and psychic distance to foreign markets in the context of small and new ventures. *International Business Review*, 24 (5), 825–835.

Oviatt, B.M. & McDougall, P.P. (2005), Defining international entrepreneurship and modeling the speed of internationalization. *Entrepreneurship Theory and Practice*, 29 (5), 537–553.

Prashantham, S. & Young, S. (2011), Post-entry speed of international new ventures. *Entrepreneurship Theory and Practice*, 35 (2), 275–292.

Reuber, A.R. & Fischer, E. (2011), International entrepreneurship in internet-enabled markets. *Journal of Business Venturing*, 26 (6), 660–679.

Riddle, L., Hrivnak, G.A. & Nielsen, T.M. (2010), Transnational diaspora entrepreneurship in emerging markets: Bridging institutional divides. *Journal of International Management*, 16 (4), 398–411.

Rousseau, D.M. & Fried, Y. (2001), Location, location, location: Contextualizing organizational research. *Journal of Organizational Behavior*, 22 (1), 1–13.

Sasaki, I. & Yoshikawa, K. (2014), Going beyond national cultures – Dynamic interaction between intra-national, regional, and organizational realities. *Journal of World Business*, 49 (3), 455–464.

Schweizer, R., Vahlne, J.E. & Johanson, J. (2010), Internationalization as an entrepreneurial process. *Journal of International Entrepreneurship*, 8 (4), 343–370.

Servantie, V., Cabrol, M., Guieu, G. & Boissin, J.P. (2016), Is international entrepreneurship a field? A bibliometric analysis of the literature (1989–2015). *Journal of International Entrepreneurship*, 14 (2), 168–212.

Shepherd, D. (2015), Party on! A call for entrepreneurship research that is more interactive, activity based, cognitively hot, compassionate, and prosocial. *Journal of Business Venturing*, 30 (4), 489–507.

Spigel, B. (2015), The relational organization of entrepreneurial ecosystems, *Entrepreneurship Theory and Practice*, doi:10.1111/etap.12167

Welter, F. (2011), Contextualizing entrepreneurship – Conceptual challenges and ways forward. *Entrepreneurship Theory and Practice*, 35 (1), 165–184.

Wright, M. & Stigliani, I. (2013), Entrepreneurship and growth. *International Small Business Journal*, 31 (1), 3–22.

Wright, M., Westhead, P. & Ucbasaran, D. (2007), Internationalization of small and medium-sized enterprises (SMEs) and international entrepreneurship: A critique and policy implications. *Regional Studies*, 41 (7), 1013–1030.

Wright, R.W. & Ricks, D.A. (1994), Trends in international business research: Twenty-five years later. *Journal of International Business Studies*, 25 (4), 687–701.

Zahra, S.A. & George, G. (2002), Absorptive capacity: A review, reconceptualization, and extension. *Academy of Management Review*, 27 (2), 185–203.

Zahra, S.A., Wright, M. & Abdelgawad, S.G. (2014), Contextualization and the advancement of entrepreneurship research. *International Small Business Journal*, 32 (5), 479–500.

Zander, I., McDougall-Covin, P. & Rose, E.L. (2015), Born globals and international business: Evolution of a field of research. *Journal of International Business Studies*, 46 (1), 27–35.

Zucchella, A., Palamara, G. & Denicolai, S. (2007), The drivers of the early internationalization of the firm. *Journal of World Business*, 42 (3), 268–280.

24

Challenges to Venture Growth in Emerging Economies

Wafa N. Almobaireek, Ahmed Alshumaimeri and Tatiana S. Manolova

INTRODUCTION

Emerging economies are countries 'with a rapid pace of economic development and government policies favouring economic liberalization and the adoption of a free market system' (Arnold & Quelch, 1998). As of 2014, they accounted for over 80% of the world's population and for over 50% of the global GDP (IMF, 2014). The establishment and growth of the private sector has greatly accelerated emerging economies' transition from overwhelmingly state-centred economies to competitive markets and has propelled the pace of their economic development. New and small businesses constitute the majority of firms operating in emerging economies, generate over 60% of GDP in countries such as Turkey, Thailand, or Vietnam and are, collectively, the largest employers in many low-income countries (Ayyagari, Beck & Demirgüç-Kunt, 2007; Beck & Demirgüç-Kunt, 2006).

The sizeable economic contribution of the SME sector, however, may be due to the proliferated number of individually small and limited growth private enterprises rather than the linear translation of entrepreneurial firm growth. This is because new and small players face considerable challenges to growth, both externally and internally. External challenges to growth include the relatively underdeveloped institutions, which significantly increase the risks and costs of doing business (Djankov et al., 2002), institutional barriers to industry entry which are disproportionately high for new players (Chang & Wu, 2014), and sceptical societal attitudes towards entrepreneurship (Spencer & Gomez, 2004; Ahlstrom, Bruton & Yeh, 2008). Internal challenges stem from the ineffective organizational routines (Shane & Foo, 1999) exacerbated by the inadequate resource endowments (Aulakh, Rotate & Teegen, 2000) and lack of managerial sophistication (Lyles, Saxton & Watson, 2004). In sum, growth continues to be an elusive target for most new and small ventures in emerging economies (Peng & Heath, 1996; Wright et al., 2005; Aidis, Estrin & Mickiewicz, 2008; Tracey & Phillips, 2011; Batjargal et al., 2013).

In our review of the literature, we explore both the external and the internal challenges to new and small business growth in emerging economies, bringing in empirical evidence across different economic and institutional contexts. Next, we compare the challenges to growth early in the life cycle of an entrepreneurial venture to the growth challenges small firms in emerging economies face later in their life cycle. We theorize that external challenges are particularly detrimental early in the life of new ventures in emerging economies, whereas internal deficiencies stump growth at later stages of development.

To illustrate our argument, we use findings from the statistical analysis of a large-scale survey of the state of small business in Saudi Arabia, commissioned in 2011 by the Saudi Ministry of Labor (n = 1,126). We augment the discussion with interview data from six Saudi entrepreneurial ventures.

The chapter is organized as follows. We start by presenting our theoretical argument and literature review, followed by results from the statistical analysis of our survey data, and insights from our fieldwork. We conclude by formulating five directions for future research and outlining some managerial and public policy implications.

THEORETICAL PERSPECTIVES AND OVERVIEW OF THE LITERATURE

Entrepreneurial Growth

Growth is a popular measure of firm performance, and is considered by many to manifest the essence of entrepreneurship (Drucker, 1985; Covin & Slevin, 1997). Although not all small firms choose to grow (Wiklund & Shepherd, 2003; Leitch, Hill & Neergaard, 2010), it is generally agreed that some growth over time (i.e. growth in sales, employees, new products or market share) is desirable for

continued survival (Delmar, Davidsson & Gartner, 2003). The decision to grow is usually the choice of the entrepreneur whose growth expectancies ultimately affect the growth of the business over time (Cliff, 1998; Wiklund & Shepherd, 2003; Cassar, 2007).

Prior research has established that the vast majority of newly established ventures around the world, across economic and institutional contexts, do not achieve substantial levels of growth (Wong, Ho & Autio, 2005). Growth-oriented ventures follow different trajectories (McKelvie & Wiklund, 2010), influenced by demographics such as industry, size, age and governance (Delmar et al., 2003); 'management, marketing and money' (Brush, Ceru & Blackburn, 2009); the gender of the founder/manager (Cliff, 1998); the CEO's specific competencies and motivations (Davidsson, 1991; Baum, Locke & Smith, 2001); the firm's competitive strategies (Baum et al., 2001), resource base (Wiklund & Shepherd, 2003), or the availability of outside resources for growth (Dobbs & Hamilton, 2007). On the basis of the empirical analysis of 1, 501 high-growth Swedish SMEs over a ten-year period (1987–1996), Delmar et al. (2003, p. 5) concluded that:

> There is no such thing as a *typical* growth firm. Rather, there are many different types of growth firms with different growth patterns. Recognizing that 'high growth' is multidimensional in nature, and that 'high growth' can occur in a variety of ways, is an important insight for researchers and practitioners.

Entrepreneurial Growth in Emerging Economies

The majority of new and small businesses in emerging markets have a no-growth or low-growth orientation (Peng & Heath, 1996; Wright et al., 2005; Aidis et al., 2008; Manolova, Eunni & Gyoshev, 2008; Tracey & Phillips, 2011; Batjargal et al., 2013; Estrin, Korosteleva & Mickiewicz, 2013). A major reason for the no-growth or low-growth orientation is that a large portion of the entrepreneurial activity in emerging economies is necessity-based, rather than opportunity-based. Necessity-based entrepreneurship occurs when individuals participate in entrepreneurial activities because all other employment options are either absent or unsatisfactory (Acs, 2006). Directed at income substitution, necessity entrepreneurship rarely has a high-growth motivation. In the context of the transition economies of Central and Eastern Europe, for example, Scase (1997) differentiated between 'entrepreneurship' and 'proprietorship' and argued that the principal component of the small business sector is composed of those whose motivation is solely to carve out niches of personal autonomy. At higher levels of economic development, technological and institutional sophistication gives rise to opportunity entrepreneurs, i.e. those who are driven by the achievement of success through exploiting an opportunity for some form of gain, often believed to be economic. Opportunity-driven entrepreneurship is more likely to be technology or innovation-based and high-growth oriented and thus contributes to economic growth and development. As the level of economic development of the country increases, the ratio of necessity-to-opportunity entrepreneurship goes down and the growth ambitions of the entrepreneurs similarly increase. The 2015–16 *Global Entrepreneurship Monitor* (GEM) reports that

> at a regional level, necessity-driven entrepreneurship is highest in Africa and Latin America and the Caribbean, where 30% of entrepreneurs, on average, cite this motive. Particularly high levels of necessity motives can be seen in economies from these regions: Guatemala, Panama, Brazil and Egypt (more than 40%). The highest level of necessity-based activity, however, is in Macedonia, where over half the entrepreneurs started out of necessity. The other three regions report 22% with these motivations on average. In three European economies (Sweden, Luxembourg and Switzerland), 10% or fewer entrepreneurs mention necessity motives (Kelley, Singer, & Herrington, 2016, p. 23).

In addition to the predominantly necessity-based nature of entrepreneurial initiatives, new and small ventures in emerging economies face significant external and internal challenges to growth. Below, we discuss these in turn.

External challenges to growth

External challenges to venture growth in emerging economies include barriers such as high transaction costs, inefficient factor markets, inefficient capital flows, opaque regulation and weak property rights (Foss & Foss, 2008). Business scholars use the term 'institutional voids' to describe the situation where absent or weak institutional settings impact market formation, economic growth and entrepreneurship development (Khanna & Palepu, 1997; Mair, Martí & Ventresca, 2012; Webb et al., 2009). Khanna and Palepu (1997) distinguished between five major types of institutional voids in the capital, labour, and product markets, as well as voids in government regulation and contract enforcement.

Access to financial capital is perhaps the most critical impediment to entrepreneurial growth. In a study based on survey data on the business environment across 80 countries, Ayyagari et al. (2007) established that finance, crime and political instability have a direct impact on firm growth and access to finance is the most robust one among those three predictors. Similarly, Hutchinson and Xavier (2006) found that the growth of small and medium-sized enterprises (SMEs) in Slovenia is more sensitive to internal financing constraints than in a developed market economy, while Krasniqi (2007) found that inadequate financing presented a major barrier to SMEs in Kosovo. Beck & Demirgüç-Kunt (2006), presenting an earlier analysis of the World Business Environment Survey (Beck et al., 2005), reported that small firms' financing obstacles have almost twice the effect on annual growth that large firms' financing obstacles do and this difference is even stronger in the case of growth constraints related to the legal system and to corruption, where small firms suffer more than three times as much in the form of slower growth as large firms. In sum, growth financing is lacking across the majority of emerging economies, and the deficiencies in the formal institutional infrastructure exacerbate the negative effects of these liquidity constraints.

In addition to the absence of growth financing, new ventures suffer from other deficiencies in emerging economies' formal institutional infrastructure. The regulatory environment is often characterized by over-regulation combined with under-enforcement, elevating the costs of doing business while aggravating uncertainty and enticing corruption (Khanna & Palepu, 1997). According to the World Bank's *Doing Business* 2016 survey, for example, it took four years and up to 12% of the estate to resolve a case of insolvency in Brazil, compared to about 11 months at a cost of 3.5% in Finland (World Bank, 2016). As another example, it took 23 procedures and 179 days to get a construction permit in Hungary, compared to 10 procedures and 26 days in Singapore (World Bank, 2016). Opportunistic government officials often take advantage of the obscure regulatory regimes in order to exploit new and small players' vulnerabilities for personal gain. In their study of the entrepreneurial growth aspirations across individuals and institutional contexts, based on GEM data, Estrin et al. (2013) documented that growth-oriented entrepreneurs benefit from strong intellectual property rights protection and small government, and are constrained by corruption. Social networks alleviate some, but not all, of the institutional deficiencies.

Overall, the institutional barriers to industry entry and growth in emerging economies are disproportionately high for new and small players. These barriers not only suppress growth opportunities, but also have a compounding negative effect, in that they propel the emergence of a vast 'informal' sector (Chang & Wu, 2014; Djankov et al., 2002). According to some estimates, the 'informal' economy accounts for 30% of national GDP in Mexico, 44% in Russia, and over 65% in Georgia, as opposed to 8–10% in Austria, Switzerland or the US (Buehn & Schneider, 2012). By staying outside the realm of the formal economy, entrepreneurs in emerging

markets cannot avail themselves of important resources and benefits, such as police and judicial protection, access to formal credit, the ability to use formal labour contracts, or greater access to foreign markets (La Porta & Shleifer, 2008; Klapper, Lewin & Quesada Delgado, 2009). All of these informal sector disadvantages further stunt venture growth.

In addition to the restrictive formal institutions, emerging market ventures face informal institutional challenges. The predominantly state-centred institutions confer higher status to large businesses and government agencies, while entrepreneurship is often associated with opportunism and profiteering. In many societies, entrepreneurship is viewed as having practical appeal, but less status or visibility (Spencer & Gómez, 2004). In the former centrally-planned economies of Central and Eastern Europe, socialist ideology associated private proprietorship with parasitism, exploitation and profiteering, leaving a lasting stigma on individuals pursuing entrepreneurial opportunities (Aidis et al., 2008). In addition, the relatively underdeveloped institutions escalate the risks and the transaction and opportunity costs of starting a business, resulting in high failure rates (Djankov et al., 2002). The high failure rates reinforce the already sceptical social attitudes towards entrepreneurial initiatives.

Many emerging economies have undertaken institutional reforms aimed at facilitating entrepreneurial entry and small business growth. In the World Bank's 2016 *Doing Business* survey, Armenia, Georgia, Azerbaijan and Lithuania (former members of the Soviet Union), as well as Macedonia, FYR, all rank in the top 10 countries for the ease of starting a business among the 189 economies included in the study (World Bank, 2016). However, Armenia ranks 99th in the ease of getting electricity, Lithuania ranks 70th and Georgia ranks 101st in the ease of resolving insolvency, Azerbaijan ranks 114th in dealing with construction permits, while Macedonia, FYR, ranks 50th in the ease of registering property. Thus the progress has not been uniform and new and small business owners still face multiple challenges and hurdles.

Although the institutional environment is deemed overall not particularly entrepreneur-friendly across emerging economies, there is substantial variability in the underlying institutional dimensions. In a comparative study of the institutional environment for entrepreneurship across the major emerging economies, Brazil, India, China and Russia (the so-called BRIC countries), Eunni and Manolova (2012) documented no significant differences in the perceived favourability of the regulatory environment, but significant differences in the perceived favourability of the cognitive and normative environments. Kshetri and Dholakia (2011), in their investigation of the differences between the regulative institutions affecting entrepreneurship in China and India, found that the Chinese firms perceived their court system and bureaucratic support to entrepreneurship at the local/regional level more favourably compared to Indian firms, while the shift of business perceptions of the relation between government, bureaucracy and private firms in the three-year period of the study was higher in India than in China. Thus, broad comparisons of the institutional regimes across countries need to be taken as a first approximation only, and a more nuanced exploration and problematization of entrepreneurial context, regulatory and market voids and of different institutional logics is well warranted.

Internal Challenges to Growth

Internal challenges to growth are equally formidable. New and small ventures in emerging markets are less resource-endowed relative to their counterparts from developed market economies (Aulakh et al., 2000), and have few internally generated sources of competitive advantage that can be exploited in a growth-oriented strategy. Human capital, derived from investments in formal education, occupational experiences and training, in particular, is a critical resource endowment which allows the entrepreneur to spend less time seeking, gathering or analysing information about availability of opportunities, but more time obtaining financial resources or developing entrepreneurial skills, and thus improving the survival and growth chances for the new venture (Cooper, Gimeno-Gascon & Woo, 1994). Human capital is particularly important for new and small business in environments characterized by rapid change (Honig, 1998), such as the environments in emerging economies.

Empirical evidence supports the critical role of managerial experience and sophistication. A large-scale study on the state of small business in Saudi Arabia (Al-Hajjar & Presley, 1992), for example, documented that the low levels of managerial sophistication and efficiency are major constraints to the development of the small business sector. As one example, almost half of the small-turnover and single-and-family ownership firms do not use strategic planning tools and techniques (Al-Ghamdi, 2005). Another study reported that SMEs face a lack of workforce skills and management capabilities, and effective legal and regulatory procedures (Merdah & Sadi, 2011).

In the context of the formally centrally-planned economies of Central and Eastern Europe, entrepreneurs are often educationally well qualified and have some management experience, but have no prior entrepreneurial experience in a market context (Lyles et al., 2004; Wright et al., 2005; Smallbone & Welter, 2006). Some scholars have even directly questioned the relevance of education and experience gained under the socialist system in a market environment (Lyles & Baird, 1994). Focusing on entrepreneurial cognition in China, Lau and Busenitz (2001) demonstrated how perceived difficulties in sales and labour thwart growth intentions, while difficulties in procuring operational facilities and borrowing are positively related to growth intentions (a more detailed review of the challenges faced by entrepreneurs in transitional economies is presented by Manev and Manolova, 2010). In all, growth-oriented entrepreneurs in emerging economies face significant internal challenges, in addition to the formidable external challenges to growth.

Growth Strategies of New and Small Ventures in Emerging Economies

Given the considerable internal and external challenges, what competitive and growth-oriented strategies are available to emerging market entrepreneurs? Peng and Heath (1996) combined institutional theory, transaction cost economics, strategic choice theory and the resource-based view of the firm to develop a model of firm growth in transition economies. These authors posited that due to the formal and informal constraints in the institutional environment, the growth strategies of firms in the formerly planned economies rely on boundary blurring through extensive networking with other firms.

Other research has explored what competitive strategies (such as low-cost-based, differentiation-based, or a hybrid between the two) are associated with the higher growth and/or performance of emerging market firms. For example, Malo and Norus (2009), in their case studies of two biotechnology firms (one in Poland and one in Lithuania), documented that the production of low-cost, high-quality products can drive the companies' growth dynamics. Kim and Choi (1994) studied 79 small firms in four industries in Korea and found that a hybrid ('versatile') strategy was associated with positive performance. Similarly, in his study of SMEs in retail (129 establishments in Argentina, 113 in Peru, and 167 in the USA), Parnell (2013) established a 'U'-shaped relationship between strategic clarity and performance, which lends support to the idea that some SMEs may be able to successfully deploy a combination strategy that incorporates facets from two or more generic competitive strategies (pure low cost

or pure differentiation). In sum, research linking the competitive strategies of new and small ventures in emerging economies to their performance and growth tends to suggest that the majority of these firms adopt hybrid or multifaceted strategies, and, even more importantly, that hybrid rather than pure strategies are more likely to be associated with better performance. Importantly, in relation to Peng and Heath's (1996) model of firm growth, recent research has suggested that with the advent of pro-market reforms in emerging economies, growth strategies based on intense personal networking gradually give way to market-based strategies based on clear competitive positioning and economic value creation (Danis, Chiaburu & Lyles, 2010).

External and Internal Challenges Along the Venture Life Cycle

Another important question concerning the challenges to growth of emerging market ventures is the relative importance of different types of challenges (external or internal) along the life cycle of the entrepreneurial venture. Stage models (Greiner, 1972; Churchill & Lewis, 1983; Scott & Bruce, 1987) conceptualize small business growth as a series of stages, each with its own distinctive characteristics. For example, Churchill and Lewis (1983) modelled the stages of small business growth as existence, survival, success, take-off and resource maturity. Regardless of the economic and institutional context in which they come into existence, new ventures experience a turbulent and chaotic period of initial organizing, during which they are particularly prone to failure (Stinchcombe, 1965; Aldrich, 1999; Eisenhardt & Schoonhoven, 1990; Zimmerman & Zeitz, 2002). This period roughly maps out what Churchill & Lewis (1983) identify as the 'existence' and 'survival' stages of small business growth. During the 'existence' and 'survival' stages, the primary concern of the entrepreneur is to secure the viability of the new entity. For those new ventures that survive the perilous early years of their existence and reach what Churchill and Lewis (1983) call the 'success' stage, the key decision becomes whether to exploit the company's accomplishments for expansion, or keep the company stable and profitable.

Early in the life of a new venture, external challenges are particularly threatening. If key social constituencies are reluctant to recognize the new organization's right to exist or are unwilling to accept its outputs, its viability and growth prospects will be seriously jeopardized (Ahlstrom et al., 2008). Attaining legitimacy, or a social licence to operate, is a critical precursor for gaining resources needed for new venture growth (Zimmerman & Zeitz, 2002; Delmar & Shane, 2004).

As new ventures mature, and move into the 'success' stage of small business growth, they need to establish a cost-effective and efficient way of operating so they can compete successfully against established organizations. They also need to marshal resources for growth and to create administrative structures and processes that direct and monitor the organization's activities. In the process, growth-oriented ventures often engage in costly experimentation under conditions of significant resource constraints (Choi & Shepherd, 2005). Thus, internal challenges to growth become critical.

Emerging economies show great variability in their level of economic development, industrial structure, institutional heritage or cultural norms. Just as Delmar et al. (2003) noted that 'There is no such thing as a *typical* growth firm' in the context of developed economies, we contend that there is no such thing as a typical emerging economy SME. In the following section, we illustrate the temporal dynamics of the challenges to new and small business growth using empirical evidence from the SME sector in Saudi Arabia. Saudi Arabia provides an interesting context in which to illustrate the role of external and internal challenges to venture growth in emerging economies, because SMEs constitute over 96% of all firms, but account for only one-third of GDP (Al-Jaseer, 2010). Encouraging SME growth, therefore, is

essential, not only for job creation but also for the continued diversification of the Saudi economy. Our empirical exploration brings in fresh evidence from a context that has so far stayed at the periphery of scholarly attention.

CHALLENGES TO NEW AND SMALL BUSINESS GROWTH: ILLUSTRATIVE EVIDENCE FROM SAUDI ARABIA

The Country Context

Saudi Arabia has a factor-driven economy with strong government controls over major economic activities. The petroleum sector contributes 80% of the budget revenues, 45% of GDP and 90% of the export earnings (World Factbook, 2014). As mentioned above, SMEs with fewer than 60 employees constituted 96.2% of all enterprises in Saudi Arabia as of 2009, but contributed only about 33% to the country's GDP (Al-Jaseer, 2010). This modest contribution can be attributed to the immensity of the oil and the public sectors. Indeed, SMEs in Saudi Arabia are predominantly concentrated in commerce (34.3%), construction (32.3%), with only about one-sixth (14.6%) operating in the manufacturing sector. According to the World Bank's *Doing Business* 2016 report (World Bank, 2016) Saudi Arabia ranks 82nd in the overall ease of doing business, but 130th in the ease of starting a business (out of the 189 economies included in the report).

Sources of Data

Data for the study came from a nationally representative large-scale survey on the state of small business in Saudi Arabia, commissioned in 2011 by the Saudi Ministry of Trade. The study covered six cities that collectively account for 84% of all registered firms in Saudi Arabia (81% response rate). The survey respondents were all Saudi nationals, firm owners, and all male. The firms were small, with fewer than 10 employees on average, and

Table 24.1   Factor analysis for investigated firms

Internal challenges		External challenges	
Item	Loading	Item	Loading
Inefficient management	0.68	Difficult procedures	0.69
Weak skills and abilities of the owner	0.74	No intellectual protection law	0.63
Owner does not work full-time in venture	0.72	High labour turnover	0.71
The owner has no experience	0.73	Negative attitude towards business	0.67
Weak managerial skills of the owner	0.76	Lack of market information	0.56
Absence of technical knowledge	0.71	Unclear roles for sponsors/suppliers	0.62
Number of factors extracted	1		1
Eigen-value	3.15		2.525
Cumulative variance explained	52.45%		42.09%
Reliability (coefficient alpha)	0.82		0.72

about two-thirds of them (63.44%) operated in the trade sector. Firms in manufacturing, services and real estate accounted for around 12% for each sector, whereas firms in agriculture comprised only 4.23% of the sample. Missing data in some of the categories led to a usable sample size of n = 1,126 (92%), for which we report the results from statistical testing.

To garner deeper insights into the phenomena of interest to the study and to contextualize its findings, we supplemented the quantitative analysis with qualitative data from six interviews with Saudi entrepreneurs. The interviews were conducted in January and February of 2014 in Riyadh with small firm owners who were also full-time managers of their firms. The firms were between three and ten years old and represented a diverse array of industries, such as manufacturing, construction and services. Three of the companies were eight or more years old and three of the companies were less than eight years old.

Survey Data Analysis

Our dependent variable, *growth*, was measured as the percentage increase in full-time employees between the start of the firm and the time of the survey (Gilbert, McDougall & Audretsch, 2006). *Internal challenges* were measured using six five-point Likert-type

scaled questions ('completely disagree' to 'completely agree' with a defined neutral point), loading on a single factor (coefficient alpha = 0.818). *External challenges* were also measured using six five-point Likert-type scaled questions, loading on a single factor (coefficient alpha = 0.724). Table 24.1 reports the composition of the two multi-item scales and the results from the factor analysis.

To account for the effects of *venture age*, we followed the definition of an entrepreneurial venture as a venture less than eight years old (Zahra, 1996; Wang & Bansal, 2012), and split our sample into two groups: ventures younger than eight years (n = 808, or 66% of the sample) and ventures eight years or older (n = 414, or 34% of the sample). Ventures younger than eight years can be assumed to be going through the 'existence' and 'survival' stages of their life course, whereas ventures older than eight years of age can be assumed to have survived the perilous years of initial existence and to be setting up for either rapid or measured growth. *Control variables* included industry sector (manufacturing, services, agriculture and real estate) against the baseline of trade, the most populous industry sector; entrepreneur characteristics (self-reported age and level of education, on a six-point ordinal scale); and the venture's size (sales revenues, on a five-point ordinal scale); level of initial capitalization (on an eight-point ordinal scale); availability

Table 24.2   OLS regression estimates on predictors of new venture growth (n = 1,126)

Variable	Model 1		Model 2		Model 3	
	Coefficient	S.E.	Coefficient	S.E.	Coefficient	S.E.
Controls						
Manufacturing	0.22†	0.13	0.23†	0.13	0.25†	0.13
Services	−0.11	0.07	−0.09	0.07	−0.08	0.07
Agriculture	−0.15	0.14	−0.16	0.13	−0.16	0.13
Real estate	0.15	0.10	0.16	0.10	0.17	0.10
Owner age	0.01†	0.01	0.01	0.01	0.01	0.01
Owner education	0.05*	0.02	0.05*	0.02	0.04*	0.02
New venture capital	0.09***	0.02	0.09***	0.02	0.08***	0.02
New venture sales	−0.06*	0.03	−0.06*	0.03	−0.06*	0.03
New venture finance	0.09	0.07	0.09	0.07	0.09	0.07
New venture business network	0.05*	0.02	0.05*	0.02	0.05*	0.02
New venture age	0.12*	0.06	0.12*	0.06	0.25	0.28
Independent variables						
Internal challenges			−0.01	0.04	−0.08†	0.05
External challenges			−0.09*	0.04	−0.02	0.05
Interactions						
Age * Internal challenges					0.16*	0.08
Age * External challenges					−0.19*	0.07
Regression function						
F(d.f.)	5.846(11)***		5.510(13)***		5.336(15)***	
Adjusted R^2	0.05		0.05		0.06	

† significant at p<.1, * significant at p<.05, ** significant at p<.01, *** significant at p<.001

of outside financial support (binary); and diversity of the business network (a count of the venture's inter-firm partnerships with large companies). The results from the statistical testing are presented in Table 24.2.

Consistent with our predictions, we found that both internal and external challenges were negatively associated with employee growth. The coefficient for external challenges was significant in Model 2, whereas the coefficient for internal challenges was significant in the fully subscribed Model 3. In the fully subscribed model (Model 3), as expected, the relationship between internal challenges and business growth was stronger for more established ventures (those older than eight years), while the relationship between external challenges and business growth was stronger for new ventures.

Among other variables, owner age and education, as well as the age of the venture,

the level of its initial capitalization and the diversity of the business network were all positively and significantly associated with the increase in the number of employees. Firms in the manufacturing sector had a significantly higher growth in employees compared to the baseline sector, trade. Surprisingly, the sales level was negatively associated with the increase in the number of employees.

As mentioned in our literature review, prior research has established a 'no growth' or 'low growth' orientation among new and small ventures in emerging economies. To address this issue, we further explored the size and growth patterns of the firms in our sample. We found that the average employee growth rate was 66%, with a range from −94% to 900%. At the same time, the average employee count at the time of founding was

4.91 employees, rising to 7.65 employees at the time of the survey. In other words, the firms in our sample had registered substantial growth, but from a very low base, and continued to operate as micro-enterprises.

Insights from fieldwork

Our six interviewees identified numerous problems they encountered both at the time of founding and at the time of the interview. Recurring external problems included the 'cumbersome', 'slow', 'constantly changing' and 'difficult to follow' government procedures, particularly with respect to hiring expatriate employees, access to financing, access to appropriate business locations, as well as problems with licensing. Internal problems included difficulties in marketing, managing cash flow and product quality, as well as in 'finding good employees'.

As the summary of interview data (Table 24.3) illustrates, and consistent with our expectations, external problems prevailed during the founding stage of the companies. For example, the owner of a coffee shop established in 2009 (Respondent 4) complained about the regulations of the labour ministry, exclaiming, 'They change the regulations every year!' He also emphasized the importance of written contracts in order to protect the interests of all parties, both small and large companies. As he shared, 'Usually large companies do not like to write specific contracts with small companies. This may lead to the abuse of the smaller partner'. The owner of a project management and consulting company, established in 2010 (Respondent 5) was mostly concerned with finding financial capital, and with the extremely high rents for office space and the high salaries that specialist consultants commanded.

While our respondents continued to struggle with hard-to-follow government regulations and the financial squeeze, some of the more established ventures (i.e. beyond the 'existence' and 'survival' stages of development) also reported problems with marketing and management. For example, the owner of an animal fodder factory (Respondent 1) shared that vocational education was very important for success in business, particularly knowledge of English, because 'it is helpful to understand general terms in business'. Other critical factors included having a business plan, because 'it shows how we are organized and makes our partners more secure when they deal with us because it shows that we have calculated our risk'; having a formal organizational structure, because 'having a formal structure means a more organized company', and generally 'good quality and being reliable'. The importance of reliability was shared by the owner of a logistics and shipment company (Respondent 3), who, when asked what factors were important for a new and/or small company to work as a partner with a large business, responded, 'Telling the truth all the time and shipping when promised'. Respondent 3 also reflected on his education and skills, noting, 'I have a bachelor's degree. But, I have a problem with the English language. I wish I had studied intensive English. Most large companies use English as first language'. In other words, internal challenges to growth were becoming more critical beyond the founding stage of the ventures.

THEORETICAL IMPLICATIONS AND DIRECTIONS FOR FUTURE RESEARCH

The review of the extant literature on the growth of new and small ventures in the emerging economy context, complemented with empirical evidence from both a large-scale survey and interview data in the context of SMEs in Saudi Arabia, can be summarized as follows. First, in various degrees, attenuated by the level of economic development, industrial structure, institutional heritage or cultural norms, emerging economies share certain characteristics that are not conducive

Table 24.3   Interview data: respondent profiles and major themes

No.	No. of employees		Major problems at founding	Major problems currently
Line of business, year established				
	At founding	Currently		
1 Animal fodder factory, 2005	4	9	Government procedures, quality	Marketing, access to quality raw materials
2 Construction, 2003	20	25	Government procedures, hiring employees	Failure to follow legislations
3 Shipment and logistics, 2006	2	7	Finding a suitable company location, government procedures	Slow government services, slow passport procedures (for expatriate employees)
4 Coffee shop, 2009	2	3	Labour ministry regulations	Changing regulations every year
5 Project management and consulting, 2010	4	8	Capital financing, high office rents, high salaries for specialist consultants	Cash flow
6 DNA lab, 2008	1	3	Financing	Finding good employees, licences

for venture growth. Second, the challenges to venture growth are both external (stemming from the level of economic development and the formal and informal institutional infrastructure) and internal (stemming from the inadequate resource base of the new and small venture, particularly with respect to managerial capabilities). Third, external challenges to growth are particularly detrimental early in the life cycle of emerging economy ventures, whereas internal challenges to growth become more significant as the new venture matures.

The insights gleaned from both the literature review and the evidence from primary data in the context of an emerging economy also leads us to the formulation of several directions for future research. They are outlined below.

Growth opportunities versus challenges to growth

We note that research on entrepreneurial growth in the context of developed market economies has focused on the *drivers* of growth (for recent comprehensive reviews of the new venture and small business growth literature, see Gilbert et al., 2006; Dobbs & Hamilton, 2007), whereas research on entrepreneurial growth in emerging economies (this study included) has focused on the *barriers* to growth (Ayyagari et al., 2007; Peng & Heath, 1996; Wright et al., 2005; Aidis et al., 2008; Tracey & Phillips, 2011; Batjargal et al., 2013). There is a sizeable corpus of work accumulated in both literature streams. The theoretical insights and cumulative empirical evidence present interesting opportunities for cross-fertilization of ideas and future cross-national studies of the phenomenon of entrepreneurial growth.

Universal versus context-specific challenges to growth

As noted in our literature review, the economic and institutional environments across emerging economies present a fascinating collage of contrasts. Context matters, and future research could go deeper into disentangling and differentiating among: (1) challenges to growth that may be common to all new and small ventures worldwide, (2) challenges that are germane to the institutional environment in emerging economies, and (3) challenges that are unique to new and small ventures in the specific country, or even local context. As Welter (2011, p. 165) argued,

> There is growing recognition in entrepreneurship research that economic behavior can be better understood within its historical, temporal, institutional, spatial, and social contexts, as these contexts provide individuals with opportunities and set boundaries for their actions.

Our illustrative evidence in the context of Saudi Arabia provided examples of all three types of challenges. An example of the first type of problem is the lack of access to appropriate locations, a classic barrier to new entry (Djankov et al., 2002). Cumbersome and inconsistent government regulation coupled with slow government services and inefficient capital markets are germane to emerging markets' institutional environments and have a disproportionately harmful effect on new and small players (Djankov et al., 2002; Ayyagari et al., 2007). Examples of issues unique to the Saudi (and possibly other Gulf countries) include expatriate employee quotas, licensing, immigration status and 'passport procedures'. The comparison of the relative importance of 'universal', 'emerging market-specific' and 'location-specific' challenges to entrepreneurial growth will be a fruitful extension of this line of work.

Size growth versus profitability growth

As noted in our literature review, there are many different types of growth firms with different growth patterns. Recall from our illustrative evidence from the context of Saudi SMEs that the sales level of the SMEs in our sample was negatively associated with the increase in the number of employees,

suggesting that at least some of the new and small ventures might have pursued intensive growth driven by higher efficiencies and productivity, rather than extensive growth driven by an increase in employee count. We call on future research to further explore the temporal dynamics of the different aspects of entrepreneurial growth.

Formal sector versus informal sector growth

The informal sector accounts for a sizeable portion of economic activities in emerging economies (Webb et al., 2009; Godfrey, 2011). Moreover, there is a considerable gendered effect of informality. This is because in certain areas, such as the Middle East and North Africa (MENA) region, many women-owned businesses are informal and home-based (Alturki & Braswell, 2010). As just one example, recall from our illustrative evidence that although the data came from a nationally representative study, the study represented *formally registered male-owned* SMEs. We need to know more about the 'invisible' entrepreneurs. What are the growth paths in the emerging markets' informal sector? What are the major challenges to growth? Who are the most important formal and informal institutional players that affect informal entrepreneurs' growth aspirations and accomplishments? Last, but not least, what are the differences in the growth strategies of men-led versus women-led businesses in both the formal and informal sector of the economy?

Growth through market interactions versus growth through social networking

Entrepreneurial social capital, or personal connections, are extremely important for competitive success in the context of emerging economies (Peng, Wang & Jiang, 2008; Batjargal, 2013). Personal connections, known as '*wasta*' in Arabic, '*guanxi*' in Chinese or '*svyazi*' in Russian, form to a large extent 'the cultural matrix' (Weir & Hutchings, 2005) for business and management interactions in many societies. Peng (2004) demonstrated that kinship networks in China facilitate the growth of private ventures (but not collectively owned enterprises). Also in China, both Zhao and Aram (1995) and Tan (2006) reported that managers in high-growth entrepreneurial ventures had greater range and intensity of business networking than their counterparts in low-growth firms. Recent theorizing and empirical evidence, however, has suggested that with the progress of pro-market reforms, network-based growth strategies may gradually wane in importance or morph in structure (Peng & Zhou, 2005; Danis et al., 2010; Danis, De Clercq & Petricevic, 2011). We call on future research to further explore the role of personal connections as precursors and facilitators of new venture growth in the context of emerging markets.

CONCLUSION: MANAGERIAL AND PUBLIC POLICY IMPLICATIONS

For practising business managers in emerging economies, our findings strongly suggest that lack of managerial sophistication, inadequate managerial skills and inefficient management are likely to stump business development even if the new venture survives the turbulent years of its initial existence; whereas the education of the owner, on the other hand, has a direct positive effect on employee growth. Our study also suggests that simplifying regulations and alleviating some of the government procedures will facilitate the growth and enhance the economic contribution of the small business sector in emerging economies. In sum, better managerial training, coupled with business-friendly institutions and administrative practices, will enhance the growth potential of new and small ventures in emerging economies.

REFERENCES

Acs, Z.J. (2006). How is entrepreneurship good for economic growth? *Innovations*, *1*(1), 97–107.

Ahlstrom, D., Bruton, G.D. & Yeh, K.S. (2008). Private firms in China: Building legitimacy in an emerging economy. *Journal of World Business*, *43*(4), 385–399.

Aidis, R., Estrin, S. & Mickiewicz, T. (2008). Institutions and entrepreneurship development in Russia: A comparative perspective. *Journal of Business Venturing*, *23*(6), 656–672.

Aldrich, H.E. (1999). *Organizations Evolving*. Thousand Oaks, CA: Sage.

Al-Ghamdi, S.M. (2005). The use of strategic planning tools and techniques in Saudi Arabia: An empirical study. *International Journal of Management*, *22*(3), 376–395.

Al-Hajjar, A. & Presley, J.R. (1992). Constraints on development: Small businesses in Saudi Arabia. *Middle Eastern Studies*, *28*(2), 333–351.

Al-Jaseer, M. (2010). Opening speech to the 'Small and Medium Enterprises' Symposium organized by the Institute of Banking. 2 November. URL: http://sama.gov.sa/sites/samaen/News/Pages/SMEIOB.aspx (accessed 6 April 2014).

Alturki, N. & Braswell, S. (2010). *Businesswomen in Saudi Arabia: Characteristics, Challenges, and Aspirations in a Regional ConTABtext*. Jeddah, Saudi Arabia: Al-Sayedah Khadijah Bint Khuwailid Businesswomen Center and Riyadh, Saudi Arabia: Monitor Group.

Arnold, D.J. & Quelch, J.A. (1998). New strategies in emerging economies. *Sloan Management Review*, *40*(1), 7–20.

Aulakh, P.S., Rotate, M. & Teegen, H. (2000). Export strategies and performance of firms from emerging economies: Evidence from Brazil, Chile, and Mexico. *Academy of Management Journal*, *43*(3), 342–361.

Ayyagari, M., Beck, T. & Demirgüç-Kunt, A. (2007). Small and medium enterprises across the globe: A new database. *Small Business Economics*, *29*(4), 415–434.

Batjargal, B., Hitt, M.A., Tsui, A.S., Arregle, J.L., Webb, J.W. & Miller, T.L. (2013). Institutional polycentrism, entrepreneurs' social networks, and new venture growth. *Academy of Management Journal*, *56*(4), 1024–1049.

Baum, J.R., Locke, E.A. & Smith, K.G. (2001). A multidimensional model of new venture growth. *Academy of Management Journal*, *44*(2), 292–303.

Beck, T. & Demirgüç-Kunt, A. (2006). Small and medium-sized enterprises: Access to finance as a growth constraint. *Journal of Banking and Finance*, *30*(11), 2931–2943.

Beck, T., Demirgüç-Kunt, A. & Maksimovic, V. (2005). Financial and legal constraints to firm growth: Does firm size matter? *Journal of Finance*, *60*(1), 137–177.

Brush, C.G., Ceru, D.J. & Blackburn, R. (2009). Pathways to entrepreneurial growth: The influence of management, marketing, and money. *Business Horizons*, *52*(5), 481–491.

Buehn, A. & Schneider, F. (2012). Shadow economies around the world: Novel insights, accepted knowledge, and new estimates. *International Tax and Public Finance*, *19*(1), 139–171.

Cassar, G. (2007). Money, money, money? A longitudinal investigation of entrepreneur career reasons, growth preferences and achieved growth. *Entrepreneurship and Regional Development*, *19*(1), 89–107.

Chang, S.J. & Wu, B. (2014). Institutional barriers and industry dynamics. *Strategic Management Journal*, *35*(8), 1103–1123.

Choi, Y.R. & Shepherd, D.A. (2005). Stakeholder perceptions of age and other dimensions of newness. *Journal of Management*, *31*(4), 573–596.

Churchill, N.C. & Lewis, V.L. (1983). The five stages of small business growth. *Harvard Business Review*, *61*(3), 30–50.

Cliff, J.E. (1998). Does one size fit all? Exploring the relationship between attitudes towards growth, gender, and business size. *Journal of Business Venturing*, *13*(6), 523–542.

Cooper, A.C., Gimeno-Gascon, F.J. & Woo, C.Y. (1994). Initial human and financial capital as predictors of new venture performance. *Journal of Business Venturing*, *9*(2), 127–143.

Covin, J.C. & Slevin, D.P. (1997). High growth transitions: Theoretical perspectives and suggested directions. In Sexton, D.L., & Smilor, R.W. (eds.), *Entrepreneurship 2000*, pp. 99–126. Chicago: Upstart.

Danis, W.M., Chiaburu, D.S. & Lyles, M.A. (2010). The impact of managerial networking intensity and market-based strategies on firm growth during institutional upheaval: A study of small and medium-sized enterprises in a transition economy. *Journal of International Business Studies*, *41*, 287–307.

Danis, W.M., De Clercq, D. & Petricevic, O. (2011). Are social networks more important for new business activity in emerging than developed economies? An empirical extension. *International Business Review*, *20*(4), 394–408.

Davidsson, P. (1991). Continued entrepreneurship: Ability, need and opportunity as determinants of small firm growth. *Journal of Business Venturing*, *4*, 211–226.

Delmar, F. & Shane, S. (2004). Legitimizing first: Organizing activities and the survival of new ventures. *Journal of Business Venturing*, *19*(3), 385–410.

Delmar, F.P., Davidsson, P. & Gartner, W. (2003). Arriving at the high-growth firm. *Journal of Business Venturing*, *18*(2), 189–216.

Djankov, S., La Porta, R., Lopez-de-Silanes, F. & Shleifer, A. (2002). The regulation of entry. *Quarterly Journal of Economics*, *117*(1), 1–37.

Dobbs, M. & Hamilton, R.T. (2007). Small business growth: Recent evidence and new directions. *International Journal of Entrepreneurial Behavior and Research*, *13*(5), 296–322.

Drucker, P.F. (1985). *Innovation and Entrepreneurship*. New York: Harper & Row.

Eisenhardt, K.M. & Schoonhoven, C.B. (1990). Organizational growth: Linking founding team, strategy, environment, and growth among US semiconductor ventures, 1978–1988. *Administrative Science Quarterly*, *35*(3), 504–529.

Estrin, S., Korosteleva, J. & Mickiewicz, T. (2013). Which institutions encourage entrepreneurial growth aspirations? *Journal of Business Venturing*, *28*(4), 564–580.

Eunni, R.V. & Manolova. T.S. (2012). Are the BRIC economies entrepreneur-friendly? An institutional perspective. *Journal of Enterprising Culture*, *20*(2), 171–202.

Foss, K. & Foss, N.J. (2008). Understanding opportunity discovery and sustainable advantage: The role of transaction costs and property rights. *Strategic Entrepreneurship Journal*, *2*(3), 191–207.

Gilbert, B.A., McDougall, P.P. & Audretsch, D.B. (2006). New venture growth: A review and extension. *Journal of Management*, *32*(6), 926–950.

Godfrey, P.C. (2011). Toward a theory of the informal economy. *The Academy of Management Annals*, *5*(1), 231–277.

Greiner, L.E. (1972). Evolution and revolution as organizations grow. *Harvard Business Review*, *50*(4), 37–46.

Honig, B. (1998). What determines success? Examining the human, financial, and social capital of Jamaican microentrepreneurs. *Journal of Business Venturing*, *13*(5), 371–394.

Hutchinson, J. & Xavier, A. (2006). Comparing the impact of credit constraints on the growth of SMEs in a transition economy with an established market economy. *Small Business Economics*, *27*(2), 169–179.

IMF (International Monetary Fund). (2014). *World Economic Outlook*. Retrieved from http://www.imf.org/external/pubs/ft/weo/2014/01/weodata/index.aspx (accessed December 2014).

Kelley, D., Singer, S. & Herrington, M. (2016). *Global Entrepreneurship Monitor: 2015/16 Global Report*. Wellesley, MA: Babson College.

Khanna, T. & Palepu, K.G. (1997). Why focused strategies may be wrong for emerging markets. *Harvard Business Review*, *75*(4), 3–10.

Kim, Y. & Choi, Y. (1994). Strategic types and performances of small firms in Korea. *International Small Business Journal*, *13*(1), 13–25.

Klapper, L., Lewin, A. & Quesada Delgado, J.M. (2009). *The Impact of the Business Environment on the Business Creation Process*. Policy Research Working Paper 4937. Washington, DC: The World Bank.

Krasniqi, B.A. (2007). Barriers to entrepreneurship and SME growth in transition: The case of Kosova. *Journal of Developmental Entrepreneurship*, *12*(1), 71–94.

Kshetri, N. & Dholakia, N. (2011). Regulative institutions supporting entrepreneurship in emerging economies: A comparison of China and India. *Journal of International Entrepreneurship*, *9*(2), 110–132.

La Porta, R. & Shleifer, A. (2008). *The Unofficial Economy and Economic Development* (No. w14520). Cambridge, MA: National Bureau of Economic Research.

Lau, C.-M. & Busenitz, L.W. (2001). Growth intentions of entrepreneurs in a transitional economy: The People's Republic of China. *Entrepreneurship Theory and Practice*, *20*(1), 5–20.

Leitch, C., Hill, F. & Neergaard, H. (2010). Entrepreneurial and business growth and the quest for a 'comprehensive theory': Tilting at windmills? *Entrepreneurship Theory and Practice*, *34*(2), 249–260.

Lyles, M. & Baird, I. (1994). Performance of international joint ventures in two Eastern European countries: The case of Hungary and Poland. *Management International Review*, *34*(4), 313–329.

Lyles, M.A., Saxton, T. & Watson, K. (2004). Venture survival in a transitional economy. *Journal of Management*, *30*(3), 351–375.

Mair, J., Martí, I. & Ventresca, M.J. (2012). Building inclusive markets in rural Bangladesh: How intermediaries work institutional voids. *Academy of Management Journal*, *55*(4), 819–850.

Malo, S. & Norus, J. (2009). Growth dynamics of dedicated biotechnology firms in transition economies. Evidence from the Baltic countries and Poland. *Entrepreneurship and Regional Development*, *21*(5–6), 481–502.

Manev, I.M. & Manolova, T.S. (2010). Entrepreneurship in transitional economies: Review and integration of two decades of research. *Journal of Developmental Entrepreneurship*, *15*(1), 69–99.

Manolova, T.S., Eunni, R.V. & Gyoshev, B.S. (2008). Institutional environments for entrepreneurship: Evidence from emerging economies in Eastern Europe. *Entrepreneurship Theory and Practice*, *32*(1), 203–218.

McKelvie, A. & Wiklund, J. (2010). Advancing firm growth research: A focus on growth mode instead of growth rate. *Entrepreneurship Theory and Practice*, *34*(2), 261–288.

Merdah, W.O.A. & Sadi, M.A. (2011). Technology transfer in context with Saudi Arabian small-medium enterprises. *International Management Review*, *7*(1), 30–37.

Parnell, J.A. (2013). Uncertainty, generic strategy, strategic clarity, and performance of retail SMEs in Peru, Argentina, and the United States. *Journal of Small Business Management*, *51*(2), 215–234.

Peng, Y. (2004). Kinship networks and entrepreneurs in China's transitional economy. *American Journal of Sociology*, *109*(5), 1045–1074.

Peng, M.W. & Heath, P.S. (1996). The growth of the firm in planned economies in transition: Institutions, organizations, and strategic choice. *Academy of Management Review*, *21*(2), 492–528.

Peng, M.W., Wang, D.Y.L. & Jiang, Y. (2008). An institution-based view of international business strategy: A focus on emerging economies. *Journal of International Business Studies*, *39*(5), 920–936.

Peng, M.W. & Zhou, J.Q. (2005). How network strategies and institutional transitions evolve in Asia. *Asia Pacific Journal of Management*, *22*(4), 321–336.

Scase, R. (1997). The role of small businesses in the economic transition of Eastern Europe: Real but relatively unimportant? *International Small Business Journal*, *16*(1), 13–21.

Scott, M. & Bruce, R. (1987). Five stages of growth in small business. *Long Range Planning*, *20*(3), 45–52.

Shane, S. & Foo, M.D. (1999). New firm survival: Institutional explanations for new franchisor mortality. *Management Science*, *45*(2), 142–159.

Smallbone, D. & Welter, F. (2006). Conceptualizing entrepreneurship in a transition context. *International Journal of Entrepreneurship and Small Business*, *3*(2), 190–206.

Spencer, J.W. & Gómez, C. (2004). The relationship among national institutional structures, economic factors, and domestic entrepreneurial activity: A multicountry study. *Journal of Business Research*, *57*(10), 1098–1107.

Stinchcombe, A.L. (1965). Social Structure and Organizations. In J.G. March (ed.), *Handbook of Organizations*, pp. 142–193. Chicago, IL: Rand-McNally.

Tan, J. (2006). Growth of industry clusters and innovation: Lessons from Beijing Zhongguancun Science Park. *Journal of Business Venturing*, *21*(6), 827–850.

Tracey, S.L.P. & Phillips, N. (2011). Entrepreneurship in emerging markets. *Management International Review*, *51*(1), 23–39.

Wang, T. & Bansal, P. (2012). Social responsibility in new ventures: Profiting from a long-term orientation. *Strategic Management Journal*, *33*(10), 1135–1153.

Webb, J.W., Tihanyi, L., Ireland, R.D. & Sirmon, D.G. (2009). You say illegal, I say legitimate: Entrepreneurship in the informal economy. *Academy of Management Review*, *34*(3), 492–510.

Weir, D. & Hutchings, K. (2005). Cultural embeddedness and contextual constraints: Knowledge sharing in Chinese and Arab cultures. *Knowledge and Process Management*, *12*(2), 89–98.

Welter, F. (2011). Contextualizing entrepreneurship: Conceptual challenges and ways forward. *Entrepreneurship Theory and Practice*, *35*(1), 165–184.

Wiklund, J. & Shepherd, D. (2003). Aspiring for, and achieving growth: The moderating role of resources and opportunities. *Journal of Management Studies*, *40*(8), 1919–1941.

Wong, P.K., Ho, Y.P. & Autio, E. (2005). Entrepreneurship, innovation, and economic growth: Evidence from GEM data. *Small Business Economics*, *24*(3), 335–350.

World Bank (2016). *Doing Business*. Retrieved from http://www.doingbusiness.org (accessed May 2016).

World Factbook, The (2014). *Saudi Arabia*. Retrieved from: https://www.cia.gov/library/publications/the-world-factbook/geos/sa.html (accessed 6 April 2014).

Wright, M., Filatotchev, I., Hoskisson, R.E. & Peng, M.W. (2005). Strategy research in emerging economies: Challenging the conventional wisdom. *Journal of Management Studies*, *42*(1), 1–33.

Zahra, S.A. (1996). Technology strategy and new venture performance: A study of corporate-sponsored and independent biotechnology ventures. *Journal of Business Venturing*, *11*(4), 289–321.

Zhao, L. & Aram, J.D. (1995). Networking and growth of young technology-intensive ventures in China. *Journal of Business Venturing*, *10*(5), 349–370.

Zimmerman, M.A. & Zeitz, G.J. (2002). Beyond survival: Achieving new venture growth by building legitimacy. *Academy of Management Review*, *27*(3), 414–431.

25

Learning and Educational Programs for Entrepreneurs

Luke Pittaway, Louisa Huxtable-Thomas
and Paul Hannon

INTRODUCTION

Since the 1990s, researchers in entrepreneurship have been developing and testing new concepts within the subject of entrepreneurial learning. Consequently, our understanding of learning during entrepreneurial efforts has advanced significantly (Harrison & Leitch, 2008). Yet despite these advances we contend that entrepreneurial learning researchers have largely failed to demonstrate the practical implications of their work within entrepreneurship education, particularly within the context of educational design and its implications for entrepreneurship education (Pittaway & Thorpe, 2012). This chapter addresses this oversight by reviewing current concepts and empirical work in entrepreneurial learning and explores implications from this work on the development of educational programs for entrepreneurs. Our starting point is Pittaway and Thorpe's (2012) summary of Cope's 'entrepreneurial learning framework'. We use this framework to review current concepts and ideas, recent studies and the latest empirical contributions and discoveries in entrepreneurial learning. Finally, we outline how this body of work can inform the design of programs for entrepreneurs. We thus begin this chapter by outlining past conceptual thought in the subject.

EARLY CONCEPTS IN ENTREPRENEURIAL LEARNING

The development of thinking in entrepreneurial learning has been mapped previously (Pittaway & Thorpe, 2012) following prior observations that entrepreneurs had to 'learn on the job' (Rae & Carswell, 2000). This 'active' component of entrepreneurial learning was conceptualized in different ways. 'Adaptive learning' was conceived to explain how entrepreneurs must adapt to change and 'learn as they go' as the circumstances warranted (Watts, Cope & Hulme, 1998). Different researchers have described it as 'learning by doing' (Jones, Macpherson & Woollard, 2008), 'learning as they go' (Gartner, 1988) and 'experiential learning' (Rae, 2002). While there are nuances between definitions, the general stance is that entrepreneurs are action-orientated people who make decisions and undertake actions, as they navigate ongoing business activities, which leads to the accumulation of a 'stock of experience' (Reuber & Fischer, 1999; Smilor, 1997). Adaptive learning highlights the importance of an entrepreneur's willingness and/or aptitude to change their personal behaviors and business strategies as the context requires (Deakins & Freel, 1998). It was widely noted that making recoverable mistakes and engaging in experimental behavior could also contribute to an entrepreneur's capacity to learn (Cope & Watts, 2000). The nature of experience, in this research, was characterized as either a 'general stock of experience', which entrepreneurs apply to their future actions, or a 'specific stock of experience' that was acquired from the highly contextual nature of the entrepreneurial process encountered (Reuber & Fischer, 1999).

Initial research confirmed entrepreneurs' anecdotal experiences and observations of practice by researchers (Pittaway & Thorpe, 2012). Entrepreneurial learning represented a gradual process of knowledge accumulation (Deakins & Freel, 1998) that led to a change in orientation over time (Cope & Watts, 2000), rather than a sudden shift. Researchers, however, began to notice two problems with this conceptualization of entrepreneurial learning.

First, it was noted that 'one can experience something and yet learn nothing' (Cope, 2003; Taylor & Thorpe, 2004). This view drew on adult learning theory which emphasized both 'action' and 'reflection' as important factors in the learning process (Preskill, 1996; Gibb, 1997; Cope, 2003). Reflection included the meaningful assessment of past action as a way to consider alternative courses of future action, the retention of good practice and the avoidance of repeated mistakes.

Researchers began to include 'action', 'experience' and 'reflection' in their thinking on entrepreneurial learning and they noted that effective entrepreneurs appeared to be more 'reflective' (Rae & Carswell, 2000; Taylor & Thorpe, 2004). Reflection, however, is a complex concept (Cope, 2003, 2005). For example, Cope (2003), drawing on others (Senge, 1990; Mezirow, 1991; Daudelin, 1996), began to highlight differences between reflection on 'ongoing experience' and 'critical reflection' that led to significant reconsideration of personal viewpoints. Later he highlighted four forms of reflection: 'inward', 'outward', 'backward' and 'forward' (Cope, 2005; Pittaway, Gazzard, Shore & Williamson, 2015), which included reflections on self, reflections on the context and on others, reflections on past events and reflections on experiences that can be 'taken forward' into future situations (Minniti & Bygrave, 2001).

Second, researchers noted that entrepreneurial ventures experience significant 'crises' and highly emotionally charged situations, which sometimes included outright failure of the business (West & Wilson, 1995). Researchers proposed that 'critical periods', 'mistakes' and 'failure' contributed to learning in heightened ways (Cope & Watts, 2000; Cope, 2003, 2005) challenging the position that all experience was equal. These seminal moments were considered as a pathway to transformative learning (Shepherd, 2003; Politis & Gabrielsson, 2009) and, as such, could change the individual's orientation to themselves, to others and to their venture. Learning from entrepreneurial failure consequently became a key aspect of thinking in the subject (Cope, 2010; Pittaway & Thorpe, 2012).

As researchers began to appreciate the 'dynamic learning contexts' that could be encountered by entrepreneurs and considered the extent to which contexts could influence learning acquisition, it became evident that concepts had been too focused on the individual learner (Harrison & Leitch, 2008;

Jack, Drakopoulou Dodd & Anderson, 2008). 'Social learning' and 'situated learning', based on Lave and Wenger's (1991) work, became more important in thinking (Taylor & Thorpe, 2004; Karataş-Özkan, 2011). Here it was noted that learning is a social process that involves multiple people within a context of ongoing activity (Jack et al., 2008). Social practice and relationships are, therefore, considered to play an integral role. Relationships with key people (e.g. spouses and mentors) were widely noted as influencers in the learning process (Hamilton, 2004). The 'situated' nature of learning became more of a focus (Cope, 2010) and researchers concluded that learning differed depending on the learning challenges encountered and thus learning outcomes differed between phases (Karataş-Özkan, 2011). Certain characteristics of the learning context were viewed as playing a pivotal role in learning acquisition. So, for example, the degree of 'emotional exposure', 'financial exposure', 'social engagement' and 'relationship conflict' (Pittaway & Thorpe, 2012) experienced could play an important role and impact on learning processes (Jack et al., 2008). Figure 25.1 summarizes these early concepts in entrepreneurial learning, as highlighted previously in Pittaway & Thorpe (2012, p. 850).

The framework presented in Figure 25.1 introduces key components from prior studies. First, all individuals come to a learning event with a prior 'stock of experience' (Smilor, 1997; Reuber & Fischer, 1999). This can be acquired from multiple contexts not related to entrepreneurship but these may contribute to people's 'entrepreneurial preparedness' or their readiness, ability and competence to act in entrepreneurial ways (Reuber & Fischer, 1999). An individual engaging in an entrepreneurial process will enter 'dynamic temporal phases' specific to their situation, context and to the endeavor they are pursuing (Cope, 2010). Even where the temporal phases are the same, the situated nature of the effort will make the experience highly unique and different. Every entrepreneur

has an inherently different experience due to temporal phase, context and levels of support provided by other people. As such, each learning situation is unique because of both its historical context and situational dynamic (Pittaway et al., 2015). Despite this uniqueness, researchers have been able to observe some common interrelated processes of learning that both describe the learning process and help explain an individual's capacity to learn. These include 'adaptive learning', 'reflective learning', 'situated learning' and 'transformative learning' (Cope, 2005). Researchers have recognized characteristics of the entrepreneurial context that can lead to a heightened sense of learning potential and some argue that these are uniquely experienced within entrepreneurial processes (Macpherson, Kofinas, Jones & Thorpe, 2010; Cope, 2010). For example, higher chances for 'social risk', 'social conflict', 'relationship conflict', 'emotional exposure' and 'financial exposure' have all been associated with entrepreneurial learning during failure events (Shepherd, 2003; Politis & Gabrielsson, 2009). Likewise, heightened sense of 'trial and error learning' and 'experimentation', have been associated with start-up processes (Dalley & Hamilton, 2000; Johnston, Hamilton & Zhang, 2008). In addition to common characteristics of learning there also appear to be common learning tasks that entrepreneurs need to accomplish. These include: learning about oneself; learning about the venture; learning about important relationships; and learning about the dynamic phase being experienced. The framework outlined presents a complex picture of entrepreneurial learning, being both uniquely embedded within the specific situation while having some common processes, characteristics and learning tasks that might be experienced by all entrepreneurs. Next we expand this picture by reviewing the latest conceptual and empirical research (2005–15) in the field. At the end of the chapter we then explore how this research can guide practice in educational design for entrepreneurs.

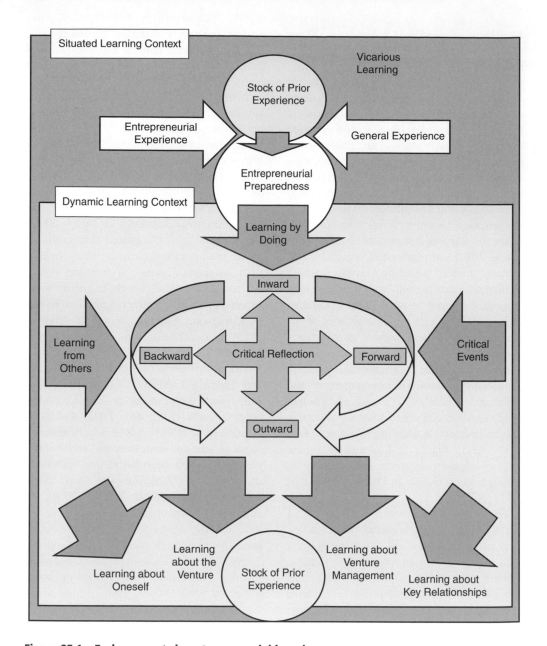

Figure 25.1 Early concepts in entrepreneurial learning

REVIEW OF CONTEMPORARY RESEARCH IN ENTREPRENEURIAL LEARNING

The review was conducted, using some of the basic principles of the Systematic Literature Review (SLR) (Pittaway, Holt & Broad, 2014). First, leading journals were selected. From these journals the search string '*entre* AND learn**' was applied to a search of abstracts between 2000 and 2015. This step produced 27 relevant research papers. Next the researchers reviewed the citation list of all of the papers identified in the first step and identified a further 44 papers for review (for a total of 71 articles). Abstracts for every paper were then reviewed and the boundaries of the review period were revised to 2005–15. During this step 16 papers were removed either because they lacked relevancy or were outside of the review period (25 removed from the review). In total 46 papers were drawn on for this review, as outlined in Tables 25.1 and Appendix 25.1 The papers were categorized according to whether they made an empirical or conceptual contribution to the subject. Finally, papers were reviewed and considered based on the themes presented in this chapter and new themes that emerged from the review were highlighted.

Papers found making conceptual contributions are summarized in Table 25.1 while all articles making empirical contributions are summarized in Appendix 25.1 (which, because of its length, appears at the end of the chapter). The review conducted mirrors a recent SLR published on entrepreneurial learning by Wang and Chugh (2014). From the two studies a number of key observations can be highlighted.

1   Observation 1 – Entrepreneurial learning as a topic has grown considerably, but is often limited to conceptual or theoretical, rather than empirical or applied approaches (Kempster & Cope, 2010).
2   Observation 2 – Entrepreneurial learning research since 2005 has increasingly diversified and as a consequence there remain definitional problems (Wang & Chugh, 2014). Consequently, studies have largely failed to recognize that learning from one context may differ substantively from another context (Taylor & Thorpe, 2004; Cope, 2005, 2010).
3   Observation 3 – There are two clear 'schools of thought' developing in entrepreneurial learning. A North American school that focuses on 'entrepreneurial orientation' (EO) and forms of learning, such as exploratory and exploitative learning (Holcomb, Ireland, Holmes & Hitt, 2009), and a European school that emphasizes the subjective nature of knowledge and has adopted qualitative methods (Cope, 2003, 2005). This 'split' between two schools may result in different and non-complementary conceptions regarding the design

and development of educational programs for entrepreneurs.
4   Observation 4 – Entrepreneurial learning research draws on multiple concepts but without much clarity regarding the relationship between individual and collective learning. Although some efforts towards synthesis have been attempted (Cope, 2005; Pittaway & Thorpe, 2012) there remains much to do to encourage conceptual clarity.

These observations suggest that there is still an incomplete picture of entrepreneurial learning, and as it continues to be researched the potential for differences of position widen. Next we explore some of these details by outlining the latest conceptual and empirical contributions in the subject.

Conceptual Contributions

The recent conceptual contributions in the subject are summarized in Table 25.1. New concepts within this literature have gained heightened attention in recent years. 'Vicarious learning', for example, has gained more attention in the conceptual literature in the last decade (Holcomb et al., 2009). As researchers have recognized that entrepreneurs can learn from the situation as well as from their own experiences, an acknowledgement has grown that entrepreneurs learn from others 'vicariously'. In other words, mentors and other entrepreneurs play a role in helping individuals as they engage with the dynamic phases of the venture process (Harrison & Leitch, 2005).

'Liability of newness' has been highlighted to explain that entrepreneurs must learn to cope with ambiguity and uncertainty and that this aptitude for coping with new experiences can in fact itself be learnt (Politis, 2005). 'Self-management' and 'self-monitoring skills' have been added to our understanding of the role of reflection in learning (Tseng, 2013). The capability of an individual to monitor and manage themselves relative to the situation and others is now considered to be an important aspect of self-directed learning. 'Exploratory and exploitative learning' (Kreiser, 2011; Zhao,

Table 25.1   Conceptual studies in entrepreneurial learning (2005–15)

Author/s (date)	Key conceptual contribution of each study
Baron & Henry (2010)	Proposes that expert performance gained from deliberate practice enhances cognitive resources (such as memory, perception and metacognition), which impacts on new venture performance.
Berglund et al. (2007)	Presents two generic approaches described as the hypothesis-testing mode and the hermeneutic mode. The model offers four categories of entrepreneurial learning: experimentation, evaluation, unreflective action and unverified assumptions.
Cardon et al. (2009)	Concludes that certain mechanisms of experience can be drawn from entrepreneurial passion concepts and explains how these might influence goal-directed cognitions and behaviors and entrepreneurial effectiveness.
Cardon et al. (2012)	Considers entrepreneurial emotion as an antecedent, which can occur concurrently and can be a consequence of the entrepreneurial process.
Cope (2005)	Proposes three elements of entrepreneurial learning, dynamic temporal phases, interrelated processes and overarching characteristics. Highlights reflective learning and transformative learning.
Corbett (2005)	Provides an in-depth explanation of experiential learning theory and shows how it might be useful for understanding learning that occurs in the entrepreneurial process. Understands the connections between entrepreneurial learning and opportunity identification and exploitation.
Dutta & Crossan (2005)	Applies the 4I organizational learning framework to entrepreneurial opportunities and presents learning as a multi-stage process. Considers entrepreneurial learning as a wider organizational effort.
Fletcher & Watson (2007)	Shows that entrepreneurial learning can include the development of an interpersonal identity formation process. Illustrates that in teaching entrepreneurship we need to consider how identity is formed.
Harrison & Leitch (2005)	Defines how the entrepreneurial context provides a unique and novel activity within which to explore organizational learning. Argues for a stronger examination of contextual and situational factors.
Holcomb et al. (2009)	Considers how people assimilate and organize knowledge. Introduces three concepts about heuristics – the availability heuristic, the representative heuristic and the anchoring heuristic. Expands on how these heuristics can influence judgments in conditions of uncertainty.
Jones et al. (2010)	Introduces three key concepts associated with strategic space; 'social capital', 'absorptive capacity' and 'mediating artefacts'. Offers a conceptual model on the creation of strategic space.
Lecler & Kinghorn (2014)	Develops four learning patterns: expert honing and aligning; entrepreneurial shaping and configuring. Argues that entrepreneurial learning is critical for the development of dynamic capabilities.
Lumpkin & Lichtenstein (2005)	Argues that organizational learning can strengthen the firm's ability to see opportunities and allows them to pursue new ventures. Develops a typology of organizational learning and opportunity identification
Macpherson & Holt (2007)	Considers how human and social capital, organizational systems and knowledge networks combine to influence firm growth. Highlights the role of experience and learning within the growth process.
Morris et al. (2012)	A model and a set of propositions is developed that links pre-venture experience, key events, experiential processing, learning, affective outcomes and decision-making.
Pittaway & Thorpe (2012)	Explores the initial implications of entrepreneurial learning theory on the development of executive education programs for entrepreneurs.
Politis (2005)	Identifies three components, entrepreneurs' career experiences, the transformation process and entrepreneurial knowledge, which includes coping with liability of newness.

(Continued)

Table 25.1   (Continued)

Rerup (2005)	Argues that mindfulness influences how entrepreneurs choose to use prior experiences to discover and exploit opportunities.
Shepherd & Kuratko (2009)	Argues that emotions generated from failure can interfere with the learning process but also shows how it can enhance learning.
Tseng (2013)	Suggests that entrepreneurs who learn and develop their self-management and self-monitoring skills have more opportunities to enhance their entrepreneurial knowledge.
Ucbasaran et al. (2013)	Examines the financial, social and psychological costs of failure and explains how entrepreneurs make sense and learn from failure.
Wang & Chugh (2014)	Highlights a need to focus more on 'individual and collective learning', 'exploratory and exploitative learning' and 'intuitive and sensing learning'.

Li, Lee & Chen, 2011) characterizes differences in entrepreneurial orientation (EO) and learning between ventures. Exploratory learning describes learning that leads to the observation of new opportunities (e.g. starting a technology-based university spinout) while exploitative learning involves learning that is accrued from exploiting existing opportunities (e.g. starting a restaurant business).

'Intuitive and sensing learning' (Wang & Chugh, 2014) considers differences in individual learning styles between intuitive and sensing learning. Intuitive learning being the association of concepts that are not inherently connected in order to consider new possibilities while sensing learning is focused on learning from an environment by understanding what is going on in a particular context or market (Bingham & Davis, 2012). It is thought different learning styles may influence an entrepreneur's approach to opportunity recognition. These concepts are somewhat similar to the 'hypothesis-testing' and 'hermeneutic' modes of entrepreneurial learning presented by Berglund, Hellström and Sjölander (2007).

'Passion' and 'emotion' also begin to enter thinking in terms of how enthusiasm, passion and engagement with entrepreneurial efforts can influence a willingness or ability to learn (Cardon, Wincent, Singh & Drnovsek, 2009; Cardon, Foo, Shepherd & Wiklund, 2012). Here, passion and emotion have been viewed as both enablers and inhibitors of learning, particularly during

venture failure (Shepherd & Kuratko, 2009; Ucbasaran, Shepherd, Lockett & Lyon, 2013). Aspects of 'social capital', such as 'absorptive capacity', and aspects of 'human capital', such as prior education, are increasingly viewed to be important antecedents and mediators within the entrepreneurial learning context (Macpherson & Holt, 2007; Jones, Macpherson & Thorpe, 2010).

Conceptual advances in the field have recently developed in a number of ways. They have further sought to explain the 'situated' nature of entrepreneurial learning emphasizing what differs within different forms of entrepreneurship (e.g. opportunity creation versus opportunity recognition). They have explored factors that provide individuals with different aptitudes for learning within these different contexts and they have considered the affective dimension of learning more thoroughly. Next, we consider how empirical contributions have advanced the subject.

Empirical Contributions

Recent empirical contributions in the subject naturally tend to lag behind the conceptual thinking. Here there are also some identifiable trends. Many studies, for example, focus on entrepreneurial orientation (EO) as a construct and consider how it might impact on learning capability of an organization. Often the focus here is on organizational learning rather than individual learning (Wang, 2008;

Anderson, Covin & Slevin, 2009; Brettel & Rottenberger, 2013; Real, Roldán & Leal, 2014). Increasingly, studies are examining wider variables in this relationship, such as human capital (Corbett, 2007), internationalization (De Clercq, Sapienza & Crijns, 2005) and different forms of learning (Hughes, Hughes & Morgan, 2007; Kreiser, 2011; Zhao et al., 2011).

Other studies seek to highlight and understand the situated nature of entrepreneurial learning and identify factors that influence how the situation can influence the learning process (Kempster & Cope, 2010; Voudouris, Dimitratos & Salavou, 2010; Karataş-Özkan, 2011). These include a focus on industry entry timing (Lévesque, Minniti & Shepherd, 2009) and the entrepreneurial team (Sardana & Scott-Kemmis, 2010). One empirical paper explores how to measure 'entrepreneurial passion' and 'emotion' and considers how this might impact on the development of ventures (Cardon, Gregoire, Stevens & Patel, 2013). Other studies have used methods more usually associated with recovery from grief to measure how entrepreneurs learn from venture failure and these also consider the emotional aspects of learning (Huovinen & Tihula, 2008; Cope, 2010).

Researchers have considered how learning and knowledge are distributed within the firm, once again taking an organizational learning perspective (Jones & Macpherson, 2006). Within this group there is a focus on how external factors, such as shocks, impact on learning capabilities (Newey & Zahra, 2009) and how new knowledge is sought and/or used by firms (Ravasi & Turati, 2005; Parker, 2006). The final group digs deeper into 'social capital' and 'human capital' attributes and how these might impact on entrepreneurial capability (Thorpe, Gold, Holt & Clarke, 2006; Zhang, Macpherson & Jones, 2006; Stinchfield, Nelson & Wood, 2012).

In comparison to the conceptual studies which emphasize individual learning concepts, the empirical contributions have

a strong focus on organizational learning. Entrepreneurial orientation (EO) as a construct and its impact on how firms engage in strategic learning and development seems to be a strong focus for studies but these would appear to have little interconnectivity with other studies (as highlighted in Observation 3). Empirical studies have only recently begun to focus on the emotional and situational aspects of learning. Based on the conceptual papers one would expect this focus to continue to grow along with more studies on the role of failure and other 'shocks' in entrepreneurial learning. Finally, within organizational learning the extent to which the small firm uses knowledge and draws on the different forms of capital available to enhance the firm's learning posture also seem to have gained some momentum.

Overall this review provides further evidence for Observation 4, that there is somewhat of a disconnect between individual and collective learning within this field of study (Wang & Chugh, 2014). Having set out the prior work in entrepreneurial learning and having reviewed in more detail the most recent studies, this chapter will now consider how this research can be used to inform and guide executive education programs for entrepreneurs.

EXECUTIVE EDUCATION FOR ENTREPRENEURS

Like research in entrepreneurial learning there is a fairly extensive history of research into management development in small firms (Curran, Blackburn, Kitchins & Worth, 1997; Fuller-Love, 2006). Research has identified many challenges and in general there has been a lack of connectivity between the research on entrepreneurial learning and thinking on educational practice for entrepreneurs (Pittaway & Thorpe, 2012). We first highlight the issues identified in the wider research on management development for small firms and then discuss the implications of the entrepreneurial learning research for the design of educational programs (Pittaway, Missing, Hudson & Maragh, 2009), aiming to link these two subjects more closely together. During the second part we will consider both the implications for individual learning and the transfer of learning to the firm itself. The key issues for management development that are usually highlighted in the literature include:

a. Engagement – many countries consider management development for entrepreneurs to be important and, despite the fact they regularly offer free or cheap programs funded by the state, there is a low level of engagement in programs (Stanworth & Gray, 1991; Storey, 1994; Westhead & Storey, 1996). Two factors often prevent engagement and these are time and cost (Gibb, 1990). Small firms typically have only limited funds and any costs can prove challenging. Likewise the opportunity cost for attending training and taking time out from revenue-generating activities is higher for smaller firms (Patel, 1994).

b. Context – programs have been traditionally led by what external organizations think entrepreneurs need (Dalley & Hamilton, 2000) rather than being led by what entrepreneurs themselves say they want. As a consequence programs are poorly designed for what they are trying to achieve (Gibb, 1990).

c. Value – entrepreneurs report that they do not see immediate value in management development programs and consider them to be too costly both in terms of time and money (Perren & Grant, 2001; Thomson, Storey, Mabey, Gray, Farmer & Thomson, 1997; Deakins, 1999).

d. Culture – smaller firms attract leaders and managers with less formal education (Curran et al., 1997; Smith, Whittaker, Loan Clark & Boocock, 1999). Lack of positive experience of education can lead to a distrust of training, compounding the issue of value.

e. Independence – entrepreneurs often choose to start businesses because they distrust authority or wish to have independence from others (Chell, 1985; Bosworth & Jacobs, 1989). Consequently, they do not necessarily wish to engage in programs led by people they do not consider experienced in their life-world (Gibb, 1997).

f. Isolation – managing an entrepreneurial venture itself can prove isolating for an entrepreneur (Clarke, Thorpe, Anderson & Gold, 2006) and they are often reluctant to release control of the business to others in order to pursue learning (Jones, Sambrook, Pittaway & Henley, 2014), which becomes a vicious cycle as they struggle to delegate when they do recruit senior employees (Scase & Goffee, 1987).

g. Complexity – entrepreneurs and those involved in running entrepreneurial ventures have to face considerable complexity and have to simultaneously undertake multiple aspects of management of the venture (Fuller-Love, 2006). Traditional management development programs have focused too much on program designs developed within traditional business education or for larger organizations to be relevant in this context (Deakins & Freel, 1998; Devins, Johnson, Gold & Holden, 2002).

h. Team development – it has been noted previously that many small businesses fail to grow because of the entrepreneur's inability to develop a leadership team (Leach & Kenny, 2000) and that training programs rarely focus on this aspect of an entrepreneur's skill set (Vyakarnam, Jacobs & Handelberg, 1996).

Due to these factors it is widely acknowledged that engaging entrepreneurs in management development can be extremely difficult. Yet the research also shows that it is essential. Managerial competence has been linked to higher failure rates of firms and to higher growth rates. Owners often ascribe their failure to operational management issues (Hall & Young, 1991), lack of capitalization compounded by a lack of managerial experience (Birley & Niktari, 1995) and weak selling skills with too few customers or too much reliance on a single customer. It is thought that such failures can be partly offset by improvements in managerial competence (Fuller-Love, 2006). Failure to grow has also been ascribed to poor leadership skills, including the poor management of employees (Leach & Kenny, 2000), an inability to build teams (Vyakarnam et al., 1996) and weak delegation skills (Stanworth & Curran, 1973). So, there is a paradox in education for entrepreneurs. It is important and yet existing provision is largely ignored by entrepreneurs themselves. This paradox has led researchers to acknowledge that part of the problem is the design and development of management development itself (Jones et al., 2014) and led them to argue that programs have to be better aligned with the lifeworld of the entrepreneur and the form of learning they need to acquire to be effective at running businesses (Pittaway & Thorpe, 2012). In the next part, therefore, we apply the current knowledge in entrepreneurial learning to explain key philosophies and/or components that we suggest should be included within designs of educational programs for

entrepreneurs and these are summarized in Table 25.2.

Prior Experience, Social and Human Capital

The personal prior experience of an individual contributes to their engagement with new situations where entrepreneurial action is required. Entrepreneurs bring a stock of experience with them when they act (Smilor, 1997; Reuber & Fischer, 1999). This stock of experience is both 'technical', from the field within which they have worked, and 'entrepreneurial', derived from prior entrepreneurial efforts (Corbett, 2005). Likewise,

Table 25.2   Key philosophies and components of programs for entrepreneurs

Concept	Forms of learning	Example methods
Prior experience	• Cohort-based learning • Interactive learning • Sharing of personal experience	• Interviewing • Storytelling • Reflective accounts • Live case studies
Social capital	• Networked-based learning	• Speaker recruitment • Informal mentoring • Advisory boards • Shadowing others
Human capital	• Open design learning	• Participant program design • Peer-to-peer delivery
Learning by doing	• Context-based learning • Problem-based learning • Experiential learning • Experimental learning	• Observing, analyzing and addressing real problems • Assessing, planning, acting and reflecting on challenges as addressed • Testing out and experimenting with new products, services and operating procedures
Reflection	• Reflective learning	• Reflective diaries • Learning logs • Portfolios of evidence • Interviewing • Coaching
Learning from others	• Vicarious learning	• Mentoring • Peer-to-peer mentoring • Shadow boards of directors • Masterclasses
Situation	• Situated learning • Team-based learning • Family-based learning	• Team-building techniques • Outdoor team-building • Consultant-based within the firm
Emotion	• Affective learning • Action learning	• Action learning sets • Support groups • Counselling

entrepreneurs bring existing social capital – relationships, networks and mentors – to each new entrepreneurial endeavor (Jones & Macpherson, 2006). Finally, they also have education training and developmental experiences, which account for their personal human capital (Jones et al., 2010). These personal resource endowments of experience, social capital and human capital can significantly impact on the success and performance of the firms they create (Zhang et al., 2006). This aspect suggests that design of learning would benefit from cohort models that encourage peer learning. Maximizing opportunities for peer or 'interactive' methods that encourage individuals to share personal prior experiences would allow programs to access this 'shared stock of experience'. Methods can vary and include interviewing, storytelling techniques, reflective accounts and live case studies.

The existence of a 'stock of social capital' cannot be overlooked either. Entrepreneurs within a program bring with them existing networks and their own social capital. Learning designs and mechanisms that utilize this could be highly productive and many are already in use. A few options include: entrepreneurs recruiting course speakers; formalizing informal relationships for mentoring; utilizing social networks to create advisory boards; and using social networks to help program participants 'shadow' established entrepreneurs. There is also in existence a 'stock of human capital' that can be leveraged effectively in program design. Participants may have had formal education, engaged in training programs and/or had on the job technical training. These prior experiences can be used effectively, alongside the available social capital, by utilizing 'open design' or 'co-creation' methodologies where the participants of a program are involved directly in designing the program or even being actively engaged in aspects of delivery where their expertise and prior knowledge is appropriate. Such approaches could allow entrepreneurs more control and

ensure programs align more closely with the identified needs of participants (Dalley & Hamilton, 2000; Jones et al., 2014).

Action and Problem-Based Learning

The 'learning by doing' and 'learning by experimentation' aspects of how entrepreneurs prefer to learn are well documented (Deakins & Freel, 1998; Watts et al., 1998). Although there have been criticisms of this thinking few researchers dispute that it remains an important aspect of entrepreneurial learning (Taylor & Thorpe, 2004; Cope, 2005). This clearly has implications for program design. It suggests that entrepreneurs will find more value in learning when it is related to ongoing practice within their firms (Thomson et al., 1997; Deakins, 1999; Perren & Grant, 2001) while abstract, academic, theories and learning will likely be seen as having less value (Clarke et al., 2006). Three forms of learning design have been identified. The first is problem-based learning, where aspects of learning are connected to specific problems or challenges within their context. Designs using this approach might, for example, engage teams of entrepreneurs in setting about investigating and proposing approaches for addressing a significant problem experienced by one or more of their businesses. The second is experiential learning, where program designs engage entrepreneurs in deliberate efforts to assess, plan, act and reflect on changes that they wish to progress within their own businesses. Finally, there is inquiry-based learning or experimental learning that allows participants to hypothesize and test new markets or products. The research suggests that entrepreneurs value the opportunity to engage in solving salient problems for their ventures, in a safe environment where they can experiment and try out new actions (Pittaway et al., 2009); where they can 'do' rather than 'listen'.

Reflective Learning

Research has identified that the focus on action needs to be consolidated with active reflection (Cope, 2005, 2010). Typically, entrepreneurs do not practice reflection as they are often embedded in the ongoing action. Life is busy, business demands are high and time is a major commodity; few entrepreneurs take time out from the business for a vacation, let alone management development education (Curran et al., 1997; Smith et al., 1999). This lack of reflection is widely considered to be a weakness within the entrepreneurial context and yet effective entrepreneurs have been observed to be capable reflective learners (Rae & Carswell, 2000; Taylor & Thorpe, 2004). Program designs should enable entrepreneurs to practice reflection more readily (Jones et al., 2014) while simultaneously recognizing the potential opportunity cost this represents to the entrepreneur (Gibb, 1990). This presents one of the more challenging aspects of program design and warrants further research. The act of engaging an entrepreneur in a program itself has been seen to encourage more reflection on learning (Jones et al., 2014). Methods that may be of use include any form of reflective learning, such as reflective diaries, learning logs, portfolios of evidence, interviewing (such as the critical incidence interview) and coaching. Embedding such approaches in designs that are focused on the activities associated with the entrepreneur's ongoing efforts would seem to have the most likely impact on perceptions of value (Deakins, 1999).

Vicarious Learning

Only in the more recent study of entrepreneurial learning has vicarious learning been in full focus (Holcomb et al., 2009). Possibly overlooked because of the entrepreneur's perceived desire for independence from others (Chell, 1985; Bosworth & Jacobs, 1989), it does seem important within learning designs. It has, for example, been noted that entrepreneurs want to learn from authentic experts (i.e. other entrepreneurs) and that those running businesses often have a feeling of isolation, particularly when making key decisions (Clarke et al., 2006; Jones et al., 2014). Both aspects of the entrepreneurial context can be offset by a focus on vicarious learning. Certain methods that might be of relevance include mentoring, peer-to-peer mentoring, shadow boards of directors and shadowing other entrepreneurs, as well as engaging successful entrepreneurs in masterclasses. Mentoring and peer-to-peer mentoring in particular have been highlighted as beneficial in encouraging vicarious learning in the entrepreneurial context (Clarke et al., 2006).

Situated Learning and Learning Transfer

Learning in the entrepreneurial context can be viewed as highly situated, i.e. fully embedded in the unique context of the venture, the entrepreneur's critical relationships and the industry/marketplace within which the firm operates (Jack et al., 2008). The context is ambiguous, uncertain and also highly social in that key relationships with others can have a disproportionate impact on the entrepreneur and the firm itself (Politis & Gabrielsson, 2009). Likewise, the learning must be transferred to others for it to influence firm development (Jones et al., 2014). Coping with this complexity is time-consuming and as a result entrepreneurs rarely allow time to engage in management development (Fuller-Love, 2006). This aspect of the research on entrepreneurial learning opens up questions about the 'individualized' nature of management development education for entrepreneurs. There is an assumption that if entrepreneurs are given support and education then there will be benefits for the firm but recent research suggests that this may not be the case if the learning is not transferred into the organizational development path of the venture as a collective effort (Leach & Kenny, 2000). This is just one area of research that requires more consideration to determine how 'learning' can be collective across a wider group of participants associated with a venture (e.g. team-based learning) and how learning might engage other critical stakeholders alongside the entrepreneur (e.g. spouses or key investors). Learning designs focused on 'collective learning' for the team and the venture more broadly may assist the transfer of learning from the individual into organizational development for the venture itself (Vyakarnam et al., 1996). Methods that might be of value include designs that incorporate more consultant-like interventions that include the entire family associated with the business or engage all key members of the leadership team. The situated nature of learning also requires thought to ensure all learning is fully embedded in the context from which it derives (e.g. through problem-based learning) and includes methods that acknowledge the level of ambiguity and uncertainty that entrepreneurs face (e.g. experimental methods).

Emotion and Affective Learning

Much recent research has begun to focus on emotion and passion in entrepreneurial learning (Cardon et al., 2009; 2012). This research stream is fairly new and it is difficult at this point to fully outline how these aspects of learning could impact on the most effective mechanisms for executive development for entrepreneurs. There are a number of initial implications that can be highlighted. First, it has been widely acknowledged that running businesses can be isolating (Chell, 1985; Bosworth & Jacobs, 1989) and that emotional, financial and social exposure is a very real danger for entrepreneurs when they experience major

crises in the business (Cope, 2005, 2010). Prolonged uncertainty and the psychological costs of running businesses can lead to negative psychological, business and social outcomes (Shepherd & Kuratko, 2009). From this early research it already seems clear that the creation of support networks for entrepreneurs that removes them from isolation and encourages them to share experiences and emotions may hold value beyond the development of managerial skills and the business. Action learning sets have already been shown to provide a support network for entrepreneurs (Clarke et al., 2006; Pittaway et al., 2009) and have been recommended as a means to help entrepreneurs during insolvency or other significant periods of difficulty (Jones et al., 2014). As research expands on entrepreneurial failure it seems likely that approaches may emerge that would allow the development of more effective support mechanisms to help entrepreneurs deal with the emotional consequences of failure. Such approaches may enhance entrepreneurial learning and help offset some of the psychological outcomes of failure events (Jones et al., 2014). Methods that could be of value within this theme include action learning sets, counselling, peer-to-peer mentoring and other group-based support (e.g. group counselling).

Approaches to management development education for entrepreneurs based on current knowledge about entrepreneurial learning are summarized in Table 25.2. Next we will conclude the chapter by explaining the wider implications of research in this subject area and by highlighting implications for future research, educational design and government policy.

CONCLUSIONS

This chapter has reflected on the historical development of research examining entrepreneurial learning and shown how the field has developed. It has then conducted a review of the contemporary subject exploring both the recent conceptual and empirical contributions (from 2005 until 2015). The implications of prior study in entrepreneurial learning are considered in some depth and from these the chapter explains how this research stream could be used to inform and develop educational program designs for entrepreneurs.

This chapter shows how the early study of entrepreneurial learning has developed from the simplified stance of 'learning from doing' (Watts et al., 1998) to incorporate deeper personal development, including reflection (Cope, 2003; Taylor & Thorpe, 2004), learning from crises (Cope, 2005; Politis & Gabrielsson, 2009) and social learning (Jack et al., 2008). Current and recent studies build on these dimensions, as well as looking at the impact of environment or situation (Politis, 2005), learning method (Kreiser, 2011; Zhao et al., 2011) and emotion (Cardon et al., 2012; Cope, 2010; Shepherd, 2003). It was clear that research in the entrepreneurial learning domain is gaining traction and growing as a subject of interest, that a degree of diversification had occurred, with the field splitting into at least two 'schools of thought', and that there is a need to further connect individual learning with collective learning outcomes (Wang & Chugh, 2014).

We argue that more consideration is needed to understand how entrepreneurial learning should inform the development of learning programs for entrepreneurs. Problems still persist of low engagement (Stanworth & Gray, 1991), poor perceived value (Perren & Grant, 2001) and an inability to design programs in a way that entrepreneurs want (Dalley & Hamilton, 2000). The chapter highlighted aspects of design based on the prior research that might help, as highlighted in Table 25.2. From this work it is clear that current knowledge on entrepreneurial learning could improve our ability to design and implement development

programs for entrepreneurs. As yet, we conclude, it has only had limited impact and it is an area that is ripe for considerable empirical research.

The main outcome of this work is a call to all researchers in entrepreneurial learning to begin to think more deeply, and thoroughly consider, the applications of this body of work. Increasing numbers of researchers have advanced the field conceptually and empirically, yet few have considered how findings can be used in practice. Researchers also need to study how conceptual and empirical studies connect. Conceptual studies tend towards a focus on individual learning while empirical studies focus more on organizational learning. Yet it is clear from this review that the nexus of the two – how individual learning is transferred into the organization and/or how the team or family learns together – is of value. Likewise, trends towards the role of emotion and passion in learning are interesting lines of inquiry that merit more work and may lead to important applied outcomes when considering how to support entrepreneurs during periods of venture difficulty.

Finally, the chapter highlights some important practical and policy considerations. Prior work shows that traditional educational designs do not reflect how entrepreneurs learn. The expansive and growing research on entrepreneurial learning confirms this mismatch between learning designs and learning needs. Those who are involved with developing or commissioning programs for entrepreneurs need to recognize the different requirements of entrepreneurs from other types of learners. Learning needs: (1) to be embedded in its context; (2) to focus on finding solutions to salient problems; (3) to be delivered by authentic and credible experts; and (4) to encourage reflective and experimental learning. Utilizing the existing research to design more effective programs is likely to have far-reaching consequences, taking learning beyond the individual and having a direct impact on the performance of businesses.

REFERENCES

Anderson, B.S., Covin, J. and Slevin, D.P. 2009. Understanding the relationship between entrepreneurial orientation and strategic learning capability: an empirical investigation. *Strategic Entrepreneurship Journal*, 3 (6), 218–240.

Baron, R.A. and Henry, R.A. 2010. How entrepreneurs acquire the capacity to excel: insights from research on expert performance. *Strategic Entrepreneurship Journal*, 4 (1), 49–65.

Berglund, H., Hellström, L. and Sjölander, S. 2007. Entrepreneurial learning and the role of venture capitalists. *Venture Capital: An International Journal of Entrepreneurial Finance*, 9 (3), 165–181.

Bingham, C.B. and Davis, J.P. 2012. Learning sequences: their existence, effect, and evolution. *Academy of Management Journal*, 55 (3), 611–641.

Birley, S. and Niktari, N. 1995. *The Failure of Owner-Managed Businesses: The Diagnosis of Accountants and Bankers*. London: Institute of Chartered Accountants in England and Wales.

Bosworth, D. and Jacobs, C. 1989. Management attitudes, behaviour and abilities as barriers to growth. In Barber, J., Metcalfe, J.S. and Porteous, M. (eds), *Barriers to Growth in Small Firms*. London: Routledge, pp. 20–38.

Brettel, M. and Rottenberger, J.D. 2013. Examining the link between entrepreneurial orientation and learning processes in small and medium-sized enterprises. *Journal of Small Business Management*, 51 (4), 471–490.

Cardon, M.S., Foo, M., Shepherd, D. and Wiklund, J. 2012. Exploring the heart: emotion is a hot topic. *Entrepreneurship Theory and Practice*, 36 (1), 1–11.

Cardon, M.S., Gregoire, D.A., Stevens, C.E. and Patel, P.C. 2013. Measuring entrepreneurial passion: conceptual foundations and scale validation, *Journal of Business Venturing*, 28 (3), 373–396.

Cardon, M.S., Wincent, J., Singh, J. and Drnovsek, M. 2009. The nature and experience of entrepreneurial passion. *Academy of Management Review*, 34 (3), 511–532.

Chell, E. 1985. The entrepreneurial personality: a few ghosts laid to rest? *International Small Business Journal*, 3 (3), 43–53.

Clarke, J., Thorpe, R., Anderson, L. and Gold, J. 2006. It's all action, it's all learning: action learning in SMEs. *Journal of European Industrial Training*, 30 (6), 441–455.

Cope, J. 2003. Entrepreneurial learning and critical reflection: discontinuous events as triggers for 'higher-level' learning. *Management Learning*, 34 (4), 429–450.

Cope, J. 2005. Toward a dynamic learning perspective of entrepreneurship. *Entrepreneurship Theory and Practice*, 29 (4), 373–397.

Cope, J. 2010. Entrepreneurial learning from failure: an interpretative phenomenological analysis. *Journal of Business Venturing*, 26 (6), 604–623.

Cope, J. and Watts, G. 2000. Learning by doing: an exploration of experience, critical incidents and reflection in entrepreneurial learning. *International Journal of Entrepreneurial Behaviour and Research*, 6 (3), 104–124.

Corbett, A.C. 2005. Experiential learning within the process of opportunity identification and exploitation. *Entrepreneurship Theory and Practice*, 29 (4), 473–491.

Corbett, A.C. 2007. Learning asymmetries and the discovery of entrepreneurial opportunities. *Journal of Business Venturing*, 22 (1), 97–118.

Curran, J., Blackburn, R., Kitchins, J. and Worth, J. 1997. Small firms and workforce training: some results, analysis and policy implications from a national survey. In Ram, M., Deakins, D. and Smallbone, D. (eds), *Small Firms: Enterprising Futures*. London: Paul Chapman, pp. 90–101.

Dalley, J. and Hamilton, B. 2000. Knowledge, context and learning in the small business. *International Small Business Journal*, 18 (3), 51–59.

Daudelin, M.W. 1996. Learning from experience through reflection. *Organisational Dynamics*, 24 (3), 36–48.

Deakins, D. 1999. *Entrepreneurship and Small Firms*, 2nd edn. Maidenhead: McGraw-Hill.

Deakins, D. and Freel, M. 1998. Entrepreneurial learning and the growth process in SMEs. *The Learning Organisation*, 5 (3), 144–155.

De Clercq, D., Sapienza, H.J. and Crijns, H. 2005. The internationalization of small and medium-sized firms: the role of organizational learning effort and entrepreneurial orientation. *Small Business Economics*, 24 (4), 409–419.

Devins, D., Johnson, S., Gold, J. and Holden, R. 2002. *Management Development and Learning in Micro Businesses: A 'Missing Link' in Research and Policy*. London: Research and Evaluation Unit, Small Business Service.

Dutta, D.K. and Crossan, M.M. 2005. The nature of entrepreneurial opportunities: understanding the process using the 4I organizational learning framework. *Entrepreneurship Theory and Practice*, 29 (4), 425–449.

Fletcher, D.E. and Watson, T.J. 2007. Entrepreneurship, management learning and negotiated narratives: 'making it otherwise for us – otherwise for them'. *Management Learning*, 38 (1), 9–26.

Fuller-Love, N. 2006. Management development in small firms. *International Journal of Management Reviews*, 8 (3), 175–190.

Gartner, W.B. 1988. 'Who is an entrepreneur?' is the wrong question. *American Journal of Small Business*, 13 (4), 11–32.

Gibb, A.A. 1990. Training the trainers for the small business. *Journal of European Industrial Training*, 14 (1), 17–25.

Gibb, A. 1997. Small firms' training and competitiveness. Building upon the small business as a learning organisation. *International Small Business Journal*, 15 (3), 13–29.

Hall, G. and Young, B. 1991. Factors associated with insolvency amongst small firms. *International Small Business Journal*, 9 (2), 54–63.

Hamilton, E. 2004. Socially situated entrepreneurial learning in family business. In Proceedings of the 27th ISBA National Small Firms Policy and Research Conference, Newcastle, November.

Harrison, R.T. and Leitch, C.M. 2005. Entrepreneurial learning: researching the interface between learning and the entrepreneurial context. *Entrepreneurship Theory and Practice*, 29 (4), 351–371.

Harrison, R.T. and Leitch, C.M. 2008. *Entrepreneurial Learning: Conceptual Frameworks and Applications*. London: Routledge.

Holcomb, T.R., Ireland, R.D., Holmes, R.M., Jr and Hitt, M.A. (2009). Architecture of entrepreneurial learning: exploring the link among heuristics, knowledge, and action. *Entrepreneurship Theory and Practice*, 33 (1), 167–192.

Hughes, M., Hughes, P. and Morgan, R.E. 2007. Exploitative learning and entrepreneurial orientation alignment in emerging young firms: implications for market and response performance. *British Journal of Management*, 18 (4), 359–375.

Huovinen, J. and Tihula, S. 2008. Entrepreneurial learning in the context of portfolio entrepreneurship. *International Journal of Entrepreneurial Behaviour and Research*, 14 (3), 152–171.

Jack, S., Drakopoulou Dodd, S. and Anderson, A. 2008. Change and the development of entrepreneurial networks over time: a processual perspective, *Entrepreneurship and Regional Development*, 20 (2), 125–159.

Johnston, L., Hamilton, E. and Zhang, J. 2008. Learning through engaging with higher education institutions: a small business perspective. *International Small Business Journal*, 26 (6), 651–660.

Jones, K., Sambrook, S., Pittaway, L. and Henley, A. 2014. Action learning: how learning transfers from entrepreneurs to small firms. *Action Learning: Research and Practice*, 11 (2), 131–166.

Jones, O. and Macpherson, A. 2006. Inter-organizational learning and strategic renewal in SMEs: extending the 4I framework. *Long Range Planning*, 39 (2), 155–175.

Jones, O., Macpherson, A. and Thorpe, R. 2010. Learning in owner-managed small firms: mediating artefacts and strategic space. *Entrepreneurship and Regional Development*, 22 (7–8), 649–673.

Jones, O., Macpherson, A. and Woollard, D. 2008. Entrepreneurial ventures in higher education: analysing organisational growth. *International Small Business Journal*, 26 (6), 683–708.

Karataş-Özkan, M. 2011. Understanding relational qualities of entrepreneurial learning: towards a multi-layered approach. *Entrepreneurship and Regional Development*, 23 (9–10), 877–906.

Kempster, S. and Cope, J. 2010. Learning to lead in the entrepreneurial context. *International Journal of Entrepreneurial Behaviour and Research*, 16 (1), 5–34.

Kreiser, P.M. 2011. Entrepreneurial orientation and organizational learning: the impact of network range and network closure. *Entrepreneurship Theory and Practice*, 35 (5), 1025–1050.

Lave, J. and Wenger, E. 1991. *Situated Learning: Legitimate Peripheral Participation*. Cambridge: Cambridge University Press.

Leach, T. and Kenny, B. 2000. The role of professional development in stimulating changes in small growing business. *Continuing Professional Development Journal*, 3 (2), 7–22.

Lecler, C.J. and Kinghorn, J. 2014. Dynamic capabilities, expert and entrepreneurial learning. *South African Journal of Business Management*, 45 (2), 65–81.

Lévesque, M., Minniti, M. and Shepherd, D. 2009. Entrepreneurs' decisions on timing of entry: learning from participation and from the experiences of others. *Entrepreneurship Theory and Practice*, 33 (2), 547–570.

Lumpkin, G.T. and Lichtenstein, B.B. 2005. The role of entrepreneurial learning in the opportunity-recognition process. *Entrepreneurship Theory and Practice*, 29 (4), 451–472.

Macpherson, A.A. and Holt, R. 2007. Knowledge, learning and small firm growth: a systematic review of the evidence. *Research Policy*, 36 (2), 172–192.

Macpherson, A., Kofinas, A., Jones, O. and Thorpe, R. 2010. Making sense of mediated learning: cases from small firms. *Management Learning*, 41 (3), 303–323.

Mezirow, J. 1991. *Transformative Dimensions of Adult Learning*. San Francisco, CA: Jossey-Bass.

Minniti, M. and Bygrave, W. 2001. A dynamic model of entrepreneurial learning, *Entrepreneurship Theory and Practice*, 25 (3), 5–16.

Morris, M.H., Kuratko, D.F., Schindehutte, M. and Spivack, A.J. 2012. Framing the entrepreneurial experience. *Entrepreneurship Theory and Practice*, 36 (1), 11–40.

Newey, L.R. and Zahra, S. 2009. The evolving firm: how dynamic and operating capabilities interact to enable entrepreneurship. *British Journal of Management*, 20 (1), S81–100.

Parker, S.C. 2006. Learning about the unknown: how fast do entrepreneurs adjust their beliefs? *Journal of Business Venturing*, 21 (1), 1–26.

Patel, A. 1994. Assessing total quality training in Wales. *Training for Quality*, 2 (2), 13–21.

Perren, L. and Grant, P. 2001. *Management and Leadership in UK SMEs: Witness Testimonies from the World of Entrepreneurs and SME Managers*. London: Council for Excellence in Management and Leadership.

Pittaway, L., Gazzard, J., Shore, A. and Williamson, T. 2015. Student clubs: experiences in entrepreneurial learning. *Entrepreneurship and Regional Development*, 27 (3–4), 127–153.

Pittaway, L., Holt, R. and Broad, J. 2014. Synthesising knowledge in entrepreneurship research: the role of systematic literature reviews. In Chell, E. and Karataş-Özkan, M. (eds), *Handbook of Research on Small Business and Entrepreneurship*. London: Edward Elgar, pp. 83–105.

Pittaway, L., Missing, C., Hudson, N. and Maragh, D. 2009. Entrepreneurial learning through action: a case study of the six-squared program. *Action Learning: Research and Practice*, 6 (3), 265–288.

Pittaway, L. and Thorpe, R. 2012. A framework for entrepreneurial learning: a tribute to Jason Cope. *Entrepreneurship and Regional Development*, 24 (9/10), 837–859.

Politis, D. 2005. The process of entrepreneurial learning: a conceptual framework. *Entrepreneurship Theory and Practice*, 29 (4), 399–424.

Politis, D. and Gabrielsson, J. 2009. Entrepreneurs' attitudes towards failure: an experiential learning approach. *International Journal of Entrepreneurial Behaviour and Research*, 15 (4), 364–383.

Preskill, H. 1996. The use of critical incidents to foster reflection and learning in HRD. *Human Resource Development Quarterly*, 7 (4), 335–347.

Rae, D. 2002. Entrepreneurial emergence: a narrative study of entrepreneurial learning in independently owned media businesses. *International Journal of Entrepreneurship and Innovation*, 3 (1), 53–59.

Rae, D. and Carswell, M. 2000. Using a life-story approach in researching entrepreneurial learning: the development of a conceptual model and its implications in the design of learning experiences. *Education and Training*, 42 (4/5), 220–227.

Ravasi, D. and Turati, C. 2005. Exploring entrepreneurial learning: a comparative study of technology development projects. *Journal of Business Venturing*, 20 (1), 137–164.

Real, J.C., Roldán, J.L. and Leal, A. 2014. From entrepreneurial orientation and learning orientation to business performance: analysing the mediating role of organizational learning and the moderating effects of organizational size. *British Journal of Management*, 25 (2), 186–208.

Rerup, C. 2005. Learning from past experience: footnotes on mindfulness and habitual entrepreneurship. *Scandinavian Journal of Management*, 21 (4), 451–472.

Reuber, A.R. and Fischer, E.M. 1999. Understanding the consequences of founders' experiences. *Journal of Small Business Management,* 37 (2), 30–45.

Sardana, D. and Scott-Kemmis, D. 2010. Who learns what? A study based on entrepreneurs from biotechnology new ventures. *Journal of Small Business Management*, 48 (3), 441–468.

Scase, R. and Goffee, R. 1987. *The Real World of the Small Business Owner*. London: Routledge.

Senge, P.M. 1990. *The Fifth Discipline: The Art and Practice of the Learning Organisation*. London: Century Business.

Shepherd, D.A. 2003. Learning from business failure: propositions of grief recovery for the self-employed. *Academy of Management Review*, 28 (2), 318–328.

Shepherd, D.A. and Kuratko, D.F. 2009. The death of an innovative project: how grief recovery enhances learning. *Business Horizons*, 52 (5), 451–458.

Smilor, R.W. 1997. Entrepreneurship: reflections on a subversive activity. *Journal of Business Venturing*, 12 (5), 341–346.

Smith, A., Whittaker, J., Loan Clark, J. and Boocock, G. 1999. Competence based management development provision to SMEs and the providers' perspective. *Journal of Management Development*, 18 (6), 557–572.

Stanworth, J. and Curran, J. 1973. *Management Motivation in the Smaller Business*. Epping: Gower Press.

Stanworth, J. and Gray, C. 1991. *Bolton 20 Years On: The Small Firm in the 1990s*. London: Small Business Research Trust, Paul Chapman.

Stinchfield, B.T., Nelson, R.E. and Wood, M.S. 2012. Learning from Levi-Strauss' legacy: art, craft, engineering, bricolage, and brokerage in entrepreneurship. *Entrepreneurship Theory and Practice*, 37 (4), 889–921.

Storey, D.J. (1994). *Understanding the Small Business Sector*. London: Routledge.

Taylor, D.W. and Thorpe, R. 2004. Entrepreneurial learning: a process of co-participation. *Journal of Small Business and Enterprise Development*, 11 (2), 203–211.

Thomson, A., Storey, J., Mabey, C., Gray, C., Farmer, E. and Thomson, R. 1997. *A Portrait of Management Development*. London: Institute of Management/Open University.

Thorpe, R., Gold, J., Holt, R. and Clarke, J. 2006. Immaturity: the constraining of entrepreneurship. *International Small Business Journal*, 24 (3), 232–252.

Tseng, C. 2013. Connecting self-directed learning with entrepreneurial learning to entrepreneurial performance. *International Journal of Entrepreneurial Behaviour and Research*, 19 (4), 425–446.

Ucbasaran, D., Shepherd, D.A., Lockett, A. and Lyon, S.J. 2013. Life after business failure: the process and consequences of business failure for entrepreneurs. *Journal of Management*, 39 (1), 163–202.

Voudouris, I., Dimitratos, P. and Salavou, H. 2010. Entrepreneurial learning in the international new high technology venture. *International Small Business Journal*, 29 (3), 238–258.

Vyakarnam, S., Jacobs, R.C. and Handelberg, J. 1996. Building and managing relationships: the core competence of rapid growth business. Paper presented at the 19th ISBA Small Firms Policy and Research Conference, Nottingham.

Wang, C.L. 2008. Entrepreneurial orientation, learning orientation, and firm performance. *Entrepreneurship Theory and Practice*, 32 (4), 635–656.

Wang, C.L. and Chugh, H. 2014. Entrepreneurial learning: past research and future challenges. *International Journal of Management Reviews*, 16 (1), 24–61.

Watts, G., Cope, J. and Hulme, M. 1998. Ansoff's matrix, pain and gain: growth strategies and adaptive learning among small food producers. *International Journal of Entrepreneurial Behaviour and Research*, 4 (2), 101–111.

West, G.P. and Wilson, E.V. 1995. A simulation of strategic decision making in situational stereotype conditions for entrepreneurial companies. *Simulation and Gaming*, 26 (3), 307–327.

Westhead, P. and Storey, D. 1996. Management training and small firm performance: why is the link so weak? *International Small Business Journal*, 14 (4), 13–24.

Zhang, M., Macpherson, A. and Jones, O. 2006. Conceptualizing the learning process in SMEs: improving innovation through external orientation. *International Small Business Journal*, 24 (3), 299–323.

Zhao, Y., Li, Y., Lee, S.H. and Chen, L.B. 2011. Entrepreneurial orientation, organizational learning, and performance: evidence from China. *Entrepreneurship Theory and Practice*, 35 (5), 293–317.

Appendix 25.1   Empirical studies in entrepreneurial learning (2005–15)

Author/s (date)	Empirical contribution
Anderson et al. (2009)	Explores the relationship between entrepreneurial orientation and strategic learning capability. The paper presents data from 110 manufacturing firms.
Brettel & Rottenberger (2013)	Samples 3,062 SMEs via an e-mail survey with a 10.7% response rate. Measures entrepreneurial orientation and organizational learning. Finds that having an entrepreneurial orientation can promote organizational learning.
Cardon et al. (2013)	Seeks to develop a measure for entrepreneurial passion. Undertakes a series of empirical studies, including three pilot studies sent to 4,000 participants to validate the instrument and a final study including 158 participants. Finds that there are distinct aspects of entrepreneurial passion.
Cope (2011)	Develops a conceptualization of the process and content dimensions of learning from venture failure. Undertakes a purposive sample using interpretative phenomenological analysis with eight entrepreneurs who have experienced venture failure.
Corbett (2007)	Examines the relationship between opportunity identification and learning by examining data from 380 technology professionals. A random sample of 1,592 founders, owners and top management team members was used (Colorado). Findings show that an individual's specific human capital has an impact on their ability to discover opportunities and specifically technical knowhow.
De Clercq et al. (2005)	Considers notions of organizational learning and entrepreneurial orientation and how these ideas might impact on the internationalization of small firms. Draws on a sample of independent firms with a sample of 92 surveys. Concludes that learning efforts towards internationalization and entrepreneurial mindsets of firms will influence the success of internationalization efforts.
Hughes et al. (2007)	Explores exploitative learning and entrepreneurial orientation amongst young firms and considers the impact on performance. Specifically examines firms in incubators that are emerging and focused on technology. Sample 211 firms responded to a mail survey.
Huovinen & Tihula (2008)	Examines entrepreneurial learning in the context of portfolio entrepreneurship. Uses a case study method to explore one portfolio entrepreneur. Data included interviews and a written description of the entrepreneur's career. Proposes that failures lead to entrepreneurial knowledge.
Jones & Macpherson (2006)	Study explores how mature small firms use external knowledge to assist strategic renewal. Highlights the role of proactivity in learning across networks and the role of certain key external organizations in enabling the institutionalization of learning.
Karataş-Özkan (2011)	Presents a multilayered relational framework of entrepreneurial learning. Conducts a longitudinal study using participant observation and in-depth qualitative interviews examining the entrepreneurial learning processes of five new entrepreneurs. Highlights how individual learning is embedded within their relationships with the broader venture community.

(Continued)

Appendix 25.1   (Continued)

Kempster & Cope (2010)	Explores 'leadership learning' within the entrepreneurial context. Uses qualitative phenomenological interviews with nine entrepreneurs to inductively build theory. The paper finds that there are situated leadership patterns that are unique to the entrepreneurial context.
Kreiser (2011)	Explores the relationship between entrepreneurial orientation and an organization's acquisitive and experiential learning capacities. They present an empirical model.
Lévesque et al. (2009)	Researches entry timing to an industry and the implications for entrepreneurial learning and competitive advantage. An empirical model is presented.
Newey & Zahra (2009)	Considers operating and dynamic capabilities and how these help firms cope with risks following external shocks. Undertakes a comparative analysis of two firms that are collaborating.
Parker (2006)	Measures how entrepreneurs adjust beliefs after being presented with new information rather than simply responding to past experiences. The model is tested using the British Household Panel Survey on 700+ self-employed people.
Ravasi & Turati (2005)	Undertakes a comparative study exploring the factors that influence the learning process supporting innovation in products and services. Uses a comparative case study method analyzing two development processes in one organization and collects data using semi-structured interviews.
Real et al. (2014)	Draws on organizational learning theory and the knowledge-based view of the firm to study entrepreneurial orientation and learning orientation. Model is tested on 140 Spanish industrial companies.
Sardana & Scott-Kemmis (2010)	Seeks to better understand the context and content of learning in the entrepreneurial process. Focuses on ventures selected from 96 biotech start-ups (India and Australia). The findings suggest that prior experience plays an important role in subsequent entrepreneurial learning.
Stinchfield et al. (2012)	Uses grounded theory methods to explore bricolage and brokerage in a study of 23 entrepreneurs. A five-category typology of entrepreneurial behavior is developed.
Thorpe et al. (2006)	Highlights the concepts of 'enacted cognition', 'practical authorship' and 'maturity' and uses them to investigate entrepreneurial activity. An e-postcard method is used with 44 UK entrepreneurs.
Voudouris et al. (2010)	Examines entrepreneurial learning in a high-technology firm that internationalized from the outset. A case study method is adopted and one company is followed over a seven-year period.
Wang (2008)	Considers both entrepreneurial orientation and learning orientation. Uses data from 213 firms in the UK to study the relationship between the two concepts. The findings suggest that learning orientation is an important prerequisite for firms to act entrepreneurially.
Zhang et al. (2006)	Seeks to develop an understanding of the unique organizational learning processes relevant to small firms. Data is obtained from interviews with 26 owner-managers.
Zhao et al. (2011)	Explores relationships between entrepreneurial orientation, experimental learning and acquisitive learning and their links to firm performance. Undertakes a survey with 607 firms.

26

The Use of Case Studies in Entrepreneurship Education

Thomas M. Cooney[1]

INTRODUCTION

It is now widely accepted that entrepreneurship education does not fit neatly into conventional models of education that are assessed by means of examination. It is also increasingly recognised that the teaching of entrepreneurship requires a practical approach, where information and knowledge are generated among participants and an action-orientated teaching philosophy assists them in understanding more thoroughly the overall concepts of entrepreneurship. This means that traditional methods of student examination must also be reconsidered, and evaluation techniques appropriate to the curricula and the student learning experience must be custom-designed for entrepreneurship programmes.

One of the key challenges facing entrepreneurship education is the lack of entrepreneurial experience among educators/trainers, combined with a general absence of entrepreneurial experience amongst students.

This situation in turn tends to produce classroom situations which focus heavily on what participants feel is a comfortable working and studying environment whereby the attention is on theory rather than practice. Another challenge faced by educators is the difficulty in making clear definitions between entrepreneurship and enterprise (and between education and training) when it comes to this subject matter. Currently, teaching entrepreneurship is frequently centred on improving a student's ability to write a business plan and therefore students are taught to see the formulation of their potential business idea as sequential by going through a number of phases. However, this is not how entrepreneurship happens 'in the real world' and so progressive educators have sought to identify more suitable methodologies for teaching entrepreneurship that can develop the capabilities of students tailored to the modern business environment. One such methodology is the use of case studies.

The ambition of this chapter is to enlighten the reader about the use of case studies in entrepreneurship education, and to encourage the reader to write case studies and use them in the classroom. The chapter begins by explaining the background to case studies and then moves on to highlighting the benefits that such a teaching approach offers both students and educators/trainers. The chapter explores how one might teach using case studies and thereafter it breaks down the challenges that many educators believe exist when seeking to write one's own cases. The chapter concludes by investigating some of the other key issues involved in the use of case studies in entrepreneurship before drawing a number of conclusions on the current position of this form of pedagogy.

WHAT ARE CASE STUDIES?

The history of case studies begins in the early nineteenth century with their usage in medicine, psychology and law. Indeed, it is understood that case studies for the purposes of business education were used in the early 1900s in Harvard University (Naumes & Naumes, 2006). It has also been found that case studies were used in teacher education programmes on the East Coast of the United States of America from the 1920s and that by the mid twentieth century, the success of such an approach was being recognised in a number of academic fields (Merseth, 1999). From the 1950s to the 1980s, some journal articles were published on the merits of case studies for teaching purposes and in the early 1990s, books of case studies started to be published and educators began to have greater access to case studies for use in their classrooms. It is suggested that the market for business cases is now dominated by Harvard Business Publishing which claims that it sells to approximately 4,000 schools globally and that its cases account for about 80 per cent of case studies used annually (Levy, 2015).

Case studies are usually based on real events (or circumstances that could reasonably have taken place) and they tell the stories of conflicts, issues or situations which need to be resolved by certain identified characters. Traditionally, case studies have contained detailed historical information which may be supported by graphs, tables, financial information or other forms of support data. Generally, the reader of the case study is invited into the role of a central character and requested to analyse the situation and offer prescriptive solutions to the given conditions. As Boehrer and Linsky (1990, p. 45) stated:

> a good case presents an interest provoking issue and promotes empathy with the central characters. It delineates their individual perspectives and personal circumstances well enough to enable students to understand the characters' experience of the issue. The importance of the compelling issue and the empathetic character reflects the fact that cases typically focus on the intersection between organisational and situational dynamics and individual perception, judgement and action.

Naumes and Naumes (2006) suggested that case studies are designed to provoke discussion and analysis of a particular situation and therefore it is an active pedagogical process as opposed to the passive process that occurs via traditional lectures. Through the use of case studies, entrepreneurship educators seek to offer students experiential learning opportunities that are highly applicable to the environment that they will one day inhabit, plus challenge them to critically analyse and offer solutions to circumstances that occur regularly within the world of entrepreneurial activity. The case studies can also be used to bring to life abstract and disparate issues by encouraging students to address problems and make decisions that occur within the complexities of business environments.

Before venturing into the examination of case studies for the purposes of entrepreneurship education, it is important that the reader first understands the difference between a case study and a case history. A case study is generally forward-focused, it invites the reader into a specific role and the primary task is to recommend what the central character or organisation should do next. A case history is generally backward-looking; it invites judgement and the primary task is to reflect upon that which has occurred in the past. Both types of case studies have their merits and each will have their strengths and weaknesses in various learning situations, but the focus of this chapter is solely on case studies (not case histories) since anecdotal evidence would suggest that they are the more widely used form within entrepreneurship education.

BENEFITS TO STUDENTS AND TEACHERS

A frequently asked question relating to case studies enquires about the benefits of using such an approach to education. Anecdotal evidence from educators will highlight that the benefits for students are wide-ranging and that they include learning by doing, the application of prior learning, learning from peers (and even teaching peers) the ability to structure their own working environment and the value of working with others as part of a team. But it is also important to note that research exists which has highlighted that case-based pedagogy enables students to develop skills such as critical analysis, problem-solving and strategic thinking (e.g. Doyle, 1990; Lundeberg & Fawver, 1994; Wasserman, 1994), and, dependent on the learning environment, they may also be required to develop their presentation skills. Students are also trained to structure their own learning environment and to develop clear roles and responsibilities if working in a group scenario (Mauffette-Leenders, Erskine & Leenders, 2001). More recently, Boud, Lawson and Thompson (2014) highlighted how students benefit through peer learning, cooperative problem-solving and metacognitive strategies, while Davis and Wilcock (2015) emphasised that the

case-based approach was a useful teaching method in developing transferable skills such as: (1) group working, (2) individual study skills, (3) information gathering and analysis, (4) time management, (5) presentation skills, and (6) practical skills. Indeed, case studies also allow the application of theoretical concepts to be demonstrated which obviously leads to a bridging of the gap between theory and practice.

Bonwell and Eison (1991) and Sivan, Wong Leung, Woon and Kember (2000) argued that students can learn more effectively when dynamically involved in the learning process and viewed the case study approach as an effective method through which active learning can take place. Grant (1997) suggested that case studies shift the learning process from teacher-centred to student-centred, while Mustoe and Croft (1999) emphasised how case studies have been linked to increased student motivation. Within this approach of self-directed learning, case studies force students to cope with ambiguities in the business environment and they will initially struggle with the fact that there is 'no right answer' to the case study. Explaining to students that any number of decisions could be equally valid in a given situation commonly leads to debate and evidence might be produced (e.g. from a company website) to reinforce their belief that their solution was the best since that is the decision that was taken by the company. Rationalising to a class that 'because the company made that decision does not necessarily make it correct' is always a challenge and student access to information on a case through the internet exacerbates this particular problem. However, over time, students will learn that good analysis can lead to optimal decision-making which is supported by a logical and evidence-based rationale, and that decisions that have been taken by case study companies may themselves be open to question. Because students do not 'live with the decision', they can be more impetuous with their choices and habitually will be ready to spend significant amounts of an organization's finances since they are not responsible for (or even conscious of) the challenges in accessing or repaying such monies. However, the emphasis on self-directed learning will eventually bring about a realisation by the student that they need to consider all angles within a case study and by the end of the course they will be offering solutions that are more measured and considerate of all elements of a business.

Not only does the use of case studies benefit students by bridging the gap between theory and practice, but case studies are also of benefit to teachers as they enable greater interaction to take place between the teacher and the students. Classes are no longer an environment whereby a subject expert imparts knowledge to the gathered audience, but instead discussions and cross-communication occurs, leading to debate and more developed reasoning around various learning points. Indeed Golich, Boyer, Franko and Lamy (2000)[2] argued that case teaching promotes good practice in teaching in the following ways:

- Encourages contact between students and faculty – especially contact focused on the academic agenda.
- Develops reciprocity and cooperation among students – teaching them to work productively with others.
- Encourages active learning – thinking, doing and thinking about what they are doing.
- Gives prompt feedback on performance – helps students figure out what to do in response.
- Emphasises time on task – provides lots of useful, productive, guided practice.
- Communicates high expectations – and encourages students to have high self-expectations.
- Respects diverse talents and ways of learning – engenders respect for intellectual diversity.

According to Barnes, Christensen and Hanson (1994), the primary task with the case method is not to teach but rather to encourage learning. Therefore, the educator becomes a facilitator of learning as the discussion leader rather than merely a disseminator of knowledge as found in a traditionally styled lecture. Depending on the level of ability of the students and the nature of the course being taught, an educator also has the ability to vary the format of the class discussion to meet the needs of a specific case or simply to keep the format from being repetitive. For example, an educator may break the students into groups in the classroom and ask them to solve the problems identified in the case, or to develop their own scenarios, or maybe invite a student to take the role of facilitator so as to create an alternative approach to the learning opportunity. It is important to appreciate that the benefits of using case studies for teaching purposes are not confined to the student but also apply to the educator. The ability of teachers to effectively enable students to truly grasp the key learning points put before them is greatly enhanced by this pedagogy and consequently one attains a greater sense of achievement as an educator. Therefore, the increasing preference of educators to move closer to case studies and problem-based learning, and to identify methodologies that heighten self-directed learning, has created a strong demand from educators who want to be taught how to teach using case studies. Unfortunately, the provision of courses on teaching with case studies remains highly underdeveloped.

TEACHING WITH CASE STUDIES

It is generally forgotten that entrepreneurship is a relatively new subject within the field of education and therefore its advancement has been quite remarkable given its short history. As Solomon, Duffy and Tarabishy (2002) highlighted, the most common teaching methods used in entrepreneurship education in recent years have been the development of business plans, entrepreneurs as guest speakers and supervised reading programmes. Within the stream of various learning methodologies, teaching with case studies has occurred frequently but not with the level of regularity preferred in today's university programmes. However, educators in earlier times had difficulty in introducing such a methodology because the case discussion teacher has to master questioning, listening and response (Christensen, Garvin & Sweet, 1991). There is also a high level of flexibility required in the case teaching process, depending on a variety of factors such as the nature and length of a case study and the role of the teacher at different stages of the process (Erskine, Leenders & Mauffette-Leenders, 1998). Over the past decade there has been an increase in the number of teaching resources (websites, books, training courses, etc.) available to educators who wish to develop the skills required to teach with case studies, plus an expansion in the number of people writing case studies for use in the classroom. However, as previously highlighted, there remains a significant gap between the demand and supply of these resources and so many educators still do not feel well-equipped to teach with case studies.

How Students Should Learn

When teaching with case studies, it is important to understand that the process of learning contains multiple layers. The learning begins at the level of the individual when a student reads the case study and attempts to make sense of it for themselves. The case study is then discussed within a student's case study group (which is either self-selected or pre-assigned by the teacher) on a number of different occasions, as initially they will analyse the key issues involved in the case and later they will identify potential solutions. It would also be normal practice for the group to prepare a presentation for class and this would ideally require a meeting solely dedicated to this purpose.

The next stage of the process is when a group (or groups) are called to present in class and are challenged by the other students and the teacher with regard to their analysis and prescriptive solutions. The teacher will then

open up the case study to the full classroom for further discussion and analysis to ensure that all students have an opportunity to participate in the dialogue, plus to safeguard that all key learning points from the case study have been brought to the attention of the class. The final layer in the learning process is when the teacher offers their own reflections on the case study and how they might have addressed the main issues highlighted.

This layered approach to learning, with its emphasis on the student being very well-prepared coming into the classroom, changes the learning process from passive to proactive, which in turn requires a different teaching approach by the teacher. It is critical that the teacher provides practical advice to students at the start of a course regarding how to analyse and prepare case studies. McDade (1988) offered the following hints for students preparing case studies:

(a) Skim the case first.
(b) What are the broad issues?
(c) Are there data appendices to consider?
(d) Reread the case carefully. Make margin notes.
(e) What are the key problems in the case? Make a list.
(f) Prioritise these problems.
(g) Develop a list of recommendations.
(h) Evaluate your recommendations versus alternatives.
(i) Discuss your analysis with others in the class.

It is not enough for a student to have simply read the case study prior to class, which is why having them work in groups and preparing presentations in advance of class enables a richer learning experience. According to Golich et al. (2000), this process ensures that students must read, assimilate, question and speculate prior to class and this will enable them to move quickly to a sophisticated level of analysis when the teacher becomes involved.

Christensen et al. (1991) argued that students learn at three distinct levels and that these need to be captured through the class discussions. At the first level, students explore a problem by sorting out the relevant facts, developing some logical conclusions, and presenting them to others. At the second level, students can be assigned specific roles within a case study and required to argue from that person's perspective. At the third level, the students begin to take ownership of the case and will discuss what they would do if they were in a similar 'real world' situation. To enable the students to work their way through these levels, it is helpful to provide them with some theoretical models that will assist them to make sense of the information in the case study. Providing them with a choice of theoretical models also allows them to bridge the gap between theory and practice, plus it assists them in identifying which models are appropriate given different analytical and prescriptive ambitions.

How Teachers Should Facilitate

A key element of teaching with case studies is the preparation and structuring of the class by the teacher. Garvin (2004) advises that a teacher should have prepared a structured timetable for the discussion of a case study in class to ensure that each specified goal is achieved and that none are neglected due to a lack of time. Timing is an issue that is constantly raised by teachers and students alike as both parties wish to secure enough time in class to have their viewpoint aired (particularly if students are being graded on their participation in class). Garvin also highlighted that the use of a whiteboard/flipchart is essential for engaging students as it reinforces that their points have been heard and it helps them to visually confirm the main issues arising from the case. The teacher may also wish to use the whiteboard/flipchart to draw circles, arrows or underline specific points as a way of connecting the different fragments of the class discussion.

During the course of the discussion on a case study, it is important to allow the analysis to flourish before attempting to undertake any form of problem-solving. As students raise different areas of discussion they can be challenged by either shifting the points of view (from person X to person Y), shifting the levels of abstraction, shifting the timeframe or by shifting the situation to another context. Equally, a teacher can facilitate the discussion by asking for the advantages and disadvantages to a given response, or by asking follow-up questions to gain greater insight or detail to the point of view being offered. Once the analysis of the case has been exhausted within the context of the specified goals for that class, it will then be time to move on to a discussion regarding the prescriptive solutions being proposed by the students. During the earlier weeks of a module/course, a teacher will find that the solutions being offered are frequently not workable as they do not consider other aspects of the business (particularly finance). To ensure that this situation is not prolonged, it is essential in the earlier case studies to focus strongly on such solutions so that students will quickly understand that their proposed solutions must be workable within the constraints faced by the individual or organisation that is the subject of the case study.

One useful technique for drawing out different perspectives is to identify different solutions through discussion and then take a vote. Not only is this a fun thing to do in class but it also offers the opportunity for students to publicly commit to their positions and this can be used to create debate between different students in the classroom. According to Garvin (2004), the vote will also allow a teacher to assess where the class stands on a particular solution and how the discussion might need to be moved or shaped differently if a teacher is seeking to ensure that specific learning goals are to be achieved. Another way of continuing the debate is to create discussion boards on class websites so that the debate can continue post class and it will also offer them the opportunity to reflect on their initial positions (Pyatt, 2006). When wrapping up the discussion, it is important for a teacher to offer his/her own perspective on the case study, to give an update on the subject of the case study (if available) and to reinforce the main learning points that were to be achieved through that particular case study in that particular class. It is also helpful if the teacher gives feedback on the performance of the class in terms of the class discussion, the quality of the analysis and the viability of the proposed solutions as this will help students develop their techniques and strategies for future case studies.

Selecting a Case Study

Over the full period of the module/course, it is important for the teacher to use a mix of case studies. A teacher might consider a range of local, national or international case studies, small and large organisations, business-to-business and business-to-customer enterprises, commercial and not-for-profit enterprises, plus a span of different topics. Across the discussions on these cases, a teacher can return to a discussion point from a previous case study and invite comparisons to be made. There are a number of different websites (e.g. www.thecasecentre.org; https://hbr.org/store/case-studies; https://www.gsb.stanford.edu/faculty-research/case-studies; www.cases.insead.edu; www.eecsrc.eu; http://businesscasestudies.co.uk) which offer a large database of case studies from which a teacher can select. Some of these websites require payment for using a case study while others make them freely available as a resource so as to encourage the greater use of case studies in the classroom. To aid the learning process for a student, a teacher must be very clear regarding the specific learning goals that they wish to achieve with a particular case study in a given classroom (Herreid, 1998). The nature of the class, the module/course being taught, the degree programme that students are studying and the topic being addressed within that precise moment of the course are all significant criteria when determining the explicit goals for that individual

class. These criteria and associated learning goals will also feature prominently when deciding what case study to select since the case study must be a perfect fit for what the teacher is seeking to achieve for that occasion. Angelo and Boehrer (2002) have suggested that the best cases are those that allow for several assessments of the same situation, which lead to several equally plausible and compelling conclusions, each with different implications for action. A good-quality case such as this promises multiple discussion points and provides no single correct answer that every student group is agreed upon.

When using cases, it is important to encourage constructive discussion, appropriate use of earlier learning, thinking 'outside of the box', detailed consideration of the available options and clear strategies for future action. It is equally important to discourage regurgitation of the history of the case study, the use of theoretical models as an end in themselves, a lack of discrimination of the information in the case study, use of outside or updated material, and sloppy presentations. However, it should also be remembered by the teacher that a number of caveats exist with regards to the use of case studies as a teaching methodology. As previously mentioned, students do not have to 'live with the decision' and this obviously changes the perspective from which they will make decisions. Also, it was previously mentioned that there is no single correct answer and this can make grading of submissions or class participation a little more challenging than more formatted approaches. Other caveats relating to cases include the fact that case studies are now dating much more quickly (primarily due to the internet) since it is increasingly easier to get access to other material that might be relevant to the case (including teaching notes and previous presentations). This has meant that the useful lifespan of a case study has eroded significantly over the past decade. Therefore, educators are increasingly finding it difficult to identify suitable case studies, although one solution to this problem is to write one's own case studies.

WRITING CASE STUDIES FOR TEACHING PURPOSES

For a variety of reasons, there remains a dearth of high-quality case studies in entrepreneurship and small business (with the exception of the USA). Many academics believe that undertaking such work is not highly rewarding in terms of career advancement or that it is too time-consuming for relatively little recognition, while others feel that they are not skilled enough to write case studies or that organisations will be reluctant to provide the information required to write a case study. According to Molian and Leleux (1997) and Leenders, Mauffette-Leenders and Erskine (2001), writing 'good' case studies can be a difficult challenge but academics can develop the skill through practice. Ultimately, a writer should remember that a case study is a story that a reader can follow and possibly enjoy (just like reading a book). The case study is usually incomplete and decisions will have to be taken with imperfect information but in many ways, this reflects the reality of the business environment. A good case study will deal with a number of different and substantive issues which will create a variety of discussion and decision points. While it is helpful if the student can engage with the case study (not the same as 'liking' it), the issues being addressed should be current as that will enable the reader to better understand the context of the case study. A good case study should also be realistic in terms of what it is seeking to achieve and be very clear about its target audience.

Structuring Your Case Study

In writing a fresh case study, a writer will need to make a number of broad decisions such as: (1) what is the central business issue being addressed; (2) what is the choice of timing; and (3) who is the focal person in the case? The central issue could be something such as opportunity recognition and evaluation,

finance, marketing, management, operations, growth or a range of other possibilities. Within these considerations also lie other factors such as the size of the business, its stage of development, the industry in which it operates and other such matters. The choice of timing determines when the case takes place and how much time the focal person has available to them in which to make a decision (e.g. hours, days, weeks or months). Finally, the focal person might be an entrepreneur, CEO/Managing Director, Marketing/Finance/Operations Manager, or an external person such as a consultant who is working with the organisation. When given a case study, it usually will be the responsibility of the reader to assume the role of the focal person and for them to address the issues highlighted in the case within the timeframe available.

It is frequently suggested that a primary reason that people will not write a case study is because they do not feel skilled enough to undertake such a task. However, a case study can be given a formatted layout which enables the writer to take a structured approach to writing cases until such time as they become competent enough to try different approaches and structures to a case. A typical structure to a case study would be as follows:

- Introduction – this sets the scene and the context, it introduces the focal person, highlights the key issues to be addressed, and offers a timeframe for the scenario.
- Organisation/Person Background – after initially presenting the focal person and context, it will be necessary to give historical background to the organisation or person (or maybe both). This offers the reader an opportunity to build up a profile of the person and the organisation which should help the reader when they assume the role of the focal person later in the case.
- Background Environment – the writer will need to present information regarding the industry and the market in which the organisation is operating. As should happen throughout the case study, a writer may include some information which may have no benefit or secondary benefit in terms of its usefulness in making a decision as it is important for a student to develop the

skill of determining the value of information, and being able to differentiate between helpful and unhelpful information.

- Outline of Key Issues – the writer will introduce the various issues that might exist within the organisation. It is helpful if the writer creates a number of different substantive issues as this will create multiple discussion points, plus it will require the reader to prioritise which issues they deem to be of greatest or most immediate importance.

- Range of Potential Solutions – it is usual (but not necessary) that a case might suggest a range of potential actions that could be taken to solve the issues being faced. However, it is critically important that none of the potential solutions should present a clearly obvious answer since this creates no discussion point as everyone will be in agreement regarding the future action needed to be taken.

- Closing – it is a regular tactic in case studies that the closing paragraph will revert back to the opening scene at the beginning of the case study. This reinforces matters such as timing, the key issues and the focal person of the case. It also acts as a reminder of what actions need to be taken by the focal person in the case study.

It is very important to highlight that the suggested structure given above is just a basic format that can be used by those writing cases for the first time. Once a person becomes more skilled and confident in writing case studies, then they will develop their own structural style and format for case studies. However, the layout given has proven to be very robust and has been successfully adopted by experienced and inexperienced case writers alike. In contrast, a poorly structured case study lacks a consistent flow or coherency to the story, the material may be repetitive or too dense in terms of understanding, and it will likely struggle in terms of identifying the relationship between the position of the organisation in the value chain and the issue under consideration. To reduce the prospect of releasing into the public domain a poorly structured case study, it is highly advisable to ask a colleague to review the case and offer feedback on areas requiring improvement,

plus it is certainly a good idea to use the case study in a classroom setting as using the case will always draw out the strengths and weaknesses of a case study.

Developing Your Case Study

The most frequent question asked regarding case studies relates to its length. There is no simple answer to this question as one-page cases can be as effective as 30-page cases, although it is equally true to say that both lengths can be highly ineffective. The secret to deciding the appropriate length for a case is to begin by identifying the target audience and the key learning objectives. A first-year class of students who are inexperienced in using case studies might benefit from a short case study while a group of MBA students might require a case study that is longer and more challenging than an average-sized case study (an average-sized case would be approximately 5,000 words). It is critically important that the case provides enough information for the reader to address the issues identified and that the key learning objectives can be achieved.

It is highly beneficial to include tables, figures, financial data (where possible) and diagrams as these offer a great deal of information and the student will have to discern which elements of the information may or may not be of benefit in tackling the key issues. On some occasions, the information may need to be altered or disguised due to market sensitivities or because the organisation does not wish to make itself known to the reader (this happens quite rarely). Any changes regarding the information (particularly financial data) must make sense with other elements of the case study, as otherwise the content and learning objectives may lose their meaning. Some larger organisations may require the case to be signed off by more than one person as there may be some concerns about the disclosure of market information if a company is listed on the Stock Exchange. However, gathering information from a variety of sources and building an interesting story can be presented in a suitable length of case study without jeopardising any confidential intelligence which a person or organisation may wish to disclose.

Gaining access to individuals or organisations that are prepared to act as subjects for a case study is not as challenging as many people imagine. At a basic level, a case writer can use secondary data from sources such as newspapers, magazines, websites and promotional materials from which to build a case study. All such information may already be widely available and therefore may not require the approval of the subject for use in the public domain. However, if a writer wishes to generate new information or input from a person or organisation, then approaching past students, friends/relatives, people whom you have met at a conference or meeting, or even by cold calling, can all result in a positive outcome. Once personal contact has been made and the process explained, it is hugely important that the person or organisation who will be the subject of the case understands that the case study will be sent to them for consideration and review after each draft. You can certainly reassure the subject by highlighting that ultimately, they will make the final decision regarding the release of the case study into the public domain and so they are entitled to stop the process at any time. Having this reassurance is an excellent way in which to get buy-in from the subject and enable a case study writer to work with them in a constructive fashion.

Teaching Notes

When composing a case study, it is beneficial for the writer to also write a teaching note. Cases with teaching notes are far more likely to be purchased from case centres than those case studies that are not accompanied by a teaching note. The teaching note also helps the writer to clarify in their mind the key learning objectives for the case and how the case is meant to be taught. The teaching note should contain a brief summary of the case study, a listing of the learning objectives and

the target audiences, a suggested teaching approach and strategy, recommended techniques for analysis (preferably worked through) and any additional readings or references that may be helpful. It is a regular occurrence that a writer will undertake another revision of their case study once they have written the teaching note as they will inevitably have learned some things about the case that will require editing or modification. Of course, the teaching note should never be available publicly (only through a reserved system) because the case study will become unusable should students ever get access to the teaching note and ready-made answers.

Writing a case study is very beneficial to one's teaching as an educator can then mould a case study specifically for the needs of a particular class or programme. It regularly occurs that a person will spend a substantial amount of time looking at existing case studies that might fit the needs of a class without ever being truly satisfied with the outcome. However, it is wonderfully empowering to be able to tailor one's own case so that it will fit with a precise set of learning objectives at an exact moment in a programme for a particular cohort of students in a given country or context. Additionally, more and more academic journals are now beginning to include case studies which will offer case writers more channels through which they can have their work published and receive academic recognition. Good case writing is time-consuming, but then so is any other form of writing that is done properly. The only way in which a person can become more proficient at case writing is to get writing and through experience they will develop and hone their skills, which in turn will enable them to write cases better and faster than previously experienced.

OTHER CONSIDERATIONS

Recent research by Hartshorn and Hannon (2005) has found that significantly more higher education institutions are now making entrepreneurship education available to their students. But embedded within these offers are fundamental and diverse beliefs about the meaning of entrepreneurship and how it should be taught. While the use of case studies has been ever more recognised as a progressive approach to teaching entrepreneurship, there are significant organisational resource issues relating to this teaching methodology as it can be amongst the costliest pedagogical approaches utilised. For case study teaching to work effectively, class sizes need to be manageable and this might require classes being broken into smaller groupings which will require additional classroom and teacher resources. There is also more time required by the teacher in terms of grading the participation of students after each class, plus grading the presentations and submissions by the groups. Therefore, to ensure that case studies are employed as a positive learning experience, the educational institution must recognise their value and give the teaching of case studies appropriate resourcing (particularly relating to staff timetabling).

Another consideration within the realm of case studies is the use of new forms of case studies such as videos, live cases, business simulations and other modern approaches that might be adopted. The modern student is more accustomed to gathering their information from social media channels than from traditional newspapers, plus they tend to have a shorter attention span than students of previous decades. The use of modern technology can be an excellent way of engaging with students and getting them to 'buy into' the learning process. Such content delivery mechanisms can also enable greater fluidity in terms of the teaching and in the way in which knowledge is absorbed by the student. Video case studies could be particularly useful for part-time or distance learning programmes where more of the information and learning process is done online.

With reference to any review of case studies as a teaching methodology, it is important to also recognise some of the common pitfalls that might arise. Chief amongst these is the breakdown of communication or working relationship within a group, an issue that will happen on a regular basis for any teacher who uses case studies on their courses. If groups are self-selected then a teacher can highlight that the students decided themselves whom they wanted to work with and therefore they need to resolve their own issues. However, if the teacher selected the groups randomly, then a diligent, hard-working student might find oneself disadvantaged by being a member of a group where the other members are not contributing their fair share of output. This is always a more challenging issue for a teacher to resolve and will require careful negotiation and communication with the group members. Another pitfall for teachers of case studies is grading presentations (this was mentioned previously) and so clear guidance on how marks will be allocated is important for the students' understanding of what is required of them. An additional drawback is that many teachers do not recognise that using case studies gives you less time to introduce new materials and therefore a teacher should ensure that adequate time is kept across a module/course for the delivery of new lecture material which complements the lessons being drawn out through the case studies. Furthermore, it is usually more effective if case studies are used in the later years of a degree programme when the student has already acquired sufficient basic knowledge on their chosen subject area (case histories can be used in earlier years to illustrate specific learning points).

CONCLUSION

There is a significant learning curve to both writing and teaching case studies but the strongest advice one can be offered is simply to jump in and get started. It is helpful to find a mentor who can offer you advice as you develop your skills in each of these areas and such mentors can either be found through colleagues with prior experience or through networks where people of common interest or subject area gather to share their experiences (e.g. www.ecsb.org). It is inevitable that the early days of writing and teaching with case studies will be challenging and that mistakes will be made, but even those who are considered experts on such matters initially suffered through the same form of learning experience. What is important is to keep to the forefront of one's thoughts during such challenging times the firm belief that the learning experience and outcomes from this work will be positive. As a consequence of this approach, you will ensure that your students will receive an enhanced opportunity to maximize their learning potential. You will also become a more accomplished teacher by adding further skill sets to your established abilities and ultimately that can only enrich your long-term teaching and career opportunities.

It is important to the development of the field that experienced academics reconsider the value of case studies and how they might increase the manner in which they are used. Undoubtedly case studies remain under-utilised as a research methodology for business studies even though they frequently offer highly insightful contributions and add to the existing body of knowledge of a topic. Such a research methodology could also be used as the basis for the writing of a case study for teaching purposes, thereby increasing the breadth of publications emanating from a single piece of research. If more academics were to use case study as a research methodology then it may also raise the perceived value of case studies as a publication output, a factor that is increasingly important in today's academic environment. The fact that a number of academic journals now publish case studies as part of their issues (e.g. *Small Enterprise Research*) should encourage more people to utilise this methodology and participate in the writing of case studies. Indeed, it has occasionally happened that people have gathered so much information for the writing of their case study for teaching purposes that a qualitative research paper

targeted at an academic journal also became possible. Therefore, while using case study methodology for an academic paper can lead to the publication of a case study for teaching purposes, researching for a case study for teaching purposes can conversely lead to the publication of an academic paper. Furthermore, it would be highly beneficial to the entrepreneurship academic community if more senior/high-quality academics were to engage in such activity as it would raise the profile and value of case studies for everybody within the community.

Finally, as a separate activity, there is significant need for research on the challenges and benefits of using case studies as there is a dearth of literature on this topic. For example, it would be very interesting for more academics to undertake research on the reward system (or lack of it) for writing case studies and how universities might rebalance the inequities that currently exist against case writing. Another potential research topic is to compare case study types (e.g. written, video, business simulation, live) as a pedagogy and which format is the most effective under which circumstances. Indeed, there are so many research opportunities regarding the value of business case studies that academics should view this topic as a highly fertile ground for future research output. Actually, whichever way one wishes to look at this topic (writing, teaching, researching), then a multitude of opportunities awaits those who may wish to engage!

ACKNOWLEDGEMENT

I wish to acknowledge the work of Gerry Mortimer (Dublin Institute of Technology) who was a wonderful teacher and writer of marketing case studies. He was also a hugely supportive mentor and friend as I developed my skills in case writing and teaching. He has recently retired and his presence and encouragement are missed.

Notes

1 The author has taught using case studies for over two decades, has published four books of case studies and has presented approximately 20 workshops across the globe on 'How to Write Case Studies'. Much of the content is based on his personal experiences in addition to reviewing the literature on the topic.
2 It should be noted that this list was adapted from A. Chickering and Z. Gamson (1987), Seven Principles for Good Practice in Undergraduate Education, *AAHE Bulletin*, March, pp. 3–7.

REFERENCES

Angelo, T. and Boehrer, J. (2002). Case Learning: How Does It Work? Why Is It Effective? *Case Method Website: How to Teach with Cases*. University of California, Santa Barbara, CA. http://www.soc.ucsb.edu/projects/casemethod/teaching.html

Barnes, L.B., Christensen, C.R. and Hanson, A.J. (1994). *Teaching and the Case Method: Text, Cases and Readings*. Harvard Business Review Press, Boston, MA.

Boehrer, J. and Linsky, M. (1990). Teaching with Cases: Learning to Question. In M.D. Svinicki (ed.), *The Changing Face of College Teaching: New Directions for Teaching and Learning*. Jossey-Bass, San Francisco, CA.

Bonwell, C.C. and Eison, J.A. (1991). Active Learning: Creating Excitement in the Classroom. *ASHE-ERIC Higher Education Report No. 1*, George Washington University, School of Education and Human Development, Washington, DC.

Boud, D., Lawson, R. and Thompson, D.G. (2014). Does Student Engagement in Self-Assessment Calibrate Their Judgement over Time? *Assessment and Evaluation in Higher Education*, Vol. 38, No. 8, pp. 941–956.

Christensen, C.R., Garvin, D.A. and Sweet, A. (eds) (1991). *Education for Judgement: The Artistry of Discussion Leadership*. Harvard Business School Press, Boston, MA.

Davis, C. and Wilcock, E. (2015) *Teaching Materials Using Case Studies*. UK Centre for Materials Education, Higher Education Academy. http://www.materials.ac.uk/guides/casestudies.asp

Doyle, W. (1990). Case Methods in the Education of Teachers. *Teacher Education Quarterly*, Vol. 17, No. 1, pp. 7–15.

Erskine, J., Leenders, M.R. and Mauffette-Leenders, L.A. (1998). *Teaching with Cases*. Richard Ivey School of Business, University of Western Ontario, London, Ontario.

Garvin, D. (2004). *Participant-Centered Learning and the Case Method: A Case Study Teacher in Action*. Harvard Business School. http://Garvin, 2004/multimedia/pcl/pcl_1/start.html

Golich, V.L., Boyer, M., Franko, P. and Lamy, S. (2000). *The ABCs of Case Teaching*. Pew Case Studies in International Affairs, Georgetown University, Washington, DC.

Grant, R. (1997). A Claim for the Case Method in the Teaching of Geography. *Journal of Geography in Higher Education*, Vol. 21, No. 2, pp. 171–185.

Hartshorn, C. and Hannon, P.D. (2005). Paradoxes in Entrepreneurship Education: Chalk and Talk or Chalk and Cheese? A Case Approach. *Education and Training*, Vol. 47, No. 8/9, pp. 616–627.

Herreid, C.F. (1998). Return to Mars: How Not to Teach a Case Study. *Journal of College Science Teaching*, Vol 27, No. 6, pp. 379–382.

Leenders, M.R., Mauffette-Leenders, L.A. and Erskine, J.A. (2001). *Writing Cases*. 4th edition. Ivey Publishing, Ivey Business School, University of Western Ontario, London, Ontario.

Levy, F. (2015). *Harvard Business School Has the Market Cornered on Case Studies*. Bloomberg Businessweek. http://www.bloomberg.com/news/articles/2015-04-09/harvard-s-case-study-monopoly

Lundeberg, M.A. and Fawver, J. (1994). Thinking like a Teacher: Encouraging Cognitive Growth through Case Analysis. *Journal of Teacher Education*, Vol. 45, No. 4, pp. 289–297.

Mauffette-Leenders, L.A., Erskine, J.A. and Leenders, M.R. (2001). *Learning with Cases*. Richard Ivey School of Business, University of Western Ontario, London, Ontario.

McDade, S. (1988). *An Introduction to the Case Study Methods: Preparation, Analysis and Participation*. Harvard College, Cambridge, MA.

Merseth, K.K. (1999). Foreword: A Rationale for Case-Based Pedagogy. In M.A. Lundeberg,

B.B. Levin and H.L. Harrington (eds), *Teacher Education: Who Learns What from Cases and How*. Lawrence Erlbaum Associates, Mahwah, NJ.

Molian, D. and Leleux, B. (1997). *European Casebook on Entrepreneurship and New Ventures*. Prentice Hall, London.

Mustoe, L.R. and Croft, A.C. (1999). Motivating Engineering Students by Using Modern Case Studies. *European Journal of Engineering Education*, Vol. 15, No. 6, pp. 469–476.

Naumes, W. and Naumes, M.J. (2006). *The Art and Craft of Case Writing*. M.E. Sharpe Inc, Armonk, NY.

Pyatt, E.J. (2006). *Using Cases in Teaching. Teaching and Learning with Technology*. Penn State University. http://tlt.its.psu.edu/suggestions/cases/

Sivan, A., Wong Leung, R., Woon, C. and Kember, D. (2000). An Implementation of Active Learning and Its Effect on the Quality of Student Learning Innovations. *Education and Training International*, Vol. 37, No. 4, pp. 381–389.

Solomon, G.T., Duffy, S. and Tarabishy, A. (2002). The State of Entrepreneurship Education in the United States: A Nationwide Survey and Analysis. *International Journal of Entrepreneurship Education*, Vol. 1, No. 1, pp. 65–86.

Wasserman, S. (1994). *Introduction to Case Method Teaching: A Guide to the Galaxy*. Teachers College Press, New York.

27

Enterprise Education Pedagogy and Redesigning Learning Outcomes: Case of a Public Reform School

Ulla Hytti and Sirpa Koskinen

INTRODUCTION

Enterprise education is a research area in the fields of entrepreneurship and education. This duality holds significant potential, but also conflicts, prejudices and even misunderstandings, if entrepreneurship education is understood only in the business context (Kyrö, 2015). Existing research suggests that teachers mostly understand and implement entrepreneurship education within a business-related framework by offering opportunities to practise entrepreneurship; for example, as a small-scale kiosk business in schools (Hietanen & Kesälahti, 2016; Ruskovaara & Pihkala, 2013). This business focus is questioned especially by teachers in compulsory education, and can thus act as a barrier to the promotion of entrepreneurship education in schools (Rönkkö & Lepistö, 2015) if and when teachers oppose the business realm entering the classroom.

In this chapter, we suggest a way forward by maintaining a sharper focus on enterprise education as *pedagogy*, as opposed to business and enterprise education as *content*. The focus on pedagogy as opposed to content is emphasised when acknowledging that the goal for enterprise education is not supporting venture creation but active citizenship (Jones & Iredale, 2010). It is also pertinent to accept that not all pupils are equally motivated to attend school and learn. Sometimes, enterprise education is suggested as a potential remedy against absenteeism, juvenile delinquency or school dropout (e.g. Smith, 2009; Yamane, 2002). For any enterprise educator this may seem intuitively logical, but few studies have discussed this in practice. One of the reasons for this is because most enterprise education studies have been conducted in higher education with self-selected and highly motivated students, whereas only a few studies, at least those published internationally, have addressed the compulsory primary or secondary school context (Kyrö, 2015).

In this chapter, we address this gap by discussing how enterprise education pedagogy can be implemented in compulsory education and how it can positively affect school motivation and learning. Overall, the entrepreneurship education research has evinced enthusiasm for experimenting with new pedagogic or didactic models, but insufficient effort has gone into describing their rationale or offering significant evidence of whether the models are capable of achieving their aims (Pittaway & Cope, 2007). Thus, we contribute to the discussion about developing new learning outcomes that can be aspired to and measured in enterprise education (Hytti, Stenholm, Heinonen & Seikkula-Leino, 2010; Scott, Penaluna & Thompson, 2016).

ENTREPRENEURSHIP EDUCATION PEDAGOGY

Enterprise education has been introduced in the school curricula in many countries (Jones & Iredale, 2010), including Finland. The new school curricula from 2014 emphasise work–life skills and entrepreneurship together as one of the seven broad learning outcomes that are seen as necessary for facing the ever-changing environment and that every pupil in basic education should therefore learn (Board of Education, 2015).

In this chapter, we develop the case for entrepreneurship education pedagogy and its ability to influence learning positively by focusing on and developing pupils' self-regulation skills. We do so by drawing from an entrepreneurship education pedagogy case conducted within a reform school. Reform schools are literally the last resort for pupils often after years of truancy and different unsuccessful interventions from the school and various social authorities. These pupils, in general, do not find school or a degree meaningful. Therefore, the departure for developing enterprise education pedagogy began when the second author of this chapter began teaching at this school in 2007 and soon realised that her learned, customary way of teaching did not work in this context. Thus, she faced a situation where it was necessary to change the pedagogy and approach to teaching, and this offered her an opportunity to research and reflect upon her own work (following an ethnographic action research project; see Carr & Kemmis, 1986) (Koskinen, 2015). These experiences are discussed in this chapter from the perspective of understanding what enterprise education pedagogy means (Jones & Iredale, 2010; Jones & Iredale, 2014; Kyrö, 2008; Kyrö, 2015) and what the potential learning outcomes can be in compulsory education, especially in demanding educational contexts.

Entrepreneurship education is described as having three alternative aims: educating and developing awareness *about* entrepreneurship; educating *for* entrepreneurship and working as an entrepreneur; and educating *through* entrepreneurship in terms of developing learning situations that call for entrepreneurial behaviour (Hytti & O'Gorman, 2004; Kirby, 2004). Whilst acknowledging the diversity of aims that entrepreneurship education may have, and therefore also the methods that it may deploy, its connections to business have remained strong (Blenker, Frederiksen, Korsgaard, Müller, Neergaard & Thrane, 2012; Jones & Iredale, 2010), for example, in terms of pupils engaging in mini-businesses or related projects even in primary school. In this chapter, our focus is on highlighting an enterprise education pedagogy that refuses to regard business as the content, and even as the context, for teaching and learning. Thus, we acknowledge the role of enterprise education in contributing to active citizenship (Fayolle & Toutain, 2013; Jones & Iredale, 2014). This is also linked to the suggestion of Sarasvathy and Venkataraman (2011, p. 130) that we understand entrepreneurship as 'a method of human action, comparable to social forces such as democracy and the scientific method, namely, a powerful way of tackling large and abiding problems at the heart of advancing our species'. In our case, the interest is in understanding how entrepreneurship – or enterprise education pedagogy – can be helpful in combatting existing problems in schools: dropout, truancy, demotivation and the failure to learn and engage in further education and in society.

Although the discussion on enterprise education began in the 1980s, its ideals of supporting learners in shouldering responsibility and self-initiative belong to a much longer tradition of citizenship education with a focus on supporting the (financial) autonomy and life skills of citizens and their civic responsibilities (Jones & Iredale, 2010). Enterprise education pedagogy emphasises difference from customary didactic learning and therefore from the familiar ways of teaching and learning. Enterprise education pedagogy suggests developing a bridge between entrepreneurship and education science (Kyrö, 2015) and focuses on active learning and learning by doing, and on renegotiating the terms and conditions of the teaching and learning experience (Jones & Iredale, 2010; Seikkula-Leino, 2007). Thus, enterprise education can be seen as a kind of reform pedagogy (Kyrö, 2015) that can help transform our schools. It is not just a marginal add-on or elitist approach targeted for the few interested in entrepreneurship as a career.

Enterprise education pedagogy always includes the human being, and human behaviour is the essential foundation for it. This view also departs from solely cognitive aspects of learning to the affective dimensions (emotions, values, attitudes), as well as to the conative aspects of motivation and volition. In this view, life and knowledge are constructed by action, and the learner is an active agent. Thus, one has a holistic relationship to oneself, one's own activities and the environment. Learners are actors in the learning process, and their interests guide the process. In enterprise education pedagogy, creative action is a guiding principle. This brings the learners' experiences to the centre of learning (Kyrö, 2008; Kyrö, 2015). Autonomy is an important element in enterprise education (van Gelderen, 2010). Thus, defining one's own learning goals and the

means to achieve these goals is essential when following enterprise education pedagogy. It further emphasises encouraging the pupils to take responsibility for their own learning, take risks and be innovative. The freedom to decide and choose entails responsibility for learning, and therefore entails risk and insecurity (Kyrö, 2015).

Adopting enterprise education pedagogy, thus, challenges the role of the teacher in the learning process (Koskinen, 2015; Kyrö, 2015) and calls upon the teacher to exhibit entrepreneurial behaviour (Gibb, 2011; Hietanen, 2012; Jones & Iredale, 2010; Rae & Carswell, 2001; Remes, 2007). The principles – the idea of the human being, action orientation, autonomy and interplay between risk and responsibility – challenge teachers to apply new pedagogies in their teaching (Gibb, 2005; Rae, 2011; Rae & Carswell, 2001; Ristimäki, 2004; Swierczek & Ha, 2003), adapted for their school environment. Blenker et al. (2012) suggest that enterprise education pedagogy calls for juxtaposing universalistic and idiosyncratic approaches to entrepreneurship education (Figure 27.1).

The idiosyncratic approach calls for understanding entrepreneurship as an everyday practice that is related to the particular cultural context and circumstances of each pupil. The teacher alone cannot decide what is relevant; this decision is made jointly with the pupil, where the teacher's role is to facilitate the process (Blenker et al., 2012). In particular, the teacher has the task of creating a safe and comfortable learning environment to support the pupil's entrepreneurial behaviour – taking risks and assuming responsibility for their learning – and acting in unconventional ways. In a safe environment, the pupil has the courage to act without the fear of being embarrassed. Restlessness, disturbing others and not learning are often consequences of feelings of insecurity (Lehtonen & Lehkonen, 2008). The teacher is responsible for addressing issues relating to the process rather than the content, and for planning and facilitating a good learning process and developing a

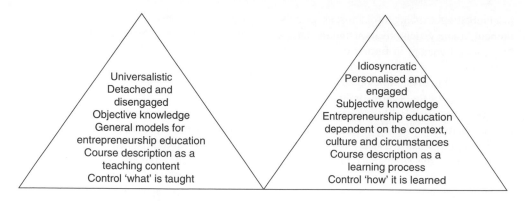

Figure 27.1   Juxtaposing universalistic and idiosyncratic approaches to entrepreneurship education (Blenker et al., 2012)

personalised learning experience with emancipatory effects for the learner (Blenker et al., 2012).

Trust and safety, which form the basis of entrepreneurship education pedagogy, are important for supporting active learning and for the pupil to embrace the new situations and activities together with familiar people in the learning environment. These activities foster the pupils' confidence that they can influence things which will support their future orientation and strengthen their beliefs in their own abilities. In compulsory education – with the aim of supporting active citizenship – the pupils need to be encouraged to envision alternative options for the future and alternative ways of behaving, should obstacles appear. Their dreams and persistence create the foundation for enterprising behaviour (Lehtonen & Lehkonen, 2008). Thus, the overall aim of the enterprise education pedagogy is fostering such enterprising behaviour and helping the person be an enterprising individual – at school, in the community, at home and in the workplace (Jones & Iredale, 2010). However, as Blenker et al. (2012, p. 426) articulate, the 'real challenge is to translate this general idea [of entrepreneurship education pedagogy] into the particular demands of the classroom and translate the ideals into a specific pedagogical practice'.

REDESIGNING LEARNING OUTCOMES: SELF-REGULATION SKILLS

The entrepreneurship education research has evinced enthusiasm for describing new entrepreneurship education models, but limited attention has been paid to the outcomes (Pittaway & Cope, 2007; Jones & Iredale, 2010). Most impact studies have focused on either changes in entrepreneurial attitudes or intentions and/or actual venturing behaviour, or related skills (Duval-Couetil, 2013; Hytti et al., 2010). We argue that these outcomes have little relevance if entrepreneurship is understood as a process and when implementing enterprise education pedagogy in compulsory education. Several authors have suggested that the goals and aims of enterprise education programmes should be aligned with the expected learning outcomes and that this match should form the basis for the course- and programme-level assessments and in evaluating the broader social outcomes (Duval-Couetil, 2013; Hytti & O'Gorman, 2014; Scott et al., 2016).

Existing reviews (e.g. Duval-Couetil, 2013; Scott et al., 2016) offer limited guidance on what kind of learning outcomes we can and should expect from applying enterprise education pedagogy in compulsory education. In this chapter, we aim to fill this gap by suggesting that enterprise education pedagogy can be particularly beneficial in supporting the self-regulation skills of the pupils (Zimmerman, 1998; Zimmerman, 2000) because they are connected to their motivation, self-efficacy and future orientation. These skills are particularly important in the case of special education, such as in reform schools, where neglecting school is often the primary reason why the pupils are placed in this environment, and hence they are not motivated by attending school or learning. In this context, most pupils have a long history of failing in school and have developed a view of themselves as poor learners (Koskinen, 2015).

We have established that enterprise education pedagogy emphasises the idea of a holistic human being, action orientation, autonomy and interplay between risk and responsibility (Kyrö, 2015). Thus, entrepreneurship education pedagogy pays particular attention to a personalised and engaged approach that is connected to the context and circumstances surrounding the learner. The teacher facilitates the process, focuses on creating a safe and comfortable learning environment and is in charge of 'how' to learn (Blenker et al., 2012; Lehtonen & Lehkonen, 2008).

Self-regulation refers to self-generated thoughts, feelings and behaviours that are oriented towards attaining goals (Zimmerman, 2000). The development of self-regulation skills can be presented as a three-phase cyclical model (Cleary, Callan & Zimmerman, 2012; Zimmerman & Campillo, 2003), including forethought, performance and self-reflection. Next, we will discuss how enterprise education pedagogy supports learners and their development of self-regulation skills as the learning outcome.

The Forethought Phase

This focuses on task analysis and self-motivation beliefs. The *task analysis* is about goal-setting – dividing the task into smaller, more specific tasks that are integrated and appropriately challenging for the learner – and about strategic planning – choosing the best strategy to achieve the goal(s) (Carver & Scheier, 2000; Locke & Latham, 1990; Locke & Latham, 2002; Schunk, 2001). In the reform school context, most pupils are reactive learners who lack self-regulation skills. They set very imprecise goals or none at all, and even refute the idea of setting goals.

Enterprise education pedagogy engages the pupil in goal-setting; for example, the pupil may have the freedom to choose what subjects to study and in which order, whether to study alone or with someone else, where to study and if they will study one subject or several subjects at the same time. The plan may also be altered during the day. The teacher and pupil discuss the study plan for the day, and then the teacher provides instant feedback on the accomplished tasks. The plan includes all the accomplishments that are considered necessary for passing the subject satisfactorily. These may include computer-aided assignments, watching videos and other recordings, tasks that involve retrieving information from the Internet and other sources as well as completing assignments in the textbooks. This contributes to the creation of a safe learning environment. Long-term plans are also important, as the benefits of self-regulation accumulate over time. These practices differ considerably from traditional pedagogy in primary schools, where the pupils normally follow the same curriculum designed by the teacher following the national guidelines, and where the teacher decides if the studying is done alone or in groups. The teacher is also normally in charge of the place of study.

Self-motivation beliefs influence the learner's commitment; self-efficacy beliefs motivate a commitment to self-regulation (Ruohotie, 2008); outcome expectations become positive if the learner is rewarded; the task value and goal orientation are connected to the goal-setting; and all motivational beliefs can influence the learner's commitment to reaching the goals, but the goals also influence the learning methods (Schunck, 1984; Zimmerman, 2008). Thus, in order for the learners to engage in action following the enterprise education pedagogy, it is important that they find the task in question motivating and valuable and believe in their own ability and skills to accomplish the task.

If the pupil's motivation to study is low and his/her self-efficacy beliefs are weak due to previous poor experiences of school and learning, it will be insufficient to only offer autonomy. The teacher's role is pivotal in guiding the pupil. Autonomy and freedom cannot be taken literally as suggesting that the pupils can always decide what they will do; on the contrary, the use of individualised and detailed learning plans, for example, may be a necessary condition. The plans can support self-regulation in time management and using the physical learning environment and methods as flexibly as possible.

Without guidance, the pupils would resort only to doing, without using any strategic planning. Feelings guide their actions, and previous experiences and their acquired reputation as poor learners hinder them from setting sufficiently high goals. Setting inspiring goals for themselves contributes to their self-satisfaction and fosters their self-efficacy beliefs. Although the pupil is in a key role and participates in setting the goals, which contributes positively to his/her experience of being able to influence things, the teacher has a crucial role in facilitating and guiding this process, for example, in making sure that the outcome expectations are realistic (Bandura, 1986; Zimmerman, 2008).

The performance phase

This is divided into two main categories: self-control and self-observation. Task strategies as part of *self-control* enable the learner to avoid entities that are too broad or too complex and optimise their performance through appropriate task strategies. By removing external disturbances it is possible to increase concentration. Self-instruction facilitates thinking and activity; for example, written strategies, thinking aloud and self-appraisal are all part of self-instruction (Boekaerts & Niemivirta, 2000; Schunk, 2001). *Self-observation* is first about metacognitive self-monitoring, which refers to the awareness and knowledge of one's own thinking. Without specific goals, metacognition becomes impossible. Second, self-observation is about self-recording one's learning; for instance, in learning diaries or portfolios that foster self-regulation and learning (Zimmerman & Kitsantas, 1997). Thus, while engaging in action, the learners should be able to monitor themselves in terms of their concentration, for example, and then they can identify learning environments that support concentration. To sustain performance, recording learning to make the accomplishment visible is important.

In this performance phase, self-control and self-observation are generally difficult for the pupils in reform school. This is particularly so for the pupils with neurological disorders and learning problems, as these disorders contribute negatively to self-regulation. Creating a peaceful work environment is essential to both comfort and safety. Reducing the uncertainty related to studying is part of the pupils' feeling of security. The detailed working plan for each day described earlier, developed jointly with the pupil, is one of the means. Having this plan and allowing studying in a quiet space, such as in one's own room, contributes positively to the pupil's learning. The individualised approach is also necessary in extracurricular activities, as the health conditions of some pupils may inhibit their participation in excursions; instead, the trips could be done through searching information on the Internet and familiarising oneself with the places. With the individualised approach, it is necessary to acknowledge, however, that the use of computers and the Internet could strengthen gaming addictions, and in such high-risk situations, these kinds of assignments need to be avoided.

The plan also includes follow-up on progress. The accomplished tasks form part of the evaluation together with other written exams, essays or project work. Furthermore, the plan includes excursions and visits to sites that relate to the subject or overall teaching. The detailed recording of accomplishments has proved to be a key element of the plan. If only written assignments are recorded, the pupils are not motivated by the visits and excursions, for example, even if they are seen as beneficial for learning and personal development from the outside. The individualised approach means that the plans are also amended to fit the pupil's personal preferences or to reflect the actual skills of the pupil, for example. Flexibility is important in that the plans are further elaborated to fit the personal circumstances. For example, if the pupil is about to go on a trip or an excursion, this will be included in the plan. It is also necessary to incorporate the pupil's history, and particularly the reasons for previously poor school attendance, into the plan.

In traditional compulsory education, the pupils study as a yearly cohort, and failing to reach the learning goals for the eighth grade (age 14–15), for example, means that the pupil must fall back and redo the whole eighth grade, and any achievements in the failed class are lost. Adopting enterprise education pedagogy also means that teaching is carried out individually and not tied to the particular year class. This flexibility is important due to the pupils' low study motivation. Class failure, including the lapse of all study accomplishments from that year, creates enormous barriers for pupils to even dreaming about obtaining a leaving certificate. Compulsory education and placement in reform school end when the pupil turns 18 years old. The individualised teaching allows pupils who are nearing their eighteenth birthday to complete their remaining studies on a faster schedule than normal in the compulsory education schools.

The role of the teacher is important in sustaining the performance; for example, by guiding the pupil in finding a quiet work environment and in recording the pupil's accomplishments. The teacher also facilitates group work; for example in pairing together pupils with similar learning styles and constructing assignments that are suitable for the group, so the interest is kept alive and working peace is sustained.

The Self-Reflection Phase

This can be divided into self-judgement (evaluation) and self-reaction. A self-regulated learner is capable of *self-evaluating* his/her learning outcomes against the set goals (Zimmerman & Kitsantas, 2005). Causal attributions are interpretations of one's learning outcomes, and failures are seen to be related either to external consequences, insufficient skills or inefficient learning strategies (Zimmerman & Kitsantas, 1997). *Self-reaction* includes both self-satisfaction and adaptiveness. Satisfaction or dissatisfaction relates to feelings about one's own activity: either joy from achievement or depression due to failure. If the learner feels that he/she has failed and is dissatisfied with him/herself, he/she will start avoiding the tasks that are connected to failure (Zimmerman & Bandura, 1994). Adaptiveness becomes a problem for the defensive learner if it leads to avoiding failure that appears in the form of learned helplessness, delaying and avoiding tasks, cognitive withdrawal or even apathy (Boekaerts & Niemivirta, 2000; Garcia & Pintrich, 1994). Hence, the ability to realistically reflect on one's learning and the reasons behind both the successes and failures in learning is important.

In the reflection phase, many pupils in the reform school context seek external reasons for their problems or are of the opinion that their capabilities are insufficient. If he/she has poor self-regulation skills, the pupil may avoid self-evaluation in order to avoid 'bad news'. Due to a lack of successful experiences in the past, a pupil is not always able to derive joy from his/her successful learning experiences. Hence, the evaluations are often unrealistic (too positive/negative). The role of the teacher is to guide the evaluation on a realistic path and provide helpful feedback and realistic interpretations. It is also about matching the task difficulty with each pupil so that he/she has sufficiently challenging tasks that he/she will not try to avoid because of the fear of failure. The ability to influence tasks and complete them successfully generates satisfaction with learning.

DISCUSSION

This chapter contributes to entrepreneurship education by emphasising entrepreneurship education pedagogy as a way forward from viewing entrepreneurship education as content (Jones & Iredale, 2010; Jones & Iredale, 2014; Kyrö, 2008; Kyrö, 2015). Thus, contrary to most entrepreneurship education approaches, we suggest that the business focus, such as organising pupils to run mini-businesses, is not the only approach in entrepreneurship education. In this chapter, we have also discussed what the potential learning outcomes can be in compulsory education, especially in demanding educational contexts, such as in reform schools. Entrepreneurship education has been suggested as a remedy for many problems which schools face, such as absenteeism or school dropout (e.g. Smith, 2009; Yamane, 2002). In this chapter, we have provided one account of one school following the principles of enterprise education pedagogy (Blenker et al., 2012; Jones & Iredale, 2010; Kyrö, 2008; Lehtonen & Lehkonen, 2008).

The chapter has demonstrated how entrepreneurship education pedagogy that applies a personalised and engaged approach, contextualised in the particular circumstances of the learner, assumes responsibility for the pupils and views them and their lives holistically in the learning environment, contributing to their learning in the reform school context. The chapter was aimed at meeting the challenge of translating the general idea of entrepreneurship education pedagogy in the classroom (Blenker et al., 2012), and has given concrete examples that were developed in the class on the basis of such pedagogy.

By relying on Zimmerman's (1998) theory of self-regulation, the chapter contributes to making sense of why entrepreneurship education pedagogy is efficient in supporting learning. We have argued that enterprise education pedagogy supports the development of self-regulation skills, and that through their improvement, the learning is also enhanced. The entrepreneurship education pedagogy interventions that were developed in the action research project (Koskinen, 2015) – personal learning plans, teaching that was not tied to a particular year class, making use of extracurricular activities and flexible weekly and daily organisation of study subjects – contributed positively to the self-regulation skills of the pupils and thus enabled them to learn and finish their schooling with a leaving certificate, allowing them to continue on their educational path. In this sense, this educational pedagogy seems to support social inclusion and prevent exclusion, which is one of the main challenges facing many young people seeking to understand their place in the world and in their society. Interestingly, when adapted to the pupils' personalised needs in particular, the pedagogy showed promise also in the case of pupils with diagnosed neurological and learning disorders. Thus, a personalised and contextualised approach that was connected to the particular circumstances of the learner supported the development of self-regulation skills and the learning (Blenker et al., 2012).

While most researchers of enterprise education have adopted an unreflexively positive view of enterprise education, some critical voices in the field are questioning the approach and its benefits (Komulainen, Korhonen & Räty, 2009). We wish to take their suggestion seriously and reflect on whether enterprise education pedagogy is the cure for all illnesses and solution to all problems in enterprise education. We warn against such a view. Even in reform schools, the pupils are not homogeneous; they can be divided into different groups that benefit from the entrepreneurship education pedagogy to different degrees (Koskinen, 2015). First, it is possible to distinguish a group of independent learners who do not have any diagnosed learning disorders, and they may have generally better self-regulation skills than others. They are motivated by the leaving certificate and not only by getting out of the reform school, and they can also complete their studies relatively fast, even if they have previously faced problems in finishing school work. Second, we can distinguish a group of pupils in need of strong guidance from the teacher; for example, they benefit especially from having a very detailed learning calendar before being left to work independently. In this group, the pupils generally have diagnosed learning or neurological disorders, such as ADHD or autism spectrum disorder, that impede their concentration. This group benefits from carefully recording their learning accomplishments, as its members are generally convinced that they will not be able to finish the tasks. Finally, the third group consists of pupils who have multiple problems, including substance abuse or mental health problems, and thus need other kinds of care and support before coming back to school. They do not benefit from entrepreneurship education pedagogy in their current life phase. In the first two groups, we believe benefits can be shown, although setbacks are not uncommon. Thus, adopting enterprise education pedagogy does not automatically solve all the problems in the school, if pupils have low motivation and poor school history. The pedagogy is not a quick fix or a one-size-fits-all solution, since some of the pupils facing mental health problems or suffering from addiction need to work with those problems before they can return to school.

CONCLUSION: THE WAY FORWARD: ENTERPRISE EDUCATION PEDAGOGY AS A REFORM PEDAGOGY

In this example, we have used one case from a reform school that can be seen as an extreme context. However, we suggest that enterprise education pedagogy can be seen as a reform pedagogy (Kyrö, 2015) that is applicable to all schools. Rather than being experimentation by some of the more adventurous entrepreneurship education enthusiasts and something that is radically different from a traditional school with a teacher-centred approach and fixed and mutual curricula for the pupils, we argue that enterprise education pedagogy has the potential to become the 'new normal'. Following the learner-centred approach that views the individual in his/her context with his/her history and current experiences and interests, engaging the individual in designing his/her own learning path and propelling him/her into action and allowing freedom and autonomy in the process, in our view, benefits all pupils (Kyrö, 2015), not just those with particular challenges in their study and learning paths. For example, the flexibility included in enterprise education pedagogy may help prevent minor school problems from escalating into bigger problems. When the teaching progresses at the same pace for the whole year cohort, pupils who skip classes for one month may find it impossible to catch up or be discouraged from trying to catch up even if they decide to return to school. This perceived impossibility may decrease their motivation to study and they may decide to skip even more classes. After a longer period of absence, the threshold for returning to school may be considerably higher. Thus, if the pupils could return to class and be reassured that they could pick up where they left off, this might be helpful throughout the school system. In addition, the individualised pace for learning will probably work well for high-achievers wishing to progress faster than the cohort or concentrate more closely on one particular subject. In addition, pupils who are active in sports or in other activities might benefit from going away to training camps, as this will place more focus on learning from extra-curricular activities.

We also argue that supporting the development of self-regulation skills is an appropriate new metric – learning outcome – for enterprise education pedagogy and related assessments. Thus, enterprise education pedagogy should enable pupils to get involved in setting motivating, challenging, yet appropriate, goals for learning and in choosing the best strategies for achieving those goals. It should strengthen their belief in their own abilities and skills to accomplish the tasks, and provide the tools they require; for example, by identifying practices and environments that support concentration and learning. Finally, enterprise education pedagogy should help pupils to realistically reflect on their learning and the reasons for their successes and failures (Zimmerman, 2000; Zimmerman & Campillo, 2003).

Making the pupils more responsible for their learning does not make the teacher's role futile. On the contrary, as our case demonstrates, the teacher needs to be very active in facilitating the process and in making sure that the pupil gets, and stays, on the right track. This case also illustrates that it is not possible to change the pedagogy and assume that the pupils will automatically follow it. They soon develop ideas about what the school is about and what they are like as learners. If they dislike and are not motivated by the school, do not trust their own ability to learn and have low self-regulation skills, the teacher must be persistent. The teacher is in a pivotal role, first, in explaining the new pedagogy and in guiding the pupils to set realistic goals for their learning both in terms of allocating the tasks and establishing the expectations and in supporting their belief that they can learn. The teacher also has a very important role in sustaining the pupils' performance, helping them find environments that allow them to learn and keeping records of their learning, especially if the intrinsic motivation to learn is weak. Finally, the teacher is needed to encourage and guide the pupils in carrying out realistic self-evaluations, and to support the pupils in identifying successful experiences and expressing joy from them. Thus, in line with the idiosyncratic approach to entrepreneurship education and entrepreneurship

education pedagogy, the role of the teacher is to focus on *how* the learning takes place (Blenker et al., 2012). This calls for the teacher to exhibit entrepreneurial behaviour to depart from the customary ways, to start investigating and experimenting with ways that might work better than the current ways. Furthermore, entrepreneurial persistence is required from the teacher, as the pupils' ability to design their day and possibly choose to do 'nothing' means that there is no constant progress, and setbacks can occur. Therefore, the teacher must persist with the pedagogy and continuously develop new approaches in order to overcome any challenges that arise.

REFERENCES

Bandura, A. (1986). *Social Foundations of Thought and Action: A Social Cognitive Theory*. Englewood Cliffs, NJ: Prentice-Hall.

Blenker, P., Frederiksen, S.H., Korsgaard, S., Müller, S., Neergaard, H. & Thrane, C. (2012). Entrepreneurship as everyday practice: Towards a personalized pedagogy of enterprise education. *Industry and Higher Education*, 26(6), 417–430.

Board of Education (2015). *Perusopetuksen opetussuunnitelman perusteet 2014*. [Guidelines for curricula in basic education 2014], Opetushallitus. [Board of Education]. Juvenes Print – Suomen Yliopistopaino Oy, Tampere 2015 http://www.oph.fi/download/163777_perusopetuksen_opetussuunnitelman_perusteet_2014.pdf

Boekaerts, M. & Niemivirta, M. (2000). Self-regulated learning: Finding a balance between learning goals and ego-protective goals. In M. Boekaerts, P.R. Pintrich & M. Zeidner (eds), *Handbook of Self-Regulation: Theory, Research, and Applications*, pp. 417–450. San Diego, CA: Academic Press.

Carr, W. & Kemmis, S. (1986). *Becoming Critical. Education, Knowledge and Action Research*. Helsinki: Falmer Press.

Carver, C.S. & Scheier, M.F. (2000). On the structure of behavioral self-regulation. In M. Boekaerts, P.R. Pintrich & M. Zeidner (eds), *Handbook of Self-Regulation: Theory,*

Research, and Applications, pp. 41–84. San Diego, CA: Academic Press.

Cleary, T.J., Callan, G.L. & Zimmerman, B.J. (2012). Assessing self-regulation as a cyclical, context-specific phenomenon: Overview and analysis of SRL microanalytic protocols. *Education Research International*, https://www.hindawi.com/journals/edri/2012/428639/cta/ [accessed July 24, 2017].

Duval-Couetil, N. (2013). Assessing the impact of entrepreneurship education programs: Challenges and approaches. *Journal of Small Business Management*, 51(3), 394–409.

Fayolle, A. & Toutain, O. (2013). Four educational principles to rethink ethically entrepreneurship education. *Revista de economía mundial*, 35, 165–176.

Garcia, T. & Pintrich, P.R. (1994). Regulating motivation and cognition in the classroom: The role of self-schemas and self-regulatory strategies. In D.H. Schunck & B.J. Zimmerman (eds), *Self-Regulated Learning: From Teaching to Self-Reflective Practice*, pp. 20–41. New York: Guilford Press.

Gibb, A. (2005). The future of entrepreneurship education: Determining the basis for coherent policy and practice. In P. Kyrö and C. Carrier (eds), *The Dynamics of Learning Entrepreneurship in a Cross-Cultural University Context*, pp. 44–67. Tampere: University of Tampere, Research Centre for Vocational and Professional Education.

Gibb, A. (2011). Concepts into practice: Meeting the challenge of development of entrepreneurship educators around an innovative paradigm: The case of the International Entrepreneurship Educators' Programme (IEEP). *International Journal of Entrepreneurial Behavior and Research*, 17(2), 146–165.

Hietanen, L. (2012). 'Tänään soitin vain kitaraa, koska innostuin': tapaustutkimus yrittäjämäisestä toiminnasta perusopetuksen 7. luokan musiikin oppimisympäristössä [I played only guitar today because I got carried away: A case study of entrepreneurial action in music education at the seventh grade in the basic education]. Acta Universitatis Lapponiensis 225. PhD thesis. Rovaniemi: Lapin yliopistokustannus.

Hietanen, L. & Kesälahti, E. (2016). Teachers in general education defining and implementing work-related and entrepreneurial approaches in learning environments. *Periodical of Entrepreneurship Education 2016*. Turku: Publications of the Scientific Association for Entrepreneurship Education, Painosalama Oy.

Hytti, U. & O'Gorman, C. (2004). What is 'enterprise education'? An analysis of the objectives and methods of enterprise education programmes in four European countries. *Education and Training*, 46(1), 11–23.

Hytti, U., Stenholm, P., Heinonen, J. & Seikkula-Leino, J. (2010). Perceived learning outcomes in entrepreneurship education: The impact of student motivation and team behaviour. *Education and Training*, 52(8/9), 587–606.

Jones, B. & Iredale, N. (2010). Enterprise education as pedagogy. *Education and Training*, 52(1), 7–19.

Jones, B. & Iredale, N. (2014). Enterprise and entrepreneurship education: Towards a comparative analysis. *Journal of Enterprising Communities: People and Places in the Global Economy*, 8(1), 34–50.

Kirby, D.A. (2004). Entrepreneurship education: Can business schools meet the challenge? *Education and Training*, 46(8/9), 510–519.

Komulainen, K., Korhonen, M. & Räty, H. (2009). Risk-taking abilities for everyone? Finnish entrepreneurship education and the enterprising selves imagined by pupils. *Gender and Education*, 21(6), 631–649.

Koskinen, S. (2015). Yrittäjyyskasvatuksen pedagogiikkaa vaativassa erityisopetuksessa Itsesäätelytaitojen kehittäminen ja tulevaisuusorientaation vahvistaminen yrittäjyyskasvatuksen pedagogiikan keinoin. [Entrepreneurship pedagogy in demanding special education. Developing the self-regulation skills and the future orientation with entrepreneurship pedagogy. An ethnographic study of a reform school.] Dissertation. Acta Universitatis Tamperensis 2028. Suomen Yliopistopaino Oy – Juvenes Print. Tampere 2015.

Kyrö, P. (2008). Yrittäjyyskasvatuksen laajenevat näköalat [Expanding horizons of entrepreneurship education]. In E. Poikela & S. Poikela (eds), *Tutkimustarinoita Ounaksen varrelta [Research stories from the river Ounas]*, pp. 139–160. Rovaniemi: Lapin yliopistokustannus.

Kyrö, P. (2015). The conceptual contribution of education to research on entrepreneurship education. *Entrepreneurship and Regional Development*, 27(9–10), 599–618.

Lehtonen, H. & Lehkonen, H. (2008). Avauksia perusopetuksen yrittäjyyskasvatukseen [Openings for entrepreneurship education in basic education]. In H. Lehtonen (ed.), *Sytykkeitä syrjäytymisen ehkäisemiseen [Tools for preventing exclusion]*, pp. 48–67, University of Tampere, Teacher Education, Hämeenlinna.

Locke, E.A. & Latham, G.P. (1990). *A Theory of Goal Setting and Task Performance*. Englewood Cliffs, NJ: Prentice-Hall.

Locke, E.A. & Latham, G.P. (2002). Building a practically useful theory of goal setting and task motivation: A 35-year odyssey. *American Psychologist*, 57(9), 705–717.

Pittaway, L. & Cope, J. (2007). Entrepreneurship education: A systematic review of the evidence. *International Small Business Journal*, 25(5), 479–510.

Rae, D. (2011). Yliopistot ja yrittäjyyskasvatus: vastaus uuden aikakauden haasteisiin. [Universities and entrepreneurship education: A response to the challenges in the new era] In J. Heinonen, U. Hytti & A. Tiikkala (eds), Yrittäjämäinen oppiminen: Tavoitteita, toimintaa ja tuloksia, [Entrepreneurial learning: Aims, activities and outcomes] Turun yliopisto, Turun kauppakorkeakoulu & Kasvatustieteiden tiedekunta [University of Turku, Turku School of Economics & Faculty of Education]. Turku, Uniprint.

Rae, D. & Carswell, M. (2001). Towards a conceptual understanding of entrepreneurial learning. *Journal of Small Business and Enterprise Development*, 8(2), 150–158.

Remes, L. (2007). Yrittäjyyskasvatus ja oppimismenetelmät [Entrepreneurship education and learning methods]. In M. Suvanto, J. Halme & S. Leväniemi (eds), *Yrittäjyyskasvatus kouluissa [Entrepreneurship education in Schools]*, pp. 21–27. Rauma: Turun yliopisto.

Ristimäki, K. (2004). *Yrittäjyyskasvatus [Entrepreneurship education]*. Hamina: Oy Kotkan Kirjapaino Ab.

Rönkkö, M.L. & Lepistö, J. (2015). Finnish student teachers' critical conceptions of entrepreneurship education. *Journal of Enterprising Communities: People and Places in the Global Economy*, 9(1), 61–75.

Ruohotie, P. (2008). Ammatillisen kompetenssin juuret [Roots of vocational competences]. In

A. Kallioniemi, A. Toom, M. Ubani, H. Linnasaari & K. Kumpulainen (eds), *Ihmisiä kasvattamassa: Koulutus, arvot, uudet avaukset* [Cultivating Humanity: Education, Values, New Discoveries]. Suomen Kasvtustieteellinen Seura. Kasvatusalan tutkimuksia 40.

Ruskovaara, E. & Pihkala, T. (2013). Teachers implementing entrepreneurship education: Classroom practices. *Education and Training*, 55(2), 204–216.

Sarasvathy, S.D. & Venkataraman, S. (2011). Entrepreneurship as method: Open questions for an entrepreneurial future. *Entrepreneurship Theory and Practice*, 35(1), 113–135.

Schunk, D.H. (1984). Self-efficacy perspective on achievement behavior. *Educational Psychologist*, 19(1), 48–58.

Schunk, D.H. (2001). Social cognitive theory and self-regulated learning. In B.J. Zimmerman & D.H. Schunk (eds), *Self-Regulated Learning and Academic Achievement: Theoretical Perspectives*, pp. 119–144. Mahwah, NJ: Routledge.

Scott, J.M., Penaluna, A. & Thompson, J.L. (2016). A critical perspective on learning outcomes and the effectiveness of experiential approaches in entrepreneurship education: Do we innovate or implement? *Education and Training*, 58(1), 82–93.

Seikkula-Leino, J. (2007). Opetussuunnitelmauudistus ja yrittäjyyskasvatuksen toteuttaminen. [Renewal of school curricula and implementing entrepreneurship education] Opetusministeriö, koulutus-ja tiedepolitiikan osasto [Ministry of Education, Department for education and science policy]. 2007:28, Helsinki: Yliopistopaino.

Smith, R. (2009). Entrepreneurship: A divergent pathway out of crime. In K. Jaishankar (ed.), *International Perspectives on Crime and Justice*, pp. 162–184. Newcastle-upon-Tyne, Cambridge Scholars Publishing.

Swierczek, F.W. & Ha, T.T. (2003). Entrepreneurial orientation, uncertainty avoidance and firm performance: An analysis of Thai and Vietnamese SMEs. *International Journal of Entrepreneurship and Innovation*, 4(1), 46–58.

van Gelderen, M. (2010). Autonomy as the guiding aim of entrepreneurship education. *Education and Training*, 52(8/9), 710–721.

Yamane, E. (2002). Entrepreneurship education in the 'period for integrated study' in elementary and lower secondary schools in Japan. *Citizenship, Social and Economics Education*, 5(1), 44–52.

Zimmerman, B.J. (1998). Developing self-fulfilling cycles of academic regulation: An analysis of exemplary instructional models. In D.H. Schunk & B.J. Zimmerman (eds), *Self-Regulated Learning: From Teaching to Self-Reflective Practice*, pp. 1–19. New York: Guilford Press.

Zimmerman, B.J. (2000). Becoming a self-regulated learner: An overview. *Theory into Practice*, 41(2), 64–70.

Zimmerman, B.J. (2008). Goal setting: A key proactive source of academic self-regulation. In D.H. Schunk & B.J. Zimmerman (eds), *Motivation and Self-Regulated Learning: Theory, Research, and Applications*, pp. 267–296. New York: Lawrence Erlbaum Associates.

Zimmerman, B.J. & Bandura, A. (1994). Impact of self-regulatory influences on writing course attainment. *American Educational Research Journal*, 31(4), 845–862.

Zimmerman, B.J. & Campillo, M. (2003). Motivating self-regulated problem solvers. In J. E. Davidson and R.J. Sternberg (eds), *The Psychology of Problem Solving*, 233–262. New York: Cambridge University Press.

Zimmerman, B.J. & Kitsantas, A. (1997). Developmental phases in self-regulation: Shifting from process goals to outcome goals. *Journal of Educational Psychology*, 89(1), 29.

Zimmerman, B.J. & Kitsantas, A. (2005). The hidden dimension of personal competence: Self-regulated learning and practice. In A.J. Elliot and C.S. Dweck (eds), *Handbook of Competence and Motivation*, pp. 509–525. New York: Guilford Press.

PART IV

Researching Small Business and Entrepreneurship

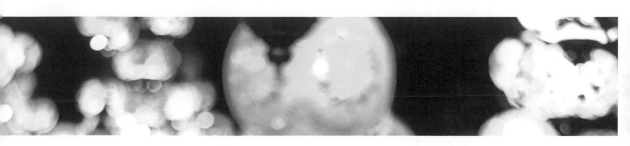

28

In Search of Causality in Entrepreneurship Research: Quantitative Methods in Corporate Entrepreneurship

Aaron F. McKenny, Miles A. Zachary,
Jeremy C. Short and David J. Ketchen Jnr.

INTRODUCTION

Uncovering the determinants of the performance of entrepreneurial firms is a key goal of entrepreneurship and small business research (e.g. Hitt, Ireland, Camp, & Sexton, 2001; Sheehan, 2014; Short, McKelvie, Ketchen, & Chandler, 2009). Unfortunately, identifying causal relationships empirically is challenging due to the complexity of organizational phenomena and incomplete control over alternative explanations for hypothesized relationships (Colquitt, 2008). It is not surprising therefore that scholars have debated the causal nature of key relationships, such as the strategic-resources–firm-performance link (e.g. Priem & Butler, 2001), the diversification–firm-performance link (e.g. Keats, 1990), and the corporate-social-responsibility–firm-performance link (e.g. Peloza, 2009).

Quantitative research methods play a key role in causal inference (Cook & Campbell, 1979; Schwab, 2005). In particular, experimental

methods have been highlighted for their ability to identify causal links because they offer researchers granular control over the stimuli and environment (e.g. Colquitt, 2008; Fromkin & Streufert, 1976). However, many entrepreneurship research questions are difficult to test using experiments (McCaffrey, 2014; Patel & Fiet, 2010). As a result, scholars frequently rely on field methods such as surveys and archival studies when examining the determinants of entrepreneurial firm performance. When methodological decisions in field research are made well, this can enhance confidence in the causal nature of uncovered relationships (Antonakis, Bendahan, Jacquart, & Lalive, 2010). To date, however, little is known regarding how well entrepreneurship scholars are making the methodological decisions that are tied to causal claims.

To help close this gap, this chapter examines the methods used in studies of the relationship between corporate entrepreneurship and firm performance. Corporate entrepreneurship refers to how individuals within an existing organization recognize and seize opportunities to bring about organizational innovation, rejuvenation, and new business development (Ahuja & Lampert, 2001). Focusing our review on a single relationship enables us to provide a detailed assessment of whether scholars are building a compelling case for the causal nature of this relationship. As a result, our study is able to address both how quantitative methods are being used to facilitate causal inference and the substantive question of whether the selected relationship is likely to be causal based on the methodological rigor in extant corporate entrepreneurship studies.

We draw from John Stuart Mill's (1843) criteria for causal inference to understand how methodological decisions influence confidence in identified relationships. Mill's work on causality has been influential in the philosophy of science literature on causation and serves as an intellectual foundation for theories of causal attribution (Ahn, Kalish, Medin, & Gelman, 1995; Pearl, 2000). Three criteria must be met to infer a causal relationship: the independent and dependent variables must covary, the independent variable must temporally precede the dependent variable, and alternative explanations must be eliminated (Cook & Campbell, 1979; Van de Ven, 2007). We use these criteria to examine the methodological decisions made within 66 studies published between 1980 and 2012 that relate corporate entrepreneurship to firm performance.

It is impossible to conclusively prove that two variables are causally related (Blalock, 1964). However, rigorous use of quantitative research methods can increase the likelihood of identifying causal relationships (Colquitt, 2008; Schwab, 2005; Stinchcombe, 1968). Given the significant theoretical and practical importance of the relationships tested in entrepreneurship and small business research, any inattention to causality undermines the relevance of our research. In sum, we seek to identify the appropriate level of confidence in a causal relationship between corporate entrepreneurship and firm performance to date while providing guidance for future research in this area.

EXAMINING CAUSALITY IN CORPORATE ENTREPRENEURSHIP RESEARCH

Research methods play an important role for scholars seeking to make causal inferences from their data. Historically, entrepreneurship research has not employed research methods with the rigor of peer fields, such as strategic management or organizational behavior (Dean, Shook, & Payne, 2007; Low & MacMillan, 1988; Short, Ketchen, Combs, & Ireland, 2010). In particular, while entrepreneurship research has been lauded for its rich qualitative studies, methods scholars have critiqued the quantitative methods employed in this literature (Short, Ketchen, Combs, & Ireland, 2010). For entrepreneurship scholars, this presents a salient challenge because rigorous quantitative methods are key to causal inference (e.g. Cook & Campbell, 1979; Schwab, 2005). To assess the extent to which the rigor of quantitative methods has impacted our ability to infer causality in a relationship of interest to entrepreneurship and small business scholars, we examine the literature linking corporate entrepreneurship to firm performance outcomes.

We collected relevant studies from 12 leading organizational/management journals: *Academy of Management Journal*, *Administrative Science Quarterly*, *Journal of Applied Psychology*, *Journal of Management*, *Journal of Management Studies*, *Journal of Organizational Behavior*, *Management Science*, *Organization Science*, *Organization Studies*, *Organizational Behavior and Human Decision Processes*, *Personnel Psychology*, and *Strategic Management Journal*; as well as three top entrepreneurship journals: *Entrepreneurship: Theory and Practice*, *Journal of Business Venturing*, and *Strategic Entrepreneurship Journal* (cf. Short, Ketchen, & Palmer, 2002; Short, Ketchen, Shook, & Ireland, 2010) over a 33-year period (1980–2012). We selected this period for three key reasons. First, this allows us to compare changes over three decades of research. Second, *Strategic Management*

Journal, the premier journal focused on strategic management, was founded in 1980, providing a convenient starting point for the assessment of corporate entrepreneurship. Third, this window captures the bulk of articles published in the entrepreneurship journals: *Entrepreneurship: Theory & Practice* (founded in 1978), *Journal of Business Venturing* (founded in 1985), and *Strategic Entrepreneurship Journal* (founded in 2007).

We used ABI/Inform and EBSCOhost to identify all articles published in the selected journals using the terms 'corporate entrepreneurship', 'firm-level entrepreneurship', 'intrapreneurship', 'corporate venturing', 'entrepreneurial orientation', or variants of these terms in the title, abstract, or keywords. The first two search terms reflect two key conceptualizations of entrepreneurship in corporate settings (Covin & Slevin, 1991). 'Intrapreneurship' was included because it has been used synonymously with 'corporate entrepreneurship' (Pinchot, 1985). 'Corporate venturing' was included because it is one of the primary ways corporations engage in entrepreneurial behavior (Burgelman, 1983). Finally, 'entrepreneurial orientation' was included because it has become one of the most widely used constructs in corporate entrepreneurship research (Rauch, Wiklund, Lumpkin, & Frese, 2009). As shown in Table 28.1, after eliminating all conceptual articles, qualitative studies, studies that were not actually focused on corporate entrepreneurship, studies without a firm-level performance dependent variable, and meta-analyses, a total of 66 studies were identified.

Table 28.1   Empirical studies of the corporate entrepreneurship–performance relationship

Academy of Management Journal	*Journal of Business Venturing*	*Journal of Management*
*Richard, Barnett, Dwyer, & Chadwick, 2004	Allen and Hevert, 2007	*Zahra, Neubaum, & Huse, 2000
	*Anderson and Eshima, 2011	
*Stam and Elfring, 2008	Antoncic and Hisrich, 2001	*Strategic Management Journal*
	*Bradley, Wiklund, & Shepherd, 2011	
Entrepreneurship: Theory and Practice	Covin, Slevin, & Heeley, 2000	Covin and Slevin, 1989
	De Clercq, Dimov, & Thongpapanl, 2010	Dushnitsky and Shapira, 2010
Barrett and Weinstein, 1998		*Keil, Maula, Schildt, & Zahra, 2008
Becherer and Maurer, 1997	Dushnitsky and Lenox, 2006	*Lee, Lee, Pennings, 2001
*Bierly and Daly, 2007	Hill and Birkinshaw, 2008	Lu and Beamish, 2001
Bruneel, Van de Velde, & Clarysse, 2013	Keh, Nguyen, & Ng, 2007	*Park and Steensma, 2012
Chandler, Keller, & Lyon, 2000	Lin and Lee, 2011	Shortell and Zajac, 1988
*Covin, Green, & Slevin, 2006	Lumpkin and Dess, 2001	*Wales, Parida, & Patel, 2013
Hitt, Nixon, Hoskisson, & Kochhar, 1999	MacMillan and Day, 1987	Wiklund and Shepherd, 2003
Kollman and Stockmann, 2014	*Park and Kim, 1997	
Lichtenthaler, 2012	Shrader and Simon, 1997	*Organization Science*
Marino, Strandholm, Steensma, & Weaver, 2002	Sorrentino and Williams, 1995	*Benson and Ziedonis, 2009
	Sykes, 1986	
Miller and Le-Breton-Miller, 2011	Thornhill and Amit, 2001	*Strategic Entrepreneurship Journal*
Moreno and Casillas, 2008	Walter, Auer, & Ritter, 2006	
Pearce, Fritz, & Davis, 2010	Wiklund and Shepherd, 2005	*Chirico, Sirmon, Sciascia, & Mazzola, 2011
Steffens, Davidsson, & Fitzsimmons, 2009	Zahra, 1991	Danneels, 2012
	Zahra, 1993	*Hill, Maula, Birkinshaw, & Murray, 2009
*Tang, Tang, Marino, Zhang, & Li, 2008	Zahra, 1995	
Wang, 2008	Zahra and Covin, 1995	Levitas and Chi, 2010
Wiklund, 1999	*Zahra and Garvis, 2000	Simsek and Heavey, 2011
Wiklund and Shepherd, 2011		*Siren, Kohtamaki, & Kuckertz, 2012
*Yiu and Lau, 2008	*Journal of Management Studies*	
Zahra, Neubaum, & El-Hagrassey, 2002		
*Zhao, Li, Lee, & Chen, 2011	Coombes, Morris, Allen, & Webb, 2011	
	*Li, Wei, & Liu, 2010	

* Met all three baseline methodological criteria for causal inference: corporate entrepreneurship and firm performance were related, firm performance was lagged, and included at least one theoretically justified control variable.

To examine how corporate entrepreneurship scholars build a case for causality using quantitative methods, we identified guidelines that influence one of the three conditions that must be met to infer causality (i.e. Mill, 1843). First, the cause and effect must covary. Second, the cause must precede the effect in time. Finally, alternative explanations for the covariance between cause and effect variables must be eliminated (Cook & Campbell, 1979; Mill, 1843). We organized our coding around these three criteria. Two coders examined each study, and differences in the initial codes were discussed until agreement was reached (cf. Short et al., 2002).

Covariance

Demonstrating that the cause and effect variables covary is the first criterion required to infer causality (Van de Ven, 2007). Covariance suggests that a change in one variable is accompanied by a change in another variable (Kerlinger & Lee, 2000), and most analytical techniques used to test hypotheses in organizational research rely on the concept of covariance (e.g. Dean et al., 2007; Scandura and Williams, 2000). One of the most common ways to demonstrate covariance is to present correlations among the variables in a manuscript. This provides the reader with information regarding all interrelationships present in the data and enables them to replicate the analysis (Crook, Shook, Morris, & Madden, 2010; Shook, Ketchen, Hult, & Kacmar, 2004). While providing covariances or correlations among all variables is ideal, some studies present statistics for a subset of variable combinations (e.g. Simsek & Heavey, 2011). To capture both possibilities, we coded each article to identify whether at least one covariance or correlation statistic was presented and whether these statistics were provided for all variable pairs used in the study.

Table 28.2 displays our findings. Fifty-nine (89 percent) studies included correlation or covariance statistics for at least one variable combination. Surprisingly, only 36 studies (55 percent) included correlations for all variables included in the study. Our review revealed that omitted control variables, in particular industry dummy variables, were the most frequent cause of incomplete correlation/covariance statistics (e.g. Danneels, 2012; Walter, Auer, & Ritter, 2006). The proportion of studies that include some correlations decreased from 100 percent in the 1980s to 73 percent in the 1990s; however, a t-test indicated that this decrease was not statistically significant ($t = -1.14$, $p = 0.27$). Over the same period, the proportion of studies that include correlations for all variables decreased from 50 percent to 27 percent; this decrease also was not significant ($t = -0.79$, $p = 0.45$). The proportion of studies that include at least one correlation increased from 73 percent in the 1990s to 88 percent in the 2000s ($t = 1.14$, $p = 0.26$) and those that include all correlations increased from 27 percent to 56 percent ($t = 1.67$, $p = 0.10$); however, neither increase was statistically significant. Finally, we compared studies from the 2000s to the 19 studies published between 2010 and 2012 to examine the current trajectory. Although we found an increase from 88 percent to 100 percent for the inclusion of at least one correlation ($t = 1.61$, $p = 0.11$) and an increase from 56 percent to 68 percent for the inclusion of all correlations ($t = 0.85$, $p = 0.40$), these increases were not statistically significant.

Providing covariance statistics provides the reader with valuable information regarding relationships in the data (Crook et al., 2010). Standard practice in organizational research is to only interpret relationships as being statistically significant when the associated p-value is less than 0.05 (Orlitzky, 2012). To provide evidence that there is a causal relationship between corporate entrepreneurship and firm performance, there must be statistically significant covariance between the two variables. However, a significant zero-order correlation between two variables does not necessarily mean that the relationship remains statistically significant when controlling for other factors (Breaugh, 2008). Accordingly, we assessed whether a

Table 28.2 Summary of methodological decisions in corporate entrepreneurship research

	Time period			t-value (1980s vs 1990s)	t-value (1990s vs 2000s)
	1980–9	1990–9	2000–9		
Number of studies	4	11	32		
Condition 1: covariance					
Some correlations presented	4 (100%)	8 (73%)	28 (88%)	−1.14	1.14
All correlations are presented	2 (50%)	3 (27%)	18 (56%)	−0.79	1.67
CE and performance covary	4 (100%)	11 (100%)	29 (91%)	N/A	−1.04
Condition 2: temporal ordering					
Performance is lagged	1 (33%)	3 (33%)	9 (30%)	0.00	−0.19
Longitudinal analyses are used	1 (25%)	4 (36%)	6 (19%)	0.39	−1.18
Tested for reverse causality	0 (0%)	1 (9%)	1 (3%)	0.59	−0.80
Condition 3: alternative explanations					
Sampling					
Random sample used	1 (25%)	0 (0%)	9 (28%)	−1.78	2.03*
Average sample size/number of variables	13.67	15.55	40.92	0.22	0.76
Control variables					
At least one control variable is included	0 (0%)	5 (45%)	26 (81%)	1.70	2.38*
Number of control variables per paper	0	1.36	4.19	1.43	2.89*
Basis for inclusion					
No rationale	N/A	0 (0%)	2 (8%)	N/A	0.62
Might influence CE or performance	N/A	1 (20%)	5 (19%)	N/A	−0.04
Theory/previous empirical findings	N/A	4 (80%)	19 (73%)	N/A	−0.31

$^{*} p < 0.05. ^{**} p < 0.01.$ CE: corporate entrepreneurship

statistically significant relationship between corporate entrepreneurship and firm performance is found in the analyses used to test the study hypotheses (e.g. regression weights, structural equation modeling path coefficients). Many studies include more than one aspect of corporate entrepreneurship (e.g. Lumpkin and Dess, 2001) or test more than one model (e.g. Stam & Elfring, 2008). If at least one corporate entrepreneurship variable was related to firm performance in one or more models, the article was coded as having found a relationship.

We found that 62 studies (94 percent) identified a statistically significant relationship between corporate entrepreneurship and firm performance. No *t*-test was possible to compare the 1980s and 1990s because all

studies from both decades found support for the relationship. The proportion of studies finding support for the relationship decreased from 100 percent in the 1990s to 91 percent in the 2000s ($t = -1.04$, $p = 0.30$); however, this decrease was not significant. We also examined whether support for the relationship changed between the 2000s and the 2010s. Despite an increase from 91 percent to 95 percent, the change was not statistically significant ($t = 0.52, p = 0.60$).

Temporal Ordering

Establishing that the purported cause precedes the effect in time is the second criterion required to infer causality (Van de Ven,

2007). For a change in an independent variable to cause a change in the dependent variable, the processes connecting the two must be given time to unfold (Van de Ven & Huber, 1990). Thus, a change in the dependent variable that occurs before or at the same time as a change in the independent variable cannot be confidently attributed to the independent variable (Black, 1956).

A common way of providing evidence for the temporal precedence of the independent variable is measuring an independent variable during an earlier time period than the measurement of a dependent variable (e.g. Lee, Lee, & Pennings, 2001; Zahra, Neubaum, & Huse, 2000). By providing a lag between the variables, researchers ensure that changes to the independent variable take place before the associated change in the dependent variable (Bergh, Hanke, Balkundi, Brown, & Chen, 2004).

The coders identified eight studies where insufficient information was provided to determine whether a lag was used. Of the remaining 58 articles, only 20 (34 percent) indicated that a lag was used. In both the 1980s and 1990s, 33 percent of studies used a temporal lag. This number decreased to 30 percent in the 2000s; however, the decrease was not statistically significant ($t = -0.19$, $p = 0.85$). While the use of temporal lags increased to 44 percent in the first three years of the 2010s, this return to previous levels was not statistically significant ($t = 0.92$, $p = 0.36$).

Longitudinal designs have grown in popularity for their ability to overcome the limitations of cross-sectional methods (Ketchen, Boyd, & Bergh, 2008). Cross-sectional methods examine the relationships among variables based on observations at a single point in time for both independent and dependent variables. Without multiple observations over time for each variable, cross-sectional studies are susceptible to biases arising from sample selection (Bergh et al., 2004). While sample selection bias can occur in longitudinal methods as well, by analyzing multiple observations over time these techniques increase confidence that the relationship is not spurious and build a stronger case for the direction of causality by showing that that variance in the independent variable is associated with variance in the dependent variable consistently (Bergh & Holbein, 1997). To assess the prevalence of these methods, we identified whether each study used at least one longitudinal analytic technique (e.g. panel regression, random coefficient modeling, 3SLS) or relied solely on cross-sectional analyses (e.g. regression, ANOVA, correlation analysis).

We found that 15 studies (23 percent) published from 1980–2012 used longitudinal methods. The use of longitudinal methods remained relatively constant across the three decades assessed. In the 1990s, 36 percent of studies used longitudinal methods; however, this was not a significant change from the 25 percent that used longitudinal methods in the 1980s ($t = 0.39$, $p = 0.71$). The proportion of studies using longitudinal methods decreased from 36 percent in the 1990s to 19 percent in the 2000s; however, this decrease was not significant ($t = -1.18$, $p = 0.24$). In the first three years of the 2010s, 21 percent of studies used longitudinal analyses. This was not a significant increase over the 19 percent that used longitudinal methods in the 2000s ($t = 0.20$, $p = 0.85$).

While longitudinal analyses provide strong evidence for the hypothesized temporal ordering of independent and dependent variables, explicit testing for reverse causality can provide important additional support. When scholars include discussion regarding the causal nature of hypothesized relationships in published manuscripts, the possibility of reverse causality is often an area of concern (e.g. Paauwe, 2009). For example, the social issues literature has questioned whether social performance causes financial performance or whether this relationship is reversed or reciprocal (e.g. Hillman & Keim, 2001). Finding that the independent variable predicts the dependent variable but the dependent variable does not predict the independent variable provides compelling evidence for the direction of causality (Echambadi, Campbell, & Agarwal, 2006).

Only three (5 percent) of the 66 studies reviewed provided an explicit test for reverse causality. No studies published in the 1980s did so. In the 1990s, 9 percent of studies tested for reverse causality. However, this was not a significant increase from the absence of reverse causality testing in the 1980s ($t = 0.59$, $p = 0.57$). In the 2000s, 3 percent of studies tested for reverse causality; however, this was not a significant decrease from the 9 percent that did so in the 1990s ($t = -0.80$, $p = 0.43$). Finally, 5 percent of the studies published from 2010 through 2012 tested for reverse causality. This was not a significant increase from the 3 percent testing for reverse causality in the 2000s ($t = 0.37$, $p = 0.71$).

Elimination of Alternative Explanations

The final criterion required to infer causality is to eliminate plausible alternative explanations for the relationship between the independent and dependent variable (Van de Ven, 2007). In the social sciences, many variables will covary regardless of whether there is an actual causal relationship linking them (Meehl, 1990). Two variables may covary due to biases in their distributions, intervening phenomena, shared antecedents, or a number of other factors (e.g. Brett, 2004; Simon, 1954). When researchers eliminate plausible alternative explanations, this improves the likelihood that a causal relationship is the best remaining explanation for an identified covariance.

Two common methods are used to control for alternative explanations: elimination and control variables (Pedhazur & Schmelkin, 1991). Elimination requires the researcher to eliminate variance in confounding factors through the research design (Pedhazur & Schmelkin, 1991). For example, researchers

using laboratory experiments can exercise great control over the environment, manipulations, and assignment of participants into test groups to control for unmeasured factors that may influence the dependent variable (Colquitt, 2008; Kerlinger & Lee, 2000). When variance cannot be eliminated, researchers can introduce control variables to account for the effect that they may have on the dependent variable (Pedhazur & Schmelkin, 1991). If a relationship is significant despite the inclusion of control variables, it is more likely that the relationship is causal (Becker, 2005).

Sampling design is a valuable method used by strategy and entrepreneurship researchers for eliminating alternative explanations (Short et al., 2002). Good sampling practices enable researchers to collect data from a subset of a population and use this data to identify relationships that generalize to the population (Kerlinger & Lee, 2000). However, poor sampling practices can introduce spurious relationships. For example, a bias in the sample may create a significant relationship between the independent and dependent variables when this relationship does not exist in the population (Short et al., 2002). Completely unbiased sampling is generally not possible without collecting a census of the population; however, careful sampling design can mitigate sampling biases (Scheaffer, Mendenhall, & Ott, 1996).

One technique for minimizing biases is random sampling. Random sampling minimizes the probability that the sample will be systematically biased by unmeasured variables (Short et al., 2002). Randomness in sampling suggests that all samples of a given size are equally likely to be selected (Kerlinger & Lee, 2000). Drawing large random samples generally selects a distribution of entities with unmeasured characteristics in proportion to their prevalence in the overall population. Consequently, random sampling contributes to building a case for causality by maximizing the degree of correspondence between the sample and population.

We coded each study according to the scheme used by Short et al. (2002). Studies using simple random, stratified random, cluster, or systematic sampling (all of which rely on randomness) were coded as random, while those using purposive, quota, or availability (i.e. 'convenience') sampling were coded as nonrandom. Random sampling was used in 15 (23 percent) of the 66 studies. No studies in the 1990s used random sampling; however, a t-test indicates that this was not a statistically significant decrease from the 25 percent that used random sampling in the 1980s ($t = -1.78, p = 0.10$). The proportion of studies using random sampling significantly increased from 0 percent in the 1990s to 28 percent in the 2000s ($t = 2.03, p = 0.05$). Finally, 26 percent of studies in the first three years of the 2010s used random sampling; this is not a significant departure from the 28 percent that used random sampling in the 2000s ($t = -0.14, p = 0.89$).

In addition to randomness, sample size also plays an important role in eliminating alternative explanations. The law of large numbers suggests, all else being equal, that the closer a sample size is to the population it is drawn from, the more representative that sample is of its population (Tversky & Kahneman, 1971). Large sample sizes are also associated with greater statistical power, facilitating the detection of relationships with smaller effect sizes (Cohen, 1992). Thus, larger sample sizes are generally favorable for identifying causal relationships (Short et al., 2002). Hair, Black, Babin, and Anderson (2010) suggest that ten cases per variable is a good baseline for ensuring adequate statistical power.

To determine whether studies had an appropriate sample size, we divided the total number of observations by the number of variables estimated (cf. Short et al., 2002). For studies where more than one sample was used, the largest sample size was used in this calculation. The average ratio of sample size to number of variables over the 32 years reviewed was 40.5. Even after removing two

outlier studies, the average was 20.4, well above the 10 data points per variable heuristic. The average number of cases per variable did not change significantly, going from 13.67 in the 1980s to 15.55 in the 1990s ($t = 0.22, p = 0.83$), and increasing to 40.92 in the 2000s ($t = 0.77, p = 0.45$). In the first three years of the 2010s, there was an average of 67.69 cases per variable. This was not significantly different from the 40.92 cases per variable in the 2000s ($t = 0.63, p = 0.53$).

Organizational research has identified several organizational and environmental factors that influence firm performance, providing multiple plausible alternative explanations for phenomena that predict firm performance (Kotha & Nair, 2007). While some of these factors can be eliminated through sampling (e.g. industry membership), others are not easily eliminated and are generally controlled statistically (e.g. firm size, firm age). Accordingly, the inclusion of one or more control variables that provide plausible alternative explanations for the corporate entrepreneurship–firm performance relationship is warranted. We tracked whether studies used any controls as well as how many controls were used.

Overall, 48 of the studies (73 percent) examining the corporate entrepreneurship–firm performance relationship included at least one control variable. The average number of control variables included across all studies was 3.67. The use of at least one control variable increased from 0 percent to 45 percent ($t = 1.70, p = 0.11$) and the average number of control variables increased from 0 to 1.36 ($t = 1.43, p = 0.18$) between the 1980s and 1990s; however, these changes were not significant. In contrast, there was a significant increase from 45 percent to 81 percent in the use of control variables ($t = 2.38, p = 0.02$) and from 1.36 to 4.19 for the average number of control variables included ($t = 2.89, p = 0.01$) between the 1990s and 2000s. The early years of the 2010s have seen an increase from 81 percent to 89 percent in the use of control variables ($t = 0.77, p = 0.45$) and from 4.19 to 4.90

for the average number of control variables ($t = 0.81$, $p = 0.42$), but these changes were not statistically significant.

Including more control variables does not always equate to better elimination of alternative explanations (Spector & Brannick, 2011). Control variables increase confidence in causal assertions by eliminating plausible alternative explanations for a relationship. However, reviews of organizational research suggest that scholars frequently include control variables without justifying their use (Atinc, Simmering, & Kroll, 2012; Becker, 2005). When control variables are used without justification, they decrease the statistical power of the analysis but do not necessarily eliminate an alternative explanation for the hypothesized relationship (Becker, 2005). As a result, methodologists have called for researchers to include only those control variables that are theoretically relevant to the relationship in question (e.g. Becker, 2005; Spector & Brannick, 2011).

Following Atinc et al. (2012), the justification for each control variable was categorized into one of four groups from least to most justified: (1) no justification provided, (2) because past studies have controlled for it, (3) because it may influence firm performance, or (4) based on theoretical reasons/empirical evidence that it influences firm performance. Because some studies include more than one control variable, the best justified control variable in each study was used to code the overall level of justification for control variables in each article (cf. Atinc et al., 2012).

Of the 48 studies that included at least one control variable, three (6 percent) provide no justification for the inclusion of any control variables, ten (21 percent) suggest that at least one control variable influences firm performance, and 35 (73 percent) use theory or cite empirical findings to justify at least one control variable. No studies had 'because others controlled for it' as the explanation for the best justified control variable. None of the four studies from the 1980s used control variables. In the 1990s, all five studies that used

control variables provided rationale for their inclusion. Of these, 80 percent provided theoretical or empirical justification and 20 percent suggested that the control variable might influence firm performance. In the 2000s, 8 percent did not provide rationale for including control variables; however, this was not a significant increase from the 1990s, where all studies provided rationale ($t = 0.62$, $p = 0.54$). In the 2000s, 73 percent of studies provided theoretical or empirical rationale for including control variables; however, this was not a significant decrease from the 80 percent that did so in the 1990s ($t = -0.31$, $p = 0.76$). In the 2000s, 19 percent of studies justified control variables by noting that they may influence firm performance; however, this was not a significant decrease from the 20 percent that used this justification in the 1990s ($t = -0.04$, $p = 0.97$). Similarly, results comparing the first three years of the 2010s to the 2000s indicate no significant changes in the justification for control variables. Specifically, we found that 6 percent of studies from the 2010s failed to provide a justification, compared to 8 percent in the 2000s ($t = -0.22$, $p = 0.83$). Similarly, 24 percent of studies from the 2010s asserted that the control variables may influence firm performance, compared to 19 percent in the 2000s ($t = 0.33$, $p = 0.74$). Finally, 71 percent of studies from the 2010s provided an empirical or theoretical reason for including the control variables, compared to 73 percent in the 2000s ($t = -0.17$, $p = 0.86$).

Summary

To build the strongest confidence in a causal relationship between corporate entrepreneurship and firm performance, all of the criteria coded above should be fulfilled. Unfortunately, none of the 66 studies met all of these criteria. However, a reasonable case for causality can still be made without meeting all of the criteria. To provide a baseline assessment of the studies' treatment of causality, we looked at three basic issues: whether corporate entrepreneurship and firm performance were related in the hypothesis tests, whether the measurement of firm performance was lagged from the measurement of corporate entrepreneurship, and whether at least one theoretically justified control variable was used.

Fourteen studies (21 percent) met these three standards. Twenty-six studies (39 percent) met two of the three. Of these, six did not include any theoretically justified control variables, and the other 20 did not include a lag between corporate entrepreneurship and performance. The latter group is problematic given that some corporate entrepreneurship activities such as corporate venturing may take up to eight years to break even (Biggadike, 1979).

Overall, our analysis of the research designs used to test the corporate entrepreneurship–firm performance relationship does not provide strong confidence that past research has established a causal relationship. Further, our decade-by-decade analysis suggests that while improvements have been made with respect to eliminating alternative explanations, the prevalence of methods that establish covariance and temporal ordering have remained unchanged. To better understand these trends, we examined the correlation between the year each article was published and each of our coding criteria. Our correlational analysis revealed that only the use of at least one control variable (ρ = 0.52, p < 0.01) and the number of control variables ($\rho = 0.49$, p < 0.01) showed an upward trend over time. As such, future research examining this relationship should increasingly attend to the temporal ordering and elimination of alternative explanations criteria to build confidence in causality claims.

DISCUSSION

Our findings should be viewed in light of the limitations of our review. We assessed the extent to which entrepreneurship and small

business scholars infer and test causality in a prominent and growing stream of literature. The situation within other research streams could be different. However, Antonakis et al.'s (2010) examination of 110 articles on leadership found that authors failed to adequately address between 66 percent and 90 percent of the necessary conditions to make causal arguments. Thus, it seems likely that our findings reasonably characterize the overall state of entrepreneurship and small business research and that both studies reflect an overall trend within organizational research in general. Another possible limitation is that we focused on only the leading management and entrepreneurship journals. While the approaches used in articles published in other journals or book chapters theoretically could be better than what we found, the difficulty of publishing in the journals that we reviewed suggests that these articles likely reflect the most rigorous attempts to argue for and test causal relationships.

Despite these limitations, our investigation offers potentially important implications. Over the last three decades, studies of the corporate entrepreneurship–firm performance relationship have progressed from the use of simple techniques such as level-zero correlations to more sophisticated techniques involving panel data and longitudinal analyses. While these analytical advances are promising, we found that none of the 66 extant studies met all of the criteria necessary to have maximum confidence in causal inferences. We also found that progress in adopting the methods that strengthen the case for causality has been slow. Below we address these areas of concern and offer suggestions directed at improving future practice.

We found that most studies included at least a subset of the covariances or correlations among variables. However, considerably fewer studies reported the correlations among all variables. Under the temporal ordering condition for testing causal relationships, our findings suggest that most research on the corporate entrepreneurship–performance relationship has yet to fully embrace lagged performance measures and longitudinal analytical techniques. As a result, it is unclear whether changes in firm performance are a function of corporate entrepreneurship efforts. While there is considerable theoretical support for expecting changes in firm-level entrepreneurial policies and practices to lead to changes in firm performance, the opposite is also plausible. For instance, slack created by strong past performance has been found to be positively related to risk-taking behaviors (Zahra & Covin, 1995). Without examining corporate entrepreneurship activity and firm performance at multiple time periods or testing for reverse causality, scholars are only able to infer a non-causal association between variables, limiting the explanatory and predictive power of their findings.

Our investigation of the criterion for evaluating causal arguments revealed somewhat mixed results. Random sampling was seldom used across the three decades of interest, with most studies relying primarily on nonrandom sampling techniques. Other methods of controlling for alternative explanations showed substantial improvement over time. Sampling problems are not confined to research on corporate entrepreneurship. Short, Ketchen, Combs, and Ireland's (2010) survey of research methods experts identified sampling as being one of the most salient problems with entrepreneurship scholarship more broadly.

While random samples are relatively sparse in the corporate entrepreneurship literature, Richard, Barnett, Dwyer, and Chadwick's (2004) study of the moderating role of the dimensions of entrepreneurial orientation on the corporate entrepreneurship–performance relationship stands out as an exemplar for future research. They sent questionnaires to the presidents of 700 randomly selected banks with $100 million or less in total assets, 700 randomly selected banks with $100–499 million in total assets, and 700 randomly selected banks with $500 million or more in total assets. This stratified random sampling ensured that the authors tested their model across a variety of banks,

reducing sampling error by allowing each subpopulation of banks to be represented.

While scholars frequently address sampling and control variable issues explicitly, other aspects of eliminating alternative explanation often go unmentioned. Key among these is the threat of endogeneity. Endogeneity occurs when the independent variable is influenced by factors that influence other variables in the model (Antonakis, Bendahan, Jacquart, & Lalive, 2012). Unaddressed, endogeneity can bias both the estimated coefficients and the direction of the relationship found, undermining confidence in the causality of the study's findings. The threat of endogeneity increases as choice variables are incorporated into models. This is problematic for corporate entrepreneurship researchers because managers make strategic choices to engage in entrepreneurial initiatives in an effort to improve firm performance (cf. Hamilton & Nickerson, 2003). This suggests that such managerial choices are not random but rather endogenous to firm performance.

The findings of our review of causality in the corporate entrepreneurship literature can also inform research into other entrepreneurship and small business phenomena. For instance, following earlier calls for understanding and explaining the nature of the franchising–performance relationship (e.g. Combs & Ketchen, 1999), scholars in franchising research have become actively engaged in establishing a causal relationship between franchising and firm performance (e.g. Barthélemy, 2008; Clarkin, 2008; Srinivasan, 2006; Yin & Zajac, 2004). Similar to corporate entrepreneurship, franchising represents a strategic choice on behalf of management, and therefore may not only influence but be influenced by firm performance. Likewise, franchising scholars should be careful to demonstrate covariation between variables, sufficiently lag performance, and include a number of control variables (among other techniques that minimize endogeneity threats) when exploring the franchising–performance relationship.

Some research streams may benefit from coupling experiments with field research. Experiments are commonly seen as the gold standard for causal inference because they are better able to block the effects of confounding variables and maximize variance in the independent variable (e.g. Colquitt, 2008; Fromkin & Streufert, 1976). In particular, research in crowdfunding and opportunity recognition have much to benefit from experimental designs. Unlike traditional sources of new venture funding, crowdfunding facilitates investments from casual investors into new ventures. This facilitates participant selection, overcoming the difficulty of soliciting participation by professional investors such as venture capitalists. Similarly, in opportunity recognition, the individual recognizing and evaluating an opportunity does not need to be an entrepreneur because opportunity recognition is frequently discussed as taking place before an individual becomes an entrepreneur.

Best Practices for Entrepreneurship and Small Business Research

Given the importance of uncovering causal relationships in entrepreneurship and small business research, our findings highlight opportunities for scholars to strengthen their designs. To identify best practices for studies investigating causal relationships, such as those that consider the effects of corporate entrepreneurship on firm performance, we examined guidance from relevant methodological works with respect to Mill's (1843) three criteria for causal inference. These best practices are presented in Table 28.3.

To provide evidence that the independent and dependent variables covary for all variable combinations should be presented (Crook et al., 2010). While most studies include some correlations, many studies omit control variables, particularly industry dummy variables (e.g. Danneels, 2012;

Walter et al., 2006). Reporting all correlations provides a better understanding of the relationships present in the data that may not be directly modeled in the hypothesis tests and enables other scholars to replicate the analyses (Crook et al., 2010; Shook et al., 2004). Second, researchers should note whether the hypothesis tests found a relationship between the independent and dependent variables with a p-value of less than 0.05. This provides direct evidence that the two variables covary with respect to the broadly accepted norms for statistical significance (Orlitzky, 2012).

To establish temporal ordering, theory should be used to identify an appropriate lag between the independent and dependent variables. For instance, scholars have used lags ranging from 90 days (e.g. Barnett, Mischke, & Ocasio, 2000) to ten years (e.g. Baysinger & Butler, 1985) when investigating the determinants of firm performance. If the lag length is too short, then the processes that relate the independent variable to the dependent variable will not have completed by the time firm performance is measured (e.g. Van de Ven & Huber, 1990). However, lag lengths that are too long increase the risk that other intervening phenomena will explain the change in dependent variable. Thus, scholars should draw from theory to identify an appropriate lag. For example, Lee et al. (2001) note the role of the product lifecycle in driving firm performance and arrive at a two-year lag based on the length of the product lifecycles of the firms in their sample.

Second, scholars should use longitudinal analyses to test for reverse and reciprocal causality. For instance, several studies noted the possibility that the corporate entrepreneurship–firm performance relationship may be reversed or reciprocal and called for longitudinal tests of the relationship (e.g. Bradley, Wiklund, & Shepherd, 2011; Danneels, 2012). Databases such as COMPUSTAT and techniques such as computer-aided text analysis facilitate the collection of large longitudinal datasets while

Table 28.3   Best practices for identifying causal relationships in entrepreneurship research

Condition	Best practice
Covariance	1. Present a correlation matrix including all variables used in the study. 2. Identify whether the independent variable was related to the dependent variable with a p-value less than 0.05.
Temporal ordering	3. Draw from theory to identify an appropriate lag between the independent and dependent variables. 4. Use longitudinal data and methods to test for reverse and reciprocal causality.
Eliminating alternative explanations	5. Use random sampling. 6. Control for cross-level effects on the dependent variable. 7. Control for past values of the dependent variable (where theoretically justified). 8. Provide theoretical or empirical justification for all control variables. 9. Address endogeneity concerns.

avoiding missing data issues common to self-report methods (e.g. Short, Broberg, Cogliser, & Brigham, 2010). This data can then be analyzed using structural equation modeling or simultaneous equation modeling (e.g. 3SLS), both of which can be used to test the direction of causality. For example, Levitas and Chi (2010) used panel regression in conjunction with performance data from COMPUSTAT and the Center for Research in Security Prices (CRSP) to provide a longitudinal analysis of the corporate entrepreneurship–firm performance relationship.

Five practices are useful to minimize the risk of alternative explanations. First, studies should use random sampling where possible (Kerlinger & Lee, 2000). By increasing the use of random sampling, scholars can reduce the threat of unmeasured variables influencing the findings of the study (Short et al., 2002), increasing the likelihood that an identified relationship is causal. Where random sampling techniques are not possible, purposive sampling offers a valuable alternative (e.g. Short et al., 2002). Purposive sampling is a nonrandom sampling technique where a sample is chosen based on the reasoned judgment of the researcher (Kerlinger & Lee, 2000). For example, because corporate venture capital is not broadly implemented across organizations, many researchers investigating

this phenomenon rely on databases such as VentureOne (e.g. Benson & Ziedonis, 2009) and Venture Economics (e.g. Dushnitsky and Shapira, 2010) to generate samples. While less desirable than a random sample, purposive samples enable the creation of large datasets where a random sample might be prohibitively expensive.

Second, researchers should consider controlling for phenomena from all relevant levels of analysis that may confound the hypothesized relationship. The firm performance variance decomposition literature suggests that both industry- and firm-level factors influence firm performance (McGahan & Porter, 2002; Short, Ketchen, Bennett, & Du Toit, 2006). Accordingly, studies examining the antecedents of firm performance should identify and control for alternative explanations at both of these levels. Many studies examining the corporate entrepreneurship–firm performance relationship included both industry- and firm-level control variables (e.g. Lee et al., 2001; Wiklund & Shepherd 2005). Techniques such as random coefficient modeling can be used to control for cross-level effects because they split the variance in the dependent variable into components attributable to each level of analysis (e.g. Short et al., 2006). Control variables can also be used to model how higher-level phenomena influence the dependent variable.

For instance, 50 percent (36) of the studies we reviewed controlled for industry-level factors. Of these, 65 percent (20) found that at least one industry-level variable explained variance in firm performance. Similarly, 61 percent (44) of studies included a measure of firm size, and 47 percent (34) of studies included a measure of firm age. Of these, 53 percent (23) found that firm size, and 47 percent (16) found that firm age explained variance in firm performance.

Third, scholars should mitigate variance in their dependent variable explained by historical values. Indeed, for many dependent variables, such as firm performance, theory suggests that past values of the variable are a predictor of future values (e.g. Naser, Karbhari, & Mokhtar, 2004). As a result, controlling for past values may eliminate a powerful alternative explanation for the relationship between the independent variable and the dependent variable. Ten studies (14 percent) examining the relationship between corporate entrepreneurship and firm performance controlled for past performance. Of these ten, six studies (60 percent) identified a significant relationship between past and future performance. One of the best ways to control for past values of the dependent variable is to specify an autoregressive covariance model in a longitudinal data analytic technique such as hierarchical linear modeling (e.g. Raudenbush, Bryk, Cheong, & Congdon, 2000) or generalized linear models (e.g. Liang & Zeger, 1986). However, past dependent variables can also be used as control variables in cross-sectional analyses (e.g. McKenny, Short, & Payne, 2013).

Fourth, all control variables should be justified using either theory or citing empirical evidence that it influences the dependent variable (Atinc et al., 2012; Becker, 2005). For example, Anderson and Eshima (2011) justify controlling for firm size and industry by noting that a recent meta-analysis found that they influence the entrepreneurial orientation–firm performance relationship. Alternatively, Chirico, Sirmon, Sciascia, & Mazzola (2011) justified controlling for firm size by noting that larger firms generally have better access to resources, which can influence firm performance. Inadequately justified control variables reduce the power of the analysis without addressing plausible alternative explanations. Thus, in many cases, control variables not supported by theory or previous empirical evidence should be removed from the study (Becker, 2005).

Finally, scholars should address the possibility of endogeneity. A first step is determining the extent of the endogeneity problem. A popular approach for determining if endogeneity is a problem is testing an augmented regression model commonly referred to as the Durbin–Wu–Hausman test (Davidson & MacKinnon, 1993). In the test, the residuals of an endogenous variable, measured as a function of all exogenous variables, are included in the original regression model. If the estimated coefficient for the endogenous residuals in the original regression model are statistically different from zero, endogeneity is a potential problem in the model (Davidson & MacKinnon, 1993).

If endogeneity is identified to be a problem, researchers should seek an alternative technique for estimating coefficients such as 2- and 3-stage least squares regression or using instrumental variables. An instrumental variable is an alternative to the endogenous explanatory variable and can be factored into the OLS regression in its place such that the instrumental variable is (1) correlated with the endogenous variable and (2) uncorrelated with the disturbance term. Two-stage (2SLS) and three-stage (3SLS) least squares estimators are special cases of instrumental variable techniques where the instrumental variable is a linear combination of all the exogenous variables. The adoption of these techniques should be driven by theory; however, each is more likely to produce coefficient estimates unbiased by endogenous variables and will further help scholars rule out endogeneity as an alternative explanation for a causal relationship.

Mill's (1843) three criteria for causal inference provide a valuable framework for assessing the likelihood that a relationship is causal. However, there are additional considerations beyond the scope of this framework that may also influence causal inference in quantitative research. One particularly important consideration is measurement. Measurement links the constructs used in hypotheses to the variables used to test the hypotheses (Kerlinger & Lee, 2000). Mill's three criteria assume that the variables used in the analysis accurately reflect the phenomena of interest to the researcher. However, the phenomena of interest to organizational researchers are frequently complex, making accurate measurement difficult (e.g. Aguinis, Pierce, Bosco, & Muslin, 2009).

Addressing measure reliability and validity concerns improves the likelihood of identifying a hypothesized causal relationship. Reliability is defined as the precision of measurement or the absence of measurement error (Kerlinger & Lee, 2000). Reliability is important to causal inference because the presence of measurement error deflates estimated correlations between variables, making hypothesized relationships more difficult to detect (Nunnally & Bernstein, 1994). Indeed, many scholars have incorrectly attributed non-findings to poor theorizing when the hypothesis should have been supported due to the attenuating effects of measurement error (Cote & Buckley, 1988). Validity addresses whether the data collected by a measure is reflective of what the researcher intended to measure (Kerlinger & Lee, 2000). Validity is important to causal inference because a relationship that is found using invalid measures describes a relationship that is different from the researcher's hypothesis. As a result, the researcher cannot claim support for a causal hypothesized relationship.

Considerable guidance exists for scholars looking to ensure the reliability and validity of their measures (e.g. DeVellis, 2012; Hinkin, 1998; Short, Broberg, Cogliser, & Brigham, 2010). Most of this guidance emphasizes steps to be taken in the development of new measures, such as pilot testing and refining a questionnaire before using it in hypothesis testing (e.g. Hinkin, 1998). However, researchers can also ensure reliability and validity by using measures that have already been developed and validated in previous studies. For example, the Covin and Slevin (1989) entrepreneurial orientation scale is a well-known and validated scale in the corporate entrepreneurship literature.

Ideally, researchers conducting quantitative entrepreneurship research would be able to address all nine criteria in Table 28.3 as well as measurement concerns. However, in practice, trade-offs must be made due to resource constraints associated with conducting empirical research. For instance, survey methods tend to be viewed as state-of-the-art with respect to psychometric measurement precision. Unfortunately, low survey response rates are a challenge in entrepreneurship and small business research (Bartholomew & Smith, 2006). As a result, non-response bias can provide a viable alternative explanation for a hypothesized causal explanation. Non-response can also result in small sample sizes, reducing statistical power and making hypothesized relationships harder to detect. Techniques such as content analysis can be used to overcome these limitations by relying on organizational texts that do not have to be provided by the focal firm (Short, Borberg, Cogliser, & Brigham, 2010). For example, McKenny et al. (2012) examined the goals of private family firms based on the language used in website and press releases posted by each firm.

Scholars are increasingly examining how organizational and entrepreneurial phenomena change over time (Bliese, Chan, & Ployhart, 2007). Despite this growing interest, the collection of time-variant data can be tedious and time-consuming. However, an advantage of archival quantitative approaches to investigating research questions in entrepreneurship is the ability to obtain repeated observations over time. For example, Allison, McKenny, and Short (2013) examine how

Table 28.4   Empirical challenges and possible solutions in empirical entrepreneurship research

Research question	Anticipated challenge	Possible solution	Exemplar(s)
Do social entrepreneurs' use of identity claims in fundraising campaigns influence resource acquisition?	Bias arising from self-report methods (e.g. recall bias)	Content analysis of social entrepreneur campaigns on crowdfunding sites	(Allison, McKenny, and Short, 2013; Moss, Short, Payne, and Lumpkin, 2011)
Do family business managers' affective states influence their performance evaluations of family and non-family employees differently?	Affect changes considerably over time within a day	Use cell phone experience sampling to capture affect and employee evaluations at multiple points during the day	(Foo, Uy, and Baron, 2009; Uy, Foo, and Aguinis, 2010)
How does the importance of exploration change for entrepreneurial firms over time?	The use of difference scores to assess change has been discouraged	Use random coefficient modeling to examine the growth or decline in exploration over time	(Allison, McKenny, and Short, 2014)
How do different configurations of firm ownership/governance affect growth in entrepreneurial firms?	Numerous forms of ownership and governance likely complicate clustering methods	Develop ideal types using fuzzy set analysis, which is more flexible when identifying groupings	(Bell, Filatotchev, and Aguilera, 2014)

ambidexterity changes over time in a longitudinal sample of family firms drawn from the S&P 500. Using random coefficient modeling, the authors model time explicitly, considering both continuous and discontinuous forms of change in ambidexterity. In Table 28.4, we highlight several common challenges associated with entrepreneurship and small business research as well as possible research designs that overcome these challenges.

CONCLUSION

Identifying the causal antecedents of entrepreneurial firm performance lies at the heart of entrepreneurship and small business research. To build a better understanding of the nature of the corporate entrepreneurship–performance relationship, increased attention to establishing temporal precedence and eliminating alternative explanations is needed. It is our hope that scholars use the findings and guidelines presented here to build stronger cases for causality in entrepreneurship research, both in corporate entrepreneurship

research and beyond. Ideally, a future review conducted after the next 66 articles are published on the corporate entrepreneurship–performance relationship will find that scholars' quantitative methods provide the basis for greatly improved confidence in the causal nature of studies' findings.

REFERENCES

Aguinis, H., Pierce, C.A., Bosco, F.A., and Muslin, I.S. (2009) 'First decade of Organizational Research Methods: Trends in design, measurement, and data analysis topics', *Organizational Research Methods*, 12(1): 69–112.

Ahn, W.K., Kalish, C.W., Medin, D.L., and Gelman, S.A. (1995) 'The role of covariation versus mechanism information in causal attribution', *Cognition*, 54(3): 299–352.

Ahuja, G. and Lampert, C.M. (2001) 'Entrepreneurship in the large corporation: A longitudinal study of how established firms create breakthrough inventions', *Strategic Management Journal*, 22(6–7): 521–43.

Allen, S.A. and Hevert, K.T. (2007) 'Venture capital investing by information technology companies: Did it pay?', *Journal of Business Venturing*, 22(2): 262–82.

Allison, T.H., McKenny, A.F., and Short, J.C. (2013) 'The effect of entrepreneurial rhetoric on microlending investment: An examination of the warm-glow effect', *Journal of Business Venturing*, 28(6): 690–707.

Allison, T.H., McKenny, A.F., and Short, J.C. (2014) 'Integrating time into family business research: Using random coefficient modeling to examine temporal influences on family firm ambidexterity', *Family Business Review*, 27(1): 20–34.

Anderson, B.S. and Eshima, Y. (2011) 'The influence of firm age and intangible resources on the relationship between entrepreneurial orientation and firm growth among Japanese SMEs', *Journal of Business Venturing*, doi: 10.1016/j.jbusvent.2011.10.001.

Antonakis, J., Bendahan, S., Jacquart, P., and Lalive, R. (2010) 'On making causal claims: A review and recommendations', *The Leadership Quarterly*, 21(6): 1086–120.

Antonakis, J., Bendahan, S., Jacquart, P., and Lalive, R. (2012) 'Causality and endogeneity: Problems and solutions', in D.V. Day (ed.), *The Oxford Handbook of Leadership and Organizations*. New York: Oxford University Press. pp.93–117.

Antoncic, B. and Hisrich, R.D. (2001) 'Intrapreneurship: Construct refinement and cross-cultural validation', *Journal of Business Venturing*, 16(5): 495–527.

Atinc, G., Simmering, M.J., and Kroll, M.J. (2012) 'Control variable use and reporting in macro and micro management research', *Organizational Research Methods*, 15(1): 57–74.

Barnett, W.P., Mischke, G.A., and Ocasio, W. (2000) 'The evolution of collective strategies among organizations', *Organization Studies*, 21(2): 325–54.

Barrett, H. and Weinstein, A. (1998) 'The effect of market orientation and organizational flexibility on corporate entrepreneurship', *Entrepreneurship Theory and Practice*, 23(1): 57–70.

Barthélemy, J. (2008) 'Opportunism, knowledge, and the performance of franchise chains', *Strategic Management Journal*, 29: 1451–63.

Bartholomew, S. and Smith, A.D. (2006) 'Improving survey response rates from chief executive officers in small firms: The importance of social networks', *Entrepreneurship: Theory and Practice*, 30(1): 83–96.

Baysinger, B.D. and Butler, H.N. (1985) 'Corporate governance and the board of directors: Performance effects of changes in board composition', *Journal of Law, Economics, & Organization*, 1(1): 101–24.

Becherer, R.C. and Maurer, J.G. (1997) 'The moderating effect of environmental variables on the entrepreneurial and marketing orientation of entrepreneur-led firms', *Entrepreneurship Theory and Practice*, 22(1): 47–58.

Becker, T.E. (2005) 'Potential problems in the statistical control of variables in organizational research: A qualitative analysis with recommendations', *Organizational Research Methods*, 8(3): 274–89.

Bell, R.G., Filatotchev, I., and Aguilera, R.V. (2014) 'Corporate governance and investors' perceptions of foreign IPO value: An institutional perspective', *Academy of Management Journal*, 57(1): 301–20.

Benson, D. and Ziedonis, R.H. (2009) 'Corporate venture capital as a window on new technologies: Implications for the performance of corporate investors when acquiring startups', *Organization Science*, 20(2): 329–51.

Bergh, D.D., Hanke, R., Balkundi, P., Brown, M., and Chen, X. (2004) 'An assessment of research designs in strategic management research: The frequency of threats to internal validity', in D.J. Ketchen and D.D. Bergh (eds.), *Research Methodology in Strategy and Management*. Oxford: Elsevier. pp.349–71.

Bergh, D.D. and Holbein, G.F. (1997) 'Assessment and redirection of longitudinal analysis demonstration with a study of the diversification and divestiture relationship', *Strategic Management Journal*, 18(7): 557–71.

Bierly, P.E. and Daly, P.S. (2007) 'Alternative knowledge strategies, competitive environment, and organizational performance in small manufacturing firms', *Entrepreneurship Theory and Practice*, 31(4): 493–516.

Biggadike, R. (1979) 'The risky business of diversification', *Harvard Business Review*, 57(3): 103–11.

Black, M. (1956) 'Why cannot an effect precede its cause?' *Analysis*, 16(3): 49–58.

Blalock, H.M. (1964) *Causal Inferences in Nonexperimental Research*. New York: WW Norton.

Bliese, P.D., Chan, D., and Ployhart, R.E. (2007) 'Multilevel methods: Future directions in measurement, longitudinal analyses, and nonnormal outcomes', *Organizational Research Methods*, 10(4): 551–63.

Bradley, S.W., Wiklund, J., and Shepherd, D.A. (2011) 'Swinging a double-edged sword: The effect of slack on entrepreneurial management and growth', *Journal of Business Venturing*, 26(5): 537–54.

Breaugh, J.A. (2008) 'Important considerations in using statistical procedures to control for nuisance variables in non-experimental studies', *Human Resource Management Review*, 18(4): 282–93.

Brett, M.T. (2004) 'When is a correlation between non-independent variables "spurious"?' *Oikos*, 105(3): 647–56.

Bruneel, J., Van de Velde, E., and Clarysse, B. (2013) 'Impact of the type of corporate spin-off on growth', *Entrepreneurship Theory and Practice*, 37(4): 943–59.

Burgelman, R.A. (1983) 'A process model of internal corporate venturing in the diversified major firm', *Administrative Science Quarterly*, 28(2): 223–44.

Chandler, G.N., Keller, C., and Lyon, D.W. (2000) 'Unraveling the determinants and consequences of an innovation-supportive organizational culture', *Entrepreneurship Theory and Practice*, 25(1): 59–76.

Chirico, F., Sirmon, D.G., Sciascia, S., and Mazzola, P. (2011) 'Resource orchestration in family firms: Investigating how entrepreneurial orientation, generational involvement, and participative strategy affect performance', *Strategic Entrepreneurship Journal,* 5(4): 307–26.

Clarkin, J.E. (2008) 'Channel changes: An examination of ownership change in franchise firms', *Journal of Marketing Channels,* 15(1): 23–41.

Cohen, J. (1992) 'A power primer', *Psychological Bulletin,* 112(1): 155–9.

Colquitt, J.A. (2008) 'From the editors: Publishing laboratory research in AMJ: A question of when, not if', *Academy of Management Journal,* 51(4): 616–20.

Combs, J.G. and Ketchen, D.J. (1999) 'Can capital scarcity help agency theory explain franchising? Revisiting the capital scarcity hypothesis', *Academy of Management Journal,* 42(2): 196–207.

Cook, T.D. and Campbell, D.T. (1979) *Quasi-Experimentation: Design & Analysis Issues for Field Settings.* Boston, MA: Houghton Mifflin.

Coombes, S.M., Morris, M.H., Allen, J.A., and Webb, J.W. (2011) 'Behavioural orientations of non-profit boards as a factor in entrepreneurial performance: Does governance matter?', *Journal of Management Studies,* 48(4): 829–56.

Cote, J.A. and Buckley, M.R. (1988) 'Measurement error and theory testing in consumer research: An illustration of the importance of construct validation', *Journal of Consumer Research,* 14(4): 579–82.

Covin, J.G., Green, K.M., and Slevin, D.P. (2006) 'Strategic process effects on the entrepreneurial orientation -sales growth rate relationship', *Entrepreneurship Theory and Practice,* 30(1): 57–81.

Covin, J.G. and Slevin, D.P. (1989) 'Strategic management of small firms in hostile and benign environments', *Strategic Management Journal,* 10(1): 75–87.

Covin, J.G. and Slevin, D.P. (1991) 'A conceptual model of entrepreneurship as firm behavior', *Entrepreneurship: Theory & Practice,* 16(1): 7–24.

Covin, J.G., Slevin, D.P., and Heeley, M.B. (2000) 'Pioneers and followers: Competitive tactics, environment, and firm growth', *Journal of Business Venturing,* 15(2): 175–210.

Crook, T.R., Shook, C.L., Morris, M.L., and Madden, T.M. (2010) 'Are we there yet?: An assessment of research design and construct measurement practices in entrepreneurship research', *Organizational Research Methods,* 13(1): 192–206.

Danneels, E. (2012) 'Second-order competences and Schumpeterian rents', *Strategic Entrepreneurship Journal,* 6(1): 42–58.

Davidson, R. and MacKinnon, J.G. (1993) *Estimation and Inference in Econometrics.* New York: Oxford University Press.

De Clercq, D., Dimov, D., and Thongpapanl, N.T. (2010) 'The moderating impact of internal social exchange processes on the entrepreneurial orientation -performance relationship', *Journal of Business Venturing,* 25(1): 87–103.

Dean, M.A., Shook, C.L., and Payne, G.T. (2007) 'The past, present, and future of entrepreneurship research: Data analytic trends and training', *Entrepreneurship: Theory & Practice,* 31(4): 601–18.

DeVellis, R.F. (2012) *Scale Development: Theory and Applications.* 3rd ed. Thousand Oaks, CA: Sage.

Dushnitsky, G. and Lenox, M.J. (2006) 'When does corporate venture capital investment create firm value?', *Journal of Business Venturing,* 21(6): 753–72.

Dushnitsky, G. and Shapira, Z. (2010) 'Entrepreneurial finance meets organizational reality: Comparing investment practices and performance of corporate and independent venture capitalists', *Strategic Management Journal,* 31(9): 990–1017.

Echambadi, R., Campbell, B., and Agarwal, R. (2006) 'Encouraging best practice in quantitative management research: An incomplete list of opportunities', *Journal of Management Studies,* 43(8): 1801–20.

Foo, M.D., Uy, M.A., and Baron, R.A. (2009) 'How do feelings influence effort? An empirical study of entrepreneurs' affect and venture effort', *Journal of Applied Psychology,* 94(4): 1086–94.

Fromkin, H.L. and Streufert, S. (1976) 'Laboratory experimentation', in M.D. Dunnette (ed.), *Handbook of Industrial and Organization Psychology.* Chicago, IL: Rand McNally. pp.415–65.

Hair, J.H., Black, W.C., Babin, B.J., and Anderson, R.E. (2010) *Multivariate Data Analysis.* 7th ed. Upper Saddle River, NJ: Prentice Hall.

Hamilton, B.H. and Nickerson, J.A. (2003) 'Correcting for endogeneity in strategic management research', *Strategic Organization,* 1(1): 51–78.

Hillman, A.J. and Keim, G.D. (2001) 'Shareholder value, stakeholder management, and social issues: What's the bottom line?' *Strategic Management Journal,* 22(2): 125–39.

Hill, S.A. and Birkinshaw, J. (2008) 'Strategy -organization configurations in corporate venture units: Impact on performance and survival', *Journal of Business Venturing,* 23(4): 423–44.

Hill, S.A., Maula, M.V., Birkinshaw, J.M., and Murray, G.C. (2009) 'Transferability of the venture capital model to the corporate context: Implications for the performance of corporate venture units', *Strategic Entrepreneurship Journal,* 3(1): 3–27.

Hinkin, T.R. (1998) 'A brief tutorial on the development of measures for use in survey questionnaires', *Organizational Research Methods,* 1(1): 104–21.

Hitt, M.A., Ireland, R.D., Camp, S.M., and Sexton, D.L. (2001) 'Strategic entrepreneurship: Entrepreneurial strategies for wealth creation', *Strategic Management Journal,* 22(6–7): 479–91.

Hitt, M.A., Nixon, R.D., Hoskisson, R.E., and Kochhard, R. (1999) 'Corporate entrepreneurship and cross-functional fertilization: Activation, process and disintegration of a new product design team', *Entrepreneurship Theory and Practice,* 23(3): 145–67.

Keats, B.W. (1990) 'Diversification and business economic performance revisited: Issues of measurement and causality', *Journal of Management,* 16(1): 61–72.

Keh, H.T., Nguyen, T.T.M., and Ng, H.P. (2007) 'The effects of entrepreneurial orientation and marketing information on the performance of SMEs', *Journal of Business Venturing,* 22(4): 592–611.

Keil, T., Maula, M., Schildt, H., and Zahra, S.A. (2008) 'The effect of governance modes and relatedness of external business development activities on innovative performance', *Strategic Management Journal,* 29(8): 895–907.

Kerlinger, F.N. and Lee, H.B. (2000) *Foundations of Behavioral Research.* 4th ed. Orlando, FL: Harcourt.

Ketchen, D.J., Boyd, B.K., and Bergh, D.D. (2008) 'Research methodology in strategic management: Past accomplishments and future challenges', *Organizational Research Methods,* 11(4): 643–58.

Kollmann, T. and Stöckmann, C. (2014) 'Filling the entrepreneurial orientation -performance gap: The mediating effects of exploratory and exploitative innovations', *Entrepreneurship Theory and Practice,* 38(5): 1001–26.

Kotha, S. and Nair, A. (2007) 'Strategy and environment as determinants of firm performance: Evidence from the Japanese machine tool industry', *Strategic Management Journal,* 16(7): 497–518.

Lee, C., Lee, K., and Pennings, J.M. (2001) 'Internal capabilities, external networks, and performance: A study on technology-based ventures', *Strategic Management Journal,* 22(6–7): 615–40.

Levitas, E. and Chi, T. (2010) 'A look at the value creation effects of patenting and capital investment through a real options lens: The moderating role of uncertainty', *Strategic Entrepreneurship Journal,* 4(3): 212–33.

Li, Y., Wei,Z., and Liu, Y. (2010) 'Strategic orientations, knowledge acquisition, and firm performance: The perspective of the vendor in cross-border outsourcing', *Journal of Management Studies,* 47(8): 1457–82.

Liang, K. and Zeger, S.L. (1986) 'Longitudinal data analysis using generalized linear models', *Biometrika,* 73(1): 13–22.

Lichtenthaler, U. (2012) 'Technological turbulence and the impact of exploration and exploitation within and across organizations on product development performance', *Entrepreneurship Theory and Practice.* Doi: 10.1111/j.1540-6520.2012.00520.x.

Lin, S.J. and Lee, J.R. (2011) 'Configuring a corporate venturing portfolio to create growth value: Within-portfolio diversity and strategic linkage', *Journal of Business Venturing,* 26(4): 489–503.

Low, M.B. and MacMillan, I.C. (1988) 'Entrepreneurship: Past research and future challenges', *Journal of Management,* 14(2): 139–61.

Lu, J.W. and Beamish, P.W. (2001) 'The internationalization and performance of SMEs', *Strategic Management Journal,* 22(6–7): 565–86.

Lumpkin, G.T. and Dess, G.G. (2001) 'Linking two dimensions of entrepreneurial orientation to firm performance: The moderating role of environment and industry life cycle', *Journal of Business Venturing,* 16(5): 429–51.

MacMillan, I.C. and Day, D.L. (1987) 'Corporate ventures into industrial markets: Dynamics of aggressive entry', *Journal of Business Venturing,* 2(1): 29–39.

Marino, L., Strandholm, K., Steensma, H.K., and Weaver, K.M. (2002) 'The moderating effect of national culture on the relationship between entrepreneurial orientation and strategic alliance portfolio extensiveness', *Entrepreneurship Theory and Practice,* 26(4): 145–60.

McCaffrey, M. (2014) 'On the theory of entrepreneurial incentives and alertness', *Entrepreneurship: Theory & Practice,* 38(4): 891–911.

McGahan, A.M. and Porter, M.E. (2002) 'What do we know about variance in accounting profitability?' *Management Science,* 48(7): 834–51.

McKenny, A.F., Short, J.C., and Payne, G.T. (2013) 'Using CATA to elevate constructs in organizational research: Validating an organizational-level measure of psychological capital', *Organizational Research Methods,* 16(1): 152–84.

McKenny, A.F., Short, J.C., Zachary, M.A., and Payne, G.T. (2012) 'Assessing espoused goals in private family firms using content analysis', *Family Business Review,* 25(3): 298–317.

Meehl, P.E. (1990) 'Why summaries of research on psychological theories are often uninterpretable', *Psychological Reports,* 66(1): 195–244.

Mill, John S. (1843) *A System of Logic, Ratiocinative and Inductive.* London: Longmans, Green and Co.

Miller, D. and Le Breton-Miller, I. (2011) 'Governance, social identity, and entrepreneurial orientation in closely held public companies', *Entrepreneurship Theory and Practice,* 35(5): 1051–76.

Moreno, A.M. and Casillas, J.C. (2008) 'Entrepreneurial orientation and growth of SMEs: A causal model', *Entrepreneurship Theory and Practice,* 32(3): 507–28.

Moss, T.W., Short, J.C., Payne, G.T., and Lumpkin, G.T. (2011) 'Dual identities in social ventures: An exploratory study', *Entrepreneurship Theory and Practice,* 35(4): 805–30.

Naser, K., Karbhari, Y., and Mokhtar, M.Z. (2004) 'Impact of the ISO 9000 registration on company performance: Evidence from Malaysia', *Managerial Auditing Journal,* 19(4): 509–16.

Nunnally, J.C. and Bernstein, I.H. (1994) *Psychometric Theory.* 3rd ed. New York: McGraw-Hill.

Orlitzky, M. (2012) 'How can significance testing be deinstitutionalized?' *Organizational Research Methods,* 15(2): 199–288.

Paauwe, J. (2009) 'HRM and performance: Achievements, methodological issues and prospects', *Journal of Management Studies,* 46(1): 129–42.

Park, S.H. and Kim, D. (1997) 'Market valuation of joint ventures: Joint venture characteristics and wealth gains', *Journal of Business Venturing*, 12(2): 83–108.

Park, H.D. and Steensma, H.K. (2012) 'When does corporate venture capital add value for new ventures?', *Strategic Management Journal*, 33(1): 1–22.

Patel, P.C. and Fiet, J.O. (2010) 'Enhancing the internal validity of entrepreneurship experiments by assessing treatment effects at multiple levels across multiple trials', *Journal of Economic Behavior & Organization*, 76(1): 127–40.

Pearce, J.A., Fritz, D.A., and Davis, P.S. (2010) 'Entrepreneurial orientation and the performance of religious congregations as predicted by rational choice theory', *Entrepreneurship Theory and Practice*, 34(1): 219–48.

Pearl, J. (2000) *Causality: Models, Reasoning, and Inference*. Cambridge: Cambridge University Press.

Pedhazur, E.J. and Schmelkin, L.P. (1991) *Measurement, Design, and Analysis: An Integrated Approach*. Hillsdale, NJ: Lawrence Erlbaum.

Peloza, J. (2009) 'The challenge of measuring financial impacts from investments in corporate social performance', *Journal of Management*, 35(6): 1518–41.

Pinchot, G. (1985) *Intrapreneurship*. New York: Harper and Row.

Priem, R.L. and Butler, J.E. (2001) 'Is the resource-based "view" a useful perspective for strategic management research?' *Academy of Management Review*, 26(1): 22–40.

Rauch, A., Wiklund, J., Lumpkin, G.T., and Frese, M. (2009) 'Entrepreneurial orientation and business performance: An assessment of past research and suggestions for the future', *Entrepreneurship: Theory & Practice*, 33(3): 761–87.

Raudenbush, S., Bryk, A., Cheong, Y.F., and Congdon, R. (2000) *HLM 5: Hierarchical Linear and Nonlinear Modeling*. Chicago, IL: Scientific Software International.

Richard, O.C., Barnett, T., Dwyer, S., and Chadwick, K. (2004) 'Cultural diversity in management, firm performance, and the moderating role of entrepreneurial orientation dimensions', *Academy of Management Journal*, 47(2): 255–66.

Scandura, T.A. and Williams, E.A. (2000) 'Research methodology in management: Current practices, trends, and implications for future research', *Academy of Management Journal*, 43(6): 1248–64.

Scheaffer, R.L., Mendenhall, W., and Ott, R.L. (1996) *Elementary Survey Sampling*. 5th ed. New York: Duxbury Press.

Schwab, D.P. (2005) *Research Methods for Organizational Studies*. 2nd ed. Mahwah, NJ: Lawrence Erlbaum.

Sheehan, M. (2014) 'Human resource management and performance: Evidence from small and medium-sized firms', *International Small Business Journal*, 32(5): 545–70.

Shook, C.L., Ketchen, D.J., Hult, G.T.M., and Kacmar, K.M. (2004) 'An assessment of the use of structural equation modeling in strategic management

research', *Strategic Management Journal*, 25(4): 397–404.

Short, J.C., Broberg, J.C., Cogliser, C.C., and Brigham, K. (2010) 'Construct validation using computer-aided text analysis (CATA): An illustration using entrepreneurial orientation', *Organizational Research Methods*, 13(2): 320–47.

Short, J.C., Ketchen, D.J., Bennett, N., and Du Toit, M. (2006) 'An examination of firm, industry, and time effects on performance using random coefficients modeling', *Organizational Research Methods*, 9(3): 259–84.

Short, J.C., Ketchen, D.J., Combs, J.G., and Ireland, R.D. (2010) 'Research methods in entrepreneurship: Opportunities and challenges', *Journal of Management*, 13(1): 6–15.

Short, J.C., Ketchen, D.J., and Palmer, T.B. (2002) 'The role of sampling in strategic management research on performance: A two-study analysis', *Journal of Management*, 28(3): 363–85.

Short, J.C., Ketchen, D.J., Shook, C.L., and Ireland, R.D. (2010) 'The concept of "opportunity" in entrepreneurship research: Past accomplishments and future challenges', *Journal of Management*, 36(1): 40–65.

Short, J.C., McKelvie, A., Ketchen, D.J., and Chandler, G.N. (2009) 'Firm and industry effects on firm performance: A generalization and extension for new ventures', *Strategic Entrepreneurship Journal*, 3(1): 47–65.

Shortell, S.M. and Zajac, E.J. (1988) 'Internal corporate joint ventures: Development processes and performance outcomes', *Strategic Management Journal*, 9(6): 527–42.

Shrader, R.C. and Simon, M. (1997) 'Corporate versus independent new ventures: Resource, strategy, and performance differences', *Journal of Business Venturing*, 12(1): 47–66.

Simon, H.A. (1954) 'Spurious correlation: A causal interpretation', *Journal of the American Statistical Association*, 49(267): 467–79.

Simsek, Z. and Heavey, C. (2011) 'The mediating role of knowledge-based capital for corporate entrepreneurship effects on performance: A study of small-to medium-sized firms', *Strategic Entrepreneurship Journal*, 5(1): 81–100.

Sirén, C.A., Kohtamäki, M., and Kuckertz, A. (2012) 'Exploration and exploitation strategies, profit performance, and the mediating role of strategic learning: Escaping the exploitation trap', *Strategic Entrepreneurship Journal*, 6(1): 18–41.

Sorrentino, M. and Williams, M.L. (1995) 'Relatedness and corporate venturing: Does it really matter?', *Journal of Business Venturing*, 10(1): 59–73.

Spector, P.E. and Brannick, M.T. (2011) 'Mythological urban legends: The misuse of statistical control variables', *Organizational Research Methods*, 14(2): 287–305.

Srinivasan, R. (2006) 'Dual distribution and intangible firm value: Franchising in restaurant chains', *Journal of Marketing*, 70(1): 120–35.

Stam, W. and Elfring, T. (2008) 'Entrepreneurial orientation and new venture performance: The moderating role of intra- and extraindustry social capital', *Academy of Management Journal,* 51(1): 97–111.

Steffens, P., Davidsson, P., and Fitzsimmons, J. (2009) 'Performance configurations over time: Implications for growth-and profit-oriented strategies', *Entrepreneurship Theory and Practice*, 33(1): 125–48.

Stinchcombe, A.L. (1968) *Constructing Social Theories*. New York: Harcourt, Brace and World.

Sykes, H.B. (1986) 'The anatomy of a corporate venturing program: Factors influencing success', *Journal of Business Venturing*, 1(3): 275–93.

Tang, J., Tang, Z., Marino, L.D., Zhang, Y., and Li, Q. (2008) 'Exploring an inverted U-Shape relationship between entrepreneurial orientation and performance in Chinese ventures', *Entrepreneurship Theory and Practice*, 32(1): 219–39.

Thornhill, S. and Amit, R. (2001) 'A dynamic perspective of internal fit in corporate venturing', *Journal of Business Venturing*, 16(1): 25–50.

Tversky, A. and Kahneman, D. (1971) 'Belief in the law of small numbers', *Psychological Bulletin,* 76(2): 105–10.

Uy, M.A., Foo, M.D., and Aguinis, H. (2010) 'Using experience sampling methodology to advance entrepreneurship theory and research', *Organizational Research Methods*, 13(1): 31–54.

Van de Ven, A.H. (2007) *Engaged Scholarship*. Oxford: Oxford University Press.

Van de Ven, A.H. and Huber, G.P. (1990) 'Longitudinal field research methods for studying processes of organizational change', *Organization Science,* 1(3): 213–19.

Wales, W.J., Parida, V., and Patel, P.C. (2013) 'Too much of a good thing? Absorptive capacity, firm performance, and the moderating role of entrepreneurial orientation', *Strategic Management Journal*, 34(5): 622–33.

Walter, A., Auer, M., and Ritter, T. (2006) 'The impact of network capabilities and entrepreneurial orientation on university spin-off performance', *Journal of Business Venturing,* 21(4): 541–67.

Wang, C.L. (2008) 'Entrepreneurial orientation, learning orientation, and firm performance', *Entrepreneurship Theory and Practice*, 32(4): 635–57.

Wiklund, J. (1999) 'The sustainability of the entrepreneurial orientation -performance relationship', *Entrepreneurship Theory and Practice*, 24(1): 37–48.

Wiklund, J. and Shepherd, D. (2003) 'Knowledge-based resources, entrepreneurial orientation, and the performance of small and medium-sized businesses', *Strategic Management Journal*, 24(13): 1307–14.

Wiklund, J. and Shepherd, D. (2005) 'Entrepreneurial orientation and small business performance: A configurational approach', *Journal of Business Venturing*, 20(1): 71–91.

Wiklund, J. and Shepherd, D.A. (2011) 'Where to from here? EO-as-experimentation, failure, and distribution of outcomes', *Entrepreneurship Theory and Practice*, 35(5): 925–46.

Yiu, D.W. and Lau, C.M. (2008) 'Corporate entrepreneurship as resource capital configuration in emerging market firms', *Entrepreneurship Theory and Practice*, 32(1): 37–57.

Yin, X. and Zajac, E.J. (2004) 'The strategy/governance structure fit relationship: Theory and evidence in franchising arrangements', *Strategic Management Journal,* 25(4): 365–83.

Zahra, S.A. (1991) 'Predictors and financial outcomes of corporate entrepreneurship: An exploratory study', *Journal of Business Venturing*, 6(4): 259–85.

Zahra, S.A. (1993) 'Environment, corporate entrepreneurship, and financial performance: A taxonomic approach', *Journal of Business Venturing*, 8(4): 319–40.

Zahra, S.A. (1995) 'Corporate entrepreneurship and financial performance: The case of management leveraged buyouts', *Journal of Business Venturing*, 10(3): 225–47.

Zahra, S.A. and Covin, J.G. (1995) 'Contextual influences on the corporate entrepreneurship-performance relationship: A longitudinal analysis', *Journal of Business Venturing,* 10(1): 43–58.

Zahra, S.A. and Garvis, D.M. (2000) 'International corporate entrepreneurship and firm performance: The moderating effect of international environmental hostility', *Journal of Business Venturing*, 15(5): 469–92.

Zahra, S.A., Neubaum, D.O., and El-Hagrassey, G.M. (2002) 'Competitive analysis and new venture performance: Understanding the impact of strategic uncertainty and venture origin', *Entrepreneurship Theory and Practice*, 27(1): 1–28.

Zahra, S.A., Neubaum, D.O., and Huse, M. (2000) 'Entrepreneurship in medium-size companies: Exploring the effects of ownership and governance systems', *Journal of Management,* 26(5): 947–76.

Zhao, Y., Li, Y., Lee, S.H., and Chen, L.B. (2011) 'Entrepreneurial orientation, organizational learning, and performance: Evidence from China', *Entrepreneurship Theory and Practice*, 35(2): 293–317.

29

Qualitative Research in Entrepreneurship

Anne Kovalainen

INTRODUCTION

In the last ten years, qualitative methods have become one of the mainstream methods used in much of entrepreneurship research (e.g. Shepherd, 2015). The use of qualitative methods is growing, but is it diversifying in the ways the method selection within qualitative research makes possible? How qualitative research and its methods are used is not uniform, even within a single, uniting topic in entrepreneurship research. The adaptations of qualitative research methods to the subject field of entrepreneurship vary considerably. This chapter will, for its part, try to explain the reasons for the great variation within the field – and ask whether any unity is actually desirable. The aim is not to take examples of all qualitative research methods used in entrepreneurship but rather to explore the topic more widely.

Furthermore, the chapter will discuss the meanings given to qualitative research, the methods used and implemented, the analyses obtained and the overall content of qualitative research, with the focus on entrepreneurship studies all the while. The field of entrepreneurship research is wide, so this chapter will be delimited to more general aspects in the use of the methods. Furthermore, I will point out some of the strengths and pitfalls of using qualitative research strategy and qualitative research methods, as well as the strengths of qualitative research in excavating the issues in and around entrepreneurship. The chapter has two main goals: to provide the readers an overview of the variety of different methods and make them cognisant of the basic tenets of those methods.

The topic itself, *qualitative research in entrepreneurship*, would require a book instead of a short review, as qualitative research is not one thing, nor is qualitative method one method, but a family of many qualitative methods and qualitative research approaches. This *Handbook* in general aims for a comprehensive view but in reality it can only compile key elements. Therefore, only some insights into the multiple uses of qualitative methods can be given. In order for the coverage to be fair, further references to books and papers published in the field will be made.

In the chapter, I will use the term 'qualitative research strategy' as an umbrella concept to cover the whole variety of *qualitative methods*. In research methodology literature, 'method' most often implies a research 'tool', such as interviewing, document reading or observing. What makes qualitative research so interesting is that qualitative research uses a variety of methods, e.g. in case studies, and that the use of the method is never a singular adaptation: there are several ways of using one method as a research tool and several ways of combining different methods in one study or research project, for example. Hence, it is not only the variety of methods that brings in variety, but also that one single method can be used in a very different way in qualitative research. And all this leads to the importance of a research strategy. As a term, 'methodology' widens the conceptual category of 'qualitative method': in the literature, methodology refers both to the particular method and to the theoretical framework that informs the use of a particular method. *Qualitative research repertoires* can thus accommodate several types of research strategy and a great variety of specific methods and techniques.

KEY POINTS OF DEPARTURE FOR QUALITATIVE ENTREPRENEURSHIP RESEARCH

As a general research approach or strategy, qualitative research is often closely aligned with specific epistemological and ontological assumptions made in the research and/or in the disciplinary field. These relations are not fixed or predetermined. Common to research employing qualitative methods is that the central ideas guiding research differ usually, but not always, from those in quantitative research. This chapter, when canvassing the

qualitative methods in entrepreneurship, opens up and straightens some misconceptions often related to qualitative research and through this contributes to the discussion on the role, position and possibilities of qualitative research methods in entrepreneurship research. The questions of how to choose the 'right kind' of research method or approach, and how to decide for or against a specific method or approach related to the topic, will be discussed briefly in the following. The chapter will also briefly valorise the general evaluation criteria for qualitative research in entrepreneurship.

Qualitative research settings – irrespective of the disciplinary field in question – usually operate without preset modelling on variables and their mutual correlational or causal relationships. The qualitative research setting can of course use pre-formulated theoretical propositions and follow a coding system of materials based on propositions in the analysis (e.g. Yin, 2014). An inductively oriented research strategy allows variation in the analysis. The way qualitative research works its way through the empirical material in research is not usually via preset and precise existing models and connections between variables. Therefore, as a result of research, totally new types of connection and outcome may come forward in empirical analysis.

David Silverman notes that qualitative research often seeks generalisations about *processes* (Silverman, 2014). Qualitative research does not necessarily relate to unified theoretical and methodological conceptual frameworks: a variety of different theories, methods and methodological thinking are indeed possible within qualitative research. The methods may vary, and so also does the philosophical thinking connected to qualitative research methods. The linkages between theory–method–empirical material–analysis and results are built on a different understanding of knowledge creation than in positivist research. This understanding of the new knowledge creation in qualitative research is not without tensions: for some, qualitative research serves as a springboard for 'proper' research, while for others it serves both as the means and the end of the research. The difference in the orientation to knowledge may explain the rather problematic questions of emphasising the number, such as of 'how many cases' or 'how many interviews' are enough to answer adequately the research question. The answer should be based on the research design and research question and not on numerical quantities. Also, the spectre of qualitative methods and the variation in the ways one specific qualitative method is being used in the entrepreneurship research explain why it is not possible to achieve a single unified method and its unequivocal relation to disciplinary knowledge.

Much of the literature in entrepreneurship aims to contribute to a theory of entrepreneurship, or even to establish one, through empirical 'evidence' (e.g. Suddaby, Bruton & Si, 2015; Jännäri & Kovalainen, 2015), either by linking theories to observations through bridging principles or correspondence rules (hypothetico-deductive model, positivism, where deduction cannot tell us more than what is logically implied by the premises) or through reasoning from statements about the observed cases to statements about other, non-observed cases (inductive model, and different forms of induction, such as enumerative induction, abduction or probative induction). Even in the qualitative research of entrepreneurship, the reasoning from particularities aims to put forward a single encompassing theory, which is called 'indigenous', as recently proposed by Suddaby et al. (2015, p. 1).[1] If we take this to mean 'inherent' instead of 'indigenous', we can see that in this thinking, the relation between 'theory' and 'empirical world' is held constant and objectively defined, with the aim of 'better' or more informed disciplinary theory. However, if we are to accept that subjectivities and differing understandings of theories, concepts and empirics are inherently part of any research, as they are part of qualitative social research, entrepreneurship included, it

means that there also exists a wide difference in the ways of using data materials, theories and understanding the boundaries between theories. Such views seem to be growing in the studies of entrepreneurship.

Following on from this, instead of aiming for the one definition of the 'qualitative research' in any field of social science, entrepreneurship included, it makes more sense to use an inclusive definition covering the process of research, which for its part explains the commonalities and differences in definitions. The process of research includes the problem formulation, data gathering and the ways analysis is designed and implemented, as well as the interpretation of the data and results – these are all inherently part of qualitative research. Let us start with three commonalities.

Researchability is the first common feature for any research topic in qualitative research, prior to the method selection. The discursive turn in social sciences has transferred the traditional idea of a transparent, unmediated researchable object of study into a reflective, mediated and constructed object. The second feature common to most qualitative research is *reflexivity/interpretation*. Reflexivity/interpretation means in practice that the researcher does not – or should not – take the 'data', whether it is interviews, people's accounts, narratives or texts, at face value as a research result but reflect, interpret and rearrange it in the analysis. The third feature common to most qualitative research is the *circularity* of the research process. Circularity refers to the process of understanding and constructing a meaning in the interpretative process during research activities. The prior knowledge is interpreted by the researcher and in that process the knowledge can be modified and changed.

There is also the question of theories, not only in entrepreneurship but also in the social sciences in general. First of all, as entrepreneurship by nature looks at empirical constructions and facts, it is crucial to note that not all data relates to theoretical concepts in a similar way. This is where *research design* becomes crucial, as the research design should state the materials and, conceptual frame used and the relationships between the materials and concepts more explicitly. The wide array of methods which are all labelled as qualitative methods easily disguises the fact that different methods are characterised by and aligned with different epistemological knowledge claims, as well as different starting points and differing targets in the actual research. Within qualitative research, the different qualitative methods differ in their understanding of the object under study and more profoundly in their epistemological and ontological starting points and commitment (e.g. Poutanen & Kovalainen 2009; Flick, 2002).

PHILOSOPHY OF SCIENCE AND ENTREPRENEURSHIP RESEARCH – OPENING UP SOME MISCONCEPTIONS

How to define literature on entrepreneurship? Methods play a crucial role in the 'canonising' of any disciplinary field, entrepreneurship included. In this, the major journals play a crucial role. When looking at the entrepreneurship journals, a variety of topics can be found but is there a similar variety of research methods? Entrepreneurship literature seems to be rather united in the ways of using qualitative methods and diversified in the range of qualitative methods used. It is rather split in the ways of understanding knowledge formation and the implicit or explicit relationships between theories and knowledge formation (epistemic questions and even ontologies). How is this visible in the research on entrepreneurship?

In entrepreneurship literature, many types of argument concerning research methods and methodologies of entrepreneurship literature have been brought forward over the years, including the justified notions of the bias in the object of study, leading to biased or problematic

sampling techniques (e.g. Neergaard, 2007). The questions of the 'method' or 'methodology' ignore the question of 'research interest and topic selection': where do the topics and research interests arise for the research in entrepreneurship? How long do the enduring empirical objects remain 'intact' and to what extent does the knowledge then become part of the knowledge of society and the economy? As this would require proper and wider analysis than is possible within the realm of one chapter (e.g. Blackburn & Kovalainen, 2009), I focus here only on some methodological and method issues.

It has been argued that the vast majority of entrepreneurship literature does not explicate its epistemic, ontological and, even less so, ideological assumptions. This claim carries an interesting point in itself. The failure to explicate this relationship – the epistemic, ontological or ideological relationship of an individual research project – is then said to be the reason the research is dominant (Lindgren & Packendorff, 2009; Hlady-Rispal & Jouison-Laffitte, 2014). Furthermore, based on the Bourdieuan theory of reflexivity (1999), it has been suggested that a researcher should break her or his own presuppositions on ontology, epistemology and methodology (Tatli, Vassilopoulou, Özbilgin, Forson & Slutskaya, 2014, p. 627) in order to become more pluralistic in research methodology. Entrepreneurship research is argued on the one hand to be 'multi-paradigmatic' but on the other to be 'lacking methodological diversity' (Karatas-Ozkan, Anderson, Fayolle, Howells & Condor, 2014). Canonising the research field and its methods uses rhetorical devices, such as talking about disciplinary development as linear development and stating that it is slow, 'slower-than-it-needs-to-be development of our field' (Davidsson, 2016, p. 300).

As a remedy to this 'epistemic blindness', some authors have recommended that after choosing the research question(s), the researcher 'chooses her or his ontological and epistemological stances and follows the method aligned with those knowledge assumptions' (Neergaard & Ulhoi, 2007, p. 436; Ahl, 2007). The argument extends further with more specific claims: 'we need to have editors and reviewers who *share our* epistemological and ontological *view of the world* and the processes that happen within it' (Neergaard & Ulhoi, 2007, p. 436).

Given the parade of differing, partly conflictual and partly unsubstantiated claims such as those above, one thing is clear: confusion reigns as to what to think about entrepreneurship research, its research topics, methodologies and connection to the philosophy of science. Epistemology and ontology have indeed become part of the vocabulary – almost a must – of all (qualitative) research in entrepreneurship, more so than one would assume given the empirical emphasis of the research. Ontologies and epistemologies are often presented as stable entities, something that a researcher 'chooses herself from the bookshelf of research philosophy', or alternatively can keep in the 'method toolbox' (Ahl, 2007).

From the philosophy of science and research methodology points of view, claims such as the ones above are based on rigid conceptualisations and normative assumptions of relations between concepts. The above quotations show that understanding the epistemic and ontological questions in research can be problematic, as they assume the epistemology and ontology are exchangeable commodities. They are described as having a practical and interchangeable nature, or as qualities that can only be understood by those who share the same belief: 'the author shares with editors and reviewers [of the journal]' (Neergaard & Ulhoi, 2007, p. 3).

In other words, these ways of understanding the key concepts of the philosophy of science easily conflate the ideas of ontology and epistemology as narrow and commodified entities, which they are not. Furthermore, with such instructions, we need to ask the question: is it really possible for a researcher to pick and choose her or his ontological and epistemological stances? More importantly, we may ask, why in entrepreneurship research is it assumed

that epistemologies are commodities, clear-cut 'things', exposed to being 'picked up' as if they were apples? Another worry is the normativity of wishing to 'share the same view of the world'. Rather, should it not be about possessing adequate, up-to-date, robust and reliable knowledge of the method, methodology and philosophy in order to be able to act as competent editor and reviewer? We can ask if these claims reflect the underdeveloped theoretical field more generally.

Neither epistemolog(y)ies nor ontolog(y)ies are 'of choice' types of philosophical concept. Not only the methods and their use but also the theories and conceptual frames in research are embedded in epistemic and ontological presuppositions. For these reasons, but also more generally, the concepts of ontology and epistemology are not separate 'entities' to be chosen, replaceable units in the toolbox of the qualitative researcher, or detachable from the research questions, methods and theories. In fact, there are several epistemological assumptions and possibilities inscribed in the various research methods, in their adaptations and in the knowledge claims based on methods and methodologies. Postpositivism, constructionism, critical theory research and feminist research, to mention some epistemologies, all have commitments which vary within the inquiry in question: not all postpositivist research commits to critical realism, and not all constructionism commits to the co-creation of findings as its major epistemological stance. The implication drawn by such authors as Silverman (2014, p. 27) is that doing qualitative research should offer 'no protection from the rigorous, critical standards' that should be the concern of any research.

RESEARCH DESIGN AS AN INTEGRAL PART OF QUALITATIVE RESEARCH

The research method(s) are inherently part of the research design, but they do not necessarily dictate the formation of the disciplinary field, even if they do have an effect on the questions being asked and analysed. For example, Clifford Geertz notes that in research, knowledge is not a matter of formal methods or simply detailing the selection of interviews, note keeping and record taking. 'It is not these things, techniques and received procedures that define the enterprise' (of research) (Geertz, 2000, p. 214). For Geertz, research was first and foremost research on culture, but this notion can be extended to any qualitative research on society or economy: what is at the focus of research. Here the research settings (research strategy) and the aim of the research come into the play.

Operationalising theory is thus not a methodological dogma in qualitative research, but rather an understanding of the ways in which qualitative analysis amounts to a form of knowledge. In much qualitative research the analysis is about sorting out the structures and processes of signification. Some methods do this 'sorting out' more formally than others. It is generally held that qualitative methodologies have most to offer in terms of theory and model building, as opposed to theory testing, in the formalisation of research. In addition, the explorative aspect of qualitative research is equally crucial: no unified theory building needs to (or is even able to) follow.

Research based on the ideas of social constructionism challenges both the demand to have factual knowledge of the object of study before doing research, and the demand to develop theory based on empirical study. Through a close relation between the researcher and object of study, qualitative research is at its best able to offer a nuanced and complex view of the subject. This does not, however, mean that the researcher needs to be closely or intimately related to the field or topic of study, as some books on the qualitative method recommend (e.g. Stake, 1995, 2005). Doing qualitative research on unfamiliar or complex topics usually requires several research methods, an ethnographic approach, nuanced selection of repertoires for interpretation and a longitudinal research

plan in order to unfold the complexity or difficulty of the topic (e.g. Hobbs, 1988, 2011; Fadahunsi & Rosa, 2002; Bratu, 2012).

For the reasons described briefly above, qualitative research methods are not mere 'methods': at best they extend to the research design, to the topics explored and to the disciplinary field in general, as discussed in the following. Qualitative research and, more precisely, qualitative methods are not only attached to 'new research questions' (Shepherd, 2015, p. 503); more integrally, qualitative research should be seen as a way of analysing and revisiting 'old' research topics and questions anew. Through these revisits, qualitative research should be able to offer new interpretations and re-readings of the established research field and previous research results. Much of the macro-level empirical entrepreneurship research elaborates further the classical demand-and-supply approach to entrepreneurship (e.g. Acs & Szerb, 2009; Braunerhjelm, 2011) – for example, in relation to knowledge and innovation (Carlsson, 2011) – but these results have not yet been revisited or scrutinised through new qualitative research settings.

Research design includes planning for and decisions on the whole research process, from selecting the topic to planning the data gathering, analysing and writing. Research design usually also includes time planning for the project and the modes and ways of data collection, as well as the method choices available for the given topic. According to most qualitative research method books, ranging from Yin (2002) and Silverman (2014) to Eriksson and Kovalainen (2016), the planning through of the rough idea, the outlining of the plan and the organising of the structure of inquiry for fulfilling that plan are crucial parts of the qualitative research design. This matters for quantitative research as well. In some method books, the standard recommendation is indeed that any combination between qualitative and quantitative methods is possible and enriches the research. There are, however, differences in the ways most quantitative and major qualitative research methods relate to knowledge commitments. De Vaus (2001, p. 16) states that as the research design refers to the whole structure of an enquiry, the crucial choices and implementation decisions between qualitative and quantitative research methods are different and thus differentiate the methodological choices.

Owing to the philosophical and methodological connections of different methods and methodology, qualitative research allows changes and reformulations during the research process as well as in the data collection and analysis. In qualitative research, the methods can work simultaneously as both practical tools for the analysis of the empirical data and as frameworks for research setting and for engaging with empirical analysis. Even if the data gathering and data analysing processes can be distinguished from each other, they are often closely related and entangled in the actual research process. Research design is sometimes described as 'methodology' – for example, as in Fischer and Reuber's analysis of online entrepreneurial communication (2014). However, methodology seldom seems to enter the theoretical frame of the study in any serious manner.

In entrepreneurship studies, the research tradition stems from Austrian economics and economic sociology. Business studies have for their part been traditionally based on quantitative methods grounded along the positivist-science ideals and, as such, are not different from other social science disciplinary fields, such as sociology or education. According to some analyses, the heavy reliance on quantitative methods has meant qualitative research has failed 'to develop an indigenous theory' (Suddaby, 2014, p. 407) and, as a result, failed to generate 'a defining theoretical question' in its field (Suddaby et al., 2015). History shows that thinking only in terms of dichotomies (qual./quant.) is misleading and highly problematic, as polarities seldom touch the diversity, and the process of inquiry and thinking is not – or should not be – method-dependent (e.g. Hammersley, 1992).

Even if the burden of proof was not this high for qualitative research in entrepreneurship, there are other reasons for the diversity of the theory corpus and lack of 'indigenous theory of entrepreneurship'. It is true that qualitative research can and will be able to identify and reflect new conceptual categories and theoretical connections through openness to inductive reasoning irrespective of the epistemic or ontological commitments of the qualitative research as such. Thus, both constructivist and realist approaches can achieve new insights and bring in new theoretical approaches and concepts, but they can also fail to do so, irrespective of the qualitative nature of research.

KEY MAINSTREAM AND SOME OFF-THE-WALL RESEARCH METHODS IN ENTREPRENEURSHIP RESEARCH

Contemporary entrepreneurship research recognised the suitability of qualitative approaches a long time ago (e.g. Jennings, Edwards, Devereaux-Jennings & Delbridge, 2015; Baron, 2008; Blackburn & Kovalainen, 2009) – for example, when emphasising the importance of interactions of agencies, processes and malleable boundaries in the analysis. The theoretical tradition of Austrian economics and continental philosophical tradition that emphasised the Verstehen tradition have historically built a strong historical connection between entrepreneurship research and qualitative methods, even if this connection does not come up in contemporary research (Kovalainen, 1989, 1995, 1998). However, the adoption of qualitative research as a mainstream method in the disciplinary field is still to a large extent missing (e.g. Shane, 2012; Shane & Venkataraman, 2000) from entrepreneurship studies. Is it possible to identify the mainstream qualitative methods and approaches in entrepreneurship studies, keeping in mind that methods are not bound to a particular discipline, as well as the qualitative methods and approaches that are in the process of becoming the future mainstream?

In the following section, I will briefly discuss some key mainstream methods and take up some methods not so often used and which may open up new avenues for entrepreneurship research and theory construction. The only advice for the reader is that, as with any qualitative research, any definition of qualitative research methods needs to be explored within the complex historically built field of research traditions and method developments. Thus, simply, qualitative research means different things at different times. At its most general, I define any qualitative research as a situated activity that locates both the research and the researcher in some defined specific time, process, discourse or place.

THE CASE STUDY APPROACH IN ENTREPRENEURSHIP RESEARCH

Case study as a qualitatively oriented research approach has a long history in entrepreneurship studies (Eriksson & Kovalainen, 2016; van Maanen, 2011; Alvarez, Young & Woolley, 2015). The case study can indeed be regarded as a 'natural' and common approach for entrepreneurship research, where generally the aim is to analyse the creation, start-up, growth and change of a business as well as an entrepreneur's individual development. The case is an in-depth investigation that uses several sources, data and analyses. Cases can consist of an individual, a group, an organisation or an institution. Also, a restricted process can be analysed as a case. Historical in-depth single cases, such as the work by Alvarez et al. (2015) on entrepreneurial opportunity, can extend from a detailed single case description with multiplicity of data into a process-related theory.

When the aim in research is not verification of the deductive model but a more inductively built analysis, the case study most often covers several method choices. The case study is an excellent approach for

generating holistic and contextual knowledge through the use of multiple sources of data and multiple methods. Indeed, case studies should be seen more as a research approach or research strategy than a method (Eriksson & Kovalainen, 2016, p. 132). Depending on the research aim, the case study approach can be intensive or extensive: there are several ways for case study research in entrepreneurship, depending on the purpose. Stoecker (1991) and Stake (2005) have proposed the distinction between intensive and extensive case studies based on the aims of the exploration and the use of the cases. The intensive case design draws from a single case or a few cases and aims at understanding the case from the 'inside'; and the analysis usually provides a thick or holistic and contextualised description and interpretation. The intensive case study can be longitudinal, process-related or even historical.

Marion, Friar and Simpson (2012) and Marion, Eddleston, Friar and Deed (2015) conducted fourteen longitudinal case studies over a ten-year period in emerging entrepreneurial ventures, collecting extensive ethnographic data: interviews, meetings, notes, e-mails, archival and documentary materials. Ethnographies with such an enduring data collection are a rarity within entrepreneurship studies – and in almost all the social sciences today. The extensive case study (also labelled as a collective case study by, e.g. Denzin & Lincoln, 2005) aims at testing, extending and generating theory by comparing a number of cases, with the primary focus on elaborating and explaining a specific phenomenon and not the cases themselves. The number of cases, then, is dependent on the theoretical aims of the study. Eisenhardt (1989), for example, suggests limiting the number of cases to the point where the incremental contribution of additional cases is only marginal.

The more usual length of an ethnographic data collection is that in Greenman's (2011) research on the venture creation process, where the researcher became involved in the process through working in formal and informal roles over a two-year period during which the empirical data was gathered. The sensitising concepts (Silverman, 2000) provided the frame, themes for the interviews and categories for analysis, together with entrepreneurship theories.

In entrepreneurship studies, the case is often defined through a 'naturally occurring' incident, such as an individual aiming for a business start-up (classical entrepreneurship theory of an omnipotent individual, Kovalainen 1989), entrepreneurial opportunity, creative occupational group, industry, growth, internationalisation process (individual, team or group, such as family or a broader notion of the environment, e.g. Jaskiewicz, Combs & Rau, 2015; Breugst, Paztel & Rathegeber, 2015; McKeever, Jack & Anderson, 2015) or, less likely, an institution with porous boundaries. The definition for the case often comes as a given entity.

The case study is indeed an exploration of a complex, 'bounded system' (Cresswell, 2012), which can be defined in terms of time and place and which usually involves multiple sources of information. If the research design requires, triangulation is part of the process, but not necessarily. Interviews, observations, textual materials such as documents and other written, visual and digital materials are all used in qualitative case studies. As an approach, the case study does not exclude the use of quantitative data within the method repertoire. However, combining qualitative and quantitative data and analyses requires a motivated approach. The use of mixed methods in case studies in entrepreneurship seems to emphasise the superiority of the quantitative approach and the use of the qualitative approach only as a pre-study for survey.

Grounded theory approach as an analysis device

Grounded theory (GT) has provided practices for data organising and analysis that are adopted in many qualitative analysis

traditions (Eriksson & Kovalainen, 2016), even if the 'methodological slurring' (Goulding, 1998, 2002), that is, several positivist practices, have at the same time been criticised. Many of the qualitative studies in entrepreneurship use and take advantage of some tenets of GT, often without paying attention to it and very often without setting clear programmatic criteria for its use (see, e.g. Mäkelä & Turcan, 2007). The renewal of GT is based on its development towards constructivist and interpretative views. This renewal has drawn a line between the positivist tradition of GT and newer, reflexive modes of GT, i.e. it has confirmed the existence of different forms of GT (Charmaz, 2006, 2014; Glaser & Strauss, 1967). Both GT and the *action research* approach have been implicitly adapted in entrepreneurship research more often than they have been mentioned or explicated in the analysis. The classification of data according to the GT classification coding schemes (e.g. Cope, 2011) and participating in the case study of entrepreneurs' activities as an employee or shadowing member of the group (e.g. Dodd, 2002) slide the approach from a mainstream case study into action research and GT. Naming the research, data gathering and analysis in the process of planning the research design is crucial, as it may bring out the connections that were not thought of earlier.

Dominance of interviews

It is notable that in business studies in general and to a large extent in entrepreneurship studies interviews are often introduced as the only or main qualitative data and research material (also in case studies). Indeed, in the 'interview society' (Gubrium & Holstein, 2001, 1997; Silverman, 2010), interviews are seen and used as mirroring or reflecting reality, and archival and documentary sources are being used to a lesser extent. It seems, based on the systematic reviewing of the major entrepreneurship outlets, such as JBV,

ETP, JSBM and ISBJ, that case studies, which would rely mainly on archival data and historical documents and not on interviews, are a rare exception from the dominance of interviews. While this may not hold true for research in entrepreneurship in general, it may reflect the publication policies of the journals more generally. As a data source, interviews dominate both for realist accounts and narratives but also for discourse analyses. In the articles, though, there are fewer rigorous, theoretically informed interpretations. The heavy reliance on interviews as the key data in qualitative entrepreneurship research gets further support from the popularity of focus groups as the key data source.

THE GROWTH OF NARRATIVES, METAPHORS AND DISCOURSE ANALYSIS IN ENTREPRENEURSHIP RESEARCH

The approaches in qualitative research range from realist to poststructuralist philosophy, but most often the variation in the approach is not explicated in the research. The elements of and activities belonging to entrepreneurship (individuals, groups, institutions) are most often taken for granted (Hardy & Maguire, 2008), even if they are explained as 'constructed'. Typical of any qualitative research in business studies is the use of interviews as a source of information and, very often, for truth claims. The otherwise rather usual intertextuality exists less systematically, but through researchers' interpretations and re-readings it creates new linkages. Narrative is one such approach which relies heavily on interviews when describing individual level stories, but it can be built on other materials as well. 'Narrative' is an umbrella term for research that acknowledges subjective storytelling and ranges from narratives as vignettes constructed around a set of significant entrepreneurial events, as in Jennings et al. (2015), to narrative analysis of non-narrative texts

(Bold, 2011) and co-constituted narratives (Hamilton, 2014; Gabriel, 2004).

It has been argued that entrepreneurial narratives provide a unique contribution to narrative scholarship (Gartner, 2007; Keats, 2009). More than that, narratives have their own tenet in entrepreneurial research, and interestingly so, less than critical research or critical theory (e.g. Poutanen & Kovalainen, 2009). Narrative research has at least four different forms (Eriksson & Kovalainen, 2016, p. 216): writing narratives for research purposes (e.g. case stories), collecting data as stories told by people, conceptualising aspects of life as story-making and narrating (e.g. disciplinary reflection). The methodologically diverse ways of using and implementing narratives range from realist to constructionist approaches. The use of metaphors also ranges from realist to constructionist approaches and is by no means a settled form of data or method in entrepreneurship research. In Dodd (2002), the metaphors used by entrepreneurs when telling their life narratives were analysed using GT analysis.

Discourse analysis in entrepreneurship research has increasingly focused on identity construction but also, more theoretically, on the discursively constructed phenomenon of the enterprising self (e.g. du Gay, 1996; Armstrong, 2005; Watson, 2009; Down, 2006; Nadin, 2007). The term 'discourse analysis' refers, depending on the context, to many and differing approaches, ranging from uncovering the features of the texts to revealing the ways in which different kinds of positional power and inequality relations are produced and articulated. There are fewer historically built discourse analyses in entrepreneurship research, and those taking Foucault as a source of inspiration or key theorist of the study have used it mainly in a methodical sense rather than adopting Foucault's theoretical stance (e.g. 1972, 1980). The qualitative analyses in entrepreneurship that are based on discursive approaches and discourse theories exemplify methods that are not inscribed into one disciplinary field but transcend its boundaries.

PARTICIPANT OBSERVATIONS, ACTION RESEARCH AND VERSIONS OF ETHNOGRAPHY IN ENTREPRENEURSHIP

Participant observation as part of data collection in social sciences relates to research on culture and cultural meanings, usually in ethnography but also to some extent action research. It is interesting that the tradition of action research is not stronger in entrepreneurship studies, even if the positive ethos is strongly present. In action research, more than in other research approaches, the aim is to transcend the usual and sometimes almost elitist boundary of research in entrepreneurship to bring about a change through subjective views and the participation of researchers in solving actual problems in entrepreneurial lives and livelihoods. Thus, action research usually follows emancipatory research and design and consists of the participation in and implementation of solutions in addition to a traditional research trajectory. Emancipatory research aims to empower the subjects of inquiry. This type of research design can be found in those entrepreneurship studies where gender, minorities or some social aspects such as poverty are at the core of the focus. The societal relevance of research topics has stepped up, and rather interestingly, no longer from economic growth, but from the perspectives of societal cohesion and inclusion. These types of topics may require novel social science methodology to be adopted.

Both action research and ethnographic research share the understanding that engagement with the subject is the key to understanding a specific culture or context. Ethnography is often described as an 'extremely broad church' (e.g. Atkinson, Goffey, Delamont, Lofland & Lofland, 2001), and this means in practice that showing one best way is hugely difficult: the two things the different approaches have in common are the importance of the fieldwork and intense, often time-consuming data collection. Besides observation, narratives, interviews, life histories, the conventional data collection methods for any ethnographic research approach are documents and site documentations. In entrepreneurship research, ethnographic research may require longitudinal data, which is both time- and money-consuming and thus difficult to obtain. The entrepreneurship research that is advocating ethnography as a research method relates ethnography to case study, which is the most usual connection.

Several method books critically remark on the naturalism which is the reigning thinking in relation to ethnography (e.g. Silverman, 2014). Ethnography is not a ticket to get inside social reality (naturalist assumption) but it can offer a way to analyse how 'reality' is assembled (constructionist assumption). Thus, in the latter the aim is not to understand the meanings of people but to examine the narrative constructions in the meanings.

HOT DATA AND COOL METHODS – FUTURE MATERIALS, BIG DATA AND METHODS IN ENTREPRENEURSHIP RESEARCH

The current and inevitably the future 'hot data' is *big data*. My claim is that big data in all its forms will inevitably transform the understanding of 'entrepreneurship' as a research field and topic and build new alignments with other disciplinary fields, partly in contrast to the current trends of own identity and own theory-building.

Why is that? For the simple reason that big data is currently building its momentum. It is everywhere, and its generating and collection have both grown tremendously. As one result for social sciences in general, the quality of the big data is often beyond the disciplinary control. It is currently almost beyond the ability of commonly used software tools to capture, manage, and process the existing big data. As a consequence, the complex and evolving relationships within the big data may require new tools for analysis.

Big data does not only transform the idea of 'data' in research but also the ways of understanding the role and meaning of data in entrepreneurial activities and in business start-ups. Big data is everywhere, and it is gathered increasingly by others than researchers, and for other purposes. Big data has thus other than directly research-related aspects, which then transfer into the research objects of entrepreneurial studies.

One example of the ways big data allows for totally new research questions and research designs to appear is with the help of the IoT: internet of things. As big data is increasingly compiled and gathered by others, rather than researchers themselves, the boundaries between 'primary' and 'secondary' data become increasingly blurred, but no longer due to the linquistic and constructionist raison d'etres but due to the multiplicity of sources for data. This adds the weight for the basics of data collection, which should be kept in mind: that data is never just numbers and figures, but increasingly data is a cultural product. As a cultural product the analysis of data should carry the meta-politics of data, that is, clarity in tracking the sources of data, and ways to use and analyse the data. This concerns qualitative as well as quantitative analyses and can be related to questions such as whose data becomes relied on in the analyses, or whose narrative becomes told, by whom and for what purposes. In any qualitative analysis, the encoding and decoding of the data is a process of translation. For the big data, the process of translation can become of importance in new ways as it can consist of several old and new methods.

Taking a more traditional qualitative stance on the current and future 'cool methods', there are of two types: research methods that relate to big data and research methods stemming from a variety of cultural research methods. These cool methods should not be merely used as 'fashionable labels' to build disciplinary theory identity, but rather they should be seen as enriching the knowledge of the topic.

Big data, through digitalisation, will challenge the traditional research methods in many ways, as big data allows for more variety in research settings and makes many research settings 'old-fashioned' due to new unexplored openings. As a phenomenon, digitalisation transforms existing economic and societal activities and intensifies the creation of new forms and types of business through new forms of entrepreneurialism. The traditional qualitative research methods using interviews as the main data source will undoubtedly be challenged, as the massive databases of materials of different kinds become available for research and analyses. One of the 'cool' challenges for research will be how the new, computationally based qualitative research methods can be applied to search, analyse and understand these materials in entrepreneurship research in the poststructuralist paradigm, where entrepreneurship is not mediated through language but resides and is situated in it. This is indeed both a theoretical and methodological challenge to the paradigmatic building up of entrepreneurship as a disciplinary field, despite the fact that big data is not a single uniform entity.

Internet-based research methods are among the cool methods. In entrepreneurial studies, a form of ethnography that is used even less, *netnography*, is growing as a research approach, due to the exponential growth of digital data. Netnography is conducted on the internet and uses the principles of ethnography (Kozinets, 1998; Silverman, 2014), but it is based on observations of textual discourses online instead of 'corporeal' activities and discussions. In netnography, the data exists in two forms: data which is directly copied from the CMC (computer-mediated communications) of online community members, and data which is inscribed by the researcher.

Netnography in entrepreneurship research is relatively new and its use is still not widespread, despite it being timelier and less costly than traditional face-to-face focus groups. The newness and scarcity of the use of netnography in entrepreneurship research may relate to its limitations of representative data and narrow focus on online communities and discussions. On the other hand, the online environment calls for readjustment of 'traditional' research settings, methods and data sources, and may open up new avenues for research where previous categories and socio-economic markers such as gender, race, class and occupation are no longer explanatory. How to adopt and adapt online ethnography/netnography into entrepreneurship studies is a challenge, as the method detaches and removes the core of the discipline from the categories and markers that surround the core: the entrepreneur and/or enterprise. The 'thick description' (Geertz, 1973; Greenblatt, 1997) of particular events, rituals and customs, which is a key part of ethnography, transforms in netnography into internet life stories, narratives, texts and blurred disciplinary genres.

Among the cool methods are several that are new to entrepreneurship as a field. Data mining of the big data typically requires computational units for data analysis and comparisons. This challenges the position of qualitative methods, and puts methods in new positions vis-à-vis quantitative analysis.

Visual analysis opens up new modes of knowing for entrepreneurship research. Ethnographies usually transform the visual into words, but increasingly visual materials have become part of the research, as data and as cultural representations. Visuality as a research approach has become a possible framework also for business studies (Eriksson & Kovalainen, 2016, p. 279). Historically, visual materials have provided information to support the realist idea of traditional ethnography as facts constituting and repeating the truth. Besides relying on positivist or realist epistemologies, visual materials can be analysed through cultural interpretations and intertextualities. Analysis in visual anthropology, semiotics and cultural studies blurs the disciplinary boundaries even further by requiring visual literacy and cultural competence to write the visual as part of the

research (Pauwels, 2010; Rose, 2012). The studies of visual cultures in entrepreneurship research are still missing but may prove to be a powerful arena, where the methods drawn from semiotics, art history, aesthetics and cultural studies are adapted in analyses of entrepreneurial activities. One way of approaching the visual method is to consider the objects of enquiry as ways of visualising the culture. The contexts of viewing and producing the visual image, and the semiotic and social conventions are part of the analysis.

It may be fair to note that the 'crisis of representation' and 'a triple crisis' have not been at the centre of the qualitative research conducted in entrepreneurship: different ways of using qualitative methods have lived parallel lives in qualitative entrepreneurship research and only a few articles can be found under the topic. Entrepreneurship research mostly uses discourses as 'method' in the sense meant by postmodern and postcolonial theories, but also in a pragmatic and realist sense. This wide variation is exemplified in the use of GT: in the US research tradition, GT aims towards theory-building in the spirit of Glaser and Strauss (1967), and very often this discussion is related to the case study approach. The European tradition seems to build the GT research strategy more in the constructivist approach presented by Charmaz (2006, 2014).

The fragmentation of research methods and growing complexity of the ways research topics and their exploration take place is visible also in research in entrepreneurship. Qualitative entrepreneurship research has broken new ground partly by borrowing concepts from social sciences to study institutional complexes. Among the hot topics and cool approaches in entrepreneurship will be the application of concepts such as 'complex systems', 'ecological niches' and 'resilience'. These concepts refer to new systemic and multifaceted analyses of the effects of institutions on entrepreneurial ecosystems and the ways in which these shape the birth and development of new enterprises. Other types of hot topic and cool approach are 'visual analysis', which requires cultural analysis and re-reading of culture in a new way, deviating from previous exercises of cultural analysis in entrepreneurship research. These will undoubtedly bring new insights to entrepreneurship research.

One of the general misconceptions related to qualitative research and to entrepreneurship is the thought that a researcher needs to have 'a clear sense of the real-life settings of the domain… studied' (Ulhoi & Neergaard, 2007, p. 440), or that it would be of particular value to know the field. We can start with the rather blatant question of what does it mean to 'know the field' and where does such a requirement come from? The assumption that the 'closeness to the matter is essential' and that 'some degree of first or second hand experience [of entrepreneurship] is necessary' (Ulhoi & Neergaard, 2007, p. 461) for understanding the various dimensions of entrepreneurship is a rather common but unfortunately also a rather naïve idea. This type of claim draws a misleading and untenable equation between the 'closeness of the subject field' and the analytical rigour of the research.

Another general misconception in qualitative research is that research using qualitative methods mainly comprises an individual's subjective experiences (Silverman, 2014, p. 323). This assumption becomes apparent in research that relies on the interview data alone and draws conclusions from other individuals and their experiences. The emphasis on the interview data is exceptionally strong in qualitative business studies, entrepreneurship research included. Interviews as the main source of information puts emphasis on the 'originality' and 'authenticity' of the talk at the interviews. Interviews are even assumed to mirror people's experiences. If this is the case, then the task of the qualitative analysis and research is only to report the experiences.

One possible explanation for the expressed needs of strict definition and strong claims for the articulation of epistemic and ontological knowledge stance may stem from the relative 'youth' of qualitative research in entrepreneurship, where the discipline has

for a very long time been rather normatively built up (Blackburn & Kovalainen, 2009; Poutanen & Kovalainen, 2009). During the last two decades, qualitative research has gained a stronger foothold in business studies, entrepreneurship research included (Neergaard & Ulhoi, 2007), but still with some underlying assumptions of the inferiority of qualitative approaches in comparison to quantitative approaches (e.g. Bygrave, 2007). Entrepreneurship research is amalgamating and intersecting several fields of business and social sciences, with the Schumpeterian approach implicitly or explicitly part of the theorisation. This has led to the fragmentation of the disciplinary field and the search for 'new' and 'unexplored' research topics. The cool methods would therefore include theoretically informed research methods with a bolder understanding of the disciplinary field of entrepreneurship, not as one outcome or function of the economy but as a complex set of questions that extend beyond the business-as-usual theories in entrepreneurship.

FUTURE OF QUALITATIVE RESEARCH IN ENTREPRENEURSHIP

Relatively 'old' social science concepts such as bricolage (MacMaster, Archer & Hirth, 2015; Baker & Nelson, 2005), trust (e.g. Nooteboom, 2002) and social capital (e.g. Coleman, 1988, 1990) have grown and matured in their use in entrepreneurship research. In entrepreneurship literature, the concepts are often connected to qualitative research strategies more explicitly than in the tradition they stem from. The entrepreneurship research surrounding these concepts provides excellent examples of the ways entrepreneurship research has expanded its field. The strength of the disciplinary field is in the adoption of new methods and fertile use of new concepts and theories.

One of the methodological and method-related pitfalls for qualitative research in entrepreneurship is that as a disciplinary field entrepreneurship turns inwards and tries to develop 'solid' or 'indigenous' theory with its own qualitative methods toolbox. The strength of qualitative research – also in entrepreneurship – is its flexibility and the methods developing across social sciences and humanities, which cross-fertilise and develop new variations of research methods and strategies. My assumption is that the fragmentation of qualitative research methods and their use will grow in the future, and this is largely due to method-related developments in the humanities and in social sciences in general. Recent analysis of published qualitative articles in three US-based entrepreneurship journals (ETP, JBV, ERD) in 2007–12 shows the growth of diversity in the method selection and in the epistemic and methodological solutions (Hlady-Rispal & Jouison-Laffitte, 2014).

The fragmentation of research methods will grow also as part of and due to the 'methodologically contested present', which results in competitive tensions within the disciplines but also within the 'qualitative research communities and journals' (e.g. Karatas-Ozkan et al., 2014; Denzin & Lincoln, 2005). These trends and developments should not be seen as a 'threat' or be interpreted as representing a 'non-mature phase' of entrepreneurship research paradigm, as sometimes has been the case. Rather, the disciplinary development should be interpreted through flexibility and porousness. The ability to have flexibility in the use of qualitative methods and the acceptance of porous boundaries between disciplinary fields is strengthening entrepreneurship as a discipline. Hence, there is not a single theory or disciplinary field, but several.

In addition to the changes triggered by the new developments in qualitative methods in general, other changes that are external to methods but internal to disciplinary developments will take place. My assumption is that the trends external to method, but integral to social sciences in the future, such as digitalisation and, with that, a new type of big data and the new methods that follow it, will also challenge the traditional ways of gathering and analysing qualitative data and writing qualitative research. In future entrepreneurship studies, the 'coming of age' of qualitative research will see the maturing of qualitative data and qualitative methods into a new set of practices with porous boundaries vis-à-vis other disciplinary fields.

Note

1 'Indigenous' refers in qualitative methodology literature to colonialist and anti-colonialist discourses which embody the critical politics of research and resistance (e.g. Sandoval, 2000; Denzin, 2005). Traditionally, indigenous research is seen as resisting the positivist and post-positivist methodologies of Western science, as these are used to continue colonising knowledge practices (Denzin, 2005).

REFERENCES

Acs, Z. and Szerb, L. (2009) The global entrepreneurship index. *Foundations and Trends in Entrepreneurship*, 5: 341–435.

Ahl, H. (2007) A Foucauldian framework for discourse analysis. In Neergaard, H. and Ulhoi, J.P. (eds.) *Handbook of Qualitative Methods in Entrepreneurship*. Cheltenham: Edward Elgar, 216–42.

Alvarez, S.A., Young, S.L. and Woolley, J.L. (2015) Opportunities and institutions: A co-creation story of the king crab industry. *Journal of Business Venturing*, 30: 95–112.

Armstrong, P. (2005) *Critique of Entrepreneurship: People and Policy*. London: Palgrave Macmillan.

Atkinson, P., Goffey, A., Delamont, S., Lofland, J. and Lofland, L. (eds.) (2001) *Handbook of Ethnography*. London: Sage.

Baker, T. and Nelson, R. (2005) Creating something from nothing: Resource construction through entrepreneurial bricolage. *Administrative Science Quarterly*, 50(3): 329–66.

Baron, R.A. (2008) The role of affect in the entrepreneurial process. *Academy of Management Review*, 33: 328–40.

Blackburn, R. and Kovalainen, A. (2009) Researching small firms: Past, present, future trends. *International Journal of Management Reviews*, 11(2): 127–48.

Bold, C. (2011) *Using Narrative in Research*. London: Sage.

Bratu, R. (2012) Actors' practices and networks of corruption: The case of Romania's accession to European Union funding. Unpublished PhD thesis in Sociology, London School of Economics: London. http://etheses.lse.ac.uk/891/1/Bratu_Actors%20practices%20and%20networks%20of%20corruption.pdf. Accessed: 14 October 2015.

Braunerhjelm, P. (2011) Entrepreneurship, innovation and economic growth: Interdependencies, irregularities and regularities. In Audretsch, D.B., Falck, O., Heblich, S. and Lederer, A. (eds.) *Handbook of Research on Innovation and Entrepreneurship*. Cheltenham, Northampton: Edward Elgar, 161–213.

Breugst, N., Patzel, H. and Rathgeber, P. (2015) How should we divide the pie? Equity distribution and its impact on entrepreneurial teams. *Journal of Business Venturing*, 20(1): 66–94.

Bygrave, W.D. (2007) The entrepreneurship paradigm (I) revisited. In Neergaard, H. and Ulhoi, J.P. (eds.) *Handbook of Qualitative Methods in Entrepreneurship*. Cheltenham: Edward Elgar. Reprint of Bygrave, W.D. (1989) article,17–47.

Carlsson, B. (2011) New knowledge: The driving force of innovation, entrepreneurship and economic development. In Audretsch, D.B., Falck, O., Heblich, S. and Lederer, A. (eds.) *Handbook of Research on Innovation and Entrepreneurship*. Cheltenham, Northampton: Edward Elgar, 214–28.

Cresswell, J. (2012) *Qualitative Inquiry and Research Design*. Thousand Oaks, CA: Sage.

Charmaz, K. (2006) *Constructing Grounded Theory*. London: Sage.

Charmaz, K. (2014) *Constructing Grounded Theory*. 2nd ed. London: Sage.

Coleman, J. (1988) Social capital in the creation of human capital. *American Journal of Sociology*, Supplement 94: S95–120.

Coleman, J. (1990) *Foundations of Social Theory*. Cambridge, MA: Harvard University Press.

Cope, J. (2011) Entrepreneurial learning from failure: An interpretative phenomenological analysis. *Journal of Business Venturing*, 26: 604–23.

Davidsson, P. (2016) *Researching Entrepreneurship: Conceptualization and Design*. 2nd ed. Heidelberg: Springer.

Denzin, N.K. (2005) Emancipatory discourses and the ethics and the politics of interpretation. In Denzin, N.K. and Lincoln, Y.S. (eds.) *The Sage Handbook of Qualitative Research*. Thousand Oaks, CA: Sage, 933–58.

Denzin, N.K. and Lincoln, Y.S. (eds.) (2005) *The Sage Handbook of Qualitative Research*. Thousand Oaks, CA: Sage.

De Vaus, D. (2001) *Research Design in Social Research*. London: Sage.

Dodd, S.D. (2002) Metaphors and meaning: A grounded cultural model of US entrepreneurship. *Journal of Business Venturing*, 17: 519–35.

Down, S. (2006) *Narratives of Enterprise: Creating Entrepreneurial Self-Identity in a Small Firm*. Cheltenham: Edward Elgar.

Du Gay, P. (1996) *Consumption and Identity at Work*. London: Sage.

Eisenhardt, K. (1989) Building theories from case study research. *Academy of Management Review*, 14(4): 620–7.

Eriksson, P. and Kovalainen, A. (2016) *Qualitative Methods in Business Research*. 2nd ed. London: Sage.

Fadahunsi, A. and Rosa, P. (2002) Entrepreneurship and illegality: Insights from the Nigerian cross-border trade. *Journal of Business Venturing*, 17, 397–429.

Fischer, E. and Reuber, A.R. (2014) Online entrepreneurial communication: Mitigating uncertainty and increasing differentiation via Twitter. *Journal of Business Venturing*, 29: 565–83.

Flick, U. (2002) *An Introduction to Qualitative Research*. London: Sage.

Foucault, M. (1972) *The Archaeology of Knowledge*. London: Tavistock.

Foucault, M. (1980) *Power/Knowledge. Selected Interviews and Other Writings, 1972–1977*. New York: Pantheon.

Gabriel, Y. (2004) Narratives, stories and texts. In Grant, D., Hardy, C., Oswick, C. and Putnam, L. (eds.) *The Sage Handbook of Organizational Discourse*. London: Sage, 309–44.

Gartner, W.B. (2007) Entrepreneurial narrative and a science of the imagination. *Journal of Business Venturing*, 22: 613–27.

Geertz, C. (1973) *The Interpretation of Cultures*. New York: Basic Books.

Geertz, C. (2000/1983) Thick description: Towards an interpretive theory of culture. In Martin, M. and MacIntyre, L.C. (eds.) *Readings in the Philosophy of Social Science*. Cambridge, MA: MIT Press, 213–32.

Glaser, B. and Strauss, A. (1967) *The Discovery of Grounded Theory: Strategies for Qualitative Research*. Chicago, IL: Aldine Publishing Co.

Goulding, C. (1998) Grounded theory: The missing methodology of the interpretivist agenda. *Qualitative Market Research*, 1(1): 50–7.

Goulding, C. (2002) *Grounded Theory: A Practical Guide for Management, Business and Market Researchers*. London: Sage.

Greenblatt, S. (1997) The touch of the 'real'. *Representations*, 59: 14–29.

Greenman, A. (2011) Entrepreneurial activities and occupational boundary work during venture creation and development in the cultural industries. *International Small Business Journal*, 30(2): 115–17.

Gubrium, J. and Holstein, A. (1997) Active interviewing. In Silverman D. (ed.) *Qualitative Research: Theory, Method and Practice*, 2nd ed. London: Sage, 140–61.

Gubrium, J. and Holstein, A. (2001) From the individual interview to the interview society. In Gubrium, J.F. and Holstein, J.A. (eds.) *Handbook of Interview Research: Context and Method*. London: Sage, 2–32.

Hamilton, E. (2014) Entrepreneurial narrative identity and gender: A double epistemological shift. *Journal of Small Business*, 52(4): 703–12.

Hammersley, M. (1992) *What's Wrong with Ethnography? Methodological Explorations*. London: Routledge.

Hardy, C. and Maguire, S. (2008) Institutional entrepreneurship. In Greenwood, R., Oliver, C., Suddaby, R. and Salin-Anderson, K. (eds.) *Handbook of Organizational Institutionalism*. Thousand Oaks, CA: Sage, 198–217.

Hlady-Rispal, M. and Jouison-Laffitte, E. (2014) Qualitative research methods and epistemological frameworks: A review of publication trends in entrepreneurship. *Journal of Small Business Management*, 52: 594–614.

Hobbs, D. (1988) *Doing the Business: Entrepreneurship, the Working Class and Detectives in the East End of London*. Oxford: Oxford University Press.

Hobbs, D. (2011) Introduction. In Hobbs, D. (ed.) *Ethnography in Context, Sage Series: Benchmarks in Social Research Methods*. London: Sage.

Jaskiewicz, P., Combs, J.G. and Rau, S.B. (2015) Entrepreneurial legacy: Toward a theory of how some family firms nurture transgenerational entrepreneurship. *Journal of Business Venturing*, 30(1): 29–49.

Jennings, J.E., Edwards, T., Devereaux-Jennings, P. and Delbridge, R. (2015) Emotional arousal and entrepreneurial outcomes: Combining qualitative methods to elaborate theory. *Journal of Business Venturing*, 30: 113–30.

Jännäri, J. and Kovalainen, A. (2015) The research methods used in 'doing gender' literature., *International Journal of Gender and Entrepreneurship*, 7(2): 214–31.

Karatas-Ozkan, M., Anderson, A., Fayolle, A., Howells, J. and Condor, R. (2014) Understanding entrepreneurship: Challenging dominant perspectives and theorizing entrepreneurship through new postpositivist epistemologies. *Journal of Small Business Management*, 54(4): 703–12.

Keats, P.A. (2009) Multiple text analysis in narrative research: Visual, written, and spoken stories of experience. *Qualitative Research*, 9(2): 181–95.

Kovalainen, A. (1989) The concept of entrepreneurship in business studies. *The Finnish Journal of Business Economics*, 2: 82–93.

Kovalainen, A. (1995) *At the Margins of the Economy. Women's Self-Employment in Finland 1960–1990*. Ashgate: Avebury.

Kozinets, R.V. (1998) On netnography: Initial reflections on consumer research investigations of cyberculture. In Albam, J. and Hutchinson, W. (eds.) *Advances in Consumer Research. Vol. 25*. Provo, UT: Association for Consumer Research, 366–71.

Lindgren, M. and Packendorff, J. (2009) Social constructionism and entrepreneurship: Basic assumptions and consequences for theory and research. *International Journal of Entrepreneurial Behaviour & Research*, 15(1): 25–47.

MacMaster, B., Archer, G. and Hirth, R. (2015) Bricolage. Making do with what is at hand. In Baker, T. and Wellter, F. (eds.) *The

Routledge Companion to Entrepreneurship. London: Routledge, 149–65.

Mäkelä, M.M. and Turcan, R.V. (2007) Building grounded theory in entrepreneurship research. In Neergaard, H. and Ulhoi, J.P. (eds.) *Handbook of Qualitative Methods in Entrepreneurship*. Cheltenham: Edward Elgar, 122–40.

Marion, T.J., Eddleston, K.A., Friar, J.H. and Deed, D. (2015) The evolution of inter-organizational relationships in emerging ventures: An ethnographic study within the new product development process. *Journal of Business Venturing*, 30: 167–84.

Marion, T.J., Friar, J.H. and Simpson, T.W. (2012) New product development and early-stage firms: Two in-depth case studies. *Journal of Production Innovation Management*, 29(4): 639–54.

McKeever, E., Jack, S. and Anderson, A. (2015) Embedded entrepreneurship in the creative re-construction of place. *Journal of Business Venturing*, 30(1): 50–65.

Nadin, S. (2007) Entrepreneurial identity in the care sector: Navigating the contradictions. *Women in Management Review*, 22(6): 456–67.

Neergaard, H. and Ulhoi, J.P. (2007) Introduction. In Neergaard, H. and Ulhoi, J.P. (eds.) *Handbook of Qualitative Methods in Entrepreneurship*. Cheltenham: Edward Elgar.

Nooteboom, B. (2002) *Trust: Forms, foundations, functions, failures and figures*. Cheltenham: Edward Elgar.

Pauwels, L. (2010) Visual sociology reframed: An analytical synthesis and discussion of visual methods in social and cultural research. *Sociological Methods & Research*, 38(4): 545–81.

Poutanen, S. and Kovalainen, A. (2009) Critical theory. In Mills, A.J., Durebos, G. and Wiebe, E. (eds.) *Encyclopedia of Case Study Research*. London, Thousand Oaks, CA, New Delhi: Sage.

Rose, G. (2012) *Visual Methodologies. An Introduction to Researching with Visual Materials*. London: Sage.

Sandoval, C. (2000) *Methodology of the Oppressed*. Minneapolis, MN: University of Minnesota Press.

Shane, S. (2012) Reflections on the 2010 AMR decade award: Delivering on the promise of entrepreneurship as a field of research. *Academy of Management Review,* 37: 318–29.

Shane, S. and Venkataraman, S. (2000) The promise of entrepreneurship as a field of research. *Academy of Management Review*, 25: 217–26.

Shepherd, D.A. (2015) Party on! A call for entrepreneurship research that is more interactive, activity based, cognitively hot, compassionate, and prosocial. *Journal of Business Venturing*, 30: 489–507.

Silverman, D. (2000) *Doing Qualitative Research: A Practical Handbook*. Thousand Oaks, CA: Sage.

Silverman, D. (Ed.) (2010) *Qualitative research*. London: Sage.

Silverman, D. (2014) *Interpreting Qualitative Data. Methods for Analysing Talk, Text and Interaction*. 5th ed. London: Sage.

Stake, R. (1995) *The Art of Case Study Research*. Thousand Oaks, CA: Sage.

Stake, R. (2005) Case studies. In Denzin, N.K. and Lincoln, Y.S. (eds.) *Handbook of Qualitative Research.* Thousand Oaks, CA: Sage, 435–54.

Stoecker, R. (1991) Evaluating and rethinking the case study. *Sociological Review*, 39(1): 88–112.

Suddaby, R. (2014) Why theory? *Academy of Management Review*, 39(4): 407–11.

Suddaby, R., Bruton, G. and Si, S.X. (2015) Entrepreneurship through a qualitative lens: Insights on the construction and/or discovery of entrepreneurial opportunity. *Journal of Business Venturing*, 30: 1–10.

Tatli, A., Vassilopoulou, J., Özbilgin, M., Forson, C. and Slutskaya, N. (2014) A Bourdieuan relational perspective for entrepreneurship research. *Journal of Small Business Management*, 52(4): 615–32.

Ulhoi, J.P. and Neergaard, H. (2007) Postscript. In Neergaard, H. and Ulhoi, J.P. (eds.) *Handbook of Qualitative Methods in Entrepreneurship*. Cheltenham: Edward Elgar.

Van Maanen, J. (2011) *Tales of the Field: On Writing Ethnography*. Chicago, IL: University of Chicago Press.

Watson, T.J. (2009) Entrepreneurial action, identity work and the use of multiple discursive resources. *International Small Business Journal*, 27(3): 251–74.

Yin, R.K. (2002) *Case Study Research: Design and Methods*. Beverly Hills, CA: Sage.

Yin, R.K. (2014) *Case Study Research*. Thousand Oaks, CA: Sage.

30

Gender and Entrepreneurship at the Crossroads: Where Do You Want to Go?

Cristina Díaz-García

INTRODUCTION

According to Blackburn and Kovalainen (2009), women's entrepreneurship is becoming an 'enduring area of research', since it has longevity in terms of need for both empirical and theoretical developments. Hughes et al. (2012, p. 429) classify this area 'at the brink to adolescence'. However, research designs have not kept pace with the theoretical developments in feminist theory. This might have prompted Ahl and Marlow (2012, p. 543) to state that 'the current entrepreneurial research agenda is in danger of reaching an epistemological dead end in the absence of a reflexive critical perspective to inform the idea of who can be and what might be an entrepreneur'. What seems to be commonly agreed is that we still know comparatively little about women entrepreneurs despite their economic and social contribution (Brush & Cooper, 2012). This might be because researchers engage in an

epistemological focus that does not question the normative underpinnings of the debate; embedded and hegemonic assumptions presume that the deficit and lack rests within women who fail to assimilate and reproduce male norms. As such, 'it becomes axiomatic to question the attitude and behaviours of the subject rather than their constructed subject position'. (Ahl & Marlow, 2012, p. 544)

In this vein, whereas many studies have emphasized the distinction between the socially constructed gender and the biological sex, and that gender is context-specific and relative to time and place, it is still operationalized in many studies with a dichotomous variable which measures sex (male/female). Whereas some of the latter studies acknowledge the more complicated context, others believe the two categories sum it up. In this line of research, although sex and gender conceptualizations have implications for research design, they are rarely made explicit by researchers. Furthermore, a unique and invariable association is frequently made between women and femininity and men and masculinity, the aim being to study masculine males versus feminine females. This example provides only one instance of analyzing a complex situation that can be examined in many ways, since assuming this as the only approach overrides all the diversity that exists within and among these categories.

Yet it is not only gender that is socially constructed; research is too, since the questions we ask and/or the methodologies we use vary over the years according to societal changes (in institutions, behaviours and relations). Therefore, within research there are power dynamics that result in certain disciplines and certain approaches having more legitimacy than others. Grant and Perren (2002), for example, report that the majority of research has a structural functionalism approach, which renders theory development problematic. In order to gain legitimacy, studies have tended to focus on testing theories from more established areas (like strategy) and have emphasized the use of quantitative techniques. As Ahl describes it:

> Researchers may be more likely to publish a study in which a statistically significant difference can be found, however insignificant, than one that shows no such result... Researchers' careers depend on being published in mainstream journals. If these encompass the practices outlined earlier, this means that articles submitted will also conform. (Ahl, 2006, pp. 608–9)

This leads Blackburn and Kovalainen (2009, p. 142) to assert that 'too often, research in the field is naïve in these respects, and hence unaware of the limitations of their contribution, no matter how "technically" correct'. Therefore, some studies have been published recently intending to provide guidelines for future research in this area (Carter & Shaw, 2006; Ahl, 2006; De Bruin, Brush & Welter, 2007; Calás, Smircich & Bourne, 2009; Brush, de Bruin & Welter, 2009; Neergaard, Frederiksen & Marlowe, 2011; Ahl & Nelson, 2010; Sullivan & Meek, 2012; Ahl & Marlow, 2012; Jennings & Brush, 2013).

This chapter aims to contribute to the discussion: first, by linking the evolution of research perspectives in social sciences (with regards to ontology and epistemology) to that of feminist positions; second, by analyzing the publication tendency; and, finally, by providing some cues for future research, including the proposal of a sociological framework that allows a multilayered and, therefore, contextual analysis to examining gender and entrepreneurship issues. In sum, the purpose of this chapter is to provide guidance for researchers, particularly new ones to the field, who are trying to move their work forward in this area, considering certain challenges for future research.

The chapter is structured as follows. First, theoritical perspectives in social sciences are reviewed relating them to the positions within feminist theory[1] that adopt that perspective. Second, a discussion of the publication tendency is presented: published articles have been classified according to the approach adopted by the researcher, differentiating between the dominant research perspective – 'gender as a variable' – and the alternatives. Subsequently, how these perspectives represent new lines for future research is discussed, highlighting the challenges that have to be taken into account. Finally, the chapter provides some conclusions and implications for future research directions on female entrepreneurship.

LINKING RESEARCH PERSPECTIVES IN SOCIAL SCIENCES AND FEMINIST POSITIONS

All research is based on some underlying assumptions about what constitutes 'valid' research. It is important to know these in order to conduct and/or evaluate research, since they influence the questions we seek to address, including: what exactly do we mean by gender? Which issues are worthy of study? Which research methods are appropriate? What importance has the context in this phenomenon? What are the implications for theory, practice and policy support? Hence, the underlying assumptions structure researchers' thinking (the possibilities for and restrictions on the conduct of the analysis) and influence the research design and results obtained. Therefore, reflecting upon the implicit ideological assumptions of our research agenda has to be our starting point.

Any research approach is underpinned by specific assumptions about the nature of social science at the ontological (beliefs and ideas about the nature of being, reality and truth), epistemological (knowledge and the relationship of the knower to the known) and methodological (how the researcher approaches the research process) levels (Lincoln, Lynham & Guba, 2011).

Western philosophy remains divided by two opposing ontological traditions: a Heraclitean ontology of *becoming* (emphasis on formlessness, chaos, processes of change) and a Parmenidean ontology of *being* (emphasis on a permanent and unchanging reality composed of clearly formed entities with identifiable properties), it is the latter that is widely accepted (Gray, 2013). According to Chia (2002), only relatively recently has postmodern epistemology challenged traditional being ontology with notions of a becoming orientation and the limitations of truth-seeking.

Although Burrell and Morgan (1979) have proposed four different categorizations of alternative inquiry paradigms, others, such as Chua (1986), prefer to label the different alternatives as 'perspectives', not considering them mutually exclusive paradigms which are based on 'dichotomic features'. Similarly, Miles and Huberman (1994, pp. 4–5) propose that the barriers between different research paradigms are not necessarily insurmountable and that there may be a blurring of epistemologies. Also, Watkins-Mathys and Lowe (2005) propose an interpretative paradigmapping which avoids paradigm incommensurability, enabling them to coexist without divisions and even learn from each other. That is, while research epistemologies are *philosophically* distinct (as ideal types), in the practice of social research

these distinctions are not always so clear cut. None of the worldviews are considered to be unconditionally superior to the others, since they may be appropriate for some purposes and insufficient or overly complex for others.

Therefore, in Table 30.1 and in line with Gray (2013), different epistemologies (objectivism, constructionism and subjectivism) and their related theoretical perspectives (positivist, interpretivisim, critical inquiry and post-modernism) are presented. Their main characteristics will be described later on. As previously discussed (Chua, 1986; Miles & Huberman, 1994; Watkins-Mathys & Lowe, 2005), this labeling does not aim to construct the idea that these are discrete and clearly defined approaches with little fluidity between them. Furthermore, it has to be stated that a discussion of the distinctions between research approaches is beyond the scope of this chapter, and the review does not intend to cover all the literature (see the previously mentioned articles for more discussions).

Many women's entrepreneurship studies do not refer to a feminist position. However, it is important to draw on feminist theory since it has a major role in changing social inequality and removing the power imbalance between genders, which otherwise is reflected in the androcentric research frameworks. The different feminist positions, as outlined by Alvesson and DueBilling (1997), have evolved parallel to the paradigmatic perspectives of research in social sciences as detailed briefly in the following lines. In this line, studies within the positivist research approach tend to take a feminist 'gender as a variable' perspective, and those who contend that women have a specific standpoint based on their experiences – feminist standpoint – tend to have a constructivism epistemology. Studies with a social constructionist or interpretive stance understand 'gender as a process', as a performance, or 'doing'. Those with a critical-interpretative perspective aim not only to interpret the world but also seek to change it. Finally, those that adopt a postmodernist perspective focus on language and

Table 30.1 Epistemology, theoretical perspectives and positions within feminism

Epistemology	Objectivism	Constructivism		Subjectivism
	One objective truth. Only knowledge that can be tested can be considered true knowledge	Actions, institutions and conditions are constructed through the interactions and interpretations of people: that is, a socially constructed reality. Reality as an internal product of the mind		Anti-ontological Avoiding trust, de-constructing
Theoretical perspective	**Positivism** (Easterby-Smith et al., 2008)	**Constructionism** (Easterby-Smith et al., 2008) **Interpretivism** (Bryman & Bell, 2003; Gray, 2013)	**Critical inquiry** Questions currently held values and assumptions and challenges conventional social structures	**Post-modernism** (Gray, 2013)
Positions within feminism	**'Gender as a variable'** (Alvesson & DueBilling, 1997) **Feminist standpoint** (Alvesson & DueBilling, 1997)	Gender as a social construction	**Critical-interpretive perspective** (Alvesson & DueBilling, 1997)	**Feminist Post-structuralism** (Alvesson & DueBilling, 1997; Calas et al., 2009)

representation, in the production of subjectivities and gender power relations, this stream being labeled feminist post-structuralism.

Positivist Research

Grant and Perren (2002), in their systematic meta-theoretical analysis of articles published in 2000 in key small business and entrepreneurship journals, found that positivism (functionalist) is the primary paradigm for organizational study in terms of publications and research. Research may be classified as positivist if there is a proposal of hypotheses for testing theories, quantifiable measures of variables and the drawing of inferences about a phenomenon from the sample to a stated population. This epistemology is concerned with explaining and predicting.

The literature on women's entrepreneurship within this research perspective is based on the liberal feminism political standpoint, according to which all human beings are equal, since men and women are both rational individuals that look for their own interest. The conceptualization of gender is dualistic, using 'sex' as a synonym for 'gender', since gender is presumed to be an essential attribute differentiating between women and men. This ideology states that because of direct discrimination or systemic factors, women have been deprived of the same access to opportunities in the labor market as men (Calás et al., 2009). If there was no discrimination between men and women, the latter would fulfil their potential to the same level. The aim is to highlight 'gender' difference in order to achieve justice through the removal of 'gender-based barriers', and the research examines and measures essential sex differences. If women-owned businesses have poorer economic performance, the conclusion is that this difference is a result of unequal access to resources and public services (family policies) and/or to the essential differences in their personality (too sensitive, emotional, etc.).

The theoretical approaches underpinning this paradigm are often based on economic rationality and 'equality of opportunity'. Research designs usually compare men and women, since it seems that if there is no 'difference' there is no problem to study. Many articles depart from the aim of reducing structural gender barriers to achieve equality, but the finding of differences is explained with an assumed essentialism of men and women's characteristics and by using discourses of choice and merit at the individual level. For example, Du Rietz and Henrekson state:

> Strictly speaking, the female underperformance hypothesis is only true if the economic performance of female entrepreneurs is inferior to the performance of their male counterparts with *identical* preferences... women are found to regard proprietorship as a mechanism for achieving independence and control over their working lives... If it is true that female entrepreneurs on average have weaker preferences for sales growth, while we consistently find that they do not underperform in terms of profitability, it is clearly the case that our study provides no support for female underperformance according to a strict interpretation of the hypothesis. (Du Rietz & Henrekson, 2000, pp. 9–10)

As a result, this approach to research has two unwanted consequences (Ahl & Marlow, 2012). On the one hand, a construction of women as the 'other' in the business realm is produced, with the devaluation of their approaches and performances. On the other hand, the audience interprets that gender issues have been solved and any disadvantage can be attributed to the individual. In the same vein, Calás et al. (2009) qualify that many studies, compatible with liberal feminist goals of overcoming women's disadvantages and discrimination in male contexts, fail to take a real feminist approach.

Another positivist approach is the feminist standpoint perspective, which seeks to highlight the existence of specific and shared experiences and interests of women that differ from those of the majority of men. Traditional research is influenced by masculine priorities and notions that have been established as the norm and are taken for granted. Therefore, the authors within this perspective propose that the marginal status of women, as an excluded group, enables them to develop certain kinds of insight that are needed if an inclusive science is the aim of the academic community (Alvesson &

Due Billing, 1997). Calás et al. (2009) refer to this perspective as psychoanalytic/cultural feminism. In line with liberal feminism, this perspective attempts to hold equal rights but argues for recognition of women's different sex roles and experiences. The studies with this feminist approach are sensitive to essentialism: that is, to defining women as members of a group with a universal and stable quality. However, although trying to avoid biological explanations, at the same time they imply that biology has some significance when they defend that women and men are different in their ways of doing and being and that this is biologically determined.

Positivism has been criticized for adopting a 'naïve realism' in which reality can be comprehended and knowledge can be captured and generalized in a context-free form (Guba & Lincoln, 1994). Reacting to these critiques, post-positivism paradigms have emerged trying to correct these flaws.

Critical-Realism Research

One of the post-positivist perspectives is 'critical realism' (Bhaskar, 1997[1975]), which can be seen in between positivism and interpretivism, since it accepts a realist ontology, but pairs that with an anti-realist epistemology. That is, even though it accepts that there is a 'real' (worldfacts are real independently of the 'human mind', there is a reality independent of our thinking about it that science can study), researchers are not able to observe every aspect of it. That is, the critical realist is critical of humans' ability to know reality with certainty. The 'actual' world is formed by observable events, which are causally generated from complex interactions of mechanisms. Research objects form part of structures which allow them to hold different levels of power, and by behaving in particular ways they cause changes. These observable events can give some information on the existence of unobservable entities: that is, the 'empirical' dimension of knowledge. Critical analyses of gender will be needed for as long as gendered relations are hierarchical (Bradley, 2007), since 'critical pragmatism and positive action' implications have to be taken seriously (Alvesson & Deetz, 2000). One example of this type of approach is the study by Rouse and Kitching (2006) in which they observe that a start-up program for young working-class participants does not enable parents to combine business trading with childcare responsibilities, which were rendered a private matter, and that this affects women more negatively, since men relied on the children's mother for caring.

Interpretive Research

According to this inquiry perspective, access to reality is only available through social constructions, such as language, consciousness and shared meanings (Alvesson & Due Billing, 1997; Calás et al., 2009). Therefore, these constructions are not absolutely true, or correct, as they are differently modeled depending on the observer. Hence, reality – social and cultural structures – is actively constructed through negotiation or interaction with others and depending on the actor's values. These studies do not predefine dependent and independent variables but focus on the full complexity of human sense-making in specific situations. The aim is to try to understand, rather than to rationalize, the social world, which differs from the natural world. The studies attempt to understand human action searching, which is the meanings that people assign to specific issues and how they influence everyday life context and in turn are influenced by it.

Gender is conceptualized as a social construction and a multilevel structure (Risman, 1998; Ridgeway & Correll, 2004) which includes: 1) cultural beliefs and distributions of resources at the macro level, 2) patterns of behaviour at the interactional level and 3) roles and identities at the micro level. Because processes at each level simultaneously reinforce

each other, it is an overdetermined system that powerfully reinforces inequality. Furthermore, as a social construct, the meanings associated with it are not fixed but vary over time and from culture to culture. From this perspective, gender is constructed and performed in contrast to theories that situate it as a stable or inherent quality. The methodology within this strand is a qualitative one, developing new theoretical insights about unexplained phenomena. In these studies, female business-owners' context is very important, and two issues are related to this: intersectionality (with other social identities: race, age, etc.) and power relations between men and women (Bradley, 2007). Power and discourse shape the individuals' social field of action, regulating 'what is possible to be' and guiding them into a normalized social order which is also gendered, perpetuating gender relations. In society, and particularly in the business realm, the discourses operate to reproduce masculinity as preferred values, while presented as gender-neutral (Bruni, Gherardi & Poggio, 2005). This is achieved because the discursive forces have a profound effect on how individuals experience their gender identity (Bradley, 2007). However, these studies also claim for the agency of the participants in their self-identity construction.

According to Gray (2013), there are five examples of the interpretivist approach: symbolic interactionism, phenomenology, realism, hermeneutics and naturalistic inquiry.

Recently Klyver, Nielsen and Evald (2012) relied on symbolic interactionism for their study on how gender equality at national level impacted the gender gap in self-employment and on the impact of context (developed countries, male-oriented industries). Symbolic interactionism is based on the ontological assumption that reality is 'socially constructed': that is, what we believe to be true is based on how we – and others – talk about what we believe to be true. They explain that according to this theory the self 'is constructed from constant, multifaceted and closely interrelated conversations between the "I" and the "Me'" (Klyver et al., 2012, p. 474). The 'I' is the part of the individual that has the opportunity to raise his/her choice above the institutionalized individual, whereas the 'Me' is the socially directed part of the individual, the one that considers institutional discourses. People form groups in which they share symbols and their accompanying meanings in order to communicate and, at the same time, this fosters those people to utilize the shared symbols/meanings to gain acceptance in the group.

Post-Modernism

Post-modernism questions objectivity and emphasizes subjectivity, since the observer has to interpret how things happen. Along these lines, if individuals perceive truth differently, it becomes important to listen to and understand their individual perceptions, which are not static facts but subject to change and flexibility. Therefore, there is no theory capable of describing all phenomena and there is no preferred method to study a phenomenon, since there might be many valid approaches.

Feminism within poststructuralist theory is focused on subverting stable meanings of gender, highlighting how women encapsulate multiple subjectivities from other status characteristics (that position them differently in power relations: that is, the importance of intersectionality (Marlow, 2016, p. 3)) and deconstructing authoritative models and practices. It is a critical perspective 'for the analytical purpose of identifying (liberal) feminist and feminine discourses, which play out in contemporary organizations' (Lewis, 2014, p. 1848).

Within this stream of research, the interpretation of text is very important. The deconstruction of text exposes many contradictions with regards to female subordination that have been hidden by discourse strategies (words, metaphors, binaries), generating an appearance of objectivity. This is why some researchers propose that reality is rhetorically constructed rather than discovered by social researchers (Alvesson & Due Billing, 1997) and, therefore, 'these premises are anti-ontological in that there is no actual ground to justify the stability of knowledge claims other than the processes of knowledge production themselves' (Calás et al., 2009, p. 25). This would be an extreme position since, as Ahl and Marlow (2012, p. 548) explain, local narratives (produced after experience is deconstructed and linguistic construction analyzed) 'cannot be produced or analysed unless they draw upon and are reflective of encompassing discourses, which command a broad subscription'. That is, these researchers are 'sensitive to the micro-constructed nature of gender identity whilst acknowledging how this coagulates into collective subordinating assumptions'.

Some studies aim to illustrate how the representations of 'gender' are constructed in distinct structural and institutional circumstances, contributing towards a dominant discourse of entrepreneurship that is gender-biased (Ogbor, 2000; Hamilton, 2006). There are socially constructed and taken-for-granted assumptions about the meanings of 'woman' and 'man' in society, which underpin structural and discursive powers that perpetuate gendered relations. These assumptions have to be unveiled in order to 'do gender' in a more equalitarian way, for example, Lewis' (2014) review of 33 studies of gender and entrepreneurship through a post-modernism lens, facilitating a better understanding of contemporary existence of multiple femininities, moving away from the unique femininity constructed in terms of exclusion through the notion of 'the other'.

Different Questions from Different Perspectives

It is interesting to pose some questions about women entrepreneurs and their ventures from the different research approaches

Table 30.2   Questions about women entrepreneurs and their ventures regarding two issues from the different research perspectives

	Social capital	Innovation
Positivism	What problems do women face in networking? How do these impact their entrepreneurial activity?	What barriers do women face for creating their firms within innovative industries? How many women-owned businesses engage in technological innovation? What are the determinants that make more women innovate?
Interpretivism	Situated networking: who networks with whom, where, when and with which rationality?	How is innovation interpreted/constructed? Do power relations impact the construction? Whose knowledge is regarded as valuable to innovation?
Post modernism	How does the discourse within boards of business-owners' associations mobilize gender biases that hamper women from achieving decision-making positions?	How is innovation constructed/perceived in public policy? How does this construction influence the value of women's contribution to innovation and the funds received?

discussed above (Table 30.2). These questions show how all of them could be employed usefully building our knowledge of women entrepreneurs, their ventures and society.

Since the majority of research has a structural functionalist approach, or positivist perspective (Grant & Perren, 2002), it is of interest to analyze if the same pattern of publication tendency is followed within women's entrepreneurship research. Therefore, the research following the dominant approach – 'gender as a variable', in line with the positivist research perspective – is now compared with other feminist positions.

PUBLICATION TENDENCY

Greene et al. (2003) reviewed the literature on women's entrepreneurship published in entrepreneurship and small business journals from 1991 to 2001. They found 173 articles, showing an increasing tendency in the number of articles published during the 90s. However, they warn that this increase can be a result of, at least in part, the increase in the number of publication outlets and volumes

during these years. Their analysis concludes that, despite larger attention being paid to women's entrepreneurship, the number of articles remains small (with regards to the total number of published articles) in absolute terms, numbers which are shown in the vertical axis of Figure 30.1. Their analysis does not include some European journals which have also paid attention to this strand of research, including the *International Journal of Entrepreneurial Behaviour and Research* and the *International Journal of Gender and Entrepreneurship*.[2]

In order to follow up the study by Greene et al. (2003), the same journals have been reviewed for 2002–15, adding the *International Journal of Entrepreneurial Behaviour and Research*. Within them, all the articles about 'women-owned business enterprises' and 'gender' were reviewed and classified within the 'gender as a variable', or dominant, approach or 'other perspectives'. The number of articles on women's entrepreneurship per year is shown in Figure 30.1 and summed up per journal for the whole period in Table 30.3.

Figure 30.1 shows that the publication tendency declines after 2006 and 2007, when three special issues were published in

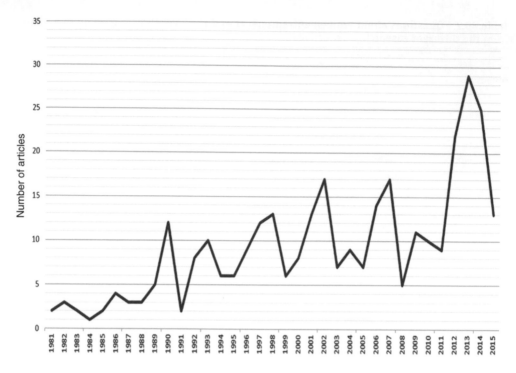

Figure 30.1   Tendency of publication in women entrepreneurship

Entrepreneurship Theory and Practice and *International Small Business Journal*, but starts to increase again in 2012, achieving a peak in 2013 before slowing down. Jennings and Brush's (2013) review shows an increasing tendency, but, as the authors explain, it is due to the inclusion of other outlets, such as academic books, beside top-tier journals. Some aspects already point to the improvement of its positioning within academia, like specific publishing outlets, conferences and special issues.

In order to analyze the publication tendency of women-entrepreneurship articles within the different feminist positions, as stated previously, the articles have been put into two categories: 'gender as a variable' and other perspectives, based on a review of their full text (see Figure 30.2). Observing the tendency, there has been an increase in studies with an alternative perspective to the dominant one: that is, from 'gender as a variable' and 'a stable category' to gender as 'an

unstable and fluid doing'. In 2011 they comprised 23.5%, and this increased to 37% in 2013 and 42.3% in 2015.

Despite this increase, 'gender as a variable' research remains the dominant approach in the majority of publications, despite the criticism by Ahl (2006) about the dominant objectivist ontological and epistemological position behind most women's entrepreneurship scholarship published to that date. The tendency has not reverted. These findings may be interpreted as 'gender as a variable' research being valuable and interesting for many scholars. Thus, despite the evolving socio-economic circumstances, the pervasive gender inequalities in the home, the labor market and business still require monitoring. Furthermore, in addressing these issues from a positivist approach, the studies have developed their levels of sophistication over the years both in terms of the theoretical framework, including issues such as gender roles and the influence of context, and in its

Table 30.3 Publications about female entrepreneurship

Publication name	Foundation date	Number of issues[1] per year	Greene et al. (2003) 1991–2001			2002–15		
			Total of reviewed issues	Number of articles about female entrepreneurship[2]	Percentage of numbers that have an article about female entrepreneurship	Total of reviewed issues	Number of articles about female entrepreneurship per journal for the whole interval	Percentage of numbers that have an article about female entrepreneurship
Entrepreneurship Theory and Practice[3]	1976	4	104	7	6.7%	56	30	53.6%
Journal of Small Business Management	1976	4	104	31	30%	56	22	39.3%
International Small Business Journal[4]	1981	4	84	11	13%	56	22	39.3%
Frontiers of Entrepreneurship	1981	1	20	18	Not available	13 (2014)	29	—
Journal of Business Ethics	1982	7	120	7	5.8%	98	5	5.1%
Journal of Business Venturing	1985	6 (3 prev.)	87	20	23%	84	15	17.9%
Entrepreneurship & Regional Development	1989	4	52	11	21.2%	56	13	23.2%
Small Business Economics	1989	6	78	14	18%	84	28	33.3%
Journal of Developmental Entrepreneurship	1996	2	12	10	83%	56 (4 issues per year)	47	83.9%
International Journal of Entrepreneurial Behaviour and Research	1995	6 (3 until 1999)	33	2	6.7%	84	26	30.9%

1. Greene et al. (2003) labeled this column 'numbers per year', but they were referring to 'number of issues per year'. Accordingly, they labeled the following column 'total of reviewed numbers', but they were referring to 'total of reviewed issues'.

2. The words 'entrepreneur', 'entrepreneurship', 'women', 'woman', 'female' and 'gender' were searched for in all the issues' abstracts.

3. Previously named: *American Journal of Small Business* (1976–88)

4. Previously named: *European Small Business Journal* (1981–2)

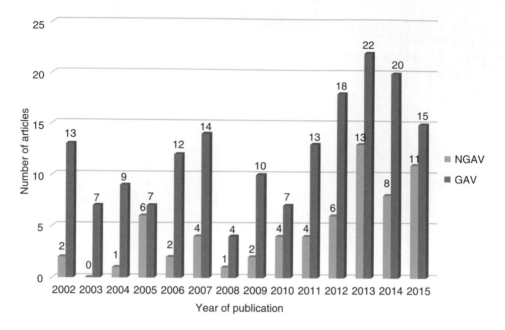

Figure 30.2   Tendency of publication by research perspective 2002–15

discussions and statistical analysis. However, in line with Ahl (2006), it can be argued that in considering entrepreneurship as an engine for growth, and especially within women due to the gender gap, researchers have inadvertently privileged some questions over others.

There has been a qualitative appreciation of the field regarding the growth in scope (theoretical underpinnings, research designs) and depth (longitudinal, cross-cultural and more sophisticated analyses and techniques) within these years; therefore, it is clearly demonstrated that entrepreneurship as a gendered phenomenon has gained considerable attention. However, there is still a lack of use of feminist theory, at least explicitly, since the majority of studies from a 'gender as a variable' orientation have a highly individualistic orientation and, therefore, little attention has been paid to contextual and historical variables that lead to gendered power structures (Hughes et al., 2012). Therefore, despite considerable diversity, the main lines of research have been until now: entrepreneurial intention and action, financial

resources, managerial practices and performance growth. There are some connections with other fields (sociology, psychology, geography) but still not many.

DISCUSSION OF FUTURE RESEARCH DEVELOPMENT

In developing research in the field of gender and entrepreneurship it is important to undertake credible social research. This means 'that the questions asked and the designs employed are shaped by the researcher's underlying, ontological and epistemological assumptions' and 'the choice of methodology becomes a matter of aptness: different types of research question are best answered by different types of study employing appropriate methods' (Leitch, Hill & Harrison, 2010, pp. 69, 71). In line with this view, two issues have to be emphasized. First, the appropriateness of a particular perspective depends on the purpose of the research. And, second, studying the phenomena through different lenses can enrich the area of research; however, certain challenges have to be taken into account in future lines of research within each perspective.

Researching from a 'Gender as a Variable' Approach

Although social structures evolve, there are still gender-based inequalities, and, drawing on the 'gender as a variable' perspective enable researchers to continue monitoring gender difference with the aim of informing policy and practice. If a positivist approach is the choice of the researcher, he or she might be aware of some aspects.

Normally, gender is conflated with sex, even though it refers to constructions of masculinity and femininity that reflect social arrangements not by necessity tied to a certain type of biological body (Borna & White, 2003). This assumption that the human population can be neatly divided into two is no longer supportable; however, within this perspective there are few attempts to quantify gender instead of sex. *There is a need to avoid essentialism in discussion of results*, since presuming the existence of measurable 'male' and 'female' attributes contributes to the reproduction of gender differences. One way might be using gender-role orientation, which is an established measure from psychology and is likely to prove useful in teasing out the heterogeneity among women entrepreneurs or finding differences that are not observed when taking into account sex (Watson & Newby, 2005; Mueller & Dato-on, 2011). Westbrook and Saperstein (2015) show that researchers are beginning to test alternative measures, including answer options beyond 'male' and 'female' in surveys. They contend that it is important in order to reflect the diversity in gendered lives and to align gender measurement practice with contemporary gender theory.

Another main criticism of this research approach is that it does not pay attention to structural barriers producing discrimination and, therefore, does not question how their implications might reproduce stereotypes about women. In this regard, research should concentrate on *utilizing theories that emphasize the conditions for entrepreneurship for both men and women*, since they are more responsible for differences than the individuals per se. For example, drawing on institutional theory, gender embeddedness can be researched on different levels: social, economic and cultural, observing how socio-economic forces cause the differences between genders (i.e. labor markets, organizational practices, welfare-state legislation concerning motherhood and childcare). The use of this theory, acknowledging the critiques of certain methodological approaches (Ahl, 2008; Foss, 2010), will lead to the inclusion of structural variables (context) in the research design and the study of different levels of embeddedness (Elam, 2008). It might be that by taking context into account it is easier to focus on questions that deviate from the dominant discourse on entrepreneurship as motor of economic growth. Hughes et al. (2012), for example, criticize the fact that the former discourse has triggered much research explaining the performance and growth of women's ventures while avoiding other types of research questions.

Finally, in using quantitative research methods, the aim is to provide an objective and neutral assessment of a phenomenon by eliminating prejudiced elements such as gender stereotypes. However, there has to be *awareness that the research methodologies often embed power relations*, either hidden in the research design and/or the ways of reasoning that are not challenged, and they usually guide researchers towards functionalist explanations of gender differences when interpreting the results (Haynes, 2008). Therefore, researchers have to be more careful of this limitation when interpreting quantitative results.

On the other hand, gender research can *draw in feminist theory with a critical view of knowledge*. A growing number of researchers are gaining a better understanding of the nuances of researching gender with a critical feminist focus. They are also illustrating the great potential that this perspective has to contribute in advancing the research field and establish a political agenda which fosters social and cultural change.

Recently, there has been a call to use multilevel theories of entrepreneurship (Ruef & Lounsbury, 2007; Elam, 2008; Brush et al., 2009). This call is related to showing the importance of the impact of different levels of the context in women's experiences, thereby precluding methodologies and interpretations of results influenced by essentialism. Another avenue for future research on gender is *designing multilevel studies with a more holistic understanding of the phenomena*. The work by Thébaud offers two good examples of multilevel designs. One of her recent studies (Thébaud, 2015a) focuses on linking the macro-social and organizational context to micro-level cognitive processes, testing how cultural beliefs about gender frame social interactions that ultimately determine whether a new organization will be deemed worthy of support and survive. Gender-status beliefs lead most people to doubt women's entrepreneurial ability, but women may be able to mitigate this status-based bias by being innovative. This effect is higher in settings in which gender is quite salient as a status characteristic for entrepreneurs (a male-dominated industry or a country in which women have a lower rate of participation in entrepreneurship than men). A further study by Thébaud (2015b) shows how, in the presence of institutional arrangements to mitigate work–family conflict (paid leave, subsidized childcare and part-time employment opportunities), women are less likely to opt for business ownership as an employment strategy. As a result, women in these contexts are relatively less well represented among entrepreneurs as a whole but better represented in growth-oriented forms of entrepreneurship (smaller gender gaps in terms of business size, growth aspirations and propensity to innovate or use new technology; less likely to report pursuing entrepreneurship because they lacked attractive employment options). In institutional contexts characterized by salient work–family conflict women's aggregate representation in business activity is larger but their segregation into less growth-oriented (and thus lower-status) ventures is reinforced.

Researching from a Non-Positivistic Approach

The interpretive perspective that considers 'gender as a process' provides evidence that gender is a complex phenomenon. Whether at the individual or at the social level, the question has to be whether the processes of gender are so rigid that we cannot change these ways of 'doing gender' in our interactions. Undoubtedly, entrepreneurship is a gendered process and, therefore, context is crucial in doing gender in one way or other. Subsequently, *the structural realms must be studied and articulated in terms of gender dynamics*, although this presents greater difficulty in doing so, as they are less tangible and explicit than individuals' traits (Hovorka & Dietrich, 2010, pp. 55–6). For example, a recent study by Marlow, Greene and Coad (2016) focuses on testing if socio-economic discrimination arising from sexual orientation prompts individuals to create their own employment. Therefore, they compared the incidence of self-employment among hetero- and homosexual entrepreneurs, finding no significant differences.

Focusing on gender as a construction in social interaction, an important issue is *how men and women interact and the impact of the relations of power*: that is, how women internalize or resist the normative heteropatriarchal discourses to construct their identity, leading to different types of femininity (Lewis, 2014). The mentioned discourses contribute to the maintenance of the gender status quo;

therefore, women strategize differently to contest them. For example, most entrepreneurial activity occurs within family and household copreneurship (Carter, 2011; McAdam & Marlow, 2013), since team-led ventures are common and have greater viability (Harper, 2008), and, therefore, it is important to analyze how gendered role ascriptions define the competencies between those involved in the team (Bruni & Perrotta, 2014; Marlow, 2016).

Another avenue for future research can be how other categories of 'difference' (race, class, etc.) and contextual circumstances (political, cultural and cognitive levels of embeddedness) interact with gender, incorporating further complexity in how individuals experience their lives and construct their identities. A challenge that needs to be avoided in this line of research is to present gender as a *heterogeneous set of practices and experiences*, since this would result in research findings being a conglomerate of knowledge that makes it difficult to develop coherent theory and provide political implications. Therefore, studies should give primacy to gender even when taking other sources of difference among women into account. A recent article by Dy, Marlow and Martin (2016) using an interpretative approach reveals how the privileges and disadvantages arising from intersecting social positions of gender, race and class are experienced by women business owners of digital firms in the UK. Social positionality and the associated resource constraints are produced and reproduced on the internet. Along these lines, Marlow (2016, p. 8) proposes that researching the way intersectional positionality, drawing upon gender in relation to other social ascriptions, shapes entrepreneurial propensity offers much scope for further interrogation.

In other areas of research (like organizational behaviour) there is *a concern for masculinity*, since men also have to negotiate gender roles. However, within entrepreneurship literature we have not focused yet on that issue, as it seems that gender concerns are widely interpreted as pertaining to women

only. This might happen because researchers assume that previous gender-blind work was already about male entrepreneurs. In order to broaden our focus, it might be useful to include constructions of masculinity, since in doing so gender power relations have to be made visible, which means we have to unveil the male-advantage position within socio-economic structures. Otherwise, we run the risk of 'reproducing a patriarchially based vision, which reinforces their privileges and re-excludes women and femininities' (Broadbridge & Simpson, 2011, p. 476).

Furthermore, because of its complexity it can be advisable that we *engage with a range of other disciplines* (geography, psychology and sociology, among others) in order to develop conceptual and theoretical work that enables us to fully understand all the facets of gender and their implications in individuals' experience.

CONCLUSION

This literature review provides an overview of the research on women entrepreneurship published since 2002. This provides an analysis of the women-entrepreneurship domain and reflects on future lines of research. Researchers have to be aware of the different research paths and select the most appropriate research design, since otherwise it will not matter which path they take: they will not reach their goal, be it either publication in academic journals and/or transfer of knowledge to practitioners. It has become more and more difficult to be published in indexed journals (outlets that are more likely to have been noticed and read by others) (Marlow, 2016), and apart from biases in the editorial process, this might imply that we have to renew and rethink the ways that we – as researchers on female entrepreneurship – are researching this topic.

With regards to the positions within feminism, researchers have to question themselves:

does the research design assume that a simple sex-based disaggregation of data (binary categories of males and females) is enough? Or does the research design imply a gender analysis? According to the research question, we have to choose the method, taking into account that some methods or combination of them may be more useful than others for particular research questions. The design of research will impact the nature and scope of the research, the parts of the phenomenon on which it focuses and the quality of the knowledge that we generate.

Regarding the publication tendency of women-entrepreneurship articles within the different feminist positions, the findings show a decline since 2007 (because of the effect of previous publication of special issues) followed by an increase until 2013. Hughes et al. (2012) report an expansion of scholarly interest and activity in the field of women's entrepreneurship in recent years, especially since 2006. This suggests that more work has to be done to increase the awareness of gender issues and move women's entrepreneurship research from the margins to become a more central body of work.

Besides this, there is a gentle 'turn' in the literature from 'gender as a variable' research to 'gender as a process'. Hence, the dominant perspective still represents the majority of research. This can be interpreted as 'gender as a variable' research, with special attention to significant gender differences being considered useful in providing evidence of gender inequality, which informs gender policies. On the one hand, these findings could be explained by the journals reviewed, which were selected in order to follow up the study by Greene et al. (2003). They are high-ranked journals that might be more prone to publish papers from the objectivist position (Ahl, 2006). The main criticism of this perspective is that it is often focused on exploring gender differences but that it allows them to persist, since it does not explore the constructed gendered notions – based on social, cultural and political issues – underpinning

those differences (Haynes, 2008; Hovorka & Dietrich, 2010). Therefore, the analysis has found that the dominance of the 'gender as a variable' approach is still evident but that it has been complemented in recent years with gender research based on a feminist theory with a more critical overtone.

Research through multiple lenses is needed for progress in a relatively young area. That is, the dominant approach discussed above has to be complemented with other research approaches that examine the social, cultural and political context of gender relations with the aim of challenging gender divisions and inequalities. Once the term *gender* was introduced, gender analysis encouraged identification of situational and temporal characteristics across cultures and time. This means understanding gender as a social process generated by relational issues between males and females in the context of social institutions (Oliffe & Greaves, 2011). These issues will be better captured with qualitative or mixed-method research approaches, to help gain a more comprehensive picture of the phenomenon of interest and to contribute results more meaningful and relevant to practitioners. Along these lines, Dunning (2007, p. 294) proposes that functional and causal explanatory paradigms need to be modified or at least complemented with more experimental and less empirical ones. The latter are more suited to an understanding of entrepreneurial activity, and the merit of this type of research has to be more fully acknowledged.

Recognizing that a young area of research can benefit from studying the phenomenon through multiple lenses, a call for future research would be that research designs should exploit the evolution of feminist theory to explain women's experiences in entrepreneurship. To advance knowledge accumulation within this field, researchers should either explore conventional questions with unconventional approaches or propose unconventional questions that raise new matters. Consequently, a focus on gender with a feminist theoretical underpinning could offer new approaches and insights to entrepreneurship and small-business research. It can shift the focus from women as individuals, responsible for their apparent 'shortcomings' in the entrepreneurial field, to gender power structures embedded in social arrangements as explanations of the differences.

Notes

1   Alvesson and Due Billing (1997) differentiate between political feminist standpoints (liberal, radical, socialist) and feminist researchers' view on knowledge ('gender as a variable', feminist standpoint, critical-interpretive perspective and post-structuralist feminism). The latter are the categories analyzed in this study.
2   The former has been included in this analysis, except for Figure 30.1, in order to have a proper comparison with the data from Greene et al. (2003). The latter has not been included, since it has a gender-specific focus differing from the journals analyzed, where articles related to that subject have lower coverage. However, reviewing the publication tendency of this journal, since its inception in 2009, could be interesting as a future line of research.

REFERENCES

Ahl, H. (2006). 'Why research on women entrepreneurs needs new directions', *Entrepreneurship Theory and Practice*, 30 (5), 595–621.

Ahl, H. (2008). 'The problematic relationship between social capital theory and gender research', in Aaltio-Marjosola, I., Kyrö, P. and Sundin, E. (eds.), *Women entrepreneurship and social capital*. Copenhagen: Copenhagen Business School Press, pp. 167–89.

Ahl, H. and Marlow, S. (2012). 'Exploring the dynamics of gender, feminism and entrepreneurship: Advancing debate to escape a dead end', *Organization*, 19 (5), 543–62.

Ahl, H. and Nelson, T. (2010). 'Moving forward: Institutional perspectives on gender and entrepreneurship', *International Journal of Gender and Entrepreneurship*, 2 (1), 5–10.

Alvesson, M. and Deetz, S. (2000). *Doing critical management research*. London: Sage.

Alvesson, M. and Due Billing, Y. (1997). *Understanding gender and organizations*. London, Thousand Oaks, CA, New Delhi: Sage.

Bhaskar, R. A. (1997 [1975]). *A realist theory of science*. London: Verso.

Blackburn, R. and Kovalainen, A. (2009). 'Researching small firms and entrepreneurship: Past, present and future', *International Journal of Management Reviews,* 11 (2), 127–48.

Borna, S. and White, G. (2003). '"Sex" and "gender": Two confused and confusing concepts in "women in management literature"', *Journal of Business Ethics*, 47 (2), 89–99.

Bradley, H. (2007). *Gender: Key concepts*. Cambridge: Polity Press.

Broadbridge, A. and Simpson, R. (2011). '25 years on: Reflecting on the past and looking to the future in gender and management research', *British Journal of Management*, 22, 470–83.

Bruni, A. and Perrotta, M. (2014). 'Entrepreneuring together: His and her stories', *International Journal of Entrepreneurial Behavior & Research*, 20 (2), 108–27.

Bruni, E. A., Gherardi, S. and Poggio, B. (2005). *Gender and entrepreneurship. An ethnographical approach*. London and New York: Routledge.

Brush, C. and Cooper, S. (2012). 'Female entrepreneurship and economic development: An international perspective', *Entrepreneurship & Regional Development: An International Journal*, 24 (1–2), 1–6.

Brush, C. G., de Bruin, A. and Welter, F. (2009). 'A gender-aware framework for women's entrepreneurship', *International Journal of Gender and Entrepreneurship*, 1 (1), 8–24.

Bryman, A. and Bell, E. (2008). *Business research methods*. New York: Oxford: Oxford University Press.

Burrell, G. and Morgan, G. (1979). *Sociological paradigms and organizational analysis*. London: Heinemann.

Calás, M. B., Smircich, L. and Bourne, K. A. (2009). 'Extending the boundaries: Reframing "entrepreneurship as social change" through feminist perspectives', *Academy of Management Review*, 34 (3), 552–69.

Carter, S. (2011). 'The rewards of entrepreneurship: Exploring the incomes, wealth, and economic well-being of entrepreneurial households', *Entrepreneurship Theory and Practice*, 35 (1), 39–55.

Carter, S. and Shaw, E. (2006). *Women's business ownership: Recent research and policy development*. London: DTI Small Business Service Research Report.

Chia, R. (2002). 'The production of management knowledge: philosophical underpinnings of research design', in Partington, D. (ed.), *Essential Skills for Management Research* (1st ed). London: Sage, pp. 1–19.

Chua, W. F. (1986). 'Radical developments in accounting thought', *The Accounting Review*, 61 (4), 601–32.

De Bruin, A., Brush, C. and Welter, F. (2007). 'Advancing a framework for coherent research on women's entrepreneurship', *Entrepreneurship Theory and Practice*, 31 (3), 323–39.

Dunning, J. H. (2007). 'A new zeitgeist for international business and scholarship', *European Journal of International Management*, 1 (4), 278–301.

Du Rietz, A. and Henrekson, M. (2000). 'Testing the female underperformance hypothesis', *Small Business Economics*, 14 (1), 1–10.

Dy, A., Marlow, S. and Martin, L. A. (2016). 'Web of opportunity or the same old story? Women digital entrepreneurs and intersectionality theory', *Human Relations*, 70 (3), 286–311.

Easterby-Smith, M., Thorpe, R. and Jackson, P. (2008). *Management research* (3rd ed.). London: Sage.

Elam, A. (2008). *Gender and entrepreneurship: A multilevel theory and analysis*. Cheltenham: Edward Elgar.

Foss, L. (2010). 'Research on entrepreneur networks: The case for a constructionist feminist theory perspective', *International Journal of Gender and Entrepreneurship*, 2 (1), 83–102.

Grant, P. and Perren, L. (2002). 'Small business and entrepreneurial research: Meta-theories, paradigms and prejudices', *International Small Business Journal*, 20 (2), 185–211.

Gray, D. E. (2013). *Doing research in the real world* (3rd edition). London: Sage.

Greene, P. G., Hart, M., Gatewood, E., Brush, C. G. and Carter, N. (2003). *Women entrepreneurs: Moving front and center. An overview of research and theory*. Coleman White Paper Series 3 (1), 1–47. Available at: www.unm. edu/~asalazar/Kauffman/Entrep_research/e_ women.pdf (accessed 20 October 2016).

Guba, E. G. and Lincoln, Y. S. (1994). 'Competing paradigms in qualitative research', in Denzin, N. K. and Lincoln, Y. S. (eds.), *Handbook of qualitative research* (pp. 105–17). London: Sage.

Hamilton, E. (2006). 'Whose story is it anyway? Narrative accounts of the role of women in founding and establishing family businesses', *International Small Business Journal*, 24 (June), 253–71.

Harper, D. A. (2008). 'Towards a theory of entrepreneurial teams', *Journal of Business Venturing*, 23 (6), 613–26.

Haynes, K. (2008). 'Power and politics in gender research: A research note from the discipline of accounting', *Gender in Management: An International Journal*, 23 (7), 528–32.

Hovorka, A. J. and Dietrich, D. (2010). 'Entrepreneurship as a gendered process', *Entrepreneurship and Innovation*, 12 (1), 55–65.

Hughes, K., Jennings, J., Brush, C., Carter, S. and Welter, F. (2012). 'Extending women's entrepreneurship research in new directions', *Entrepreneurship Theory and Practice*, 36 (3), 429–42.

Jennings, J. E. and Brush, C. G. (2013). 'Research on women entrepreneurs: Challenges to (and from) the broader entrepreneurship literature?', *The Academy of Management Annals*, 7 (1), 663–715.

Klyver, K., Nielsen, S. L. and Evald, M. R. (2012). 'Women's self-employment: An act of institutional (dis) integration? A multilevel, cross-country study', *Journal of Business Venturing*, 28 (4), 474–88.

Leitch, C. M., Hill, F. M. and Harrison, R. T. (2010). 'The philosophy and practice of interpretivist research in entrepreneurship: Quality, validation, and trust', *Organizational Research Methods,* 13 (1), 67–84.

Lewis, P. (2014). 'Postfeminism, femininities, and organization studies: Exploring a new agenda', *Organization Studies*, 35 (12), 1845–66.

Lincoln, Y., Lynham, S. and Guba, E. (2011). 'Paradigmatic controversies, contradictions and emerging confluences', in Denzin, N. and Lincoln, Y. (eds.), *The Sage handbook of qualitative research* (pp. 97–128). Los Angeles, CA: Sage.

Marlow, S. (2016). 'Rethinking the gender agenda in entrepreneurship: Time to "queer the pitch"?', paper presented at RENT XXX, Antwerp, November.

Marlow, S., Greene, F. and Coad, A. (2016). 'Queering the agenda? A critical evaluation of contemporary assumptions underpinning the influence of gender', paper presented at the BCERC Babson Conference, Bodo.

McAdam, M. and Marlow, S. (2013). 'A gendered critique of the copreneurial business partnership: exploring the implications for entrepreneurial emancipation', *International Journal of Entrepreneurship and Innovation*, 14 (3), 151–63.

Miles, M. and Huberman, A. M. (1994). *Qualitative data analysis: A source book of new methods*. Beverly Hills, CA: Sage.

Mueller, S. L. and Dato-on, M. C. (2011). 'A cross-cultural study of gender-role orientation and entrepreneurial self-efficacy', *International Journal of Entrepreneurship and Management*, doi: 10.1007/s11365-011-0187-y.

Neergaard, H., Frederiksen, S. H. and Marlow, S. (2011). 'The emperor's new clothes: Rendering a feminist theory of entrepreneurship visible', paper presented at ICSB, Stockholm.

Ogbor, J. O. (2000). 'Mythicizing and reification in entrepreneurial discourse: Ideology critique of entrepreneurial studies', *Journal of Management Studies*, 37 (5), 605–35.

Oliffe, J. L. and Greaves, L. (2011). *Designing and conducting gender, sex, and health research*. Thousand Oaks, CA: Sage.

Ridgeway, C. L. and Correll, S. J. (2004). 'Unpacking the gender system: A theoretical perspective on gender beliefs and social relations', *Gender and Society,* 18 (4): 510–31.

Risman, B. (1998). *Gender vertigo*. New Haven, CT: Yale University Press.

Rouse, J. and Kitching, J. (2006). 'Do enterprise support programmes leave women holding the baby?', *Environment and Planning C: Government and Policy*, 24 (1), 5–19.

Ruef, M. and Lounsbury, M. (2007). 'Introduction: The sociology of entrepreneurship', in *The sociology of entrepreneurship*. Bingley: Emerald Group Publishing, pp. 1–29.

Sullivan, D. M. and Meek, W. R. (2012). 'Gender and entrepreneurship: A review and process model', *Journal of Managerial Psychology*, 27, 428–58.

Thébaud, S. (2015a). 'Status beliefs and the spirit of capitalism: Accounting for gender biases in entrepreneurship and innovation', *Social Forces*, 94, 61–86.

Thébaud, S. (2015b). 'Business as plan b: Institutional foundations of gender inequality in entrepreneurship across 24 industrialized countries', *Administrative Science Quarterly*, 60 (4), 671–711.

Watkins-Mathys, L. and Lowe, S. (2005). 'Small business and entrepreneurship research: The way through paradigm incommensurability', *International Small Business Journal*, 23 (6), 657–77.

Watson, J. and Newby, R. (2005). 'Biological sex, stereotypical sex-roles and SME owner characteristics', *International Journal of Entrepreneurial Behaviour and Research*, 11 (2), 129–43.

Westbrook, L. and Saperstein, A. (2015). 'New categories are not enough: Rethinking the measurement of sex and gender in social surveys', *Gender and Society*, 29 (4), 534–60.

31

Making Entrepreneurship Research Matter: The Challenging Journey to an Academic Identity

Bengt Johannisson

INTRODUCTION

With the digital revolution the world has become increasingly ambiguous, or 'liquid', as Zygmunt Bauman (2000) puts it. The world is a social construction emerges in strange ways, combining repetitions and serendipitous encounters in a crazy-quilting mode. In a social world that is in constant motion, little can be taken for granted. Such ambiguity, though, does not just produce anxiety. It also carries freedom. There is no path to follow, but neither is there organized resistance against any initiative taken. Thus, if we hold on to the belief that the environment is enactable, mobilize our imagination and then persistently (inter)act with trusted allies, our ideas may actualize (Daft & Weick, 1984; Smircich & Stubbart, 1985; Gartner, Bird & Starr, 1992). Recognizing entrepreneurship as a mode of dealing with ambiguity by constantly enacting ventures obviously announces a Kuhnian paradigm shift in how entrepreneurship is comprehended. Rather than being associated with instigating change, entrepreneurship becomes a way of arresting change by channelling its energy into temporary social constructs or ventures that produce economic, social and/or ecological value. In contributing to a platform for future entrepreneurship research, it thus seems more productive to reflect upon the implications of this view than to take stock of research carried out within an old paradigm. Accordingly, as well as due to space restrictions, the review of existing research is here kept very brief, with most chapters in this *Handbook* naturally attending to significant texts on their respective subjects.

The purpose of this chapter is, first, to provide some further signs of a paradigm shift in entrepreneurship research. Second, a bibliometric analysis is reported that maps how entrepreneurship research presents itself in the perspective of management studies, a field usually considered to embrace entrepreneurship. A third ambition is to show that the entrepreneurship research community can strengthen its identity by promoting 'originality' as another dimension of quality in research besides the established two – rigour and relevance.

First, though, a few comments concerning the state of the art in the field of entrepreneurship. In the beginning of empirical research into entrepreneurship and small business, many scholars took advantage of their background in applied statistics and mathematics to do quantitative studies of populations of new ventures and established firms. This interest in objectivist approaches has certainly remained within small-business and entrepreneurship research communities. It has also inspired the creation and use of rich databases such as the General Entrepreneurship Monitor (GEM). In parallel, however, many researchers have become even more intrigued by 'entrepreneuring' as a social and processual phenomenon (Steyaert, 2007), which dressed differently appears in all contexts where there is human activity. This reorientation has also triggered the development of qualitative methodologies able to reveal entrepreneurship as a cultural phenomenon (see, for example, Hjorth & Steyaert 2004; Gartner, 2007). In addition, there is at present an urge among entrepreneurship scholars to find a way to reconcile two contrasting views: on the one hand, inquiring into the everyday practising of entrepreneuring and its need for detailed accounts and, on the other, into abstracted images of the phenomenon and associated operationalized models that pave the road to generalization. This desire probably explains why Saras Sarasvathy's (2001, 2008) notion of the 'logic of effectuation' has been well received in the field of entrepreneurship research and is now about to be recognized as a theoretical breakthrough (Arend, Sarooghi & Burkemper, 2015). Further contemporary studies into entrepreneurial practices contribute to creating a link between the rather mundane down-to-earth everyday occurrences of entrepreneurship and the spectacular outcome of these processes in terms of radical innovations (see, for example, Plowman, Baker, Beck, Kulkarni, Solansky & Travis, 2007).

The chapter is organized as follows. Next, I present three critical issues that announce a need for changing our understanding and modes of researching entrepreneurship. In the third section I use bibliometrics to demonstrate how entrepreneurship, as well as small-business research, is still submitting to an omnipotent management research community. In the fourth section I outline a perspective on entrepreneurship that recognizes it as a processual phenomenon and practice that invites an 'enactive' methodology and 'originality' as a dimension of research quality. Reflecting on the topical notion of 'the entrepreneurial university', in the last section I propose a way of enabling academia to provide more responsible research and adequate education for entrepreneurship.

REDESIGNING ENTREPRENEURSHIP RESEARCH: BASIC POSTULATES

Forty years ago James March upset the organizational-research community with his challenging text 'The Technology of Foolishness' (1976). His argument was that 'foolishness' must exist in parallel with reason in order to create learning organizations. He highlights that adults take their own objectives for granted but tell children that they do not know what is for their own good. March's call for playfulness also includes, besides treating goals as hypotheses, treating intuition as real, hypocrisy as a transition, memory as an enemy and experience as a theory (1976, pp. 78–9). Luckily, children's playful approach to life resists the attempts of adults to curb it. What is more, children's play is part of an experiential learning process, including changing without fuss the rules when they need to adapt to the situation. Also, children's play is undertaken in a community spirit. When adults play in their leisure time, the atmosphere becomes quite competitive and the rules are definitive (Huizinga, 1950). In children's worlds being and doing are inseparable, as they are to the existentially and instrumentally driven entrepreneur. Their world is a world of entrepreneurial practice (Johannisson, 2010).

I want to make three statements which provide the terms for making entrepreneuring as a practice intelligible, thereby providing a platform for future research in the field: *A. Entrepreneuring is not about instigating change but about temporarily arresting it; B. Entrepreneuring is a processual phenomenon that crosses boundaries in time and space; C. Entrepreneuring is a multi-coloured science.*

A. Entrepreneuring is not about instigating change but about temporarily arresting it

Since the days of Schumpeter, it has been taken for granted that entrepreneuring carries change (Schumpeter, 1912) and ultimately creates new worlds (Spinosa, Flores & Dreyfus, 1997). Opposing frameworks, such as Kirzner's (1973), that view the entrepreneur as an alert mediator between suppliers and customers, aiming at stabilizing markets, are seldom discussed. Both these views were, however, developed in an industrial era when environmental complexity was discernible and the dynamics foreseeable. In present post-industrial times, these forces, supported by digital information technology, have brought the economy and hence society to the edge of chaos. Within a world that *is* change – that is, in a constant state of becoming (Tsoukas & Chia, 2002) – there is no need to unchain further forces that create alterations. This means that the image of entrepreneurs as change-makers has to be revised. The challenge is now rather to find ways of mobilizing human capabilities that can stem ongoing change, at least temporarily, so that value can be created.

Accordingly, we have to focus on entrepreneurs as sense-makers and doers, able to trigger enactments while in the driving seat. Alternatively stated, the very role of entrepreneuring in contemporary society is to interpret and tame the energy that external changes create. In this perspective, typical entrepreneurial behaviours such as constant improvising, spontaneous action and bricolaging are not irrational but mirror the only feasible way to deal with ambiguous environments. Incessant and nearsighted micro-eventing reveals an ability to mobilize situated knowledge and to take action, rather than becoming paralysed or, equally bad, resigned to analysis, not to mention conceptualization (Nayak & Chia, 2011). The institutionalization of an emergence process into a new venture means that an abode for diverse further enactments has been established. Organizations are becoming increasingly impermanent (Weick, 2009), making ephemeral organizing (Lanzara, 1983) a norm. Economies of size and scope do not even guarantee the survival of the few corporations that today (still) appear as global institutions.

B. Entrepreneuring is a processual phenomenon that crosses boundaries in time and space

In a recent publication Gartner (2016) summarizes his many contributions to the field by stating that entrepreneurship is about creative 'organizing'. This means that a state materializes where neither institutionalized stability nor chaos rules. This processual perspective calls for an ontology of becoming, presenting entrepreneuring as an emerging activity that is closely related to mundane and spontaneous doings: 'It is through [these] everyday practical coping actions and sense-making interactions, prior to the existence of any form of explicit conceptualization and representation, that we collectively forge out a more coherent and liveable world' (Nayak & Chia, 2011, p. 289; see also Chia & Holt, 2006). This is a view that definitely challenges dominant objectivist approaches to entrepreneurship.

Process philosophy provides us with different perspectives on time. Usually, time is referred to as chronological or linear, which makes change appear as a series of consecutive phases. The process philosopher Henri Bergson instead refers to time as 'duration', which associates with lived experience, which in turn means that the present always carries the past in terms of memories and expectations about the future in terms of intentions and visions (Linstead, 2014). When these meet an unknowable environment constant improvisation (Barrett, 1998) and associated bricolaging (Garud & Karnøe, 2003; Baker & Nelson, 2005) are called for. This makes the venture emerge along a path defined by critical incidents (*kairos*, according to Aristotle) rather than by linear time: that is, chronologically (*chronos*, according to Aristotle) (see Rämö, 1999). Surprises and coincidences have to synchronize with available resources into opportunities that are enactable if the right moment arises. In order to survive, the organization thus has to find a way to change concurrently with the environment. Sarasvathy's (2001, 2008) observation that habitual/expert entrepreneurs are as much concerned with exit as with growth strategies reflects this general condition for 'entrepreneuring' in a changing world.

A framework that puts a lot of emphasis on individuals and opportunities with a bearing on the future is carried by a strong belief that the world can be controlled by technical advancements. However, the new information and communication technology (CIT), once welcomed as the creator and explorer of the knowledge and experience economy, has now brought the world into a state that is neither controlled nor out of control. The traditional separation of producers and consumers has become blurred because product development has progressed from in-house via customer-driven to open innovation. The financing of new ventures has moved from 'friends, family and fools' via bootstrapping (Winborg, 2015) to crowd-funding (Shneor & Flåten, 2015). Practising entrepreneuring is today, thanks to CIT, closely integrated in everyday life, as prophesied by Steyaert (2004). This suggests a universally increased involvement of people in entrepreneuring, which is confirmed by the GEM annual panel study. A comparison of new-firm creation in 2000 with that in 2015 in terms of TEA (Total Entrepreneurship Activity) shows that the number of countries where TEA has increased is several times larger than where there has been a decline (GEM, 2000, 2015/16).

C. Entrepreneuring is a multi-coloured science

Dolly Parton sings that as a child she was very proud of her coat of many colours that her mother sewed out of small pieces of cloth. Ongoing improvisations also make any venture appear as a patchwork of actions and interactions – a practice indeed. Likewise, there are many understandings/ostensive definitions of entrepreneurship/ing. Some argue that the existence of many definitions of entrepreneurship reveals the field as immature or 'pre-paradigmatic' (see, for example, Davidsson, 2004), while others assert that the multiple definitions signal a vibrant arena that attracts different discourses and disciplines with associated vocabularies. These contrasting claims signal a need to reconsider the very constitution of entrepreneuring as a science. Here I want to bring up four constructs, namely entrepreneuring as a science of *the artificial*, as a science of *the concrete*, as a science of *the imagination* and as a science of *unique events*.

One of the few things that entrepreneurship scholars seem to agree upon is that entrepreneuring is about producing artefacts, whether discursive, social or material. One reason for this silent agreement when it comes to defining entrepreneurship may be an interest in stressing its affinity with innovation. Drawing upon Herbert Simon's work, some scholars, however, argue that this perspective, that sees entrepreneurship as a designed product of human endeavour, as *a science of the artificial*, should direct future research (see Venkatamaran, Sarasvathy, Dew & Forster, 2012; Sarasvathy, 2003; Selden & Fletcher, 2015).

A popular image of the entrepreneur and entrepreneuring over the last decade has been the notions of bricoleur and bricolage (see above). Lévi-Strauss recognizes that a 'bricoleur' in modern times is 'someone who works with his hands and uses devious means compared to those of a craftsman' (1966, pp. 16–17) and 'bricolage' is using what is at hand, usually a heterogeneous set of resources. Lévi-Strauss argues that the practice of 'bricolaging' activates knowledge that is different from the abstract notion adopted by the social sciences. This alternative view he addresses as 'a science of the concrete' (1966, p. 16). Using concrete experiences to make sense of the world is, according to Lévi-Strauss, no less scientific than sciences carried by concepts.

There are different ways of making sense of how entrepreneurs deal with their experiences. Recognizing entrepreneuring as a personal mode of experiencing the world, Morris, Kuratko, Schindehutte and Spivack (2011) structure extant research in the field. The comprehensive review follows strictly the logico-scientific approach of providing hypotheses and a comprehensive model based on ostensive definitions (compare Latour, 1986). There are, however, other ways of making sense of entrepreneurial experience and learning. Metaphors, analogy and storytelling relate experiences to the local setting where they originate at the same time as transferring them to other sites. A favourite disparaging response to stories from the world of entrepreneuring is that such testimonies 'only' represent 'anecdotal evidence'. Researchers' unconscious and therefore uncontrollable embodied tacit knowledge, however, seems to confirm that such stories with all their concrete details literally 'make sense': that is, communicate what entrepreneuring 'really' may be/is about. Research also demonstrates the potential of narrative approaches when it comes to elucidating different appearances of entrepreneurial phenomena (Hjorth & Steyaert, 2004). Gartner (2007) consequently calls for entrepreneurship as a *science of the imagination*.

Lévi-Strauss argues that the 'science of the concrete' is founded in culture and thus that myths and not objective facts bring order to disparate objects and their use. This creates a bridge between the science of the concrete and the understanding of inquiry into entrepreneurship as *a science of unique events*. Referring to Weber, Agevall (1999) argues that cultural sciences stand out due to their focus on unique events. This means that phenomena are studied because they are significant to us as members of society and not because they are assumed to be 'instances under a law' (Agevall, 1999, pp. 234–5).

Associating entrepreneuring with value creation makes any single micro-event unique that contributes to the venture as a patchwork. This importance of details has been extensively dealt with in 'second-order cybernetics' (Maruyama, 1963) and in chaos theory (see, for example, Stacey, 1992). These frameworks have taught us that the future is unknowable and that the trajectory of a venture is contingent on random events, however paltry. Agency, then, has to focus on interaction, language and symbols in order to enforce and exploit the powers released by uncontrollable forces (Plowman, Baker, Beck, Kulkarni, Solansky & Travis, 2007). Still, again, as anything goes in an ambiguous environment, a strong-willed person is able to enact an idiosyncratic idea, since resistance is difficult to mobilize.

The postulates stated above urge us to study entrepreneurial 'irrationalities' such as acting (intuitively) before thinking, the rationalization of spontaneous action and the incorporation of improvisations into an envisioned action repertoire. The question remains how the entrepreneurship research community can draw upon the proposed postulates to enhance its prospects. I argue and elaborate upon that below. First, entrepreneurship scholars have to be more concerned with joining forces than with pursuing personal agendas when it comes to what to research and how. Second, methodologies have to be developed that take their point of departure in the idiosyncrasies of any entrepreneurial phenomenon, as outlined above. Third, we have to prepare coming generations of researchers, our students, for upcoming challenges by offering them a truly 'entrepreneurial university' as a playground.

A BIBLIOGRAPHIC PROFILE OF ENTREPRENEURSHIP RESEARCH

When it comes to showing the state of the art as regards a research field, its institutionalization in terms of publishing is a major indicator. Then bibliometric analyses are convenient. Table 31.1 thus reports the five journals in the field of entrepreneurship and small business that have, after the turn of the millennium, published the most review articles (as defined by the Web of Science), 112[1] in total. A search on topics using the keywords 'entrepreneurship OR small business' was made in the Web of Science Core Collection for the years 2000–15. The result was limited to articles categorized as reviews, according to the Web of Science, as these are assumed to have a stronger influence on the development of the field of research. The data set was supplemented with impact factors from JCR – Journal Citation Report (Social Sciences Edition), 2014.

The table shows, not surprisingly, that only American and European journals qualify and the former were established ahead of the latter (*Small Business Economics* and *Entrepreneurship & Regional Development*) and probably therefore have a lead with respect both to taking responsibility for publishing review articles and to influencing the research community.

A straight classification based on the abstracts of these articles tells us that about half of them are analytically/methodologically oriented, while the other half focuses on reporting empirical studies. A closer, yet 'impressionistic', reading and content analysis of the subjects covered by these 112 articles (in effect 104, since it was not possible

to clarify eight of them) showed that many articles report on social entrepreneurship and associated subjects. However, none of the 15 journals that, according to the Ulrich database, specialize in this field was at the time of the analysis (March 2016) included in the Web of Science. Process and complexity frameworks are quite often presented as appropriate when researching entrepreneuring. It is, however, alarming that only a handful of the review articles concern how entrepreneurship and small business deal with CIT and/or contribute to the emerging knowledge and experience economy (Shneor & Flåten, 2015). Neither ethical issues nor the practice turn in social sciences are treated.

Management's dominance wherever there is organized activity makes it important for the field of entrepreneurship to accentuate its own distinctive feature, i.e. the practice of unique and concrete events. The message is simple: the members of the entrepreneurship research community must unite to communicate the idiosyncrasies of entrepreneuring as a phenomenon and research area. So far, entrepreneurship researchers have submitted to rules of the academic game that favour management. Priority is given to publishing in journals with high impact factors, where management journals have a lead over entrepreneurship journals. Management can thus, through its journals, control the criteria for what should be considered as proper research in the field of entrepreneurship.

Table 31.2 shows that management journals dominate as outlets for published research in the field of entrepreneurship. A topic search with the keywords 'entrepreneurship OR entrepreneur OR entrepreneurial' was made in the Web of Science Core Collection for the years 2000–15. After records had been sorted on number of times cited, the 100 most cited articles were included in the analysis. In the table, impact factors from JCR – the Journal Citation Report (Social Sciences Edition), 2014 – are included for journals with more than three articles. Almost half of the one hundred most quoted articles on entrepreneurship published

Table 31.1   The contemporary community of research in entrepreneurship and small business – influential journals

Journal (Title and Foundation year)	Number of articles	Impact factor
Journal of Business Venturing (1985)	14	3.678
Entrepreneurship Theory and Practice (1988/1976)(1)	40	3.144
International Small Business Journal (1982)	29	1.800
Small Business Economics (1989)	14	1.795
Entrepreneurship and Regional Development (1989)	15	1.519
Total	112	—

Source: Web of Science (January 2016)

Impact factor: JCR – Journal Citation Reports (Social Sciences Edition), 2014

Note: (1) The journal was established in 1976 as the American Journal of Small Business.

Table 31.2   The exodus of advanced entrepreneurship research to the promised land of management – the bibliometric picture

Journal	Number of articles	Impact factor
Strategic Management Journal	16	3.341
Academy of Management Journal	10	6.448
Journal of Business Venturing	9	3.678
Research Policy	8	3.117
Journal of Management	6	6.071
Academy of Management Review	5	7.475
Entrepreneurship Theory & Practice	4	3.144
Harvard Business Review	3	1.574
(Other journals)	(39)	
Total	61 (100)	—

Source: Web of Science (February 2016)

Impact factor: JCR – Journal Citation Reports (Social Sciences Edition), 2014

over the 2000–15 period appeared in highly ranked management journals, according to the Web of Science.[2] The table also informs us that only two of the five entrepreneurship and small-business journals which published the most review articles during the same period (Table 31.1) – that is, *Journal of Business Venturing* and *Entrepreneurship Theory & Practice* – were among those journals which over the 2000–15 period frequently published top articles in the field of entrepreneurship.

Obviously, few frequently quoted articles concerning entrepreneurship appear in journals publishing organization research. This is surprising considering that as early as 1988 William B. Gartner published a seminal article in the field, arguing that entrepreneurship is basically about organization creation (see also Gartner, 2016). The negligence of entrepreneurship's unique organizational characteristics may explain why it has taken such a long time for researchers to apply processual and practice perspectives to entrepreneuring. On the one hand, the visibility of entrepreneurship research in established management journals may have increased its legitimacy. On the other, potential impulses for creative and/or critical perspectives and appropriate methodologies in the pursuit of insight into entrepreneuring have probably been held back.

The challenge for the entrepreneurship-research community is to balance the legitimacy that publishing in highly ranked (management) journals brings and to protect the uniqueness of the field of inquiry as outlined in the previous section. The increased awareness of this uniqueness, together with bibliometric analyses, suggests that it is time for entrepreneurship researchers to give priority to publishing in the field's own journals. Taking a greater responsibility for the development of our own field is, however, not mainly a question of streamlining the understanding of entrepreneuring and of negotiating a clear-cut and conclusive definition of the phenomenon. We should demonstrate loyalty by communicating entrepreneuring in unison as a social/cultural phenomenon which opens up for many forms of inquiry. Prioritizing entrepreneurship journals when publishing would create both focus and diversity as well as generate the critical mass needed to become visible on one's own terms in the social-science research community at large. One way to accomplish that is to put some of the lessons we have learnt from researching entrepreneuring into action. How that may be done is brought up in the next section.

ENTREPRENEURSHIP RESEARCH AS AN ENTREPRENEURIAL PRACTICE

Introducing his eye-opening 1985 text, *Innovation and Entrepreneurship,* Peter Drucker stated that entrepreneurship is neither art nor science but practice (Drucker, 1985, p. viii). Drucker's style of writing about entrepreneurship, though, revealed a relaxed playfulness and creativity that signalled its kinship with art rather than with science. Scholars, including Schumpeter (1943, p. 132), had already pointed out that entrepreneuring, as the process of 'getting

things done', calls for 'actionable' knowledge (Jarzabkowski & Wilson, 2006). Although other scholars such as Polanyi (1974) and Schön (1983) had earlier stressed the importance of embodied knowledge and experiential learning, the practice perspective was not much discussed within the research community. Pierre Bourdieu's *The Logic of Practice* appeared in English only in 1990 (Bourdieu, 1990), and it took practice theory another decade to emerge into a research field (Schatzki, 2001, 2002). Although it took another decade before a practice-theoretical perspective on entrepreneuring was adopted (see Johannisson, 2011), Drucker's abolishment of entrepreneurship as a science was obviously premature. Sarasvathy and Venkataraman (2011) are even clearer on this point in presenting an analogy between the entrepreneurial and the scientific methods.

Here I propose that entrepreneuring should not only be associated with practice and science but also with art. I consider practice, science and art as complementary perspectives on the world in general, and entrepreneuring as an object of study in particular. Therefore, rather than cross-examining the implications of considering entrepreneuring as a practice, art *or* science, I think that the features and potentialities of the *interrelationships* between these three aspects should be explored. This means that the philosophical, methodological and ethical implications of recognizing entrepreneurship as a science, and equally as a practice and art, have to be reviewed. It also seems appropriate to bring together Drucker's seminal, yet essayist, contributions to the field, presented one and a half decades before the turn of the century, with trends appearing during the first 15 years of the new millennium into a proposed methodology that pays due respect to the idiosyncrasies of entrepreneuring.

Organization researchers have become increasingly interested in the philosophical bases of inquiry in their field. The publication of *The Oxford Handbook of Process Philosophers & Organization Studies* (Helin,

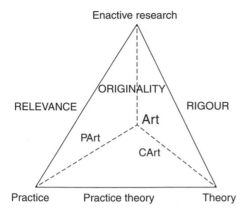

Figure 31.1   Originality as a complementary quality criterion in (social) research triggering enactive research as an appropriate methodology

Hernes, Hjorth & Holt, 2014) confirms this development. This anthology offers a variety of intellectual aperitifs for deeper inquiry into entrepreneurial venturing and its existential challenges. The other way around, the handbook reveals that entrepreneuring provides many examples, such as different perspectives on time and change, which connect philosophical ideas and empirical phenomena. It goes without saying that many of the often futile attempts to adopt a process perspective in entrepreneurial studies would have been more successful if studies into its paradigmatic basis had been enforced earlier. For example, ideas about the environment as being unknowable and ambiguous yet enactable have already – for example, through Karl Weick (1979) – inspired entrepreneurship researchers such as William B. Gartner (see, for example, Gartner et al., 1992). The philosophical ideas and concepts have been further developed by also including as interpreters organization researchers such as Robert Chia (see, for example, Chia & Holt, 2006; Nayak & Chia, 2011; Tsoukas & Chia, 2002). Recognizing the world as being continuously (re)constructed has fundamental implications for the understanding of both the constitution of opportunities and the ways

of actualizing them – a core issue in entrepreneurship research (Shane & Venkataraman, 2000; Venkataraman et al., 2012).

Keeping Vesper's (1990) statement in mind – that successful business entrepreneurs launch their venture in a domain that they know well – we should apply to our own trade, our academic practice, what we have learnt from researching entrepreneuring. The argument is thus that as professional researchers we should appropriate an entrepreneurial mindset but use it in the academic context. Schumpeter certainly provided scholars and practitioners with innovative insights into entrepreneuring, but he was not a successful commercial entrepreneur (Swedberg, 1991). My argument is thus that *originality*, the key feature of making entrepreneuring into a science of the unique, should be the contribution of entrepreneurship scholarship to how to define quality in social research. I also argue that an original conceptualization is not enough to advance a research field: it has to be complemented with an appropriate methodology that bridges to the empirical world.

Figure 31.1 summarizes the reasoning so far, also proposing 'enactive research' (Johannisson, 2011, 2014; see also Steyaert, 2011) as a methodological contribution by entrepreneurship scholarship to include 'originality' as a criterion for evaluating social science inquiries, supplementing the established ones: that is, 'rigour' and 'relevance' (Frank & Landström, 2016). I will return to enactive research, but first some comments on the pyramidal figure. Its basis is constituted by the Druckerian catchwords 'practice', 'science' and 'art', with proposed interconnections.

Beginning with the relationship between practice and theory, *practice theory* as commented upon above is already established in the social sciences (Schatzki, 2001, 2002). Management (for example, Mintzberg, 1973) as well as entrepreneurship (Carter, Gartner & Reynolds, 1996) researchers have looked into what managers and entrepreneurs actually do. *Art* as the materialization of ideas is in the research literature often linked to entrepreneurship (see, for example, Scherdin & Zander, 2011), and creativity is an interest common to art and entrepreneurship (see, for example, Sternberg & Krauss, 2014). *Conceptual art (CArt)* inquires into contemporary discourses in society, using text as much as other modes to trigger reflexivity among different audiences (see, for example, Corris, 2004). Some argue that science is a kind of art and craftsmanship (Tengblad, Solli & Czarniawska, 2005). *Performative art (PArt)*, which brings together aesthetic experiences and doings into happenings, has for long been an institutionalized field. Art, both as production and consumption, also reminds us of the need to balance the overly cognitive approaches in both research and practice. Affection and conation are also forces that trigger, energize and enact not only human (inter)action in general (Hilgard, 1980) but entrepreneurial (inter)action in particular. The role of affection in the entrepreneurial process is, for example, discussed by Baron (2008) and Cardon, Wincent, Singh and Drnovsek (2009). The importance of conation – that is, desire and willpower – was brought up already by Knight (1921) and Schumpeter (1912). Both entrepreneuring and artistry have always been associated with existential commitment. Lévi-Strauss (1966), with reference to the science of the concrete, as well as Agevall (1999) in the context of science of the unique, bring up art as an associated field of inquiry.

Figure 31.1 proposes that each of the three ways of framing entrepreneuring – science, practice and art – provides an anchorage point for each quality criterion in research: *rigour*, *relevance* and, thus, *originality*. However, *rigour* as associated only with systematic, preferably replicated, studies aiming at law-like generalizations is a criterion that does not make much sense when applied to research into entrepreneurial phenomena as unique occurrences. When *rigour* is applied to qualitative research it is reflected in a call for multilevel reflexivity (Steier, 1991; Alvesson & Sköldberg, 2009), which is as applicable to entrepreneuring as to any other social science. As regards *relevance*, entrepreneurs learn by listening to and observing equals and then by analogy, sensitively translating these experiences into appropriate lessons for how to deal with their own challenges (Johannisson, 2011). A call for relevant knowledge means that emic research, i.e. studies from the perspective of the entrepreneurs themselves, has to be stimulated.

Original research is needed to move the research frontier in entrepreneurship forward both with respect to *what* is studied and *how*. Elsewhere I argue that an appropriate way to establish how a venturing process and the practices that constitute it are enacted is that the scholar designs the research project as an entrepreneurial journey and embarks upon it himself (see Johannisson, 2014). This methodology I accordingly address as 'enactive research'. Only through this personal commitment and authentic being will it be possible for the researcher to explore the unique trajectory of the venture in all its details while it still is emerging (compare the notion of *modus operandi* by Bourdieu, 1990, p. 12). Accounts have to be caught in real time because the emergence of the venture is an outcome of a dialogue between intended (inter)actions and situations produced by the environment. Shadowing entrepreneurs and their mobility in social space in the way Mintzberg (1973) did – see also Czarniawska (2007) – will not do because entrepreneurs' (inter)actions are often triggered intuitively, i.e. for reasons that cannot be explicated. Neither are conventional methods such as interviews and participant observation appropriate as it is a methodology aiming at catching institutionalized behaviour, such as habits and cultural norms, and the meanings attached to them (see, for example, Feldman 2000). Oral statements in research settings, whether delivered as life stories or as interviews of different depth, are usually contaminated by rationalizations and justifications, even if this does not necessarily mean that the interlocutor is intentionally manipulating the researcher. Thus, only the researcher's own personal involvement in the enactment of a venture will make it possible to catch those social and embodied actions that craft its emergence.

Enactive research is thus guided by the three-dimensional quality indicator – rigour, relevance and originality – which seems to be especially relevant in entrepreneurship research as an inquiry into processes and practices. Unique phenomena are then studied in their real-life setting, where the researcher also takes on the identity of an entrepreneur. S/he must rigorously keep track of the current intended and spontaneous actions and interactions that enact the venture. Rigour is also reflected in paying systematic attention to and taking account of shared experiences as the process evolves. Relevance is not reduced to generally addressing issues that are important to society and to disseminating findings to stakeholders once the study is closed. The very realization of the venture calls for close collaboration with different stakeholders, which guarantees the relevance of the research.

This proposed 'enactive' research (Johannisson, 2014, forthcoming) belongs to the family of *interactive research* methods that invite representatives from communities of practice outside the academic to participate in joint knowledge creation (Adler, Shani & Styhre, 2004). Andrew Van de Ven (2007) proposes a mode of interactive research addressed as 'engaged scholarship'. It is:

> a participative form of research for obtaining the different perspectives of key stakeholders (researchers, users, clients, sponsors, and practitioners) in studying complex problems. By involving others and leveraging their different kinds of knowledge, engaged scholarship can produce knowledge that is more penetrating and insightful than when scholars or practitioners work on the problems alone. (Van de Ven, 2007, p. 9)

Van de Ven's approach, however, keeps the scholar in the driver's seat when it comes to directing the problem-solving process whose aim is general theorizing. Accordingly, Van de Ven presents a 'diamond' model linking the elements: problem formulation, theory-building, research design and problem-solving (the order of them may vary). This resembles a managerial approach to knowledge creation in the sense that steps are taken according to a negotiated plan. In contrast, enactive research means that the scholar takes charge of and responsibility for the initiation, organizing and closure of a venture, while making actions and interactions sensitively dependent on the locally evolving context in order to gain situated insight: 'Only by placing ourselves at the center of an unfolding phenomenon can we hope to know it from within' (Tsoukas & Chia, 2002, p. 571). The authentic involvement of the researcher that enactive research calls for immerses her/him in the venturing process.

Summarizing the argument: enactive research is a methodology that is tailor-made for tracking the detailed practices and processes turning the entrepreneurial journey into a road lined with enacted opportunities. First, this research design makes a unique contribution by recognizing that entrepreneurial opportunities are actualized by enacting the venture and the environment in parallel. Second, the methodology makes it possible not only to register and reflect upon the micro-events that construe entrepreneurial processes; it also offers the opportunity to experiment in a real-world context, to the extent that the researcher's reflections are fed back into the research/enactment process. This makes every enactment project unique. Third, there is no need for special arrangements to create a participatory research project as the stakeholders' contributions are organically integrated into the evolving project. Thus, such studies provide an arena for a genuine spontaneous interaction between the academic community, staff as well as students, and adjacent communities of practice. Fourth, in every enactive project, the researcher/entrepreneur, considering that knowledge is situated, has to reinvent the proper approach both as a practical challenge and as a scientific inquiry. This means that the entrepreneurial process being enacted is dealt with on its own terms. The research community is offered a narrative open to further interpretation, and practitioners are provided with an example ready for translation into and use in their own setting.

CONCLUSION: THE LEGACY OF ENTREPRENEURSHIP RESEARCH TO THE MAKING OF THE ENTREPRENEURIAL UNIVERSITY

The 'entrepreneurial university' is a topical subject in the academic discourse, on which two anthologies with different foci have been recently published (Fayolle & Redford, 2014; Foss & Gibson, 2015). The former volume provides a bouquet of images of the entrepreneurial university, while the Foss and Gibson contribution adopts a stricter approach where the contributors are told not to adopt a narrative approach but reflect upon the same concept – 'entrepreneurial architecture' as the 'collection of internal factors that interact to shape entrepreneurial agendas at the universities' (Foss & Gibson, 2015, p. 5) – when reporting on how the entrepreneurial university is enacted in their national setting. Although the two publications complement each other with respect to both design and contents, they both provide a rather fragmented picture of what an entrepreneurial university may look like. The main reason, from the perspective of what has been argued above, is that those who inquire into the notion of the entrepreneurial university are either stuck with regard to how universities structure their activities (see also Pinheiro & Stensaker, 2013; Greenwood, 2015) and/or are occupied by alternative modes of diffusing/translating research findings to, mainly, the business community. Researching about, training for and supporting entrepreneurship are generally considered as three separate activities.

I argue instead that the very integration of research, education and society should be made into the unique feature of the entrepreneurial university. Enactive research is then one way of accomplishing this, as projects can be designed that include students as contributors to value creation in the interest of different stakeholders. This is what enactive research provides as a bridge between Humboldtian ideals, with researchers as masters and students as disciples, on one hand, and the exchange of different kinds of knowledge with external stakeholders, on the other (compare Sam & van der Sijde, 2014). The ambition to help students develop an entrepreneurial mindset then becomes embedded in responsible research and committed external communities. In this way we can as scholars actively deal with the responsibility we have as pathfinders in contemporary rough social settings (Nayak & Chia, 2011).

Obviously, the travel of entrepreneurship research from a remote and dark corner of management research in order to reach, 'by dawn', the promised land of being a recognized science on its own merits will be arduous. The entrepreneurship research community has to mobilize broadly in order to establish a shared identity by promoting close-up studies of the very practice of entrepreneuring. Other researchers have already expressed worries and called for action in entrepreneurship as an academic discipline (see, for example, Wiklund, Davidsson, Audretsch & Karlsson, 2010). Zahra and Wright (2011) even see entrepreneurship research as mainly affiliated with management studies and policymaking. However, they also point out the need for studying the 'micro-foundations of entrepreneurial phenomena' (2011, pp. 77–8), which to my mind invites a practice approach that is best studied by enactive research as it includes researchers and practitioners as well as students in a joint learning process.

However relevant, rigorous and original university research into entrepreneuring becomes, its direct impact on society is almost negligible if compared with the potential impact through the students we educate. Thus, it could even be argued that the ability of research to make an impact on society through education should be added to rigour, relevance and originality research, thus providing a fourth quality criterion (compare Sarasvathy & Venkataraman, 2010). However, it is not at all self-evident that our business schools would then become the main contributors.

Even before the CIT revolution, influential researchers in the field of entrepreneurship education questioned the ability of business schools to train their students for entrepreneuring (Gibb, 2002, 2007; see also Greenwood, 2015). The foundation for knowledge creation in the practice of entrepreneuring as stated above suggests that art schools may provide a more appropriate site for entrepreneurship education. At those institutions, the dialogue between students' own original work and art theory as embedded in a practice perspective has always formed the centre of attraction.

Notes

1 The reason for including also 'small business' in the search profile is the fuzzy boundary between entrepreneurship and small business in these specialized journals. In July 2016 a parallel search for the number of review articles published 1985–99 was carried out. Then 46 articles were identified, signalling a considerable expansion of the research field after the turn of the century.

2 On the recommendation of the library at Linnaeus University, the Web of Science was used in the analyses reported here. Like the database Scopus, Web of Science has a bias towards the natural sciences and covers fewer data sources than the Ulrich's database (see Mongeon & Paul-Hus, 2016), but is nevertheless generally practised.

REFERENCES

Adler, N., A.B. Shani, and A. Styhre (eds) 2004 *Collaborative Research in Organizations: Foundations for Learning, Change and Theoretical Development*. Thousand Oaks, CA: Sage.

Agevall, O. 1999 *A Science of Unique Events. Max Weber's Methodology of the Cultural Sciences*. PhD dissertation. Uppsala: Uppsala University.

Alvesson, M., and K. Sköldberg. 2009 *Reflexive Methodology. New Vistas for Qualitative Research*. Second edition. London: Sage.

Arend, R.L., H. Sarooghi, and A. Burkemper 2015 "Effectuation as Ineffectual? Applying the 3E Theory-Assessment Framework to a Proposed New Theory of Entrepreneurship." *Academy of Management Review* 40(4): 630–51.

Baker, T., and R. Nelson 2005 "Creating Something from Nothing: Resource Construction through Entrepreneurial Bricolage." *Administrative Science Quarterly* 50(3): 329–66.

Baron, R.A. 2008 "The Role of Affect in the Entrepreneurial Process." *Academy of Management Review* 33(2): 328–40.

Barrett, F.J. 1998 "Creativity and Improvisation in Jazz and Organizations: Implications for Organizational Learning." *Organization Science* 9(5): 605–22.

Bauman, Z. 2000 *Liquid Modernity*. Polity: Cambridge.

Bourdieu, P. 1990 *The Logic of Practice*. Cambridge: Polity Press.

Cardon, M.S., J. Wincent, J. Singh, and M. Drnovsek 2009 "The Nature and Experience of Entrepreneurial Passion." *Academy of Management Review* 34(3): 511–32.

Carter, N.M., W.B. Gartner, and P.D. Reynolds 1996 "Exploring Start-up Event Sequences." *Journal of Business Venturing* 11: 151–66.

Chia, R., and R. Holt 2006 "Strategy as Practical Coping: A Heideggerian Perspective." *Organization Studies* 2: 635–55.

Corris, M. (ed.) 2004 *Conceptual Art. Theory, Myth, and Practice*. Cambridge: Cambridge University Press.

Czarniawska, B. 2007 *Shadowing and other Techniques for Doing Fieldwork in Modern Societies*. Malmö: Liber.

Daft, R.L., and K.E. Weick 1984 "Toward a Model of Organizations as Interpretation Systems." *Academy of Management Review* 9(2): 284–95.

Davidsson, P. 2004 *Researching Entrepreneurship*. Boston, MA: Springer.

Drucker, P. 1985 *Innovation and Entrepreneurship*. New York: Harper & Row.

Fayolle, A., and Redford, D.T. (eds) 2014 *Handbook on the Entrepreneurial University.* Cheltenham: Edward Elgar.

Feldman, M.S. 2000 "Organizational Routines as a Source of Continuous Change." *Organization Science* 11(6): 611–29.

Foss, L., and D.V. Gibson (eds) 2015 *The Entrepreneurial University. Context and Institutional Change.* Abingdon: Routledge.

Frank, H., and H. Landström 2016 "What Makes Entrepreneurship Research Interesting? Reflections on Strategies to Overcome the Rigour-Relevance Gap." *Entrepreneurship and Regional Development* 28(1–2): 51–75.

Gartner, W.B. 1988 "'Who Is An Entrepreneur?' is the Wrong Question." *American Small Business Journal* 12(4): 11–31.

Gartner, W.B. 2007 "Entrepreneurial Narrative and a Science of the Imagination." *Journal of Business Venturing* 22: 613–27.

Gartner, W.B. 2016 *Entrepreneurship as Organizing. Selected Papers by William B. Gartner.* Cheltenham: Edward Elgar.

Gartner, W.B., B.J. Bird, and J.A. Starr 1992 "Acting 'as if': Differentiating Entrepreneurial from Organizational Behavior." *Entrepreneurship Theory and Practice* (Spring): 13–31.

Garud, R., and P. Karnøe 2003 "Bricolage vs. Breakthrough: Distributed and Embedded Agency in Technology Entrepreneurship." *Research Policy* 32(2): 277–300.

GEM 2000 *2015/6 General Entrepreneurship Monitor* (GEM). Annual Reports.

Gibb, A. 2002 "In Pursuit of a New 'Enterprise' and 'Entrepreneurship' Paradigm for Learning: Creative Destruction. New Ways of Doing Things and New Combinations of Knowledge." *International Journal of Management Reviews* 4(3): 223–69.

Gibb, A. 2007 "Entrepreneurship: Unique Solutions for Unique Environments. Is It Possible to Achieve This with the Existing Paradigm?" *International Journal of Entrepreneurship Education* 5: 93–142.

Greenwood, D.J. 2015 "Competing the Cycle in Entrepreneurial Research: Action Research to Link Entrepreneurs and Researchers and Reform the University." *Entrepreneurship Research Journal* 5(4): 269–92.

Helin J., T. Hernes, D. Hjorth, and R. Holt (eds) 2014 *The Oxford Handbook of Process Philosophy & Organization Studies.* Oxford: Oxford University Press.

Hilgard, E.R. 1980 "The Trilogy of Mind: Cognition, Affection and Conation." *History of the Behavioral Sciences* 16(April): 107–17.

Hjorth, D., and C. Steyaert (eds) 2004 *Narrative and Discursive Approaches in Entrepreneurship.* Cheltenham: Edward Elgar.

Huizinga, J. 1950 *Homo Ludens – A Study of the Play Element in Culture.* Boston, MA: Beacon Press.

Jarzabkowski, P., and D.C. Wilson 2006 "Actionable Strategy Knowledge. A Practice Perspective." *European Management Journal* 24(5): 348–67.

Johannisson, B. 2010 "In the Beginning Was Entrepreneuring." In Bill, F., B. Bjerke, and A.W. Johansson (eds) *[De]mobilizing the Entrepreneurship Discourse. Exploring Entrepreneurial Thinking and Action.* Cheltenham: Edward Elgar. pp. 201–21.

Johannisson, B. 2011 "Towards a Practice Theory of Entrepreneuring." *Small Business Economics* 36(2): 135–50.

Johannisson, B. 2014 "The Practice Approach and Interactive Research in Entrepreneurship and Small-Scale Venturing." In Carsrud, A., and M. Brännback (eds) *Handbook of Research Methods and Applications in Entrepreneurship and Small Business.* Cheltenham: Edward Elgar. pp. 228–58.

Johannisson, B. (forthcoming) *Doing Enactive Research – Disclosing Entrepreneurship as Practice.* Cheltenham: Edward Elgar.

Journal Citation Reports: Social Science Edition 2014, Thomson Reuters. http://wokinfo.com/products_tools/analytical/jcr/.

Kirzner, I.M. 1973/1978 *Competition and Entrepreneurship.* Chicago, IL: The University of Chicago Press.

Knight, F.H. 1921/2006 *Risk, Uncertainty and Profit.* Mineola, NY: Dover.

Lanzara, G.F. 1983 "Ephemeral Organizations in Extreme Environments: Emergence, Strategy, Extinction." *Journal of Management Studies* 20(1): 71–95.

Latour, B. 1986 "The Powers of Association." In J. Law (ed.) *Power, Action and Belief. A New Sociology of Knowledge.* London: Routledge and Kegan Paul. pp. 264–80.

Lévi-Strauss, C. 1966 *The Savage Mind.* Chicago, IL: The University of Chicago Press.

Linstead, S. 2014 "Henri Bergson." In Helin J., T. Hernes, D. Hjorth, and R. Holt (eds) *The Oxford Handbook of Process Philosophers & Organization Studies.* Oxford: Oxford University Press. pp. 218–35.

March, J.G. 1976 "The Technology of Foolishness." In March, J.G. and J.P. Olsen *Ambiguity and Choice in Organizations.* Oslo: Universitetsförlaget. pp. 69–81.

Maruyama, M. 1963 "The Second Cybernetics. Deviation-Amplifying Mutual Causal Processes." *American Science* 51: 164–79.

Mintzberg, H. 1973 *The Nature of Managerial Work.* New York: Harper & Row.

Mongeon, P., and A. Paul-Hus 2016 "The Journal Coverage of Web of Science and Scopus: A Comparative Analysis." *Scientometrics* 106: 213–28.

Morris, M.J., D.F. Kuratko, M. Schindehutte, and A.J. Spivack 2011 "Framing the Entrepreneurial Experience." *Entrepreneurship Theory & Practice* (January): 11–40.

Nayak, A., and R. Chia 2011 "Thinking Becoming and Emergence: Process Philosophy and Organization Studies." *Philosophy and Organization Theory. Research in the Sociology of Organizations* 32: 281–309.

Pinheiro, R., and B. Stensaker 2013 "Designing the Entrepreneurial University: The Interpretation of a Global Idea." *Public Organization Review* 14: 497–516.

Plowman, D.A., L.D. Baker, T.E. Beck, M. Kulkarni, S.T. Solansky, and D.V. Travis 2007 "Radical Change Accidentally: The Emergence and Amplification of Small Change." *Academy of Management Journal* 50(3): 515–43.

Polanyi, M. 1974 *Personal Knowledge. Towards a Post-Critical Philosophy.* Chicago, IL: The University of Chicago Press.

Rämö, H. 1999 "An Aristotelian Human Time–Space Manifold. From Chronochora to Kariotopos." *Time & Society* 8(2): 309–38.

Sam, C., and P. van der Sijde 2014 "Understanding the Concept of the Entrepreneurial University from the Perspective of Higher Education Models." *Higher Education* 68: 891–908.

Sarasvathy, S.D. 2001 "Causation and Effectuation: Toward a Theoretical Shift from Economic Inevitability to Entrepreneurial Contingency." *Academy of Management Review* 26(2): 243–63.

Sarasvathy, S.D. 2003 "Entrepreneurship as a Science of the Artificial." *Journal of Economic Psychology* 24: 203–20.

Sarasvathy, S.D. 2008 *Effectuation. Elements of Entrepreneurial Expertise*. Cheltenham: Edward Elgar.

Sarasvathy, S.D., and S. Venkataraman 2011 "Entrepreneurship as Method: Open Questions for an Entrepreneurial Future." *Entrepreneurship Theory & Practice* (January): 113–35.

Schatzki, T.R. 2001 "Introduction: Practice Theory". In Schatzki, T.R., K. Knorr Cetina, and E. von Savigny (eds) *The Practice Turn in Contemporary Theory*. London: Routledge. pp. 1–14.

Schatzki, T.R. 2002 *The Site of the Social – A Philosophical Account of the Constitution of Social Life and Change*. University Park, PA: Pennsylvania State University.

Scherdin, M., and I. Zander (eds) 2011 *Art Entrepreneurship*. Cheltenham: Edward Elgar.

Schön, D. 1983 *The Reflective Practitioner. How Professionals Think in Action*. New York: Basic Books.

Schumpeter, J.A. 1912/1934 *The Theory of Economic Development*. Oxford: Oxford University Press.

Schumpeter, J.A. 1943/1987 *Capitalism, Socialism and Democracy*. Sixth edition. London: Unwin.

Selden, P.D., and D.E. Fletcher 2015 "The Entrepreneurial Journey: An Emergent Hierarchical System of Artifact-Creating Processes." *Journal of Business Venturing* 30: 603–15.

Shane, S., and S. Venkataraman 2000 "The Promise of Entrepreneurship as a Field of Research." *Academy of Management Review* 25(1): 217–226.

Shneor, R., and B.T. Flåten 2015. "Opportunities for Entrepreneurial Development and Growth through Online Communities, Collaboration, Value Creation and Co-Creation Activities." In Kaufman, H.R., and R. Shams (eds) *Entrepreneurial Challenges in the 21st Century*. Basingstoke: Palgrave Macmillan. pp. 178–99.

Smircich, L., and C. Stubbart 1985 "Strategic Management in the Enacted World." *Academy of Management Review* 10(4): 724–36.

Spinosa, C., F. Flores, and H. Dreyfus 1997 *Disclosing New Worlds – Entrepreneurship,*

Democratic Action and Cultivation of Solidarity. Cambridge, MA: MIT Press.

Stacey, R.D. 1992 *Managing the Unknowable. Strategic Boundaries between Order and Chaos in Organizations.* San Francisco, CA: Jossey-Bass.

Steier, F. 1991 "Reflexivity and Methodology: An Ecological Constructionism." In Steier, F. (ed.) *Research and Reflexivity.* London: Sage. pp. 163–85.

Sternberg, R., and G. Krauss (eds) 2014. *Handbook of Research on Entrepreneurship and Creativity.* Cheltenham: Edward Elgar.

Steyaert, C. 2004 "The Prosaics of Entrepreneurship." In Hjorth, D. and C. Steyaert (eds) *Narrative and Discursive Approaches in Entrepreneurship*, Cheltenham and Northampton, MA: Edward Elgar. pp. 8–21.

Steyaert, C. 2007 "Entrepreneuring as a Conceptual Attractor? A Review of Process Theories in 20 Years of Entrepreneurship Studies." *Entrepreneurship & Regional Development* 19(6): 453–77.

Steyaert, C. 2011 "Entrepreneurship as In(ter) vention: Reconsidering the Conceptual Politics of Method in Entrepreneurship Studies." *Entrepreneurship and Regional Development* 23(1–2): 77–88.

Swedberg, R. 1991 *Schumpeter. A Biography.* Princeton, NJ: Princeton University Press.

Tengblad, S., R. Solli, and B. Czarniawska (eds) 2005 *The Art of Science.* Malmö: Liber.

Tsoukas, H., and R. Chia. 2002 "On Organizational Becoming: Rethinking Organizational Change." *Organization Science* 13(5): 567–82.

Van de Ven, A.H. 2007 *Engaged Scholarship. A Guide to Organizational and Social Research.* New York: Oxford University Press.

Venkataraman, S., S.D. Sarasvathy, N. Dew, and W.R. Forster 2012 "Reflexions on the 2010 AMR Decade Award: Whither the Promise? Moving Forward with Entrepreneurship as a Science of the Artificial." *Academy of Management Review* 37(1): 21–33.

Vesper, K.H. 1990 *New Venture Strategies.* Second edition. Englewood Cliffs, NJ: Prentice-Hall.

Weick, K.E. 1979 *The Social Psychology of Organizing.* Second edition. Reading, MA: Addison-Wesley.

Weick, K.E. 2009 *Making Sense of the Organization. The Impermanent Organization. Volume 2.* Chichester: Wiley.

Wiklund, J., P. Davidsson, D. Audretsch, and C. Karlsson 2010 "The Future of Entrepreneurship Research." *Entrepreneurship Theory & Practice* (January): 1–9.

Winborg, J. 2015 "The Role of Financial Bootstrapping in Handling the Liability of Newness in Incubator Businesses." *The International Journal of Entrepreneurship and Innovation* 16(3): 197–206.

Zahra, S.A., and M. Wright 2011 "Entrepreneurship's Next Act." *Academy of Management Perspectives* 25(4): 67–83.

32

Critical Perspectives in Entrepreneurship Research

Seppo Poutanen

INTRODUCTION

To introduce critical perspectives in entrepreneurship research in a short chapter of a handbook requires two basic things. First, the meanings attached to the concept of 'critical' must do some reasonable justice to the rich and multifaceted research field in question. Second, certain significant scientific uses of the concept must be bypassed due to the relative lack of space. It is easy to find scientific articles with titles like 'Management capabilities and environmental characteristics in the critical operational phase of entrepreneurship – a comparison of Finnish family and nonfamily firms' (Littunen, 2003), or 'Critical success factors for e-commerce entrepreneurship: an empirical study of Thailand' (Sebora, Lee & Sukasame, 2009), for example, but uses like these are ignored here.

Furthermore, the critical perspective on entrepreneurship and its research that might be judged the most devastating will be assessed in some other context. The ideas of entrepreneurship and its research commonly presuppose the existence of a freely choosing, acting and innovating *entrepreneur*, but if such an individual cannot exist, then surely these common ideas should also be abandoned? The truly devastating criticism derives from certain defensible philosophical arguments against the existence of authentic free will in a causally deterministic natural world (see, e.g. Kane, 2002; Pink, 2004). Nevertheless, if such arguments indeed win the day, the conventional understanding of entrepreneurship will become a rather small piece of what they sweep away. On the other hand, the gloomy sketch of a world inhabited by puppet-like creatures with delusions of (entrepreneurial) freedom still anticipates the most radical perspective of criticism I will introduce. What I call the 'avant-garde' of critical entrepreneurship research constructs, through complex philosophical arguments, a remarkably analogous image of our world, although in the avant-garde case it is meant for whole-hearted positive adoption with nothing gloomy about it.

The critical standpoints relevant to this chapter are characterised by *relationality* and *explicit value-ladenness*. Criticism necessarily concerns something; it has a target, and criticism typically aims to reveal the target's more-or-less implicit value-ladenness and to suggest something presumably better. The subject of the critical perspectives in question can be broadly defined as 'mainstream' entrepreneurship research, but the relationality indicates that neither the criticism nor the mainstream are stable and monolithic 'blocks' with sharp boundaries. In reality, the contents of the blocks and their mutual relations continuously change over time in numerous ways, and so the introductory text at hand is a limited, transient snapshot. No absolute guarantees protecting us from the mistake of introducing empty criticism exist, which means that the 'mainstream' may be accused of doing things it is not actually doing, and vice versa. See Roscoe (2011) for illuminating comments on this. I strive to dispense with such useless critical perspectives. Moreover, the general problem of value-ladenness involves the choice of subject matter, empirical materials, methods, theories and various meta-perspectives[1] in entrepreneurial research, but questions of a very specific or technical nature have been omitted.

The sections of this chapter proceed as follows. I start from the many meanings given to 'entrepreneurship' in research literature and various methodological difficulties involved in doing research on entrepreneurship. The arguments presented here may well be seen as part of the self-reflective mainstream research itself, but in the next section the mainstream research as a whole is seen to advocate a problematic ideology, called 'entrepreneurialism'. Criticism is first explicated through feminist studies of gender systems, and then one key theoretical problem in entrepreneurship research, the nature of 'entrepreneurial opportunity', is analysed with the conceptual tools of critical realism. Critical realism is at heart a general metatheory of society, but it tends to endorse the same type of political values of emancipation and empowerment of the oppressed as feminism does. However, concerning entrepreneurship research, no such clearly political values have been at the forefront in studies applying critical realism. Finally, and farthest away from the mainstream research, I introduce what I call the 'avant-garde'. The term is justified by the powerful radicalism with which the avant-gardists rethink both entrepreneurship and its analysis. They gain their main inspiration from the long and rich tradition of processualist thinking in Western philosophy, and I bring out certain key ideas of their thoroughly *positive* criticism.

THE MANY MEANINGS OF ENTREPRENEURSHIP AND FLAWS IN ITS EMPIRICAL STUDIES

What is the subject of entrepreneurship research, i.e. entrepreneurship? To begin with a clarifying simplification, I see mainstream definitions of the concept as striving for scientific objectivity, finality and inclusiveness, and so the obvious tasks of critical entrepreneurship research would seem to be to analyse these characteristics and demonstrate their problematic nature. However, before any such analysis can be done, one general observation is necessary: mainstream researchers themselves agree remarkably little on a comprehensive and definitive definition of 'entrepreneurship'.

For example, in his effort at a taxonomy, Gedeon (2010) highlights 32 different definitions of 'entrepreneurship' from research literature, which extend from the Enlightenment[2] to the founding fathers of modern economics[3] and, finally, to contemporary key figures in entrepreneurship research.[4] Kim (2015) lists 34 varying meanings from practising entrepreneurs (e.g. Richard Branson), popular media (e.g. the *New York Times*), fiction and the arts (e.g. the TV series *Breaking Bad*) and textbooks (e.g. Kuratko, 2009; Gartner & Bellamy, 2010). Already in the title of his book chapter, Kim states, evidently correctly, that 'entrepreneurship means something different to everyone' (Kim, 2015, p. 59).

That the concept of 'entrepreneurship' both stimulates intensive efforts to define it and scatters those efforts in many directions evokes important critical questions in itself. The familiar activity of combining 'entrepreneurship' with countless other terms just multiplies potential subjects of a critical perspective – for example, social, academic, corporate, innovative, necessity, startup or grassroots entrepreneurship (Gedeon, 2010, p. 27).Yet to focus and delimit the type of criticism dealt with in this chapter – that is, to problematise the subject matter, empirical materials and methods of mainstream entrepreneurship research – I relate the discussion to *one* explicit definition of 'entrepreneurship', which comes from a recent review article on the evolving domain of entrepreneurship research (Carlsson, Braunerhjelm, McKelvey, Olofsson, Persson & Ylinenpää, 2013). The authors' definition summarises many representative features of its mainstream kind in a helpfully detailed manner:

> Entrepreneurship refers primarily to an economic function that is carried out by individuals, entrepreneurs, acting independently or within organizations, to perceive and create new opportunities and to introduce their ideas into the market, under uncertainty, by making decisions about location, product design, resource use, institutions, and reward systems. The entrepreneurial activity and the entrepreneurial ventures are influenced by the socioeconomic environment and result ultimately in economic growth and human welfare. (Carlsson et al., 2013, p. 915)

Perhaps the most clearly value-laden feature in the definition hinges on the use of the term 'ultimately'. The suggestion seems to be that, even if entrepreneurial activity and entrepreneurial ventures may not immediately result in economic growth and human welfare, we should postpone our judgement until they 'ultimately' do so. Strongly positive expectations are thus built into the definition, and a preponderance of similar affirmative statements is familiar from public political discourse in Western countries, for example.

In contrast to this image, several critical studies have shown that only a small group of high-performing entrepreneurial firms actually drive growth, wealth and job creation in an economy, whereas an overwhelming majority of all entrepreneurs contribute only modestly or practically nothing to growth or welfare (e.g. Hamilton, 2000; Moskowitz & Vissing-Jorgensen, 2002; Blanchflower, 2004; Bartelsman, Scarpetta & Schivardi, 2005; Audretsch, 2007; Santarelli & Vivarelli, 2007; van Praag & Versloot, 2007; Shane, 2008; Hall & Woodward, 2010). Yet a realistic definition of 'entrepreneurship' should presumably also cover barely managing, bankrupt and even criminal entrepreneurs. Nonetheless, instead of paying attention to potential differences between entrepreneurial individuals, for example, I find it more useful to review empirical and methodological problems in the kind of mainstream entrepreneurship research that helps to sustain the strongly and one-sidedly positive views of entrepreneurship. I will follow Nightingale and Coad's (2013) informative treatment, which focuses on research into small and medium-sized enterprises (SMEs).

Poor Data Quality, Unrepresentative Samples

Small firms typically move so quickly – they emerge and die quickly; the death rate of new companies can be as high as 50 per cent in their first three years (Frankish, Roberts, Coad, Spears & Storey, 2013) – that official statistics or conventional datasets can find it difficult to make these firms visible. Accordingly, there may simply not exist any data, or the available data may be inaccurate or unrepresentative. Firms struggling to survive are less likely to serve government officials or researchers than successfully growing enterprises, and thus a misleadingly positive overview tends to result, where bad and literally hopeless enterprises are under-represented. Some researchers aware of these problems have rejected the demand of statistical representativeness and have opted for rich case studies, but as these cases commonly concern only elite businesses, the picture of entrepreneurship has generally remained skewed to the positive side (Nightingale & Coad, 2013, p. 120.)

Skewed Statistics, Definitional Vagueness

Entrepreneurial firms in general differ so drastically from each other that random inclusion or exclusion of even one particular firm in or from a statistical sampling can decisively change the results (e.g. Hall & Woodward, 2010). The implied huge dispersion in the hypothesized whole set thus makes any reference to 'average' economic effect from an 'average' firm meaningless. The rationality of talking about both the small minority of mammoth engines of the economy (GE, Google, Apple, etc.) and the huge majority of small struggling businesses with the same 'entrepreneurial' concepts hence becomes questionable. From a more technical perspective, lack of reliable and comprehensive statistics often means that attempts to define SMEs and distinguish them from different enterprises become haphazardly dependent on what kind of information is available (e.g. Dennis, 2011). Comparison of studies on what is seemingly the same subject thus become difficult (Nightingale & Coad, 2013, pp. 120–2).

Meagre Job Creation, Productivity, Innovation

In spite of these empirical and methodological problems, reasonably well-crafted empirical studies on the performance of SMEs have been published (e.g. Disney, Haskel & Heden, 2003; Santarelli & Vivarelli, 2007; Hvide, 2009; Ortega-Argiles, Vivarelli & Voigt, 2009). The results of these studies, however, offer a complex and rather negative picture, especially if juxtaposed with creating economic growth and human welfare, which Carlsson and his colleagues (2013) underline. First, SMEs' oft hailed ability to create employment has been elaborated by such matters as the typically short span of these jobs and the relatively low level of experience and education they require. Second, productivity growth in economies is mainly driven by large established firms, whereas entrepreneurial start-ups usually need many years to achieve comparable productivity levels, or anything like them. Furthermore, in the contemporary knowledge economy, an enterprise's ability to create profitable innovations[5] is a major key to its prosperity. Although numerous successful SMEs operate in the fields of computing and biotechnology around the world, for example, large firms with access to considerable venture capital, effective R&D resources, diverse markets, etc. tend to eventually win the day (Nightingale & Coad, 2013, pp. 124–9).

Basically, noteworthy parts of mainstream entrepreneurship research appear, from the critical perspective summarised above, biased towards conceptualising, studying and highlighting entrepreneurship, including self-employment, as something to be favoured and endorsed. Core scientific values nonetheless become compromised if empirical material is gathered without appropriate care, unsuitable research methods are applied or conclusions not soundly based on empirical results are derived. In economic and political conditions where governments eagerly want 'scientific' support for their optimistic (i.e. one-sided) entrepreneurship policies, actualisation of scientific values in research may become harmfully influenced by political and related interests.

Whether the kind of criticism introduced in this section might be considered 'radical' naturally depends on the evaluator's point of view. Many researchers would claim that Nightingale, Coad, etc. produce nothing genuinely radical – that they too belong to the mainstream of entrepreneurship research. Nightingale, Coad and their like-minded colleagues can indeed be said to be acting merely as realisers of standard, narrowly understood scientific values of self-criticism and self-correction who do not challenge any profound assumptions of mainstream research. As a way of transitioning towards a different type of value-laden criticism, the lack of deeper reflection on concepts like 'growth' or 'entrepreneur' in Nightingale and Coad's analysis thus deserves attention. Contrary to the usual conceptions, important critical paradigms aspire to reconstruct entrepreneurship research in varying ways and also give it more ambitious practical tasks than operating as a supplier of valid information to policymakers.

'ENTREPRENEURIALISM' AS IDEOLOGY AND SOME CONCEPTUAL QUESTIONS: FEMINIST ENTREPRENEURSHIP RESEARCH AND CRITICAL REALISM

A major volume of critical entrepreneurship research that goes beyond upholding common ideals of good scientific practice is united by a core, value-laden thesis. This thesis claims that entrepreneurship and its related economic system, i.e. capitalism, are not necessarily anything good; quite often, they are something remarkably bad. Nightingale and Coad have already shed light on the kind of political and societal scheme where positive entrepreneurship ideology (practically propaganda) pushes great numbers of people into dead-end careers as entrepreneurs (Nightingale & Coad 2013, 135–6; see also, e.g. Armstrong, 2005; Blackburn & Kovalainen, 2009; Rehn, Brännback, Carsrud & Lindahl, 2013). Similar examples are easy to find. Wealth and well-being produced by enterprises for some individuals, groups and nations can be argued to mean, more or less directly, poverty and misery for other people somewhere else (e.g. Jones & Murtola, 2012, pp. 129–33; Sveiby, Gripenberg & Segercrantz, 2012, pp. 61–84). In the broadest picture, the ecological system of the earth has apparently become damaged beyond repair because of humankind's relentless entrepreneurial activities in the capitalist mode over the last two hundred years.

Damage from 'entrepreneurialism' deserves an independent review of relevant empirical analyses, but in this general section, I outline the objectives of certain critical theories in entrepreneurship research on the basis of Spicer's (2012) useful summary. First, because the relationships of power and domination inherent in capitalist societies are now seen by many as fundamentally asymmetrical and unjust, criminal business activity, exploitation of workforces, degradation of the environment, etc. are not considered aberrations from some ideal type of well-functioning capitalism, but outcomes of its normal entrepreneurial functions (Spicer, 2012, pp. 150–1). The fact that mainstream researchers do not much study these kind of things does not stem from their commitment to some imaginary value-free objectivity of science but from their implicit or explicit political values, which critical theorists urge us to reject.

Challenging the conventionally understood value-neutrality of science leads critical theorists to analyse the assumptions behind knowledge production that tend to reduce entrepreneurship into a relatively simple engine of the economy, for example. More precisely, and following Fournier and Grey's (2000) influential account, Spicer elaborates three critical measures that should enable destabilization of our routine knowledge claims in entrepreneurship research:

a reflexive epistemology that questions how our methodological assumption structure and in some ways shape how we see our very object of inquiry (i.e. entrepreneurship), a de-naturalizing ontology that seeks to show how objects of inquiry (entrepreneurs) are constructed through ongoing social processes and a political anti-performativity that seeks to un-tether knowledge production from means–ends calculation. (Spicer 2012, p. 151)

In the following subsections, I detail two notable models for specifying the three critical measures, and I title these models 'feminist entrepreneurship research' and 'critical realism'.

Feminist Entrepreneurship Research

In its effort at scientific objectivity, finality and inclusiveness, the definition of 'entrepreneurship' by Carlsson and his colleagues states that this 'primarily… economic function… is carried out by individuals, entrepreneurs, acting independently or within organizations' (Carlsson et al., 2013, p. 915). This may look self-evident to us, but, in the light of Spicer's (2012) critical account, it just means that a lot of conceptual, theoretical and ideological work has gone into making the definition look like a truism. Why not, for example, view entrepreneurship more broadly as a generator of social change and analyse both its positive and negative effects on people's social, cultural, economic and ecological realities in their particular contexts (e.g. Steyaert & Hjorth, 2006; Calás, Smircich & Bourne, 2009; Williams & Nadin, 2013; Verduijn, Dey, Tedmanson & Essers, 2014; Peredo, 2015)?

Tenable analysis of social change related to entrepreneurship requires us, in critical theorists' view, to reject the conception of 'entrepreneur' included in common mainstream definitions: a remarkably atomistic, abstract and attribute-free character who differs from other individuals by his/her extraordinary capability of entrepreneurism. Probably the most influential critical approach to challenge this kind of image is feminist entrepreneurship research, which has a history of several decades of rich, varied scholarship. Accordingly, my brief review only gives a few compressed insights of recent feminist

entrepreneurship research and related feminist theory. The most straightforward thing to realise from the feminist perspective is that abstract mainstream definitions bypass actual global reality, where *female* entrepreneurs suffer various modes of economic, social and cultural oppression and subordination that do not affect *male* entrepreneurs (e.g. Calás et al., 2009; Pines, Lerner & Schwartz, 2010; Ahl, 2012; Kwong, Jones-Evans & Thompson, 2012; Kariv, 2013; Al-Dajani & Marlow, 2015).

Contemporary feminist theory principally sees female and male entrepreneurs as important nodes inside pervasive gender systems, where asymmetrical relationships of power and domination typically favour males through socially and culturally embedded processes and practices. However, as recent theoretical feminism problematises all our apparently natural and self-evident understandings in these matters, a more precise formulation is to state that the gender system socially, culturally and materially constructs and interprets individuals as inhabiting differing and asymmetrically power-infused social-economic-cultural positions. In and through these positions, individuals are expected to *perform femininity* and *masculinity*, among many other things (e.g. Butler, 1990; Evans, 2003; Gherardi, 2014).

'Performance' does not mean something clearly distinguishable that could be easily abandoned, as actors leaving the stage do with their performances. On the contrary, 'performance' in the intended sense is a continuing and multidimensional process in which we, through our everyday practices of life, repetitiously and routinely act and produce our ostensibly stable *personality* and, for example, ethnic and gendered identity into reality. In our interactions with other people, we also constantly monitor how well we and others succeed in the performances in question. This penetrating constructionism rejects the common interpretation that humans have two objectively natural and biological *sexes*, whereas *constructed gender* qualities are, more or less freely, attached to individuals of the two sexes. The radical performance constructionism counters this kind of dualism by remarking that our own biology too becomes understandable and manipulable only through some historically and culturally specific conceptualizations and other activities that *we* attach to it (e.g. Lorber, 1996; Evans, 2003).

Nonetheless, it must be emphasised that mainstream entrepreneurship research has not ignored women entrepreneurs in recent decades, rather the contrary. Feminist criticism pinpoints, however, the specific kind of *problem of female entrepreneurship and entrepreneurs* that mainstream research typically constructs. This problem originates in statistics that reveal, for example, how in 2012 only 29 per cent of all entrepreneurs in 37 European countries were women (European Commission, 2014, p. 7). Under the influence of positive entrepreneurship ideology, this kind of statistic is taken to mean that women should be encouraged to become entrepreneurs, because entrepreneurship is considered their best option, especially in the Global South, to gain independence, break away from poverty and contribute to the economic growth of their nation (World Bank, 2015).

One implication of focusing on non-entrepreneurial women is the conviction that they need help to become more entrepreneurial, which basically means that they need help to become more like men. Feminist research has shown that attributes linked to 'entrepreneur' in, for example, news media, fiction and entrepreneurship education are consistently the same attributes that Westernised global culture constructs as (white) male[6] (e.g. Vavrus, 2002; Ahl, 2006, 2012; Lewis, 2006, 2013; Achtenhagen & Welter, 2011; Dahl, Keränen & Kovalainen, 2011; Heilman, 2012; Wee & Brooks, 2012; Katila & Eriksson, 2013; Hanappi-Egger, 2014). The dominant image of a woman as a defective man helps to reinforce gendered power asymmetries in entrepreneurship and thus hampers the economic prospects of a great number of women, whether 'entrepreneurial' in the prescribed sense or not, around the world.

Feminist entrepreneurship research aims to promote women's emancipation and empowerment, for which purpose it formulates alternative concepts of entrepreneurship, uses different methods and strives to make research results practicable on women's own terms. First, in place of the narrowly economic means–ends logic of the mainstream definitions (Spicer, 2012), feminist research understands 'entrepreneurship' as a broadly creative activity that can advance positive social change (Calás et al., 2009). Second, socially and materially constructed processes of becoming a gendered entrepreneur are often considered more responsive to, for example, narrative and action research methods than to surveys and related statistics (Ahl & Marlow, 2012). Third, research-informed, context-sensitive practical projects of empowerment are prolifically realised around the world (Brush, de Bruin, Gatewood & Henry, 2010; Al-Dajani & Marlow, 2015). Furthermore, in the rapidly globalising reality, the often considerable differences in needs, resources and ambitions of women in the West and in the Global South have received increasing attention from feminist critical approaches to entrepreneurship.

Critical Realism

Separation of critical realism as a distinct perspective on entrepreneurship and its research does not mean that feminism and critical realism have nothing in common; there are distinguished researchers who are both feminists and critical realists (e.g. New, 1998, 2005; Lawson, 1999, 2003; Clegg, 2006). Critical realist feminists, however, challenge the penetrating constructionism that characterises the kind of feminist research introduced before.[7] If an individual is just thoroughly constructed to 'perform' some deeply gendered and other repetitious roles in society, a critical realist asks, then how can there exist any comprehensible space for this individual to embark on emancipatory and empowering acts? Obviously, such value-laden action, essential to practical and political feminism, conflicts with the picture of closely monitored performers of, for example, *femininity* and *masculinity*. From where could the desired routine-breaking acts then stem (e.g. Lawson 1999, 2003)?

Critical realism is basically a metatheory[8] that sees social reality as constituted by ongoing dynamic interactions between relatively free human agents and relatively independent social (cultural, economic, involved material/biological) structures (e.g. Bhaskar, 1979, 1986; Archer, 1995, 2000; Archer, Bhaskar, Collier, Lawson & Norrie, 1998; Sayer, 2000; Danermark, Ekström, Jakobsen & Carlsson, 2002; Carter & New, 2004; Cruickshank, 2007; Fullbrook, 2008).[9] Carlsson and his colleagues consequently present an obvious research subject to critical realists when they state, in the designated mainstream definition of entrepreneurship, that 'entrepreneurial activity and the entrepreneurial ventures are influenced by the socioeconomic environment' *(*Carlsson et al., 2013, p. 915). Such influences look real enough, but surely people who launch enterprises and entrepreneurial ventures are not just passive targets but reciprocally affect their 'socioeconomic environment'? Relationships of presumably complex nature between entrepreneurs and the settings of their entrepreneurial actions hence ask for scientific analyses.

As a matter of fact, certain critical realist arguments have entered the general discussion of the theory of entrepreneurship research, but, at least thus far, critical realism has been adopted from a notably restricted viewpoint. One central problem under debate is comfortably passed over by Carlsson and his colleagues when they note that 'entrepreneurship refers primarily to an economic function that is carried out by individuals, entrepreneurs, acting independently or within organizations, to perceive and create new opportunities'

(Carlsson et al., 2013, p. 915). In their classic article 'The promise of entrepreneurship as a field of research', Shane and Venkataraman (2000) define the nature of entrepreneurial opportunities as an essential theoretical subject of the field. To put the puzzle most plainly, would it be reasonable to consider entrepreneurial opportunities as something that exist independently in reality, waiting for an entrepreneurial person to perceive and discover them? Or is it more justifiable to think that entrepreneurial people create and enact those opportunities through their unique understanding of their socio-cultural-economic environment (Shane & Venkataraman, 2000; Gartner, Carter, Hills, Steyaert & Hjorth, 2003; McMullen & Shepherd, 2006; Alvarez & Barney, 2007, 2010; Klein, 2008; Cardon, Wincent, Singh & Drnovsek, 2009; Venkataraman, Sarasvathy, Dew & Forster, 2012; Fiet, Norton & Clouse, 2013)?

Critical realists position entrepreneurial opportunities as part of relatively independent social (cultural and material) structures, which means that the opportunities can be, in some sense, *discovered* by human agents. Choosing thus the discovery side entails tricky theoretical problems, but the features of critical realism as metatheory offer argumentative strategies to solve the three paradoxes usually associated with the discovery side:

1   Entrepreneurship can clearly bring something new into the world: marketable innovations and pathbreaking business models, for example. The novelty of such things becomes difficult to explain if they are seen to proceed from some detected entrepreneurial opportunities, because, if they already exist in the world, what real novelty can opportunities breed? An entrepreneur's creativity may now look a necessary input to the mix, but the more the importance of creativity is emphasised, the more unclear becomes the nature of what an entrepreneur is supposed to discover (Kirzner, 1997; Gielnik, Frese & Kampschulte, 2012; Martin & Wilson, 2016).

2   A clarifying division of labour for opportunity and creativity has been suggested, whereupon entrepreneurial opportunity is a discoverable possibility to recombine resources in a profit-

able way, and creativity equates to a business idea of doing the recombining (Shane, 2012, pp. 10–20). This distinction may be useful, but it shifts the theoretical puzzle to the business idea. If a business idea has to reflect the related entrepreneurial opportunity, then evidently the idea's attributes also must be held as *discovered*, with nothing crucially new in them. The paradox thus appears to lead to the conclusion that the true novelty of entrepreneurial opportunity or a business idea means creating something out of nothing, virtually drawing rabbits out of hats. Not all theorists, though, want to push interpretation of the key concepts in such a mysterious-looking direction (Klein, 2008; Martin & Wilson, 2016).

3 Lastly, our common intuitions about things that exist independently in reality and can be routinely found there clearly contradict the conceptual nature of 'opportunity'. The real furniture of the world appears tangible and measurable, whereas opportunity is, by definition, 'the potential for something not yet in existence' (Martin & Wilson, 2016, p. 265). Opportunities are accordingly oriented towards the future, of which no observations or discoveries can be made at the present. Moreover, the presumed world of customary and stable objects seems to conflict with the essential uncertainty that characterises many entrepreneurs' work and life experiences (Fletcher, 2006; Dimov, 2011; Martin & Wilson, 2016).

Against the paradoxes, Martin and Wilson utilise critical realism's layered ontology[10] to argue that a thing discoverable as an entrepreneurial opportunity is always causal potentiality for something new, and this potentiality resides in pre-existing structured mechanisms and their causal powers. For example, because of their particular internal constitution, steel and the combustion engine can actualise causal powers to make bridges bear loads and factories run, among other things. Most motor cars are likewise built on steel and the combustion engine, but the emergence of the first motor car depended on certain inventors using their creative minds to discover (i.e. to *realise conceptually* and not directly *observe* anything in the world) the potential causal power of steel to provide a durable body for a self-moving vehicle and the potential causal power of the combustion engine to become

the mover (Martin & Wilson, 2016, p. 268). To draft a contemporary example, the triumphal march of social media obviously stems from some valid insights concerning the massive causal potential of relatively simple apps to draw millions of people into virtual online communities.

So, from the perspective of critical realist theory, entrepreneurial opportunities are not created by entrepreneurs, even though a creative and agile mind is usually needed to trace the kind of mechanism, with potential causal powers that might be harnessed for a worthwhile enterprise. This potentiality arguably satisfies the conceptual core of 'opportunity', because possible actualisation of causal power is always a matter of the future in relation to its state of potentiality. Reality in general is considered a complex and open dynamic system, where structured mechanisms of material, cultural and other kinds in varying combinations both merge to produce distinctive effects and contradict each other to freeze some causal powers to the level of potentiality. An enterprise in a strong market-leader position may indeed permanently suppress its smaller competitors' real potential for innovation and growth. In this world, an entrepreneur has no guarantees of success in finding real opportunities or grasping the intricate interplay of an opportunity with other involved factors. The uncertainty of entrepreneurial life thus looks like the norm.

The critical contribution of critical realists to entrepreneurship research has, at least thus far, mainly consisted of reconceptualising the term 'entrepreneur' and its broadly understood social, cultural and economic setting of conduct with specific theoretical tools. In this work, both strong constructionism and certain assumptions associated with mainstream entrepreneurship research have been rejected.[11] Yet moving from rather complex metatheoretical abstractions towards originally and distinctively critical realist empirical research of entrepreneurship has not proved to be an easy task; it is a work in progress (e.g. Best, 2001; Porter, 2002; Bowey & Easton,

2003; Leca & Naccache, 2006; Blundel, 2007; Gilman & Edwards, 2008; Edwards, Sengupta & Tsai, 2010; Mole & Mole, 2010; Mole, 2012; Kitching, Hart & Wilson, 2015).

In conclusion, and especially from the standpoint of the founders of critical realism, critical realism in entrepreneurship research appears curiously *neutered*. This evaluation derives from the fact that theorists like Bhaskar (1986), Sayer (2000) and Collier (2003) are driven by a powerful ideal of political emancipation; in the last resort, the value of critical realism to them should be proven by its ability to help people understand and practically change the social structures that dominate and oppress them. Not much of this general spirit seems to have inspired the specialised critical realist studies of entrepreneurship, but the future remains open (see, e.g. Mingers 2014).

FREEING ENTREPRENEURSHIP FROM ALL BOUNDARIES: THE AVANT-GARDE OF CRITICAL ENTREPRENEURSHIP RESEARCH

The great enthusiasm for discussing 'entrepreneurship' and 'entrepreneur' shown by both academic researchers (Gedeon, 2010) and various quarters of the public (Kim, 2015) can be taken in two critical but still very different modes. The first, *negatively* critical, standpoint sees in this zeal proof of how the entrepreneurialist ideology of capitalism has thoroughly permeated societies. This ideology considers economic enterprises the engine for almost everything good in the world and nudges individuals into thinking of themselves as one-person enterprises, who must calculatedly plan their life projects, coolly search for means of achieving their goals, carefully nurture their personal brand, etc. As a central consequence of this, capitalism can continue its production of injustices and misery uninterrupted, because any potential source of failure or success in life other than an individually managed

life-enterprise is becoming hard to perceive or picture (e.g. Ogbor, 2000; Armstrong, 2001, 2005; du Gay, 2004; Jones & Spicer, 2009; Bröckling, 2007; Rose & Miller, 2008; Costa & Saraiva, 2012; Jones & Murtola, 2012; Tedmanson, Verduyn, Essers & Gartner, 2012; Vallas & Cummins, 2015).

However, intensive academic and popular interest in entrepreneurship can be given an essentially more *positive* reading, too. Maybe the common need to understand 'entrepreneurship' has simply escaped the narrow meanings and contexts of traditional economic and business studies, in which case theorists and researchers should also wake up to the new reality. The expected awakening has occurred already in numerous ways, clear signs of which include vibrant empirical research on types of entrepreneurship (e.g. social, cultural or academic), kinds of entrepreneurial agent (e.g. organisational, domestic or immigrant), as well as on the how, why, when and where of entrepreneurship (e.g. innovative, imitative, necessity, lifestyle, nascent, startup, grass-roots or diaspora entrepreneurship) (Gedeon, 2010, p. 28).

The evident dispersion of conceptualisations and subfields of entrepreneurship research in multiple directions gives rise to the theoretical problem of whether anything meaningful at all can be claimed about the research and concepts in question. What I call the avant-garde of the critical research under review has its own solution to the problem. To explicate in a preliminary way, the avant-garde can be argued as detecting in the dispersion referred to a gradually developing and largely shared sense of entrepreneuring as a unifying positive force that ultimately gives *processes of life itself* the creative spark they need to keep on going (e.g. Sorensen, 2006; Steyaert, 2007, 2011, 2012; Nayak, 2008; Styhre, 2008; Weiskopf & Steyaert, 2009; Hjorth & Steyaert, 2009; Beyes & Steyaert, 2012; Hjorth, 2015; Hjorth, Holt & Steyaert, 2015).

What Steyaert (a key figure in the field) calls 'radical process philosophy' (Steyaert 2007, p. 468) represents the avant-garde in this review, and I justify choosing it by the fact that, acquiring inspiration and concepts from the centuries-long processualist tradition in Western philosophy,[12] the avant-garde thoroughly aims to rethink not only entrepreneurship but also our styles of studying, analysing and theorising it. Concentrated in a relatively small group of active and visible researchers, the radical process philosophy represents a true minority position with scant prospects of becoming integrated and domesticated into mainstream entrepreneurship research, even compared to critical realism.

Grasping the Core of Radical Process Philosophy

In place of itemising complex and occasionally obscure concepts of the radical process philosophy, it is more useful here to aspire to some intuitive grasp of what it is that the radicals are striving to achieve. The aspiration can start from a simple-looking question: what is reality like according to a survey questionnaire? Survey questionnaires map such things as gender, age, marital status, income, type of enterprise and, specifically, the quality and strength of respondents' attitudes to countless matters, with the Likert scale. Methodologists typically ponder whether the Likert scale finds independently existing attitudes or creates them on the spot, but, to the radical process philosophy, the true problem lies in the *static ontology of being* that survey questionnaires imply. Complying with certain mainstream logic, the research instrument gives a frozen portrait of nailed-down and atomistic individuals who somehow carry remarkable gradual entities called 'attitudes' in their heads. 'Attitudes' are supposed to 'cause' individuals to act in certain ways, but attitudes may change, and so follow-up surveys often acquire material for statistical analysis to reveal all kinds of new connections between units.

However, is reality at all like survey questionnaires present it? Does dualistic 'gender' or five alternatives of 'marital status' make

sense when women are increasingly adopting characteristics traditionally considered masculine and vice versa, when many kinds of sexual and asexual identities demand to be heard and when people living in informal intimate relationships may commit themselves to the ideal of being faithful more strongly than people switching from one marriage to another? When individuals are enmeshed in the concrete interactions of their everyday lives, could entities of a particular sort (e.g. attitudes) really be isolated as engines of their actions? The more inclined we are to answer questions like these negatively, the more open we might become to the ontological alternative that the radical process philosophy offers, with implications for understanding 'entrepreneurship' and its research included.

The radicals replace the static ontology of being with a *dynamic ontology of becoming*, according to which key characteristics of reality include 'movement, change and flow… the world is restless, something underway, becoming and perishing, without end' (Hjorth et al., 2015, p. 599). Hjorth, Holt and Steyaert offer the following intuitively enticing image of a commercial enterprise's processualist life:

> what might seem fixed becomes loose. Buildings are outgrown, symbols are updated, personnel change, the products and services being delivered change, mergers occur, best forgotten histories are repressed, stakeholders loosen their stakes or hold on to them jealously, assets are stripped, tectonic shifts of wider institutional settings are acknowledged, revolts are resented or embraced, and all the while money flows, in and out. Through time, there are breaks in coherence or consistency of these patterns as various groups ignore or advocate different interests and desires. Indeed, we ask, can there be an organization to which employees, resources, prospects and responsibilities can belong? (Hjorth et al., 2015, 599–600)

Instead of considering an enterprise or organisation as a spatially and temporally durable entity, it would be more fruitful to think of enterprising, or organising, which is an incessant process of becoming. If this kind of change into a verbal or functional mode looks odd or incomprehensible, the puzzlement might well be caused by the structure and functioning of language itself. By dividing reality essentially into subjects, objects, verbs, etc., language seems to construct a world filled by stable but qualitatively different kinds of thing with supposedly causal interrelationships that offer, for example, the very problems for the sciences to solve. Interestingly therefore, probably the toughest resistance to switching from the *being* ontology to the *becoming* ontology may be intensively ingrained in our thinking.

Nonetheless, as reality from the processualist ontological viewpoint is constituted of neither distinctive things nor spaces between things to be filled with causality, an intriguing problem surfaces: language profoundly distorts our understanding of reality, but evidently we cannot replace language with anything crucially different, or even reform it radically. The processualists understand the irreplaceability of language, and in dealing with the problem they: 1) emphasise the verbal, adverbial and functional nature of reality (i.e. the world is becoming in countless ways) and there are always qualities to this becoming (e.g. intensively, haphazardly, strikingly, porously, etc.); and/or 2) invent novel concepts and vocabularies to better catch the true nature of the world (e.g. Whitehead, 1978; Deleuze, 1988; Steyaert, 2007, 2012; Weiskopf & Steyaert, 2009; Halewood, 2011; Poutanen, 2013; Hjorth, 2015.)

Entrepreneuring as a Mode of the World's Creative Becoming

To state that key characteristics of reality are 'movement, change and flow' (Hjorth et al., 2015, p. 599) does not imply the view that reality consists of nothing but a formless and limitless stream of life. On the contrary, continuously bringing new, though temporary, events and figurations into existence is the crux of the matter (e.g. Gartner, 2012). *Entrepreneuring* is a special kind of organising, where desire for value potential – that is,

the 'pull' of an evolving business idea, for example – imaginatively transforms some 'proto-organizational forms into an organization that becomes productive in actualizing the imagined value potential' (Hjorth et al., 2015, p. 604). Importantly, entrepreneuring is distinguished from *managing*, because 'entrepreneuring ends when desire is coded into interest, when an organization is in place the purpose of which is to capture value as much as possible, for this is when management will do a better job' (Hjorth et al., 2015, p. 604; see also Hjorth, 2015; Steyaert, 2012).

Arguably, reality comes into existence often just managerially, for most of the world's substance emerges into being only as minimally different reproductions of already existing material. Entrepreneuring in the sense of 'desire for value potential' (Hjorth et al., 2015, p. 604) thus may not be a very general phenomenon. Nonetheless, entrepreneuring appears as a fundamental force for creative novelty, whose leverage exceeds any conventionally economic function. Concerning the already analysed problem of entrepreneurial opportunity, to the radical process philosophy true novelty can lie neither in thing-like characteristics of the world, nor in the creative/constructive mind of an aspiring entrepreneur; instead, through eventful movement from desire for value potential into actualisation of this potential, both a particular entrepreneurial opportunity and a creative entrepreneur utilising this opportunity are understood to come into their temporary existence *at the same time*. The dynamic and diverse constituents in this becoming (e.g. cultural, corporeal, affective, artefactual constituents), in their mutual absorption through ongoing processes, are clearly challenging to capture.

Research into entrepreneurship is still possible but, as there basically exists nothing stable or delimited for empirical description or theoretical representation to correspond with, the radicals aim to 're-create (re-form) … studies in entrepreneurship as (participation in) creative processes of world-making, as acts of creation rather than as attempts of discovering the truth about entrepreneurship' (Weiskopf & Steyaert, 2009, p. 15). A kind of 'double act' is therefore required: scientific research should become inventive, imaginative, creative etc. in the true entrepreneurial sense, and research should also maintain some non-descriptive and non-representative relationship to entrepreneurship 'on the outside'. Steyaert, Hjorth and Gartner (2011) formulate six strategies for enforcing this double act:

a *Othering words and concepts.* Inventing concepts can create new venues for research, as terms like 'glocalization', 'entrepreneurial ecosystem' or 'mumpreneur' show. In this mode, Gartner (2011) suggests 'otherpreneur' to refer to 'person who is not the primary "founder" of an organization, yet plays an important role in the creation of the organization' (Gartner, 2011, p. 9; Steyaert et al., 2011, p. 4).
b *Exploring boundaries.* Ideas of 'business climate' or 'entrepreneuring as a way of life', for instance, were once novel, and a similar rethinking of ostensibly incommensurate things must be encouraged (Steyaert et al., 2011, p. 4).
c *Affecting community scholarship.* Critical research has replaced the myth of a lone, cool and heroic entrepreneur with the reality of the messy and emotional sociality of entrepreneuring. The community of entrepreneurship scholars needs constant myth-breaking in the same mould (Steyaert et al., 2011, p. 5; Campbell, 2011).
d *Affecting entrepreneurship education.* Entrepreneurial education should not be about memorising scientific 'results' or 'theories'; it must use any means available (e.g. provocation, fabulation, paralogy) to push students into states where creative thinking and doing becomes possible (Steyaert et al., 2011, p. 5; Hjorth, 2011).
e *Contextualising through participation.* There exist no backgrounds or contexts in relation to which the 'objectivity' of research results could be stabilised. Instead, scientists with their research subjects – for example, business entrepreneurs – always enact the presumed context of a research project in multiple ways. Boundaries between ostensibly different practices (researching and entrepreneuring, for example) are fuzzy (Steyaert et al., 2011, pp. 5–6; Fletcher, 2011).
f *Reconceptualizing method.* Scientific research methods consider world-making (ontology)

more than knowledge-producing (epistemology). Therefore, methods should be understood as 'method-assemblages that help us to make visible the complex social process in which methods co-figure with other actants' (Steyaert, et al., 2011, p. 6). To study entrepreneuring by launching and running a business evidently offers one opening towards reconceptualization.

To try to discuss, for example, 'empirical applications' of the radical process philosophy would be misleading, because the world is not seen to cut its joints into any strict categories like 'empirical' or 'theoretical'. Furthermore, as researchers, we cannot inhabit any detached and durable position from where such distinctions could be meaningfully made; we are always already tangled in the manifold processes of life. In some constellations of these, we may transiently become what could be reasonably called 'free actors', although we often lose our entrepreneurial momentum and freedom to managerially routine churning out of everyday banalities. The critically positive mission of the avant-gardists is to create space and time for freedom and entrepreneurialism in the broadest sense to emerge. They have put their mission into practice via various educational and methodological experiments, which have included theatre-like multimedia performances and processualist reconstructions of conventional research, among other things (e.g. Steyaert & Hjorth, 2002; Hjorth & Steyaert, 2006; Sorensen, 2006; Steyaert, 2011).

CONCLUSION

In this chapter, I have introduced certain critical perspectives in entrepreneurship research in relation to what I call 'mainstream' entrepreneurship research. I have intentionally left details of this baseline vague, because boundaries between the 'mainstream' and the 'non-mainstream' are obviously fluid and constantly moving. The methodological criticism discussed in the second section can be argued to belong to the mainstream, but it also shows awareness of the narrow ideology of entrepreneurialism. This ideology comes into sharp focus in feminist entrepreneurship research, discussed in the third section, which also includes critical realism, whose position in entrepreneurship research reveals certain peculiarities. Taken as a whole, critical realism belongs to the Marxist tradition in social theory and endorses political values of emancipation, empowerment and removal of oppression in society. It seems that entrepreneurship researchers inspired by critical realism have not yet been very interested in its political heart; they have mainly adopted some helpful critical realist concepts to analyse 'entrepreneurial opportunity', for example.

What I call the 'avant-garde' of critical entrepreneurship research in the fourth section builds on complex ontological theories of processualist reality and unties 'entrepreneurship' from narrow economy- and business-centred meanings. Instead, even if the avant-gardists often study ordinary businesses and enterprises, 'entrepreneurship' to them concerns any innovative turning point in the processualist flow of the world, or events of true creativity where something genuinely novel is brought into existence. With their imaginative methods of research and teaching, the avant-gardists consider their critical task as resisting 'managerialism', i.e. the (often dominant) routine and banal repetitiveness of human conduct. Obviously, the bold reconceptualisation of 'entrepreneurship' in relation to, for example, 'creativity' could offer meaningful openings for dialogue between the avant-gardists and more conventionally oriented researchers of entrepreneurship.

Notes

1   Values operate in many functions and at many levels, and what I call 'meta-perspectives' cover, for example, questions of scientific methodology and general theories of social reality.

2   The entrepreneur is the bearer of risks inflicted by changes in market demand (Cantillon, 1755, quoted in Thornton, 2005; Gedeon, 2010, p. 19).

3   Carrying out new combinations we call 'enterprise'; the individuals whose function it is to carry them out we call 'entrepreneurs' (Schumpeter, 1961; Gedeon 2010, p. 20).

4   Entrepreneurs innovate. Innovation is the specific instrument of entrepreneurs (Drucker, 1985; Gedeon 2010, p. 20).

5   The distinction between *innovation* and *invention* is conventionally made. For example, referring to Ahmed and Shepherd (2010), Gripenberg, Sveiby and Segercrantz state that 'invention stands for the generation of a new idea, whereas innovation stands for the fruitful commercialization/exploitation/market capitalization of that idea' (Gripenberg et al., 2012, p. 5).

6   Attributes associated both with 'entrepreneur' and 'masculinity' include 'self-centered', 'independent', 'strong-willed', 'energetic', 'resolute', 'visionary', 'detached', 'achievement-oriented' and 'foresighted' (Ahl, 2006).

7   On efforts at dialogue between critical realists and strong feminist constructionists, see Poutanen, 2007.

8   Metatheory concerns the most general questions of how social reality exists (the question of ontology), how something could be known about this reality (the question of epistemology) and suitable methods to obtain this knowledge (the question of methodology). Metatheory does not itself describe or explain any substantial or concrete phenomena; it aims to create the space to do so.

9   From the ontological perspective, reality for critical realism is multiply layered, that is, entities at a certain level emerge, i.e. they become more than the sums of their parts, from entities at a lower level of complexity. Social life is constituted by countless dynamic unions of i) human beings with their multiple capabilities, ii) their cultural and material world 'ready-to-hand' with artefacts included, and iii) the non-human natural world. However, social life itself is much more complex than its constituents (e.g. Bhaskar, 1986; Archer et al., 1998; Cruickshank, 2007).

Entities existing at different levels (bacterium, stone, human individual, book, commercial enterprise, etc.) carry their own specific structures, which involve mechanisms capable of producing causal effects into reality. In other words, entities carry causal powers, which are real even when they are not exercised (an enterprise keeps its capability to make products and profit through its staff's holidays). They may also be real only as potentialities (an enterprise cannot operate internationally at the moment, but it has prospects of doing so in future). Individuals' freedom of action emerges as joint effects from interaction between their 'inner' constitution and their environment. This freedom is relative, significantly because there are general and particular limits to what we can do (nobody can fly by themselves, only some individuals can become top musicians or successful entrepreneurs, etc.). On the other hand, social structures, i.e. the way our material/biological, cultural and economic conditions of living have been built and moulded by human activity over the centuries, exist independently in the sense that we encounter a kind of ready-made social world. Here, we do not need to build everything from scratch. This world both hinders and enables our lives in countless ways, and we can affect and change it with our own actions, because we too carry causal powers as complexly structured entities. Still, the independence of the social world is relative too, because without humankind there would not exist any social structures.

10 The analytically abstracted, ontological layers of reality include: 1) *the real layer* of entities' structured mechanisms with their causal powers, which may be exercised, non-exercised or potential; 2) *the actual layer* of causal effects brought about by exercised causal powers; and 3) *the empirical layer* of such actual causal effects that can be observed, measured and made direct sense of. To entrepreneurship research, this layered model implies that just collecting and combining empirical data is rarely, if ever, enough to understand and explain phenomena. In addition, conceptual and theoretical work to link the different layers is needed (e.g. Bhaskar, 1986; Archer et al., 1998; Cruickshank, 2007).

11 Against strong constructionism is put the relative independence of social reality and individuals' relative freedom of action. Mainstream research is seen as flawed by its flat ontology, i.e. by its biased concentration only on the empirical layer. Furthermore, the mainstream's common ideas of human agency are considered simplified, atomistic and ahistorical (e.g. Archer & Tritter, 2000).

12 Key historical figures include the philosophers Baruch Spinoza, Friedrich Nietzsche, Henri Bergson and A. N. Whitehead.

REFERENCES

Achtenhagen, L. and Welter, F. (2011). 'Surfing on the ironing board' – the representation of women's entrepreneurship in German newspapers. *Entrepreneurship & Regional Development,* 23(9–10), 763–86.

Ahl, H. (2012). Gender, organizations and entrepreneurship. In D. Hjorth (ed.), *Handbook on Organisational Entrepreneurship*. Cheltenham: Edward Elgar Publishing, pp. 134–50.

Ahl, H. (2006). Why research on women entrepreneurs needs new directions. *Entrepreneurship Theory and Practice*, 30(5), 595–621.

Ahl, H. and Marlow, S. (2012). Exploring the dynamics of gender, feminism and entrepreneurship: advancing debate to escape a dead end? *Organization*, 19(5), 543–62.

Ahmed, P. K. and Shepherd, C. D. (2010). *Innovation Management*. Essex: Pearson.

Al-Dajani, H. and Marlow, S. (2015). Empowerment, place and entrepreneurship: women in the Global South. In T. Baker and F. Welter (eds.), *The Routledge Companion to Entrepreneurship*. Abingdon: Routledge, pp. 343–57.

Alvarez, S. A. and Barney, J. B. (2010). Entrepreneurship and epistemology: the philosophical underpinnings of the study of entrepreneurial opportunities. *Academy of Management Annals,* 4, 557–83.

Alvarez, S. A. and Barney, J. B. (2007). The entrepreneurial theory of the firm. *Journal of Management Studies,* 44, 1057–63.

Archer, M. S. (2000). *Being Human: The Problem of Agency*. Cambridge: Cambridge University Press.

Archer, M. S. (1995). *Realist Social Theory: The Morphogenetic Approach*. Cambridge: Cambridge University Press.

Archer, M. S. and Tritter, J. Q. (eds.) (2000). *Rational Choice Theory: Resisting Colonisation*. London: Routledge.

Archer, M. S., Bhaskar, R., Collier, A., Lawson, T. and Norrie, A. (eds.) (1998). *Critical Realism: Essential Readings*. London: Routledge.

Armstrong, P. (2005). *Critique of Entrepreneurship: People and Policy*. Basingstoke: Palgrave Macmillan.

Armstrong, P. (2001). Science, enterprise and profit: ideology in the knowledge-driven economy. *Economy and Society,* 30(4), 524–52.

Audretsch, D. B. (2007). Entrepreneurship capital and economic growth. *Oxford Review of Economic Policy*, 23(1), 63–78.

Bartelsman, E., Scarpetta, S. and Schivardi, F. (2005). Comparative analysis of firm demographics and survival: evidence from micro-level sources in OECD countries. *Industrial and Corporate Change,* 14(3), 365–91.

Best, M. H. (2001). *The New Competitive Advantage: The Renewal of American Industry*. Oxford: Oxford University Press.

Beyes, T. and Steyaert, C. (2012). Spacing organization: non-representational theory and performing organizational space. *Organization,* 19(1), 43–59.

Bhaskar, R. (1986). *Scientific Realism and Human Emancipation*. London: Verso.

Bhaskar, R. (1979). *The Possibility of Naturalism: A Philosophical Critique of the Contemporary Human Sciences*. Hassocks: Harvester.

Blackburn, R. and Kovalainen, A. (2009). Researching small firms and entrepreneurship: past, present and future. *International Journal of Management Reviews,* 11(2), 127–48.

Blanchflower, D. G. (2004). Self-employment: more may not be better. *Swedish Economic Policy Review,* 11(2), 15–73.

Blundel, R. (2007). Critical realism: a suitable vehicle for entrepreneurship research? In H. Neergaard and J. P. Ulhoi (eds.), *Handbook of Qualitative Research Methods in Entrepreneurship*. Cheltenham: Edward Elgar Publishing, pp. 49–74.

Bowey, J. and Easton, G. (2003). A critical realist framework for explaining changes in entrepreneurial relationships. In *Proceedings of the 19th IMP International Conference*, University of Lugarno, Switzerland.

Bröckling, U. (2007). *Das Unternehmerische Selbst: Soziologie einer Subjektivierungsform (Suhrkamp Taschenbuch Wissenschaft)*. Berlin: Suhrkamp.

Brush, C., de Bruin, A., Gatewood, E. and Henry, C. (eds.) (2010). *Women Entrepreneurs and the Global Environment for Growth: A Research Perspective*. Cheltenham: Edward Elgar Publishing.

Butler, J. (1990). *Gender Trouble: Feminism and the Subversion of Identity*. Abingdon: Routledge.

Calás, M. B., Smircich, L. and Bourne, K. A. (2009). Extending the boundaries: reframing 'entrepreneurship as social change' through feminist perspectives. *Academy of Management Review,* 34(3), 552–69.

Campbell, K. (2011). Caring and daring entrepreneurship research. *Entrepreneurship and Regional Development,* 23(1–2), 37–47.

Cardon, M. S., Wincent, J., Singh, J. and Drnovsek, M. (2009). The nature and experience of entrepreneurial passion. *Academy of Management Review,* 34, 511–32.

Carlsson, B., Braunerhjelm, P., McKelvey, M., Olofsson, C., Persson, L. and Ylinenpää, H. (2013). The evolving domain of entrepreneurship research. *Small Business Economics,* 41(4), 913–30.

Carter, B. and New, C. (eds.) (2004). *Making Realism Work: Realist Social Theory and Empirical Research*. London: Routledge.

Clegg, S. (2006). The problem of agency in feminism: a critical realist approach. *Gender and Education,* 18(3), 309–24.

Collier, A. (2003). *In Defence of Objectivity and Other Essays: On Realism, Existentialism and Politics*. London: Routledge.

Costa, A. S. M. and Saraiva, L. A. S. (2012). Hegemonic discourses on entrepreneurship as an ideological mechanism for the reproduction of capital. *Organization,* 19(5), 587–614.

Cruickshank, J. (ed.) (2007). *Critical Realism: The Difference It Makes*. London: Routledge.

Dahl, H. M., Keränen, M. and Kovalainen, A. (eds.) (2011). *Europeanization, Care and Gender: Global Complexities*. Basingstoke: Palgrave.

Danermark, B., Ekström, M., Jakobsen, L. and Carlsson, J. C. (2002). *Explaining Society: Critical Realism in the Social Sciences*. London: Routledge.

Deleuze, G. (1988) [1966]. *Bergsonism*. New York: Columbia University Press.

Dennis, W. J. (2011). Entrepreneurship, small business and public policy levers. *Journal of Small Business Management,* 49(1), 92–106.

Dimov, D. (2011). Grappling with the unbearable elusiveness of entrepreneurial opportunities. *Entrepreneurship Theory and Practice,* 35(1), 57–81.

Disney, R., Haskel, J. and Heden, Y. (2003). Restructuring and productivity growth in UK manufacturing. *Economic Journal,* 113(489), 666–94.

Drucker, P. (1985). *Innovation and Entrepreneurship*. New York: Harper Perennial.

du Gay, P. (2004). Self-service: retail, shopping and personhood. *Consumption, Markets and Culture,* 7(2), 149–63.

Edwards, P., Sengupta, S. and Tsai, C.–J. (2010). The context dependent nature of small firms' relations with support agencies: a three-sector study in the UK. *International Small Business Journal,* 28(6), 543–65.

European Commission (2014). *Statistical Data on Women Entrepreneurs in Europe*. Luxembourg: Publications Office of the European Union.

Evans, M. (2003). *Gender and Social Theory*. Buckingham: Open University Press.

Fiet, J. O., Norton, W. I. Jr. and Clouse, V. G. H. (2013). Search and discovery by repeatedly successful entrepreneurs. *International Small Business Journal,* 31, 890–913.

Fletcher, D. E. (2011). A curiosity for contexts: entrepreneurship, enactive research and autoethnography. *Entrepreneurship and Regional Development*, 23(1–2), 65–76.

Fletcher, D. E. (2006). Entrepreneurial processes and the social construction of opportunity. *Entrepreneurship and Regional Development,* 18(5), 421–40.

Fournier, V. and Grey, C. (2000). At the critical moment: conditions and prospects for critical management studies. *Human Relations,* 53(1), 7–32.

Frankish, J., Roberts, R., Coad, A., Spears, T. and Storey, D. (2013). Do entrepreneurs really learn? Or do they just tell us that they do? *Industrial and Corporate Change,* 22(1), 73–106.

Fullbrook, E. (ed.) (2008). *Ontology and Economics: Tony Lawson and His Critics*. London: Routledge.

Gartner, W. B. (2012). Entrepreneurship as organization creation. In D. Hjorth (ed.), *Handbook on Organisational Entrepreneurship*. Cheltenham: Edward Elgar Publishing, pp. 21–30.

Gartner, W. B. (2011). When words fail: an entrepreneurship glossolalia. *Entrepreneurship and Regional Development,* 23(1–2), 9–21.

Gartner, W. B. and Bellamy, M. G. (2010). *Enterprise*. Mason, OH: South-Western Cengage Learning.

Gartner, W. B., Carter, N., Hills, G., Steyaert, C. and Hjorth, D. (2003). The language of opportunity. In C. Steyaert and D. Hjorth (eds.), *New Movements in Entrepreneurship*. Cheltenham: Edward Elgar Publishing, pp. 103–125.

Gedeon, S. (2010). What is entrepreneurship? *Entrepreneurial Practice Review,* 1(3), 15–35.

Gherardi, S. (2014). Organizations as symbolic gendered orders. In S. Kumra, R. Simpson and R. Burke (eds.), *The Oxford Handbook of Gender in Organizations*. Oxford: Oxford University Press, pp. 76–94.

Gielnik, M. M., Frese, M. and Kampschulte, A. (2012). Creativity in the opportunity identification process and the moderating effect of diversity of information. *Journal of Business Venturing,* 27, 559–76.

Gilman, M. W. and Edwards, P. K. (2008). Testing a framework of the organization of small firms. *International Small Business Journal,* 26(5), 531–58.

Gripenberg, P., Sveiby, K.-E. and Segercrantz, B. (2012). Challenging the innovation paradigm: the prevailing pro-innovation bias. In K.-E. Sveiby, P. Gripenberg and B. Segercrantz (eds.), *Challenging the Innovation Paradigm*. London: Routledge, pp. 1–12.

Halewood, M. (2011). *A. N. Whitehead and Social Theory: Tracing a Culture of Thought*. London: Anthem Press.

Hall, R. E. and Woodward, S. E. (2010). The burden of the nondiversifiable risk of entrepreneurship. *American Economic Review,* 100(3), 1163–94.

Hamilton, B. H. (2000). Does entrepreneurship pay? An empirical analysis of the returns to self-employment. *Journal of Political Economy,* 108(3), 604–31.

Hanappi-Egger, E. (2014). 'Homo economicus' and 'his' impact on gendered societies. In M. Evans, C. Hemmings, M. Henry, H. Johnstone, S. Madhok, A. Plomien and S. Wearing (eds.), *The SAGE Handbook of Feminist Theory*. London: Sage, pp. 397–412.

Heilman, M. E. (2012). Gender stereotypes and workplace bias. *Research in Organizational Behavior,* 32, 113–35.

Hjorth, D. (2015). Sketching a philosophy of entrepreneurship. In T. Baker and F. Welter (eds.), *The Routledge Companion to Entrepreneurship*. New York: Routledge, pp. 41–58.

Hjorth, D., Holt, R. and Steyaert, C. (2015). Entrepreneurship and process studies. *International Small Business Journal,* 33(6), 599–611.

Hjorth, D. and Steyaert, C. (eds.) (2009). *The Politics and Aesthetics of Entrepreneurship*. Cheltenham: Edward Elgar Publishing.

Hjorth, D. and Steyaert, C. (2006). American Psycho/European Schizo: stories of managerial elites in a hundred images. In P. Gagliardi and B. Czarniawska (eds.), *Management Education and Humanities*. Cheltenham: Edward Elgar Publishing, pp. 67–97.

Hvide, H. K. (2009). The quality of entrepreneurs. *The Economic Journal*, 119(539), 1010–35.

Jones, C. and Murtola, A.-M. (2012). Entrepreneurship, crisis, critique. In D. Hjorth (ed.), *Handbook on Organisational Entrepreneurship*. Cheltenham: Edward Elgar Publishing, pp. 116–33.

Jones, C. and Spicer, A. (2009). *Unmasking the Entrepreneur*. Cheltenham: Edward Elgar Publishing.

Kane, R. (ed.) (2002). *Oxford Handbook on Free Will*. New York: Oxford University Press.

Kariv, D. (2013). *Female Entrepreneurship and the New Venture Creation: An International Overview*. New York: Routledge.

Katila, S. and Eriksson, P. (2013). He is a firm, strong-minded and empowering leader, but is she? Gendered positioning of female and male CEOs. *Gender, Work and Organization*, 20(1), 71–84.

Kim, P. H. (2015). Action and process, vision and values. Entrepreneurship means something different to everyone. In T. Baker and F. Welter (eds.), *The Routledge Companion to Entrepreneurship*. London: Routledge, pp. 59–74.

Kirzner, I. M. (1997). Entrepreneurial discovery and the competitive market process: an Austrian approach. *Journal of Economic Literature*, 35(1), 60–85.

Kitching, J., Hart, M. and Wilson, N. (2015). Burden or benefit? Regulation as a dynamic influence on small business performance. *International Small Business Journal*, 33(2), 130–47.

Klein, P. (2008). Opportunity discovery, entrepreneurial action, and economic organization. *Strategic Entrepreneurship Journal*, 2(3), 175–90.

Kuratko, D. F. (2009). *Entrepreneurship: Theory, Process and Practice*. Mason, OH: South-Western Cengage Learning.

Kwong, C., Jones-Evans, D. and Thompson, P. (2012). Differences in perceptions of access to finance between potential male and female entrepreneurs: evidence from the UK. *International Journal of Entrepreneurial Behavior & Research*, 18(1), 75–97.

Lawson, T. (2003). Ontology and feminist theorizing. *Feminist Economics*, 9(1), 119–50.

Lawson, T. (1999). Feminism, realism, and universalism. *Feminist Economics*, 5(2), 25–59.

Leca, B. and Naccache, P. (2006). A critical realist approach to institutional entrepreneurship. *Organization*, 13(5), 627–51.

Lewis, P. (2013). The search for an authentic entrepreneurial identity: difference and professionalism among women business owners. *Gender, Work and Organization*, 20(3), 252–66.

Lewis, P. (2006). The quest for invisibility: female entrepreneurs and the masculine norm of entrepreneurship. *Gender, Work and Organization*, 13(5), 453–69.

Littunen, H. (2003). Management capabilities and environmental characteristics in the critical operational phase of entrepreneurship – A comparison of Finnish family and nonfamily firms. *Family Business Review*, 16(3), 183–97.

Lorber, J. (1996). Beyond the binaries: depolarizing the categories of sex, sexuality, and gender. *Sociological Inquiry*, 66(2), 143–59.

McMullen, J. S., and Shepherd, D. A. (2006). Entrepreneurial action and the role of uncertainty in the theory of the entrepreneur. *Academy of Management Review*, 31, 132–52.

Martin, L. and Wilson, N. (2016). Opportunity, discovery and creativity: a critical realist perspective. *International Small Business Journal*, 34(3), 261–75.

Mingers, J. (2014). Helping business schools engage with real problems: the contribution of critical realism and systems thinking. *University of Kent Working Paper No. 301*. Kent: University of Kent.

Mole, K. (2012). Critical realism and entrepreneurship. In K. Mole and M. Ram (eds.), *Perspectives in Entrepreneurship: A Critical Approach*. Basingstoke: Palgrave Macmillan, pp. 137–48.

Mole, K. and Mole, M. (2010). Entrepreneurship as the structuration of individual and opportunity: a response using a critical realist perspective. Comment on Sarason, Dean and Dillard. *Journal of Business Venturing*, 25, 230–37.

Moskowitz, T. J. and Vissing-Jorgensen, A. (2002). The returns to entrepreneurial investment: a private equity premium puzzle? *American Economic Review*, 92(4), 745–78.

Nayak, A. (2008). On the way to theory: a processual approach. *Organization Studies,* 29(2), 173–90.

New, C. (2005). Sex and gender: a critical realist approach. *New Formations,* 56(4), 54–70.

New, C. (1998). Realism, deconstruction and the feminist standpoint. *Journal for the Theory of Social Behaviour,* 28(4), 349–72.

Nightingale, P. and Coad, A. (2013). Muppets and gazelles: political and methodological biases in entrepreneurship research. *Industrial and Corporate Change*, 23(1), 113–43.

Ogbor, J. (2000). Mythicising and reification in entrepreneurial discourse: ideology – critique of entrepreneurial studies. *Journal of Management Studies*, 37, 605–35.

Ortega-Argiles, R., Vivarelli, M. and Voigt, P. (2009). R&D in SMEs: a paradox? *Small Business Economics*, 33(1), 3–11.

Peredo, A. M. (2015). Poverty, reciprocity and community-based entrepreneurship: enlarging the discussion. In T. Baker and F. Welter (eds.), *The Routledge Companion to Entrepreneurship*. London: Routledge, pp. 263–80.

Pines, A. M., Lerner, M. and Schwartz, D. (2010). Gender differences in entrepreneurship: equality, diversity and inclusion in times of global crisis. *Equality, Diversity and Inclusion,* 29(2), 186–98.

Pink, T. (2004). *Free Will: A Very Short Introduction*. Oxford: Oxford University Press.

Porter, S. (2002). Critical realist ethnography: the case of racism and professionalism in a medical setting. In S. Ackroyd and S. Fleetwood (eds.), *Critical Realism in Action in Organization and Management Studies*. London: Routledge, pp. 141–60.

Poutanen, S. (2013). From gendered research interview toward ontologized co-creativity: reformulating the methodological underpinnings of the well-worn practice with metaphorizing. *The International Journal of Communication and Linguistic Studies,* 10(3), 1–15.

Poutanen, S. (2007). Critical realism and post-structuralist feminism: the difficult path to mutual understanding. *Journal of Critical Realism,* 6(1), 29–53.

Rehn, A., Brännback, M., Carsrud, A. and Lindahl, M. (2013). Challenging the myths of entrepreneurship? *Entrepreneurship & Regional Development,* 25(7–8), 543–51.

Roscoe, P. (2011). The unbearable emptiness of entrepreneurship. *Ephemera Reviews: Theory & Politics in Organization,* 11(3), 319–24.

Rose, N. and Miller, P. (2008). *Governing the Present: Administering Economic, Social and Personal Life*. Cambridge: Polity Press.

Santarelli, E. and Vivarelli, M. (2007). Entrepreneurship and the process of firms' entry, survival and growth. *Industrial and Corporate Change*, 16(3), 455–88.

Sayer, A. (2000). *Realism and Social Science*. London: Sage.

Schumpeter, J. (1961) [1934]. *The Theory of Economic Development: An Inquiry into Profits, Capital, Credit, Interest, and the Business Cycle*. New York: Oxford University Press.

Sebora, T. C., Lee, S. M. and Sukasame, N. (2009). Critical success factors for e-commerce entrepreneurship: an empirical study of Thailand. *Small Business Economics,* 32(3), 303–16.

Shane, S. (2012). Reflections on the 2010 AMR decade award: delivering on the promise of entrepreneurship as a field of research. *Academy of Management Review,* 37(1), 10–20.

Shane, S. (2008). *The Illusions of Entrepreneurship: The Costly Myths that Entrepreneurs, Investors and Policy Makers Live By*. New Haven, CT: Yale University Press.

Shane, S. and Venkataraman, S. (2000). The promise of entrepreneurship as a field of research. *Academy of Management Review,* 25, 217–26.

Sorensen, B. M. (2006). Identity sniping: innovation, imagination and the body. *Creativity and Innovation Management,* 15(2), 135–42.

Spicer, A. (2012). Critical theories of entrepreneurship. In K. Mole and M. Ram (eds.), *Perspectives in Entrepreneurship: A Critical Approach*. Basingstoke: Palgrave Macmillan, pp. 149–60.

Steyaert, C. (2012). Making the multiple: theorising processes of entrepreneurship and organisation. In D. Hjorth (ed.), *Handbook on Organisational Entrepreneurship*. Cheltenham: Edward Elgar Publishing, pp. 151–68.

Steyaert, C. (2011). Entrepreneurship as in(ter)vention: reconsidering the conceptual politics of method in entrepreneurship studies. *Entrepreneurship & Regional Development,* 23(1–2), 77–88.

Steyaert, C. (2007). 'Entrepreneuring' as a conceptual attractor? A review of process theories in 20 years of entrepreneurship studies. *Entrepreneurship & Regional Development,* 19(6), 453–77.

Steyaert, C. and Hjorth, D. (2006). *Entrepreneurship as Social Change.* Cheltenham: Edward Elgar.

Steyaert, C. and Hjorth, D. (2002). Thou art a scholar, speak to it: on spaces of speech. A script. *Human Relations,* 55(7), 767–97.

Steyaert, C., Hjorth, D. and Gartner, W. B. (2011). Six memos for curious and imaginative future scholarship in entrepreneurship studies. *Entrepreneurship & Regional Development,* 23(1–2), 1–7.

Styhre, A. (2008). Transduction and entrepreneurship: a biophilosophical image of the entrepreneur. *Scandinavian Journal of Management,* 24(2), 103–12.

Sveiby, K.-E., Gripenberg, P. and Segercrantz, B. (2012). The unintended and undesirable consequences: neglected by innovation research. In K.-E. Sveiby, P. Gripenberg and B. Segercrantz (eds), *Challenging the Innovation Paradigm.* London: Routledge, pp. 61–84.

Tedmanson, D., Verduyn, K., Essers, C. and Gartner, W. B. (2012). Critical perspectives in entrepreneurship research. *Organization,* 19(5), 531–41.

Thornton, M. (2005). The origin of economic theory: a portrait of Richard Cantillon (1680–1734). Retrieved 12 August 2015 from www.mises.org/content/cantillon.asp.

Vallas, S. P. and Cummins, E. R. (2015). Personal branding and identity norms in the popular business press: enterprise culture in an age of precarity. *Organization Studies,* 36(3), 293–319.

van Praag, C. M. and Versloot, P. H. (2007). What is the value of entrepreneurship? A review of recent research. *Small Business Economics,* 29, 351–82.

Vavrus, M. D. (2002). *Postfeminist News: Political Women in Media Culture.* Albany, NY: State University of New York Press.

Venkataraman, S., Sarasvathy, S. D., Dew, N. and Forster, W. R. (2012). Reflections on the 2010 *AMR* decade award: whither the promise? Moving forward with entrepreneurship as a science of the artificial. *Academy of Management Review,* 37(1), 21–33.

Verduijn, K., Dey, P., Tedmanson, D. and Essers, C. (2014). Emancipation and/or oppression? Conceptualizing dimensions of criticality in entrepreneurship studies. *International Journal of Entrepreneurial Behaviour & Research,* 20(2), 98–107.

Wee, L. and Brooks, A. (2012). Negotiating gendered subjectivity in the enterprise culture: metaphor and entrepreneurial discourses. *Gender, Work and Organization,* 19(6), 573–91.

Weiskopf, R. and Steyaert, C. (2009). Metamorphoses in entrepreneurship studies: towards an affirmative politics of entrepreneurship. In D. Hjorth and C. Steyaert (eds.), *The Politics and Aesthetics of Entrepreneurship.* Cheltenham: Edward Elgar Publishing, pp. 183–201.

Whitehead, A. N. (1978) [1929]. *Process and Reality. An Essay in Cosmology (Gifford Lectures Delivered in the University of Edinburgh during the session of 1927–28),* corrected edition (D. Griffin and D. Sherburne, eds.). New York: The Free Press.

Williams, C. C. and Nadin, S. J. (2013). Beyond the entrepreneur as a heroic figurehead of capitalism: re-representing the lived practices of entrepreneurs. *Entrepreneurship & Regional Development,* 25(7–8), 552–68.

World Bank (2015). Gender and development. Retrieved 1 September 2015 from http://datatopics.worldbank.org/gender/.

Author Index

Page numbers in **bold** indicate tables and in *italic* indicate figures.

Subject Index

Page numbers in **bold** indicate tables and in *italic* indicate figures.